PROCEEDINGS OF THE ELECTORAL COMMISSION AND OF CONGRESS RELATIVE TO THE PRESIDENTIAL ELECTORAL VOTES CAST DECEMBER 6, 1876

PROCEEDINGS OF THE

ELECTORAL COMMISSION

AND OF THE TWO

HOUSES OF CONGRESS IN JOINT MEETING

RELATIVE TO THE

COUNT OF ELECTORAL VOTES CAST
DECEMBER 6, 1876

FOR

THE PRESIDENTIAL TERM COMMENCING
MARCH 4, 1877

DA CAPO PRESS • NEW YORK • 1970

A Da Capo Press Reprint Edition

This Da Capo Press edition of the *Proceedings of the Electoral Commission and of the Two Houses of Congress in Joint Meeting Relative to the Count of Electoral Votes Cast December 6, 1876, for the Presidential Term Commencing March 4, 1877,* is an unabridged republication of the first edition published in Washington, D. C., in 1877.

Library of Congress Catalog Card Number 69-11322
SBN 306-71185-0

Published by Da Capo Press
A Division of Plenum Publishing Corporation
227 West 17th Street, New York, New York 10011

ELECTORAL COUNT OF 1877.

PROCEEDINGS

OF THE

ELECTORAL COMMISSION

AND OF THE

TWO HOUSES OF CONGRESS IN JOINT MEETING

RELATIVE TO THE

COUNT OF ELECTORAL VOTES CAST DECEMBER 6, 1876,

FOR

THE PRESIDENTIAL TERM COMMENCING MARCH 4, 1877.

———→◆←———

WASHINGTON:
GOVERNMENT PRINTING OFFICE.
1877.

IN THE HOUSE OF REPRESENTATIVES,
March 3, 1877.

Resolved by the House of Representatives, (the Senate concurring,) That there be printed 10,000 copies of the proceedings of the Electoral Commission, embracing all of the said proceedings and arguments and briefs of counsel, together with the proceedings of the joint convention regarding all States the returns from which were submitted to said commission, 7,500 copies for the use of the House of Representatives and 2,500 copies for the use of the Senate.

Attest:

G. M. ADAMS, *Clerk.*

IN THE SENATE OF THE UNITED STATES,
March 3, 1877.

Resolved, That the Senate concur in the foregoing resolution of the House of Representatives.

Attest:

GEO. C. GORHAM, *Secretary.*

IN THE SENATE OF THE UNITED STATES,
March 15, 1877.

Resolved, That the volume containing the proceedings of the Electoral Commission and of the two Houses in the counting of electoral votes, directed to be printed by a concurrent resolution of March 3, be prepared for publication under the direction of the Committee on Printing.

Resolved, That of the number of copies of said publication allotted to the Senate by said concurrent resolution 200 copies be furnished to the justices of the Supreme Court who were members of the Electoral Commission.

Attest:

GEO. C. GORHAM, *Secretary.*

ELECTORAL COUNT OF 1877.

The disputes as to the votes cast in some of the States by the respective sets of persons claiming to have been chosen electors at the popular elections held therein on the 7th day of November, A. D. 1876, were of such a nature as to lead to grave fears that difficulty might ensue if there were no further provision for the case than was contained in some of the sections of the act of Congress of March 1, 1792, and the act of March 26, 1804, embodied in the Revised Statutes from section 135 to 143, which sections contained all the legislation that had been provided for any such contingency and that seemed to be entirely inadequate. When the second session of the Forty-fourth Congress convened, the subject immediately attracted attention in both Houses. On the 14th of December, 1876, the House of Representatives passed a resolution for the appointment of a committee of seven, with power to act in conjunction with any similar committee appointed by the Senate, to prepare and report without delay a measure for the removal of differences of opinion as to the proper mode of counting the electoral votes for President and Vice-President of the United States and as to the manner of determining questions which might arise as to the legality and validity of the returns of such votes made by the several States, to the end that the votes should be counted and the result declared " by a tribunal whose authority none can question and whose decision all will accept as final."

On the 18th of December the Senate referred the message of the House of Representatives communicating its resolution, to a select committee, to be composed of seven Senators, with power " to prepare and report, without unnecessary delay, such a measure, either of a legislative or other character, as may, in their judgment, be best calculated to accomplish the lawful counting of the electoral votes and best disposition of all questions connected therewith, and the due declaration of the result," and also with power " to confer and act with the committee of the House of Representatives."

The committees provided for by these resolutions were composed, on the part of the Senate, of George F. Edmunds of Vermont, Oliver P. Morton of Indiana, Frederick T. Frelinghuysen of New Jersey, Roscoe Conkling of New York, Allen G. Thurman of Ohio, Thomas F. Bayard of Delaware, and Matt. W. Ransom of North Carolina, and on the part of the House of Representatives of Henry B. Payne of Ohio, Eppa Hunton of Virginia, Abram S. Hewitt of New York, William M. Springer of Illinois, George W. McCrary of Iowa, George F. Hoar of Massachusetts, and George Willard of Michigan.

On the 18th of January, 1877 these committees submitted a report to the respective Houses, signed by all their members except Senator Morton, recommending the passage of a bill, which, after discussion in both Houses, became a law on the 29th of January, in the precise words reported, as follows:

AN ACT to provide for and regulate the counting of votes for President and Vice-President, and the decision of questions arising thereon, for the term commencing March fourth, anno Domini eighteen hundred and seventy-seven.

Be it enacted by the Senate and House of Representatives of the United States of America in Congress assembled, That the Senate and House of Representatives shall meet in the hall of the House of Representatives, at the hour of one o'clock post meridian, on the first Thursday in February, anno Domini eighteen hundred and seventy-seven; and the President of the Senate shall be their presiding officer. Two tellers shall be previously appointed on the part of the Senate, and two on the part of the House of Representatives, to whom shall be handed, as they are opened by the President of the Senate, all the certificates, and papers purporting to be certificates, of the electoral votes, which certificates and papers shall be opened, presented, and acted upon in the alphabetical order of the States, beginning with the letter A; and said tellers having then read the same in the presence and hearing of the two houses, shall make a list of the votes as they shall appear from the said certificates; and the votes having been ascertained and counted as in this act provided, the result of the same shall be delivered to the President of the Senate, who shall thereupon announce the state of the vote, and the names of the persons, if any, elected, which announcement shall be deemed a sufficient declaration of the persons elected President and Vice-President of the United States, and, together with a list of the votes, be entered on the journals of the two houses. Upon such reading of any such certificate or paper when there shall be only one return from a State, the President of the Senate shall call for objections, if any. Every objection shall be made in writing, and shall state clearly and concisely, and without argument, the ground thereof, and shall be signed by at least one Senator and one Member of the House of Representatives before the same shall be received. When all objections so made to any vote or paper from a State shall have been received and read, the Senate shall thereupon withdraw, and such objections shall be submitted to the Senate for its decision; and the Speaker of the House of Representatives shall, in like manner, submit such objections to the House of Representatives for its decision; and no electoral vote or votes from any State from which but one return has been received shall be rejected except by the affirmative vote of the two houses. When the two houses have voted, they shall immediately again meet, and the presiding officer shall then announce the decision of the question submitted.

SEC. 2. That if more than one return, or paper purporting to be a return from a State, shall have been received by the President of the Senate, purporting to be the certificates of electoral votes given at the last preceding election for President and Vice-President in such State, (unless they shall be duplicates of the same return,) all such returns and papers shall be opened by him in the presence of the two houses when met as aforesaid, and read by the tellers, and all such returns and papers shall thereupon be submitted to the judgment and decision as to which is the true and lawful electoral vote of such State, of a commission constituted as follows, namely: During the session of each house on the Tuesday next preceding the first Thursday in February, eighteen hundred and seventy-seven, each house shall, by viva voce vote, appoint five of its members, who with the five associate justices of the Supreme Court of the United States, to be ascertained as hereinafter provided, shall constitute a commission for the decision of all questions upon or in respect of such double returns named in this section. On the Tuesday next preceding the first Thursday in February, anno Domini eighteen hundred and seventy-seven, or as soon thereafter as may be, the associate justices of the Supreme Court of the United States now assigned to the first, third, eighth, and ninth circuits shall select, in such manner as a majority of them shall deem fit, another of the associate justices of said court, which five persons shall be members of said commission; and the person longest in commission of said five justices shall be the president of said commission. The members of said commission shall respectively take and subscribe the following oath: "I, ———— ————, do solemnly swear (or affirm, as the case may be) that I will impartially examine and consider all questions submitted to the commission of which I am a member, and a true judgment give thereon, agreeably to the Constitution and the laws: so help me God;" which oath shall be filed with the Secretary of the Senate. When the commission shall have been thus organized, it shall not be in the power of either house to dissolve the same, or to withdraw any of its members; but if any such Senator or member shall die or become physically unable to perform the duties required by this act, the fact of such death or physical inability shall be by said commission, before it shall proceed further, communicated to the Senate or House of Representatives, as the case may be, which body shall immediately and without debate proceed by viva voce vote to fill the place so vacated, and the person so appointed shall take and subscribe the oath hereinbefore prescribed, and become a member of said commission; and, in like manner, if any of said justices of the Supreme Court shall die or become physically incapable of performing the duties required by this act, the other of said justices, members of the said commission, shall immediately appoint another justice of said court a member of said commission, and, in such appointments, regard shall be had to the impartiality and freedom from bias sought by the original appointments to said commission, who shall thereupon immediately take and subscribe the oath hereinbefore prescribed, and become a member of said commission to fill the vacancy so occasioned. All the certificates and papers purporting to be certificates of the electoral votes of each State shall be opened, in the alphabetical order of the States, as provided in section one of this act; and when there shall be more than one such certificate or paper, as the certificate and papers from such State shall so be opened, (excepting duplicates of the same return,) they shall be read by the tellers, and thereupon the President of the Senate shall call for objections, if any. Every objection shall be made in writing, and shall state clearly and concisely, and without argument, the ground thereof, and shall be signed by at least one Senator and one member of the House of Representatives before the same shall be received. When all such objections so made to any certificate, vote, or paper from a State shall have been received and read, all such certificates, votes, and papers so objected to, and all papers accompanying the same, together with such objections, shall be forthwith submitted to said commission, which shall proceed to consider the same, with the same powers, if any, now possessed for that purpose by the two houses acting separately or together, and, by a majority of votes, decide whether any and what votes from such State are the votes provided for by the Constitution of the United States, and how many and what persons were duly appointed electors in such State, and may therein take into view such petitions, depositions, and other papers, if any, as shall, by the Constitution and now existing law, be competent and pertinent in such consideration; which decision shall be made in writing, stating briefly the ground thereof, and signed by the members of said commission agreeing therein; whereupon the two houses shall again meet, and such decision shall be read and entered in the journal of each house, and the counting of the votes shall proceed in conformity therewith, unless, upon objection made thereto in writing by at least five Senators and five members of the House of Representatives, the two houses shall separately concur in ordering otherwise, in which case such concurrent order shall govern. No votes or papers from any other State shall be acted upon until the objections previously made to the votes or papers from any State shall have been finally disposed of.

SEC. 3. That while the two houses shall be in meeting, as provided in this act, no debate shall be allowed and no question shall be put by the presiding officer, except to either house on a motion to withdraw; and he shall have power to preserve order.

SEC. 4. That when the two houses separate to decide upon an objection that may have been made to the counting of any electoral vote or votes from any State, or upon objection to a report of said commission, or other question arising under this act, each Senator and Representative may speak to such objection or question ten minutes, and not oftener than once; but after such debate shall have lasted two hours, it shall be the duty of each house to put the main question without further debate.

SEC. 5. That at such joint meeting of the two houses, seats shall be provided as follows: For the President of the Senate, the Speaker's chair; for the Speaker, immediately upon his left; the Senators in the body of the hall upon the right of the presiding officer; for the Representatives, in the body of the hall not provided for the Senators; for the tellers, Secretary of the Senate, and Clerk of the House of Representatives, at the Clerk's desk; for the other officers of the two houses, in front of the Clerk's desk and upon each side of the Speaker's platform. Such joint meeting shall not be dissolved until the count of electoral votes shall be completed and the result declared; and no recess shall be taken unless a question shall have arisen in regard to counting any such votes, or otherwise under this act, in which case it shall be competent for either house, acting separately, in the manner hereinbefore provided, to direct a recess of such house not beyond the next day, Sunday excepted, at the hour of ten o'clock in the forenoon. And while any question is being considered by said commission, either house may proceed with its legislative or other business.

SEC. 6. That nothing in this act shall be held to impair or affect any right now existing under the Constitution and laws to question, by proceeding in the judicial courts of the United States, the right or title of the person who shall be declared elected, or who shall claim to be President or Vice-President of the United States, if any such right exists.

SEC. 7. That said commission shall make its own rules, keep a record of its proceedings, and shall have power to employ such persons as may be necessary for the transaction of its business and the execution of its powers.

Approved, January 29, 1877.

ORGANIZATION OF THE ELECTORAL COMMISSION.

Under the provisions of the second section of this act, each house of Congress on Tuesday, January 30, proceeded by *viva voce* vote to designate five of its members to be members of the Electoral Commission therein provided for, and the following-named gentlemen were selected by their respective houses:

Senators Edmunds, Frelinghuysen, Morton, Thurman, and Bayard.

Representatives Payne, Hunton, Abbott, Hoar, and Garfield.

On the same day, the Associate Justices of the Supreme Court of the United States, designated in the act, met and selected Associate Justice Joseph P. Bradley to be a member of the Commission, thus completing its constitution, which fact was communicated to both houses of Congress on the morning of the 31st of January.

WEDNESDAY, *January* 31, 1877.

The members of the Commission appointed for the decision of certain questions relating to the counting of the electoral votes for the offices of President and Vice-President of the United States, under an act entitled "An act to provide for and regulate the counting of votes for President and Vice-President, and the decision of questions arising thereon, for the term commencing March 4, A. D. 1877," approved January 29, 1877, met in the Supreme Court room at the Capitol, at eleven o'clock in the forenoon, this 31st day of January, 1877.

Present: Mr. Justice Clifford, Associate Justice assigned to the first circuit; Mr. Justice Miller, Associate Justice assigned to the eighth circuit; Mr. Justice Field, Associate Justice assigned to the ninth circuit; Mr. Justice Strong, Associate Justice assigned to the third circuit; Mr. Justice Bradley; Senators Edmunds, Morton, Frelinghuysen, Thurman, and Bayard; Representatives Payne, Hunton, Abbott, Garfield, and Hoar.

The appointment on the Commission of Associate Justice BRADLEY by the other four Associate Justices of the Supreme Court above named was presented and read, as follows:

Hon. JOSEPH P. BRADLEY,
  Associate Justice of the Supreme Court of the United States:

Pursuant to the provisions of the second section of the act of Congress entitled "An act to provide for and regulate the counting of votes for President and Vice-President, and the decision of questions arising thereon, for the term commencing March 4, A. D. 1877," approved January 29, 1877, the undersigned, Associate Justices of the Supreme Court of the United States assigned to the first, third, eighth, and ninth circuits, respectively, have this day selected you to be a member of the commission constituted by said act.

Respectfully,

NATHAN CLIFFORD.
SAM. F. MILLER.
STEPHEN J. FIELD.
W. STRONG.

WASHINGTON, *January* 30, 1877.

The certificate of the appointment of the Senators above named as members of the Commission was read, as follows:

IN THE SENATE OF THE UNITED STATES,
  Tuesday, January 30, 1877.

The Senate proceeded in compliance with its order of this day to the appointment by *viva voce* vote of five Senators to be members of the Commission provided for in the act entitled "An act to provide for and regulate the counting of votes for President and Vice-President, and the decision of questions arising thereon, for the term commencing March 4, A. D. 1877," approved January 29, 1877; and

On taking and counting the votes it appeared that the following Senators were duly and unanimously chosen members of the said Commission, namely: Mr. George F. Edmunds, Mr. Oliver P. Morton, Mr. Frederick T. Frelinghuysen, Mr. Allen G Thurman, and Mr. Thomas F. Bayard.

Attest:

GEO. C. GORHAM, *Secretary.*

The certificate of the appointment of the Representatives above named as members of the Commission was read, as follows:

FORTY-FOURTH CONGRESS, SECOND SESSION,
CONGRESS OF THE UNITED STATES,
IN THE HOUSE OF REPRESENTATIVES, *January* 30, 1877.

The House of Representatives, by a *viva voce* vote, appointed Mr. Henry B. Payne, of Ohio; Mr. Eppa Hunton, of Virginia; Mr. Josiah G. Abbott, of Massachusetts; Mr. George F. Hoar, of Massachusetts, and Mr. James A. Garfield, of Ohio, members of the Commission on the part of the House of Representatives provided for in the act approved January 29, 1877, entitled "An act to provide for and regulate the counting of votes for President and Vice-President, and the decision of questions arising thereon, for the term commencing March 4, A. D. 1877."

Attest:
[SEAL OF THE HOUSE OF REPRESENTATIVES.] GEORGE M. ADAMS, *Clerk.*

Associate Justice Clifford having made oath, as required by the said act, before the clerk of the Supreme Court of the United States, and the same having been filed with the Secretary of the Senate, the other members of the Commission severally took and subscribed before Mr Justice Clifford the oath required by the act, and the Commission was organized and called to order, Associate Justice Clifford presiding.

On motion of Mr. Commissioner THURMAN, it was

Resolved, That a committee of two Justices, two Senators, and two Representatives be appointed to consider and propose such rules of proceeding, and officers and employés as may be proper for the Commission, the committee to be appointed by the President.

The PRESIDENT appointed Commissioners Edmunds, Bayard, Field, Payne, and Hoar as the committee.

On motion of Mr. Commissioner HOAR, it was

Resolved, That the President appoint a temporary clerk until the committee above appointed report.

The President appointed James H. McKenney temporary clerk to the Commission.

On motion of Mr. Commissioner HOAR, it was

Resolved, That the proceedings of the Commission, until otherwise ordered, be considered confidential, except as to the fact of the organization.

The certificates of the oaths of the members of the Commission were delivered to the clerk, who was directed to file them with the Secretary of the Senate.

On motion of Mr. Commissioner EDMUNDS, the Commission adjourned until four o'clock p. m.

———

The Commission met at four o'clock p. m., pursuant to adjournment. Present all the members.

The report of the Committee on Rules was presented by Mr. Commissioner Edmunds.

On motion of Mr. Commissioner BRADLEY, the rules reported were considered *seriatim,* and, after being amended, were adopted as follows, namely:

RULE I. The Commission shall appoint a secretary, two assistant secretaries, a marshal and two deputy marshals, a stenographer, and such messengers as shall be needful; to hold during the pleasure of the Commission.

RULE II. On any subject submitted to the Commission a hearing shall be had, and counsel shall be allowed to conduct the case on each side.

RULE III. Counsel, not exceeding two in number on each side, will be heard by the Commission on the merits of any case presented to it, not longer than two hours being allowed to each side, unless a longer time and additional counsel shall be specially authorized by the Commission. In the hearing of interlocutory questions, but one counsel shall be heard on each side, and he not longer than fifteen minutes, unless the

Commission allow further time and additional counsel; and printed arguments will be received.

Rule IV. The objectors to any certificate or vote may select two of their number to support their objections in oral argument and to advocate the validity of any certificate or vote the validity of which they maintain; and in like manner the objectors to any other certificate may select two of their number for a like purpose; but, under this rule, not more than four persons shall speak, and neither side shall occupy more than two hours.

Rule V. Applications for process to compel the attendance of witnesses or the production of written or documentary testimony may be made by counsel on either side. And all process shall be served and executed by the marshal of the Commission or his deputies. Depositions hereafter taken for use before the Commission shall be sufficiently authenticated if taken before any commissioner of the circuit courts of the United States, or any clerk or deputy clerk of any court of the United States.

Rule VI. Admissions to the public sittings of the Commission shall be regulated in such manner as the President of the Commission shall direct.

Rule VII. The Commission will sit, unless otherwise ordered, in the room of the Supreme Court of the United States, and with open doors, (excepting when in consultation,) unless otherwise directed.

On motion of Mr. Commissioner HOAR, the President of the Commission was requested, on consultation with Commissioners Edmunds and Payne, to nominate officers to the Commission.

On motion of Mr. Commissioner GARFIELD, the Committee on Rules were authorized to report rules to regulate the order of business of the Commission.

On motion of Mr. Commissioner FRELINGHUYSEN, the Commission adjourned until to-morrow at eleven o'clock a. m.

Thursday, *February* 1, 1877.

The Commission met for consultation at eleven o'clock a. m.; and, on motion of Mr. Justice CLIFFORD, the following-named gentlemen were selected as officers of the Commission:

Secretary—James H. McKenney.
Assistant Secretaries—B. E. Cattin and George A. Howard.
Marshal—William H. Reardon.
Deputy Marshals—Albert S. Seely and J. C. Taliaferro.
Stenographer—D. F. Murphy.

On motion, the Commission adjourned till three o'clock p. m., after having sent the following communications to the respective Houses of Congress, which were there read and ordered to be placed on their journals:

WASHINGTON, D. C., *February* 1, 1877.

SIR: I have the honor to inform the Senate that the Commission constituted under the act of Congress approved January 29, 1877, entitled "An act to provide for and regulate the counting of votes for President and Vice-President, and the decision of questions arising thereon, for the term commencing March 4, A. D. 1877," has met and (the members thereof having taken and subscribed the oath prescribed by law) organized, and is now ready to proceed to the performance of its duties.

Very respectfully, yours,

NATHAN CLIFFORD,
President of the Commission.

To the PRESIDENT OF THE SENATE.

WASHINGTON, *February* 1, 1877.

SIR: I have the honor to inform the House of Representatives that the Commission constituted under the act of Congress approved January 29, 1877, entitled "An act to provide for and regulate the counting of votes for President and Vice-President, and the decision of questions arising thereon, for the term commencing March 4, A. D. 1877," has met and (the members thereof having taken and subscribed the oath prescribed by law) organized, and is now ready to proceed to the performance of its duties.

Very respectfully,

NATHAN CLIFFORD,
President of the Commission.

Hon. SAMUEL J. RANDALL,
Speaker of the House of Representatives.

JOINT MEETING OF THE TWO HOUSES.

THURSDAY, *February* 1, 1877.

Prior to the hour fixed for the joint meeting of the two Houses, the appointment of the tellers for each House was announced by the presiding officer thereof. The Speaker of the House of Representatives (Mr. Samuel J. Randall, of Pennsylvania) appointed as tellers on the part of the House Mr. Philip Cook, of Georgia, and Mr. William H. Stone, of Missouri ; and the President *pro tempore* of the Senate (Mr. Thomas W. Ferry, of Michigan) appointed Mr. William B. Allison, of Iowa, and Mr. John J. Ingalls, of Kansas, tellers on the part of the Senate.

In the Senate, at twelve o'clock and fifty-eight minutes,

The PRESIDENT *pro tempore.* The Chair will announce that by the provisions of an act approved on the 29th instant, known as the electoral act, the Senate is required to appear in the Hall of the House of Representatives at one o'clock on this day. It is now within two minutes of that time.

Mr. Senator EDMUNDS. I move that the Senate proceed to the House of Representatives.

The motion was agreed to ; and the Senate, preceded by the Sergeant-at-Arms, thereupon proceeded to the Hall of the House of Representatives.

In the House of Representatives, at one o'clock the Doorkeeper announced the Senate of the United States.

The Senate entered the Hall, preceded by its Sergeant-at-Arms and headed by its President *pro tempore* and its Secretary, the members and officers of the House rising to receive them.

In accordance with the law, seats had been provided as follows : For the President of the Senate, the Speaker's chair ; for the Speaker, immediately upon his left ; for the Senators, in the body of the hall upon the right of the presiding officer ; for the Representatives, in the body of the hall not provided for the Senators ; for the tellers, Secretary of the Senate, and Clerk of the House of Representatives, at the Clerk's desk ; for the other officers of the two Houses, in front of the Clerk's desk and upon each side of the Speaker's platform.

The PRESIDENT *pro tempore* of the Senate took his seat as presiding officer of the joint convention of the two Houses, the Speaker of the House occupying a chair upon his left.

Senators INGALLS and ALLISON, the tellers appointed on the part of the Senate, and Mr. COOK and Mr. STONE, the tellers appointed on the part of the House, took their seats at the Clerk's desk, at which the Secretary of the Senate and the Clerk of the House also occupied seats.

The PRESIDING OFFICER. The joint meeting of the two Houses of Congress for the counting of votes for President and Vice-President of the United States will now come to order. In obedience to the Constitution, the Senate and House of Representatives have met to be present at the opening of the certificates, the counting and the declaring of the result of the electoral votes for President and the Vice-President of the United States for the term of four years commencing on the 4th day of March next. In compliance with law, the President of the Senate will now proceed, in the presence of the two houses, to open all the certificates of the several States, in alphabetical order, beginning with the State of Alabama.

Having opened the certificate of the State of Alabama, received by messenger, the Chair hands to the tellers the certificate, to be read in the presence and hearing of both Houses.

Mr. Senator ALLISON (one of the tellers) read in full the certificate of the electoral vote of the State of Alabama, giving 10 votes for Samuel J. Tilden, of New York, for President, and 10 votes for Thomas A. Hendricks, of the State of Indiana, for Vice-President of the United States.

The PRESIDING OFFICER. The certificate of the vote of the State of Alabama having been read, the Chair has opened and hands to the tellers the duplicate certificate received by mail from the same State, which will likewise be read.

Mr. Representative STONE (one of the tellers) proceeded to read the duplicate certificate.

Mr. Senator CONKLING. I venture to interrupt the reading to suggest that it can hardly be necessary to read *in extenso* the duplicate certificates received by mail; and, if that should be the impression of the Presiding Officer and of the two Houses, I make the further suggestion that hereafter when tellers read a certificate the tellers not reading had better overlook the duplicate certificate at the same time, in order that a comparison may thus be made.

The PRESIDING OFFICER. The suggestion of the gentleman from New York has been heard. Is there objection to following that suggestion? The Chair hears none and it will be followed hereafter.

Mr. Representative STONE (one of the tellers) then concluded the reading of the duplicate certificate of the State of Alabama.

The PRESIDING OFFICER. Are there any objections to the certificate of the State of Alabama? The Chair hears none, and the votes of the State of Alabama will be counted. One of the tellers will announce the vote, so that there can be no mistake.

Mr. Representative COOK, (one of the tellers.) The State of Alabama gives 10 votes for Samuel J. Tilden, of New York, for President of the United States, and 10 votes for Thomas A. Hendricks, of Indiana, for Vice-President.

The PRESIDING OFFICER. The Chair hands to the tellers the certificate of the electoral vote of the State of Arkansas, received by messenger, and the corresponding one received by mail. In accordance with the suggestion of the Senator from New York, but one will be read, and the other will be examined as the original is read. The tellers will follow the reading of the one received by messenger in every case with the one received by mail.

The tellers then proceeded, in the manner indicated, to announce the electoral votes of the States of Arkansas, California, Colorado, Connecticut, and Delaware, it being mentioned in each case that the certificate of the election of the electors was signed by the governor and countersigned by the secretary of state, and in each case the Presiding Officer asked whether there were any objections to the certificate; and, there being none, the vote in each case was thereupon counted.

The PRESIDING OFFICER. The Chair hands to the tellers a certificate from the State of Florida, received by messenger, and the corresponding one by mail.

Mr. Representative STONE (one of the tellers) read the certificate, as follows:

FLORIDA.

CERTIFICATE No. 1.

EXECUTIVE OFFICE,
Tallahassee, Florida, December 6, 1876.

STATE OF FLORIDA:

Pursuant to laws of the United States, I, Marcellus L. Stearns, governor of Florida, do hereby certify that Frederick C. Humphreys, Charles H. Pearce, William H. Holden, and Thomas W. Long have been chosen electors of President and Vice-President of the United States, on the part of this State, agreeably to the provisions of the laws of the said State and in conformity to the Constitution of the United States of America, for the purpose of giving in their votes for President and Vice-President of the United States, for the term prescribed by the Constitution of said United States, to begin on the fourth day of March, in the year of our Lord one thousand eight hundred and seventy-seven.

Given under my hand and the seal of the State, at Tallahassee, this sixth day of December, A. D. one thousand eight hundred and seventy-six, and in the one hundredth year of the Independence of the United States of America.

[SEAL.]   M. L. STEARNS, *Governor.*

By the governor.

Attest: SAML. B. McLIN,
                          Secretary of State.

STATE OF FLORIDA:

We, whose names are mentioned in the annexed certificate of appointment, having, pursuant to the Constitution and laws of the United States of America, and in the manner directed by the laws of the State of Florida, been appointed electors of President and Vice-President of the United States of America, and having assembled at the State capitol in Tallahassee, being the seat of government of said State, and the place designated by law for that purpose, on the first Wednesday in December, A. D. one thousand eight hundred and seventy-six, being the sixth day of said month, and in the one hundredth year of the Independence of the United States of America, have voted, by ballot, for President and Vice-President, having named in our ballots the person voted for as President and in distinct ballots the person voted for as Vice-President, and in the same ballots there were four (4) votes for President of the United States of America, all of which four (4) votes were cast for Rutherford B. Hayes, of Ohio.

In testimony whereof we have hereunto set our hands on the first Wednesday, being the sixth day of December, in the year of our Lord one thousand eight hundred and seventy-six.

             F. C. HUMPHREYS.
             C. H. PEARCE.
             W. H. HOLDEN.
             THOS. W. LONG.

STATE OF FLORIDA:

We, whose names are mentioned in the annexed certificate of appointment, having, pursuant to the Constitution and laws of the United States of America, and in the manner directed by the laws of the State of Florida, been appointed electors of President and Vice-President of the United States of America, and having assembled at the State capitol, in Tallahassee, in the State aforesaid, being the seat of government of said State, and the place designated by law for that purpose, on the first Wednesday in December, A. D. one thousand eight hundred and seventy-six, being the sixth day of said month, and in the one hundredth year of the Independence of the United States of America, have voted, by ballot, for President and Vice-President, having named in our ballots the person voted for as President, and in distinct ballots the person voted for as Vice-President, and in the same ballots there were four (4) votes cast for Vice-President of the United States of America, all of which four (4) votes were cast for William A. Wheeler, of New York.

In testimony whereof we have hereunto set our hands on the first Wednesday, being the sixth day of December, in the year of our Lord one thousand eight hundred and seventy-six.

F. C. HUMPHREYS.
C. H. PEARCE.
W. H. HOLDEN.
THOS. W. LONG.

The PRESIDING OFFICER. The Chair hands another certificate received by messenger from Florida and the corresponding one received by mail.

Mr. Representative STONE (one of the tellers) read the certificate, as follows:

CERTIFICATE No. 2.

STATE OF FLORIDA, ATTORNEY-GENERAL'S OFFICE,
Tallahassee, —— —, 18—.

List of electors of President and Vice-President of the United States for the State of Florida.

I, William Archer Cocke, attorney-general of the State of Florida, and as such one of the members of the board of State canvassers of the State of Florida, do certify that, by the authentic returns of the votes cast in the several counties of the State of Florida, at the general election held on Tuesday, November 7, 1876, said returns being on file in the office of the secretary of state, and seen and considered by me, as such member of the board of State canvassers of the said State of Florida, it appears and is shown that Wilkinson Call, James E. Yonge, Robert B. Hilton, and Robert Bullock were chosen the four electors of President and Vice-President of the United States; and I do further certify that under the act of the legislature of the State of Florida establishing said board of State canvassers, no provision has been enacted, nor is any such provision contained in the statute law of this State, whereby the result shown and appearing by said returns to said board of State canvassers can be certified to the executive of the said State.

Witness my hand and seal this 6th day of December, 1876, at the capitol in Tallahassee.

[SEAL.]

WM. ARCHER COCKE,
Attorney-General, State of Florida.

STATE OF FLORIDA, *County of Leon:*

I, Robert Bullock, and I, Wilkinson Call, and I, James E. Yonge, and I, Robert B. Hilton, do solemnly swear that I will support, protect, and defend the Constitution and Government of the United States and of the State of Florida against all enemies, domestic or foreign, and that I will bear true faith, loyalty, and allegiance to the same; and that I am entitled to hold office under the constitution of this State; that I will well and faithfully perform all the duties of the office of elector of President and Vice-President of the United States, on which I am about to enter.

WILKINSON CALL.
J. E. YONGE.
ROBERT BULLOCK.
ROBERT B. HILTON.

Sworn to and subscribed before me this sixth day of December, A. D. 1876.
[SEAL.]

FRED. T. MYERS,
Clerk Supreme Court of the State of Florida.

STATE OF FLORIDA:

We, the undersigned, electors of President and Vice-President of the United States of America for the next ensuing regular term of the respective office thereof, being electors duly and legally appointed by and for the State of Florida, as appears by the annexed list of electors, made, certified, and delivered to us by William Archer Cocke, attorney-general of the State of Florida, and, as such, one of the members of the State board of canvassers of said State, having met and convened in the city of Tallahassee, at the capitol, in pursuance of the direction of the legislature of the State of Florida, at twelve o'clock m., on the first Wednesday, the sixth day, of December, in the year of our Lord one thousand eight hundred and seventy-six, the same being the seat of government of the State of Florida, do hereby certify that, being so assembled and duly organized, we proceeded to vote by ballot, and balloted first for such President, and then for such Vice-President, by distinct ballots.

And we further certify that we, and each of us, are duly qualified, under the Constitution and laws of the United States, to hold the said office of elector of President and Vice President, and that we have each of us taken the oath of office prescribed by the laws of the State of Florida for electors of President and Vice-President, and that we have complied with all and singular the other requirements of the laws of this State prescribing, declaring, and establishing the duties of such electors.

And we further certify that the following are two distinct lists; one of the votes for President and the other of the votes for Vice-President.

List of all persons voted for as President, with the number of votes for each:

For President of the United States, Samuel J. Tilden, of the State of New York. Whole number of votes, four, (4.)

List of all persons voted for as Vice-President, with the number of votes for each:

For Vice-President of the United States, Thomas A. Hendricks, of the State of Indiana. Whole number of votes, four, (4.)

In witness whereof we have hereunto set our hands. Done at the capitol, in the city of Tallahassee and State of Florida, the sixth day of December, in the year of our Lord one thousand eight hundred and seventy-six, and of the Independence of the United States of America the one hundred and first, at the seat of government of the said State of Florida.

> WILKINSON CALL, *Elector.*
> ROBERT BULLOCK, *Elector.*
> ROBERT B. HILTON, *Elector.*
> J. E. YONGE, *Elector.*

And we further certify that, having met and convened as such electors, at the time and place designated by law, we did notify the governor of the State of Florida, the executive of said State, of our appointment as such electors, and did apply to and demand of him to cause to be delivered to us three lists of the names of the electors of the said State, according to law, and the said governor did refuse to deliver the same to us.

> WILKINSON CALL, *Elector.*
> ROBERT BULLOCK, *Elector.*
> ROBERT B. HILTON, *Elector.*
> J. E. YONGE, *Elector.*

The PRESIDING OFFICER. Still another certificate from the State of Florida has been received by messenger, January 21, and it is now handed to the tellers, with the corresponding one received by mail, January 30.

Mr. Senator ALLISON (one of the tellers) read the certificate, and Mr. Senator INGALLS (another of the tellers) the papers accompanying the certificate, as follows:

CERTIFICATE No. 3.

EXECUTIVE OFFICE, *Tallahassee, Fla.*

Whereas, in pursuance of an act of the legislature of this State entitled "An act to procure a legal canvass of the electoral vote of the State of Florida, as cast at the election held on the 7th day of November, A. D. 1876," approved January 17th, 1877, a canvass of the returns of said votes on file in the office of the secretary of state was, on the 19th day of January, A. D. 1877, made, according to the laws of the State and the interpretation thereof by the supreme court, and Robert Bullock, Robert B. Hilton, Wilkinson Call, and James E. Yonge were duly determined, declared, and certified to have been elected electors of President and Vice-President of the United States for the State of Florida, at said election held on the 7th day of November, A. D. 1876, as shown by said returns; and whereas, in a proceeding on the part of the State of Florida, by information in the nature of a *quo warranto*, wherein the said Robert Bullock, Robert B. Hilton, Wilkinson Call, and James E. Yonge were relators, and Charles H. Pearce, Frederick C. Humphries, William H. Holden, and Thomas W. Long were respondents, the circuit court of this State for the second judicial circuit, after full consideration of the law and the proofs produced on behalf of the parties respectively, by its judgment determined that said relators were, at said election, in fact and law, elected such electors as against the said respondents and all other persons:

Now, therefore, and also in pursuance of an act of the legislature entitled "An act to declare and establish the appointment by the State of Florida of electors of President and Vice-President of the United States," approved January 26, A. D. 1877, I, George F. Drew, governor of the State of Florida, do hereby make and certify the following list of the names of the said electors chosen, appointed, and declared as afore-said, to wit: Robert Bullock, Robert B. Hilton, Wilkinson Call, James E. Yonge.

In testimony whereof I have hereunto set my hand and caused the great seal of the State to be affixed, at the capitol, at Tallahassee, this the 26th day of January, A. D. 1877.

[SEAL.]
Attest:

GEO. F. DREW,
Governor.
W. D. BLOXHAM,
Secretary of State.

STATE OF FLORIDA, *Leon County,* 88:

The executive of the State of Florida having caused three lists of the electors of this State for President and Vice-President of the United States to be made and certified and delivered to us—one of which said lists is hereto annexed—from which lists it ap-pears that we, the undersigned, were duly appointed on the seventh day of November, A. D. eighteen hundred and seventy-six, electors of President and Vice-President for and in behalf of the said State of Florida:

Now, therefore, be it remembered, and we do hereby certify and make known, that we, the undersigned, Robert Bullock, Robert B. Hilton, Wilkinson Call, and James E. Yonge, electors as aforesaid, did, on the first Wednesday of December, A. D. eighteen hundred and seventy-six, being the sixth day of said December, at 12 o'clock m., meet as such electors, in the capitol, at Tallahassee, to give our votes as such electors for President and Vice-President of the United States; and did then and there give and cast our votes, as such electors, by ballot, for President of the United States; and did then and there give and cast our votes, as such electors, by distinct ballots, for Vice-President of the United States; and the said ballots having been opened, inspected, and counted, it did there and then appear that on four of said ballots was the name of Samuel J. Tilden, of the State of New York, for President of the United States, and that upon four other of said ballots was the name of Thomas A. Hendricks, of the State of Indiana, for Vice-President of the United States. We, the undersigned, do there-fore and hereby certify and make known as follows:

1. That, at the said election and voting by us as aforesaid, the number of electoral votes cast for Samuel J. Tilden, of the State of New York, for President of the United States, was four votes.

2. That, at the said election and voting by us as aforesaid, the number of elelectoral votes cast for Thomas A. Hendricks, of the State of Indiana, for Vice-President of the United States, was four votes.

Done at Tallahassee, on this the 26th day of January, A. D. 1877.

In testimony whereof we have hereto set our hands and affixed our seals.

WILKINSON CALL,   [SEAL.]
JAMES E. YONGE,   [SEAL.]
ROBT. BULLOCK,   [SEAL.]
ROBERT B. HILTON,   [SEAL.]
Electors of President and Vice-President of the United States.

AN ACT to procure a legal canvass of the electoral vote of the State of Florida as cast at the election held on the seventh day of November, A. D. 1876.

The people of the State of Florida, represented in senate and assembly, do enact as follows:

SECTION 1. The secretary of state, attorney-general, and the comptroller of public accounts, or any two of them, together with any other member of the cabinet who may be designated by them, shall meet forthwith at the office of the secretary of state, pursuant to notice to be given by the secretary of state, and form a board of State canvassers, and proceed to canvass the returns of the election of electors of President and Vice-President, held on the 7th day of November, A. D. 1876, and determine and declare who were elected and appointed electors at said election, as shown by such re-turns on file in the office of the secretary of state.

SECTION 2. The said board of State canvassers shall canvass the said returns accord-ing to the fourth section of the statute approved February 27, 1872, entitled "An act to amend an act to provide for the registration of electors and the holding of elections," approved August 6, 1868, according to the construction declared, and the rules defining the powers and duties of the board of State canvassers under said law, prescribed in and by the supreme court of this State in the case of The State of Florida on the rela-tion of Bloxham *vs.* Jonathan C. Gibbs, secretary of state, *et al.,* decided in January, A. D. 1871, and in the case of The State of Florida on the relation of George F. Drew *vs.* Samuel B. McLin, secretary of state, William Archer Cocke, attorney-general, and Clayton A. Cowgill, comptroller of public accounts of the State of Florida, decided De-cember 23, A. D. 1876.

SECTION 3. The said board shall make and sign a certificate, containing, in words written at full length, the whole number of votes given at said election for each office of elector, the number of votes given for each person for such office, and therein declare the result, which certificate shall be recorded in the office of the secretary of state, in a book to be kept for that purpose, and the secretary of state shall cause a certified copy of such certificate to be published once in one or more newspapers printed at the seat of government, and shall transmit two certified copies of such certificate, one to the presiding officer of the senate and one to the presiding officer of the assembly of the State of Florida.

SECTION 4. This act shall take effect from and after its passage.

Approved January 17, 1877.

I, W. D. Bloxham, secretary of state of State of Florida, do hereby certify that the foregoing is a true and correct copy of the original on file in my office.

In testimony whereof I have hereunto set my hand and affixed the great seal of the State.

Done at Tallahassee, the capital, this 26th day of January, A. D. 1877.

[SEAL.]   W. D. BLOXHAM,
                                             Secretary of State.

[Official.]

STATE OF FLORIDA.

Certificate of State canvassers of the election held November 7, 1876.

We, W. D. Bloxham, secretary of state of the State of Florida, Columbus Drew, comptroller of public accounts of said State, and Walter Gwynn, treasurer of said State, constituting the board of canvassers of the State of Florida, do hereby certify that we met at the office of the secretary of state, at the capitol, in the city of Tallahassee, on the 19th day of January, 1877, and proceeded to canvass the returns of a general election held in said State on the 7th day of November, A. D. 1876, for presidential electors, in accordance with the provisions of an act entitled "An act to procure a legal canvass of the electoral vote of the State of Florida, as cast at the election held on the 7th day of November, A. D. 1876." From said canvass we arrived at the following result, which we do hereby certify:

The whole number of votes cast for presidential electors in the county of Alachua was as follows, viz:

TILDEN ELECTORS.

Wilkinson Call received twelve hundred and sixty-seven, (1,267.)
James E. Yonge received twelve hundred and sixty-seven, (1,267.)
Robert B. Hilton received twelve hundred and sixty-seven, (1,267.)
Robert Bullock received twelve hundred and sixty-seven, (1,267.)

HAYES ELECTORS.

F. C. Humphries received nineteen hundred and eighty-four, (1,984.)
C. H. Pearce received nineteen hundred and eighty-four, (1,984.)
W. H. Holden received nineteen hundred and eighty-four, (1,984.)
T. W. Long received nineteen hundred and eighty-four, (1,984.)

The whole number of votes cast for presidential electors in the county of Baker was as follows, viz:

Wilkinson Call received two hundred and thirty-eight, (238.)
James E. Yonge received two hundred and thirty-eight, (238.)
Robert B. Hilton received two hundred and thirty-eight, (238.)
Robert Bullock received two hundred and thirty-eight, (238.)
F. C. Humphries received one hundred and forty-three, (143.)
C. H. Pearce received one hundred and forty-three, (143.)
W. H. Holden received one hundred and forty-three, (143.)
T. W. Long received one hundred and forty-three, (143.)

The whole number of votes cast for presidential electors in the county of Brevard was as follows, viz:

Wilkinson Call received one hundred and eleven, (111.)
James E. Yonge received one hundred and eleven, (111.)
Robert B. Hilton received one hundred and eleven, (111.)
Robert Bullock received one hundred and eleven, (111.)
F. C. Humphries received fifty-eight, (58.)
C. H. Pearce received fifty-eight, (58.)

16 ELECTORAL COUNT OF 1877.

W. H. Holden received fifty-eight, (58.)
T. W. Long received fifty-eight, (58.)
The whole number of votes cast for presidential electors in the county of Bradford
was as follows, viz:
Wilkinson Call received seven hundred and three, (703.)
James E. Yonge received seven hundred and three, (703.)
Robert B. Hilton received seven hundred and three, (703.)
Robert Bullock received seven hundred and three, (703.)
F. C. Humphries received two hundred and two, (202.)
C. H. Pearce received two hundred and two, (202.)
W. H. Holden received two hundred and two, (202.)
T. W. Long received two hundred and two, (202.)
The whole number of votes cast for presidential electors in the county of Calhoun
was as follows, viz:
Wilkinson Call received two hundred and fifteen, (215.)
James E. Yonge received two hundred and fifteen, (215.)
Robert B. Hilton received two hundred and fifteen, (215.)
Robert Bullock received two hundred and fifteen, (215.)
F. C. Humphries received sixty-three, (63.)
C. H. Pearce received sixty-two, (62.)
W. H. Holden received sixty-three, (63.)
T. W. Long received sixty-three, (63.)
C. H. Humphries received one, (1.)
The whole number of votes cast for presidential electors in the county of Columbia
was as follows, viz:
Wilkinson Call received nine hundred and three, (903.)
James E. Yonge received nine hundred and three, (903.)
Robert B. Hilton received nine hundred and three, (903.)
Robert Bullock received nine hundred and three, (903.)
F. C. Humphries received seven hundred and eighteen, (718.)
C. H. Pearce received seven hundred and eighteen, (718.)
W. H. Holden received seven hundred and eighteen, (718.)
T. W. Long received seven hundred and eighteen, (718.)
The whole number of votes cast for presidential electors in the county of Clay was
as follows, viz:
Wilkinson Call received two hundred and eighty-six, (286.)
James E. Yonge received two hundred and eighty-seven, (287.)
Robert B. Hilton received two hundred and eighty-seven, (287.)
Robert Bullock received two hundred and eighty-seven, (287.)
F. C. Humphries received one hundred and twenty-two, (122.)
C. H. Pearce received one hundred and twenty-one, (121.)
W. H. Holden received one hundred and twenty-two, (122.)
T. W. Long received one hundred and twenty-two, (122.)
The whole number of votes cast for presidential electors in the county of Duval was
as follows, viz:
Wilkinson Call received fourteen hundred and thirty-six, (1,436.)
James E. Yonge received fourteen hundred and thirty-seven, (1,437.)
Robert B. Hilton received fourteen hundred and thirty-seven, (1,437.)
Robert Bullock received fourteen hundred and thirty-seven, (1,437.)
F. C. Humphries received twenty-three hundred and sixty-seven, (2,367.)
C. H. Pearce received twenty-three hundred and sixty-six, (2,366.)
W. H. Holden received twenty-three hundred and sixty-seven, (2,367.)
T. W. Long received twenty-three hundred and sixty six, (2,366.)
Marcellus L. Stearns received one, (1.)
The whole number of votes cast for presidential electors in the county of Dade was
as follows, viz:
Wilkinson Call received five, (5.)
James E. Yonge received five, (5.)
Robert B. Hilton received five, (5.)
Robert Bullock received five, (5.)
F. C. Humphries received nine, (9.)
C. H. Pearce received nine, (9.)
W. H. Holden received nine, (9.)
T. W. Long received nine, (9.)
The whole number of votes cast for presidential electors in the county of Escambia
was as follows, viz:
Wilkinson Call received fourteen hundred and twenty-six, (1,426.)
James E. Yonge received fourteen hundred and twenty-six, (1,426.)
Robert B. Hilton received fourteen hundred and twenty-six, (1,426.)
Robert Bullock received fourteen hundred and twenty-six, (1,426.)

F. C. Humphries received sixteen hundred and two, (1,602.)
C. H. Pearce received sixteen hundred and two, (1,602.)
W. H. Holden received sixteen hundred and two, (1,602.)
T. W. Long received sixteen hundred and two, (1,602.)
The whole number of votes cast for presidential electors in the county of Franklin
was as follows:
Wilkinson Call received one hundred and sixty-seven, (167.)
James E. Yonge received one hundred and sixty-seven, (167.)
Robert B. Hilton received one hundred and sixty-seven, (167.)
Robert Bullock received one hundred and sixty-seven, (167.)
F. C. Humphries received ninety-one, (91.)
C. H. Pearce received ninety-one, (91.)
W. H. Holden received ninety-one, (91.)
T. W. Long received ninety-one, (91.)
The whole number of votes cast for presidential electors in the county of Gadsden
was as follows, viz:
Wilkinson Call received eight hundred and thirty-five, (835.)
James E. Yonge received eight hundred and thirty-five, (835.)
Robert B. Hilton received eight hundred and thirty-five, (835.)
Robert Bullock received eight hundred and thirty-five, (835.)
F. C. Humphries received thirteen hundred, (1,300.)
C. H. Pearce received thirteen hundred, (1,300.)
W. H. Holden received thirteen hundred, (1,300.)
T. W. Long received thirteen hundred, (1,300.)
The whole number of votes cast for presidential electors in the county of Hamilton
was as follows, viz:
Wilkinson Call received six hundred and seventeen, (617.)
James E. Yonge received six hundred and seventeen, (617.)
Robert B. Hilton received six hundred and seventeen, (617.)
Robert Bullock received six hundred and seventeen, (617.)
F. C. Humphries received three hundred and thirty, (330.)
C. H. Pearce received three hundred and thirty, (330.)
W. H. Holden received three hundred and thirty, (330.)
T. W. Long received three hundred and thirty, (330.)
The whole number of votes cast for presidential electors in the county of Hernando
was as follows, viz:
Wilkinson Call received five hundred and seventy-nine, (579.)
James E. Yonge received five hundred and seventy-nine, (579.)
Robert B. Hilton received five hundred and seventy-eight, (578.)
Robert Bullock received five hundred and seventy-nine, (579.)
F. C. Humphries received one hundred and forty-four, (144.)
C. H. Pearce received one hundred and forty-four, (144.)
W. H. Holden received one hundred and forty-four, (144.)
T. W. Long received one hundred and forty-four, (144.)
The whole number of votes cast for presidential electors in the county of Hillsborough
was as follows, viz:
Wilkinson Call received seven hundred and ninety, (790.)
James E. Yonge received seven hundred and ninety, (790.)
Robert B. Hilton received seven hundred and ninety, (790.)
Rober Bullock received seven hundred and eighty-nine, (789.)
F. C. Humphries received one hundred and eighty-six, (186.)
C. H. Pearce received one hundred and eighty-six, (186.)
W. H. Holden received one hundred and eighty-six, (186.)
T. W. Long received one hundred and eighty-six, (186.)
The whole number of votes cast for presidential electors in the county of Holmes was
as follows, viz:
Wilkinson Call received three hundred, (300.)
James E. Yonge received three hundred, (300.)
Robert B. Hilton received three hundred, (300.)
Robert Bullock received three hundred, (300.)
F. C. Humphries received sixteen, (16.)
C. H. Pearce received sixteen, (16.)
W. H. Holden received sixteen, (16.)
T. W. Long received sixteen, (16.)
The whole number of votes cast for presidential electors in the county of Jackson was
as follows, viz:
Wilkinson Call received thirteen hundred and ninety-seven, (1,397.)
James E. Yonge received thirteen hundred and ninety-seven, (1,397.)
Robert B. Hilton received thirteen hundred and ninety-seven, (1,397.)
Robert Bullock received thirteen hundred and ninety-seven (1,397.)

F. C. Humphries received twelve hundred and ninety-nine, (1,299.)
C. H. Pearce received twelve hundred and ninety-nine, (1,299.)
W. H. Holden received twelve hundred and ninety-nine, (1,299.)
T. W. Long received twelve hundred and ninety-nine, (1,299.)
The whole number of votes cast for presidential electors in the county of Jefferson
was as follows, viz:
Wilkinson Call received seven hundred and thirty-seven, (737.)
James E. Yonge received seven hundred and thirty-seven, (737.)
Robert B. Hilton received seven hundred and thirty-seven, (737.)
Robert Bullock received seven hundred and thirty-seven, (737.)
F. C. Humphries received twenty-six hundred and sixty, (2,660.)
C. H. Pearce received twenty-six hundred and sixty, (2,660.)
W. H. Holden received twenty-six hundred and sixty, (2,660.
T. W. Long received twenty-six hundred and sixty, (2,660.)
The whole number of votes cast for presidential electors in the county of La Fay-
ette was as follows, viz:
Wilkinson Call received three hundred and nine, (309.)
James E. Yonge received three hundred and nine, (309.)
Robert B. Hilton received three hundred and nine, (309.)
Robert Bullock received three hundred and nine, (309.)
F. C. Humphries received sixty-two, (62.)
C. H. Pearce received sixty-two, (62.)
W. H. Holden received sixty-two, (62.)
T. W. Long received sixty-two, (62.)
The whole number of votes cast for presidential electors in the county of Leon was
as follows, viz:
Wilkinson Call received one thousand and three, (1,003.)
James E. Yonge received one thousand and three, (1,003.)
Robert B. Hilton received one thousand and three, (1,003.)
Robert Bullock received one thousand and three, (1,003.)
F. C. Humphries received three thousand and thirty-five, (3,035.)
C. H. Pearce received three thousand and thirty-five, (3,035.)
W. H. Holden received three thousand and thirty-five, (3,035.)
T. W. Long received three thousand and thirty-five, (3,035.)
The whole number of votes cast for presidential electors in the county of Levy was
as follows, viz:
Wilkinson Call received four hundred and eighty-seven, (487.)
James E. Yonge received four hundred and eighty-eight, (488.)
Robert B. Hilton received four hundred and eighty-seven, (487.)
Robert Bullock received four hundred and eighty-seven, (487.)
F. C. Humphries received two hundred and seven, (207.)
C. H. Pearce received two hundred and seven, (207.)
W. H. Holden received two hundred and seven, (207.)
T. W. Long received two hundred and six, (206.)
The whole number of votes cast for presidential electors in the county of Liberty
was as follows, viz:
Wilkinson Call received one hundred and forty-seven, (147.)
James E. Yonge received one hundred and forty-seven, (147.)
Robert B. Hilton received one hundred and forty-seven, (147.)
Robert Bullock received one hundred and forty-seven, (147.)
F. C. Humphries received eighty-three, (83.)
C. H. Pearce received eighty-three, (83.)
W. H. Holden received eighty-three, (83.)
T. W. Long received eighty-three, (83.)
The whole number of votes cast for presidential electors in the county of Madison
was as follows, viz:
Wilkinson Call received one thousand and seventy-eight, (1,078.)
James E. Yonge received one thousand and seventy-eight, (1,078.)
Robert B. Hilton received one thousand and seventy-eight, (1,078.)
Robert Bullock received one thousand and seventy-eight, (1,078.)
F. C. Humphries received one thousand five hundred and twenty-four, (1,524.)
C. H. Pearce received one thousand five hundred and twenty-four, (1,524.)
W. H. Holden received one thousand five hundred and twenty-four, (1,524.)
T. W. Long received one thousand five hundred and twenty-four, (1,524.)
The whole number of votes cast for presidential electors in the county of Manatee
was as follows, viz:
Wilkinson Call received two hundred and sixty-two, (262.)
James E. Yonge received two hundred and sixty-two, (262.)
Robert B. Hilton received two hundred and sixty-two, (262.)
Robert Bullock received two hundred and sixty-two, (262.)

F. C. Humphries received twenty-six, (26.)
C. H. Pearce received twenty-six, (26.)
W. H. Holden received twenty-six, (26.)
T. W. Long received twenty-six, (26.)
The whole number of votes cast for presidential electors in the county of Marion was as follows, viz :
Wilkinson Call received nine hundred and fifty-eight, (958.)
James E. Yonge received nine hundred and fifty-eight, (958.)
Robert B. Hilton received nine hundred and fifty-eight, (958.)
Robert Bullock received nine hundred and fifty-eight, (958.)
F. C. Humphries received fifteen hundred and fifty-two, (1,552.)
C. H. Pearce received fifteen hundred and fifty-two, (1,552.)
W. H. Holden received fifteen hundred and fifty-two, (1,552.)
T. W. Long received fifteen hundred and fifty-two, (1,552.)
The whole number of votes cast for presidential electors in the county of Monroe was as follows, viz :
Wilkinson Call received ten hundred and forty-seven, (1,047.)
James E. Yonge received ten hundred and forty-seven, (1,047.)
Robert B. Hilton received ten hundred and forty-seven, (1,047.)
Robert Bullock received ten hundred and forty-seven, (1,047.)
F. C. Humphries received nine hundred and eighty, (980.)
C. H. Pearce received nine hundred and eighty, (980.)
W. H. Holden received nine hundred and eighty, (980.)
T. W. Long received nine hundred and eighty, (980.)
The whole number of votes cast for presidential electors in the county of Nassau was as follows, viz :
Wilkinson Call received six hundred and sixty-seven, (667.)
James E. Yonge received six hundred and sixty-seven, (667.)
Robert B. Hilton received six hundred and sixty-six, (666.)
Robert Bullock received six hundred and sixty-seven, (667.)
F. C. Humphries received eight hundred and two, (802.)
C. H. Pearce received eight hundred and two, (802.)
W. H. Holden received eight hundred and two, (802.)
T. W. Long received eight hundred and two, (802.)
The whole number of votes cast for presidential electors in the county of Orange was as follows, viz :
Wilkinson Call received nine hundred and eight, (908.)
James E. Yonge received nine hundred and eight, (908.)
Robert B. Hilton received nine hundred and eight, (908.)
Robert Bullock received nine hundred and seven, (907.)
F. C. Humphries received two hundred and eight, (208.)
C. H. Pearce received two hundred and seven, (207.)
W. H. Holden received two hundred and eight, (208.)
T. W. Long received two hundred and six, (206.)
The whole number of votes cast for presidential electors in the county of Putnam was as follows, viz :
Wilkinson Call received six hundred and five, (605.)
James E. Yonge received six hundred and five, (605.)
Robert B. Hilton received six hundred and five, (605.)
Robert Bullock received six hundred and five, (605.)
F. C. Humphries received five hundred and eighty-six, (586.)
C. H. Pearce received five hundred and eighty-six, (586.)
W. H. Holden received five hundred and eighty-six, (586.)
T. W. Long received five hundred and eighty-five, (585.)
The whole number of votes cast for presidential electors in the county of Polk was as follows, viz :
Wilkinson Call received four hundred and fifty-six, (456.)
James E. Yonge received four hundred and fifty-six, (456.)
Robert B. Hilton received four hundred and fifty-six, (456.)
Robert Bullock received four hundred and fifty-six, (456.)
F. C. Humphries received six, (6.)
C. H. Pearce received six, (6.)
W. H. Holden received six, (6.)
T. W. Long received six, (6.)
The whole number of votes cast for presidential electors in the county of Santa Rosa was as follows, viz :
Wilkinson Call received seven hundred and sixty-eight, (768.)
James E. Yonge received seven hundred and sixty-eight, (768.)
Robert B. Hilton received seven hundred and sixty-eight, (768.)
Robert Bullock received seven hundred and sixty-eight, (768.)

F. C. Humphries received four hundred and nine, (409.)
C. H. Pearce received four hundred and nine, (409.)
W. H. Holden received four hundred and nine, (409.)
T. W. Long received four hundred and nine, (409.)
The whole number of votes cast for presidential electors in the county of Sumter was as follows, viz:
Wilkinson Call received five hundred and six, (506.)
James E. Yonge received five hundred and six, (506.)
Robert B. Hilton received five hundred and six, (506.)
Robert Bullock received five hundred and five, (505.)
F. C. Humphries received one hundred and seventy-three, (173.)
C. H. Pearce received one hundred and seventy-three, (173.)
W. H. Holden received one hundred and seventy-three, (173.)
T. W. Long received one hundred and seventy-three, (173.)
The whole number of votes cast for presidential electors in the county of Saint John's was as follows, viz:
Wilkinson Call received five hundred and one, (501.)
James E. Yonge received five hundred and one, (501.)
Robert B. Hilton received five hundred and one, (501.)
Robert Bullock received five hundred and one, (501.)
F. C. Humphries received three hundred and thirty-eight, (338.)
C. H. Pearce received three hundred and thirty-eight, (338.)
W. H. Holden received three hundred and thirty-eight, (338.)
T. W. Long received three hundred and thirty-eight, (338.)
The whole number of votes cast for presidential electors in the county of Suwannee was as follows, viz:
Wilkinson Call received six hundred and twenty-six, (626.)
James E. Yonge received six hundred and twenty-six, (626.)
Robert B. Hilton received six hundred and twenty-six, (626.)
Robert Bullock received six hundred and twenty-six, (626.)
F. C. Humphries received four hundred and fifty-eight, (458.)
C. H. Pearce received four hundred and fifty-eight, (458.)
W. H. Holden received four hundred and fifty-eight, (458.)
T. W. Long received four hundred and fifty-eight, (458.)
The whole vote cast for presidential electors in the county of Taylor was as follows, viz:
Wilkinson Call received two hundred and forty-two, (242.)
James E. Yonge received two hundred and forty-two, (242.)
Robert B. Hilton received two hundred and forty-two, (242.)
Robert Bullock received two hundred and forty-two, (242.)
F. C. Humphries received seventy-three, (73.)
C. H. Pearce received seventy-three, (73.)
W. H. Holden received seventy-three, (73.)
T. W. Long received seventy-three, (73.)
The whole number of votes cast for presidential electors in the county of Volusia was as follows, viz:
Wilkinson Call received four hundred and sixty, (460.)
James E. Yonge received four hundred and fifty-nine, (459.)
Robert B. Hilton received four hundred and fifty-nine, (459.)
Robert Bullock received four hundred and sixty, (460.)
F. C. Humphries received one hundred and eighty-six, (186.)
C. H. Pearce received one hundred and eighty-six, (186.)
W. H. Holden received one hundred and eighty-six, (186.)
T. W. Long received one hundred and eighty-six, (186.)
The whole number of votes cast for presidential electors in the county of Wakulla was as follows, viz:
Wilkinson Call received three hundred and sixty-one, (361.)
James E. Yonge received three hundred and sixty-one, (361.)
Robert B. Hilton received three hundred and sixty-one, (361.)
Robert Bullock received three hundred and sixty-one, (361.)
F. C. Humphries received one hundred and eighty-two, (182.)
C. H. Pearce received one hundred and eighty-two, (182.)
W. H. Holden received one hundred and eighty-two, (182.)
T. W. Long received one hundred and eighty-two, (182.)
The whole number of votes cast for presidential electors in the county of Walton was as follows:
Wilkinson Call received six hundred and twenty-six, (626.)
James E. Yonge received six hundred and twenty-eight, (628.)
Robert B. Hilton received six hundred and twenty-eight, (628.)
Robert Bullock received six hundred and twenty-eight, (628.)

F. C. Humphries received forty-six, (46.)

C. H. Pearce received forty-six, (46.)

W. H. Holden received forty-seven, (47.)

T. W. Long received forty-six, (46.)

The whole number of votes cast for presidential electors in the county of Washington was as follows, viz:

Wilkinson Call received four hundred and seven, (407.)

James E. Yonge received four hundred and seven, (407.)

Robert B. Hilton received four hundred and seven, (407.)

Robert Bullock received four hundred and seven, (407.)

F. C. Humphries received one hundred and nineteen, (119.)

C. H. Pearce received one hundred and nineteen, (119.)

W. H. Holden received one hundred and nineteen, (119.)

T. W. Long received one hundred and nineteen, (119.)

Now, therefore, we, the said W. D. Bloxham, secretary of state, Columbus Drew, comptroller, and Walter Gwynn, treasurer, constituting the board of canvassers as aforesaid, do hereby certify that, having completed said canvass in conformity to law, have ascertained and determined, and do declare and proclaim, as follows, viz:

The whole number of votes cast for presidential electors was as follows, viz:

Wilkinson Call received twenty-four thousand four hundred and thirty-seven, (24,437.)

James E. Yonge received twenty-four thousand four hundred and forty, (24,440.)

Robert B. Hilton received twenty-four thousand four hundred and thirty-seven, (24,437.)

Robert Bullock received twenty-four thousand four hundred and thirty-seven, (24,437.)

F. C. Humphries received twenty-four thousand three hundred and forty-nine, (24,349.)

C. H. Pearce received twenty-four thousand three hundred and forty-five, (24,345.)

W. H. Holden received twenty-four thousand three hundred and fifty, (24,350.)

T. W. Long received twenty-four thousand three hundred and forty-four, (24,344.)

Now, therefore, we, the said William D. Bloxham, secretary of state, Columbus Drew, comptroller of public accounts, and Walter Gwynn, treasurer, constituting the State board of canvassers as aforesaid, do hereby certify that, having completed said canvass in conformity with the provisions of said act entitled "An act to procure a legal canvass of the electoral vote of the State of Florida, as cast at the election held on the 7th day of November, A. D. 1876," we have ascertained and determined, and do hereby declare and proclaim, that, from said canvass, Wilkinson Call, James E. Yonge, Robert B. Hilton, and Robert Bullock are duly elected, chosen, and appointed electors of President and Vice-President of the United States for the State of Florida.

In testimony whereof we do hereunto affix our official signatures, at Tallahassee, this the 19th day of January, 1877.

W. D. BLOXHAM,
Secretary of State and Chairman Canvassing-Board.
C. DREW,
Comptroller Public Accounts, State of Florida.
WALTER GWYNN,
Treasurer, State of Florida.

Tabulation.

Counties.	Democratic electors.				Republican electors.				C. H. Humphries.	Marcellus L. Stearns.
	Wilkinson Call.	James E. Yonge.	Robert B. Hilton.	Robert Bullock.	F. C. Humphries.	C. H. Pearce.	W. H. Holden.	T. W. Long.		
Alachua	1,267	1,267	1,267	1,267	1,984	1,984	1,984	1,984	.....	......
Baker	238	238	218	238	143	143	143	143	.....	......
Brevard	111	111	111	111	58	58	58	58	.....	......
Bradford	703	703	703	703	202	202	202	202	.....	......
Calhoun	215	215	215	215	63	62	63	63	1	......
Columbia	903	903	903	903	718	718	718	718	.....	......
Clay	286	287	287	287	122	121	122	122	.....	.
Duval	1,436	1,437	1,437	1,437	2,367	2,366	2,367	2,366	.....	1
Dade	5	5	5	5	9	9	9	9	.....	......
Escambia	1,426	1,426	1,426	1,426	1,602	1,602	1,602	1,602	.....	......
Franklin	167	167	167	167	91	91	91	91	.....	......
Gadsden	835	835	835	835	1,300	1,300	1,300	1,300	.....	......
Hamilton	617	617	617	617	330	330	330	330	.....	......
Hernando	579	597	578	579	144	144	144	144	.....	......
Hillsborough	790	790	790	789	186	186	186	186	.....	......
Holmes	300	300	300	300	16	16	16	16	.....	......
Jackson	1,397	1,397	1,397	1,397	1,229	1,299	1,299	1,299	.....	......
Jefferson	737	737	737	737	2,660	2,660	2,660	2,660	.....	......
La Fayette	309	309	309	309	62	62	62	62	.....	......
Leon	1,003	1,003	1,003	1,003	3,035	3,035	3,035	3,035	.....	......
Levy	487	488	487	487	207	207	207	206	.....	......
Liberty	147	147	147	147	83	83	83	83	.....	......
Madison	1,078	1,078	1,078	1,078	1,524	1,524	1,524	1,524	.....	......
Manatee	262	262	262	262	26	26	26	26	.....	......
Marion	958	958	958	958	1,552	1,552	1,562	1,552	.....	......
Monroe	1,047	1,047	1,047	1,047	980	980	980	980	.....	......
Nassau	667	667	666	667	802	802	802	802	.....	......
Orange	908	908	908	907	208	207	208	206	.....	......
Putnam	605	605	605	605	586	586	586	585	.....	......
Polk	456	456	456	456	6	6	6	6	.....	......
Santa Rosa	768	768	768	768	409	409	409	409	.....	......
Sumter	506	506	506	505	173	173	173	173	.....	......
Saint John's	501	501	501	501	338	338	338	338	.....	......
Suwannee	626	626	626	626	458	458	458	458	.....	......
Taylor	242	242	242	242	73	73	73	73	.....	......
Volusia	460	459	459	460	186	186	186	186	.....	......
Wakulla	361	361	361	361	182	182	182	182	.....	......
Walton	626	628	628	628	46	46	47	46	.....	......
Washington	407	407	407	407	119	119	119	119	.....	......

TOTAL RESULT.

Wilkinson Call	24,437	F. C. Humphries	24,349
J. E. Yonge	24,440	C. H. Pearce	24,345
R. B. Hilton	24,437	W. H. Holden	24,350
Robert Bullock	24,437	T. W. Long	24,344

OFFICE OF THE SECRETARY OF STATE,
　　　Tallahassee, Florida:

I, W. D. Bloxham, secretary of state of the State of Florida, do hereby certify that the foregoing is a true and correct copy of the certificate of the board of State canvassers, at a canvass of the votes cast at the election held on the 7th day of November, A. D. 1876, for electors of President and Vice-President of the United States, for and on behalf of the State of Florida, and of the result thereof, as the same appears of record in my office.

In attestation whereof I hereunto set my hand and affix the seal of my office, at Tallahassee, the capitol, this twenty-sixth day of January, A. D. 1877.

　　　　　　　　　　　　　　　　　W. D. BLOXHAM,
　　　　　　　　　　　　　　　　　Secretary of State.

EXECUTIVE OFFICE,
　　　Tallahassee, Florida:

I, George F. Drew, governor of the State of Florida, do hereby certify that the above attestation of W. D. Bloxham, secretary of state of the State of Florida, is in due form, and that it is made by the proper officer, to whose act as such full faith and credit are due.

In testimony whereof I have hereunto set my hand and caused the great seal of the State to be affixed, at the capitol, at Tallahassee, this 26th day of January, A. D. 1877.

[SEAL.]

GEO. F. DREW,

Governor.

An act to declare and establish the appointment by the State of Florida of electors of President and Vice-President.

Whereas at the general election held in this State on the 7th of November, 1876, according to the returns from the several counties on file in the office of the secretary of state, and according to a canvass and a statement and a certification thereof, made by the secretary of state, treasurer, and comptroller of public accounts, under an act of this legislature, entitled "An act to procure a legal canvass of the electoral vote of the State of Florida, as cast at the election held on the 7th day of November, A. D. 1876,"

Robert Bullock received twenty-four thousand four hundred and thirty-seven votes for the office of elector of President and Vice-President of the United States,

Robert B. Hilton received twenty-four thousand four hundred and thirty-seven votes for the said office,

Wilkinson Call received twenty-four thousand four hundred and thirty-seven votes for the said office,

James E. Yonge received twenty-four thousand four hundred and forty votes for the said office,

Charles H. Pearce received twenty-four thousand three hundred and forty-five votes for the said office,

Frederick C. Humphries received twenty-four thousand three hundred and forty-nine votes for the said office,

William H. Holden received twenty-four thousand three hundred and fifty votes for the said office,

Thomas W. Long received twenty-four thousand three hundred and forty-four votes for the said office ;

And whereas, as shown by the said returns, the said Robert Bullock, Robert B. Hilton, Wilkinson Call, and James E. Yonge were duly chosen and appointed electors of President and Vice-President of the United States by the State of Florida, in such manner as the legislature of the said State had directed ;

And whereas the board of State canvassers constituted under the act approved February 27, 1872, did interpret the laws of this State defining the powers and duties of the said board in such manner as to give them power to exclude certain regular returns, and did, in fact, under such interpretation, exclude certain of such regular returns, which said interpretation has been adjudged by the supreme court to be erroneous and illegal ;

And whereas the late governor, Marcellus L. Stearns, by reason of said illegal action and erroneous and illegal canvass of the said board of State canvassers, did erroneously cause to be made and certified lists of the names of the electors of this State containing the names of the said Charles H. Pearce, Frederick C. Humphries, William H. Holden, and Thomas W. Long, and did deliver such lists to said persons, when in fact the said persons had not received the highest number of votes, and on a canvass conducted according to the rules prescribed and adjudged as legal by the supreme court, were not appointed as electors or entitled to receive such lists from the governor, but Robert Bullock, Robert B. Hilton, Wilkinson Call, and James E. Yonge were duly appointed electors, and were entitled to have their names compose the lists made and certified by the governor, and to have such lists delivered to them :

Now, therefore, the people of the State of Florida, represented in senate and assembly, do enact as follows:

SECTION 1. That Robert Bullock, Robert B. Hilton, Wilkinson Call, and James E. Yonge were, on the 7th day of November, 1876, duly chosen and appointed by and on behalf of the State of Florida, in such manner as the legislature thereof has directed, electors of President and Vice-President of the United States, and were, from the said 7th day of November, 1876, and are, authorized and entitled to exercise all the powers and duties of the office of electors as aforesaid, and had full power and authority, on the 6th day of December, 1876, to vote as such electors for President and Vice-President of the United States, and to certify and transmit their votes as provided by law, and their acts as such electors are hereby ratified, confirmed, and declared to be valid to all intents and purposes ; and the said Robert Bullock, Robert B. Hilton, Wilkinson Call, and James E. Yonge are hereby appointed such electors as on and from and after the said 7th day of November, 1876.

SEC. 2. The governor of this State is hereby authorized and directed to make and certify in due form, under the great seal of this State, three lists of the names of the said electors, to wit, Robert Bullock, Robert B. Hilton, Wilkinson Call, and James E.

Yonge, and to transmit the same, with an authenticated copy of this act, to the President of the Senate of the United States; and said lists and certificates shall be as valid and effectual to authenticate in behalf of this State the appointment of such electors by this State as if they had been made and delivered on or before the 6th day of December, 1876, and had been transmitted immediately thereafter, and the lists and certificates containing the names of Charles H. Pearce, Frederick C. Humphries, William H. Holden, and Thomas W. Long are hereby declared to be illegal and void.

SEC. 3. The governor of this State is further authorized and required to cause three other lists of the names of said electors, to wit, Robert Bullock, Robert B. Hilton, Wilkinson Call, and James E. Yonge, to be made and certified, and forthwith delivered to the said electors; and the said electors shall thereupon meet at the capitol in Tallahasse, and make and sign three additional certificates of all the votes given by them on the said sixth day of December, each of which certificates shall contain two distinct lists, one of the votes for President and the other of the votes for Vice-President, and annex to each of the certificates one of the lists of the electors which shall have been furnished to them by the governor pursuant to this section, and the certificates so made shall be sealed up, certified, and one of them transmitted by messenger and the other by mail to the President of the Senate, and the third delivered to the judge of the district, as required by law.

SEC. 4. An authenticated copy of this act shall be transmitted by the secretary of state to the President of the Senate of the United States, and another copy to the Speaker of the House of Representatives of the United States.

SEC. 5. This act shall take effect from and after its passage.

Approved *January 26*, 1877.

OFFICE OF THE SECRETARY OF STATE,
Tallahassee, Florida:

I, W. D. Bloxham, secretary of state of the State of Florida, do hereby certify that the foregoing is a true and correct copy of the original on file in my office.

In testimony whereof I have hereunto set my hand and affixed the great seal of the State. Done at Tallahassee, the capital, this 26th day of January, A. D. 1877.

[SEAL.]   W. D. BLOXHAM,
                                                                Secretary of State.

The PRESIDING OFFICER. Are there objections to the certificates from the State of Florida?

Mr. Representative FIELD. The following is an objection to the votes, certificates, and lists mentioned in the return first read. I send it to the desk.

The PRESIDING OFFICER, (having examined the paper sent up.) The objection complies with the law, having attached the signatures of Senators and Representatives. The Clerk of the House will read the objection.

The Clerk of the House read as follows:

OBJECTION TO No. 1.

The undersigned, Charles W. Jones, Senator of the United States from the State of Florida; Henry Cooper, Senator of the United States from the State of Tennessee; J. E. McDonald, Senator of the United States from the State of Indiana; David Dudley Field, Representative from the State of New York; J. Randolph Tucker, Representative from the State of Virginia; G. A. Jenks, Representative from the State of Pennsylvania, and William M. Springer, Representative from the State of Illinois, object to the counting of the votes of Charles H. Pearce, Frederick C. Humphries, William H. Holden, and Thomas W. Long as electors of President and Vice-President of the United States in, for, or on behalf of the State of Florida; and to the paper purporting to be a certificate of M. L. Stearns, as governor of the said State, that the said Charles H. Pearce, Frederick C. Humphries, William H. Holden, and Thomas W. Long were appointed electors in, for, or on behalf of the said State; and to the papers purporting to be the lists of votes cast by the said Charles H. Pearce, Frederick C. Humphries, William H. Holden, and Thomas W. Long for President and Vice-President of the United States; and to the votes themselves, in the reasons and upon the grounds following, among others, that is to say:

1. For that the said Charles H. Pearce, Frederick C. Humphries, William H. Holden, and Thomas W. Long were not appointed by the said State of Florida in such manner

as its legislature had directed, or in any manner whatever, electors of President and Vice-President of the United States.

2. For that Wilkinson Call, James E. Yonge, Robert B. Hilton, and Robert Bullock were appointed by the said State in such manner as its legislature had directed electors of President and Vice-President of the United States.

3. The manner of appointing electors of President and Vice-President of the United States in, for, or on behalf of the State of Florida was by the votes of the qualified electors at a general election held in said State on the 7th day of November, 1876 ; and the qualified electors of the said State did, on the said 7th day of November, 1876, execute the power by appointing Wilkinson Call, James E. Yonge, Robert B. Hilton, and Robert Bullock to be such electors, which appointment gave to the appointees an irrevocable title that could not be changed, or set aside, or conferred on any other person.

4. For that the pretended certificate, or paper purporting to be a certificate, signed by M. L. Stearns, as governor of said State, of the appointment of Charles H. Pearce, Frederick C. Humphries, William H. Holden, and Thomas W. Long to be electors, was and is in all respects untrue, and was corruptly procured and made in pursuance of a conspiracy between the said M. L. Stearns, the said Charles H. Pearce, Frederick C. Humphries, William H. Holden, and Thomas W. Long, and other persons to these objectors unknown, with intent to deprive the people of the said State of their right to appoint electors, and to deprive Wilkinson Call, James E. Yonge, Robert B. Hilton, and Robert Bullock of their title to said office, and to assert and set up fictitious and unreal votes for President and Vice-President, and thereby to deceive the proper authorities of this Union.

5. For that the said papers, falsely purporting to be the votes for President and Vice-President of the State of Florida, which are now here objected to, are fictitious and unreal, and do not truly represent any votes or lawful acts, and were made out and executed in pursuance of the same fraudulent conspiracy by the said persons purporting to have cast said votes.

6. For that the said pretended certificate, and the pretended lists of electors connected therewith, so made by the said M. L. Stearns, if the said certificates and lists ever had any validity, which these objectors deny, have been annulled and declared void by a subsequent lawful certificate of the executive of the State of Florida, duly and lawfully made, in which the said Wilkinson Call, Robert Bullock, James E. Yonge, and Robert B. Hilton are truly and in due form declared to have been duly appointed by the said State in the manner directed by its constitution, and also by an act of the legislature of the said State, in which the title of the said Wilkinson Call, James E. Yonge, Robert B. Hilton, and Robert Bullock as such electors is declared to be good and valid, and, further, by the judgment of the circuit court of the said State of Florida for the second judicial circuit, that being a court of competent jurisdiction, upon an information in the nature of *quo warranto* brought on the 6th day of December, 1876, before said pretended electors in any form voted for President or Vice-President, as aforesaid, by the State of Florida on the relation of the said Wilkinson Call, Robert Bullock, James E. Yonge, and Robert E. Hilton against the said Charles H. Pearce, Frederick C. Humphries, William H. Holden, and Thomas W. Long, whereby the defendants, after having appeared, pleaded, and put in issue the question of their own right and title, and that of the relators, to act as such electors, and after full hearing, it was duly and lawfully adjudged by said court that the said Charles H. Pearce, Frederick C. Humphries, William H. Holden, and Thomas W. Long were not, nor was any one of them, elected, chosen, or appointed, or entitled to be declared elected, chosen, or appointed, as such electors or elector, or to receive certificates or certificate of election, or appointment, as such electors or elector ; and that the said respondents were not, upon the said 6th day of December, or at any other time, entitled to assume or exercise any of the powers and functions of such electors or elector, but that they were, upon the said day and date, mere usurpers, and that all and singular their acts and doings as such were and are illegal, null, and void.

And it was further considered and adjudged that the said relators, Robert Bullock, Robert B. Hilton, Wilkinson Call, and James E. Yonge, all and singular, were, at said election, duly elected, chosen, and appointed electors of President and Vice-President of the United States ; and were, on the said 6th day of December, 1876, entitled to be declared elected, chosen, and appointed said electors, and to have and receive certificates thereof, and upon the said day and date, and at all times since, to exercise and perform all and singular the powers and duties of such electors, and to have and enjoy the pay and emoluments thereof.

For that the four persons last named did, as such electors, on December 6, 1876, cast the four votes of Florida for Mr. Tilden as President and Mr. Hendricks as Vice-President ; and, as well in that respect as in all others, acting in entire and perfect conformity with the Constitution of the United States, they certified the same votes to the President of the Senate.

They did everything toward the authentication of such votes required by the Constitution of the United States or by any act of Congress, except the section 136 of the Revised Statutes. And, in conformity with the aforesaid judgment of the Florida court, a governor of Florida who had been duly inducted into office subsequently to December 6, 1876, did, on the 26th day of January, 1877, give to the last-named four electors the triplicate lists prescribed by said act of Congress, (R. S. of U. S., § 136,) which they forwarded, as prescribed by the acts of Congress, as a supplement to their former certification in that behalf.

And in support of the said objections and claims, the undersigned beg leave to refer to the reasons and documents submitted herewith, and to such petitions, depositions, papers, and evidence as may be hereafter produced, and as may be competent and pertinent in considering the said objections and claims.

Among the papers herewith submitted are the following:

1st. So much of the official Congressional Record of February 1, 1877, as contains the report of the House committee on the recent election in Florida.

2d. The original report of said committee.

3d. The certified copy of the act of the legislature of Florida, approved January 17, 1877, entitled "An act to procure a legal canvass of the electoral vote of the State of Florida as cast at the election held on the seventh (7th) day of November, 1876."

4th. The certificate of the State canvassers of the election held November 7, 1876, dated January 19, 1877.

5th. The certified copy of the act of the legislature of Florida, approved January 26, 1877, entitled "An act to declare and establish the appointment by the State of Florida of electors of President and Vice-President."

6th. The certificate of George F. Drew, governor of the State of Florida, of the names of the electors chosen on the 7th day of November, 1876, bearing date January 26, 1877.

7th. The certificate of Wilkinson Call, James E. Yonge, Robert Bullock, and Robert B. Hilton, electors appointed by the State of Florida, of the votes cast for President and Vice-President by them, bearing date January 26, 1877.

8th. The record of the proceedings and judgment of the circuit court of Leon County, second judicial circuit, State of Florida, on the information in the nature of *quo warranto* in the name of the State of Florida *ex rel.* Wilkinson Call, Robert Bullock, Robert B. Hilton, and James E. Yonge *vs.* Charles H. Pearce, F. C. Humphries, W. H. Holden, and T. W. Long.

Also, the certified copy of the act of the legislature of Florida, approved January 26, 1877, aforesaid, and the certificate of State canvassers, aforesaid, and the proceedings and judgment on the information aforesaid, transmitted to and received by the House of Representatives on the 31st day of January, 1877.

CHAS. W. JONES.
HENRY COOPER.
J. E. McDONALD.
DAVID DUDLEY FIELD.
J. R. TUCKER.
G. A. JENKS.
WILLIAM M. SPRINGER.

WASHINGTON, *February* 1, 1877.

The PRESIDING OFFICER. Are there further objections to the certificates from the State of Florida?

Mr. Senator SARGENT. In behalf of certain Senators and members of the House of Representatives who have signed the same, I present three papers containing objections, the first one of which I send to the Clerk's desk and ask to have now read.

The Secretary of the Senate read as follows:

OBJECTION TO No. 2.

An objection is interposed to the certificates, or papers purporting to be certificates, of the electoral votes of the State of Florida, as having been cast by James E. Yonge, Wilkinson Call, Robert B. Hilton, and Robert Bullock, upon the ground that the said certificates or papers are not authenticated according to the requirements of the Constitution and laws of the United States, so as to entitle them to be received or read, or votes stated therein, or any of them, to be counted, in the election of President of the United States or of Vice-President of the United States.

S. B. CONOVER,
A. A. SARGENT,
JOHN SHERMAN,
H. M. TELLER,
Senators.
WILLIAM WOODBURN,
MARK H. DUNNELL,
JOHN A. KASSON,
GEO. W. McCRARY,
Members House of Representatives.

The other papers presented by Senator SARGENT as objections were read by the Secretary of the Senate, as follows:

OBJECTION TO NO. 2.

An objection is interposed to the certificates, or papers purporting to be certificates, of the electoral vote of the State of Florida, as having been cast by James E. Yonge, Wilkinson Call, Robert B. Hilton, and Robert Bullock, upon the ground that said certificates or papers do not include, and are not accompanied by, in the package or inclosure in which they are produced and opened by the President of the Senate in the presence of the two Houses of Congress, any certificate of the executive authority of the State of Florida of the list of the names of said electors, James E. Yonge, Wilkinson Call, Robert B. Hilton, and Robert Bullock, or of any of them, as being said electors. Nor are said certificates or papers objected to accompanied by any valid or lawful certification or authentication of said electors, James E. Yonge, Wilkinson Call, Robert B. Hilton, and Robert Bullock, or any of them, as having been appointed, or as being electors to cast the electoral vote of the State of Florida, or entitling the votes of said James E. Yonge, Wilkinson Call, Robert B. Hilton, and Robert Bullock, or of either of them, to be counted in the election of President of the United States or of Vice-President of the United States.

S. B. CONOVER,
A. A. SARGENT,
JOHN SHERMAN,
H. M. TELLER,
Senators.
WILLIAM WOODBURN,
MARK H. DUNNELL,
GEO. W. McCRARY,
JOHN A. KASSON,
Members House of Representatives.

OBJECTION TO NOS. 2 AND 3.

An objection is interposed to the certificates, or papers purporting to be certificates, of the electoral votes of the State of Florida, as having been cast by James E. Yonge, Wilkinson Call, Robert B. Hilton, and Robert Bullock, upon the ground that, by a certificate of the electoral vote of the State of Florida, in all respects regular and valid and sufficient under the Constitution and laws of the United States, and duly authenticated as such and duly transmitted to and received by and opened by the President of the Senate in the presence of the two Houses of Congress, it appears that Frederick C. Humphreys, Charles H. Pearce, Thomas W. Long, and William H. Holden, and each of them, and no other person or persons, were duly appointed electors to cast the electoral vote of the State of Florida, and that said above-named electors did duly cast the electoral vote of the State of Florida and did duly certify and did transmit the said electoral vote of the State of Florida to the President of the Senate, by reason whereof the said certificates or papers purporting to be certificates objected to are not entitled to be received or read, nor are the votes therein stated, or any of them, entitled to be counted, in the election of President of the United States or of Vice-President of the United States.

S. B. CONOVER,
A. A. SARGENT,
JOHN SHERMAN,
H. M. TELLER,
Senators.
WILLIAM WOODBURN,
MARK H. DUNNELL,
GEO. W. McCRARY,
JOHN A. KASSON,
Members House of Representatives.

The PRESIDING OFFICER. Are there further objections to the certificates from the State of Florida?

Mr. Representative KASSON. I present a further objection, duly signed by members of the Senate and House of Representatives, to the last paper purporting to be a certificate read at the Clerk's desk.

The Clerk of the House read as follows:

OBJECTION TO NO. 3.

The undersigned object to the last paper read, purporting to be a certificate of electors and of electoral votes of the State of Florida, and to the counting of the votes named therein:

1st. Because the same is not certified as required by the Constitution and laws of the United States—the certificate being by an officer not holding the office of governor or any other office in said State with authority in the premises at the time when the electors were appointed, nor at the time when the functions of the electors were exercised, nor until the duties of electors had been fully discharged by the lawful college of electors having the certificates of the governor of Florida at the time, and the action of said lawful college duly transmitted to the President of the Senate as required by law.

2d. Because the proceedings as recited therein as certifying the qualifications of the persons therein claiming to be electors are *ex post facto*, and are not competent under the law as certifying any right in the said Call, Yonge, Hilton, and Bullock, to cast the electoral vote of the said State of Florida.

3d. Because the said proceedings and certificates are null and void of effect as retroactive proceedings.

A. A. SARGENT,
JOHN SHERMAN,
Senators.
JOHN A. KASSON, *M. C.*
S. A. HURLBUT, *H. R.*

The PRESIDING OFFICER. Are there any further objections to the certificates from the State of Florida?

Mr. Senator JONES, of Florida. I send up to be read a further objection.

The Secretary of the Senate read as follows:

OBJECTION TO ELECTOR HUMPHREYS.

The undersigned object to the counting of the vote of F. C. Humphreys as an elector from the State of Florida, upon the ground that the said Humphreys was appointed a shipping-commissioner under the Government of the United States at Pensacola, Florida, heretofore, sct., on the 3d day of December, 1872, and qualified as such thereafter, sct., on the 9th day of December, 1872, and continued to hold the said office continuously from the said last-named day until and upon the 7th day of November, 1876, and thereafter until and upon the 6th day of December, 1876. Wherefore, and by reason of the premises, the said F. C. Humphreys held, at the time of his alleged appointment as an elector for the said State, and at the time of casting his vote as elector therefor, an office of trust and profit under the United States, and could not be constitutionally appointed an elector as aforesaid.

CHAS. W. JONES,
Of the Senate.
CHARLES P. THOMPSON,
Of the House.

The PRESIDING OFFICER. Are there further objections to the certificates from the State of Florida? [A pause.] If there are none, the certificates and papers, together with other papers accompanying the same, as well as the objections presented, will now be transmitted to the electoral commission for judgment and decision. And the Senate will now withdraw to its chamber.

Accordingly (at three o'clock and five minutes p. m.) the Senate withdrew.

ELECTORAL COMMISSION.

THE FLORIDA CASE.

THURSDAY, *February* 1, 1877.

The Commission met at 3 o'clock p. m., pursuant to adjournment.

Present, the President and Commissioners Miller, Field, Strong, Bradley, Edmunds, Morton, Frelinghuysen, Thurman, Bayard, Payne, Hunton, Abbott, Hoar, and Garfield.

The journal of the preceding sessions was read, corrected, and approved.

Mr. GEORGE C. GORHAM, Secretary of the Senate, appeared (at 3 o'clock and 15 minutes p. m.) and submitted a communication from the President of the Senate presiding over the two Houses of Congress in joint meeting.

The communication was received and handed to the Secretary of the Commission, who read it as follows:

HALL OF THE HOUSE OF REPRESENTATIVES,
February 1, 1877.

To the President of the Commission:

More than one return or paper purporting to be a return or certificate of electoral votes of the State of Florida having been received and this day opened in the presence of the two Houses of Congress, and objections thereto having been made, the said returns, with all accompanying papers, and also the objections thereto, are herewith submitted to the judgment and decision of the Commission, as provided by law.

T. W. FERRY,
President of the Senate.

Mr. Commissioner BRADLEY. Mr. President, I understand there are three certificates from the State of Florida that have been sent to us. I should think that the proper course would be to have those three certificates read, and then as each is read let the parties be called upon to state whether it is objected to and who are the objectors. Until we read those certificates, or hear them read, we do not know what we have before us. After that it will be time to take such other order in regard to proceeding as may be necessary.

The PRESIDENT. I will adopt that suggestion without a vote.

Mr. Commissioner MILLER. I had the pleasure, sir, if it was a pleasure, of listening to the reading of those documents in the House of Representatives. If the papers about the State of Florida are read, it will take an hour to read them. The objectors' names are to the papers making the objections. I presume they will be printed; they certainly ought to be printed; and then everybody can read them without our consuming an hour of time in doing that which every man will want to do for himself more carefully. I think if Brother Bradley had known as I do the length of these papers, he would perhaps withdraw his motion.

The PRESIDENT. Does Justice Bradley withdraw his motion?

Mr. Commissioner BRADLEY. I did not make a motion; I merely made a suggestion.

Mr. Commissioner PAYNE. Now I move that the certificates, with the papers, be printed at as early an hour as possible.

The PRESIDENT. The motion before the Commission is that the three certificates in the case of Florida be printed, and the objections thereto. If that is your pleasure you will say ay, [putting the question.] It is a vote.

Mr. Commissioner FIELD. Should we not have copies of the papers presented?

The PRESIDENT. I suppose the certificates and objections may be printed in a very short time. The Secretary will understand that the motion is intended to include the certificates and the objections and the papers that accompany the certificates, and nothing else. It is desirable that they should be printed with as little delay as possible.

That matter being disposed of, I am requested to inquire if there are counsel present who will take part after the managers or objectors have stated the case on the one side and the other.

Mr. EVARTS. Mr. President, Mr. Senator Sargent has come in and will state what he has to say in that regard.

The PRESIDENT. I will withdraw the inquiry as put, and say to Mr. Sargent that inquiries have been made as to the objectors.

Mr. Senator SARGENT. The objectors on our side, the persons whose names are signed to the papers, are Senators Conover, Sargent, Sherman, and Teller, and Mr. McCrary, Mr. Kasson, Mr. Woodburn, and Mr. Dunnell, Members of the House. There has been no opportunity up to this moment of consulting with these gentlemen to ascertain which of them will state their objections to the Commission.

The PRESIDENT. Two objectors may represent the case in this tribunal.

Mr. Senator SARGENT. So we understand by the rules.

The PRESIDENT. Who are the two?

Mr. Senator SARGENT. There has been no opportunity to consult to ascertain which of the objectors will present the matter to the court.

The PRESIDENT. Please make it known to the Commission as soon as convenient.

Mr. Senator SARGENT. We will.

The PRESIDENT. Will Mr. Field state the names of the objectors on the other side?

Mr. Representative FIELD. The objectors to the first return are Senators Jones of Florida, McDonald, and Cooper, and Representatives Thompson, Jenks, Tucker, Springer, and myself.

Mr. Commissioner ABBOTT. Mr. President, I desire to inquire whether the motion made in reference to printing covers the printing of all papers that are sent here with the objections, because it seems to me that we are to consider all papers sent with the objections, and it is just as material for us to have those papers printed, so that we can consider them, as it is to have the objections themselves.

The PRESIDENT. I do not understand the vote in that way at present. It is that the certificates, with the objections and the papers which accompany the certificates, shall be printed; not all the papers that may have been sent.

Mr. Commissioner ABBOTT. I suggest, then, that at some point of time, if we are to consider the papers accompanying the objections, they may be so made part of the cause. The objections themselves would hardly be understood without the papers; and we should have those papers printed, or put in some form that we can act on them.

The PRESIDENT. There is no motion on that subject.

Mr. Commissioner ABBOTT. I move, then, that the papers accompanying the objections be also printed.

Mr. Commissioner EDMUNDS. Mr. President, I submit that it is possible under the statute under which we are acting that there may be no papers, lawfully and within the statute, accompanying an objection. The statute provides for papers that accompany certificates; but, as I remember at this moment—I speak subject of course to correction—it does not provide for papers accompanying the objections; so that I think it will be a matter for the consideration of the Commission in consultation how far in printing the testimony that may be offered, whether by objectors or anybody else, we ought to go. It may be a question for consideration whether time would warrant us in receiving and printing everything that may be proposed on either side.

Mr. Commissioner THURMAN. Mr. President, it is true that the statute requires the papers accompanying certificates to be laid before the Commission; but it also authorizes the Commission to take into view all documents, depositions, and other papers that may be competent and pertinent in this inquiry; and, if we have received papers from either of the Houses which in the estimation of the Houses it is proper to send to us, it seems to me we must look at them and see whether they are competent and pertinent. I think, therefore, that the motion to print ought to be adopted. That will not delay us in having by to-morrow morning, as early as we see fit to meet, a print of the certificates and the objections. We can give directions that they shall be sent to us immediately; and the printing of these other papers could go on; and, knowing the great rapidity with which work is done at the Government Printing-Office, I do not think we should have to wait very long to get them all.

Mr. Commissioner ABBOTT. Mr. President, I think on looking at the law that objections only are to be sent here; and I fancy that those papers, if they are sent here at all, must come as part of the objections, so that perhaps the motion to print the objections would carry with it, necessarily, the printing of those papers. I do not see how they get here except as papers accompanying the certificates or as part of the objections. Of course, I have no desire to impede the printing of the objections and certificates, but I wish to get them as soon as possible.

Mr. Commissioner EDMUNDS. Mr. President, in order that we may consider that topic, I move that the motion of Judge Abbott be for the time being laid upon the table, so that we may consider about it a little afterward.

The PRESIDENT. The motion is to lay the motion of Judge Abbott upon the table.

Mr. Commissioner ABBOTT. I withdraw the motion for the time, to be renewed at a subsequent time.

The PRESIDENT. The motion is withdrawn. [A pause.] I am requested now to call for the names of counsel who appear in the case on each side.

Mr. Representative FIELD. We have several counsel on our side. We have Mr. O'Conor of New York, Judge Black of Pennsylvania, Judge Trumbull of Illinois, Mr. Merrick of Washington, and Mr. Green of New Jersey.

The PRESIDENT. Counsel not exceeding two in number on each side are allowed to participate in argument.

Mr. Representative FIELD. We have not selected those two. I only mention to you in answer to the question how many there are who are concerned in the case. We shall arrange that matter in the course of the evening.

The PRESIDENT. That will answer. Who are counsel on the other side?

Mr. EVARTS. As representing objectors to other certificates than those that have been represented in the enumeration by Mr. Field, I will state that Mr. Stoughton, Mr. Stanley Matthews, Mr. Shellabarger, and myself are expected to represent objectors in some of the cases which will appear, and I would ask the instruction of the court—it is pertinent now to make the inquiry—as to what is included in the phrase "on the merits of any case presented to it;" whether that means any issue joined on objections to any particular certificate or whether it includes all that arises in the case of a particular State.

The PRESIDENT. I think the counsel will have to judge of that matter for themselves. Unless they have some question to submit to the Commission, it is hardly within the province of the Presiding Justice to determine that.

Mr. EVARTS. We understand, then, if the Commission please, that the designation of two counsel will be sufficiently early enough made when the case is up?

Mr. Commissioner EDMUNDS. That is merely for the final argument.

The PRESIDENT. After the objectors have opened the case.

Mr. EVARTS. So we understand.

Mr. Commissioner BRADLEY. I suggest to Mr. Evarts that probably the construction of that would be "the case on its merits;" the principal question would be included in that term; and all interlocutory or other motions would not be included in that phrase.

Mr. Commissioner EDMUNDS. It covers the whole subject of a particular State.

Mr. Senator SARGENT. In reply to the question of the Commission as to which of the objectors would present the case on behalf of the objectors to certificates Nos. 2 and 3, aside from counsel, on conference it is determined that Mr. McCrary and Mr. Kasson will so appear.

Mr. Commissioner EDMUNDS. I move that the public sitting of the Commission be now adjourned until half past ten in the morning unless counsel or objectors have something further to say at this present time.

Mr. Commissioner GARFIELD. I think there was one objection filed that no action has been taken in regard to—an objection, I believe from Senator Jones; and as I have heard the President of the Commission make no allusion to it, I inquire whether there is any special hearing on that objection. I think it was different from the other objections which have been filed. I refer to it because it makes a distinct case, being a different objection in its character from either of the other two that have been referred to.

The PRESIDENT. My impression is—although I do not make that decision in behalf of the Commission—that the several objections to the returns from a State constitute one case, and two objectors will be heard upon one side and two on the other; and after they shall have been heard, two counsel will be heard upon one side and two upon the other. Unless otherwise advised by the Commission, that will be the ruling.

Mr. Representative FIELD. Will you allow me to say that perhaps there may be some misunderstanding in regard to that rule unless I state to you precisely the facts?

The PRESIDENT. Proceed, sir.

Mr. Representative FIELD. There are objections to the 4 votes of Florida on each side; that is to say, we object to the 4 votes mentioned in the first return——

Mr. Commissioner EDMUNDS. Which are they?

Mr. Representative FIELD. They are, if I may use the names of the candidates, the Hayes electors. We object on our part to those votes, certificates, and lists.

Mr. Commissioner EDMUNDS. And the other gentlemen object to the others?

Mr. Representative FIELD. Mr. Sargent, Mr. Kasson, and the gentlemen on the other side specifically object to ours. Then there is the additional objection made by Senator Jones, of Florida, and others, to one of the Hayes electors as ineligible under the Constitution. That is a distinct matter, and we supposed it would be taken up quite distinctly. It is a minor affair and should not encumber the principal one. And if the Commission will allow us, we will designate Mr. Thompson and Mr. Jenks. I suppose the discussion of that will not take up much of the time of the Commission; but at all events, as a matter of form, if you will allow us, we will suggest that Mr. Thompson and Mr. Jenks be the objectors in those, and then as to counsel we will advise to-night and inform the Commission to-morrow what counsel represent us.

The PRESIDENT. When you are advised what you desire, you will submit a motion to the Commission and I will have it determined. At present. I am not prepared to rule otherwise than I have. If there be no further suggestion to be presented, I will put the question to the Commission on the motion that when this Commission adjourns it adjourn to meet at half past ten o'clock to morrow morning.

Mr. Commissioner EDMUNDS. I will move—so that we shall not keep here gentlemen who wish to prepare their matters—that the public sittings of the Commission be now adjourned until half past ten o'clock to morrow.

Mr. Commissioner THURMAN. But the Commission to continue in session?

Mr. Commissioner EDMUNDS. Yes, for consultation.

The PRESIDENT. Under the circumstances I will put the motion, with the consent of the mover, that when the Commission adjourns it adjourn until to-morrow at half past ten o'clock.

The motion was agreed to.

The PRESIDENT. I will notify all who are present that there will be no more public business transacted by the Commission to-day.

Mr. Commissioner FRELINGHUYSEN. I was about to suggest that it would be well to understand from the objectors and counsel whether they will be prepared to go on to-morrow morning.

Mr. Representative FIELD. On our part we are prepared to go on at any moment—to go on now if you wish.

The PRESIDENT. The gentlemen present may understand that there will be no further public business transacted by the Commission to-day. The Commission will remain for private consultation.

The room having been cleared, the Commission remained for consultation.

On motion of Mr. Commissioner EDMUNDS, it was—

Ordered, That Mr. Abbott and Mr. Hoar be a committee to consider and report whether certain papers referred to in the objections of C. W. Jones and others ought to be printed for the use of the Commission.

On motion of Mr. Commissioner HOAR, it was

Ordered, That no action be taken by the committee referred to in the resolution of Mr. Commissioner Edmunds until the next meeting of the Commission for consultation.

Mr. Commissioner MILLER moved that the objections to certificates in the Florida case be heard as one objection to each set of electors, and be argued together; which was adopted.

The Secretary of the Commission, on motion of Mr. Commissioner EDMUNDS, was directed to prepare and have printed on slips the names of the members of the Commission in alphabetical order for the purpose of being used in taking the votes.

Mr. Commissioner HOAR moved that the Secretary have printed for the use of the Commission such laws as may be directed by the President of the Commission.

Mr. Commissioner MORTON moved an amendment to include the election-laws of the States of Florida, Louisiana, Oregon, and South Carolina.

The amendment was agreed to.

The motion, as amended, was agreed to.

On motion of Mr. Commissioner STRONG, (at four o'clock and forty-five minutes p. m.,) the Commission adjourned.

FRIDAY, *February* 2, 1877.

The Commission met at half past ten o'clock a. m., pursuant to ad-journment, all the members being present.

The journal of yesterday was read and approved.

The PRESIDENT. The case before the Commission is that of Florida. Inquiries were made yesterday "what is the case?" to which I beg leave to respond that it consists of three certificates with the accompanying papers, and the objections to the same. Two of the objectors on each side will be allowed to speak in the opening of the case. Those representing the objections to certificate No. 1 will speak first, and I would remind them that the fourth rule allows them two hours in which they will state the case in the opening arguments in support of their objections, and also in support of any other certificate which they claim to be valid. When they have concluded, two objectors on the other side will speak under the same rules and limitations. I will not give any direction now as to counsel; that will come afterward.

Mr. Representative FIELD. Allow me to ask whether after the two objectors have spoken on the other side, we shall not be allowed the opportunity of a reply within our two hours?

The PRESIDENT. The rules make no provision for any reply on the part of the objectors. Applications for further time or further counsel must be made to the Commission, the Presiding Justice having no dis-cretion in the matter whatever. When counsel speak, it will be under different regulations; perhaps they need not be stated now; but as it seems that I am rather expected to state it, I will say that my view is that one of the counsel in favor of the objections to certificate No. 1 should open; two counsel in favor of the certificate No. 1 and against the objections should reply; and then the other counsel in favor of the objections to certificate No. 1 should have the close.

Mr. Representative TUCKER. May I ask whether the two hours of the objectors to the first-named certificate must be consumed in the opening?

The PRESIDENT. If at all. There is no provision made for a reply. One of the objectors to certificate No. 1 may proceed. I am told that some time would be spent in reading the certificates and accompanying papers and the objections, if they were read; but they will soon be printed and laid on our tables, and it is suggested that unless it produces inconvenience the statement or opening should proceed without read-ing the papers. If it is desired I will direct that they shall be read, though I understand the reading will consume some time. If that is not desired, the statement of the case will proceed.

Mr. Representative KASSON. If the Commission please, I ought to state on behalf of the objectors on this side that, while we have no objection to the proceeding this morning as far as the objectors to the first certificate are concerned, my associate and myself find that so many more questions are involved in the objections to that certificate than it was supposed would be found—we not having had the oppor-tunity to examine them until this morning—that it is probable we shall be obliged to ask the court for some time before proceeding on our behalf.

I make that statement now, not desiring to object to gentlemen going on this morning who are ready, but simply to save our right to make that suggestion to the tribunal at the completion of the argument on that side on behalf of the objectors.

The PRESIDENT. The suggestion calls for no ruling on the part of the presiding officer. You will proceed, gentlemen on the side of the objectors to certificate No. 1 ; I shall designate them as Nos. 1, 2, and 3, for convenience.

Mr. Representative FIELD. Before proceeding, if you will allow me, I beg to speak to a preliminary matter. I observe that Rule 5 speaks of evidence. Now, I am in some doubt about the course of proceeding. If evidence is admissible it should be stated, we suppose, before beginning the argument. We are prepared with witnesses from Florida to show at the bar or in any manner that the court may indicate, by deposition or otherwise, all that is necessary to prove the allegations of our objection. We suppose that the papers which have been presented here contain sufficient evidence and are receivable ; but I ought to state *in limine* that I do not wish to proceed with the argument under the impression that we have not other evidence. Of course, saving the question whether the evidence is competent, I wish to say that we have the evidence and we can produce it here or anywhere that the Commission may direct, and offer to do it now or at any other time or in any other manner.

I thought I ought not to proceed with my statement without making that preliminary suggestion.

Mr. Commissioner STRONG. Mr. President, it seems to me that the rules which we have adopted place the objectors in precisely the same position that counsel are placed in who open a case before it is submitted to a jury. We propose—such is my understanding of the rule—that the objectors shall occupy exactly that position in their statement of their objections—state what the objections are, and how they propose to support them. The other questions will come up afterward in regard to the admissibility of evidence.

Mr. Representative FIELD. That is quite satisfactory.

Mr. Commissioner STRONG. That is my understanding at this time.

The PRESIDENT. You can proceed, Mr. Field, with the case at a quarter before eleven. Your side will have two hours.

Mr. Representative FIELD. Mr. President and gentlemen of the Electoral Commission : It will be my endeavor, in the statement which I shall make, to set forth with as much conciseness as I may the facts that we expect to prove and the propositions of law which we hope to establish.

The power devolved by the Federal Constitution upon the States of this Union was, in the State of Florida, exercised by the legislature of the State directing the appointment of presidential electors to be made by the qualified voters of the State at a general election. That election was held on the 7th of November, 1876. It was quiet and orderly, so far as we are informed, throughout the State, and it remained only to gather the result of the voting. That result was a majority in favor of the electors who, for convenience sake, I will designate as the Tilden electors. Nevertheless, a certificate comes here signed by the then governor of the State certifying that the Hayes electors had a majority of the votes. By what sort of jugglery that result was accomplished I now take it upon me to explain.

By the laws of the State the counties are divided into polling-precincts and the votes of the polling-precincts are returned to the county clerk at the county-seat, where they are canvassed, and the county canvassers certify to the State canvassers. I have occasion to mention canvassers only in one county. That county was decisive of the result ; but if it were not, *ex uno disce omnes.* The county to which I refer is Baker County. The canvassers were by law to be the county judge, the county clerk, (or rather I think he is called the clerk of the circuit court for the county, but I call him for convenience the county clerk,) and a justice of the peace to be by them called in for their assistance. In case either the judge or the clerk is absent or cannot attend, the sheriff of the county is to be called in his place. The law provides that the canvass by the county canvassers shall be on the sixth day after the election, or sooner if the returns are all received.

In this county there were but four precincts, and the returns from them were all received in three days. On the 10th of November the county clerk, considering that the returns being in, further delay in the canvass might be embarrassing—for what reasons it does not devolve on me to say—requested the county judge to join him in the canvass. The county judge refused. The clerk then asked the sheriff to join him, but he declined. The clerk thereupon called to his assistance a justice of the peace and made the canvass, and a true canvass it was, as all parties agree, I think. I have never heard anywhere the suggestion that the votes as certified by them were not the true votes. But it so happened that the county judge, on the same day, the 10th, issued a notice to the county clerk and to a justice of the peace to attend him at the county seat on the 13th, which, as you will remember, was just six days after the election, at noon, for the purpose of making the count. On that day and hour the county clerk and the justice thus requested attended. The county judge, however, absented himself, though he had given the notice. He was invited and urged to go on with the canvassing. The record shows that he laughed, and said he thought that what had been already done was enough. The sheriff was then applied to and he refused. Thereupon the county clerk and a justice of the peace—another justice called in—recanvassed the votes, giving the same result precisely, and certified them to the State canvassers, stating in the certificate the reasons why neither the county judge nor the sheriff was present. The office of the clerk was then closed for the day.

In the evening of that day the same county judge and the same sheriff, taking to their assistance a justice of the peace who had been commissioned by Stearns only on the 10th, and who had never acted before, entered the office surreptitiously, opened a drawer, and took out the returns, threw aside two precincts, certified the two remaining, and sent that certificate to the State canvassers. You are now to say whether this certificate of these men, under these circumstances, in the darkness of the night, throwing out two precincts, and certified to the State canvassers without any reason why the county clerk was not present, shall be taken as the voice of that county of Florida. That I do not misrepresent the exact state of facts let me read you the testimony as it will appear upon the record to be laid before you. Here is the testimony in respect to this third canvass, this false and fraudulent canvass, which I will read as given by the sheriff.

He testified that he first received notice from Judge Drieggers to assist him in making the canvass of Baker County probably between four and five o'clock in the afternoon of the 13th; that they went to the clerk's office; that the clerk's office was closed when they got there. He thinks this was about six o'clock, "it might have been seven o'clock." That they lit up the office; that they knew that the clerk had made the canvass on that afternoon; that there was no one then in the office.

The law providing that the canvass should be public, the record thus proceeds, as follows, and I give it verbatim:

Question. What did you do then?—Answer. We just made the return, throwing away two precincts in the county.

Q. What two precincts in the county did you throw away ?—A. One was Darbyville precinct and the other was Johnsville precinct.

Q. Which did you throw away first ?—A. The Johnsville precinct.

Q. And then you threw away the Darbyville precinct ?—A. Yes, sir.

Q. Did you have any witnesses at all before you ?—A. None at all.

Q. Did you have anything before you except the returns ?—A. No, sir.

Q. Why did you throw away Johnsville precinct ?—A. We believed that there was some intimidation there : that there was one party prevented from voting.

Q. Did you have any evidence before you to that effect ?—A. No, sir ; there was only his statement.

Q. Did you not have a particle of evidence before you ?—A. No, sir.

Q. You believed that one party had been intimidated and prevented from voting ?—A. Yes, sir.

Q. And therefore you threw out the Johnsville precinct ?—A. Yes, sir.

Q. Was there any reason for throwing it out ?—A. No, sir.

Q. None whatever ?—A. No, sir.

Q. No other reason suggested but that, was there ?—A. No, sir.

Q. You next threw out Darbyville precinct ?—A. Yes, sir.

Q. For what reason did you do so ?—A. We believed that there was some illegal votes cast there.

Q. Did you have any evidence before you at all ?—A. No, sir.

Q. Not a particle ?—A. No, sir.

Q. But you had an impression that some illegal votes were cast there ?—A. Yes, sir.

Q. You had no proof of it at all ?—A. No, sir.

Q. How many illegal votes did you have an impression were cast there?—A. About 7, I think, as well as I can recollect.

Q. Therefore you threw out the precinct without any evidence at all ?—A. Yes, sir.

Q. Then you made up your returns ?—A. Yes, sir.

Q. Who wrote those returns ?—A. I did.

Q. You wrote them yourself ?—A. Yes, sir.

Q. And the judge signed them ?—A. Yes, sir.

Q. Mr. Green signed them ?—A. Yes, sir.

Q. You made return to the secretary of state that you had canvassed the vote ?—A. Yes, sir.

Q. And also sent one to the governor that you had canvassed the vote ?—A. Yes, sir.

Q. The returns, so far as you knew, appeared to be regular from the different precincts, did they ?—A. Yes, sir.

Q. Who was the chairman of the board of canvassers ?—A. The judge.

Q. Who made the suggestion to throw out Johnsville ?—A. He did himself.

Q. Who made the suggestion to throw out the Darbyville precincts ?—A. He did.

Q. And you sustained him in it ?—A. Yes, sir.

Q. Mr. Green sustained him in it also ?—A. Yes, sir.

Mr. Green was the justice appointed by Stearns on the 10th.

Q. How did you know that one man was intimidated at Johnsville precinct ?—A. Well, we just heard it rumored around at the time.

Q. Was there any other cause operating in your mind in rejecting the Johnsville return but the fact that you had heard that one party was intimidated ?—A. No, sir ; that was all.

Q. Where did you and the judge and the justice of the peace, Green, find the returns when you went to the clerk's office to make the canvass ?—A. After we got the light, when I saw them first, the judge had them in his hands.

Q. Do you know where he got them ?—A. I do not; I think he got them out of a desk.

Q. Out of what desk ?—A. In the clerk's desk, in the clerk's office.

Q. Was the desk unlocked that contained these papers ?—A. Yes, sir.

Q. And nobody was in the clerk's office ?—A. No, sir.

Now let me go from this county canvass to the State canvass. When the State canvassers were at work there were certain significant telegrams passed between Florida and Washington; I omit the names of the correspondents except that of the governor, Stearns, the same whose certificate is before you certifying to the election of the Hayes electors. The examination is thus reported :

Q. Do you recollect any telegram at Lake City about the 25th of December, asking—

(I will say the chairman of the national republican committee)—

any questions about attacking the returns ?—A. I remember one dispatch (I cannot give the date) asking on what grounds they should assail these counties, or words to that effect.

Q. What was the answer?—A. There was a dispatch subsequently received, (whether or not it was the answer to it, you must draw your own conclusion.) The words in it were "fraud, intimidation." There was another word which may have been "violence;" but I am not sure that it was "violence."

Thereupon the State canvassers did what? They took the third canvass from Baker County and amended it, as appears in the CONGRESSIONAL RECORD of February 1, page 65, and added "amended by canvassing all the precinct returns," and that statement in the full canvass is the true one as to Baker County; that is, they got at a true result in respect to that county by taking the false certificate and amending it so as to take in all the returns. But what did they then do? Stearns was a candidate for the office of governor. He was then governor and he was a candidate for the succession. His opponent was Mr. Drew. The canvassers were Stearns's appointees, to go out of office with him and to remain in office if he was counted in. They took the returns from the other counties and threw out enough to give the State to the Hayes electors and to Stearns as governor.

Thus the matter stood upon the State canvass thus made. You will observe that it gave the true vote of Baker County, but eliminated from the votes of other counties certain precincts enough to elect their patron Stearns. But it did not remain so, as I will show in a moment; for this elimination being declared by the supreme court illegal, the canvassers thereupon, in order to prevent a majority appearing for the Tilden electors, recalled their amendment of the Baker County false return, and used it in all its falsehood.

These are all facts, which we offer to make good by evidence as the Commission may prescribe, by a cloud of witnesses and by a host of documents.

This monstrous fraud being thus far accomplished, the people of the State took it upon themselves to see if they could right the wrong, and they did it with a spirit and a success which does them all honor. Not even your own native State of New Hampshire, Mr. President, could have more manfully stood up for its rights. If such a fraud had been perpetrated there, you would have heard a voice from her people that would have shaken the everlasting foundations of her granite hills. From peak to peak, and from the easternmost peak to the shining sea, you would have heard a roar of dissent and of indignation. So their brethren of Florida raised their voices through all the flowery peninsula, and they accomplished the result which I will now give. First, Drew, the candidate for governor on the other side, went into the courts of law as a law-abiding citizen should do and will ever do so long as he can get justice in the courts, but when he finds that he cannot get it there he will get it elsewhere. He went into the supreme court of the State and applied for a mandamus to compel this canvassing-board to restore to their canvass the eliminated precincts, and the supreme court decided that the State canvassers had no power under the laws of Florida to eliminate votes, but they were bound to count every lawful vote put into the ballot-box; that they were neither electors nor judges otherwise than of what votes were put in; and in obedience to that they restored to the canvass the rejected precincts and certified a majority for Drew, and Drew took his place and is now the lawful and accepted governor of the State.

What did the Tilden electors do? They commenced in a circuit court of Florida, which had competent jurisdiction, an information in the nature of *quo warranto* against the Hayes electors. They charged in the information that they, the relators, were the lawful claimants of the office, and that the others were usurpers. That information was commenced before the Hayes electors voted on the 6th of December. The case proceeded in the regular course of legal proceedings until it came to trial and judgment, first upon a demurrer, and then, the demurrer being overruled and an answer interposed, upon the issues and proofs; and here is the judgment of the court. After the recitals—

It is, therefore, considered and adjudged that said respondents—

Who were the Hayes electors, Humphreys and so on—

were not, nor was any one of them, elected, chosen, or appointed as such electors or elector, or to receive certificates or certificate of election or appointment as such electors or elector, and that the said respondents were not, upon the said 6th day of December, or at any other time, entitled to assume or exercise any of the powers and functions of such electors or elector; but that they were, upon the said day and date, mere usurpers.

Mr. Representative KASSON. Will the objector allow me to state to the court that I presume we are not considered as agreeing to the presentation of those as being in the case at all?

Mr. Commissioner EDMUNDS. They are merely referred to for information.

The PRESIDENT. We are hearing the statement of one side now.

Mr. Representative FIELD. The whole record is certified and exemplified in due form.

I will go on with the reading:

And it is further considered and adjudged that the said relators, Robert Bullock, Robert B. Hilton, Wilkinson Call, and James E. Yonge—

These are the Tilden electors—

all and singular, were at said election duly elected, chosen, and appointed electors of President and Vice-President of the United States, and were, on the said 6th day of December, 1876, entitled to be declared elected, chosen, and appointed as such electors, and to have and receive certificates thereof, and upon the said day and date, and at all times since, to exercise and perform all and singular the powers and duties of such electors, and to have and enjoy the pay and emoluments thereof. It is further adjudged that respondents pay to relators the costs of the action.

So much for the action of the judicial department of Florida. Everything was done, I take it upon me to say, which it was possible to do; so that I am warranted in asserting that if there be any way known to the law by which in such a case a defrauded State can right itself through the courts of the State, that way has been taken.

In the mean time the Hayes electors had voted and sent their lists of votes to the President of the Senate, with the certificate of Stearns to their appointment.

There was no canvass or certificate of the State canvassers to their appointment, other than that first made, which the supreme court had ordered to be rectified on the application of Mr. Drew, and the rectification of which, therefore, could go no further than the canvass of the governor's vote. The same rectification, applied to the electoral votes, would of course give the majority to the Tilden electors, but to avoid the appearance of this the canvassers pretended to alter the vote first given by them to Baker County, and reduce it to the two precincts mentioned in the third and false return of the county canvassers. This attempt was rebuked by the supreme court, in an order directing the State canvassers to confine their action under the mandamus to the votes for governor; so that there really appears upon the records of the State canvassers no semblance of any authority for Stearns's certificate other than the first canvass, which the supreme court branded as illegal and false.

Now look at what the legislature of Florida has done. The legislature is the department of the Florida government which could alone direct how the power devolved by the Federal Constitution could be performed. This legislature has passed two acts to which I call your attention. In view of the fact that the supreme court had made the decision which I have mentioned, the legislature passed—

An act to provide for a canvass according to the laws of the State of Florida, as interpreted by the supreme court, of the votes for electors of President and Vice President cast at the election held November 7, 1876.

The law was approved January 17. It provides that the secretary of state, attorney-general, and the comptroller of public accounts, or any two of them, together with any other member of the cabinet who may be designated by them, shall meet forthwith at the office of the secretary of state, pursuant to a notice to be given by the secretary of state, and proceed to recanvass the votes. They did meet and recanvass pursuant to that law, and they certified the result according to the fact, giving the majority to the Tilden electors. The second law declared that the Tilden electors, naming them, were elected on the 7th day of November, and that they had voted; and directed that the same electors should meet, that the governor should give them a certificate of their election, pursuant to the recanvass, and that they should make out duplicate lists of the votes, and transmit them to the President of the Senate at Washington; and the proceedings under that law make up the third return which has been read.

Mr. Commissioner BRADLEY. What was the second return?

Mr. Representative FIELD. The second return to the President of the Senate was the return of the Tilden electors.

The return No. 1 was made by the Hayes electors and sent with the certificate of Stearns as governor. Return No. 2 contains the certificates of the Tilden electors without the certificate of the governor, but with a certificate of the attorney-general, the only dissenting member of the board of State canvassers, certifying that they were elected. Then return No. 3 contains the action of the State authorities subsequently to the two first, for the purpose of ratifying and confirming, so far as it was possible for the State authorities to do it, the second return; and they therefore not only passed a law for the recanvass of the votes, which recanvass took place and resulted in a certificate of the election of the Tilden electors, but they passed another act, reciting that the election had been in favor of the Tilden electors, and that the Tilden electors had met and voted on the 6th of December, but without a certificate of the governor, and directing the governor of the State to forward a supplementary certificate for its confirmation; and directing, moreover, for abundant caution, that there should be new lists made out and a new certificate by these electors who were to be re-assembled for the purpose, the certificates all to be forwarded to the President of the Senate, as they would have been, but for the conspiracy, in November. Those papers make the third return. I will read the recital in this act of the legislature of Florida:

And whereas the board of State canvassers constituted under the act approved February 27, 1872, did interpret the laws of this State defining the powers and duties of the said board in such manner as to give them power to exclude certain regular returns, and did in fact under such interpretation exclude certain of such regular returns, which said interpretation has been adjudged by the supreme court to be erroneous and illegal;

And whereas the late governor, Marcellus L. Stearns, by reason of said illegal action and erroneous and illegal canvass of the said board of State canvassers, did erroneously cause to be made and certified lists of the names of the electors of this State, containing the names of the said Charles H. Pearce, Frederick C. Humphreys, William H. Holden, and Thomas Long—

Being the Hayes electors—

and did deliver such lists to said persons, when in fact the said persons had not received the highest number of votes, and, on a canvass conducted according to the rules prescribed and adjudged as legal by the supreme court, were not appointed as electors or entitled to receive such lists from the governor, but Robert Bullock, Robert B. Hilton, Wilkinson Call, and James E. Yonge—

Those are the Tilden electors—

were duly appointed electors, and were entitled to have their names compose the lists made and certified by the governor, and to have such lists delivered to them:

Now, *therefore, the people of the State of Florida, represented in senate and assembly, do enact, &c.*

The certificate is in effect that the electors who met and voted on the 6th of December were the true choice of the people of Florida; and the same electors re-assembled and made new lists; they did not vote anew because they were to vote on the 6th of December, but they did certify anew that they had thus voted on the 6th of December, and that certificate, with the other certificate, was forwarded in due form, as I have stated, to the President of the Senate at this Capitol.

Now, if the Commission please, we are told that the certificate of the governor, Stearns, which has been forwarded to Washington annexed to the lists of votes of the Hayes electors, countervails all this evidence, and that no matter what amount of testimony we may offer, documentary or oral, we can never invalidate the signature of Marcellus L. Stearns; and it is to that question that I shall devote what remains of my address. It is putting the question in an erroneous form to put it thus, "You cannot go behind the certificate." The form should be reversed, Can the certificate go before the truth and conceal it? I prove these facts or offer to prove them. On the other side—if I have rightly understood the objections made yesterday in the joint convention—on the other side there is no suggestion that we are not right in the facts; there is no averment that the true and lawful vote of the State of Florida was not given for the Tilden electors; but the claim is that "there is the certificate of M. L. Stearns, and that stands as a barrier against all these witnesses, and the truth cannot be proven. The truth is buried under this certificate. Neither you exercising for this occasion the powers of the two Houses of Congress, nor the two Houses themselves, acting separately or together, can consider any fact whatever to the contrary of which Stearns has certified."

Let me ask in the first place upon what foundation that doctrine rests? Who tells you that you are to take that certificate as conclusive evidence against anything that can be proved on the other side? By what rule of evidence, by what precept of law, are you deprived of the right to investigate the truth? Is it not a universal rule that every judge is invested *ex necessitate* with the power to take into consideration all pertinent evidence in respect to the facts upon which his judgment is to be pronounced, unless there is some positive law declaring that certain certificates or other documentary evidence shall be conclusive? I venture to say that that is the universal rule, and that there is no court of general jurisdiction known to American or Anglo-Saxon law in which it is not a fundamental principle that whenever a court can inquire into facts necessary to its judgment, it may take all the pertinent evidence, that is to say all evidence that tends to prove the fact, unless it is restricted by some positive law. Now, then, show me a positive law that makes the certificate of Stearns evidence against the truth? Where is it? In what book? It is not in the Constitution. It is not in the laws of Florida. Is it in any law of Congress? The only act of Congress applicable is that which provides that the executive of the State shall deliver to the electors a certificate that they are such electors, but that act does not declare that his certificate shall be conclusive—neither declares it, nor implies it. Suppose I offer to prove that the certificate is wholly false, fabricated for the purpose of cheating the State out of its vote and the other States out of their rights. Take the State, one of the oldest and proudest in this Union of States—the State of Massachusetts, of which my friend Mr. Commissioner Abbott is so worthy a representative, and suppose that the honored governor of that State were so debased as to certify that the Tilden electors had received the votes of a majority of the good and true voters of Massachusetts; will any man tell me that it must be taken as absolutely true, that you cannot prove it to be false? Where is the law for that? Nay, more, I venture to affirm that if an act of Congress had declared that that certificate should be conclusive, the act would have been unconstitutional. For what reason? For this reason: The Constitution, as if the foresight of the fathers grasped the conflicts of future years, declares that the person having the highest number of votes shall be the President, not that the person declared to have the highest number of votes, but "the person having the highest number." No certificate can be manufactured to take that away. If you had declared by act of Congress in the most express and positive terms that the certificate of the governor delivered to the electors should be conclusive against all proof, you would have transcended the limits of the organic law. You cannot say that the certificate of the governor of Massachusetts shall override the votes of the electors of Massachusetts in their choice of President. Therefore it is I say not only that you have not done it, but you could not do it; you could not do it if you would, as I am sure you would not if you could.

The language of the act of Congress is not as strong as the language of the State laws generally respecting the canvass of votes. Take the case in Wisconsin, which arose in the courts, of the contest for the office of governor. There a law of the State had declared that the State canvassers should determine—I think that is the language—should determine, certify, and declare who was governor. A person came into the office of governor upon such a certificate declaring that he was elected, and a rival claimant went into the courts with a writ of *quo warranto*, and was met there by the ablest counsel in the State with the argument, "You cannot inquire, because the certificate of the State canvassers is conclusive." "No," said the court, in an opinion which does them great honor and will stand as a record of their learning, their patriotism, and their inflexible firmness; "the title of governor depends upon the votes of the people, upon those little ballots that declare their supreme will; the question is not who have certified but who have voted;" and the court declared the claimant entitled and threw out the usurping governor.

Is not your right to inquire into the very truth implied by the law under which you act? What are you to do? You are to declare whether any and what votes are the votes provided by the Constitution, not to declare what are the votes certified by Governor Stearns. That was known well enough beforehand. You are to certify what are the lawful votes upon which a President of forty-five millions of people is to be inducted into office.

Is not the same right implied in the notion which I find to prevail everywhere, that Congress might authorize a writ of *quo warranto* to try the title of President within the purview of the Constitution? Can that be doubted? The Constitution has declared that the person having the highest number of votes shall be the President; not the one certified. Congress has not as yet invested any tribunal with the power to try the title to the Presidency by *quo warranto.* No such law exists, I am sorry to say. Such a law, if I might be permitted to say so, ought to be made. It is no small reproach to our statesmanship that for a hundred years no law has been provided for this great exigency. I know that one eminent member of this Commission has labored assiduously to procure the passage of such a law, and of all his titles to respect I am sure that will be especially remembered hereafter.

Mr. Commissioner BRADLEY. Does not the law of the District apply to the case?

Mr. Representative FIELD. I think not, sir. I should be very glad to learn that it does. The judiciary act of 1789, as if *ex industria,* omitted to mention writs of *quo warranto.* It gave the several courts power to issue writs of mandamus and certain other writs, but not that of *quo warranto.* I know that the statutes lately passed give a right to a *quo warranto* in respect to certain offices, enumerating them, arising out of the amendments to the Constitution providing for the emancipated slaves; but I do not find any provision whatever for a writ of *quo warranto* to try the title to any such office as that of President or presidential elector.

Mr. Commissioner BRADLEY. You are aware, of course, that the whole body of the Maryland law as existing in 1801 is the municipal law of this District, so far as not modified.

Mr. Representative FIELD. I am.

Mr. Commissioner BRADLEY. I do not know whether there is any such provision in those laws or not.

Mr. Representative FIELD. Of course I speak entirely under submission to the better knowledge of the court. I have not been able to satisfy myself that there is any provision for a writ of *quo warranto* in the case of President. But my argument is that, whether there be a law now existing or not, it is competent to Congress to pass such a law, and if a law to provide for a writ of *quo warranto* would be constitutional, then it is constitutional to impose a like duty on any other tribunal to investigate the title. That is to say, if you could devolve that duty upon any tribunal by means of a writ of *quo warranto,* you can devolve it by other means. If the governor's certificate would not be conclusive there, it is not conclusive here. The right to inquire into the fact exists somewhere, and, if nowhere else, it must be here.

Thus thinking that Congress could devolve upon some tribunal the authority to inquire into the title of the President, and that such authority would necessarily give to the tribunal investigating the right to go into the truth notwithstanding any certificate to the falsehood, I argue that here before this Electoral Commission, invested with all the functions of the two Houses, you can inquire into the truth, no matter what may have been certified to the contrary.

Furthermore, I submit to the Commission that there is another rule of law which necessarily leads us to answer affirmatively the question whether the truth can be given in evidence notwithstanding the certificate; and that is that fraud vitiates all transactions and can always be inquired into in every case except possibly two. I will not argue now that the judgment of a court of record of competent jurisdiction can be impeached collaterally for fraud in the judge. Opinions differ. If it cannot be impeached, it must be because such an impeachment would lead to an inquiry that would be against public policy. It would be a scandal to inquire into the bribery or corruption of a judge while the judge is sitting to administer justice; and, therefore, from motives of public policy, it may be the rule that until the judge is impeached and removed you cannot inquire into the corruption of his acts. And it may also be true that you cannot inquire into the validity of an act of a legislature upon the ground of fraud or bribery. But, with those two exceptions, I venture to claim that there is no act and no document anywhere that you cannot impeach for fraud. Now, this canvassing-board and this governor were not invested with any such sanctity as are judges of courts of record. They were not dispensing justice between litigating parties, and it would not be against public policy to inquire into the corruption or invalidity of their acts. Not a single consideration that I have ever heard of or which I can imagine would lead us to the conclusion that you cannot inquire into the truth of their certificates; and I put it to the Commission that if they corruptly acted, if they were bribed or led astray by hunger for office, or the thirst for power, or the thirst for gold, you can impeach their acts. Who is it whose acts we are now seeking to impeach? It is the then governor of Florida, Stearns; Stearns, the man who sent the telegram asking on what grounds the votes of counties could be thrown out, and who received for answer, fraud, intimidation, or something else; Stearns, the man who controlled the canvassing-board sitting to certify whether he and they were to continue in office.

Is it a true proposition of law that you cannot inquire whether he has acted fraudulently? If it be true that the certificate of the governor is conclusive evidence that these persons were elected, then it follows that the certificate would be sufficient if there were no election at all. Yes; suppose I prove or offer to prove that in point of fact on the 7th day of November there was no election at all in the State of Florida, that no man cast a vote, no polls were opened, no man thought of voting, would this certificate, signed "M. L. Stearns," prove that the four Hayes electors were duly chosen?

To that complexion must it come at last.

There is no middle ground. If you can inquire into the truth of that certificate, you can inquire into every certificate of fact and show whether it be true or false.

Such, Mr. President and gentlemen of the Commission, is as brief a statement as I could make of the facts and the law as we understand them to be. The greatness of the question in respect to the dignity of the presidential office and the vast interests depending upon it, is as nothing compared with the moral elements involved; for true as it is that the person upon whom your decision will confer the office for four years will be the Chief Magistrate of forty-five millions of people, Commander-in-Chief of your Army and Navy, the organ between you and all foreign states, the bestower of all offices, the fountain of honor and the distributer of power, the executor of your laws, that is as nothing compared with the greater question whether or not the American people stand powerless before a gigantic fraud. Here is the certificate; one feels reluctant to touch it. Hold it up to the light. It is black with crime. Pass it round; let every eye see it; and then tell me whether it is fit to bestow power and create dignity against the will of the people. One of the greatest poets of the palmy days of English literature, writing of the coming of our Saviour, has said:

—— And ancient Fraud shall fail,
Returning Justice lift aloft her scale.

Ancient fraud! Was there ever fraud like this? In previous ages fraud has succeeded only because it has been supported by the sword, and protesting peoples have been powerless before armed battalions. Never yet in the history of the world has a fraud succeeded against the conscience and the will of a self-governing people. If it succeeds now, let us hang our heads for shame; let us take down from the dome of this Capitol the statue which every morning faces the coming light; let us clothe ourselves with sackcloth and sit in ashes forever.

Mr. Representative TUCKER. With submission to the Commission, the objections which are made by members of the two houses of Congress to the counting of the votes of the electors who voted for Messrs. Hayes and Wheeler are to be found printed this morning in a form to which I call the attention of the Commission for a moment. The first objection is:

That the said Charles H. Pearce—

And others—

were not appointed by the said State of Florida in such manner as its legislature had directed.

The second is:

That Wilkinson Call—

And others, the Tilden electors—

were appointed by the said State in such manner as its legislature directed.

The third states that the qualified electors of the said State, in manner as provided by the law of Florida, did elect Wilkinson Call and others, the Tilden electors.

The fourth is:

That the pretended certificate, or paper purporting to be a certificate, signed by M. L. Stearns as governor of said State, of the appointment of the said Charles H. Pearce * * * was and is in all respects untrue, and was corruptly procured and made in pursuance of a conspiracy between the said M. L. Stearns—

And the said Pearce and others, and so on—

to assert and set up fictitious and unreal votes for President and Vice-President.

The fifth is:

That the said papers falsely purporting to be the votes for President and Vice-President of the State of Florida, which are fictitious and unreal and do not truly represent any votes or lawful acts, * * * were made out and executed in pursuance of the same fraudulent conspiracy.

The sixth states at length what I will state succinctly, that by a *quo-warranto* proceeding initiated prior to the vote given for Hayes and Wheeler by these pretended electors on the 6th of December, and which resulted in a judgment on the 25th or 26th of January, their election their title to the office of electors for the State of Florida, was declared, utterly null and void, and that they were usurpers and pretenders to the said office.

Mr. Commissioner MORTON. May I inquire of the counsel, who were made parties to that proceeding?

Mr. Representative TUCKER. The State of Florida *ex relatione* Wilkinson Call and others, the Tilden electors, as plaintiffs, against Pearce and others, the Hayes electors.

Mr. Commissioner MORTON. Was the governor a party to the proceeding?

Mr. Representative TUCKER. No; he was not a party. Now, sirs, these are succinctly the objections made, and they may be summarized thus: We object to these votes being counted, because we say that these men were not elected according to the law of Florida, and not being so elected can have no title to the office; secondly, we hold that, even if they had been elected according to the forms of the law of Florida, their election was tainted with fraud and is void; and the whole question presented to this tribunal, the question presented to the two Houses of Congress, and which they have substituted this tribunal in their stead to decide, is simply this: Is there any power in the Constitution under which we live by which a fraudulent and illegal title to the office of President can be prevented? Must a man that everybody knows to be a usurper be pronounced by the two Houses of Congress, or by this tribunal in their stead, to have a valid title to the office when all the world knows he has not? I will not ask whether the decision of a returning-board is to screen the illegality and fraud from your vision, but whether the returning-boards can run their fingers into the eyes of this tribunal and prevent their seeing what all the world sees? Shall the two Houses of Congress, the sentinel-guards appointed by the Constitution against the usurpation of this high office, shall this tribunal as the substitute for those sentinel-guards, permit fraud to crawl with slimy trail into the executive seat, whence it may spring from its coil and sting with fatal fang the life-blood of the grandest republic in the world? Is the power of a returning-board, tainted with fraud, based upon lawlessness, to conclude the judgment of the American people and put a usurper in the seat of Washington? That is the question.

Now, sirs, whatever may be the decision of this tribunal, I shall die in the faith of my fathers, that the fathers of the Constitution never framed an instrument of that kind and said that their posterity were to live under it.

What is the power of these two Houses? I have discussed that question elsewhere. If your honors will save me the labor of repeating it here, I will, as soon as I can get advance sheets of it, lay before your honors a copy of the speech delivered by me in the House of Representatives on that point; but I take it, summarizing the proposition, that when the Constitution declared that these votes were to be counted in the presence of the two Houses of Congress, when it declared that they were to be counted, they were the votes of electors to be counted, they were the votes of electors, real electors, not pretended electors, to be counted; it was intended that the two Houses of Congress, and therefore that this tribunal in their place, should see that there was no fraudulent counting of pretended votes for President of the United States.

Now, taking up the line of argument which was presented by my able and distinguished friend on my left, [Mr. Field,] I apprehend that the powers of the two Houses of Congress and of this tribunal as their substitute are not less in this inquiry than the powers of a court upon a *quo-warranto* proceeding. We are now standing as the guards to the entrance of the executive department, and we are to let no man pass that has not the pass-word of the people of the United States. We have a right to question his title, and if he has no title never to permit him to enter.

What says a distinguished authority upon this subject, which I found this morning on the table? I must beg the pardon of the Commission that what I shall say shall not be overloaded with learning, for I have had no opportunity of looking into this question. In High on Extraordinary Legal Remedies, section 760, it is stated:

Judgment of ouster may be given against one who was not duly elected to the office claimed, notwithstanding the return or certificate of a board of canvassers of the election in his favor, since such return is by no means conclusive and the courts may go behind it and examine the facts as to the legality of the election. Nor will the holding of a commission for the office prevent the court from giving judgment of ouster if the incumbent was not legally elected, since the title to the office is derived from the election and not from the commission. Even though the incumbent were properly elected in the first instance, yet if he was never sworn into the office judgment of ouster may be given.

That is the key-note of the remarks that I shall make to your honors. Who appoint electors? The Constitution declares that each State shall appoint so many electors as it is entitled to Senators and Representatives in Congress. "Each State shall appoint." What is the meaning of that? I apprehend that the word "State" in the Constitution has three or four meanings, one indicating the territory in which the population lives; another the people themselves as an organic body-politic, a sovereign power—I trust I trench upon no proprieties in saying that a State is a sovereign power and a body-politic—and another is the State government. In this particular case, I apprehend it means the State as a body-politic, as an organic society, not its government, because the next sentence says that each State shall appoint "in such manner" as its "legislature may direct." There you have the functional power of election in the State as a body-politic; the manner of the election to be prescribed and directed by its legislature. The law-making power of the State directs the manner; the substantial power is in the State.

Now, let us look at this for a moment, and I beg the Commission to bear with me in making a distinction which I have not seen made as clearly as it appears to my mind; and if there is any value in it, I hope I may be permitted to make it clear. It is this: In every appointment or election two elements enter: first, the exercise of the elective function; second, the exercise of the determining function. The elective function is in the State; is, in Florida, in the body of the sovereign. The determining function is in a returning-board. Now, wherever the determinant power usurps the elective function, then it must be set aside and adjudged void; that is to say, wherever, under the name of determining and deciding who is elected, the board or the body which so decides really elects, then it is a usurping power and it has transcended its authority; it has acted *ultra vires;* and its act must be declared void by any tribunal before whom its action comes for adjudication. I therefore say that in Florida the elective function was in the body of the people of the State; whoever the body of the people of the State elected to be its electors were its electors and had title to the office, according to the language of the authority I have read. The question of whether they should be determined to have been elected by the board of canvassers is an entirely different question. If the board of canvassers, either contrary to law, or transcending their legal authority, or under their legal authority, fraudulently counted in as elected those who were not elected by the people, their act was void.

I will go no further in this controversy than just to say that if it can be shown that the returning-board or the executive of the State of Florida transcended their legal authority in giving the return to these electors, then their action is simply *ultra vires* and a nullity; or if, acting within the limits of their authority, they used their legal power fraudulently and falsely, then that also is a usurpation of the elective function and is void, because I apprehend that if I can show, as it has been shown or seems to have been shown in some part of this Capitol very recently, that if a returning-board tells its clerk to take 178 votes bodily from one side, for Tilden, and put them over to Hayes, that is not a determining power; that is the elective function; and if this tribunal permitted such a thing as that to stand, it would permit an oligarchic board in Louisiana or Florida to elect the electors against the law of the State and against the will of the people. The power of determination can never be valid where it usurps the elective function which is vested by the law in any other body.

I go a step further. I apprehend that if the primary determinant, if I may invent a term, should decide in favor of certain electors and there should be provided by the proper authority an ultimate determinant authority, or, to come down to the concrete proposition, if the primary determinant authority in Florida was the returning-board and there was provided by the laws of the State an ultimate determinant authority in the form of a judicial tribunal, then your honors are not going behind State authority to pick a flaw in the election of their electors if you give force and validity to the action of the returning-board as reviewed by the judicial authority and as adjudged by the judicial authority. In other words, the judicial procedure in that case becomes a part of the determinant authority in the election provided by the State, and therefore you say that a man is elected in the manner prescribed by the State law, when he is determined to be elected by the State law, and that determination is revised and adjudged upon by the State judiciary.

I apprehend, therefore, that unless the primary determinant authority, that is, the board under State law, is conclusive, not only in its action, but conclusive as to the extent of its own powers, then we must regard the judicial proceedings in Florida upon the action of these electors as a part of that determinant power which the State has provided against fraud and illegality in the exercise of the elective function; and therefore I apprehend that, if there was nothing in the law of Florida which gave a judicial power of supervision to the action of the board, the two Houses of Congress, and this Commission as substituted for the two Houses of Congress with all the powers vested in both or either of them, have a right to plunge down into this mass of corruption and unkennel fraud; and that this tribunal has not only the power, but it is its solemn duty under God and before this people to see whether these pretended electors are mere pretenders or the real representatives of the voice of Florida.

There can be no plainer proposition, in my judgment, than that all action in court even, particularly a court of inferior and limited jurisdiction, which is *ultra vires*, is void, and that every act done by an inferior tribunal, even within the forms of law, if it be fraudulent, is void. To say that the two Houses of Congress—I will not use the illustration in reference to this honorable Commission—that the two Houses of Congress, in the presence of whom these votes are counted, are to sit with their fingers in their mouths and see a fraud which they cannot prevent, and witness an illegality the triumph and victory of which they have only to countenance, is to say that our fathers meant that their posterity should be handed over to the power of those who would practice a fraud and an illegality upon their rights.

I need not refer your honors to any authority upon these points. The great leading authority of the Duchess of Kingston's case as to the validity or invalidity of a fraudulent judgment, of course is familiar to you all. Your honors will find that case elaborately discussed in Smith's Leading Cases.

I state these propositions as clear law:

First, that where a determinant power in these elections transcends its authority, it usurps the elective function and is void. It elects instead of determining.

Second, where the determinant power fraudulently decides, it assumes to elect and its act is void.

I beg this Commission to keep distinctly in their minds, as I have no doubt they will, what to my mind is perfectly clear and lies at the very root of this whole controversy, the distinction between the power of election and the power of determining on the election. The power of election is in the suffragans of Florida and the power of determining on the election was in this board of three. Now, if the board of three transcend their merely determining power and under color of determining really exercise the elective power, it is an usurpation that must be trampled upon not only by this tribunal but by the two Houses of Congress.

I hold that every illegal or fraudulent act of a returning-board or of any determining board in an election is open to inquiry. We may inquire into their jurisdiction. If they have not transcended their jurisdiction, then the question is have they executed it *bona fide* or *mala fide?* If they have not transcended their jurisdiction and have exercised it in bad faith, it is void. Fraud taints the whole act. I beg your honors and the other gentlemen of the Commission to refer to what is very familiar to your honors, that class of cases that began in a decision of the case of Pearce *vs.* Railroad Company, 21 Howard, p. 442,* where the court take the distinction between the exercise of a corporate power *ultra vires* and the exercise of a corporate power *infra vires*, and against the internal order of the board. In every case where a corporate act is *ultra vires*, no matter whether with the whole sanction and faith of all the corporators, it is void, as the corporation can only act under the powers of its charter. So I hold here. Here is a petty corporation, this trio of oligarchs, who are set there to determine upon an election, and if they trench upon the elective function and transcend their authority, their act is void.

This being so, I advance another proposition. If the election is determined by a board, and a State court of competent jurisdiction decides its action to be illegal or fraudulent, decides that it was an usurped authority, or an authority *infra vires*, but exercised fraudulently, I say that that judgment is conclusive upon these two Houses and upon this tribunal, unless the court so deciding was itself without jurisdiction or acted *mala fide.* Therefore I say to gentlemen here, if they want to stand upon the ground of not being permitted to go behind State authority in these matters, they must take the whole of the State authority; and the trio of oligarchs, with Governor Stearns at their head, making a quartette, are not the only authority of the State of Florida, but the authority of its judiciary pronouncing upon the title of this trio, and the authority of its supreme court must be taken into consideration as a part of that State authority which we are called upon so to respect.

Now I say that this *quo warranto* by the supreme court in the case of the State of Florida *ex relatione* Drew against Stearns and others——

Mr. Commissioner HOAR. Mr. Tucker, do your papers contain the petition for the writ of *quo warranto* or the writ itself? I see here the judgment.

Mr. Representative TUCKER. The original papers are here. They are not printed; only the judgment was printed.

Mr. Commissioner HOAR. I was looking to see whether the application was for a writ of *quo warranto* to determine a title to an office which

---

* See, also, Knox County *vs.* Aspinwall, 21 Howard, p. 539; Zabriskie *vs.* Railroad Company, 23 Howard, 381.

the respondent formerly held, or one which he held at the time of issuing the writ.

Mr. Representative TUCKER. I cannot go into that just now, if you please. My time has nearly run out. It was served on the 6th, before the parties had perfected their act, while they were performing their function, and therefore before they had cast their vote. It was served upon them then; and my idea, my belief is in the doctrine of law that by relation the judgment rendered in January goes back to the first stage in the proceeding and avoids the whole. I beg Judge HOAR to understand me. This writ of *quo warranto* was served upon Pearce and others, the Hayes electors, five minutes after twelve o'clock on the 6th of December, before they had performed the function of voting for President and Vice-President, and therefore by relation now the judgment sweeps away the whole of the action of those electors under their pretended right and title. But the judgment of the supreme court in the case of Drew *vs.* Stearns settles the question of the power of this board, that their duty was merely ministerial; that they had no right to throw out votes; that they had a right merely to enumerate the votes as they were sent up from the counties, but that they had no right to reject on the idea that there was fraud or intimidation, or on such loose evidence as my friend read this morning, that they had heard somewhere the air was full of rumors of bull-dozing "and intimidation, and therefore we threw out any amount of votes."

Then I say that the proceeding in the *quo warranto* of Call *vs.* Pearce settles the question of the title of Pearce and others, the Hayes electors; utterly avoids it; declares that they are usurpers and that all their acts are void. That decision is unreversed, is the decision of a court of competent jurisdiction, and is conclusive as we maintain, and has stamped as the stamp of the State "usurpation" upon the power of these men who claim to have voted for President.

But we are told that the executive of the State has certified, M. L. Stearns has certified, and that is conclusive. Who made him a ruler or a judge over us? The act of Congress, it is said, says that the executive shall send on three certificates. Can the act of Congress make his certificate conclusive against the voice of the State? Then if it can, I beg gentlemen to follow to its legitimate conclusion their proposition. If the act of Congress has the effect (I think not by a fair interpretation of the statute) of giving conclusiveness to the return by the executive of the election in the State, then Congress has usurped the function of determining the manner of the election and determining the elective function of the State. "Each State shall appoint, in such manner as the legislature thereof may direct;" and the manner of election must include the manner of determining the election. There can be no such power in the executive of a State.

Now I apprehend that the thing just comes down to this: that whether this be a Federal or State office (and I believe it to be a State office) the elector must be appointed by the State in such manner as the legislature directs, and that we must refuse—I speak now of the two Houses and of this Commission as a substitute for them—we must refuse effect to any certificate which belies the fact; and to assert that we have no right to say a thing is a lie when we see it is a lie is to say you might as well disband and go to your respective functions prior to the organization of the Commission.

As I have but a few moments left, I will, as preachers say sometimes, give practical application to this discourse. The question is, are the Hayes electors appointed, not are they returned by the trio or by Mr.

Stearns, but are they appointed by the people of Florida; not who gave them commission, but who gave them title to speak for Florida? The title comes from the body of the people. The commission may come from the trio of oligarchs. Do I hear "yes"? Who say so? The board and governor. Have they the legal right to say it? The judgment of the court answers no. Did they fraudulently make the return? The court answers they did. Now shall this tribunal, in the teeth of this ultimate State determinant power, give title to any such commission, or give title under the voice of the people? Shall you hold the commission which the State court of Florida has declared to be invalid, to be valid, in order to stifle the elective power of the people and give power to the determinant functions of the oligarchy? That is the question.

May it please the Commission, there is only one other question that I desire to speak to, and that is one which it is proper I should mention before I sit down. I will not go into the facts of this case any further. Baker County was never thrown out for any informality until the exigency of the second count required. Upon the first count there was no informality or irregularity in Baker County, and its return was counted; but when the court ordered them to count those counties that they had thrown out, they found that the only way to procure the election to the Hayes electors was then to throw out Baker County instead of those that they had already thrown out and were now ordered to count.

Now I come to this point only about Mr. Humphreys, who was an officer of the Government. On page 70 of the document as to the recent election in Florida, the testimony taken before the select committee of the House of Representatives, the Commission will find the evidence is:

United States circuit court, northern district of Florida.

And that evidence is here printed from the original certificate of the clerk of the court.

Ordered, By the court, that Frederick C. Humphries, of Pensacola, be, and he is hereby, appointed shipping-commissioner for the port of Pensacola.

That is with the objection made by two gentlemen.

Mr. Commissioner EDMUNDS. Is that the objection of Mr. Jones and Mr. McDonald?

Mr. Representative TUCKER. Yes, sir, that Frederick C. Humphreys was appointed, and then there is a certificate that he took the oath to discharge the duties of shipping-commissioner to the best of his ability, sworn to and subscribed, &c., and then here is the certificate of the clerk:

I, M. P. De Rioboo, clerk, &c., do hereby certify the foregoing to be a true copy as the same remains on file in my office. I further certify that no resignation of said office of shipping-commissioner has been filed in my office by the said Frederick C. Humphries.

So that here is a man who was appointed in 1872 shipping-commissioner; continued to hold the office on the day of election; continued to hold the office on the day he voted, contrary to the Constitution of the United States, and continues to hold it now, as far as I know; and upon that point, I refer to page 425 of the testimony taken by the House committee:

He has been United States shipping-commissioner.

So that a man who was an elector was United States shipping-commissioner. Let me refer you to one single fact. The question is whether he was an officer of the United States. In the Revised Statutes, page 876, you will find the section providing for the appointment of such shipping-commissioner by the court.

Thanking the Commission for their kind attention and having exhausted my time, I have only to say that we are prepared, as soon as the court shall advise us of the mode in which we shall unkennel this fraud, to go into the evidence in any shape or form that either the tribunal will indicate or that the gentlemen on the other side may desire. We have the evidence that has been taken by the committees of both Houses. We apprehend that, as both Houses would have been entitled to use this upon the determination of the question, this Commission has the same power. There may be evidence in reference to these other counties, but not knowing what would be the rules established by this tribunal—of course, it was impossible to know—we have not submitted it. I only mean to say that of course all the evidence taken before either House and now in the hands of either House, which they could have used in the determination of this question, is before this tribunal, and we apprehend that this tribunal is competent to go into any further evidence that may be necessary to elucidate the subject for decision, and to unearth the fraud and illegality which affects the title of either of these parties to the election. It relates to Duval County and Clay County, as well as Baker.

Mr. Commissioner ABBOTT. I want to ask you if your last reference—I have not the book before me—tended to show that this person who was an elector was the person appointed shipping-commissioner?

Mr. Representative TUCKER. No, sir; it only showed what was the nature of his office under the Revised Statutes.

Mr. Commissioner ABBOTT. I alluded to the reference in the evidence.

Mr. Representative TUCKER. The last reference to the evidence was to show that he was the very man and performed the duties.

Mr. Representative FIELD. He has been acting as such.

The PRESIDENT. One of the objectors on the other side will now be heard.

Mr. Representative KASSON. On consultation, Mr. President, as I intimated before the opening of the argument on the other side, my associate [Mr. McCrary] and myself have thought it due to the interests represented that we should ask further time to examine the certificates which are all involved in these objections, asking it specially upon this ground, that instead of the certificates and papers to which the objections apply appearing in print in the RECORD this morning as we expected them to do, so that they might be directly considered by us, they have not yet been in print; the certificates are not before us; we have had no access to them until counsel in this printed document just this moment laid them upon the table before us.

In addition to that I have only to say that the magnitude of the questions presented by the argument here, also, is a reason why we should attempt to aid the Commission more than we can do by hastily proceeding now to the consideration of these great constitutional questions. My colleague and myself only saw the objections yesterday and were only notified after the meeting of this Commission that we were to present them on our part.

The PRESIDENT. How much delay do you ask? I have no authority to grant it; I must have something definite to submit to the Commission.

Mr. Representative KASSON. I think it will be sufficient, inasmuch as we can have access to the original papers now, they being in possession of the Commission, to ask to be allowed to go on to-morrow morning.

The PRESIDENT, (to the members of the Commission.) The objectors to the second certificate, and who support the first one, ask for a postponement of their reply to the two objectors who have already spoken this morning, until to-morrow morning. The question before the Commission is whether the delay shall be granted. Are you ready for the question?

Mr. Commissioner STRONG. I should like to inquire whether it would not be possible for one of the objectors to go on this afternoon, and then the Commission might possibly assent to a postponement of the hearing of the other one until morning.

Mr. Representative KASSON. That would be practicable, except for the fact that we are both in the same situation, and we have not been able to distribute the two branches of the subject between us.

Mr. Commissioner EDMUNDS. Can you not go on at three o'clock?

Mr. Representative KASSON. That would exhaust the time of the objectors with ten minutes additional.

Mr. Commissioner MILLER. Mr. Kasson, much as I would like to oblige you, for myself I must say that looking to the emergency and the necessity of getting along and the number of persons to be heard in all these cases, if we set this example the Commission probably would never get through. I must for myself vote against any delay unless it be till three o'clock, so as to allow an opportunity to take lunch in the mean time.

Mr. Representative KASSON. If that be the disposition of the Commission I certainly interpose no objection, and we shall avail ourselves of the time.

The PRESIDENT. You only ask now for delay until three o'clock?

Mr. Commissioner MILLER. Mr. President, I move that these objectors have till three o'clock to present their statement.

The PRESIDENT. The question before the Commission is whether a delay until three o'clock shall be granted to the objectors on the other side.

The motion was agreed to.

Mr. Commissioner MILLER. Now I move that the Commission take a recess until three o'clock.

Mr. Representative KASSON. Before that vote is put may I inquire whether the Commission has in its possession the certificates and the objections?

The PRESIDENT. It has. It is moved that the Commission take a recess until three o'clock.

The motion was agreed to; and (at twelve o'clock and fifty-two minutes p. m.) the Commission took a recess until three o'clock.

The Commission re-assembled at 3 o'clock p. m.

The PRESIDENT. One of the objectors to the second certificate will now be heard on the same rules and conditions prescribed in respect to objectors to the first.

Mr. SHELLABARGER. Mr. President and gentlemen, I am requested to lay before the Commission the Senate report upon Florida containing the laws of Florida and other matters pertinent to this discussion.

Mr. Commissioner EDMUNDS. We take it as part of the statement, not as evidence.

The PRESIDENT. We will take it as part of the statement on that side.

Mr. Representative KASSON. Mr. President and gentlemen of the Commission, in what I have to say I shall be mindful of one of the traditions of that very honorable court which usually occupies the bench now filled by this Commission. It is said of Chief-Justice Marshall that, after listening for a day and far into the second day to a young counselor who had by that time only passed Littleton, and Coke, and Blackstone, and got down to Kent's Commentaries, the Chief-Justice ventured to remind him that it must be presumed that the Supreme Court of the United States itself was partially cognizant of the law, and he might be able to abbreviate his argument. In that spirit I shall to-day endeavor as early as possible to free our part of the case from the charges, allegations, and arguments which have been presented and which do not seem to us pertinent to the question to be considered by the Commission.

What is the case before the Commission? First, a certificate, as required by the Constitution and laws of the United States and in conformity with the statutes of the State of Florida, certifying the electoral votes of one of these States which my honorable friend who last spoke before the recess [Mr. Tucker] was pleased to call "sovereign States" of this Union. That certificate is the one which was first opened and read in the joint session. There is a second so-called certificate opened in the joint meeting of the two Houses of Congress in which the persons signing the same preface their own certificate by one signed by an officer not recognized by the laws of the United States nor by the statutes of Florida as a certifying officer, being the attorney-general of the State of Florida. He certifies that there is no provision of the law of Florida "whereby the result of said returns can be certified to the executive of said State," admitting by that certificate, if it has any force at all, that his action is without the law and without any sanction of the statutes of the State. Next, the self-styled electors certify to their own election and their own qualifications, and that they themselves notified the governor of their own election. That is the certificate No. 2, a certificate of unauthorized persons and uncertified persons in the view of the laws, State and national, and that was presented and opened in pursuance of the recent act of Congress for what it is worth.

There is a third certificate still more extraordinary, still more wanting in all the legal elements of electoral verification, and which asks for itself consideration. It is a certificate which is thoroughly *ex post facto*, certified by an officer not in existence until the functions of the office had been exhausted; a certificate which recites or refers to posterior proceedings in a subordinate court and in a superior State court, the latter expressly excluding the electoral question; a certificate which is accompanied by that sort of a return which a canvassing board might under some circumstances report to the State officers, but which has never been sent to the Congress of the United States or to the President of the Senate for their consideration in the one hundred years in which we have been a Republic. Every date of the judicial orders and of the laws authorizing the executive acts certified, the official existence of the very officers who certify them, the proceedings in the court as recited in them, are all subsequent to that time which by the Constitution and laws of the United States is the date fixed for the final performance of electoral functions.

These two certificates, therefore, are wanting in all the elements of constitutional and legal validity which should exist to give them audience before this Commission. They conform in no respect to the laws of the country as they now are, or to the laws of the State as they were on the 6th day of December, when the functions of the electors were ended. More than that, if the first certificate, designated as certificate No. 1, is a constitutional and legally certified expression of the vote of the State of Florida, that question being settled in favor of this certificate obviates the necessity for considering the certificates numbered 2 and 3. I ought, perhaps, to say to the honorable Commission that it is fortunate they did not grant the request of our objectors for an adjournment till to-morrow. The next mail might have brought to you certificate No. 4 or 5, reciting to you new proceedings, a new action before the courts, and no end would come to the papers that might be presented in party or personal interest as establishing a retroactive right to exercise an electoral function in the State of Florida.

I shall. therefore, cheerfully confine the argument to certificate No. 1, because if the objections to that certificate are invalid, and the certificate itself is valid, of course that dismisses all need of consideration of the other certificates, and we shall have ascertained what is the constitutional and legal electoral vote of the State of Florida.

The objections to this certificate are substantially one, namely, that there was fraud, or conspiracy, or both somewhere behind it, and behind the college, not by reason of anything which appears in connection with the electoral college or its proceedings or on the face of the certificate, but because of action on the part of local or State canvassing officers, or of the people, and away behind all action of the presidential electors themselves. Hence it is that we have heard this morning, chiefly, instead of a constitutional and legal presentation of the question within your jurisdiction, a speech before this Commission as if it were a jury in a court having original jurisdiction to determine law, to determine fact, to establish titles to office, to oust and to install officers, to decide rights between parties, to decide State rights, to decide national rights, an assertion that State or county officials, wholly outside of national control, have somehow acted fraudulently under State law, and that this electoral return has been vitiated thereby.

Now, it is not within the scope of my purpose to answer otherwise than generally that argument which took up most of the time of the objectors who opened this discussion. I must affirm, however, to this Commission that the first objector was in error in saying that we on this side had nothing to say contradicting his assertions of fraud. We say everything in denial of fraud in the State officers. We affirm fraud in directly the reverse sense, and frauds which you would ascertain in the very steps to which he calls your attention, in the action of certain county canvassers certifying results for Tilden electors. For example, when he refers to Baker County, I entirely dissent from his view of the facts as existing of record in that case; but if you go into that question in Baker County to verify his assertions, we should inevitably ask that you go into Jackson County, where, under other political domination, they rejected 271 votes actually cast for the Hayes electors. We should ask you to go into Alachua County and find at one precinct a railroad train of non-resident passengers getting off on their passage through and voting the ticket which was supported by the objector [Mr. Field] who made the allegation against Baker County. We should invoke your attention to Waldo precinct of the same county to find that they had vitiated that poll also by what is called stuffing the ballot-box. And so on with other counties passed upon by the State board.

We answer, then, the allegation that their charges of fraud have not been denied by us, by stating that if they are ever reached in the exercise of your jurisdiction, we propose to show, and shall show in that contingency, that there was such a case of fraud in the incipiency of that vote which they claim should elect their candidate as would astonish not only this Commission, but the whole country by its presentation. I unite with my friends in condemning fraud wherever it exists. It should not only vitiate the result which it produced when it is ascertained by the proper tribunals, but it should also condemn every man, public or private, who participated in it. We are not here to defend fraud. We are here, however, to say not only that the allegation of it as made on the other side is not correct, but that the very next step behind the county canvassers confronts you with some of the grossest cases of the violation of the popular right to freely cast the vote, and to have that vote counted, which have ever been found in the history of this country.

If we go for fraud, let us go to the bottom of it; let us go where that fraud is found in such a degree and with such force, in more than one State, North and South, as to penetrate the very foundation of the popular sovereignty of this country, and to lead every patriot to consider whether the highest duty of legislators is not first to put their guards where alone fraud is essentially to be feared, namely, at the ballot-box, because it is further removed from the sight of the general public and from the control of supervising authority.

I leave that question now. I do not believe that this Commission by the Constitution or laws was ever intended, or has the power, to go to the extent that would be required if it attempted to probe these mutual allegations of fraudulent voting and fraudulent canvassing to the bottom by judicial investigation and judicial decision.

It seems to me that our honorable friends on the other side have been misled by the judicial atmosphere of this hall, consecrated usually to the jurisdiction of a constitutional court of justice. Under the influence of these columns as pillars of a supreme court, and with the judicial associations of this chamber, they have addressed you, honorable gentlemen of the Commission, as if you were a constitutional court, vested with the power to try causes without a jury, vested both with the powers of a subordinate and an appellate court in a proceeding by *quo warranto*, and vested with unlimited discretion in the determination of rights to hold the electoral office. They have presented to you the following questions upon which it is absolutely necessary to come to a decision, upon their theory of your jurisdiction:

First. Is this Commission a general canvassing-board with power to recanvass the popular vote of the State of Florida?

Second. Is this Commission a national court of appeal from the State canvassing-boards?

Third. Is this Commission a judicial court of appeal from the State circuit court of Florida in proceedings by writ of *quo warranto?*

The gentlemen on the other side affirmed that your jurisdiction was co-extensive with that of a court in a proceeding by *quo warranto;* and I add in response to the alleged decision of this subordinate court, Judge White's court in Florida, that it is not a final determination of that proceeding by *quo warranto.* We are informed, and so claim the fact to be, that it is now pending on appeal in the supreme court of the State of Florida. Hence I ask the question whether this Commission can take jurisdiction from the supreme court of Florida, after regular appeal from the circuit court, of the proceedings in *quo warranto.*

The affirmative of all these propositions is taken by our opponents. They do affirm that you are a canvassing-board with power to recanvass the vote of Florida cast by the people; they do affirm that you are not merely a canvassing-board, but a national court of appeal from the action of the canvassing-board of Florida; they do affirm that you are a court so judicial that from the action of the State circuit court of Florida you can take jurisdiction by reviewing that action; and they do affirm that there is no limit to your power to investigate into the honesty and integrity of the action of the returning-board of Florida, and to determine originally, with the powers of a court, to whom the certificate of election should have been awarded.

This represents the legal position of our opponents. I ask, therefore, what are the powers of this Commission? I need not remind the honorable gentlemen composing it that the assumption of these powers implies that we are to have no election of a President and Vice-President of the United States by the time limited for the commencement of the functions of their offices. You cannot say to those gentlemen, "We will go behind the regular certificates provided by the Constitution and the law just so far as will accommodate you to find whether it is true or not that what you allege to be fraud was done against your interest in one or two counties. We must, if we go behind the electoral college, go where all the allegations of fraud on both sides assert its existence." It is the popular vote that those gentlemen say you are to review, to recanvass, and to ascertain. Where does this Commission get its power for that? By the act organizing the Commission you are vested with the right to consider just so much of this alleged case as Congress might consider; and when I say "Congress," I include, of course, the two Houses. Let me ask then what is that limit? We must clear our minds from what has grown within the later years to be most dangerous to the reserved rights of the States and to the rights of the people, namely, the assertion of unlimited universal power of each House, or of both Houses, to assume jurisdiction over all things or questions having a national aspect or relation. No such undefined grasp was intended by the Constitution. Suppose this act—and I beg the attention of gentlemen to it—suppose this act had provided that, instead of surrounding the President of this Commission with these gentlemen and conferring these indefinite powers, Congress had chosen to surround the President of the Senate with only the representatives of the Senate and of the House, would you have thought of attributing judicial power to them? The same power that justifies Congress under the Constitution of the United States in providing that the counting should be done by this Commission would have justified them in providing that the counting should be done by the President of the Senate alone. Admitting that Congress has power to that extent to regulate the counting, you must guide yourselves by the same principles in determining your jurisdiction that you yourselves would decide limited the jurisdiction of the President of the Senate as sole counting agent were he designated by this act to count the votes alone.

Now suppose that act in existence, and you have it by law that the Vice-President shall not only open, but shall himself count the votes. If the Constitution had said " and the votes shall then be counted *by him*," the same result would have been attained. If instead of "by him" you add the two words " by Congress," you do not vary the power at all. Whatever counting is to be done is to be done either by the President of the Senate or by the two Houses of Congress. In either case it is only to " count." That is the substance. The rest is agency. Would you maintain for one moment, if that were the provision, either of Constitution or law, that the President of the Senate should count the votes, that he had the right to send out commissioners to take depositions, " to take into view " all other papers, to reach evidence at will, to recanvass the popular vote of the State of Florida, to organize the whole machinery alike of executive canvassing-boards of a State and of all the judicial courts of the State ? Is there a gentleman on this Commission from either House of Congress or from the Supreme Bench who would tolerate for a moment the exercise of such power under the simple language " shall count the votes ? " If not, then the act has given no additional power to fifteen men beyond that power which by the like terms would have been conferred upon one man ; and hence I affirm that there is in this law no power whatever to do more than is necessarily implied in the words " and the votes shall then be counted."

If that be so, then we come to the next question, What does the word " count " mean ? and is the power of that sort that implies something not ministerial, or within the narrow circuit of discretion that belongs to the ministerial power ? Does it imply, as gentlemen on the other side claim, the unlimited circuit of the judicial power ? If it does, your Constitution in its very frame-work and organization is violated.

The first three articles of the Constitution divide the functions of this Government into legislative, executive, and judicial. The third article affirms positively that the judicial power is vested in one Supreme Court and in inferior courts to be established. So the first article says that all legislative power granted is vested in the Congress of the United States. So the second article says that the executive power is vested in the President. Your limits are drawn by the Constitution of your country, which tells you that the several powers of this Government, the three great powers, shall not by any contrivance be merged or mingled in any tribunal, whether constituted of the three divisions, or of any or either of the three. The safety of our people hangs on it ; the safety of our States hangs upon it ; all the elements of national safety hang upon the observance of that division of the functions of government. It is the greatest act in the progress of modern civilization as contrasted with the ancient and the Eastern, which combined all functions in one supreme head. It withholds each department of power from assuming either of the other essential powers of the Government, that the people may be saved from the tyranny of irresponsible authority.

The claim made on the other side confuses and merges them in so far as you are asked to exercise judicial functions in the determination of rights. The very language used this morning was that your powers were co-extensive in this matter with those of a court trying a proceeding by *quo warranto*. Are you, then, a court under the third article of the Constitution ?

I therefore think it may be assumed that the indefinite language of this act of Congress confers no such powers as claimed upon this delegated Commission, organized to tide over a difficulty, and to do the ministerial act of counting the votes in the stead of the President of the Senate.

I have spoken of the narrow circuit of discretion that surrounded the ministerial act of counting. I beg to renew the distinction that there is no difference made by adding, as this act implies, the words " by Congress " at the end of the constitutional clause, so that it would read " shall then be counted by Congress." It is the same as if the words were added " shall then be counted by him," meaning the President of the Senate. The essential factor of the phrase is the " count."

Now what is that narrow circuit of discretion ? It is broad enough to ascertain whether the papers before you as certificates are genuine and not counterfeit, and are duly and truly verified by State authority, as required under the Constitution and laws. It is broad enough to ascertain whether the electoral college has complied with the law. This is a ministerial examination. Do the papers upon their face contain evidence of fraud, of doubt, of irregularity, of error ? Is certificate number two on its face more regular, more free from apparent fraud, more worthy of being received in evidence than certificate number one ? Is certificate number three a truer certificate, more in compliance with law, and bearing upon its face greater evidences of its authenticity ? Which is the authentic certificate and the authenticated vote ? These are the questions to be ministerially settled. Neither Congress nor any officers created by it have the right to recount popular votes; for the Constitution says expressly, it is the *electoral votes* that are to be counted, not the popular vote. Over this Congress has no power under the presidential clauses of the Constitution.

Every phase of the discussion confronts us in a narrower or broader circle of reasoning with this one question: Are you to revise and adjudicate all the proceedings of State elections for electors of President and of all State tribunals relating thereto appointed by State laws ? We always come around to that. Or are you to count what is properly certified and presented to you ? If you affirm the first proposition, you must declare the Constitution amended by this tribunal, *ipso facto* amended, so that it shall read : " Each State shall appoint, in such manner as the legislature thereof may direct, a number of electors equal," &c., *subject, however, to revision by the Congress of the United States, who shall have power to overrule the State authorities in determining the college of electors*. Would the Constitution ever have been adopted with that construction ?

We are brought inevitably to such an amendment by construction. Yet the Constitution sought to preserve absolutely the right of the State to appoint its electors without Federal dictation. It required every ballot to be cast on the same day throughout the Union, that it might be free from every centralized influence. Every member of the Commission knows what the history of the adoption of this clause is, and yet we are brought perpetually by the claims of the other side to this one question: Shall we now go on and complete the absorption of this most absolute, independent, and unquestioned right of the States to appoint their electors in their own way, and hold that it is subject to revision and change by the two Houses of Congress?

The objectors ask are we, then, to take the certificate of the proper State officers against the truth ? Is there any reason why, on the other hand, it should not be asked, are we to take the certificate of these fifteen gentlemen against the truth ? There is a necessity in public affairs and, in the very organization of society and of political communities, an absolute necessity to have some final jurisdiction. There must be somewhere an authority by which we stand, even if it be impeached by charges of fraud. Where is that authority ? Is it here ? Is it in the governor ? Is it in the canvassing-board ? Is it in the State legislature ? Is it in the State judiciary ? Where is it ? I submit that for the purposes of this case, and under the Constitution and laws, it is found where the State authority concludes, and that if the Constitution and laws of the United States in manner, in time, in substance, so far as shown by the duly-certified results, are conformed to, there is the determination of the case.

I regret to pause, may it please the Commissioners, to repel the suggestions made against this returning-board. It was said that the court had found their return fraudulent. There is no evidence in the records of the court that that allegation is true. I have read the decision, and in answering their argument I must say there is not an allusion to the fact that that canvassing-board acted fraudulently. It was alleged that their action, which had conformed to the action two years before, was a misinterpretation of their rights under the law; and in the document submitted a few moments ago to the commissioners, I think, on the second page, there is a copy of the essential section of the law. The important language of the act to which I wish to call the attention of the Commissioners in the statutes of Florida regulating the powers of this board is this:

If any such returns shall be shown or shall appear to be so irregular, false, or fraudulent that the board shall be unable to determine the true vote for any such officer or member, they shall so certify, and shall not include such return in their determination and declaration.

Mr. Commissioner EDMUNDS. Can you give us the date of that statute?

Mr. Representative KASSON. That is the old statute, under which the election was held, passed February 27, 1872, and was the law in force at the time of the canvass, at the time of the certificate of the electors, at the time of the voting of the electors, and until the 17th of January, 1877.

Mr. Commissioner GARFIELD. Has the paper been filed?

Mr. Commissioner EDMUNDS. Not as evidence.

Mr. Representative KASSON. I simply use it for reference, because in it is found this statute of Florida. I refer to it here and for that purpose. This document was handed to the Commissioners for the law-references in it.

Thus it will be seen that the canvassing-board of Florida were to inquire if these returns appeared to be so irregular, false, or fraudulent that the board was unable to ascertain the true vote. That was their function. In exercising that function they not merely passed upon the returns of the county canvassers but upon the certified results in precincts.

The court said they had overstepped the law. And here I must remind the gentlemen composing the Commission that, when they made the recanvass which I have styled canvass number two under order of the supreme court of Florida, it will appear they then reported not only the result in respect to governor, but they also reported the result in respect to electors. That result of the second canvass showed the election of the Hayes electors, but by a reduced majority. These electors appear to have run two or three hundred votes ahead of the State ticket, and the recanvass left them still some two hundred majority. That appeared on the record. It does not appear on the printed document which has been submitted on the other side here, I suppose because the court ruled that they intended their order to only apply to State officers; and therefore they struck out, after it had once gone in the record, the result as to the electors; but it was originally a part of the proceedings under order of the court, which, if gone into, will disclose the fact that not only canvass number one showed the election of the Hayes electors, but canvass number two "had under the order and in accordance with the ruling of the supreme court" showed both the election of the democratic State ticket and the election of the Hayes electors.

Mr. Commissioner ABBOTT. Was that called in question at all in that case of Drew against the other party?

Mr. Representative KASSON. It was said not to be raised by the pleadings or by the order, but was in the return of the canvass as to the election of governor. The canvass had under the order of the court in that case showed both classes of elections, that of the electoral college and that of the State officers. The result of that count, when made under that ruling, was what I have stated, and then objection was taken to its record, and the court said they were not considering the electoral count, and struck it out.

Mr. Commissioner ABBOTT. My only desire was to learn whether that was ruled at all in the case.

Mr. Representative FIELD. Please to state that in the recanvass this canvassing-board put back Baker County so as to include only two precincts.

Mr. Representative KASSON. That is only to say that the gentlemen on the other side want to take just so much of that action under order of the court as suits their case, and reject all the rest. They applied the rule and determined the result, and they made changes in several counties both ways; they put back some democratic votes, they put back some republican votes. I only allude to it in answer to the statement here, because the printed proceedings do not contain all the proceedings in that case. This is left out. But if the case is gone into those facts must also appear.

Then we come to canvass No. 3, made after the college was *functus officio*, and here you find that, not satisfied at all, they appointed a new board of State canvassers. From that new board they left out the attorney-general of the State. This I suppose was owing to the fact that his opinion had been, as to the law of the case in many points of the canvass, with the republican members of the board. These papers which have been laid on your desk show that, instead of the attorney-general being a member of the new State canvassing-board, the treasurer of the State was substituted.

Now, I ask, if you are to recognize canvass after canvass and the changing results of partisan affiliations, the changing desires of individuals, the changing influences surrounding the canvassing-board and the whole political aspect of the State? Are you to change your rules of law, and to say that canvass after canvass may be made after the electoral function was exhausted, and that the last canvass made under the circumstances should prevail, *ex post facto* entirely, *ex post facto* by law authorizing it, *ex post facto* by executive authority, *ex post facto* by the constitution of the board, *ex post facto* by the exhaustion of the functions of the officers themselves elected, *ex post facto* because the very terms of the officers elected had expired?

This *ex post facto* certificate No. 3 is dated January 26, 1877, and when opened in the joint meeting of the two houses was stated by the President of the Senate to have been received only the day before the joint meeting. This certificate recites a law of January 17, 1877, and also a law of January 26, 1877, as the authority for the certificate. It recites the third canvass of which I have already spoken, and which was made on the 19th of January, 1877, and the copy of that canvass is certified under date of January 26, 1877. Then this canvass No. 3 was legislated to be the canvass by act dated January 26, 1877. These are the essential points of certificate No. 3.

The objector next me [Mr. Field] proposed at the opening to explain in his argument what he styled the "jugglery" by which the Hayes electors got their certificates. I ask this Commission, if there be a *prima facie* presumption of fraud, whether it exists against those officers elected before fraud could have been contemplated, against a board that acted at the time required by the State law, against a board that acted

at the time provided by congressional law, against a board that acted in
ignorance of the electoral vote in other States, as it was contemplated
by our fathers they should do; *or* does that presumption of fraud exist
against the men who knew the importance of a change of the result
in Florida, against men who acted in full knowledge of the necessity of
the action they took to accomplish their result, against men who
organized a new tribunal and enacted a new law to accomplish that
result?

If there be fraud, if there be conspiracy as alleged, where does the
presumption of law under these circumstances place it? Inevitably it
places it where the motive of the act, the knowledge requisite to give
the motive effect, and the purpose to be accomplished, were all before
the eyes of the persons participant in it. Fraud cannot be so presumed
against the parties who acted in conformity with law and in discharge
of duty at the time required by law, and in the mode required by law,
and in the presence of a political opponent, as that presumption would
exist against those who do it at irregular times, outside the provisions
of the law, and with the full knowledge of the effect which would be
produced upon the general result. The conspiracy is not with the first,
but with the last canvass.

A few words more before I close. I believe I have expressed already
my great regret that we have not been able on both sides to argue these
questions exclusively on points where we all see and all know are to be
found the hinges on which this decision is hung. But my honorable
friend from Virginia [Mr. Tucker] in his argument not only spoke of the
fact, which was unsupported by any evidence, but which he said he
could support by some evidence, that there was bad motive and fraudulent conduct on the part of the canvassing-board, of which I have seen
no evidence whatever; but he went further and asked, are we to submit
this great question of the supreme Magistrate of the United States to
the determination of a trio of oligarchs in Florida? Trio of oligarchs!
What shall I say of the quartette of oligarchs in my State who exercise
corresponding functions? What shall I say of the quartette or the quin-
tette of oligarchs that exist in every State of this Union, save perhaps
two or three, who are empowered in the same manner to preserve the
rights of their respective States as canvassing-boards? Nay, more, I
should like to ask my honorable friend, what shall I say of the solo of
oligarchy in Oregon and his right to determine the election of Chief
Magistrate? Is there any significance in giving a name of this sort to
a tribunal which is acting under and because of the provisions of the
Constitution and laws of the United States or of the State? I answer
to all that, that the question is, where does the law put the power to arrive at that determination on which action is based? Whether that be
one man or five men, or three men, that determination is *prima facie*
valid, and can be vitiated only in the modes provided by the laws of the
local or general jurisdiction, as the case may be.

The case is made when it is found to be in accordance with Constitution and law in time, manner, and due certification of authenticity. Can
it be upset? Yes, if legal provision is made therefor. Where? asks the
gentleman. I answer, within the jurisdiction where the laws provide
for the appellate or original determination of rights. But, says the
gentleman, suppose no such provision of law is made? Then, I answer
that a *casus omissus* of proper authority is no reason for the usurpation
of that authority where not a scintilla of constitutional law has placed
it. If the allegation were true, it simply shows the necessity of further

legislation where that legislation ought to exist. If it be untrue, the whole ground and fabric of the argument here falls to the ground.

The Constitution says that we have very little to do with this matter of elections by States. The history of it shows that it was intended that we should have very, very little to do with the determination of the result. It gave us no authority to overrule State action; and the alleged right to change a duly certified result contains within itself a claim of right, and without appeal, to deny to the States that exclusive right which the Constitution took such extraordinary pains to confirm to them.

If you have the right to say that another set of votes must be counted in Florida, you have the right to say that another set of votes must be counted in New York; and if you take jurisdiction to allow the mere ninety votes which constitute the alleged majorities in Florida, and which would change the electoral college of that State, a partisan Congress may assert that the sixty thousand majority of my State shall be overthrown, and we cannot question it nor take appeal.

I speak to you as if you were Congress, because the act says that whatever Congress might do in the consideration of certain questions you may do. I say that Congress itself in no element of its character contains a justification for such a construction of its power as it is proposed now to give to it. It is the legislative body of the country, and may inquire into all these facts, which they have perhaps in both branches inquired into, because they may be needed to amend the Constitution or amend the law.

But the act which creates the board of fifteen says, not that you have the same powers which Congress has, but you have the same powers which Congress has "*for this purpose.*" What purpose? For counting the votes, as the President of the Senate would do it if Congress had chosen to give him that power. There stand the great bulwarks of the Constitution, where they divide the three powers of the Government, and they cannot be overthrown.

You cannot be judges of this or any other question for judicial action. If both Houses were unanimous, it would be usurpation for them to determine judicially who was entitled to the vote of the State of Florida as constituting its electoral college; and without that power this Commission is limited to the determination of the relative validity and authentication of these three certificates, which is the certificate that is duly certified to be counted. Go behind this certificate, unless simply to determine the verity of the several authentications and their conformity to law, and you launch yourselves into a tumultuous sea of allegations of fraud, irregularity, and bad motive, and, as my honorable friend on the other side says, greed of office or undue ambition to secure the honors of the State. There is no limit unless we draw the constitutional line narrowly. You cannot expand it without launching this vessel of our Constitution upon a sea full of rocks and dangers, where there is every prospect that it will be shattered, and the very structure preserving the rights of the States and the nation will go to pieces.

Mr. Commissioner THURMAN. Will it interrupt your argument, Mr. Kasson, if I make an inquiry? Do I understand your argument to go to this length, that if the State of Florida had elected four members of Congress or four persons under the disability of the fourteenth amendment, and they had cast their votes for President, we should be bound to count them?

Mr. Representative KASSON. I have borne in mind that a question would arise as to Tennessee and some other States touching individual electors, as it is also presented in one of the objections that have been submitted in the House. I have not had time since last evening to do more than to become possessed in my own mind of the general arguments and the results of those arguments applicable to the general principles of this case.

I have no doubt that the provision of the Constitution touching offices of trust, profit, and emolument, and that also relating to persons disqualified by participation in the rebellion, are imperative upon the several States, and it is expected that they will conform to them. Whether we can go behind, whether it was intended that we should go behind, the action of the States upon the assumption that they had violated that constitutional duty, or to prove that they had violated it, is a question that I leave to the consideration of those who shall follow me.

Of course I understand that one of the objections in Florida, if you do permit yourselves to go behind and examine it, does involve that point; but as my time has now nearly expired, I have not the opportunity to go into it and will leave it to counsel.

The PRESIDENT. You have five minutes of your hour.

Mr. Representative KASSON. May it please the Commission, I have said all that I regard essential in that part of the case which has fallen to me, and I trust my honorable friend who is associated with me will address himself still more effectually to points which I have alluded to and to the remaining points of the case.

My great anxiety and my belief in the great importance of this case all rest upon the fact that it is proposed that Congress shall, through you, usurp judicial powers for the first time in the history of this country. It is a usurpation which loses sight of the great divisions of authority in the Constitution of the United States and of the original reserved rights of the States.

I wish, in addition, to simply call the attention of the Commission to the recent decision in Florida, which has been published, and in which that court bases its decision against a judicial quality in the returning-board of Florida upon the constitution of Florida, which has the same division of powers to which I have referred as existing in the Constitution of the United States. The court therefore says that this canvassing-board cannot do anything except the ministerial act of determining upon the face of the returns irregularity, fraud, &c.; and by a strange inconsistency of argument, the gentlemen on the other side, coming to Washington in the case of Florida, ask this Commission to take the other ground, which has been overruled as law in Florida, and say that we, who have not the powers conferred by statute upon the Florida board, have immensely larger powers, which have not been hinted at in the Constitution and laws of the United States, and do have the right to exercise judicial functions.

I commend to the consideration of the Commission that decision, to which I refer, in the case of Drew vs. Stearns. And with that I submit this part of the case to the consideration of the Commission.

The PRESIDENT. The second objector will be heard on the same conditions and limitations.

Mr. Representative McCRARY. Mr. President and gentlemen of the Commission, I think I ought to say in justice to myself that perhaps no counsel ever appeared in so important a case upon so short a notice and with such inadequate opportunity for preparation. It was not until about four o'clock yesterday that I was made aware of the rule which the Commission had promulgated during the day, providing that gentlemen of either House uniting in objections to these votes should be heard before the tribunal; but appreciating the great importance of dispatch in the conduct of this case, I have not felt at liberty to ask for any greater indulgence than that which the tribunal has already awarded.

The question which this Commission is to decide is tersely and clearly set forth in the act of Congress under which it has been organized, and it is "by a majority of votes" to "decide whether any, and what, votes from such State, are the votes provided for by the Constitution of the United States."

How broad is the jurisdiction given by this act? How far can the Commission go in this inquiry? It has been asserted by counsel who addressed the tribunal this morning that you sit here as a court possessing all the functions and powers of a judicial tribunal clothed with authority to hear, try, and determine a case of *quo warranto*, in order to settle the title to an office. The announcement of the learned counsel of this proposition, I must confess, was a startling one to me. If it be true, what are to be the consequences? If this tribunal shall so construe the Constitution, and shall hold that it sits here as a court with these judicial powers to try the title of every one of the three hundred and sixty-nine presidential electors chosen at the recent election or at any election, it will follow that the two Houses of Congress sit as a court clothed with this great power to review and revise and set aside and hold for naught the action of all the States of this Union. If one case can be made against one elector in the United States, requiring Congress or this tribunal to go down among the forty-five millions of people and decide how many votes were legally cast for this candidate or that, a case can be made against every one of the members of the electoral college of the United States, and the result is—I say it with deliberation—that, unless the two Houses of Congress shall consent, the people of the United States can never again be allowed to choose a President and Vice-President. It is not necessary for me to say to this tribunal that it is utterly impossible for the two Houses of Congress to exercise such a jurisdiction as this. It is utterly impossible for this tribunal to exercise it with any degree of discretion or deliberation even in the few cases that will be brought to your attention and adjudication. If the Constitution clothes the two Houses with the power now asserted to try the title of all the electors, not upon the credentials that come here under the seal of the States of the Union, not upon the evidence which the laws of the land prescribe as evidence of title to this office, but by an inquiry into the question how many people have voted for this candidate and that, and in all the States of the Union, I say it is utterly impossible for either the two Houses of Congress or this tribunal to exercise a jurisdiction like that.

How are we to determine what are the votes of a State provided for by the Constitution? The Constitution has provided the extent of this inquiry, has limited and defined it:

Each State shall appoint, in such manner as the legislature thereof may direct, a number of electors, equal to the whole number of Senators and Representatives to which the State may be entitled in the Congress.

The election of President of the United States is by the States, and the States appoint the electors. Gentlemen have argued, and their whole case rests upon the argument, that the appointment of electors is by the votes of the people at the polls; that that constitutes the appointment; and that, therefore, the Commission must inquire how the people have voted at the polls in order that Congress may decide who have been appointed electors. But, may it please the Commission, the appointment of the electors is not by the votes of the people at the polls. That may possibly be one of the steps required by the laws of the State, but the appointment of the electors is by the vote of the people cast at the polls, by the action of such tribunals as the State laws have created, canvassing, determining, and ascertaining the result of that vote, and by the issuing in pursuance of that canvass of the evidence showing the election of the electors. The State acts through its officials, through its constituted authorities, and the State declares who has been appointed. Therefore when the Constitution says that we shall inquire who have been appointed electors by the State in accordance with the laws of the State or as directed by the legislature of the State, we are simply to inquire what persons have been declared to be electors by the tribunal and the authority which the State law has created for that purpose. Now, the law of Florida, which has already been called to the attention of the Commission, provides:

On the thirty-fifth day after the holding of any general or special election for any State officer, member of the legislature, or Representative in Congress, or sooner, if the returns shall have been received from the several counties wherein elections shall have been held, the secretary of state, attorney-general, and the comptroller of public accounts, or any two of them, together with any other member of the cabinet who may be designated by them, shall meet at the office of the secretary of state, pursuant to notice to be given by the secretary of state, and form a board of State canvassers, and proceed to canvass the returns of said election, and determine and declare who shall have been elected to any such office or as such member, as shown by such returns. If any such returns shall be shown or shall appear to be so irregular, false, or fraudulent that the board shall be unable to determine the true vote for any such officer or member, they shall so certify, and shall not include such return in their determination and declaration.

By that statute this tribunal was created with the power to canvass the votes and declare the result. The tribunal did canvass the votes and the canvass will be found on the third page of the same document, which I will not take the time now to read; but acting under the authority given them by that statute, they ascertained the result. How far they went in the exercise of the discretionary power which is given them by the statute, may not be material; but it is a fact, which will appear if this Commission shall go into the inquiry, that on three separate occasions, the first and regular canvass, the second canvass made under the mandamus proceedings and in relation to the office of governor, and on a third canvass made subsequently, this board constituted by the laws of the State of Florida ascertained and declared that the gentlemen known as the Hayes electors had a majority of all the votes cast.

Now, Mr. President and gentlemen, what law of Florida is to be looked at in order to determine the mode prescribed by the legislature of that State for appointing these electors? Are we to look at the law as it existed at the time of their appointment, or may we consider statutes that have been passed since? One of the papers which is presented is based entirely upon an adjudication of one of the inferior courts of that State and upon an act of the legislature of that State made long after the appointment of these electors, and long after they had discharged the functions of their office. It appears that a proceeding in *quo warranto* was commenced by the filing of a petition on the 6th day of December, the day upon which the electors met to cast their votes; that a summons was served upon that day at an hour in the day which is named in the papers; and that the electors were cited to appear and answer on the 18th day of the same month. The suit thus commenced continued and passed through various stages until the latter part of January, when a judgment was finally rendered in favor of the gentlemen known as the Tilden electors; but in the mean time—whether before or after the commencement of the original suit does not appear; I have seen nothing in the record that shows at what time in the day the votes were canvassed, but it is entirely immaterial—the electors appointed according to the laws of Florida proceeded to discharge their duties; they cast their votes; they adjourned *sine die.*

It is claimed by counsel that this *quo warranto* proceeding, which went into judgment nearly two months after the casting of the vote of Florida for President and Vice-President by the electors, relates back to the date of the filing of the petition and vacates and vitiates everything that was done in the mean time. That I think is not the law. The writ of *quo warranto* is a proceeding to test the right of an incumbent of an office. It does not restrain him from acting from the time that the original summons may be served. It does not oust him from the office until there is a final judgment of ouster; and there is no authority for the declaration of counsel, I undertake to say, that the judgment in *quo warranto* relates back to the time of the filing of the original petition and vitiates the acts of the officer in the mean time. The authorities are the other way, and I beg to cite a few cases upon that point.

I refer to section 756 of High on Extraordinary Legal Remedies:

> The effect of judgment of ouster upon the officer himself, where the information is brought to test the right of one usurping an office, is to constitute a full and complete amotion from the office and to render null and void all pretended official acts of the officer after such judgment, and the party thus amoved is entirely divested of all official authority and excluded from the office as long as the judgment remains in force.

In 55 Illinois Reports, page 173, will be found the case of The People *vs.* Whitcomb, and there the court say:

> The question sought to be raised by the information in this case is, whether the city officers can extend the city government beyond the original limits of the town, and can levy taxes and enforce ordinances in the portion of territory annexed by the act of February 23, 1869, and which is used exclusively for agricultural purposes, and whether that act is not unconstitutional and void. The demurrer to the answer of respondents brought the whole record, as well the information as the answer, before the court to determine its sufficiency. The first question presented by the demurrer is, whether the remedy, if any exists, has not been misconceived; whether the question of power to extend the city government over this territory thus annexed can be raised by *quo warranto.*
>
> This writ is generally employed to try the right a person claims to an office, and not test the legality of his acts. If an officer threatens to exercise power not conferred upon the office, or to exercise the powers of his office in a territory or jurisdiction within which he is not authorized to act, persons feeling themselves aggrieved may usually restrain the act by injunction.

I next refer to 2d Johnson's Reports, page 184. The whole opinion is very brief, and I will read it:

> This court has a discretion to grant motions of this kind or to refuse them, if no sufficient reasons appear for allowing this mode of proceeding. The office of Sweeting, the acting supervisor, will expire in April, and before the remedy now prayed for can have any effect. There must be an issue joined, and a trial, which could not take place before the next election, so that it would be impossible to restore Teel to his office. It would, therefore, be idle and useless to grant the motion.

That was an application for the writ of *quo warranto* to try a title to this office.

> If the justices have been guilty of any misdemeanor, the party aggrieved must seek a different remedy.

Here, if the Commission please, is a case in Florida, where at the time of the judgment every function of the office of presidential elector had been exercised. The office had ceased to be. The officer had ceased to be and was *functus officio*. What is the extent of the term of office of a presidential elector ? There is no period of time given in the statute during which he shall act ; but he is an officer chosen for the discharge of a particular public duty. When that duty has been performed the term of his office has expired.

I call attention also to a case in Massachusetts decided as early as 1807, the case of Commonwealth *vs.* Athearn, 3 Massachusetts Reports, page 285 :

At the last July adjournment in Suffolk, B. Whitman filed a motion for a rule of court against the respondent to show cause why an information in the nature of a *quo warranto* should not be awarded against him for claiming to hold the office of town clerk of Tisbury, in Dukes County. The court granted a rule, *de bene esse*, returnable at this term.

And now the chief-justice suggested to Whitman that since granting the rule to show cause the court had considered the subject more fully and doubted whether, from the impracticability of giving a remedy in the case, an information ought to be awarded against an officer holding by election for a year only. Whatever may be the authority of the court to issue process of this kind, from the present organization of the terms of the court, it will in no case be possible to come to a decision of the question until a year has expired. In the mean time another election will pass, and the respondent will be either out of office or lawfully in by virtue of a new choice.   *   *   *

PARKER, J. I should not be for granting an information in any case where the judgment of the court upon the information can have no effect. The officer may be liable to a fine in case judgment of amotion be rendered, but not otherwise, as I now recollect. When the information comes to a hearing, this man's tenure in the office he claims will have expired.

And therefore they refused to grant the writ, because the functions of the officer would have ceased before there could be a judgment of ouster, and because a judgment of that character, if the man had ceased to act in his official capacity, would be null and void.

I refer also to the case of the State upon the relation of Newman *vs.* Jacobs, 17 Ohio Reports, and I read a sentence from page 153 :

But further, there is an objection to the proceeding in this case, even as to the appointment of February the 28th, because the term of office has at this time expired. In England it seems not to be considered necessary that the person should continue to hold the office at the time of applying for the information. In New York, however, and Massachusetts, the information has been refused when the time must expire before the inquiry would have any effect, leaving the parties to their common remedies.

I next cite a case decided by the supreme court of Georgia, and read from 19 Georgia Reports, page 563, the case of Morris *et al. vs.* Underwood *et al.* :

In England, notwithstanding the term of office has expired for which the incumbent has been elected who is sought to be removed, still the courts of that country will grant leave to file the information for the purpose of inflicting a fine for the usurpation ; and that, too, perhaps, where no judgment of ouster can be awarded. It will be found, however, that even this is only done in those cases where the office illegally held is one of a public nature, such as mayor, &c. But the American courts, from the peculiarity of their constitutions, laws, and forms of government, or for some other cause, have, with great unanimity, repudiated this doctrine of imposing a penalty. It has never been enforced in this State, even where the proceeding was directly at the instance of the State. Much less would it be in a case like this, where the effort making is not to forfeit the charter of the bank, but to redress the wrongs of the relators within the corporation. In such a case it is strictly a civil proceeding.

In this case, the term for which these directors were elected had expired by efflux of time six months before the rule was made absolute. There could, therefore, be no judgment of amotion rendered.

There was an attempt in this *quo warranto* proceeding in Florida to render a judgment of amotion or of ouster nearly two months after the expiration of the term of office by the discharge of every duty and every function which belongs to an elector under the laws of the land.

And if no fine could be inflicted, why order the information to be filed ? Why trouble the country with a trial which could result in nothing beneficial to the applicants or prejudicial to their opponents ? In New York and Massachusetts, the information has been refused when the time must expire before the inquiry would have any effect, leaving the parties to their common remedies. (Angell and Ames on Corporations, 436–7.) Much less, then, will the suit be entertained where the term of office has already expired.

The case of The People on the relation of Koerner *et al. vs.* Ridgley *et al.*, in the supreme court of Illinois, is to the same purport, but I will not detain the Commission by reading it. It is in volume 21 of Illinois Reports, page 65. That goes to the point that the proceeding in *quo warranto* must be against a person who holds and executes the functions of an office. It is not against the man, not against the individual, it is against the officer; and when he ceases to be the officer the action falls to the ground as much as a personal suit against an individual falls when the individual dies.

Mr. Commissioner THURMAN. Do I understand Mr. McCrary to say that the case cited decides that an action of *quo warranto* properly commenced against the incumbent of an office abates by reason of the expiration of his term ?

Mr. Representative McCRARY. That is not the point in the case precisely. It is stated in the syllabus thus :

The information should allege that the party against whom it is filed holds and executes some office or franchise, describing it, so that it may be seen whether the case is within the statute or not.

Mr. Commissioner THURMAN. At the time of the commencement ?

Mr. Representative McCRARY. At the time of the commencement; but these other cases do hold that no judgment can be rendered in a *quo warranto* proceeding against a party out of office, and there is no authority to the contrary so far as I can find, after a somewhat diligent search through the Library, to be discovered in this country, although a different rule has sometimes been followed in England.

Mr. Commissioner EDMUNDS. Is there any English case in which a judgment of amotion has been rendered after the expiration of the term ?

Mr. Representative McCRARY. I have not consulted the English authorities; I only judge of their character from what I see in the American cases.

Mr. Commissioner EDMUNDS. The cases of fine are reasonable enough; but my inquiry is whether there is one of amotion.

Mr. Representative McCRARY. I think perhaps there is no case of that kind even in England. They retain jurisdiction for the purpose of assessing the fine, and for no other purpose whatever, after the expiration of the term of office.

Mr. Commissioner THURMAN. How about the judgemnt for costs ?

Mr. Representative McCRARY. The judgment for costs would go against the party perhaps, though I have not gone into that question.

Now, in the very nature of things, this whole proceeding in the courts of Florida must have been after the functions of the electors had been fully discharged. The Constitution of the United States does not prescribe the time when the electors in the States shall cast their votes; it does prescribe that Congress may fix the time, and that it shall be upon the same day in all the States of the Union. In pursuance of this power, Congress has fixed the time by an act passed in 1792 fixing the first Wednesday in December as the time for the casting of the votes.

The record which has been filed in the *quo warranto* case shows that the petition was filed on the 6th of December; that the appearance was

ordered for the 18th of December; that the order was that the respondents should demur or answer by the 28th of December. Those were in
the original orders, and it was at a much later period when the case
finally came to judgment, late in January.

Now, I wish to call the attention of the Commission to the acts of
Congress passed in pursuance of the power conferred upon Congress by
the Constitution, to show how impossible it is that such proceedings as
these can have any force or validity whatever. I refer to sections 135
and 136 of the Revised Statutes. The first declares:

> The electors for each State shall meet and give their votes upon the first Wednesday
> in December in the year in which they are appointed, at such place, in each State, as
> the legislature of such State shall direct.

Section 136 provides that—

> It shall be the duty of the executive of each State to cause three lists of the names
> of the electors of such State to be made and certified, and to be delivered to the electors
> on or before the day on which they are required, by the preceding section, to meet.

The electors, then, are to be appointed; they are to receive from the
executive authority of the State the evidence of their appointment on
or before the first Wednesday in December. How can it be possible
that any court in Florida could have jurisdiction in the last days of
January to decide a question who were the electors in that State?
The gentlemen who exercised these functions on the 6th of December
under the credentials given to them by the regular State authorities of
Florida met on that day, in accordance with the Constitution and the
laws. They cast their votes. They made their return. They certified
their proceedings. They transmitted them to the President of the Senate. They discharged every function that belonged to them under the
Constitution and the laws on the 6th day of December; and it was impossible for them to have discharged it after that date, unless in a certain contingency which is provided for in another section, and which it
is not pretended arose in this case. Section 140 provides, among other
things:

> The electors shall dispose of the certificates thus made by them in the following
> manner:
> One. They shall, by writing under their hands, or under the hands of a majority of
> them, appoint a person to take charge of and deliver to the President of the Senate,
> at the seat of Government, before the first Wednesday in January then next ensuing,
> one of the certificates.
> Two. They shall forthwith forward by the post-office to the President of the Senate,
> at the seat of Government, one other of the certificates.
> Three. They shall forthwith cause the other of the certificates to be delivered to the
> judge of that district in which the electors shall assemble.

That is a statute passed in pursuance of the provision of the Constitution which requires, for the greatest and most important of public
reasons, that the electors in all the States shall assemble and discharge
their duties upon the same day. Now, if it be true that after the college in any State has in accordance with the law assembled upon that
day and discharged its duties, it remains to any court in the State to
review its decision after its action has been transmitted to the seat of
Government, then I say the Constitution in one of its most vital provisions has been trampled upon and violated, for in that case, after the
time fixed by the law, after the result of the election in the whole Union
has been ascertained, after it has been discovered that by changing the
vote of a single State the result of the election in the whole nation may
be changed, parties may institute their proceedings, may bring their
action of *quo warranto*, may proceed to try the case, and may determine

that the electors who have discharged this duty on the day fixed by the Constitution and the laws were not the legal electors. In one State an inferior court having power to issue the writ of *quo warranto*, being attached to one side of the question, will entertain a petition of this character and will decide in favor of one set of electors, and send up to the President of the Senate the record of its proceedings declaring that the men who had voted on the day fixed by the law were not the electors. In another State another judge will perhaps render a judgment in favor of a set belonging to the other side. And so we shall be called upon, instead of counting the votes provided for by the Constitution of the United States and the laws of the land, to investigate the decisions of all these courts in all the States.

I come back then to the position with which I started, and I repeat what my associate has said, in substance, that the Constitution devolves upon the two Houses, or upon the President of the Senate, or upon the person who counts the votes, whoever that may be, the narrowest possible ministerial duty. The framers of the Constitution chose that word which better than any other word in the English language expresses the idea of ministerial duty, contradistinguished from judicial power and authority: "the votes shall then be counted." What do we mean by the word "counted"? To count is to enumerate one by one. It is a narrower term than the word "canvass," which we find used in laws that regulate proceedings of this character, for to canvass implies the right to examine into; but the word "count" expresses the idea of a ministerial duty far more strongly than any other word in our language, or as strongly certainly as any other word.

I will add one other word with reference to this *quo warranto* proceeding. I feel confident that this Commission will determine that the whole proceeding is wholly null and void in so far as the duties of this Commission are concerned. But if that question is to be gone into, we propose to present to this Commission the record of the fact that an appeal has been regularly taken in that case and that it is now pending in the supreme court of the State of Florida; and whatever may have been the value or the force of the original judgment of the circuit court, it is vacated by that appeal; and I presume to say that this Commission will not undertake to decide a case that is now pending before the supreme court of Florida. I will not presume to anticipate what might be the result if this tribunal, entertaining jurisdiction of that case, should decide it one way, and the supreme court of Florida when they reach it in order should decide it the other way. Whether it would form a ground for that proceeding in *quo warranto* under which one of my learned friends proposes to contest or thinks he might contest the right of the President of the United States to hold his office, is a matter that I need not discuss.

I come to the objection that one of the electors of Florida was a shipping commissioner at the time he cast his vote. I am advised that such is not the fact, and that if the Commission will go into an inquiry as to the facts, it will appear that the gentleman referred to had resigned his office at the time of the election. Of that I have no personal knowledge, but I have no doubt from the information I have received that such is the fact. But how does that question come before this tribunal? The objection states that it has been proven by some testimony taken before a committee. The act under which this tribunal is organized and acting prescribes what papers shall come before it:

When all such objections so made to any certificate, vote, or paper from a State shall have been received and read, all such certificates, votes and papers so objected to, and all papers accompanying the same, together with such objections, shall be forth with submitted to said commission.

Now, there are no papers accompanying any of the votes, or papers purporting to be votes, that relate at all to this matter of the alleged ineligibility of one of the electors. I apprehend that it is not competent under this act for any member of either House to make any objection he pleases and refer to any papers he pleases. He must base his objection upon the papers accompanying the votes or the certificates alleged to be votes. Upon this question I think that all we have said with regard to the finality of the action of State tribunals will apply, perhaps not with the same force as to the question whether we can inquire as to the individual votes of the citizens; but still the State authorities have certified that these parties are their electors; they present the evidence which the Constitution and the laws require; they have discharged the functions of that office; they have cast their votes; the State through them has voted; it is not the vote of the elector, it is the vote of the State that has been registered; and I hold that no inquiry can now be made even upon that question. The vote of a State when deposited in the hands of the President of the Senate, certified and evidenced as required by the legislature of that State, "shall," in the language of the Constitution, "be counted."

I desire, if the Commission please, to yield the residue of my time, which I think is some six or seven minutes, to my colleague, who has another suggestion to make.

Mr. Representative KASSON. I do not, Mr. President, desire the time, except a very brief portion of it, to answer after a little reflection the question put to me by the honorable Commissioner from Ohio, and I wish to say that I answer it according to my best judgment, submitting it very deferentially to the able counsel who are likely perhaps to consider the same question, for I understand it is presented by an objection, though not in any proper form appearing upon any of the certificates. I answer the question in accordance with the spirit of the division of powers of the different branches of Government. Congress, under its power to give effect by legislation to constitutional provisions, might probably provide by law for investigation of the question of personal and constitutional disqualification by judicial adjudication, because it is a judicial proceeding in its nature, not executive or legislative; but without such legislation, it is not, in my judgment, a question to be considered in counting, and the question cannot be tried as an incident of count by either an executive or legislative board.

I think I have enabled the Commissioner to understand the principle on which I consider the question as decided, that it is in its nature the determination of a judicial right, and cannot be taken up as an incident to a ministerial function of counting, nor is it within the narrow range of discretion associated with the phrase "ministerial count."

The PRESIDENT. For the information of the Commission I desire to inquire of the objectors to the first certificate whether they propose before the argument by counsel to offer evidence. I inquire of counsel for the information merely of the Commission, that we may know how to act in consultation, do you propose to offer evidence before proceeding to the argument?

Mr. Representative KASSON. While the other side are considering that question I desire to state the position of our side on another matter that was omitted. We regard as not within the act the concluding part of the objection to certificate No. 1, and I simply want to state that we waive no right to exclude that objection as not within the jurisdiction of the tribunal.

The PRESIDENT. I think the Commission prefer that the answer to my inquiry should come from the counsel rather than from the objectors.

Mr. Representative FIELD. It is our opinion, if the Commission please, that we should offer at some stage of the proceedings evidence, and we will do it if the Commission desire——

Mr. Commissioner EDMUNDS. Are you speaking now as an objector, Mr. Field?

Mr. Representative FIELD. I am speaking as an objector.

Mr. Commissioner EDMUNDS. I submit, as one member of the Commission, that the objectors have exhausted their functions, and the rest of the case belongs to counsel.

Mr. Representative FIELD. I was simply answering the question put to me.

The PRESIDENT. In the first place I addressed it to the objectors, but I changed it and asked counsel whether they proposed to offer evidence before proceeding with the argument.

Mr. MERRICK. Mr. O'Conor requests me to answer your honor that we expect to offer evidence, which is now here, before proceeding with the argument. We have been under the impression that the evidence was already before the Commission, without any necessity for a further offer on our part.

The PRESIDENT. That is sufficient, sir. What is the proposition of counsel on the other side?

Mr. Commissioner MILLER. Before proceeding with that, I wish to say, as one of the Commissioners, that I do not understand that any evidence has yet been admitted in this case; and I suggest to the counsel who propose to offer evidence to-morrow morning, that they make a brief synopsis or a brief statement of what it is they propose to offer altogether, instead of offering it in detail and having objections raised to every particular piece of testimony. This is a mere suggestion from myself.

The PRESIDENT. Now we will hear the reply of the counsel on the other side.

Mr. EVARTS. We have no evidence to offer, unless there should be a determination to admit evidence inquiring into facts, and evidence should be produced against us which we should then need to meet.

The PRESIDENT. Should the Commission decide to receive evidence, you expect to have the privilege of offering it afterward?

Mr. EVARTS. We do. To apply it to this particular fact of Humphreys, whenever it is made to appear by evidence which is admitted by this Commission that Mr. Humphreys at any time held an office, we shall need to give evidence, perhaps, that he resigned it before the election.

The PRESIDENT. Of course no such question would arise if the Commission should decide that it was not admissible.

Mr. EVARTS. Undoubtedly; and we suppose we may say on this point that if there is to be an inquiry which adduces evidence, that evidence is to be proved according to the rules which make its production evidence—by the system of the common law.

The PRESIDENT. I did not put the inquiry by direction of the Commission. It was merely, as we are to have private consultation, that we might know what was expected on one side or the other.

Mr. Commissioner THURMAN. I beg leave to make a suggestion. I suppose it is the inclination of counsel to aid the Commission and facilitate its labors as much as possible. There are a number of facts, I suppose, about which there is really no controversy; I mean as to the existence of the facts themselves. Whether proof of them is admissible in this proceeding is a question of law, and wholly different from the question of whether the facts exist or not. Now, if counsel would agree, as far as they can, in respect to those facts of which there can be no controversy, leaving the question of their admissibility as a question of law to the decision of the tribunal, it would very much tend to save our time, much more than to have proof of the facts offered piecemeal and objections argued *pro* and *con*. I should suppose that counsel would be inclined to aid our deliberations and facilitate our investigations by agreeing, as far as they possibly can, upon what are the facts of the case without at all prejudicing themselves upon the question whether they are legally applicable to this investigation.

Mr. Commissioner EDMUNDS. Mr. President, I move that the Commission adjourn until half past ten o'clock to-morrow.

The motion was agreed to; and (at five o'clock and three minutes p. m.) the Commission adjourned.

SATURDAY, *February* 3, 1877.

The Commission met at half past ten o'clock a. m. pursuant to adjournment, all the members being present. There were also present:

Hon. Charles O'Conor, of New York,
Hon. Jeremiah S. Black, of Pennsylvania,
Richard T. Merrick, esq., of Washington, } Of counsel in opposition
Ashbel Green, esq., of New Jersey, to certificate No. 1.
William C. Whitney, esq., of New York,

Hon. William M. Evarts, of New York,
Hon. E. W. Stoughton, of New York, } Of counsel in opposition to
Hon. Stanley Matthews, of Ohio, certificates Nos. 2 and 3.
Hon. Samuel Shellabarger, of Ohio,

The journal of yesterday's proceedings was read and approved.

The PRESIDENT. I will state to the counsel at the bar that the proceedings under rule 4 are concluded. Proceedings will now take place under rule 3, two counsel on a side being allowed.

Doubtless some question will arise as to the best mode of proceeding. It occurs to the Chair, without speaking for the Commission, that a convenient and just mode may be that counsel representing the objectors to certificate No. 1 should make their offers of proof in a concise, well-arranged, classified form, and then that the counsel representing the objectors to the second certificate should make their offers of proof, based of course upon the condition that proof should be admitted, it being understood by the Chair that they probably may object to all proofs on the part of the counsel representing objections to certificate No. 1. They can therefore make their provisional offers of proof in case there shall be a decision that proofs are admissible. Then the Commission will have before it a case, and so will the bar. The case then would be, if that course should be adopted and pursued, the certificates with the accompanying papers, the objections, and the offers of proof, upon which the counsel on the one side and the other would be heard. Then the Commission would in a great degree have before it the whole case and all the questions that arise under it.

Mr. O'CONOR. Mr. President and gentlemen of the Commission,

advised of the position which this controversy stood in and the stage of it at which we had arrived, by the question somewhat suddenly propounded last evening to us before the adjournment, I have endeavored in the *interim* to adjust a statement of what seemed to me to be desirable matter in the nature of evidence to be laid before this Commission—as distinct, and as succinct, and as brief, and as explanatory and intelligible a statement as, by the utmost efforts I could possibly make, having in view the act of Congress under which this Commission is acting, which seems to contemplate great promptitude, or at least a great effort at celerity upon the part of all concerned, so that the possibly numerous matters of investigation that may be presented may be gotten rid of within the limited time allowed by the circumstances, and the many observations that have fallen from the bench evincing on the part of the honorable Commissioners a strong desire to second this object on the part of Congress, and to accelerate as much as possible the proceedings.

I did not prepare that exactly in the form of an offer of evidence; but, although that be not its form, that is the substance of what I have written, which presently I will read, there not having been time even to make a fair copy of it, much less to have it printed.

Mr. EVARTS. Mr. O'Conor, will you allow me to say a word?

Mr. O'CONOR. Certainly.

Mr. EVARTS. Mr. President and gentlemen, if we are to assume that the intimations of the President are the order of the Commission as to the manner of the conduct of the trial, it is the first knowledge we have that that order will be the method of this trial.

The PRESIDENT. It is not the order of the Commission; it was a suggestion from the presiding officer.

Mr. EVARTS. No objection was made by any of your associates; and if Mr. O'Conor was to proceed I supposed it was upon that idea; and I do not question that fact; I only wish to say that if that is the order of this Commission as to the method of this trial, it is the first instruction which we as counsel have received that that would be the method, and we have not prepared and are not ready to proceed upon that method of trial so far as affirmative action on our part is to go.

Mr. Commissioner EDMUNDS. I do not think it is understood, Mr. Evarts, certainly it is not by myself, that supposing you object to the proofs offered by Mr. O'Conor you are necessarily called upon at the same time to state what you expect to prove in reply if his proofs shall be received. That comes later.

Mr. EVARTS. That comes later, of reply to their proofs; but the President laid down a proposition that we were to propose——

The PRESIDENT. No proposition.

Mr. EVARTS. That is our first instruction that we should have that right or authority.

Mr. Commissioner EDMUNDS. I think all we need do to-day, Mr. Evarts, is to hear any objections you may make to the proofs offered on the other side.

Mr. EVARTS. And we shall not be called upon to proceed further to-day?

Mr. Commissioner EDMUNDS. You will not be called upon to offer proofs on your own side, so far as I understand, because it may not be necessary.

Mr. O'CONOR. With great respect, I hope the learned Commission is not committed to any of the propositions which have been casually mentioned either by counsel or by any one of its members.

The PRESIDENT. Or by the presiding officer.

Mr. O'CONOR. Or by the presiding officer, who I understood rather hastily to rule——

The PRESIDENT. I have no authority to make any ruling until the Commission instruct me, and they have not instructed me.

Mr. O'CONOR. I was not instructed, nor had I any earlier notice nor had any of us any earlier notice than the learned counsel upon the other side, of the probable course of things this morning, save what sort of instruction we might conceive we had in drawing our own inferences from the observations that fell from the Chair and from the learned Commissioners on both sides of the Chair yesterday. And my object in framing what I propose to read to the court—which I have not myself read a second time yet—was not to conform to any particular view that I have heard exactly from any quarter, but to place the Commission in possession of the general facts of the case in this brief and condensed form, so that the proper course of proceeding might go on and that proper course be adjudged of and determined in a fair view of the matter by the Commission.

The chief consideration which induced me to adopt this course was this: One of your rules indicates that something like a general argument upon this whole case and its merits was to be presented to this court by opposing counsel, each being allowed a period of two hours on the main question and, say, fifteen minutes to present their views on any incidental question that might arise. With these rules before me and the record proper, consisting of the certificates opened by the President of the Senate and the objections to them, and I may add as part of the record the statements made to this honorable Commission by the managers on both sides, I was led to believe that there would be something possibly quite incongruous and unprofitable, owing to the special condition of this proceeding, in such a course as takes place ordinarily in the subordinate courts before a jury, who are presumed to be entirely incapable of discriminating and apt to be led astray if they hear anything which is not to be taken into judgment in the final consideration of the case. It would be very inconvenient if such a course were to be taken here, because the issue as made by these papers to which I have referred—the certificates and the objections—the issue as made at least by the counsel in favor of the Hayes electors, as I will take the liberty of calling them, makes the question whether any evidence outside of that record shall be received the whole question in controversy. No other can arise except only some possible infirmity in the extrinsic evidence or some possible contradiction. I have supposed, from a careful though very recent view of this case, that there was neither any infirmity in any evidence which the supporters of the Tilden electors desire to present, nor any desire to offer evidence to contradict that evidence, so as to raise a question; and thus I am led to conclude that the admissibility of this so-called extrinsic evidence, its effect, and the final merits of the point which you have to decide on this trial between two sets of electors or two classes of certificates—that is, these three heads, fairly resolve themselves into one and the same question. Whenever a piece of evidence of this extrinsic character shall be offered, there will be literally nothing which the supporters of the Hayes electors can desire to say or desire to present to this Commission in any branch of this controversy that will not then be relevant.

Nor can I perceive that a decision interlocutory upon one of these incidental questions would not, if favorable to the exceptant or the objector, be conclusive as to the whole case; because that decision would almost to a certainty go upon an affirmation of the principal point, or the so-called merits on which the supporters of the Hayes electors rely. Consequently, in this debate of fifteen minutes about the admissibility of particular evidence, we should have to argue the whole case. There would be then a difficulty which from the flexibility of your honors' rules could be obviated by your giving additional time. But it has not appeared to me that that was the true course. On the contrary, with great respect to the better judgment of my learned opponents, if they shall differ with me, or to any honorable member of this Commission who may have taken a different view of it, my conception of the matter is, that all the needful evidence should come in subject to such questions as to its competency and its effect as may exist, for the reason that they necessarily incorporate themselves with the main question that you have finally to decide.

And I would just take leave to add here, before reading the paper which I mean to present, that such is the usual course of all tribunals where the matter of fact is judged of by judicial experts, such as your honors must all be deemed; and the rule of snapping promptly an exception to some bit of possibly irrelevant testimony in order to prevent an ignorant jury being misled by some improper considerations growing out of it has no application to a proceeding before learned experts, learned judges. It is unusual, according to the practice of those courts in which the judges determine the fact as well as the law, to hear any argument in relation to the admission of a particular piece of evidence before the final hearing, unless it should chance to be found quite convenient to take some very simple and isolated point by a motion to suppress a particular deposition; as, for instance, if counsel had been examined whose deposition ought not be read, or something of that kind.

I have said that I conceive the true remedy would not be to enlarge the time under the fifteen-minute rule; but to pursue the other course, to take the evidence that may be offered subject to the exceptions, to be considered with the whole case, and for the reasons which I have already stated——

The PRESIDENT. Mr. O'Conor, I am obliged to ask you to submit your propositions.

Mr. O'CONOR. I will submit them in one minute. I merely wish to state one single proposition: you would have to listen over and over again to the same precise, identical arguments in the final hearing as in this fifteen-minute hearing enlarged. Now if the——

Mr. EVARTS. Shall we be heard on this preliminary inquiry or await the submission of the proposition?

The PRESIDENT. I think you had better wait until you hear the proposition.

Mr. O'CONOR. The learned counsel has said something to the court under his view of what was convenient to be said, and your honors have extended the privilege to me. That is all I consider that I am doing.

The PRESIDENT. We will hear your proposition first.

Mr. O'CONOR. I am not speaking to any order of the court, but making a suggestion which your honors have been pleased to permit. I will speak no longer than may be agreeable. I now proceed to read the paper on which I have written our propositions:

"First. On December 6, 1876, being the regular law day, both the Tilden and the Hayes electors respectively met and cast their votes, and transmitted the same to the seat of Government. Every form prescribed

by the Constitution, or by any law bearing on the subject, was equally
complied with by each of the rival electoral colleges, unless there be a
difference between them in this : The certified lists provided for in section 136 of the Revised Statutes were, as to the Tilden electors, certified
by the attorney-general; and were, as to the Hayes electors, certified by
Mr. Stearns, then governor. All this appears of record, and no additional evidence is needed in respect to any part of it."

Perhaps I convey no new light by saying that, but it is for the sake
of presenting as distinct matter the view we take.

" Secondly. A *quo warranto* was commenced against the Hayes electors in the proper court of Florida on the said 6th day of December,
1876, before they had cast their votes, which eventuated in a judgment
against them on the 25th of January, 1877. It also determined that
the Tilden electors were duly appointed. The validity and effect of
this judgment is determinable by the record ; and no extrinsic evidence
seems to be desirable on either side, unless it be thought (1) that the
Tilden electors should give some supplemental proof of the precise fact
that the writ of *quo warranto* was served before the Hayes electors cast
their votes, or (2) unless it be desired on the other side to show the entry
and pendency of an appeal from the judgment in the *quo warranto*."

With these two possible and very slight exceptions the whole case on
this branch of it depends upon the record.

" Thirdly. To show what is the common law of Florida and also the
true construction of the Florida statutes, the Tilden electors desire to
place before the Commission the record of a judgment in the supreme
court of that State on a mandamus prosecuted on the relation of Mr.
Drew, the present governor of that State, by force of which Mr. Stearns
was ousted and Mr. Drew was admitted as governor. This judgment,
together with the court's opinion, is matter of record, and they require
no other proof; nor is there any technical rule as to the manner in which
this Commission may inform itself concering the *law* of Florida."

If I may be permitted to interject, it will be seen that I am endeavoring to show how very little there is in the shape of proof to delay this
Commission in proceeding directly to an argument on the merits.

" Fourthly. The legislation of Florida subsequently to December 6,
1876, authorizing a new canvass of the electoral vote, and the fact of
such new canvass, the casting anew of the electoral votes, and the due
formal transmission thereof to the seat of Government, in perfect conformity to the Constitution and laws except that they were subsequent
in point of time to December 6, 1876, are all matters of record and already regularly before the Commission.

" Fifthly. The only matters which the Tilden electors desire to lay
before the Commission by evidence actually extrinsic will now be stated.

" I. The board of State canvassers, acting on certain erroneous views
when making their canvass, by which the Hayes electors appeared to
be chosen, rejected wholly the returns from the county of Manatee and
parts of returns from each of the following counties, to wit : Hamilton,
Jackson, and Monroe."

I trust I have omitted none, but I have had no consultation.

" In so doing the said State board acted without jurisdiction, as the
circuit and supreme courts in Florida decided. It was by overruling
and setting aside as not warranted by law these rejections, that the
courts of Florida reached their respective conclusions that Mr. Drew
was elected governor, that the Hayes electors were usurpers, and that
the Tilden electors were duly chosen. No evidence that in any view
could be called extrinsic is believed to be needful in order to establish

the conclusions relied upon by the Tilden electors, except duly authenticated copies of the State canvass," [that is the erroneous canvass as we consider it,] " and of the returns from the above-named four counties, one wholly and others in part rejected by said State canvassers.

" II. Evidence that Mr. Humphreys, a Hayes elector, held office under the United States."

What is next stated may be deemed anticipatory and perhaps not proper to come from me.

" Sixthly. Judging from the objections taken by those supporting the Hayes electors and the opening argument offered in their behalf, the supporters of the Tilden electors are led to believe that no evidence is needed or intended to be offered by the supporters of the Hayes electors unless it be: first, that the above-mentioned appeal was taken, and, secondly, that Mr. Humphreys had resigned before the election."

If I may be permitted to say a word, the Commission will perceive that I have acted here with a view to support my idea that the facile method is to take these proofs subject to all question; that there is not enough of matter to produce delay or confusion or conflict in respect of those extrinsic proofs that could give rise to a judgment in discretion that the course proposed might be inconvenient. On the contrary, there is so little, and that is almost all matter that might be called of record, that we can give evidence very promptly and easily and beneficially as to time and as to results. We therefore trust that the Commission will not adopt such a method as will force us, on the first little scrap of testimony being offered, to present our whole case on both sides and have the whole merits decided on a mere preliminary exception.

I will cause this paper to be printed, and will deliver it up as quickly as it can be printed.

Mr. BLACK. If your honors please, I think the suggestions that have come from the Commissioners and what has been said by Mr. O'Conor, as well as what has fallen from the gentlemen on the other side, relate to the most important duty that you have to perform; and, therefore, I shall be pardoned, I trust, for making a remark or two at this moment.

The PRESIDENT. Do you desire to make further offers of proof?

Mr. BLACK. No, sir; I desire to suggest the course of proceeding which I think this tribunal is bound by its legal duties to take for the purpose of reaching the justice of this cause.

The PRESIDENT. Mr. Black, I think we ought to give Mr. Evarts an opportunity to explain his views before we hear you.

Mr. EVARTS. I waive my privilege to precede.

Mr. BLACK. I am perfectly willing that he shall be heard.

The PRESIDENT. Mr. Evarts waives his privilege. I have indicated to him that he would be heard.

Mr. EVARTS. I waive the privilege to precedence.

Mr. BLACK. If your honors please——

The PRESIDENT. It is not the moment for argument now.

Mr. BLACK. It is the moment for suggesting the course of proceeding and our rights with reference to the evidence which is to be given. I insist upon it that the evidence is in, and that we are not bound to make any offer at all.

The PRESIDENT. That, I think, is part of your argument after the cause is set down for argument, and not a preliminary statement.

Mr. BLACK. Then is it to be decided that this evidence is out or in now?

The PRESIDENT. Not by the presiding officer.

Mr. Commissioner MILLER. Let me suggest that Mr. O'Conor has made a proposition to submit certain evidence. If counsel on the other side have no objection to it, there is no occasion for further argument. If counsel on the other side submit to have that evidence come in, it will come in, and we can go on. I do not understand precisely what it was that Mr. Evarts waived.

Mr. EVARTS. I waived my privilege of preceding Judge Black.

Mr. Commissioner MILLER. If you want to object to this proposition for evidence, now is the time to object, certainly.

Mr. EVARTS. That I understand, if the Commission please.

The PRESIDENT. I think Judge Black had better defer until we hear from Mr. Evarts; otherwise there may be misunderstanding. We will hear Mr. Evarts.

Mr. EVARTS. The question whether the certificates transmitted from the States, that fall within the warrant of such transmission by the Constitution and laws of the United States, constitute the material upon which the duty of counting the vote of the State is to proceed, or whether the authority vested by the Constitution with the power to count can seek or receive extrinsic evidence of any kind, in any form, to be added to the certificates in the hands of the President of the Senate under the Constitution, is no doubt a principal inquiry of law and of jurisdiction in this Commission, which, once settled upon principle and by your decision, will go to a certain extent in superseding or predetermining your action upon the merits.

Mr. Commissioner STRONG. Mr. Evarts, allow me to suggest that perhaps I do not understand Mr. O'Conor's position. I have not understood Mr. O'Conor as offering evidence at all. He has suggested what he supposes to be in evidence and suggested what he might offer; but there has been no offer made, so far as I have understood him. If there has been an offer made, your province, it seems to me, is simply to withhold objection or to object to the admission of the evidence so offered.

Mr. EVARTS. Am I to understand that my objection cannot be accompanied with any observation?

Mr. Commissioner MILLER. If you object we will hear argument. We cannot hear argument before anything is offered.

Mr. Commissioner BRADLEY. I understand Mr. O'Conor to suggest that the extrinsic evidence mentioned by him be received provisionally for the purpose of the argument, and not to be decided upon by the Commission at present. If that is his position, then it is simply a question of convenience whether that would be the better course or whether we had better have an argument upon the question of the admissibility of evidence now alone, before going into an argument on the merits. As the argument on the admissibility of evidence would necessarily greatly involve the merits, it seems to me, unless counsel on the other side have forcible objections to that plan, Mr. O'Conor's suggestion is a good one, because it would then unify the argument, make one argument of the whole case; and the court upon the close of it would decide both questions: first, whether the evidence was admissible, and if it was, then as to its effect.

Mr. Commissioner HOAR. Mr. President, suppose Mr. O'Conor's offer of testimony be objected to by the other side, and then the Commission hear the argument of the case as it then stands, resembling, more nearly than any other judicial proceeding that I think of, an argument made on a demurrer to the plaintiff's evidence, the evidence not being considered as in, but as offered?

The PRESIDENT. That was the view of the Chair.

Mr. Commissioner HOAR. Now if we should hear the counsel on both sides on the case presented by the certificates which are before the Commission, upon the offer of evidence made by Mr. O'Conor and objected to by the other side, it seems to me that that would present (I do not know what other questions may arise in the case) one principal question of the case in the most clear, convenient, and quick form.

Mr. Commissioner THURMAN. Mr. President, I should like to inquire of counsel who support certificate No. 1, what objection they have to all the evidence being received subject to all exceptions, not precluding any objection to it whatsoever? It appears from the statement of Mr. O'Conor that the testimony to be produced by him is in a very small compass. How great may be the volume of testimony, if any, produced on the other side, I do not know. But what objection is there, as this is a trial not by jury but by a court, to receiving all this testimony subject to all exceptions, and then arguing its admissibility with the main argument in the cause, allowing counsel, if it become necessary by the adoption of that course, more time than the third rule allows, such further time as may be necessary, in order to consider the question of the admissibility of the evidence as well as the main question? What objection is there to that? I should like Mr. Evarts to answer.

The PRESIDENT. In the absence of other discussion I will state the view of the Chair. I shall regard the paper read by Mr. O'Conor as an offer of proof. Nothing, therefore, remains to the other side except to object or waive objections.

Mr. EVARTS. Then I am not permitted to reply to Mr. Commissioner THURMAN?

The PRESIDENT. It is hardly necessary, because you are to have full argument as well as a brief explanation of the objection.

Mr. EVARTS. I rose to speak to the precise point——

The PRESIDENT. Do you object to the offer of proof?

Mr. Commissioner THURMAN. I suggest that Mr. Evarts ought to answer my inquiry.

Mr. EVARTS. I rose originally to speak to the very point to which Mr. Commissioner THURMAN has drawn my attention.

The PRESIDENT. Very well, sir; you may reply to that inquiry. I wished to get at the case as soon as may be. That was my purpose.

Mr. EVARTS. I will be as brief as I can, and certainly fall quite within the fifteen minutes. The proposition is that the preparation of the case as ready for argument upon its exhausted and completed merits on either alternative of the views of this Commission as to the exclusion or admission of evidence, shall be made up by provisional acceptance of the mass of proof, whatever it may be, to be discussed as to admissibility and pertinency and efficacy in the conclusions of the tribunal as a part of the final argument. That I understand to be the proposition.

The difficulty with that is it requires the inclusion of all the countervailing proof that we, opposing their certificate or supporting ours, have a right to present under some determination of this court as to that right; for if you go beyond the evidence furnished from the hands of the President of the Senate into an inspection and scrutiny of the election in the State as upon a trial of right to the office, then we say that the tribunal that accepts that task and is to fulfill that duty is to receive evidence that will make the scrutiny judicial and complete from the primary deposit of the votes to the conclusion of the election. Now this Commission, as I suppose, does not contemplate a provisional introduction of all that evidence, oral, documentary, record, and otherwise, on our part, which comes in without objection and subject only to the sifting of a final argument. That is my suggestion in reference to this intimation of convenience of a *de bene esse* introduction of evidence. The evidence by which under the instruction of this Commission that we have the right, we are let into a scrutiny of the election in Florida is a scrutiny which can only be exhausted by oral testimony and by the fundamental original transactions of the election. That is the difficulty in selecting a part of the evidence to be admitted provisionally as furnishing the ground and area of a final discussion, because it does not include the evidence upon both sides which under some *post hac* determination of the court on the final argument may be properly introducible.

I object to the evidence now offered.

Mr. BLACK. Am I in order to say a word or two in reply to Mr. Evarts?

The PRESIDENT. A brief explanation. I wish to get to the argument as soon as may be.

Mr. BLACK. We insist that the whole of the evidence, including that mentioned by Mr. O'Conor in this paper of his, has been given already, and is a part of the record. A question arose before the two Houses of Congress whether certain votes offered for President and Vice-President ought to be counted or not. Whether they ought or not depended upon the question whether they were votes or papers falsely fabricated. Not with any purpose of going behind the appointment of the electors, but for the purpose of ascertaining what electors had been appointed, who were the true agents of the State in casting its vote, the two Houses proposed to use their verifying power. Their purpose was not to entertain an appeal from the decision of the State, but to ascertain what that decision was. This involved a question of fact. It was absolutely necessary that the conscience of the two Houses should be informed concerning the truth of the case which they were to decide, and accordingly they took a perfectly legitimate and proper mode of ascertaining it. They sent their committees and had evidence taken. These committees collected the documents, put the whole thing into a proper form, and then came back and offered it to the two Houses, by whom it was received and made part of the record of this case. And when you were appointed as a substitute for them and became the keepers of their conscience, they required you to tell them what they ought to do and to make the decision which upon the evidence that was before them they ought to make. That evidence I say was put in, and the portion of it which was taken by committees of the House of Representatives was laid before that House after a fierce struggle and the filibustering of half a night to keep it out.

The President of the Senate, the president of the two bodies, handed this evidence, all of it, over in bulk to be used here by this Commission. You have seen it. I cannot conceive of anything more unjust or more wrong than to talk about the necessity of our producing this evidence piecemeal, here a little and there a little, line upon line, in order that it may be submitted to the scrutiny of counsel who will apply to it those snapperadoes of *nisi prius* practice which might do if this case, instead of concerning the rights of a whole nation, related to the price of a sheep. If your honors suppose that it is to be taken up *de novo* and that everything is to be done, then of course you are to proceed, how? According to some approved rule of fair play and natural justice. What is that? The rule that prevails in courts of chancery, and not the artificial rules that are provided for by the common law of England in cases of trial by jury. You know surely, I need not say, that when a party files his bill in chancery, he may put in along with it all the evidence that he has in his possession. There can be no objection to the evidence in a court of equity. There is no such thing known as objecting to the admissibility of evidence there. The defendant cannot object to it because he is not in court at the time the bill is filed. And when the defendant puts in his answer he may accompany it with all the evidence he has. If either of the parties needs any more, the court does exactly what the two Houses have done in this case. They appointed their own agents to take the evidence and report it. An examiner, a master in chancery, an auditor, or other assessor of the court who takes evidence for the court, is doing precisely the office for the court that these committees have done for the two Houses of Congress. There is no such thing when the evidence is taken, as objecting to it before it is made a part of the record. It is as a matter of course filed whenever it is offered by the party if he does it regularly upon a rule day. He need not even come into the court and get a special *allocatur* of the chancellor for it.

Now the rule about admitting and rejecting evidence, the rule of procedure for that purpose always throws the burden of proving that it ought to go out upon the party who does not like to have it in. The question of materiality or relevancy, what its value and weight are, as well as what probative force ought to be given to it by the court, is a question which, as one of the judges said a moment ago, is always to be discussed upon the hearing, and determined by the final decree of the court. Evidence may come from an improper source or it may come through an illegal channel. There it is the duty of the party who makes any objection to it to move for its suppression, but it is never in order for him to make objection to it when it is filed or when it comes before the court and is made a part of the record.

If your honors please, you cannot safely adopt an artificial rule of the common law which prevails in a trial by jury, and where evidence is offered piece by piece to the court, and is there sifted and scrutinized before it is allowed to go to the jury. That rule is made necessary by two considerations: First, that it is deemed most important to the interests of justice that the jury, so far as possible, should be kept in utter ignorance of everything that is not material, lest their judgments might be misled. The court looks at the evidence when it is offered, and refuses to let anything be heard which is not a necessary and proper element of a just verdict. This rule prevails nowhere, even in the common-law courts, except where the trial is before a jury. In all other cases, causes in chancery as well as in all equity and ecclesiastical cases, and in all admiralty cases, the doctrine is, that whenever the evidence is offered it becomes a part of the record by the fact that it is put on the record. I do not say that you are bound to believe whatever is here; I do not say that you are bound to give to it more force or weight than it is entitled to; not more force and weight perhaps than a judge at a court of *nisi prius* would give to evidence which he rejects; but you are to sift it and scrutinize it and to separate the chaff from the wheat upon the final hearing of the cause, and it is impossible for you to proceed otherwise without a very great amount of trouble, without an expenditure of more time than you have got to expend upon this subject.

For every reason, for purposes of justice as well as the purposes of convenience, it is necessary that you should pursue the course of courts of equity and not come the quarter-sessions rule over us.

The PRESIDENT. Judge Black, I must regard this as an interlocutory question. The third rule is that—

In the hearing of interlocutory questions but one counsel shall be heard on ach side, and he not longer than fifteen minutes.

Your time has expired.

Mr. BLACK. Has already expired?

The PRESIDENT. Yes, sir.

Mr. Commissioner MILLER. Mr. President, I move that counsel on each side be allowed two hours to discuss the question raised by Mr. Evarts's objection to testimony, as to whether any other testimony will be considered by this Commission than that which was laid before the two houses by the presiding officer of the Senate.

Mr. Commissioner THURMAN. Mr. President, suppose then that the Commission should decide that further evidence should be considered, we should not have determined one thing as to what that further evidence should be. We should only have decided that evidence beyond the mere face of the papers presented by the President of the Senate to the two Houses should be received, but we should not have advanced one single step toward deciding what kind of evidence should be received. Here the two Houses have sent this inquiry to this Commission with all the powers that the two Houses acting separately or together possess, and obviously on that bare statement the question arises what powers have the Houses; what may the Houses, not by main force, but what may they constitutionally receive as testimony, and that question is for us to decide; for whatever they may constitutionally receive as testimony in deciding this question, it will be certainly admitted that we, having their powers, may receive. And that brings up the question suggested by the counsel who last spoke. I think, therefore, while I am perfectly willing that this question shall be argued, and indeed it ought to be argued, that the scope of the argument must go much further than that suggested by Mr. Justice Miller, and it must embrace the question of whether or not we are to take into consideration the testimony which has been taken by either of the Houses, and also the question what further testimony may be offered here. Therefore, I think the question to be submitted for argument ought not to be narrowed to the mere question of whether we can go beyond the face of the papers that were handed in and opened by the President of the Senate, for when we have decided that, if it be decided one way that we can go further, we have not advanced one single step toward deciding what we can receive, and we should have to have another argument.

Mr. Commissioner MILLER. I have no objection to the argument taking the scope that the Senator suggests. My only object was to give ample time for the argument of this proposition, whatever it may be, which is of very great importance, as to whether any evidence shall be received, and what evidence. Let there be one argument to determine it.

The PRESIDENT. First I will state the motion as made. Judge Miller moves that counsel be allowed two hours on each side to discuss the question whether any evidence will be considered by the Commission that was not submitted by the President of the Senate to the Houses of Congress.

Mr. Commissioner MILLER. I am willing to modify the motion in accordance with the suggestion of the Senator from Ohio.

Mr. Commissioner GARFIELD. I suggest that in the modification the Justice so enlarge it that we may hear from the counsel on the scope of our powers under the law. It seems to me that is as vital as the question of the mere rule of evidence that we shall adopt. I offer that suggestion to the Justice.

The PRESIDENT. I will state the question as soon as the motion is modified by the mover, and then it will be open to amendment.

Mr. Commissioner HOAR. I desire, if it be a proper time, to suggest a substitute for the motion of Judge Miller.

The PRESIDENT. As soon as the modified motion is presented to the Chair, you will have an opportunity. The motion as modified is as follows:

"That counsel be allowed two hours on each side to discuss the question whether any evidence will be considered by the Commission that was not submitted to the two Houses by the President of the Senate; and if so, what evidence can properly be considered, and also the question what is the evidence now before the Commission."

Mr. Commissioner HOAR. I will read what I had drawn up:

"That counsel be now heard for two hours on each side upon the effect of the matters laid before the two Houses by the President of the Senate and of the offer of testimony made by Mr. O'Conor and objected to by Mr. Evarts."

The PRESIDENT. Do you offer that as a substitute?

Mr. Commissioner HOAR. Yes, sir. The result of that will be that if the effect of these two matters were to require us to go into further evidence, we should say that. If the effect were a final and total decision of the whole case, we should also say that.

Mr. Commissioner EDMUNDS. Mr. President, I wish to suggest that it appears to me the proposition of Judge Miller, as modified at the suggestion of Judge Thurman, covers the whole ground. There are two points for consideration. The first is whether anybody, the Houses or this tribunal, has the power to go behind the formal certification of the State authorities. The second is, if so, by what species of evidence and inquiry below that may be sustained or affected. It is claimed by Judge Black that it may be sustained and affected by evidence in the nature of testimony taken by committees, &c., and reported to either of the Houses, and I suppose it is contended on the other side that it cannot be. Now I think that Judge Miller's suggestion covers all these grounds, and I suggest to my learned friend that he had better withdraw his amendment.

Mr. Commissioner HOAR. In view of the suggestions made by the honorable Senator, I will withdraw it. I do not think there is much difference practically between the two.

Mr. Commissioner FIELD. I renew the amendment.

The PRESIDENT. Mr. Justice Field renews the amendment as a substitute. I must put the question first on the substitute. Are you ready for the question?

Mr. Commissioner BAYARD. Please let it be stated again.

The PRESIDENT. The amendment offered as a substitute reads as follows:

That counsel be now heard for two hours on each side on the effect of the matters laid before the two Houses by the President of the Senate and of the offer of testimony made by Mr. O'Conor and objected to by Mr. Evarts.

The question is on adopting the substitute.

The question being put, it was determined in the negative.

The PRESIDENT. The question recurs on the original motion of Mr. Justice Miller, as modified.

The motion was agreed to.

Mr. EVARTS. We must ask the instruction of the Commission as to whether there is also an allowance of the division of this labor between two counsel, if this is to be treated as interlocutory argument.

The PRESIDENT. Of course, the two hours can be divided between counsel.

Mr. EVARTS. Then you will allow us to suggest that the two hours that Mr. Justice Miller's proposition allowed for one discussion are now extended over what is undoubtedly very much additional in area and consideration—I speak of that in respect to time—so that if two hours were thought by the proposer of this first resolution, before it received Mr. Commissioner Thurman's modification, as a suitable time for the single question——

The PRESIDENT. A single word, Mr. Evarts. Notwithstanding the resolution is adopted, I think it is quite in order for you to ask for additional time.

Mr. EVARTS. So I understand. I do not think it requires any modification for that purpose.

The PRESIDENT. How much do you ask in addition? Another hour?

Mr. EVARTS. I think we should desire another hour on our side.

The PRESIDENT. The usual course in the Supreme Court is, if we allow it on one side to allow it to both.

Mr. EVARTS. Of course.

Mr. Commissioner EDMUNDS. What time would be agreeable to the gentlemen opposing the first certificate?

Mr. O'CONOR. We shall be obliged to conform to the view of the court, as a matter of course.

The PRESIDENT. Is one hour additional on a side enough? [A pause.] Shall an additional hour be allowed on each side? The Chair will submit that question to the Commission.

The question, being put, was decided affirmatively.

The PRESIDENT. The extension of time is allowed. The order of speaking will be that indicated yesterday, unless otherwise instructed by the Commission. One of the counsel supporting the objections to certificate No. 1 will open. Both the counsel supporting the objections to certificate No. 2 will follow. Then the other counsel supporting the objections to certificate No. 1 will close. The case is before you under the motion of Mr. Justice Miller already adopted by the Commission, and, if the counsel are ready, the Commission is ready to hear them.

Mr. O'CONOR. As this view has been presented somewhat suddenly, we are a little embarrassed about the array, as to who shall proceed first.

Mr. Commissioner BRADLEY. I have no doubt the court will take a recess of half an hour, if you desire it, before commencing.

The PRESIDENT. I think fifteen minutes should be sufficient.

Mr. EVARTS. On our part, if the Commission please, we will say that this introduces a very important and principal inquiry, no doubt, and under the previous intimations that these questions of an interlocutory nature might precede what would be called an argument on the substantive merits of the case, we should, if it is at all comfortable to your sense of duty, prefer not to go on until a day is given us; but we of course submit that simply as our indication of what we regard our duty.

The PRESIDENT. Several members of the Commission suggest to me that we take a recess for half an hour.

Mr. EVARTS. Allow me to ask whether any hour has been fixed as the purpose or habit of the Commission at which to adjourn daily.

The PRESIDENT. Not regularly. I am still under the direction of the Commission.

Mr. Commissioner MILLER. Allow me to say, Mr. Evarts, that we set a precedent yesterday by refusing to the objectors themselves half a day for preparation. This Commission is of opinion that it cannot delay, but must go on with the hearing of the case. It is willing, however, to take a short recess now.

The PRESIDENT. It seems to be the view of the Commission that it will now take a recess until half past twelve o'clock. I now declare a recess till that time.

The Commission (at twelve o'clock noon) accordingly took a recess till half past twelve o'clock, at which time it re-assembled and was again called to order.

The PRESIDENT. The counsel will be allowed three hours on each side to discuss the question whether any evidence will be considered by the Commission that was not submitted to the two Houses by the President of the Senate, and, if so, what evidence can properly be considered; and also the question what is the evidence now before the Commission. Counsel representing the objectors to the first certificate will now be heard.

Mr. EVARTS. Mr. President, it has been a subject of consideration among the counsel, and if it would be at all suitable to the views of the Commission that one counsel on each side should be heard to-day, and that we should have until Monday for the replies on each side, or for the further reply on our side and the final reply on the other, we should feel that we were able to present the matter in better form.

Mr. Commissioner BRADLEY. Mr. President, I move that that be the course to be pursued.

The PRESIDENT. Will that be agreeable to the other side, that one counsel on each side only be heard to-day?

Mr. Commissioner HOAR. What is the understanding as to the length of time that one counsel on each side will occupy?

The PRESIDENT. They have three hours on a side. What portion of it they will use to-day, I do not know; and two will have the right to reply afterward.

Mr. Commissioner HUNTON. Mr. President, would not that allow the counsel who address the Commission to-day to address them for fifteen minutes each, and throw the whole bulk of the argument into Monday?

The PRESIDENT. They are to occupy half the time to-day—make a full opening.

Mr. Commissioner HUNTON. It is satisfactory, if that is understood.

Mr. Commissioner THURMAN. Let it be understood that three hours shall be consumed in the argument to-day; otherwise there might be one hour or half an hour occupied to-day and the argument practically put off until Monday.

The PRESIDENT. The understanding of the Chair is that half the time is to be occupied to-day.

Mr. O'CONOR. I have understood from the beginning of this case, and it has repeatedly fallen from the Chair, that the two counsel assigned to speak might divide the time between themselves as they pleased.

The PRESIDENT. That is subject always to this condition, that there shall be a full opening.

Mr. O'CONOR. I agree. If your honors please, I understand that it would be indecorous and unbecoming and unprofessional not to present a full opening in the commencing argument; but I do not perceive that it would be expedient to lay down any such distinctive rule as that the counsel speaking must speak an hour and a half.

The PRESIDENT. No; that is not it; but there must be a full opening.

Mr. O'CONOR. It is as fair for the other side as it is for us. I presume it is very possible that they might have an hour apiece, about as much as was necessary for the opening for the purposes of the argument; but I do not know anything about it.

Mr. EVARTS. We understand ourselves to be subject to that professional obligation, here as well as elsewhere, to make a proper division of the matter between the counsel; but beyond that we can hardly agree.

Mr. Commissioner EDMUNDS. That is satisfactory.

The PRESIDENT. That is entirely satisfactory. The motion is that there be two arguments to-day, one on each side. [Putting the question.] The motion is carried.

Mr. BLACK. Is it understood that three counsel may speak, provided they do not take more time than is assigned to the two?

The PRESIDENT. There has been no request of that sort, and consequently no such understanding. Usually, in the Supreme Court, such an application is granted on the condition that they take no more time; but there has been no request of the kind offered.

Mr. EVARTS. We should concur, perhaps, in that wish.

Mr. BLACK. I ask the court, inasmuch as there is no other way under the heavens by which we can do what your honors seem to require, that is, make a full opening and give the gentlemen on the other side full notice of the grounds upon which we sustain our side of the case, to permit me to make some general remarks which it is desired by my colleagues that I should make, and then allow Mr. Merrick to go fully into the details of the case by way of opening; that is, let us splice the opening.

Mr. O'CONOR. I hope I may be allowed to say, Mr. President, that your direction to proceed immediately in an argument which appears to us to involve essentially the whole merits, has rather confused our order of battle. We bow to it, however, most respectfully; but it somewhat embarrasses us; and it has not been thought that it would answer any useful purpose to make the counsel who is expected to deliver the reply to also deliver an opening. It would be clumsy and inconvenient in a great many respects; and we have had some difficulty in arranging so as to present a fair and proper argument covering the whole ground to-day, without consuming too much of our three hours. It appears to us that Judge Black and Mr. Merrick should be allowed to divide the time that we consider it proper to occupy to-day, if that is agreeable to the Commission.

The PRESIDENT. I will submit the question to the Commission on the condition that two counsel shall speak in the opening, and that only one is to reply.

Mr. EVARTS. We shall have the same privilege of division, I presume?

The PRESIDENT. Certainly. [To the Commission.] Shall three counsel be allowed to speak on each side if they desire, without enlarging the time? That is the motion.

The motion was agreed to.

Mr. MERRICK. Mr. President and gentlemen of the Commission, the order passed by the honorable Commission this morning, as remarked by Mr. O'Conor, has somewhat changed our order of battle, and we are compelled, though but indifferently prepared, to enter upon the discussion of the grave and important questions which you have required us to argue. We came into court expecting to proceed regularly with the Florida case; and believing that the testimony taken by the committees of the Senate and House of Representatives upon this subject was regularly before the Commission as testimony in the case, without being liable to any objection on account of its formality, supposed that its effect and ultimate admissibility would be considered by the court when it came finally to determine the main questions involved in the cause. But that case is practically suspended for the present, and the counsel are required to argue an abstract proposition of law submitted by the Commission, involving an inquiry into the general powers of this Commission under the organic act, and as to what evidence is now before you, and what further evidence it may be competent for counsel to offer and introduce.

First, then, may it please your honors, as to the powers of the Commission.

The law of the United States under which this Commission has been established and organized, provides as follows in regard to electoral certificates from States which have sent up duplicate or triplicate certificates, and to any of which objections may be made at the time such certificates are opened in the presence of the two Houses:

When all such objections so made to any certificate, vote, or paper from a State shall have been received and read, all such certificates, votes, and papers, so objected to, and all papers accompanying the same, together with such objections, shall be forthwith submitted to said Commission, which shall proceed to consider the same, with the same powers, any, now possessed for that purpose by the two Houses acting separately or together, and, by a majority of votes, decide whether any and what votes from such State are the votes provided for by the Constitution of the United States, and how many and what persons were duly appointed electors in such State, and may therein take into view such petitions, depositions, and other papers, if any, as shall by the Constitution and now existing law be competent and pertinent in such consideration.

The language that I have read from the law embraces a succinct and clear declaration of the powers of this Commission, and is the only part, I believe, that has direct reference to the testimony which we regard as at present before the Commission. As to the formal regularity of the evidence that is already before you, I presume there can be no objection. A question was raised in each of the two Houses of Congress after the late presidential election, early in their session, as to what votes, if any, should be counted from the States of Florida, Louisiana, South Carolina, and Oregon. Upon that question committees were duly appointed under the authority of the respective Houses to take testimony. In reference to the case of Florida, the committees from the two Houses respectively proceeded to that State and took testimony in accordance with the uniform methods and custom adopted by committees representing Congress and discharging duties similar to those imposed upon these committees. That testimony having been so taken, was returned to the two Houses of Congress, and when objection was made to the counting of the votes from that State at the time the certificates were opened by the President of the Senate, in pursuance of the mandate of that portion of the law to which I have referred, the certificates from the State of Florida, being three in number, with the papers accompanying those certificates and the objections and the evidence that had been taken by the Committees of the House in reference to the regularity and the legality of the vote contained in these certificates, were all transmitted to this Commission. I respectfully submit that this evidence so transmitted is now before this Commission and properly in the cause. Wherever either House of Congress has assumed to exercise the power of instituting an inquiry into a disputed fact, it has uniformly appointed special committees or invested standing committees with authority to summon witnesses and take testimony in regard to that fact; and in this case each of the two Houses appointed its committee to take testimony upon the issue raised in reference to the electoral vote of Florida. That testimony was regularly returned to the two Houses, that were to act upon that vote under the Constitution of the United States, and such as was taken by the committee of the House has been transmitted by the Houses in joint session to this Commission, which possesses and is to exercise all the power of the two Houses, or either of them, in the premises.

I therefore presume, may it please your honors, that there can be no question in reference to the regularity of that testimony, whatever question may be raised in reference to its admissibility under the issues you are to try and in reference to its effect upon those issues. I speak now of the mass of testimony, generally, that was laid upon this table, and respectfully submit that it is now before the Commission, and, so far as I am advised, there is no other evidence, with the exception, possibly, of that relating to the particular hour of the day at which the writ of *quo warranto* was served upon the persons called the Hayes electors; and, with that exception, as stated in the paper read by Mr. O'Conor this morning, I believe there is no question upon which the counsel for the objectors propose to offer any extrinsic evidence whatever.

This evidence, which has thus been sent to the Commission by the two Houses, is of two separate and distinct characters. First, there is the evidence that was inclosed in the certificates returned from the State of Florida. There were, as I have stated, three certificates; the first certificate being that of the Hayes electors, accompanied by the certificate of the governor of Florida given to those electors. The second certificate was accompanied by the certificate of the attorney-general of Florida; and the third was accompanied by certain judicial records, which, under the express language of the organic act, were referred to this body for its consideration.

The other testimony to which I have already referred was extrinsic evidence, taken by the committee acting under the authority of, and in obedience to the mandate of, the House of Representatives.

And I may remark that when the House committee took this testimony there was full opportunity given to all parties interested in the result of the inquiry to summon whatever witnesses they might desire to have examined and to cross-examine all that were brought forward. The examination-in-chief was taken subject to the established rules of evidence, and cross-examination was permitted with the broadest latitude those rules allow. And if we were required to repeat the experience of that committee under the authority of this Commission and retake that evidence, there would probably be no witness summoned who was not before the committee, possibly no question propounded that was not propounded by some of the members of that committee, and no cross-interrogatory propounded that was not propounded and the answer to which is not now before this honorable tribunal.

But as this Commission is invested with all the powers of Congress, under the law, the question recurs upon the materiality and admissibility of the evidence without regard to its form, and this brings me to the inquiry as to what are its powers. I owe your honors an apology for undertaking to argue so important a subject, for I did not come into court prepared to perform that duty, and in assuming to discharge it now I am submitting myself to that subordination which prevails in the profession and obey the orders of my senior counsel.

It was said in the opening statement made by the objectors upon the other side that this Commission possessed no other than simply a power to perform a ministerial duty; that it possessed no other than a power to enumerate the votes; that the certificate of the governor of the State was final and conclusive; and that there was no authority in this Commission, whatever might be the proof, to correct that certificate for mistake or vacate it for fraud. They told you that it imported absolute verity beyond the reach of any evidence, however strong and however conclusive, and beyond the reach of the power of the State itself either to correct, modify, or annul it; and, carrying out the position assumed by the objectors on the other side, it would follow that if, in reference to the certificate of Governor Stearns, Governor Stearns himself had, subsequent to the date of that certificate, come before the two Houses of Congress in sackcloth and ashes, begging on behalf of his State to have some error in that certificate corrected, it could not be done. If he had come with penitential sorrow, confessing himself to have been guilty of any fraud, however enormous—I am merely supposing a case—and made it patent that that certificate was the representative of a falsehood and a fraud, and not of truth, yet the certificate was beyond reach of the truth and that it was necessary to canonize its falsehood into a practical fact.

May it please your honors, in view of that position upon the other side, as well as in taking appropriate positions in the opening of this argument, it becomes necessary to look at that paper and see what it is, and whence it derives this extraordinary sanctity; infinitely holy, beyond any judicial record, and beyond any record that can be made between nations in their most solemn compacts. By the act of Congress, section 136 of the Revised Statutes, it is provided as follows:

It shall be the duty of the executive of each State to cause three lists of the names of the electors of such State to be made and certified, and to be delivered to the electors on or before the day on which they are required by the preceding section to meet.

There is nothing in this section declaring that the certificate to which it refers shall be conclusive evidence of anything. There is nothing in this section declaring in words as to what particular fact that certificate shall be directed. There is nothing in this section making it mandatory upon the governor to issue that certificate; and if there had been it would have been something transcending the powers of Congress under the Constitution to put there, for Congress could not reach the executive of a State by any enactment as to his official duty. It is not within the power of Congress to make it mandatory upon the governor to issue that certificate; and if it is not within the power of Congress to make it mandatory upon the executive of a State to issue that certificate, can it be possible that it is within the power of Congress to say that the certificate, if issued, should be conclusive, or that the certificate should be necessary evidence in the absence of which the electoral vote should not be counted? Congress could not have required the executive to issue the certificate, and could not have declared that the certificate should be the conclusive and only evidence of the election of the electors, because, in addition to what I have already submitted, the Constitution of the United States itself provides for the authentication of those electors, and that requirement is for an authentication from themselves; and if Congress superadds to that authentication an additional authentication which it makes a condition-precedent to counting the vote, it would be an act in violation of that provision of the Constitution, as well as in contravention of the relations of the Federal to the State government. I do not question the power of Congress to require authentication, and to specify whatever manner of authentication it desires, in order to relieve any difficulty in determining who are the agents appointed by a State to cast its electoral vote; but the power that I deny to exist is the power to specify some authentication as an absolute condition-precedent to counting the vote, and to declare that, in the absence of that authentication so required by Congress, the electoral vote shall not be counted at all.

Recurring to that section of the law in the Revised Statutes which I have read, I respectfully submit, as a proposition of law, that where certificates are required as matters of evidence, or where the law specifies evidence of any kind going to a particular fact with which the law so specifying the evidence is dealing, such evidence is never regarded in any court of law as conclusive beyond the power of rebuttal, unless the law specially provides that it shall be conclusive. Where the law says that such and such a paper or fact shall be evidence of a certain conclusion, that fact and that paper so specified as evidence of that conclusion are never beyond the power of rebuttal, unless the law has declared in specific terms that it shall be the only evidence and shall be unimpeachable.

I have referred to that clause of the Constitution which requires the electors to certify to their own appointment, and the manner in which they have executed their office; and I submit in this connection that it is not within the power of Congress to tie its hands so that it can never inquire into the truth of the due appointment of the electors and the true electoral vote. It is not within the power of Congress to estop the two Houses from ascertaining what is the true vote. The language of the article referred to requires the return of the vote by the electors, requires them to name in their ballots the persons voted for as President and Vice-President, to make distinct lists, to return the certificate of their vote to the President of the Senate, and then it proceeds as follows:

The President of the Senate shall, in the presence of the Senate and House of R pre-sentatives, open all the certificates, and the votes shall then be counted.

The learned objectors upon the other side stated yesterday that the word "counted" was the controlling word in the sentence, and that giving that word its proper and only signification, the clause that I have read conferred no other power upon the two Houses of Congress than the power of enumeration. I respectfully submit that the controlling word in that sentence is "*votes*"—"the votes shall then be counted"— and that the word "votes" controls the word "counted;" and when you refer to the word "counted" you have to go back and see what it is that you are required to count. What is it, may it please your honors, that is to be counted? It is "the votes," and if those votes are cast by persons not duly appointed electors under the law of the State, they are not votes, and when you count them you count something the Constitution did not authorize you to count. Therefore, in executing your duties under this clause, you must, before you count, ascertain what are votes. Having ascertained what are votes, you count those votes, throwing aside whatever ballots you may find that are not votes. Under this article of the Constitution, and this particular clause of the article, I respectfully submit that there is in the two Houses of Congress a power to determine what are votes.

Then the question arises as to how far you shall go in taking testimony to determine what are votes; but as preliminary to that question I beg leave to add that if the Constitution has devolved upon the two Houses of Congress the duty of counting the votes, the true votes, and the necessary power of determining what are the true votes, Congress possesses no power to say what shall be conclusive and unimpeachable evidence of those votes; but, in the performance of their high function, the two Houses must ascertain what are the true votes, without any limitation placed upon them by Congress, and without being so restrained that they cannot go into the inquiry as to the truth. Congress may prescribe modes of authentication, but merely modes of authentication as aids and not as conclusive evidence or restraints upon the Houses in their action. We therefore submit that any legitimate evidence going to determine what are the true votes is proper and competent evidence before this tribunal.

And, may it please your honors, upon the question of whether you can go behind the certificate of the executive of the State, and whether the certificate is conclusive or not upon Congress, I beg to refer you to a high and most responsible authority, an authority that has the sanction of some of the most distinguished names that now adorn the passing history of the Republic. In 1873 the question came before Congress as to the counting of the Louisiana vote. The electors met; they vôted; they sent up to the President of the Senate the certificate required by the twelfth article of amendments to the Constitution, stating for whom they had voted, and inclosed in that certificate so sent up the certificate of the recognized governor of Louisiana certifying to their due apointment; and all their proceedings were regular on their face from beginning to end. There was no objection made, and none intimated, to those proceedings, because of their non-conformity to the statutes of the United States. When that vote was opened, objection was made to it; but prior to the time when the vote was opened, it was understood that there was some difficulty in reference to that vote, of some kind or other. The Senate of the United States directed its Committee on Privileges and Elections to inquire into the circumstances attending the election of the electors of that State. That committee entered upon the inquiry; it examined witnesses, and they were also cross-examined. All the facts that were needed and desired lying behind that certificate were gone into fully by that committee. Having gone into all those facts, they made their report to the Senate. In that report, made February 10, 1873, (which is to be found on page 1218 of the Congressional Globe, part 2, third session of the Forty-second Congress,) the chairman of the committee, one of the honorable Commissioners whom I have now the privilege of addressing, states as follows:

If Congress chooses to go behind the governor's certificate, and inquire who had been chosen as electors, it is not violating any principle of the right of the States to prescribe what shall be the evidence of the election of electors, but it is simply going behind the evidence as prescribed by an act of Congress; and, thus going behind the certificate of the governor, we find that the official returns of the election of electors, from the various parishes of Louisiana, had never been counted by anybody having authority to count them.

In the conclusion of the report Senator MORTON says:

Whether it is competent for the two Houses, under the twenty-second joint rule, (in regard to the constitutionality of which the committee here give no opinion,) to go behind the certificate of the governor of the State, to inquire whether the votes for electors have ever been counted by the 'legal returning-board created by the law of the State, or whether, in making such count, the board had before them the official returns, the committee offer no suggestions, but present only a statement of the facts as they understand them.

Now, in reference to the power of the joint rule of the two Houses, it is proper, before I proceed further, that I should make a single remark. That joint rule could give to the two Houses no power they did not possess under the Constitution. It could neither enlarge nor abridge their constitutional powers. It is beyond the authority of Congress or of any other tribunal to enlarge or abridge the powers with which the Constitution has vested that body. A joint rule might formulate that power; a joint rule might indicate the manner in which that power should be exercised; a joint rule might prescribe the methods of proceeding in the execution of that power; but it could neither give power nor diminish power. In this report the only objection made to the vote of Louisiana is that the returns for electors in that State had never been canvassed or counted. It was conceded that the certificate of the governor was regular, perfectly regular on its face; and the honorable chairman of the committee, after stating those facts, says that he declines to make any suggestion to Congress as to what disposition ought to be made of the vote.

May it please your honors, the evidence taken by that committee was before the two Houses of Congress when they met to count the vote four years ago. The intimation of the objection in the report was before those two Houses, and that intimation found shape and substance and form in a motion made by the Senator from Wisconsin, that the vote of Louisiana should not be counted. I am aware that that Senator, at the time, maintained that Louisiana was not a State bearing such relation to the Federal Union as authorized her to participate in the election of a Chief Magistrate, but in that position it is a well-known political and historical fact that few or none of the Senators sympathized. He made his motion, stating different grounds for the motion, but the only ground before the Senate, conceding that Louisiana was a State and could participate in that election, the only ground before the two Houses of Congress upon which her vote could be excluded by any possibility, or under the process of any sophistry or logic, was that, although the certificate of the governor to the election of the electors was regular in form, yet the return lying behind that certificate, and upon which that certificate purported to be founded, had never been canvassed. The question came up for determination in the Senate on the 12th day of February, 1873, (as will be seen by reference to page 1293 of the same volume,) and it was voted upon. Mr. Carpenter's resolution that the vote should not be counted was determined in the affirmative and the vote was not counted.

Mr. Commissioner EDMUNDS. Have you there, and will you read, the resolution adopted by the Senate on that occasion?

Mr. MERRICK. The only one I have been able to find is Mr. Carpenter's resolution "that the vote should not be counted." He objected to the vote, stating various grounds, but the only resolution I have been able to find is a simple resolution that the vote of Louisiana should not be counted.

Mr. Commissioner EDMUNDS. Without stating in terms the grounds on which it proceeded?

Mr. MERRICK. Yes, sir; I indicated that.

Mr. Commissioner EDMUNDS. I was only inquiring for information.

Mr. MERRICK. But I supplemented the indication by this further statement: that there was no ground before the Senate upon which the vote could have been excluded, as far as I can ascertain from the record, except that the vote for electors had not been canvassed. If there is any other ground stated in the report of the committee I have been unable to find it. Mr. Carpenter entertained a different opinion from nearly every Senator as to the peculiar relations of Louisiana to the Federal Union. He may have voted upon that ground; but I believe that no other Senator, or not more than one or two, shared his opinion. I believe his honor who made the inquiry of me voted in the affirmative on the resolution that the vote should not be counted.

Now, may it please your honors, I refer to this precedent as authority for two propositions: First, that the testimony taken by a committee of either of the Houses inquiring into the regularity and legality of an electoral vote is competent testimony to be considered when the question arises as to what disposition you shall make of that vote; secondly, that it is competent for Congress, under the Constitution of the United States, to go behind the certificate of the governor and throw out a vote, where the testimony proves that that certificate does not properly indicate the wishes of the people in the individuals that certificate designates as the agents of the State, and those facts being established, it is competent to discard the vote.

But, may it please your honors, in the case of the State of Florida we shall not ask for evidence going behind the certificate. This case presents itself to the court in a peculiar aspect. The evidence which we shall offer and which we claim to be admissible as to that State, is evidence furnished by the State herself as indicated in the proposition read by the distinguished gentleman with whom I have the honor to be associated, [Mr. O'Conor.]

Two propositions as to evidence, then, come before your honors.

First, whether the United States, through its Congress, or either or both Houses of Congress, can, in reference to an electoral vote, institute an original inquiry itself, and by a committee of either House take testimony going behind the certificate of the State, and invalidate that certificate on its own motion, when the State still adheres to the regularity of that certificate. That is one question, and a very important one; but there is another totally different from that.

Second, whether when the Houses of the Congress of the United States come to inquire into the electoral vote, and ascertain which vote shall be counted, it is competent for them to receive evidence furnished by the State herself in reference to the certificate her governor may have given.

Your honors perceive at once the wide difference in the two cases; and I respectfully submit in connection with this proposition, that if the power does not exist in the two Houses of Congress as a primary and original power separately to take testimony going behind the certificate, then it must exist in the State to correct its own certificate or impeach it for fraud or falsehood; else we may be irrevocably tied to an accident or mistake, and a presidential election may turn upon a certificate which is known to all the world to be an accident, a falsehood, or a fraud, which can neither be impeached by the State that gave it, because of fraud, accident, or mistake, nor interfered with in any way by the Federal Government to which it is addressed, but must become a substantial and perpetual truth in the presence of convincing evidence that it is an active and living lie.

In the case of the State of Florida, taking up the second proposition, the State herself, after the meeting of the electors, ascertaining that this certificate given by Governor Stearns, was given either in mistake or fraud, and founded upon an irregular and illegal canvass of the votes according to the laws of Florida, by her legislature passed a law directing another canvass to be made. But she did not pass that law, even, until she had appealed to her judicial tribunals to interpret the laws previously existing, and relating to the subject. Having appealed to those tribunals to interpret those laws, and in the mandamus case having received from her tribunal of last resort an opinion giving construction to those previously existing laws, by which opinion it became apparent that the returning-board had transcended its jurisdiction and made a return which was erroneous under the law, her legislature then, on the basis of that opinion, directed another canvass of the vote to be made in accordance with the judicial construction of the law. When that canvass was made and returned to the legislature, her legislature passed another act on the basis of that canvass, declaring that the parties to whom the certificate had been issued by Governor Stearns, had not been appointed, and designating the persons who had been chosen as the agents of the State to speak her voice in the electoral college. But she has gone further. A *quo warranto* was issued against these parties who assumed to exercise the electoral office under the certificate granted by Governor Stearns, and that *quo warranto* having come before her judicial tribunals, they, in the exercise of a jurisdiction given to them by the State laws of Florida, decided that the men who had received that certificate were not elected, but that other men were elected; and those other men so elected received a certificate from the governor of Florida, and, in the execution of the office to which they had been appointed by the people in the previous November, discharged their duties as electors and voted for President and Vice-President on the day designated by the law of the United States.

Now, then, may it please your honors, you have from that State this mass of evidence—evidence from her legislature, evidence from her executive, evidence from her judicial tribunals—that the electors to whose vote we object, were not the duly appointed electors of Florida; and, through all the departments of her government, Florida therefore comes to the United States Congress and begs that you (for you now exercise that power and it is vested in you) will protect her people from the enormity of having their voice simulated by parties never appointed to speak in her behalf. Is not that competent evidence to go before the Houses of Congress? If it is not, and if Congress itself cannot in the exercise of its original power go forward and inquire into the due election of these electors, then you have placed the whole Government and administration of the United States in the power of any executive who may issue his certificate to a party never voted for at all, while the unanimous vote of the State may have been in favor of another party. You may take the whole population of Florida, and although they may never have voted for A and B at all, and though the vote may have been unanimous in favor of other parties, if the governor chooses to issue his certificate to A and B, that certificate becomes binding upon Congress and may determine a presidential election. If this be the law, may it please your honors, then *who will deliver us from the body of this death?* It is beyond the power of Congress to grant relief; and relief is beyond the power of the State.

I find that I have consumed, may it please your honors, more than the time allotted me.

The PRESIDENT. Fifty minutes you have occupied.

Mr. BLACK. Mr. President and gentlemen of the Commission, the time allowed for the opening of this argument on our side is nearly consumed. I do not presume to do more than merely supplement or enforce by a few general propositions Mr. Merrick's admirable statement of our case, which is as well calculated to impress the true nature of it on the minds of this court and to give a full notice to the gentlemen on the other side of what we intend to rely upon as anything that could possibly have been said. I am only "gilding refined gold" when I attempt to add anything to it.

You have before you the question whether this case is to be decided by you upon the evidence taken for the purpose of enabling the Senate and House of Representatives to do the duty which the Constitution cast upon them of counting the votes and of seeing that votes only were counted. For all the reasons that I gave this morning, and for many other reasons which I might add if I had time, I insist upon it that the evidence being once reported and filed in the cause is to be treated as a court of equity treats evidence in the same condition. You may throw it out; you are not required to give it, because you have admitted it, any particular amount of force or weight or value in your final judgment; but you are to look at it and determine the case upon all that is in it. And I can give you an assurance, founded upon some little experience, that a judge never decides upon any subject much the worse for knowing a little about it before he does decide. This notion of determining the whole case upon an offer to admit evidence is a thing that you have got to forget. It is impressed upon those who practice the common law very strongly by that peculiar and anomalous system which is adopted in the common-law courts upon jury-trials. It is not natural; it does not belong to any other kind of tribunal. If there be any evidence here which comes through illegal channels, or from any improper source, let the other side move to suppress it. But being in already, and therefore part of the case now, you cannot ask us to offer it over again.

I need not certainly produce Chitty's Pleading, Daniell's Chancery Practice, or Starkie on Evidence, or any of the rest of the books in which these rules are laid down. I need not show you what is the code of procedure in courts of admiralty and courts of equity; for I take it for granted that these are things on which I may speak as unto wise men. One of the gentlemen who spoke yesterday repeated what had been said by Judge Marshall, and which I am glad he did. We have heard it before, but it cannot be told too often, for it contains a very wholesome moral. The judge said to a counselor who was addressing him that a judge of the Supreme Court was presumed to know something. I hope that no decision which you make in this case will repel that presumption. Indeed, I think it will be extended and enlarged, and that the presumption after this will be not only that the judges of the Supreme Court know something, but that members of the Senate and House of Representatives also know something.

There has been much talk here about getting behind the action of the State. I do believe firmly in the sovereign power of the State to appoint any person elector that she pleases, if she does it in the manner prescribed by the legislature; and, after she has made the appointment in that manner, no man has a right to go behind her act and say that it was an appointment not fit to be made. A man, whether he be an officer of the State or an officer of the General Government, who undertakes to set aside such an appointment is guilty of a usurpation and his act is utterly void. Therefore, if the governor of the State of Florida, after this appointment of electors was made by the people, undertook to certify that they were not elected and to put somebody else in the place which belonged to them, his act was utterly void and false and fraudulent. We are not going behind the action of the State; we are going behind the fraudulent act of an officer of the State whose act had no validity in it whatever.

This is a question of evidence. Who are the electors? Two sets of persons come here, each of them pretending to be the agents of the State of Florida, for the purpose of performing that important function of the State, the election of a President and Vice-President of the United States. It is the business of the two Houses to count the votes. Now, remember the argument that Mr. Merrick made upon that Constitution; let it sink into your hearts, and do not forget it, because it is the God's truth. The word "votes" it is that controls the meaning of it. "The *votes* shall then be counted;" the *votes*, mind you; not the frauds nor the forgeries. But they on the other side tell us that if the President of the Senate lays before the two Houses when the votes are to be counted a false paper, a paper which was absolutely counterfeited, that is an end of it; you cannot produce any extrinsic evidence for the purpose of showing that it is a forgery or any evidence to show that it is not genuine. The doctrine goes that far if it is to be adopted at all. Carry that proposition to its logical consequences, and where does it take you? That you must simply receive whatever anybody chooses to fabricate and lay before Congress through the President of the Senate, and that neither the President of the Senate, nor either of the two Houses, nor both of them together, can do anything but just take what is given to them, without inquiring into its genuineness at all. I affirm, everybody affirms, and I hope to God that nobody here, even on the other side, will attempt to deny, that the Congress of the United States has the verifying power, the power that enables it to inquire whether this is a forgery or not; and, if you have the right to inquire whether it is counterfeit, you have a right to inquire whether it is or is not invalidated by the base fraud in which this thing was concocted. The work of the counterfeiter is as well entitled to be received for truth as this spawn of a criminal conspiracy got up to cheat the State and the Union, overturning and overthrowing the great principle that lies at the foundation of all our security.

Why, this doctrine that a thing which is false, willfully false, is utterly void and good for nothing, has been by this court (I mean by the Supreme Court) asserted a thousand times. Nay, I undertake to say that the contrary doctrine has never yet been set up by any judge or any lawyer whose authority is worth one straw. Suppose you have a case of a patent issued by the Secretary of the Interior or the Commissioner of the General Land Office, the validity of which depends upon a confirmation by the court, and he falsely recites that the court delivered a judgment which the record shows it never did pronounce, and upon that basis puts the patent. Is the patent worth anything? Why is it worthless? Because it is based upon a fact which is untrue. "False" is "fraudulent" in all cases of this kind. When a man undertakes to say "I certify to this fact," and at the time he does it there glares upon him from the record that lies before him the evidence that the fact is the other way, is not that a fraudulent certificate? And if it be fraudulent, is it not as void in law and as corrupt in morals as if it were a simple counterfeit?

In this case we show that it was fraudulent. How? By producing the evidence which the governor was as well aware of as we are, which every man and woman and child in this whole nation knew or had reason to believe was true, namely, that the other set of electors had a decisive and clear majority of the votes that were received and counted at the polls. He knew it, because it was recorded in every county of his State; the votes were collected together and filed in the office of the secretary of state. That is one way in which we show the falsehood and the fraud ; but we show it again by the evidence of an act of the legislature containing the solemn protest of the· State against the cheat which her *de facto* governor attempted to palm off upon her and upon the nation. We prove it again by showing that the governor himself—not the same person but the same officer—rebuked this fraud, declaring that the other parties, and not those whose votes are now offered, were elected and chosen and authorized exclusively to cast the vote of the State.

Thus acted two departments of the State government of the State. But the State, determined not to be cheated out of her vote and determined that she would ascertain it in some undeniable form by a proceeding the correctness and truth of which could never be impeached, took these usurpers by the throat and dragged them into a court of justice, and there, in the presence of a competent tribunal, she impleaded them, charged them with the offense, brought the other parties who also claimed to be her agents for this purpose and set them face to face. The proofs were given upon both sides, and it ended in a solemn adjudication by that court of competent jurisdiction that the persons who claimed to cast these votes for Hayes and Wheeler had no right, nor authority, nor power whatever to do that thing.

Now look at this. Whenever a cause has been decided by a court of competent jurisdiction, the determination of that court, as a plea is a bar, as evidence is conclusive of every fact and every matter of law which was or could have been adjudged there, and neither law nor fact there determined shall ever afterward collaterally or directly be drawn into controversy again. Is not that the rule? It was so laid down in the Duchess of Kingston's case, which has been followed in every court in Christendom from that day to this. There is not in England or America one judge or one lawyer who has undertaken to assert that the law is otherwise stated nor has it ever been attempted to be clothed in any other words than the clear and felicitous language used by Chief-Justice De Grey in that case.

This doctrine has been applied over and over again to election-returns, as well as to all other things. It would be perfectly absurd to say that, when the title to a horse is in question before a justice of the peace, the doctrine that makes the title void may be applied so as to save the horse to the honest owner of it, and should not be applied to a case in which the rights of a whole nation are involved.

False returns have been made many times; false counts have been made at the polls; election-officers have altered the count afterward. No man that I know of has ever said that an election fraud ought to be held to be successful merely because it was put into the forms of law; never before this time, except on two occasions. In New Jersey the governor of that State stamped the broad seal upon a commission as members of Congress for five gentlemen whom he knew not to be elected. Congress said that certificate was void. Then the House of Representatives did precisely what we ask the two Houses of Congress and you, their substitute, to do in this case. It was contended then, as now, that the certificate of the governor was conclusive evidence of the right of the commissioned men to take their seats in the first place and participate in the organization of the House. Do not let it be said that this arose out of the right of a legislative body to pass on the qualifications of its own members. They had no right to pass on the qualifications of their own members until they were organized. The right of those men to hold their seats until the time when their seats were declared vacant upon a petition of their adversaries to unseat them was as conclusive as anything can be, supposing it to be honest. But it was not honest, and that made it all void.

Mr. Commissioner STRONG. Were those persons who held the certificate of the governor of New Jersey admitted to their seats at all?

Mr. BLACK. They were not.

Mr. Commissioner STRONG. Not allowed to take seats and participate in the organization?

Mr. BLACK. Not allowed to take seats at all.

Mr. Commissioner STRONG. I understood you to say that they were.

Mr. BLACK. I do not know but that your honor was in Congress at that time.

Mr. Commissioner STRONG. No, sir.

Mr. BLACK. I supposed you were. That was in 1839. You were not in Congress then. There was a very great struggle over it and it lasted for four or five weeks, one set of men pressing the fraud with as much vigor as any of our friends can press this one, and it being resisted at the same time with perhaps more firmness than we are resisting now.

There is another case, however, that one of the judges upon this bench will recollect more distinctly. I do not say that there was any judicial or legislative determination of that question which makes it authority in this case, but it is an illustration of the condition in which we are to be thrown if a mere fraud, a counterfeit, is to be accepted as sufficient to carry everything before it.

In 1838 Mr. Porter was elected governor of Pennsylvania by a majority of about fourteen thousand. It was thought desirable that the election should be set aside and treated as though it had not been held, and in order to do that, it was necessary that his opponents should have possession not only of the senate and executive, which they had already, but of the other house of the legislature, the lower house; and in order to effectuate that, they just simply manufactured, fabricated impudently and boldly, a fraudulent and false return of eleven members from the county of Philadelphia. The law was that the returns were to be made to the secretary of the commonwealth and he was to make out from those returns a list of the persons who were entitled to be members of the house. They said that certificate was conclusive evidence, and it was conclusive evidence if the fourth section of the act of Congress in this case makes the governor's certificate conclusive of the electors' election, because it is very nearly in the same language. You know what came of it—the Buckshot war. They intended to carry that out at the expense of covering the whole commonwealth with blood and ashes, and would have done it only they could not get General Patterson and his men to fire on the people who were there assembled.

Until now, except in those two cases, nobody in this country has ever had the portentous impudence to offer a fraudulent vote and insist that the fraud could not be inquired into because forsooth it came wrapped in the forms of law.

I believe my time is out, and I am not going to trespass upon your honors any further.

Mr. MERRICK. May it please the Commission, I desire to file a brief prepared by Hon. Ashbel Green, of New Jersey, associated with us in the case, which is a clear, full, and able discussion of the question now before the Commission and which brief counsel have unanimously adopted.

The PRESIDENT. It will be received and filed.*

Mr. BLACK. There is one thing which I omitted to mention and which it is necessary to call the attention of the court to; and that is the evidence which we have produced here to show that one of the Hayes electors was ineligible on account of his being an officer of the Federal Gouernment on the day the election took place. I suppose that makes a clear case as against him.

Mr. EVARTS. Judge Black, will you allow me to ask a single question? A certain mass of evidence not otherwise described than generally in argument, and which we have never seen and inspected, is argued to be already in, upon some chancery notion that it has been attached to something that has brought it in. What is it contended that it is attached to?

Mr. BLACK. O, it is in the record, a part of the record in this case made up by the House of Representatives before the case was sent over here.

Mr. EVARTS. What is it attached to?

Mr. BLACK. "Attached to." Do you mean to ask me the bookbinder's question, whether it is stiched?

Mr. EVARTS. No. What is it? A bill in chancery?

Mr. MERRICK. It was attached to the objection made when the vote was offered in the House, and is recited in the objection as being the basis upon which the objection rests.

Mr. EVARTS. The question is answered.

Mr. Commissioner EDMUNDS. Mr. Evarts will find it on page 3 of the objection signed by Charles W. Jones and others. It comes in in support of the objection and is referred to as evidence to support it.

The PRESIDENT. The side that has been opened has spoken one hour and twenty minutes. We will now hear the other side.

Mr. MATTHEWS. Mr. President and gentlemen of the Commission, unused as I am to appearing before tribunals so unprecedented and august as this, and equally unused to handling such high themes as form the subject of the jurisdiction of this Commission, I rise with the most unaffected diffidence to undertake the discharge of that duty which has been assigned to me by my learned associates; and while I hope that I may say something which will assist the Commission in solving the questions which are submitted for argument, I shall be only too happy if, after I take my seat, I shall be able to recollect that I have said nothing which may injure the cause I represent.

I take the earliest opportunity to correct a serious misapprehension on the part of the learned gentlemen who have argued as counsel in the opening of this question, in respect to the position which they seem to assume has been already taken upon our side. I refer to the conclusive effect that they suppose we attribute to the certificate of the governor of a State accompanying a list of those whom he certifies as having been duly appointed electors for that State. I am authorized to say, by the gentlemen who are objectors to the second and third certificates, that that statement is an incorrect representation of their position, and I respectfully submit that when I have stated ours the gentlemen on the other side will understand our case differently.

I think I may also take this immediate opportunity of relieving the apprehensions of my very learned friend [Judge Black] who spoke last

_____
* This brief will be found in the appendix containing the briefs, as Brief No. 1.

and has spoken so often, in respect to the possible effect of excluding the consideration of what he has been pleased to call exhibits or evidence, upon the judgment of this tribunal. It is, Mr. President and gentlemen, the fortunate feature of your legal constitution that you can make no mistakes. It was a quaint saying, I believe, of Selden, in an essay on papal councils, where he was treating of the doctrine that they were enlightened by the presence of the Holy Ghost, that he had generally found that the Spirit dwelt in the odd man. So, in the exercise of the constitutional function, whatever that may be, devolved upon Congress in its participation in the count of the electoral votes, effectual provision has been made against the defeat of the transaction by referring it to a tribunal that cannot be equally divided.

And now, Mr. President and gentlemen, allow me to state in very general terms, and yet as precisely as I have been able to accomplish it, the various propositions by which and through which we lead ourselves, and hope to lead you, to the conclusion for which we contend in respect to the point to which you, as the representatives of congressional jurisdiction, may go in this inquiry, and that point where you must stop.

What is the transaction that is the subject of the general investigation? It is stated, in its final result, as the election of a President and Vice-President of the United States. In what does that consist? It is not a single act; it is a series of acts. The election of those two high officers is not a popular election, according to the spirit of the Constitution, the meaning of its framers, the interpretation of the generation which adopted it, or the practice under it. There is a selected body of men in each State who compose the constituent body which is to make that election; and I need not remind the tribunal that they have a right to make a *selection* as well as an *election;* and it is altogether a mistake, in my judgment, to consider this electoral body as delegates representing a State or the people of a State, as agents accomplishing their will. They not only have *power* in the sense of *might*, but they have *power* in the sense of *right*, to vote, on the day named, for the persons who, in their judgment, ought to be, all things considered, the chief executive officers of the nation.

Each State under the Constitution has the right to prescribe the mode in which these electors shall be appointed. No one else has any right or authority in that business. They may elect by the general assembly or legislature; they may appoint by the governor, or any other officer whom they may choose to designate; they may cause that appointment to be based on the result of a popular election; and that, in the case of Florida and now in all the States, except the new State of Colorado, is, I believe, the universal practice; so that the appointment of electors in a State is based on a popular election.

Now, what is that election? That also consists not of one act, but of a series of acts, beginning with the deposit in the ballot-box, if it be by ballot, as we may assume it to have been, in each locality prescribed by law, called a parish, or a precinct, or a township, or a school-district, or whatever small division of territory may be adopted. The voter deposits his written or printed ballot into the hands of one, or two, or three judges of election, who inscribe his name in a list of voters, and put his ballot into the box, and then at the conclusion of the election make a return of the result, showing how it has been attained. That is carried from the primary voting-places to the county-seat, and there county officers compile these various returns, acting with more or less powers according to the statutes of the State from which they derive their appointment; and the result of that choice in that county as it appears to them, based on the returns which they have received from the primary officers, is reported by them again to a third and highest and last returning-officer or canvassing-board, who, receiving these returns from all the counties in the State, exercise the powers conferred upon them by law and make that which in my judgment is *the completion and the consummation of this appointment.* That board sitting upon these returns make their final return of the fact, as it appears to them, sitting under their responsibility as public officers and in the exercise and discharge of public functions and public duties; and having accomplished their task, they deposit the record of their finding and declaration in the public archives of the State, and there they remain in perpetual memorial of the fact which they have found.

Up to that point the State alone acts in the appointment. That last act completes the appointment, and that appointment completed and finished is unchangeable except by State authority exerted upon that act within an interval of time; and what is that? Congress, under the Constitution of the United States, has had reserved to it control in certain particulars over this appointment; that is to say, it may designate the day on which the appointment shall be made, and it shall designate the day on which the electors so appointed shall deposit their ballots for President and Vice-President. In that interval I do not know and I do not care to discuss, I will neither deny nor affirm, but I am willing to admit, any and everything that may be claimed on the other side as to the existence of State authority to inquire into and affect that record. But when the day has passed when in pursuance of the authority of law conferred by that appointment under the statutes of the State, on the day named by Congress, the body which has, according to the forms of law, been invested with the apparent title to act as the constituents of that great electoral body, and when they are required by Constitution and law to accomplish the act for which and for which alone they have been brought into being, then that transaction, so far as State authority is concerned, has passed beyond the limit of its control. It then becomes a Federal act. It then becomes one of those things which pass into the jurisdiction, whatever that may be, of Federal power. It is the deposit of the vote of the elector in the ballot-box of the United States, and the nation takes charge of its ballot-box. Whatever power, then, may be exerted after that must be exerted under that power which is conferred by the Constitution upon any constitutional national authority which is invested with authority over the subject. These electoral votes so given are to be sealed and transmitted to the seat of Government, delivered into the custody of the President of the Senate, the Vice-President of the United States, who is *ex officio* President of the Senate, by him kept unopened until the day named when he is to open the certificates, and *then the votes shall be counted.*

What, then, are we engaged in doing? What, then, is this Commission organized to effect? It is to assist in that business which under the Constitution is called counting the electoral vote. This is all the power that Congress has on that subject. It makes no difference who is to do it. The debate up to the passage of this act was whether the President of the Senate should do it or whether the two houses of Congress should participate with him in it; and a variety of opinions from the year 1800 up to now has been entertained and expressed by distinguished statesmen on both sides as to where the power was lodged. But it is immaterial now. The question is not *who does it,* but *what is it that is to be done.*

It was said by the objectors on our side—I think it cannot be controverted—that counting in its primary meaning is merely enumeration, and is limited to that, in all caseswhere the subjects of the count are definitely ascertained. To be sure, it is an important question as put by the learned counsel on the other side, what is to be counted? There is no dispute on that. It is the electoral votes; and the cases which are referred to this tribunal are those of two sets of votes, and the power, therefore, is implied to distinguish between these several sets of votes and ascertain which is the vote lawfully to be counted.

What is the nature and extent of that implied power, incident to this right to separate the lawful from the unlawful electoral votes? for upon the question of the limit of the inquiry which this body is authorized to make under the act which organizes it, depends the solution of the question as to what evidence it may look to for the purpose of determining the fact which is the subject of its inquiry. I think it involves undoubtedly the exercise of certain discretion and judgment. It may involve the decision of some questions of fact not determinable merely by inspection of the paper purporting to contain the vote or to constitute the vote; as, for example, the very case put by one of the learned gentlemen on the other side, its genuineness or whether it be a forgery; whether, if it be proven by a seal, the seal be the genuine seal. It may also involve the decision of some question of law, as for example whether the paper offered is one known to the law or made in conformity with the law.

But this power, however described, whether as ministerial, administrative, political, or otherwise, must be carefully distinguished from that judicial power which is exerted by judicial courts under the jurisdiction to try the title to an office by the prerogative writ of *quo warranto*. In the exercise of that jurisdiction, the court, armed with its proper forms and the machinery of trial by jury and for the enforcement of evidence, goes *to the very truth and right of the matter* without regard to the paper title. It ascertains by a scrutiny and the testimony of witnesses who in fact received the legal number of legal votes to vest him with actual title to the office. Is it proposed here to do that? Why, if your honors please, what length of time would be required to investigate by recounting and recanvassing the popular vote that lies at the foundation of the electoral vote in every State in the Union, or even in those which are the subjects of dispute in this count? And if you cannot go down to the bottom, if you cannot in probing and searching for frauds and errors and mistakes go through the long and black catalogue of crime, why stop at the first in order to take advantage of all the rest? If this work is the work of this tribunal, then it is to be made thorough and searching; certainly there is not any principle of law or good morals which, if the door be opened to that inquiry, requires you to stop before you have got through.

I think it is plain that this Commission is not engaged in the exercise of that jurisdiction. It is not invested with any portion of that judicial power which is conferred or constituted by the Constitution of the United States; and Congress, not possessing it itself, could not confer it upon such a body as this, which is created for the mere purpose of assisting in the count of the votes, because it is not such a court as Congress is authorized to create for the purpose of receiving a grant of the judicial power of the Constitution. I do not doubt that the jurisdiction to try the title to the office of President and Vice-President, being judicial and properly exercised under the power to issue writs of *quo warranto*, may be vested by law in the Federal courts, as a case at common law arising under the Constitution and laws of the United

States; but until vested it remains dormant. Whether in point of fact such legislation exists, either by a direct act of Congress or indirectly by the adoption of the Maryland statutes in the District of Columbia, is a question upon which I am not advised; but the fact that such a jurisdiction either has been or may be evoked out of the Constitution is an unanswerable reply to the doctrine that Congress, or this tribunal sitting in its stead, has a right to make judicial inquiry as in *quo warranto* into the title of any office. I claim, provided there be no actual legislation such as I have spoken of by Congress in respect to *quo warranto* in regard to President and Vice-President, that there is no law, either State or Federal, in reference to the office and function of an elector; I maintain that there is no law, either State or Federal, whereby that title can be judicially investigated and determined after he has cast his vote.

I maintain that no State can exercise such jurisdiction after that event, because although by the terms of the Constitution of the United States each State by its legislature may determine the mode of the appointment and in fact make the appointment of its electors, yet the function of voting for President and Vice-President is exercised under the authority of the Constitution of the United States; and if it were possible that such jurisdiction existed in State tribunals under the authority of State laws, it would be an easy matter in the great strife and struggle of political parties in the various States that constitute the Union, after the election to interpose by judicial process such delays in respect to the quieting of the title of the parties having the regular and formal appearance of election as to defeat by an injunction as well as a *quo warranto* the right to cast the vote at the time when by the Constitution and laws of the United States it is necessary that it should be cast. And so it would be in the power of party and faction at any time, when beaten at the polls by the popular vote, to resort to these extraordinary writs under State authority and defeat their adversaries by the interminable delays of litigation.

It was the policy of our fathers, it is the policy of the Constitution, to provide a machinery which, let it work as it will, must nevertheless by the 4th day of March after the election necessarily work out the result of having some President and some Vice-President. It was of far more consequence, and was so esteemed by the framers of the Constitution, as it will be by every lover of law and order, that we should have some constituted authority, far more important that the line of continuous authority should be preserved, than that either A or B should hold the place and receive the power and the emoluments of the office.

I say, therefore, that although I admit that the State may provide as it pleases any mode by which the appointment may be made, and by which the fact of appointment may be verified, so as to furnish such machinery and mode of proof as it may choose to verify its own appointment, yet, nevertheless, it must take effect, if it have any power whatever, prior to the time when, by the Constitution of the United States, those who have the *indicia* of office and the color of office are called upon, as the appointed electors of a particular State, to discharge the constitutional duty of depositing their vote for President and Vice-President; so that when the person appointed, or who appears to have been appointed, having in his possession formal evidence of his appointment, in fact exercises the authority conferred upon him under the Constitution of the United States, actually discharges the duty of casting the vote which it is his business to deliver, the transaction to which he has been a party has passed beyond the control of State power and authority.

Then, Mr. President, if I be right, the actual question before this Commission is not which set of electors in Florida received a majority of popular votes; it is not which set appears from the return of the votes made at the primary voting-places to have had a majority of votes so returned; it is not which set, by looking at the county-returns, appears to have had a majority of the votes so compiled; but it is this: Which set, by the actual declaration of the final authority of the State charged with that duty, has become entitled to and clothed by the forms of law with actual incumbency and possession of the office. That body of electors which, with an apparent right and a paper title, and in possession of the function, franchise, or office, actually exercises it, is for the purposes of this tribunal the lawful body whose votes must be counted. It is not necessarily the body which upon subsequent proceedings may be ascertained to have had *de jure* title; but it is that body which, by color of office, having the formal external proofs of authority, was in point of fact inducted into possession of the power to cast that vote, and who did it; in other words, who, under the law of Florida, were on the 6th day of December, 1876, *de facto* electors for that State.

The gentlemen say there were two sets. Why, Mr. President and gentlemen, it is as absurd to say that there are or can be two sets of *de facto* officers in the same office as it is to say that there or can be two sets of *de jure* officers. It is as absurd in law as it would be in physics to say that two bodies can occupy the same space in the same moment of time. The man who is in the office, who has possession of it, who has been inducted into it, who exercises its authority, who does the thing which that office authorizes whomsoever is in it to do, is the man for whom we are inquiring, for he is the man that votes. Nobody else votes. Everybody else is a mere volunteer, unorganized, illegal, without authority, no matter although his ultimate and final right be better than that of the man who has intruded.

There is no safety and there is no sense—I speak it with great respect to this tribunal and to the gentlemen who differ with me; I am bound to say it—there is neither safety nor sense in any other doctrine. You may talk as eloquently as may be on questions of fraud. It is said, "Fraud vitiates everything." No, it does not. It makes things voidable, but it does not vitiate everything. If my friend, [Mr. Black,] by the arts and stratagems of other people, (which I know his guileless soul does not possess,) should hoodwink me by fraudulent misrepresentation into voting for his candidate—if that be a possible supposition—I cannot retract my ballot, nor can the scrutiny set aside the result, because fraud upon private persons is sometimes insignificant when compared with public interests. Frauds by trustees or persons in fiduciary capacities do not make void their fraudulent transactions. They may be avoided, but only by judicial process, and the defense of laches is always a sufficient answer; and lapse of time may be an element in a matter of such transcendent public interest as this, that no man, after the time had elapsed, can be heard to allege it.

And, Mr. President, the only alternative, as I think I have already once said, is, upon the doctrine of our learned friends on the other side, that if the inquiry is opened, it must be opened to all intents and purposes; it must be opened for all inquiries and investigations; it must be opened for all possible proofs. It will not do to stop at the first stage in the descent; but you must go clean to the bottom. And, although it be not pertinent to a forensic discussion, perhaps the example set to me by the learned gentlemen on the other side will warrant the expression, on my part, of my personal confidence that if that true result, setting aside all the forms and the fictions of the law, could be ascertained, there would be no question here as to who ought to be entitled to have counted in his favor the vote of Florida.

Mr. President and gentlemen, an argument has been made upon the effect of the act of Congress of 1792, which provides for the certification by the governor of a State of those who have been duly appointed electors in that State. I have already corrected the misapprehension of the learned gentlemen on the other side that we regard that as so conclusive as that inquiry might not be made into its falsity, whether a forgery or genuine; but, nevertheless, it is evidence; it is evidence provided by existing law; it is the evidence which Congress, of which you are the advisers and constituent parts in this matter, has made and declared to be regular, ordinary, usual, formal evidence of the facts which it contains, and if it be not conclusive, yet it is sufficient.

I admit that the mere certifying act is not conclusive. It may be dispensed with. Congress, who provided it, furnished it, made it a part of the transaction, may disregard it. They need not tie themselves hand and foot; they need not estop themselves; but they have directed this Commission to receive only that which is competent and pertinent by existing law, and the existing law makes the governor's certificate pertinent and competent and sufficient.

But, Mr. President and gentlemen, if you go behind the certificate what are you limited to by the necessity of the thing? In my judgment, you are limited to this: to an inquiry into what are the facts *to which he should have certified and did not;* not what are or may be the ultimate and final facts and right of the case. The facts to be certified by the governor in this or in any case are the public facts which by law remain and constitute a part of the record in the public offices and archives of the State, and of which, being governor for the time being, he has official knowledge. So, then, the case stands, that on the day and at the time when, if ever, the title and right to the possession and incumbency of this function became complete, Governor Stearns was the lawful governor of Florida, and the fact to be certified was just what appeared at that time in his office or in the office of the secretary of state, to wit, that by the judgment and finding of the final authority of the State canvassing that election the gentlemen whom he certified to be electors had, in fact and according to law, been appointed.

How shall I treat the pretense that a subsequent governor coming in at an after-time, or that a court, acting upon the *status* of the parties subsequently when it rendered its judgment—if it rendered any at all— could, by relation, change the *de facto* situation, or the pretense, more groundless still, that an act of legislation could unsettle and otherwise determine that which had already passed beyond the control of mortal power? For, Mr. President and gentlemen, I believe it is a saying of one of the sages of the common law that though Parliament be omnipotent, it cannot alter a fact, and *facts are rights.* All our rights are founded on facts. All the theory and practice of our law and of judicial tribunals and all that system of government and society under which we live, depend not upon abstractions, however beautifully they may be defined, but upon the facts of human nature and of human life. *Stare decisis!* where does that come from? You perpetuate *an error* because if you do not, *you will commit a wrong.*

Will the President inform me how much time I have consumed?

The PRESIDENT. You have spoken forty-five minutes. I will notify you when the hour is up.

Mr. MATTHEWS. The *quo warranto* proceedings in Florida which seem to be relied upon in this matter, in my judgment, cannot be alleged against the truth of the facts recited in Governor Stearns's certificate, mainly for the reason which I have already given, because all State power had passed away. But the record of that proceeding does not in anywise correspond with the description of what constitutes an estoppel by judgment, according to the decision of Chief-Justice De Grey in the Duchess of Kingston's case. In the *quo warranto* in Florida the inquiry was not what it is here. The inquiry there was what was the actual, real, final right; not who in fact according to law on the day exercised the power and was entitled to possession. One man may be entitled to possession; another man may have the right. Nothing is more common than that. Gentlemen have sat in both Houses of Congress upon a certificate of election and they had the right of possession, when perhaps some unnamed person outside the area and not entitled to the privileges of the floor may have had residing within him all the time the real right.

That leads me to say that the analogy drawn between this case and the celebrated New Jersey case, by my distinguished friend from Pennsylvania, [Mr. Black,] fails utterly, because by the express terms of the Federal Constitution the House of Representatives was the judge not only of the qualification and return of the members but of their election. Therefore it could set aside the broad seal of the State of New Jersey and the *prima facie* right, to inquire into the real right. I have already undertaken to show to this Commission that they are not sitting here with any such jurisdiction as that.

But so far from availing anything as proof against the position which I deem to be the right and constitutional one here, that record establishes for us, by the very verity which is claimed for it on the other side, the essential fact on which, in my judgment, rest all the rights involved in this discussion; and that is, that on that day, on the 6th of December, the day appointed by law, the respondents in that proceeding, who are certified in certificate No. 1, were *in possession of, and exercising, and discharging the functions* and duties of the office of elector, and that the complainants or relators *were not*, because, as they said, we kept them out, we were unlawfully intruding and had ousted them, and thereupon they asked to have themselves re-instated. But the fact is, that on that day, the critical day, the day of days, the respondents in that record are shown by the gentlemen to have been in the undisturbed exercise of the actual franchise of electors for the State of Florida, and hence they cast their votes and hence their votes are entitled to be counted; and inasmuch as the relators appear by the record *not to have been in possession*, not to have been situated so that by law they could exercise that function, they complain and admit that the form of their vote was mere dumb-show without meaning or significance and without the least particle of legality or constitutional force.

Mr. President, I am exceedingly obliged to yourself and the gentlemen of the Commission, and will now suspend the argument so far as I am concerned.

The PRESIDENT. You have occupied fifty-five minutes. Is there another gentleman to be heard on the same side this afternoon?

Mr. EVARTS. It was agreed that Mr. Stoughton and myself would divide the remaining two hours and five minutes, but we were not expecting to proceed to-day.

The PRESIDENT. The understanding of the Chair was that during this day two would speak on each side, if three were to speak altogether.

Mr. Commissioner ABBOTT. There is to be but one closing argument on each side on Monday, as I understood the arrangement.

The PRESIDENT. There is only one person to close on each side on Monday. That was my understanding.

Mr. EVARTS. That was the arrangement when there were but two on each side to speak; but then when there were three introduced, it was required that two should open.

The PRESIDENT. On each side, I meant.

Mr. EVARTS. We all three speak, one after the other?

The PRESIDENT. I think two had better speak to-night.

Mr. EVARTS. If it is your honor's instruction, we will submit.

Mr. STOUGHTON. Mr. President and gentlemen of the Commission, although my brother Evarts and myself propose to divide between us the remainder of our time, I shall occupy, I think, but a very small portion of it.

The question which the court or rather this tribunal has directed us to argue, as I understand it, is whether any, and, if any, what, testimony can be received in this case of any nature, independent of the documents which were transmitted to the President of the Senate, and opened in the presence of the two Houses.

In the first place it seems to me appropriate to ask what is the jurisdiction of this tribunal and what are its powers? Upon it is devolved by legislation of Congress such power, if any, to count the electoral vote, in the special cases referred to it, as is possessed by the two Houses of Congress acting separately or together. The jurisdiction as conferred is, therefore, an unknown quantity until it shall be ascertained what are the powers of the two Houses acting separately or together; and the purpose of this Commission is—assuming the power of the two Houses or of either to be to count the electoral vote—to ascertain what duties, what powers are involved in the exercise of that function. The purpose to be attained is the count of the electoral vote. The power devolved upon this tribunal is to count that vote in special cases. It is to count the electoral vote, and not to count the votes by which the electors were elected. That is a discrimination which I think hardly need be enforced by argument. The electoral vote is to be counted, and this tribunal has no power, it has no duty to count the vote by which the electors were elected. If it has, it will be compelled to descend into an unfathomable depth and to grope its way in paths hitherto untrodden by judicial feet and amid voting-polls and places whence it cannot emerge in many days.

Now, what is proposed by the testimony in question? The general inquiry which counsel are to answer is, what, if any, testimony is admissible in this case; and, for the purpose of ascertaining this, it is well to learn precisely what this case is and what is the purpose of the testimony proposed. There are some facts of which this tribunal can take judicial notice. One is, the laws of the State of Florida. What are they in reference to this subject, and what was done in pursuance of them, and what is proposed to be done by testimony—as it is called—for the purpose of overthrowing what was done in pursuance of the laws of that State?

In the first place, its statute, by a clause a part of which I will take the liberty of reading, authorized the creation of an ultimate returning-board having capacity to certify the number of votes cast for electors and who were elected; and, if that board performed its duty, however mistaken, however crowded with error, however, if you please, tainted by fraud, if that board discharged the duty cast upon it by law, and did ascertain and did declare how many votes for particular sets of electors were cast, and did certify and declare who were the persons elected electors, that ends all inquiry here, assuming that you may go behind the governor's certificate, unless, indeed, you may retreat behind the action of the returning-board, the final tribunal for that purpose created by the laws of the State, and ascertain whether it did or did not, according to your judgment, faithfully return the votes cast and faithfully declare who were the persons elected. I read as to the constitution of the returning-board, may it please this tribunal, from the fourth section of the act of 1872, which will be found on page 2 of the report made by Mr. Sargent of the Senate. It provides that:

On the thirty-fifth day after the holding of any general or special election for any State officer, member of the legislature or Representative in Congress, or sooner, if the returns shall have been received from the several counties wherein elections shall have been held, the secretary of state, attorney-general, and the comptroller of public accounts, or any two of them, together with any other member of the cabinet who may be designated by them, shall meet at the office of the secretary of state, pursuant to notice to be given by the secretary of state, and form a board of State canvassers, and proceed to canvass the returns of said election—

Will your honors mark the language—

and determine and declare who shall have been elected to any such office or as such member, as shown by such returns. If any such returns shall be shown or shall appear to be so irregular, false, or fraudulent that the board shall be unable to determine the true vote for any such officer or member, they shall so certify, and shall not include such return in their determination and declaration.

There was committed to this board by that statute a capacity to determine and decide—finally and conclusively—how many lawful votes were cast and who were elected electors. A majority of that board were authorized to perform that duty; and it appears here, before this tribunal, that, in the discharge of that duty, a majority of its members—omitting the attorney-general—did, in the exercise of the discretion thus confided to them, certify and declare that the Hayes electors, so called, were duly elected by the lawful voters of that State. If we go behind that finding we disregard the determination of a tribunal which the State of Florida has declared by her legislature to be empowered to determine what persons she has constituted to declare her will in the electoral college; for it is her will as a sovereign State—wise or foolish—which is to be thus expressed.

Now, it seems to me that if this Commission shall go behind the finding of that board it will go behind it upon the theory that it may exercise its will, irrespective of judicial power, upon some theory that it has the capacity of both Houses or of either House to do as it pleases, not in subjection to the Constitution of the country, but in obedience to an unlicensed will and purpose; and I expect, as my brother Black did, a conclusion which will rescue this tribunal from falling into so fatal an error as that of undertaking to interfere with the final declaration of the tribunal which the legislature of a State has declared shall finally and at last certify who may deposit the expression of its will in the national ballot-box, as it has been called.

I suppose it will not be denied—I presume no one will deny—that a State of this Union, by its legislature, may in any mode it pleases declare who shall be its instrument for selecting electors. I suppose that, if the State of Florida had declared that one of its sheriffs should select the electors, that would be final when done. Peradventure some theorist, upon the notion that you should go to the people as the source of power to elect judges as well as all other officers, might say such a mode of selection and appointment would hardly be in harmony with republican institutions; but I think he who would venture to go behind the expressed will of the State as to the method in which the electors should be appointed would find himself engaged in an effort to invade its sovereignty and interfere with the supremacy of a State.

I am perfectly aware that, if this tribunal were empowered to appoint committees by which it could through them proceed to different States and, irrespective of the rules of evidence or of law, gather together testimony, and then if it had the capacity upon that to do as it should please, it might go behind and overset any final lawful declaration of any returning-board in any State in the country. But Congress, while it conferred in the shape of an unknown quantity a jurisdiction upon this tribunal—declaring it should possess the powers, *if any*, possessed by the two Houses, or either, for the purpose of performing the duty of counting the vote—took care not to permit it to found its conclusion upon testimony inadmissible in a court of justice. The distinction between the uncertainty of language which conferred jurisdiction and the certainty and precision of language which conferred power to receive testimony is marked and apparent, and I will, with your honors' permission, refer to it.

All such certificates, votes, and papers so objected to, and all papers accompanying the same, together with such objections, shall be forthwith submitted to said Commission, which shall proceed to consider the same, with the same powers, if any, now possessed for that purpose by the two Houses acting separately or together, and, by a majority of votes, decide whether any and what votes from such State are the votes provided for by the Constitution of the United States, and how many and what persons were duly appointed electors in such State, and may therein take into view such petitions, depositions, and other papers, if any, as shall, by the Constitution and now existing law, be competent and pertinent in such consideration.

"Competent and pertinent" in view of what? In view of the action of Congress through its committees? I mean no disrespect when I say that such mode permits the breath of calumny to be blown in a way which, thank God, courts of justice take care to prevent; and your honors, being endowed with power to hear depositions, papers, and petitions competent and pertinent within the meaning of the Constitution and existing laws—it being not expressed precisely what they are—will look at those rules of law which guide in administering justice upon the bench, and will determine what are the depositions and papers which you may thus receive. Turning over the pages of the law, you find, printed in characters unmistakable, your utter incapacity to receive other proof than that which the common law has sanctified by usage and through the lips of its judges as fit to be employed to affect the rights of men, to say nothing of the rights of States and nations. Here we have a tribunal of special and limited jurisdiction, incapable of moving out of the narrow orbit in which it is placed, proceeding for a particular purpose, liable in the language of the act, theoretically but not practically, to have its decision overturned by a concurrent órder of the two Houses acting finally, and therefore a tribunal thus created exerts no powers not specially conferred, and can receive no testimony not in harmony with principles of law long since settled.

Then, may it please your honors, your jurisdiction is to count the electoral votes; your power is in counting to resort to such proof, if any, as the Constitution and laws permit. You are dealing with a delicate subject when the question of jurisdiction is reached. You are dealing with the supremacy of a State when you undertake to touch its final tribunal for the purpose of overhauling and upsetting its action.

Now I have in a general way, perhaps very imperfectly, presented my view of the jurisdiction and the power and the purpose of this tribunal. I propose to say a very few words in addition.

I have said that the purpose of the testimony offered is to go behind, not merely the governor's certificate—for that undoubtedly, upon questions of forgery, upon questions of mistake, upon many questions, this tribunal could deal with—but, designing to get behind that, the purpose is to get behind the action of that tribunal which the State has set up, and to cancel its finding; or else the testimony offered is senseless and worthless. What is specially offered? To maintain the right to have the votes counted for Mr. Tilden, we have before us the certificate of the attorney-general of Florida, who dissented from the majority of the returning-board, stating in that certificate—with frankness, as he does—that there is no method of authenticating their title beyond his mere certificate, by obtaining the certificate of the governor, because it would be in violation of the laws of Florida for him to certify to the election of electors who had been returned as such by but a minority of the board empowered to perform that duty.

What next do we find? We find a statute of the State of Florida thrust upon us, passed on the 17th of January—long after these electors had voted—authorizing a new canvass—of what? In harmony with the authority to canvass previously authorized? No, but a canvass of the votes, precisely indicating them, then in the office of the secretary of state; and we find under that act a board of canvassers meeting; a canvass made and certified, stating the Tilden electors to have been found by that board on the 25th of January to have been elected in the November previous. That is the authority for going behind the certification of the electors by the lawful returning-board. Coupled with this is a proceeding by *quo warranto*, ultimating in a judgment on the 25th of January declaring that these persons who performed all their duties on the 6th of December were not then electors, but that all their acts were illegal and invalid; and the learned gentleman from Virginia [Mr. Tucker] who yesterday addressed this tribunal said that decision swept away all prior acts of these officers *de facto;* but for this he gave us no authority. My memory immediately carried me to case after case in which it had been held that where an officer *de facto* is ousted by such a proceeding, all his prior acts are necessarily considered as valid and binding. Society could not exist without the application of such a rule. Judges go upon the bench, property passes under their decrees, men are hung by their judgments, and finally some one after a litigation of years obtains possession of the office. Is the virtue of that decree to sweep away the past, restore to life, yield back property? No. So here the act of the electors lawfully appointed, declared to be such in the mode prescribed by the legislature of Florida, doing what they were commanded to perform, is valid and irreversible.

Not content with this effort to succeed by *quo warranto* through the aid of an active and willing court, or with the finding of the new returning-board, the legislature passed another act declaring the canvass of the latter board valid and binding, and the Tilden electors by it declared elected to be duly qualified electors of the State. These judicial and statutory contrivances are unavailing and cannot disturb the electoral votes duly cast.

The alleged fault of the lawful returning-board was not fraud—at which my friends are so shocked—but mistake. After electors are thus appointed lawfully, but possibly by a mistaken view of the law by the board declaring their election, its conclusion must forever stand. The electors who by virtue of such an appointment have cast their votes are not to allow the day prescribed by Federal law to cast the vote of the State to pass, and the vote of the State to be lost, upon the theory that possibly their work may be undone by subsequent judicial action or *ex post facto* legislation.

It seems to me, may it please your honors, in view of the jurisdiction and capacity of this tribunal, in view of its powers to take testimony, in view of the purpose of introducing this testimony, which I have undertaken to state, that the application to introduce testimony should be overruled.

The PRESIDENT. One hour and thirty-two minutes are left, Mr. Evarts, of the time allotted to your side.

On motion of Mr. Commissioner STRONG, the Commission adjourned until eleven o'clock on Monday morning, the 5th instant.

MONDAY, *February* 5, 1877.

The Commission met at eleven o'clock a. m., pursuant to adjournment, all the members being present.

The following counsel also appeared:

Hon. Charles O'Connor, of New York,
Hon. Jeremiah S. Black, of Pennsylvania,
Richard T. Merrick, esq., of Washington, D. C.,
Ashbel Green, esq., of New Jersey,
William C. Whitney, esq., of New York,

} Of counsel in opposition to certificate No. 1.

Hon. William M. Evarts, of New York,
Hon. E. W. Stoughton, of New York,
Hon. Stanley Matthews, of Ohio,
Hon. Samuel Shellabarger, of Ohio.

} Of counsel in opposition to certificates Nos. 2 and 3.

The Journal of Saturday's proceedings was read and approved.

The PRESIDENT. The concluding counsel on the part of the objectors to the first certificate is entitled to an hour and forty minutes. Mr. Evarts, on the other side, who will speak first, is entitled to an hour and thirty-two minutes.

Mr. EVARTS. Mr. President and gentlemen of the Commission, the order of the Commission inviting the attention of counsel lays out for their consideration three topics:

First, whether, under the powers possessed by the Commission, any evidence beyond that disclosed in the three certificates from the State of Florida, which were opened by the President of the Senate in the presence of the two Houses of Congress and under the authority of the recent act of Congress are transmitted to this Commission, can be received;

Second, if any can be received, what that evidence is; and

Third, what evidence other than these certificates, if any, is now before the Commission.

I will dispose of the last question in the order of the Commission first. It requires but brief attention to express our views sufficiently, and will, I think, require but little consideration, in point of time, however important it may be in substance, from the Commission.

It is suggested that certain packages of papers which were borne into the presence of the Commission by the messenger that brought the certificates and objections are *already* evidence in the possession of the Commission. What those packages contain, what degree of authenticity, or what scope of efficacy is to be imputed to or claimed for them as particular matters of evidence and particular forms of proof, is unknown to us and unknown to the Commission. The proposition upon which it is claimed that this evidence, whatever it may be—subject, undoubtedly, to discussion and to rejection by the Commission as not pertinent and not important and not authentic—the proposition is that, being mentioned in one of the objections interposed against the first certificate as matter on which the objection was founded, instead of being a warrant as it were to the objector which he vouches, he, the objector, thereby makes it a part of the evidence before the Commission; and our learned friend, Judge Black, has proposed that, except as against objectors who prevail in their arts and efforts in common-law courts and whom he has been polite enough to designate as "*snapperadoes*," this evidence is, by authentic principles of jurisprudence, made evidence by this attachment to this objection. He instances the case of a bill in equity which may append exhibits and which, of course, brings the exhibits, as a part of itself, into the possession of the court. But that, thereby, they were made evidence any more than his bill, except upon such weight as should be imputed to them by the answer of the defendant admitting, or not denying, or establishing a rule of necessary contradiction by two witnesses, instead of one, I have never heard that the plaintiff made the exhibits evidence in the cause by appending them to his bill.

Now, the provisions of the recent act that at all touch this matter are very few. In the first place, the objections are not conclusive of anything. They bind nobody. They are merely the occasion upon which the reference to this Commission arises. If there be no objection, the case provided for the exercise of your authority is not produced. If the objection is made, however inartificial or imperfect, the case has arisen; but that the objection narrows and limits and provides the issue or affects the controversy upon which your jurisdiction attaches, is a pure fabrication out of utterly unsubstantial and immaterial suggestions in the law. Certainly, if volunteer objectors on one side and the other were permitted to lay down the issues, and adduce the evidence, and make up the packages of the evidence, it would be a strange commitment of your great authority to casual, to rash, to disingenuous suggestion.

So much, I think, entirely disposes of the question of whether there is any evidence here. The other question, as to whether evidence in the possession of either or both of the Houses of Congress, in the shape of committees' reports or conclusions of either of those great bodies, in any form, is transmissible, and may be proposed to this Commission and may be accepted and received by it after it is unfolded, after it is understood, after the paper is scrutinized and is opposed, is a question that is but a subordinate part of the main question, whether any evidence beyond the certificates can be received.

I wish to preclude, at the outset, anything that should carry for a moment the impression that there has been overpassed by some stroke of astuteness or of diligence the question of what you can receive and what you must reject. I find myself, then, unimpeded in the inquiry, as open to me as it is open to you, whether *any* evidence can be received, and, if any, what, beyond the certificates opened by the President of the Senate. On that question I shall think it quite attentive to the instruction of the Commission and much more suitable to a practical and definite discussion and a practical and definite determination by this

Commission, that whatever of general principles, and however far-reaching the decision on those general principles in this matter of evidence may be, the evidence that is now actually proposed should be taken as the apparent limit of the inquiry whether evidence should be received, not from any particular defect as to form or manner of proffer, but as to whether it falls within evidence that may be received extraneous to, in addition to, the certificates opened by the President of the Senate. I am enabled by the memorandum presented by the learned counsel, Mr. O'Conor, which is found on the forty-second page of the Congressional Record of yesterday, to present the quality and character, the office and effort, of extraneous evidence that it is supposed might be, within the powers of this Commission, received and entertained by it.

In the first place, he excludes from the area of consideration one of the certificates, to wit, that which contains the vote of the Tilden electors; for that they need no extrinsic proof, and it is mentioned only that it may be excluded. Then, secondly, there are statements concerning the *quo warranto* suit in Florida, commenced on the 6th of December and ending on the 25th of January. In regard to that the record is supposed to contain in itself the particular means of its use according to established rules of jurisprudence as a record or as an authority. It is suggested in respect to that, therefore, that extraneous proof only would need to reach the point of the precise hour of the day on the 6th of December on which the writ commencing that action was served, and on our part perhaps proof that an appeal had been taken from that judgment and is still pending.

Then are enumerated some other matter sthat require no proof, as it is supposed. Again, the acts of the legislature mentioned are public acts and matters of record; and it is supposed that they are regularly before the Commission, so far at least as they appear in the third certificate, by virtue of that transmission, and besides I suppose that they are matters of public record as the action of the legislature of the State.

We come now to the following:

Fifthly. The only matters which the Tilden electors desire to lay before the Commission by evidence actually extrinsic will now be stated.

1. The board of State canvassers, acting on certain erroneous views when making their canvass, by which the Hayes electors appeared to be chosen, rejected wholly the returns from the county of Manatee and parts of returns from each of the following counties—

Naming them.

In doing so the said State board acted without jurisdiction, as the circuit and supreme courts in Florida decided.

That is, by their recent judgments in mandamus and *quo warranto.*

"It was by overruling and setting aside as not warranted by law these rejections, that the courts of Florida reached their respective conclusions that Mr. Drew was elected governor, that the Hayes electors were usurpers, and that the Tilden electors were duly chosen. No evidence that in any view could be called extrinsic is believed to be needful in order to establish the conclusions relied upon by the Tilden electors, except duly authenticated copies of the State canvass," (that is—

Mr. O'Conor adds—

the erroneous canvass as we consider it,) "and of the returns from the above-named four counties, one wholly and others in part rejected by said State canvassers."

Mr. O'CONOR. That is your canvass that you rely on.

Mr. EVARTS. So I understand. I was reading your language.

And of the returns from the above-named four counties, one wholly and others in part rejected by said State canvassers.

It is proposed, therefore, as the matter extraneous that it is desired to introduce, and that it is claimed is open to your consideration, not that the certificate of Governor Stearns falsifies the fact he was to certify; not that it falsifies the record that makes the basis of the fact which he was to certify; but that the record at the time on which by law he was to base his certificate, departing from which his certificate would be false, is itself to be penetrated or surmounted by extraneous proof, showing that by matters of substance occurring in the progress of the election itself errors or frauds intervened. This means that somewhere in the steps of the election between the deposit of the ballots in the boxes at the precincts and the original computation of the contents of those boxes there, and the submission to a correct canvass in a county of the precincts thus canvassed at their own ballot-boxes, or between the returns of the county canvass to the State canvassers, or in the action of the State canvassers in the final computation of the aggregates to ascertain the plurality of votes as for one or the other candidate, and so declare the result of the election, frauds or mistakes occurred. In other words, that in the process of the election itself, from stage to stage, on the very matter of right and on the question of the title *de jure* there has occurred matter of judicial consideration which should be inquired into here. For I need not say that, however simple and however limited the step to be taken behind the record of the final State canvass, to serve the needs and to accomplish the justice as proposed by the learned counsel for the objectors against the Hayes certificate, the *principle* upon which this evidence is offered, if their occasions required it, if justice required it, if the powers of this commission tolerated it, would carry the scrutiny and the evidence to whatever point this complete correction or evisceration of the final canvass would demand.

I am at once, therefore, relieved from any discussion as practical in this case, except so far as illustration or argument may make it useful, *pro* or *con*, of any consideration whether a governor's certificate could be attacked as itself being not a governor's certificate, but a forgery. That is not going *behind* the governor's certificate. That is going in front of the governor's certificate and breaking it down as no governor's certificate. That is not the question you are to consider here. There is certainly no reason, on principle, that when a governor's certificate is required for any solemnity or conclusiveness of authentication, a forged paper should be protected because it is called a governor's certificate. Neither does their offer of proof suggest any debate as to whether *the fact to be certified by the governor*, the substance that his certificate is to authenticate, can be made the subject of extraneous evidence with a view to show that the fact to be certified is discordant with the certificate, and that the fact must prevail over the interpolated false certificate of the fact.

There can be no escape from this criticism on their offer of proof, unless our learned opponents ask your assent to a claim that when the act of Congress requires the governor's certificate as to the list of per-sons that have been appointed electors it requires from the governor a certificate that every stage and step of the process of *the election* has been honest and true and clear and lawful and effectual, and free from all exception of fraud. Unless you make *that* the fact to be certified by the governor, you lay no basis for introducing evidence of discord between the fact to be certified and the fact that has been certified. Without disguise, therefore, the proposition is that, whether or no there might be occasion for extraneous proof to falsify a governor's certificate on the ground of its own spurious character, or on the ground of its falsely setting forth the fact professed to be stated, and admitting the governor's certificate to be genuine, and admitting the final canvass, duly filed and recorded, to be in accord with the certificate, this Commission stands at the same stage of inquiry and with the same right to investigate the election itself to the bottom as a judicial court exercising the familiar jurisdiction of *quo warranto.*

There is also a suggestion that extraneous proofs may be necessary on the point "that Mr. Humphreys, one of the Hayes electors, held office under the United States;" and, in our behalf, it is then suggested by the learned counsel that we might need to introduce evidence that he had resigned. The interposition of this objection was a surprise to us; for it was a matter of inquiry before the Florida State canvassing-board on the 4th day of December, 1876, antecedent to the completion of the final and conclusive canvass. The evidence thus taken I am able to read from page 32 of the Congressional Record of Saturday, in the report of the minority of the House committee :

Extract from testimony before the Florida State canvassing-board, Monday, December 4, 1876.

FREDERICK C. HUMPHREYS sworn for the republicans.

Examined by the CHAIRMAN :

Question. Are you shipping-commissioner for the port of Pensacola ?—Answer. I am not.

Q. Were you at one time ?—A. I was.

Q. At what time ?—A. Previous to the 7th of November.

Q. What time did you resign ?—A. The acceptance of my resignation was received by me from Judge Woods about a week or ten days before the day of election, which I have on file in my office. I did not think of its being questioned, or I would have had it here. He stated in his letter to me that the collector of customs would perform the duties of the office, and the collector of customs has since done so.

On the nature of an objection for *disqualification* as a subject of proof before the two Houses or the President of the Senate, in their attribution of authority under the clause of the Constitution governing their joint meeting, a word needs to be said; and I will attempt at the same time to answer the inquiry made very pertinently and forcibly by Mr. Commissioner THURMAN the other day.

There is, as I understand the matter, (and I will not anticipate a discussion that must come later in this argument,) a consideration in the first place of whether the Houses of Congress in the matter of the count, at the time of the meeting for the constitutional duty of opening and counting the votes, have any power by law for any intervention or any methods of extraneous proof. Whatever may be thought as to whether disqualifications of this nature were proper for the scrutiny of the votes to be counted, and however proper it might have been for Congress to provide by law for the production of extraneous proof in that transaction, and for the manner in which it might be adduced and considered, there is no act of Congress on the subject. Our proposition is that, at that stage of the transaction of the election, the two Houses cannot entertain any subject of extraneous proof. The process of counting must go on. If a disqualified elector has passed the observation of the voters in the State, passed the observation of any sentinels or safeguards that may have been provided in the State law; when these are all overpassed and the vote stands on the presentation and authentication of the Constitution—that is, upon the certificate of the electors themselves and of the governor—it must stand unchallengeable and unimpeachable in the count. Of course, the provision of means of inquiry at that stage by Congress, if they had thought fit to provide means, would have involved the delays of such inquiry, the proof of the alleged infirmity in the elector, and the counter-proof of its removal, all matters ordinarily manageable, perhaps in point of time not leading to much prolixity, but still, in supposable cases, involving contradiction of witnesses and discussion as to the effect of testimony which would involve delay.

Mr. Commissioner Thurman asked this question : " Suppose that the electoral vote, when opened, disclosed the fact that the four electors were then present members of Congress, and had been such members at the time of appointment as electors, what then ? " That involves an element, you will perceive, that is not touched by the considerations that belong to proof. That impeachment of qualification in the electors supposed is of ocular and personal observation at all times by the President of the Senate and by the two Houses of Congress, and is of record at the Capitol. But if the instance is merely that of a member of Congress not presently a member and thus involving extraneous proof of his retirement from the office in season to qualify him for appointment as elector, then the case falls back into the class of cases which I have just considered, where there has been no provision for extraneous proof, and where the office accorded to the governor's certificate cannot be overpassed without extraneous proof. There is, as we suppose, no safe rule, except to say that this injunction laid upon the States, that they shall not appoint the excluded persons, does not execute itself under the Constitution, and if unexecuted in the laws of the State, is only to be executed by laws of Congress providing the means and time and place for proof and determination on the fact of disqualification. This is all that I need to say on the question of personal disqualification.

I have said that this Commission cannot receive evidence in addition to the certificates, of the nature of that which is offered ; that is, evidence that goes behind the State's record of its election, which has been certified by the governor as resulting in the appointment of these electors. One reason of this proposition, and on which sufficiently it rests, is that that is a judicial inquiry into the very matter of right, the title to office. This inquiry accepts the prevalence of the formal, the certificated, the recorded title of the electors, and proposes then to investigate as *inter partes*, as a matter of right, which of two competing lists of electors is really elected on an honest and searching canvass and scrutiny of the State election. It undertakes a function that is judicial ; and the powers for its exercise are attempted to be evoked by their necessity for the exercise of the function assumed. What are adequate means ? Adequate means for that judicial investigation are plenary means. No means are adequate for that inquiry that are not plenary. But no plenary judicial powers, no plenary powers for inquiry into fact and determination of law judicially, can be communicated by Congress except to tribunals that are courts inferior to the Supreme Court. and that are filled by judges appointed by the President of the United States and confirmed by the Senate. Will any lawyer, expert or inexpert, mention a topic or method of judicature, of jurisprudence, that involves the possession of means of larger reach and a more complete control of powers than the trial of a *quo warranto* for an office that is to search an election ? But not only is it beyond the power of Congress to transfer to this Commission the powers of a court of this plenary reach and efficiency, but on the topic of *quo warranto* to try the title of an office they would find a *subject* of jurisdiction in regard to which the Constitution had interposed an insurmountable barrier to its devolution on a court like this. The *quo warranto* is a matter and an action of the common law. It involves as matter of right the introduction of a jury into its methods of trial. No title to office on a contested election was ever tried without a jury. The seventh article of amendments to the Constitution requires that in suits at common law the right of trial by jury shall be preserved, and their verdict shall never be re-examined in any court of the United States except by the rules of the common law.

I may ask your attention, in connection with the topic that I last discussed, and in pertinent relation to the present, to the case of Groome *vs.* Gwynn, in 43 Maryland Reports, 572, especially at page 624. This case shows that this argument, that a duty attributed by law or the Constitution, must carry to itself, in the functionary charged with its exercise, all the powers necessary, upon the ground that the duty must involve the powers, finds no place in our jurisprudence; the argument is the other way. If the functionary, if the Commission has not been clothed with the necessary faculties, then the duty is not accorded or, the means of its exercise not being furnished, it cannot be discharged. There the governor had, by the State constitution, the power to determine a contest for the elective office of attorney-general of the State of Maryland. The governor, finding by his own inspection of the constitution that he lacked the means of carrying out the scrutiny that must decide, held that he could not exercise it and he would not exercise it, unless compelled by judicial authority. The court of appeals, on an application for a mandamus to compel the governor to give the certificate to the candidate appearing to be elected by the canvass, held that he was vested by the constitution with an authority to decide the contest, but that the laws of Maryland had not executed the constitution by furnishing him with powers to perform the duty assigned to him, and that the mandamus must go against him to compel him to deliver the certificate to the candidate that, on the fraudulent election, was returned as having the plurality of votes. Thus the preliminary contest before the governor that might have been effectual to redress the frauds of the election, was defeated for want of necessary legislation. The contest could only be had under the judicial powers of the State lodged in the courts, and in the shape of *quo warranto* on a suit against the inducted candidate that the governor might or would have decided not to be entitled to take the office.

I find in this act of 1877 no such purpose in the arrangement of this Commission or its endowment with powers as to make it a court under the Constitution. I find no appointment of these judges to this court under the powers of the Constitution. I find no means provided for writs and their enforcement, nor for the methods of trial that must belong to a discussion on a *quo warranto*. Now, I understand that the proponents of this proof lay out as the nature and the limit of your inquiries, of your duties and your powers, that of judicial investigation upon *quo warranto*. Mr. Representative Field assigned to you what he described as "powers at least as great as of a court on *quo warranto*," and, of course, in that nature. Mr. Merrick claimed the same. Judge Black did not in terms, yet in assigning the nature and the searching character of the transaction that you are to enter upon, gave it that character and implied that demand. The brief handed in by Mr. Green, in the praise of which I am happy to join with his learned associates, makes the claim distinctly that you are not adequate as a revising canvassing-board, but you must have the powers of a court on *quo warranto*. And why this claim if anything less magnificent and anything less intolerable could have been found sufficient area for your action as desired? It is because in the methods and machinery of elections, as they insist, the steps are onward, from one canvass to the next, and if you are made only a superior canvassing-board to determine whether Governor Stearns's certificate that these electors were appointed is valid, and you are nothing but a returning-board, surmounting the final returning-board to see whether their returns justified that certificate, that, at once, you must find that it does, that the *de-facto* title and'possession are complete, and that nothing but a jurisdic-tion that concedes the *de-facto* title and possession can begin, can find the case for beginning, the consideration of the question of right. This *quo-warranto* suit in the Florida court, if it becomes a subject of evidence; declares absolutely, on the petition of the Tilden electors, that the Hayes electors are in possession of the faculty, the office, or whatever it may be, and are exercising it, and they ask that an inquiry may then proceed in due course of law to inquire whether that possession and that exercise, as matter of right, between them and the Hayes electors, are or are not according to law and truth.

And the Commission will be good enough to look at an act, not re-printed in the little collection of the acts so usefully laid before us, of February 2, 1872, in the laws of Florida, in relation to the proceeding upon writs of *quo warranto*. The general statute of procedure excludes any possible writ of *quo warranto* except by the State through the action of the attorney-general, and this *quo-warranto* suit begins by evidence that the attorney-general refused to bring the writ for the State, and that led to an inquiry how it happened that it was brought at all, and to the discovery of this law of 1872, providing that when the attorney-general refuses, then claimants may make themselves relators and use the name of the State ; but in such case the suit is a mere private suit, that is good between the parties, but does not affect the State. It is in terms so provided, and it is provided that the judgment shall not be a bar to a subsequent suit by the attorney-general in the public right. So much to explain that situation.

Mr. Commissioner BRADLEY. Will you give us the page of the session laws?

Mr. EVARTS. Page 28 of the session laws of 1872.

There is but one other point that I wish to call to the attention of the Commission in the legislation of Florida, for I can spend no time to rehearse the statutes. On page 53 of the pamphlet that has been printed for the use of the Commission there are found sections 31 and 32. One is a provision that—

The secretary of state shall make and transmit to each person chosen to any State office immediately after the canvass—

showing that the canvass as completed is the basis of the State's authen-tication of the right of every State officer—

a certificate showing the number of votes cast for each person, which certificate shall be *prima facie* evidence of his election to such office.

That gives him the office. Subsequent inquiry is as to the final right. Then section 32 :

When any person shall be elected to the office of elector of President and Vice-Pres-ident, or Representative in Congress, the governor shall make out, sign, and cause to be sealed with the seal of the State, and transmit to such person a certificate of his election.

That is the State's final designation of the person that has been appointed an elector under the Constitution of the United States. Had these contestants any such authentication of their right, and have they proposed any such evidence of right as in existence on the 6th day of De-cember? Have they questioned the completeness of the Hayes electors' warrant to attend and discharge their duty that clothes the vote when cast with the complete qualification under the State laws and the State's action? We have the governor's certificate—and he is the very person that passed officially upon that question which furnishes the authority to the electors to meet and act—that this is the list of the electors appointed. *Omnia præsumuntur rite acta;* but there is no presumption needed here. These certificates under the State law form no part of the return to the President of the Senate; but when the same governor executes under Federal law the same duty and upon the same evidence as under State law, we have in his certificate, now here, adequate authentication of the completion of the transaction by which the State appointed the Hayes electors.

Now we come to consider the general doctrine as to what the powers are, and what the arrangement and disposition of those powers are, under the Constitution of the United States in the transaction of choosing a President. In the first place, the only transaction of choosing a President begins with the deposit, so to speak, in the Federal urn of the votes of certain persons named and described in the Constitution as electors. From the moment of that deposit the sealed vote lies protected against destruction or corruption in the deposit provided for it, the possession of Federal officers in Federal offices. The only other step, after that, is the opening of those votes and their counting. All that precedes the deposit of the votes by electors relates to their acquisition of the qualifications which the Constitution prescribes. Those qualifications are nothing but *appointment by the State,* and with that the act of Congress and the Federal Constitution, with due reverence to State authority, do not interfere. It has been provided under a rule of prudence that the electors shall all be appointed on the same day in all the States. It has been provided that they shall meet and cast their votes on the same day. The latter provision fixes a duty in the transaction of *voting for President.* The other is the only intrusion upon State authority in the absolute choice of the time and manner of appointment; Congress may prescribe that the time of voting shall be the same in all the States, and Congress has so prescribed.

What are we to gather in respect to the stage of this transaction which is the deposit of the Federal vote for President by the qualified electors? It is their own vote. They are not delegates to cast a vote according to the instruction of their State. They are not deputized to perform the will of another. They are voters that exercise a free choice and authority to vote, or refrain from voting, and to vote for whom they please; and from the moment that their vote is sealed and sent forward toward the seat of Government no power in a State can touch it, arrest it, reverse it, corrupt it, retract it. Nothing remains to be done except count it, and count it as it was deposited. The wisdom of the secret ballot and of its repose in the possession of the President of the Senate secures the object, *ut nihil innovetur.* The vote is to be opened and counted, in contemplation of law, as freshly as if it had been counted on the day it was cast, in the State.

These electors, at our present election three hundred and sixty-nine citizens in number, not being marked and designated by any but political methods, are by the Constitution made dependent for their qualification upon the action of the State. If the State does not act there are no qualified electors. If the State does act, whatever is the be-all and the end-all of the State's action up to the time that the vote is cast is the be-all and the end all of the qualification of the elector, and he is then a qualified elector depositing his vote to accomplish its purpose, and to be counted when the votes are collected.

Our ancestors, whom we revere—let us not at the same time despoil them of their right to our reverence—were not wanting either in forecast or in circumspection in this provision. Every solicitude, every safeguard that a not very credulous view of human nature could exact for the supremacy of the Constitution in this supreme transaction under it was provided. At the bottom of everything was a determination that this business should proceed to fill the office; that that terror of monarchies and of republics alike, a vacant or a disputed succession to the occupancy of the Chief Magistracy, should not possibly exist.

Let me find for you those constitutional limitations upon the supposed *quo warranto* procedures that were to cover investigations into thirteen or thirty-eight States before the votes could be counted. Why, the *second substituted election*, on the failure of the first, must end by the 4th of March. What room is there to interpolate *quo warranto* proceeding in any stage from the deposit in the primary ballot-box in the State up to the counting of the votes which declares a President elected, or the failure to elect, upon which the States resume their control through their delegates in the lower House of Congress upon the basis of State equality? The substituted election must come to an end by the 4th of March; and whoever introduces judicial *quo warranto* anywhere in the transaction introduces a process of retardation, of baffling, of obscuring, of defrauding, of defeating the election, and gives to the Senate, by mere delay, the present filling of the Presidency with an acting officer and *compels* a new election. That much for delay. Now it is an absolutely novel proposition that judicial power can put its little finger into the political transaction of choosing anybody to an elective office.

The bringing into office a President, bringing into office a governor, bringing into office any of the necessary agents of the frame and structure of the State, without which in present action it will be enfeebled and may fall, is a political action from beginning to end. It comes to furnish a subject of judicial *post hac* investigation only after it has been completed. If judges are to intrude and courts with their proceedings at the various stages that are to be passed in the business of filling the office, so that there shall be no vacant and no disputed succession *de facto*, who does not see that you introduce the means of defrauding and defeating the political action entirely, and turning it into a discussion of the mere right that shall leave the office vacant till the mere right is determined?

It is an absolute novelty, unknown in the States, unknown in the nation, that judicial inquiries can be interposed to stop the political action that leads up to the filling of office. The interest of the State is that the office shall be filled. Filling it is the exercise of a political right, the discharge of a political duty. Such safeguards as can be thrown about the ballot-box, about the first canvass, the second canvass, the third canvass, the final canvass in the States, about the final counting before the two Houses, and that shall not retard or defeat the progress to the necessary end, are provided. These are provided; these are useful; but you do not step with a judicial investigation into a ballot-box upon a suggestion that it has been stuffed, and stop the election till that *quo warranto* is taken; and then when you get to the first canvasser stop his count from going on, because it is a false count, and have a court decide, and so with the county canvassers, stop their transaction in the rapid progress to the result aimed at, to wit, filling the office, with a *quo warranto* there, and then in the State canvass, and then here. It is an absolute novelty. No judicial action has ever been accepted and followed except the mandamus to compel officers to act, nothing else. That was not retarding; that was ascertaining; that was compelling; that was discarding delays on the question of right.

In our supreme court in New York, not very many years ago, an attempt was made to obtain an injunction against inspectors canvassing votes, the primary deposit in the ballot-box of their election-district, because they had been sworn on the directory and not on the Bible. They had no right to discharge their function without taking an official oath, the preliminary oath. The court refused it necessarily. However much this irregularity might find play and place in a *quo warranto* investigation of the whole transaction, piecemeal inquiry cannot be made and no injunction of a court can intrude into the course of the political action of an election.

The position that I have assigned to the States is the appointment as they please. Now, let me call your attention to a provision in the act of Congress, the application of which may not have occurred to your observation. It is provided in the act that if the State shall have failed to appoint on the day for appointment, it may make a subsequent appointment as the legislature may please. It was not intended, then, that the process of finding out whether there had been an election or not should, by its method and its regular action, be exposed to frustration. Even the failure itself, disclosed by the political canvass, was the basis on which the State was renewedly to exercise its right in time for transmission here. Now, you have in this act of Congress a provision which shows that they recognized that the method of progress and result was to be cherished above all others that its success might end in time to confer the qualifications or its failure in time that the substituted appointment reserved to the States should be accomplished.

But now it is said that a failure of election may be retarded in its declaration so as to deprive the State of its power to act on that failure, and it is said that by the act of Congress the contemplated ascertainment may involve judicial proceedings in the State. Why, if there be anything that in election laws is provided in every State, it is that there shall be no reconsideration, no steps backward, no delays except of ministerial and apparently easy duty; and if discretion is given, by departures from that general policy in particular States, it is always found to have its origin in a motive of correcting a special mischief for which it is framed, some abnormal condition of the body-politic that requires a departure from the general method of absolute ministerial transaction. Our proposition, as has been laid down so well by my learned associates, is that, under the State law of Florida, that is the method, that is the purpose, that is the action, and that every step and stage of that action, rightly or wrongly, honestly or dishonestly, purely or fraudulently, has conferred qualifications such as the Federal Constitution requires in the appointment by the State through the methods that it had provided.

If support were needed for the point that the line of demarkation between the inception of the Federal authority and the culmination and consummation of the State's action precludes an inquiry, at the furthest, beyond the facts certified as of record and the accuracy of the certificate, is to be found in the legislation proposed in the Congress of 1800, when the wisdom was still of the fathers. Enlightened by their experience of the working of the great scheme they had framed, it was declared that the demarkation should be observed, and that the powers should not include nor be deemed to include *any inquiry into the votes as cast in the States.*

The novelty, as I have said, of the situation produces strange results. Never before has there been the retardation of the political transaction of counting an election, and to accomplish that almost a miracle has been needed, for the sun and the moon have been made to stand still much longer than they did for Joshua in the conflict in Judea. You will find that an attempt to bring judges—I do not now speak of judges in the official capacity that some portion of this bench occupy in the Supreme Court, but I mean judges in the nature of judicial function and its exercise—into the working of this scheme of popular sovereignty in its political action, will make it as intolerable in its working, will so defraud and defeat the popular will, by the nature and necessary consequences of the judicial intervention, that, at last, the government of the judges will have superseded the sovereignty of the people, and there will be no cure, no recourse but that which the children of Israel had, to pray for a king.

The PRESIDENT. Mr. O'Conor, the Commission will now hear you.

Mr. EVARTS. I ask your honors to take a reference to very recent cases in the seventy-eighth volume of Illinois Reports, Dickey *vs.* Reed. It is a long case and an important case. On pages 267, 268, 269, the matter pertinent to this inquiry is to be found. I refer also to 25 Maine Reports, page 566, an opinion of the supreme judicial court of that State on the powers that are included in the authority to open and count votes. In 38 Maine Reports, page 598, is a similar judicial instruction; and in 53 New Hampshire Reports, page 640, there is a similar judicial action under the constitution of that State. I refer also to a recent case, called Cæsar Griffin's case, in the district of Virginia, in Johnson's Reports, page 364, a decision of Chief-Justice Chase on the authority of *de-facto* officers proved not to have been *de jure* in all the efficacy of their conduct of affairs.

Mr. O'CONOR. Mr. President and gentlemen of the Commission: I will not say probably, because it may be said certainly, that the most important case that has ever been presented to any official authority within these United States is now brought before this honorable Commission for its investigation and decision. It is brought here under circumstances that give absolute assurance, as far as absolute assurance can exist in human things, of a sound, upright, intelligible decision that will receive the approval of all just and reasonable men. The great occasion which has given rise to the construction of this tribunal has attracted the attention of every enlightened and observing individual in the civilized world. This Commission acts under that observation. The conclusion at which it may arrive must necessarily pass into history, and, from the deeply interesting character in all their aspects of the proceedings had and the judgment to be pronounced, that history will attract the attention of students and men of culture and intelligence as long as our country shall be remembered; for it cannot be supposed that a question will ever arise and be determined in a similar manner which, by its superior magnitude, importance, delicacy, and interest, will obscure this one or cause it to be overlooked.

The selection of members to this Commission was made by a choice of five individuals equal, assumed to be equal, pronounced to be equal, if not superior to, any others to be found in the House of Representatives, and a similar choice of similar individuals taken from the Senate, thus placing the entire legislative representation of our whole country under the observation of present and future times in respect to whatever shall here be done. To that has been added a selection of five other members from the highest judicial tribunal known under our Constitution and laws, and certainly a tribunal equal in official majesty and dignity, as well as in intellectual power, to any that has ever existed. Evidently, from the whole frame of the procedure, these appointments were made with an earnest intent, and indeed a fixed resolution, to have here represented in this tribunal whatever of perfect impartiality and fairness, whatever of purity and integrity, whatever of learning and dignity of position our country could afford. This, too, is a public act of the highest authority that could be invoked to express the sovereign will of the whole people.

The questions to be considered are of a public character and of a judicial nature. Every member of the Commission has been a jurist by profession during his life, and has devoted his time and his study to the apprehension and comprehension of legal questions.

It was said by a great English judge, and an eminent writer and historian, in the highest court of that country, in a conspicuous case, that "jurisprudence is the department of human knowledge to which our brethren of the United States of America have chiefly devoted themselves, and in which they have chiefly excelled."

With all these elements affording guarantees in respect to the result, I think it may be confidently asserted that such result cannot be other than the intelligent judgment of mankind in present and future times will approve. With that assurance, and with a deep sense of my own incapacity to fulfill the part assigned me in arguing the great question presented, but a conviction that all deficiencies of this kind will be supplemented by the learning and ability of the tribunal, I proceed to lay before your honors what may seem proper to be now said on our part in relation to the issues that have been raised for consideration by the Commission's resolve adopted on Saturday.

The questions, in short, without repeating details, are expressed by the inquiry, what powers have been vested in this Commission for the purpose of enabling its members to guide through its determination the action of the political authorities as to the election of President and Vice-President? And here let me observe on a mistake which the other side has made in relation to a paper presented to the court on our part on Saturday. It has been construed as in some sense prescribing limits or giving our view of some limit proper to be assigned to the power and authority of this Commission. This is a mistake. That paper was designed for no such purpose and expresses no such idea. With a view to facilitate the action of the court, we presented in that paper a statement which we believe to be correct, and true in point of fact, showing the very narrow range of inquiry into matters of fact that would actually become necessary.

In reference to the question, what elements of inquiry are within the competency of this court, we stand in direct conflict with the other side, and the issue formed between us is this:

We maintain, as representing what are called the Tilden electors, that this tribunal has full authority to investigate by all just and legitimate means of proof the very fact, and thereby to ascertain what was the electoral vote of Florida.

On the other hand, it is claimed that this learned Commission is greatly trammeled by technical impediments, and has no power except merely to determine what may be the just inferences from the documents returned to the President of the Senate from the State of Florida. While thus contending, however, the Hayes electors mainly repose themselves on the proposition that they are officers *de facto*. Admitting for the sake of argument that their claim to be electors is without right, and is simply clothed with a false and fabricated color of title, the Hayes electors claim through their counsel that inasmuch as they cast their vote while possessed of some documents which gave to them the mere color of a right to perform that duty, the fact that they acted upon this color, and did, of their own motion, of their own personal will, through their own right of selection, cast the votes for Mr. Hayes that are sent here as the vote of Florida, completely precludes all inquiry, and that it is impossible for any earthly tribunal or any individual to investigate or to declare the invalidity of their claim.

This issue, thus I trust not too narrowly stated, raises the question, What are the powers of this Commission? I proceed to state our views on the subject.

Those powers are distinctly and briefly expressed in the electoral bill under which you are acting—that admirable act of legislation, destined to the immortal honor of those concerned in its preparation, to pass into history with your action. The language defining your powers declares that you shall possess—

The same powers, if any, now possessed—

For the purpose in hand—

by the two Houses acting separately or together.

You have then (and this is the test) all the powers of those two Houses which they could possibly exercise under the Constitution and by the pre-existing statutes, for the purpose of enabling you to determine the inquiries submitted to you. Let us see, then, what powers are possessed by the two Houses separately or together in deciding as to the electoral vote upon the facts that exist or that might exist and may be proven. And this calls upon us to say what those powers are, and requires us to answer whether, in relation to the action which has here been called counting, any powers under the laws existing when this electoral bill was passed, and which were needed to a proper ascertainment of the vote, were vested in the President of the Senate.

Now, that no power of any description deserving the name of a power to investigate and decide resided in the President of the Senate is most plain from the very words of the Constitution. He is authorized to receive certain packets, and he has no authority whatever by the Constitution save and except only to present himself to the two Houses of Congress and in their presence to open these packets. The phrase is "open the certificates," but this evidently means open the packets. He has no right to open them at any previous time; he has no power whatever to investigate what is contained in the packets before thus opening them. He has no means of taking testimony; he has no right to judge of anything; and he is positively precluded, not only by the Constitution itself but by the physical laws of nature, from knowing what may be within any packet thus received by him until the moment at which he opens that packet in the presence of the two Houses; of course the packets which he is thus authorized to open are to present the basis of subsequent action.

Nothing further is prescribed to him, and I humbly submit that it is most manifest that he has none but the merest of clerical powers nor any ability to do anything except to open the packets at that time and at that place and in that presence. He cannot even know what is in the packets until he opens the packets. But it is manifest that the packets which he thus opens may require a decision by some authority of a preliminary question, that is to say, what are the votes in respect to which a count may take place? No person or functionary or body is specially pointed out as having power to make that count. Now, a great deal has been said, which I consider not very applicable or very instructive, in reference to this word "count," as if it were the operative and principal word here and were used to determine the faculty and point out the power of those who have authority to count. Now, I humbly insist that the count itself is so purely a simple arithmetical process that in reference to it there never could be a possible difference of opinion anywhere or among any persons.

I apprehend that there is a word in this constitutional provision that ought not to be overlooked. The President of the Senate is to receive these packets. They are not required to have any note or ear-mark of any description to indicate to him what they are, and he can only learn by external inquiry or report that they are sent him by persons pretending to be electors of President and Vice-President; and the Constitution, proceeding to declare his duty, says that he shall "open all the certificates." The word "all" would perform no function, and it would be entirely useless, if it were to be confined to indicating the certificates before spoken of. The simple phrase "shall open the certificates" would suffice; but he is to "open all the certificates;" and this provision of the Constitution, not granting powers of investigation but dealing with visible facts, declares that he shall "open all the certificates." This I apprehend means all packets that may have come to him under color of being such packets as the Constitution refers to; that is, packets containing electoral votes or appearing to be of that character. He is bound to open all such packets in the presence of the Houses, and there ends his duty. But when we come to the prescription that there shall be a count, we are not told that there shall be a count of *all* the certificates presented, or of *the* certificates, or of anything in the certificates, but that there shall be a count of "the votes." This, I humbly submit, introduces a necessary implication that somehow and by some authority there shall be made, if necessary, a selection of the actual votes from the mass of papers produced and physically present before the Houses. Any investigation that the nature of the case may happen to require in order to determine what are "the votes" must be made by some functionaries having competency to make it. This is a preliminary inquiry, and whether you denominate it judicial or ministerial or executive, it is to be an inquiry, and the power to institute or carry it on is neither granted in terms, nor are there any possible means of its exercise so far as the President of the Senate is concerned. This is left to an implication that it is to be exercised by those who may have occasion to act officially on the result of the electoral vote.

Who are they that are to act officially by the terms of the Constitution in performance of duty resulting from the count of the votes? The Constitution is plain. The votes—meaning of course the legal votes—are to be counted. The count is the merest ceremony in itself; but the ascertainment of what are legal votes presented, necessarily devolves upon that body or those bodies that must act on that which is produced as a result by the count. The authorities compelled by duty to see that the count is justly and truly made and to act on the result are the two Houses.

Unquestionably the first and primary duty of the Houses, if there is a count showing the election of a person to the Presidency and another to the Vice-Presidency, is to recognize them as constituting that co-ordinate department of the Government called the Executive. As to a mere count, all the world may make it; no mortal man can doubt about the effect of a count; but I presume the general world is not called upon to act in reference to the count until that count has been officially recognized by some lawful authority. But what is more certain is this: It is the duty of the House of Representatives at that point in the process to determine whether an exigency has arisen which renders it their duty to recognize that a person has been elected as President by a majority of votes, of the legal votes, or whether there has been a failure to elect by reason of a tie; and in that event, if it should occur, that House is bound to act upon the result, and in this exigency itself is to elect a President. The same observations apply to the Senate with reference to the Vice-President; that body is bound in like manner to recognize the fact of an election, to allow it, admit it, and accept it as a fact, or to deny it and say that it is not so, and themselves to proceed in the election of a Vice-President.

I attach no importance to the word " count;" but I claim from the very nature of the thing, from the laws inwrought into the constitution of human beings and governing human transactions, that those who have thus to act officially on the count are the persons who must do whatever may be needful for the purpose of enabling a count to be made. Those who are bound to act in the one direction or in the other, as the case may require, must possess the power of making any preliminary investigation that may become necessary.

The result of this construction is that that officer who has no power but to open them is set aside from the moment he opens the packets, and the duty of exercising the higher function, preliminarily, of inquiring what are the votes, prior to this mere formal act, " counting," must devolve upon those who must take notice what are the legal votes and act upon the count of them. This no one is authorized to make or to declare unless it be themselves. This implied power is not introduced by any forced construction, but from the absolute necessity of the case. And, consequently, we claim that the needful powers of preliminary investigation were in the Houses. It cannot fairly be disputed that Congress by united action might have constituted some public body to conduct the investigation; and how far they might have gone toward making the result absolutely obligatory on the Houses themselves respectively, we need not inquire.

They did not exercise such a power prior to the election of 1876, and they have not otherwise exercised it subsequently, except by the constitution of this tribunal, and they have reserved to themselves the privilege of establishing a different determination by a concurrent vote.

The competency of each House to ascertain the truth is unquestionable. Each has complete powers of investigation; they can take proof through their committees or otherwise as to any matter on which they may be obliged to decide, and, either before or after the opening of all the votes, they can thus investigate, though not, it must be admitted, with the aid of a jury, nor in the precise forms of a judicial proceeding. They can investigate, as political and legislative bodies may, touching all the facts and circumstances that are necessary to be known in order to enlighten their judgment and guide them to a just and righteous decision.

Our construction thus recognizes in those two bodies on such a contingency as is here presented full power to do whatever may be needful to the accomplishment of justice.

What is the objection to this construction? The whole argument against it resolves itself simply into the argument *ab inconvenienti*. Those who would seek to grasp a high office by illegal, irregular, and fraudulent means claim that it would be inconvenient to take so much trouble as might become necessary in order to investigate rightly and rightly to determine, on proofs, the question of their delinquency and the falsehood of their claim. This is a common plea among persons who set up a falsely and fraudulently contrived title. When an effort is made to strip them of their pretended authority by demonstrating before a court or other appropriate tribunal the fallacy of their claims and the necessity to the ends of justice of having that fallacy declared and their pretensions set aside, they point out the trouble involved in the task. But let us see how stands that argument. Let us test it by ordinary and familiar principles.

It is suggested that it might lead, and if entered upon must necessarily lead, if the parties think fit, to an investigation of the personal qualifications of every one among millions of electors, and that if you lay down the rule or adopt the principle that you have a right to investigate at all, you open the door to that inconvenient and boundless sea of litigation. The mischief of this, they say, would be so great that it is better to let injustice triumph and permit a usurper to enter the executive office by the most unholy of avenues, that which is paved with falsehood, fraud, and corruption. They say it is better to submit to all that or any other more enormous evil, if a more enormous one can be imagined, than to submit to the shocking and monstrous inconvenience that is thus to result from any attempt to inquire into the validity of the election!

There is really nothing in this broadly presented picture of overwhelming inconvenience. They say no matter how we should limit our inquiries to a very narrow range, for if you allow any investigation you will establish the doctrine, you will open the door to intolerably protracted litigation. This suggestion is not warranted by law or the practice of courts in such investigations. True it is that in a writ of *quo warranto* to inquire into the title of an individual to an office it is competent to investigate all the particulars down to the qualifications of each individual voter, and on a point of identity similar to that which occurred in the Tichborne case one trial might take many years. This is presenting a "raw head and bloody bones" to frighten this Commission and the whole country from its propriety.

The answer to all that is as simple as can possibly be imagined. The objection you perceive applies as much to ordinary writs of *quo warranto* in reference to ordinary offices as it does to this inquiry if it should take place before Congress. For this argument *ab inconvenienti* is as fatal to the general procedure of courts of justice in actions of *quo warranto* as it is to the proceeding here suggested.

But, if the learned Commission please, the investigation which might be allowed to take place before either House of Congress or any commission appointed by them, would be governed by the same principles of general jurisprudence which apply to the determination of proceedings by *quo warranto;* and one of those principles is that no man has a right to the writ of *quo warranto* as of course or merely because he makes out an apparent title. It has always been a matter of discretion. Numerous cases are cited here for that purpose on the other side. It has always been treated as a matter of discretion in the power of the supreme tribunal, acting in the name and majesty of the sovereign power, when applied to for a writ of *quo warranto*, to allow it or not as under all the circumstances may be thought most consistent with the public interest and the ends of justice and the convenience of society; and, by consequence, this expanded inquiry could never take place in the writ of *quo warranto;* it never would be allowed; no court would ever permit the writ to issue without a statement of the points intended to be made; and, if it were necessary in allowing the writ the court would lay their restraint on the party as to what points or questions he might make.

So it appears that in all investigations, judicial or otherwise, as to the right of a particular individual to hold and exercise a public office, it is in the discretion of the tribunals how far they will go, and it is in your discretion, as it would be in the discretion of either House of Congress investigating for its own advice and direction, as to the election of President or Vice-President, to determine whether they would permit any of these intolerably prolix investigations.

So much for the argument *ab inconvenienti*. It has no application. Standing upon the ancient practices of the law, the authority that might be called upon to institute an investigation would look at the difficulty presented and say under the influence of a due regard to the argument *ab inconvenienti*, "thus far you may go; no farther shall you go."

Now in reference to the legal question presented, as to what powers each House of Congress has, under existing laws, and what powers consequently you can exercise, we say, as the learned manager from the House said in opening this case, that there is no technical legal limit or barrier, but that you exercise the same high power of the Government which has always been exercised in such questions even in the courts of the common law to which application must be made to obtain the writ of *quo warranto*. You exercise the same discretion, but you can limit the inquiry, when the point arises, within those limits that are prescribed by necessity and convenience.

Now this is our view stated as fully as it is in my power to state it in the brief time I am permitted to occupy the attention of your honors. We say that there is no limit to the power of investigation for the purpose of reaching the ends of justice, except such as a due regard for public convenience and the interests of public justice and society at large may impose in the exercise of this discretionary authority.

Well, what is our condition and the condition of all cases of this kind? There is no judicial court of the United States clothed with authority to deal with the premises. We assert that, without stopping to cite books and to prove it to you negatively. It seems to be conceded that, if such a power might have been created, it has remained dormant and has not been exercised. And consequently we are told that here we stand, in the second century of this Republic's existence, in such a condition that there is no possible remedy against the most palpable fraud and forgery that could be perpetrated or against any outrageous acts in violation of the rights of the people of the respective States and of the whole nation; that Congress must sit by blind and silent and permit an alien to be counted into office as President of the United States; they must sit by and permit a set of votes plainly and palpably fraudulent, votes given by individuals not only disqualified for want of having been chosen by the States but being themselves absolutely disqualified by the Constitution from acting in the office or casting the vote, and must permit the usurpation contemplated to take place merely because our wise fathers— one would think that the compliment was intended as a sarcasm—had so chosen to constitute the Government they created that injustice, however flagitious, might be perpetrated in open day without the possibility of having any remedy or even uttering decorously a complaint.

This, we humbly submit, cannot be the Constitution and the law. Reason forbids. All acts, however solemn, however sacred, from whatever quarter coming, by whatever body perpetrated, are liable to review in some manner, in some judicial or other tribunal, so that fraud and falsehood may shrink abashed and defeated and may fail in the attempt to trample upon the right.

It seems to be virtually conceded here that the governor's certificate is not conclusive. I have not time to say much about that. It is not required by the Constitution. It is only required by an act of Congress. The governor could not have been compelled to give it. Many circumstances might prevent his giving it, and he might have given it under circumstances of plainly flagitious falsehood, without any election, without any proceeding had to sanction it. He might have given his certificate to his own four little boys and constituted them an electoral college, and the vote which they gave pursuant to his bidding, by force of his certificate, would be absolutely conclusive, forsooth, and binding upon all the authorities of the United States that had any power to act in the premises!

I submit to your honors that this is not so, and I beg you to turn, when you come to consider this matter, to the citations of the Amistad case in Mr. Green's brief, 15 Peters, 594, where the Supreme Court, speaking by the voice of Judge Story, pronounced all decisions of every description, however solemn, impeachable for fraud and capable of being reversed. In the case of the State of Michigan *vs.* Phœnix Bank, in 33 New York—I will refer to the particular page, though I will not stop to read it—page 27, your honors will find that the most solemn judgments of any court may be overhauled and reviewed and be shown to have been procured by a trick, a deception, or a falsehood, and may be completely reversed and defeated.

The inquiry then is, How far are we to go in this case? The Florida laws to which you have been referred show that it may not be necessary to go further, and we have not asserted that it will be necessary to go further, than to make a correction of the unlawful extrajudicial acts of the canvassing-board. When you come to look at the law which is contained in the little document placed before you, at page 55, you will find that there is no such sanctity attending the action of this State board as is supposed. They have but little power in the matter.

If any such returns—

That is, the county returns to them—

shall be shown or shall appear to be so irregular, false, or fraudulent that the board shall be unable to determine the true vote for any such officer or member, they shall so certify, and shall not include such return in their determination and declaration ; and the secretary of state shall preserve and file in his office all such returns, together with such other documents and papers as may have been received by him or by said board of canvassers.

One of which must be the certificate of their action rejecting these returns. The law itself provides for and contemplates an investigation of the action of the board of State canvassers ; and turning back to the laws in relation to the county board of canvassers, and to the inspectors of elections, you find that neither of those bodies has any power whatever except simply to compute and return the vote as received. Such is the case as to the primary board of canvassers and the second board of canvassers, and the last and ultimate board of canvassers have these very limited powers, which they seem to have exercised only in respect to one single county if you are to take our assertions as an evidence of the probable line of proof before you, because they rejected some little fragments of three other counties, but did not exercise the power of rejecting the whole of these returns, which was the only power that they possessed. In one single county they seem by some human possibility to have acted within the limits of their power and authority ; I say it may be supposed rather that by some human possibility they did act within them. We purpose to show that they did not. We show it by their own certificate which the law compelled them to file and place along with the canvass which they made, and which very short, brief, and simple proof will demonstrate the monstrosity of the deed that we seek to set aside.

We claim that the *quo warranto* is admissible. You will perceive by looking at that same statute to which we have referred that unless the electors are State officers this canvassing-board had no authority whatever to deal with the subject, and you would be called upon to disregard the canvass which they made and to look at the county returns which the law does authorize to be made in reference to presidential electors as well as State officers, in terms. If they are State officers, surely they were subject to correction by the State if there were any possible means or contrivance by which they could be corrected at all; and the familiar, ordinary, regular course of proceeding by *quo warranto* was commenced in due season, before they had actually cast their vote, and their authority was determined to be utterly void, it was annulled, and that, too, long before their vote had reached the seat of Government or could possibly have been subjected to count. If they are not State officers, then we have done with the canvass of the State board, and have only to look, in case you pass by the governor's certificate, to the next element of proof, and that is the whole set of county returns, which being footed up would show the result to be as we claim, and that the governor's certificate was utterly false.

Subsequent legislation has been placed before your honors and a subsequent investigation for the purpose of a recanvass, or will be before your honors if necessary; indeed, it is before your honors already in the original documents opened by the President of the Senate and which, at least, are here.

We claim that on these principles and on these proofs and such full proofs as may be offered to you, subject only to the restraint to which I have referred that you may exercise in your discretion, you have a right to go on to investigate this matter and to determine two things: first, whether the Hayes electoral vote is valid; and, secondly, whether the Tilden electoral vote is valid. The final decision at which you may arrive might reject either or might reject both. They are not involved in precisely the same question necessarily. Different questions might possibly apply, and the vote for Mr. Hayes might be pronounced invalid and the vote for Mr. Tilden equally so. I have not time to discuss more fully the question as to the right of setting up the Tilden vote in case the Hayes vote should be rejected.

Perhaps in the little time that is left to me I have hardly an opportunity of saying one word in reference to that which is the main reliance of these parties, and that is the doctrine of officer *de facto*.

What is this doctrine of officer *de facto?* The best definition of an officer *de facto* that I have fallen in with is given by Lord Ellenborough, in The King *vs.* The Corporation of Bedford Level, 6 East, 368:

An officer *de facto* is one who has the reputation of being the officer he assumes to be, and yet is not a good officer in point of law.

One who somehow has clothed himself with a reputation of being the officer; and in relation to that person the law, with its wise conservatism, has declared that during the period that the person pretending title to the office was in apparent possession of all its powers and functions and exercised the duties of it, his acts, as it respects persons who in the ordinary course of things were obliged to recognize him and to act under him and in conformity with his directions and his power, shall be esteemed valid, that individuals may not be deceived by this species of disorder or temporary insurrection that has broken in upon the functions of government.

It is the duty of individuals, and they are under a necessity also for their own business purposes, of bowing to the existing authorities who have thus color of right and are the only authorities to which they can refer, and in that action, as a reward for their humble obedience and respect for order, regularity, and the apparent law, they are held to be entitled to protection, and in all forms, ways, and places that may be needed they are protected. The officer himself, however, is never protected. That this is the precise rule in relation to that class of officers, I would take leave to prove by referring your honors to Green vs. Burke, 23 Wendell, 502, where a very able opinion was written by one of the most elaborate investigators of legal authorities that I have known or ever heard of, Judge Cowen, formerly of the State of New York. The cases, to be sure, have gone pretty far. He examined all the authorities, and what he says is:

I know the cases have gone a great way; but they have stopped with preventing mischief to such as confide in officers who are acting without right.

A summing up of the authorities and of the principle.

Now, what is the proposition here contended for? That these officers, having acted under color of right, and having completely exercised and perfected the function with which they appeared, it is said, to be charged, and with which, if they were duly elected, they were charged, any subsequent attempt to set it aside would be contrary to that principle, contrary to convenience, and mischievous to society. Is this so? Is not that principle of necessity confined to acts affecting private persons? Is not that necessity confined to cases where the act of the officer *de facto* is consummated and perfected and has taken effect in some manner before it is ascertained that he is not entitled to his office and he is ousted? Are the bank-notes of a bank not having authority to issue them, though signed, perfected, and finished, and put in the hands of an agent, valid and effectual under this principle until some person has confided in them, has received them, and thus been misled by the appearance of right with which the bank had improperly clothed itself?

We maintain that neither the public good, nor the protection of men from deception, nor any rule of convenience or policy, requires the allowance of pretended electors, whose title, on an investigation by competent authority before the votes have been opened and counted, has been ascertained to be groundless.

Referring to the facts of the case, what do we find? These four gentlemen sat down with a false governor's certificate or a sham certificate from a board of State canvassers, and they of their own authority, certifying their acts themselves, cast four votes in a given direction, put them in a packet, and sent it to an officer, who cannot look at it until the time of its presentation for the purpose of being considered and counted. Before the time arrived at which that act of theirs could deceive anybody, could have any operation, could take any effect, could get into such a condition that its preservation and maintenance was necessary to the cause of public justice or private right, their lack of title was ascertained by a solemn writ of *quo warranto* to be groundless; it was determined that they were usurpers, had no right to the office, and that their acts were void. Is there any such principle as that the inchoate, partial action of an officer *de facto* shall be carried onward, carried forward, and given its perfection by the acceptance of the act as a due and valid act after the invalidity of that officer's claim has been established? Here we repose, upon the *quo warranto* under your honors' allowance, or repose upon the proofs which may be here offered, admitted, and passed upon by your honors, for the purpose of showing the utter invalidity of these gentlemen's claim to the office of electors. In whichever shape this matter is presented or carried forward, that the act of these officers *de facto* fails to have reached the point where it could have or take any effect, or mislead or deceive anybody, is shown and established by competent means to be an act of those who had no authority to perform it.

And the position of the thing is very striking in this singular attitude which the other side have assumed, the attitude of an undoubted, undisputed, convicted usurper. They claim to be received and that their act shall have an effect which as yet it never has had, although since the time they performed the initiatory and preliminary step they have been shown to be utterly without right to their pretended offices. It may be said that this sharpened arrow aimed at the heart of the nation, aimed for the purpose of establishing falsehood, seating a usurper, and trampling down the right of the State and of the Union—it may be said that this arrow was placed in the bow of the false elector, that adequate force and strength were imparted to it to carry it to the bosom that was to be wounded and stung to death by it; but it cannot be denied, if the *quo warranto* is effectual, or if we have a right now to prove the facts of the case, that a shield is interposed between the wrong-doer's arrow and the bosom he designed to pierce, by which that arrow, steeped in guilt and fraud, designed for the perpetration of injustice and the consummation of an atrocious wrong, has been arrested in its flight and deprived of its poison and its force.

In this connection, under this strange head of a claim to have a *de facto* President by force of a set of *de facto* electors, I would call your honors' attention to a single view of which this case is susceptible. Although there may be an officer *de facto*, it seems to be in the nature of things that there cannot be an unlawful, unauthorized tribunal or body *de facto* acting without right. These persons could not act except by constituting what has been well enough called an electoral college, of which they were to be the members. They undertook to constitute it. It was an electoral college of their own. They filled it up with their own wrongful claims and intrusive persons, and thus sought to create by wrong and without one single element of right but this mere color or reputation resting in these individuals a lawful electoral college. I would ask your honors for the purpose of showing that that distinction is entitled to considerable weight, to refer to the case of Hildreth's Heirs against McIntyre's Devisee, (1 J. J. Marshall's Kentucky Reports, 206,) where certain persons, being no doubt *de facto* officers, claimed that they had established a *de facto* court; and the determination, upon very good reasoning which I submit to your honors' consideration, was that there could not be a *de facto* court, although there might be a *de facto* judge or a *de facto* officer; and we say, by the same reasoning, there cannot be an unlawful *de facto* electoral college composed of mere pretenders to that office who have no right.

In this connection you have exactly the case that was before the court there and which, perhaps, exists in other States of this Union about this time. You have the case of two distinct bodies existing at the same time, one rightful and the other wrongful; I mean formal bodies attempted to be created. The Tilden electors who, though they had not documentary evidence to establish their title, had actually been elected, if our evidence is to be believed, convened their electoral college, performed every ceremony that the Constitution of the United States enjoined upon them, performed every ceremony that the laws of the United States enjoined upon them and that it was possible to perform, failing only in this, that they did not obtain the certificate of the governor. They met; they constituted a college; they acted; and they sent forward their votes. Thus you have two rival bodies acting at, to be sure, the right time and in the right place, as prescribed by all laws bearing on this subject; two rival colleges, one of which was composed of persons truly elected, the other of which was composed of persons who had no right, but only the mere color of pretense of right, who were usurpers, as has been ascertained in one form, and will be ascertained in any other that will be satisfactory to you, if you will permit us to present the evidence.

This, then, is the actual condition of this case. The Constitution prescribes no forms save such as have been complied with by the Tilden electors; the laws of Congress prescribe no forms that were not complied with by the Tilden electors, save and except only that they could not obtain the governor's certificate; and it is pretty much conceded, I think, that the governor's certificate is not absolutely indispensable, and might be gainsaid and contradicted even if it had been given.

So then, in this case of rivalry between these two sets of electors, it appears to me that we present the best legal title. That we have the moral right is the common sentiment of all mankind. It will be the judgment of posterity. There lives not a man, so far as I know, upon the face of this earth, who, having the faculty of blushing, could look an honest man in the face and assert that the Hayes electors were truly elected. The whole question, therefore, is whether in what has taken place there has been such an observance of form as is totally fatal to justice, and beyond the reach of any curative process of any description.

I have just about time left to say that it was not intentional that the law of Florida in relation to writs of *quo warranto* was omitted. I have copies of it, enough, I think, to deliver to the court; but I found, on looking about after an observation was made about it, that I have not any of them here. I will have them delivered to the court. They were printed long ago, with the view of having them sent up, but the gentleman who prepared the pamphlet copies of some of the laws here did not insert it. Perhaps it was because he knew it was already printed, and thought it was already here. I have not had time to inquire into that, nor is it at all necessary. That law is to be found in the laws of Florida for 1872, page 29. It will be found that it does not confine the effect of the *quo warranto* to the parties prosecuting; that it does not in any way impair or diminish or lessen the force and effect of the judgment in *quo warranto* at the suit of the rival claimant, who was justly entitled to the office, except in this: it provides in section 3 that, while the judgment is to have full effect and to entitle the relator to be placed in the office until he is ousted, the judgment in the case shall not have conclusive effect as against the State in case the State shall prosecute another *quo warranto* in its own behalf against the party who was successful in the first. That is all that that law requires. It in no way changes or diminishes the effect.

Now, I think I have observed as much as was any way needful upon the other questions as to what evidence is admissible here. I conceive that the propositions we have advanced have the effect of entitling us to produce any evidence here which either of the Houses of Congress prosecuting an investigation of this description might lawfully receive, and that we are subject here only, as we would be before one of the

Houses of Congress, to the discretion which I have before referred to, by which you can restrain us as you can restrain the other party from going into interminable and absurd inquiries.

As to what is actually here, the course of my argument has been intended to establish and, if of any value, has established that each House of Congress had jurisdiction of the matter, each of them at least of one section of it, and, therefore, that the evidence which, according to the customs and usages of legislative bodies, either House has taken and has upon its files and will consent to send in here or has sent in here at our request, is already in evidence in the case, so far as to be here, to be read if it comes within the range of subjects as of matter of fact which you will allow us to investigate; it is as good evidence as if we produced witnesses or documents here at the bar and examined them according to the usages of the common law.

Mr. EVARTS. Your honors will allow me to refer to page 32 of the Congressional Record of February 3, which I omitted to do, though I had the passage marked, to indicate the result of the different computations under the new statute and under the *quo warranto* and under the mandamus, all ending in canvasses that resulted in favor of the Hayes electors.

Mr. O'CONOR. This matter in a newspaper is certainly not to be accepted here as evidence. It is a report of a minority of a committee of Congress.

Mr. Commissioner EDMUNDS. We have not admitted any evidence of this kind yet.

Mr. O'CONOR. But your honors will permit us to say that this is brought forward as matter of fact. We have not relied on being able to establish facts by the reports of certain gentlemen in Congress. It is the evidence which they took on which we rely. If these reports as reports, the opinions of these gentlemen, are evidence, very well; let us understand it.

The PRESIDENT. The reference to it does not make it evidence.

Mr. EVARTS. I do not offer it as evidence, but I offer it for your honors' information, and in answer to the intimation of the learned counsel that every man, woman, and child knew that, if the canvass was not so, then the Hayes electors were not chosen.

Mr. O'CONOR. It will be very apparent.

Mr. EVARTS. This is the matter to which I refer:

As a summary of the various ways of estimating the vote of the State of Florida on the 7th of November, the minority submit the following:

I. If the vote be reckoned by the face of the returns which were opened by the board on the 28th of November, and unanimously declared, (Attorney-General Cocke concurring,) under the rule of the board, to be the regular returns, having all the legal formalities complied with, the majority for the Hayes electors is 43.

II. If the vote be reckoned by the official statutory declaration of the canvassing-board exercising its jurisdiction under the State statute, in accordance with the practice adopted without objection, and by the advice of the democratic attorney-general, Cocke, and never disputed until the result of this canvass was about to be determined, which declaration in the belief of the minority is final and irreversible, the majority for the Hayes electors is 925.

III. If the vote be reckoned upon the principles laid down by the supreme court in their order to recanvass in the case of Drew *vs.* Governor Stearns, of not purging the polls of illegal votes and retaining the true vote, but of rejecting the whole county return when appearing or shown to be so irregular, false, or fraudulent that the true vote could not be ascertained, the result would be, according to the declaration of the board, a majority for the Hayes electors of 211.

IV. If the board had thoroughly reconsidered, according to the decision of the supreme court, the various county returns for the purpose of throwing out *in toto* all that could be shown to be irregular, false, or fraudulent, instead of purging the returns of their illegalities and returning the true vote, there should be thrown out the returns from the following counties:

Counties.	Tilden electors.	Hayes electors.
Baker	238	143
Clay	287	122
Hamilton	617	330
Jackson	1,397	1,299
Manatee	262	26
Total	2,801	1,920

eaving a majority for the Hayes electors of 791.

V. If the vote of the State were to be estimated according to the honest and true vote of the people at the polls, without regard to precinct, county, or State canvassers, the result would be, according to the judgment of the minority, a larger majority for the Hayes electors than the declared majority of 925.

Mr. Commissioner HOAR. Can counsel on either side furnish the Commission with a copy of the Florida *quo-warranto* law mentioned to-day?

Mr. EVARTS. I have handed it to the clerk, who will have it printed. I believe the court understands that that is a law amending the general *quo-warranto* law, which is found in another place.

Mr. MERRICK. If your honors please, may we be allowed to file with the Secretary in a very short time a memorandum of authorities and citations from them, which we have had printed for the convenience of the Commission, and which was to have been here this morning, but has not yet come to hand, although we expect to receive it in the course of a very few minutes?

The PRESIDENT. Mr. Merrick asks leave to file a printed list of authorities which he hopes to receive in a few minutes. Shall he have that leave?

Leave was granted.

Mr. EVARTS. We ought to be able to place in your honors' hands a printed list of authorities.

The PRESIDENT. It is so eminently just, if allowed on one side, that the same right ought to be accorded to the other, that I will take the privilege of giving the consent without putting the question to the Commission.

On motion, the Commission took a recess for three-quarters of an hour. On re-assembling at three o'clock and fifteen minutes p. m., the Commission proceeded to deliberate with closed doors.

The room being cleared, and the doors closed, the Commission, at three o'clock and fifteen minutes, met for deliberation as to whether any, and what, evidence would be considered in the matter of the electoral vote of the State of Florida.

On motion of Mr. Commissioner THURMAN,

Ordered, That the public session of the Commission be adjourned until day after to-morrow, (Wednesday, the 7th instant,) at eleven o'clock a. m.

After some time spent in deliberation, at three o'clock and forty-five minutes the Commission adjourned until to-morrow at twelve o'clock, noon.

TUESDAY, *February* 6, 1877.

The Commission met at ten o'clock a. m. pursuant to adjournment, all the members being present.

The Journal of yesterday was read and approved.

The Commission proceeded to deliberate on the matters submitted.

After debate,

On motion of Mr. Commissioner BRADLEY, (at three o'clock p. m.,) the Commission took a recess of half an hour.

On re-assembling, the Commission resumed its session.

After debate,

Mr. Commissioner STRONG (at seven o'clock and forty minutes p. m.) moved that the vote on the question now pending be taken at an hour not later than three o'clock p. m. to-morrow ; and the motion was agreed to.

On motion of Mr. Commissioner GARFIELD, it was

Ordered, That when the Commission adjourn it be until ten o'clock a. m. to-morrow.

And, on motion of Mr. Commissioner PAYNE, (at seven o'clock and forty-five minutes p. m.,) the Commission adjourned.

WEDNESDAY, *February* 7, 1877.

The Commission met at ten o'clock a. m. pursuant to adjournment, all the members being present.

The Journal of yesterday was read and approved.

The PRESIDENT stated that on the 5th instant an order had been made requiring an open session of the Commission at eleven o'clock a. m. to-day.

On motion of Mr. Commissioner FRELINGHUYSEN, it was

Ordered, That at eleven o'clock a. m., the hour designated by the order of the 5th instant requiring an open session, the doors be considered as open, and the Commission at once adjourn the same for deliberation.

The Commission resumed its session for deliberation on the question pending in the matter of the electoral vote of the State of Florida.

After debate,

The hour of eleven o'clock a. m. having arrived, and the doors being considered as open,

On motion of Mr. Commissioner MORTON, it was

Ordered, That the public session of the Commission be adjourned until eleven o'clock a. m. to-morrow, the 8th instant.

Thereupon, the Commission resumed its session for deliberation with closed doors.

After further debate,

The hour of three o'clock having arrived, being the time designated by an order of the Commission at which the question on the matter pending should be submitted,

Mr. Commissioner MILLER moved the following order :

Ordered, That no evidence will be received or considered by the Commission which was not submitted to the joint convention of the two Houses by the President of the Senate with the different certificates, except such as relates to the eligibility of F. C. Humphreys, one of the electors.

The question being on its adoption, it was determined in the affirmative :

Yeas.. 8
Nays.. 7

Those who voted in the affirmative are: Messrs. Bradley, Edmunds, Frelinghuysen, Garfield, Hoar, Miller, Morton, and Strong.

Those who voted in the negative are: Messrs. Abbott, Bayard, Clifford, Field, Hunton, Payne, and Thurman.

So the motion of Mr. Commissioner Miller was agreed to.

Mr. Commissioner ABBOTT moved the following order :

Ordered, That in the case of Florida the Commission will receive evidence relating to the eligibility of Frederick C. Humphreys, one of the persons named in certificate No. 1, as elector.

The question being on its adoption, it was determined in the affirmative:

Yeas.. 8
Nays.. 7

Those who voted in the affirmative are: Messrs. Abbott, Bayard, Bradley, Clifford, Field, Hunton, Payne, and Thurman.

Those who voted in the negative are: Messrs. Edmunds, Frelinghuysen, Garfield, Hoar, Miller, Morton, and Strong.

On motion of Mr. Commissioner HOAR, it was

Ordered, That the proceedings of to-day's session, as entered in the Journal, be read by the Secretary at the public session of the Commission to-morrow.

On motion of Commissioner THURMAN, it was

Ordered, That the Secretary of the Commission is hereby directed to furnish immediately to counsel, on both sides, copies of the orders made to-day, and to notify them that the Commission will be ready at eleven o'clock a. m. to-morrow to proceed with the case now before them.

And on motion of Mr. Commissioner MILLER (at three o'clock and forty-five minutes p. m.) the Commission adjourned.

THURSDAY, *February* 8, 1877.

The Commission met at eleven o'clock a. m. pursuant to adjournment, all the members being present.

The following counsel were also present:

Hon. Charles O'Conor, of New York,
Hon. Jeremiah S. Black, of Pennsylvania,
Richard T. Merrick, esq., of Washington, D. C.,
George Hoadly, esq., of Ohio,
Ashbel Green, esq., of New Jersey,
William C. Whitney, esq., of New York,
} Of counsel in opposition to certificate No. 1.

Hon. William M. Evarts, of New York,
Hon. E. W. Stoughton, of New York,
Hon. Stanley Matthews, of Ohio,
Hon. Samuel Shellabarger, of Ohio,
} Of counsel in opposition to certificates Nos. 2 and 3.

The Journal of yesterday's proceedings was read and approved.

The PRESIDENT. The proceedings to-day are under the orders adopted yesterday, of which, on motion of Mr. Thurman, counsel were notified last evening. The Secretary was directed to notify counsel that at eleven o'clock to-day the Commission would proceed with the case now before it, subject of course to the two orders which have been read in the proceedings of yesterday ; one, that no evidence will be received except what was submitted to the two Houses by the President of the Senate ; and the other, that in the case of Florida this Commission will receive evidence relating to the eligibility of one elector named.

Mr. MERRICK. Mr. President and gentlemen, will you give the marshal an order to admit the witnesses for the objectors? There are two or three witnesses in attendance who are not allowed to enter without such an order.

The PRESIDENT, (to members of the Commission.) Shall the marshal be so directed? [Putting the question.] The motion is adopted. The marshal will admit the witnesses designated by the counsel who made the motion.

Mr. EVARTS. May I ask for an order that a witness in attendance on our part, Mr. Humphreys, may be admitted?

The PRESIDENT. I will give the order without putting the question. The marshal will admit the witness.

Mr. GREEN. Mr. President and Commissioners, we propose to call as a witness George P. Raney, of Florida.

The PRESIDENT. The witnesses who are called will be sworn by the Secretary.

The Secretary administered an oath to the respective witnesses in the following form :

You do solemnly swear that the evidence you shall give in the case now before the Commission shall be the truth, the whole truth, and nothing but the truth.

GEORGE P. RANEY sworn and examined.

By Mr. GREEN :

Question. Where do you reside?—Answer. I reside in Tallahassee, Florida.

Q. What is your occupation or profession?—A. I am a lawyer by profession.

Q. What official position do you hold, if any?—A. I am attorney-general of the State of Florida.

Q. Where were you on the 6th of December, 1876?—A. I was in the city of Tallahassee, in the State of Florida.

Q. Have you any knowledge as to the time of the service of the writ of *quo warranto?*

Mr. EVARTS. One moment. That is not within the license, as we understand, of the order of the Commission.

Mr. GREEN. I should like to hear the objection stated.

Mr. EVARTS. The objection is that it is not within the order of the Commission admitting evidence concerning the eligibility of Mr. Humphreys and excluding all other evidence.

Mr. GREEN. We propose to prove by this witness the simple fact as to the precise time when the writ of *quo warranto* was served upon Messrs. Humphreys and others, known as the Hayes electors. It is apprehended upon our side that the order which has been made by the Commission does not in its spirit exclude the consideration of the *quo warranto* proceedings which have been laid upon the table, and it is in aid of what may be perhaps considered a question as to the precise moment when the writ of *quo warranto* was served upon Humphreys and others, that we desire to make this proof this morning.

The PRESIDENT. I will submit the question to the Commission. Gentlemen of the Commission, is the objection well taken ? [Putting the question.] The ayes have it, and the objection is sustained. Proceed with the examination of the witness.

Mr. GREEN. We can now dispense with this witness and will call James E. Yonge.

JAMES E. YONGE sworn and examined.

By Mr. GREEN:

Question. Where do you reside ?—Answer. At Pensacola, Florida.

Q. Do you know Frederick C. Humphreys ?—A. I do.

Q. Where does he reside ?—A. At Pensacola, Florida.

Q. How long have you known him ?—A. I have known him for about ten years.

Q. What is his business or occupation ?—A. Agent for an express company, and has been United States shipping-commissioner.

Q. Have you known him to act in the capacity of United States shipping-commissioner ?—A. I have.

Mr. EVARTS. We submit that if an official position is to be proved as by authority communicated from the Government, in the absence of some reason to the contrary, the official appointment should be given.

The PRESIDENT. Perhaps it is about to be produced.

Mr. GREEN. This is evidence of his use of the office.

Mr. EVARTS. That is my objection, that use is not sufficient on a matter depending upon authority.

Mr. GREEN. We propose to follow that——

The PRESIDENT. You had better introduce the commission at once, to save time.

Mr. GREEN. I offer in evidence an order of the United States circuit court for the northern district of Florida at the December term, 1872:

United States circuit court, northern district of Florida. December term, 1872.

DECEMBER 3, 1872.

In the matter of the appointment of Frederick C. Humphreys, shipping-commissioner of the port of Pensacola.

Ordered by the court that Frederick C. Humphreys, of Pensacola, be, and he is hereby, appointed shipping-commissioner for the port of Pensacola.

Further ordered that said commissioner may enter upon the duties of his said appointment upon taking and filing the oath prescribed by law. And it is further ordered that the clerk of this court do furnish said commissioner with a certified copy of this order.

I. J. E. Townsend, clerk of the circuit court of the United States for the northern district of Florida, do certify that the above and foregoing is a true copy of the original order as of record in this office.

[SEAL.]   J. E. TOWNSEND, *Clerk.*

I do solemnly swear that I will support the Constitution of the United States; and that I will truly and faithfully discharge the duties of a shipping-commissioner to the best of my ability and according to law.

F. C. HUMPHREYS.

Sworn and subscribed before me this 9th day of December, A. D. 1872.

GEO. E. WENTWORTH,
United States Commissioner for the United States Circuit Court,
Northern District of Florida.

Filed December 9, 1872.

M. P. DE RIOBOO, *Clerk.*

Northern District of Florida:

I, M. P. De Rioboo, clerk United States circuit court, in and for said district, at Pensacola, do hereby certify the foregoing to be a true copy as the same remains on file in my office. I further certify that no resignation of said office of shipping-commissioner has been filed in my office by the said Frederick C. Humphreys.

Given under my hand and seal of said court, at Pensacola, this January 24, 1877.

[SEAL.]   M. P. DE RIOBOO, *Clerk.*

Q. (By Mr. Green.) Do you know Frederick C. Humphreys, one of the persons who was voted for as an elector for President and Vice-President of the United States at the election in November, 1876?—A. I do.

Q. Is he, or is he not, the same Frederick C. Humphreys of whom you have spoken as being United States shipping-commissioner?—A. He is the same person.

Q. Have you seen Mr. Frederick C. Humphreys in the exercise of any acts as United States shipping-commissioner?—A. I have had transactions with him in that capacity.

Q. How late and when?—A. I had transactions with him from time to time from the early part of 1873 up to the date of my leaving Pensacola, some time between the middle and latter part of August of last year.

Q. Describe the business you had with Mr. Humphreys as shipping-commissioner.—A. I frequently had occasion to communicate with him on the subject of the discharge of American seamen. His duties in the capacity of shipping-commissioner related to such matters between American seamen and shipping-masters.

Q. Did you testify as to your occupation?—A. I did not.

Q. What is your occupation?—A. I am a lawyer.

Q. Engaged in the practice of your profession where?—A. In Pensacola.

Q. And as a lawyer have you from time to time had transactions with Mr. Humphreys as United States shipping-commissioner?—A. I have.

Q. Have you appeared before him from time to time?—A. Yes, sir.

Q. How late?—A. From time to time, as I answered before, up to the date of my leaving Pensacola, which was between the middle and latter part of August of last year, 1876.

Q. Did Mr. Humphreys, as United States commissioner, take cognizance of any, and, if so, what, questions which may have been from time to time presented to him?—A. The ordinary questions of difference between seamen and masters of vessels—questions of the right to their discharge and the right to receive their wages.

Q. Did he hold court there for that purpose?—A. It was a sort of informal court.

Q. In which parties appeared before him?—A. Yes, sir.

Q. Did he hear evidence?—A. He heard the testimony.

Q. And arguments of counsel?—A. When arguments were presented. It was seldom that arguments were presented in such cases.

Mr. GREEN. That is all.

The PRESIDENT. Do the other side desire to cross-examine?

Mr. EVARTS and Mr. STOUGHTON. No.

Mr. GREEN. That is all that we propose to offer on that point by way of affirmative evidence, unless there may be something which may be required to be offered by way of rebuttal when the other side shall have presented their testimony.

The PRESIDENT. Is there anything to be offered on the other side?

Mr. EVARTS. Without commenting upon the state of the proof thus far reached as calling upon us to offer any evidence in rebuttal, principally upon the point that as yet no evidence has been adduced which shows that he held and exercised the office of shipping-commissioner at the date of the November election, we will introduce the proof on our part and leave any question for discussion hereafter.

F. C. HUMPHREYS sworn and examined.

By Mr. STOUGHTON:

Question. Where do you reside?—Answer. In Pensacola.

Q. Were you a candidate for elector?—A. I was.

Q. On the republican ticket?—A. Yes, sir.

Q. Had you prior to being such candidate held any office?—A. Yes, sir.

Q. What?—A. I was United States shipping-commissioner for the port of Pensacola.

Q. When did you cease to act as such?—A. On the 5th day of October, when acceptance of my resignation was received from Judge Woods.

Q. Did you resign your office?—A. I did.

Q. By resignation to whom?—A. By resignation through the mail.

Q. To whom?—A. To Judge Woods.

Q. Have you the acceptance of that resignation?—A. I have.

Q. Have you that in your possession?—A. I have.

Q. Be kind enough to let me see it.—A. [Producing a paper.] That is the paper.

Q. Judge Woods is one of the circuit judges of the United States?

The PRESIDENT. The court is aware of that.

Mr. MERRICK. We object, if your honors please, to the production of this paper as the acceptance of a resignation, as it is the act of an individual and not the act of the court.

The PRESIDENT. The simple question now is whether you object to its admissibility. Its effect will be a subject of argument afterward.

Mr. EVARTS. Its authenticity is not objected to.

Mr. MERRICK. It is hardly anticipating the main question, but of course I will waive it at the suggestion of the President of the Commission for the present.

The PRESIDENT. Its effect can be judged of afterward.

Mr. MERRICK. If I shall not be understood as waiving my objection, very well.

The PRESIDENT. The question of its effect will be considered as reserved.

Q. (By Mr. Stoughton.) You received from Judge Woods, in reply to your resignation, this paper?—A. Yes, sir.

Mr. Commissioner MILLER. It had better be read.

Mr. STOUGHTON. I will read it.

NEWARK, *October*, 1876.

DEAR SIR: I inclose the acceptance of your resignation as shipping-commissioner. The vacancy can only be filled by the circuit court, and until I can go to Pensacola to open court for that purpose, the duties of the office will have to be discharged by the collector.

Respectfully, yours,

W. B. WOODS.

Major F. C. HUMPHREYS,
Pensacola, Fla.

To F. C. HUMPHREYS, Esq.,
Pensacola, Fla.:

Your letter of the 24th of September, 1876, resigning your office of United States shipping-commissioner for the port of Pensacola, in the State of Florida, has been received, and your resignation of said office is hereby accepted.

Very respectfully, your obedient servant,

W. B. WOODS,
United States Circuit Judge.

Oct. 2, 1876.

Mr. MERRICK. What place is it dated?

Mr. STOUGHTON. Newark.

Mr. EVARTS. What State?

Mr. STOUGHTON. There is no State on it.

The PRESIDENT. If no objection be made, the paper will be filed with the Secretary.

Mr. STOUGHTON. I have another, may it please your honors. [To the witness.] Did you receive the paper I now hold in my hand, dated October 1, 1876, from Hiram Potter, collector of customs at Pensacola? A. I did.

Q. Is this his signature?—A. It is.

Mr. MERRICK. We object to that paper being received.

Mr. STOUGHTON. It connects itself with the other two, as the Commission will see.

Mr. MERRICK. I make the objection, reserving the consideration of the question.

The PRESIDENT. It will be received subject to the decision of the Commission as to its effect.

Mr. MERRICK. Yes, sir; and as to its admissibility, also.

The PRESIDENT. Yes.

Mr. STOUGHTON. This letter is:

CUSTOM-HOUSE, PENSACOLA, FLORIDA,
Collector's Office, October 5, 1876.

F. C. HUMPHREYS, Esq.,
Pensacola, Fla.:

SIR: I am informed by Judge Woods that he has accepted your resignation as U. S. shipping-commissioner, and that it devolves upon me to assume the duties of the office until a regular appointment shall be made by the circuit court. I respectfully request, therefore, that you will turn over to me such public books, papers, records, &c., as may pertain to the business.

I remain, very respectfully, your obedient servant,

HIRAM POTTER, JR.,
Collector of Customs.

(To the witness.) Was he the collector?

The WITNESS. Yes, sir.

Q. (By Mr. STOUGHTON.) Did you cease to act in your office from the time of the receipt of the letter accepting your resignation?—A. I did.

Q. Have you acted at all in that capacity since?—A. No, sir.

Q. Has the collector acted in your place?—A. Yes, sir.

Q. Did you turn over to the collector whatever you had of public papers or property connected with the office, if you had any?—A. I had none. The blanks were my personal property, bought and paid for with my own money.

Cross-examined by Mr. HOADLY:

Q. Have you a copy of your letter of resignation?—A. Yes, sir.

Q. How did you convey it to Judge Woods?—A. Through the mail.

Q. To what point did you address that?—A. To Newark, in the State of Ohio. He was there on a visit.

Q. Judge Woods was on a visit to Newark, Ohio?—A. Yes, sir.

Q. Has there been any open session of the circuit court of the United States for the northern district of Florida since the date of that resignation?—A. No, sir.

Q. When did you receive Judge Woods's reply to your letter ?—A. On the 5th of October.

The PRESIDENT. Is there anything further ?

Mr. STOUGHTON. Nothing further.

The PRESIDENT. Anything in rebuttal ?

Mr. MERRICK. Nothing further.

The PRESIDENT. The testimony is closed. The third rule is as follows:

Counsel, not exceeding two in number on each side, will be heard by the Commission on the merits of any case presented to it, not longer than two hours being allowed to each side, unless a longer time and additional counsel shall be specially authorized by the Commission.

I consider myself instructed to say that the whole case is now open for argument under that rule. If members of the Commission entertain a different view they will suggest it. That is my understanding on the construction I give. I think the order should be as before, that one counsel representing the objections to certificate No. 1 should open, that two on the other side should reply, and then the other counsel having the affirmative should have the close.

Mr. MERRICK. Mr. President, we would ask, if it be agreeable to the Commission, that there should be allowed three counsel to be heard for the objectors to certificate No. 1.

The PRESIDENT. I will allow that without submitting the question to the Commission, provided no additional time is asked.

Mr. MERRICK. We were going to ask for some slight addition to our time.

The PRESIDENT. That is for the Commission.

Mr. MERRICK. The reason for asking that three be heard is that there is a new and quite important question raised by the testimony this morning in reference to Mr. Humphreys, and it enlarges very considerably the sphere of the argument.

The PRESIDENT. How much more time do you want?

Mr. MERRICK. An hour. We desire to have that question in its first presentation to the court fully presented, and it is a question upon which Mr. Hoadly has prepared himself with some careful examination, and it is one which before the Commission finally disperses may again arise ; and we deem it important that it should be fairly, fully, and ably discussed when first presented to your consideration.

Mr. Commissioner MILLER. Mr. Merrick, nearly all the other questions were discussed in the first argument. The effect of the papers submitted by the President of the Senate was fully discussed in the opening argument by counsel on both sides, and it does seem to me, as we must get along and discharge this business, that we should get through with the argument to-day.

The PRESIDENT. What, if anything, is said on the other side ? What are the views of the other side ? Do they wish to be heard by three counsel ?

Mr. EVARTS. We shall not want more than two hours, even if three should be allowed to speak.

The PRESIDENT. Will more than two counsel speak on your side ?

Mr. EVARTS. I think not.

The PRESIDENT. The question submitted to the Commission is whether an additional hour shall be allowed to counsel for the time of argument.

The question being put, it was determined in the affirmative.

Mr. HOADLY. May it please the Commission, it has been established by the proof that Frederick C. Humphreys held the office of shipping-commissioner by appointment of the circuit court of the United States in Florida. It has been established by the proof that before the November election he attempted to divest himself of this office by forwarding to the city of Newark, in the State of Ohio, a paper resignation of the office, and by receiving from the judge, not the court, acting not in Florida but in Ohio, an acceptance of that resignation.

The powers of this office are derived from section 4501 of the Revised Statutes:

> The several circuit courts within the jurisdiction of which there is a port of entry, &c., shall appoint, &c.

The resignation cannot be made except to the same authority that appointed. The resignation could not, therefore, be made by letter addressed to the judge in Ohio. The acceptance of the resignation could not emanate from the judge in Ohio. The court has not since held a session. The court which clothed the officer with the power has not relieved him from the performance of the duty, and I respectfully submit that this proposition is sustained by a cause recently decided in the Supreme Court of the United States, the opinion in which has just been placed in my hands, the case of Badger and others *vs.* The United States on the relation of Bolton, a copy of the decision in which will be furnished to your honors. It is also, I am advised, according to the practice of the Government as shown by Document No. 123, Twenty-sixth Congress, second session, House of Representatives, and by the second volume of the Opinions of the Attorneys-General, pages 406 and 713. Therefore, considering that Frederick C. Humphreys had been duly appointed to this office, that by the laws of the United States it is shown to be an office of profit and trust, is by the Revised Statutes so made; considering that the judge of the circuit court acting in Ohio was not the circuit court and was not the power that clothed him with the authority, and could not relieve him from the performance of the duty with which he had been intrusted by another power; considering that the judge of the circuit court of the United States acting in chambers could not in Ohio release him from a trust with which the court not in chambers clothed him in Florida; considering these circumstances, we respectfully submit that he held an office of profit and trust on the day of the November election for electors of President and Vice-President, and that therefore the vote that he cast as an elecctor in December cannot be counted.

The provision of disqualification contained in the first section of the second article of the Constitution I will read, that I may have freshly before my own mind the text in reference to which this debate must proceed.

Mr. Commissioner THURMAN. Before you proceed with that, will you state whether this was an office a resignation of which must be accepted, or could the officer resign of his own motion at any time?

Mr. HOADLY. There is nothing in the statute with regard to the resignation of this office at all. Having accepted the office, given bond, and taken oath to perform its duties, we submit that he could not divest himself of it by his own act. I will read the whole section which authorized the appointment:

> The several circuit courts within the jurisdiction of which there is a port of entry which is also a port of ocean navigation shall appoint a commissioner for each such port which in their judgment may require the same, such commissioners to be termed shipping-commissioners; and may, from time to time, remove from office any commissioner whom the court may have reason to believe does not properly perform his duties,

and shall then provide for the proper performance of his duties until another person is duly appointed in his place.

I submit that where the legislative body have created an office, and the judicial authority has, according to the law, clothed a person with the trusts of that office, public policy requires that it should not be held at his will and pleasure, it being an office of public convenience and necessity, for the performance of which bond is required to be given, and the filling of which may be at all times essential to the performance of public duty.

Turning to the constitutional provision, I read :

> Each State shall appoint, in such manner as the legislature thereof may direct, a number of electors equal to the whole number of Senators and Representatives to which the State may be entitled in the Congress ; but no Senator or Representative, or person holding an office of trust or profit under the United States, shall be appointed an elector.

The form is mandatory; it is negative; that is, the provision of disqualification is negative. It is coupled with the grant of power by the word " but," which, together with the words of the context, shows that it is a limitation, a qualification, a diminution of the grant of power. The grant of power is to the State, not to the people of the State, but to the State as a legal entity, as an organized body-corporate in its character; and to this grant thus given to the State is attached a limitation introduced by words of exception, " *but* no Senator or Representative shall be entitled." It is clothed in negative language. " Negative language," it is said, " will make a statute imperative ; and this is incontestable. Negative words will make a statute imperative. Affirmative words may ; negative must," as is stated in Sedgwick on Constitutional and Statutory Law, page 370 ; Cooley on Constitutional Limitations, 75 ; Potter's Dwarris on Statutes, 228 ; Rex *vs.* Justices of Leicester, 7 Barnewall & Cresswell, 6, 12.

But what is of more consequence than the form, although the form is indicative of the purpose of the authors in using the words of substance, the provision is in substance imperative and admits of no evasion. Lord Mansfield distinguishes mandatory from directory clauses in statutes by reference to " circumstances which are of the essence of a thing required to be done" as distinguished from circumstances which are " merely directory." Rex *vs.* Loxdale, 1 Burr., 447.

Having relation, as Lord Mansfield says, to that which is essential as different from that which is merely directory, I suggest that several circumstances show that our fathers, who framed this provision, considered it essential. It seems to have been first adopted into the Constitution on the motion of Mr. Gerry and Mr. Gouverneur Morris, in a slightly different form from that in which it now appears. On July 19, 1787, Mr. Gerry and Mr. Gouverneur Morris moved " that the electors of the Executive shall not be members of the National Legislature, nor officers of the United States, nor shall the electors themselves be eligible to the Supreme Magistracy. Agreed to *nem. con.*" (*Madison Papers*, 343.)

On September 6, Mr. Rufus King and Mr. Gerry moved to insert in the fourth clause of the report, after the words " may be entitled in the Legislature," the following :

> But no person shall be appointed an elector who is a member of the Legislature of the United States, or who holds any office of profit or trust under the United States.— *Madison Papers*, 515.

It passed *nem. con.* It was the unanimous will of our fathers, therefore, that this disqualification should attach; that it should attach in the nature of an exception or proviso to the grant of power to the States to elect electors; that it should attach by disqualification of the persons who might be appointed electors; that it should attach by disqualification of the State in the appointment of electors. The State is disqualified from appointing, the elector from accepting the trust. The disqualification, therefore, is imposed both upon the appointing power and upon the candidate, and the effect of such disqualification, it is respectfully submitted, is to render the action of the State in the appointment null and void. The disqualification is of the action of the State; of the State in all its departments; of the voters of the State as well as of the government of the State. The disqualification binds every citizen of the State, every functionary of the State, and attaches to and qualifies and limits the corporate action of the State, and is equivalent to saying "the State may appoint from among the number of qualified persons." I submit that the substance and real meaning of the sentence, although it is cast in the negative and inhibitory form, is that from among the number of those who do not occupy positions of profit and trust the State may appoint electors. The object of our fathers in introducing, without dissent, this provision, was to prevent the Federal power, the officers controlling Federal agencies, from continuing their power through the influence of the offices of trust with which they were clothed for Federal and State benefit. It was not merely to protect the State in which the candidate might be elected from the intrusion of a Federal office-holder into the electoral office, but it was to protect every other State, each State, all the States, and the people of each and every State by a mutual covenant in the form of a limitation of power, that no State should appoint a disqualified person. Each State, therefore, through the agencies of the Federal Government, is entitled to be protected from the illegitimate use of Federal power in any State. Delaware, Oregon, the smallest of our States, are entitled to ask, through their Senators and Representatives, that the Federal power shall enforce this provision for their protection against the corruption of the elections in the larger States by means of the election of disqualified persons.

If it be said—but I do not think it will—that the remedy which our fathers provided for the evil which they apprehended has but little value, and that their forecast was not great, so much the more reason for rigidly insisting upon such value as it possesses now; for surely time has not proved, experience has not shown that the evils which our fathers apprehended, as they clearly manifested and showed by the text of the provision itself, are any less than they supposed they would be. The influence of Federal power through the candidacy of Federal officers for electors is explicitly here prohibited. The object is to diminish and prevent and restrict Federal interference in the election of electors. It is the duty, not of the States, in purging the votes of electors, but of the Federal Government, for the protection of each State, to insist upon and carry into full force this provision.

Again, the occasions upon which this provision has been considered during our history emphasize this suggestion as to the purpose of our fathers in adopting it. In 1837 five postmasters, or five persons bearing the same names as certain postmasters, were appointed or attempted to be appointed electors. Mr. Clay submitted, on January 27, 1837, this instruction, which he asked to be given to the joint committee of the Senate and House appointed to ascertain and report a mode of examining the votes for President and Vice-President of the United States, namely, that they should

Inquire into the expediency of ascertaining whether any votes were given at the recent election contrary to the prohibition contained in the second section of the second article of the Constitution; and if any such votes were given, what ought to be done with them; and whether any and what provision ought to be made for securing the faithful observance, in future, of that section of the Constitution.

The members of this committee on the part of the Senate were Felix Grundy, Henry Clay, and Silas Wright; on the part of the House, Francis Thomas, Churchill C. Cambreleng, John Reed, Henry W. Connor, and Francis S. Lyon, the latter of whom, I was informed in Mobile a few days since, is the only survivor, now living in Alabama at a great age, and deeply interested in this discussion. Mr. Grundy submitted a report of the committee on February 4, from which I desire to read the following quotation:

That the short period at which they were appointed, before the day on which the votes for President and Vice-President of the United States have to be counted, has prevented them from investigating the facts submitted to their examination as fully as might have been done had more time been allowed. The correspondence which has taken place between the chairman of the committee and the heads of the different departments of the executive branch of the government accompanies this report, from which it appears . . . that in two cases persons of the same names with the individuals who were appointed and voted as electors in the State of North Carolina held the office of deputy-postmaster under the General Government.

I suggest, in passing, that the course taken by this committee of the most eminent men of that generation indicates that I am right in the suggestion that the duty was then considered, as we now claim it should be, as imposed on the Federal power to take testimony so as to ascertain the facts and by Federal agencies enforce the prohibition for the protection not merely of the State in which the disqualified elector has voted, but of the States in which the disqualified elector has not voted for the election of President and Vice-President, and thus that it concerns all the States, and relates to the deepest and most vital interests of all the States. The disqualification cannot therefore be permitted to be evaded in one State without a blow struck at every other State.

I will continue reading the report:

It also appears that in New Hampshire there is one case; in Connecticut there is one case; in North Carolina there is one case in which, from the report of the Postmaster-General, it is probable that at the time of the appointment of electors in these States respectively the electors or persons of the same name were deputy postmasters. The committee have not ascertained whether the electors are the same individuals who held or are presumed to have held the office of deputy postmasters at the time when the appointment of electors was made; and this is the less to be regretted, as it is confidently believed that no change in the result of the election of either the President or Vice-President would be effected by the ascertainment of the fact in either way, as five or six votes only would, in any event, be abstracted from the whole number, for the committee cannot adopt the opinion entertained by some, that a single illegal vote would vitiate the whole electoral vote of the college of electors in which it was given, particularly in cases where the vote of the whole college has been given for the same persons.

From this sentence it appears that at that time, forty years ago, the question in debate was whether the single illegal vote vitiated more than the vote itself, and the committee were of opinion that it did not.

The committee are of opinion that the second section of the second article of the Constitution, which declares that "no Senator or Representative, or person holding an office of trust or profit under the United States, shall be appointed an elector," ought to be carried, in its whole spirit, into rigid execution, in order to prevent officers of the General Government from bringing their official power to influence the elections of President and Vice-President of the United States. This provision of the Constitution, it is believed, excludes and disqualifies deputy postmasters from the appointment of electors; and the disqualification relates to the time of the appointment, and that a resignation of the office of deputy postmaster after his appointment as elector would not entitle him to vote as elector under the Constitution.

I submit that when it appears that two such minds as those of Henry Clay and Silas Wright, statesmen of such opposite political education and modes of thought, concur in a statement with reference to the reasons and meaning of the Constitution, it comes to us with a weight and with an authority that is not to be gainsaid. Fortunately or unfortunately, however, our American habit of not bridging chasms until we reach them prevented any action by Congress such as Mr. Clay suggested; and accordingly the question re-presents itself to-day without any further elucidation by legislation than it had then.

Mr. Commissioner EDMUNDS. What did the committee say ought to be done, Mr. Hoadly, if anything?

Mr. HOADLY. Only this, "that the article ought to be carried in its whole spirit into rigid execution;" but, inasmuch as the disqualification, if admitted in its whole spirit and carried into rigid execution, did not change the result of that election, as Martin Van Buren was elected President, and the election of Vice-President went to the Senate, they reported no steps as necessary to be taken, and no steps were taken.

Mr. Commissioner EDMUNDS. Have you read the conclusion of the report?

Mr. HOADLY. I cannot answer the question. I think I have read the conclusion of the report, but unfortunately copying not from the Congressional Globe but from an excerpt which, working in great haste, I had to use for my own convenience, I cannot answer the question.

Mr. Commissioner EDMUNDS. I had the impression that the committee had added something else.

Mr. Commissioner BRADLEY. What is the date of the report?

Mr. HOADLY. February 4, 1837.

If we are right in our proposition with regard to the facts, Humphreys held the office at the time when he cast his vote. The only two questions, therefore, which present themselves for debate are, first, did he hold at the time an office of profit or trust; secondly, as to the effect of the holding, provided the fact has been shown. As the questions thus present themselves, we are not concerned to consider the authorities decided in cases of resignation after the election, except so far as they indicate the views of courts with regard to the effect of the disqualifying facts. In Rex *vs.* Monday (Cowper, page 536,) Sergeant Buller, afterward Mr. Justice Buller, states the rule thus, *arguendo* :

Two requisites are necessary to make a good election: first, a capacity in the electors; second, a capacity in the elected; and unless both concur the election is a nullity. With respect to the capacity of the electors, their right is this: They cannot say there shall be no election, but they are to elect. Therefore, though they may vote to prefer one to fill an office, they can not say that such a one shall not be preferred, or by merely saying, "We dissent to every one proposed," prevent any election at all. Their right consists in an affirmative, not a negative declaration. Consequently there is no effectual means of voting against one man but by voting for another; and even then, if such other person be unqualified and the elector has notice of his incapacity, his vote will be thrown away.

Such is the well-settled English rule, as affirmed by a multitude of cases since.

Lord Chief-Justice Wilmot, in the same volume, note-to page 393, in the case of Harrison *vs.* Evans, discussing the statute of 13 Charles II, which enacted that no person should be elected into any corporation-office who had not received the sacrament within a twelvemonth preceding his election, and in default of doing so the election and choice should be void, said:

The provision is not only addressed to the elected and a provision upon them, but a provision laid down upon the electors if they have notice. The legislature has commanded them not to choose a non-conformist, because he ought not to be trusted. Consequently, with respect to any legal effect of operation, it is as if there had been no election.

So in a multitude of cases in England since, as I said, which need not be here more particularly referred to, but with a reference to which your honors will be furnished in my brief. The same doctrine is applied in many American cases also, and it is respectfully submitted that there is no case to the contrary. American cases have differed widely upon the question whether the non-eligibility of the candidate receiving the largest vote has the effect to elect the next highest competing candidate; but no American case, it is respectfully submitted, treats the election of one who at the time was non-qualified and who attempted to act as other than an absolutely null appointment. To this effect is the case of Searcy vs. Grow, 15 California, 118, which was a contest for the office of sheriff of Siskiyou County, where Grow was returned as having been elected and was found to be the holder of an office of profit and trust under the constitution of California, to which a disqualification was attached by the constitution, and who had resigned after the election and before induction into the shrievalty, but was holding the disqualifying office at the time of the election. Mr. Justice Baldwin (Cope, J., and Field, C. J., concurring) said:

The people in this case were clothed with this power of choice. Their selection of a candidate gave him all the claim to the office which he has. His title to the office comes from their designation of him as sheriff. But they could not designate or choose a man not eligible—that is, not capable of being selected. They might select any man they chose, subject only to this exception: that the man they selected was capable of taking what they had the power to give. We do not see how the fact that he became capable of taking office after they had exercised their power can avail the appellant. If he was not eligible at the time the votes were cast for him, the election failed.

Of course your honors will see the pertinency of this quotation to other questions that may arise in other cases, and I am compelled to read portions of the opinion which do not refer to the particular case in hand, in order to use intelligently those portions that do:

If he was not eligible at the time the votes were cast for him, the election failed. We do not see how it can be assumed that by the act of the candidate the votes which, when cast, were ineffectual because not given for a qualified candidate, became effectual to elect him to office.

So in the case of the State of Nevada on the relation of Nourse vs. Clarke, (3 Nevada, 566,) which, it is true, may be treated as obiter dictum, because it was found there that the resignation had been effectually made before the election, the court discussed this question with this result: "That a person holding the office of United States district attorney on the day of election was incapable of being chosen to the office of attorney-general of the State, because of a provision in the State constitution to the effect that no Federal office-holder ' shall be eligible to any civil office of profit under this State.' 'Which word eligible,' says this learned court, ' means both capable of being legally chosen and capable of legally holding.' "

The word here is "appointed;" that no person holding an office shall be appointed an elector. Who appoints? The State appoints; not the voters of the State; not the legislature of the State; not the governor of the State; but the State appoints. The State appoints from among qualified persons; or, which is the same thing, the State appoints, but may not appoint a disqualified person. Now the State does appoint a disqualified person, and the disqualification is one contained in the same constitutional provision as a qualification, limitation, restriction of the

same constitutional clause which gives the right to appoint, a part of
the same sentence attached to the grant of power. The appointment
refers to the act of the State, the act of the State on the day which Congress has named as the day upon which only the choice of elector can
be made. On that day the State shall appoint, but shall not appoint
a person not legally qualified to hold the office.

In Commonwealth *vs.* Cluly (56 Pennsylvania State Reports, 270) the
election went back to the people. In the Indiana cases the next highest
competing candidate was declared elected—going beyond the rule we ask
to be applied to the Florida electoral college. In Searcy *vs.* Grow, I suppose the result of the contest was to unseat the disqualified person without seating the next highest competing candidate. In all the cases
which are commented upon in the decision of Gulick *vs.* New, in 14
Indiana, 93, and by the various authorities and text-writers on this
subject, no one, I submit, will be found which favors the idea that the
election of one constitutionally disqualified can by any possibility result,
if it do not elect the next highest candidate, in anything else than a
failure to elect; and Congress by its legislation on the subject has indicated its purpose in the same direction. Thus the one hundred and
thirty-third section of the Revised Statutes provides for a case of vacancy
occurring when the college of electors shall meet to cast their votes.
Section 134 provides for a case where the State shall fail to elect ; that,
where the State shall fail to elect on the day provided, the electors may
be appointed on a subsequent day in such manner as the legislature of
such State may direct. These provisions of law, which have been in
force since the act of January 23, 1845, in that statute were attached,
and not separated as in the Revised Statutes and thrown into two separate sections ; these two provisions of law, which were then attached to
each other, indicate the meaning of the law-makers of this generation
and the last to furnish a remedy in case of the election of one disqualified under the Constitution.

If it be shown that the State of Florida has acted under the one hundred and thirty-fourth section of the Revised Statutes, then the vote of
Florida is not diminished by reason of the fact that on the 7th of November one of the persons voted for was disqualified.

SEC. 134. Whenever any State has held an election for the purpose of choosing electors, and has failed to make a choice on the day prescribed by law, the electors may be
appointed on a subsequent day in such a manner as the legislature of such State may
direct.

If it were true, as ruled in Furman *vs.* Clute, 50 New York Reports ;
in Commonwealth *vs.* Cluly, 56 Pennsylvania State Reports ; in Searcy
vs. Grow, in 15 California Reports ; if it were true, as ruled in all the
American cases, which have held that the next highest competing candidate was not elected, that the case was one of non-election, and
rendered necessary a new election, then I respectfully submit that the
one hundred and thirty-fourth section of the Revised Statutes provided for the State of Florida a remedy for the mischief to which she
was found on the 7th of November to have been subjected. She could
have provided by law, as I shall presently show to your honors was
done in the State of Rhode Island, to meet the exact contingency. It
is not the case of an absolute non-election, or one where there has been
no attempt to hold an election, to which this section refers. This provision of law operates whenever any State has held an election for the
purpose of choosing electors and has failed to make a choice on the day
prescribed by law. Then the electors may be appointed on a subsequent day in such manner as the legislature of such State may direct.

If every elector in every State in the United States were disqualified, would it not be true that there was an election held and a failure to make choice? If every elector in the State of Florida was disqualified, would it not be true that there was an election held, but without choice? If, in the State of Pennsylvania, in the case of Cluly, the people had again to elect; if, in New York, in Furman *vs.* Clute, the people had again to elect; if, in California, in the case of Searcy *vs.* Grow, the people had again to elect, then it would follow that, if all the four electors of the State of Florida were disqualified, it would be clearly a case of failure to make choice, and the people would have to elect again, provided the legislature confided to the people, under section 134, the function of electing for the second time and did not exercise it themselves, as was done in Rhode Island. *Omne majus continet in se minus.*

If it be a failure to make choice where a single disqualified candidate runs against another officer, if it be a failure to make choice so that he can be ousted and a new election is required to be held, and if there be a provision of statute law of the United States contemplating the emergency and providing a remedy, and if the power of appointment be with the State, and if the opportunity of remedy be with the State, then I submit that it must be shown that the State has taken advantage of this provision of the Revised Statutes, section 134, or the single vote is lost.

The question came directly before the judges of the supreme court of Rhode Island, in the case of George H. Corliss, who held the office of member of the Centennial Commission under the United States on the day of the presidential election. The governor, under the authority of the statutes, submitted to the judges of the supreme court of that State five questions: First, whether the office of centennial commissioner was an office of trust and profit, which they answered, by a majority of voices, it was, such as disqualified the holder for the office of elector of President and Vice-President. Secondly, whether the candidate who received a plurality of votes created a vacancy by declining the office. Thirdly, whether the disqualification was removed by the resignation of the said office of trust or profit. Fourthly, whether the disqualification resulted in the election of the candidate next highest in number of votes, or in failure to elect. Fifthly, if by reason of the disqualification of the candidate who received the plurality of the votes given there was no election, could the general assembly in grand committee elect an elector?

The judges answered the first question, as I said, by a majority of voices, that it was a disqualifying fact, this office of commissioner of the United States Centennial Commission, and, by all their voices agreeing, answered that "such candidate who received a plurality declining the office did not create a vacancy; that the disqualification was not removed by the resignation of the office, but that the disqualification did not result in the election of the candidate next in vote, but did result in a failure to elect, and that there was no election, so that the general assembly in grand committee might elect, and the general assembly in grand committee did elect."

The opinion is signed by all the judges, Thomas Durfee, W. S. Burges, E. R. Potter, Charles Matteson, and Stiness. It was a question submitted under the constitution and laws of that State. I read it at this time in order that I may if possible satisfy the Commission that the construction which I place on section 134 of the Revised Statutes is the correct construction.

In answer to the fourth question, which was this, "If not, does the disqualification result in the election of the candidate next in vote or in a failure to elect ?" the court answered :

We think the disqualification does not result in the election of the candidate next in vote, but in a failure to elect.

In England it has been held that where electors vote for an ineligible candidate, knowing his disqualification, their votes are not to be counted any more than if they were thrown for a dead man or the Man in the Moon, and that in such a case the opposing candidate, being qualified, will be elected, although he has had a minority of the votes.

And such is the rule in Indiana and as was established at an early day in Maryland by Chief-Justice Samuel Chase, of that State, and has continued in force, as I am informed, down to this time, and been enforced very recently. The judges of Rhode Island sustain this by the following references : King *vs.* Hawkins, 10 East., 210 ; Reg. *vs.* Coaks, 3 El. & B. 253.

But even in England, if the disqualification is unknown, the minority candidate is not entitled to the office, the election being a failure. (Queen *vs.* Hiornes, 7 Ad. & E., 960 ; Rex *vs.* Bridge, 1 M. & Selw., 76.) And it has been held that to entitle the minority candidate to the office it is not enough that the electors knew of the facts which amount to a disqualification, unless they likewise knew that they amount to it in point of law. (The Queen *vs.* The Mayor, &c., Law Rep., 3 Q. B., 629.)

In this country the law is certainly not more favorable to the minority candidate. (State *vs.* Giles, 1 Chandler, (Wis.,) 112; State *vs.* Smith, 14 Wis., 497 ; Saunders *vs.* Haynes, 13 Cal., 145; People *vs.* Clute, 50 N. Y., 451.) The question submitted to us does not allege or imply that the electors, knowing the disqualification, voted for the ineligible candidate in willful defiance of the law ; and certainly, in the absence of proof, it is not to be presumed that they so voted. The only effect of the disqualification, in our opinion, is to render void the election of the candidate who is disqualified, and to leave one place in the electoral college unfilled.

The answer to the fifth question, " If, by reason of the disqualification of the candidate who received a plurality of the votes given, there was no election, can the general assembly, in grand committee, select an elector," was in the affirmative. The court, in discussing another question, had cited the seventh section of the General Statutes of Rhode Island, chapter 11, to wit :

If any electors, chosen as aforesaid, shall, after said election, decline the said office, or be prevented by any cause from serving therein, the other electors, when met in Bristol in pursuance of this chapter, shall fill such vacancies.

They had decided that disqualification did not create a case of vacancy. They then considered another statute of Rhode Island, which they held to have been passed under the authority confided to the State of Rhode Island by the one hundred and thirty-fourth section of the Revised Statutes of the United States :

Our statutes (General Statute, chapter 11, section 5) provides that "if, by reason of the votes being equally divided, or otherwise, there shall not be an election of the number of electors to which the State may be entitled, the governor shall forthwith convene the general assembly at Providence for the choice of electors to fill such vacancy by an election in grand committee." We think this provision covers the contingency which has happened, and that, therefore, the general assembly in grand committee can elect an elector to fill up the number to which the State is entitled. The law of the United States provides that " whenever any State has held an election for the purpose of choosing electors, and has failed to make choice on the day prescribed by law, the electors may be appointed on a subsequent day, in such manner as the legislature of the State may direct."

We have, then, the unanimous opinion of all the judges of Rhode Island to the effect that the distinction on which we insist is well taken, that the acts of Congress are furnished for the purpose of covering all the cases that may arise, in order that the constitutional provision may have full force and effect, and yet that the State may not be deprived of its opportunity to be fully represented in the electoral college. The inhibition of the constitution being peremptory, and like all the inhibitions, whether express or implied, self-enforcing, were there no such provision as that contained in section 134, the vote of the State would necessarily be lost, unless it could be shown by some principle of law, by the authority of some decided case, that the election of a disqualified candidate is possible, notwithstanding the disqualification contained in a constitutional inhibition of the character here referred to.

But peradventure by mistake, and without the intent to violate the spirit of the constitutional provision, by mere misadventure the State may have selected as one of its electors, or as all of its electors, persons holding disqualified offices, and, therefore, said Congress, whenever there be a case of non-election in any State the legislature may provide a method of supplying the defect; and whenever there be a case of vacancy the legislature may provide a method of supplying the defect; a vacancy which occurs when the college of elected electors meets, a non-election which occurs when an election has been held. If no election has been held, there is no provision of statutory law to meet the case at all; but the one hundred and thirty-third section provides for the case of a vacancy when there has been a qualified person elected, and the one hundred and thirty-fourth section provides for the case of non-election when an election has been held. It does not contemplate the case where no election at all has been held, but it explicitly provides for a case where an election has been held which has not resulted in the choice of a competent and qualified candidate, and furnished to the people of the State of Florida, as it did to the State of Rhode Island, ample opportunity to save themselves from all misadventure, from all the consequences of mistake, or ignorance, or innocent evil, by enabling them to have a second opportunity, notwithstanding the constitutional provision that Congress may determine the time of choosing the electors.

Mr. GREEN. Mr. President and gentlemen of the Electoral Commission, that portion of the duty which has been assigned to me consists in submitting, by way of opening, the views which the counsel for the objectors to return No. 1 feel it necessary to make under the order of the Commission read to them this morning. That portion of the opening argument which relates to the second branch of the order has been disposed of by my friend, Judge Hoadly, and we leave it just there with a single additional suggestion which I have been desired to make, namely, that this office of shipping-commissioner, being one to be filled by the court, could be only surrendered up or resigned to the court itself; that the so-called letter of resignation sent to Judge Woods, and for aught this Commission knows by him still retained, fails to perform the office sought to be imputed to it until it reaches the records of the court or receives some official recognition from the court itself. If that letter had been sent by mail, it could have no effect until it reached its destination. Had it been sent by messenger, no effect could have been given to it until it reached the archives of the court; and the mere fact of its reception by Judge Woods himself gives it no other or greater validity than if it had been in the pocket of the messenger or in the mail-bag.

Moreover, I am desired to call the attention of the Commission to the certificate of the clerk of the circuit court read in evidence this morning. I have not the paper before me, and therefore may not state its date with accuracy; but my recollection of it is that it contains a certificate that up to a very recent period, certainly subsequent to the time when Humphreys acted as an elector, no resignation of his office had yet reached the archives of the court; and with these suggestions I pass to the other branch of the case.

The order which has been read to us this morning directs the reception and consideration of all evidence submitted to the joint convention of the two Houses by the President of the Senate, together with the certificates which were also presented by him to the joint convention; and in order that we may distinctly understand where we have arrived in the progress of the discussion of this great question, it is proper for us to consider what were the papers presented by the President of the Senate to the joint convention of the two Houses.

They were, first, what is known as return No. 1, which has been printed for the use of the Commission. It consists of three documents. The first one is the certificate of Governor Stearns, dated 6th December, 1876, under the seal of the State, and attested by the secretary of state. It purports to be the list which is contemplated by the act of Congress. Although that list may not state the exact and true fact, it would seem to be not objectionable in point of form. Next follows the certificate signed by Humphreys, Pearce, Holden, and Long, the Hayes electors, stating that they had, pursuant to the Constitution and laws of the United States, been appointed electors, and had assembled at the State capitol and had voted by ballot for President and Vice-President in two distinct ballots, stating in the first certificate the result for President, and with a like preamble stating the result for Vice-President in the second certificate. This, if the Commission please, is all that is contained in what is known as certificate or return No. 1.

Certificate or return No. 2 consists of a certificate of Mr. Cocke, the attorney-general of the State of Florida, to the effect that he is attorney-general of the State of Florida and a member of the State board of canvassers, and that by the authentic returns of the votes cast in the several counties of the State of Florida at the election held in November, 1876—

Said returns being on file in the office of the secretary of state, and seen and considered by me, as such member of the board of State canvassers of the said State of Forida, it appears and is shown that Wilkinson call—

And the other Tilden electors, naming them—

were chosen the four electors of President and Vice-President of the United States.

And he further certifies—

That, under the act of the legislature of the State of Florida establishing said board of State canvassers, no provision has been enacted, nor is any such provision contained in the statute law of this State, whereby the result shown and appearing by said returns to said board of State canvassers can be certified to the executive of the said State.

Next follows an oath of office on the part of Call and the other so-called Tilden electors, and then the certificate of Call and the other electors of their having met according to law and having balloted for President and also Vice-President by distinct ballots, and certifying that the result is that Samuel J. Tilden, of the State of New York, received 4 votes for President, and Thomas A. Hendricks, of the State of Indiana, 4 votes for Vice-President. Attached to this certificate is another one:

And we further certify that, having met and convened as such electors, at the time and place designated by law, we did notify the governor of the State of Florida, the executive of said State, of our appointment as such electors, and did apply to and demand of him to cause to be delivered to us three lists of the names of the electors of the said State, according to law, and the said governor did refuse to deliver the same to us.

This return No. 2, made by the attorney-general and by the electors, accompanied by the oath of office on the part of the electors, being an official document under the sanction of an official oath, being a declaration made by these electors and by the attorney-general, who was also a member of the board of State canvassers, solemnly in this manner, is at least some evidence before this Commission to support the facts which are stated in it. It appears from this official certificate, thus made by the attorney-general, that by the returns of the election on file in the office of the secretary of state, seen and considered by him as a member of the board of State canvassers, Call and the other Tilden electors were duly chosen and appointed electors for the State of Florida; and it also supplies the evidence necessary to satisfy the inquiry why the attorney-general should make this certificate and why the governor did not, because the electors themselves certify that they made an application to the governor for a proper certificate and that he refused to give it to them.

Certificate or return No. 3, which was received, as it appears from the statement made by the Presiding Officer of the joint convention, on the 31st day of January, 1877, and so stated by him to the joint convention on Thursday last, consists of several papers, and I proceed now to call the attention of the Commission to what those papers are.

First in order is a certificate of Governor Drew, the governor of the State of Florida, bearing date the 26th day of January, 1877, under the great seal of the State and attested by the secretary of state. It recites first an act of the legislature of the State of Florida of the 17th of January, 1877, being an act to procure a recanvass of the electoral vote of the State of Florida, as cast at the election held on the 7th of November, 1876. It recites the making of the canvass under the authority of the act, according to the laws and the interpretation thereof by the supreme court of the State of Florida. It recites that by the said canvass the Tilden electors were duly determined, declared, and certified to have been elected electors at the election held in November, 1876, as shown by the returns of the votes on file in the office of secretary of state. It recites that in *quo-warranto* proceedings wherein the said Robert Bullock and others, the Tilden electors, were relators, and Pearce and others, the Hayes electors, were respondents—

The circuit court of this State for the second judicial circuit, after full consideration of the law and the proofs produced on behalf of the parties respectively, by its judgment, determined that said relators were, at said election, in fact and law, elected such electors as against the said respondents and all other persons.

So that, with whatever force, as to its weight or as to the sufficiency of its mode of proof, this Commission has before it this day such evidence as must carry conviction to the mind of every member of the commission that in a court of the State of Florida in *quo-warranto* proceedings, by the judgment of that court upon the pleadings and upon the proofs, it was held and determined, not merely as matter of law but also as matter of fact, that the Tilden electors were entitled to office as against the Hayes electors and all the world beside. The governor then, in pursuance of another act of the legislature of the State of Florida of the 26th of January, 1877, makes and certifies a list of the names of the electors chosen, appointed, and declared as aforesaid, which contains the names of the Tilden electors. That is the first paper in what is known as return No. 3.

The second paper consists of a certificate under date of the 26th of January, 1877, signed by the Tilden electors, reciting that the executive had caused three lists of electors to be made, certified, and delivered to them, one of which was thereto annexed, by which it appeared that they had on the 7th of November, 1876, been duly appointed electors, and then that they did on the first Wednesday of December, 1876, meet at the capitol at Tallahassee to give and cast their votes as electors, and did as such electors by ballot vote for President and Vice-President of the United States, and, the ballots having been opened, inspected, and counted, the ballots were given for what are called the Tilden electors, and then follow the distinct lists of votes cast for President and Vice-President in the form required.

The next paper in order in this return is an act of the State of Florida under the date of the 17th of January, 1877, certified by the secretary of state under the great seal. This act provides for a board of State canvassers, and directs them to meet forthwith at the office of the secretary of state and to proceed to canvass the returns of the election of electors and determine and declare who were elected and appointed electors at the election, as shown by the returns on file in the office of the secretary of state. It then goes on to provide that the mode which shall be adopted by this board of canvassers for determining and declaring the votes shall be the law as prescribed by the supreme court of the State of Florida in two cases named, the case of Bloxham *vs.* Gibbs and the case of Drew *vs.* McLin, the latter one of which has been known as the mandamus proceeding instituted by Governor Drew as against McLin and the other members of the State canvassing-board, and which proceedings by mandamus and the opinion of the court in regard thereto the Commission have before them and will find in House Document No. 35, part 3, and known as the exhibits.

These documents of course are not in evidence before the Commission in the strict sense of that word; but we respectfully submit to the Commission that inasmuch as in order to determine this question they must arrive at a construction of the statutes of the State of Florida, it is their duty, as it is the rule of every court in the United States, to consider such decisions as binding and conclusive upon them, and to follow the construction given by the State courts to the State statutes. Therefore, in considering what are the powers of this State board of canvassers originally, the law creating it and defining its duties is to be taken into consideration in connection with the determination of the highest court of the State of Florida; and it is with a view that the Commission may be informed as to the precise facts which were under consideration in this mandamus case, that I call your attention to the exhibits mentioned in that document. It will be found, upon inspection of the document and of the record, that it arose out of transactions of the same board of canvassers at the same election, and passes directly upon the legality of the same action of the board of canvassers as is involved in the presidential contest. The Commission will learn from the opinions and from the exhibits that the decision of the supreme court of the State of Florida is full upon the point which has been argued before them heretofore. They clearly demonstrate that the action of the State board of canvassers in November last, by which the Hayes electors claimed to have been rightfully elected, has been solemnly pronounced by adjudication of the supreme court of that State to be unauthorized, illegal, and void.

Now, is it necessary for me to interject just here any authority upon the point as to the binding effect of this decision of the State courts? And yet, perhaps, it will be as convenient to do so here as at any other time. If the Commission please, from the time of the case of Shelby *vs.* Gray, in 11 Wheaton, 361, through Green *vs.* Neal, 6

Peters, 291; Christy *vs.* Pritchett, 4 Wallace, 201; Tioga Railroad *vs.* Blossburg Railroad, 20 Wallace, 137, down to Elmwood *vs.* Macy, 2 Otto, 289, an unbroken line of decisions will be found; and, if we correctly apprehend the force and effect of this current of judgment in the Supreme Court of the United States, it is that the adjudications of the highest tribunal of the State are to be deemed and taken as a part of the very statute itself, and that other courts, in considering what is meant by the statute, what is the legislative intent, exercise no independent judgment or criticism upon the language itself, or upon its scope, meaning, or effect, but accept, as if it were incorporated into the very body of the legislative act, the construction thus placed upon it by the highest judicial authority in the State. The court say, in the case of Green *vs.* Neal:

The decision of this question by the highest tribunal of a State should be considered as final by this court, not because the State tribunal in such a case has any power to bind this court, but because a fixed and received construction by a State in its own court makes it a part of the State law.

Returning now to the consideration of this return No. 3, the Commission will find that by the third section of the act the board is to "make and sign a certificate containing in words written at full length" the result of that election, and that that certificate is to be recorded in the office of the secretary of state in a book kept for that purpose.

Next following this act of the legislature is the certificate of the board of State canvassers organized under this law which I have just read, and dated the 19th day of January, 1877, and which presents to the consideration of this tribunal, county by county, all the returns for presidential electors on file in the office of the secretary of state, with all the details of the number of votes cast in each county for each one of the persons voted for, and at the end of it is a summary or tabulation, the result of which shows the election of the Tilden electors, one and all.

So that the Commission thus far have not only the certificate of the governor of the State to the main fact at issue before this tribunal, but they have in detail, county by county, all the votes cast for electors of President and Vice-President, and a tabulated statement showing the election of the Tilden electors. It is true that they have not all this mass of documents, sent in with the objections filed to the returns; it is true they have not all the original precinct-returns before them; but they have that before them which answers practically the same purpose. They have a certificate made in due form of law by the State authority showing, so far as needs to be inquired into just here and now, precisely how many votes were cast for the Hayes electors and precisely how many votes were cast for the Tilden electors in every county of the State of Florida.

Then follows another act of the legislature. The executive has spoken; the canvassing-board erected under State authority has spoken; and now the legislature, another branch of the government, speaks in the same unmistakable tones by an act of the legislature of the 26th of January, 1877. The preamble recites that according to the returns from the several counties on file in the secretary of state's office, that according to the canvass made by the board, the Tilden electors were chosen in such manner as the legislature of the State had directed; that the original canvassers had interpreted the law defining their powers and duties in such a manner as to give them power to exclude certain regular returns, and did under such erroneous interpretation exclude certain returns, which interpretation had been solemnly adjudged by the supreme court to be improper and illegal. It also recites that Governor Stearns by means of such illegal action misled, deceived —no allegation of fraud it is true there, but misled, deceived—by this erroneous interpretation of the board of State canvassers, founded upon their erroneous interpretation of the law, and deceived by the illegal and erroneous canvass of the canvassers, did erroneously cause to be made a certified list containing the names of the Hayes electors, when in fact such persons had not received the highest number of votes, and on a canvass conducted according to the rules prescribed and adjudged by the supreme court, were not appointed electors or entitled to receive such lists from the governor, and that the Tilden electors were truly appointed electors and entitled to have their names made upon a list and certified by the governor. This is the preamble to this confirmatory act.

It then, in section 1, declares that the Tilden electors were duly appointed and authorized to act, and their acts are ratified and confirmed and declared to be valid, and that they were appointed on, from, and after the 7th of November, 1876. The second section authorizes the governor to make and certify three lists of electors; to transmit them in the manner therein mentioned; provides that the electors are to meet at Tallahassee, and that they are to give an additional certificate of the votes which had been cast by them on the 6th of December, and to send that to the President of the Senate as required by law.

So then, if the Commission please, in this return No. 3 we have practically all the branches of the government of the State of Florida speaking with unanimous and united voice to the same effect, and certifying to the same fact which is the question now before this tribunal for decision.

It is upon this evidence that this question is now to be determined; and the different kinds of evidence may be thus classified: They consist, first, of lists purporting to be made by the electors under the twelfth article of amendments to the Constitution, the certificates and lists made out under and in pursuance of that article of the Constitution. If these prove themselves, they both have the same force and effect, and this Commission would be at a loss to determine which one of these pieces of conflicting evidence is to be potential, and in any event this testimony must be deemed inconclusive. The second class of evidence are the lists of the executive under the one hundred and thirty-sixth section of the United States Revised Statutes. I shall not presume at this stage of the case to re-argue the question as to the conclusiveness of the governor's certificates. It would not be necessary to do so after what has already been said. Moreover I conceive that the order itself practically determines that question in the negative, for it permits other evidence. These governor's certificates are not essential. They are not made indispensable or conclusive or exclusive or invested with any particular force or effect by the statute. Their permanent absence would not be fatal to the validity of the vote of the electors. They are mere requests, not obligatory on the executive; there is no mode of compelling the performance of the duty imposed on him. And here, if the Commission please, I beg leave to call attention to the message of Governor Hancock of the commonwealth of Massachusetts, which will be found appended to a brief which we shall hand up, bearing the date of the 8th day of November, 1792. It is as follows:

Gentlemen of the Senate and the House of Representatives:

By the Constitution of the United States of America, each State is to appoint, in such manner as the legislature shall direct, electors of President and Vice-President. By a late act of Congress it is enacted " that the supreme executive of each State shall cause three lists of the names of the electors of such State to be made and certified, and to be delivered to the electors on or before the first Wednesday in December."

I feel the importance of giving every constitutional support to the General Government, and I also am convinced that the existence and well-being of that Government depends upon preventing a confusion of the authority of it with that of the States separately. But that Government applies itself to the people of the United States in their natural, individual capacity, and cannot exert any force upon, or by any means control, the officers of the State governments as such; therefore, when an act of Congress uses compulsory words with regard to any act to be done by the supreme executive of this commonwealth, I shall not feel myself obliged to obey them, because I am not, in my official capacity, amenable to that Government.

My duty as governor most certainly oblige me to see that proper and efficient certificates are made of the appointment of electors of President and Vice-President; and perhaps the mode suggested in the act above mentioned may be found to be the most proper. If you, gentlemen, have any mode to propose with respect to the conduct of this business, I shall pay every attention to it.

Gentlemen, I do not address you at this time from a disposition to regard the proceedings of the General Government with a jealous eye, nor do I suppose that Congress could intend that clause in their act as a compulsory provision; but I wish to prevent any measure to proceed through inattention, which may be drawn into precedents hereafter to the injury of the people or to give a constructive power where the Federal Constitution has not expressly given it.

This injunction, therefore, is not mandatory in its character; it is not obligatory upon the State officers; it is not addressed to the electors who cast the votes or to the tribunal which counts them; but to a third party to do an act for the convenience of the electors and of the counting tribunal. But it has been intimated, and it may be argued perhaps, that this certificate or return No. 3 did not arrive at the seat of Government before the first Wednesday in January, according to a forced construction, as it seems to us, of the one hundred and fortieth section of the Revised Statutes of the United States. We respectfully submit to the Commission that this provision of the Revised Statutes of the United States in section 140, as well as the direction contained in section 136 as to the delivery of the lists by the executive to the electors, is merely directory. Upon that subject I desire to call the attention of the Commission—I shall not stop to read it—to what is said in Sedgwick on Statutory and Constitutional Law, page 368 of the edition of 1857, and also to recall to the attention of the Commission what was said by Lord Mansfield in the case of the King *vs.* Loxdale in 1 Burrows's Reports, page 447.

There is a known distinction between the circumstances which are of the essence of the thing required to be done by an act of Parliament and clauses merely directory. The precise time in many cases is not of the essence.

Now, if the Commission look at the purpose of this enactment, if they will consider what were the reasons which induced the Congress of the United States to prescribe the times therein mentioned, we submit that they will come to the conclusion that the time or times mentioned therein within certain prescribed limits are not of the essence, and that they are not essential to the purpose which the legislature had in view when they made the enactment. Delay in the transmission of the certificates within proper limits cannot produce any invalidity or work any legal consequences. The reason the governor is directed in section 136 to furnish the list on or before the meeting of the electoral college was doubtless that the college may not be hindered in annexing the lists on the first day of their meeting if they choose then to annex them to their statements of the votes they cast for President and Vice-President. There is no express direction anywhere which requires that the electoral college, after it shall have met and cast its ballots, shall immediately proceed to make out the lists which are to be transmitted to the President of the Senate. There is no express declaration anywhere, either in the Constitution or in the laws, that if they do not immediately proceed to make out and certify their lists, which are to be sent to the President of the Senate, their action shall be nugatory. The main fact which is to be determined is, did the electors vote according to the constitutional requirement? If they did so vote, the lists which they are to send to the President of the Senate may as soon as can conveniently be done be made out and sent; but there is no absolute requirement that they shall be so made out and sent immediately.

The first Wednesday in December is fixed by the statute for the meeting of the electors. The delivery of the statement by the electors of their votes by messenger to the President of the Senate at the seat of Government is to be made at any time before the first Wednesday in January. Thirty days are thus allowed for transmission and delivery. No doubt, we submit, it would be a perfect compliance with this provision if the electors' statement of their votes were made out and the list of the governor obtained and annexed at any time so that the delivery should be made within the thirty days. It is true that the statement of the votes to be forwarded by mail and the statement to be deposited with the district judge are required to be sent forthwith; but the one transmitted by messenger would be good whether the others reached the seat of Government or not. And practically it is matter of public notoriety that the occasion has never, or if ever very seldom, arisen when the certificate deposited with the district judge has been called in requisition or has reached the seat of Government. No time is fixed by any of the statutes of the United States for the arrival at the seat of Government of the certificate deposited with the district judge. If it was received at any time before it was to be used in the counting of the votes, we submit that that would be sufficient. The vote could not be objected to because it had not arrived earlier.

Now, taking all these statutory provisions together, they exhibit careful precautions that the votes shall be received before the count. That is the point to be arrived at, that the votes shall be received before the counting takes place. Whether they get here one day after the meeting of the electoral college or thirty days after the meeting of the electoral college is immaterial. The point to be arrived at is that they get to the seat of Government before the count.

The specifications of the times at which or before which acts shall be done to furnish evidence to the counting tribunal as to who have been appointed electors and for whom those electors have voted are merely directory. The times are fixed so that each act shall be done in season to enable the next step to be promptly taken and in season to enable any failures to be remedied. These limitations of the time are precautionary and remedial; they are intended to save and give effect to the votes. They are not snares to betray and destroy the votes.

This line of argument is carried out more fully in the printed brief which we shall submit to the Commission, and I therefore pass to another point. We contend that these certified lists which are contained in return No. 3, and furnished afterward, are effectual. We submit the proposition that such acts of public officers, if not done within the time prescribed by law, do not thereby become incapable of being done afterward. They do not only remain capable of being done, but the duty of public officers to do them subsists in full vigor and operation, and the right to compel their performance by public officers accrues for the very reason that the time limited by the law has passed.

I beg to call the attention of the tribunal upon that point to what is said by the court of Queen's Bench in 11 Adolphus and Ellis:

It would be too great a triumph for injustice if we should enable it to postpone forever the performance of a plain duty only because it had done wrong at the right season.

This same idea is illustrated by the doctrine of the courts in regard to mandamus. It is often invoked on the very ground that the time fixed by law for specific acts has expired. In the case of The Mayor of Rochester *vs.* The Queen, in 1 Blackburn and Ellis, page 1024, the court say:

We are of opinion that the court of Queen's Bench was right, and ought to be affirmed. It seems to us that Rex *vs.* Sparrow, 2 Strange, 1123, and Rex *vs.* Mayor of Norwich, 1 B. and Adolphus, 310, are authorities upon the point, and that the principle of those cases establishes the doctrine that the court of Queen's Bench ought to compel the performance of a public duty by public officers, *although the time prescribed by statute for the performance of them has passed.*

And in particular I refer to what is said by the supreme court of New York in the case of *ex parte* Heath, 3 Hill R., 42, which was an election case coming up on proceedings for mandamus:

Ward inspectors of New York City were required by statute to certify the result of the ward election " on *the day subsequent* to the closing of the polls, or sooner." A ward election was held on the 12th of April; the result was not certified until the 14th.

The return was held valid notwithstanding, and the mandamus was directed to go commanding the mayor to administer the oath to the persons·returned as elected. In the opinion of the court it is said:

The idea which we understood to be thrown out in argument, that the return from the sixth ward was void because not completed till the 14th of April instead of the 13th, is altogether inadmissible. Nothing is better settled, as a general rule, than that where a statute requires an act to be done by an officer *within a certain time,* for a public purpose, the statute shall be taken to be merely directory; and though he neglects his duty by allowing the precise time to go by, if he afterward perform it, the public shall not suffer by the delay.

I next call the attention of the tribunal to another piece of evidence which is of the third class, namely, the act of the legislature of January 17, 1877. This is a curative act, simply allowing and requiring a piece of evidence to be supplied after the time within which the law required the public officers to furnish it. I shall not trouble the Commission with going over it again. I simply call their attention to the fact that this is what it seeks to accomplish. It is a curative act. It simply allows and requires this piece of evidence to be supplied after the time within which the law required the public officers to furnish it, but before it is needed for the use intended; it is allowing an act to be done *nunc pro tunc* in furtherance of right and justice, as courts sometimes do, curing a defect of form, which the law-making power has a large discretion to do and frequently and habitually does.

It has been suggested to this Commission, rather than gravely argued, that this act, as well as the other act of the State of Florida, is to be considered in some sense as an *ex post facto* law. I submit to this tribunal that neither of these laws comes within the definition of *ex post facto* laws. They are retrospective and retroactive, but not *ex post facto* laws. It certainly will not be necessary for me to do more than to refer the Commission to what is said upon that subject by Mr. Justice Chase in 3 Dallas, in the celebrated case of Calder *vs.* Bull, more particularly to what he says on the three hundred and ninetieth page:

I will state what laws I consider *ex post facto* laws, within the words and the intent of the prohibition. First. Every law that makes an action done before the passing of the law, and which was innocent when done, criminal; and punishes such action. Second. Every law that aggravates a crime, or makes it greater than it was when committed.

The PRESIDENT. Mr. Green, it is hardly necessary to cite authorities to us that that is not an *ex post facto* law within the meaning of the Constitution.

Mr. GREEN. I am very happy to be relieved from further discussion of the character of these legislative acts.

The PRESIDENT. I do not suppose anybody in the Commission has any doubt about that.

Mr. GREEN. Then the next piece of evidence is the actual canvass on file in the secretary of state's office, showing in detail the votes of the several counties and the election of the Tilden electors. Superadded to all this, we submit to the Commission, that even under the order which was read to us this morning, in the light of the governor's certificate, this Commission has a right to look into these *quo warranto* proceedings with a view of seeing what they are. I shall not discuss that; I shall simply call the attention of the Commission in passing to the fact that they will find noted on the brief already handed up that the jurisdiction of the circuit court of the State of Florida is ample and full, that the authorities are there cited, and I beg leave to ask the Commission to refer to them. I only allude to it now in order that our learned friends on the other side may take notice that we conceive and shall insist that, even under the order of the Commission read to us this morning, by virtue of the governor's certificate which is the commencement of return No. 3, this Commission may look into and consider the *quo warranto* proceedings and their effect upon the question now before us.

The only additional authorities that we desire to call the attention of the Commission to on the subject of that *quo warranto* are, the Commonwealth *vs.* Smith, 45 Pennsylvania State Reports, page 59, where Mr. Justice Woodward, delivering the opinion of the court, held this language:

I have no doubt that *quo warranto* brought within the term of an office may be well tried after the term has expired.

And the case of Hunter *vs.* Chandler, 45 Missouri, page 435, where the court held that an information in the nature of a *quo warranto* to try the right to a public office may be tried after the term has expired or the officer holding has resigned, if the information was filed or the proceedings begun before resignation took place or the term had expired.

The sixth class of evidence is the confirmatory act of January 26, 1877. I shall say nothing on that subject, except to ask the attention of the tribunal to what is stated on the brief which we shall hand up.

Now, if the Commission please, we rest here upon the testimony before you, and we humbly submit to the tribunal that even upon that testimony, meager as it is contended to be, there is but one proper conclusion to be arrived at, namely, that this voice of the State of Florida which is uttered not only by its executive and legislative, but by its judicial departments, shall be respected, and that this Commission cannot come to any other determination than that the vote of the State of Florida is truly contained in the returns 2 and 3, and is not correctly returned in the return No. 1.

No one can be more aware than I am how inadequately I have endeavored to rise to the height of this great argument. If I have failed to convince your judgments as judges, I shall not appeal to your patriotism as statesmen; but here in this place consecrated by the memories of those early senatorial conflicts which resulted so often in the preservation of the Union and the maintenance of the Constitution, as well as by the recollection of the decisions of the most august tribunal upon earth which is accustomed here to assemble in favor of human freedom and of human rights; in the name of the American people; in the name of that Constitution which we all have sworn to uphold and maintain; in the name of that Union to form and perpetuate which the Constitution was framed, and of that liberty which is at once the origin and the result of that Union; not as a partisan; not as an advocate of Mr. Tilden or Mr. Hendricks; nor yet as an opponent of Mr. Hayes or Mr. Wheeler, but as an American citizen, speaking to American citizens, I demand your judgment for the right.

The PRESIDENT. We will now hear the other side.

Mr. SHELLABARGER. Mr. President and gentlemen of the Commission, this morning before I knew how thoroughly all that part of the papers that were laid before this Commission which relate to those matters occurring subsequently to the date of the electoral vote had been disposed of by your order, I had arranged to speak a very few minutes in regard to those matters—their competency in this case. Since I came into court and heard the decision of the Commission excluding the offer of testimony touching the date of the service of process in the *quo warranto* case, all that part of the case of Florida which I had proposed to discuss seems to me to be thoroughly disposed of and such discussion rendered unnecessary. It is only because on the other side discussion has been indulged in with regard to the effect of matters subsequent to the electoral vote that I venture to do what I would not otherwise do, make some few remarks in regard to the legal value of those matters that follow in point of time the date of that vote.

It will be observed by reading what has been here called certificate No. 3, that there can reasonably be no possible claim that the record in the proceedings in *quo warranto* is in any sense or way before this Commission. The only papers before the Commission are those which were submitted to the Commission by the President of the Senate or submitted to the Houses and thence here. In those papers, thus submitted, there is but one allusion to this proceeding in *quo warranto*, and that is where the governor, Drew, states that—

In a proceeding on the part of the State of Florida, by information in the nature of *quo warranto*, wherein the said Robert Bullock, Robert B. Hilton, Wilkinson Call, and James E. Yonge were relators, and Charles H. Pearce, Frederick C. Humphreys, William H. Holden, and Thomas W. Long were respondents, the circuit court of this State for the second judicial circuit, after full consideration of the law and the proofs produced on behalf of the parties respectively, by its judgment determined that said relators were, at said election, in fact and law, elected such electors as against the said respondents and all other persons.

That being the only thing that is before this Commission, it will not be claimed, I think, even on the other side, that there is any evidence in the record before this body that any judgment in *quo warranto* was ever pronounced. The governor cannot make you acquainted with the existence of the record in that way. The action of the Commission in excluding that manuscript copy of the record of such judgment tendered as evidence, in moreover excluding all evidence about the date of service of process, taken in connection with all else which has transpired, makes it entirely and utterly certain that we have reached a stage in the case where at least that proceeding and judgment in *quo warranto* are excluded. So, too, in regard to the certificates No. 2 and No. 3. These are, as we regard the matter, and for precisely the same reasons which exclude the *quo warranto* case, now excluded by the order that has already been made. Still, since discussion by the other side in regard to the effect of these papers, Nos. 2 and 3, has been indulged in, I desire to make a few statements in the way of mere propositions rather than of extended argument, in regard to the whole matter of the legal effect upon the electoral vote of transactions of the State functionaries occurring after the date of such vote.

Now I state my foundation proposition in regard to all these post-election matters—whether it be the mandamus, the legislation of January, the *quo warranto*, the canvass by the improvised returning-board, or any other act post-dating the electoral vote—in these words, that "this power bestowed by the Constitution upon the State, of appointing an electoral college for the election of a President and Vice-President of the United States, is such, in its very nature, and by the necessities of the case, that every act of the State in accomplishing the 'appointment' must antedate the performance of that one single function which the appointee is competent to discharge under the Constitution." If that proposition is sound, then of course all that the gentlemen say in regard to the effect of the decisions of the courts in determining the signification of their own statutes, all the decisions which have been referred to in regard to the obligation of all Federal tribunals to follow the interpretation which the State courts put upon their own statutes, lose all significance in this case. In other words, if when the electoral vote of a State has once been cast by men endowed with every muniment of title to the office of elector which the laws of the State enabled them to hold at the date when they must do their first and last official act, the power of the State to manipulate that vote, its jurisdiction over it. has gone away from the State to the nation, then, of course, these acts of Florida done after the electoral vote, in the frantic effort to change the result of a national election, lose every semblance of legal significance.

The strongest statement I have heard of the position of the gentlemen on the other side in regard to the grounds on which they rest their claim of right in these States to handle, by means of *quo warranto* and the like, the electoral vote after it has gone under seal to the President of the Senate is in its substance this: It is, they say, competent for the States, not to appoint electors after the voting-day, not to qualify them after the voting-day, but competent for them through their courts, after the voting-day has passed, to make interpretations of their own election laws which shall act backward, shall throw light on and bindingly decide the question who of rival claimants were the true functionaries of the State on that voting-day and thus competent for the States to settle the question which of the two rival bodies were really the lawful electors of the State. That is, I think, about the substance of the strongest statement I have seen of this claim, so zealously pressed by the other side, alleging power in the State after the electoral vote is cast to destroy it, and to unseat a President, though elected by electors who held in favor of their title every judgment, determination, and certificate which it was *possible* for the State to bestow under her existing laws, *before* the time when the electoral vote must be cast and sent off, under seal, to its Federal custody.

Let us analyze that claim for a moment, and see if it is not utterly unsound. The Constitution in its express terms *limits* the powers of the State to that matter which it has denominated tersely by the word "appoint." About this first point there *can* be no debate. The utmost power, the furthest reach of the State in regard to this matter of making a President stops when "*appointment*" stops; not a hair's breadth beyond that anywhere can the State go in creating your President by the popular vote. Then when we get the true sense of the word "*appoint*" we know the boundary of the powers of the State in this regard.

Now, sirs, what gentleman of this Commission, so learned as it is in all these great constitutional and legal ideas, will say to me, "There are *some* functions in the nature of 'appointment'—functions which go to make up 'appointment'—which the States may exercise *after* the office has passed away and all its duties are done forever ?" Such a proposition as that simply reduces the Constitution and this whole debate, I submit, to the most intense and unmitigated absurdity. Therefore every act of the State in the way of exercising power must be " appointment," and " appointment " in the very nature of the case cannot follow the day when the first and the last and the only act of the functionary must, by the Constitution and law, be completely and forever discharged. Is it not plain, therefore, thus far, that it was the design of the Constitution, is the express requirement of the Constitution, that every act of the State, being all appointment and appointment only, shall antedate the vote ?

Mr. Commissioner THURMAN. If it does not interrupt you, let me ask this : Suppose it to be granted that every act which constitutes the appointment must be done before the day when the electors cast their votes, does it follow that there can be no inquiry afterward as to whether any appointment was made ?

Mr. SHELLABARGER. I shall come to that in a moment, and I thank the Senator and member of the Commission for the suggestion. It is really the same idea to which I alluded when I undertook to state the position of the other side as well as I could, as to whether acts subsequently to the day of voting and to the appointment may not be looked to as throwing light or deciding upon the matter as to who the appointee really was, as made on the day of the vote. That is a fair question. It deserves a fair, frank, and square answer, and I shall make it as I proceed, as well as I can.

First of all, when the Constitution is confessed to design that the power of the State over the votes shall stop at the moment it puts them under seal, then that confession involves the admission that that is the moment at which the State must have completed all the scrutinies and trials it can employ in adjudging who are its electors. In other words, if an elector on the voting-day is endowed with all the insignia of right, with all the apparent title of office that *can*, according to the then existing State machinery, be held on that day, he *is*, to every possible legal intent, *as against the State*, the elector both *de facto* and *de jure*. If after that any power can try the title, it is not the State, but the nation. That arises out of the very nature of this *sui generis* thing with which we deal, this dual government of ours, having no likeness anywhere else in the governments of the world or in the law-books of the world. It is a case where two sovereignties combine, not in the mere process of making an election—for it is more than that—combine their powers in the process of inaugurating government and of creating the executive branch of a powerful people, in transmitting succession; a process wherein the boundary-line between the powers of the two sovereigns is carefully marked in the Constitution. That boundary is at the point where the vote is sealed and goes to the capital. At that time, before that vote, the State must have done her last act in adjudging who are her electors and bestowing the evidences of their title.

When that process is complete on the part of the State, when all that she is permitted to transact in the way of appointing her electors has been discharged according—to repeat what I said a moment ago, and I wish to state it with the utmost care about my words—when that political transaction by the State has been discharged according to the requirements of the law of the State as it existed upon the day of voting, then the power of the State over the subject-matter is an accomplished process of government on the part of the State, and the power of the

State over the subject-matter has passed forever away. It becomes from that moment a matter of Federal care and solicitude, and not of State. In other words, and to state my proposition in still another form, every part of the machinery of a State which it proposes to make use of in the business of making a Federal elector must be placed in point of time in front of the exercise of the office of an elector. No part of it can be placed behind, because on that day the power of the State over the subject-matter is completely and forever ended.

Now, in the way of enforcing this view, let me take some propositions that seem to me to be exceedingly conclusive in regard to it. In the first place take the common, plain, practical, every-day, non-lawyer sense of the thing, and how does it look then? Everybody agrees that the trial of the matter as to who is appointed is a *part of the appointment itself*. Therefore I concede that it is within the power of the State to try the title of her electors. She can try it by *quo warranto;* she can try it by any machinery she pleases. It is within the province of the State to try the question by her own machinery as to whom she has selected to cast her vote; but if she makes any part of that machinery up in such a way that the trial cannot come until after the office is performed, then she must content herself with such scrutinies as she has arranged in advance of the discharge of the function of the elector. How would an act of a legislature sound which read: "*Be it enacted,* That this State reserves to herself the power to try by *quo warranto* who were her Federal electors after the time when they are compelled to cast the electoral vote?" Would not such an act be, on its very face, simply a monstrosity? Would it help it any to add the proviso: "*Provided,* That somebody shall start the *quo warranto* suit before the vote is cast?"

Suppose you should see a system of government that deliberately placed any part of the trial or "contest" of an election to an office after the office by the very organic law must have been performed and passed away! You would say, would you not, that such a system was simply insane? To give to the States the power here claimed would be not only this degree of insanity, but would also enable the States to contest an election after every possible function of the office must have been discharged, and also it places this contest and destruction of the vote by the State after the time when all the State's power over the vote is carefully withdrawn. More even than this; it enables any one who can manipulate the courts of the States to render an election by the people impossible, or, at best, within the mercy of the courts. Surely, such is not the insanity of the Constitution. In *this* view, therefore, I repeat that the State *must,* by the very nature of the case, place her election machinery for testing or determining, whether by her returning-board, or by courts in *quo warranto,* or in whatever tribunal she may please, the question whom she has selected, before the time when the office expires, her powers over the vote have ended, and her act has become an investiture of government by act of the State.

But take another step. Everybody agrees—the Constitution's terms and its history both combine to make everybody agree—that the reasons why the Constitution held back from the State and kept within the nation the power to fix the day for counting the vote, also the requirement that the day shall be the same in all the States, also the requirement that the vote shall be by ballot and that it shall remain under seal from the moment of its casting until the day of its counting—those requirements are confessed all to be in the Constitution for the vital purpose of rendering it impossible for the States to intrigue after they knew the votes of sister States, for the changing of the result of the election. They meant that no *post hac* judgments, no political intrigues, no subsidized courts, should be enabled to destroy the votes of States and unseat a President after they had found out just how many votes must be destroyed, by purchased judgments in *quo warranto*, in order to unseat a President elected and even inaugurated according to all the forms of law. And here let it be remembered forever that in order to unseat Presidents by this modern plan of post-election *quo warranto*, it is not necessary that any rival electors should have voted on the election-day. All that is needed is that enough *quo warrantos* shall be got to adjudge bad enough of the electors of the successful party to change the result.

The third volume of Elliot's Debates, page 101, Story on the Constitution, section 1475, and every other commentator on that subject, state the reason of the stopping the power of the States over the votes at election-day, sealing them up, and casting of them on the same day, just as I have stated it now. No debate is possible with regard to that vital object, or about that being the design, or at least the leading design, of these provisions. Now, what will be the effect upon these provisions of the Constitution of suffering the States, by judgment in *quo warranto* or acts of legislation or any other act destructive of a State's vote *after they have found out* how their sister States have voted, to change the result by placing *some part* of the machinery of the State for contesting this election after the election is over, and all power over the subject-matter of the election has passed over to the nation? Plainly, most manifestly, right on its face, it completely destroys every object for which those provisions making the voting-day the same, and the like, were put into the Constitution.

Your honors, if I, in my own State, being an earnest partisan, after I have found out how my sister States have voted and after I have learned that it only requires, say, nineteen votes to be destroyed in order to change the presidential election, can go to work in my local *nisi prius* court, and get a judgment in *quo warranto*, and this in my own name, and without the leave of my State, (as is done in Florida,) that will unseat the electors of my State and unseat a President, then I have turned the Government into a farce and the Constitution into a sham. I know such a caricature of our form of government is revolting to every mind that I now address; and yet I defy the ingenuity of counsel to devise a reply which will show that these opportunities for mischief, nay, sir, these mischiefs themselves, will not come if you suffer the determination by the States of who were their electors to come after they have found out how the other States have voted.

But the reply is made to that, "We commenced our *quo warranto* before the vote was cast." Pray, gentlemen of the Commission, tell me how does that relieve the subject of its difficulties? It puts you just in this position: Mark you, this was an information (and so it may be in every State if they so enact) upon the part, not of the State, but of a set of defeated candidates. It therefore puts it in the power of every individual who is disappointed, who is unhappy about results, or who is "enterprising," to attack and destroy the title to the greatest office of the world, and to precipitate the nation in revolution and unutterable disaster. The mere fact that such a one chooses to launch such a speculative—a private, speculative, or tentative *quo warranto*, before the voting is done, and thus putting himself in the position of preparing for emergencies after he finds out how his sister States have voted—putting himself in the position of "commanding the situation," in the situation of taking time by the forelock, of getting hold of the reins, puts him in the position of defeating and defying the provisions of the Constitution setting bounds to the power of the States over the votes, thereby causing them all to be trampled down.

All this is to be done by the simple act of a private individual in a *nisi-prius* court, in a partisan court, starting a suit that cannot be tried until long after the election is over—starting a suit for the purpose of holding the reins and commanding the situation. How does that launching of a suit before the vote relieve the subject of its difficulties? Not in the slightest degree. I submit with the utmost deference both to the learned counsel on the other side and to the Commission, not the slightest. You cannot travel an inch in that direction without destroying the guarantees that the Constitution has so wisely furnished whereby a presidential election is an accomplished fact so far as the States are concerned contemporaneously throughout the Union. Was that not wise—do not the debates on the Constitution show you the sagacity and the marvelous foresight of your fathers when they made it so that it was impossible for the States to find out, in advance of their own action, how their sisters had voted? Do not the perils of this hour, nay, the appalling dangers which now we trust in God are passing away, in which we see these attempts to overthrow the votes of the States because so few overthrown will change the result, impress us anew with the wisdom of the provision which requires all the States to take off all their hands at the same hour from all presidential votes?

But, gentlemen of the Commission, there is another part of this great theme that is equally conclusive; and indeed I have not followed the points that I had marked in my brief at all. I have gone over as many of them as I care to go over at this time, except the one that I now come to.

In the very able argument that was offered by Mr. O'Conor, he stated what seemed to me to be the strongest proposition on his side that he did state at all. It was stated in reply to our proposition that the elector who on the election-day was endowed with all the insignia of office which the State laws enabled him to hold on that day, and who thus endowed cast the vote of the State, that such an officer, so endowed, had in *fact* and in law then and thereby *accomplished an act of government;* that whether he were an officer *de jure* or *de facto*, still being upon that day so endowed, so IN OFFICE, so acting in the actual occupancy of office, with all apparent right, that in such case such act constituted *an act of government*, that thereby the act of the State was accomplished in law—it was *government*, not mere *election*, but *government*—government inaugurated, accomplished, endowed. That was our proposition, and that, therefore, whether *de jure* or *de facto* an elector, provided he had all the evidences and insignia of right, the act was good as the act of the State, and I stand by that. But it was met by what, I say, was the strongest position that can be taken against it, and it was about this, as near as I can state it; I shall be pardoned if I state it with less strength than it was stated by the distinguished author of it. It was about this: "You are mistaken, gentlemen; that is not an act of government; it is not an exercise of official power by one in office, which, if not sustained, if stricken down, would hurt some third person, some public, some other person." "That is not your case," says Mr. O'Conor, "but this is your case: your case is that of an attempted vote, that vote by a man having no power to cast it, and it is arrested on its way to Government *in transitu;* it is arrested by our process in the nature of a *quo warranto*, and therefore it is not at all the case of a *de facto* exercise of authority."

One of the errors of that position, the one that strikes me as the fatal one, and I submit it with the utmost deference, is that it misstates the nature of the legal characteristics of this business of a State casting its vote by its electors. That is government, bless you; that is more than an election; it is government. It is the last act of the State in exercising its part of the creation of a President. It is, therefore, when done, government accomplished, irrevocably done.

My friend's position is, if I conceive the truth of this point, utterly fallacious in that it assumes a legal status that does not belong to the case you are dealing with, a case where a State has endowed her elector with all the right which her machinery enables that elector to hold on the day that he must vote. He has it all; every appearance of right. Now the law says, the Constitution says, the necessities of the case say that a man thus endowed on that day when the act must be accomplished, if ever, can perform an act of government, and he does do it. Therefore the public is hurt, the community is hurt, your country is hurt, the Constitution, all its designs are hurt, if you strike down an act of government performed and forever performed on the only day that it could be performed, by men who had every insignia of right that the State laws enabled them to have on the day when it was performed. Therefore it is the act of a man *de facto*, an officer whether *de jure* so or not, and his act is government accomplished when it is performed under all the apparent rights of office that our electors were surrounded with.

In enforcement of that view, suffer me to call your attention to some language in the case of Potter *vs*. Robbins, in Clarke and Hall's Contested Elections, pages 900 and 901. I ought to say in regard to this case what, if I am in error about, the very learned gentlemen of the Commission will correct me, that I understand that ever since its announcement it has been admitted and held to be, in so far as it goes in the way of exposition, the law of the Constitution upon the subject to which it relates. It was pronounced in the year 1834 by the Senate of the United States, in one of the most celebrated debates that ever occurred, so far as I know, in the history of the Senate, in regard to the question of a right to a seat in that body. Among the men who debated it and who sustained the position that is here stated that I am about to read, you will find such names as Bell, Calhoun, Clay, Clayton, Ewing, Frelinghuysen, Kent, Mangum, Poindexter, Preston, Webster, and others, embracing of course some of the most illustrious names of our country, nearly all of whom participated in this debate and who voted to sustain the proposition that I am about to read. It was a case where the legislature of Rhode Island, after it had elected Mr. Robbins to the Senate, undertook at a subsequent meeting of the legislature to declare that election worthless, to take it back, to put in the place of Mr. Robbins Mr. Potter, whom they elected six months after they had elected Mr. Robbins. The report in the case discusses the power of the State to withdraw the act of election on the one hand and the power of the Senate on the other hand to look into the question whether or not some members of that legislature were or were not entitled to vote. Upon the question of the power of the State to take back any part of its act in creating a Senator, and also the question of the power of the Senate to look into the question of the individual right of members to vote in the body that composed the legislature, the report in that case used language that I now read:

In the performance of this duty, the State acts in its highest sovereign capacity, and the causes which would render the election of a Senator void, must be such—

And I call attention to this language because it is the most terse, the best stated that I have seen on the subject—

as would destroy the validity of all laws enacted by the body by which the Senator was chosen.

It must go to the destruction of the body itself, and cannot inquire into the eligibility of the persons that made the election. Now, omitting some, I read this:

But where the sovereign will of the State is made known through its legislature, and consummated by its proper official functionaries in due form, it would be a dangerous exertion of power to look behind the commission for defects in the component parts of the legislature, or into the peculiar organization of the body for reasons to justify the Senate in declaring its acts absolutely null and void. Such a power, if carried to its legitimate extent, would subject the entire scope of State legislation to be overruled by our decision, and even the right of suffrage of individual members of the legislature, whose elections were contested, might be set aside. It would also lead to investigations into the motives of members in casting their votes, for the purpose of establishing a charge of bribery or corruption in particular cases. These matters, your committee think, properly belong to the tribunals of the State, and cannot constitute the basis on which the Senate could, without an infringement of State sovereignty, claim the right to declare the election of a Senator void, who possessed the requisite qualifications and was chosen according to the forms of law and the Constitution.

What now is the application of that to this occasion? Manifestly this: The closest analogy which we have at all under our system of government to this choice by the States of electors is the one I have just read from, is the choice of a Senator. The language of the Constitution in regard to the election of Senators is that they shall be chosen by the legislature, and that that choice shall be in such manner as the legislature shall prescribe—almost the precise words of the Constitution in regard to the manner of choosing electors.

It is true that the Senate itself, having the large, unlimited range of vision that belongs to courts when trying *quo warrantos*, having the power of trying the election of its members, cannot without invading the rights of the States go behind the action of the legally-constituted legislature for the purpose of inquiring into the eligibility of the men who created the appointment, cannot strike down that act of the legislature except, to adopt the words of this report, for causes that would render the laws passed by the legislature invalid. If that be so, I say, in regard to this limitation on the powers of the Senate on one side to overthrow the action of the States in making the election, and also on the other side limiting the powers of the States to take back an election that is accomplished according to the forms of law, if that be true in this case, as it is, then it must be true, I submit, utterly true beyond fair room for debate, that when the States, whose power is limited to a single act of appointing according to the requirements of the legislature electors, have made that appointment, have made it on the only day that they could, have made it by the men who held on that day every vestige and indication of right which it was possible to hold on the day of election—if it be true, I say, that such is the limitation as between the Senate and its members, how much more thoroughly true must it be that this body having no power but the power to count— I care not now how latitudinary you may make that word signify for the purposes of this Commission, still it is but a power to count—how much more true must it be that under your power to count you cannot assume that these officers, appointed according to the form of every law that existed on election-day, holding all the authority that the legislature enabled them to hold on that day, certified by every certificate that it was possible to hold under the laws of the States on that day, you, with no other power than the power to count, cannot go back and destroy by *quo warranto* or anything else that act after the accomplishment of the election of a President, and thus throw away, destroy, overthrow an election accomplished according to all the forms of law.

Gentlemen, I say without exaggeration and without falling into any extravagance that comes from heat of debate, that it is inevitably true that if you suffer men to start away down in the piepoudre courts of our country, on their own private motion, quo warrantos, or bills in the legislature, or any act that shall unseat the President of the United States before the day of counting, you can unseat him after. I challenge gentlemen to show where that rule of law is that shall say, "thus far thou mayest go, and no farther." If you can unseat Mr. Tilden to-day, he being the President, by a judgment of a republican court in my republican State you can do it after he is in office, for there is no limitation upon the power; and there is no principle that compels the courts that have jurisdiction in *quo warranto*, and whose case is simply started before the vote, to make their decision before the count in February; no principle that compels them to make their decision before the inauguration-day; and you establish that rule, and you have at once put it in the power of the States, as I have already remarked, to overthrow the Constitution, to destroy it in this, its very citadel, and to end the life of the state.

I thank you, gentlemen, for the very singular kindness with which I have been listened to.

Mr. EVARTS. Mr. President and gentlemen of the Commission, the wisdom of the method and order of this examination adopted by the Commission has fully proved itself in its execution. The intelligent and experienced and learned minds acting in the Commission saw at once that the decisive lines of the controversy were to be determined upon the limitation of their powers and the limitation of the subjects and the means for producing those subjects upon which those powers were to act. In the full discussion accorded to counsel, and in the deliberations of the Commission extended during the periods of their private session, the result is disclosed in this form and to this effect, that this Commission will receive no evidence, and will merely inspect the certificates that the Constitution and the laws of the United States have authorized for transmission, and as such, received by the President of the Senate, have been opened to the two Houses, save in one particular, that in aiding them to inspect these certificates, and, within the limits of the information there disclosed, determine and advise the two Houses of Congress how many and what votes shall be counted for the State of Florida, it will receive evidence touching the eligibility of one of the named electors appointed. In that determination I do not understand the Commission to have overpassed the question, what the effect is as to the acceptance or rejection of a vote thus challenged for ineligibility, but to have decided that on that point they will receive the evidence that may be offered in order that they may determine in the first place whether upon the facts the exception taken to Humphreys's vote is maintainable; and secondly, whether, if maintainable and maintained upon the facts, the methods of the Constitution and the duty now presently being discharged permit of any rejection from the certificated vote transmitted and opened of the vote of an elector upon that ground.

I will first deal with the question of fact. I call the attention of the Commission to the proposition that the point of exception under the Constitution, the matter proposed of disqualification under the Constitution, is simply this: that at the time of his appointment he filled an

office of honor or emolument under the United States. I except to the
mode of proof as to its effect when it stops where it did, that was used
by the excepting party to his qualification, that they used a commission
of the date of 1872 and proved no occupation of the office later than
August, 1876. I understand that when, under the certificate of a governor the vote of a State is in the very process of counting, to be questioned in the presence of the two Houses of Congress, no exception that
shall proceed for its prosperity upon the power of the exceptor to find an
old commission and then take advantage of the unreadiness or want of
notice that the exception was to be raised is admissible, to argue from the
ancient case that all things remain as they were until contradicted. The
danger of that proposition in a transaction of this nature can be at once
discerned. Let whosoever take up the burden of proving that on the 7th
day of November one of these certified electors having the warrant of the
seal and authority of the State as having been elected was disqualified
for that election, he must prove it down to and as of that day. But
when the proof stops there, the neighbor, the friend, the lawyer whose
dealings are to fill out with living effect the dead commission, stops with
his necessary proof in the month of August, you have failed to find that
actual possession and use of the office, even presumptively, beyond the
date, for no reason was given in the witness's evidence why his knowledge stopped there unless the action of the officer stopped there.

You must dispose of this question of fact upon some method of strictness suitable to the nature of the transaction in which you are engaged
and suitable to the exercise of the duty, not under an organized and arranged Commission like this, but as an ordinary discharge of constitutional duty by the two Houses in their joint convention; and I submit
that there is no claim, the proof there stopping, that it is to be regarded
as a challenge which requires the fact that he was in office on the 7th
of November to be presumed.

I now come to the counter-proof, supposing that that step is passed;
and the counter-proof, not challenged in form, comes to this, that, early
in October, Humphreys resigned in writing his office to the circuit judge
of that circuit, and received from him an acceptance of the resignation,
such judge proceeding to instruct him to turn over whatever of public
means for the exercise of the office he held to the collector of customs,
who would discharge the office, such judge at the same time advising
the collector of the accepted resignation and of the devolution of the
office upon him, followed by the evidence of Mr. Humphreys that thereafter, from the early day in October, he himself discharged no part of
its duties and held out no professions of capacity to discharge them,
and moreover that the collector from that time thenceforth until after the
period of inquiry, the 7th of November, and perhaps till now, occupied
the office and discharged its duties.

Upon this plenary and apparently conclusive proof, an objection is
made that as the appointment was made by the circuit court, the
resignation could only be made to and received by the court in session,
and that no such session having taken place, within the meaning of
the Constitution of the United States which prescribes as a qualification
for an elector that he should not exercise an office under the United
States, Mr. Humphreys was an officer of the United States on the 7th
day of November. Now, this office had no term whatever prescribed
by statute; it had no enlargement by necessity or by prescription
beyond the present will of resignation. The office itself was secured
for the public by no clause requiring it to be occupied and exercised
until a successor was qualified. There was no need of the office being

refilled. The act took care of the service by prescribing that when there was no officer of this kind the collector should discharge the duty of this act of Congress.

Upon that state of law, in view of the existing legislation of Congress on the subject of resignations to which I shall call your attention, is it to be pretended for a moment that there was any power to hold an occupant of that office to the performance of its duties one moment beyond his will? Can it be pretended that, beyond the necessity of the conveyance of the resignation as determining that will, executed and placed in the power of the authority thus made its depositary, he could be held under any law, if there had been any, or his sureties under any law or jurisprudence enforcing the obligations of sureties, for the failure to perform acts or to do duties after his office was thus resigned?

Besides, look at the nature of this disqualification as proposed to the voters in the State of Florida and those who produce the candidates and name them to be voted for. Is the title, the paper-title back in the archives of courts or offices, to be searched for by electors in determining whether their fellow-citizen Mr. Humphreys shall receive their votes? They know who are in the possession and in the exercise of offices under the Government of the United States by their action, by their public possession and exercise of office; and now when Mr. Humphreys, to the knowledge of his neighbors in Pensacola and the community throughout the State of Florida, is out of his office, and its constant duties are performed by another from and after the date in October, are they to lose the effect of their suffrage by the production of a certificate that in 1872 he held the office? I think not.

I have said I would ask your attention to the only provisions in the statutes of the United States that bring their bearing upon the question of resignation; and they are found at three pages of this volume—233, 251, and 277.

Mr. Commissioner ABBOTT. Are you quoting by pages or sections?

Mr. EVARTS. Pages.

Mr. Commissioner ABBOTT. The Revised Statutes?

Mr. EVARTS. Yes. They relate only to resignations of military officers or enlisted soldiers in the nature of desertion. Now, under a scheme of law that from the foundation of the Government until now has never lifted finger to restrict the right of citizens to retire from office at their mere will, who shall say that within the property of this electoral qualification and this count of it on this evidence any question is to be made?

But the authorities seem to be very clear as to the right of resigning without even acceptance. In section 260 of Mr. McCrary's book I read:

Where the law requires an officer resigning to do so by a written resignation—

Where the law in terms requires an officer resigning to do so by a written resignation—

to be sent to the governor, it is not necessary that the governor should signify his acceptance of a resignation to make it valid. The tenure of office, in such a case, does not depend upon the will of the executive, but of the incumbent.

Mr. Commissioner ABBOTT. Is not that a case where the law expressly provides that the office may be resigned by the party by a written resignation without any acceptance?

Mr. EVARTS. I have not examined the law.

Mr. Commissioner ABBOTT. I think you will find it so.

Mr. EVARTS. It is spoken of as a law which requires a resignation in writing. This careful commentator quotes it as a law that requires " an officer resigning to do so by a written resignation."

A civil officer has the absolute right to resign his office at pleasure, and it is not within the power of the executive to compel him to remain in office.

And the authorities for this are given in the first volume of McLean's Reports, page 512, where that learned judge says:

There can be no doubt that a civil officer has a right to resign his office at pleasure; and it is not in the power of the executive to compel him to remain in office. It is only necessary that the resignation should be received to take effect; and this does not depend upon the acceptance or rejection of the resignation by the President. And if Fogg had resigned absolutely and unconditionally, I should have no doubt that the defendant could not be held bound subsequently as his surety.

This was a question of suretyship. There is a case in California, The People *vs.* Porter, 6 California Reports, 27. " Resignation of office" is the head-note. "A resignation is effectual without its acceptance by the appointing power." You will observe that under this condition of law, all the circumstances of this office making its application a necessary result from the nature of the office and the tenure not limited in any way, all that was necessary was to make a permanent vacation of the office, evidenced by the conduct of the resigning officer, and followed not necessarily by any necessary proof, but if followed by the public possession and discharge of the office by another, it took the officer out of his place within the disqualification or qualification concerning it.

I might refer to a very important proposition made by Mr. Manager Hoar on the impeachment of Mr. Belknap, found on page 62 of the Record, volume 4, part 7, of this Congress, the two concluding paragraphs on the first column of that page. I will not occupy time by reading them; but it was there laid down by the authority of the House of Representatives through their managers that in this country the acceptance of a resignation was not essential to vacate office, and that the English authorities to the contrary turned upon the peculiarity of their laws and their system which exacted maintenance of office against the will of an officer.

Mr. Commissioner HOAR. With the exception there stated, that of the class of offices which a person could be compelled by mandamus to accept.

Mr. EVARTS. So I understood; but that was drawn from the English cases.

Mr. Commissioner HOAR. And the early New England cases. The office of constable a person could be compelled by mandamus to accept.

Mr. EVARTS. But there it was I believe contended, certainly it is matter of public knowledge and history, that in the United States service there are no such civil officers; and no pretense of any such obligation has been set forth. We have been satisfied to rest upon the working maxim of our politics that none resign.

Now, I will consider, and very briefly, the question of ineligibility made apparent by proof *aliunde*, as bearing upon the question whether the vote is to be omitted in the count. That question, if not open for discussion, will nevertheless occupy me but a very brief period, and I must assume that it is open, that there has been no determination that ineligibility made to appear by extraneous proof would lead to the rejection of the vote. This clause of the Constitution, which simply prescribes an exclusion from the office of elector, left open to the appointment of the States, of persons filling seats in Congress or occupying office under the United States, is a clause of the Constitution not executing itself and not executed by law; and when, therefore, in the presence of the two Houses, the transaction commences of counting the presidential votes, no objection of that kind can be heard or entertained, because Congress has not filled out the legislation necessary to provide the means of adducing proof in advance, one way and the other, and the effect that is to be given to the presence of a disqualified elector. Let me call your attention to a case of the greatest weight in all our discussions of matters before the Supreme Court—the case of Groves vs. Slaughter, in 15 Peters; I read from page 500. Look at that question as it was presented. The constitution of Mississippi contained this provision:

The introduction of slaves into this State as merchandise or for sale shall be prohibited from and after the 1st day of May, 1833.

After that date they were imported for sale; they were sold; and the buyer gave his notes for the price; and the question was whether the notes could be collected. The courts of Mississippi held that they could not; and the Supreme Court of the United States, with but two dissenting judges, held that the constitution did not execute itself and that until legislation was provided that was to have that effect, it was not executed. The court had the advantage in their decision of the arguments of the ablest men at the bar; Mr. Clay and Mr. Webster both appeared in this case and other very eminent lawyers. At pages 500 and 501, Mr. Justice Thompson, giving the opinion of the court, said:

Admitting the constitution is mandatory upon the legislature, and that they have neglected their duty in not carrying it into execution, it can have no effect upon the construction of this article. Legislative provision is indispensable to carry into effect the object of this prohibition. It requires the sanction of penalties to effect this object. How is a violation of this prohibition to be punished? Admitting it would be a misdemeanor, punishable by fine, this would be entirely inadequate to the full execution of the object intended to be accomplished. What would become of the slaves thus introduced? Will they become free immediately upon their introduction or do they become forfeited to the State? These are questions not easily answered. And although these difficulties may be removed by subsequent legislation, yet they are proper circumstances to be taken into consideration when we are inquiring into the intention of the convention in thus framing this article. It is unreasonable to suppose that, if this prohibition was intended, per se, to operate without any legislative aid, there would not have been some guards and checks thrown around it to secure its execution.

Now, suppose this injunction of the Constitution is mandatory on the States not to appoint as electors those who are within the prescribed disqualification, Congress has not undertaken to execute it; the States have not undertaken to execute any procedure by which votes for disqualified persons shall cause the failure of the vote of the State. They have provided no means; none have been exercised here; and I submit to this Commission that, laying down, as you must, a rule that is suitable to the ordinary and orderly and unretarded progress of the proceedings of the two Houses, when the President of the Senate opens the certificates, and, dealing only with the certificates as your judgment about evidence is they must deal unless in this particular, you must hold that in this particular also, unless there be statutory provisions of the United States or of the State purging the lists, you must count the vote that the State sends forward and that its governor certifies, where there is no question of objection of any other nature, which, of course, the case now being considered contains. You are undertaking to deal, in the process of counting the vote, with a question to be settled by fact antecedent to the appointment, and you are exposed to a final and irrevocable rejection of a vote from the mere casual impression or uncertainty of evidence.

This subject, then, being rejected from a further consideration, I under-

stand there is no matter left but for the execution by this Commission
of the duty accorded to it by the act of Congress under which it is
organized, to determine out of the materials of these three certificates
what and how many votes are to be counted for the State of Florida.
The first certificate is subject to no criticism. You have rejected all
means whatever of questioning it by evidence as to what occurred before
the vote was cast, before the vote was certified by the governor, or after
either of those parts of the transaction up to the time of the counting.
No fact can intervene. This vote, then, is to be counted, not because
it is the best that is seen, but by the absolute fullness of its title in complying with all the laws that have been imposed by Congress concerning
the complete verification of a certificate. The fact certified is not gainsaid by proof, for it is excluded. There was no offer of proof between the
fact of the canvass closed and recorded and the governor's certificate.

This certificate then includes, with every degree of certainty and assurance, the votes of the State of Florida, and there are four votes here,
and there is room for no more. To make it, therefore, of any practical
importance in the further discussion, there must be apparent on the two
other certificates either such disparagement of the first or such authenticity in the latter as should displace the one and substitute the other,
or there must be such production of rival and competing certificates as
leaves the Commission to rest in doubt and uncertainty as to which
votes are to be counted.

Now, as you will not allow evidence outside of this first certificate as
bearing directly upon its actual affirmative authenticity and sufficiency,
you will not allow any evidence collaterally on the mere presentation or
support of any other certificate. If another certificate comes here that,
by its own credit, is made superior to ours, it displaces it. If it is made
equal to ours, then there are two certificates, and then you must determine which of the two, or whether either, is entitled to consideration.
That leads me to ask attention to these other certificates, so called. By
the only certificate that relates to an apparent act in the election of
President of the United States on the part of the State of Florida, it is
shown to have been wholly without authority of law, and this second
certificate, so far from competing with the first or disparaging the
first, confirms it in all respects; in the first place negatively, for it
wants the certificate of the executive that is prescribed; in the second
place, by an entirely superfluous and worthless paper, so far as the
Constitution and laws of the United States are concerned and so
far as the laws of Florida are concerned, of an attorney-general of that
State, having no more power or authority to certify anything about the
election than the commander of the militia of the State, carrying therefore on its face no invitation to your hospitality and excluding itself
from consideration by its being wholly without legal support in the laws
of Florida and wholly unrecognized under the Constitution and laws of
the United States.

But if you treat it as a paper, read it for what it says. It shows you
that the recorded canvass as it lay in the secretary of state's office was
the only transaction in that election that the governor of the State by
its laws could certify to, and that his certificate rested upon that fact
and could not be questioned for reason of its not observing the executive duty. Let me ask your attention to the true result of this certificate, as was well and firmly stated by my associate, Mr. Stoughton,
when he said that it showed that it would have been a violation of duty
on the part of the governor of the State of Florida to have certified or
looked at anything else, provided you take this attorney-general's cer-

tificate of what the law is. He describes himself as an attorney-general, and by virtue of that office one of the members of the board of State canvassers of the State of Florida, and he undertakes to certify " that, by the authentic returns of the votes cast in the several counties of the State of Florida, * * * said returns"—that is, the county returns— " being on file in the office of the secretary of state, and seen and considered by me as such member of the board of State canvassers of the said State of Florida, it appears and is shown" that the four gentlemen named " were chosen the four electors of President and Vice-President of the United States,"

And I do further certify that, under the act of the legislature of the State of Florida establishing said board of State canvassers, no provision has been enacted, nor is any such provision contained in the statute law of this State, whereby the result shown and appearing by said returns—

That is, the county returns—

to said board of State canvassers can be certified to the executive of the said State.

If that is not as complete an exclusion of the possibility of there being any reliance or resort by the laws of Florida on the part of the executive to any of this evidence, these returns, or any part of them, what could supply such a conclusion? And when you look at the law of Florida already brought to the attention of the Commission, you find that, as a part and the final part of the transaction of appointing electors, the canvassers having made their report, it is the governor's duty thereupon to issue his certificate to the electors thus shown to be elected, which is the final warrant by the State of Florida of their appointment and the justification of their action in voting.

I come now to a third certificate, so called, and we are to proceed to inquire whether there is anything on that which disparages or overtops the paramount authority of the first certificate. In regard to this certificate, I say that it is a paper having no warrant whatever under the Constitution or laws of the United States or of the State of Florida—I mean the laws of the State of Florida as they existed when the appointment was completed and when the vote was cast and certified and transmitted here. It is a posthumous certificate of *post-mortem* action, never proceeding from any vital or living college of electors, but only by the galvanic agency of interested party purpose, taking effect after the whole transaction was ended. I submit to your honors, without making any imputation as between political parties, that the inspection of this certificate shows that, the transaction having gone on and been completed within the purview of the Constitution and the laws of the United States and the laws of the State of Florida, a government, coming into being on the subsequent 1st of January by the change of political parties, undertakes to undo what has already been done.

That proposes (without offense to the arrangement of the two parties in this transaction) that one party was in possession of power during the procedure of the transaction and was succeeded by a change of party. It would be just the same if the reverse situation in the names of the parties were concerned. If it can be done, then all the care and all the wisdom and all the contrivances that are to make this transaction in the States final at some point, certifiable at some point, and in some manner and by some officer, are to go for nothing, if when there are new officers, new interests, new legislators, by either or all the powers of the changed government, the vote that has been deposited can be corrupted, subtracted, obscured, or substituted; if legislature, governor, judiciary, all enter into the transaction that is to substitute for the deposited vote of the State a vote that they then presently seek to deposit, or that its efficacy, if not adequate for its own counting, shall displace the counting of the completed transaction.

This certificate, opened by the President of the Senate, and by that mere act therefore laid before the Houses of Congress, and transmitted here, when the contents are opened and read, is shown to be no certificate under the Constitution of the United States or the act of Congress or the laws of Florida in existence at the time of the casting of the electoral vote of that State within its borders. It is, under the aspect and the cover of a certificate, transmitted to the President of the Senate, connected with the election, made the vehicle of carrying into the physical presence and power of the two Houses, and thus of this Commission, what is utterly nugatory, utterly ineffectual, utterly unauthorized by any provision of the Constitution.

You cannot count that, then, as an electoral vote. Nobody pretends that that certificate, coming here on the 31st of January, reciting legislation not completed, I think, until the 26th, and some *quo warranto* judgment referred to that was terminated on the 23d or 17th—the dates are utterly immaterial—is a paper that the President of the Senate was by the Constitution required to receive. It is not a paper that is a certified vote of a State. It is not a paper that can carry any means of furnishing you with the vote of the State to be counted. So in respect of evidence it is wholly without authority.

It will be observed that the certificate of Governor Drew, by public knowledge shown to have come into his office on the 1st of January or later perhaps, but the term of his office dates from then, undertakes by authority of an act passed January 17, 1877, which had ordered a new "canvass of the returns of said votes on file," which canvass "was, on the 19th day of January, made according to the laws of the State and the interpretation thereof by the supreme court," to recite that four gentlemen named "were duly determined, declared, and certified "— that is, by these canvassers taking up the transaction in January under a law passed in January, and making a scrutiny ending on the 17th— "to have been elected electors of President and Vice-President of the United States for the State of Florida " at the past election in November, " as shown by said returns;" and it further recites that—

In a proceeding on the part of the State of Florida by information in the nature of *quo warranto* wherein the said Robert Bullock, Robert B. Hilton, Wilkinson Call, and James E. Yonge were relators, and Charles H. Pearce, Frederick C. Humphreys, William H. Holden, and Thomas W. Long were respondents, the circuit court of this State for the second judicial circuit, after full consideration of the law and the proofs produced on behalf of the parties respectively, by its judgment determined that said relators were, at said election, in fact and in law, elected such electors as against the said respondents and all other persons:

Now, therefore, and also in pursuance of an act of the legislature entitled "An act to declare and establish the appointment by the State of Florida of electors of President and Vice-President of the United States," approved January 26, A. D. 1877, I, George F. Drew, governor of the State of Florida, do hereby make and certify the following list of the names of the said electors chosen, appointed, and declared as aforesaid, to wit:

The certificate required was a certificate to be delivered to the college of electors at or before the day, and that is the only certificate which can have any force; and here we have a certificate of a governor who was not governor at that time.

Then, besides, we have all that is here stated, absolutely *post hac*, subsequent to the transaction, and only allowed to present itself on the 31st day of January just past, to have some influence upon the transaction that had been completed and been certified; and that when the two competing certificates of the rival electors had been finished and placed in possession of the President of the Senate long before this authority arose. What becomes of the authority in Congress, exercised under the Constitution, to say that the votes shall all be delivered on the part of the States on the same day? Is not that a substantive provision? Is not that a hold that Congress by the Constitution was given concerning the deposit of the electoral vote? Certainly it was. What becomes of the provision of the act of Congress, justified by the Constitution, that the elections or other methods of appointment that the State may use shall be on the same day? What does it mean? Does it mean anything? Did our fathers trifle upon questions of punctilio and order? No. If it means anything, it means that it must be done on one day, that it shall not be undone on any other day. It is to be done on one day; it is to be finished on one day; and they would laugh at the triviality of the wisdom of their successors in the great places of the Constitution, the Senate and the House and the great judges of the land, if on the first occasion that it became necessary or at all effectual to undo, it should be held as constitutional law that when it was provided it should all be done on one day, that meant that after what was done was known, and after the importance of undoing it was understood, and after the change of parties or the ambition of human nature made it important to undo in separate parcels and at various times what had been supposed to have been concluded and made sacred in the deposit that the Constitution had assigned for a finished transaction, that courts, that legislatures, that governors remote from responsibility, or seconded in their transgressions by the opinion of party and the applause of political interests, should have the fingering of every vote for President until the counting was concluded.

What are the prodigious claims here? That by a lawsuit, and a lawsuit in a State court, begun and ended it may be afterward, begun if you please before but ended afterward, by virtue of that transaction the State's completed vote is to be retrieved and reversed; and that when a justice's court of the first instance has so decided, as my learned brother, Mr. Green, has said, the courts of the United States make a low obeisance to Mr. Justice White, and say, "That is the end of the law; that is the *fiat* of the State." Well, supposing that we had succeeded in counting a President in under *quo warranto*, justified under the Constitution and the laws as they now are or that shall be opened by legislation to the tribunals of the country, and suppose that then a *quo warranto* is started to prove that the President in his seat should be dislodged because some of the votes counted for him were not by *de-jure* electors, and then it is proposed that the decision of the State court is "the be-all and the end-all" of that inquiry; that whichever of these candidates takes his seat as President of the United States in a situation of evenly-balanced elections, his continued possession of the Federal office upon the judgment *post hac* of a State court that holds, whenever a *quo warranto* comes to an end by due procedure of their laws, that the title of the President that acquired the count of the votes of Ohio or of New York was a miscount, a count of spurious votes, so held and determined by the State in the independence of its judiciary passing upon the question. What sort of a government, what sort of a presidency, what sort of muniments and protections of regularity and permanence of authority under the Constitution are provided by a scheme of perpetual four years' dependence upon a *quo warranto* in the State of Nevada or of Florida?

You then must never lose sight of the matter that you are to advise what votes and how many shall be counted by the two Houses that

stand in a present duty, never intended by the Constitution to be interrupted by a day or by an hour. When you have determined that evidence shall not invade the regularity of the finished transaction of the
State or defeat the regularity of the certification under the acts of Congress at the time when the votes are sealed up in their packages and
transmitted—when you have determined that that shall not be invaded
by extraneous evidence, you have determined as by a double decision
that it shall not be invaded, disparaged, or exposed to any question by
a mere certificate that is its own agent and author and volunteer in disturbance of the counting of the votes.

The PRESIDENT. Will any other gentleman speak on your side,
Mr. Evarts?

Mr. EVARTS. We have, I believe, a little unoccupied time.

The PRESIDENT. O, yes.

Mr. EVARTS. We do not propose to occupy it.

The PRESIDENT. The case is submitted on your side?

Mr. EVARTS. Yes, sir.

The PRESIDENT. There are fifty-five minutes left for reply to the
other side.

Mr. MERRICK. Mr. President and gentlemen of the Commission, the
duty of closing this argument has, I regret to say, been imposed upon
me, and I especially regret that its performance should be required at
so late an hour of the day and after so protracted a session of the Commission; but, may it please your honors, I know the importance of a
speedy termination of the labors of this Commission, and shall proceed
to the discharge of my duty as best I can without asking the indulgence of any delay.

The counsel on the other side in their arguments to-day seem to have
taken a step even in advance of that taken on the occasion of the
preceding argument, and now seek to exclude even any inquiry whatever into the subject-matter submitted to this Commission for their consideration; and while the learned counsel who has just closed has so
eloquently called your attention to the painful condition that might follow should we proceed to an election of a President of the United States
subject to the delays that would be incident to the various judgments
that might be rendered on *quo warrantos* instituted in different States
for the purpose of ascertaining the truth of the due election of electors,
he omitted to call your attention to the counterpart of that picture, viz:
the condition of government we should have with a President walking
up to the presidential chair along a pathway strewn with recognized
frauds, perjuries, and crime, into which the people of this country are
neither allowed to inquire through their representatives in the Federal
Congress nor through their representatives in the governments of the
States. I apprehend that this Commission, in considering the picture
the learned gentleman has presented to you, will find in the counterpart
a picture more painful to contemplate than that which he has drawn,
and one from which the mind and the heart of every patriotic citizen
will start back pained and shocked and agonized.

All that we have asked, may it please your honors, and all that we
ask now, under the rules of evidence prescribed by this tribunal, is that
the truth shall be ascertained in these matters in regard to which you
are to act, and that when that truth is ascertained it may become in its
necessary and legal results substantially and practically incorporated
into the political history of the country.

The point to which the learned gentleman first addressed himself was
that raised by the counsel for the objectors this morning to the vote of

Humphreys because of his position as an official under the Federal Government, and both gentlemen have taken the position that we are so fastened to fraud and illegality, if either should exist in this matter, that there can be no inquiry by the Congress of the United States, or this Commission, or the two Houses of Congress, to ascertain whether an elector coming forward and depositing his ballot is within the class of persons inhibited from holding the office of elector by the Constitution of the United States. I beg pardon, may it please your honors, for using the word "inhibited," for to speak of a person as inhibited by the Constitution from holding a certain Federal office or to speak of a person as ineligible for certain reasons is to convey a very erroneous impression of the provision of the Federal Constitution on the subject now under consideration.

This provision is not directed immediately to any personal disability of the individuals to whom it refers, nor is it directed immediately to any personal disqualification under which such person may be, but the limitation operates upon the power given to the State, and disables the State from appointing such persons, rather than disables the person from holding the office. This, probably, is the only article in the Constitution of the United States in which there is anything in the nature of a grant from the Federal Government to the States. Throughout our entire system the Federal Government becomes the recipient of power from the States, and is the grantee of powers and not the grantor, or to speak more correctly in the phraseology of the law, is the donee and not the donor; but in this particular instance a power is given to the States to appoint electors in such manner as their legislatures respectively may think proper. But, says the article, in its further provision limiting the power granted:

No Senator or Representative, or person holding an office of trust or profit under the United States, shall be appointed an elector.

You will see from the phraseology of the article that it is a limitation upon the power of appointment rather than a specification of any disability in the appointee. A State has the power to appoint whom it pleases within certain limitations; and when it transcends those limitations it does not execute a power which is given to it, but assumes to act beyond the given power, and the attempted appointment is therefore absolutely null and void. And yet the learned counsel on the other side contend that, whether the State regards this requirement of the Federal Constitution or not, whether the State in the execution of the power delegated to her shall appoint one whom it is beyond her power to appoint or not, we are not permitted to enter into the inquiry, but must accept as final and conclusive in a presidential election the vote of one whom the Constitution of the United States has declared the State shall under no circumstances appoint.

In contrast with this provision of the Constitution, and by analogy to develop more distinctly the view I have presented, recur, may it please your honors, to those provisions that relate to the personal disqualification of citizens of the United States to occupy the offices of Representatives and Senators in Congress. Those provisions ordain that no person who has a certain disability, or who fails to have certain qualifications, shall be a Senator or Representative; for instance, no person shall be a Representative until he attains the age of twenty-five years; no person shall be a Senator until he attains the age of thirty. Under the clauses of the Constitution referred to, if an individual is elected to the House of Representatives before he is twenty-five years of age, but reaches that age prior to the time of taking his seat, he is capable of occupying the position; and if a Senator is elected before he reaches the age of thirty, but attains that age before he takes his seat, he is capable of occupying that position. But in the case of a State as to its electors, it is not a personal disability that either the lapse of time or anything on earth can cure, remove, or dispense with, for it is a limitation upon the power, and if the State exceeds the power granted, the act is void from the very day it was attempted to be performed, and the individual who assumes to cast the ballot, when appointed in excess of the power of appointment, casts a piece of paper that must, in every view of constitutional law, and under every ordinary and known principle relating to the law of powers, be regarded as a blank.

Now, may it please your honors, we maintain that the State of Florida, if it should be that you hold the first certificate valid, has appointed as one of her electors an office-holder under the Federal Government, and thus exceeded her power. Upon that question there are two matters of fact arising—first, was the elector referred to an office-holder, and, second, if so, was he such at the time of the appointment? The learned counsel on the other side require that we should be limited to the strictest possible proof of the fact of his incumbency on the day of the appointment. I apprehend that, as far as legal principles are known and recognized, when you have once proved the incumbency of an individual, the presumption of law follows and goes with you, and the burden of proof is upon him to show that that incumbency has ceased to exist. It is not for us to trace the fact of his continuing in office down from the day of his appointment. If we prove the commission under the broad seal by which he holds the office, and then superadd to that commission the fact that he has discharged the functions of the office at a period of time somewhat near in date to the period of his appointment, the presumption of law is that he acted under the commission from the date of his appointment and up to the present time.

But the learned counsel on the other side had the officer himself upon the stand; and if the resignation as proved by that officer is not a sufficient resignation, then, as a matter of course, he did not resign at all according to his own evidence, and was still in office on the day of his pretended appointment as elector. The resignation, as shown by him, was a private letter addressed to the judge of the circuit court, who was then in Ohio—I forget the particular locality in Ohio to which the letter was addressed——

Mr. STOUGHTON. Newark.

Mr. MERRICK. Newark, Ohio; and the receipt of a letter by him from the judge indicating his acceptance of that resignation. The statute of the United States requires that this appointment shall be made by the circuit court, and if any resignation is necessary at all, as we hold that it is, that resignation can only be made to the power that gave the appointment, and the power that gave the appointment is the only power capable of accepting the resignation and relieving the party from the incumbency of the official position.

The circuit court being the power that gave the appointment, it was to the circuit court that the resignation should have been sent; and if an acceptance was necessary it was the circuit court that should have given that acceptance, and the acceptance should have appeared upon the records of that court, if ever given, alongside of the commission, nullifying the commission by the same sanctity of record which the commission possessed that bestowed the office. But it is in proof before this honorable Commission that there is no record of that resignation;

that the commission stands upon the records of the court to-day unimpeached and unimpaired by any recorded resignation of the officer that it clothed with official power; and I respectfully submit that, until that resignation is there recorded, until that resignation is accepted by the power which gave it and appears of record, this party still continues in office.

Mr. Commissioner HOAR. Mr. Merrick, I should like to ask you a question which perhaps it will be convenient to state now, and you can answer it at such time as you choose. Section 6 of article 1, to which you have just referred, provides that no person holding any office under the United States shall be a member of either House during his continuance in office. Now if this gentleman had been elected a Senator or Representative of the United States, and the judge of the circuit court had refused to accept his resignation as shipping-commissioner, do you hold that he never could have taken the office of Senator or Representative? If not, how do you distinguish the case from the present one?

Mr. MERRICK. I will answer the question. I do not hold that if his resignation had never been accepted he would not have been competent to act as a Senator of the United States; but when elected to the Senate of the United States the acceptance by the Senate of the United States of that individual as a Senator would have been his discharge from that office, provided he had, prior to that time, tendered his resignation to the court.

Mr. Commissioner HOAR. Then if taking upon himself the incompatible office be a sufficient discharge from the other one in that case, is not the taking upon himself the office of elector?

Mr. MERRICK. If this were a personal disability it would have been. If it were a personal disqualification in the man, it would have effected that result. But where the difficulty in taking the office is not a personal disqualification in the individual, but a limitation upon the power that is to give the office, it does not have that effect.

Mr. Commissioner ABBOTT. The acceptance in that way would be at a time very much later than the appointment, would it not?

Mr. MERRICK. Necessarily so. It rests upon the distinction that in the one case there is a limitation upon the power and in the other there is a disqualification of the person.

Mr. Commissioner ABBOTT. Mr. Merrick, I understand you to claim in this case that an acceptance is not necessary, but still the resignation must be to the party or court or person appointing.

Mr. MERRICK. It must be, unquestionably. If a resignation even is not necessary, as I stated to Judge HOAR, I think, in my reply, yet if he had resigned, whether his resignation had been accepted or not, the offer of the resignation is necessary, and that offer must be made to the power that gave the appointment. Suppose he had resigned to the clerk of the court, addressed the clerk at Newark, Ohio, a private letter saying, "I as shipping-commissioner beg leave to tender my resignation to you," or "beg leave to tender my resignation," how would it have been understood? It would have been understood as a resignation intended for the clerk to present to the court, and until it got to the court it could not operate as a resignation of his office, either with or without any acceptance.

The PRESIDENT. Mr. Merrick, if a commissioner of the circuit court tenders his resignation to the judge and the judge directs it to be filed in the court, is that an acceptance?

Mr. MERRICK. When the court is in session it is an act of the court; and if the commissioner sends that resignation to the clerk's office it is there to wait for the sitting of the court, and is then filed during the session.

Mr. Commissioner GARFIELD. Mr. Merrick, allow me to ask you, do you hold that in case there should be a long vacation of the court, or the court should be abolished by law, or the judge should die and for a year or two no appointment be made in his place, this commissioner could never have resigned?

Mr. MERRICK. I should refer that case to one of the returning-boards of the South. I hardly know in such an extreme case what reply to make.

Mr. Commissioner GARFIELD. I understand your position to be that he cannot resign except when the court is in session.

Mr. MERRICK. He cannot resign except when the court is in session; but I presume that death and the abolition of an office and the extinction of a government and the wiping out of a country and the destruction of a whole people would make exceptions to all principles of law.

The PRESIDENT. I shall not take these interruptions out of your time, Mr. Merrick.

Mr. MERRICK. Now, may it please your honors, I pass from that branch of the case.

Mr. Commissioner MILLER. Before you pass from that, Mr. Merrick, I should like to ask you a question. You have been very much taxed, but I know your ability to reply. You say that the distinction between a man who accepts the office of Senator or Member of the House of Representatives, who is ineligible by holding another office, and the man who accepts and acts in the office of elector, being in the same situation, is that in one case the disability or inhibition goes to the power of the State and in the other it does not. Now, if the language is precisely the same, that no man shall be elected to the office of Senator unless he is thirty years old and no man shall be appointed to the office of elector who holds another office, where is the difference in the question of power in the State?

Mr. MERRICK. I am not prepared to answer that the language quoted is the exact language used in the Constitution.

Mr. Commissioner MILLER. I do not know that it is the exact language, for the text is not before me.

Mr. MERRICK. Allow me to look at the Constitution before I answer the question.

Mr. Commissioner MILLER. Are not both State officers in one sense at least; both elected by the power of the State?

Mr. MERRICK. No person of a certain description shall be a member of either House. Says the Constitution:

No Senator or Representative shall, during the time for which he was elected, be appointed to any civil office under the authority of the United States, which shall have been created, &c.

No person shall be a Representative who shall not have attained the age of twenty-five years.

No person shall be a Senator, who shall not have attained to the age of thirty years.

But in reference to the electors it is that "no person shall be *appointed*," following a previous grant of power to appoint; and according to the rules of law, wherever there is a power given to do an act, the donee of the power can only execute it legally according to the grant, and when he pursues strictly the limitations and the directions of the donor. You will perceive there is marked difference in the two cases.

I pass, then, may it please your honors, from that subject. My first inquiry in passing from it is as to what through the labors of this honorable Commission we have reached in reference to a definite conclusion with regard to the testimony before you for consideration. The learned counsel who last addressed you seemed to be under the impression, and endeavored to force that impression upon your consideration, that by the order passed no extrinsic evidence should be taken as to certificate No. 1, and therefore no evidence contained in certificates Nos. 2 and 3 could be used to invalidate certificate No. 1. I do not understand the order passed by this tribunal as the learned counsel on the other side seem to have understood it. I understand the scope and meaning of that order to be that while you, in the exercise of the powers of the two Houses of Congress, and representing the Federal Government in that regard, will not go behind the certificates, so to speak, to impeach them by extraneous evidence, yet you will consider whatever the State has sent to you in those certificates for the purpose of ascertaining which certificate represents the true wishes and will of the State. The order is:

That no evidence will be received except such as was laid before the two Houses by the President of the Senate with the different certificates.

If what is contained in the three certificates be evidence before you, it is evidence for all the purposes of this case; and whatever evidence there is in certificate No. 3 to show that that certificate contains the names of the persons duly appointed electors by the State of Florida must, either directly or indirectly, operate to invalidate or affect certificate No. 1.

Now what is before you in those certificates? In certificate No. 1 you have the statement of Governor Stearns as to the appointment of certain individuals as electors, and in certificate No. 2, which the counsel seemed to treat with a good deal of indignation, if not contempt, you have the certificate of the attorney-general of Florida as to the appointment of certain other parties as electors of the State of Florida, and the further certificate from those electors that they applied to the governor of the State for a certificate, which was refused. Now, I submit as a principle of law, sound in itself, and furnishing a full reply to the argument made by the counsel who opened for the other side, and as giving a satisfactory assurance against those serious consequences that he seemed to apprehend from the practical application and experience of the positions advanced by us, that where a party entitled to receive a piece of evidence from an official applies for it and does not get it, but is refused, he is in as good a position before a court of justice as though he had received it. You cannot and will not charge upon that individual or upon the interests and rights of the persons, the State, or the nation which that individual claims to represent, the consequences of the delinquency of an official who has failed or refused to perform his duty. It was not, as the learned counsel on the other side have intimated, that we waited until after it was seen how the election had gone. There is no danger from this case, as he would suggest, that hereafter, if the precedent of a favorable decision to the objectors should be reached, the door would be thrown open to fraud and to the bad passions of men, to the excitements of politics, and the acerbity of party hatreds, to interfere with the just result of popular expression; none whatever. On the contrary, we ask that those excitements should be suppressed by the calm voice of the reason of this august tribunal, and that men who would hereafter seek to perpetuate political power through the instrumentalities of fraud, deceit, and bad practices should find in the recorded judgment of this tribunal, as part

of the history of the Government, the declaration that all such iniqui-
tous proceedings, schemes, and designs will be utter failures and unavailing for the production of any result. Instead of waiting to see how
these elections had gone, as intimated by the counsel, or instead of its
being a case from which hereafter parties might be induced so to wait,
it is apparent to this court from these certificates that the men who
claimed to be elected as the so-called Tilden electors of Florida went to
the governor, carrying with them a majority of the votes of the electors of that State, and asked the governor to give them the certificate
which under the statute law of the United States they were entitled to
receive. That governor, possibly influenced by some of those motives
which the gentleman has so kindly ascribed as impelling the action of
other people, declined to give that certificate, and they were left to
look for the next best evidence they could find.

Mr. Commissioner THURMAN. If it does not interrupt you, I
should like, Mr. Merrick, to hear you upon this point: Suppose that
what you call the Tilden electors had never voted at all; the question
I should like to hear counsel upon is this: is it competent, by subsequent State proceedings, to show that the men who did vote, the Hayes
electors, had no title to vote?

Mr. MERRICK. Most unquestionably. The State cannot have her
voice simulated. It happens that on this occasion the true voice of the
State was spoken; but if it had not been, there could have been no
more power and vigor in the simulated tones of her voice to reach the
councils of the Federal Government than there is when those simulated
tones come ringing along with the true sentiments of her people. The
State is not to be deceived and cheated in that way. She might on the
day after her people voted have instituted her *quo warranto*, and, standing in the presence of her own judicial tribunals, clothed with the majesty
of her power, and appealing to her judicial authority, asked these men,
" By what right do you assume to exercise the power of this State ?" And
she could have stripped from them the garments they had stolen; stripped
from their shoulders her livery which they had no right to wear. She
could proceed against them, whether others spoke in her behalf or not.
In this case the proceeding was by individuals under circumstances
which the State subsequently felt constrained to recognize. But in the
case supposed by Senator Thurman the proceeding would have been
directly by the State herself in her courts or through her legislature.

Could she not have proceeded in her courts; could she not, in conjunction with proceedings in her courts, also have proceeded through her
legislature? The power is given to the State to appoint electors in such
manner as her legislature may prescribe. That power so given to appoint necessarily carries with it and implies a power to certify to that
appointment, and it is for her to authenticate the appointment which
she makes in the exercise of the power conferred upon her under that
provision of the Constitution. I do not mean to question or deny that
the United States, through its statutes, may provide also for a mode of
authentication, as it has done; but, as seems to have been concluded by
the Commission, that mode of authentication is not by any means conclusive, and, I respectfully submit, is not the best evidence of the appointment. The best evidence of the appointment is from the State
herself in obedience to her own law and in the execution of the power
of providing for the authentication of the appointment she is authorized
to make. The legislature of the State would have the right in the canvass of the vote even, as over and above any returning-board, to ascertain who were the parties really and truly appointed.

Mr. Commissioner EDMUNDS. Do you maintain that, Mr. Merrick, as an act of legislative will notwithstanding the previous law that had provided some other method?

Mr. MERRICK. Yes, may it please your honors, notwithstanding the previous law may have provided some other method. If the legislature of Florida, having the power under the Constitution to appoint electors, found that under the previous law there had been proceedings by the ministerial officers of the State out of which proceedings had come a commission authorizing individuals not appointed in fact to exercise a power instead of those who were truly appointed, she might by her legislature enact a law to proceed not to change the relation, not to divest vested rights, not to create new rights and new relations, but in the exercise of legislative authority to ascertain who had been in point of fact duly appointed according to existing laws.

Mr. Commissioner EDMUNDS. By that you mean that the legislature is the judge of who had been appointed in fact?

Mr. MERRICK. The legislature could proceed to ascertain who had been in point of fact appointed according to the law of the State, and the result of the inquiry coming from the State is evidence, the best evidence, and therefore better evidence than the mere certificate of the governor.

But I do not need to assume this position in the pending case; and the interrogatories propounded upon abstract questions evoke from me abstract answers that are applicable to those questions only, for in this case the legislature of Florida proceeded to execute the decree of the courts of the State of Florida. The question had been before her judicial tribunals and the legislature did not primarily and of its own motion enter into the consideration of this question and act upon it, but the question having come before the courts of Florida and the courts having construed the law of Florida, the legislature gave effect to that judicial construction of the State law.

Now it appears in certificate No. 3 that the governor issued this certificate in obedience to the acts of the legislature of Florida and in obedience to the decision of her courts, and this certificate No. 3 is the only certificate before this tribunal that contains a canvass of the votes of Florida.

The learned counsel spoke of the incoming of a new administration and the displacement of an old, and of their belonging to hostile political parties; but I apprehend that such a circumstance is a matter of very little importance in this inquiry, for the State as a political organization goes on forever and never dies, and whatever the governor who was governor at the time the electors voted could do after that event, his successor can do just as well. The change of the administration makes no difference whatever in the gubernatorial power.

This certificate, then, contains, as I have stated, the only canvass that is before your honors; it contains a canvass of the votes of the people of Florida made under the authority of an act of the legislature of Florida. There is no other canvass here. It states that the canvass has been made and that a certain result has been reached in virtue of a decision of the court of last resort in Florida; and these documents are here under the sanction of State authority. Now how far will this tribunal regard this paper as representing the facts in reference to the condition of these two claimants who hold these certificates, the first certificate unaccompanied, the second accompanied by this evidence?

I suppose that your honors, according to the rule you have laid down, have concluded that the right to ascertain who were really the agents of the State, who were really authorized to represent the State, was limited to the evidence laid before the two Houses of Congress and in or accompanying the certificates. According to this certificate No. 3, a canvass of the votes of Florida was made under legislative enactment in pursuance of her judicial decision. I speak not now of the *quo warranto;* I speak of a case that occurred prior to the decision of the *quo warranto.* How far are we bound in this regard by the judicial decision of the court of Florida? The learned counsel who addressed this Commission last on behalf of the other side seemed disposed somewhat to sneer at the idea that the tribunals of the United States should be bound by the decisions of the courts of the State in matters so grave as this. For my part, it seems to me that the graver the subject, and the higher it rises, the more binding become the obligations of the law; and I submit to your honors as a proposition of law that in reference to all matters having local concern of a statutory character, in reference to all local municipal laws of the States upon all subjects, the Supreme Court of the United States without exception invariably accepts as final and conclusive the decisions of the courts of the States, even although it may not approve the correctness of their logic or the wisdom of their conclusion. I beg leave to refer to one or two cases upon that subject. In the case of the Tioga Railroad Company *vs.* The Blossburg Railroad, in 20 Wallace, 143, the court uses the following language:

These decisions upon the construction of the statute are binding upon us, whatever we may think of their soundness on general principles.

In those few lines is contained the rule I have just now indicated to your honors. This was an opinion in reference to the operation under certain conditions and circumstances of the statute of limitations of New York; and the learned justice, in delivering the opinion on behalf of the court and accepting it of course for himself, announced the doctrine that the decisions of the State tribunals " upon the construction of its statutes are binding upon " the Supreme Court " whatever we may think of their soundness."

The opinion was delivered by his honor Mr. Justice Bradley, following a long line of preceding opinions of the same character.

In the case of Green *vs.* Neal's lessees, 6 Peters, the same doctrine was announced. In the case of The Township of Elmwood *vs.* Macy, 2 Otto, 294, the same rule was announced. It is unnecessary for me to read from the case, for I shall have occasion to refer presently to the dissenting opinion on another point.

In the case of Thompson *vs.* Whitman, 18 Wallace, 467, where the opinion was delivered by his honor Mr. Justice Bradley, the same general principle was announced:

Where a court has jurisdiction, it has a right to decide every question which occurs in the cause, and whether its decision be correct or otherwise, its judgment, until reversed, is regarded as binding in every other court. But, if it act without authority, its judgments and orders are regarded as nullities.

And in the case in 4 Wallace, referred to by Mr. Green in his opening to-day, the same rule is announced, his honor Mr. Justice Field, if I mistake not, giving the opinion of the court and declaring in effect that the State decision is incorporated into the State statute, and that the courts of the United States in considering and applying the statute apply it as modified, enlarged, or limited by that decision, giving to the decision the same effect as though in so many words it had been incorporated into the statute at the time of the passage of the act.

After submitting these few suggestions in reference to the authority of the State courts, I beg leave to suggest some views in reference to the time of the appointment of electors and as to what constitutes the appointment.

The learned counsel on the other side have regarded the appointment as made up of several acts reaching their culmination in the giving of the certificate by the governor at or about the time of the meeting of the electoral college. That certificate has nothing to do with the appointment whatever, and I submit is simply evidence of a previously existing fact which became a consummated fact on the day of election at the hour when the polls were closed. A certificate, whether it be the certificate of the governor, or of the attorney-general, or of the canvassing-board, is only evidence that the appointment has been made by the people, but itself is no part of the appointment, in no way essential to it, and in no way connected with it. It seems to be the theory and the basis of the argument of the counsel who preceded me that this appointment had depended in some way upon the muniment of the title, and if it did not——

Mr. EVARTS. I spoke of the governor's certificate under the law of Florida which was given to each elector as his warrant to execute his duty, and not the congressional certificate.

Mr. MERRICK. Even that has as little reference to the appointment as the certificates required by Congress; for these certificates, each of them, are only evidence that something has been done—are evidence that the individual to whom they are given has been invested with a power, not granted by the governor, not granted by the executive power of the State, but that he has been invested with a power granted by the people, and of which grant this shall be the muniment of title.

Now, may it please your honors, this principle has been very clearly stated in several cases, to one or two of which I beg leave to refer, among them the twenty-seventh volume of New York Reports, the case of The People vs. Pease, at pages 54 and 55:

It is made the duty of the board of county canvassers, upon the statement of votes given, to determine what person—

Very similar to the law organizing some of our present returning-boards—

to determine what person, by the greatest number of votes, has been duly elected to any office mentioned in said statement. (1 Revised Statutes, fifth edition, page 438, section 10.) County treasurers of the several counties of this State are to be elected at a general election, and hold their office for three years. (*Ibid*, page 406, section 17.) And the certificate of the board of canvassers authorized to canvass the votes given for any elective office is made evidence of the election of the person therein declared to have been elected.

*   *   *   *   *   *   *

What is it that confers title to the office, and the legal right to the reception of its emoluments? It surely is the fact that the greatest number of qualified voters have so declared their wishes at an election held pursuant to law. It is not the canvass, or estimate, or certificate which determines the right. These are only evidences of the right, but the truth may be inquired into, and the very right ascertained. When it is so ascertained, the legal consequences follow that the person usurping the office is ousted, the person legally entitled takes the office and its fees, &c., and recovers from the usurper the fees or emoluments belonging to the office received by him by means of his usurpation thereof.

It is not the canvass, then, or the estimates, or the certificates which determine the right. The right is determined by the vote of the people, and the canvass is only to ascertain what that vote was, and the certificate is evidence as to who received the larger majority of votes.

Mr. Commissioner EDMUNDS. Was that a *quo warranto*, Mr. Merrick?

Mr. MERRICK. It was a proceeding by *quo warranto*. There are other authorities of a similar nature to which I will refer the court, and taking a suggestion from the inquiry made by the Senator, I would remark that it is quite immaterial whether it was a proceeding by *quo warranto* or not, for the same rule would apply in all cases, barring the fact claimed by the other side in behalf of a proceeding or an action involving the acts of an officer *de facto*. The rule is the same, no matter what may be the form of action, as to whether the appointment is derived from executive appointment or derived from the people. By the act of the legislature of Florida, which legislature was authorized to appoint her electors in such a manner as it might deem proper, it was provided that the electors should be appointed by the people. They were voted for and appointed by the people. The State did not provide that her electors should be appointed by her executive or by her returning-board, but that they should be appointed by the people; and whatever other machinery of the government was dedicated to use in this direction was machinery dedicated to the office of ascertaining whom the people had appointed and providing those whom the people had appointed with the proper muniments of title in order that no one might be deceived or led astray, and no inconvenience might result from their claim to the official position.

Mr. Commissioner THURMAN. Mr. Merrick, are you not arguing a question that is settled by the Constitution and the act of Congress? The Constitution says that Congress may determine the time of choosing the electors. The act of Congress says:

Except in case of a presidential election prior to the ordinary period, as specified in sections 147 to 149, inclusive, when the offices of President and Vice-President both become vacant, the electors of President and Vice-President shall be appointed in each State, on the Tuesday next after the first Monday in November, in every fourth year succeeding every election of a President and Vice-President.

They are to be appointed on that day.

Mr. MERRICK. The Senator is correct. I am engaged in possibly a useless discussion on this point. The electors are to be appointed on the day specified, and being appointed on that day whatever transpires after that day with regard to them has relation to that appointment and is simply evidence of that appointment. It is hardly necessary that I should refer your honors to any other authorities upon that subject after Senator THURMAN'S remark.

Permit me now a word or two in reference to the writ of *quo warranto;* and I regret that my time is so nearly spent that on this important branch of the case it can only be a word or two. The counsel on the other side have stated that they considered that the *quo warranto* judgment was no longer before the Commission. I understand the order of the court to refer to the certificates and to state that all that the certificates contain is in evidence, and as certificate No. 3 makes recital of the *quo warranto* as being the basis of executive action in issuing the certificate, the judgment on this *quo warranto* is therefore before this Commission. It is before the Commission as a judgment of the court of the State, independent of this certificate. We have that judgment here in a proper form; and although it may not be proper under the order to use it before this court as evidence in this particular case as to these parties, it is before the court as evidence of what is the construction of the law of Florida by her judicial tribunals.

The PRESIDENT. I have already allowed you five minutes for interruptions. I must consider your time as closed.

Mr. Commissioner EDMUNDS. Mr. Merrick has been interrupted so much that I think he ought to have five minutes more.

Mr. MERRICK. I am much obliged to the Senator for his consideration; and while I accept with grateful acknowledgment the privilege conferred, I beg to say that the time allowed would scarcely compensate for the interruptions. They have diverted me to such an extent from the line of argument I was pursuing as to have entirely broken the direction of thought and reasoning I had intended to follow.

I submit that the *quo warranto* is then before you at least as evidence of what is the law of Florida. If it is not evidence as to the title of these particular individuals, it is before you as evidence of the law of Florida, and it tells you that according to the law of Florida the so-called Hayes electors were not appointed; it tells you that according to the law of Florida the so-called Tilden electors were appointed. It is a judgment of the court of Florida rendered upon an issue of fact to which the law of Florida was applied. If you will look into the record of this *quo warranto* you will find that it was not decided upon a simple demurrer, not upon a simple question of jurisdiction, although the court decided that it had jurisdiction, that question being directly brought before it; but it was decided upon the facts in the case. A plea having been interposed by the respondents in the *quo warranto* to the effect that they were the duly-elected electors and had received a majority of the votes of the people, and issue being joined upon that plea, a jury being waived by agreement of counsel and the cause having been submitted to the court to be tried upon the facts, it was tried upon the facts. All the facts were brought before the court. The canvass was before the court; the county returns were before the court; all the evidence that the Hayes electors desired to bring before the court to have the fact of their appointment according to law adjudicated was there; and upon all that evidence, so before the court, that court decided that according to the law of Florida as applied to the case made before it the Hayes electors were not appointed, and the Tilden electors were appointed.

I then submit, may it please your honors, in reference to this *quo warranto*, in the first instance, that it is before you as part of certificate No. 3, so intimately connected with it and interwoven with it that you cannot fail to regard it as part of the legitimate evidence to be considered when you come to determine which of these certificates you will accept, and that if it is not before you in that character it is then before you as a judicial decision of the courts of Florida bearing testimony as to what is the law of Florida, not in its general conclusion and general result, but bearing testimony as to that law in specific details found throughout the case as the various points were made and presented, and as you will find them decided upon looking into the record.

May it please your honors, I have endeavored in the remarks I have made to present this case, as far as I possibly could, as I would present any ordinary case at law, keeping far away from my heart and lips all feeling or expression of a partisan character. If, in the heat of the argument or in response to inquiries made of me, I should have broken in any particular the resolution I had formed in that regard, I can only beg pardon of the sacred traditions that cluster about this chamber of justice.

Mr. GREEN. The brief to which I alluded in my argument is now here, and, with the permission of the Commission, I will have it distributed among its members.*

---

* This brief will be found in the appendix of briefs as brief No. 2. A brief was also filed by Mr. Whitney which will be there found as brief No. 3.

The PRESIDENT. Certainly.

Mr. GREEN. I will also ask permission to state that the brief which had been prepared for what is known as the Oregon case, to which Judge Hoadly alluded in his argument, has not yet come from the printer, but that we expect to have it during the afternoon. He requests me also to state that that brief having been prepared for use in the Oregon case, necessarily contains some matters which he would not use in this argument if he had had time to prepare a brief specially for this case.

The PRESIDENT. I will state to the bar that there will be no further public business transacted to-day by the Commission.

Mr. Commissioner EDMUNDS. I move that the Commission take a recess for half an hour.

Mr. Commissioner PAYNE. I move as a substitute that the Commission adjourn until to-morrow morning at ten o'clock.

Mr. Commissioner EDMUNDS. On that motion I ask for the yeas and nays.

The PRESIDENT. The motion to adjourn takes precedence. The question is on the motion to adjourn until to-morrow at ten o'clock.

The question being taken by yeas and nays, resulted—yeas 8, nays 7; as follows:

Those who voted in the affirmative are: Messrs. Abbott, Bayard, Bradley, Clifford, Field, Hunton, Payne, and Thurman—8.

Those who voted in the negative are: Messrs. Edmunds, Frelinghuysen, Garfield, Hoar, Miller, Morton, and Strong—7.

So the motion was agreed to; and (at four o'clock and fifty minutes p. m.) the Commission adjourned until to-morrow at ten o'clock a. m.

FRIDAY, *February* 9, 1877.

The Commission met at ten o'clock a. m., pursuant to adjournment, all the members being present.

The journal of yesterday was read, corrected, and approved.

The PRESIDENT. The case in regard to Florida having been submitted, shall the doors be closed for consultation?

Mr. Commissioner MORTON. I move that the doors be now closed.

The motion was agreed to; and the Commission proceeded to deliberate with closed doors in the matter of the electoral vote of the State of Florida.

After debate,

Mr. Commissioner THURMAN (at one o'clock and thirty-seven minutes p. m.) moved that the Commission take a recess for half an hour.

The motion was agreed to.

At two o'clock and seven minutes p. m., the recess having expired, the Commission resumed its session for deliberation.

After further debate,

Mr. Commissioner STRONG moved that general debate on the question pending be closed on or before six o'clock p. m.

The motion was agreed to.

Mr. Commissioner EDMUNDS moved that after six o'clock p. m. each Commissioner be allowed to speak but once, and not longer than five minutes.

The motion was agreed to.

Mr. Commissioner THURMAN offered the following resolution:

Resolved, That F. C. Humphreys was not a United States shipping-commissioner on the 7th day of November, 1876.

After debate,

Mr. Commissioner THURMAN withdrew his resolution.

After further debate,

Mr. Commissioner EDMUNDS offered the following resolution:

Resolved, That the following be adopted as the decision of the Commission in the case of Florida:

ELECTORAL COMMISSION,
Washington, D. C., February 9, A. D. 1877.

To the President of the Senate of the United States, presiding in the meeting of the two Houses of Congress, under the act of Congress entitled "An act to provide for and regulate the counting of the votes for President and Vice-President, and the decision of questions arising thereon, for the term commencing March 4, A. D. 1877," approved January 29, A. D. 1877:

The Electoral Commission mentioned in said act having received certain certificates and papers purporting to be certificates, and papers accompanying the same, of the electoral votes from the State of Florida, and the objections thereto submitted to it under said act, now report that it has duly considered the same, pursuant to said act, and has decided, and does hereby decide, that the votes of Frederick C. Humphreys, Charles H. Pearce, William H. Holden, and Thomas W. Long, named in the certificate of M. L. Stearns, governor of said State, which votes are certified by said persons, as appears by the certificate submitted to the Commission, as aforesaid, and marked "number one," by said Commission, and herewith returned, are the votes provided for by the Constitution of the United States, and that the same are lawfully to be counted as therein certified, namely: Four (4) votes for Rutherford B. Hayes, of the State of Ohio, for President, and four (4) votes for William A. Wheeler, of the State of New York, for Vice-President.

The Commission also has decided, and hereby decides and reports, that the four persons first before named were duly appointed electors in and by said State of Florida.

The brief ground of this decision is, that it appears upon such evidence as by the Constitution and the law named in said act of Congress is competent and pertinent to the consideration of the subject that the before-mentioned electors appear to have been lawfully elected such electors of President and Vice-President of the United States for the term beginning March 4, 1877, of the State of Florida, and that they voted as such at the time and in the manner provided for by the Constitution of the United States and the law.

The Commission has also decided, and does hereby decide and report, that, as a consequence of the foregoing and upon the grounds before stated, neither of the papers purporting to be certificates of the electoral votes of said State of Florida numbered two (2) and three (3) by the Commission, and herewith returned, are the certificates or the votes provided for by the Constitution of the United States, and that they ought not to be counted as such.

Done at Washington the day and year first above written.

Mr. Commissioner HUNTON offered the following as a substitute:

That the electors named in certificate No. 2, to wit, Wilkinson Call, J. E. Yonge, Robert Bullock, and Robert B. Hilton, are the four persons who were duly appointed electors by the State of Florida on the 7th day of November, 1876, and that their votes as certified in such certificate are the votes provided for by the Constitution of the United States.

The question being on the adoption of the substitute, it was decided in the negative:

YEAS 7
NAYS 8

Those who voted in the affirmative were: Messrs. Abbott, Bayard, Clifford, Field, Hunton, Payne, and Thurman—7.

Those who voted in the negative were: Messrs. Bradley, Edmunds, Frelinghuysen, Garfield, Hoar, Miller, Morton, and Strong—8.

Thereupon the resolution offered by Mr. Commissioner EDMUNDS was withdrawn.

Mr. Commissioner GARFIELD offered the following resolutions:

Resolved, That the four persons, to wit, Frederick C. Humphreys, Charles H. Pearce, William H. Holden, and Thomas W. Long, were duly appointed electors of President and Vice-President for the State of Florida, and that the votes cast by the aforesaid four persons are the votes provided for by the Constitution of the United States.

Resolved, That Mr. Edmunds, Mr. Bradley, and Mr. Miller be appointed a committee to draft a report of the action of the Commission, as required by law.

The question being on the adoption of the first resolution, it was decided in the affirmative:

YEAS 8
NAYS 7

Those who voted in the affirmative were: Messrs. Bradley, Edmunds, Frelinghuysen, Garfield, Hoar, Miller, Morton, and Strong—8.

Those who voted in the negative were: Messrs. Abbott, Bayard, Clifford, Field, Hunton, Payne, and Thurman—7.

The question being on the adoption of the second resolution offered by Mr. Commissioner Garfield, it was decided in the affirmative.

Mr. Commissioner EDMUNDS (at six o'clock and five minutes p. m.) moved that the Commission take a recess for one hour.

The motion was agreed to; and a recess was accordingly taken until seven o'clock and five minutes p. m.

The recess having expired, the Commission resumed its session for deliberation.

Mr. Commissioner EDMUNDS, on behalf of committee appointed to prepare the report of the Commission in the matter of the electoral vote of the State of Florida, offered the following order:

Ordered, That the following be adopted as the final decision and report in the matters submitted to the Commission as to the electoral vote of the State of Florida:

ELECTORAL COMMISSION,
Washington, D. C., February 9, A. D. 1877.

To the President of the Senate of the United States, presiding in the meeting of the two Houses of Congress, under the act of Congress entitled "An act to provide for and regulate the counting of the votes for President and Vice-President, and the decision of questions arising thereon, for the term commencing March 4, A. D. 1877," approved January 29, A. D. 1877:

The Electoral Commission mentioned in said act, having received certain certificates and papers purporting to be certificates, and papers accompanying the same, of the electoral votes from the State of Florida, and the objections thereto submitted to it under said act, now report that it has duly considered the same, pursuant to said act, and has decided, and does hereby decide, that the votes of Frederick C. Humphreys, Charles H. Pearce, William H. Holden, and Thomas W. Long, named in the certificate of M. L. Stearns, governor of said State, which votes are certified by said persons, as appears by the certificate submitted to the Commission as aforesaid, and marked " number one " by said Commission, and herewith returned, are the votes provided for by the Constitution of the United States, and that the same are lawfully to be counted as therein certified, namely: four (4) votes for Rutherford B. Hayes, of the State of Ohio, for President, and four (4) votes for William A. Wheeler, of the State of New York, for Vice-President.

The Commission has also decided, and hereby decides and reports, that the four persons first before named were duly appointed electors in and by said State of Florida.

The ground of this decision, stated briefly, as required by said act, is as follows:

That it is not competent under the Constitution and the law, as it existed at the date of the passage of said act, to go into evidence *aliunde* the papers opened by the President of the Senate in the presence of the two Houses to prove that other persons than those regularly certified to by the governor of the State of Florida, in and according to the determination and declaration of their appointment by the board of State canvassers of said State prior to the time required for the performance of their duties, had been appointed electors, or by counter-proof to show that they had not, and that all proceedings of the courts or acts of the legislature or of the executive of Florida subsequent to the casting of the votes of the electors on the prescribed day, are inadmissible for any such purpose.

As to the objection made to the eligibility of Mr. Humphreys, the Commission is of opinion that, without reference to the question of the effect of the vote of an ineligible elector, the evidence does not show that he held the office of shipping-commissioner on the day when the electors were appointed.

The Commission has also decided, and does hereby decide and report, that, as a consequence of the foregoing, and upon the grounds before stated, neither of the papers purporting to be certificates of the electoral votes of said State of Florida, numbered two (2) and three (3) by the Commission, and herewith returned, are the certificates or the votes provided for by the Constitution of the United States, and that they ought not to be counted as such.

Done at Washington the day and year first above written.

The question being on the adoption of the report of the committee, it was decided in the affirmative:

YEAS 8
NAYS 7

Those who voted in the affirmative were: Messrs. Bradley, Edmunds, Frelinghuysen, Garfield, Hoar, Miller, Morton, and Strong—8.

Those who voted in the negative were: Messrs. Abbott, Bayard, Clifford, Field, Hunton, Payne, and Thurman—7.

So the report of the Commission was adopted; and said decision and report was thereupon signed by the members agreeing therein, as follows:

> SAM. F. MILLER,
> W. STRONG,
> JOSEPH P. BRADLEY,
> GEO. F. EDMUNDS,
> O. P. MORTON,
> FRED'K T. FRELINGHUYSEN,
> JAMES A. GARFIELD,
> GEORGE F. HOAR,
> *Commissioners.*

Mr. Commissioner EDMUNDS offered the following order:

Ordered, That the President transmit a letter to the President of the Senate, in the following words:

WASHINGTON, D. C., *February 9,* 1877.

SIR: I am directed by the Electoral Commission to inform the Senate that it has considered and decided upon the matters submitted to it, under the act of Congress concerning the same, touching the electoral votes from the State of Florida, and herewith, by direction of said Commission, I transmit to you the said decision, in writing, signed by the members agreeing therein, to be read at the meeting of the two Houses, according to said act. All the certificates and papers sent to the Commission by the President of the Senate are herewith returned.

The Hon. THOMAS W. FERRY,
    President of the Senate.

And that he deliver to him therewith the written decision of the Commission this day made, and all the certificates, papers, and objections in the case of Florida.

The order was adopted; and the letter was thereupon signed accordingly by "Nathan Clifford, President of the Commission."

Mr. Commissioner EDMUNDS offered the following order:

Ordered, That the President of the Commission transmit to the Speaker of the House of Representatives a letter, in the following words:

WASHINGTON, D. C., *February 9,* 1877.

SIR: I am directed by the Electoral Commission to inform the House of Representatives that it has considered and decided upon the matters submitted to it under the act of Congress concerning the same, touching the electoral votes from the State of Florida, and has transmitted said decision to the President of the Senate, to be read at the meeting of the two Houses, according to said act.

The Hon. SAMUEL J. RANDALL,
    Speaker of the House of Representatives.

The order was adopted; and the letter was thereupon signed accordingly by "Nathan Clifford, President of the Commission."

On motion of Mr. Commissioner ABBOTT, it was

Ordered, That the injunction of secrecy imposed on the action had to-day as entered in the Journal be removed.

On motion of Mr. Commissioner BRADLEY, it was

Ordered, That when the Commission adjourn it be until three o'clock p. m. to-morrow, the 10th instant.

On motion of Mr. Commissioner EDMUNDS, (at eight o'clock and five minutes p. m.,) the Commission adjourned.

PROCEEDINGS OF THE TWO HOUSES.

IN SENATE, *Saturday, February* 10, 1877.

The recess taken on Friday, February 9, having expired, the Senate resumed its session at ten o'clock a. m. of Saturday, February 10.

The PRESIDENT *pro tempore* laid before the Senate the following communication; which was read:

WASHINGTON, D. C., *February* 9, 1877.

SIR: I am directed by the Electoral Commission to inform the Senate that it has considered and decided upon the matters submitted to it, under the act of Congress concerning the same, touching the electoral votes from the State of Florida, and herewith, by direction of said Commission, I transmit to you the said decision in writing, signed by the members agreeing therein, to be read at the meeting of the two Houses, according to said act. All the certificates and papers sent to the Commission by the President of the Senate are herewith returned.

NATHAN CLIFFORD,
President of the Commission.

Hon. THOMAS W. FERRY,
President of the Senate.

On motion of Mr. Senator BOUTWELL, the Senate took a recess until twelve o'clock noon, at which hour it re-assembled; when, on motion of Mr. Senator HAMLIN, it was

Resolved, That the Secretary be directed to inform the House of Representatives that the President of the Electoral Commission has notified the Senate that the Commission had arrived at a decision of the question submitted to them in relation to the electoral votes of the State of Florida; and that the Senate is now ready to meet the House to receive the same, and to proceed with the count of the electoral vote for President and Vice-President.

IN THE HOUSE OF REPRESENTATIVES,
Saturday, February 10, 1877.

The House of Representatives resumed its session at ten o'clock a. m., the recess taken on Friday, February 9, having expired, and immediately, on motion of Mr. Representative CLYMER, took a further recess until eleven o'clock and fifty-five minutes a. m., when, after some formal business, the House, by unanimous consent, took a further recess till twelve o'clock noon, when the Speaker laid before the House the following communication; which was read:

WASHINGTON, D. C., *February* 9, 1877.

SIR: I am directed by the Electoral Commission to inform the House of Representatives that it has considered and decided upon the matters submitted to it, under the act of Congress concerning the same, touching the electoral votes from the State of Florida, and has transmitted said decision to the President of the Senate, to be read at the meeting of the two Houses, according to said act.

NATHAN CLIFFORD,
President of the Commission.

Hon. SAMUEL J. RANDALL,
Speaker of the House of Representatives.

Mr. Representative SAYLER moved that the Clerk be directed to notify the Senate that the House of Representatives will be prepared at one o'clock p. m. to receive them for the purpose of proceeding further with the counting of the electoral vote for President and Vice-President.

Mr. Representative HALE submitted the following resolution as an amendment, viz:

Resolved, That the Clerk of the House notify the Senate that the House of Representatives is now in session and ready to meet the Senate in the hall for further proceedings under the provisions of the act to provide for and regulate the counting of votes for President and Vice-President.

Mr. Representative SAYLER demanded the previous question; which was seconded and the main question ordered,

And being put,

First, upon the resolution submitted by Mr. Representative Hale as an amendment to the motion of Mr. Representative Sayler,

The same was not agreed to.

The question then recurring on the motion of Mr. Representative Sayler,

The same was agreed to.

JOINT MEETING.

SATURDAY, *February* 10, 1877.

The action of each House having been communicated to the other,

At one o'clock p. m. the appearance of the Senate was announced to the House of Representatives.

The Senate entered the hall of the House, preceded by its Sergeant-at-Arms and headed by its President *pro tempore* and its Secretary, the members and officers of the House rising to receive them.

The PRESIDENT *pro tempore* of the Senate took his seat as Presiding Officer of the joint convention of the two Houses, the Speaker of the House occupying a chair upon his left.

The PRESIDING OFFICER. The joint meeting of Congress for counting the electoral vote resumes its session. The two Houses, having separated pending the submission to the Commission of objections to the certificates from the State of Florida, have re-assembled to hear and to coincide or otherwise with the decision of that tribunal, by a majority of the Commission, in writing and signed by the members agreeing therein, which will now be read by the Secretary of the Senate and be entered in the Journal of each House.

The Secretary of the Senate read as follows:

ELECTORAL COMMISSION,
Washington, D. C., February 9, *A. D.* 1877.

To the President of the Senate of the United States, presiding in the meeting of the two Houses of Congress, under the act of Congress entitled "An act to provide for and regulate the counting of the votes for President and Vice-President, and the decision of questions arising thereon, for the term commencing March 4, A. D. 1877," approved January 29, 1877:

The Electoral Commission mentioned in said act having received certain certificates and papers purporting to be certificates, and papers accompanying the same, of the electoral votes from the State of Florida, and the objections thereto, submitted to it under said act, now report that it has duly considered the same, pursuant to said act, and has decided, and does hereby decide, that the votes of Frederick C. Humphreys, Charles H. Pearce, William H. Holden, and Thomas W. Long, named in the certificate of M. L. Stearns, governor of said State, which votes are certified by said persons, as appears by the certificate submitted to the Commission, as aforesaid, and marked "number one" by said Commission and herewith returned, are the votes provided for by the Constitution of the United States, and that the same are lawfully to be counted as therein certified, namely: Four votes for Rutherford B. Hayes, of the State of Ohio, for President, and four votes for William A. Wheeler, of the State of New York, for Vice-President.

The Commission has also decided, and hereby decides and reports, that the four persons first before named were duly appointed electors in and by said State of Florida.

The ground of this decision stated briefly, as required by said act, is as follows:

That it is not competent under the Constitution and the law, as it existed at the date of the passage of said act, to go into evidence *aliunde* the papers opened by the President of the Senate in the presence of the two Houses, to prove that other persons than those regularly certified to by the governor of the State of Florida, in and according to the determination and declaration of their appointment by the board of State canvassers of said State prior to the time required for the performance of their duties, had been appointed electors, or by counter-proof to show that they had not, and that all proceedings of the courts or acts of the legislature or of the executive of Florida, subsequent to the casting of the votes of the electors on the prescribed day, are inadmissible for any such purpose.

As to the objection made to the eligibility of Mr. Humphreys, the Commission is of the opinion that, without reference to the question of the effect of the vote of an ineligible elector, the evidence does not show that he held the office of shipping-commissioner on the day when the electors were appointed.

The Commission has also decided, and does hereby decide and report, that, as a consequence of the foregoing, and upon the grounds before stated, neither of the papers purporting to be certificates of the electoral votes of said State of Florida, numbered two (2) and three (3) by the Commission and herewith returned, are the certificates, or the votes provided for by the Constitution of the United States, and that they ought not to be counted as such.

Done at Washington the day and year first above written.

> SAM. F. MILLER,
> W. STRONG,
> JOSEPH P. BRADLEY,
> GEO. F. EDMUNDS,
> O. P. MORTON,
> FRED'K T. FRELINGHUYSEN,
> JAMES A. GARFIELD,
> GEORGE F. HOAR,
> *Commissioners.*

The PRESIDING OFFICER. Are there objections to this decision?

Mr. Representative FIELD. I submit an objection to the decision and report just read.

The PRESIDING OFFICER. The member from New York [Mr. Field] submits an objection to the decision; which will be read by the Clerk of the House.

The Clerk of the House read as follows:

An objection is interposed by the undersigned Senators and Representatives to the decision made by the Commission constituted by the act entitled "An act to provide for and regulate the counting of the votes for President and Vice-President, and the decision of questions arising thereon, for the term commencing March 4, A. D. 1877," as to the true and lawful electoral vote of Florida, upon the following grounds:

First. For that the decision determines that the vote cast by Charles H. Pearce, Frederick C. Humphreys, William H. Holden, and Thomas W. Long, as electors of President and Vice-President of the United States in and for or on behalf of the State of Florida, is the true and lawful electoral vote of said State, when, in truth and in fact, the vote cast by Wilkinson Call, James E. Yonge, Robert B. Hilton, and Robert Bullock is the true and lawful vote of said State.

Second. For that said Commission refused to receive competent and material evidence tending to prove that Charles H. Pearce, Frederick C. Humphreys, William H. Holden, and Thomas W. Long were not appointed electors in the manner prescribed by the legislature of the State of Florida, but were designated as electors by the returning-board of said State corruptly and fraudulently, in disregard of law, and with the intent to defeat the will of the people expressed in the choice of Wilkinson Call, James E. Yonge, Robert B. Hilton, and Robert Bullock, who were legally and regularly appointed electors by the State of Florida in the manner directed by the legislature thereof.

Third. For that the decision aforesaid was founded upon the resolution and order of said Commission previously made, as follows:

" *Ordered,* That no evidence will be received or considered by the Commission which was not submitted to the joint convention of the two Houses by the President of the Senate with the different certificates, except such as relates to the eligibility of F. C. Humphreys, one of the electors."

Fourth. For that said decision excludes all the evidence taken by the two Houses of Congress and by the committees of each House concerning the frauds, errors, and irregularities committed by the persons whose certificates are taken as proof of the due appointment of electors.

Fifth. For that said decision excludes all evidence tending to prove that the certificate of ——— Stearns, governor, as also that of the board of State canvassers, was procured or given in pursuance of a fraudulent and corrupt conspiracy to cheat the State of Florida out of its rightful choice of electors and to substitute therefor those who had not been chosen or appointed electors by said State in the manner directed by the legislature thereof.

Sixth. For that said Commission refused to recognize the right of the courts of the State of Florida to review and reverse the judgment of the returning-board or board of State canvassers, rendered through fraud and without jurisdiction, and rejected and refused to consider the action of said courts after their decision that Charles H. Pearce, Frederick C. Humphreys, William H. Holden, and Thomas W. Long were not entitled to cast the electoral vote of Florida; which said decision was rendered by a court of said State in a case lawfully brought before said court, which court had jurisdiction over the subject-matter thereof and whose jurisdiction over the said Charles H. Pearce, Frederick C. Humphreys, William H. Holden, and Thomas W. Long had attached before any act was done by them as electors.

Seventh. For that said decision excludes all evidence tending to prove that the State of Florida, by all the departments of its government, legislative, executive, and judicial, has repudiated as fraudulent and void the certificate of ——— Stearns, governor, as well as that of the State canvassers, upon which certificate of the said governor the said Commission has acted, and by means of which the true electoral votes of Florida have been rejected and false ones substituted in their stead; and

Eighth. For that to count the votes of Charles H. Pearce, Frederick C. Humphreys, William H. Holden, and Thomas W. Long as electors for President and Vice-President would be a violation of the Constitution of the United States.

> CHS. W. JONES, *Florida,*
> HENRY COOPER, *of Tennessee,*
> FRANCIS KERNAN, *of New York,*
> ELI SAULSBURY, *Delaware,*
> J. E. McDONALD, *Indiana,*
> W. H. BARNUM, *Connecticut,*
> > *On the part of the Senate.*
>
> J. PROCTOR KNOTT,
> DAVID DUDLEY FIELD, *of New York,*
> W. S. HOLMAN, *of Indiana,*
> J. R. TUCKER,
> CHARLES P. THOMPSON,
> G. A. JENKS, *of Pennsylvania,*
> J. J. FINLEY,
> MILTON SAYLER,
> E. JNO. ELLIS,
> W. R. MORRISON,
> ABRAM S. HEWITT,
> WILLIAM M. SPRINGER,
> > *On the part of the House.*

The PRESIDING OFFICER. Has the member from New York, who submitted this objection, a duplicate, so that each House may have a copy?

Mr. Representative FIELD sent to the Clerk's desk a copy of the objections.

The PRESIDING OFFICER. Are there further objections to the decision? [A pause.] If there be none, the Senate will retire to its chamber, that the Houses respectively may consider and determine on the objection.

The Senate then withdrew.

IN SENATE, *Saturday, February* 10, 1877—1.30 p. m.

The Senate having returned to its chamber at half past one o'clock p. m., the PRESIDENT *pro tempore* took the chair and called the Senate to order.

The objection to the decision of the Electoral Commission submitted in the joint meeting of the two Houses was read by the Secretary.

Mr. Senator SHERMAN submitted a resolution; which (after debate and the rejection of various amendments thereto) was agreed to by a vote of yeas 44, nays 25, in the following words:

Resolved, That the decision of the Commission upon the electoral vote of the State of Florida stand as the judgment of the Senate, the objections made thereto to the contrary notwithstanding.

On motion of Mr. Senator SARGENT, it was

Ordered, That the Secretary notify the House of Representatives thereof, and that the Senate is now ready to meet the House to resume the counting of the electoral votes for President and Vice-President.

The Senate, being advised that the House of Representatives had taken a recess, took a recess (at three o'clock p. m.) until Monday, February 12, at ten o'clock a. m.

IN THE HOUSE OF REPRESENTATIVES,
Saturday, February 10, 1877—1.20 p. m.
The Senate having retired,

Mr. Representative LYNDE moved that the House take a recess until ten o'clock a. m. of Monday, February 12.

Mr. Representative HALE made the point of order that under the act of Congress of January 29, 1877, known as the electoral act, no such recess could be taken, and that therefore the motion was not in order.

The SPEAKER overruled the point of order; from which decision Mr. Representative HALE appealed.

On motion of Mr. Representative COX, the appeal was ordered to lie on the table.

The question recurring on the motion of Mr. Representative LYNDE, it was agreed to—yeas 162, nays 107; and the House (at two o'clock and fifty-five minutes p. m.) took a recess until Monday, February 12, at ten o'clock a. m., the action of the Senate being communicated to the House during the call of the roll on the motion for a recess.

ELECTORAL COMMISSION.

SATURDAY, *February* 10, 1877.

The Commission met at three o'clock p. m., pursuant to adjournment. Present: The President of the Commission and Commissioners MILLER, FIELD, STRONG, BRADLEY, EDMUNDS, MORTON, FRELINGHUYSEN, GARFIELD, HUNTON, and HOAR.

The Journal of yesterday was read, corrected, and approved.

On motion of Mr. Commissioner EDMUNDS, the Commission (at three o'clock and twenty-eight minutes p. m.) adjourned till Monday next at half past two o'clock p. m.

PROCEEDINGS OF THE TWO HOUSES.

IN SENATE, *Monday, February* 12, 1877.

The Senate resumed its session at ten o'clock a. m., transacting no business, and at two o'clock and twenty minutes p. m., being notified of the action of the House of Representatives on the objection to the decision of the Commission as to the electoral votes of Florida, it proceeded to the hall of the House of Representatives.

IN THE HOUSE OF REPRESENTATIVES,
Monday, February 12, 1877.

The House of Representatives resumed its session at ten o'clock a. m. After a suspension of business for half an hour by unanimous consent, Mr. Representative FIELD submitted the following resolution :

Ordered, That the counting of the electoral votes from the State of Florida shall not proceed in conformity with the decision of the Electoral Commission, but that the votes of Wilkinson Call, James E. Yonge, Robert B. Hilton, and Robert Bullock be counted as the votes of the State of Florida for President and Vice-President of the United States.

After debate, and the rejection of amendments proposed, the resolution of Mr. Representative FIELD was adopted—yeas 168, nays 103 ; whereupon it was

Ordered, That the Clerk inform the Senate of the action of the House, and that the House is now ready to meet the Senate in this hall to proceed with the counting of the electoral votes for President and Vice-President.

JOINT MEETING.

MONDAY, *February* 12, 1877.

The Senate, at two o'clock and twenty-five minutes p. m., entered the hall of the House of Representatives, preceded by its Sergeant-at-Arms and headed by its President *pro tempore* and its Secretary, the members and officers of the House rising to receive them ; and the Senators, tellers, Secretary of the Senate, Clerk of the House of Representatives, and officers of the two Houses took the seats provided for them.

The PRESIDING OFFICER. The joint meeting of Congress resumes its session. The two Houses separately have considered and determined the objection submitted by the member from the State of New York [Mr. FIELD] to the decision of the Commission upon the certificates from the State of Florida. The Secretary of the Senate will now read the decision of the Senate.

The Secretary of the Senate read as follows :

Resolved, That the decision of the Commission upon the electoral vote of the State of Florida stand as the judgment of the Senate, the objections made thereto to the contrary notwithstanding.

The PRESIDING OFFICER. The Clerk of the House will now read the decision of the House.

The Clerk of the House read as follows :

Ordered, That the counting of the electoral vote from the State of Florida shall not proceed in conformity with the decision of the Electoral Commission, but that the votes of Wilkinson Call, James E. Yonge, Robert B. Hilton, and Robert Bullock be counted as the votes of the State of Florida for President and Vice-President of the United States.

The PRESIDING OFFICER. The two Houses not concurring in ordering otherwise, the decision of the Commission stand, unreversed, and the counting will now proceed in conformity with the decision of the Commission. The tellers will announce the vote of the State of Florida.

Mr. Senator ALLISON, (one of the tellers.) The State of Florida gives 4 votes for Rutherford B. Hayes, of Ohio, for President, and 4 votes for William A. Wheeler, of New York, for Vice-President.

UNDISPUTED STATES.

The PRESIDING OFFICER. The Chair having opened the certificate of the State of Georgia, the tellers will read the same in the presence and hearing of the two Houses. A corresponding certificate received by mail is also handed to the tellers.

Mr. Representative COOK (one of the tellers) read in full the certificate of the electoral vote of the State of Georgia.

The PRESIDING OFFICER. Are there objections to the certificate of the State of Georgia? [A pause.] There being none, the vote of that State will be counted. The tellers will announce the vote.

Mr. Representative STONE, (one of the tellers.) The State of Georgia casts 11 votes for Samuel J. Tilden, of New York, for President of the United States, and 11 votes for Thomas A. Hendricks, of the State of Indiana, for Vice-President.

The PRESIDING OFFICER. The Chair having opened the certificate from the State of Illinois, one of the tellers will read the same in the presence and hearing of the two Houses. A corresponding certificate received by mail is also handed to the tellers.

Mr. Senator ALLISON (one of the tellers) read the certificate of the electoral vote of the State of Illinois.

The PRESIDING OFFICER. Are there objections to the certificate of the State of Illinois? If none, the vote will be counted. The tellers will announce the vote of that State.

Mr. Senator ALLISON, (one of the tellers.) In the State of Illinois 21 votes were cast for Rutherford B. Hayes, of Ohio, for President, and 21 votes for William A. Wheeler, of New York, for Vice-President.

The PRESIDING OFFICER. The certificate of the State of Indiana having been opened, one of the tellers will read the same in the presence and hearing of the two Houses. The Chair hands to the tellers the corresponding certificate received by mail.

Mr. Representative STONE (one of the tellers) read the certificate.

The PRESIDING OFFICER. Are there objections to the certificate of the State of Indiana? There being none, the vote of that State will be counted. The tellers will announce the vote of Indiana.

Mr. Representative STONE, (one of the tellers.) The State of Indiana casts 15 votes for Samuel J. Tilden, of the State of New York, for President of the United States, and 15 votes for Thomas A. Hendricks, of Indiana, for Vice-President of the United States.

The PRESIDING OFFICER. Having opened the certificate from the State of Iowa, the Chair directs the reading of the same by the tellers in the hearing and presence of the two Houses. A corresponding certificate received by mail is also submitted to the tellers.

Mr. Senator ALLISON (one of the tellers) read the certificate.

The PRESIDING OFFICER. Are there objections to the certificate of the State of Iowa? If there be none, the vote of that State will be counted. The tellers will announce the vote of Iowa.

Mr. Senator ALLISON, (one of the tellers.) The State of Iowa casts 11 votes for Rutherford B. Hayes, of Ohio, for President, and 11 votes for William A. Wheeler, of New York, for Vice-President.

The PRESIDING OFFICER. The certificate from the State of Kansas having been opened, it will now be read by one of the tellers. A corresponding one received by mail is also submitted.

Mr. Senator INGALLS (one of the tellers) read the certificate.

The PRESIDING OFFICER. Are there objections to the certificate from the State of Kansas? If there be none, the vote of that State will be counted. The tellers will announce the vote.

Mr. Senator INGALLS, (one of the tellers.) The State of Kansas casts 5 votes for Rutherford B. Hayes, of Ohio, for President of the

United States, and 5 votes for William A. Wheeler, of New York, for Vice-President.

The PRESIDING OFFICER. Having opened the certificate from the State of Kentucky received by messenger, the Chair hands the same to the tellers to be read in the presence and hearing of the two Houses. A corresponding certificate received by mail is also delivered to the tellers.

Mr. Representative COOK (one of the tellers) read the certificate.

The PRESIDING OFFICER. Are there objections to the certificate from the State of Kentucky? If there be none, the vote of that State will be counted. It will be announced by the tellers.

Mr. Representative COOK, (one of the tellers.) The State of Kentucky casts 12 votes for Samuel J. Tilden, of New York, for President, and 12 votes for Thomas A. Hendricks, of Indiana, for Vice President.

LOUISIANA.

The PRESIDING OFFICER. The Chair opens a certificate from the State of Louisiana received by mail, no corresponding one by messenger. One of the tellers will read the same in the hearing and presence of the two Houses.

Mr. Senator ALLISON (one of the tellers) read as follows:

CERTIFICATE No. 1.

THE UNITED STATES OF AMERICA,
STATE OF LOUISIANA, EXECUTIVE DEPARTMENT,
New Orleans, December 6, 1876.

I, William Pitt Kellogg, governor of the State of Louisiana, hereby certify, pursuant to the laws of the United States, that at a general election duly held in accordance with law in the State of Louisiana, on Tuesday, the seventh day of November, 1876, for electors for President and Vice-President of the United States, the following-named persons were duly chosen and appointed electors of President and Vice-President of the United States for the State of Louisiana:

William Pitt Kellogg, for the State at large.
J. Henri Burch, for the State at large.
Peter Joseph, for the first congressional district.
Lionel A. Sheldon, for the second congressional district.
Morris Marks, for the third congressional district.
Aaron B. Levissee, for the fourth congressional district.
Orlando H. Brewster, for the fifth congressional district.
Oscar Joffrion, for the sixth congressional district.

In testimony whereof I have hereunto affixed my signature and caused the seal of the State to be attached, at the city of New Orleans, this sixth day of December, in the year of our Lord one thousand eight hundred and seventy-six, and in the year of the Independence of the United States of America the one hundred and first.

WM. P. KELLOGG.

By the governor:
[SEAL.] P. G. DESLONDE,
Secretary of State.

THE UNITED STATES OF AMERICA, STATE OF LOUISIANA, STATE-HOUSE,
New Orleans, December 6, 1876.

We, the electors of President and Vice-President of the United States for the State of Louisiana, do hereby certify that on this, the sixth day of December, in the year of our Lord eighteen hundred and seventy-six, we proceeded to vote by ballot for President of the United States, on the date above; that Rutherford B. Hayes, of the State of Ohio, received eight votes for President of the United States, being all the votes cast; and that we then immediately proceeded to vote by ballot for Vice-President of the United States, whereupon William A. Wheeler, of the State of New York, received eight votes for Vice-President of the United States, being all the votes cast.

In testimony whereof we, said electors, have hereunto signed our names, on this the first Wednesday, being the sixth day, of December, in the year of our Lord eighteen hundred and seventy-six, and of the Independence of the United States the one hundred and first.

> WILLIAM P. KELLOGG.
> J. HENRI BURCH.
> PETER JOSEPH.
> LIONEL A. SHELDON.
> MORRIS MARKS.
> AARON B. LEVISSEE.
> ORLANDO H. BREWSTER.
> OSCAR JOFFRION.

UNITED STATES OF AMERICA,
  State of Louisiana, City of New Orleans :

Be it remembered, that on this Wednesday, the sixth day of December, A. D. eighteen hundred and seventy-six, that the following-named persons, having been duly chosen and appointed by the people of the State of Louisiana electors of President and Vice-President of the United States, according to the certificate of William P. Kellogg, governor of the State of Louisiana, hereto attached, namely: William P. Kellogg, elector for the State at large; J. Henri Burch, elector for the State at large; Peter Joseph, elector for the first congressional district; Lionel A. Sheldon, elector for the second congressional district; Morris Marks, elector for the third congressional district; Oscar Joffrion, elector for the sixth congressional district, met at the State-house, at the city of New Orleans, the seat of government of the State of Louisiana, as required by law, on the first Wednesday of December, A. D. eighteen hundred and seventy-six, being the sixth day of said month.

The certificate of the governor was read, and the following persons answered to their names: William P. Kellogg, J. Henri Burch, Peter Joseph, Lionel A. Sheldon, Morris Marks, Oscar Joffrion. Not answering: Aaron B. Levissee and Orlando H. Brewster.

On motion of Peter Joseph, J. Henri Burch was elected to preside ; and on motion of Oscar Joffrion, Morris Marks was appointed secretary.

On motion of Lionel A. Sheldon, a recess was taken till the hour of three-thirty p. m., when the electors re-assembled.

On the roll being called, it was found that Aaron B. Levissee and Orlando H. Brewster were not present. At the hour of four p. m. the said Aaron B. Levissee and Orlando H. Brewster having failed to attend, the electors present proceeded to supply such vacancies by ballot, in accordance with the statute of the State of Louisiana in such case made and provided, which is in words and figures as follows :

"If any one or more of the electors chosen by the people shall fail from any cause whatever to attend at the appointed place at the hour of four p. m. of the day prescribed for their meeting, it shall be the duty of the other electors immediately to proceed by ballot to supply such vacancy or vacancies."

Lionel A. Sheldon and Peter Joseph were appointed tellers, when, after balloting, it was found that Aaron B. Levissee received six votes, being all the votes cast, to supply the vacancy in the fourth congressional district occasioned by the failure of Aaron B. Levissee to attend, and Orlando H. Brewster received six votes, being all the votes cast, to supply the vacancy in the fifth congressional district occasioned by the failure of Orlando H. Brewster to attend. The said Aaron B. Levissee and Orlando H. Brewster were thereupon declared elected to supply the vacancies in the fourth and fifth congressional districts respectively, and being sent for, soon after appeared and were in attendance as electors.

The said electors then proceeded to vote by ballot for President of the United States, when William P. Kellogg and Lionel A. Sheldon were appointed tellers, and upon counting the ballots for President of the United States, Rutherford B. Hayes, of the State of Ohio, did receive eight votes for President of the United States, being all the votes cast.

The said electors then proceeded to vote by ballot for Vice-President of the United States, when Peter Joseph and Oscar Joffrion were appointed tellers, and upon counting the votes for Vice-President of the United States, William A. Wheeler, of the State of New York, did receive eight votes for Vice-President of the United States, being all the votes cast, whereupon the said electors signed three certificates, one of which is hereto attached, which certificates are herewith placed separately in envelopes and sealed up carefully, and on each envelope was indorsed that " The within contains a list of all the votes cast by the electors for the State of Louisiana for President and Vice-President of the United States," one of which is given to the person appointed to convey the vote to the President of the Senate of the United States, and another indorsed in the same way is put in the post-office, and the other deposited with the judge of the district court of the United States for the district of Louisiana.

On motion of Peter Joseph, the electors proceeded to appoint a person to take charge of and deliver to the President of the Senate at the seat of the Government, before the first Wednesday in January next ensuing, one of said certificates, when Thomas C. Anderson was appointed to the above service, and said electors made and signed a certificate of such appointment in the following form:

UNITED STATES OF AMERICA, STATE OF LOUISIANA, STATE-HOUSE,
New Orleans, Wednesday, December 6, 1876.

We, the undersigned, electors of President and Vice-President of the United States for the State of Louisiana, do hereby appoint Thomas C. Anderson to take charge of and deliver to the President of the Senate of the United States, at the seat of Government at Washington, D. C., before the first Wednesday in January next, one of the certificates of the votes cast by the undersigned for President and Vice-President of the United States, on Wednesday, the sixth day of December, A. D. 1876.

In testimony whereof we have hereunto signed our names, on this sixth day of December, in the year of our Lord eighteen hundred and seventy-six, and of the Independence of the United States of America the one hundred and first.

WILLIAM P. KELLOGG.
J. HENRI BURCH.
PETER JOSEPH.
LIONEL A. SHELDON.
MORRIS MARKS.
A. B. LEVISSEE.
O. H. BREWSTER.
OSCAR JOFFRION.

UNITED STATES OF AMERICA, STATE OF LOUISIANA,
OFFICE SECRETARY OF STATE,
New Orleans, December 6, 1876.

I, P. G. Deslonde, secretary of state of the State of Louisiana, hereby certify that the following is a true and correct extract from an act of the legislature of the State of Louisiana, being act No. one hundred and ninety-three, approved October thirtieth, eighteen hundred and sixty-eight, the original of which act is on file among the records of my office, and is still in force and unrepealed:

"SEC. 8. *Be it further enacted, &c.*, That if any one or more of the electors chosen by the people shall fail from any cause whatever to attend at the appointed place at the hour of four p. m. of the day prescribed for their meeting, it shall be the duty of the other electors immediately to proceed by ballot to supply such vacancy or vacancies."

In testimony whereof I have hereunto set my hand and caused the seal of the State to be affixed this sixth day of December, in the year of our Lord eighteen hundred and seventy-six, and of the Independence of the United States the one hundred and first.

[SEAL.]   P. G. DESLONDE,
Secretary of State.

UNITED STATES OF AMERICA, STATE OF LOUISIANA,
OFFICE SECRETARY OF STATE,
New Orleans, December 6, 1876.

I, P. G. Deslonde, secretary of state for the State of Louisiana, hereby certify that at a general election held in the State of Louisiana, on Tuesday, the seventh day of November, eighteen hundred and seventy-six, the following-named persons were elected, chosen, and appointed electors for President and Vice-President of the United States, as appears from the returns of said election now on file in my office, and which have been duly promulgated according to law by the legal returning-officers of the State, to wit: William P. Kellogg, for the State at large; J. Henri Burch, for the State at large; Peter Joseph, for the first congressional district; Lionel A. Sheldon, for the second congressional district; Morris Marks, for the third congressional district; Aaron B. Levissee, for the fourth congressional district; Orlando H. Brewster, for the fifth congressional district; Oscar Joffrion, for the sixth congressional district. And I further certify that the names appended to the certificates of votes cast for President of the United States and for Vice-President of the United States, on Wednesday, the sixth day of December, A. D. eighteen hundred and seventy-six, and to the *procés-verbal* of the proceedings of said electors accompanying said certificates, are the true and proper signatures of the before-mentioned persons elected, chosen, and appointed electors of President and Vice-President of the United States for the State of Louisiana.

In testimony whereof I have hereunto signed my name and caused the seal of the State to be affixed this sixth day of December, in the year of our Lord eighteen hundred and seventy-six, and of the Independence of the United States the one hundred and first.

[SEAL.]   P. G. DESLONDE,
Secretary of State.

The PRESIDING OFFICER. Having opened a certificate received by messenger from the same State, the Chair hands it to the tellers, to be read in the presence and hearing of the two Houses. A corresponding one received by mail is also handed to the tellers.

Mr. Representative STONE (one of the tellers) read as follows:

CERTIFICATE NO. 2.

UNITED STATES OF AMERICA,
State of Louisiana :

This is to certify that the following is a true and correct list of the names of the electors of the President and Vice-President of the United States for the next ensuing regular term of the respective offices thereof, being electors duly and legally appointed by and for the State of Louisiana, having each received a majority of the votes cast for electors at the election in the State of Louisiana held in accordance with law; this certificate being furnished as directed by law, by the executive authority of said State of Louisiana.

List of names of electors: Robert C. Wickliffe, John McEnery, Louis St. Martin, Felix P. Poché, K. A. Cross, Alcibiade De Blanc, R. G. Cobb, William A. Seay.

In witness whereof I have hereunto signed my name and caused the great seal of the State of Louisiana to be affixed, at the city of New Orleans, the seat of government of said State, on this 6th December, 1876, being the first Wednesday in said month of December, in the year of our Lord one thousand eight hundred and seventy-six, and of the Independence of the United States the one hundred and first.

[SEAL.]
JOHN McENERY,
Governor of the State of Louisiana.

STATE OF LOUISIANA, *ss :*

We, the undersigned, electors of President and Vice-President of the United States of America for the next ensuing regular term of the respective offices thereof, being electors duly and legally appointed by and for the State of Louisiana, as appears by the annexed list of electors, made, certified, and delivered to us by the direction of the executive of the State, having met and convened in the city of New Orleans and the seat of government, at the hall of house of representatives, in pursuance of the laws of the United States, and also in pursuance of the laws of the State of Louisiana, on the first Wednesday, the sixth day of December, in the year of our Lord one thousand eight hundred and seventy-six—

Do hereby certify that, being so assembled and duly organized, we proceeded to vote by ballot, and balloted first for such President, and then for such Vice-President, by distinct ballots.

And we further certify that the following are two distincts lists; one of the votes for President, and the other of the votes for Vice-President.

List of persons voted for as President, with the number of votes for each.

Names of persons voted for.	Number of votes.
Samuel J. Tilden, of the State of New York......................	Eight votes.

List of all persons voted for as Vice-President, with the number of votes for each.

Names of persons voted for.	Number of votes.
Thomas A. Hendricks, of the State of Indiana....................	Eight votes.

In witness whereof we have hereunto set our hands.

Done at the hall of the house of representatives, in the city of New Orleans, and State of Louisiana, the sixth day of December, in the year of our Lord one thousand eight hundred and seventy-six, and of the United States of America the one hundred and first.

ROBERT C. WICKLIFFE.
JOHN McENERY.
L. ST. MARTIN.
F. P. POCHÉ.
ALCIBIADE DE BLANC.
K. A. CROSS.
R. G. COBB.
WM. A. SEAY.

[Indorsement.]

We hereby certify that the lists of all votes of the State of Louisiana given for President, and of all the votes given for Vice-President, are contained herein.

ROBERT C. WICKLIFFE.
JOHN McENERY.
L. ST. MARTIN.
ALCIBIADE DE BLANC.
F. P. POCHÉ.
R. G. COBB.
WM. A. SEAY.
K. A. CROSS.

To the PRESIDENT OF THE SENATE,
    At the seat of Government, Washington, District of Columbia.

The PRESIDING OFFICER. The Chair having opened another certificate from the State of Louisiana, received by messenger, one of the tellers will read the same in the presence and hearing of the two Houses. A corresponding certificate received by mail is also handed to the tellers.

Mr. Senator INGALLS (one of the tellers) read as follows:

CERTIFICATE NO. 3.

THE UNITED STATES OF AMERICA,
STATE OF LOUISIANA, EXECUTIVE DEPARTMENT,
    New Orleans, December 6, 1876.

I, William Pitt Kellogg, governor of the State of Louisiana, hereby certify, pursuant to the laws of the United States, that, at a general election duly held in accordance with law in the State of Louisiana, on Tuesday, the seventh day of November, 1876, for electors for President and Vice-President of the United States, the following-named persons were duly chosen and appointed electors of President and Vice-President of the United States for the State of Louisiana:

William P. Kellogg, for the State at large.
J. Henri Burch, for the State at large.
Peter Joseph, for the first congressional district.
Lionel A. Sheldon, for the second congressional district.
Morris Marks, for the third congressional district.
Aaron B. Levissee, for the fourth congressional district.
Orlando H. Brewster, for the fifth congressional district.
Oscar Joffrion, for the sixth congressional district.

In testimony whereof I have hereunto affixed my signature and caused the seal of the State to be attached, at the city of New Orleans, this sixth day of December, in the year of our Lord one thousand eight hundred and seventy-six, and in the year of the Independence of the United States of America the one hundred and first.

WM. P. KELLOGG.

By the governor:
    [SEAL.]   P. G. DESLONDE,
        Secretary of State.

————

THE UNITED STATES OF AMERICA,
STATE OF LOUISIANA, STATE HOUSE,
    New Orleans, December 6, 1876.

We, the electors of President and Vice-President of the United States, for the State of Louisiana, do hereby certify that, on this the sixth day of December, in the year of our Lord one thousand eight hundred and seventy-six, we proceeded to vote by ballot for President of the United States, on the date above; that Rutherford B. Hayes, of the State of Ohio, received 8 votes for President of the United States, being all the votes cast; and that we then immediately proceeded to vote by ballot for Vice-President of the United States, whereupon William A. Wheeler, of the State of New York, received 8 votes for Vice-President of the United States, being all the votes cast.

In testimony whereof we, said electors, have hereunto signed our names, on this the first Wednesday, being the sixth day of December, in the year of our Lord eighteen hundred and seventy-six, and of the Independence of the United States the one hundred and first.

WILLIAM P. KELLOGG.
J. HENRI BURCH.
PETER JOSEPH.
LIONEL A. SHELDON.
MORRIS MARKS.
AARON B. LEVISSEE.
ORLANDO H. BREWSTER.
OSCAR JOFFRION.

UNITED STATES OF AMERICA,
       State of Louisiana, City of New Orleans :

Be it remembered that, on this Wednesday, the sixth day of December, A. D. eighteen hundred and seventy-six, that the following-named persons, having been duly chosen and appointed by the people of the State of Louisiana electors of President and Vice-President of the United States, according to the certificate of William P. Kellogg, governor of the State of Louisiana, hereto attached, namely, William P. Kellogg, elector for the State at large; J. Henri Burch, elector for the State at large; Peter Joseph, elector for the first congressional district; Lionel A. Sheldon, elector for the second congressional district; Morris Marks, elector for the third congressional district; Oscar Joffrion, elector for the sixth congressional district, met at the State-house, at the city of New Orleans, the seat of government of the State of Louisiana, as required by law, on the first Wednesday of December, A. D. eighteen hundred and seventy-six, being the sixth day of said month.

The certificate of the governor was read, and the following persons answered to their names: William P. Kellogg, J. Henri Burch, Peter Joseph, Lionel A. Sheldon, Morris Marks, Oscar Joffrion. Not answering: Aaron B. Levissee and Orlando H. Brewster.

On motion of Peter Joseph, J. Henri Burch was elected to preside; and on motion of Oscar Joffrion, Morris Marks was appointed secretary.

On motion of Lionel A. Sheldon, a recess was taken till the hour of three-thirty p. m., when the electors re-assembled.

On the roll being called, it was found that Aaron B. Levissee and Orlando H. Brewster were not present. At the hour of four p. m., the said Aaron B. Levissee and Orlando H. Brewster having failed to attend, the electors present proceeded to supply such vacancies by ballot, in accordance with the statute of the State of Louisiana in such cases made and provided; which is in words and figures as follows:

"If any one or more of the electors chosen by the people shall fail from any cause whatever to attend at the appointed place at the hour of four p. m., of the day prescribed for their meeting, it shall be the duty of the other electors immediately to proceed by ballot to supply such vacancy or vacancies."

Lionel A. Sheldon and Peter Joseph were appointed tellers, when, after balloting, it was found that Aaron B. Levissee received six votes, being all the votes cast, to supply the vacancy in the fourth congressional district occasioned by the failure of Aaron B. Levissee to attend, and Orlando H. Brewster received six votes, being all the votes cast, to supply the vacancy in the fifth congressional district occasioned by the failure of Orlando H. Brewster to attend. The said Aaron B. Levissee and Orlando H. Brewster were thereupon declared elected to supply the vacancies in the fourth and fifth congressional districts respectively, and being sent for, soon after appeared and were in attendance as electors.

The said electors then proceeded to vote by ballot for President of the United States, when William P. Kellogg and Lionel A. Sheldon were appointed tellers, and upon counting the ballots for President of the United States, Rutherford B. Hayes, of the State of Ohio, did receive 8 votes for President of the United States, being all the votes cast.

The said electors then proceeded to vote by ballot for Vice-President of the United States, when Peter Joseph and Oscar Joffrion were appointed tellers, and upon counting the votes for Vice-President of the United States, William A. Wheeler, of the State of New York, did receive 8 votes for Vice-President of the United States, being all the votes cast. Whereupon the said electors signed three certificates, one of which is hereto attached, which certificates are herewith placed separately in envelopes and sealed up carefully, and on each envelope was indorsed that "The within contains a list of all the votes cast by the electors for the State of Louisiana for President and Vice-President of the United States," one of which is given to the person appointed to convey the vote to the President of the Senate of the United States, and another indorsed in the same way is put in the post-office, and the other deposited with the judge of the district court of the United States for the district of Louisiana.

On motion of Peter Joseph, the electors proceeded to appoint a person to take charge of and deliver to the President of the Senate, at the seat of the Government, before the first Wednesday in January next ensuing, one of said certificates, when Thomas C. Anderson was appointed to the above service, and said electors made and signed a certificate of such appointment in the following form:

STATE OF LOUISIANA, STATE-HOUSE, UNITED STATES OF AMERICA,
New Orleans, Wednesday, December 6, 1876.

We, the undersigned electors of President and Vice-President of the United States, for the State of Louisiana, do hereby appoint Thomas C. Anderson to take charge of and deliver to the President of the Senate of the United States, at the seat of Government at Washington, D. C., before the first Wednesday in January next, one of the certificates of the votes cast by the undersigned for President and Vice-President of the United States, on Wednesday, the sixth day of December, A. D. 1876.

In testimony whereof we have hereunto signed our names on this sixth day of December, in the year of our Lord one thousand eight hundred and seventy-six, and of the Independence of the United States of America the one hundred and first.

WILLIAM P. KELLOGG.
J. HENRI BURCH.
PETER JOSEPH.
LIONEL A. SHELDON.
MORRIS MARKS.
A. B. LEVISSEE.
O. H. BREWSTER.
OSCAR JOFFRION.

UNITED STATES OF AMERICA, STATE OF LOUISIANA,
OFFICE SECRETARY OF STATE,
New Orleans, December 6, 1876.

I, P. G. Deslonde, secretary of state of the State of Louisiana, hereby certify that the following is a true and correct extract from an act of the legislature of the State of Louisiana, being act No. one hundred and ninety-three, approved October thirtieth, eighteen hundred and sixty-eight, the original of which act is on file among the records of my office, and is still in force and unrepealed:

"SEC. 8. *Be it further enacted, &c.,* That if any one or more of the electors chosen by the people shall fail from any cause whatever to attend at the appointed place at the hour of four p. m. of the day prescribed for their meeting, it shall be the duty of the other electors immediately to proceed by ballot to supply such vacancy or vacancies."

In testimony whereof I have hereunto set my hand and caused the seal of the State to be affixed this sixth day of December, A. D. eighteen hundred and seventy-six, and of the Independence of the United States the one hundred and first.

[SEAL.]   P. G. DESLONDE,
                                        Secretary of State.

UNITED STATES OF AMERICA, STATE OF LOUISIANA,
OFFICE SECRETARY OF STATE,
New Orleans, December 6, 1876.

I, P. G. Deslonde, secretary of state for the State of Louisiana, hereby certify that at a general election held in the state of Louisiana, on Tuesday, the seventh day of November, eighteen hundred and seventy-six, the following-named persons were elected, chosen, and appointed electors for President and Vice-President of the United States, as appears from the returns of said election now on file in my office, and which have been duly promulgated according to law by the legal returning officers of the state, to wit: William P. Kellogg, for the State at large; J. Henri Burch, for the State at large; Peter Joseph, for the first congressional district; Lionel A. Sheldon, for the second congressional district; Morris Marks, for the third congressional district; Aaron B. Levissee, for the fourth congressional district; Orlando H. Brewster, for the fifth congressional district; Oscar Joffrion, for the sixth congressional district. And I further certify that the names appended to the certificates of votes cast for President of the United States and for Vice-President of the United States, on Wednesday, the sixth day of December, A. D. eighteen hundred and seventy-six, and to the *procès verbal* of the proceedings of said electors accompanying said certificate, are the true and proper signatures of the before-mentioned persons elected, chosen, and appointed electors of President and Vice-President of the United States for the State of Louisiana.

In testimony whereof I have hereunto signed my name and caused the seal of the State to be affixed this sixth day of December, A. D. eighteen hundred and seventy-six, and of the Independence of the United States the one hundred and first.

[SEAL.]   P. G. DESLONDE,
                                                         Secretary of State.

The PRESIDING OFFICER. This closes the reading of the certificates from the State of Louisiana. Are there objections to the certificates which have been read?

Mr. Senator McDONALD. On behalf of the Senators and Representatives whose names are subscribed thereto, I submit the following objections to the counting of the electoral vote of the State of Louisiana as cast for Hayes and Wheeler.

The PRESIDING OFFICER. The objections to counting the vote will be read by the Secretary of the Senate.

The Secretary of the Senate read as follows:

OBJECTION No. 1.

The undersigned Senators and Members of the House of Representatives of the United States object to the lists of the names of electors made and certified by William P. Kellogg, claiming to be, but who was not, the lawful governor of the State of Louisiana, and to the electoral votes of said State, signed by W. P. Kellogg, J. H. Burch, Peter Joseph, L. A. Sheldon, Morris Marks, A. B. Levissee, O. H. Brewster, and Oscar Joffrion, being the two several certificates, the first and third presented by the President of the Senate to the two Houses of Congress in joint convention, for the reasons following;

I.

Because, on the 7th day of November, 1876, there was no law, joint resolution, or other act of the legislature of the State of Louisiana in force directing the manner in which electors for said State should be appointed.

II.

Because, if any law existed in the State of Louisiana, on the 7th day of November, 1876, directing the manner of the appointment of electors, it was an act of the legislature which directed that electors should be appointed by the people of the State in their primary capacity at an election to be held on a day certain, at particular places, and in a certain way; and the people of the State, in accordance with the legislative direction, exercised the power vested in them at an election held in said State November 7, 1876, in pursuance of said act and of the laws of the United States, and appointed John McEnery, R. C. Wickliffe, L. St. Martin, F. P. Poché, A. De Blanc, W. A. Seay, R. G. Cobb, and K. A. Cross to be electors, by a majority for each of six thousand and upward of all the votes cast by qualified voters for electors at said election, and said electors received a certificate of their due appointment as such electors from John McEnery, who was then the rightful and lawful governor of said State, under the seal thereof; and thereupon the said McEnery, Wickliffe, St. Martin, Poché, De Blanc, Seay, Cobb, and Cross became and were vested with the exclusive authority of electors for the State of Louisiana, and no other person or persons had or could have such authority or power, nor was it within the legal power of any State or Federal officer, or any other person, to revoke the power bestowed on the said McEnery, Wickliffe, St. Martin, Poché, De Blanc, Seay, Cobb, and Cross, or to appoint other electors in their stead, or to impair their title to the offices to which the people had appointed them.

III.

Because the said Kellogg, Burch, Joseph, Sheldon, Marks, Levissee, Brewster, and Joffrion were not, nor was either of them, duly appointed an elector by the State of Louisiana in the manner directed by the constitution and laws of said State and of the United States, and the lists of names of electors made and certified by the said William P. Kellogg, claiming to be, but not being, governor of said State, were false in fact, and fraudulently made and certified by said Kellogg, with full knowledge at the time that the said Kellogg, Burch, Joseph, Sheldon, Marks, Levissee, Brewster, and Joffrion were not duly appointed electors by the qualified voters of the State, and without any examination of the returns of the votes cast for electors as required by the laws of the State.

IV.

Because the pretended canvass of the returns of said election for electors of President and Vice-President by J. Madison Wells, T. C. Anderson, G. Casanave, and Louis Kenner, as returning officers of said election, was without jurisdiction and void, for these reasons:

First. The statutes of Louisiana, under which said persons claim to have been appointed returning officers, and to have derived their authority, gave them no jurisdiction to make the returns, or to canvass and compile the statement of votes cast for electors of President and Vice-President.

Secondly. Said statutes, if construed as conferring such jurisdiction, give the returning officers power to appoint the electors, and are void, as in conflict with the Constitution, which requires that electors shall be appointed by the State.

Thirdly. Said statutes, in so far as they attempt to confer judicial power, and to give to the returning-officers authority, in their discretion, to exclude the statements of votes, and to punish innocent persons without trial, by depriving them of their legal right of suffrage, are in conflict with the constitution of the State of Louisiana, and are anti-republican and in conflict with the Constitution of the United States, in so far as they leave it to the discretion of the returning-officers to determine who are appointed electors.

Fourthly. If said Louisiana statutes shall be held valid, they conferred no jurisdiction on said Wells, Anderson, Casanave, and Kenner as a board of returning-officers to make the returns of said election, or to canvass and compile the statements of votes made by the commissioners of said election, for the reason that they constituted but four of the five persons to whom the law confided those duties; that they were all of the same political party; and that there was a vacancy in said board of returning-officers, which the said Wells, Anderson, Casanave, and Kenner failed and refused to fill as required by law.

Fifthly. Said board of returning-officers had no jurisdiction to exercise judicial functions and reject the statement of the votes at any poll or voting-place, unless the foundation for such jurisdiction was first laid as required by the statute, which the papers and records before said board of returning-officers show was not done to such an extent as to change the result of the election as shown on the face of the returns.

Sixthly. Said returning-officers, with the full knowledge that a true and correct compilation of the official statements of votes legally cast November 7, 1876, for presidential electors in the State of Louisiana, showed the following result, to wit:

	Votes.
John McEnery	83,723
R. C. Wickliffe	83,859
L. St. Martin	83,650
F. P. Poché	83,474
A. De Blanc	83,633
W. A. Seay	83,812
R. G. Cobb	83,530
K. A. Cross	83,603
W. P. Kellogg	77,174
J. H. Burch	77,162
Peter Joseph	74,913
L. A. Sheldon	74,902
Morris Marks	75,240
A. B. Levissee	75,395
O. H. Brewster	75,479
Oscar Joffrion	75,618

And that said McEnery, Wickliffe, St. Martin, Poché, De Blanc, Seay, Cobb, and Cross were duly and lawfully elected electors, illegally and fraudulently changed, altered, and rejected the statements of votes made by the commissioners of election and the returns of supervisors of registration, and declared the following to be the state of the vote, to wit:

John McEnery	70,508
R. C. Wickliffe	70,509
L. St. Martin	70,553
F. Poché	70,335
A. De Blanc	70,536
W. A. Seay	70,525
R. G. Cobb	70,423
K. A. Cross	70,566
W. P. Kellogg	75,135
J. H. Burch	75,127
Peter Joseph	74,014

L. A. Sheldon 74,027
Morris Marks 74,413
A. B. Levissee 74,003
O. H. Brewster 74,017
Oscar Joffrion 74,736

And the said returning-officers thereupon falsely and fraudulently certified that said Kellogg, Burch, Joseph, Sheldon, Marks, Levissee, Brewster, and Joffrion were duly elected electors, when the fact was that, omitting the statements of votes illegally withheld by supervisors, those before the returning-officers, which it was their duty to, but which they did not canvass and compile, showed majorities for McEnery, Wickliffe, St. Martin, Poché, De Blanc, Seay, Cobb, and Cross, ranging from three thousand four hundred and fifty-nine to six thousand four hundred and five.

Seventhly. That said returning-officers, before making any declaration of the vote for electors, offered for a money consideration to certify and declare the due election of the persons who, according to the face of the returns, received a majority of the votes and were duly and properly elected. Failing to find a purchaser, they falsely, corruptly, and fraudulently certified and declared the minority candidates elected, after having first applied for a reward for so doing.

Wherefore the undersigned object to the certificate or declaration of the election of electors made by said returning-officers as utterly void by reason of the fraud and corruption of said board of returning-officers in thus offering said certificate or declaration for sale.

V.

The undersigned respectfully object to counting the vote cast by the said A. B. Levissee, for the reason that the State of Louisiana was forbidden by the Constitution of the United States to appoint the said A. B. Levissee an elector, because he was, at the time of the appointment of the electors in said State, to wit, on the 7th day of November, 1876, and for a number of days previous and subsequent thereto, holding an office of trust or profit under the United States, to wit, the office of commissioner of the United States circuit court for the district of Louisiana, and his subsequent appointment by the electors was not only without authority of law and void, but it was knowingly and fraudulently made for an illegal and fraudulent purpose.

VI.

The undersigned especially object to counting the vote cast by the said O. H. Brewster, for the reason that the State of Louisiana was forbidden by the Constitution of the United States to appoint the said Brewster an elector, because he was, at the time of the appointment of electors in said State, to wit, on the 7th day of November, 1876, and for a number of days previous and subsequent thereto, holding an office of trust or profit under the United States, to wit, the office of surveyor-general of the land-office of the land-district of the State of Louisiana; and any subsequent appointment of the said Brewster as an elector by the other electors was not only without warrant of law and void, but was made knowingly and fraudulently for an illegal and fraudulent purpose.

VII.

The undersigned object and insist that under no circumstances can more than six of the eight electoral votes cast in Louisiana for Rutherford B. Hayes and William A. Wheeler be counted, for the reason that at least two of the persons casting such votes, to wit, A. B. Levissee and O. H. Brewster, were not appointed electors by said State; and they further object, especially to the vote given and cast by William P. Kellogg, one of the pretended electors of said State of Louisiana, because the certificate executed by himself as governor of that State to himself as elector of that State is void as to him and creates no presumption and is no evidence in his own favor that he was duly appointed such elector, and there is no other evidence whatever of his having been appointed an elector of said State. And they further object to the said William P. Kellogg, that by the constitution of Louisiana he was not entitled to hold both offices, but was disqualified therefrom, and that on the day of casting the vote aforesaid, and on the day of the election for electors, and before and after those days, he continued to act as governor of the State, and that his vote as elector is null and void.

VIII.

Because the certified lists of the names of the said Kellogg, Burch, Joseph, Sheldon, Marks, Levissee, Brewster, and Joffrion, as the duly appointed electors for the State of

Louisiana by W. P. Kellogg, claiming to be, but who was not, governor of said State, were falsely, fraudulently, and corruptly made, and issued as part of a conspiracy between the said Kellogg and the said returning-officers Wells, Anderson, Casanave, and Kenner, and other persons, to cheat and defraud the said McEnery, Wickliffe, St. Martin, Poché, De Blanc, Seay, Cobb, and Cross, of the offices to which they had been duly appointed as aforesaid, and to defraud the State of Louisiana of her right to vote for President and Vice-President according to her own wish, as legally expressed by the vote of their people at the election aforesaid.

For which reasons the said lists of names of the said Kellogg, Burch, Joseph, Sheldon, Marks, Levissee, Brewster, and Joffrion, as electors, and the votes cast by them, are utterly void, in support of which reasons the undersigned refer to the Constitution and laws of the United States and of the State of Louisiana, and among other, to the evidence taken at the present session of Congress by the Committee and subcommittees on Privileges and Elections of the Senate, the Select Committee and subcommittees of the House of Representatives on the Recent Election in the State of Louisiana, and the Committee of the House of Representatives on the Powers, Privileges, and Duties of the House of Representatives in Counting the Electoral Vote, together with the papers and documents accompanying said evidence.

ELI SAULSBURY,
J. E. McDONALD,
JOHN W. STEVENSON,
LEWIS V. BOGY,
Senators.
DAVID DUDLEY FIELD,
G. A. JENKS,
R. L. GIBSON,
J. R. TUCKER,
WILL M. LEVY,
E. JNO. ELLIS,
WM. R. MORRISON,
Representatives.

The PRESIDING OFFICER. Are there further objections to the certificates from the State of Louisiana?

Mr. Representative GIBSON. I have the honor to offer objections to the certificates of the electoral vote of the State of Louisiana signed by William Pitt Kellogg on behalf of the State of Louisiana.

The PRESIDING OFFICER. The Clerk of the House will read the objections presented by the member from the State of Louisiana (Mr. Gibson.)

The Clerk of the House read as follows:

OBJECTION No. 2.

The undersigned Senators and members of the House of Representatives of the United States object to the certificates and electoral votes of the State of Louisiana, signed by W. P. Kellogg, J. H. Burch, Peter Joseph, L. A. Sheldon, Morris Marks, A. B. Levissee, O. H. Brewster, and Oscar Joffrion, for the following reasons:

First. The government of the State of Louisiana as administered at and prior to the 7th day of November, 1876, and until this time, was and is not republican in form.

Second. If the government of the State of Louisiana was and is republican in form, there was no canvass of the votes of the State made on which the certificates of election of the above-named alleged electors were issued.

Third. Any alleged canvass of votes on which the certificate of election of said alleged electors is claimed to be founded was an act of usurpation, was fraudulent and void.

Fourth. The votes cast in the electoral college of said State by Oscar Joffrion, W. P. Kellogg, J. H. Burch, and Morris Marks are not electoral votes, for that the said Oscar Joffrion, W. P. Kellogg, J. H. Burch, and Morris Marks are and were ineligible by the laws of Louisiana, are and were disqualified; for by the constitution of Louisiana (sec. 117) it is provided, "No person shall hold or exercise at the same time more than one office of trust or profit, except that of justice of the peace or notary public." Whereas on and prior to the 7th day of November, 1876, and until after the 6th day of December, 1876, W. P. Kellogg was acting *de facto* governor of said State; Oscar Joffrion was supervisor of registration for the parish of Pointe Coupée, in said State; Morris Marks was a district attorney for one of the districts of said State, and canid-date for district judge and was elected at said election; and J. H. Burch was a member of the senate of said State, also a member of the board of control of the State penitentiary, administrator of the deaf and dumb asylum, both salaried offices, and treasurer of the school board of the parish of East Baton Rouge.

Fifth. In addition thereto, said Oscar Joffrion was specially disqualified by the thirteenth section of the act of the legislature of said State, dated 24th day of July, 1874, which provides that no supervisor of registration shall be eligible for any office at any election when said supervisor officiates, and the said Oscar Joffrion, at the election held on the 7th day of November, 1876, did act and officiate as supervisor of registration for the parish of Pointe Coupée, in said State.

In support hereof *inter alia* there is herewith submitted the testimony taken before the special committee of the House of Representatives to investigate the election in Louisiana; also, the testimony taken before the Committee on Powers and Privileges of the House of Representatives; also, the testimony taken before the Committee on Privileges and Elections of the Senate.

> ELI SAULSBURY,
> J. E. McDONALD,
> FRANCIS KERNAN,
> > *Senators.*
>
> G. A. JENKS,
> J. R. TUCKER,
> R. L. GIBSON,
> DAVID DUDLEY FIELD,
> WILL. M. LEVY,
> E. JNO. ELLIS,
> > *Representatives.*

The PRESIDING OFFICER. Are there further objections to the certificates from the State of Louisiana?

Mr. Representative WOOD, of New York. I present, on behalf of the Senators and Representatives who have signed it, a further objection.

The PRESIDING OFFICER. The objection submitted will be read by the Clerk of the House.

The Clerk of the House read as follows:

OBJECTION No. 3.

> HOUSE OF REPRESENTATIVES,
> *Washington, D. C., February 12,* 1877.

The undersigned Senators and Representatives object to the counting of the votes of O. H. Brewster, A. B. Levissee, W. P. Kellogg, Oscar Joffrion, Peter Joseph, J. H. Burch, L. A. Sheldon, and Morris Marks, as electors for the State of Louisiana, for the reason that the said persons were not appointed electors by the State of Louisiana in the manner directed by its legislature.

> M. I. SOUTHARD,
> > *Representative from the State of Ohio.*
> CHAS. E. HOOKER, of Mississippi.
> JOHN W. STEVENSON, of Kentucky.
> WM. PINKNEY WHYTE, of Maryland.
> FERNANDO WOOD,
> > *Representative from the State of New York.*
> ERASTUS WELLS,
> > *Representative of Missouri.*
> A. G. EGBERT,
> > *Representative of Pennsylvania.*
> R. A. DE BOLT, of Missouri.
> R. P. BLAND, of Missouri.

The PRESIDING OFFICER. Are there further objections to the certificates from the State of Louisiana?

Mr. Senator HOWE. I submit some concise objections to counting the vote certified here by John McEnery and his associates.

The PRESIDING OFFICER. The objections will be read by the Secretary of the Senate.

The Secretary of the Senate read as follows :

OBJECTION No. 4.

The undersigned respectfully object to the counting of any vote for President and Vice-President of the United States given or purported to have been given by John McEnery, R. C. Wickliffe, L. St. Martin, F. B. Poché, A. De Blanc, W. A. Seay, R. G. Cobb, and K. A. Cross, of Louisiana, or by either of them, for the reason that there is no evidence that either of said persons has been appointed an elector of said State in such manner as the legislature thereof has directed ; and for the further reason that there is evidence conclusive in law that neither of said persons has been appointed to be an elector for the State of Louisiana in such manner as the legislature thereof has directed.

They respectfully object to the reading, the recording, or acknowledging of any commission, license, certificate of appointment, or of authentication signed or purporting to be signed by John McEnery as governor of the State of Louisiana, for the reason that there is no evidence that John McEnery is now, or ever was at any time during the year 1876, governor of the State of Louisiana, and for the further reason that there is conclusive evidence that William P. Kellogg was, during the whole of the year 1876, and for several years prior thereto, governor of that State ; was recognized as such by the judicial and legislative departments of the government of that State and by every department of the Government of the United States.

T. O. HOWE.
R. J. OGLESBY.
JOHN SHERMAN.
J. R. WEST.
S. A. HURLBUT.
W. TOWNSEND.
CHARLES H. JOYCE.
L. DANFORD.
WM. W. CRAPO.
EUGENE HALE.
WILLIAM LAWRENCE.

The PRESIDING OFFICER. Are there further objections to the certificates from the State of Louisiana ? If there be no further objections, all the certificates from that State, and the papers accompanying the same, together with the objections thereto, will now be submitted to the Electoral Commission for its judgment and decision. The Senate will now retire to their Chamber.

Accordingly (at four o'clock and thirty-four minutes p. m.) the Senate withdrew.

ELECTORAL COMMISSION.

LOUISIANA.

MONDAY, *February* 12, 1877.

The Commission met at half past two o'clock p. m. pursuant to adjournment.

Present: The President, and Commissioners Miller, Field, Strong, Edmunds, Bradley, Morton, Frelinghuysen, Bayard, Payne, Hunton, Abbott, Garfield, and Hoar.

On motion by Mr. Commissioner HOAR, the Commission took a recess until four o'clock p. m.

The Commission re-assembled at four o'clock p. m.

The Journal of Saturday's proceedings was read and approved.

At four o'clock and forty minutes p. m., a communication from the two Houses of Congress in joint session was presented by Mr. GORHAM, Secretary of the Senate, and read as follows:

HALL OF THE HOUSE OF REPRESENTATIVES,
February 12, 1877.

To the President of the Commission :

More than one return or paper purporting to be a return or certificate of electoral votes of the State of Louisana having been received and this day opened in the presence of the two Houses of Congress and read, and objections thereto having been made, the said returns, with all accompanying papers, and also the objections thereto, are herewith submitted to the judgment and decision of the Commission, as provided by law.

T. W. FERRY,
President of the Senate.

Mr. Commissioner FIELD. I move that the certificates and papers accompanying the same, and the objections thereto, be printed.

The motion was agreed to.

The PRESIDENT. Who represent the objectors ?

Mr. Representative FIELD. Mr. President, Mr. McDonald of the Senate and Mr. Jenks of the House will represent the objectors. I understand they are coming now.

Mr. Commissioner EDMUNDS. The objectors to which certificate ? I assume that there are several.

Mr. Representative FIELD. They will explain for themselves.

Mr. TRUMBULL. There are three certificates.

The PRESIDENT. And an objection to each, I presume ?

Mr. TRUMBULL. Yes, sir. The objections to the first and third are represented by Senator McDonald and by Mr. Jenks of the House of Representatives.

Mr. EVARTS. The objections to the second certificate will be represented by Mr. Howe of the Senate and Mr. Hurlbut of the House.

Mr. Commissioner MILLER. Will the gentlemen be prepared to go on this evening ?

Mr. Commissioner MORTON. Senator Thurman sent word to me that he would not be able to be here to-day, and preferred that the argument be not commenced until to-morrow.

The PRESIDENT. I will then, with the consent of the Commission, state that two objectors to certificates numbered 1 and 3, if I am correctly informed, may be heard in oral argument in support of their objections and to advocate the validity of any certificate the validity of which they maintain. In like manner two objectors to certificate No. 2— as I now assume it to be without having looked at the papers—will also be heard under like circumstances and to the same extent. " Under this rule not more than four persons shall speak, and neither side shall occupy more than two hours."

Mr. Commissioner MORTON. I move an adjournment to 10 o'clock to-morrow.

Mr. Commissioner FIELD. I should prefer eleven.

The PRESIDENT. I will put the longest time first. The motion of Mr. Justice Field is that the Commission adjourn until to-morrow at eleven o'clock in the forenoon.

The motion was agreed to; there being on a division—ayes 8, noes 3; and (at four o'clock and forty-five minutes p. m.) the Commission adjourned until to-morrow at eleven o'clock a. m.

[It is understood that the following counsel appear :

Hon. John A. Campbell, of Louisiana,
Hon. Lyman Trumbull, of Illinois,
Hon. Matt. H. Carpenter, of Wisconsin,   In opposition to certi-
Richard T. Merrick, esq., of Washington, D. C.,   ficates Nos. 1 and 3.
George Hoadly, esq., of Ohio,
Ashbel Green, esq., of New Jersey,

Hon. William M. Evarts, of New York,
Hon. E. W. Stoughton, of New York,   In opposition to certificate
Hon. Stanley Matthews, of Ohio,   No. 2.]
Hon. Samuel Shellabarger, of Ohio,

TUESDAY, *February* 13, 1877.

The Commission met at eleven o'clock a. m. pursuant to adjournment.

Present: The President, and Commissioners Miller, Field, Strong, Bradley, Edmunds, Morton, Frelinghuysen, Bayard, Payne, Hunton, Abbott, Garfield, and Hoar.

The various objectors to the certificates from Louisiana and the respective counsel were also present.

The Journal of yesterday was read and approved.

The PRESIDENT. Three certificates are before the Commission, to each of which there are objections. For my own convenience I have numbered them one, two, and three. Two of the objectors to certificates numbered one and three will now be heard under the fourth rule.

Mr. Commissioner GARFIELD. Are the certificates numbered in the order they were presented to the two Houses?

The PRESIDENT. I have so numbered them, as I am assured by the Stenographer.

Mr. Commissioner GARFIELD. I wish to understand if they are in the chronological order of their presentation.

The PRESIDENT. They are. Each side will be entitled to two hours. Two who support the views of the objectors to certificates numbered one and three will be heard, and two of the objectors who support the objections to certificate number two. First those supporting the objections to numbers one and three will be heard.

Mr. Senator McDONALD. Mr. President, as the Commission is not full, I would prefer to wait a few moments to see whether it cannot be filled before proceeding.

The PRESIDENT. If there be no objection, we shall wait a few moments. We cannot wait long, I suppose.

Mr. Senator McDONALD. If a member of the Commission is absent, what is the rule in reference to proceeding?

The PRESIDENT. There is no rule on the subject; but the law provides for cases of physical inability to attend, and points out measures for filling the vacancy. There is nothing in the rules on the subject.

Mr. Senator McDONALD. I have understood, but do not know personally, that Senator Thurman has been ill for some days, at least not very well able to give his attention to business. If it is not likely that he will be present this morning, I would rather some action should be taken in regard to his absence, before proceeding.

Mr. Commissioner EDMUNDS. Mr. McDonold must be aware that we can scarcely assume that Judge Thurman is physically unable to be present and proceed to notify the Senate in order that the place may be filled, without some sort of proof. Undoubtedly, I presume, if Judge Thurman thought himself unable to attend, he would so inform the Commission in writing.

Mr. Senator McDONALD. I should judge so; and, therefore, I suppose if he is able he will be here in a short time, unless the Commission receives a message from him to the contrary.

Mr. Commissioner EDMUNDS. It does not appear to me that we should be justified in waiting on account of the absence of a single member of the Commission or of any number less than a quorum, in the present state of affairs. We have only reached the second of what are understood to be four causes submitted to us. The first one having occupied nine or ten days, we have now only sixteen days, including this one, before the presidential office begins; so that it appears to me we should avoid our duty under the statute if we were not to proceed. Of course, if Senator Thurman be ill, we ought to be advised, so that his place may be filled; but without any evidence of that, it appears to me due to all parties concerned that we should proceed, as we have done occasionally when one or more gentlemen may have been temporarily absent.

Mr. Commissioner MILLER. We have constantly proceeded in the discharge of the duties of this Commission with members of it absent for the time; it is no reason for delaying proceedings.

Mr. Commissioner BAYARD. I have just sent a message to the Senate Committee room on Private Land-Claims, of which Mr. Thurman is chairman, to ask the clerk there in regard to the probability of his presence. The last communication he made was to Mr. Commissioner Morton yesterday, to whom he sent some message asking that the argument might not proceed yesterday afternoon in his absence. From that I presume he expected to be here this morning.

The PRESIDENT. By general consent we can wait a few minutes until the messenger returns from his committee-room.

Mr. EVARTS. Mr. President, allow me to ask the attention of the Commission to certain laws of Louisiana which are not included in the compilation we have received that was printed under the direction of the Commission, and which are important for the consideration of the principal questions of law.

The PRESIDENT. Would it be convenient for you to make a note of them and hand it to us?

Mr. EVARTS. I simply ask, by giving a note to the Clerk, that they may be printed in season for to-morrow morning.

The PRESIDENT. I take it all the members of the Commission desire the laws to be printed, and if you will furnish a note to the Secretary, any omissions will be supplied.

Mr. EVARTS. We supposed it was proper we should ask the consent of the Commission.

The PRESIDENT. I suppose it is hardly necessary to submit it to the Commission.

Mr. EVARTS. One law was printed last night since the compilation, but the other it seems had been printed and was omitted from the compilation under the notion that it was repealed; but we still desire its use, and it may be there are copies of it already in print.

The PRESIDENT, (after the expiration of five minutes.) Senator Thurman's clerk reports that Senator Thurman is suffering from neuralgia, but will be out to-day. Shall the business of the Commission proceed? [Putting the question.]

The question was determined in the affirmative.

The PRESIDENT. One of the objectors to certificates Nos. 1 and 3 will now be heard.

Mr. Senator McDONALD. Mr. President and gentlemen of the Commission, the certificates announced by the President as first under consideration embrace the electoral votes cast for Hayes for President and Wheeler for Vice-President.

The PRESIDENT. You may not only support the objections, but any other certificate which you claim to be valid within the allotted time—two hours for your side.

Mr. Senator McDONALD. If the votes contained in these certificates are the votes provided for in the Constitution, then they are to be counted. To constitute them the votes provided for in the Constitution, they must have been cast by electors who were competent and who had been appointed electors in the manner prescribed by the legislature of the State. The objections that we make to these votes are—

First. That the legislature did not provide the manner of the appointment of the electors who cast them ;

Second. That they were fraudulently returned by the officers intrusted with the canvass and return of the votes ;

Third. That two of them were incompetent under the Constitution of the United States ;

Fourth. That others of them were disqualified from serving or acting by the constitution and laws of the State of Louisiana ; and

Fifth. That at the time of their appointment the State of Louisiana did not have a government republican in form.

With respect to the laws of the State authorizing the appointment of electors, I shall call the attention of the Commission to the statutes which have been heretofore enacted, and which are understood to stand still upon the statute-book. It will be found in the session laws of 1868 that a special law was enacted for the appointment of presidential electors ; and that this special law was re-enacted in the revised code of 1870, and it will be found at page 550 of that revised code. It is also printed in one of the compilations of laws that have been printed under the order of this Commission, at page 93.

Mr. Commissioner GARFIELD. Which one, the first or the second print ? We have had two.

Mr. Senator McDONALD. I am not able to determine, but the second, I think. It is entitled in this revision "Presidential Electors, Session Laws, 1868, No. 193," Revised Statutes of Louisiana of 1870, page 550.

Mr. TRUMBULL. It is the last publication of the compilation.

(Mr. Commissioner Thurman appeared and took his seat,)

Mr. Senator McDONALD. It will be observed that this special law does make specific provision for the appointment of presidential electors by a popular vote. It also provides for the manner of the return and canvass of that vote. It will be seen by section 2826 that—

Immediately after the receipt of the return from each parish, or on the fourth Monday of November, if the returns should not sooner arrive, the governor, in the presence of the secretary of state, the attorney-general, a district judge of the district in which the seat of government may be established, or any two of them, shall examine the returns and ascertain therefrom the persons who have been duly elected electors.

At the session at which this revision was adopted, there was another act passed. It is also published in one of these compilations at page 924.

Mr. Commissioner ABBOTT. That is in the compilation without a cover.

Mr. Senator McDONALD. There are two sets of compilations without covers and one of them is the same as the covered pamphlet to which I previously referred ; the other has this act of 1870 ; and it will be necessary to obtain the proper copy in order to follow these citations. Your honors will see by the first section of this act that the elections provided for in it are styled "the general elections of the State." Section 35 specifically provides for the election of presidential electors. That section is as follows :

That in every year in which an election shall be held for electors of President and Vice-President of the United States, such election shall be held on the Tuesday next after the first Monday in the month of November in such year, in accordance with an act of the Congress of the United States, approved January 23, 1845, entitled "An act to establish a uniform time for holding elections for electors for President and Vice-

President in all of the States of the Union," and such elections shall be held and conducted and returns made thereof in the manner and form prescribed by the law for general elections.

Not merely the elections shall be held and conducted and returns made, but the returns shall also conform to the provisions prescribed in the laws for general elections. The repealing section of this act, which is the eighty-fifth section, reads as follows:

That all laws or parts of laws contrary to the provisions of this act, and all laws relating to the same subject-matter, are hereby repealed, and this act shall take effect from and after its passage.

It was approved March 16, 1870; and so your honors will see that two laws covering the same subject seem to have been enacted or recognized at the same session; the special law of 1868 carried forward into the code of 1870 and the session act of 1870. By the enacting clause attached to the code, the provisions of the code were to take effect on the 1st day of April, 1870, and this was after the close of the session of 1870, at which this general law was passed. And to meet any questions that might arise out of a conflict between the session act of 1870 and the provisions embodied in the code, another act was passed, one to which the gentleman from New York [Mr. Evarts] called the attention of the court.

Mr. Commissioner BRADLEY. When you speak of " the code," you refer to the revised statutes?

Mr. Senator McDONALD. Yes, sir; it is called in Louisiana, I believe, the code.

Mr. Commissioner BRADLEY. No; the code is a different thing.

Mr. Senator McDONALD. The revised statutes.

Mr. Commissioner EDMUNDS. Can you give us the date of the approval of the revising act?

Mr. Senator McDONALD. March 14; and to take effect on the 1st of April.

Mr. Commissioner EDMUNDS. That I understood; but I did not get the date of the approval before.

Mr. Senator McDONALD. It will be found in the revised statutes. I have not the volume here. The act I now refer to is an act printed this morning to be a part of this compilation of statutes that have been printed under the direction of the Commission. It is entitled "An act giving precedence in authority to all the other acts and joint resolutions passed by the general assembly at this session over the acts known as the Revision of the Statutes and of the Civil Code and Code of Practice, when there exists any conflict in the provisions of said acts and revisions." It is a single section, and is as follows:

That all the acts and resolutions passed during the present session of the general assembly which may be contrary to or in any manner in conflict with the acts of the present session known as the "revision of the statutes of a general character," and of the Civil Code and Code of Practice, shall have precedence of said revisions, and be held as the law in opposition thereto, and as repealing those acts so far as they may be in conflict therewith.

This presents a question, and a very grave one, as to which of these acts was in force at the close of the session of the legislature of 1870, (and upon the taking effect of the revised statutes,) and upon that fact depend very important questions arising hereafter. If the session laws of 1870 had the operation which the legislature enacting those revised statutes expressly determined that they should have, and repealed the provisions of the revised statutes wherever there was a conflict between the session laws and the revised statutes—if the repealing statute has this effect, then the special law providing for the election of electors, first enacted in 1868 and carried forward into the revised statutes, was thereby repealed. Ordinarily, and perhaps almost universally, the last expressed will of the legislature must stand; and where several acts are passed at the same session of the legislature and they are in such conflict that they cannot be reconciled, the last act must stand and the first give place. But this presents a little different question from that. These acts embraced in the revised statutes were a revision of laws compiled by the authority of the legislature and to take effect by its will, and at the same session in which it acted upon that revision it was passing laws. Its session acts were from day to day considered and passed by it, and in contemplation that there might be conflicts between those session acts and this revision of laws that was being prepared they declared the force and effect of their session acts with respect to those revised statutes, so that it is not to be said that when they passed this act thus restricting the operation and effect of the revised statutes, yet, notwithstanding the clear intent and purpose of the legislature in so doing that, the revised statutes contained the last will of the legislature, because they took effect in April at a later period than the passage of this law.

I have not time to elaborate this proposition, and can but state it for the consideration of the Commission. But if it has the effect which the will of the legislature designed it should have, then the act of 1870 (and I call it the act of 1870 to distinguish it from the special law of 1868) went upon the statute-book as the election law of the State of Louisiana, and provided the mode and manner which the State designed to carry into effect the provisions of the Constitution with reference to her right and authority to appoint electors, for the section of that law to which I have called your honors' attention fully covers this question, and in point of fact it was so considered by the authorities in the State of Louisiana; and when the election for the appointment of electors in 1872 took place it was conducted under the session act of 1870, both as to the election and the returns. The act of 1868 carried forward into the revised statutes was ignored, and the act of the session of 1870 was the one regarded as in force, and so regarded until the 20th day of November, 1872, when another act was passed to which I shall call your honors' attention. Your honors perhaps know the fact judicially that at that time the legislature of Louisiana was not in session. The act had been passed at the previous session, but had not been signed by the governor, and was not signed by him until the 20th of November, 1872. This he was authorized to do under their constitution. The law took effect from the date of his signature. This act is found on page 96 of this second compilation of statutes. That is entitled:

An act to regulate the conduct and to maintain the freedom and purity of elections; to prescribe the mode of making returns thereof; to provide for the election of returning-officers, and defining their powers and duties; to prescribe the mode of entering on the rolls of the Senate and House of Representatives; and to enforce article 103 of the constitution.

The first section declares that the elections therein provided for shall be styled the general elections. The seventy-first section, which is the repealing clause, is as follows:

That this act shall take effect from and after its passage, and that all others on the subject of election laws be, and the same are hereby, repealed.

This unquestionably repealed the session act of 1870. It is an act upon the same subject throughout, so far as the general elections of the State of Louisiana are concerned, but it omits to make any provision for the appointment of electors. Section 29 is the only section that makes any reference to the subject of presidential electors, and it is as follows :

That in every year in which an election shall be held for electors of President and Vice-President of the United States, such election shall be held at the time fixed by act of Congress.

But it fails to provide, as the act of 1870 did in the section that applied to the same subject, that such election should be held under the provisions of this act or that the canvass and return should be under the provisions of this act. Your honors will see, by comparing this section with the one I have already quoted in the session acts of 1870, that while it refers to presidential electors and their appointment it makes no provision, as the other act does, for their election or appointment.

Mr. Commissioner MORTON. Have you looked at the thirty-second section?

Mr. Senator McDONALD. I have noted the thirty-second section. It is—

That the provisions of this act, except as to the time of holding elections, shall apply in the election of all officers whose election is not otherwise provided for.

If the act of 1868 stood unaffected by the legislation of 1870, then this section would have something to apply to; but if the session laws of 1870 repealed the act of 1868, if that was their force and effect both in reference to the conflict between them and as to the proper construction of the repealing act passed in the session of 1870, then this could not be held to apply; for there can be no question but what the act of 1870 *in toto* was repealed by this act of 1872. If the provisions had not been such as to bring them in conflict, the repealing clause of 1872 unquestionably embraced it.

Again, I may state to your honors that the authorities of Louisiana regarded the act of 1872 and the amendments subsequently made as the only laws in force regulating the election of all officers and of all persons; and if it should be held that under this twenty-sixth section and the reference there made there might be held an election for electors, still it leaves this difficulty yet unprovided for, that there is not anywhere in the act of 1870 or in the act of 1872 or its amendments any provision whatever for filling vacancies in the electoral college, as it is termed, except by election. No other provision exists in either of these laws for filling vacancies of this class except by popular election.

I will simply place these statutes before your honors for your due consideration, and shall not undertake further to discuss their bearing at present. I have already stated that the election of 1872 for the appointment of electors took place under the session acts of 1870, and that the election of 1876 took place under the act of 1872 and the amendments that have been since made. So far as a construction has been given to these statutes by the authorities of the State, it has been to hold that the act of 1870 took the place of all other laws on the subject of the appointment or election of officers, and the act of 1872 took its place and repealed all other laws on the subject—" all election laws," to use the language of the repealing clause; and there is not to be found in the act of 1872 any provision, specific or otherwise, providing for the election of presidential electors; and if there is any provision that could be under any circumstances made to embrace that subject, then there is no provision whatever for filling any vacancies that may exist in the electoral college except by popular election.

Mr. Commissioner THURMAN. Were there any vacancies filled in this case?

Mr. Senator McDONALD. Yes, sir; two vacancies were filled by electing the same persons who, it was claimed, had been elected by the popular vote.

Mr. Commissioner BRADLEY. Why do you say "except by popular election?" Is there a section that provides for that?

Mr. Senator McDONALD. Yes, sir; section 24 is, "All elections to be held in this State to fill any vacancies shall be conducted," &c.

Then, as the fact was that the officers in charge of the administration of the laws in the State of Louisiana, with respect to her elections, did hold the election under the act of 1872, I propose to consider in what manner they held it, for we charge that the persons who have undertaken to cast the electoral votes now under consideration were fraudulently returned by the officers intrusted with the canvass of the votes cast by the people. In considering this branch of the subject it will be only necessary for me to examine the acts and conduct of those who are termed "the returning-officers of the State of Louisiana.". Their powers and duties are defined in sections 3 and 26 of the act of 1872. They are the same precisely as those conferred upon similar officers by the law of the session of 1870. First, however, your honors, as to the constitution of this board, the second section provides:

That five persons, to be elected by the senate from all political parties, shall be the returning-officers for all elections in the State, a majority of whom shall constitute a quorum, and have power to make the returns of all elections. In case of any vacancy by death, resignation, or otherwise, by either of the board, then the vacancy shall be filled by the residue of the board of returning-officers.

Your honors will see that the board herein provided consists of five, and that in its political caste it shall represent all the political parties, and if a vacancy occurs, the remaining members of the board shall fill it. This is a very peculiar statute, a very singular law. Here a board, organized with powers over the election-returns of all elections, is made perpetual, with the power within itself to continue that perpetuity. When once established, the board has gone out from the State authorities, from the people, from the popular control, into the hands of these men, and they continue on and on and on forever.

I have already said that their duties were prescribed and their authority circumscribed; and you honors will see that it is very necessary to circumscribe such authority. The sections to which I have made reference have been under review before; they are not here to be considered for the first time. Such has been the condition of affairs in Louisiana, that it has become the duty on former occasions of Congress, on the part of the Senate and on the part of the House, to investigate the matter of popular elections there and the powers of this board. The powers so far as canvass and return are concerned, I have already stated, as embraced in the act of 1872, are the same as those embraced in the act of 1870.

Now let us see what construction has been given to those powers heretofore. I will first call your honors' attention to the report made by the Senate Committee on Privileges and Elections, (Report 417 of the Forty-second Congress, third session, under date of February 10, 1873,) submitted by Senator Morton, the chairman, in which the following language is used:

The statute of Louisiana authorizes the supervisors of registration in the parishes, or the commissioners of election, to make affidavit in regard to any violence, tumult, fraud, or bribery by which a fair election had been prevented, which shall be forwarded to the returning-board, along with the returns, and upon which the returning-board may reject the vote of a poll in making the count; and if the evidence of the officers of the election is not sufficient to satisfy the minds of the returning-board in regard to the matter charged, they are authorized to send for persons and papers and take further testimony upon the matter; but they have no authority to make such investigation unless the foundation is first laid by the sworn statements of the officers of the election, as before mentioned.

That report was made to the Senate of the United States, and upon that report and the facts therewith connected the Senate acted in 1873 upon the electoral vote of that State.

In the House of Representatives also a committee report was made on the 23d of February, 1875, signed by honorables George F. Hoar, William A. Wheeler, and W. P. Frye, members of the committee. They quote at length sections 3 and 26, and I will read them as they have quoted them:

SEC. 3. *Be it further enacted, &c.* That in such canvass and compilation the returning-officers shall observe the following order: They shall compile first the statements from all the polls or voting-places at which there shall have been a fair, free, and peaceable registration and election. Whenever, from any poll or voting-place, there shall be received the statement of any supervisor of registration or commissioner of election, in form as required by section 26 of this act, on affidavit of three or more citizens, of any riot, tumult, acts of violence, intimidation, armed disturbance, bribery, or corrupt influences, which prevented, or tended to prevent, a fair, free, and peaceable vote of all qualified electors, entitled to vote at such poll or voting-place, such returning-officers shall not canvass, count, or compile the statement of votes from such poll or voting-places until the statements from all other polls or voting-places shall have been canvassed and compiled. The returning officers shall then proceed to investigate the statements of riot, tumult, acts of violence, intimidation, armed disturbance, bribery, or corrupt influences at any such poll or voting-place; and if from the evidence of such statement they shall be convinced that such riot, tumult, acts of violence, intimidation, armed disturbance, bribery, or corrupt influences did not materially interfere with the purity and freedom of the election at such poll or voting-place, or did not prevent a sufficient number of qualified voters thereat from registering or voting to materially change the result of the election, then, and not otherwise, said returning-officers shall canvass and compile the vote of such poll or voting-place with those previously canvassed and compiled; but if said returning-officers shall not be fully satisfied thereof, it shall be their duty to examine further testimony in regard thereto, and to this end they shall have power to send for persons and papers. If, after such examination, the said returning-officers shall be convinced that such riot, tumult, acts of violence, intimidation, armed disturbance, bribery, or corrupt influences did materially interfere with the purity and freedom of the election at such poll or voting-place, or did prevent a sufficient number of the qualified electors thereat from registering and voting to materially change the result of the election, then the said returning-officers shall not canvass or compile the statement of the votes of such poll or voting-place, but shall exclude it from their returns: *Provided,* That any person interested in said election by reason of being a candidate for office shall be allowed a hearing before said returning-officers upon making application within the time allowed for the forwarding of the returns of said election.

There is their authority; there is the direction by which they are to be guided; and section 26 provides for the character of these papers that are thus to assail and attack these polls; and that is:

SEC. 26. *Be it further enacted, &c.* That in any parish, precinct, ward, city, or town in which, during the time of registration or revision of registration, or on any day of election, there shall be any riot, tumult, acts of violence, intimidation, and disturbance, bribery, or corrupt influences at any place within said parish, or at or near any poll or voting-place or place of registration, or revision of registration, which riot, tumult, acts of violence, intimidation, and disturbance, bribery, or corrupt influences shall prevent, or tend to prevent, a fair, free, peaceable, and full vote of all the qualified electors of said parish, precinct, ward, city, or town, it shall be the duty of the commissioners of election, if such riot, tumult, acts of violence, intimidation and disturbance, bribery, or corrupt influences occur on the day of election, or of the supervisor of registration of the parish if they occur during the time of registration, or revision of registration, to make in duplicate and under oath a clear and full statement of all the facts relating thereto, and the effect produced by such riot, tumult, acts of violence, intimidation, and disturbance, bribery, or corrupt influences, in preventing a fair, free, peaceable, and full registration or election, and of the number of qualified electors deterred by such riots, tumult, acts of violence, intimidation, and disturbance, bribery, or corrupt influences from registering or voting, which statement shall also be corroborated under oath by three respectable citizens, qualified electors of the parish.

When such statement is made by a commissioner of election or a supervisor of registration, he shall forward it in duplicate to the supervisor of registration of the parish. if in the city of New Orleans to the secretary of state, one copy of which, if made to the supervisor of registration, shall be forwarded by him to the returning-officers provided for in section 2 of this act when he makes the returns of elections in his parish. His copy of said statement shall be so annexed to his returns of elections by paste, wax, or some adhesive substance that the same can be kept together, and the other copy the supervisor of registration shall deliver to the clerk of the court of his parish for the use of the district attorney.

After quoting these sections as I have read them, the report proceeds:

Upon this statute we are clearly of the opinion that the returning-board had no right to do anything except to canvass and compile the returns which were lawfully made to them by the local officers, except in cases where they were accompanied by the certificate of the supervisor or commissioner provided in the third section. In such cases the last sentence of that section shows that it was expected that they would ordinarily exercise the grave and delicate duty of investigating charges of riot, tumult, bribery, or corruption on a hearing of the parties interested in the office. It never could have been meant that this board of its own motion, sitting in New Orleans, at a distance from the place of voting, and without notice, could decide the rights of persons claiming to be elected.

But an examination of the law will clearly disclose that such was its purpose and intent; for when you consider the second section, as to what these officers shall do, it will be seen that their primary duty is to canvass and compile the votes returned to them. They are first required to take an oath of office that "they will faithfully and diligently perform the duties of a returning-officer as prescribed by law; that they will carefully and honestly canvass and compile the statements of the votes, and make a true and correct return of them, so help them God."

Mr. Commissioner THURMAN. Is there any evidence now before us that they threw out returns that were not accompanied by a protest?

Mr. Senator McDONALD. I shall call the attention of the Commission, before I am through, to what I claim to be evidence on that subject.

Within ten days after the closing of the election said returning-officers shall meet in New Orleans to canvass and compile the statements of votes made by the commissioners of election, and make returns of the election to the secretary of state.

They are to canvass and compile "the statements of votes made by the commissioners of election," those primary officers who receive the ballots from the people, and then to make a sworn statement of them.

Mr. Commissioner MORTON. What section do you read that from?

By Senator McDONALD. Section 2. That is what they are to do; canvass the statements of the votes made by the commissioners of election. Then, when they have made this canvass according to law and followed the law, their act gives a *prima facie* right to the party receiving a certificate, and but a *prima facie* right by the express terms of the statute itself.

These constructions of the authority of the returning-board in Louisiana have been affirmed by each House of Congress in its dealings with the popular elections there; and in the case of the presidential electors of 1872 the vote of the State of Louisiana was cast out and not counted because there had been a failure to comply with the law of the State on the part of these officers; not that there had not been an election, not that the people had not voted there, but that there had been a failure on the part of those intrusted, as it is termed, with the "machinery of the election" in that State to make that kind of return that gave faith and credit to their acts. (See pages 396–407 Compilation of Proceedings of Counting the Electoral Votes.)

Of the votes actually cast at the late election for the appointment of electors in Louisiana, the democratic electors received majorities ranging from 5,300 to 8,990 ; on the face of the returns, as made by the supervisors of registration to the board of returning-officers, their majorities ranged from 3,459 to 6,405, but by the canvass and the return made by the returning-officers majorities were certified in favor of the republican electors ranging from 3,437 to 4,800. To produce this result sixty-nine polls were rejected, embracing twenty-two parishes in whole or in part.

In the canvass thus made by the returning-officers there were actually frauds committed by them in this, that they failed and refused to canvass and compile the statements of votes made by the commissioners of election, and pretended to consider only the consolidated statements made by the supervisors of elections. In this manner the parish of Grant was rejected entirely, because the statement of votes made by the commissioners of elections, although before them, had not been returned by the supervisor of registration. They also refused for the same reasons to consider 2,914 votes cast for the democratic electors and 651 votes cast for the republican electors, mainly in the parishes of East Baton Rouge and Orleans. They transposed 178 votes from democratic electors cast in the parish of Vernon to the republican electors, which transposition has never been corrected. They rejected poll No. 4 in the parish of Iberia, in which were cast 322 votes for the democratic electors, and 11 votes for the republican electors, for no other alleged cause than that the commissioners' statement did not show that the word "voted" had been written or stamped on the certificates of registration presented by the voters. They rejected polls 1, 3, and 10 in the parish of Vernon, aggregating 179 votes for the democratic electors and none for the republican electors, upon affidavits fraudulently made and filed after they had closed their public sessions, and they added to the votes as returned by the supervisors of registration over 500 votes to five of the eight republican electors in the parish of Concordia, and over 500 votes in the parish of Natchitoches, upon no sufficient proof that such votes had been actually cast, and without the knowledge of the democratic electors interested in the question.

In some instances polls were rejected because, from the necessities of the case, commissioners of elections at such polls were democrats, the supervisors of election not being able to find qualified republicans to fill such positions.

From these and other facts of a like nature, it is charged and claimed that the action of the board of returning-officers was so corrupt and fraudulent as to destroy all faith and credit in their canvass and return.

Again, in rejecting the polls the board of returning-officers acted without lawful authority, there being but few, if any, cases in which the returns made to them had been accompanied by any proper certificate or statement of the supervisors of registration or commissioners of election, as provided for in the law under which they claimed to act, contesting the fairness of the registration or election, but arbitrarily, and without any sufficient foundation being laid therefor and upon false and fraudulent affidavits manufactured for that purpose, rejected such polls on charges of riot, tumult, bribery, &c., without any proper hearing on the part of the parties interested.

The election laws of 1870 and 1872 had placed under control of the governor of the State all the machinery of election and vested in him an authority and power "scarcely exercised by any sovereign in the world." He appointed the State superintendent of registration and the supervisors of registration in each parish in the State, and they in turn fixed the polling-places in the several parishes and appointed the commissioners or judges of election, who received the ballots of the people. All of these appointees, with but very few exceptions, were members of the republican party, and in this instance all this vast power was aided by Federal officers, civil and military, and particularly by the United States marshal for the district of Louisiana, who, claiming to act under the instructions from the Department of Justice, increased the number of his deputies to over eight hundred, and distributed them through the different parishes under the pretense of aiding in preserving order and protecting the purity of the ballot-box. All of these combined official forces acted in unison and harmony with the republican State committee in conducting the canvass and in controlling the election.

HEADQUARTERS REPUBLICAN PARTY OF LOUISIANA,
ROOMS JOINT COMMITTEE ON CANVASSING AND REGISTRATION,
MECHANICS' INSTITUTE, *September* 25, 1876.

DEAR SIR: It is well known to this committee that, from examination of the census of 1875, the republican vote in your parish is 2,200 and the republican majority is 900.

You are expected to register and vote the full strength of the republican party in your parish.

Your recognition by the next State administration will depend upon your doing your full duty in the premises, and you will not be held to have done your full duty unless the republican registration in your parish reaches 2,200 and the republican vote is at least 2,100.

All local candidates and committees are directed to aid you to the utmost in obtaining the result, and every facility is and will be afforded you; but you must obtain the results called for herein without fail. Once obtained, your recognition will be ample and generous.

Very respectfully, your obedient servant,

D. J. M. A. JEWETT, *Secretary.*

SUPERVISOR OF REGISTRATION,
Parish of Assumption, Louisiana.

Notwithstanding this immense power wielded for the purpose of procuring in the returns to be made a majority for the republican electors and republican State ticket, the local returning-officers were compelled to and did return the majorities heretofore stated in favor of the democratic electors. It was then that the duties of the returning-officers, in the language of J. Madison Wells, president of the board, "augmented the magnitude of the destiny of the two great parties," and, by the fraudulent and unlawful means already charged, reversed the popular verdict, and fraudulently issued the certificates, which are the foundation of the authority for the vote cast for Hayes and Wheeler, and which this Commission is called upon to pronounce to be the true and lawful vote of the State of Louisiana.

The evidence to support these charges of fraud and illegality on the part of the canvassing-officers of Louisiana has already been taken by the Senate of the United States, in pursuance of the resolution adopted December 4, 1876, requiring the Committee on Privileges and Elections, among other duties, to inquire whether the appointment of electors, or those claiming to be such, in any of the States had been made either by force, *fraud,* or other means, otherwise than in conformity with the Constitution and laws of the United States and the laws of the respective States; and by the House of Representatives through a special committee appointed to investigate the recent election and the action of the canvassing or returning board of the State of Louisiana in reference thereto, and report all the facts essential to an honest return of the votes received by the electors of said State for President and Vice-President of the United States.

The PRESIDENT. I do not know, Mr. McDonald, what the arrangement between you and your associate is, but half the time has elapsed. One hour has been consumed.

Mr. Senator McDONALD. I shall not take up his time, but I shall leave him to present *in extenso* these questions. I will only occupy a few minutes further.

It is the duty of this Commission, under the law creating it, *exercising for that purpose all the powers now possessed by the two Houses of Congress acting separately or together*, to determine and decide whether any and what votes from the State of Louisiana are the votes provided for by the Constitution of the United States, and how many and what persons were duly appointed electors in said State, and it may therein take into view such petitions, depositions, and other papers, if any, as shall, by the Constitution and now existing laws, be competent and pertinent in such consideration.

In vesting these powers in this Commission Congress created a judicial, and not a clerical, board.

As a judicial board, this Commission is not bound to accept as "the votes provided for in the Constitution of the United States" such as may have been cast by persons fraudulently certified as electors nor to accept them as duly appointed electors, and must consider, in reaching its determination, such proof as would be admissible in either branch of Congress if engaged in the consideration of the same question; and, therefore, the proofs already taken by either of said Houses with respect to these questions are to be deemed "depositions and other papers pertinent in such consideration."

If these proofs, or any other evidence which the Commission may properly receive, shall establish the fact that the electors who cast the votes in question had been appointed by fraud or other means otherwise than in conformity with the Constitution and laws of the United States and the laws of the State of Louisiana, or that any of them were incapable of being chosen, then the votes cast by such must be rejected, for they are not "the votes provided for in the Constitution."

Mr. President and gentlemen of the Commission, may I in conclusion conjure you to meet these questions on their merits?

Say that the charges are true or false.

Here are charges of fraud against the perpetration of which every honest instinct of our nature rebels—a villainy in their perpetration that is ringing through the land.

Do not, by closing your eyes to them, exhibit a degree of judicial blindness that all good men must deprecate and the whole country condemn.

Mr. Commissioner BAYARD. I should like to ask you to refer to the statute of Louisiana providing for filling vacancies in the college of electors, recited in the certificate of Mr. Kellogg.

Mr. Senator McDONALD. That is the act of 1868.

Mr. TRUMBULL. It will be found in the pamphlet at page 93.

Mr. Commissioner HUNTON. Allow me to ask a question, Mr. McDonald. You have stated that the electoral vote of Louisiana was discarded in 1872 on the ground that there was no regular machinery for counting the electoral vote.

Mr. Senator McDONALD. No, sir; not that; but that there had been a fraudulent return of that vote. That was one of the grounds of objection made at the time the certificates were opened. It does not appear upon which one of the several grounds the action was based, but there were quite a number. The Senate and House acted, and they each passed resolutions that it was not the electoral vote of the State.

Mr. Commissioner HUNTON. I am aware of that. I only wanted to ask you to furnish the Commission with that evidence.

Mr. Senator McDONALD. In the book entitled Presidential Counts you will find the whole of it.

Mr. Representative JENKS. I would ask, Mr. President, how much time I have?

Mr. Commissioner ABBOTT. I move, if Mr. Jenks desires it, that he may have a full hour. Some ten minutes of it, I think, were taken by Senator McDonald and interruptions of him, and there are many questions to be discussed here which are of importance.

Mr. Senator McDONALD. I trust, Mr. President and gentlemen, it may be so. The questions put to me necessarily led me to occupy more time than I intended.

The PRESIDENT. Are you satisfied, Mr. Jenks, to take five minutes in addition to the time left?

Mr. Representative JENKS. I prefer a full hour; I do not know that I shall consume it.

The PRESIDENT. I will submit the question to the Commission: Shall Mr. Jenks have an hour?

The question was decided in the affirmative.

Mr. Commissioner ABBOTT. And of course the same time will be extended to the other side if they wish it.

Mr. Representative JENKS. Mr. President and gentlemen of the Commission, by the organic act under which this tribunal is constituted, with the decision that has been rendered thereon and adopted by the Houses, the principle has been established that the Houses of Congress shall count the votes. That being fixed as a fact from which to start, the inquiry is, what is implied in counting the votes? Counting any given thing implies two different actions of the mind; one of discrimination or determination to find that the thing to be counted is generically of the kind that is to be counted, and the counting an act of enumeration or finding the result from these acts of determination. To throw out either word from the sentence, "the votes shall then be counted," would be to destroy its sense.

Now I will assume that the Constitution has said the Houses of Congress shall count the votes. When a power is conferred by the Constitution, every power that is necessarily implied to perform that power is also granted; and when a power is granted and the emergency arises when that power should be exercised, the execution of that power becomes a duty, and when that emergency has arisen, the implied powers, whatever are necessary to discharge that duty, are granted; and if they are a necessary implication from the Constitution, they are as much a part of it as though there written; and if the Constitution has written therein that they have the power to intelligently do the act, neither Congress nor any one else can lawfully deprive them of that power. Hence, if the act of Congress which says that the executive certificate shall be the only evidence received contravenes the grant of power which is necessarily implied to find the truth, that statute is a simple nullity, because here are the legislative bodies of a great nation; they are required to attest by their journals a fact which is to go down through all history as the truth over their signatures, and no power on earth can say that you shall put upon those journals that which you and every one else knows to be false. So there can be no such thing as blinding the eyes. If Congress had passed an act that the members of the Senate and House of Representatives with bandages over their eyes, under the superintendence of the President of the Senate, bandaged in a like manner, should count the votes, you would say that absurdity cannot be tolerated; and the same fact exists here. Truth is the moral sunlight of the world, and if you dare cut out the truth from the physical eye, you dare from the moral eye or the mind's eye; but you cannot from one more than from the other unless you propose to defy the intelligent judgment of the world.

Then, this being the duty of the Houses, to count the votes, and the counting implying the fact that there must be an intelligent judgment and an accurate enumeration, no power can deprive the Houses of the necessary intelligence to do that duty.

Then I wish to call the attention of the Commission to another distinction. It has been rather assumed that this is a judicial tribunal. I am unable to concur in this view. It is essentially legislative to determine the succession of the Chief Executive; nothing more and nothing less. A merchant turns to his clerk and says to him, " Go to yon pile of goods and determine which are the calicoes and count the number of webs." It is not a judicial act for that clerk to obey the order. There are no parties to it. The merchant is the owner; he is to do it for himself, and not another; it is not a judicial act at all. The United States says to her two Houses of Congress, "All certificates, true and false, being opened, you are required to make a truthful count of those which are genuine, and repudiate those which are false." It is the nation doing it for herself. It is not parties.

This discussion has been somewhat depreciated in its character, I apprehend, in that it has been to some extent assumed that this is a contest between parties. It is forty-five millions of people speaking for themselves through their own representatives, and saying "you, for me, and in my name and stead, count these votes." It is legislative action, and not judicial, but it must be truthful; and it was conferred upon the legislative power from the very fact that the Senate representing the States, the Representatives representing the people of the whole nation, the question of succession being known as the question that would ultimately involve the greatest danger to our institutions, and that there could be no human foresight that could conceive of every possible emergency that might arise, and in order that there might be no *casus omissus*, it was put into the hands of the States and the people, intending that from the broad view of the legislator, from the broad range of evidence that he takes into view, and from his mode of thought, he should decide upon this counting on principles of original justice with discretionary application, which is the definition given by Mr. Burke of legislative power. So that from original justice, not as a court with discretionary application, intended by those who conferred the power upon the States and the people, you are to count this vote, not for candidates, but for your country, and count it truly. There should be no blinding of the eyes before we assume to count it.

With these preliminary views, we will proceed to consider the count of the votes. Here are two certificates presented, each of which represents eight electors, each of which bears the seal of a State, each of which bears the signature of a governor. Shall both be counted? Shall either? Or shall neither? If I ask whether both shall not be counted, what is the response? The response is in the language of the Constitution, very simple, very short. Both cannot be counted, because the Constitution provides that a number of electors equal to the whole number of Senators and Representatives to which the State may be entitled in the Congress, only, shall be appointed. The Constitution at once meets you, because the number is prescribed therein. You immediately say, " Both cannot be counted." Then that is disposed of, and disposed of because the Constitution says that only a fixed number shall be counted; but the Constitution in identically the same clause fixes the other qualifications. It fixes as to the manner of their choosing and as to the qualifications these men shall have who shall be chosen. If you settle it peremptorily and speedily when the Constitution meets you in reference to the number, have you a right on some man's certificate to say, " I will ponder awhile whether I will recognize the Constitution as to manner or as to qualification?" The answer should be equally prompt. All that the legislatures of the States direct is the manner, with the qualification that no person holding an office of trust or profit under the United States shall be appointed an elector. Then let us meet the question, if we find the facts to show a violation of the provision of the Constitution as to manner or as to qualifications, with the same promptness with which we would meet it with reference to the number.

Then let us proceed to the count. You cannot count both, because the Constitution limits the number. Then they must be chosen as the legislature directs. They are not both genuine, then, is the conclusion you come to. The inquiry would be, if you were investigating something else and found some real and some false, which is the genuine? And the same principle you would apply to such an inquiry should be applied here now; which is genuine? If either one conforms to the law of the land in all essential particulars, that is genuine. If either fails to conform to the law of the land in any essential particular, that is false. Then it necessarily involves the inquiry as to which conforms to the law of the land. If either does, it is to be counted; but if neither does, you cannot count either.

Then, what are the provisions of the law of the land? With reference to the McEnery certificate, the certificate No. 2, as it has been designated by the Commission, we claim and are prepared to prove that those electors were elected in the manner prescribed by the State of Louisiana. Second, we are prepared to prove that the electors that are certified to by Mr. Kellogg were not elected in conformity to the laws of Louisiana. Will you accept the proof? That is our offer, and we can establish it.

Then, if we establish that the one is elected according to the legislative provisions of the State of Louisiana, you have it precisely on the same principle on which you rule that both shall not be counted. The constitutional provision is identical and equally imperative. We are also prepared to prove that, in pursuance of the statutes of the United States, the one set, the McEnery electors, were elected on the 7th day of November, and the other, the Kellogg electors, were not elected until the 6th day of December; so that affirmative law, in addition to the Constitution, will be in favor of counting certificate No. 2. We are also prepared to show that those who claim under certificate No. 2 voted, exercised their right of office, on the day prescribed by law.

Thus, in every essential particular, certificate No. 2 is in precise conformity to law. Certificates Nos. 1 and 3 lack, first, the qualification that the men named therein were not elected in pursuance of the mode prescribed by the legislature, and they were not elected on the day prescribed by the act of Congress. It would seem, if these facts are established, that certificate No. 2 most nearly conforms; but we may consider whether it is sufficiently evidenced hereafter, because the questions of evidence arise even after the real merits shall have been established;

but if we establish these facts, certificate No. 2 is that which most nearly conforms to law, and, as we claim, in every essential particular.

If these two certificates come in collision, shall the provision which says the executive shall certify override the provision of the Constitution which prescribes the mode of choice, and override that provision of the act of Congress which fixes that the time of election shall be on a given day, the 7th day of November in this case? It seems to me it ought not, and if the formal be preferred to the substantial, it ought not to be. Then suppose the element of fraud enter into the formal, and we propose to prove that the certificate as signed by Governor Kellogg was procured through the fraudulent acts of a returning-board. But it may be objected that we have no right to inquire into that. I was struck somewhat with the argument made concerning the successive steps in an election, as they were announced a day or two since by one of the honorable gentlemen, and the peculiar feature which marked it was that he stopped just at the place that suited his argument, and thereby eliminated the whole power of the United States Government. He stepped right up until the electors have cast their votes, and then announced, "Then the thing is ended;" then every avenue of truth is cut off. A State may do what she pleases, fraudulently, and the United States cannot inquire into it. Is this true? Is it intended that the Senate and House of Representatives of the United States shall be compelled to certify to what they know to be false, and transmit it into history in this way? It does not seem to me to be possible. Has the State of Louisiana, or Florida, or any other State, the right to put in the food, that we all must eat, poison, and require us to eat it? It seems to me we have some say-so in such a matter. The thirty-seven other States have an interest, as well as Louisiana, or Florida, or any single State; and the United States Government, until the votes are opened in the Houses, has no opportunity to know whether it is food or poison. If a State violates the Constitution of the United States by force, we call a million of men to crush her; but if by fraud, we are to take the poison and let the nation die. Is that true or is it false? It is not true. This nation has power to guard against fraud as she has against force; and when it is our duty to count, the two great bodies, representing the States and representing the people, have a right to say, when fraud is injected therein, "We will exclude that, and accept only that which is honest and *bona fide.*"

But suppose the certificate of the governor had been procured by a band of buccaneers sailing up the river to New Orleans, capturing Governor Kellogg, taking him on board their ship, and forcing him to sign his name to that certificate, and thus perpetrating it upon the United States, would you hesitate a moment to inquire concerning that? If, instead of that, a band of more insidious scoundrels deceive him and induce him to sign that certificate, does that render it more sacred? It seems to me Mars, the god of war, was more respectable than Mercury, the god of thieves. Insidious villainy does not commend itself to us as much as actual force. In no judicial tribunal nor in any legislative tribunal ought it to be accepted as worthy of any more sanctity. But suppose, in addition (and this we expect to prove) to the returning-board poisoning these returns, that the governor who issued the certificate was himself a party to it; does the fact that he was dishonest, a member of the same band of conspirators, render it more sacred than if he had been an honest man? Can he by his own villainy sanctify his villainous act? Can he take advantage of it himself for his own aggrandizement?. It seems to me these propositions need no argument; hence I merely state them.

I may here call attention to the only explanation I know of giving any sufficient probability by which to account for the "certificates" 1 and 3, as found in the evidence as taken before the congressional committee. Each member of the returning-board had sworn that the canvass of votes on which they promulgated their result was not obtained earlier than eight o'clock in the evening of the 5th of December. A newspaper reporter by the name of Smith, investigating, as is their wont, around the State-house, discovered that in the afternoon of the 5th, about two or three o'clock, the certificate of election for the republican electors had been made out; and yet the returning-board swore they never knew nor had any idea until after they had finished their counting that there was a majority for one side or the other; but their certificates were already prepared. This passed into the newspapers, and as a consequence it became necessary to make two certificates, and they were made, we say the second set as well as the first, so that if you have difficulty in arriving at the fact, why there are these double certificates. That is the only explanation I find in the evidence.

But I will proceed with the facts, for it was not my intention to have entered on a legal discussion at all, because the facts are sufficiently important as a groundwork for future action to be laid before the Commission. With reference to the facts, the first fact we present would be this: that the legislature has directed that the electors shall be appointed by a popular vote. I need not refer to the statute to establish that; the evidence is in the revised statutes. The second fact is that on the popular vote cast in that State, undisputed by any one, and as proven from the only record-evidence of the State, there is a majority of between 6,000 and 9,000 in favor of the Tilden electors, an average of 7,639, I believe, depending upon which you compare with the others; but the majority is not less than 6,000 and it is not in excess of 9,000. That is the second fact.

Here I may call attention to the only mode of arriving at the truth of this case in reference to this point. The papers that pass into the hands of the returning-board are only ephemeral. They are not made records. There is no place for their preservation. They pass into the hands of this board, and where they go from that no one knows by law. As a fact they distribute themselves pretty miscellaneously; but the law provides no place for their preservation, and they are only intended for the temporary purpose of a canvass. Then from the returning-board there is no record-evidence or mode of testing the veracity of their acts; but the law has provided a record-evidence, and that is this: Every commissioner of election shall file his statement with the supervisor of registration in duplicate. The supervisor of registration shall make out his statements in duplicate. Of those duplicates of the commissioners of election and supervisors of registration, one is to be sent to the clerk of the court in the parish, and the other to the returning-board. That of the returning-board is temporary; the other goes as a standing muniment in evidence of title. Then from these, the only muniments of title, placed on record in that State with the several courts of record, this is the result; but the result was changed in some way, and it was changed so that a certificate was given by Governor Kellogg; it was done by the excluding of 13,236 democratic votes and 2,178 republican votes, a difference of 11,058.

In this connection, in order that I may answer the question suggested by the honorable Senator from Ohio, I will give a statement of the different parishes and the facts with reference to them. So far as protest is concerned, it has already been elaborated before the Commission that where there is a protest filed, if the law be constitutional, there is power on the establishment of certain facts to exclude certain votes or certain polls. Now, this is a law conferring special jurisdiction, and, as we know, it must receive a strict construction. If there be any element that is necessary to give this jurisdiction not in the evidence before it, it has no jurisdiction, and its acts so far as this extraordinary power is concerned are entirely void. In order to obtain jurisdiction there must be a protest filed by the supervisor of registration if there be intimidation or fraud during the period of registration or revision of registration. He has no power to file a protest with reference to violence or anything of the kind on election-day; but it is only during the registration and revision of registration that he has any authority to file any protest. Then the commissioners of election on election-day may file protests for violence on election-day. If it be not done by one of these parties, there is no power to inquire concerning it, and if inquiry be made it is a usurpation; and in addition to that we will prove the exercise of such power is a fraud which was intentionally perpetrated in the alleged canvass by the returning-board of Louisiana in this case.

Of these protests there must be duplicates; of the duplicates one is transmitted to the returning-board, the other filed in court. That filed in court is placed there in order that there may be a prosecution by the district attorney for the crime, and for the additional purpose that the people of a parish, poll, or whatever may be objected to, may know what is charged against them, in order that they may stand for their rights; because it is not possible that the right of suffrage of the people of a whole parish may be taken from them by the inquisitorial proceedings before such a board as this, and of which they never had notice, when the law says duplicates shall be filed in the courts. Hence if there be no duplicate filed in court there is no jurisdiction; and I may now state, as a generality, that with the exception of the parishes of Bossier and Concordia there was not a single protest filed in court in the State of Louisiana. In Concordia there was not a single vote thrown out, because it was republican in all its polls. In Bossier there were some one hundred votes or so thrown out, because there were democratic polls in that parish. We will now go over the several parishes.

Here it may be necessary to explain that the supervisor of registration is to receive the returns of the commissioners of election, and within twenty-four hours of the date of their receipt send them by mail, sealed up, to the returning-board. He has no more power or discretion concerning the votes that are cast, their reception or their exclusion, than has the mail-boy to determine whether the letters in his mail-bag are such as should be carried or not—not a mite of discretion, but simply that of an instrument of transmission; nothing more and nothing less. Although the constitution of the State requires that all her officers shall be citizens of the State, and the parish officers citizens of the parish in which they officiate and citizens of the State, F. A. Clover was appointed a supervisor of registration for East Baton Rouge, being a citizen of Mississippi, holding two offices in the State of Mississippi until the 1st of January, 1876, and it takes one year to acquire a residence in Louisiana. After that he came some time in March to Louisiana, and engaged as a runner, or in the techinal parlance of that vicinity he became a roper-in for a snake-show; that is, a caller-in to a gambling tent on the wharf. He continued in that vocation until the

27th of August, when he was appointed supervisor of East Baton Rouge, because East Baton Rouge it was known was becoming strongly democratic.

Clubs had been organized there in which there were from five hundred to seven hundred colored voters, and it became necessary to put this parish under the charge of a particularly appropriate supervisor of registration. This supervisor of registration of East Baton Rouge filed no protest with the clerk of the court; none is found on file; it is so proven by the testimony as taken according to law, because we say that the testimony taken by Congress is a part of this record. This is a legislative tribunal as to practice in proceeding. The law says you shall receive petitions, depositions, &c., as provided by the law of the land. What law? The law with reference to legislative bodies who have the counting of this vote. If all the citizens of the United States who choose send a petition in, it would be your duty to receive it in evidence, giving it its proper weight. If the different Houses of Congress have taken testimony, it is your duty to receive it, because by the law of the land, through all time, that has been the mode of taking testimony in the several Houses of Congress, and this body is acting with the powers and under the obligations substantially as though it were a congressional body. Then the supervisor of registration of East Baton Rouge threw out 1,147 democratic votes and 47 republican votes, making a change of 1,100 in that parish.

Mr. Commissioner THURMAN. The supervisor of registration, not the returning-board?

Mr. Representative JENKS. Not the board; it was before they got to the board that this roper-in for the snake-show did this, and the evidence was before the returning-board as to what the true vote was; and they, with that fidelity which was indicated by a dispatch sent by their attorney, John Ray, that by throwing out five parishes the State would be republican, (and this was one of them,) accepted his act and never inquired concerning it. Eleven hundred were thrown out by an officer with no more power than a mail-carrier; and with notice to the board that he had done it, with the actual vote placed before them, they by their act reply, "that takes that much burden off our shoulders and we leave it so."

After the supervisor of registration had thrown out 1,100 votes, that is, 1,100 of a difference, the board then took two polls, 12 and 14, and at poll No. 12 threw out 162 democratic votes and 4 republican votes; at poll No. 14 they threw out 144 democratic votes and 6 republican votes in that parish, making a difference of 1,396; and no protest filed in court, no notice to a single citizen of East Baton Rouge, and yet they were being disfranchised by the thousand; and this purports to be a free government!

The next is West Feliciana. There was no protest filed in court in that parish. There were 1,010 democratic votes thrown out and 154 republican; no protest filed, no opportunity for the citizens to know the truth; making a difference of 856.

In East Feliciana there was no protest filed with the clerk of the court. There were 1,736 democratic votes thrown out and 1 republican, and this is the parish over which they rejoice as conclusive evidence of intimidation. The governor of the State, we are prepared to prove, had notice in advance that the colored people were passing into the democratic party in large masses. The supervisor of registration it was first contemplated should not go there at all, and thereby prevent an election. But in consequence of hoping to carry two members of the legislature he was instructed to go back and did go back; but there were no republican tickets sent there, and hence there was but 1 republican vote cast. The arrangement was made to keep the tickets away; they did not go, and the consequence of it was 1 republican vote and 1,736 democratic, and that was intended as evidence of intimidation. But we stand on the legal proposition that there was no protest filed, and being without jurisdiction the act of throwing out was usurpation.

The next was New Orleans. There were none thrown out by the board, but there were three polls thrown out by the supervisors of registration, these mail-carriers. There were 993 democratic votes thrown out and 346 republican votes, making 647 of a difference in New Orleans. They were thrown out on very different pretexts. One was thrown out because for the single elector De Blanc it was uncertain on the commissioner's statement whether the number of votes cast was 247 or 249; that is, the figure 7 was not made with sufficient accuracy by the commissioner of election to know certainly whether it was a 7 or a 9; and because the supervisor of registration could not decipher that figure he threw out the whole poll; and although that fact was called to the attention of the returning-board, they went over it, and excluded it in their count. If this is not an abomination that a great nation is not bound to submit to, I would ask you what you would call an abomination?

The next is Claiborne. There was no protest filed of any kind with the board or elsewhere, and 184 votes were thrown out. In Caldwell there was no protest filed whatever, and 141 democratic votes were thrown out and 74 republican, making 67 of a difference. In Franklin 74 democratic and 28 republican votes were thrown out, a difference of 46, and there was no protest. In Catahoula there was no protest whatever, and 97 democratic votes were thrown out and 20 republican, making 77 of a difference. In Richland there was no protest filed with the clerk of the court, and there was no protest filed, either, with the returning-board until the 30th day of November. When the supervisor of registration brought in his returns, instead of sending them by mail he carried them, and that brought him in connection with the custom-house, and the custom-house was in need of witnesses, as they stated. The consequence was they gave this supervisor of registration $150 to pay witnesses, and he filed a protest on the 30th of November with the returning-board, and the consequence was that they excluded 770 democratic votes and 157 republican votes, making 613 of a difference in majorities; and you are asked to sanction that. The supervisor of registration received $150 under the nominal pretext of searching for witnesses, and some seventeen days after he has made his original return his conscience then becomes enlightened, and he files a protest with the board, but not in court; and you are to count the votes as so manipulated and say it is right!

Mr. Commissioner THURMAN. Was the protest in regard to registration?

Mr. Representative JENKS. The protest was a general one, that there was intimidation. There is not a single one of these protests that in a legal tribunal or before an honest board comes up to the requisition of the law.

Mr. Commissioner THURMAN. If I understood your statement before, the supervisor of registration has no duty to perform in protesting in respect to the election, but only in respect to registration.

Mr. Representative JENKS. None at all in reference to election-day, but during the period of registration and the revision of registration.

His official right to protest began on the 28th of August and terminated on the evening before election-day, and only extends to such acts as interfered with registration and revision, and whenever election-day comes his power is exhausted and the commissioners of election then make the protest. That is the way the law divides the duty.

The next parish is Morehouse. There was no protest filed of any kind. The number of democratic votes thrown out by the board was 985, of republican 357, making a difference of 628. In Ouachita Parish there was a protest filed with the board, but not in court. There were 1,517 democratic votes thrown out and 48 republican, making a difference of 1,469. In Madison there were 63 votes added to the republican vote as returned by the commissioners of election to the supervisor of registration. That was an act of extended discretion, I presume. Whenever a vote was not what they (the board) conceived it ought to be, they assumed the right, as in Vernon Parish, to make it what they thought it should be; and if this be republican in form, how will you define a republic? If a board has a right to say how an election shall result at its own discretion, without regard to the vote actually cast, how are you to define what a republic is?

Then in Webster there was no protest filed whatever. There were 436 democratic votes thrown out and 194 republican, making 242 of a difference. In Bossier there was a protest by the supervisor of registration, but not by the commissioners of election. Bossier, as I stated before, and Concordia are the only two parishes where there were any protests filed with the clerks of the courts. Here was a protest filed by the supervisor of registration, but it related to acts of violence on election-day, over which he had no jurisdiction, and hence that action was void. The number thrown out there against the democracy was 342 of a majority.

In Natchitoches there was no protest of any kind. The number of democratic votes thrown out was 343, republican 7, making a difference of 336. No protest was filed whatever; that is, no protest filed with the clerk of the court. There was a protest filed with the board, made after the election by the supervisor of registration, with reference to transactions that occurred on election-day principally and after the time limited by law for him to make protest.

Here it is claimed the statute is directory as to the time of the protest. As the duty of the supervisor of registration is a simple one, he only being empowered to pack up the statements and put them in an envelope and mail them, he has but twenty-four hours to do it, and the statute required that he should send them from the place where they were received and not carry them in person, in order that there might not be a comparison of results at the capital, as there was in this case, and then go to cutting and fitting to match results as they might desire. So that that part of it is not directory. It is not necessary it should be so considered; but if it be directory and they violated it unnecessarily, that is presumptive evidence of fraud.

In Vernon there was no protest whatever. They took jurisdiction without evidence. They threw out 178 democratic votes and added 179 to the republican side—a difference of 357. In Iberia there was no protest and 333 democratic and 11 republican votes were thrown out, making a difference of 322. The reason these votes were thrown out was that the law requires that when the voter shall have voted there shall be written on the back of his certificate of registration "voted." In the morning the officers of election at one poll did not write on the back of the certificate of the electors "voted" until about one hundred votes had been cast. After that, finding it was their duty to so do, they did write it. This fact was communicated to the board, and the upshot of it was that they threw out the whole poll because it gave 322 of a democratic majority.

Then in La Fayette there was no protest filed in court. Two polls were rejected by the supervisor of registration. The number thrown out was 518 democratic and 7 republican.

In La Fourche no protest was filed in court. Two polls were thrown out by the supervisor of registration, in one of which 142 votes were democratic as against 104 republican, making 38 of a difference, and in the other 127 of a difference in majorities against the democratic electors.

In Livingston there was no protest filed of any character. The democratic majority of 328 was thrown out. In Saint Landry there was no protest filed, and poll No. 9 was thrown out with a democratic majority of 82. In Tangipahoa there was no protest filed in court. Poll No. 10 was not compiled; that is, it was thrown out by the supervisor of registration; and poll No. 3 was excluded, making 76.

There is a coincidence that I wish to call attention to here. If accidents do happen, it is a little singular that they always happen in one direction; and if you find this fact to exist that the accidents happen in the direction that the person who occasions their happening would desire accidents to happen, it is a ground for suspicion that possibly it may not have been an accident. Then when you take the fact into consideration that the acting governor of the State was a republican, that he appoints the State supervisors of registration and he also appoints every supervisor of registration in the State, the supervisors of registration appoint every commissioner of elections in the State, (the clerks of the supervisors of registration were usually republicans,) I believe there were one or two instances in which there were exceptions—every single mistake that was made happened to cut just one way. That suggests the possibility that there might be design in it so strong, that when we give some additional facts which we will state directly, it seems to me almost conclusive of design.

But it is probably now my duty to answer what they may say. I have stated that there were no protests at all in certain cases. That is evaded by a proposition that parties in interest may have a hearing before the board under the provisions of the third section of the act. After stating that the supervisor of registration shall file protests, &c., it proceeds:

Provided, That any person interested in said election by reason of being a candidate for office shall be allowed a hearing before said returning-officers upon making application within the time allowed for the forwarding of the returns of said election.

That provides for a hearing. This tribunal cannot entertain an original pleading between parties, because if it did it would be clearly and wholly judicial. If the claimant of an office has a right to come before this board and allege that he was elected, of course his opponent has a right to deny that allegation. We then find every element constituting a court. There are the *actor*, the *reus*, the *judex*, full judicial characteristics in all particulars; and yet the constitution of Louisiana says that all judicial powers shall be vested in certain courts, and that none shall be exercised by any other authority. So it is not possible that the "hearing" contemplated was that certain men might go over the State and file protests, as they did in this case, against nearly every parish in the State; so that when I say there was no protest, I say the protest by the officers who claimed to have been elected was no protest at all as contemplated by this act, and was a nullity; and if you count the others who filed no protests in court, and throw out every vote that was thrown out under them, and say that this general protest was not lawfully filed— and you can say nothing else as to this alleged general protest as I understand the law—it still leaves a very considerable majority in favor of the McEnery electors.

I have gone through *seriatim* the statements of the several parishes. I will now pass to more general evidence of fraud. However, there is another system of facts which it is my duty to call the attention of the Commission to, in order that there may be a full opening. There are certain persons who are alleged to be disqualified. A. B. Levissee and O. H. Brewster are disqualified under the Constitution of the United States. We will prove that Levissee was a commissioner appointed by a circuit court of the United States holding at the time of the election. We will prove that Mr. Brewster was surveyor of the land-office for the land-district of Louisiana. He swears himself that three or four days after the election he wrote a letter resigning and asking that it might take effect as of the 4th of November. This letter was written on the 10th or 11th of November. It was mailed to Washington and received at Washington on the 18th. On the 23d he received a reply accepting his resignation as of the 4th. Hence on the day of the election he was disqualified from holding this office; and as we decide very promptly when the number is limited by the Constitution, it is our duty to decide equally promptly that the qualification is equally as binding on us.

The disqualification of the Constitution does not extend to the officer alone, but it goes down and pervades the whole country. The voter who casts his vote for a disqualified person does the same as though he cast a blank vote, for he is as much bound by the Constitution as is the officer who claims to be elected. It pervades all. It is the supreme fundamental law, reaching every citizen from the lowest to the highest, and the disqualification made it equivalent to the absolute not voting of the party who threw a vote for a constitutionally disqualified man.

Then, in reference to the other officers, we find that J. H. Burch was a State senator of the State of Louisiana. By the constitution of the State of Louisiana it is provided that no person shall hold any two offices under the said State except those of justice of the peace and notary public. Burch was a State senator, we will prove, prior to the election, and continues so up to this day by virtue of the holding under which he held before. Then the disqualification of the State constitution rendered the vote of the citizen as to this Burch the same as though it had not been cast. He was not elected, even if he had a majority of the votes.

Morris Marks, another elector in certificates Nos. 1 and 3, was district attorney for the district in which the parish of Saint James is, prior to the election and has continued to hold down to this day. He is disqualified by the State constitution. We will also show that Oscar Joffrion was supervisor of registration for Point Coupee Parish. He is disqualified by the constitution of the State, article 117, and he is also disqualified by express enactment, because in the registration law, section 13, you will find that a supervisor of registration is expressly disqualified from being a candidate for any office being voted for during the time of his officiating as supervisor of registration. The language is:

That no supervisor of registration appointed under this act, and no clerk of such supervisor of registration, shall be eligible for any office at any election when said officers officiate.

So that, in addition to the constitutional disqualification, there is express statutory disqualification with reference to Joffrion, and we will prove that he was acting and did act clear through this election as supervisor of registration for the parish of Point Coupee. These are disqualifications, and we will establish all of them by affirmative evidence.

Then with reference to actual fraud we have some testimony to offer, to which I will call your attention very briefly and from memory. In the first instance we are prepared to prove that prior to the election those who had the conduct of the campaign on behalf of the republican party alleged in advance that, no difference how the election went by the people, the returning-board would make it all right. This was declared by Mr. Lewis and by Judge Dibble, the acting attorney-general. Lewis is the one who claims to have been elected to the United States Senate by the late legislature created by virtue of the action of this returning-board. We will show that in addition to this, prior to the meeting of the returning-board, there was a telegram sent by John Ray, who was attorney for the returning-board and went through all of its sessions, public and private, in which he states:

NEW ORLEANS, *November* 16, 1876.

Hon. J. R. WEST, *Washington, D C.:*

Returns to date leave us majority, throwing out five parishes.

JOHN RAY.

That is dated on the 16th of November, before the returning-board met, showing that the attorney that they selected to discharge the functions of their adviser stated in advance that five parishes were to be thrown out. We will corroborate that by predictions coming from many sources. On the 17th of November, 1876, J. R. G. Pitkin, United States marshal, who used the funds of the Government with a very generous hand in reference to procuring witnesses to upset the right in that State, telegraphed J. R. West as follows:

NEW ORLEANS, *November* 17, 1876.

Hon. J. R. WEST, *Washington, D. C.:*

Louisiana is safe. Our northern friends stand firmly by us. The returning-board will hold its own.

J. R. G. PITKIN.

Showing that there was no reliance upon the votes of the people, but their hopes concentrated in the returning-board. Then on the 3d of December, prior to the time that Governor Wells swears he knew anything about what the results were, we have the following telegram:

NEW ORLEANS, *December* 3, 1876.

Hon. J. R. WEST, *Washington, D. C.:*

Democratic boast entire fallacy. Have northern friends on way North—answer telegram of this morning; also, have Senate anticipate House in sending committee to investigate outrages. Have seen Wells, who says, " Board will return Hayes sure. Have no fear."

J. R. G. PITKIN.

And Mr. Pitkin swore before the congressional committee that Wells did tell him before he sent the telegram that the board would return Hayes sure, to have no fear.

Then, taking these predictions and taking their action, we will add, besides, to many other things that I have not time to recapitulate, that this board offered by some of its members to sell the result in that State to two different men, to one for a consideration of $200,000, to another asking a million. The price was changed in conformity to the probabilities of the purchase. The constant succession of accidents all on one side would be sufficient in itself. Then, again, the attention of the board was called to the fact that it was their duty to fill the board to deliver themselves from suspicion. Every one felt and knew that prior to this these very men had been found guilty of doing dishonest acts with reference to elections. They were asked to fill the board. The law was laid before them; they admitted it was the law, but said it was directory. Assuming that they were not bound to obey a directory law, but had a discretion to regard or disregard it as they pleased, they interpreted the word "directory" as discretionary; they used their discretion to exclude any person from knowing what they did who would have an interest in contradicting any false assertion which they might make or dishonest trick which they might perform with reference to the canvass of the election.

Then their attention was called to the fact in reference to making their compilations from the statements of the votes. They made, in violation of law, their compilations from the supervisors of registration, and thereby threw out the whole parish of Grant, and excluded the statements which were not returned by the supervisors of registration, by which they made 2,900 of a difference in their action in favor of their own party.

Now, is a great nation to submit to all this? Must forty-five millions of people drink from a foul sink the ordure that flows through such a fetid sewer? It is not right. Truth should be admitted to shine upon this. You cannot erect a false god and bow down to it and worship it, and be blameless. Truth ought to be permitted to shine upon this transaction; and if truth shine upon it, but one single result can possibly be attained. The wisest of men or the strongest of men cannot make that which is false true. Solomon, the wisest of men, set up the false god Moloch, and in the glowing arms of the monster children wailing died; but his wisdom, his power, and his glory have not been able to efface the stain or to prevent posterity ever since from regarding it as pollution on his name and his character. If you set up the false for the true, if you attempt to blind the eyes of a mighty nation, and to say the Senate of the United States and the House of Representatives of the United States shall put upon their journals as a perpetual memorial to all generations that which they know to be false, and command all to bow down and worship it, your edict will be vain; because history will judge and will know the truth. We ask now that the simple truth, the great moral light of the universe, may be permitted to shine upon this transaction, to clear out all this pollution, and to let our country be free from the disgrace of being poisoned by the act of this vile returning-board.

Mr. Representative HURLBUT. Mr. President and gentlemen of the Commission, I wish my mind could be relieved of the difference of opinion expressed by the several members who objected in advance of me, and that the important question could be determined either as claimed by Senator McDonald, that this is a judicial tribunal, or as claimed by Mr. Jenks, of the House, that it is a legislative tribunal. If indeed there be any claim of special and peculiar jurisdiction belonging to this Commission, it comes under the act of Congress. The judicial power is limited by the Constitution, and you certainly possess not that. The legislative power is equally limited by the Constitution to Congress, and you certainly possess not that. I apprehend that the constitution of this Commission is as a means, as a committee, if I may call it so, appointed by the two Houses, as a convenience to them, to determine upon certain questions which have arisen with regard to this presidential election, and that this committee or this Commission is bound to pass upon these questions in conformity to well-settled and regularly-established law, and· not at all in conformity to any vague suggestions of matter which is *dehors* the record, which is not among the things committed to you by the President of the Senate, and which already, if I understand the decision of this Commission, is barred by the spirit and reason of the decision made in the Florida case.

I am here in the discharge of the duty which has been cast upon me, to do two things: first, to object to the paper known as No. 2, the McEnery certificate. That may be done, as I understand it, in two ways: first, by showing that the certificate itself is not good; second, by showing that McEnery himself is not governor. That is an attacking process to the certificate and to the title of the man who gives it. The attack may be made just as well by supporting by the law and the evidence the existence and legal effect of the other and counter-certificate purporting to be given by William P. Kellogg as governor, and the establishment of the fact to the satisfaction of this Commission and of the world that William P. Kellogg was at the time the certificate was given the only legal and recognized governor in the State of Louisiana. Fortunately, there is an abundance of proof upon that question. There is no governor who has held office in these United States that is so abundantly bolstered up by proof of his existence as governor, not only *stricti juris* by the fact of election, but by the fact of the declaration of that election by the only legal returning-officers of the State, by the fact of the counting of the votes by the only legal legislature of the State, by the fact of the entrance into office under that count, by the fact that when in pursuance of the system which prevails in that most wretched State the course of law, sovereign and supreme as it ought to be in every republican government, was violently overthrown, when in 1874 rebellion by arms was inaugurated and civil war brought into the streets of the capital city, armed forces organized deliberately to overthrow it, and a skirmish which bore a near approach to the dimensions of a battle took place, the avowed object being to overthrow the existing government, and to substitute the other one, of which this man McEnery was the figure-head, the intervention of the United States was asked under the Constitution. The United States was asked to lend her strong arm to sustain the right. Which was the government to be sustained there in the case of these two conflicting governments, was by the act of 1795 delegated by Congress to the President of the United States, and that delegation gives until his decision is overthrown by both branches of Congress absolute validity to his recognition on the part of this Government in determining which was the rightful government of the State. The President of the United States so recognized it. The President of the United States did more; he used the military arm of the country, put down the rebellion by force of arms, by conquest, and placed Kellogg back again in the seat from which he had been deposed.

This is not the end of the record. I allude to these facts without giving the dates, which I will do hereafter for the consideration of the tribunal. It does not end here. The question comes up, as to the propriety of the President's action, in the Senate of the United States. The Senate of the United States adopted eventually a resolution offered by Mr. Anthony in terms as follows; I quote from the Senate Journal of 1874-'75, page 475:

Resolved, That the action of the President in protecting the government in Louisiana, of which W. P. Kellogg is the executive, and the people of that State against domestic violence, and in enforcing the laws of the United States in that State, is approved.

There is the senatorial recognition of the determination made by the President of the United States, under the power delegated to him in the law of 1795, and the approval of his action, and the committal of one branch, at all events, of Congress to the validity of Kellogg's tenure of office.

But in reading through that record I find a still more pointed action of the Senate, because the negativing of a proposition sometimes, which is antagonistic to the main proposition, adds peculiar vigor and force to the proposition itself. I find, that resolution being pending, Senator Thurman offered an amendment, which appears on page 473 of the Journal, that nothing in that resolution should be considered as recognizing Kellogg as *de jure* governor of Louisiana; and that amendment was rejected by the vote of the Senate.

The House also has taken some action on this matter. The committee of the House known as the Louisiana Committee, which has been referred to by Mr. Jenks in his argument, reported certain resolutions, and in the Journal of the House of Representatives, page 603, of the session of 1874–'75, this resolution appears:

Resolved, That William Pitt Kellogg be recognized as the governor of the State of Louisiana until the end of the term of office fixed by the constitution of that State.

That resolution was adopted by a vote of 165 to 89. The same committee, of which Mr. Hoar and Mr. Wheeler were members, were anxious, as all true men ought to be, to put an end to the bad state of things which confessedly prevailed there in Louisiana, and to that end they undertook, at the request of these parties—John McEnery, this contesting governor, being one—to make an award which was to be carried out by certain changes, by resignations on the one side and putting men into office on the other, in the legislature of that State; in other words, they undertook to do equity, and an award was made by them, and in pursuance of that award the legislature of Louisiana passed a resolution by which—I am quoting from memory—they agreed that the tenure of office of William Pitt Kellogg during the term for which he had been elected and until his successor should be appointed, should not in any way be interfered with by that legislature of the State of Louisiana in consideration of this award.

Now I will come back, first, to the question of his election. In 1872 the contest was between John McEnery and William P. Kellogg for governor of the State of Louisiana. Governor Warmoth, who undertook to manipulate more things than he could carry, endeavored to complicate the matter by breaking up the legal board of returning-officers, which existed under the act of 1870, and create a board, creatures of his own, so that in fact at that election of 1872 there were two conflicting boards of returning-officers of election of the State of Louisiana; one of them known as the Lynch board and the other as the Forman board. The supreme court of the State of Louisiana has settled all that question. The supreme court of the State of Louisiana, in 25 Louisiana Annual Reports, in the case of The State *ex rel. vs.* Wharton *et al.,* rendered this decision; I read from page 14:

It is therefore ordered and adjudged that the board of returning-officers composed of H. C. Warmoth, F. J. Herron, John Lynch, James Longstreet, and Jacob Hawkins was the legal board of returning-officers of elections of the State of Louisiana.

And that was the board by whose certificate of election Kellogg derived his title. Now, if it be true that William P. Kellogg was governor of the State of Louisiana on the 6th day of December, 1876, it is manifestly true that John McEnery was not; and whatever virtue or value in the way of evidence this Commission may attach to the certificate of a governor must be given to the governor who, by election, recognition, and all other steps known to the law, was at the time the actual governor, and not to a mere pretender who retired from that contest, of his own will, in 1874 and has not in any way undertaken to assert or exercise any possible control over the office of governor of that State from that day to this.

Again, I call the attention of the Commission to the peculiar wording of the certificate given by John McEnery. He was careful, as far as he could, not to commit himself to a statement of any essential fact appearing by evidence:

This is to certify that the following is a true and correct list of the names of the electors of the President and Vice-President of the United States for the next ensuing regular term of the respective offices thereof, being electors duly and legally appointed by and for the State of Louisiana, having each received a majority of the votes cast for electors at the election in the State of Louisiana, held in accordance with law; this certificate being furnished as directed by law, by the executive authority of said State of Louisiana.

There is no reference there to any source known to the laws from which he derives his information; there is no reference there to any returns appearing on file in his office, because he had no office; he had no returns; he had no secretary of state; he had no man in all Louisiana who would come forward and verify the seal of the State and the signature of the governor by signing, " By the governor: So-and-so, secretary of state."

This brings me to consider, in the line of argument which I have marked out for myself, what are the evidences that ordinarily in the regular course of law in all cases of election come up before a canvassing or determining tribunal. Does any one contend for a moment that this Commission has the power, the authority, or the means or time to purge the election in Louisiana, to pass through the whole system as it was displayed there on the 7th day of November, to examine into every poll, or even to read that mass of balderdash under the name of evidence that is sent up here and half yet unprinted? Is it not true that this Commission is exercising to a certain extent a political and not a judicial power, that you are exercising it as all determining bodies pass upon elections, not upon the very facts that may have taken place away down to the remotest poll in the different parishes, but upon the regular returns of the officers constituted for that purpose and sent forward to you? In other words, I draw very clearly in my own mind this distinction—the distinction between the power of a political tribunal to determine an election upon the apparent right, the *prima-facie* right, as it appears upon the papers that are sent up, and the right of a judicial tribunal when two parties are properly before it, one claiming to have been veritably elected and that the other has not been. In that case no man denies that the judicial tribunal, if clothed by law with that power, can pass behind the returns and papers and inquire into the veritable fact of the case and determine according to the very right. Now, I do not believe that either by any fair construction of the law, or by any proper construction of the powers of the two Houses as given by the Constitution, there exists either in the two Houses or in this tribunal the power of examining into the very right as if you were a court sitting to-day to try the case of a *quo warranto* brought by one candidate for the presidency against another in occupation, if such a proceeding be known to the laws, on which I confess I do not propose to give any opinion.

It was stated, and stated correctly, by the distinguished counsel who argued another cause before your tribunal, [Mr. Matthews,] that an election necessarily consists of certain steps moving forward. It does so everywhere; in all States, in all governments where elections are and where they involve anything larger than the single political unit; and, if the Commission will excuse me, I will endeavor to show the distinction that exists under the laws of Louisiana in their mode of scrutinizing their elections and of handling elections from what exists, so far as I know, in any other State in the Union, and the reasons for it.

Where you have a community in which general education is diffused, in which there is a general desire to maintain fair dealing and support of law, as prevails fortunately in most of the States of this Union, but not in Louisiana, then the election processes begin from the bottom; they commence in the unit, the lowest possible subdivision of political power; the people themselves are trusted, are fit to be trusted, and ought to be trusted with the power of determining in those little local communities, under the inspection of their neighbors, who shall be judges of their elections. And so you have and can have judges of election; and from that base the election processes go up by returns from township to county, from county to district, from district to the State canvassing-board; and in every one of those processes the subordinate election tribunals, every one of them, have and exercise the power properly meant by the power of making returns. They are returning-officers; and, as a rule, in the States with which I am most acquainted, the State board of canvassers has no duty to perform excepting a ministerial one. All questions of eligibility of voters, of their right to vote, and all those matters, are in such communities safely intrusted to the local tribunals. But in Louisiana the case is altogether different, and it is different because of the difference of the population, the difference of the character of the people. The laws which they have there are as good laws as the people will permit themselves to have. All laws reflect the condition of society. Thus in Louisiana the election processes, instead of beginning from the bottom and coming up, begin from the top. There is not in that community that diffused education—and I am saying these things with no unkindness to that community, but as a matter of fact—there is not that diffused education, above all things there is not that reverence for law, which permits trusting local neighborhoods with this power. And so, in recognition of that fact, in recognition of the fact that by the processes of reconstruction a vast body of uneducated men had been suddenly elevated to the position of citizenship and of eligibility to office, in recognition of the fact that from the beginning in that most unfortunate State there has been armed, deliberate resistance to the law, there has been deliberate, settled, persistent resolution to crush out by violence and force all those things, no matter what they were, which stood in the way of the party that sought to make itself dominant by force when it was not dominant by numbers, the legislature commenced in 1868 by first creating a sort of returning-board, consisting of the governor and certain officers, but using a judge for the purpose of determining these facts of intimidation.

This Commission is acquainted with the history of this country, and even of that remote part of it. It knows as part of the current history of the country that that change in the system of election laws in the State of Louisiana was brought about by the murders, the assaults, the violent breaking into the regular course of law which swept that State in 1868 and compelled the legislature which sat in 1868 to undertake to devise some remedy. That was one of the remedies they devised.

But that did not answer; and so, in 1870, the legislature of the State went a step further, and they took all the power of making returns in any sense of the word from all these local and subordinate ministers of election, and they did not allow them even to say in a ward-district whether a police-justice or a constable had been elected, the lowest form of subdivision in that State being these precincts or polls in parishes. They took all that away, and took away any power on the part of the commissioners of election even to pass upon the right of a voter to vote. They gave by that law to the supervisor of registration controlling power to determine whether or not a man was a legal voter in a parish, and his determination once made bound every officer of the election. There was positively nothing left to these local commissioners of election except to examine and determine whether the man who offered his vote was the identical man registered by the supervisor of registration. That was all. So their office became simply ministerial and clerical. Their returns were no longer dignified by the name of "returns," but dropped down in the law to what they ought to be, "statements of votes." These statements of votes passed up to the supervisor, who is also— Mr. Jenks has stated it correctly in that particular—deprived of any judicial power whatsoever. He is simply a compiler of the statements, and is bound by the law to send forward his compilation and all the original papers he receives—he passes no judgment on them—to the re-turning-board of elections for the State of Louisiana; and the entire power and faculty all over the State of giving any declaration whatso-ever which should amount to *prima facie* evidence on which the governor could commission is solely and exclusively vested in this State board of returning-officers. All this appears from the very terms of the law itself, and if it were worth while I could read the decision of the supreme court of that State which sustains, as it could not help sustaining, the plain, emphatic, and undeniable words of the law.

Having constituted them judges, not of all State elections—that is not what they say, but they make them the final judges and only tribunal which has the right to give a *prima facie* certificate of elec-tion for all elections held in the State—the question gravely resolves itself back to this: whether the presidential election of 1876, in which certain persons were chosen as electors, was an election held within the State of Louisiana. If it was, these men had jurisdiction. I shall not have time to follow all the points that have been made. I shall leave that to be done far more ably and better by the counsel. Permit me, however, to follow this one.

There is another consideration. The point having been raised, as I understand, by the objectors on the other side, that as a matter of fact there exists no law to-day by which the right of appointing electors in Louisiana was delegated to the people, that is a question to be deter-mined on the inspection of the laws themselves, and I will simply read from the list of all the laws on this point, section 29 of the act of 1872, though I believe it has been read before:

Be it further enacted, That in every year in which an election shall be held for elect-ors of President and Vice-President of the United States, such election shall be held at the time fixed by act of Congress.

The presidential election—that is, the election of electors by the peo-ple—stands in Louisiana upon two statutes; not one, but two. There is one statute in the revised code—I do not know where it is printed in this compilation—which is on the question of elections; it makes the provision :

SEC. 1410. That in every year in which an election is to be held for electors of Presi-dent and Vice-President of the United States, such election shall be held on the Tuesday next after the first Monday in the month of November; and such election shall be held and conducted in the same manner and form provided by law for general and State elections.

That is the general-election law under the revised statutes.

Mr. Commissioner ABBOTT. Is that section put in in any of these compilations that we have?

Mr. Representative HURLBUT. I have not been able until a few minutes since to obtain a copy of the compilations, and cannot say.

Mr. Representative HOAR. It is on the ninety-fourth and ninety-fifth pages of the pamphlet with the paper cover.

Mr. Representative HURLBUT. Now there is another law that is in the revised statutes under the title of "Presidential electors" on page 551; it is section 2823. It is simply a repetition of section 1410; and section 2824 proceeds to direct the manner in which they shall vote, and sections 2826 and 2827 and others relate to a special mode of return pro-vided by that revision.

Mr. Commissioner BRADLEY. What is the date of that book on the title-page?

Mr. Representative HURLBUT. This volume is the Revised Statutes of Louisiana of 1870 that I am quoting from.

I apprehend that in considering the effect of statutes that are claimed to repeal the one or the other, the first question is what the probable intent and meaning of the legislature was. No man pretends that it was the probable intent and meaning of the legislature of Louisiana at any time, that it was their purpose, to repeal the right of the people to cast their votes for electors of President and Vice-President. Why? Be-cause it is inconsistent with the actual state of things that has prevailed since that time, for there has been a presidential election held since that, held in 1872, and held by this same process of voting by the people. There has been a presidential election held in 1876, and held in the same manner and by the same process of ascertaining the choice of the people in this matter of the appointment of electors. So the construc-tion to be derived by the usage of the Government itself is against the theory of repeal.

Besides, there comes in another great principle of interpretation, that subsequent laws repeal only so much of the preceding law as is incon-sistent with the one to be enacted; and hence it has been held in prac-tice in Louisiana, and undoubtedly is the clear law of the case, that the repealing act of 1872 creating this returning-board only interfered with the act in regard to presidential electors so far as to do away with the special tribunal provided under the former act, and to submit that elec-tion as all other elections held in the State to the arbitrament and deter-mination of this board of returning-officers.

Now, I may perhaps be pardoned in saying that whatever may be the amplitude of the power committed by these statutes under the will of the people of Louisiana to this board of returning-officers, whatever may be the peril (and I can see it) of giving so large a jurisdiction to any board, the thing which was behind it, the cause of the enactment, is infinitely worse and deserves the condemnation of every man who loves his country or believes in the right of the down-trodden and the oppres-sed ; for I say here from some knowledge of the fact and close investiga-tion, that the history of Louisiana since reconstruction has been nothing

more nor less than a series of deliberate attempts to overthrow existing
law by force. The old Anglo-Saxon method by which existing evils are
corrected in the form of law never seems to have entered into the imagination of that hot-headed, rash, and impetuous people. They have
adopted rather the Latin form that their neighborhood to Mexico brings
about, sending *pronunciamientos* of revolution followed up by confiscation and forced loans on the commerce and interests of the country to
support an illegal and irregular armed force in breaking down that
which the Constitution and the laws have given to the people of that
State; and therefore the board, with all its powers, came into existence.

The mode in which that board may have discharged its duties, the
detail, if you please, of the various steps which it took to acquaint
itself with the condition of the various parishes, all these things are
evidence *aliunde*, outside; and the simple and direct proposition is made
by the objectors upon the other side that this Commission shall resolve
itself into a tribunal to try the question who did vote and who did not
vote yonder at every poll in Louisiana. You cannot rest upon *ex parte*
testimony taken by a congressional commission; for although I have
the honor to be a member of one branch of Congress, my experience
is that, of all tribunals or pretended tribunals that ever were gotten up
by the ingenuity of man for the purpose of inquiring into political
questions, there is not any so likely to be unfair and to do injustice as
a congressional committee. It is necessarily so. Look at the time.
Does this Commission expect to read several thousand pages of the
results of the so-called investigation held by the committee of which I
had the honor to be a member, down in Louisiana? There are only
four thousand pages printed. The other three thousand will be printed
when your printer gets money enough. You cannot read intelligently
the mass that is there within the time that lies between now and the
4th of March. You cannot take the synopsis of any gentleman as the
existing fact in the case. You have no right to do so. If you undertake to try, you must try by law, and as the law prescribes. This tribunal, at all events, it is to be trusted and believed, will not suffer itself
to be the mere vehicle of wholesale and continuous slander against men,
and giving them no opportunity for rebuttal or explanation.

So much for the idea of opening up this entire matter, passing into
the reasons which guided the returning-board, passing behind their
judgment as given and recorded under the forms of law in pursuance
of the constitution of their State and the power granted to them by
this legislature. You are asked to pass behind all that and inquire.
Well, if you undertake to do that, you will do what the supreme court
of the State of Louisiana has declined to do; for the supreme court of
that State has decided—I read from the case of Collin *vs.* Knoblock, 25
Louisiana Annual Reports, page 265:

The returns made by a legal State board and officially promulgated—

Mr. Commissioner HOAR. When was that decision given?
Mr. Representative HURLBUT. In March, 1873.

To determine the validity of a commission, they cannot, under this act, go beyond
the returns and report of the legal returning-officers for all the elections of the State.
The returns made by a legal State board and officially promulgated by that board as
the general returning-officers for the State at large, constitute the basis upon which
the governor is authorized to issue commissions. These returns are, by the act of 16th
March, 1870, made "*prima facie* evidence in all courts of justice and before all civil
officers until set aside after a contest according to law of the right of any person
named therein to hold and exercise the office to which he shall by such return be declared elected."

Mr. Commissioner EDMUNDS. What was the nature of that action?

Mr. Representative HURLBUT. An action under their statute for intrusion into office.

Mr. Commissioner ABBOTT. Was it not, therefore, in the nature of a *quo warranto?*

Mr. Representative HURLBUT. It is a modified form of *quo warranto.*

Mr. Commissioner ABBOTT. Who gave the opinion there?

Mr. Representative HURLBUT. The opinion was given by Judge Taliaferro. The same opinion is repeated in other cases which I do not desire now to take up the time of the Commission in quoting, as a reference to them will be printed.

Mr. Commissioner STRONG. Has that case reference to an election conducted under the act of 1870 or under the act of 1872?

Mr. Representative HURLBUT. This is a case in which they decide, as of course they had to do, that the election of November, 1872, was governed by the law of 1870, a proposition which seems so self-evident that I hardly thought it would require the decision of a court, inasmuch as an act approved fourteen days after an election takes place could not, I think, anywhere outside of Louisiana, be claimed to have anything to do with the election that took place fourteen days before.

Thus the supreme court of the State itself, as regards its own local elections, has decided that the returns made by this board and required by the law to be filed with the secretary of state, and also required to be promulgated by publication in the newspapers, are the evidence on which the governor gives commissions to all officers of the State, and that those returns and declarations are *prima facie* evidence which can only be gone behind in a judicial trial touching the right to hold and enjoy office. I apprehend that the case here is somewhat analogous to that. I apprehend that this Commission is not sitting, nor can it sit, as a judicial tribunal, to try which of the two gentlemen named for President has actually been elected, which is entitled to hold and enjoy the office. You are not sitting as a judicial tribunal for that; you are sitting to determine what, on the regular mode of authorization established by each State according to its own act and pleasure under a delegated right in the Constitution, appears. Is there any end to the inquiry if the other view be taken? Is there any possibility of ever deciding this question of the presidential election that occurred last fall? Is it not manifestly not only contrary to law, but impossible in fact, that this immense mass of allegations *pro* and *con* can be gone into? Where are you to stop?

My friend, Mr. Jenks, I recollect, was very pointed in his remarks about an innocent person of the name of Clover, who acted as supervisor of the parish of East Baton Rouge; and, in order to show that Mr. Tilden got the votes of Louisiana, he proposed to this Commission, as a matter of proof, that this man once kept a snake-show, or was a roper-in for a snake-show, as he called him. Will the Commission inform me whether that is a traversable fact that we can take issue with? If so, every other allegation connected with this matter, all these points that are made, some under the law, some under a misconception of the law, require evidence; they are to be sustained by testimony *pro* and *con*, and I confess that on deliberate study of the law which organized this Commission I do not know any means that this Commission has of testimony on these questions, or to compel its production, or to judge of its validity.

Now, all this is simply a repetition—and I am glad of it—on a modified and far more respectable scale before this tribunal, of the utterances with which we have been favored for the last four weeks in direct prejudgment of the whole question that is submitted to this tribunal; and I deeply regret that the echo of those utterances, bad enough and ill enough even in the license of debate in deliberative bodies, should come within this hall whose memories are all sanctified by adherence to great principles of justice, and most of all I regret that the speech of my distinguished friend from Pennsylvania [Mr. Jenks] should have closed with a style of warning to this Commission that amounted to an implied menace. That sort of thing may do yonder in Louisiana, where the physical force and organized deviltry of a whole race are on the one side, and God and the law and a clear majority of humble American citizens are on the other; but it is infinitely bad taste that here, catching his inspiration from his clients, he should venture to attempt to bulldoze this Commission. I pray you, gentlemen, to do simply what I know you will do, and what you need no prayers from me to do, pass upon this question, not in obedience to any popular clamor got up by self-interest and repeated time after time by a ribald press, but determine this question on your oaths according to the tenor of the Constitution and the law, and the event will justify the confidence that all sound and well-judging men repose in the integrity and the stern purpose of duty of the Commission itself.

Mr. Senator HOWE. Mr. President and gentlemen of the Commission: I am somewhat mortified, I confess, coming to the discharge of the duty which has been assigned me, of saying something in support of objection No. 4, to find how very small a thing it is in comparison with this volume of objections which has been urged on the other side. It is a very small piece of paper to put in here. I feel bound to say of it as, I believe, Mercutio said of his sword-cut, that it really is not as capacious as a well, but I am inclined to think "'twill serve." We respectfully object that you shall not count the votes for President and Vice-President of the United States tendered here by John McEnery and Robert C. Wickliffe and by their associates, any of them, for this reason, to begin with : You have no evidence before you, none whatever, that either of those was ever appointed as directed by the legislature of Louisiana to vote for President and Vice-President of the United States. You ought to have some evidence before you receive those votes, ought you not? The statute—not of Louisiana, but the statute of the United States—commands that you should seek for and should find their authority so to vote, certified to you by the governor of that State. Can you dispense with that evidence, substitute anything else for it? It is conceded all about me on all these papers that no man can have his vote counted for President and Vice-President of the United States unless his right so to vote is certified by the governor of the State. Those gentlemen who urge you to accept the votes tendered here by McEnery and Wickliffe do not seek to derogate from the authority of the statute of the United States nor to dodge it at all; their effort is, you find, to elevate John McEnery himself to the dignity of governor of Louisiana ; and so you find him certifying, as governor of that State, to the authority of that board of electors at the head of which you find his own name. There is a practical difficulty which imperils the success of that effort, and it is this : John McEnery was not in November last, he never was, governor of Louisiana. How do we know that? Simply because we are rational beings, and, as such, we are bound to know it. We may be ignorant of a great many things in this world, and we are, God knows; but there is one thing of which we are not permitted to be ignorant. We are bound to know who is the governor of a State in this Union; and being bound to know that no State can have more than one governor, when we come to know who that man is, then we know that all the rest of God's beings are not.

But I do not content myself merely with the proposition that we are bound to take, as I believe the lawyers say, judicial notice of who is the governor of a State; a sort of notice that every man must take, no matter whether he be judge, or statesman, or citizen, a lighterman on the Atlantic coast or a lumberman in the forests of Michigan. I say we are not only bound to take this sort of notice, but every one of you sitting there has helped to give notice, has served notice on the world that John McEnery was not governor of Louisiana and that William Pitt Kellogg was. So many of you as occupy seats there and who belong to the Senate of the United States have often seen this signature of John McEnery attached to the credentials of some aspiring citizen of that State knocking for admission to the Senate; but you never have opened your doors to any such demand. So many of you as belong to the other House of this National Legislature have seen that same name appended to the credentials of those who asked to be admitted to the deliberations of that body, and you have uniformly turned them away and said, "We do not know you, John McEnery." I do not know that in the character of governor he has ever appeared before the Supreme Court of the United States; but another man has appeared before that court, has been impleaded before it as the governor of Louisiana, and judgment has been given in that court upon the issue there formed. The justices of that court will remember the case to which I refer. I think it is the Board of Liquidation vs. McComb. So that you have all in your several capacities been called upon directly to pass judgment upon this pretended governor and have all given judgment against him. When a committee of one House of Congress went to Louisiana a few years ago and undertook to compose that State by compiling a government for it, no such calico as John McEnery got into that patch-work; another man was recognized as the governor then and there.

And yet that man comes here again, now in these last days, and undertakes to certify to the right of men to vote for President and Vice-President of the United States in the name of Louisiana. I have heard something said here in this presence this morning about fraud and corruption. Do you know, have you heard, of any indication of fraud anywhere or in anybody so bald and palpable as this of John McEnery's attempting to pass himself off, not only upon this high Commission, but upon the nation itself, as governor of Louisiana? Very cunning men, I know, sometimes attempt to pass and do pass upon business men spurious notes as genuine, and you take it as the trick of a knave, to be sure, but of a smart knave. What would you say of a man who should bring to a bank of issue a note pretending that it was manufactured on its own plates, but which had actually been stamped "counterfeit" by half the receiving tellers in the United States, and offer that as genuine to the bank from which it purported to be issued? You would not say that was the effort of a smart knave, would you? But here this man comes again, this man whose pretentions, as I say, have been repudiated just as often as they have been thrust forward; he comes in here once more, once again, with all the sprightliness and vivacity with which a half eagle is thrown out that has just come from the mint. "Here we come again, sirs," he says, " Governor John Mc-

Enery, of Louisiana." No, Mr. President, no; I think I will not spend more time on Mr. John McEnery.

I said you have determined that another man was governor of L uis-iana, William Pitt Kellogg. For good or for ill, for four years past, William Pitt Kellogg has presided over that State as its governor, recognized as such both by the legislative and judicial departments of that State, recognized expressly as such by the Senate of the United States, more than once by the Senate, recognized expressly as such by the House of Representatives when the pretensions of both men, Kellogg and McEnery, were before the House, one certifying that Spencer was entitled to a seat, and another certifying that Morey was entitled to a seat. This House of Representatives said: "We know Kellogg; we do not know McEnery; therefore Morey shall take his seat in the House and Spencer must stand back." The. President more than once has recognized him. He is the man who has signed the enactments of the legislature of Louisiana, or he has refused to sign them. If he has approved them, they became laws; if he has vetoed them, they did not become laws unless passed in spite of his veto. He has granted pardons or he has refused to grant pardons; and almost ten millions of the bonds of Louisiana bearing his signature are afloat to-day in the money-markets of the world. Kellogg, I think, will pass here, as elsewhere through creation, as the governor of Louisiana in November last; and he tells you who were the constituted electors of that State, appointed in accordance with the directions of the legislature, to vote for that State in the choice of a President and Vice-President. Do you want more evidence? Can you contradict that? That is the very evidence which our statute tells you to look for, and all it tells you to look for.

I know the Constitution says that each State shall appoint a pre-scribed number of electors in any such way as the legislature of the State shall direct, and perhaps you may feel authorized to go a little back of this certificate of the governor of a State in order to see whether he has acted in accord with the direction of the legislature or has not. In other words, even if the statute of the United States does not have respect to the authority of the legislature as clearly as it ought, you are bound to keep your eyes upon the legislature of the State and see what it has done, see if it has told the governor he may say what he has said or if he has said something which the legislature did not permit him to say. If you feel called upon to make that inquiry, just one step behind the certificate of the governor you will find that certain officers created by the laws of Louisiana for canvassing the vote given by the people of that State at the election in November last, declared that those people voted, a majority of them, for the electoral ticket headed by Kellogg and Burch, and a minority of them, alone, voted for the ticket headed by McEnery and Wickliffe. You find that board by the law of that State directly instructed to canvass the votes given at all elections and to declare the result of them. "The returning-officers of the State," they are called, and the statute of the State tells you in the most unqualified terms that their determination, when made and promulgated, is *prima facie* evidence of the right of every man to hold office whose right is so determined by their certificate; and if the statute had not said so, you know such would have been the effect of their certificate and is in law the effect of every such certificate given by every similar board in every State we have in the Union.

Will you then go further than this in that direction? The governor of the State has told you who were the electors of the State, and going back you find he has spoken upon the authority of the returning-officers of that State, the only tribunal known to its laws which can inform the executive by authority what has been the result of an election. Will you go further back? I heard you just now rather affectionately invited to go back further still. I think it was intimated that if you would go still further back, behind the certificate of the governor, and behind the certificate of the returning-officers, some impressive testimony would be laid before you. I am aware, and I ought to say in passing, out of respect to those who have urged that view, that objections are taken to the legal character of this board as it was constituted in November. I thought to spend some time on those objections. I had really taken the trouble to look into some law-books and read some adjudications, and thought I would offer to this Commission some authorities on the subject; but I shall spare myself any such labor and you any such infliction. I see those who are to follow me and I know they will suffer no jot, no tittle of the law to fail. If they do, it is because they have lost their grip, for they have been masters of the law for many years. I think I may be saved some trouble by letting the counsel in this case do the very easy thing, as I think it is, of giving you the constitutional view of that returning-board.

I said that I had heard you rather earnestly entreated to open these seals which are claimed to close in the certificate of the returning-officers and the certificate of the governor of the State, to break those seals, and to go back and listen to what can be proved to you if you will be good enough to listen not only to what all the lawyers in the United States may urge, but to what all the citizens of Louisiana may see fit to swear. I do not undertake to tell you by authority precisely what you would find if you were to throw those doors wide open. I think I can give you a lively hint of what you will find. I have myself been making, under the instructions of the Senate of the United States, some inquiries in that direction.

The gentleman from Illinois [Mr. Hurlbut] who just addressed you was pleased to say that, judging from his experience, a legislative investigation was the poorest instrumentality he knew of for arriving at the truth. If I might be allowed to refer to my own very limited experience, it would not corroborate that of the gentleman to whom I have just referred. A committee of the Senate went to Louisiana. It represented both political opinions which are found in that body, and they went there instructed to ascertain, if they could, whether the right of suffrage in that State had been abridged in any way either by fraud or by force, either by excluding votes from the ballot-box or by refusing to count the votes illegally after they had been deposited in the ballot-box. We did investigate these questions so far as a portion of the State was concerned; we spent all the time we had and all the money the two Houses would furnish us, not by way of an *ex parte* inquiry, by any manner of means. We took up parish after parish; and when we had entered upon the examination of one parish we did not quit that until we supposed we had every fact concerning it which witnesses could establish before us, not witnesses called on one side, but called on both sides. I know that one political opinion was represented by the larger number of members on that committee; but I believe that when that committee closed its labors a majority of the witnesses who had been sworn in that whole examination—I do not assert this as a fact, but I believe that a majority of those who had been sworn had been called by the minority of that committee.

The first parish of which we made inquiry happened to be the parish of Ouachita, which is on the river of that name almost classic in our history. It was upon that river, I believe, that Blennerhassett and Burr made their purchase of the Baron de Bastrop, whose appellation gives name to the shire town of the adjoining parish; and I think I shall venture to tell the Commission something of what we discovered touching the election in Ouachita Parish.

You have heard it said here, that those returning-officers did not count the votes which were actually cast by the voters of Louisiana at the last election, did not canvass them at all, rejected some from their count. How do you know that? Louisiana has not told you that. They say they will prove it to you if you will be good enough to step behind both the certificate of the governor and the certificate of the returning-officers. Possibly; but as yet you do not know that. Counsel say it is so. I agree with them, it is so; but then it is not Louisiana tells you; it is only what we tell you. You are good enough to hear us argue; I trust you will be altogether too good to hear us testify. Perhaps we are entitled to some consideration while we are merely reasoning; when we come to state facts, to very little. But while you are told that these returning-officers rejected votes that were cast, you may have been told, you can be if you open the statutes of that State, that that board was not only authorized to reject such votes upon certain conditions, but that the statute expressly commanded it. It is said here that certain steps must be taken by the commissioners of election or by the parish supervisors in order to give to that tribunal jurisdiction to reject votes. I wanted to speak upon that, but I leave that to those who shall come after me.

They did reject certain votes. I concede it. The statute told them in express terms that if they were convinced there was not in a given parish or in a given precinct within a parish a fair election, that either fraud or force was employed so as materially to change the result of the election, they should exclude from count the vote of that precinct or of that parish. They did reject portions or the whole of twenty-two parishes. Portions or the whole of seventeen parishes were rejected upon the ground of intimidation, which these returning-officers said they found satisfactorily proved to them.

I have noticed in certain quarters a disposition to ridicule this idea that voters can be induced by intimidation and fear to withhold the vote they want to give, much less made to give the vote they do not want to give; and it does seem a little incredible to a free citizen of the United States in the habit of opening his mouth and lifting his hand on all occasions freely, to believe that such results can be wrought by intimidation. After all, in the light of history, no such incredulity becomes us. We know that Henry of Navarre and his cousin the Prince of Condé were, through intimidation, induced to abjure the Protestant faith. We know that Galileo on his knees promised, under the influence of fear, that he never again would teach the doctrine of the earth's motion. And we know that one of the chiefest of the apostles, moved by fear, swore that he never knew his own Master, that Saviour whom we all make believe now to adore. If great soldiers and great scientists and great apostles can be forced by fear to abjure cherished convictions, are we permitted to doubt that the poor and ignorant freedman of Louisiana may be compelled by fear, either to withhold his vote from the ballot-box or to put a vote therein which he does not choose to put in?

Then again, this theory is assailed by those who speak on behalf of Louisiana and say that Louisiana is occupied by respectable men, by Christian men, men who pray and who hear prayer, men who acknowledge their relations to other men and who acknowledge their obligations not only to this world but their relations to that world which is to come. They say it is a foul libel on the fair name of Louisiana to say any such thing; that Louisiana would not permit force or intimidation to be employed. Would she not? Are we sure of that? Was not force, was not fraud ever employed in the history of the world by men as white, by men as chivalrous, by men as decent, by men as Christian as any who occupy Louisiana to-day?

It is not two hundred years since Louis XIV was induced to revoke that edict, the Edict of Nantes, which for something like a hundred years had performed the part in the constitution of the French Empire which we humbly hope the fourteenth amendment will perform yet for the people of the United States, even the blacks of the United States. I say he revoked that edict, and by that revocation he let loose the iron hand of persecution, not on black men, but white men and white women; that iron hand which drove out of France or slaughtered in France more than half a million of Huguenots. Do you think they were monsters who came to that act? The charming Madame de Sévigné clapped her hands in approval of that act of revocation. Bossuet, the most eloquent preacher of his time I suppose, applauded it, and churches stooped to render thanks to the mistress of the king, through whose influence it was believed that revocation was obtained. Has humanity changed so radically and utterly since then?

I need not go outside of Louisiana for an illustration; the known history of Louisiana. All remember the 14th of September, 1874. Louisiana then had a government as regular, as well recognized, as well known to all the people of the United States as New York has to-day, and as respectably filled, I may say, in all its departments. An armed band of men took possession of the streets of New Orleans, the capital of the State; in a moment, almost in the twinkling of an eye, suddenly drove the constituted governor of the State from his seat, and would have driven him out of existence had he not found protection. I know they say that Kellogg was only a make-believe governor. Who says that? Whoever says it in Louisiana or outside of Louisiana is disloyal to the law of Louisiana. All the authority there was in Louisiana said that Kellogg was governor. If he was not the lawful as well as the *de facto* governor of Louisiana, there was some tribunal in the land which could declare by authority who was. That tribunal was not the White League with arms in their hands to drive him from his office; there should have been an inquisition found of some kind, I think, before the white-leaguers of New Orleans went for him.

I was about to call attention to what took place in January last. It was only a repetition of the same thing. I must pass over it. I wanted to say something to you about what took place in the single parish of Ouachita at the last election, and I must be very brief. Let me introduce Ouachita Parish to you. In 1868 that parish gave for the republican candidate for governor 1,418 votes, and for the democratic candidate but 347. There was a republican majority of 1,071. In 1870 there was a republican majority of 798. In 1872 there was a republican majority of 798, precisely the same figures as two years before. In 1874, but two years ago, there was a republican majority in the parish of 927. In 1876 there were 2,392 colored voters registered, and there were 992 white voters registered; and in November last that parish returned to its supervisor 1,865 democratic votes to 793 republican votes, giving a democratic majority of 1,072, where two years ago there was a republican majority of 927. There are men uncharitable enough in the world to believe that intimidation was employed to produce that result. There are men, on the contrary, who say that intimidation was not employed at all; it was mere solicitation, it was artifice, persuasion, bargaining, and the like. But the campaign in Louisiana started out early in June, started out with a circular issued by Mr. Patton, chairman of the democratic State committee, in which he said—a confidential circular, it is said, and it was so marked; it is denied that it was intended to be confidential; the fact is it did not get to the public until some time in August, through the columns of a republican newspaper—in that circular Mr. Patton informed his friends of various things, and this among others, that the negro could not be reasoned with, but he could be impressed. I do not use his language; it has been often quoted; but one of the methods he recommended for impressing the negro was that they should not only organize themselves into clubs, but that they should mount their clubs, and as frequently as possible they should make processions mounted in order to make a demonstration of their strength.

During the months of July and August, the evidence shows that the white people of Ouachita Parish were organized into clubs, mounted clubs, and they did better than the instructions of the chairman of the democratic central committee. They not only mounted the clubs, but they armed them. The republican party was also organized into clubs, not mounted and not armed; into such political clubs as are organized all over the country. So in that way, during the month of August, the organization of both parties was completed. On the 30th of August, an event took place in that parish which gave a material coloring to the election in that parish. On the 30th of August, Bernard H. Dinkgrave, a white man, a cultivated man, a native Louisianian, a man against whose character no one has breathed a word except that the chairman of the democratic committee for Ouachita Parish said that he was a violent partisan—Bernard H. Dinkgrave was shot down, about four o'clock in the afternoon, going from his office in Monroe to his house just outside of the town. It is said that that was not done for political effect. It has been suggested that the death grew out of a difficulty he had in 1870 with a man by the name of Wemberly, or it grew out of an arrest that he made two years before, when he was sheriff of Ouachita Parish, of a man by the name of Allen.

Upon that single point a great deal of evidence was taken. I must content myself with saying that, weighing the evidence as carefully as I could, I have no more doubt that Bernard H. Dinkgrave was killed for political effect than I have that he was killed at all. But no matter whether he was killed for political effect or not, his death had a political effect. The people of Ouachita Parish, the colored people at all events, believed that he was killed for political effect. Republican effort was paralyzed at once. Another republican meeting was not held in the parish until some time in October, and after troops had been stationed at Monroe; and no meeting I think was held by the republican party afterward, unless troops of the United States were near the place of meeting.

I ought to have preceded this allusion to the death of Dinkgrave by giving an idea of the state of the canvass on the 19th of August. I read from the Vienna Sentinel a letter directed to that newspaper by the editor, written from Monroe, in this parish of Ouachita:

Politics in Ouachita are gaining more attention than at any previous election since 1860. In fact every man, woman, and child seems to have his or her whole soul in the contest. This is encouraging, and a good sign of state of hope in the democratic mind is that there are, or rather were, numerous candidates for parish offices. I say were, because they are now reduced to one candidate for each office, the democrats having held their parish nominating convention on Saturday last. If the democrats are hopeful in this parish, they have good cause to be so. While they present an unbroken front and an admirable organization, the radicals are wavering, disheartened, and *scared*. There are a few bold, empty-headed orators among the latter who either have not sense enough to appreciate the situation or are willing to draw us on to any extremes in order that their elevation may be secured. It is human nature to admire boldness, but when boldness is united to rascality it is Louisiana's nature to deal summarily with it. These inflammatory spouters, demagogues in the truest sense of the word, are using their best efforts to instill bad principles into the minds of the colored people, and seem to be anxious to precipitate a violent conflict between the two races. Nothing could be further removed from the wishes of the whites of this community; but if anything of the kind should come about, there is a stern resolve that the foolish cat's-paw, the negro, shall not be the only sufferer. The promoters of these murderous principles are well known and well watched, and the halter for their necks is already greased.

That was written on the 8th of August, and it appeared in the Sentinel on the 19th. It appeared in Monroe on the 21st. A witness swore that up to this time only three republicans had taken part in the canvass in that parish. One was this Bernard H. Dinkgrave; one was his nephew, John H. Dinkgrave; one was George B. Hamlet, a colored man and sheriff of the parish. On the 30th of August following this publication in this newspaper, Dinkgrave, one of the three, was assassinated; Hamlet fled to New Orleans; and no further attempts were made to organize or to rally the republican party in that parish until in October following. On the 10th of October another tragic event occurred. I have got to pass over a multitude. I have here among my papers a schedule of eighty-odd different outrages committed upon persons or property, including, I think, five murders; I do not know the number of whippings; I do not know the number of robbings; I must pass over all these; but on the 10th of October another event occurred.

Eaton Logwood, in the broad daylight, was visited by a party of mounted men, was shot, severely wounded. His brother-in law at the same place and at the same time was shot dead. Either from the influence of these visitations, where red-handed murder traveled at noonday, or under the influence of the barbecues and the speeches to which we are referred on the other side, there was a very marked effect produced upon the colored population of Ouachita Parish. A great number of them had been induced up to that time to join democratic clubs. Great numbers of them had not been induced to join democratic clubs even up to that time; but a letter I wanted to refer to, but must pass by, written to one of the organs of the party in New Orleans, and written from Monroe later in October, spoke quite hopefully of the result; said they could not calculate it accurately; it was liable to a great many contingencies and accidents; but that already a great many colored men had joined their clubs and they were inclined to think would stick. But two difficulties were still in the way. There were still a great many colored men who had not joined their clubs, and there was not absolute certainty that those who had joined would stick. For these or other reasons a demonstration seemed to be thought necessary, and that demonstration was made on the Saturday night before the election, which took place on Tuesday.

On that night the house of one Abraham Williams was visited by a party of mounted disguised men, and he was taken from his bed and his house, and he was stripped, and he was whipped brutally. He was a man sixty years old. The house of his son was visited the same night and unquestionably by the same party. He was sleeping in a cotton-field, not daring to sleep under his own roof, and not finding him his wife was taken out of the house and she was whipped. The house of Willis Frazier was visited on the same night and undoubtedly by the same party of men, mounted men, disguised men, and he was taken out from his house and he was whipped brutally. The house of Randall Driver was visited, and he had been admonished over and over again by democrats that he was exposing himself to peril. On this night his house was visited and he was taken out and whipped. The house of Henry Pinkston was visited and he was killed, and his child was killed, and his wife was nearly killed.

I see that I cannot stop to dwell upon any one of these cases. I can speak of the effects produced in a moment. While speeches and barbecues were the order of the day, Willis Frazier, Alexander Williams, Abraham Williams, Henry Pinkston, and Randall Driver had not joined democratic clubs. The Tuesday after they were whipped three of these men went submissively to the polls and voted the democratic ticket. Henry Pinkston did not go to the polls on that day; he had settled his accounts with the world. Randall Driver did go to the polls. Whipped till he could not stand, he had his wife anoint his body, his sores, with kerosene oil and lay him out before the fire on a cot, and there he lay till morning, and then he told his wife to help him on to a chair; he told his wife to help him on with his clothes; he told his wife to help him to his stick; and when she asked him where he was going he said he was going to Monroe to vote " dat " ticket if it took him three days to get there, and he started, and he did get to Monroe. He reached it in the afternoon of Tuesday, and he did vote the republican ticket, and he was the only man visited that night who did. Knowing that they could not vote at any other polls than those in Monroe, the negroes, so many of them as had not been forced into democratic clubs, made up their minds to make their way to Monroe, and to vote there; and against that poor privilege there was an organized effort made. The mayor of the town issued a proclamation to those who had come in to leave, and rifle-clubs picketed the highways leading into the city of Monroe to keep men who had not come in from coming in.

The election was held, and the next step was to get affidavits that the election had been fair.

Mr. Commissioner PAYNE. Mr. Howe, before you pass to that point, will you be good enough to say whether the facts you have narrated were found to be such by the united report of the committee, or was there a difference of opinion?

Mr. Senator HOWE. There has been no report of the committee. I am stating the impressions the evidence made on my mind—evidence not introduced by one party only. In this very parish of Ouachita, I think forty-eight witnesses were sworn on the part of the republicans and forty-nine witnesses were sworn on the part of the democrats.

But these are my views of the testimony, that I am giving you, and nobody else's. I have only spoken, and briefly spoken, of some very few of the incidents which transpired in a single parish. I shall not allude to any other parish; but I want to submit to the Commission one table which I think is quite suggestive of what would be ascertained if there was a careful examination made of every parish, as was made of this one and of several other parishes.

There are seventeen parishes, as I remarked to the Commission, from which votes were excluded upon the ground of intimidation. In those seventeen parishes there was a white vote registered of 20,320; there was a colored vote registered of 27,269. The colored registration was in a majority in those seventeen parishes, in which the returning-officers said intimidation was employed, of 6,949. In the other forty parishes of the State there was a colored registration of 87,899 and a white registration of 72,034, leaving a colored majority of 15.965. In those forty parishes where no intimidation is alleged the result of the vote I give you. Kellogg's vote in those forty parishes was 65,747 and McEnery's vote was 59,392. Where intimidation is not alleged, in forty parishes, a colored registration of 15,965 majority yields a republican majority on the vote of over 6,000; but in the seventeen parishes where intimidation is alleged the result is very different. One would suppose that, if a colored registered majority of 15,000, where the election is fair, yields a republican majority of nearly 7,000, a colored registered majority of 6,949 would yield some republican majority. On the contrary, in those seventeen parishes 21,123 votes were returned for the democratic ticket and but 10,970 for the republican ticket, making a democratic majority of 10,153 in the seventeen parishes.

I see that I have exceeded my time.

The PRESIDENT. There were seven minutes extended to Mr. Jenks and I proposed to extend the same to you, so that you have a minute or two more. When the time is extended to one side, I always extend it to the other.

Mr. Senator HOWE. I will occupy that minute in stating that I am clear upon the point that in those parishes where you hear so much complaint that votes were rejected from the count, notwithstanding the rejection the democratic ticket has a larger comparative vote in those parishes than it had in the same parishes two years ago.

I close with one other reflection. I remember, and you have not forgotten, how you were invoked just now to exert all the authority you have or could find to save the nation from drinking waters from these filthy pools which it is said are concocted there by the political tricksters who manage politics in Louisiana. I make no such appeal to this Commission. I ask this Commission to listen to the lawful voice of Louisiana as it would listen to the lawful voice of any other State. Give weight to it. Hear it. There is more than one foul stream to be found in the State of Louisiana. That to which you have been pointed may be dirty. Coming right from that State, I know of other and larger streams which are not merely dirty, but are very bloody. I would be glad if in this tribunal or in any there was power to say that only pure water should run anywhere; but the power does not reside in any human tribunal. I want your streams all purified as soon as it can be done. If you can aid in that direction, cleanse the bloody before you attempt the muddy streams.

The PRESIDENT. Who are the counsel in support of the objection to certificates Nos. 1 and 3?

Mr. CAMPBELL. Mr. Carpenter, Mr. Trumbull, and myself.

The PRESIDENT. Who are the counsel in support of the objection to certificate No. 2?

Mr. EVARTS. Mr. Stoughton, Mr. Shellabarger, and myself.

The PRESIDENT. Three on each side.

Mr. CAMPBELL. I would ask, may the Commission please, that the time be extended. I understand that there is an allowance of three hours. I would ask permission that the time be extended to six hours for either side, and I would state the reason——

Mr. PRESIDENT. Excuse me a moment. By the rule the allowance is two hours on each side.

Mr. CAMPBELL. We ask for six hours on a side, twelve hours in all. The Commission must perceive that on the objections which have been presented, probably every question that can ever arise under the existing laws of the United States and its present Constitution will come up for the examination of this Commission. It comprehends nearly everything that can probably take place in a presidential election and be the cause of any question. Under such circumstances it seems to me that a full and frank discussion ought to be permitted and a sufficient time allowed in order that that discussion may be made.

The PRESIDENT. Would not four hours on a side possibly answer your purpose?

Mr. CAMPBELL. My friends think not.

Mr. EVARTS. On our part, Mr. President, we had supposed that the instruction given to counsel already by the determination of the Commission as announced upon the discussions heretofore had in the Florida case had greatly reduced the possible area of discussion; that the principal and preliminary considerations common to all the cases in the nature of the reach and effect of evidence had already been passed upon; and that we certainly should have no occasion to ask more than the time of an hour for each counsel. We shall submit to your honors' direction in that regard.

Mr. CARPENTER. The court will pardon a suggestion. The great difficulty in arguing this case is to determine in the first place what statute law was in force when the election was held in Louisiana. That requires an examination of a great many statutes and is a question of great intricacy. Then the other questions arising in the case are, as we understand them, totally different from the questions arising in the Florida case. Of course the learned counsel on the other side will not be compelled to speak six hours; it is only permission, not compulsion; and if they do not think it necessary, of course they will not avail themselves of the privilege. But regarding this as the most important case ever heard in this country, regarding it as a case in which the attempt is made to disfranchise 10,000 legal voters of a State, we submit that to ask twelve hours' hearing on 10,000 disfranchisements is not an unreasonable request.

Mr. Commissioner ABBOTT. Mr. President, I move you that the time be extended to six hours on each side, as desired. I think it is very much more important that we should have all these questions, which are so numerous and so very important, discussed fully than to shorten the time and not have all the light there is on them that can possibly be given.

The PRESIDENT. The motion submitted by Judge Abbott is that the time for discussion be extended to six hours on a side.

Mr. Commissioner GARFIELD. I move to amend by making it four hours on each side.

The PRESIDENT. Do you move to strike out "six" and insert "four?"

Mr. Commissioner GARFIELD. Yes, sir.

Mr. Commissioner HOAR. Mr. President, the questions of the character to which Mr. Carpenter alluded, of the existing laws of the State of Louisiana, can certainly be discussed with great convenience upon printed briefs. Counsel have the fullest opportunity to submit printed briefs in addition to their oral arguments. It does not seem to me that there is any case made for any extension whatever.

Mr. CARPENTER. Pardon me a suggestion. If this court could hear on printed briefs and settle that question so that we should know——

Mr. Commissioner HOAR. I do not think counsel should take part in the discussions of the tribunal after they have been heard.

The PRESIDENT. I presume not. The matter is now between members of the tribunal.

Mr. Commissioner EDMUNDS. I move that this Commission take a recess for thirty minutes,

Mr. Commissioner ABBOTT. I think we can afford to sit here later at night for the purpose of having this matter fairly and fully discussed.

The PRESIDENT. Mr. Edmunds moves that the Commission take a recess for thirty minutes. I must regard that as preceding the other question, as it may be for the purpose of consultation. The question is on the motion that there be a recess for thirty minutes.

Mr. Commissioner EDMUNDS. I will say until half past four; that will be three-quarters of an hour.

Mr. Commissioner FIELD. I ask for the yeas and nays.

The yeas and nays were ordered; and being taken, resulted—yeas 11, nays 4; as follows:

Those who voted in the affirmative were: Messrs. Bayard, Bradley, Clifford, Edmunds, Frelinghuysen, Garfield, Hoar, Miller, Morton, Strong, and Thurman—11.

Those who voted in the negative were: Messrs. Abbott, Field, Hunton, and Payne—4.

So the motion was agreed to; and the Commission (at three o'clock and forty-seven minutes p. m.) took a recess until four o'clock and thirty minutes p. m.

The Commission re-assembled at four o'clock and thirty minutes p. m.

The PRESIDENT. The Commission has decided to allow four and a half hours for argument on each side. The Commission has also voted to continue the session to-night until nine o'clock.

Mr. Commissioner STRONG. I move that the recess be continued half an hour longer.

The motion was agreed to; and (at four o'clock and thirty-five minutes) the Commission took a recess until five o'clock and five minutes p. m.

The Commission re-assembled at five o'clock and five minutes p. m.

Mr. CARPENTER. If the court please, of the four and a half hours' time assigned to each side, if the court will permit it, we ask indulgence to be allowed to make an argument for an hour or so upon these laws and upon the general question which the case involves before offering our evidence; of course with the distinct understanding that we are not closing the case, but that we are opening preparatory to offering our proof.

The PRESIDENT. Occupying a portion of the four hours and a half?

Mr. CARPENTER. Whatever time we take of course to come out of our four hours and a half.

The PRESIDENT. I see no objection to that. If no objection be made, that may be understood.

Mr. CARPENTER. Mr. President, and gentlemen of the Electoral Commission: Permit me to state in the outset why I appear here. It is not because Mr. Tilden was my choice for President; nor is my judgment in this case at all affected by friendship for him as a man, for I have not the honor of a personal acquaintance with him. I voted against him on the 7th of November last, and if this tribunal could order a new election I should vote against him again; believing as I do that the accession of the democratic party to power at this time would be the greatest calamity that could befall our country, except one, and that one greater calamity would be to keep them out by falsehood and fraud. I appear here professionally, to assert, and if possible, establish the rights of ten thousand legal voters of Louisiana, who, without accusation or proof, indictment or trial, notice or hearing, have been disfranchised by four persons incorporated with perpetual succession, under the name and style of "The returning-board of Louisiana." I appear, also, in the interest of the next republican candidate for President, whoever he may be, to insist that this tribunal shall settle principles by which, if we carry Wisconsin for him by 10,000 majority, as I hope we may, no canvassing-board, by fraud, or induced by bribery, shall be able to throw the vote of that State against him and against the voice and will of our people.

I beg your honors to pause a moment and consider the lesson to be taught to the politicians of this country by this day's work. This is no ordinary occasion, no ordinary tribunal, no ordinary cause. An emergency has arisen which has induced Congress to create a tribunal never before known in this country; a tribunal composed of whatever is most distinguished for integrity, for learning, for judicial and legislative experience, to conduct the nation through a great crisis. Your decision will stand as a landmark in the history of this country. Prior to the election in November last the question was, who ought to be elected. That was purely a political question, and every voter was bound to support the candidate whose election would, in his judgment, best promote the public good. Since the election the question has been, not who ought to be elected, but who in fact was elected; and that is the question the determination of which you are to aid. Before that election no honest man could have supported the candidate he thought ought not to be elected. Since that election no honest man can refuse his support to the one he believes to have been elected. And you have all taken an oath to decide the matters submitted to you—not according to your political preferences, nor in the interest of any political party— but impartially and according to the Constitution and laws.

The case, as we offer to establish it, by evidence entirely satisfactory in the popular sense and conlusive in the legal sense, is this: At the general election in the State of Louisiana on the 7th day of November last, the Tilden electors received of the votes cast for electors about 8,000 majority. This is conceded. The questions upon which the case must turn arise out of proceedings subsequent to the election. By the general election law of that State, (clearly unconstitutional, but at present concede its validity—not applicable to this election, as we shall contend hereafter, but at present concede its applicability, so as to state the case most strongly against ourselves,) it is provided that whenever the return from any poll or voting-place shall be accompanied by a certain statement, in the form provided by the act, supported by the oaths of three citizens, that riot, violence, intimidation, bribery, &c., materially affected the result at such poll or voting-place, the returning-board may inquire into the facts, and if they find it so, they may exclude all the votes given at such poll or voting-place. But the fact is, as we will prove by the returns themselves, that not a single return was accompanied by this statement, which alone confers upon the returning-board the jurisdiction to exclude votes. The reason is obvious. There was no riot, intimidation, tumult, or bribery at the election in question. The election machinery was in the hands of republicans. The State administration was republican. Every sheriff, every deputy sheriff, every constable, every police-officer, every supervisor of registration, and every commissioner of election, and many thousand special officers appointed and charged with the duty of guarding the freedom and purity of the election—every one was a republican appointee. And back of them stood the Federal administration and the Army and Navy of the United States. Yet, not an arrest was made throughout the State for riot, intimidation, or bribery committed on that day. And it is not alleged that even a knock-down occurred in the State on that day. But the returning-board, without the semblance of jurisdiction, threw out about 10,000 Tilden votes, and declared the Hayes electors elected by about 2,000 majority. We shall offer to prove that this proceeding of the returning-board was not erroneous merely, not the result of inadvertence or mistake, or error of judgment; but that it was willful, fraudulent, and corrupt.

Again, we shall offer to prove that of the Hayes electors thus fraudulently declared to have been elected, two, Brewster and Levissee, were on the day of the election holding offices of trust and profit under the Government of the United States. The Constitution of the United States, Art. II, sec. 1, provides that—

No Senator, or Representative, or *person holding an office* of *trust or profit* under the United States, shall be *appointed* an elector.

Another of the Hayes electors was William Pitt Kellogg, governor of the State, both on election-day and on the 6th day of December when he sat in the electoral college and cast a vote for Mr. Hayes; and three others, both on election-day and when they voted in the electoral college, were holding other salaried offices under the State government. The constitution of the State of Louisiana, Art. 147, declares—

No person shall at the same time hold more than one office, except that of justice of the peace and notary public.

Therefore, if electors are to be considered as Federal officers, two of the Hayes electors in this college were constitutionally incapable of being electors; and if they are State officers, then four others were constitutionally incapable of being electors.

And William Pitt Kellogg, as governor, certified that he, *himself*, Brewster, Levissee, and associates, had been *duly* appointed electors; and they met on the appointed day as an electoral college and cast their votes for Mr. Hayes. The Tilden electors, McEnery and others, who received a majority of the votes cast at the election, but were counted out by the returning-board and were refused a certificate by the governor, met on the same day and cast their votes for Mr. Tilden. Both bodies, each claiming to be the electoral college of that State, have certified their proceedings to the President of the Senate as required by the constitution.

This being the case, the two Houses of Congress, whose duty it is to count the votes for President and Vice-President, and who must ascertain which are the electoral votes of that State before they can be counted, find themselves confronted with several important questions:

(1.) Whether the Hayes electors, who were not elected, but were counted in; or the Tilden electors, who were elected, but were counted out, constitute the legal electoral college of that State;

(2.) And in case the Hayes electoral college is held to have a better title, founded upon false certificates without votes, than the Tilden college with the votes but without certificates; whether Levissee and Brewster, two electors in the Hayes college, were duly appointed; and

(3.) Whether conceding that the Hayes electors were not duly appointed, and that Levissee and Brewster were incapable of appointment, yet having received the official certificates of election, and having in fact acted—whether their votes should be counted, upon the principle that the acts of officers *de facto* but not *de jure* are binding upon the public and third persons?

The two Houses have referred these questions to this Commission for an opinion, after which the two Houses must pass finally upon the matter.

The importance of the opinion you shall give upon these questions cannot be exaggerated. If you shall say of the Hayes electors, for instance, that although they were actually defeated by the people by eight thousand majority, and although two of them were forbidden by the Constitution of the United States to be electors, and four others were so forbidden by the constitution of the State, yet having been counted in by fraud, and having in fact acted, although in violation of express constitutional provision, State and Federal, they were *duly appointed*, and their votes must be accepted, you will thereby declare that a fraud is as good as a majority and that the Constitution of the Union and of every State may be violated in the methods of a presidential election without affecting the result; and you might as well write out a full license for the perpetration of all the frauds which ingenuity can suggest or self-interest induce.

Since the last election the democrats have been and now are in possession of Florida. Say to them, by your decision in this case, that no matter what frauds are committed by a canvassing-board, this high tribunal will take no notice of them, and if you cannot, neither can the two Houses of Congress, for you have all the power of each House and of both Houses in that behalf; and if the democratic returning and certifying officers of that State do not, in the next campaign, certify 10,000 democratic majority, without regard to the fact, it will be because they have not profited by the lesson you will have taught them. If a governor can certify that an elector has been duly appointed who did not receive a vote, and that, upon the certificate of a returning-board, bribed or coerced to certify a falsehood—a falsehood known to both Houses of Congress from investigations carried on through their respective committees—a falsehood boasted of by its perpetrators and known of all men, who is so hopeful as to believe that there ever will be another President elected by anything but fraud? Why go through with all the tremendous labor of a political campaign; why send your orators upon the stump, and spend thousands of dollars in circulating documents to convince the people that a certain candidate ought to be elected, when you, with a third of that money, can bribe a canvassing-board, and carry an election without a vote?

Your honors will see I am not overstating the case contended for by our opponents. The fraud mentioned would be greater in degree, but not different in character, from the one which is now before you for consideration, and I ought to apologize for saying, for your approval. You are expected to say to the politicians and caucus managers of the country, "No matter what frauds you commit, no matter how glaring and damnable, we see nothing;" as the German colonel, when he went with a regiment from Illinois into Alabama said to the boys, "Now, boys, I shuts my eyes; I opens them at three o'clock;" so this tribunal is expected to shut its eyes to all the frauds committed in the canvass of these votes by which I will show your honors, not by declamation and assertion, but by argument which in any court of justice could not be gainsaid, that this result was reached; disfranchisement was imposed upon 10,000 legal voters by a tribunal which had no jurisdiction to exclude a vote; if these things can be done in the green tree, what may we not expect to see in the dry? If in the centennial year only of the life of our nation such frauds can pass unwhipped of justice, and not only pass unwhipped, but win the prizes, what may we not expect when the degeneracy of this nation shall come?

I.

The first questions naturally suggested by this discussion are, what is the character of this tribunal, and what is the *nature* of the powers conferred upon it?

The Constitution of the United States embodies the American conception of a republic. It creates a government to exercise the powers of sovereignty as to certain enumerated subjects. It proceeds upon the fundamental idea that the rights, privileges, and liberties of the people can only be secured against encroachment on the part of those charged with the execution of governmental powers by a careful separation of legislative, executive, and judicial powers, and a distribution of such powers among three great, equal, and co-ordinate departments. The legislative power is vested in the Congress, the executive power is vested in the President, and the judicial power is vested in one Supreme Court, and in such inferior courts as the Congress may from time to time ordain and establish. "The judges, both of the Supreme and inferior courts, shall hold their offices during good behavior, and shall, at stated times, receive for their services, a stated compensation, which shall not be diminished during their continuance in office."—*Const., article 3, sec. 1.*

It is well settled that "the judicial power" cannot be vested elsewhere than in courts composed of judges holding their offices during good behavior.

It is therefore certain that no part of "the judicial power" can be vested in a tribunal organized as this tribunal is. No tribunal created by act of Congress, whose decisions are subject to review except by other judicial courts of superior jurisdiction, can be considered as judicial courts. The Court of Claims, as originally constituted, could render judgments so called; but such judgments were submitted to the approval and ultimate action of Congress. For this reason, the Supreme Court of the United States held that no appeal would lie from the decisions of that court to the Supreme Court of the United States.—*Gordon* vs. *The United States*, 2 Wall., 561.

After this decision, Congress remodeled that court, and gave conclusive effect to its judgments; since which appeals have been entertained by the Supreme Court.

In *The United States* vs. *Ferriera*, 13 How., 40, acts of Congress had conferred upon the district judge of the United States for Florida authority to adjudicate upon certain claims arising under the treaty with Spain; which claims, when adjudicated by him, should be paid, *if the Secretary of the Treasury* should, on a report of the evidence, deem it equitable. The court, by Taney, C. J., say:

The powers conferred by these acts of Congress upon the judge as well as the Secretary are, it is true, *judicial in their nature*, for judgment and discretion must be exercised by both of them. But it is nothing more than the power ordinarily given by law to a commissioner appointed to adjust claims to lands or money under a treaty, or special powers to inquire into or decide any other particular class of controversies in which the public or individuals may be concerned. A power of that description may constitutionally be conferred on a Secretary as well as on a commissioner. *But it is not judicial* in either case *in the sense* in which judicial power is granted by the Constitution to the courts of the United States.

See also Hayburn's case, 2 Dall., 405.

It is therefore plain that "the judicial power" could not be vested in this tribunal, and it is equally clear that the bill organizing this tribunal does not pretend to clothe it with such power, because the decision, so called, which this tribunal may render is submitted to the approval of and may be reversed by the two Houses of Congress.

What, then, is this tribunal? It is, we submit, a mere legislative commission, exercising political power pertaining to the jurisdiction of Congress. Congress finds itself charged with the duty of ascertaining who, if any one, has been elected President of the United States, by the votes cast in the several electoral colleges on the 6th of December last. And to aid it in the performance of this duty, the exercise of this political power, it has created this commission to investigate and decide and report to the two Houses of Congress upon certain matters embraced in the performance of that duty; and the bill creating this commission provides that its report shall be made to the two Houses, and shall be conclusive, unless reversed by the Houses themselves.

There is no doubt of the power of both Houses of Congress by law, or perhaps by a joint resolution, to create a commission to investigate and report upon any subject falling within the scope of ordinary legislation, or relating to the performance of any duty cast upon Congress by the Constitution. Similar parliamentary commissions have frequently been ordered in England; sometimes raised by the Houses themselves, and sometimes authorized by statute and appointed by the Crown.

For instance, by statute 15 and 16 Vict., chap. 57, a commission was authorized, which was appointed by the Crown to inquire into alleged corrupt practices in elections of members of the House of Commons; which commission was authorized by the statute to send for persons and papers, administer oaths, examine witnesses, &c. And false swearing before such commission would have been perjury under the laws of Great Britain. This commission made report, which became the foundation for legislation upon that important subject.—May's Parl. Prac., p. 593.

The Constitution, amendment XII, provides, in regard to the votes given in the several electoral colleges, that they shall be certified and returned to the President of the Senate, and then provides as follows:

The President of the Senate shall, in the presence of the Senate and House of Representatives, open all the *certificates,* AND THE VOTES SHALL THEN BE COUNTED.

But by whom the votes shall be counted the Constitution does not declare. Most of the powers conferred by the Constitution of the United States are vested in some designated department or officer. Other powers are conferred upon the United States generally. For instance, article 4, section 4, provides as follows:

The United States shall guarantee to every State in this Union a republican form of government, and shall protect each of them against invasion, and, on application of the legislature, or of the executive, (when the legislature cannot be convened,) against domestic violence.

The last clause of the legislative article confers upon Congress the power—

To make all laws which may be necessary and proper for carrying into execution the foregoing powers, and all other powers vested by this Constitution in the Government of the United States, or in any department or officer thereof.

Congress has provided by law for the execution by the President of the power as to protection against domestic violence.

The constitutionality of the bill creating this Commission may be considered upon one or the other of two grounds.

(1.) If the power to count the votes is vested in the two Houses of Congress, then this Commission is a proper instrumentality for making the investigation necessary to enable the two Houses intelligently to execute the power. If, on the other hand, the case is to be treated as one of power granted generally, that is, without designation as to who shall count the votes, then it falls within the power of Congress to make laws for its execution, as a power vested by the Constitution in the Government of the United States, or in some department or officer thereof. If the latter is the true view of the Constitution, then Congress might pass a law creating a commission or court, to be appointed by the President, to count the votes, and leave the matter entirely to such court or commission.

But, evidently, the bill proceeds upon the theory that the votes are to be counted by the two Houses of Congress, because by the bill power is reserved to the two Houses to set aside the report, called the decision, to be made by this Commission. And, considering the matter in this light, it is manifest that Congress may impose upon the Commission such duties, that is, order it to investigate such questions—as it may see fit. It may direct the Commission to report what is the *prima facie* right of candidates upon certain papers, or it may direct this Commission to ascertain and report upon the *de jure* right of the several candidates.

What duty, then, does the law creating this tribunal impose upon it? The law declares that you shall—

(1.) "By a majority of votes decide whether any and what votes from such State are the votes provided for by the Constitution of the United States; and

(2.) "How many and what persons were *duly appointed* electors in such State."

And to enable you to perform this duty, the act clothes you with all the powers of the two Houses of Congress. What this means may be inferred from the fact that the two Houses of Congress in the last count of presidential votes concurred in deciding that the electoral vote of the Louisiana college ought to be excluded, because the votes cast at the popular election for electors had not been canvassed according to the laws of that State; thus going behind a regular certificate of the governor that the electors had been duly appointed, and a regular return of the votes cast by said college. This is at least a construction by the two Houses themselves of their power to go behind the certificate of the governor to ascertain whether the electors were duly appointed. It will be said that this was under the 22d joint rule of the two Houses. It seems now to be a matter of dispute between the two Houses whether or not that rule is now in force; but whether it is or not, is wholly immaterial. Either House, or the two Houses, may regulate practice in the exercise of their constitutional authority; but neither, nor both, can add to that authority by rules of their own. If this joint rule added to the Constitution, it was void; if it took from the Constitution, it was void; if it did neither, it was useless. And the concurrent action of both Houses of Congress in rejecting the vote of Louisiana four years ago must be regarded as a declaration by them of their power in the premises, and that power they have conferred upon this tribunal.

This tribunal has been created to meet a great national emergency. The public welfare and business interests alike require a speedy, final, and satisfactory settlement of the presidential question. The people will be content with, and the rival candidates will acquiesce in, any determination of the question founded upon the full merits of the case. But no one will be content with, no candidate will acquiesce in, a determination of this great question which ignores the merits and rests upon technicalities or false certificates.

It is a total error to suppose that this tribunal can make any decision which, in the judicial sense of that term, can settle this question. And it is an equal error to suppose that Congress has pretended to clothe this tribunal with any such power. On the contrary, section 6 of this bill reserves to the defeated candidate the right—if any such right now exists by law—to prosecute a writ of *quo warranto* against the candidate who may be counted in.

Mr. Commissioner BRADLEY. Mr. Carpenter, I do not think there is a difference of opinion in the Commission on that subject. I have not heard any. It has been universally considered, so far as I am informed, that the powers of this Commission extend so far, and so far only, as the powers of the two Houses of Congress extend.

Mr. CARPENTER. In other words, then, it is agreed on all hands that the powers of this Commission are political powers; they are legislative powers delegated by the two Houses to this Commission. Your honors would have relieved yourselves from the infliction of the last twenty minutes if that had been announced to me a little earlier.

Mr. Commissioner HOAR. I do not understand that Judge BRADLEY announces the proposition you have stated as the opinion of the Commission.

Mr. CARPENTER. The proposition is so self-evident, so thoroughly fortified by the Constitution, that I will stop with the mere suggestion which Judge BRADLEY has made on the subject. It is perfectly certain that this tribunal is exercising some power, or else we should not be wasting all these candles here to-night, the property of the United States. If its power is not judicial—and that is conceded— nobody will claim that it is executive. Then it must be legislative.

Mr. Commissioner GARFIELD. Do you hold that we can pass a bill, that we can legislate?

Mr. CARPENTER.. No; I do not. I do not hold that one of the standing committees of the Senate or House could pass a bill. But I do say that when the Judiciary Committee of the Senate, for instance, is instructed to inquire into and report upon a given subject. and has power to send for persons and papers, and examine witnesses, that committee, in doing so, is exercising the delegated power of the Senate in that behalf. That is what I maintain. Therefore I say that this Commission, sitting here under this act of Congress, is exercising a delegated political power, and that its jurisdiction is precisely what, and its duty exactly that which the law of its creation prescribes. In other words, I contend this Commission is merely a legislative committee of investigation, and it is bound to inquire into and report upon the matters which have been submitted to its determination by the act of Congress under which it is sitting.

This brings me back to consider the precise duties imposed upon this Commission, and the methods by which it may investigate the subject.

I turn now to the text of the act creating this tribunal. The papers are to be sent to the Commission, "which shall proceed to consider the same, with the same powers, if any, now possessed for that purpose by the two Houses, acting separately or together, and, by a majority of votes, decide whether any and what votes from each State are the votes provided for by the Constitution of the United States, and how many and what persons were *duly appointed* electors in such State." The duty imposed on this Commission is to decide, not how many and what electors have a *prima facie* title, not how many and what electors appear from certain papers and certificates to have been appointed, but "how many and what persons were *duly* appointed electors in such State." That is precisely the duty of the common-law courts in trying a case commenced by information in the nature of *quo warranto*. I concede that you are not trying a *quo warranto;* I concede that your decision will not bind either party who may be defeated by your determination from maintaining his *quo warranto*. Nevertheless, considering the public necessities—considering the evils to result from a further contest over this presidential question, Congress has seen fit to direct you to investigate and decide—that is, report, for there can be no *decision* in the judicial sense of that term—"how many and what persons were *duly* appointed electors in such State." And for this purpose you are clothed with all the power possessed by the two Houses of Congress. If you cannot go to the bottom of this subject it is bottomless, and there is no power to defeat the greatest fraud ever attempted in our political history.

To investigate this subject you have the powers of the two Houses of Congress. What are those powers; or, in other words, what methods of investigation may legislative bodies adopt? Sir George Cornwal Lewis, in his work entitled "Methods and Reasonings in Politics," says:

The subject of judicial evidence has been treated by jurists with more or less fullness since jurisprudence became a science; but it has, perhaps, been elaborated in more detail, and has received a more systematic form, in England than in any other country. This has been owing to peculiarities in the procedure of our courts of common law, which need not be here noticed. With respect to our present subject, the most important rule of evidence in the law of England is that which prescribes the exclusion of *hearsay testimony;* that is to say, of statements of fact made by the witness, not from his own observation but from the observation of others.

* * * * * * *

In judicial proceedings, therefore, where the facts are determined, not by official agents of the Government, but by the testimony of witnesses taken casually from the midst of the community, the general principle is recognized by our law that the witness must speak to an event which occurred under his notice, and within the reach of his senses.

* * * * * * *

The process of ascertaining facts for legislative purposes is not, in general, so formal, or subject to such strict rules of evidence as the procedure of executive departments, whether administrative or judicial. Petitions, complaints, remonstrances, statements of grievances, are presented to a legislature, or, if it consist of a deliberative body, individual members of that body may represent facts upon their own authority. It may then either proceed at once to legislate upon the faith of such suggestions, or it may take them as raising merely a presumption, and may institute an inquiry of its own. It may call for papers, accounts, correspondence, and other documents; it may likewise, by proper means, examine witnesses, and thus ascertain, by original testimony, the facts bearing upon the subject under consideration.

Upon this authority, I assert that the testimony taken by the committees of the two Houses of Congress upon this subject is before you, and should be considered in this inquiry; and that you can proceed in the methods usual in legislative bodies, and act upon any information which would authorize a legislative body to act. It is not expected, as the law creating this tribunal clearly shows, that you are to proceed only in the judicial method of investigating facts, by examination of witnesses, &c.

Four years ago the subject of the electoral vote of the State of Louisiana was referred by the Senate to a committee. The committee reported, although the governor had certified in regular form that the electors were duly appointed, and they had met on the proper day and cast their votes for President and Vice-President, that the votes cast at the election for the electors had not been canvassed according to law; and the two Houses of Congress, without further investigation, each by itself, the Senate by the vote of every republican Senator, and the House without a division, decided to reject the electoral vote of that State.

At this point let me refer to the remedy of *quo warranto*, touching the matter in question.

It has been settled in England for more than one hundred years, and is perfectly well settled in this country, that information in the nature of *quo warranto* is in its *nature* a civil proceeding, and must be so classified in the distribution of cases between courts of civil and courts of criminal jurisdiction. Rex *vs.* Francis, 2 D. & E. 484. In State Bank *vs.* The State, 1 Blackford, 272, the court said: "We have no need of resorting to the general doctrine or information, for a *quo warranto* on information is a criminal proceeding only in name and in form;·in its *nature* it is *purely a civil proceeding.*" Citing 2 Kid on Corpo., 439; King *vs.* Francis, 2 T. R., 484. "The proceeding by information in the nature of a *quo warranto* is essentially a civil proceeding, and the pleadings in it are as much subject to amendment as they are in ordinary civil actions. It is criminal only in form." (State of Florida *vs.* Gleason, 14 Flor., 109.)

In Brison *vs.* Lingo, 26 Mo., 496, the supreme court said: "The inquiry arises, is this a criminal case? For a great while it has been applied to the simple purpose of trying civil right, and regarded as a remedy to try the right to office." The court held it was a civil case. See also State *vs.* Kupfurle, 44 Mo., 154. "A proceeding by *quo warranto* is not a criminal proceeding." Ensminger *vs.* Peo., 47 Ill., 384. In Commonwealth *vs.* Browne, 1 S. & R., 382, it was held that "an information in the nature of a *quo warranto*, although a *criminal* proceeding in *form*, is in *substance* but a *civil* one, and is therefore not within the prohibition of the tenth article of the constitution of Pennsylvania." In State *ex rel.* Bashford *vs.* Barstow, 4 Wis., 467, the attorney-general, after some proceedings, filed a formal discontinuance on the part of the State, but the court held the suit must proceed as between the relator and the defendant, and the court proceeded and rendered judgment in favor of the relator; and he thereupon entered into and held the office for the balance of the term.

The Constitution of the United States, article 3, section 2, declares that the judicial power of the United States "shall extend to all cases arising under this Constitution, the laws of the United States, and treaties made under their authority," &c. A contest between Mr. Tilden, if he shall be counted out, and Mr. Hayes, if he shall be counted in, touching the right to exercise the office of President, would undoubtedly be a case arising under the Constitution and laws of the United States.

Now let us see whether any court has jurisdiction to try the case.

The act of Congress March 3, 1875, 18 Statutes at Large, part 3, provides as follows:

That the circuit courts of the United States shall have original cognizance, concurrent with the courts of the several States, of all suits of a *civil nature* at common law or in equity, where the matter in dispute exceeds, exclusive of costs, the sum or value of five hundred dollars, and arising under the Constitution or laws of the United States, or treaties made, or which shall be made, under their authority, &c.

It is well settled that where the title to an office is in dispute, the amount involved, for the purpose of jurisdiction, is the salary of the office. (U. S. *vs.* Addison, 22 How., 174.)

It is true the act of Congress quoted above says nothing about writ or information of *quo warranto*. But when an act of Congress confers upon a circuit court jurisdiction of a case or controversy, the power of the court to issue the proper writ, or entertain the proper proceedings to bring the case or controversy before the court, cannot be questioned.

It is well settled that in proceedings by *quo warranto* the court will ascertain the right to the office, and go through all forms, fictions, certificates of canvassing-boards and commissions of office, to ascertain that right.

> *People* vs. *Van Slyck*, 4 *Cow.*, 297.
> *People* vs. *Ferguson*, 8 *Cow.*, 102.
> *Jeter* vs. *State*, 1 *McCord*, 233.
> *People* vs. *Vail*, 20 *Wend.*, 12.
> *Bashford* vs. *Barstow*, 4 *Wis.*, 567.
> *Hill* vs. *State*, 1 *Ala.*, (*N. S.*,) 559.

As a determination of this question by this tribunal based upon the broad merits of the case would give peace to the country, and set the obstructed wheels of enterprise once more in motion, so, on the other hand, a narrow and technical decision which would throw the question into a judicial controversy, to continue for months, would be a calamity to the country, and raise a doubt as to the efficiency of free institutions.

This is undoubtedly the reason why Congress has directed this Commission to inquire into the ultimate, final fact as a court of law would do on a *quo warranto*—reserving to itself, however, the right to adopt or reject such conclusion in the final counting of votes, which is to be done by the two Houses themselves after this Commission shall have performed its functions. The duty cast upon this Commission to inquire and decide—that is, report—what persons were "*duly* appointed electors" can be performed in no way but by an inquiry into the ultimate fact; that is, the legality of such appointment. This commission must take judicial notice of the laws of Louisiana. (Pennington *vs.* Gibson, 16 How., 65.) It must, therefore, ascertain whether any law of that State directs the manner in which electors shall be appointed; whether such State law is in accordance with the constitution of that State, and whether, in fact, the electors were appointed according to such law. Without this it is impossible to say whether or not they were *duly* appointed.

II.

I come now to another question which I think is one of considerable difficulty, and that is to ascertain what was the statute law of Louisiana on the 7th day of November last. It very rarely happens that in investigating a case you are unable to find out what the statute is. There may be differences about the meaning of a statute, but you can generally ascertain what statute was in force; but anything that comes from Louisiana is full of difficulty to a lawyer; that is, everything that has come up from it except my honorable friend on the left here, [Mr. Campbell.]

The legislature of the State of Louisiana, October 19, 1868, (Laws 1868, p. 218,) passed a general election law for the election of governor, lieutenant-governor, members of the legislature, and other State and parish officers.

Section 32 of that act is as follows, (page 223 :)

SEC. 32. *Be it further enacted, &c.*, That in every year in which an election shall be held for electors of President and Vice-President of the United States, such election shall be held on the Tuesday next after the first Monday in the month of November, in accordance with an act of the Congress of the United States, approved January twenty-three, one thousand eight hundred and forty-five, entitled "An act to establish a uniform time for holding elections for electors of President and Vice-President in all States of the Union." And such elections shall be held and conducted in the manner and form provided by law for general State elections.

SEC. 33. *Be it further enacted, &c.,* That the foregoing provisions, except as to time and place of holding elections, shall apply to the election of all officers whose election is not otherwise provided for.

Eleven days afterward, October 30, 1868, the legislature proceeded to, and " otherwise provided for," the election of presidential electors, thus taking that election out of the operation of the general election law. The latter act is a complete regulation of presidential electors, and is as follows:

No. 193.—An act relative to presidential electors.

SECTION 1. *Be it enacted by the senate and house of representatives of the State of Louisiana in general assembly convened,* That in every year in which an election is to be held for electors of President and Vice-President of the United States, such election shall be held on Tuesday next after the first Monday in the month of November in such year, in accordance with an act of the Congress of the United States approved January twenty-three, eighteen hundred and forty-five, entitled "An act to establish a uniform time for holding elections for electors of President and Vice-President in all of the States of the Union," and such elections shall be held and conducted in the manner and form provided by law for general State elections.

SEC. 2. *Be it further enacted, &c., That every qualified voter* in the State shall vote for seven persons, as follows: Two persons shall be selected from the State at large, and one person shall be chosen from each congressional district in this State ; and in case any ticket shall contain two or more names of persons residing in the same district (except the two chosen from the State at large) the first of such names only shall be considered as duly voted for.

SEC. 3. *Be it further enacted, &c.,* That no person shall be an elector who is not a qualified voter in the district for which he is chosen, or in case of being elected for the State at large, then of some parish of the State.

SEC. 4. *Be it further enacted, &c.,* That immediately after the receipt of a return from each parish, or on the fourth Monday of November, if the returns shall not sooner arrive, the governor, in presence of the secretary of state, the attorney-general, a district judge of the district in which the seat of government may be established, or any two of them, shall examine the returns and ascertain therefrom the several persons who have been duly elected electors.

SEC. 5. *Be it further enacted, &c.,* That one of the returns from each parish, indorsed by the governor, shall be placed on file and preserved among the archives of the secretary of state.

SEC. 6. *Be it further enacted, &c.,* That the names of the persons selected, together with a copy of the returns from the several parishes, shall forthwith be published in the newspaper or papers in which the laws of the State may be directed to be published.

SEC. 7. *Be it further enacted, &c.,* That the electors shall meet at the seat of government on the day appointed for their meeting by the act of Congress, (the first Wednesday in December,) and shall then and there proceed to execute the duties and services enjoined upon them by the Constitution of the United States, in the manner therein prescribed.

SEC. 8. *Be it further enacted, &c.,* That if any one or more of the electors chosen by the people shall fail from any cause whatever, to appear at the appointed place at the hour of four p. m., of the day prescribed for their meeting, it shall be the duty of the other electors immediately to proceed by ballot to supply such vacancy or vacancies.

SEC. 9. *Be it further enacted, &c.,* That each elector shall receive the same daily compensation and allowance which at that time shall be allowed by law to the members of the general assembly, to be paid by the treasurer of the State on warrants signed by the governor.

SEC. 10. *Be it further enacted, &c.,* That all laws conflicting herewith be, and the same are hereby repealed ; that this act shall take effect from and after its passage.

March 16, 1870, the legislature passed another election law. Laws of 1870, p. 145–161.

Section 35, page 150 of this act, reads as follows:

SEC. 35. *Be it further enacted, &c.,* That in every year in which an election shall be held for the electors of President and Vice-President of the United States, such election shall be held on the Tuesday next after the first Monday in the month of November, in accordance with the act of the Congress of the United States approved January twenty-third, one thousand eight hundred and forty-five, entitled "An act to establish a uniform time for holding election for electors of President and Vice-President in all States of the Union," and such election shall be held and conducted and returns made thereof in the manner and form prescribed by law for the general elections.

Section 38 of this act is as follows:

SEC. 38. *Be it further enacted, &c.,* That the provisions of this act, except as to the time of holding elections, shall apply in the election of all officers whose election is not otherwise provided for.

The last section of said act is as follows:

SEC. 85. *Be it further enacted, &c.,* That all laws or parts of law contrary to the provisions of this act and all laws *relating to the same subject-matter* are hereby repealed, and this act shall take effect from and after the passage.

REVISED STATUTES, 1870.

This revision took effect April 1, 1870. It contains a general election-law, differing materially from the act of 1870, and made no provisions for a returning-board, and this revision also re-enacted the special act of 1868.

Section 1410 of the revision is as follows:

SEC. 1410. In every year in which an election shall be held for electors of President and Vice-President of the United States, such election shall be held on the Tuesday next after the first Monday in the month of November, in accordance with an act of Congress of the United States approved January 13th, 1845, entitled " An act to establish a uniform time for holding elections for electors of President and Vice-President in all States of the Union," and such elections shall be held and conducted in the manner and form provided by law for general State elections.

Sections 2823–2832 of the revision are the same in substance as the act of 1868. Section 2826 of the revision in relation to the canvass of votes given for presidential electors is as follows:

SEC. 2826. Immediately after the receipt of a return from each parish, or on the fourth Monday of November if the returns should not sooner arrive, the governor, in presence of the secretary of state, the attorney-general, a district judge of the district in which the seat of government may be established, or any two of them, shall examine the returns and ascertain therefrom the persons who have been duly elected electors.

Section 3990 of the revision repealed all former laws or parts of laws on the same subject-matter covered by the revision, with certain exceptions not material here.

THE ACT OF 1872.

November 20, 1872, the legislature passed another general election-law which was in force at the last November election. Sections 1, 29, 32, and 71 are as follows:

SEC. 1. *Be it further enacted,* That all elections for State, parish, and judicial officers, members of the general assembly, and for members of Congress, shall be held on the first (Tuesday after the first) Monday in November; and said election shall be styled the general elections. They shall be held in the manner and form and subject to the regulations hereafter prescribed, and no other.

By constitutional amendment, 1874, the day for holding general elections was changed from the first Monday to the first Tuesday following the first Monday in November.

SEC. 29. *Be it further enacted, &c.,* That in every year in which an election shall be held for electors of President and Vice-President of the United States, such election shall be held at the time fixed by act of Congress.

SEC. 32. *Be it further enacted, &c.*, That the provisions of this act, except as to the time of holding elections, shall apply in the election of all officers whose election is not otherwise provided for.

SEC. 71. *Be it further enacted, &c.*, That this act shall take effect from and after its passage, and that all others on the subject of election-laws be and the same are hereby repealed.

Whether the election-law of 1870 was repealed by the revision, or whether it remained in force after April 1, 1870, when the revision took effect, depends upon the effect to be given to several acts of the legislature enacted at the session of 1870.

On the 28th February, 1870, the following act was passed:

No. 50. An act giving precedence in authority to all the other acts and joint resolutions passed by the general assembly at this session over the acts known as "The Revision of the Statutes and of the Civil Code and Code of Practice" when there exists any conflict in the provisions of said acts and revisions.

SECTION 1. *Be it enacted by the Senate and House of Representatives of the State of Louisiana in general assembly convened,* That all the acts and joint resolutions passed during the *present session* of the general assembly which may be contrary to or in any manner conflict with the acts of the present session known as "*Revision of the Statutes* of a general character, and of the Civil Code and Code of Practice," shall have precedence of said revisions, and be held as the law in opposition thereto, and as repealing those acts so far as they may be in opposition or conflict.—*Promulgated March 20, 1870.*

On the 14th March, 1870, the revision was passed, and by its terms was to go into effect April 1, 1870.

On the 16th March, 1870, the election-law was passed, to take effect from its passage.

The question is whether after the 1st April the revision repealed the election-law of 1870, or whether the election-law of 1870, by virtue of the act of February 28, 1870, remained in force notwithstanding the revision, and nullified the general election-law contained in the revision. The general rule is that an act passed to take effect on a future day, has on that day the same effect as though it had been *passed on that day.* "A law speaks from the time of its going into effect." Rice *vs.* Ruddiman, 10 Mich., 125; Peo. *vs.* Johnson, 6 Cal., 673; Arthur *vs.* Franklin, 16 Ohio, N. S., 193; Lyner *vs.* Stale, 8 Ind., 490; Supervisors *vs.* Keady, 34 Ill., 293; Charless *vs.* Lamberson, 1 Clarke, (Iowa,) 435; Price *vs.* Hopkins, 13 Mich., 318.

Mr. Commissioner HOAR. Mr. Carpenter, do I understand you to claim that, if an act is passed on the 1st of April to take effect on the 1st of May, and on the 15th of April an act is passed repealing that altogether, still on the 1st of May the repealing act itself would be repealed?

Mr. CARPENTER. I do not claim so; I do not think so. This is not that case. The Revised Statutes were not repealed before they took effect, unless *pro tanto* by the inconsistent and conflicting provisions of the general election-law of 1870. Treating the revision as having been passed April 1, 1870, the time when by its own terms it was to take effect, it repealed the election-law of 1870, and also repealed all prior acts denying to it the full force and effect which would otherwise attach to it as a law. And this I believe to be the sound view of the subject.

But if it is competent for the legislature to provide that of two acts thereafter to be passed the first shall repeal the second, then the revision taking effect April 1, 1870, was subordinated to the election-law of March 16, 1870.

It is not very material to this case which view of this matter shall be taken by the court. It is certain that the act of 1868, re-enacted in the revision, *was* or it *was not* in force at the last election.

I shall present the case first upon the ground that the act of 1868 was in force, as I incline to that opinion.

1. Assuming the act of 1868 (re-enacted in the revision of 1870) as in force, it is not pretended that the votes given for electors at the last election in that State have ever been canvassed as required by this act. It is evident that the canvass which was made, and which resulted in the exclusion of over 10,000 votes in favor of the Tilden electors, was not only unauthorized by this act, but in direct violation of its express provisions.

By this law, section 2826, revised statutes, it is provided that—

Immediately after the receipt of a return from *each parish*, or on the fourth Monday of November, if the returns should not sooner arrive, the *governor*, in the presence of the secretary of state, the attorney-general, a district judge of the district in which the seat of government may be established, or any two of them, shall examine *the returns* and ascertain *therefrom* the persons who have been duly elected electors.

SEC. 2827. One of the returns *from each parish*, indorsed by the governor, shall be placed on file and preserved among the archives of the secretary of state.

SEC. 2828. The names of persons elected, together with a copy of the returns *from the several parishes,* shall forthwith be published in the newspaper or papers in which the laws of the State may be directed to be published.

Under this law, no returns whatever could be excluded. The result must be ascertained from all the returns "from each parish." No judicial power, and no discretion, is conferred by this act; the duty is purely mathematical. The returns from each parish are to be preserved among the archives of the secretary of state. It will not be pretended that if this law was in force the election was conducted and returned according to its provisions. If the election law of 1868, as re-enacted in the revision of April 1, 1870, was not repealed by the act of March 16, 1870, then it certainly was in force at the time of the election, unless repealed by the act of 1872. The history of this act of 1872 is well known. In the early part of 1872 the legislature passed this bill and sent it to Governor Warmoth for his approval. He neither approved nor vetoed the bill during the session of the legislature. But after the presidential and the State elections of November, 1872, when Governor Warmoth was engaged in a contest with Judge Durell, months after the adjournment of the legislature which passed the bill, and after Judge Durell, in the circuit court of the United States, had tied up the canvass of those elections, Governor Warmoth, as the only means of counteracting the usurpations of a Federal judge, took this act of 1872 from his pocket, and gave it his approval, and caused it to be promulgated as a law of the State.

The repealing clause contained in this act is very sweeping in terms, but was evidently intended to repeal only the general election laws of the State. An examination of these statutes will show that the legislature always treated the election of electors as a matter distinct from the general elections of the State.

In 1868 the legislature, on the 19th of October, passed an act entitled "An act relative to elections in the State of Louisiana," &c., and on the 30th day of the same month passed another act entitled "An act relative to presidential electors;" and both were published in the session laws of that year as distinct and independent acts.

In the Revised Statutes of 1870 the general election law of the State is published under the head "Elections," on pages 272–282. Under the head of "Presidential electors," on pages 550–553, is re-enacted the act of 1868.

Here the intention is manifest to treat the two elections as distinct, and they are regulated by different provisions. The election of State officers under the authority of the State constitution and the election of electors under the authority of the Constitution and laws of the United States are treated in the laws of Louisiana as distinct subjects, and, notwithstanding the repealing clause of the act of 1872 is very broad, it is evident from the whole act that it was only intended to repeal all laws relating to general elections under State authority. It is a well-established rule for the interpretation of statutes, that, for the purpose of ascertaining the intention of the legislature in any particular part of the act, the whole act must be considered; and if the general intention manifested by the whole act is clear, such intention will enable the court to control the *language* of other parts of the act.— See *Blanchard* vs. *Sprague*, 3 *Sumner*, 279.

In doubtful cases a court should compare all the *parts* of a statute, *and different statutes in pari materia*, to ascertain the intention of the legislature.—*The Elizabeth*, 1 *Paine*, 10.

Words which, standing alone in an act of Congress, may properly be understood to pass a benefical interest in land, will not be regarded as having that effect *if the context shows that they were not intended to be so used.*—*Rice* vs. *Railroad Company*, 1 *Black*, 358.

That the act of 1872 was intended as a regulation *only* of the election for *State* officers, and the repeal of former laws upon that subject is manifest from the first section of that act.

Section 1. That all elections for *State, parish*, and *judicial* officers, members of the general assembly, and for members of Congress, shall be held on the first Monday in November, and said election shall be styled the *general elections*. They shall be held in the manner and form and subject to the regulations hereinafter prescribed, *and in no other*.

Presidential electors are not State officers. As between the Union and the States, to determine whether an officer is a *Federal* or *State officer*, we have only to determine whether the *office* is created by the Constitution and laws of the Union or the constitution and laws of a State. Senators are elected by the legislatures of the States, but the office of Senator is created by the Constitution of the United States, and nobody doubts that a Senator is an officer of the United States and not of the State which elects him. The office of elector is created by the Constitution of the United States. The office is therefore a Federal office, and the fact that a State may fill the office by appointment does not change the character of the office. Suppose an amendment of the Constitution to be adopted to-morrow, providing that, in addition to the present number, each State might appoint an additional judge of the Supreme Court of the United States; would it be pretended that a judge thus appointed was any less an officer of the United States than those appointed by the President? The effect of the Constitution is simply this: It establishes an office and authorizes a State to fill it. The only power possessed by the State in regard to the electoral college for each State is the power of appointment; but in what manner the *duties of the office* shall be performed, when the electors shall meet, and how they shall vote, the manner and order of their proceedings, the authentication of their action, and how to make return to the General Government, whether they shall give bonds or take oaths and receive compensation, and indeed all things concerning the office except the filling of the office, are subjects of Federal regulation; subjects over which the State has no control whatever.

Mr. Commissioner EDMUNDS. The Constitution says that the President shall commission all officers of the United States. You would not contend, I suppose, that an elector, in order to exercise the functions of his office, should be commissioned by the President.

Mr. CARPENTER. The Constitution, as I recollect, says he shall commission all officers except otherwise provided.

Mr. Commissioner EDMUNDS. I do not remember that phrase.

Mr. CARPENTER. I think it is there; if it is not, it ought to be. At all events, I do not undertake to decide that question now. The mere fact that the President had not issued a commission certainly could not determine that he ought not to have issued it, nor could it determine that these are not Federal officers, because a judge of the Supreme Court might go on the bench and sit here twenty years and not have a commission; and yet he might be an excellent *de facto* judge.

Mr. Commissioner ABBOTT. A great many officers under the Federal Constitution have no commission from the President.

Mr. CARPENTER. I think the only provision for the President's commissioning an officer is in the case of a vacancy happening during the recess of the Senate, when he issues a commission to expire at the time provided in the Constitution. He has authority, " by and with the advice and consent of the Senate, to make treaties."

Mr. Commissioner GARFIELD. Mr. Carpenter, please read the last clause of section 3 of article 2.

Mr. CARPENTER. It does provide that he " shall commission all the officers of the United States." I had forgotten that provision, and know as a matter of fact that he does not do it. There is an act of Congress providing that the officers of the internal revenue shall be commissioned by the Secretary of the Treasury, and that is the practice to-day.

I wish now to present the view of the case and what I think are the results, if we hold that the act of 1868 embodied in the revision was repealed by the former act of March 16, 1870.

Mr. Commissioner HUNTON. Mr. Carpenter, let me call your attention to this clause:

He shall have power, by and with the advice and consent of the Senate, to make treaties, provided two-thirds of the Senators present concur ; and he shall nominate, and, by and with the advice and consent of the Senate, shall appoint ambassadors, other public ministers, and consuls, judges of the Supreme Court, and all other officers of the United States, whose appointments are not herein otherwise provided for, &c.

That is as you stated at first, as I understand.

Mr. EVARTS. That is appointment, not commission.

Mr. CARPENTER. Upon the question whether the act of 1872 was intended to repeal the act of 1868, let me call attention to what was referred to by Mr. Jenks this morning. Under the act of 1872, if that is the only act which was in force, there is no provision whatever for filling any vacancy in the electoral college except by a popular election.

Mr. Commissioner HOAR. Is there any provision for electing electors at all except that sentence which simply speaks of the time ?

Mr. CARPENTER. That is all.

Mr. Commissioner HOAR. No provision for the manner of election ?

Mr. CARPENTER. None whatever, nor for a canvass, nor for a return, nor whether the electors shall be elected on a general ticket or from the congressional districts, nor anything on the subject. So then, if the act of 1868 was not in force, there was no provision whatever in force on the 7th day of November last.

Mr. Commissioner THURMAN. Did the act of 1872 repeal the act of 1870 ?

Mr. CARPENTER. Certainly, if it was in force down to that time. If it was not repealed by the revision of the 1st of April, 1870, it certainly was repealed by the act of 1872 in the broadest and most unequivocal terms; and, besides, the provisions of the act regulated the same subject; they were both election statutes; and the repealing clause of the act of 1872 repeals all other election laws.

Mr. Commissioner ABBOTT. What do you make of the second section of the act of 1872, that the returning-board shall be the returning-officers for all elections in the State?

Mr. CARPENTER. I am aware of that section and I answer: That provision I understand to be limited; the general language employed there is limited by the whole tenor of the act, which on its face shows, I think, that it was intended to apply to nothing but the election of State officers. It is well settled that where the intention of the legislature is manifest by the whole act to be a certain way, that will authorize a court to control the express language of other provisions in conflict. You are to reach the general intention of the legislature, and for that purpose courts are often compelled to disregard language employed in particular sections.

But another thing follows, if your honors take that view of the case, and hold that these officers are returning-officers for all elections. Then the other provision, that the election to fill all vacancies shall be by the people, certainly includes the vacancy which has been filled by that same election, does it not? If one section applies to all the officers elected in the State, including electors, then certainly the provision in regard to filling vacancies of all officers applies equally, and strikes out two of the votes given by this electoral college.

Again, the act of 1872 contains no direction in regard to the manner of appointing electors. It does not declare, nor does any other law of the State, except that of 1868, whether the electors shall be chosen by the people, elected by the legislature, or appointed by the governor. The act of 1868 is a specific and complete regulation of the whole subject, and provides for the election of electors by a popular vote; and provides that, in case of the absence of any of the electors, the other electors may supply their place by ballot; that two electors shall be elected at large, and one from each congressional district; and provides how the votes given shall be canvassed and certified. The act of 1872 contains *no* provision upon any of these subjects, and only refers to electors for the purpose of fixing the *time* for the appointment—a provision wholly useless, because Congress, and not the State, must fix the time for making such appointment. All that the State can do is to direct, by its legislature, the manner in which, and not the time at which, the appointment shall be made, when the time arrives for making it as provided by Congress.

It is not to be supposed that the legislature, in the act of 1872, intended to strike down the only act regulating the manner for appointing presidential electors, without making any other provision covering the subject.

Again, the act of Congress (Rev. Stats., p. 21, sec. 133) provides as follows:

SEC. 133. Each State may, *by law*, provide for the filling of any vacancies which may occur in its college of electors when such college meets to give its electoral vote.

The act of 1868 provides ·that, when the electoral college meets, if any elector is absent, his place may be filled by the electors present, they voting by ballot. But the act of 1872 provides, (sec. 24:)

That *all elections* to be held in this State to fill *any vacancies* shall be conducted and managed, and returns thereof shall be made, *in the same manner as is provided for general elections.*

Now, if the act of 1872 be construed as repealing the act of 1868, in regard to the election and returns for election of electors, then, beyond question, a vacancy in the electoral college would be one of the vacancies provided for in the section last quoted; and *such vacancy* could only be filled by a popular election.

In the case at bar, when the electoral college in Louisiana convened, it was found that two of the electors were holding offices of "honor or trust" under the United States at the time of the election, and therefore the election as to them was void under the provisions of the Constitution of the United States. We contend here that this was not a vacancy, but was a case falling within section 134 of the Revised Statutes of the United States; in other words, as to them there had been a failure to make a choice, and no law of the State, not even the law of 1868, provided for appointment to fill their places. But the electoral college treated the case as one of vacancy, and proceeded by election to fill the places deemed vacant. Treating this as a case of vacancy, and not a case of a failure to elect, it was a regular proceeding under the act of 1868, but utterly void if that act was repealed by the act of 1872; because the language in the act of 1872, in regard to filling vacancies, is as broad as other parts of the act in regard to the election of officers. And it is impossible for this tribunal to hold that the act of 1872 repealed the act of 1868 in regard to the election of electors, but that the section last quoted did not repeal the section in the act of 1868, which authorized a different method of filling a vacancy in the particular case.

Mr. Commissioner THURMAN. Was the act of 1868 repealed by the act of 1870?

Mr. CARPENTER. Undoubtedly. The election law of 1870, if that took effect, repealed the act of 1868.

Mr. Commissioner BRADLEY. Is there anything in the revised statutes of 1870 on this subject that was not taken from the act of 1868?

Mr. CARPENTER. No, sir; it merely re-enacts it.

Mr. Commissioner BRADLEY. Then the question of Judge THURMAN amounts also to the question whether the revised statutes took effect.

Mr. CARPENTER. Certainly; it all depends on that question. The act of 1870, if that was the law after the revision took effect on the 1st of April, unquestionably repealed the revision as to this subject, because the revision embodied precisely the act of 1868.

Mr. Commissioner BRADLEY. There is no express repeal of either.

Mr. CARPENTER. No, sir; except the repealing clause in the act of 1870, and in the act of 1872, repealing all prior laws on the same subject. Now let us assume for a moment that the act of 1868 was in force. That act was a complete regulation of the whole subject of electing presidential electors. It provided how they should be elected, that is, at a popular election; it provided who should be voters at that election; it provided who should be elected—two at large, and the others elected from the different congressional districts of the State; it provided the entire machinery of the election, and then provided—and the provision is to be found in section 2826 of the revision identical in language:

Immediately after the receipt of a return from each parish, or on the fourth Monday of November, if the returns should not sooner arrive, the governor, in the presence of the secretary of state, the attorney-general, a district judge of the district in which the seat of government may be established, or any two of them, shall examine the *returns,* and ascertain *therefrom* the persons who have been duly elected electors.

SEC. 2827. One of the returns from each parish, indorsed by the governor, shall be placed on file and preserved among the archives of the secretary of state.

SEC. 2828. The names of the persons elected, together with a copy of the returns from the several parishes, shall forthwith be published in the newspaper or papers in which the laws of the State may be directed to be published.

The law of 1868 contains no provision about a canvassing-board except what I have read. The governor must open the returns from each parish, and in the presence named they must then be counted, and the returns from the parishes must then be deposited in the office of the secretary of state to remain a permanent record. No one will pretend that under that act there was any jurisdiction or discretion about excluding any votes. That never has been pretended, and it will not be now. If the act of 1868 was in force at the last election, it is not pretended that there has ever been any canvass of the votes of that election according to that statute. They did not attempt it. They acted upon the theory that the other law was in force. So that if your honors say that the act of 1868 was in force because embodied in the revision taking effect April 1, and therefore repealed the former act of the 16th of March, 1870, the case now is precisely in the attitude in which it was four years ago.

Four years ago there came up from Louisiana a regular certificate of its governor that so many persons had been duly appointed electors for the State; but the Senate, acting upon the theory which I maintain is the true and proper one, raised a committee in advance to examine into the facts about the election of that college. They sent for witnesses, brought them here in large numbers, made an examination, and the committee made a report not expressing an opinion as to whether such votes should or should not be excluded, but stating the fact that there had never been a canvass of those votes by any person authorized to canvass them, and submitting the question whether the vote of that State should be counted or not. The two Houses, acting separately, each House for itself, decided that they should be excluded.

Now, let me ask this Commission whether it will to-day decide that Congress violated its constitutional duty or usurped power in holding that the vote should not be counted four years ago. That the two Houses went back of the certificate is certain. That they went back and condemned the vote on account of infirmities in the election is certain. If they could do so because the votes had not been canvassed, can they not because they had been falsely canvassed? If they could do it for neglect, can it not be done for fraud? And will this tribunal here and now declare that the action of both Houses of Congress in excluding that vote was an outrage upon the people of Louisiana? That must be the conclusion, if you are to hold that you cannot go back of the governor's certificate. The two Houses did go back of it; and they have clothed you with all the power that they then possessed or now possess or ever will possess under the present Constitution.

Mr. Commissioner THURMAN. I understand you to say that the provision of the revised statutes is precisely the same as that of the act of 1868.

Mr. CARPENTER. Identically; so that the act of 1868, which is clearly repealed by the election-law of 1870, if that is in force, was continued by virtue of re-enactment in the revision. If the revision is to be treated as an act passed on the day when it took effect, it repealed the act of March 16, 1870.

Mr. Commissioner BRADLEY. When the revision was made there was no other statute but the act of 1868 in force, and the revisers merely took that statute and put it into the revision.

Mr. CARPENTER. Certainly; it is copied word for word.

It is clear that if the election-law of March 16, 1870, survived the effect of the revised statutes, April 1, 1870, then the act of 1868 was repealed, and there was no law in force in that State at the last election directing the manner of appointing presidential electors.

It is very clear that the election-law of 1870 repealed the act of 1868.

The act of 1870, after providing a method of holding, conducting, and returning the general elections of the State, provided, in section 35, that the election for electors should be held on the day fixed by the act of Congress, and provided as follows: " and such elections shall be held and conducted, and returns made thereof, *in the manner and form prescribed by law for the general elections.*"

And the last section of the act provided as follows:

That all laws or parts of laws contrary to the provisions of this act, *and all laws relating to the same subject-matter,* are hereby repealed, and that this act shall take effect from and after its passage.

The special act of 1868 was, by implication, in part *at least,* repealed by the 35*th section* of this act, which made different provision for holding, conducting, and returning the election. But, even conceding that the portion of the act of 1868 which declared who should be voters and who should be voted for, might *have stood with* the 35th section of this act, and therefore not have been repealed by this section, it is *impossible* to hold that *any part* of the act of 1868 escaped the effect of the repealing clause of this act of 1870, because it is evident that the 35th section of the act of 1870 and the act of 1868 were "*laws relating to the same subject-matter.*"

About all that I am willing to assert positively in regard to the act of 1868, is, that it either was or it was not in force at the last election. If it was the whole electoral vote must be excluded, as it was four years ago, because there has been no canvass of the votes, and no electors duly appointed. If it was not in force, then there was no law of the State directing the manner in which electors should be appointed, and the whole college must go down for that reason. Because it is evident that if a State has omitted through its legislature to provide the manner in which electors shall be appointed, or, having made such provision, repeals it and makes no other, no constitutional appointment can be made by such State.

And if this were otherwise, still the two votes given by the two persons elected by the electoral college to fill the supposed vacancies must be excluded, because there was no law of the State authorizing the filling of a vacancy otherwise than by a popular election.

Is the order of the court to proceed till nine o'clock inflexible, unchangeable, for health or sickness, or anything else?

The PRESIDENT. There is no qualification.

Mr. CARPENTER. I am really unable by this candle-light to read my brief and refer to these statutes.

The PRESIDENT. There was no qualification made in the private consultation. I was instructed to make the announcement which I did make, and I have no authority to qualify it.

Mr. CARPENTER. Have I authority to ask the court to indulge me till to-morrow morning?

The PRESIDENT. Certainly you have authority to ask them, and I will submit it to the Commission.

Mr. CARPENTER. I make that request.

The PRESIDENT. What is the request?

Mr. CARPENTER. That I be excused until to-morrow morning. It is now half past six o'clock.

Mr. Commissioner MILLER. Mr. Carpenter, how much time do you propose to take? You have spoken an hour and ten minutes.

Mr. CARPENTER. I meant to go up to two hours.

Mr. Commissioner MILLER. Cannot some other gentleman go on? We are ready to sit here.

The PRESIDENT. I will submit the question to the Commission. Mr. Carpenter asks that he be excused until to-morrow morning, which, in effect, is an adjournment. Are you ready for the question?

Mr. Commissioner EDMUNDS. That is, that the proceedings be suspended, if I correctly understand.

The PRESIDENT. That proceedings be suspended until to-morrow morning.

Mr. Commissioner FIELD. Mr. Carpenter, how early are you willing to come in the morning? because we may perhaps make up in the morning the time now lost.

Mr. CARPENTER. Any time after six o'clock.

The PRESIDENT. Shall the proceedings be suspended until the opening of the session to-morrow morning? [Putting the question.]

Mr. Commissioner EDMUNDS. I call for the yeas and nays.

Mr. Commissioner PAYNE. I move that the Commission adjourn until ten o'clock to-morrow morning.

The PRESIDENT. I doubt whether I ought to put that; this is in the midst of a vote.

Mr. Commissioner STRONG. I should like to inquire, Mr. Carpenter, whether you are understood as saying you are sick?

Mr. CARPENTER. I am sick, and sick from this smoke. I could sit here for several nights and not be sick; but speaking here and inhaling the smoke of these candles really makes me ill.

The PRESIDENT. The question is whether the proceedings shall be suspended until to-morrow morning at the opening of the session, upon which the yeas and nays are called for.

Mr. Commissioner HOAR. Has any hour been named?

Mr. Commissioner ABBOTT. I would suggest ten o'clock.

Other MEMBERS. Ten o'clock.

The PRESIDENT. Ten o'clock is suggested. It is moved that proceedings be suspended until ten o'clock to-morrow.

The yeas and nays being called, the result was as follows:

Those voting in the affirmative were Messrs. Abbott, Bayard, Bradley, Clifford, Field, Hunton, Payne, and Thurman—8.

Those voting in the negative were Messrs. Edmunds, Frelinghuysen, Hoar, Miller, and Strong—5.

The Commission thereupon (at six o'clock and thirty-five minutes p. m.) adjourned until to-morrow at ten o'clock a. m.

WEDNESDAY, FEBRUARY 14, 1877.

The Commission met at 10 o'clock a. m., pursuant to adjournment, all the members being present.

The respective counsel appearing in the Louisiana case were also present.

The Journal of yesterday was read and approved.

The PRESIDENT. Proceed with your argument, Mr. Carpenter.

Mr. CARPENTER. May it please your honors, before resuming my argument, I desire to make my grateful acknowledgment to the Commission for their kindness in excusing me last night. The currents of atmosphere in this chamber, like the currents of authority, proceed from the bench toward the bar with overwhelming force, and I presume your honors sitting against the wall were not aware of it; but the air in the chamber at this point was absolutely stifling, and it would have been impossible for me to stand on my feet twenty minutes more.

Recurring for a moment to the question put me by Senator EDMUNDS in that part of my argument in which I attempted to show that electors were Federal and not State officers, as to whether they were commissioned by the President, the Constitution provides that the President "shall nominate, and, by and with the advice and consent of the Senate, shall appoint embassadors, other public ministers, and consuls, judges of the Supreme Court, and all other officers of the United States, whose appointments are not herein otherwise provided for, and which shall be established by law; but the Congress may by law vest the appointment of such inferior officers, as they think proper, in the President alone, in the courts of law, or in the heads of Departments."

The construction put upon this provision has always been that those officers who were appointed by the President must be commissioned by him; those officers appointed by the heads of Departments are commissioned by such heads of Departments. For instance, all the postmasters after the first grade, which are not required to be confirmed by the Senate, are commissioned by the Postmaster-General. So all the officers of internal revenue are appointed by the Secretary of the Treasury and commissioned by him. The appointment of electors is to be by the State, and they are not confirmed by the Senate; therefore they are not commissioned by the President. Senators are not commissioned by the President; and although Senators are not civil officers within that clause of the Constitution relating to impeachment, yet in a broader sense, distributing offices between the Government of the United States and the State, nobody would claim that a Senator was a State officer; he is an officer of the United States; he is a Senator of the United States, not a Senator of the State from which he is elected. He is elected to fill an office created by the Constitution of the United States, and he is a Senator of the United States, and not of the State which elects him.

Mr. Commissioner EDMUNDS. But is the true meaning of the clause that the President shall commission all the officers of the United States, that he shall commission all officers of the United States who are appointed by him?

Mr. CARPENTER. Certainly; and that has been the uniform practice of the Government. Nobody would deny that officers under the Internal Revenue Department are officers of the United States. They have been indicted as such, and are in the States-prison as such to-day, any number of them, under statutes punishing officers of the United States; and yet they are not commissioned by the President, but by the Secretary of the Treasury.

Mr. Commissioner GARFIELD. Mr. Carpenter, are there not two grades, one called officers proper and the other inferior officers? The President commissions all officers; but the heads of Departments or courts may appoint inferior officers.

Mr. CARPENTER. There is no such distinction in the Constitution whatever.

Mr. Commissioner GARFIELD. I think you will find the language is that such inferior officers as Congress may direct may be appointed by the heads of Departments or by the courts.

Mr. CARPENTER. I see the point now, which I did not before, because I did not distinctly hear the inquiry. The question is not whether the man is an inferior or a superior officer; the question is whether he is an officer of the United States; and the clause which requires the President to commission is that he shall " commission all officers of the United States." An inferior officer is an officer, is he not? He would not be an inferior officer if he was not an officer. That clause of the Constitution is that the President shall commission all officers, which would, of course, include the inferior as well as the superior. But the interpretation always put upon it has been that the President must commission those officers who are nominated by him and appointed by and with the advice and consent of the Senate, and none others.

Now I will proceed with the argument at the point where I stopped last night.

III.

Although we are entirely confident that the vote of Louisiana must be excluded for the reasons before given, yet should the court differ with us in regard to the objections before made, and hold that the act of 1872 repealed the act of 1868 and is itself a complete regulation of the subject of appointment of electors, still we submit that the rejection of over 10,000 Tilden votes by the returning-board under the provisions of the act of 1872 was wholly unauthorized by that act, and void. This brings us to consider the act of 1872 according to its own provisions in regard to the jurisdiction and powers of the returning-board. Section 3 of this act is as follows:

SEC. 3. *Be it further enacted, &c.*, That in such canvass and compilation the returning-officers shall observe the following order: They shall compile first the statements from all polls or voting-places at which there shall have been a fair, free, and peaceable registration and election. Whenever from any poll or voting-place there shall be received the statement of any supervisor or registration or commissioner of election *in form* as required by *section twenty-six* of this act, on affidavit of three or more citizens, of any riot, tumult, acts of violence, intimidation, armed disturbance, bribery, or corrupt influences, which prevented or tended to prevent a fair, free, and peaceable vote of all qualified electors entitled to vote at such poll or voting-place, such returning-officers shall not canvass, count, or compile the statements of votes from such poll or voting-place until the statements from all other polls or voting-places shall have been canvassed and compiled. The returning-officers shall then proceed to investigate the statements of riot, tumult, acts of violence, intimidation, armed disturbance, bribery, or corrupt influences at any such poll or voting-place; and if from the evidence of such statement they shall be convinced that such riot, tumult, acts of violence, intimidation, armed disturbance, bribery, or corrupt influences did not materially interfere with the purity and freedom of the election at such poll or voting-place, or did not prevent a sufficient number of qualified voters thereat from registering or voting to materially change the results of the election, then, and not otherwise, said returning-officers shall canvass and compile the vote of such poll or voting-place with those previously canvassed and compiled; but if said returning-officers shall not be fully satisfied thereof, it shall be their duty to examine further testimony in regard thereto, and to this end they shall have power to send for persons and papers. If, after such examination, the said returning-officers shall be convinced that said riot, tumult, acts of violence, intimidation, armed disturbance, bribery, or corrupt influences did materially interfere with the purity and freedom of the election at such poll or voting-place, or did prevent a sufficient number of the qualified electors thereat from registering and voting to materially change the result of the election, then the said returning-officers shall not canvass or compile the statement of the votes of such poll or voting-place, but shall exclude it from their returns: *Provided*, That any person interested in said election by reason of being a candidate for office shall be allowed a hearing before said returning-officers upon making application within the time allowed for the forwarding of the returns of said election.

Section 26 of this act is as follows:

SEC. 26. *Be it further enacted, &c.*, That in any parish, precinct, ward, city, or town, in which, during the time of registration or revision of registration, or on any day of election, there shall be any riot, tumult, acts of violence, intimidation, and disturbance, bribery or corrupt influences, at any place within said parish, or at or near any poll or voting-place, or place of registration or revision of registration, which riot, tumult, acts of violence, intimidation and disturbance, bribery or corrupt influences, shall prevent, or tend to prevent, a fair, free, peaceable, and full vote of all the qualified electors of said parish, precinct, ward, city, or town, it shall be the duty of the commissioners of election, if such riot, tumult, acts of violence, intimidation and disturbance, bribery or corrupt influences, occur on the day of election, or of the supervision of registration of the parish, if they occur during the time of registration or revision of registration, to make in duplicate and under oath a *clear and full statement of all the facts* relating thereto, and of the *effect* produced by such riot, tumult, acts of violence, intimidation and disturbance, bribery or corrupt influences, in preventing a fair, free, peaceable, and full registration or election, *and of the number* of qualified electors deterred by such riots, tumults, acts of violence, intimidation and disturbance, bribery or corrupt influences, from registering or voting, which statement shall also be corroborated under oath by three respectable citizens, qualified electors of the parish. When such statement is made by a commissioner of election or a supervisor of registration, he shall forward it in duplicate to the supervisor of registration of the parish, if in the city of New Orleans, to the secretary of state, one copy of which, if made to the supervisor of registration, shall be forwarded by him to the returning-officers provided for in section 2 of this act when he makes the returns of election in his parish. His copy of said statement shall be so annexed to his returns of elections, by paste, wax, or some adhesive substance, that the same can be kept together, and the other copy the supervisor of registration shall deliver to the clerk of the court of his parish for the use of the district attorney.

We contend that the action of the returning-board in excluding from their canvass over 10,000 votes for the Tilden electors was void *even if* *the provisions of this act repeal the act of* 1868, and were applicable to this election, for the following reasons:

1. The Constitution of the United States provides that "each *State* shall appoint, in such manner as the legislature thereof may direct, a number of electors, equal to the whole number," &c.

When the Constitution refers to a State, it refers, of course, to a State of the Union—a community organized under a State constitution republican in form. When the Constitution of the United States was adopted, the States were communities organized according to the American idea of republics. One of the most important and essential features of a republican government, according to the American idea, is a separation of legislative, judicial, and executive functions, and a distribution of powers among separate and distinct departments. One of the duties imposed upon the Federal Government is to guarantee to every State in this Union a republican form of government. And, of course, in admitting new States, it is the duty of Congress to see that such is the form of their government. As it is the duty of the United States to guarantee—that is, see to it that every State has a republican form of government—it follows that the government of every State, its form, structure, and powers, must constantly be in the Federal mind. And the provisions of the Constitution that each State shall appoint electors must be construed to mean that such State, according to the provisions of its own constitution, shall appoint electors. No State could delegate this power to another State or to a foreign prince or power, or to individuals, by name or classifying designation. It is only *the State*—the constitutional republican State—a State of the Union under its written republican form of government, proceeding according to its constitution, which constitution is constantly subject to Federal supervision, that can appoint an elector. In other words, when the Constitution provides that each State shall appoint electors, it means, of course, that it shall appoint them according to its own constitution and laws. And what its *laws* may be must be determined by its own constitution, which, on the admission of the State, has been approved by Congress; and which, in all its mutations by amendments, continues to enjoy the approval of Congress as a republican form of government. And when the Constitution of the United States declares that "each

State shall appoint, in such manner as the legislature thereof may direct, a number of electors," &c., it does in substance provide that the State shall prescribe a manner for such appointment in accordance with its own constitution. The Federal Government knows that any act of a State legislature in violation of its own constitution is void. In yet other words, the Constitution of the United States provides that the State, in providing for the manner of appointment of electors, shall proceed according to the provisions of its own constitution. Therefore, if it can be shown that the manner provided by the legislature for the appointment of electors by a State is in contravention of its own constitution, such appointment is void under the Constitution of the United States.

Now let us examine the constitution of Louisiana, to ascertain whether the provisions of the act of 1872—if the same are applicable to the election of electors—is in conformity to or in contravention of the State constitution.

The constitution of Louisiana provides, title 4, article 73, as follows:

ART. 73. The judicial power shall be vested in a supreme court, in district courts, in parish courts, and in justices of the peace.

And then, after defining the jurisdiction of the several courts above mentioned, article 94 provides as follows:

ART. 94. No judicial powers, except as committing magistrates in criminal cases, shall be conferred on any officers other than those mentioned in this title, except such as may be necessary in towns and cities; and the judicial powers of such officers shall not extend further than the cognizance of cases arising under the police regulations of towns and cities in the State. In any case, when such officers shall assume jurisdiction over other matters than those which may arise under police regulations or under their jurisdiction as committing magistrates, they shall be liable to an action of damages in favor of the party injured or his heirs, and a verdict in favor of the party injured shall *ipso facto* operate a vacation of the office of said officer.

Thus it will be seen that the constitution of the State not only by affirmative provisions vests the whole judicial power of the State in certain designated tribunals or magistrates, but, by negative provisions, forbids the exercise of any judicial power by others.

The sections quoted from the act of 1872 undoubtedly pretend to vest judicial powers in the returning-board. The highest penalty that can be inflicted upon an American citizen for *crime* is disfranchisement. The elective franchise is not merely a right to deposit a ballot in a ballot-box, but it is a right to have such ballot counted, estimated, and made effectual in determining the result of an election.

The fifteenth amendment of the Constitution provides that "the right of citizens of the United States *to vote* shall not be denied or abridged by the United States or by any State on account of race, color, or previous condition of servitude."

What would be said of the law of a Southern State which should provide that the vote of a colored citizen should be received and deposited in the ballot-box, but that it should not be canvassed or returned? Manifestly, such provision would be in contravention of this amendment. Hence it follows that a provision of law which authorizes a canvassing-board to exclude from its return any votes legally cast is a disfranchisement of the voters casting such votes. This infliction can only be visited upon the voters by an exercise of judicial power. Consequently, any statute which authorizes the returning-board to exclude such votes authorized such board to exercise judicial power, and is void under the quoted provisions of the State constitution.

Again, it is contrary to the first principles of natural justice that one man should be punished for crimes committed by another. By the provisions above quoted from this act it is provided in effect that the votes cast by a thousand honest men in a certain parish may be excluded from the canvass in consequence of violence, intimidation, or bribery committed by a thousand other men. A law which should provide that any voter who had been guilty of violence, intimidation, or bribery in an election should on conviction thereof be forever disfranchised vould' be constitutional. But before such disfranchisement can be visited upon any voter he must be tried and convicted, according to the forms of law, in a tribunal possessing judicial power to try for the crime and declare the punishment. But by this act the full and extreme effect of judicial condemnation—that is, disfranchisement—may in effect be inflicted by a returning-board before whom the voter is not summoned to appear, has no hearing, but is condemned without appearance or hearing. A law which provides for such consequences in suc h case is not only in opposition to the constitution of Louisiana, anti-republican, opposed to natural justice, but it is too outrageous and abominable to be tolerated in any civilized country.

2. But even conceding the constitutionality of the sections above quoted from the act of 1872, they do not pretend to confer this extraordinary power upon the returning-board except when a case is made under the twenty-sixth section of the act; that is when, accompanying the return from the precinct, there is a statement made showing *the facts* relating to the alleged " riot, tumult, acts of violence, intimidation and disturbance, bribery or corrupt influences, and the *effect* produced thereby in preventing a fair, free, and peaceable and full election, and *of the number* of qualified electors deterred thereby ; said statement to be corroborated by three qualified electors of the parish."

It is well settled that whenever a *judicial court* exercises a special and statutory power outside of and apart from its general jurisdiction, it must appear, in order to sustain its jurisdiction, that it was acting in a case clearly within the statute and that it strictly pursued the statute.

In Thatcher *vs.* Powell, 6 Wheaton, 119, the court, by Marshall, C. J., says :

> In summary proceedings, when a *court* exercises an extraordinary power under a special statute prescribing its course, we think that course ought to be *exactly* observed, and those facts especially which give jurisdiction ought to appear, in order to show that its proceedings are *coram judice*. Without this act of assembly the order for sale would have been totally void. This act gives the power only on a report to be made by the sheriff. This report gives the court jurisdiction, and without it the court is as powerless as if the act had never passed.

It is too well settled to require citation of authorities in its support, that when a judicial court is proceeding under statutory provisions apart from the common law, or when a special tribunal or magistrate is exercising a special statutory jurisdiction, it must appear that the case was strictly within the statutory provision, and that the course pursued was exactly in conformity with the statute conferring the authority :

> Justices' courts, not proceeding according to the course of common law, are confined strictly to the authority given them ; they can take nothing by implication but must show the power *expressly given them in every instance.*" 3 Burr, 1366 ; 3 Term Rep., 444 ; Str., 1256 ; 2 Ld. Raym., 1144 ; Salk., 406 ; Jones *vs.* Reed, 1 Johns. Cas., 20 ; Wells *vs.* Newkirk, 1 Johns. Cas., 228 ; Powers *vs.* People, 4 Johns. Cas., 292 ; Bloom *vs.* Burdick, 1 Hill, 330 ; Adkins *vs.* Brewer, 3 Cowen, 206.

In Walker *vs.* Turner, 9 Wheaton, 541, it was held that when a magistrate was pursuing special authority, it was " essential to the validity of his judgment and of the proceedings under it that the record should show that he acted upon a case which the law submitted to his jurisdiction."

Now it is submitted, and we offer to prove, that not in a single case in which the returning-board excluded the vote of a parish was the foundation laid for such exercise of its authority.

To show this, let us refer to the machinery of elections in that State.

The method of holding the elections and making returns according to law is as follows:

The polling-place is presided over by three commissioners of election, appointed by the supervisor of registration for the parish, who is appointed by the governor. After the balloting is concluded, the commissioners count the ballots, make two statements of the result, and deliver one statement, together with the ballot-box containing all the ballots, to the clerk of the district court of the parish, and the other statement to the supervisor of registration, together with the tally-sheets, list of voters, &c. The supervisor for the parish is required, *within twenty-four hours* after the receipt of all the statements and papers from the different polling-places, to consolidate such returns or statements, to be certified as correct by the clerk of the district court, and forward the same, with the originals received by him, to the State returning-board; such statement and papers " to be inclosed in an envelope of strong paper or cloth, securely sealed, and forwarded by mail."

Section 43 makes it the duty of the supervisor to forward with his statement " a copy of any statement as to violence or disturbance, bribery or corruption, or other offenses specified in section 26 of this act, if any there be, together with all memoranda and tally-lists used in making the count and statement of the votes."

Section 26 provides that the supervisors' copy of such statement " shall be so annexed to his returns of elections by paste, wax, or some adhesive substance, that the same can be kept together, and the other copy the supervisor of registration shall deliver to the clerk of the court of his parish for the use of the district attorney."

Section 26 also provides what the statement in relation to riots, intimidations, &c., shall be; that it shall be made in duplicate and under oath; and that it shall be—

(1) "A clear and full statement of *all the facts* relating thereto;

(2) "And *of the effect* produced by such riot, tumult, acts of violence, intimidation, and disturbance, bribery or corrupt influences in preventing a fair, free, peaceable, and full registration or election;

(3) "And of the number of qualified electors deterred by such riots, tumult, &c., from registering or voting;

(4) " Which statement shall also be corroborated under oath by three respectable citizens, qualified electors of the parish." And this section 26 also provides that the supervisor shall forward this statement with his return.

The only authority pretended to be conferred by the act of 1872 upon the returning-board to exclude any return or statement of votes which comes within their power to canvass is in section 3 of the act, and is as follows:

Whenever, from any poll or voting-place, there shall be received the statement of any supervisor of registration or commissioner of election, in form as required by section 26 of this act, on affidavit of three or more citizens, of any riot, tumult, acts of violence, intimidation, armed disturbance, bribery, or corrupt influences which prevented, or tended to prevent, a fair, free, and peaceable vote of all qualified electors entitled to vote at such poll or voting-place, such returning-officers shall not canvass, count, or compile the statements of votes from such poll or voting-place until the statements from all other polls or voting-places shall have been canvassed and compiled. The returning-officers shall then proceed to investigate the statements of riot, tumult, acts of violence, intimidation, armed disturbance, bribery, or corrupt influences at any such poll or voting-place; and if from the evidence of such statement they shall be convinced that such riot, tumult, acts of violence, intimidation, armed disturbance, bribery, or corrupt influences did not materially interfere with the purity and freedom of the election at such poll or voting-place, or did not prevent a sufficient number of qualified voters thereat from registering or voting to materially change the results of the election, then, and not otherwise, said returning-officers shall canvass and compile the vote of such poll or voting-place with those previously canvassed and compiled; but if said returning-officers shall not be fully satisfied thereof, it shall be their duty to examine further testimony in regard thereto, and to this end they shall have power to send for persons and papers. If after such examination the said returning-officers shall be convinced that such riot, tumult, acts of violence, intimidation, armed disturbance, bribery, or corrupt influences did materially interfere with the purity and freedom of the election at such poll or voting-place, or did prevent a sufficient number of the qualified electors thereat from registering and voting to materially change the result of the election, then the said returning-officers shall not canvass or compile the statement of the votes of such poll or voting-place, but shall exclude it from their returns: *Provided,* That any person interested in said election by reason of being a candidate for office shall be allowed a hearing before said returning-officers upon making application within the time allowed for the forwarding of the returns of said election.

Thus it will be seen that the jurisdiction of the returning-board to pass upon this subject at all is made to depend upon the jurisdictional fact that the return which the board receives from the parish supervisor is not only accompanied with but attached to the statement provided for in the twenty-sixth section of the act in regard to riots, intimidation, &c. If such return is not accompanied by such statement, supported by the affidavit of three electors, in regard to riots, &c., the returning-board is not authorized even by this act to examine at all into the subject, much less exclude any votes. And the principle of law, universally recognized, that a statutory tribunal, as distinguished from a judicial court of general jurisdiction, can only act upon a case clearly within its jurisdiction, and must strictly pursue the methods directed by the statute in exercising such jurisdiction, applies in its full force to the returning-board acting under this act of 1872.

If we are right in this position, it is conclusive against the validity of the action of the returning-board in excluding over 10,000 votes given for the Tilden electors; because the foundation for the exercise of this power by the returning-board was not established in regard to a single parish the votes of which were excluded by the board. And we are supported upon this point by two very high authorities, sitting members of this Commission.

I refer you to the discussion in the Senate on the resolution to admit Mr. Pinchback to a seat in that body from Louisiana; especially to the very able speeches of the Senator from Vermont, [Mr. Edmunds,] where precisely the doctrine I am claiming here is enforced with that clearness and eloquence of which he is master and I only an humble and hopeless imitator. I refer you to the fountain of this doctrine. I refer you to his speeches upon it, which make it as clear as the sun at noonday.

Again, I refer you to the reports of committees on the condition of the South, second session of the Forty-third Congress, pages 21 to 29, a report signed by Hon. George F. Hoar, Hon. W. A. Wheeler, a candidate for Vice-President at the last election, and Hon. William P. Frye, the distinguished Representative from the State of Maine. From this very able report I will read a few pertinent extracts.

Speaking of affairs in Louisiana, after quoting sections 3 and 26 from the act of 1872, which I have read, they say:

Upon this statute we are all clear'y of opinion that the returning-board had no right to do anything except to canvass and compile the returns which were lawfully made to them by the local officers, except in cases where they were accompanied by the certificates of the supervisor or commissioner provided in the third section. In such cases, the last sentence of that section shows that it was expected that they would ordinarily exercise the grave and delicate duty of investigating charges of riot, tumult, bribery, or corruption on a hearing of the parties interested in the office. It never could have been meant that this board, of its own notion, sitting in New Orleans, at a distance from the place of voting, and without notice, could decide the right of persons claiming to be elected.

The board took a different view of its powers, and proceeded to throw out the votes from many polls where they found intimidation and violence to have existed. The result was to defeat persons whom on the returns they should have declared elected, and to elect persons who should not have been declared elected.

Now let us see for a moment what is that statement provided for by the twenty-sixth section which must come up within twenty-four hours, embalmed in wax or paste or some other adhesive substance, to the returning-board. The third section says that when they receive a statement in the form prescribed by the twenty-sixth section they may proceed. Now let us turn to the twenty-sixth section and see what must be shown. That must be—

A clear and full statement of all the facts relating thereto—

That is, relating to the riot, tumult, &c.—

and of the effect produced by such riot, tumult, acts of violence, intimidation and disturbance, bribery, or corrupt influences in preventing a fair, free, peaceable, and full registration or election, and of the number of qualified electors deterred by such riots, tumult, &c., from registering or voting; which statement shall also be corroborated under oath by three respectable citizens, qualified electors of the parish.

We will show this Commission that not a single parish sent up any such statement with its return, verified by the affidavit of three persons. In other words, we will show affirmatively that this statutory tribunal had no jurisdiction to exclude a vote, but that, in violation of the very statute they were pretending to proceed under, they excluded 10,000 votes given for the Tilden electors. This we are prepared to show, and show by record testimony. And this brings the present case within the opinion of the committee just read.

But our opponents say, in substance, "Yes; that is all true." My honorable friend, Judge Howe, who opened this case on the other side, did not pretend that there had not been frauds. He said there had, but he said there had been blood also. In other words, one crime was to be offset by another. If the plaintiff's witnesses commit perjury, the defendant is authorized to have his witnesses commit perjury! That is the argument. Now let me show how this was condemned by the report of the committee from which I have just read:

The returning-board claims that in this proceeding they acted under an honest belief that they were right in their construction of the law, and that they were giving effect to the true will of a majority of the people of Louisiana, and that in their construction they followed the precedent set by the democratic or fusion returning-board of 1872. We believe they did follow such a precedent. We have no doubt that they believed they were defending the people of Louisiana against a fraud on their constitutional rights. But there is no more dangerous form of self-delusion than that which induces men in high places of public trust to violate law to redress or prevent what they deem public wrongs.

We are not prepared to declare without further examination how many persons obtained a *prima facie* title to seats in the legislature through this wrongful action. In some of the cases there were defects either of form or substance in the returns themselves, which, the board claimed, required their rejection without regard to the evidence of intimidation.

But the method adopted to set right this wrong was totally objectionable.

Then they proceed to consider why it was objectionable, giving the reasons among others which I have now given, and they proceed:

We do not overlook the causes which tend to excite deep feelings of discontent in the white native population of Louisiana. There has been great maladministration; public funds have been wasted, public credit impaired, and taxation is heavy. These facts combine with the general prostration of business through the country, and with the diversion of business from New Orleans by reason of the construction of railroads northerly from Texas, to create gloom and discontent.

It is further said—

Passing on—

that this is a question which concerns the people of Louisiana alone, and that they should be left to fight out the question among themselves. But this is an erroneous view, both of the rights and duties of the people of the United States under the Constitution. They have an interest in the question whether Senators and Representatives for Louisiana, thrust into their seats by illegal means, shall sit in Congress to make laws for them, and whether electors, gaining their office in like manner, shall turn the scale in the choice of a President of the United States. The President and Congress are bound to recognize and, if need be, to support the true government of Louisiana against all usurpers; and the American people will abandon their rights and flinch from the performance of their duties when they leave these questions to be settled either by the mob or the assassin.

Again:

The American people are now brought face to face with this condition of things. In the State of Louisiana there is a governor in office—

" In office." A man who gets into land or office by forcible entry and detainer is nevertheless in.

In the State of Louisiana there is a governor in office who owes his seat to the interference of the national power, which has recognized his title to his office, not by reason of any ascertainment of the facts by legal process, but has based its action solely on the illegal order of a judge. In the same State there is a legislature one branch of which derives its authority partly from the same order, the other being organized by a majority who have been established in power by another interference of the National Government, and which majority derives its title, not from any legal ascertainment of the facts, but from the certificates of a returning-board which has misconceived and exceeded its legal authority. It is not strange that the republicans of Louisiana should delude themselves by any plausible views of laws which will enable them to occupy the places which they believe the will of a majority of the legal voters of the State, if free from violence and intimidation, would award to them. It is not strange that the democrats of Louisiana should believe the whole State government a usurpation, should give it no credit for its best acts, should seek to embarrass, and thwart, and resist it to the extent of their power, and should be unwilling to wait for the slow but sure operation of lawful remedies to cure whatever evil really belongs to it.

This report expresses the deliberate judgment of its signers: Mr. Hoar, a member of this commission; Mr. Wheeler, candidate for Vice-President, and Mr. Frye. Will not Mr. Wheeler be astonished if he shall find himself counted in as Vice-President in violation of the principles thus solemnly declared by him when he was a *disinterested* and impartial judge in the matter? Will not the American people think this is remarkable, especially if it shall be done by the casting vote of his colleague on the committee, [Mr. Hoar,] the author, I suppose, of the report from which I have read?

This report is clear and full authority in support of the proposition I am maintaining, that even under the election law of 1872 the returning-board had no authority to exclude votes, unless a case was made before them under the third and twenty-sixth sections, upon which their jurisdiction depends.

IV.

It only remains to apply these principles to the case before us.

This tribunal is required to report upon two questions:

1. How many and what persons were duly appointed electors in this State; and

2. Which are the electoral votes which ought to be counted.

Your finding will be like a special verdict, and after receiving your report, the two Houses may agree with you upon one proposition and disagree upon the other.

First. Were the Hayes electors *duly appointed ?* We contend they were not, for the following reasons:

1. If the act of 1868 was in force at the last election, then there has been no canvass of the votes according to its provisions, and there is no power, under that act, for the canvassers to exclude or reject votes under any circumstances or for any reason. Therefore, on the facts offered to be established by evidence, it is certain that the Hayes electors were defeated by about 8,000 majority.

2. If the act of 1868 was not in force, there was no law of that State in force at the last election directing the manner in which electors should be appointed ; therefore none could be appointed.

3. If the Commission shall be of opinion that the act of 1868 was not in force, then it is agreed that the act of 1872 is the only election-law of that State which was in force at the last election. And if you shall be of opinion that this act did cover the election of electors, which we deny, yet the action of the returning-board in excluding over 10,000 votes given against the Hayes electors was *coram non judice* and absolutely void ; and therefore the Hayes electors were not *duly appointed.*

It will be claimed that the certificate of Governor Kellogg is conclusive. But it is certain that it is not conclusive as to his own appointment, therefore the Commission must go back of that certificate at least as to his appointment.

It is well settled by the English cases that the king, although he is the fountain of honor and of office, cannot himself exercise an office to which he might make an appointment. An appointment is like any other grant, and the same person cannot be grantor and grantee. Therefore an officer possessing the power of appointment cannot appoint himself, and a pretended appointment is void in such case. (7 Bacon Abr., title "Offices and officers," p. 281; State *vs.* Hoyt, 2 Oregon, 246 ; Peo. *vs.* Thomas, 33 Barb. N. Y., 287.)

A sheriff cannot *certify* an excuse for his neglect, but must make his affidavit. (Rex *vs.* Bolton, Anstruther, 79.)

This rests upon the general principle of law that no officer can exercise the functions of his office for his individual benefit. And whenever a sheriff is compelled to rely upon his own return, made upon process issued in a cause between *other* parties, such return is only *prima facie* evidence. (2 Greenleaf's Ev., sec. 585.)

A distinction between the power of an officer to appoint himself to another office and his power to issue a certificate which is conclusive evidence of such appointment is too nice to be substantial. Therefore to show that Kellogg was duly appointed elector, resort must be had to other evidence of the fact. At least resort *may* be had to other evidence to show that he was *not* duly appointed. The certificate of the governor is the only evidence prescribed by act of Congress, and when, as in this instance, it is unavailing, inquiry may be made into the fact so certified. What is that fact ? Why, that Kellogg was duly appointed an elector. It is not contended by our opponents there is any law authorizing the appointment except by general election. Therefore, if the act of 1872 be held to cover this election, the question is whether Kellogg was elected at that election. This is the fact to be established, and the fact that may be controverted. This brings us to consider what evidence, back of the governor's certificate, must be resorted to to establish or controvert this fact.

It will be said that the return of the canvassing or returning board is the next evidence to be considered, and is conclusive.

I have already shown that the action of this board is void in rejecting votes, unless a case was made in each instance according to section 26 of the election-law of 1872, and that no such case was made in regard to any parish where the vote was excluded.

It would not be pretended that a decision of the Supreme Court of the United States would be of any avail unless accompanied by and attached to the complete record of the cause in which such decision was made. Without such full authenticated record it would not appear that the court had jurisdiction. It would be monstrous to hold that stronger presumption exists in favor of a statutory tribunal than in relation to the Supreme Court of the United States. And it is submitted that, to make the certificate of the returning-board evidence at all, it must be shown that returns were made by the supervisors of registration, what these returns were, and, if the board rejected any such returns, that a case was made giving the board jurisdiction in that behalf.

We submit *at least* that it may be shown affirmatively that such returning-board did not give effect to the votes as cast, and that no case was shown before them giving them jurisdiction to reject votes.

It will be borne in mind that this is not a case of accident, inadvertence, mistake, or error on the part of the returning-board, but a case of intentional, willful malfeasance—a positive, actual fraud, committed in pursuance of a conspiracy formed before the election was held. The fathers of the common law, the elementary writers, and the adjudicated cases, declare that " fraud vitiates everything." By this is meant that everything—the most solemn judgment, temporal or ecclesiastical— is void, of which fraud is an element. Therefore, when the governor's certificate is found unavailing to conclude inquiry as to his own appointment, and the certificate of the returning-board is relied upon, we meet that with the offer to prove that it is not only false in fact, but that it was made fraudulently and corruptly ; that it is not the result of error merely, but the fruit of rank fraud. The doctrine now contended for should be expressed thus : "*Fraud* triumphs over everything, and especially it paralyzes every instrumentality designed for its correction."

I submit with entire confidence that, at the very least, you must hold that Kellogg's certificate of his own appointment is only *prima facie* evidence of it and may be controverted ; and that when, to establish his due appointment, resort is had to the certificate of the returning-board, we may impeach it for fraud and show it to be false in fact.

Again, and apart from our offer to impeach it for fraud, upon what ground can it be maintained that the certificate of the returning-board is conclusive and cannot be contradicted ? Section 2 of the election-law of 1872, under which this certificate is made and promulgated, provides :

The return of the election thus made and promulgated shall be *prima facie* evidence in all courts of justice and before all civil officers, until set aside after contest, according to law, of the right of any person named therein to hold and exercise the office to which he shall by such return be declared elected.

What is *prima facie* evidence ? It is that which on its face is sufficient to establish a fact, but which may be controverted. And when the law under which this certificate is made declares that it shall be *prima facie* evidence in all courts of justice and before all civil officers, it does in effect declare that *it may be contradicted in all courts of justice and before all civil officers.*

Again, were Levissee and Brewster *duly* appointed? The act of Congress requires that all presidential electors shall be appointed on a certain day—last year, the 7th day of November. It is conceded that on that day both Levissee and Brewster were holding offices of *trust and profit* under the Government of the United States. The Constitution of the United States, article 2, section 1, is as follows:

> Each *State shall appoint, in such manner as the legislature thereof may direct,* a number of electors equal to the whole number of Senators and Representatives to which the State may be entitled in the Congress; *but no Senator or Representative, or person holding an office of trust or profit under the United States, shall be appointed an elector.*

This provision of the Constitution applied to the case in hand is this: The State of Louisiana shall appoint eight electors; but neither Levissee nor Brewster shall be appointed. This does not fix the qualification of electors; but it is an inhibition upon the State in the exercise of its power to appoint. The Constitution, article 1, section 3, declares:

> No person *shall be* a Senator who shall not have attained to the age of thirty years.

He may be *elected* before he attains to that age and take his seat, that is, become a Senator, afterward. But if the Constitution had provided that no person should be *elected* before he attained to that age, would any one contend that the election of one under that age could be legal and constitutional?

It is too plain to be questioned that the Constitution, speaking to Louisiana on the 7th day of November last, forbade the State to appoint Levissee or Brewster. Is it possible, then, that that State could on that day *duly* appoint both of them? *Duly* means legally, properly, regularly. Can *that* be done legally, properly, and regularly which the Constitution declares shall not be done at all? It has become an axiom in our constitutional jurisprudence that what the Constitution says shall not be done cannot, in a legal sense, be done. An attempt to do it is void, an absolute nullity, accomplishing nothing. It was at one time contended that an act of Congress in conflict with the Constitution was *prima facie* valid, a *de facto* law, valid as to persons acting under it, until set aside by judicial determination. But that sophism was instantly rejected. Such a law is *ab initio* and always absolutely void, mere blank paper in the statute-book. It follows that an attempt to appoint a person an elector of whom the Constitution declares that he shall not be appointed, is simply and absolutely *void; not voidable,* but *void.*

In the counting of presidential votes in 1837 the Houses raised a joint committee to consider the subject. On the part of the Senate Henry Clay, Silas Wright, and Felix Grundy, three great names in our history, were appointed. The report, in which they concurred, says:

> The committee are of opinion that the second section of the second article of the Constitution, which declares that "no Senator or Representative, or person holding an office of trust or profit under the United States shall be appointed an elector," ought to be carried in its whole spirit into rigid execution. * * * This provision of the Constitution, it is believed, *excludes* and disqualifies deputy postmasters from the *appointment* of electors; and the disqualification relates to the *time of the appointment,* and that a resignation of the office of deputy postmaster after his appointment as elector, *would not entitle him to vote as elector, under the Constitution.*

Second. Having shown, as I think, that no electors have been duly appointed in Louisiana, and, at all events, that Levissee and Brewster were not duly appointed, I come now to the second question: whether, inasmuch as these persons have in fact acted, they are to be regarded as *de facto* electors, and their votes are to be counted as the electoral vote of the State.

The ground upon which a *de facto* officer stands is that his election or appointment, though *voidable*, is not *void*. But I have attempted to show that the pretended appointment of Levissee and Brewster was in the technical sense absolutely *void*. In other words, as to them there was a failure to elect. The case was as though the voters had cast ballots with six names instead of eight, thereby appointing six instead of eight electors for the State.

The act of Congress recognizes and provides for two cases : (see Rev. Stats., sections 133 and 134.)

SEC. 133. Each State may, *by law*, provide for the filling of any vacancies which may occur in its college of electors when such college meets to give its electoral vote.

SEC. 134. Whenever any State has held an election for the purpose of choosing electors, *and has failed to make a choice* on the day prescribed by law, the electors may be appointed on a subsequent day, in such a manner as the legislature of such State may direct.

The State had by law made no provision for the case of failure to elect. Even conceding the act of 1868 to be in force it made no provision for such case, although it did provide for filling a vacancy occurring after a legal election. But upon the theory contended for by our opponents, that the act of 1872 was the only law in force at the last election, then the only provision for filling *even* a vacancy was that it should be filled by a popular election. So that the election of Levissee and Brewster by the electoral college was unauthorized and void, and their votes should be rejected.

Again, it is well settled that the principle that the acts of *de facto* public officers are valid in regard to the public and third persons, is confined to those who hold office under some color of election or appointment and are in the exercise of continuous official acts, being recognized by the public as filling the office to which they pretend. (See Vaccari *vs.* Maxwell, 3 Blackford, 368.) It is manifest that electors cannot be considered as *de facto* officers within this definition, nor within any definition ever laid down by the courts upon the subject.

V.

But again this Commission is required by the act of Congress to—

Decide whether any and what votes from such State are the votes provided for by the Constitution of the United States.

Now, conceding that this Commission cannot inquire into the regularity of the election under the constitution and laws of the State, nor redress the frauds committed by the returning-board, and conceding that this Commission is estopped by the certificates of State officials as to what persons received the greatest number of votes for electors, still it is submitted that whether the persons who were duly elected, so far as votes were concerned, were authorized to act in the electoral college and cast votes for President and Vice-President, is a question to be settled, as to Levissee and Brewster, by the Constitution of the United States; and that every Federal tribunal, the judicial courts, and the two Houses of Congress are bound, in every act they perform, to give effect to the Federal Constitution.

It is clear that no person can vote for President and Vice-President who is not an elector of the State. The provision of the Constitution, article 2, section 1, is as follows :

Each *State shall appoint, in such manner as the legislature thereof may direct,* a number of electors equal to the whole number of Senators and Representatives to which the State may be entitled in the Congress; but no Senator or Representative, or person holding an office of trust or profit under the United States, *shall be appointed* an elector.

Every lawyer will concede that a person who is forbidden by the Constitution to be appointed an elector is equally forbidden by the Constitution to be an elector or to cast a vote for President or Vice-President. The provision of the Constitution that no person holding an office of trust or profit under the United States shall be *appointed* an elector strikes at the very root of the matter, because if he cannot be appointed he cannot be an elector, cannot vote for President or Vice-President. In other words, he violates the Constitution by acting and voting in the electoral college. Every vote cast by such person in the electoral college is a violation of the Constitution. Now, it is an axiom in all constitutional discussions that an act done or vote cast in violation of the Constitution is no act, no vote. How, then, can this commission decide that the votes for Mr. Hayes which were cast by Levissee and Brewster are votes provided for by the Constitution of the United States. Their appointment and, consequently their votes, the Constitution forbids; and to hold that their votes are the votes provided for by the Constitution is to hold the Constitution contemplates its own violation. The only decision this Commission can make consistent with the judicial decisions and the universally received and sanctioned canons of constitutional law is that the votes cast by these persons are no votes, and that they must be excluded from the count. The most deliberate, carefully-considered act of Congress, approved by the President, is absolutely void, no act, a blank in the statute-book, if it be forbidden by the Constitution. And it would be simply shocking and monstrous, and a fatal blow to the Constitution itself, to hold that the votes cast by two persons forbidden by the Constitution to vote at all are votes provided for by the Constitution. This is a question independent of the appointment *in fact* by the State; it relates to the action of the college itself, which college derives its power to act at all from the Federal Constitution. How, then, can it be maintained that an act performed by one of its members, which by the Constitution he is forbidden to perform, can be a constitutional act? Can it be pretended that, when a person is forbidden by the Constitution to cast a vote, nevertheless, if he violates the Constitution and does cast it, it is a vote provided for by the Constitution?

This is the case upon which we stand, and none of the facts are seriously controverted by our opponents. Senator Howe, in substance, admits the frauds we charge; but he says that though some streams in that State are muddy with fraud, other streams run blood. I loathe the sight of blood and the thought of it. I never have vindicated nor justified the outrages committed within this State, nor shall I ever. That there have been violations of law and outrages unnumbered is unquestionable. That there have been murders, maimings, and whippings cannot be denied. But are these things to be cured by inflicting upon the State an injury more injurious to our institutions than are these bloody outrages? They fall upon individuals; if our institutions are to be stabbed, the injury falls upon the nation. If justice is to be slaughtered in her own temple, if the laws are to be sacrificed by their sworn priests, if fraud is to be solemnized and sanctioned as an instrumentality for electing a President of the United States, then farewell to hope for free institutions and for our country.

One thing more. Without making any apology for the outrages that have undoubtedly been perpetrated in this State of Louisiana, let us look for a moment at the condition of affairs there—the condition described by Messrs. Hoar, Wheeler, and Frye, the committee from whose report I have quoted. And I ask, is it a method likely to produce good feeling in that State, to keep them under a government which cannot rest upon "ascertained facts," but which is based upon nothing but fraud and falsehood? I submit it is not. The injunction of the apostle is, "Be ye first pure, and then peaceable." There is no assurance that authorizes any one to expect peace who is not himself in the right. Peace, in an American State, with a government forced upon it by the villainy of four men; peace, under a government resting not upon "ascertained facts," but upon notorious falsehoods! No. Let no man hug such delusion to his bosom. Allegiance to a government and submission to its laws in this country can only be expected when that government is the choice of the people, the government of the people. So exercise your functions as to give back to that people the rights of which they have been defrauded, and you will do more to restore harmony and peace to its citizens than could be done by all the armies of the world.

Mr. TRUMBULL. Mr. President and gentlemen, this is the time when I suppose under the ruling of the Commission we shall be required to present our evidence, and we offer now——

The PRESIDENT. That was the suggestion from the bar, that after the close of the first argument you would offer some evidence.

Mr. TRUMBULL. We propose now to prove before the Commission that William P. Kellogg, who certifies as governor of the State of Louisiana to the appointment of electors of that State, which certificate is now before this Commission, is the same William P. Kellogg who by said certificate is certified to have been appointed under said election. In other words, Kellogg certifies to his own appointment as such elector. We offer that proof.

The PRESIDENT. Do you propose now to state all your offers of proof?

Mr. TRUMBULL. We did not propose to do so at once. We proposed to offer the proof. There may be some of it that the Commission might receive and others not. Our proposition now is to prove that one fact, unless there is some objection to it.

Mr. EVARTS. We object that it is not admissible.

Mr. TRUMBULL. If the Commission please, I suppose we are entitled to be heard upon that question.

The PRESIDENT. I feel constrained to take the advice of the Commission whether they will proceed upon your separate offers of proof or upon the whole together.

Mr. Commissioner STRONG. Mr. President, if the counsel would offer in writing all that they propose to prove, offer it as a whole, and also offer it in detail, it would very much simplify the labor of the Commission. The Commission could then, on consultation, determine whether the whole or whether any part was admissible. Otherwise we might be obliged to retire for consultation again and again.

Mr. TRUMBULL. Then would the argument on the introduction of testimony be limited to fifteen minutes? because there are various branches of it. We could hardly argue the offer of testimony in fifteen minutes.

Mr. Commissioner STRONG. If the offer were all made in that way, all that was proposed to be offered as a whole and also the various elements in detail, so that the Commission could then pass upon the whole or upon the various elements and determine what was and what was not admissible, for one I should be very much disposed to give all the time that was necessary for the discussion of its admissibility.

The PRESIDENT. I will submit the question to the Commission. Perhaps without sufficient reason as yet, I derived the impression that your offer would be made altogether, but of course in subdivisions.

Mr. TRUMBULL. If the Commission will allow me I am quite willing to follow the suggestion made by Mr. Justice Strong to offer the whole of our testimony at once, with the understanding that each part may be considered separately.

Mr. Commissioner STRONG. You offer it as a whole and in parts?

Mr. TRUMBULL. As a whole and in parts. I am entirely willing to follow that suggestion if it meets the views of the Commission, and then we shall be allowed a reasonable time.

The PRESIDENT. I think I may assume that that is the general understanding of the Commission. If not, some member will express his dissent.

Mr. Commissioner BRADLEY. Have you a printed copy of the offer you mean to make?

Mr. TRUMBULL. Yes, sir; partially so.

Mr. EVARTS. The only offer of evidence that has yet been made to the Commission is to prove that Mr. Kellogg who appears in the certificate opened by the President of the Senate to be governor and Mr. Kellogg, who appears to be elector are the same person. While we regard the admission of any evidence extrinsic to the certificates that were opened by the President of the Senate as inadmissible, we should not not in argument upon those certificates contend that they were not the same person.

The PRESIDENT. The counsel are now deliberating as to the form to be taken. I understand Judge Trumbull now to accept the suggestion of Mr. Justice Strong to make all the offers at the same time.

Mr. TRUMBULL. Yes, sir; and in parts.

The PRESIDENT. Separately and together. Proceed then to state the offer.

Mr. TRUMBULL. In presenting these offers of evidence, perhaps it would be well that we should have some understanding as to how much time will be permitted. I do not wish to take any unnecessary or unreasonable time in stating what we offer.

Mr. Commissioner EDMUNDS. How much time do you think it requires?

Mr. TRUMBULL. I cannot tell, because I have not prepared an argument on this particular branch of the subject. I shall have to read the offers and briefly state what each of them is. I do not know how long it will take.

Mr. Commissioner EDMUNDS. The reading, of course, will not be counted as part of your time.

The PRESIDENT. You may proceed.

Mr. TRUMBULL. I have stated the first proposition, and, as I understand, the fact is conceded, although it is objected that we have no right to introduce it in evidence.

Mr. EVARTS. My statement was that we should not contend, on the face of the certificates as opened by the President of the Senate, that Mr. Kellogg governor and Mr. Kellogg elector were not the same person. That is satisfactory, I suppose.

Mr. TRUMBULL. The second branch of the first offer which we make is to prove that said Kellogg was governor *de facto* of said State during all the months of November and December, A. D. 1876. That is in the same category, I suppose?

Mr. EVARTS. That is in the certificate.

Mr. TRUMBULL. On this point we refer to the constitution of Louisiana:

ART. 117. No person shall hold or exercise at the same time more than one office of trust or profit, except that of justice of the peace or notary public.

We offer to prove that said William P. Kellogg was not duly appointed one of the electors of said State in A. D. 1876, and that the certificate is untrue in fact.

To show this we offer to prove—

1. By certified copies of the *lists* made out, signed, and sworn to by the commissioners of election in each poll and voting-place in the State, and delivered by said commissioners to the clerk of the district court wherein said polls were established, except in the parish of Orleans, and in that parish delivered to the secretary of state, that at the election for electors in the State of Louisiana, on the 7th day of November last, the said William P. Kellogg received for elector 6,300 votes less than were at said election cast for each and every of the following-named persons, that is to say: John McEnery, R. C. Wickliffe, L. Saint Martin, E. P. Poché, A. De Blanc, W. A. Seay, R. G. Cobb, K. A. Cross. (Section 43, act 1872.)

That offer of testimony involves the merits, to some extent, of our case. Your honors will remember that by the law of Louisiana the elections are held by persons denominated " commissioners of election." They correspond with judges of election in most of the States. There are fifty-seven parishes in the State of Louisiana, and in each parish there are a number of polls or polling-places, usually from ten to thirty. There is for each parish in the State an officer known as a supervisor of registration. This supervisor of registration is appointed by the governor of the State and he appoints all the commissioners of election throughout the State. He appoints as many places for voting as he pleases, and these voting-places are presided over by the commissioners whom he appoints. The governor appoints fifty-six supervisors, one for each parish outside of Orleans, and each of these supervisors appoints all the commissioners of election, and the commissioners of election designate as many places for holding the election as they please and fix the points where the elections are to be held. We complain very seriously of this arrangement. You will observe that it places the entire machinery of the election in the hands of the governor, and it is in evidence here that these supervisors were all of one party. The commissioners of election are required by the law to be of different parties, but they were generally all of one party. They were all selected by the supervisor of registration.

The law further provides that this canvassing-board for the State, (called returning-officers,) which under the law is to consist of five persons to be elected by the senate and composed of different political parties, shall canvass the returns of the commissioners of election. They take an oath that they will compile and canvass the statements of votes made by the commissioners of election. That is their oath and that is the statute. In the second section, if you will refer to it, you will find that they are required to canvass and compile the statements of the votes sent by the commissioners of election. Those commissioners of election are required under the law to make out duplicate returns upon the close of the polls. One of these duplicates they send to the clerk of the parish. They also send the ballot-boxes to the clerk of the parish.

I will not stop to read it; but the law is very specific as to the duties of these commissioners of election, how they are to make up their returns, and what they are to do with the ballots. They are to make up their returns, you will observe, in duplicate, and one of these duplicates goes to the supervisor of registration of the parish, from which he makes up consolidated returns and sends them to this board of returning-officers for the State. Our offer in this instance is to prove by certified copies of the lists made up, signed, and sworn to by the commissioners of election at each poll and voting-place in the State, and delivered into the clerk's offices throughout the State, except the city of New Orleans, in what is known as Orleans Parish, where they are delivered to the secretary of state; so that there is in the State of Louisiana a perfect return from every voting-place in the State, made by the commissioners of election to this board of returning-officers, and there is a duplicate in the clerk's offices, the same that the board of returning-officers have before them. From that we say it will appear that the majority given to what are denominated here as the Tilden electors varied from six to nine thousand, speaking in round numbers. We offer now to show that to this tribunal by certified copies of these papers, that you may see what the fact is.

Then the question arises, what is this tribunal? That has been gone over by all the counsel who have spoken; but I trust you will pardon me for stating very briefly my view of what this tribunal is and what its duties are.

Mr. Commissioner STRONG. Before you proceed to that consideration, allow me to ask you a question.

Mr. TRUMBULL. Certainly.

Mr. Commissioner STRONG. The action of what is said to be the canvassing-board—that is, the canvassing-board created by the act of 1872—the result at which they arrived, is not before us, I think.

Mr. TRUMBULL. Yes, sir; we propose to present those results to you; that is one of our propositions.

Mr. Commissioner STRONG. Very well. Then I understand that that is one of your propositions.

Mr. TRUMBULL. That will be one of our propositions.

Mr. Commissioner STRONG. But thus far it is not before us.

Mr. TRUMBULL. Perhaps I shall be better understood, and the Commission will better understand the state of the case, if I anticipate a little, then, what we propose in that regard.

Mr. Commissioner STRONG. Give us all your offers first, and the argument afterward.

Mr. TRUMBULL. Shall I read the whole paper through?

Mr. Commissioner STRONG. I think you had better give us all your offers at once.

Mr. TRUMBULL. I have no objection to that, if it is agreeable to the Commission.

2. In connection with the certified copies of said lists we offer to prove that the returning-board, which pretended to canvass the said election under the act approved November 20, 1872, did not receive from any poll, voting-place, or parish in said State, nor have before them, any statement of any supervisor of registration or commissioner of election in form as required by section 26 of said act, on affidavit of three or more citizens, of any riot, tumult, acts of violence, intimidation, armed disturbance, bribery, or corrupt influences which prevented or tended

to prevent a fair, free, and peaceable vote of all qualified electors entitled to vote at such poll or voting-place.

3. We further offer to show that in many instances the supervisors of registration of the several parishes willfully and fraudulently omitted from their consolidated statement, returned by them to the State returning-board, the result and all mention of the votes given at certain polls or voting-places within their respective parishes, as shown to them by the returns and papers returned to said supervisors by the commissioners of election, as required by law; and that, in consequence of this omission, the said consolidated statements on their face omitted of majorities against the said Kellogg, and in favor of each and every the said McEnery, Wickliffe, St. Martin, Poché, De Blanc, Seay, Cobb, and Cross, amounting to 2,267; but that said supervisors of registration did, as by law required, return to the said returning-board, with their consolidated statements, the lists, papers, and returns received by them according to law from the commissioners of election at the several polls and voting-places omitted as aforesaid from said consolidated statements of said supervisors.

And that the said returning-board willfully and fraudulently neglected and refused to make any canvass of the majorities so omitted, or estimate them in any way in their pretended determination that the said Kellogg was duly elected an elector at the election aforesaid.

4. We offer to show that, by the consolidated statements returned to said returning-board by the supervisors of registration of the several parishes of the State of the result of the voting at the several polls or voting-places within their parishes respectively, it appeared that said Kellogg received at said election 3,459 less votes for elector than the said McEnery, Wickliffe, St. Martin, Poché, De Blanc, Seay, Cobb, and Cross, and each and every one of them.

5. We further offer to show that the said returning-board willfully and fraudulently estimated and counted as votes in favor of said Kellogg 234 votes which were not shown to have been given at any poll or voting-place in said State, either by any consolidated statement returned to said returning-board by any of the said supervisors, or by the statements, lists, tally-sheets, or returns made by any commissioners of election to any of said supervisors, or which were before said returning-board.

6. We offer to prove that the votes cast and given at said election on the 7th of November last for the election of electors, as shown by the return made by the commissioners of election from the several polls or voting-places in said State, have never been compiled or canvassed; and that the said returning-board never even pretended to compile or canvass the returns made by said commissioners of election, but that said returning-board only pretended to canvass the returns made by the said supervisor. (Act of 1872, section 43: "Supervisor must forward;" act of 1872, section 2: "Board must canvass.")

7. We offer to prove that the votes given for electors at the election of November 7 last at the several voting-places or polls in said State have never been opened by the governor of the said State in presence of the secretary of state, the attorney-general, and a district judge of the district in which the seat of government was established, nor in the presence of any of them; nor has the governor of said State ever, in presence as aforesaid, examined the returns of the commissioners of election for said election to ascertain therefrom, nor has he ever, in such presence, ascertained therefrom, the persons who were, or whether any

one was, duly elected electors or elector, at said election; nor has he ever pretended so to do. (Revised Statutes, section 2826.)

8. We further offer to prove that the said William P. Kellogg, governor as aforesaid, when he made, executed, and delivered the said certificate, by which he certified that himself and others had been duly appointed electors as aforesaid, well knew that said certificate was untrue in fact in that behalf, and that he, the said Kellogg, then well knew that he, the said Kellogg, had not received of the legal votes cast at the election of November 7, 1876, for electors, within five thousand of as many of such votes as had at said election been cast and given for each and every of the said McEnery, Wickliffe, Saint Martin, Poché, De Blanc, Seay, Cobb, and Cross; and that he, the said Kellogg, when he made and executed the aforesaid certificate, well knew that of the legal votes cast at the popular election held in the State of Louisiana on the 7th day of November last, for the election of electors in said State, as shown by the lists, returns, and papers sent according to law by the commissioners of election, who presided over and conducted the said election at the several polls and voting-places in said State, to the supervisors of registration, and as shown by the said lists, returns, papers, and ballots deposited by said commissioners of election in the office of the clerks of the district courts, except the parish of Orleans, and deposited for the parish of Orleans in the office of secretary of state, according to law, that each and every the said McEnery, Wickliffe, Saint Martin, Poché, De Blanc, Seay, Cobb, and Cross had received more than five thousand of the legal votes cast at said election for electors more than had been cast and given at said election for the said Kellogg as elector, and that the said McEnery, Wickliffe, Saint Martin, Poché, De Blanc, Seay, Cobb, and Cross had been thus and thereby duly appointed electors for said State in the manner directed by the legislature of said State.

9. We further offer to prove that at the city of New Orleans, in the State of Louisiana, in the month of October, A. D. 1876, the said William P. Kellogg, J. H. Burch, Peter Joseph, L. A. Sheldon, Morris Marks, A. B. Levissee, O. H. Brewster, Oscar Joffrion, S. B. Packard, John Ray, Frank Morey, Hugh J. Campbell, D. J. M. A. Jewett, H. C. Dibble, Michael Hahn, B. P. Blanchard, J. R. G. Pitkin, J. Madison Wells, Thomas C. Anderson, G. Casanave, L. M. Kenner, George P. Davis, W. L. Catlin, C. C. Nash, George L. Smith, Isadore McCormick, and others entered into an unlawful and criminal combination and conspiracy to and with each other, and each to and with each of the others, to cause it to be certified and returned to the secretary of state, by the returning-board of said State, upon their pretended compilation and canvass of the election for electors to be thereafter held on the 7th day of November, A. D. 1876, that the said Kellogg, Burch, Joseph, Sheldon, Marks, Levissee, Brewster, and Joffrion had received a majority of all votes given and cast at said election for electors, whether such should be the fact or not; and

That afterward, to wit, on the 17th day of November, A. D. 1876, after said election had been held and it was well known to all of said conspirators that said Kellogg and others had not been elected at said election, but had been defeated, and their opponents had been elected at said election, the said returning-board assembled at the city of New Orleans, the seat of government of said State, to pretend to compile and canvass the statement of votes made by the commissioners of election from the several polls and voting-places in said State for presidential electors, and make returns of said election to the secretary of state, as required by an act of the legislature of that State, approved November 20, 1872; that when said returning-board so assembled, said Wells, said Anderson, said Kenner, and said Casanave, who were all members of one political party, to wit, the republican party, were the only members of said board; there being one vacancy in said board, which vacancy it was the duty of said Wells, said Anderson, said Kenner, and said Casanave, as members of said board, to fill, then and there, by the election or appointment of some person belonging to some other political party than the republican party; but that the said Wells, Anderson, Kenner, and Casanave then and there, *in pursuance of said unlawful and criminal combination aforesaid*, neglected and refused to fill said vacancy, for the reason, as assigned by them, that they did not wish to have a democrat to watch the proceedings of said board; and that, although frequently during the session of said board assembled for the purpose aforesaid, they, the said Wells, Anderson, Kenner, and Casanave, were duly, and in writing, requested by said McEnery, Wickliffe, St. Martin, Poché, De Blanc, Seay, Cobb, and Cross to fill said vacancy, they refused to do so, and never did fill the same, but proceeded, as such board, in pursuance of said combination and conspiracy, to make a pretended compilation and canvass of said election without filling the vacancy in said returning-board; and

That said Wells, Anderson, Kenner, and Casanave, while pretending to be in session as a returning-board for the purpose of compiling and canvassing the said election, and in pursuance of said combination and conspiracy, employed persons of notoriously bad character to act as their clerks and assistants, to wit, one Davis, a man of notoriously bad character, who was then under indictment in the criminal courts of Louisiana, and said Catlin, said Blanchard, and said Jewett, three of said conspirators, who were then under indictment for subornation of perjury in the criminal courts of Louisiana; the said Jewett being also under indictment in one of the criminal courts of Louisiana for obtaining money under false pretenses; and Isadore McCormick, who was then under indictment in a criminal court of said State charged with murder. And that in pursuance of said unlawful combination and conspiracy aforesaid, the said Wells, Anderson, Kenner, and Casanave, acting in said returning-board, confided to their said clerks and employés, said co-conspirators, the duty of compiling and canvassing all returns which were by said returning-board ordered to be canvassed and compiled; and, although thereto particularly requested by a communication, as follows:

To the honorable Returning-Board of the State of Louisiana:

GENTLEMEN : The undersigned, acting as counsel for the various candidates upon the democratic-conservative ticket, State, national, and municipal, with respect show :

That the returns from various polls and parishes are inspected by this board, and the vote announced by it is merely that for governor and electors ;

That the tabulation of all other votes is turned over to a corps of clerks, to be done outside of the presence of this board;

That all of said clerks are republicans, and that the democratic-conservative candidates have no check upon them, and no means to detect errors and fraudulent tabulations, or to call the attention of this board to any such wrong, if any exist ;

That by this system the fate of all other candidates but governor and electors is placed in the hands of a body of republican clerks, with no check against erroneous or dishonest action on their part ;

That fair play requires that some check should be placed upon said clerks, and some protection afforded to the said candidates against error or dishonest action on the part of said clerks :

Wherefore they respectfully ask that they be permitted to name three respectable persons, and that to such parties be accorded the privilege of being present in the room or rooms where said tabulation is progressing, and of inspecting the tabulation and comparing the same with the returns, and also of fully inspecting the returns, and previous to the adoption by this board of said tabulation, with a view to satisfy all parties that there has been no tampering or unfair practice in connection therewith.

Very respectfully,

F. C. ZACHARIE.
CHARLES CAVANAC.
E. A. BURKE.
J. R. ALCEE GAUTHREAUX.
HENRY C. BROWN.
FRANK McGLOIN.

I concur herein.

H. M. SPOFFORD,
Of Counsel—

they, the said Wells, Anderson, Kenner, and Casanave, acting as said board, expressly refused to permit any democrat or any person selected by democrats to be present with said clerks and assistants while they were engaged in the compilation and canvass aforesaid, or to examine into the correctness of the compilation and canvass made by said clerks and assistants as aforesaid; and that said returning-board, in pursuance of said unlawful combination and conspiracy aforesaid, and for the purpose of concealing the *animus* of said board and inspiring confidence in the public mind in the integrity of their proceedings, on the 18th day of November, A. D. 1876, adopted and passed a preamble and resolution, as follows:

Whereas this board has learned with satisfaction that distinguished gentlemen of national reputation from other States, some at the request of the President of the United States and some at the request of the national executive committee of the democratic party, are present in this city, with the view to witness the proceedings of this board in canvassing and compiling the returns of the recent election in this State for presidential electors, in order that the public opinion of the country may be satisfied as to the truth of the result and the fairness of the means by which it may have been attained;

And whereas this board recognizes the importance which may attach to the result of their proceedings, and that the public mind should be convinced of its justice by a knowledge of the facts on which it may be based: Therefore be it

Resolved, That this board does hereby cordially invite and request five gentlemen from each of the two bodies named, to be selected by themselves, respectively, to attend and be present at the meetings of this board while engaged in the discharge of its duties, under the law, in canvassing and compiling the returns and ascertaining and declaring the result of said election for presidential electors, in their capacity as private citizens of eminent reputation and high character, and as spectators and witnesses of the proceedings in that behalf of this board.

But that said returning-board, being convinced that a compilation and canvass of votes given at said election for presidential electors, made fairly and openly, would result in defeating the object of said conspiracy, and compelling said returning-board to certify that said McEnery, Wickliffe, St. Martin, Poché, De Blanc, Seay, Cobb, and Cross had been at said election duly chosen, elected, and appointed electors by the said State of Louisiana; and, in pursuance of said unlawful combination and conspiracy, did afterward, to wit, on the 20th day of November, A. D. 1876, adopt and pass the following rules for the better execution and carrying into effect said combination and conspiracy; that is to say:

VII.

The returning-officers, if they think it advisable, may go into secret session to consider any motion, argument, or proposition which may be presented to them; any member shall have the right to call for secret session for the above purpose.

X.

That the evidence for each contested poll in any parish, when concluded, shall be laid aside until all the evidence is in from all the contested polls in the several parishes where there may be contests, and, after the evidence is all in, the returning-officers will decide the several contests in secret session; the parties or their attorneys to be allowed to submit briefs or written arguments up to the time fixed for the returning-officers going into secret session, after which no additional argument to be received unless by special consent.

That the proceedings thus directed to be had in secret were protested against by the said McEnery, Wickliffe, St. Martin, Poché, De Blanc, Seay, Cobb, and Cross; but said board thereafter proceeded and pretended to complete their duties as such returning-board, and did perform, execute, and carry out the most important duties devolving upon said board *in secret*, with closed doors, and in the absence of any member of their board belonging to the democratic party or any person whatever not a member of said board not belonging to the republican party.

That the said Wells, Anderson, Kenner, and Casanave, acting as said returning-board, while engaged in the compilation and canvass aforesaid, were applied to to permit the United States supervisors of election, duly appointed and qualified as such, to be present at and witness such compilation or canvass.

That application was made to said returning-board in that behalf as follows:

To the President and Members of the Returning-Board of the State of Louisiana:

GENTLEMEN: The undersigned, of counsel for United States supervisors of election duly appointed and qualified as such, do hereby except, protest, and object to any ruling made this 20th day of November, 1876, or that hereafter may be made, whereby they are deprived of the right of being present during the entire canvass and compilation of the results of the election lately held in the State of Louisiana, wherein electors for President and Vice-President and members of the Forty-fifth Congress were balloted for, and the result of which said board are now canvassing.

That under the fifth section of the United States act of February 28, 1871, they are " to be and remain where the ballot-boxes are kept, at all times after the polls are open, until each and every vote cast at said time and place shall be counted, and the canvass of all votes polled be wholly completed and the proper and requisite certificate or returns made, whether said certificates or returns be required under any law of the United States or any State, territorial, or municipal law."

That under said law of the United States, District Attorney J. R. Beckwith, under date of October 30, 1872, gave his written official opinion for the instruction and guidance of persons holding the office now held by protestants, wherein said United States district attorney said:

" It cannot be doubted that the duty of the supervisors extends to the inspection of the entire election, from its commencement until the decision of its result. If the United States statutes were less explicit, there still could be no doubt of the duty and authority of the supervisors to inspect and canvass every vote cast for each and every candidate, State, parochial, and Federal, as the law of the State neither provides nor allows any separation of the election for Representatives in Congress, &c., from the election of State and parish officers. The election is in law a single election, and the power of inspection vested in law in the supervisors appointed by the court extends to the entire election, a full knowledge of which may well become necessary to defeat fraud."

In which opinion the attorney-general of the State of Louisiana coincided. Whereupon protestants claim admittance to all sessions of the returning-board, and protest against their exclusion as unwarranted by law, as informed by their attorneys has been done and is contemplated to be done hereafter in said proceedings of said board.

F. C. ZACHARIE,
E. A. BURKE,
CHAS. CAVANAC,
FRANK McGLOIN,
J. R. A. GAUTHREAUX,
H. C. BROWN,
Of Counsel.

But that said Wells, Anderson, Kenner, and Casanave, acting as such returning-board, in further pursuance and execution of said unlawful

combination and conspiracy, then and there refused to permit said
United States commissioners of election to be present for the purpose
aforesaid, but proceeded in their absence to the pretended compilation
and canvass aforesaid.

That the said returning-board, while in session as aforesaid, for the
purpose aforesaid, to wit, on the 20th day of November, 1876, adopted
the following rule to govern their proceedings; that is to say:

IX.

No *ex parte* affidavits or statements shall be received in evidence, except as a basis to
show that such fraud, intimidation, or other illegal practice had at some poll requires
investigation, but the returns and affidavits authorized by law, made by officers of
election or in verification of statements as required by law, shall be received in evidence as *prima facie.*

But that said board subsequently, while sitting as aforesaid for the
purposes aforesaid, having become convinced that they could not, upon
other than *ex parte* testimony, so manipulate the said compilation and
canvass as to declare that said Kellogg, Burch, Joseph, Sheldon, Marks,
Levissee, Brewster, and Joffrion were elected electors at said election,
and, in further pursuance of said unlawful combination and conspiracy,
did subsequently modify said rule and declare and decide that as such
returning-board they would receive *ex parte* affidavits, under which last
decision of said board over two hundred printed pages of *ex parte* testimony were received by said board in favor of said Kellogg and others;
and afterward, when the said McEnery and others offered *ex parte* evidence to contradict the *ex parte* evidence aforesaid, the said returning-
board reversed its last decision and refused to receive *ex parte* affidavits
in contradiction as aforesaid.

And that in pursuance of said unlawful combination and conspiracy
the said returning-board, in violation of a law of said State approved
November 20, 1872, neglected and refused to compile and canvass the
statements of votes made by the commissioners of election which were
before them, according to law, for canvass and compilation as aforesaid
in regard to the election of presidential electors, but that said board
did, in pursuance and further execution of said combination and conspiracy, canvass and compile only the consolidated statements and
returns made to them by the supervisors of registration of the several
parishes of said State.

And that said returning-board, in pursuance and further execution of
said unlawful combination and conspiracy, did knowingly, willfully, and
fraudulently refuse to compile and canvass the votes given for electors
at said election in more than twenty parishes of said State, as was
shown and appeared by and upon the consolidated statements and
returns made to them by said supervisors of said parishes.

And that said returning-board did, in said canvass and compilation,
count and estimate, as a foundation for their determination in the premises, hundreds of votes which had not been returned and certified to
them either by the commissioners of election in said State or by the
supervisors of registration in said State, they, the said members of said
board, then and there well knowing that they had no right or authority
to estimate the same for the purpose aforesaid.

And that said returning-board, in further pursuance and execution
of said unlawful combination and conspiracy, knowingly, willfully,
falsely, and fraudulently, did make a certificate and return to the
secretary of state that said Kellogg, Burch, Joseph, Sheldon, Marks,
Levissee, Brewster, and Joffrion had received majorities of all the

legal votes cast at said election of November 7, 1876, for presidential electors, they then and there well knowing that the said McEnery, Wickliffe, St. Martin, Poché, De Blanc, Seay, Cobb, and Cross had received majorities of all the votes cast at said election for presidential electors, and were duly elected as the presidential electors of said State.

And that the said returning-board, in making said statement, certificate, and return to the secretary of state, were not deceived nor mistaken in the premises, but knowingly, willfully, and fraudulently made what they well knew when they made it was a false and fraudulent statement, certificate, and return; and that the said false and fraudulent statement, certificate, and return, made by said returning-board to the secretary of state in that behalf, was made by the members of said returning-board in pursuance and execution of, and only in pursuance and execution of, said unlawful combination and conspiracy.

And that said returning-board, while in session as aforesaid, for the purpose aforesaid, in further pursuance and execution of said unlawful combination and conspiracy, did alter, change, and forge, or cause to be altered, changed, and forged, the consolidated statement and return of the supervisor of registration for the parish of Vernon, in said State, in the manner following, to wit: The said consolidated statement, as made and returned to said board, showed that, of the legal votes given in said parish for electors at said election of November 7, 1876, said McEnery received 647, said Wickliffe received 647, said St. Martin received 647, said Poché received 647, said De Blanc received 647, said Seay received 647, said Cobb received 647, said Cross received 647; and that said Kellogg received none, said Burch received none, said Joseph received 2, said Brewster received 2, said Marks received 2, said Levissee received 2, said Joffrion received 2, said Sheldon received 2; and said board altered, changed, and forged, or caused to be altered, changed, and forged, said consolidated statement so as to make the same falsely and fraudulently show that the said McEnery received 469, said Wickliffe received 469, said St. Martin received 469, said Poché received 469, said De Blanc received 469, said Seay received 469, said Cobb received 469, said Cross received 469; and that said Kellogg received 178, said Burch received 178, said Joseph received 178, said Sheldon received 180, said Marks received 180, said Levissee received 180, said Brewster received 180, said Joffrion received 180; and that said returning-board, while in session as aforesaid for the purpose aforesaid, to pretend to justify the alteration and forgery of said consolidated statement, procured and pretended to act upon three forged affidavits, purporting to have been made and sworn to by Samuel Carter, Thomas Brown, and Samuel Collins—they, the said members of said returning-board, then and there, well knowing that said pretended affidavits were false and forged, and that no such persons were in existence as purported to make said affidavits.

And that said members of said returning-board, acting as said board, in pursuance and execution of said unlawful combination and conspiracy, did, in their pretended canvass and compilation of the legal votes given at said election, on the 7th day of November, A. D. 1876, for presidential electors in said State of Louisiana, as shown to them by the statements, papers, and returns made according to law by the commissioners of election presiding over and conducting said election at the several polls and voting-places in said State, all of which votes were legally cast by legal voters in said State, at said election, knowingly, willfully, and fraudulently, and without any authority of law whatever, exclude and refuse to count and estimate, or compile or canvass, votes given at said election for electors, as follows, which papers, statements, and returns were before them, and which it was their duty by law to compile and canvass; that is to say, for said John McEnery, 10,280; for said R. C. Wickliffe, 10,293; for said L. St. Martin, 10,291; for said F. P. Poché, 10,280; for said A. De Blanc, 10,289; for said W. A. Seay, 10,291; for said R. A. Cobb, 10,261; for said K. A. Cross, 10,288; they, the said members of said returning-board, then and there, well knowing that all of said votes, which they neglected and refused to canvass and compile, had been duly and legally cast at said election for presidential electors by legal voters of said State; and then and there well knowing that, had they considered, estimated, and counted, compiled and canvassed said votes, as they then and there well knew it was their duty to do, it would have appeared, and they would have been compelled to certify and return to the secretary of state, that said Kellogg had not been duly elected or appointed an elector for said State, but that at said election the said McEnery, the said Wickliffe, the said St. Martin, the said Poché, the said De Blanc, the said Seay, the said Cobb, and the said Cross had been duly elected and appointed presidential electors in said State.

And that by said false, fraudulent, willful, and corrupt acts and omissions to act by said returning-board as aforesaid in the matter aforesaid, and by said nonfeasance, misfeasance, and malfeasance of said returning-board, as hereinbefore mentioned, the said returning-board made to the secretary of state of said State the statement, certificate, and return upon which the said Kellogg, as *de facto* governor of said State, pretended to make his said false certificate, certifying that himself and others had been duly appointed electors for said State, as hereinbefore mentioned; and that said statement, certificate, and return made by said returning-board, and that the said certificate made by the said Kellogg, as *de facto* governor, each, every, and all were made in pursuance and execution of said unlawful and criminal combination and conspiracy, as was well known to and intended by each and every of the members of said returning-board when they made their said false statement, certificate, and return to the secretary of state of said State, and by the said Kellogg when, as governor *de facto* of said State, he made his said false certificate hereinbefore mentioned.

III. We further offer to prove that Oscar Joffrion was, on the 7th day of November, A. D. 1876, supervisor of registration of the parish of Point Coupée, and that he acted and officiated as such supervisor of registration for said parish at the said election for presidential electors on that day; and that he is the same person who acted as one of the electors for said State, and on the 6th day of December, A. D. 1876, as an elector, cast a vote for Rutherford B. Hayes for President of the United States and for William A. Wheeler for Vice-President of the United States.

IV. We further offer to prove that, on the 7th day of November, A. D. 1876, A. B. Levissee, who was one of the pretended college of electors of the State of Louisiana, and who in said college gave a vote for Rutherford B. Hayes for President of the United States and for William A. Wheeler for Vice-President of the United States, was at the time of such election a court commissioner of the circuit court of the United States for the district of Louisiana; which is an office of honor, profit, and trust under the Government of the United States.

V. We further offer to prove that, on the 7th day of November, A. D.

1876, O. H. Brewster, who was one of the pretended electors in the pretended college of electors of the State of Louisiana, and who in sa college gave a vote for Rutherford B. Hayes for President of the United States, and for William A. Wheeler for Vice-President of the United States, was, at the time of such election as aforesaid, holding an office of honor, profit, and trust under the Government of the United States, namely, the office of surveyor-general of the land-office for the district of Louisiana.

VI. We further offer to prove that, on the 7th day of November, 1876, Morris Marks, one of the pretended electors, who in said college of electors cast a vote for Rutherford B. Hayes for President of the United States, and a vote for William A. Wheeler for Vice-President of the United States, was, ever since has been, *and now is*, holding and exercising the office of district attorney of the fourth judicial district of said State, and receiving the salary by law attached to said office.

VII. We further offer to prove that, on the 7th day of November, A. D. 1876, J. Henri Burch, who was one of the pretended electors who in said pretended electoral college gave a vote for Rutherford B. Hayes for President of the United States and a vote for William A. Wheeler for Vice-President of the United States, was holding the following offices under the constitution and laws of said State, that is to say: member of the board of control of the State penitentiary, also administrator of deaf and dumb asylum of said State, to both of which offices he had been appointed by the governor with the advice and consent of the senate of said State, both being offices with salaries fixed by law, and also the office of treasurer of the parish school-board for the parish of East Baton Rouge; and that said Burch, ever since the said 7th day of November, (and prior thereto,) has exercised and still is exercising the functions of all said offices and receiving the emoluments thereof.

VIII. We further offer to prove the canvass and compilation actually made by said returning-board, showing what parishes and voting-places and polls were compiled and canvassed, and what polls or voting-places were excluded by said returning-board from their canvass and compilation of votes given for presidential electors; and we also offer to show what statements and returns of the commissioners of election and of the supervisors of registration were duly before said returning-board.

IX. We further offer to prove that a member of said returning-board offered to receive a bribe in consideration of which the board would certify the election of the Tilden electors.

X. We offer to prove that the statements and affidavits purporting to have been made and forwarded to said returning-board in pursuance of the provisions of section 26 of the election-law of 1872, alleging riot, tumult, intimidation, and violence at or near certain polls and in certain parishes, were falsely fabricated and forged by certain disreputable persons under the direction and with the knowledge of said returning-board, and that said returning-board, knowing said statements and affidavits to be false and forged, and that none of said statements or affidavits was made in the manner or form required by law, did, knowingly, willfully, and fraudulently fail and refuse to canvass or compile more than ten thousand votes lawfully cast, as is shown by the statements of votes of the commissioners of election.

XI. We further offer to prove that said returning-board did willfully and fraudulently pretend to canvass and compile and did promulgate as having been canvassed and compiled certain votes for the following-named candidates for electors which were never cast and which did not appear upon any tally-sheet, statement of votes, or consolidated statement or other return before said board, namely: J. H. Burch, 241; Peter Joseph, 1,362; L. A. Sheldon, 1,364; Morris Marks, 1,334; A. B. Levissee, 829; O. H. Brewster, 776; Oscar Joffrion, 1,364.

Mr. EVARTS. Has the Commission given any direction as to the length of time for discussing the question of admissibility?

The PRESIDENT. I have no instructions on the subject.

Mr. Commissioner EDMUNDS. I think some time should be fixed. There being so many offers, fifteen minutes would hardly be sufficient. There ought to be some reasonable time.

The PRESIDENT. Does any one submit a motion?

Mr. Commissioner ABBOTT. I should like to know how much time the counsel would desire to argue all these objections in the mass.

Mr. Commissioner BRADLEY. I understood the decision to be that the argument on the offer of evidence would come out of the time allowed to counsel on either side. It was understood this morning that the reading of the offers should not be counted as part of the time. That was fair; but I think the presentation of the evidence is as much a part of the presentation of the case as the rest of the argument. It seems to me that we are breaking our rules, if we allow further time than four and a half hours on each side.

The PRESIDENT. Let us first hear the counsel answer the inquiry. I think we ought to have that answer.

Mr. TRUMBULL. On consultation with the gentlemen with whom I am associated, they think that we should have three hours on each side, an hour apiece to each counsel. Each of the gentlemen associated with me desires to present his views; and we think, as suggested by one of the Commissioners, or at least I do, that this does involve to a great extent any argument that will afterward take place.

Mr. Commissioner STRONG. Mr. President, I did not understand the order which the court made in regard to time, as Mr. Justice Bradley understood it. I did not understand the order we made as requiring that the time occupied in the offer of evidence, or objections that might be made to its admissibility, or arguments made in support of its admissibility, should be taken out of the four and a half hours which we agreed to allow for general argument on each side. I agree, sir, that in one aspect of the case the evidence which is offered is substantially the whole case; in another aspect of the case it is not. I think counsel ought to be allowed a reasonable time for the argument of the question whether this evidence thus proposed is admissible or not. It seems to me that three hours on this interlocutory question is rather large. I should be willing to give what we gave in the Florida case, two hours. I think counsel ought to be content with that.

The PRESIDENT. Do you move that?

Mr. Commissioner STRONG. I move that two hours be allowed.

The PRESIDENT. Mr. Commissioner Strong moves that counsel be allowed two hours on a side for the argument of the question of the admissibility of the evidence offered and objections thereto.

Mr. Commissioner THURMAN. Mr. President, I cannot help saying that it does seem to me that counsel on both sides would aid this Commission in arriving with a reasonable degree of expedition and not unreasonable haste at the conclusion to which they must arrive one time or another, and this whole thing should be settled by letting the evidence come in, subject to exception, and then arguing the question. If the four hours and a half that we have allowed are not sufficient for that purpose because of the introduction of the element of the competency or incompetency of the testimony, then that time can be enlarged;

but to fritter our time away with arguments upon the admissibility of this point of testimony or that particular item of testimony, instead of treating this subject in a large view and letting the testimony come in subject to exception on both sides, and then arguing its competency and its relevancy as well as the merits of the case, seems to me to be making of this tribunal a court of common pleas instead of the tribunal which it is.

Mr. Commissioner EDMUNDS. Mr. President——

The PRESIDENT. I will remark that there is no motion before the Commission except that of allowing two hours on a side to the counsel to argue the question. Having permitted discussion by Mr. Thurman, I will also allow Senator Edmunds to proceed.

Mr. Commissioner EDMUNDS. . That was precisely the question, Mr. President, that I was about to speak to. The length of time required for the discussion of this question depends on whether counsel are to discuss the offer of testimony as a mere technical question of whether a particular species of testimony is competent to prove a particular fact that is relevant to the matter, or whether the fact itself proposed is one which falls within the scope of the consideration of the Commission. Inasmuch as we understand from the preceding case exactly how this question arises, really, as Judge Strong has said, in one aspect of the case, the discussion of the question of the admissibility of this testimony, and so of its legal effect, or the question of its materiality in point of law, covers the whole ground. If, therefore, counsel can so manage as to argue the whole subject presented by this offer, as well its materiality as the result that must be drawn from it if the facts were proved, then if the Commission should be of opinion that it was not competent in its judgment to go into that species of proof, that would be an end of the matter. On the other hand if the Commission should be of opinion that it was competent to go into the proof or some portion of it—of course I am not speaking of everything—then we should have already determined the relevancy and effect of the facts if they should be established and not counteracted by counter-proof, and should have made, as it appears to me, more rapid progress than in any other way.

The difficulty about taking proof provisionally, as I understand the other side's attitude, is that if you take proof provisionally on the part of the objectors to certificate No. 1, then you must take proof provisionally on the part of those who support certificate No. 1, and we at once, if I correctly understood the statement of the objectors, go into an indefinite period of taking testimony on the part of the supporters of certificate No. 1 to prove that the very circumstances did exist under which, if this law of Louisiana be constitutional and applies to this case, it was the duty of this board to proceed to reject polls, and so on; and they would ask us on the same principle to waive for the time being the question as to whether preliminary steps had been taken and to take the evidence and then consider whether it was competent for this canvassing-board to receive testimony owing to a defect in the want of protest, or whatever it might be. The result, therefore, of taking evidence provisionally on both sides (for we must on both sides if on either) would be that we might find ourselves at the end of a week or ten days in the attitude of just discovering, as it is possible we might—I express no opinion about it and have none to express—that we had wasted all this time in going into a range of inquiry that we felt, under the law, we had no right to have gone into. So I think the rule which we adopted in the Florida case would be the better one, to hear this question now argued generally upon the effect of this evidence if it should be made out, and the nature of it, and what our powers are, and so on, so that we can make definite progress in the inquiry and upon the whole of the case as it would be presented on this evidence.

Mr. Commissioner BRADLEY. That is very much my view, that we should go on and have it argued as we had the Florida case. It might be considered if not as evidence in subject to objection, at least as evidence offered and demurred to on the other side.

Mr. Commissioner STRONG. We must assume then that they can prove what they offer.

Mr. Commissioner BRADLEY. Certainly. I would add that no one can shut his eyes, it seems to me, to the fact that the discussion of the admission of this evidence and going into this inquiry is the discussion of the whole case.

Mr. Commissioner MILLER. Mr. President, I would ask my brothers Edmunds and Bradley whether they mean (which I think is the better course) to give what time now may be proper on all the questions in the case, including the effect of this evidence, so that, when we retire for consultation, if we should conclude that none of this evidence is to be admitted, we could then decide the whole case without coming back for another argument, giving counsel fair time to argue all the questions in the case, including the admissibility of this evidence. Of course, if in conference we determine to receive this evidence, we shall have to come back, let it be admitted, and let counter-evidence be admitted, and hear argument on its effect. If not, can it not be so argued that when we do retire on this question, if the evidence should be excluded, (about which I have no idea what the Commission will hold,) the law will then have been argued on the other papers and we shall be prepared to make a decision.

The PRESIDENT. The only question before the Commission is the motion of Judge Strong to allow two hours on a side.

Mr. Commissioner EDMUNDS. I move to amend that by substituting the following order :

Ordered, That counsel now be heard on the whole subject as the case now stands, and that three hours on a side be allowed.

Mr. EVARTS. Three hours added to what is already allowed ?

Mr. Commissioner EDMUNDS. No, sir ; three hours now.

Mr. EVARTS. We had four and a half hours on our side yesterday. Two hours have been taken up by the other side.

The PRESIDENT. This is changing the course of the trial.

Mr. Commissioner EDMUNDS. I will modify my proposition on the suggestion that part of the time has already been occupied.

The PRESIDENT. As modified, the order is :

Ordered, That counsel now be heard on the whole subject as the case now stands, and that four hours on a side be allowed.

It makes no deduction of what is past.

Mr. Commissioner THURMAN. I should like to have the meaning of that order explained.

Mr. Commissioner EDMUNDS. It means, as I suppose, exactly what it says. If I read it to my friend again, perhaps he will understand it :

Ordered, That counsel now be heard on the whole subject as the case now stands, and that four hours on a side be allowed.

If I correctly understand the offer of Judge Trumbull, which has been carefully read and is perfectly perspicuous and understandable, it is that the objectors to certificate No. 1 and the supporters of certificate

No. 2 propose to prove certain things. The counsel on the other side object to that as irrelevant and incompetent in this consideration. So that if we now proceed on the subject as the case now stands, it opens the effect of this evidence, as we must take it to be capable of being proved as a matter of course as we now argue it; and the whole duty of this Commission upon the subject, if we decide that it is not within our power under the law to go into an inquiry of that kind, will be disposed of. If we decide that it is in our power to go into a part of the inquiry, then we go into it. If we hold that it is within our power to go into the whole inquiry, we so decide and the evidence proceeds. I think there is no difficulty in understanding it.

Mr. Commissioner THURMAN. I really meant no disrespect to my brother; but I did not understand it. If he means four hours on a side to argue the admissibility of this testimony, it is one thing.

The PRESIDENT. And its effect.

Mr. Commissioner THURMAN. If he means that the whole case is to be submitted after four hours have been exhausted on each side, then that strikes me as a singular proposition for several reasons. In the first place, one of the sides has already occupied two hours. The proposition then would give to them the advantage of two hours in the argument, give them six hours instead of four.

But again, if, without deciding whether we have anything in evidence at all, without counsel knowing whether we have anything in evidence at all, we are to fix a time to have the whole case submitted and the argument finally closed and then we retire and give our final decision, upon my word I do not know what kind of a judicial proceeding that would be.

Mr. Commissioner MILLER. Mr. President, let me suggest that the proposed order does not provide that we shall give a final decision; it does not provide that we shall give any decision at all, nor what that decision shall be. It says that we shall hear argument upon the whole case as it now stands, on the effect of the certificates and papers submitted by the President of the Senate and the effect of the offer of testimony. It is easy to see that under such an argument, whether it be long or short, (and I have nothing to say about what its length should be,) when we retire, if this testimony is to be admitted, we have got to come back and let it be submitted and argued; and if it is to be excluded, then the other question of the effect of the papers submitted and the whole of the case will have been argued, and we can then decide the whole case. That I understand to be the purport and object of the order.

Mr. Commissioner BAYARD. Mr. President, what is the precise meaning of the words " as the case now stands," if, as has been said by my brother Bradley, the case is to be treated as if on a demurrer to evidence, which considers the evidence before the court, the effect of it simply being in question? If therefore this argument is to proceed upon the basis of the facts which have been offered to be proved being proved and before the court, that is one thing. Then the argument would have for its basis the law as applied to the facts stated by counsel here to us. If that be the understanding, that we are to hear this case as if it were upon a demurrer to testimony, we know what that means; and if after that judgment there will be again argument in case it is desired, with that understanding I shall be content.

Mr. Commissioner FRELINGHUYSEN. Mr. President, I should like to know from the objectors to certificate No. 2 whether this time is satisfactory to them. If it is, I shall vote for it. If it is not, inasmuch as the other side have already occupied two hours, I should want the rule made uniform.

Mr. Commissioner ABBOTT. Mr. President, I understand, in answer to the suggestion made by Senator Bayard, that this is an argument not only upon the competency of the evidence offered as upon a demurrer to evidence, but it is in addition an argument upon the whole case, so that when this argument is once made we are to decide the whole case unless we admit the testimony. It is not an argument simply upon a demurrer to the testimony, as to the effect of the testimony, but it is an argument upon that and also upon the whole merits of the case if there is anything else outside of this question of testimony. Now, sir, I object for one to mixing up the two matters together. I am content, as suggested by Judge Strong, to take an argument upon this offer of testimony as upon a demurrer to testimony. Let us hear the effect of that testimony argued, whether we will or will not admit it; and then if we agree to admit it, very well; if we agree not to admit it, let us have the argument upon what is left of this case, distinct and independent and by itself. I think the statement made by Judge Strong on that matter covers the whole case. The course now proposed is mixing up two matters which necessarily have no sort of connection with each other.

Mr. Commissioner EDMUNDS. Mr. President, that would be true if we had unlimited time, and I should quite agree that it would be more convenient to hear the precise point argued on the offer of a particular piece of testimony, just as a court would; but we ought not to forget that time is running very fast and we only have a dozen or thirteen days more within which to dispose of this case and every other that may come to us, and that there are twenty five States, or something like that number, whose voice in this queston has not been unsealed, and cannot be until a report is made upon this case. Therefore, to save time, it appears to me that it would be better to argue the case as it now stands, upon the admissibility of this testimony and upon the attitude the case would occupy if the testimony were not admitted, in order that in one event we should be able to make proper and diligent haste and not undue haste, and in the other event we then should have eliminated difficulties and should be ready to go on with the testimony.

The PRESIDENT. I desire to say one word. If the order relates only to the evidence and its effect, I will vote for it. If it embraces not only the offer of evidence and its effect, but also the effect of the certificates and of the evidence which accompanies them and all the other papers submitted to us, I will vote against it.

Mr. Commissioner THURMAN. Mr. President, I do not understand what is meant by speaking of a demurrer to evidence before this tribunal. Do we proceed by a demurrer to evidence? If we do, we are to give judgment when we overrule that demurrer; that is an end of the case. Furthermore, if we proceed by the technical rules of a demurrer to evidence, then the party who demurs is subject to every possible inference and suggestion that can be drawn from that testimony—every one that is possible. He is subjected to the disadvantages of it. Is that meant here? What is this but a simple objection to evidence, not a demurrer to evidence? I do not understand that the technical rules as to demurrers to evidence apply in this case at all.

If the Commission think that the course pursued in the Florida case is the best way, and will now hear argument on the admissibility of this testimony and then decide that question, and if decided one way, decided in favor of the admissibility, then receive the testimony, and if decided against it, then let the argument take place upon the papers that have been laid before us and which all admit to be in evidence, well and good. Then it is only a question of how much time should be allowed to either side to argue the question of the admissibility of the evidence. I am in favor of a liberal time for that purpose; but I agree with my brother Abbott that if we are to treat the case in that way, let us keep the questions separate. I think a very much better way would be to consider all the testimony in and argue this case on its full merits with reference to the competency of the testimony, and allow ample time to do it; but if that is not agreeable to the Commission, then the only other way that I see is to allow a reasonable time to argue the question of the admissibility of this testimony.

Mr. Commissioner ABBOTT. I only desire to say that I used the term " demurrer to evidence " not in its strictest technical sense. I think the Senator from Ohio and myself do not differ as to what we desire. I suppose that the argument of this question of the offer of evidence is upon the objection to the evidence, but it is to be treated precisely as if the evidence was before us, and if it was before us what would be the effect of that evidence upon the objection to the evidence? I only used the term " demurrer to the evidence " as a convenient way of expressing what I meant. God knows I do not desire to import into this tribunal any technical rules and count in or count out a President of the United States upon a technical rule.

Mr. EVARTS. Mr. President, I have been anticipated in a great part by the observations that have fallen from Mr. Commissioner Thurman. I wished to guard against any implication by our silence that we assented to the position of counsel who were objecting to the admissibility of evidence as being equivalent to that of counsel who admitted the evidence and demurred to its effect. We certainly do not intend to place ourselves in the position of treating the evidence as if already in and arguing then.

The PRESIDENT. In arguing the question, must we not proceed on the ground that those who offer it can prove it?

Mr. EVARTS. Undoubtedly, and then you determine whether it is admissible.

The PRESIDENT. That is the exact state of the case.

Mr. EVARTS. That is the situation; but a demurrer to evidence concedes it to be already in and says, " What happens then?" We wish to guard against that implication and simply that. Now, in regard to the question that Mr. Commissioner Frelinghuysen put to us, it certainly would seem to enlarge a little the area of argument imposed upon us when, in addition to what was supposed to be the duty imposed upon counsel when four and a half hours were allowed to each side, there is now by introduction of this offer of evidence a somewhat separate consideration. But we agree entirely on our part to the method suggested of hearing the question of the admissibility of the evidence, and then also the question of what would be the result if it were excluded and the certificates opened by the President of the Senate were the only matters before the Commission. The argument of both may properly proceed together; so that if the Commission, retiring from that completed argument, should hold that this evidence was to be excluded and that all the evidence before them was included in the certificates opened by the President of the Senate, it would have heard the argument on that subject.

The PRESIDENT. The question is on the order submitted by Senator Edmunds:

Ordered, That counsel now be heard on the whole subject as the case now stands, and that four hours on a side be allowed.

Mr. Commissioner PAYNE. Mr. President, I am very much opposed, as one member of the Commission, to that order. There are eleven or twelve propositions stated by counsel of what they propose to prove; and under the rules of this Commission one counsel on a side can be heard on each one of those propositions for fifteen minutes. That would make more time than we now propose by this motion to allow for the argument of the merits as well as the argument of the interlocutory question. I do not understand the reason or the propriety of compelling counsel to argue, upon this first proposition as to the admissibility of evidence, the other questions presented in the case, to wit, the constitutionality of some of these laws. They are entitled to three hours to discuss the interlocutory questions. Now, after this statement of counsel that they require the three hours for the discussion of those questions, to require them within the same time to discuss the other questions pertaining to the constitutionality of these laws—some three or four distinct propositions made in the statement of counsel—appears to me grossly unjust and grossly unfair toward the counsel who prosecute this case. I hope, therefore, that the Commission will not so regard the pressing necessity of urgent haste, on the supposition made by Senator Edmunds that there are some twenty or thirty cases yet behind this, as a reason for inflicting this unjust requisition on counsel. I hope, therefore, that the Commission will not adopt that resolution, but will confine it to interlocutory questions.

Mr. Commissioner MORTON. Mr. President, in view of the very few days left, I shall be compelled to vote against any extension of time and that we proceed under the rule as it now stands. The order seems to me to be unequal in its character and in effect to give six hours to one side and four hours to the other. It seems to me that the ordinary way is the best way: first, let the question of the admissibility of the evidence be taken up and discussed; and if it should be decided to admit all of it or to admit none of it, then the effect of that which is admitted, what it proves, will be discussed. As far as I am concerned, I prefer to adhere to the rule as it now stands.

Mr. Commissioner ABBOTT. Mr. President, as I understand, proceeding with this case as the rule now stands would be, as suggested by Mr. Commissioner Payne, to give fifteen minutes on each single proposition, and if we are to act upon that I do not see that it can be prevented. Then if we have required, as we have, the counsel to present their objections all in a mass instead of separately, I do not see how we can say to them, "You shall expend your fifteen minutes upon one proposition," but they may take the whole time, it seems to me, upon the whole mass. We have massed the propositions, the offers of evidence, and why not consolidate and mass the time?

Mr. Commissioner EDMUNDS. May I ask Judge Abbott, supposing exactly the same principle applied to two propositions and two offers of evidence, would you hold that having heard one discussion of fifteen minutes and decided it you could hear the judgment of the tribunal discussed over again on the next one, which was exactly like it?

Mr. Commissioner ABBOTT. No, sir.

Mr. Commissioner EDMUNDS. Then it would not follow that the whole twelve would take up fifteen minutes each.

Mr. Commissioner ABBOTT. I do not understand that the decision of one offer of evidence necessarily decides all the others. I do not understand that counsel are to discuss over again the judgment of the tribunal that has once been made; but if you will be kind enough, Mr. President, to read the   ler again, I desire to move an amendment.

The PRESIDENT. I will read it again.

Ordered, That counsel now be heard on the whole subject as the case now stands, and that four hours on a side be allowed.

Mr. Commissioner STRONG. If Judge Abbott will permit me, I understand that to be an amendment offered to the order which I moved. My motion was that counsel be allowed two hours on each side to argue the question of the admissibility or inadmissibility of the evidence offered.

The PRESIDENT. I will state the question. The motion made by Judge Strong is that two hours be allowed on a side to argue the question of the admissibility of the testimony offered. Mr. Edmunds's proposition is in the nature of a motion to strike that out and insert—

Ordered, That counsel now be heard on the whole subject as the case now stands, and that four hours be allowed on a side.

The question is upon striking out and inserting.

Mr. Commissioner HOAR. Mr. President, it seems to me that it is very obvious that this is not the ordinary question of presenting evidence in a court on an issue framed. The prime question, we all know, which lies at the foundation of this whole discussion is this: Is the constitutional power vested in the two Houses, or either of them, by the provision that they shall be present at the opening of the certificates, to hear evidence to impeach those certificates? If that power be vested in the two Houses, and through them in this Commission, then there may come up the ordinary questions of detail as to the evidence which is to be introduced, its competency, and its force. If that power be not vested in the two Houses and through them in the Commission, then to ask them to exercise it is to ask them to do exactly what is imputed as a crime to the officers whose action is now laid before the Commission, to wit, to usurp power to redress what we fancy to be a public wrong. That one question cannot be separated from the question of the admissibility of the evidence. If the evidence be inadmissible, it is inadmissible in consequence of one view of that question. If it be admissible, it is admissible in consequence of another view of that question. It seems to me, therefore, that the amendment proposed by Senator Edmunds brings up practically what we already know is and must be brought up practically in the mind of the Commission in any form of the discussion.

The PRESIDENT. The question is upon striking out the motion made by Judge Strong and inserting the one made by Senator Edmunds.

Mr. Commissioner GARFIELD. I wish to make a single remark. The proposition of Judge Strong proceeds upon the supposition, which is the fact, that our order of last night, which is partially executed, has been arrested by an interlocutory question. The order last night was that we should proceed to hear counsel four and a half hours on each side, and as far as anything before us then was concerned, it was on the final question. That order is partly executed; two hours have been consumed on one side; but we are now arrested by an interlocutory question of the offer of proof and the admissibility of evidence. It seems to me much the plainest, much the easiest mode, to arrest our progress here and hear that question argued, as Judge Strong moves, for two hours on a side. That being settled, we proceed to execute the other order which has half been executed by hearing argument for two hours on one side; two hours and a half more are to be heard on that side and four and a half on the other, and that closes it. I shall vote against the amendment and in favor of Judge Strong's motion.

Mr. Commissioner THURMAN I wish there may be no misunderstanding as to the effect of this amendment or substitute. As I understand it, it is this, that after four hours of argument on each side the Commission shall go into consultation; if they decide against receiving the testimony, then without further argument they shall proceed to decide the case. I hope that that will be understood. That is the proposition.

Mr. Commissioner EDMUNDS. That is as I understand it.

Mr. Commissioner THURMAN. That we hear eight hours' argument, four on a side, and then go into consultation. Then if the decision be to receive the testimony, we come into open session again and hear it, and then argument follows, as a matter of course. If we decide not to receive it, then without any further argument we decide the whole case. That is the proposition in substance. I rather incline to think that the course suggested by Mr. Justice Strong is better than that, provided the time be extended. I do not believe that the admissibility of this testimony can be argued on either side within two hours, and, therefore, as it is in order to move to perfect the original motion before a substitute is voted on, I move to strike out "two" in Judge Strong's motion and insert "four."

Mr. Commissioner GARFIELD. Only three hours are asked for.

Mr. Commissioner THURMAN. Three, then, I will say.

The PRESIDENT. The first question is on perfecting the motion of Judge Strong by striking out "two" and inserting "three" as the number of hours. The question is on that amendment.

Mr. Commissioner PAYNE called for the yeas and nays; and being taken, they resulted—yeas 7, nays 8; as follows:

Those who voted in the affirmative were: Messrs. Abbott, Bayard, Clifford, Field, Hunton, Payne, and Thurman—7.

Those who voted in the negative were: Messrs. Bradley, Edmunds, Frelinghuysen, Garfield, Hoar, Miller, Morton, and Strong—8.

So the amendment was not agreed to.

The PRESIDENT. The question recurs on the substitute striking out all after the word "ordered" in Judge Strong's proposition and inserting the substitute of Senator Edmunds.

Mr. Commissioner PAYNE called for the yeas and nays; and being taken, they resulted—yeas 4, nays 11; as follows:

Those who voted in the affirmative were: Messrs. Edmunds, Frelinghuysen, Hoar, and Miller—4.

Those who voted in the negative were: Messrs. Abbott, Bayard, Bradley, Clifford, Field, Garfield, Hunton, Morton, Payne, Strong, and Thurman—11.

So the amendment was rejected.

The PRESIDENT. The question recurs on the motion of Judge Strong that counsel be allowed two hours on each side to argue the question of the admissibility of the offers of evidence.

The motion was agreed to.

Mr. EVARTS. Mr. President, we understand upon our part, and it is important that we should not misunderstand at this stage of the matter, that when the two hours have been consumed by each side on this interlocutory matter of the introduction of evidence, the order of yesterday proceeds to be executed by two hours and a half being allowed to the other side on the merits and four and a half hours to us.

The PRESIDENT. That is my understanding, unless the Commission otherwise direct.

Mr. EVARTS. The pertinency of this suggestion will be seen when I state what I was proceeding to ask in our behalf; that is, we might be of opinion that the argument in full and satisfactorily in point of time of this interlocutory question might well be expected to shorten our final argument upon the merits; we might be allowed to take an hour from the four and a half on the merits, lessening our time in that behalf, to speak on the interlocutory question.

The PRESIDENT. There is no such power in the Chair.

Mr. EVARTS. If the Commission should retire at the end of two hours' argument nothing in supplement to that would proceed from our general discussion of the case, while our opponents have had two hours of general discussion of the case in aid of the considerations they are now presenting.

The PRESIDENT. The present decision of the Commission is that two hours be allowed on a side to discuss the question of the admissibility of the proof offered. When that is concluded, unless the Commission decide to retire, (on which the Chair will not make any determination,) the question then will be the execution of the former order, which has been in part executed.

Mr. CAMPBELL. Allow me, Mr. President, to make a remark. I have the same opinion that was expressed by one of the honorable members of the Commission, that the whole merits of this case will be involved in the question of the admissibility of this evidence, because in the question of admissibility is involved the question of the effect; and therefore, I agree with the suggestion of counsel on the other side that if we find it necessary to discuss the question of admissibility at greater length than the two hours, we be allowed to continue the discussion and subtract the time so consumed from the four and a half hours allowed us on the merits.

The PRESIDENT. That is for the Commission, not for the Chair.

Mr. EVARTS. The Commission will see the great disparity in the position of the counsel for the two sides. Two hours have been occupied already in discussing the general merits of the case which involve all this question of admissibility. Now, they are to have two hours to discuss the specific question. We are to have but two hours to discuss the specific question, and then the Commission may retire upon that disparity of argument and preclude us from further argument.

Mr. Commissioner BRADLEY. Mr. President, I voted for two hours for a side on this question in consequence of the amount of time still left to discuss the main question; but the proposition now made by counsel on both sides seems to me to be a very fair one, that either side may take so much of their remaining time as they consider necessary in the discussion of this question of the admissibility of the evidence, and I move that they be permitted to do so.

Several MEMBERS. That is right.

The PRESIDENT. The motion of Justice Bradley is that counsel may take such time as they desire, if any, from the time previously allowed, four and a half hours, and employ it in the discussion of the question of the admissibility of the proofs, in addition to the two hours already allowed. The question is on that motion.

The motion was agreed to.

The PRESIDENT. In the absence of any direction from the Commission, the Chair rules that the objectors to the offers of proof open and close.

Mr. EVARTS. That is the opposite order to that which was adopted on the former discussion.

The PRESIDENT. Certainly; but it is the rule in court and I adopt that rule in the absence of any direction from the Commission. The objectors to evidence always speak first.

Mr. Commissioner EDMUNDS. In the Florida case it was exactly the other way. I do not know what would be more convenient to counsel.

Mr. EVARTS. We had expected that the course pursued in the Florida case would have proceeded here; we had no intimation of a change.

Mr. Commissioner EDMUNDS. I move, then, that those who offer the proof shall have the opening and the close.

The PRESIDENT. The question is on the motion of Senator Edmunds.

Mr. Commissioner MILLER. If the counsel on both sides wish that, there can be no objection to it.

Mr. Commissioner GARFIELD. If counsel can agree on that I should prefer that they should decide it. I think, if they can make a choice themselves, they ought to be permitted to do it.

Mr. TRUMBULL. We supposed it properly came from the objectors, but upon that we are entirely willing to submit to the Commission. We are willing to open ourselves.

The PRESIDENT. Very well; then there is no need of a vote. If you are agreed, the counsel making the offer of proof will open, but the rule in court is always the other way.

Mr. TRUMBULL. Mr. President, and gentlemen of the Commission——

Mr. Commissioner EDMUNDS. Before Judge Trumbull begins, as we shall have to sit quite late, I move that we now take a recess for thirty minutes.

The motion was agreed to, and the Commission took a recess.

The Commission re-assembled at one o'clock and four minutes p. m.

Mr. TRUMBULL. Mr. President and gentlemen, under the ruling of the Commission, we are brought face to face with the question whether a President of the United States is to be made by forgery and conspiracy on the part of the officials whose duty it is to certify the electoral vote of a State; and it is submitted to this Commission boldly and baldly to decide that question. The power rests nowhere else. There is no tribunal in this land, judicial or otherwise, that can inquire into this matter except this Commission; and when I speak to this Commission I consider myself as addressing the two Houses of Congress assembled together for the purpose of counting the electoral votes from the various States.

Is it true that the great Republic, founded by the wisest men and the purest patriots, has made no provision against the inauguration of its Chief Magistrate by fraud, corruption, and forgery? Is that the condition to which the people of this great country are reduced? Is this our boasted freedom? Is this our great American system that has no power to protect the seat occupied by Washington and Lincoln from being filled by a person who goes to it through the forgery, fraud, and conspiracy of those who certify to the election, and thereby thwart the will of the people? I confess myself humiliated that as a citizen of this Republic, in which we all take so much pride, I am called upon to argue such a question before a national tribunal.

In my judgment, there has been a very great misconception in regard to the powers of this Commission. It is neither a canvassing-board, with the powers usually given to persons who are to determine who is elected constable in some small town, nor is it a judicial tribunal; but it is the representative of both Houses of the Congress of the United States, vested with power to go to the bottom and investigate any question that the two Houses have a right to consider. Parliamentary law, the rules and methods of proceeding by legislative assemblies, are as well established as the rules of proceeding of the common law.

You are sitting here as legislators to decide a political question, hampered by no technical rules of evidence, but having authority conferred upon you by the organic act and by parliamentary law to inform yourselves upon any question that you have a right to consider.

It has been settled, and is not now to be questioned, that the two Houses of Congress are to count the electoral vote, and you now represent those two Houses. The question has arisen and has been submitted to you, as to how many, and what, votes shall be counted from the State of Louisiana, and there is submitted to you not only that question, but the law of your organization declares that all questions "upon or in respect" to the double returns from that State have been submitted to your consideration.

Is this tribunal a lie and a cheat, to defraud the American people? When the act passed creating it, there was great satisfaction through this whole country. We were thought by some to be upon the verge of civil war. There was great danger of collision in the land, of the inauguration of two Presidents, and the consequences were dreaded by every well-wisher to his country. When the act passed creating this Commission it was felt that, whatever might be its decision, it would receive the sanction of the whole people; for however much partisans of one candidate or the other might be disappointed, all good men felt that it was vastly more important that whoever succeeded to the Presidency should succeed as the legitimate choice of the people, than that any particular man should be installed by fraud.

Is it to turn out that this Commission was formed for the mere purpose of doing a sum in arithmetic, of adding up certain figures? When it was said to the country that it was to decide "all questions upon or in respect to such double returns," did it mean nothing more than that you should compute the number of votes appearing on the returns? When the oath was taken "to examine and consider all questions submitted," did that mean that you were simply to add up a set of figures? Do "examination and consideration" apply to a mere mathematical proposition of that kind?

But you are required by the law to proceed to consider the objections and to decide what? To decide "whether any and what votes from the State of Louisiana are the votes provided by the Constitution, and how many and what persons were duly appointed electors in that State." Can you consider how many and what persons were duly appointed electors in the State of Louisiana without inquiring whether the certificate that is read here is a forgery or the result of forgery and a conspiracy? We offer to prove that William P. Kellogg, whose certificate is before you, was a conspirator with others, fraudulently to alter the return of the election and that his certificate is false. We offer to prove that the canvassing-board, upon the action of which his certificate was based, through its president, offered the vote of the State for sale in the markets of the country, and are you only here to count that vote? Is there a man in America fit to be, I will not say President, but fit to be a constable, that would take office through such a source? What the country wants is a decision of the question as to who is *duly* elected. With that the country will be satisfied, and with nothing else.

I said you were clothed with power to investigate this subject, because it is submitted for your consideration, and I beg leave to refer to an elementary book for authority for what I have said. In Cushing's Law and Practice of Legislative Assemblies, at page 253, section 634, it is said:

> It has always, at least practically, been considered to be the right of legislative assemblies to call upon and examine all persons within their jurisdiction as witnesses in regard to subjects in reference to which they have power to act and into which they have already instituted, or are about to institute, an investigation. Hence they are authorized to summon and compel the attendance of all persons within the limits of their constituency, as witnesses, and to bring with them papers and records, in the same manner as is practiced by courts of law.

At page 295, section 747, of the same work, it is said:

> In addition to what may properly be called evidence, namely, that which is obtained by means of an inquiry instituted by the House or brought forward by a party, all the information of every description which in any way comes into the possession of the House may be regarded as evidence. Messages from the Executive, either at the commencement or in the course of the session, documents from the same source, returns from public officers or commissioners, either in pursuance of law or of the orders of the House, constitute evidence upon which legislative proceedings may be founded.

These are the usual modes of obtaining evidence by legislative bodies, and they are as well established as the rules by which testimony is obtained in courts of law. Have you, then, authority to pass upon the question submitted to you as to which of these returns from the State of Louisiana is the proper return? Have you authority to pass upon the question submitted to you in respect to those returns? Have you authority to determine "how many, and if any, what, persons were duly appointed electors in the State" of Louisiana? If you have power to make that inquiry, you are bound by parliamentary law, you are bound by the oath imposed upon you, you are bound by the proceedings of legislative bodies as old as the existence of parliaments, to investigate this question; and will you say that you will not receive this testimony that you yourselves have been two months in obtaining? The Senate sent its committee to Louisiana, and the House sent its committee to Louisiana, and these committees have taken a mass of testimony, which now lies before you, and we are prepared with that testimony, taken according to the rules of legislative assemblies, to establish the facts we allege. I call upon gentlemen on the other side to show, if they can, that the power of a legislative body does not extend to any investigation it thinks proper to make in regard to a question submitted to its consideration.

What is this State of Louisiana that has sent here these double returns, one of which is just as good as the other? Both these returns come here signed by an acting governor; both come under the great seal of the State of Louisiana, and the real seal is the one affixed to the McEnery certificate. I know it was said here yesterday by my distinguished friend from Wisconsin, [Mr. Howe,] in his quiet way, that you knew who William Pitt Kellogg was, but you did not know John McEnery; that John McEnery had given certificates to persons who came knocking at the doors of Congress for admission, but that the gate was never opened to them. If I have not forgotten, hardly twelve months have transpired since a person came knocking at the door of the Senate with a certificate signed by William Pitt Kellogg as governor of the State of Louisiana, stating that the applicant was duly elected to the Senate of the United States. Did the Senate open its doors to him; or did it shut the door in his face and send him away? From the day that Kellogg pretended to be governor, more than four years ago, no man has entered the Senate Chamber on a credential signed by him. He is in no better condition in that respect than McEnery.

Let us look at the history for a moment. In 1872 McEnery and Kellogg were opposing candidates for governor. A committee of the Senate, presided over by one of this commission, and of which I had the honor at the time to be a member, investigated that contest. The returns from the State of Louisiana were brought here and exhibited in our committee-room. After careful examination of the returns, the committee reported as follows:

Your committee are, therefore, led to the conclusion that if the election held in November, 1872, be not absolutely void for frauds committed therein, McEnery and his associates in State offices, and the persons certified as members of the legislature by the De Feriet board, ought to be recognized as the legal government of the State.

Such was the report of the committee of the Senate after the most patient investigation of all the facts, showing that McEnery, and not Kellogg, was the legitimate, lawful governor of the State. How, then, did Kellogg happen to get to be acting governor? The history of that transaction is known to the whole country.

Mr. Commissioner BRADLEY. Is that the report made by Mr. Carpenter?

Mr. TRUMBULL. Yes, sir. Kellogg succeeded in being installed as governor through the usurpation of a subordinate judge, who usurped authority and set up a legislature and a government in the State of Louisiana. Under his order no man was permitted to enter the legislative halls of the State as a member unless he had a certificate of election from a returning-board that never had a return before it, from a returning-board that counted forged affidavits by the thousand as evidence of election. The legislature thus organized, in less than twenty-four hours impeached and removed the existing governor. In a few hours more it turned out of office some of the judges of the courts, and appointed others to whom it gave the sole jurisdiction of determining all questions in regard to the right to hold office.

Mr. Commissioner EDMUNDS. You mean that they suspended the governor. They never pronounced final sentence.

Mr. TRUMBULL. Whether he was convicted and sentenced I do not know; but under the constitution and laws of Louisiana, the impeachment amounts to a suspension. They removed him in that way. His term, I understand, expired within a very short time.

Mr. Commissioner EDMUNDS. I merely meant to suggest that the word "removed" was, perhaps, inapplicable; but yet it does not affect the line of your argument.

Mr. TRUMBULL. Not at all.

Immediately a case was brought before a judge whom this legislature had created to determine as to the rightfulness of the legislature, and, of course, this judge, the creature of usurpers calling themselvs a legislature, decided that the authority from which he derived his judgeship was legitimate; and that is the way the legitimacy of the Kellogg government was established!

In regard to that usurpation, let me read a sentence from the report of the Senate committee:

Viewed in any light which your committee can consider them, the orders and injunctions made and granted by Judge Durell in this cause are most reprehensible, erroneous in point of law, and are wholly void for want of jurisdiction; and your committee must express their sorrow and humiliation that a judge of the United States should have proceeded in such flagrant disregard of his duty, and have so far overstepped the limits of Federal jurisdiction.

Mr. Morton, a member of that committee, commenting upon the acts of this judge, said in his separate report:

The conduct of Judge Durell, sitting in the circuit court of the United States, cannot be justified or defended. He grossly exceeded his jurisdiction and assumed the exercise of powers to which he could lay no claim, and his acts can only be characterized as a gross usurpation.

This same government in Louisiana underwent a review only a year or two ago, when a person bearing the certificate of Kellogg applied for a seat in the Senate as having been elected by the legislature of that State, and in the discussion upon that occasion much was said, and better than I can express it, in regard to the Kellogg government. In speaking of the usurpation of the returning-board which had counted in the Kellogg legislature and of the returns required to be transmitted to the secretary of state by the constitution, a member of this Commission, Mr. Edmunds, said:

They—

The returns—

are the returns which the various local officers take from the votes of the people, seal up, and transmit, and not the judgment of a body of men unknown to the constitution, who are to take these various papers and produce any result that in their judgment is lawful or convenient.

* * * * * *

I shall have no hesitation in saying that, no matter what returning-board had declared this to be a legislature or the other to be a legislature, it is within the competence of our duty to know, as the final and supreme judges of the election and qualification of this claimant to a seat, whether that legislature was composed of persons who appeared by the returns that the constitution speaks of to have been elected or whether they were the creation of some intermediate contrivance that either the cupidity of thieves or the ambition of politicians, or whatever, may have invented as a means of standing between the right of the people to elect their representatives and the persons who are to be authorized to meet and to organize the house.

Then, speaking of the powers of the board, Mr. Edmunds said:

The law itself gives this board no power of its own judgment or its own discretion in any way to tamper with or to change this primary and fundamental evidence, the only evidence which in any government which is to live by law can ever be received for the time being, the certificates from the people to show who have been elected members of the legislature or the governor of the State.

* * * * * *

Can any man stand up and say that it is any other thing than what the language of the law says, a compilation of results from the various sources which the law has provided and which has flowed into their hands? Such returns, it says—not those obtained by extrinsic evidence; not those obtained upon affidavit; not those obtained upon the judgment of any court; not those obtained in any other way than that they come from the separate assemblies of the people, sworn to and certified in the manner prescribed by law, their seals broken in their presence, and the results of those statements are to be proclaimed—and such results, thus proclaimed, are *prima-facie* evidence.

It is a special creation of the law; it has no finality, and it can have none that the law does not expressly or by clear implication confer upon it; and when the law says it may throw out a parish for a certain reason, it is an implied declaration of the law that it shall not throw out a parish for any other reason; and when the law says that it shall compile and canvass the returns that come to it, that is certainly a prohibition against its compiling or canvassing and getting together information, as this witness calls it, derived from his political knowledge or from any other knowledge under the sun, I do not care how sacred or how particular or complete it may be; for the moment these officers of the law, whose duties are so clearly pointed out, depart from the firm foundation of that path which the law has marked out for them, there is no security for liberty or for right or for anything for which government is instituted, for the reason that there is then no guide or limit either to their powers or their discretion; and that people, in my opinion, will make a great mistake who undertake to uphold results produced by a body acting, as this did, outside of the constitution and the laws of the State.

Every word I have read, and much more that was said on that occasion, is applicable to the canvass by which Kellogg, conspiring with the returning officers, made the certificate which is now before you and on which you are called upon to count the electoral vote for Hayes.

Not to detain you as to this government in Louisiana, I will only say that it is not a republican government, for it is a matter that I think this Commission should take official knowledge of, that the pretended officers in the State of Louisiana are upheld by military power alone. They could not maintain themselves an hour but for military support. Is that government republican which rests upon military power for support? A republican government is a government of the people, for the people, and by the people; but the government in Louisiana has been nothing but a military despotism for the last four years, and it could not stand a day if the people of the State were not overborne by military power.

Hear what an author of great credit in this country says in regard to this Louisiana usurpation. I read from Story on the Constitution, as lately published, with notes and additions by Judge Cooley.

Mr. Commissioner EDMUNDS. Is the original numbering of the sections preserved?

Mr. TRUMBULL. The original number is 1814, second volume. Judge Cooley in his note to that section says:

The recent case of Louisiana demonstrates that there may be greater wrongs than even the wrongful refusal by Congress to recognize the legitimate government of a State, and yet no speedy and effectual remedy be attainable. Such action on the part of Congress would at least be that of a proper authority, and would imply deliberation, and be supported by a presumption of due regard for the public good and for the supremacy of the law. But in the case of Louisiana in 1873, an inferior Federal judge, without a shadow of authority, and consequently in defiance of law, and for that reason supported by no presumption of correct motives, and with scarcely a pretense of observing even the usual forms, by the process of his court, aided by a military force, installed in power a State government which he sided with as against rival claimants, and in consequence of a pressure of business in Congress precluding prompt attention to the case by that body, has been enabled to sustain this government in power until the present time. Mr. Justice Story has with reason predicted that "if a despotic or monarchical government were established in one State it would bring on the ruin of the whole republic."

How prophetic. We are threatened to-day with that ruin which Mr. Justice Story foresaw.

What government can be more despotic than one elected by an injunction and continued in power by a military force under the order of a judge who, having no jurisdiction, is restrained by no law but his arbitrary will?

It is a despotism according to Judge Cooley.

For the facts of this unparalleled wrong we refer to reports made by the Judiciary Committee of the United States Senate in February, 1873. The case requires no further comment than it there receives. The dullest mind cannot fail to see that the facility with which the wrong is committed and the possible immediate advantages which individuals may derive therefrom present constant temptations to its repetition, and if suffered to pass once unrebuked a precedent will be tacitly assented to which cannot fail to threaten constant danger to our liberties, especially at those very periods of high political excitement when prudence, caution, and the strictest regard for the Constitution and the laws are most important. What party or what political leader can at such times be expected to pay scrupulous deference to the laws if a judge may ignore them with impunity? It was thought the climax of wrong had been reached when a local judge in one of the States could seize upon the property of individuals and corporations through his injunctions and mandates and plunder them through receivers; but he at least was not acting wholly without jurisdiction, and if he seized property he did not venture to go so far as to make the liberties of the people the subject of a receivership.

There is the opinion of a judge and one of the ablest elementary writers of our time in regard to this government in Louisiana. The Constitution of the United States says that each State shall appoint, in such manner as its legislature shall direct, a number of electors equal to the whole number of its Senators and Representatives in Congress; but it must be a State that does it; and what is meant by a "State?" A despotism, or a State having a republican form of government where the people, and not usurpers, rule? What has become of Durell, the Federal judge who set up the Kellogg dynasty? He resigned to escape impeachment by the House of Representatives, composed at the time of a large majority of political friends of the party he sought to serve, and is now a fugitive from the State of Louisiana, subject to the scorn and contempt of all who know him. He is receiving to-day the punishment which sooner or later will come upon all men who, clothed with official authority, betray their trust, and for party ends encroach on the rights of the people. While the author of these iniquities which have brought ruin upon the people of Louisiana goes forth a vagabond upon the face of the earth, condemned to everlasting infamy, his work stands, and this high Commission is to-day asked to uphold it and give it new force.

But you have here a certificate from a person claiming to be governor, a certified list, as it is called in the statute, of the names of the persons elected electors. What does that amount to? Did the Constitution require it? That instrument says:

The electors shall meet in their respective States and vote by ballot for President and Vice-President, one of whom at least shall not be an inhabitant of the same State with themselves; they shall name in their ballots the person voted for as President, and in distinct ballots the person voted for as Vice-President, and they shall make distinct lists of all persons voted for as President, and of all persons voted for as Vice-President, and of the number of votes for each; which lists they shall sign and certify, and transmit sealed to the seat of Government of the United States, directed to the President of the Senate. The President of the Senate shall, in the presence of the Senate and House of Representatives, open all the certificates, and the votes shall then be counted.

That is all the electors have to do. The right to appoint electors is not inherent in a State, but derivative from the Constitution of the United States, which is as much a part of the constitution of every State as it is of the United States. Every word and every letter of this Constitution is as binding on the State as on the United States. It was framed for the purpose of forming a general government and also for the purpose of protecting the States in certain national rights. This Constitution says to the State of Louisiana, "You may appoint electors in such manner as your legislature shall direct; they shall meet and cast their ballots in a certain way, and send them to the President of the Senate, and the votes shall then be counted." Tell me by what authority Congress passes a law that they shall not be counted unless certified in a particular manner. By what authority has Congress said to the governor of Louisiana or to the governor of any State, "You make three certified lists of the names of the persons appointed electors?" It may be a matter of convenience for the two Houses to have that sort of evidence; but it is entirely at the option of the governor of the State to obey that act or not; and old John Hancock, nearly a century ago, before he would make any such certificate, sent a communication to the legislature of the commonwealth of Massachusetts to know whether it would meet their approval. I will read what was said by a committee of the Senate in a unanimous report made by Mr. Morton on this subject in 1873:

The third section of the act of Congress of 1792 declares what shall be the official evidence of the election of electors, and provides that "the executive authority of each State shall cause three lists of the names of the electors of such State to be made and certified, to be delivered to the electors on or before the first Wednesday in December, and the said electors shall annex one of the said lists to each of their votes." The certificate of the secretary of state is not required, and the certificate of the governor, as provided for in this section, seems to be the only evidence contemplated by the law of the election of electors and their right to cast the electoral vote of the State. If Congress chooses to go behind the governor's certificate, and inquire who has been chosen as electors, it is not violating any principle of the right of the States to prescribe what shall be the evidence of the election of electors, but it is simply going behind the evidence as prescribed by an act of Congress; and, thus going behind the certificate of the governor, we find that the official returns of the election of electors from the various parishes of Louisiana had never been counted by anybody having authority to count them.

What was the result? On that report in 1873 the Senate and the House of Representatives voted not to count the electoral vote of the State of Louisiana, and it was rejected. Governor Warmoth had given a certificate in due form certifying to the election of the electors in that State; but what was it good for? The two Houses went behind it. A committee of the Senate reported that the votes had never been canvassed by anybody having authority to canvass them, and the result was that the vote of the State was rejected. There is authority for going behind the governor's certificate.

Mr. Commissioner BRADLEY. Who canvassed at that time? Who made the canvass?

Mr. TRUMBULL. The canvass at that time was required to be made by a returning-board consisting of the governor, the lieutenant-governor, the secretary of. state, and two persons designated by name. There was a controversy as to which was the proper canvassing-board.

Mr. Commissioner BRADLEY. And it was held that the proper board had not made the canvass?

Mr. TRUMBULL. It was not decided in this report.

Mr. Commissioner BRADLEY. I want to know the meaning of that language.

Mr. TRUMBULL. Let me read from the report:

And thus going behind the certificate of the governor, we find that the official returns of the election of electors from the various parishes of Louisiana had never been counted by anybody having authority to count them.

Mr. Commissioner MORTON. I would inquire whether Judge Trumbull has the whole report there?

Mr. TRUMBULL. I have. You will find it commencing at page 370 of this book entitled The Presidential Counts.

Mr. Commissioner MORTON. Will the Judge then state what the report says in regard to the right of Congress to go behind the evidence prescribed by the laws of the State, a little further on?

Mr. Commissioner BRADLEY. The thing has passed out of my mind and I merely ask for information.

Mr. TRUMBULL. This is the passage, I suppose:

The election of the Greeley electors was certified to by the governor of the State, but the official returns of the election have not been counted by the returning-board created by the laws of Louisiana for that purpose; and the persons who, in fact, made the examination and count had no legal authority to do so. The election of the Grant electors is certified by the Lynch returning-board, but that board did not have the official returns before them, and their election is not certified by the governor of the State, as required by the act of Congress. The committee are of the opinion that neither the Senate of the United States nor both Houses jointly have the power under the Constitution to canvass the returns of and election and count the votes to determine who have been elected presidential electors, but that the mode and manner of choosing electors are left exclusively to the States. And if by the law of the State they are to be elected by the people, the method of counting the vote and ascertaining the result can only be regulated by the law of the State. Whether it is competent for the two Houses, under the twenty-second joint rule, (in regard to the constitutionality of which the committee here give no opinion,) to go behind the certificate of the governor of the State to inquire whether the votes for electors have ever been counted by the legal returning-board created by the law of the State, or whether in making such count, the board had before them the official returns, the committee offer no suggestions, but present only a statement of the facts as they understand them.

That covers, I presume, what was asked of me.

Mr. Commissioner MORTON. That covers it.

Mr. Commissioner EDMUNDS. Do I understand you to mean, Judge Trumbull, in speaking of the action of the Senate four years ago, that the judgment of the Senate was upon the question of fact as to what the real vote of the people had been?

Mr. TRUMBULL. It would be difficult to state upon what consideration Senators voted. The vote of Louisiana was duly certified to by the governor of the State; I have the certificate here in proper form; as the honorable Senator is aware, we never can know the considerations upon which Senators vote, but for some reason or other the Senate and the House concurred in rejecting the vote of Louisiana. The certificate of the governor, however, was in due form and complete; so that it does amount to a decision thus far that the two Houses of Congress have decided that the certificate of the governor in due form, stating that certain persons are electors, is not conclusive upon the two Houses of Congress.

Mr. Commissioner EDMUNDS. Under certain circumstances. The resolution, if you will pardon me, was that all the objections presented having been received, no electoral vote purporting to be that of the State of Louisiana should be counted, in favor of which there were 33 affirmative and against it 16 negative votes. Among the objections was one by Mr. Carpenter, a Senator from Wisconsin:

I object to the counting of the votes given for U. S. Grant for President and Henry Wilson Vice-President, by the electors of Louisiana, because there is no proper return of votes cast by the electors of the State of Louisiana, and because there is no State government in said State which is republican in form, and because no canvass or counting of the votes cast for electors in the State of Louisiana at the election held in November last had been made prior to the meeting of the electors.

And another of similar purport by Mr. Senator Trumbull, of the State of Illinois.

Mr. Commissioner THURMAN. Allow me to interrupt Judge Trumbull. I understand that the decision of the Senate went on the question whether the governor's certificate was conclusive, and it was decided not only that his certificate was not conclusive, but it was decided that the decision of that returning-board on which he founded his certificate was not conclusive.

Mr. Commissioner MORTON. There was no such certificate before the Senate.

Mr. Commissioner THURMAN. There was a certificate of one returning-board.

Mr. TRUMBULL. The certificate of Governor Warmoth I had better read, that the Commission may see what the certificate was in that case:

UNITED STATES OF AMERICA,
    State of Louisiana, city of New Orleans:

I, H. C. Warmoth, governor of the State of Louisiana, do hereby certify that the foregoing signature of B. P. Blanchard, State registrar of votes for the State of Louisiana, is genuine; and I do further certify that Messrs. T. C. Manning, A. S. Herron, and C. H. Weed, for the State at large, and Hugh J. Campbell, for first district; Louis Bush, second district; Allen Thomas, third district; A. H. Leonard, fourth district, and L. V. Reeves, fifth district, were duly and legally elected presidential electors for the State of Louisiana, at an election held in said State on the 4th day of November, A. D. 1872, pursuant to the statutes of the Congress of the United States and State of Louisiana on the subject.

In faith whereof I have hereunto affixed my official signature and caused the great seal of the State to be hereto attached, at the city of New Orleans, capital of the State, this 4th day of December, A. D. 1872, and of the Independence of the United States the ninety-seventh.

                                        H. C. WARMOTH.
By the governor:
[L. S.]
                                    Y. A. WOODWARD,
                                    Assistant Secretary of State.

In the Senate report it is said:

Messrs. Woodward and Bragdon, according to the testimony, looked over the returns to ascertain who had been elected electors for President and Vice-President, and made a statement to the governor of the result of their examination; and the governor, on the morning of the 4th of December, the day fixed by the act of Congress when the electors in the several States shall meet and cast their votes, issued a paper, in which he declared that T. C. Manning, G. A. Weed, A. S. Herron, H. J. Campbell, L. Bush, A. Thomas, A. H. Leonard, and L. V. Reeves had been elected electors, and placed a copy of the said paper in the possession of each of said persons; and afterward, on the same day, they assembled in the city of New Orleans, and, as electors, voted for President and Vice-President. It clearly appears from the testimony that the official returns of the State were never examined and counted for presidential electors by any persons except Messrs. Woodward and Bragdon, and up to this time never have been examined and counted by the Lynch board or any person having authority whatever to make such examination and count. While we have no doubt that the returns sent to Governor Warmoth from the various parishes by the supervisors of registration will, upon their face, show that the aforesaid persons named as electors, and whom we shall designate as the "Greeley electors," received a majority of the votes, that fact has never been ascertained by any competent authority, and the action of Governor Warmoth depended entirely upon the unauthorized statements of Messrs. Woodward and Bragdon, who, at the time, had no right to look into the returns at all. In this matter there is no pretense that the law was complied with, and the Lynch board were never at any time permitted to see them.

That is the report made by the Senate Committee on Privileges and Elections, of which the Senator from Indiana then was, as he now is, chairman.

Mr. Commissioner BRADLEY. I now understand the point. One set of men had the returns but were not entitled to have them, and the other set who were entitled to them did not have them.

Mr. TRUMBULL. That was a disputed question, and I do not know that it has ever been settled to this day, except by the judge to whom I referred who was put in office for the purpose of settling it.

Mr. Commissioner EDMUNDS. That was the contention.

Mr. TRUMBULL. That was the contention, as is very aptly expressed. But however it may have been, one thing was settled by Congress, so far as the two Houses could settle it, that the governor's certificate in due form, the same kind of a certificate as No. 1 now before the Commission, was overruled by the concurrent action of the two Houses of Congress, and they refused to count the vote, and the report of the committee was that the vote had not been properly canvassed. Now we propose to show this Commission that the vote in November last has never been canvassed, that the pretended canvass is a fraud, that the papers were forged, that the returns were altered and falsified, and I should like to know if a count under such circumstances is any better than a true count made by persons who had no authority to make it. If the action of Congress is worth anything, unless it is to reverse its decision, and that in behalf of iniquity, this Commission can go back of the returns. Legislative bodies and courts sometimes, though very reluctantly, overrule former decisions; but in the history of legislative proceedings or of courts was it ever heard that a former decision was reversed in order to perpetuate a wrong, an iniquity, a falsehood, a forgery? If the action of Congress is good for anything, it establishes the right to go behind the certificate. That was the understanding when this Commission was created, and it will be a delusion and a snare in the estimation of this whole people if the questions submitted to this Commission are decided upon the technical ground that the Commission has nothing to do but to add up the votes as shown on the face of the certificates. It will be overturning not only the decision of Congress four years ago, it will overturn every settled principle of parliamentary law from the beginning of time, so far as we have any record of it. Is my time up?

The PRESIDENT. You commenced at five minutes past one. It is now twelve minutes past two. You have spoken one hour and seven minutes.

Mr. Commissioner ABBOTT. There were some fifteen minutes lost by a discussion of the Louisiana question which I do not think in all fairness should be taken out of Judge Trumbull's time.

Mr. Commissioner BAYARD. Mr. President, I submit that when counsel are compelled to read long papers in answer to members of the Commission and are thereby diverted from their argument, at least the time so occupied in responding to questions of individuals upon the Commission should not be charged to them in the computation of their time.

The PRESIDENT. Judge Trumbull has still time left. The question would hardly arise, unless the time should come when I might consider it my duty to stop him.

Mr. TRUMBULL. There is another principle of parliamentary law to which I desire to call attention. It is succinctly stated in an elementary work to which I refer rather than quote decisions, in section 441 in what is entitled The American Law of Elections, by McCrary, where it is said:

> Fraud, in the conduct of an election, may be committed by one or more of the officers thereof, or by other persons. If committed by persons not officers, it may be either with or without knowledge or connivance of such officers. There is a difference between a fraud committed by officers or with their knowledge and connivance, and a fraud committed by other persons, in this: the former is ordinarily fatal to the return, while the latter is not fatal, unless it appear that it has changed or rendered doubtful the result. If an officer of the election is detected in a willful and deliberate fraud upon the ballot-box, the better opinion is that this will destroy the integrity of his official acts. even though the fraud discovered is not, of itself, sufficient to affect the result, (ante, section 184, Judkins vs. Hill, 50 N. H., 104.) The reason of this rule is that an officer who betrays his trust in one instance is shown to be capable of the infamy of defrauding the electors, and his certificate is therefore good for nothing.

Now we propose to show by evidence which we have offered here that the president of the returning-board with the sanction of his confederates altered the returns of Vernon Parish, took 178 votes from one side and put them on the other by a forgery of the papers. According to this authority, a fraud committed by an officer is fatal to his return.

I see I shall have no time to go, and it is perhaps not proper that I should on this preliminary question of admitting evidence go, into the question of the want of authority in this returning-board under any circumstances to canvass the electoral vote. Assuming that it has such authority under any circumstances, still it would have no authority to reject votes, except the foundation be properly laid. The law is succinctly and clearly stated in the report already cited, made by Senator Morton, as follows:

> The statute of Louisiana authorizes the supervisors of registration in the parishes, or the commissioners of election, to make affidavit in regard to any violence, tumult, fraud, or bribery by which a fair election has been prevented, which shall be forwarded to the returning-board along with the returns, and upon which the returning-board may reject the vote of a poll in making the count; and if the evidence of the officers of the election is not sufficient to satisfy the minds of the returning-board in regard to the matters charged they are authorized to send for persons and papers and take further testimony upon the matter; but they have no authority to make such investigation unless the foundation is first laid by the sworn statements of the officers of the election, as before mentioned.

Everybody who ever looked into the Louisiana law agrees with what was stated by the Committee on Privileges and Elections of the Senate in 1873. The same committee in 1875 and the committee of the House of Representatives which visited Louisiana in 1874 both agree that the laying of a proper foundation to reject votes was a jurisdictional fact, without the existence of which the returning-board would have no authority to reject votes or to do anything except to compile the statements of votes that were made by the commissioner of election.

Mr. Commissioner MILLER. Judge Trumbull, allow me to make a suggestion to you just there. The point came up in the Florida case, and was much considered in the conference and was the ground of some of the votes then cast, and there is a great deal of importance attached to it, in my mind at least. If the only thing which that returning-board could do was to determine whether certain polls should be rejected or counted, your argument is a perfectly just one; but is it not also true that the jurisdiction of that board is commensurate with the duties and functions it is to perform, and is it not true that the one main function it is to perform is to ascertain who was elected and to declare that fact? And can it be said that if they mistake the law in some of the points that they have to determine upon in discharging that function of declaring who are elected, or if they fail properly to weigh the testimony on which they act in any of those points, that is so jurisdictional that their decision is erroneous?

Mr. TRUMBULL. No, sir; I do not contend for that.

Mr. Commissioner MILLER. Then my suggestion is that the jurisdiction of this board, the function which it is called upon to discharge, is to ascertain and declare who are elected. That is their jurisdiction, and all below it is the exercise of means and modes of procedure.

Mr. TRUMBULL. To that I cannot quite assent. I assent entirely to the proposition that upon any matter of which this board had jurisdiction and a discretion to act, their judgment is not to be disturbed; but the point I make is that while it is their duty to canvass and compile the vote—that is their sworn duty—it is also their sworn duty not to take jurisdiction of the question of rejecting votes unless a foundation is first laid for so doing. Upon the want of power of a canvassing-board to reject votes, and that its acts in so doing are without jurisdiction and void, I refer to the cases of The People *vs.* Cook, 4 Selden, 82; and 10 Bush, 743. In the case of the State *vs.* County Judge, 7 Iowa Rep., 201, it is said:

The next subject of examination is the answer that the duty had already been performed.

It was a case of mandamus to compel a returning-officer to canvass the votes.

Inasmuch as the canvassers have rejected the returns from three of the townships which they should have counted, it is legally true that duty has not been discharged; and when the writ now commands, it is not, in a proper legal sense, to recanvass, but to canvass, the returns of that election. It is to do that which was before their duty, but which they omitted. What has been done is as if it had not been done, and the judge is now commanded to proceed as if no former steps had been taken.

He had left out three returns that it was his duty to canvass. The mandamus went compelling him to make the canvass. The same principle is very forcibly stated in a recent decision by the Supreme Court of the United States in a case that is not yet reported, decided at the present term of the court. It is the case of Windsor *vs.* McVeigh. It was an action of ejectment, and there came up collaterally the validity of title derived from a sale under the confiscation acts. Some years ago a suit was instituted in Virginia to condemn property under the confiscation acts, and the owners came in and sought to defend. The judge of the court struck their answer from the files and refused to hear them at all. The case proceeded to judgment and the property was sold. An action of ejectment was brought involving the title derived under the sale. The court say in that case:

> The law is and always has been that whenever notice or citation is required, the party cited has the right to appear and be heard, and when the latter is denied the former is ineffectual for any purpose. The denial to a party in such a case of the right to appear is in legal effect the recall of the citation to him.
>
> * * * " * * *
>
> The jurisdiction acquired by the court by seizure of the *res* was not to condemn the property without further proceedings.

The jurisdiction secured by this returning-board to make the canvass was not to reject a part of the returns arbitrarily and at will. There is much in this decision illustrative of the present case:

> If a seizure is made and condemnation is passed without the allegation of any specific cause of forfeiture or offense, and without any public notice of the proceedings, so that the parties in interest have no opportunity of appearing and making a defense, the sentence is not so much a judicial sentence as an arbitrary sovereign edict.

In quoting from Mr. Justice Story in another case, with approbation, the court say—

> In another part of the same opinion the judge characterized such sentences "as mere mockeries, and as in no just sense judicial proceedings;" and declared that they "ought to be deemed, both *ex directo in rem* and collaterally, to be mere arbitrary edicts or substantial frauds."

The court held the judgment of condemnation absolutely void in a collateral proceeding. A jurisdiction to compile and canvass votes does not confer jurisdiction to reject votes. The latter jurisdiction can only be exercised when the statutory foundation is laid.

There is another point which goes to the jurisdiction of this board which we ought, I think, to be permitted to show, that it was not so constituted as to have jurisdiction of the canvass at all, for the reason that the law declares that "five persons, to be elected by the senate, of all political parties, shall constitute the returning-officers for all elections, a majority of whom shall constitute a quorum and have power to make the returns of all elections." Now, I insist that it was incompetent for four persons to act. Four or three might act if the board was full; but when a duty is required to be performed by five persons of different political parties, it cannot be lawfully performed by four persons all of the same party.

There was an object in the requirement that the board should be composed of different political parties. It is not a mere directory statute. The legislature undoubtedly had in view fairness in the canvass of the returns, and hence it committed it to returning-officers to be made up of all political parties. The fact here is, that four persons, all of one party, made the canvass. Suppose five had existed, could a majority have acted without giving notice to the others? The act of a majority would doubtless be good if the board had been full and all had been notified. Each party had the right to have the advice and the judgment of some of its friends in this board. While three might act they must give notice to all that all might have an opportunity to be present. These four had authority to fill up the board. The statute required them to do it. They were asked to fill the vacancy and refused. Every clerk engaged by them was of the same political party. I insist that this board was not constituted so as to have authority to make the canvass at all. The general rule on this subject is well stated in 21 Wendell's Reports in the case of Downing vs. Ruger, page 182:

> The rule seems to be well established that, in the exercise of a public as well as a private authority, whether it be ministerial or judicial, all the persons to whom it is committed must confer and act together, unless there be a provision that a less

number may proceed. Where the authority is public, and the number is such as to admit of a majority, that will bind the minority, after all have duly met and conferred.

I do not insist that the whole five must have been present; but I do insist that where the authority existed in the four to supply the vacancy they had no authority to go on and make the canvass without supplying the vacancy. It was not fair; it was not what the legislature intended; and they are in no better position surely, failing to obey the law and supply this vacancy, than they would have been if they had supplied the vacancy and then acted without giving the fifth man notice or affording him an opportunity to attend; and that would have been fatal.

The fact that the statute authorizes a majority to act does not change the rule. A majority could have acted in a case of this kind, if the statute had not said so, provided all had been afforded an opportunity to co-operate.

Mr. Commissioner EDMUNDS. Your point is, that no step at all could be taken until the board was full?

Mr. TRUMBULL. No step could be taken until the vacancy was filled, the four having authority to fill it.

The constituent elements of which this returning-board was to consist being wanting, I insist the four could not go on without filling up the board, particularly as one of the elements which entered into the mind of the legislature in the passage of the law was wanting in the board as it existed, the four being all of one political party.

My attention is called to the phraseology of the law. It is:

In case of any vacancy by death, resignation, or otherwise, by either of the board, then the vacancy *shall be filled* by the residue of the board of returning-officers.

The act is mandatory, and a failure to obey it I think is a fatal defect in the organization of the board.

The PRESIDENT. Excuse me for saying that you have occupied an hour and a half.

Mr. TRUMBULL. I desire to call attention to one other matter. It has been stated in another argument in the hearing of the Commission, and I have not the vanity to suppose that I can state it any more clearly, but yet I desire to press it upon your consideration. To my mind it is conclusive and unanswerable. I allude to the inability of the legislature of Louisiana to appoint Brewster and Levissee electors. The language of the Constitution is in that respect peculiar. It is an inhibition on the legislature and not a disqualification or inability on the part of the individual. The attention of the Commission was called to that the other day. The language of the Constitution, that "no person shall be a Senator who shall not have attained to the age of thirty years and been nine years a citizen of the United States," is very different from the language here. The only power that a State has to appoint an elector at all is derived from the Constitution of the United States. Most of the powers exercised by a State are inherent, belonging to the State itself, but the power to appoint electors of President and Vice-President is derived from the Constitution of the United States. That is the warrant of authority, and it reads thus:

Each State shall appoint, in such manner as the legislature thereof may direct, a number of electors, equal to the whole number of Senators and Representatives to which the State may be entitled in the Congress; but no Senator or Representative, or person holding an office of trust or profit under the United States, shall be appointed an elector.

We have here the evidence that Brewster was surveyor-general of the land-office for the district of Louisiana, an office to which he was nominated by the President and confirmed by the Senate. He held this office on the 7th of November last. The warrant of authority to the State of Louisiana is, " You may appoint as many electors as you have Senators and Representatives, but you shall not appoint O. H. Brewster." That is what the Constitution in effect says.

Mr. Commissioner MORTON. Let me ask the gentleman a question. Does he believe that the control given to the legislature in the appointment of electors can be limited, restrained, or directed by the constitution of the State?

Mr. TRUMBULL. They can determine certainly in the State whom they will appoint, and may put inhibitions on the appointment of particular persons, I should imagine.

Mr. Commissioner MORTON. My question is this: inasmuch as the Constitution of the United States gives to the legislature of the State the control of the appointment of electors, is it competent for the State by her constitution to control the legislature in the exercise of that power?

Mr. TRUMBULL. That question does not arise in this case. The power being granted by the Constitution of the United States to the legislature in terms, it may be questionable whether it is competent for the people in their constitution to regulate it.

Mr. Commissioner HOAR. Mr. Trumbull, is not the question a little deeper even than Mr. Morton has put it? When the Constitution of the United States has fixed the qualifications of presidential electors, or rather has expressed certain disqualifications, is it competent for the legislature of a State, under the mere power of fixing the manner of appointment, to impose other disqualifications?

Mr. Commissioner THURMAN. No such question arises here.

Mr. SHELLABARGER. This is a Federal officer.

Mr. Commissioner HOAR. I understand that was the point you were then arguing, but Mr. Morton called your attention to another, and you were replying to him.

Mr. TRUMBULL. The question of the Senator from Indiana, as I understand it, is whether the legislature, in the exercise of this power conferred upon it by the Federal Constitution, is bound by its State constitution? It amounts to that. I should say a legislature is bound to observe the State constitution as well as the Constitution of the United States, both, unless they conflict. If there be a conflict between them, then we all know that the Federal Constitution is paramount; but I think the legislature would be bound by the constitution of the State so far as it did not interfere with any provision of the Constitution of the United States. But that is not the case I am arguing. The case I am presenting to you is this: The Constitution of the United States in the grant of power has said to the State of Louisiana, " You may appoint certain persons as electors for President, but you shall not appoint O. H. Brewster." Now, I say, when the Constitution says that to the State of Louisiana, it is binding upon the legislature and upon every citizen of Louisiana. Any appointment, therefore, made in defiance of that provision is utterly void. It cannot be that such an appointment can stand. You are to inquire here, " Who, and how many electors, were duly appointed;" and I put it to every member of this Commission if he can say, that a man who the Constitution, which is above us all and which we all swear to support, says shall not be an elector, shall nevertheless be an elector, and that his appointment as such is according to the Constitution?

Mr. Commissioner MORTON. I ask the gentleman this question,

whether it is competent for a State by her constitution to add to the qualifications required for United States Senators?

Mr. TRUMBULL. Undoubtedly not. That has been settled. That is another question. I do not see its applicability to this point. There are some cases in Louisiana which I shall leave for my associate, Judge Campbell, to discuss, of persons inhibited by the constitution of Louisiana from holding any office; for instance, the law of Louisiana specifically and in terms declares that no supervisor of registration that is, no person who has charge of all this election machinery, shall be a candidate for an office at the election which he superintends. Yet, in defiance of that statute, one of the Hayes electors was a supervisor of registration managing the election when he himself was a candidate. I do not propose to go into that. I am speaking of the other cases of United States officers; there are two of them who claim to have been chosen electors. What is the answer to the suggestions that such persons cannot be electors? My distinguished friend [Mr. Evarts] says the Constitution does not execute itself.

Mr. Commissioner BRADLEY. Allow me, Mr. Trumbull. The proposition No. 6 is that Brewster was surveyor-general at the time of the election.

Mr. TRUMBULL. Yes, sir.

Mr. Commissioner BRADLEY. Do you include and intend to prove that he was such at the time of giving his vote?

Mr. TRUMBULL. No, sir; at the time of his appointment; he was appointed at the time of the election. I do not wish to state it stronger than it is. I understand that he tendered his resignation some time in November after the election, and it was accepted, very singularly, to date back before the election, although the resignation was not offered until some time after, as Mr. Brewster himself stated under oath.

Mr. Commissioner THURMAN. Let me ask you a question, Judge Trumbull. The law of Louisiana, as I understand, provides that if an elector who has been chosen or appointed does not appear by a certain hour, the remaining electors shall proceed to fill the vacancy?

Mr. TRUMBULL. Yes, sir; there is such a provision in the act of 1868.

Mr. CARPENTER. And nowhere else.

Mr. Commissioner EDMUNDS. I understand Judge Trumbull contends that act is not in force.

Mr. Commissioner THURMAN. But if that law is in force, and he did not appear at the time, as the certificate reads, then no matter whether he was an officer or not, there was a vacancy under that law, was there not?

Mr. TRUMBULL. No, sir.

Mr. Commissioner THURMAN. Under the law of 1868?

Mr. TRUMBULL. I do not consider that there was; I understand that there was not. The statutes of the United States make two provisions: one is for filling any vacancies which may occur in the college when such college meets to give its electoral votes; the other is when a State has held an election for the purpose of choosing electors, and has failed to make a choice on the day prescribed by law, the electors may be appointed on a subsequent day, in such manner as the legislature of the State may direct. Here was no choice. It was just as if two persons had received the same vote.

Mr. Commissioner THURMAN. I do not think you comprehend my question. Is not the real question, whether there is any power to fill a vacancy in the remaining members of the board? Suppose this man had been qualified, but did not appear.

Mr. TRUMBULL. Then, if this statute was in force, the other electors could have filled the vacancy.

Mr. Commissioner THURMAN. But suppose it were not?

Mr. TRUMBULL. Then there is no law authorizing the filling of the vacancy——

Mr. Commissioner HUNTON. Except by popular election.

Mr. TRUMBULL. That brings up complicated questions. The statute of 1872 provides for filling all vacancies by popular election. If that statute was in force, then the vacancy would have to be filled by a popular election. If the law of 1868 was in force, then one of those elected being absent would give the others authority to fill the vacancy, provided anybody had ever been elected. If you will look at the statute of 1868 you will find it says:

If any one or more of the electors chosen by the people shall fail from any cause whatever to attend—

We insist that these men, Brewster and Levissee, were never chosen by the people, and could not be chosen by the people; it was utterly out of their power to choose them. As to the other provision of the law of the United States, there is no statute in Louisiana authorizing the supplying of this want of an election on the 7th of November, unless it be the statute of 1872, and so there must be a popular election if that applies.

But I was about, when interrupted, to reply to the suggestion that the Constitution did not execute itself. That is true in reference to some things; but it is untrue in reference to a great many other things. If you will refer to the Constitution of the United States you will find that a great many of its provisions do execute themselves. Look at section 10 of article 1. You will observe that this is an inhibition on the State, and such provisions do execute themselves. No law of Congress could execute them. How could you punish a State for not obeying the Constitution of the United States? The Constitution says that no State shall appoint a public officer an elector. The Constitution of the United States says:

No State shall   *   *   *   emit bills of credit.

Suppose a State does emit bills of credit, are they not void? Did not the Supreme Court of the United States nearly half a century ago decide in the Missouri case that bills of credit issued by the State of Missouri were utterly void; and where is the statute making them void? How many times has the Supreme Court decided that a law passed by a State impairing the obligation of a contract is void? Is there any statute of the United States declaring that if a State passes a law impairing the obligation of a contract it shall be void? Would it not be an absurdity to pass such a statute? Could a United States statute impose a penalty on a State for passing an *ex post facto* law? Do you propose to put a State in prison or to fine a State? All these inhibitions on the State execute themselves. The case referred to in Mississippi in regard to the importation of slaves into that State is entirely different, governed by different considerations. The constitution of Mississippi provided that—

The introduction of slaves into this State as merchandise, or for sale, shall be prohibited from and after the 1st day of April, 1833.

That was a provision for the legislature to prohibit the importation for certain purposes after a certain time.

I certainly need not take up the time of this honorable Commission further to show that certain provisions of the Constitution are self-executing. There is not a person upon it who does not know that it has been decided over and over again that these inhibitions upon the States are self-executing.

There is only one other suggestion to be made in regard to this disqualified elector, and that is that he was not a *de facto* elector; but if he was such, his acts as a *de facto* officer are no more valid than the acts of the Tilden electors. The duties of the office of elector are all performed at one time. It is simply to cast a vote, and McEnery and his associates met together at the proper place, on the proper day, and cast their vote. They were officers *de facto* just as much as was Brewster. But neither of them was an officer *de facto* in the sense that the acts of an officer *de facto* are to stand; and why? Because the reason of the rule that gives validity to the acts of *de facto* officers has no application whatever to the act of a person who has a single duty to perform, and that act incomplete. The object of the law recognizing the acts of *de facto* officers as valid is the security of the public. The people having business before officers cannot stop to investigate their legal authority to the offices they occupy; and hence, so far as the public and business interests are concerned, their acts are valid. What act has this elector ever performed that affected the public interest until this vote is counted? The reason that has led to the adoption of the rule in regard to *de facto* officers has no application to such a case.

I have taken so much more time than I intended that I must close without discussing some other points; and I do so by saying that if a man is to be made President of the United States by counting the votes of Levissee, Brewster, and their associates from Louisiana, it will be by the mere form of law, contrary to the principles of the Constitution and in violation of the rights of the people.

Mr. MERRICK. Mr. President, I ask leave to file a brief on the subject of the validity of the acts of officers *de facto.**

The PRESIDENT. I think I may receive it.

Mr. EVARTS. Let us have copies.

Mr. MERRICK. Certainly.

Mr. TRUMBULL. If the Commission please, in justice to my associate I really think that all the time I have occupied ought not to be taken from his, as I was frequently interrupted.

The PRESIDENT. I shall submit that matter to the Commission when Mr. Campbell asks for time.

Mr. Commissioner PAYNE. I move now that the time consumed by interruptions of the Commission be not counted.

The PRESIDENT. I have no definite count of the time so consumed.

Mr. Commissioner BAYARD. I should like to ask Mr. Trumbull whether there is any statute of Louisiana requiring a certificate from the governor of the appointment of electors.

Mr. TRUMBULL. There is a statute of Louisiana which I will refer to, which requires the governor to commission all officers except certain persons who are named, of which an elector is not one.

Mr. Commissioner BAYARD. That is the law of 1872. Is there any statute requiring the governor to issue a certificate of election to the electors?

Mr. TRUMBULL. Not specifically, but there is a statute of Louis-

* This brief will be found in the Appendix of Briefs, marked Brief No. 4.

iana and a provision of the constitution. The act of 1872, section 25, provides—

That it shall be the duty of the governor to commission all officers-elect except members of the general assembly, the governor, and the members of the police-jury.

Mr. Commissioner BAYARD. Is there any other provision than that?

Mr. TRUMBULL. I do not remember any other provision. I am informed that there is no constitutional provision, and that is the only provision of the statute I can call attention to at this moment.

Mr. Commissioner STRONG. It would be a great convenience to some of us if we could have copies of the offers of evidence. I heard them read only.

Mr. CARPENTER. I will see that the judges are furnished with a copy to-night before nine o'clock.

Mr. Commissioner EDMUNDS. Only a very few of the Commission have been able to obtain copies.

Mr. CARPENTER. I will see that all of them are supplied to-night. If the Commission please, I ask permission for about five minutes to cite some authorities on some of our points, so that they may be before the counsel on the other side before they close, as I understand we have the conclusion. Is there objection to that?

The PRESIDENT. Some not in your brief?

Mr. CARPENTER. One or two not in our brief. Five minutes will suffice.

The PRESIDENT. I suppose there is no objection to that.

Mr. EVARTS. None at all. We understand they have the right to have three counsel speak if they choose, and it comes out of their time.

Mr. CARPENTER. That is the way we understood it. If for instance the discussion had proceeded under the formal rule, we should have had fifteen minutes on each offer, and could have taken the time with one counsel on one objection and another on another.

The PRESIDENT. Are there three counsel to speak on your side of this question?

Mr. CARPENTER. Yes, sir; counting me for five minutes as counsel.

The PRESIDENT. Then two are required to open.

Mr. TRUMBULL. If the Commission please, in regard to our offer of testimony, some of it is in manuscript. I would suggest, if it is proper for me to do so, that the clerk be directed to have it printed, that you may get a copy of it.

Mr. Commissioner GARFIELD. We had better have it all printed.

The PRESIDENT. I presume there will be no objection to having it printed.

Mr. CARPENTER. We offer to prove, and it is a conceded fact——

The PRESIDENT. I want it distinctly understood that the rule which I have prescribed is that, if three counsel are to be heard on a side, two shall open and only one speak in conclusion.

Mr. CARPENTER. So I understand. We offer to prove, and it is admitted as a fact, that Governor Kellogg, who issued the certificate here to the electors, is the same individual as elector Kellogg certified to by him. On page 38 of my brief I have cited the authorities to show that a person cannot appoint himself. The king is the fountain of honor and of office, but he cannot exercise the duties of an office to which he might make an appointment.

It was decided in 33 Barbour, cited on this brief, that where three officers had the power to appoint an officer, they could not appoint one of their own number, it being all an enlargement of that proverb of the law that no man can be a judge in his own case and that no man can exercise the functions of his office for his own benefit. In this case the distinction between a man's appointing himself and issuing a certificate which would be conclusive evidence that he had been appointed, is too nice to be substantial, and it falls, we think, within that well-settled principle that no public officer can certify anything for his own benefit; that is, in which he holds an interest at the time he makes the certificate. Upon that point, in addition to the cases cited in the brief, I want to call attention to the case of McKnight *vs.* Lewis, 5 Barbour's Reports, page 584. In that case a note had been protested by a notary; he afterward became the owner of the note, and the question was whether he could read in his own favor the certificate which he made as notary public of the protest of the note. This is what the court say about it:

The next objection is that the official protest and certificate of the intestate were admitted in evidence in favor of the plaintiff, who is his representative. At the time J. E. McKnight made his protest and memoranda of notice at its foot, he had no interest in the note. He had authority by law, and was competent in the particular case, to present and demand payment of it and to give the notice of refusal, and also to make officially the protest and memoranda which, in a certain contingency, the statute had declared presumptive evidence of such dishonor and notice. The certificate of an officer, when by law evidence for others, is competent testimony for the officer himself, provided he was competent, *at the time of making it,* to act officially in the matter to which it relates. This doctrine is applied daily in cases of justices of the peace, sheriffs, constables, and other officers. No one will doubt that a commissioner of deeds or judge who takes and certifies the acknowledgment of the execution of a deed conveying land, and who subsequently purchases the same land, may use his own certificate to prove the execution of the conveyance to his grantor.

Witnesses who have been examined and afterward become interested, and are made parties in the same suit, have been permitted to read their depositions in their own favor.

All stating the ground to be that, in order to make the certificate available in his own favor, it must be shown that he had no interest in it at the time the certificate was made. The case cited on the brief from Anstruther held that a sheriff could not certify his own neglect or an excuse for his neglect. He must make his affidavit to that. He could not use the functions of his office to certify anything in his own favor. Now, the doctrine applied to this case is this: Governor Kellogg's certificate to himself is worthless. It is no evidence that he was duly appointed elector at all. In the case of a sheriff, it is universally well known to all the judges that where a sheriff on process in a case between other parties makes a return which afterward becomes material in a suit against him, and he offers it in evidence, even in that case where he made it upon process between other parties, at the time merely performing his duty, when he comes to claim any benefit to himself, it is only *prima-facie* evidence.

Then to show that Kellogg was duly appointed, you have got to go behind the certificate of Kellogg. He cannot appoint himself; he cannot certify that he is appointed; and when you get behind that certificate what do you come to? You come to the certificate of this canvassing-board. It will be claimed undoubtedly by my honorable friends that there you must stop. But what is the effect of that certificate of the returning-board? Its character as evidence is determined by the law which makes it evidence. That law says that the certificate of the returning-board, when filed with the secretary of state, shall be *prima-facie* evidence in all courts and before all civil officers until set aside by contest.

What is *prima-facie* evidence? It is evidence that may be disputed; and when the legislature says a certain paper shall be *prima-facie* evidence in all courts and before all officers, it says in effect that in all courts and before all officers you may dispute it. The Supreme Court of the United States in two or three cases have defined what *prima-facie* evidence is and so defined it. It is that evidence which, of itself and uncontradicted, would be sufficient to establish the fact, but which is always controvertible. So we say this returning-board's certificate is not conclusive. The statute says it shall not be conclusive; it says it shall be *prima facie*, and *prima facie* means disputable. Then you must go back of that to the fact in order to prove that Kellogg was elected; or, if it is not necessary for them affirmatively to go back to show that he was elected, it is certainly competent for us to go back to show that he was not, or else you give that certificate, which the law says shall be only *prima-facie* evidence, the full force and effect of conclusive evidence.

I want to cite also without comment, upon the same subject, the case of Ohio *vs.* Taylor, 12 Ohio State Reports, 132.

I also call attention to the case of Sublett *vs.* Treadwell, in 47 Mississippi Reports, 266, and will read simply one clause from the syllabus:

The majority candidate, having been a registrar of voters preparatory to the election at which he was a candidate and elected, was thereby disqualified and his election was void.

The PRESIDENT. The other side may now proceed.

Mr. STOUGHTON. Mr. President and gentlemen, I have heard in the course of to-day some objections made which I think may well be disposed of first and briefly. We are somewhat surprised to hear it objected that the certificate of Governor Kellogg is inoperative for the purpose of certifying to this tribunal the electoral vote. I think it will be remembered that when the vote of Connecticut was counted, her governor, Ingersoll, was an elector at large. I think his certificate was received without objection. Such objections are hardly suitable to the dignity of the occasion.

It has been objected this morning, and argued with much zeal, that Governor Kellogg is not the governor of Louisiana. It has been said that Louisiana is governed by a military despotism, by which I suppose is meant that military force, which, on application sent by Governor Kellogg to the President, he ordered to Louisiana, for the purpose of suppressing insurrection. I think the learned counsel was right in saying that without such aid the government of which Governor Kellogg was the head would have been overturned; but is the gentleman aware that the very fact that Governor Kellogg made such an application, the very fact that it was granted, is decisive evidence here that he was, until his term expired, governor of the State of Louisiana? Need I tell the learned counsel that?

I beg leave to refer this Commission for one moment to the case of Luther *vs.* Borden, where that question was decided, and where it was held that the very fact that the President of the United States had recognized the then governor and government of Rhode Island, although he had not sent a military force for the purpose of suppressing the Dorr insurrection, was evidence conclusive of who was the governor of that State and what was its government. Has my learned friend forgotten that case?

Mr. TRUMBULL. Did the court say that was conclusive?

Mr. STOUGHTON. I mean to say conclusive until the Congress of the United States in its capacity as such shall determine otherwise.

Mr. TRUMBULL. Could not either House contradict it?

Mr. STOUGHTON. No. I am amazed at some of the doctrines which I have heard announced here, and this one of them, and I pass from it, for this tribunal is entirely familiar with the doctrine decided in the case referred to, binding upon every department of the Government, decided by a court—perhaps the counsel did not entertain the same opinion of it then that he does now—presided over by a judge eminent for his learning and for his integrity, and I may add for the greatness of his abilities, Chief-Justice Taney.

Now let me state briefly and generally what the question is that counsel here are expected to argue. I think I may say it comprehends substantially the whole case; and yet it comes up upon an offer to do what? It comes up upon an offer to prove by a search and scrutiny of many, if not all, the polls of Louisiana, what in fact was the vote of that State for electors last November. Many other facts are superadded. It comes up upon an offer to prove facts upon which it is insisted that this tribunal may overrule, disregard, go behind the action of the final returning-officers of that State and hold for naught their conclusions. They acted under a statute to which I will call the attention of the tribunal for a moment; and in the course of what I shall have to say I shall satisfy this tribunal beyond all question that that board as constituted had the power delegated to it by the State of Louisiana—as a little patience, a little intelligence, will demonstrate—to determine the number of votes cast for electors, and power to certify finally, so far as the authority of that State is concerned, who they were. Confusion rather than clearness has resulted relative to these statutes owing somewhat, I conceive, to their arrangement. I shall take some pains, for the purpose of showing that the board was a final tribunal, empowered by the State to determine who had been chosen electors, to call attention to the different statutes, after a careful examination of which it will be clear that the board, and that only, and not the governor of the State as has been suggested, was the authorized power for the purpose named; and I shall satisfy the Commission, moreover, that the objection raised yesterday by the learned counsel, [Mr. Carpenter,] that if there should happen to be a vacancy in the electoral college it must be filled by a popular election and could not be filled by the electoral college itself, has no foundation whatever.

It seems to me that the decision of this tribunal in the Florida case determines the entire question here raised as to the right to go behind the returning-board; and I beg leave, in order that we may move with chart in hand, to read what this tribunal did in that case decide and determine:

The ground of this decision, stated briefly, as required by said act, is as follows:

That it is not competent under the Constitution and the law, as it existed at the date of the passage of said act, to go into evidence *aliunde* the papers opened by the President of the Senate in the presence of the two Houses to prove that other persons than those regularly certified to by the governor of the State of Florida, in and according to the determination and declaration of their appointment by the board of State canvassers of said State prior to the time required for the performance of their duties, had been appointed electors, or by counter-proof to show that they had not, and that all proceedings of the courts, or acts of the legislature, or of the executive of Florida, subsequent to the casting of the votes of the electors on the prescribed day, are inadmissible for any such purpose.

I am unable to perceive from that determination that any question, much less the main question here directed to be argued, is open for argument. The manifest justice of that conclusion, if support can be obtained from such a source—I speak with great respect— is to be found in the report of the committee of the Senate of the United

States, of which the learned counsel, Mr. Trumbull, was a member, from
the portion of which report that I shall read he not only did not dissent,
but by expressly dissenting from other portions he did assent to this;
so that we have, before his conversion to a different doctrine, his adhesion to the opinion announced by this Commission, and that conclusion
thus stated is as follows:

> The committee are of the opinion that neither the Senate of the United States, nor
> both Houses jointly, have the power under the Constitution to canvass the returns of
> an election and count the votes to determine who have been elected presidential
> electors, but that the mode and manner of choosing electors are left exclusively to the
> States. And if by the law of the State they are to be elected by the people, the
> method of counting the vote and ascertaining the result can only be regulated by the
> law of the State. Whether it is competent for the two Houses, under the twenty-
> second joint rule, (in regard to the constitutionality of which the committee here give
> no opinion,) to go behind the certificate of the governor of the State, to inquire
> whether the votes for electors have ever been counted by the legal returning-board
> created by the law of the State, or whether, in making such count, the board had be-
> fore them the official returns, the committee offer no suggestions, but present only a
> statement of the facts as they understand them.

So careful was this committee that it doubted its power to go far
enough behind the certificate of the governor to learn whether the
votes for electors had been counted by the proper returning-board. To
going so far, we here make no objection; but when the purpose is to
go further, to violate the rule laid down by this Commission, to violate
the principle asserted in this report, to violate the fundamental law of
the Union, the Federal Constitution, which provides that electors shall
be appointed in such manner as the legislature of the State may direct;
when this tribunal is asked to go thus far, and by inquiry ascertain not
only what occurred at every poll throughout the State of Louisiana, but
to purge the polls, and not merely to do that, but to ascertain for the
purpose of enforcing the law of Louisiana, whether violence and outrage and intimidation have been in fact perpetrated, and bring on a
trial of the entire case involving every parish and every poll of Louisiana within the circumference of Federal jurisdiction, I say the objection to such testimony, to such a course, instead of being technical, becomes substantial in the last degree, and is asserted, not on behalf of
ten thousand, (for whom my learned brother Carpenter said he appeared,) but on behalf of forty-odd millions of people, every one deeply
interested to preserve the independence of the States from the aggres-
sions of Congress and the Federal power.

What is the theory on which this power is supposed to rest? We
are referred to the bill organizing this Commission, which has been
read as though the tribunal had been appointed to ascertain what
electors were duly appointed, not in the sense of the Constitution, but
in another and aggressive sense—as though this tribunal had been appointed to explore and ascertain step by step, from the time the first
voter presented himself at the ballot-box until the time when the election was over, what had been its course and what had been the votes,
how many, and for whom. The law under which this Commission was
created is an extraordinary exhibition of subtlety and of care. It had
a subject to deal with not easy of solution. We know all the surrounding circumstances; we know the causes which led to the framing of
this bill; and we know why its language was couched so inexpressively
of power delegated here. We know that conflicting opinions were to
be harmonized not by uniting upon language which had meaning, but
by using that which for certain purposes conveyed none—I mean none
as the expression of an opinion of Congress. And to this tribunal was
delegated the power to do what? To exercise such powers, if any, as

the two Houses or either of them had. For what purpose? For the purpose of counting the electoral votes.

Now, will the tribunal permit me—little entitled as I am to attempt to instruct any one, much less a member of this body—to suggest that there has been a great confusion of ideas presented upon this subject. My learned brother, Mr. Carpenter, yesterday said this tribunal had no judicial power; I suppose he was right; it had no legislative power; I suppose he was right; but had a parliamentary authority to investigate and take testimony by any means it pleased. What is a parliamentary power? It is the power of parliament. And what is the power of parliament? To legislate. And what is the purpose of taking testimony? It is that legislative bodies may be better informed as to how they should legislate upon all subjects; and when a legislative body takes testimony it takes it to inform itself, and hence its mode of taking testimony is loose, confined by no rule, guarded by no objection, often overturning the safeguards, if not of society, certainly of reputation, carefully protected always in courts of justice. So, with a wide, unlicensed discretion, and as wide, unlicensed power, it takes testimony when and where it pleases; but it discharges only its duties as a legislative body, always for the purpose of legislation only, unless for one other purpose, and that is to inquire into the qualifications of its own members, in accordance with that clause in the Constitution which provides that "each House shall be the judge of the elections, returns, and qualifications of its own members," a very familiar clause. But is each House judge of the elections, returns, and qualifications of presidential electors? Has either House that power? Are not the learned counsel here seeking to induce this body to exercise exactly that power? Is there any question that they are?

I ask every gentleman upon this Commission, are you not seeking by this course, if you concur in the views of the counsel, to ascertain by inquiry and testimony whether these electors have been properly elected, returned, and qualified? Let every man pause who undertakes to advance toward that result. I repeat, no member of the Commission can discriminate, assuming the evidence offered to be competent, between the power of the House to investigate as to the election, return, and qualification of its members, and the power here asserted.

Again, what happens if this testimony shall be admitted? Is it to be assumed that it will not be controverted by counter-proof? Certainly not. Then are you to undertake to execute the laws of Louisiana by determining as matter of fact whether there has been intimidation, violence, armed disturbance, and therefore whether this board has properly performed its duty? Is that a function which can be exercised by this tribunal? It must be if you enter upon the inquiry suggested. Is it not as well to leave that administration of State laws to the States? The power to count, transferred to this tribunal, is the power of the two Houses, or either of them. That power, if it exists, is subject to other constitutional provisions; and one is, that the electors of the several States are to be appointed in such manner as the legislatures thereof may direct. How has the legislature of Louisiana directed its electors to be appointed? By a majority of votes lawfully cast, to be ascertained and the appointment of electors finally determined and declared by the State officers appointed by its legislature, such officers having exclusive authority so to do.

The national power to count, the power to do what may be needful in counting, is subject to that power of each State to appoint. Where does that power of appointment by the State end? Where does the power to count begin? Does the power of the State end until it fully reaches the appointment by the final authority delegated by the State as the appointing power? The State of Louisiana has but one mode of expressing its will upon this subject; that is, by the returning-board. It may not have been the best way; but it is its mode of expressing its will, and cannot be here overthrown. I am glad to have my argument on this point confirmed by an eminent jurist, an honest judge, and I was about to say a spotless politician, but perhaps that would be going too far, though I think not. I allude to a letter written by the chief-justice of the court of appeals of the State of New York, who says:

I have always expressed the opinion that the authentication of the election of presidential electors according to the laws of each State is final and conclusive, and that there exists no power to go behind them.

This opinion thus concurs with that of this tribunal, and of the eminent gentlemen who made the report in the Senate in 1873.

Mr. Commissioner MORTON. I would inquire of the counsel when that was written?

Mr. STOUGHTON. It appears to have been dated on the 10th of February, 1877.

Mr. Commissioner BAYARD. A letter by Judge Church?

Mr. STOUGHTON. It purports to be signed by him, and doubtless was written as a more correct expression of his opinion than was given by an interviewer; that class of gentlemen not being always absolutely accurate, although I believe very generally so.

Mr. Commissioner ABBOTT. Do you understand that to express the opinion that it cannot be shown that fraud, that corruption, that bribery existed in obtaining that authentication? I do not so understand it.

Mr. STOUGHTON. I understand it in this way, and there is no difficulty in understanding it if one will only place his mind toward the subject and in the right road: The State, having power to appoint, is responsible for its tribunals and they are responsible to it; but the circumference of the power of Congress is limited, and that of the power to count very much circumscribed, being neither judicial, as gentlemen say, nor legislative; although legislative powers are here claimed for the purpose of taking testimony, and the broadest judicial powers in the nature of a *quo warranto* for the purpose of going behind the final returns of the returning-board. The State corrects the frauds of its officers. It does not appeal to Congress, and Congress will best perform its duty by discharging it within its authority, leaving those occasional frauds, which are sometimes assumed and sometimes for effect offered to be proven, to be taken care of by the tribunals having jurisdiction over them.

I think some of my learned friends within the hearing of my voice, who have been much engaged in contested suits, have had their trials somewhat added to by being compelled to object to testimony offered in presence of a jury (and the American people are the jury to-day) to prove frauds of the most infamous character, when peradventure the practice and performance would not come up to the proclamation! But it is the duty of counsel to make objection to the introduction of testimony beyond the function of the tribunal he is before to receive; and we make it here.

And now I proceed to look at some of the questions in this case, assuming that this is a lawful and final returning-board of the State of Louisiana, having the final powers attributed to it, not merely by this body in the decision in the Florida case, not merely in the Senate by the report which I have read, not merely by force of the opinion contained in the letter of the learned chief-justice of New York, but also by the sanction of the highest courts of the State of Louisiana. I believe that if there is one principle settled in our jurisprudence, it is that on a question of local law, on the powers of a tribunal of a local character within a State, the decision of the highest judicial tribunal of the State is a final authority.

I therefore cite the decision of the highest court of Louisiana on the subject of the powers of the returning-board, not in one case only, but in several—in 25 Louisiana Annual Reports for 1873, page 268, declaring the legality of the Lynch returning-board, which did not have before it in 1872 the electoral or other returns, but undertook to canvass and did canvass the vote in favor of the Grant electors without having the returns before it. It was therefore said, if I am not mistaken, by the committee of Congress that inasmuch as the right board did not have the returns, and therefore had not the materials for action, and the wrong board did have the returns, they could not count the votes of either set of electors. The court in Louisiana in the case to which I have referred declares:

No statute conferring upon the courts the power to try cases of contested elections or title to office authorizes them to revise the action of the returning-board. If we were to assume that prerogative, we should have to go still further, and revise the returns of the supervisors of elections, examine the right of voters to vote, and, in short, the courts would become in regard to such cases mere offices for counting, compiling, and reporting election-returns. The legislature has seen proper to lodge the power to decide who has or has not been elected in the returning-board. It might have conferred that power upon the courts, but it did not. Whether the law be good or bad, it is our duty to obey its provisions, and not to legislate. * * * Having no power to revise the action of the board of returning-officers, we have nothing to do with the reasons or grounds upon which they arrived at their conclusion.

There are one or two other cases in this same book to the same effect; and when it was sought under the so-called intrusion act to eject a person who had been returned and commissioned by force of this returning-board, the court held that the commission was conclusive, and that the court could not go behind it. There was no judicial power vested in the court so to do, unless conferred specially by legislative authority. Some courts have given very good reasons for thus maintaining the inviolability of the highest and final returning-board of a State, and I beg leave here to introduce two or three such decisions.

Mr. Commissioner THURMAN. What is the name of the case you just read from?

Mr. STOUGHTON. I beg pardon for not mentioning it. It was the case of Bonner vs. Lynch, and I read from page 268. It was decided in 1873, and it passed upon the power of the returning-board organized under the act of 1870, repealed by the act of 1872, the only difference between the two acts being in this, that the act of 1872 now in force requires that the returning-officers shall be appointed by the senate, while the act of 1870 designates the persons to act as the board, as the governor, lieutenant governor, I think, and two persons, naming them. That, I believe, is the only substantial difference between the two; and therefore, when the supreme court of the State of Louisiana held that it had no power to review or reverse or revise the action of the returning-board then existing, it said the same thing as to the returning-board now existing; and this tribunal will not disregard the highest judicial authority of a State upon a purely local question.

Mr. Commissioner GARFIELD. Were the duties of that board substantially the same as the duties of this?

Mr. STOUGHTON. Precisely almost. There is hardly the variation of a line. That act was substantially transcribed for the purpose of

making it the act of 1872. Now I refer to 47 Illinois, 169, where a stat
ute had expressly authorized a circuit court consisting of a single judge
to pass upon a contested election case on appeal from justices, and the
constitution giving judicial power to the supreme court of the State
conferred it in certain cases "and in all other cases;" and when the
supreme court on appeal in this case was asked to revise the decision of
the circuit court, it said:

> This is not a case within the meaning of the constitution, but a statutory proceeding
> to recanvass votes cast at an election, in which illegal votes may be rejected and legal
> votes may be counted and the result ascertained, and that result is not a judgment.
> It is neither a suit at law nor in chancery.

Why have sensible courts adopted views like that? For the purpose
of keeping these inflammatory cases, as far as possible, outside of the
reach of judicial authority. As was well said in a Kentucky case which
I will refer to, courts of justice have always held in dealing with these
questions that unless the legislative power expressly delegates authority
to do it, courts have no power to touch election contests. But yet here,
under a power to count electoral votes, this tribunal is expected to count
the popular votes given for the electors, and to purge the polls from the
beginning to the end of the election, upon the theory that it has the
power by implication and by a stretch, an enforced stretch, an outrage
upon language, which courts of justice take care never to commit.

I refer now to 51 Illinois, 177, where the court said that—

> The proceeding was purely statutory; that without the aid of an act of the legisla-
> ture the contest could not have been brought to the circuit court, and that jurisdiction
> can be exercised only subject to the limitations of the act.

And then in the Kentucky case, 1 Metcalfe's Kentucky Reports, 538,
the court say:

> This was a board to determine questions upon an election. A board is to be
> constituted to examine the poll-books and issue certificates of election. Another
> is to be organized in the case of contested elections for determining contests be-
> tween claimants. Upon this the law devolves the duty and confers the power of
> deciding who is entitled to the office. The courts have no right to adjudicate upon
> these questions or to decide such contests. Decisions of the contesting-board are
> final and conclusive; and this is so to accomplish a twofold purpose: a speedy and
> summary mode of deciding cases of contested elections, and determining finally and con-
> clusively which one of the claimants is entitled; and another, equally important, was
> to withdraw these contests from the jurisdiction of courts, and as was said in New-
> combe vs. Kirkley, (13 B. Monroe, 517,) to prevent the ordinary tribunals of justice
> from being harassed, and, indeed, overwhelmed, with the investigation and involved
> in the excitements to which these cases may be expected to give rise.

If there ever was an illustration of the solidity and policy of such a
view, it is to be found here before us, where this great tribunal is asked
to go into an inquiry, endless in detail, harassing by its very nature, involving the examination of hundreds of witnesses, and leading to that
excitement, to be tenfold increased, which we already perceive gather-
ing about this Commission. Here we have offers of testimony, inflamed
to the last degree by their mode of statement, involving inquiries of the
most extraordinary and painful character, leading to answers, leading to
testimony in reply, leading to testimony in justification of the returning-
board, endless, difficult of procurement; and all for what? To enable
this tribunal to violate the supremacy of the State, to determine how
many votes were cast in the State of Louisiana for electors; and all
that the public may be satisfied that we have here a tribunal anxious to
calm and allay excitement and prevent, as the learned counsel who opened
the case yesterday [Mr. Carpenter] said, a judicial proceeding to vex the
nation for years, that it may thereby be determined who is elected President. I have heard more than one threat couched under shields of lan-

guage so that it might not quite reach in plain terms its destination, but I have understood those threats, and they are unworthy of the circumstances under which this tribunal was formed, and equally unworthy of those who seek its justice and its decision.

Now, may it please your honors, I desire to say a few words on the subject of these statutes. My learned brother [Mr. Carpenter] yesterday insisted that this returning-board, as it has been called, had no power under the laws of Louisiana to ascertain the votes cast for electors or who had been elected. He said if that power existed anywhere, it existed in the governor of the State under the act of 1868 incorporated afterward into the revised laws of the State of Louisiana, and that proposition was presented as though the laws of Louisiana had at one time discriminated between the officer or tribunal to count votes for electors and the officer or tribunal authorized to count votes for other State officers. That is a misconception of that law, and I call attention to what the statute law on that subject is. But if it were not, if the governor had the power under the section referred to to count the vote, this tribunal would be bound under the certificate to consider that power as having been properly exercised, the governor having certified that—

Pursuant to the laws of the United States, at a general election held in accordance with law, the following-named persons were duly chosen and appointed electors.

If, therefore, that clause only were contained in this certificate, it would be ample evidence of the election of these electors, if the statute which declares that

Immediately after the receipt of a return from each parish, or on the fourth Monday of November, if the returns should not sooner arrive, the governor, in the presence of the secretary of state, the attorney-general, a district judge of the district in which the seat of government may be established, or any two of them, shall examine the returns and ascertain therefrom the persons who have been duly elected electors,

were unrepealed.

All who have examined the statute with care know that that provision has been repealed, however, and I will proceed to show under what circumstances it was repealed, and also that instead of that section being isolated and making a distinction between the officers authorized to count the votes for electors and those authorized to count the votes for other officers, it was a part of the scheme of the act of 1868, by which the governor, in conjunction with the district judge of the parish, counted the votes for all officers—the governor counting, subject in certain cases to a prior determination of the district judge as to whether there had not been violence, tumult, intimidation, &c., sufficient to justify the throwing out of the polls, the governor, if the district judge came to that conclusion, being inhibited by the statute from counting the vote. The governor on receiving the judge's decision, if it was to reject the poll or any number of polls, was authorized to do so and count the remainder; but he could not count the contested parish as having voted until after receiving the decision of the district judge. That was the scheme of 1868, never really to any extent put into practice; a scheme of a returning-board very imperfect, quite inadequate, and still a part of a general scheme in which the governor participated, not merely by ascertaining the votes for electors, but by ascertaining and certifying as to all votes.

Another view taken by the learned counsel, Mr. Carpenter, and very much relied upon, was this: That if a vacancy should occur in the electoral college, he did not care how this tribunal determined the question as to which statute was in force, for he could under either cast out two electoral votes and still attain his object, which seemed to me somewhat strange, his purpose being, as he told us at the outset, to appear not for Mr. Tilden, whose future supremacy he deplored as one of the greatest disasters which might befall this country, but for the ten thousand persons who had been deprived of their votes in Louisiana. A rejection, therefore, by this tribunal of two electoral votes, while it would answer his purpose, would bring upon us the calamity he so much deplored. I think he will be disappointed. Let us look at this objection. Assuming, as the learned counsel assumed, for the purpose of inquiring into this objection, that the act of 1872 is in force, let us learn whether vacancies in the electoral college are to be filled by a popular election. He referred us as authority for that to section 24, page 104 of the covered book :

That all elections to be held in this State to fill any vacancies shall be conducted and managed, and returns thereof shall be made, in the same manner as is provided for general elections.

Now, says the learned counsel, that covers the case of an election to fill a vacancy in the electoral college. But the Constitution of the United States provides that Congress may determine the time of choosing the electors and the day on which they give their votes, "which day shall be the same throughout the United States." By an act of Congress, section 133 of the Revised Statutes, each State is authorized to provide by law for the filling of any vacancy which may occur in its college of electors when such college meets to give its electoral vote. Then the Louisiana law provides—

If any one or more of the electors chosen by the people shall fail from any cause whatever to attend at the appointed place at the hour of four p. m. of the day prescribed for their meeting, it shall be the duty of the other electors immediately to proceed by ballot to supply such vacancy or vacancies.

Mr. Commissioner HUNTON.   But is not that the law of 1868 ?

Mr. STOUGHTON.   It is a law passed in 1868, an old law.

Mr. Commissioner HUNTON.   Did not the act of 1872 repeal that ?

Mr. STOUGHTON.   O, no ; it did not touch it.

Mr. Commissioner HUNTON.   This was also in the act of 1870, the revised statutes.

Mr. STOUGHTON.   It does not touch this at all.   It would be an absurdity to hold that the express purpose in the Constitution, carried out by Federal legislation, supplemented by State legislation, could be defeated by giving a violent construction to the clause, section 24, when it has abundance to feed upon in the sections that I will refer to in one moment.   Look at the vacancies provided for in section 24, to be found in sections 28, 30, and 31.

Mr. Commissioner HUNTON.   The clause that I referred to as repealing the section you have mentioned will be found in section 71 of the act of 1872.   It says that "all other acts on the subject of election laws be, and the same are hereby, repealed."

Mr. STOUGHTON.   Yes, that means all other acts on the subject of election laws, for the purpose of carrying on the machinery of elections within the State.

Mr. Commissioner HOAR.   Mr. Stoughton, I do not wish to interfere with the course of your argument, but I will venture to ask you if you think it is worth while to spend much time in the endeavor to satisfy the Commission that section 24 refers to vacancies to be filled by popular election, and can refer to nothing else ?

Mr. STOUGHTON.   I do not propose to spend a moment, only to refer to the three sections which are referred to by section 24, and which relate to vacancies which may occur, and those three sections you will find to be sections 28, 30, and 31, on page 106 of the covered book.

In the revised statutes of the State which were adopted on the 14th of March, 1870, will be found the act of 1868, originally passed in that year, containing the scheme that I have mentioned, and the scheme under which the governor was to count the electoral vote, as he was in substance all other votes. That act of 1868 in entering into the revised statutes was very much divided in space; the section authorizing the district judge to act being found at page 274, section 1386. Upon a statement made by a commissioner he was to make a duplicate, transmit one to the judge and one to the governor. If the governor thought the statement of riot and tumult was of such a character that the vote ought to be thrown out, he directed the district judge to investigate it. During the investigation the governor was prohibited from counting the vote of that poll or parish. When the district judge decided, he certified his decision to the governor; the governor could then proceed to count, and he did; but he acted always in subjection to the mandate of the statute, which was that he must not count until the decision of the district court should be presented; that is, he must not count that parish. That was found to be inefficient and the act of 1870 was passed. It was passed on the 16th of March, 1870.

A question is raised that inasmuch as the act of 1870 incorporated in the revised statutes was not to go into operation until the 1st of April, that might by its own operation repeal or stand in place of the act adopted on the 16th of March to go into operation immediately. The answer is this: The act of the 14th of March repealed all prior acts on the subject of these election laws providing for elections within the State and the mode of returning votes, but repealed nothing else. It did not repeal those clauses of the act which had always stood in substance authorizing the election of electors, only changing the mode by which their election should be ascertained after the vote of the State had been cast. Then the act of 1872 was passed, I think approved on the 20th of November, 1872, and that provided for the present returning-board, adopting substantially the prior act of 1870, adopting it in all respects with the exception of the composition of the returning-board.

I have not troubled the Commission as fully as I had marked upon my notes with the different sections of these laws. I only desire to say that it will appear by looking at page 101 of the covered book that the act of 1872 provided in a general way for the election of electors, and the returning-board having been abolished and with it the functions of the governor for the purpose of counting the votes, the returning-board provided for by the act of 1872 took their place—the act of 1872 declaring in terms that "five persons to be elected by the senate from all political parties, shall be the returning officers for all elections of the State, a majority of whom shall constitute a quorum, and have power to make the returns of all elections." And then we have at the close of the act that it "shall take effect from and after its passage, and that all others on the subject of election laws be, and the same are hereby, repealed." Will any one seriously contend that the operation of that was to blot out from the statute-book the power to elect electors when their election was provided for in a previous part of the act in a general way? Will any one pretend that section 24, which has ample means to give effect to it in other sections of the act, was intended to declare that that needful authority given to the college of electors to elect on the day they assemble, if need be, was blotted out, and that the State must lose its electoral vote because it could not possibly then go through on that day with another election? Such frivolous objections are some-times made elsewhere; but I think are entitled to but very little force.

It has been said that this board to be appointed by the senate should consist of five persons. Originally that number were appointed. Hav-ing ceased to be five and having become four only by the resignation of one, it is said it had no power to act by means of these four. The gen-tlemen who urge the objection say that although it had no power to act there being but four, if there were five it could act by three alone. "A majority of whom shall constitute a quorum and have power to make returns of all elections." Is it to be said that with the power expressly conferred upon three to act alone, they could only act alone when there were five and could not when there were four?

Then it is said that the political complexion of this board was not of the right color; there should have been a democratic infusion; and there has been read an application for the admission of a democratic member. I suppose, upon that theory, if after the election of these five, two being democrats and three republicans, the two democrats (not an improbable supposition) should have changed their faith, the board would cease to exist by that operation! This clause is directory merely. The failure to observe it in no manner interferes with the capacity or jurisdiction of the board.

I suppose that it is entirely proper and respectful to this tribunal to argue the leading questions involved here without assailing the reputa-tion of any one, and I shall follow no example of that kind. I have heard the members of this board stigmatized by the speech of counsel in a way that I have been somewhat sorry to hear. Personally they are unknown here, personally they were perhaps unknown to counsel who spoke of them. They are to be respected as officials when acting as such, and their determination is to be respected and followed.

An example of that kind was set in a very celebrated case where the question arose, in 1792, as to whether George Clinton or Mr. John Jay was elected governor of the State of New York. There, as the members of this tribunal may remember, there was a clear majority of votes de-posited in the ballot-boxes of the State of New York for Mr. Jay. The sheriff appointed to carry the votes of one county, giving a majority of some four hundred for Mr. Jay, was an officer whose term of office had expired for a few days, no one having been appointed to succeed him. Mr. King, an eminent lawyer, advised that he was a proper messenger to carry the votes, being sheriff *de facto*. Aaron Burr advised that he was not. The lineal ancestors of the democratic party of to-day adopted the views of Aaron Burr, threw out the county vote, and defeated Mr. Jay; and inasmuch as the canvassing-board had final and absolute power to determine who was elected, although an effort was made by the friends of Mr. Jay to induce him to rebel against the decision, to vex the State of New York for years perhaps with the judicial question of who was elected, he declined to do it, considering that the tribunal had final and absolute power to determine the question, and he cheerfully submitted to its exercise; and moreover, he added that no man, no set of men, did wrong who did right under the law—holding to the precept that justice is the law executed, and not that wild and unlicensed thing which we sometimes call justice, but is the law executed, whatever the law may be; and whoever executes the law, if he be empowered by it so to do, is entitled to respect, and if his determination is final, it must stand unresisted. You can no more invade the domain of State juris-diction than you can direct your marshal to enter my house and take my property or my person. And he who invites any departure from that respect for loyalty to the law and its officers is not performing his duty as a minister of justice, and he who denounces a judge who has discharged his duty because it does not suit the prejudice or political views of another, is unworthy to speak his name or to come into his presence. Such was the teaching of Mr. Jay.

I have heard it said that the law authorizing what the learned counsel calls the disfranchisement of these voters is unconstitutional. Is it? Will the Commission indulge me for a moment while I refer to the doctrine of one of the ablest, one of the purest, and one of the most distinguished of men belonging to the democratic party at this day. I find this doctrine in a report written by him—I allude to Senator Stevenson, of Kentucky—founded upon authority so solid that nothing can shake the views he presents. If it be unconstitutional to pass laws for the purpose of protecting men from violence and outrage at the polls, then we have been under a delusion for many generations. I refer for this purpose to reports of committees of the House of Representatives, second session, Thirty-sixth Congress, volume 1, 1860–'61. He is considering the question of the effect of intimidation and violence at an election where the sitting member received 10,068 votes and the contestant 2,796; and I allude to it upon the general question that such legislation as we have in Louisiana is right in all States and countries, but especially right in that State where in 1868 a lesson was taught which led to the legislation now before you; a lesson written in blood, as was said by the learned Senator [Mr. Howe] who addressed you yesterday; a lesson taught us by the death by violence, as reported authentically by committees of Congress, of two thousand people, where whole parishes were disfranchised on one side. No horror has been expressed at outrages like those. Great horror is expressed for fraud, perjury; none for violence and murder. While Louisiana was teaching the lesson that led the legislature to pass this act, the State of New York was teaching a lesson in its chief city which led the Congress of this country to pass the law to take care of the elections for members of Congress, because in 1868 25,000 votes were manufactured—we all know it; it is a matter of authentic history—in the city of New York. They were needed to carry the State; they carried it by 10,000 majority. A governor was elected by them; a President was to be. Sitting over and managing the scene was an individual as chairman of the State committee whose name I will not mention, and his instruments; in the city of New York, who actually manufactured the votes that led to the legislation we all know. Such legislation in cases of fraud and violence and murder and outrage sometimes becomes necessary.

In the report of Senator Stevenson it was said "that illegal voting was a trifling wrong—altogether a venial offense—in comparison with the overshadowing outrage of intimidation and violence upon which the burden of his evidence bears."

Mr. Commissioner MORTON. In what case was that report made?

Mr. STOUGHTON. I read from the report made by Mr. Stevenson from the committee on the Henry Winter Davis election case, in which report he cites for his propositions authorities the most eminent we have in the common law, and he says:

Indeed, there is no conflict of authority, nowhere a hint of an opposite doctrine, no intimation of a doubt that elections must be free, or they cease to have any legal validity whatever. * * * The very word *election* implies choice, the declaration of the preference, the wish, of those who have the right to make a choice, * * * but if bribery be found to have corrupted the well, if violence prevented access to the poll, or reasonable fear deterred electors from a determined effort to exercise the elective franchise, there is no question made as to the number of votes affected by this bribery, violence, or intimidation.

23 E C

In Louisiana, under the statute, it is said that 10,000 votes were thrown out by the returning-board, and my learned brother yesterday said he appeared for those men here. I will state the problem: I think after what has been said I may state the problem that was solved in Louisiana by those who managed the election there. In forty parishes there was 6,097 republican majority. In the remaining seventeen parishes there were 20,323 colored voters registered and 16,253 registered white voters. What do you suppose the problem to be solved was? How to get a majority to overcome the 6,000 republican majority in the forty parishes. That was the problem. Out of what material? Sixteen thousand white votes registered to 20,000 colored. Was the problem solved? Yes. How? Does any man in this court-room believe that the problem could have been peacefully solved by 12,000 majority with 20,000 colored republican voters to 16,000 white voters? What became of the latter in the seventeen parishes? I appear for them, in imitation of my learned friend. Were they disfranchised? How?

Again, five of these parishes had 13,244 registered colored voters and 5,134 white. The problem was what? To get a democratic majority of 4,495 by means of 5,000 white voters to 13,000 colored. Was it solved? Yes. How? Let the record of the five parishes answer. Solved by bloody hands. I hurl back the charge of fraud and disfranchisement of voters! There are two sides to this question, and if you sit here to go back and canvass votes, you sit here to administer the laws of Louisiana, and you will administer them by learning who have been disfranchised and what was the lawful vote of that State in harmony with her laws, and not in harmony with the will of any party.

I will not trouble the Commission further except to say, as to the objection made to some of the electors because they held offices under the State government when elected electors, that I conceive there is here no disqualification whatever. The constitutional provision inhibiting the holding and the exercise of two offices refers only to offices under the State constitution, to offices mentioned in it; and on that subject I desire to call attention to a case to be found in 25 Louisiana Annual Reports, page 138.

I now leave it to my learned brothers to make such further observations upon the questions presented as they may see fit.

Mr. SHELLABARGER. Mr. President and gentlemen of the Commission, I know how weary you must be, and it is with extreme reluctance that I rise to address you. There is this reflection with which we may all sustain ourselves in this protracted trial, that we shall probably never have to go through such an experience again, certainly never such an experience again so far as it relates to the matter of its dignity and its supreme importance. I know, judging by what I have already experienced and observed of your kindness, that you will be forbearing in indulging me in my part of this discussion. I shall endeavor, Mr. President and gentlemen, to eschew everything in the way of an attempt at extended elaboration, to try to state, if I can, what seem to me to be the points on which this case now, as it is presented, must turn.

Of course, at the very threshold of your inquiry now is the question, what are the statutes which have been enacted by Louisiana under the authority of the Constitution of the United States directing the appointment of electors—what are the statutes which were in force this last year governing that matter? My friend, who has just taken his seat, has gone over that subject; it has been gone over by others; I had designed to discuss it; but I think I will omit any extended analysis of the statutes. I will venture to make this statement, gentlemen, that after you have carefully gone over the statutes and have looked at them in all their parts, you will be unanimous. One of your body said to me a day or two ago that you had proven to be unanimous on one subject, and that was that this was a great Commission and that the members thereof were all great men.

The PRESIDENT. There has been no vote on that question.

Mr. SHELLABARGER. Now, I will venture the prediction that when you go over these statutes you will be unanimous upon another subject, that is, that the act of 1872 did govern in 1876 the presidential election. You will be unanimous in the opinion that that provision of the revisory act of 1870, which provided for the canvassing of the returns by the governor, &c., was repealed and was not in force in 1876. You will be unanimous upon that subject for the very plain reason that that provision which made the governor a canvasser for the purposes of the election was inconsistent with the fifty-fourth section of the session acts of 1870, which expressly provided a different tribunal for all elections, including the electoral elections.

There is not a particle of difficulty or doubt or obscurity upon either one of the propositions that I have thus far stated. You will also, I think, be unanimous upon the proposition that the election law of 1872 applies to all elections, and furnishes the machinery or means of conducting all in the State, including that for the electoral college. You will be so for several quite conclusive reasons. One is that when an act undertakes to revise and provide for a subject-matter in its totality, such a revisory act is always considered to repeal and to take the place of the acts that it revises in so far as it purports so to do. This act of 1872 purports to supply the machinery for every popular election in the State by its scope. But a more conclusive reason perhaps than even that, is that its express terms in its section 2, in so many words, declare that this returning-board shall be "the returning-board for *all* elections held in the State," and you have simply to disregard the express wording of the act, without any authority for so disregarding it, or else you have got so to treat this law.

I say I have no apprehensions in regard to either one of those propositions. Now the only other one left is the question whether the consequences of the propositions that I have now gone over lead me to any result hurtful to the position that we take in this case in regard to this, to wit, that that section of the act of 1870—I mean the revisory act which provides for filling vacancies in the electoral college—is thereby also repealed. That is the predicament that we are claimed to place ourselves in, when we say that the act of 1872 has superseded and swept away the act of 1870, including that section in regard to the governor canvassing the vote.

Now, sirs, it is never wise, it is never manly, it is never lawyerlike, it is never respectful to a court to blink or dodge any question in a great discussion or in a small one; and it would be eminently unworthy that we should undertake to avoid every possible consequence of the positions we take in this regard; and upon that subject I have not the slightest difficulty, though in that I may be deceived.

My question at the present moment is, how can I preserve and keep in force that provision of the act of 1870 revising that of 1868, which provides for filling the electoral college, consistently with what I have just been saying? I answer first of all that it is a cardinal, as it is an exceedingly benign, canon of interpretation that a law is never repealed by a new act unless either expressly so done, or unless the repugnance be such (and now I am using the very words of the Supreme Court of the United States, at least half a dozen times repeated in the most solemn judgments) that it is impossible for the two acts to stand to-gether. Those words are so familiar, so thoroughly established as law, that they have become the formula of statement upon which courts seize in stating the rule on this subject, that a succeeding act shall not, where the prior act is not expressly repealed, repeal the preceding one unless the two cannot stand together.

Another rule of interpretation equally salutary, equally well estab-lished, equally familiar, you will find stated in the case of The United States *vs.* Kirby, 7 Wallace, pages 482, 486, and 487.

I beg to impress this part of my statement upon the memory of every one of you. There is of course nothing new in that case, as you will see when I state it. It is only in cases of doubt that the office of interpre-tation comes in at all. Where the language of an act is clear, one of the maxims, one of Domat's rules, one of the American rules, as you will find it laid down in Dwarris, is that there is no place for interpre-tation except where the words are susceptible of doubt. Wherever, then, the business of the interpreter comes in at all and has play, an-other rule for his guidance is this, and it is one that I want to impress on your memories, from 7 Wallace, pages 482, 487, that wherever inter-pretation would lead to consequences that are either absurd or hurtful to the public welfare, that interpretation shall never be tolerated unless its escape is impossible.

Then keeping that in your mind, go with me the next step. Is it pos-sible to escape the conclusion that, under the legislation of Louisiana, Louisiana was disfranchised?

I invite gentlemen on the other side who may suppose that this act is repealed, by which a vacancy in the electoral college can be filled if filled at all, to show me some statute that forces upon you, either by direct provision or by any fair interpretation, the conclusion that Louis-iana has been disfranchised in these processes of legislation. There is nothing, absolutely nothing, to repeal that section which provides for the filling of vacancies under the law of 1868 and the law of 1870, except the repealing clause of 1872, which is in these words:

That this act shall take effect from and after its passage, and that all others on the subject of election laws be, and the same are hereby, repealed.

Is it possible for the act of 1870, providing for filling vacancies, to stand consistently with that repealing clause? If it is, you are bound by your oaths and by all the rules of interpretation to let it stand; first, because of the rule I have stated, that you shall not make it work a re-peal by implication if you can help it; second, because if you do make it work a repeal, you work a disfranchisement of the State. The pro-vision for filling a vacancy in the electoral college is not an election law at all in the sense that that language is used there. Taking that sec-tion by itself, it is not an election law at all. I mean in the popular and legal sense of that repealing clause. It is filling a vacancy where there was a failure, the gentlemen say, to elect; we say where there was a vacancy under the provisions of these acts of Congress on the subject of vacancy and this legislation of the State.

Mr. President and gentlemen, having said that much, you are in pos-session, without any elaboration at all of the discussion, of my views in regard to what you will find out for yourselves when you go to your chamber, and I take the next step in this discussion. The law of 1872 was in force; it governed this election; and the provision for filling the vacancy is one that was resorted to and was in force.

I ought to have added, by way of abundant caution, in the connection in which I was a moment ago, another rule of interpretation which is exceedingly valuable here, and that is where a statute has received what your Supreme Court calls a practical construction, and has been executed according to that practical construction, in every case of doubt, that is exceedingly valuable. The Supreme Court of the United States, in a decision that I will hand up—I think it is in 21 Howard, 66—says that, in a case of doubt, the practical construction that has been given to a law is conclusive. This law for filling vacancies has been practically construed as applicable to the presidential elections, because all the elections that have been held since it was upon the statute-book have been conducted under it, there being in fact two.

I take my next proposition. I have not deemed it necessary in marking out my part of the work to take these propositions up in any particular order. I therefore come at once to the question as to what opportunity there is left for doubt, dispute, or debate in regard to the question of the power of Governor Kellogg to certify this election. I want to add to what was said by Mr. Stoughton, whose argument has just been concluded, in the way of refreshing your memories, the words of the Supreme Court of the United States upon that point that are so exactly apposite, so completely conclusive here, as it seems to me, as to shut up forever, to all intents and purposes, all discussion in regard to the question which was the rightful government in Louisiana and which was entitled to make the certificate.

Mr. Commissioner PAYNE. Mr. Shellabarger, before you proceed to that point, I should like to ask you if there are any of the sections of the law of 1868, on which you have been just commenting, that you claim are not repealed by the repealing clause of the law of 1872, except the one you referred to about filling vacancies?

Mr. SHELLABARGER. I have not gone over the law of 1868 nor even the law of 1870, as it revises that of 1868, in all its parts. I therefore cannot answer that question categorically, for I do not know, not having any concern about any other parts of the law except those that were involved in this case. I answer generally that I understand that an examination will result in finding that all the provisions of 1868 are superseded without exception by the revision of 1870. Then, if your question means to ask me what part of the legislation of 1870 is left alive, I reply that my analysis has not been such as to enable me to answer except as to the case in hand, and that as to that, the section relating to vacancies has been preserved, first by the fact that it is not within the repealing clause of 1872, it not being a matter as to holding an election; and second, it has not been repealed, because to do so would disfranchise a State; third, it has not been repealed because it is possible to stand. That is my whole position on that subject.

Mr. Commissioner HOAR. The law of 1870 is an entire revision of the whole statute law of the State on this subject. It contains provision as to the presidential electors meeting, how they shall certify their acts, and a like class of provisions.

Mr. EVARTS. I rise to ask Mr. Commissioner Payne whether, in his inquiry as to the law of 1868, he referred to the general election law of 1868, or the electoral election law of 1868, which are two independent acts?

Mr. Commissioner PAYNE. May they not be "election laws?"

Mr. EVARTS. They are two independent acts, found in the session laws of the same year.

Mr. SHELLABARGER. Now, Mr. President, I take the language of the Supreme Court of the United States from a case that has been often referred to, Luther *vs.* Borden, and I apply it here. It is in these words :

It rests with Congress to decide what government is the established one in a State; * * * and when the Senators—

And it is especially to this that I invite your attention—

and when the Senators and Representatives from a State are admitted into the councils of the Union, the authority of the government under which they are appointed, as well as its republican character—

Note, for here are two objections, first, that the State has not a republican character; second, that it is not a State, or that the Kellogg government was not the government. The Supreme Court replies to that, that when members are admitted to the councils of the Union—

the authority of the government under which they are appointed, as well as its republican character, is recognized by the proper constitutional authority, and its decision is binding on every other department of the government and cannot be questioned in a judicial tribunal.

I said, gentlemen, that that language was absolutely conclusive of this whole question, and it is, unless the suggestion made by Judge Trumbull to my friend who preceded me is an answer. His suggestion was, "Well, that says it is for Congress to determine, and here we are in Congress for the purpose of having you determine the thing the other way." Now, plainly and most manifestly, the suggestion is founded in error, first, because if you were Congress, with all the sovereign powers of Congress, and could make a law, still you could not make your act *ex post facto* or retroactive. If that thing was in November, 1876, a State by the recognition of the two Houses, by the action of the Executive under the act of 1795, by the fact of its passing laws and taking the government and exercising it, by all the facts that make and create a State of this Union *de facto* and *de jure*—if that were so of Louisiana as it was in November, 1876, then will my friend have the courage, not to say the temerity, to tell this Commission that even Congress can take that *status* away and rob the State by *post hac* action of its capacity to elect, as it was held on the day when the election was made?

I come next to the question of the ineligibility that is alleged to be wrought as to certain of these electors by the fact that certain of them held State offices. Let me take now and let me make illustrious, if I can, my speech by a quotation. I know it has been quoted a hundred times, so that it has become familiar to you all; but the oftener the better, because, first, of the intrinsic excellence of the statement itself; second, because of the time whence it comes to us, away back in the very morning of our life as a nation; and, third, and perhaps especially, because it comes from one of the most illustrious of the framers of the Constitution. I mean Charles Pinckney. It is a speech that he made on the bill that was pending in Congress in 1800, proposing to make a commission something like this. I am now reading from Mr. Pinckney for the purpose of showing to you that it was not the design of the Constitution to permit the States by any method to add to or subtract from the qualifications of the presidential electors. I have now reached the point that it is said disqualifies Kellogg and one or two other men because they held State offices, and I wish to make use of what Mr. Pinckney here states upon that point. But in order that I may use what he states in other connections, I will read as well what he stated on other points as upon that one. He says:

Knowing that it was the intention of the Constitution to make the President completely independent of the Federal Legislature, I well remember it was the object, as it is at present not only the spirit but the letter of that instrument, to give to Congress no interference in or control over the election of President. It is made their duty to count over the votes in a convention of both Houses, and for the President of the Senate to declare who has the majority of the votes of the electors so transmitted.

It never was intended, nor could it have been safe, in the Constitution, to have given to Congress thus assembled in convention the right to object to any vote, or even to question whether they were constitutionally or properly given.

This right of determining on the manner in which the electors shall vote; the inquiry into the qualifications, and the guards that are necessary to prevent disqualified or improper men voting, and to insure the votes being legally given, rests and is exclusively vested in the State legislatures.

When I come to read this, it reminds me that my friend who sits before me [Mr. Trumbull] drew his wisdom from this speech, for it is almost *in hæc verba* the language of his report made in 1873.

If it is necessary to have guards against improper elections of electors and to institute tribunals to inquire into their qualifications, with the State legislatures —

That is just what you said in 1873; it is with the State legislatures—

and with them alone, rests the power to institute them, and they must exercise it. To give to Congress, even when assembled in convention, a right to reject or admit the votes of States would have been so gross and dangerous an absurdity as the framers of the Constitution never could have been guilty of. How could they expect that in deciding on the election of a President, particularly where such election was strongly contested, that party spirit would not prevail and govern every decision? Did they not know how easy it was to raise objections—

Very easy, as we have found out to-day, for there are whole piles, cart-loads of them here—

how easy it was to raise objections against the votes of particular electors, and that in determining upon these it was more than probable the members would recollect their *sides*, their favorite candidate, and sometimes their own interests?

*   *   *   *   *   *   *

These being the avowed reasons for introducing this bill, I answer them by observing that the Constitution having directed that electors shall be appointed in the manner the legislature of each State shall direct, it is to be taken as granted that the State legislatures will perform their duties, and make such directions as only qualified men shall be returned as electors. The disqualifications against any citizen being an elector are very few—

Now note—

The disqualifications against any citizen being an elector are very few indeed; they are two: the first, that no officer of the United States shall be an elector; and the other, that no member of Congress shall.

Having read that, we have the indication of the point I am now upon, that it was for very wise reasons that the disqualifications imposed upon the electors were very few; also, we have it indicated, what is plain of course upon the face of the instrument, that the Government of the United States, the Constitution itself, was the only authority upon that subject of eligibility, and that the States can exercise none whatever.

I now pass to another authority. Let me refer you to the language of Mr. Cooley, in his Constitutional Limitations, page 64:

Another rule of construction is that when the Constitution defines the circumstances under which a right may be exercised—

The electoral right here—

or a penalty imposed, the specification is an implied prohibition against legislative interference to add to the condition or to extend the penalty to other cases. On this ground it has been held by the supreme court of Maryland (4 Maryland, 189) that where the Constitution defined the qualifications of an officer, it was not in the power of the legislature to change or superadd to them, unless the power to do so was expressly or by necessary implication conferred by the Constitution.

So that, both by the most obvious reason of the case and by the authority of Mr. Pinckney, one of the framers of the Constitution, stating why it was that so few disqualifications were imposed upon the holding of the electoral office, and also by the decisions of the courts, and by every possible view that applies to the case, it is true that the holding of office under the State government neither is nor can be made to be a disqualification to hold the electoral office. I add more, that the Congress itself cannot add to or subtract from the qualifications of an elector. There they stand, broad, wide, and unlimited, except, as Mr. Pinckney states, by two solitary disqualifications.

Mr. Commissioner THURMAN. Would it be unconstitutional for a State to require its elector to be a citizen of the State?

Mr. SHELLABARGER. A citizen of the State in which he resides? I answer that in my judgment it would be. I see not why it is that a State can on any account add to or subtract from the provisions that the Constitution has made upon the subject of qualification.

Mr. Commissioner THURMAN. Could then a State select an alien for an elector?

Mr. SHELLABARGER. If the State may not choose an alien for an elector, it must be because the Constitution has prohibited it. The Constitution of the United States has not prohibited it. It has, as Mr. Pinckney has expressed it, made but two prohibitions. It was long doubted whether the States could appoint their electors by an act of the legislature, but long ago it was settled that there was no limitation, no fettering of the power of the State in regard to the methods of the appointment. That there was a provision in regard to what the qualification of the electors should be, I think is express and plain upon the very face of the Constitution, and two disqualifications being named the addition of others is excluded. Whether I am right or not upon that, is not very material for the purposes of this discussion, because the question put to me by the Senator does not arise in this case. No such extreme case has occurred here, and it is an abstract proposition.

The next question I propose to consider is whether the returning-board as it was organized was a good returning-board; I mean good as to numbers. It is said that because it had but four in it, when there ought to have been five, that spoils the board and renders it incapable of action. Now, without any elaboration, permit me to state the authorities and the propositions upon which I rely in that regard. In the case of Gildersleve vs. The Board of Education, 17 Abbott's Practice Reports, 201, you will find a case where the court held that a board composed of ten persons with power to fill vacancies could by a vote of five of its members remove a superintendent of schools at a time when there was an unfilled vacancy in the board, because they could act by a majority, and five was a majority of nine.

I have selected this case simply because, although a decision of a common pleas judge, the facts happened to be so exceedingly like those of the case we are dealing with. It was a case where the number was fixed by statute at ten; it was a case where there was a vacancy at the time of the action; it was a case where there was a power to fill the vacancy in the board; it was a case where they failed to fill the vacancy; and it was a case where had they filled the vacancy the vote by which the act was done, to wit, five, would not have accomplished the removal. There the court was brought square up to the very question whether that board thus constituted could act. It is the exact case with which we deal. There the court says that in private affairs all must meet and consider, and then proceeds:

But where the powers to be exercised are a continuous trust or duty confided to designated persons, the discharge of the public trust is not to be interrupted or fail through the death or absence or inability of any of the persons to whom the exercise of it is intrusted; provided, there is a sufficient number to confer together, to deliberate, and, in view of the possibility of the division of opinion, to decide upon what course is to be adopted.

I said that this was the decision of a common pleas judge.

Mr. Commissioner STRONG. By whom was the opinion delivered?

Mr. SHELLABARGER. By Judge Daly; but I want now to say for Judge Daly's opinion and for his authority that he has quoted what I have read from the very highest sources of the law, and I give you the cases from whence he derived it. You will find it first in the case of Blacket vs. Blizzard, decided in 1829, found in 9 Barnewall and Creswell, pages 856 to 859. You will find the same principle in Cooke vs. Loveland, 2 Bosanquet and Puller, 31; also in Rex vs. Beeston, 3 Term Reports, 592; also in Grindley vs. Baker, 1 Bosanquet and Puller, 229. You will find the same thing in its legal effect laid down in Bouvier's Law Dictionary under the title "Quorum." Precisely the same thing is decided in the great case of The People vs. Cooke, 4 Selden, 67. That was a case where the court decided that a vacancy or an absence in the election board did not vitiate the poll. That is one of the leading American cases. It is quoted everywhere ever since it was decided, on a great many different points, and it is so long that I will ask you to make a note of the place where you will find the fact especially stated as to how that board was organized in the dissenting opinion of Judge Taggart, pages 95 and 96. There you will find that the board held an election when but two out of the three were present a part of the time, and other irregularities appeared in the case.

You will find the same thing decided in The State vs. Stumpf, 21 Wisconsin, 579, where two out of three judges were held to be competent to hold an election. The same principle you will find decided in the State of Louisiana in 4 Louisiana Annual Reports, 419, decided in 1849, where it was held that when the power of a motion was conferred upon two-thirds of the body, then two-thirds of a quorum were capable of acting. So also in a case in 10 Wendell, 658, and in 16 Iowa, 284, where the same thing is laid down.

The result of all these cases is that wherever a body has a public or political duty to discharge, as distinguished from private arbitration or trial of that sort, there because it is a public tribunal exercising, as in the case at bar, political functions with the presence of a quorum, a majority of a quorum is competent to act and the public business will not be suffered to be arrested or put in peril by reason of the death or the absence of any member. The law as laid down in the case of Gildersleve is the law upon this subject.

Mr. Commissioner ABBOTT. Permit me to ask a question. Have you examined those cases so as to say whether the board was full, that is, that the number required by law had absolutely been appointed and were in existence, or whether there was a mere absence?

Mr. SHELLABARGER. I answer that, and it is a very pertinent inquiry, they are not all so directly on all-fours with the case at bar as the case I first read, because in most of them, perhaps in all for aught I know, the absence was not by reason of death so as to create an actual vacancy; and the reasoning of the court is entirely in support of our position, to wit, that the public interests will not be imperiled nor stopped

absence, whether that absence be caused by death or what not. They employ that very language, so as to show that it makes no difference what the cause of the absence is, whether it is death or what; it being a public function, a public tribunal disposing of public and political affairs, it can act by a majority when a majority is present. That is the law of this body, and it makes no difference, as you will see by reading the cases, whether the absence is caused by death or what.

Mr. Commissioner ABBOTT. I put the question, sir, because there are very respectable cases, I am sure, where the courts have holden, even with the provision of the statute that a majority may act, that, if the board is not full, the action of a majority will not bind, because that is not the board provided by law.

Mr. SHELLABARGER. I am very much obliged for the suggestion, and every one that I can answer I will, and if I cannot I will say so.

Mr. Commissioner THURMAN. If it would not interrupt you I should like to ask you a question. According to my recollection, all the authorities you have read are very good law ; but do they touch the case where the board is required to be constituted of different elements, where the statute creating it requires it to be constituted of different elements, and requires certain persons to constitute it in practice, and one element excludes the other element ?

Mr. SHELLABARGER. That question I will discuss under another head ; but my answer now to that suggestion is that that provision is, in its very nature and by the necessities of the case, directory, and it does not go to the essential power of the body. You must know that from the very common sense of the case, because how are you to test whether a man is a democrat or a republican ? How are you to find out whether his politics change yesterday, to-day, or to-morrow ? It is most obvious, I submit to your long experience and excellent learning, it must be so, that that is a directory provision to be abided by and performed in good faith, and if not performed in good faith and if there were no reason for its being omitted in this case, then it is an act reprehensible and to be condemned ; but it does not go to the jurisdiction of the body. I will state here, Mr. President and gentlemen, what I happen to know. Gentlemen have been talking about the testimony they propose to give. Now, let me state the testimony that I propose to give if you open this door. I shall prove, and say so on my professional honor, that if these gentlemen—and they seem to me to be gentlemen of the very highest character—have not falsified to me, I will prove, if you compel us to go into this door, that we tendered again and again the filling of that vacancy and it was refused by every man, and there were several to whom the application was made, because they did not want to be mixed up with the troublous affairs of Louisiana and the long labor, or some such reason as that. I only say that, in passing, to repudiate and repel these incessant inundations that we have in the way of denunciation, of invective, and of declamation about fraud. I undertake to meet it just where I have ; and if I am deceived in that, it is not my fault, but it is the fault of the gentleman who stated it to me, he being one of the leading members, not the president, of the board.

I now come to the next point that I have marked in my brief, and that is a proposition that my friend Senator Carpenter seems to attach some consequence to, though I do not know that anybody else on his side has especially discussed it ; and it is the proposition that these functions of the returning-board of Louisiana are judicial in their nature, that they could not under the constitution of Louisiana be conferred except on a court, and that hence this law goes by the board for that reason. Let me in the first place give your honors a reference to the case of The State vs. Hufty, 11 Louisiana Annual Reports, 304, decided in 1856. I give you the date of the decision in order that I may get you away back of the unhealthy influences that are alleged to have pervaded and affected these courts since the rebellion. In 1856, when the State constitution had a provision, as every constitution has, divorcing the executive, the legislative, and the judicial parts of the government, keeping them separate; away back in 1856, under a constitution that prohibited the exercise of judicial powers by anything except the courts of Louisiana, this question arose in the case of The State *vs.* Hufty. There an address was made—that was what it was called—an address by the legislature to remove Mr. Hufty from the office of sheriff to which he had been elected. One of the grounds for removal was the very ground with which we deal to-day, to wit, that his election had been carried by violence, intimidation, and fraud. It was alleged that there were organized bands of men that broke up the ballot-box, disturbed the election, and prevented its result being fair. The counsel in that case made the point directly that that was a judicial question, that it could not be tried in the legislature, and that the law providing for such address was unconstitutional. The court decided this very question that it was not a judicial but was an administrative process—that was the word of the court—and was entirely competent to be committed to the legislature, and that it was therefore constitutional.

Then I give you three other cases: the case of Collins *vs.* Knoblock, 25 Louisiana Annual Reports, 263; The State *vs.* Lynch, the same book, 267; also 13 Louisiana Annual Reports, 90, in every one of which the question of the validity of laws giving this power to the returning-board was involved, although perhaps in none of them, certainly not in all of them, was the question directly and expressly made; but it was involved in each one of these cases, the one in 13 Annual Reports being under a former constitution, because that was about 1858, the others under the present constitution and under the law of 1870, all holding and agreeing that this is a valid law, and that the judicial powers, or the quasi-judicial powers, as the court calls them, that are conferred upon this returning-board are entirely competent to be so conferred under the constitution of Louisiana.

Then upon that question—that local question of the constitution and laws of Louisiana—you have the judgment three times, nay four times over, pronounced under similar constitutions by the court of last resort of the State of Louisiana. Surely, that ought to be enough upon that. But pardon me again, by way of making "assurance double sure," for adding to them other authorities. First I take Cooley's Constitutional Limitations, page 623, and I use his words in the way of fortification of what I have said. Speaking about the proposition that boards of canvassers generally act ministerially in our States, he proceeds:

This is the general rule, and the exceptions are those where the law under which the canvass is made declares the decision conclusive, or where a special statutory board is established with powers of final decision.

So that, according to the authority of Mr. Cooley, it is perfectly competent for their legislature to confer the quasi-judicial powers upon the board, and where that is done by the State statute it is final, and neither by *quo warranto* nor by any other trial can you reverse the decision of the returning-board, as has been decided in Louisiana in the four cases that I have now given to you. I may refer also to Greer *vs.* Shackelford, Constitutional S. C. Reports, 642. There is also a case in 1 Metcalfe, Kentucky, Reports, Batman *vs.* Magowan, 533; The People *vs.* Goodwin, 22 Michigan, 496; The State *vs.* Marlow, 15 Ohio State Reports, 114; The Commonwealth *vs.* Garrigues, 28 Pennsylvania State Reports, 9; The Commonwealth *vs.* Baxter, 35 Pennsylvania State

Reports, 263; The Commonwealth *vs.* Leech, 44 Pennsylvania State Reports, 332.

In every one of these cases there were special statutory tribunals provided. In most of them they were not the courts. In my State it happened to be one of the courts; but in every one of them, whether they were special statutory tribunals or whether they were courts, it was held, just as Cooley says, that wherever or whenever a special tribunal is constituted as the one to try, as this does, it can be made final. It is administrative, to adopt the language of the supreme court of Louisiana in the old case in 13 Annual Reports, 90, and requoted in every subsequent decision. It is administrative; it is a part of the political machinery of your country; and it is perfectly competent, unless the constitution of the State otherwise provides, to confer it upon these special tribunals; and that is as well settled as anything that is settled in our law.

Mr. President, how long have I been speaking?

The PRESIDENT. One hour and eight minutes, to be exact.

Mr. SHELLABARGER. I want to add now to the authorities that were read by my friend who preceded me upon this subject of the finality of the acts of the returning-board in Louisiana, and also upon the question I have just passed over, to wit, that it is competent to bestow this power upon this special tribunal, and is not unconstitutional. He read one, The State, on the relation of John M. Bonner, *vs.* B. L. Lynch, in 25 Louisiana Annual Reports, page 267, and I add the case of Collins *vs.* Knoblock, 25 Louisiana Annual Reports, page 263, and also 13th Louisiana Annual Reports, page 90. The court go over very thoroughly and carefully, and, I think, very strongly state, the law of Louisiana upon this subject; but whether strongly or not, for the purposes of this tribunal, by the judgments of the Supreme Court of the United States, making the laws of the States and their interpretation by the local courts the law of this tribunal, you are bound to abide.

Gentlemen, I have gone over these various outlying questions as well as I could. I come now to the main question in this case, and really, as it seems to me in all frankness and fairness of statement, the only question there is; and that is decided by what you have just decided in the case of Florida, and that is whether or not it is competent for you to go behind the action of the returning-board of Louisiana for the purpose of finding out what happened in its exercise of the jurisdiction vested by the statute. I need not restate, indeed I will not, what has been decided in the Florida case. I know that the logic and law of that case has decided all there is in this, if I can appreciate legal principle at all, except the question whether that Louisiana returning-board was one authorized by valid law to exercise the jurisdiction that it undertook to exercise.

Mr. Commissioner EDMUNDS. Was it offered in the Florida case to prove that the State board of canvassers of Florida were actuated by corrupt motives in whatever mistakes they were said to have made? In this case it is directly offered to prove that the motive of the board in doing these alleged wrong things was corrupt.

Mr. SHELLABARGER. I understood, your honor, that the proposition in the Florida case offered to prove—without designating whether it went to the question of motive or not—fraud generally, corrupt action on the part of the Florida returning-board. That was the proposition, to prove conspiracy and corrupt motive or action on the part of that board.

Now I come to the consideration of that question so far as I shall discuss it at all, because I shall assume in the remarks that I am about to make that the Florida case decided nothing. That is the assumption we are compelled to adopt, because it is adopted and this debate is conducted and the whole case is conducted on the idea that nothing has been decided in the Florida case. Now let me state what I understand to be the main question or foundation-inquiry that we have reached, and it is this: It being assumed that the law of 1872 is in force and is constitutional—I have gone over that—it being assumed that this board had the functions that the second and third sections purported to give to the returning-board, then is it competent for this tribunal to inquire into the method of the exercise of the jurisdiction that the board did possess? Let me restate my proposition. It is really the same question, very much less clearly stated, that was suggested by his honor, Judge Miller, to wit: Whether there being a board competent to make these returns, competent and required by the law, as it expressly is, to find out, to declare, and certify who were duly elected to the offices in the State, including that of elector, that being the jurisdiction of the board, you have the power in this tribunal to try the question as to how they reached the result they did reach?

Upon the threshold of that inquiry, pardon me for saying to you that when we deny in this stage of inquiry and in this tribunal the power of going behind the finding of that board, the charge that we are thereby covering up fraud or seeking to escape scrutiny is, I submit, unutterably unjust. It has not even the semblance of fairness in it. Why? Simply because—and I concede his law—my friend, Mr. Carpenter, has furnished us with a reply to all the loud denunciations in which he indulged yesterday; and, with my friend Stoughton, I must say that I too was surprised at the language that was brought into this high tribunal when he undertook to denounce four men that he probably never saw, as four villains of Louisiana. I say the language was not worthy of my friend. It is surely not worthy of this tribunal. Why do I say that our position is no concealment of fraud? First of all, because it is begging the whole question to say that you have a right to try the question of fact that discloses this fraud, in this tribunal. I said a moment ago that he begged the whole question when he said we were undertaking to cover up fraud by our objection to this evidence. It just occurs to me that in a case not long ago decided by his honor, Mr. Justice Field, in 13 Wallace, 347, where Mr. Bradley sued Mr. Fisher, a judge of this District, because he fraudulently, maliciously, wantonly, and corruptly turned him away from the bar, Justice Field met that as a court, as a lawyer would, by saying that is one of the cases where you cannot show fraud for reasons that are given by the Justice in the decision. It would have been strange logic and stranger law for Mr. Carpenter to have got up and insulted the court by saying, "You are nine villains and conspirators undertaking to shut out the light of truth from the courts of the country." It would have been just as worthy, though, as this remark here to-day.

Then take the case of Field vs. Seabury, 19 Howard, 331, an action of ejectment coming up from California on a writ of error, where a law making a grant had been got through the legislature by fraud, whereby the grantee under the fraudulent deed brought himself within the category of persons whose titles to land were confirmed by an act of Congress. He got his grant by a fraud in the legislature. He brought himself within the category. His opponent sought to set up the fraud; but no, said the Supreme Court of the United States, it is not true that fraud in every forum vitiates everything; you are in the wrong forum;

you must attack this thing in the right place. So with us to-day here and now. Gentlemen, it is an insult to your intelligence to say that, because as mere counters, as mere ministerial officers, you cannot go into frauds, therefore here is an attempt to cover up fraud.

Look at it for a moment in another light. This argument of the gentlemen contains in itself an utter *felo de se*. How wide-mouthed was their declamation when they were talking to you about the fraud of the returning-board in Florida. What was the fraud? It was a fraud which was committed by them, they being mere ministerial officers, in usurping jurisdiction and going behind the returns from the counties and undertaking to throw out votes, in violation of law. There, my friends, a case of that sort could not be inquired into according to your law. Abide by your law; stand up to its logic, and take its consequences. It is right, and it is right because of what you put nto your report in 1873, to wit, that the two Houses combined have not the power of a *quo warranto* court. You could not go behind the returns. Therefore, do not talk to me about our position being one designed either in logic, law, or morality to shut out evidence of fraud. But more than that, do not forget that my friend, Senator Carpenter, said to you last night, and he read the law-books to prove it, that the courts of the United States to-day, under the existing law bestowing jurisdiction upon the circuit courts, have power to try which of these two men has been elected President of the United States. Did he not say that? Did he not read the statutes to prove it to you? Did he not take the ground that there was such power to-day; and that to-morrow, if you make your decision, after the 4th of March, he can come with his *quo warranto* and can retry the question as to who is President? I do not undertake to say whether that is law or not; but, if it be law, then it ill-becomes our friend to talk to us about this being an attempt to put a man into the presidency of the United States by fraud.

I remember reading a remark that was made by King James in regard to the *Novum Organon* of Lord Bacon. He said the book was like the peace of God, that it passed all knowledge. These objections on the other side are just of that sort. At one moment we find them saying to you that the divorcement between the judiciary and the executive and the legislative is complete, and therefore Congress cannot exercise judicial powers; but the very next moment they say to you, "Yes, you have all judicial powers; you can do the same thing that a *quo warranto* could, and because a *quo warranto* could try this thing, therefore you can try it." Thus my brother Carpenter gets *felo de se* into his argument there. Then in another place you find these gentlemen coming up and saying that Mr. Kellogg was the governor of Louisiana, and therefore he is no elector, and then the next moment you have them coming forward and saying, "No, he is not an officer at all; he is not the governor of Louisiana, but McEnery is." To such strange positions, gentlemen most eminent are driven in this frantic endeavor to escape from the familiar requirements of the law.

Now, if you will pardon me, I will read on this point one single authority and then will trouble you with no more. I read it because of its application to the point upon which I am now engaged. It is the case of Hulseman *vs.* Rems, in 41 Pennsylvania State Reports, 396. It was a bill to restrain the defendants from using election-certificates to get their seats as members of the common council from the nineteenth ward in Philadelphia, and among the grounds for the injunction were:

1. That when the returning-board met and made the canvass it was without authority

of law, and the proceedings were therefore null and void, because issued by a defunct board.

That brings squarely up your biggest question, the want of authority in the body.

2. That this defunct board counted forged returns.

That is another big thing here.

3. That even these forged returns never reached the board in any lawful way, but surreptitiously and without certificates, and the bill alleged that the certificates were therefore utterly void.

There are two things in that decision that I want to call attention to. The first proposition is in these words:

It is alleged that on the second Tuesday of November some of the return-judges refused to meet, and that those who did meet met at an unusual place to count the soldiers' votes and to issue the certificates; but the affidavits of the defendants seem to us sufficiently to account for this by showing that the duties of the return-judges were so interfered with by a disorderly crowd that they could not be performed at the usual place.

While I am on that, let me make use of it in another connection. There was a case where the returning-officers were required to meet and make their return within a certain time, and were also required to have their meeting at a certain place. It does not appear in the report whether that certain place was pointed out by statute or by usage; it is spoken of as a failure to meet at the usual place. Perhaps Judge Strong, who, I think, was on that bench at the time, will enable me to know how that was. At any rate, that is the way it appears in the report. There were two defects in the return; one was that the board met at the wrong time; the second was that they met at the wrong place. The supreme court of Pennsylvania say that it was a sufficient reason for their not meeting at that time and at that place, that they could not do so by reason of mob violence, and that they could perform that act at another time and place. I say that for the purpose of stating this, and I want to state it once for all, for I shall probably not have time to discuss the question *in extenso;* but I want to lay it down and state it carefully, that these provisions in regard to the sending up of affidavits, to their being attached with wax, in regard to the time of their taking, &c., are just like this one in the Pennsylvania State Reports relating to an election; they are directory, and they are not jurisdictional in the sense of that word as applied to the trial of private rights of the citizen. Let me restate it, and perhaps in a little different form, for I wish to leave it in your minds, if it is worthy of being left.

Because this is a political process, because it is a step in government as distinct from a trial of private rights of suitors in the courts, therefore the law is that any affirmative requirement of this kind which is either not accompanied or connected with negative words prohibiting the thing from being done at another time or in another way, or else is not of such essence of the very provision as to spoil the provision if it is not done in the time and way pointed out—in every such case the law is directory. I do not say that these acts in regard to the returning of affidavits can be dispensed with; but I say the things required can be done at other times and in other ways as soon as the violence will suffer them to be done.

Gentlemen, look at the reason of the thing. Is it possible that you are going to hold that that same violence which rendered it impossible to vote, and at the same time rendered it impossible for the officers safely to make their affidavits and their returns, shall triumph so that they cannot do it at another time? Beware before you come to such a conclusion. If you do, you will do it in the face of the law. You will find Parsons, that chief-justice who stands in his illustrious fame next to Marshall himself, and perhaps his peer, declaring in 2 Massachusetts Reports that whenever one of these laws contains no negative words and the provision as to time, place, and circumstance does not go to the essence of the transaction or affect it, in every such case the provision is directory merely.

Mr. Commissioner HOAR. Judge Shellabarger, I should like to ask you a question, whether that is not of the essence of the transaction? What do you make of the provision that "any person interested in the office by reason of being a candidate shall be allowed a hearing on making application within the time for the forwarding of the returns of said election?" In order to give the person interested in the office the opportunity for a hearing or the power of complying with the requisition that he shall make that application in time, must he not find on the copy sent to the clerk's office, notice that the validity of the voting at the particular polling-place or particular parish is to be drawn in question? In other words, can the essential right of the person interested in the office to be heard before the returning-board be preserved, if you regard this as merely directory, and not essential?

Mr. SHELLABARGER. I answer that first by saying that that is a suggestion addressed to the consideration of convenience. It is a useful provision beyond all doubt; it is a proper provision to be obeyed; but it being a mere suggestion going to convenience, it is not so of essence as that no violence or impossibility of executing it at the time shall forbid that notice being given to the candidate in some other way, or in that way at some later date, or in some way that is adequate, so that he shall have the opportunity in the language of the statute to have his hearing before the time for making returns shall have expired. That, it seems to me, is an answer. If it is not, I accept the consequences of its not being. It is not essential at all to the case that we should maintain the proposition that I am stating; still I believe it to be the law, and I submit it to this tribunal.

I was about, when Mr. Hoar kindly asked the question, to take the case of the jurisdiction conferred by the act of 1795 on the President of the United States to make proclamation and to require insurgents to disperse, and all that. There, you remember, it is a constitutional provision that interference can only occur upon a vote and request of the legislature, if the legislature be in session, or the executive, if it be not in session; but yet when the time came, as it did come sadly in our history, when that same violence that made the insurrection rendered it impossible for the legislature to send the summons, when the legislature itself went into the mischief, was a part of it, and when the executive made a part of the mischief, then came the time when the life of the State was rescued by still issuing the proclamation calling for the troops and attempting the suppression of the insurrection in the absence of all requests. I take it as entirely analogous to and confirmatory of the proposition that I now restate in the light of the case of Hulseman vs. Rems, in 41 Pennsylvania State Reports, in the light of the reason of the thing. It is that the time of making the return, the attaching of it, &c., are not jurisdictional in the sense that they cannot be done at another time; but that, wherever the mischief in fact exists, wherever the violence in fact has destroyed the election, and wherever that fact is made known in due time to the returning-officers, there their jurisdiction to exclude votes has attached and they can make the exclusion.

But that is not necessary to the purposes of our case, as I said a moment ago, and I now come back to the proposition that I stated awhile ago, that, these men having the requirement put upon them that they shall canvass and make return as to every officer and declare who is properly and duly elected, there is the scope of their jurisdiction. Under that they had power to decide who was elected and to grant these certificates; and that maxim applies which presumes that all things are done rightly by officers until the contrary is shown, which you will find decided in a number of cases that I have on my brief, but will not stop to read (see 12 Wheaton, 70) because it is not only familiar law, but it is a maxim of the law that all things done officially are presumed to be rightly done until the contrary is proved. Therefore, as suggested by the question of Judge Miller, as suggested by the manifest law of the case, these men having power to exercise this jurisdiction, the jurisdiction having been exercised, you not being a court can only count, not having judicial functions sufficient, as my friend Trumbull's report says, must stop without going behind and canvassing the votes for electors. Such being your function, I say this jurisdiction of this board thus exercised is presumed to have been lawfully exercised; and for the purposes of this count, you have rightfully decided the law as stated by Pinckney, as stated by your decision in the Florida case, and as recognized by the decisions that I have read, and I was about to conclude by reading a single one more. Lowrie, Judge, says, in the case in 41 Pennsylvania State Reports:

We have, therefore, no ground left for our interference, but the single one that the return-judges included, in their enumeration, returns purporting to be from three companies of volunteers which were mere forgeries. We admit that, in the evidence before us, it appears clear to us all that those returns are forgeries, and that it was only by their inclusion in the enumeration that the defendants have obtained certificates of their election. We admit, therefore, that the evidence proves that these certificates of the election of the defendants are founded in manifest fraud, the forgery of some unknown person, but we do not find that the defendants had any hand in it, and we trust they had not.

Can we, on this account, interfere and declare the certificates void? We think not. According to our laws, the election has passed completely through all its forms, the result has been in due form declared and certified, and the defendants have received their certificates of election, and are entitled to their seats as members of the common council. The title-papers of their offices are complete, and have the signatures of the proper officers of the law; and if they are vitiated by any mistake or fraud in the process that has produced them, this raises a case to be tried by the forms of "a contested election."

Gentlemen, this case goes all over the one at the bar; it answers all this exclamation about fraud, about our attempt to cover up fraud, about what are the functions of a counting-board and what the functions of a contesting-board:

And if they are vitiated by any mistake or fraud in the process that has produced them, this raises a case to be tried by the forms of "a contested election," before the tribunal appointed by law to try such questions, and not by the ordinary forms of legal and equitable process before the usual judicial tribunals. It is part of the process of political organization, and not a question of private rights; and therefore the Constitution does not require that the courts shall determine its validity.

The law has appointed a special tribunal to try just such a question as this, and we can have no right to step in between the case and that tribunal, and alter the return of the election judges, and annul their certificates. Plain as the fraud appears, and earnestly as we condemn it as citizens, it is no part of our functions as a court to sit in judgment on it. The common council is the proper tribunal to try cases of contested elections relative to its own members, and there the fraud and forgery must necessarily be tried and decided with final effect. They are appointed by law to try the whole case, and they alone can try it. We decided this last year at Philadelphia, in the case of The Commonwealth vs. Baxter, 11 Casey, 264, a case from Bradford County, where a commissioner of highways had received a regular certificate of election, and where we decided that it could be avoided only by a regular process of a contested-election case. Perhaps that case may be found worthy of examination.

If in this way we suffer a gross fraud to pass through our hands without remedy, it is not because we have any mercy for the fraud, but because we cannot frustrate it by any decree of ours without an act of usurpation. Another tribunal is appointed to administer the remedy, and we believe that, on proper application, it will administer it rightly, according to the evidence it may have.

And, gentlemen, I say here now and once for all that there is a proper tribunal, according to my friend Carpenter's able argument last night; that tribunal is the courts of the country, and there we invite them to go with this case, where our side can be heard as well as theirs.

I now conclude this argument by an allusion or two to what has been the weight and the burden of debate on the other side. It is in regard to this alleged outrage in the State of Louisiana. Why, gentlemen, are we to shut our eyes in scanning this question as to where this wrong and fraud and violence is going ultimately to be found when it comes to a tribunal that can try it. Can you shut your eyes to what now is the saddest—if not the saddest, certainly one of the saddest chapters of American history?

I remember, Mr. President, as you do right well, though I was then but a boy, when the Caroline was set on fire, sent adrift, and it was believed that one, two, or more American citizens were destroyed by the act of the British government. O, the thrill of indignation and of unutterable horror that pervaded the whole body-politic! It was only by the matchless diplomacy and the strange power of such intellects as Webster, who was then guiding the helm of state, that your country was rescued from universal war with the mightiest power of the earth, because we believed that by an outrage of the British government one or two lives of American citizens had been lost. So that thing struck us then; but how marvelously inured has the public mind become since those better days to this business of the destruction of American citizens! Why, gentlemen, by actual count made in an official report to the Government of the United States, through the aid of General Sheridan, it is set down as a part of your history that in this blighted and blasted State of Louisiana four thousand and odd citizens have been murdered by plan, murdered by system, by organization, murdered for the purpose of putting down the right of the black man to vote, and that thing has been going on and on and on through these dark and terrible years.

It was my misfortune to go once myself to this State, sent by the Congress of the United States. I went there in 1866, and I took the testimony of hundreds of men; and when I was taking it I literally sat with my feet in pools of human blood (clotted and dried up then, but still visible) shed there, that of Dr. Dotsie and others, in putting out the free government of the State of Louisiana, and they did put it out right well and effectually. So that thing has been going on and on in the attempt to put out the right of the black man to vote.

Gentlemen of America, you have written in the last fifteen years a grand history for your country, a grand one in its general, large aspects. I remember with gratification, and I shall till I die, that I was once thrown in company with the most illustrious man now living in Great Britain, illustrious by reason of his intellect, illustrious by reason of his great deeds, illustrious by reason of his service in the British Parliament for thirty years, illustrious because of his adhesion to the cause of human liberty in his own country and in all others; I mean John Bright, of England. I remember with gratification what he said to me in regard to the last chapters that we had written in our

American history. Said he to me: " Sir, I have been a part of the British government now for thirty years. In that time I have thought we in the British country had enacted some great affairs; and so we have. We have extended the right of the Englishman to vote; we have obliterated the rotten borough system; we have emancipated the Jews; we have elevated our colonies; we are extending the right of the children to be educated," and so he went on in a grand catalogue of the affairs that had been enacted during his time in the British government, and then he concluded by saying: " Sir, notwithstanding what I have said about my country, I say to you that you have dwarfed it," and he brought his hand down on the table with an emphasis that was startling, " you have dwarfed all that we have done in the life of the British nation by what you have enacted in the last ten years of your life. You have saved the life of the last, the one republic of the earth, and the cynosure of all eyes loving human liberty. You have done more than that; you have put out of the Constitution of your country and thereby ultimately out of the earth the chattelization of the human soul." Was it not a grand tribute? But let me say to you now, if this career of yours as a nation which began fifteen or twenty years ago in this direction by the election of Mr. Lincoln to the Presidency, then by the putting down of the rebellion, then by the extinction of slavery by the thirteenth amendment, then by your fourteenth amendment making all men equal before the law in all their civil and political rights, then making all men free to vote—if this procession of yours as a nation, and which is indeed like the procession of the gods, which in every foot-fall marks a constellation and shakes from its sandals the star-dust of the heavens—if your career of that grand description is to end by going back, turning around, and abandoning to these murderers who are drenching our country, in this part of it which is under consideration to-night, in blood for purposes of their disfranchisement, then indeed this career of yours will be like that French astronomer's, described so magnificently by one of our most gifted men, who went in search of the central sun of the universe until he found it, and then denied the existence of the God that made it, and walked back to perdition in the night of his own shadow.

I conclude this discussion by saying, gentlemen of America—that is a higher designation than gentlemen of the Commission—gentlemen of America, remember that there is on trial here to-night the question whether those laws made in Louisiana in pursuance of article 103 of her constitution and enjoining it on the legislature to make laws for the protection of the right of the freedman to vote, can be sustained and enforced. If you fail to execute these laws you will have stabbed your country in that place where by the very traditions of the children we are taught the life of the country is to be found, and is to reside, to wit, in the freedom, the purity of the ballot-box.

Mr. EVARTS. I was expecting to address the Commission, not to so great length as my associates, and I certainly would much prefer to do so to-morrow morning. I have been in the room ever since ten o'clock, not being able to leave it during the recess that was given.

Mr. Commissioner ABBOTT. I move, Mr. President, that we adjourn. It seems to be desirable to the counsel on either side. My motion is that we adjourn until to-morrow morning at ten o'clock.

Mr. Commissioner THURMAN. I propose half past ten.

Mr. Commissioner ABBOTT. I will accept the amendment; say half past ten.

Mr. Commissioner EDMUNDS. I ask for the yeas and nays.

Mr. Commissioner GARFIELD. Let us take ten o'clock, and not call the yeas and nays.

Mr. Commissioner ABBOTT. I have no choice about the hour. I will return to the original motion.

The PRESIDENT. The amendment is to strike out "ten" and insert "half past ten," I understand. I will put the question on that amendment.

The amendment was rejected.

The PRESIDENT. The question recurs on the motion that the Commission adjourn until to-morrow morning at ten o'clock.

Mr. Commissioner MORTON called for the yeas and nays, which being taken, resulted—yeas 7, nays 7.

Those who voted in the affirmative were: Messrs. Abbott, Bradley, Clifford, Garfield, Hunton, Payne, and Strong—7.

Those who voted in the negative were: Messrs. Edmunds, Field, Frelinghuysen, Hoar, Miller, Morton, and Thurman—7.

So the motion was not agreed to.

Mr. Commissioner THURMAN. I move that we adjourn until quarter past ten to-morrow.

Mr. Commissioner MORTON called for the yeas and nays, which being taken, resulted:

YEAS 8
NAYS 7

Those who voted in the affirmative were: Messrs. Abbott, Bayard, Bradley, Clifford, Field, Hunton, Payne, and Thurman—8.

Those who voted in the negative were: Messrs. Edmunds, Frelinghuysen, Garfield, Hoar, Miller, Morton, and Strong—7.

So the motion was agreed to; and (at six o'clock and fifty-two minutes p. m.) the Commission adjourned until to-morrow at ten o'clock and fifteen minutes a. m.

THURSDAY, *February* 15, 1877.

The Commission met at ten o'clock and fifteen minutes a. m., pursuant to adjournment, all the members being present.

The respective counsel appearing in the Louisiana case were also present.

The Journal of yesterday was read and approved.

Mr. EVARTS. Mr. President and gentlemen of the Commission, the general subject of controversy before the Commission is, how this Commission, under the powers conferred upon it and in discharge of the duty confided to it by the act of Congress under which it is organized, shall advise the two Houses of Congress, in the discharge of their duty under the Constitution of the United States in counting the votes for President and Vice-President, what votes shall be counted for the State of Louisiana. The Constitution has undertaken to determine that the State shall have the power to appoint electors as its legislature may direct, and no authority or argument can disparage or overreach that right of the State. That right is in the State. It is not a gift from the Federal Government, for there was no Federal Government to give it. It is not carved out of any fund of power and right that the Federal Government possessed, for the Federal Government had no general fund of power or right out of which it could carve a gift to a State. The State of Louisiana stands in this behalf as one of the original thirteen States stood. Whatever was the right of one of the original thirteen States in the election of Washington, is the right of Louisiana now in the election of a President. And, therefore, it is not to be measured as a gift, not to be measured by its relation to any general fund of authority on the subject that the United States had and which it has limited, but as one of the original conditions, one of the original limitations, one of the original distributions of power out of which and by which combined comes the Government of the United States and exists the government of each State as a member of the Union.

This topic at once leads us to consider wherein the Constitution of the United States has established and how it has distributed the authority of choosing a President of the United States, what part of it is administered and administrable as the action of the Federal Government, and what part of it is administered and administrable as a part of State action in the matter. On the terms of the Constitution is this demarkation to be drawn and adhered to? And in this regard, as well as in every other respect of power, are the maxims of the Constitution as to construction concerning the line drawn to be observed as well as in any other? The Government confers nothing upon the States. The Government comes into existence by and through the States and their people. The location of authority is primarily in the State, and is in the General Government only by its allotment in the terms of the Constitution. There is therefore the same method of construction and interpretation in drawing the line and in maintaining its defenses in this matter of the election of President as in all others. Whatever the Federal Government has in this matter of the election of a President, it has by force of terms in the Constitution; and whatever the State has, it has upon the same terms; and then the ninth and tenth articles of the amendments made soon after the adoption of the Constitution apply, that there is to be no disparagement of rights that are reserved by rights that are conferred, and that whatever is not conferred upon the Federal Government by this Constitution, and is not forbidden to the States, is reserved to the States or to the people.

It is not for me to repeat the arguments made by my learned associates so well, and by me, so far as I could aid them, in the general discussions which were presented under the Florida case. These general propositions were that the whole matter of creating the elector belonged to the State; the whole matter of ascertaining, accrediting, setting forward with credentials, belonged to the State so far as the text of the Constitution read; and that whatever the statute of 1792 had sought to prescribe in the matter of these credentials was directory and for the convenience and instruction of the body that was to count the votes, as to the fact of the action of each State; that the elector was not an officer of the State; that in no very considerable sense could he be treated as an officer of the United States; that he was an elector, having the right under the Constitution of the United States to vote for President, and that he was a representative elector, and was to be measured only to discern whether he was deputized to act as an agent or whether he was accredited with the voting power to vote as an elector having the suffrage in his hands. To say that he is a representative elector because he comes to be the elector in representation of a participation in the government of a State, comes to nothing more than to say that you, members of the two Houses of Congress, are representative legislators. You are representative legislators. You are legislators in a Government resting upon the will of the people and on its communicated authority to you as representatives; but you are not deputies to derive your instructions and authority from a principal at home. You are representatives of the legislative authority, lodged theoretically in the people, and in the theory of representation possessed by you in the same plenary power that the people themselves would have exercised it.

It was then announced as our proposition, that after the appointment of the elector, the vote, and the title to vote, and the exercise of the right, and performance of the duty to vote on the part of the elector had come under the exclusive dominion of the Federal Constitution; the representation, so far as it entered into the creation of the title and the conferring of authority, had been exhausted.

In the Florida case, as here, these considerations had their weight and were accepted or declined by the different members of the Commission, according to their estimate of the constitution and laws of their country. In that case, as in this, there were present before this Commission matters of consideration, about which, as open entirely for your inspection and necessarily forming a part of your determination, there was no question—I mean the papers that were opened by the President of the Senate, according to the Constitution, in the presence of the two Houses of Congress. They are before you under the law of 1877, as they were before that assemblage in that presence under the Constitution without the law of 1877, and now the question as to what more is or can be before you is a question under the law of 1877, as interpreted by its own terms in the light of the Constitution of the United States. It has passed beyond dispute; we did not dispute it in the Florida case; and, if we are to receive the intimation of Mr. Justice Bradley, it has passed beyond dispute in your own deliberations, as receiving the concurrence of all, that you have the powers that the two Houses have in the act and transaction of counting the votes, and no other powers; not that you have the powers that the two Houses of Congress together or separately have as the legislature of the country; not that you have any of the powers that either of them separately has in respect to what is accorded to either of them separately in the Constitution outside of legislative power.

You have no particle of any authority that is lodged in the two Houses of Congress under any of the general grants of authority to them as the legislature or to either of them separately, except what is granted by the Constitution within the very terms of this article, that the transaction being completed in the States and they having forwarded their votes hither under such authenticity as entitles them to the first reception and brings them into the presence of the two Houses of Congress that their contents may be disclosed and acted upon, whatever action thereupon proceeds by the two Houses there met or by the two Houses separating in the discharge of and in the continued exercise of the function of counting the votes, this is passed over to you that your advice may be given to them, as it would proceed out of their original, their independent deliberations and construction if they had limited themselves to the conduct of the counting of the votes in the simple terms of the Constitution. They then proceed to count. They count the votes. Having made a law unto themselves, which they cannot transcend without its repeal, this instruction as to what votes ought to be counted under the Constitution of the United States they will act upon as determining what votes under that Constitution ought to be counted unless their united judgment shall contravene this great authority they have given to you.

We insisted, therefore, in the Florida case that one great consideration in determining what the powers of Congress were in this mere procedure was what the nature of the procedure was, what the constitutional objects and solicitudes in providing for the transaction had indicated as the will of the people when they adopted the Constitution of the United States, and we were met by very learned and very authoritative statements from very eminent lawyers.

Mr. Field, in behalf of the House of Representatives, proposed to you that you had at least the powers of a court on *quo warranto*. Mr. O'Conor, with that accuracy and precision and acceptance of all logical results that proceed from his statements, demanded the same authority; insisted that otherwise the correction of frauds, the redress of violence, the curbing of excesses of authority would be remediless, and yet in their nature being festering wounds in the body-politic would work its ruin.

Those demands we met; those demands we answered. And now, without one particle of change in the law, the Constitution, or the area of this debate, we are told by the responsible representatives of the Houses of Congress through their objections and by the eminent counsel that have thus far put forth their positions, that you have no judicial power whatever; that we were quite right about that; there could not be any judicial power outside of the courts inferior to the Supreme Court, the judges whereof were appointed by the President and confirmed by the Senate, and holding their offices for life upon a stated compensation. Why might we not have been saved the former discussion if we are to enter upon this with any great trust in its soundness or its permanence? Obedience to the conclusions of this Commission as requiring this shifting of ground in our favor would be a respectable support for the maneuver, but I have not heard that assigned as the reason why the argument in the Florida case was abandoned and an independent and inconsistent one proposed here.

Now, what is the power? It is what is called a legislative power that is supposed to reside in this Commission in determining how it should advise that the votes should be counted, it being a legislative power in the two Houses. Now, there are quite as many constitutional objections to a legislative power vested in this Commission or a legislative power resting in the two Houses of Congress in the matter of counting the votes, as there are to any other form or description of power. The legislative power, the great principal power of the Government, is vested in those Houses when they act in such concurrence as the Constitution requires before any legislation is effected. It is not, therefore, in that sense that our learned friends attribute legislative power either to the two Houses or to you. It is in the sense of a political power, of political action in a political transaction, and those are the limits that we had assigned in our argument of the Florida case to any possible powers of the two Houses, to wit, that in a transaction of election which starts from the primary polling-places and proceeds to the point of developing and accrediting the elector up to the scrutiny, so far as it is open here, and the counting of the electoral votes, (not of votes *for* electors, but votes *of* electors,) it was all a part in the series of movements that had for their purpose the transaction of the political act of bringing into office a President of the United States; and that the two Houses of Congress, under the Constitution as it reads, must discharge, when the President of the Senate opened the certificates, that duty on those certificates alone, unless by some prior legislation of Congress—putting in execution, and thus interpreting, some other powers that they assumed to possess, in their construction of the Constitution—Congress had provided legal means for the exercise of such further powers. The terms of this act carefully observed the limitation that this act was not to be interpreted as carrying any congressional powers that were determined and created by the act or any interpretation to be put upon it in its own terms, but that this act was to carry only such powers as were in the two Houses under existing law, and as solely determinable by the Constitution and existing law.

As a primary consideration, then, as in the Florida case, it is to be determined not as an abstract question. Let me ask the Commission to consider that it is to determine not what hypothetical proofs might be received, but what proofs within the offers are rightfully to be received and added to the elements and funds of proof which the papers opened by the President of the Senate themselves disclose.

What then is the offer of proof, not in its details, but in its principles? What is the state of proof as presented on the certificates in aid or supplement or contradiction of which this proof *aliunde* is to be introduced? The first certificate contains in itself every certainty and every conclusive credential that the laws and the Constitution of the United States or of the State of Louisiana prescribe. This certificate also discloses a special state of facts concerning two of the electors who cast their votes; I mean Levissee and Brewster; this special state of facts, that being among the electors that were voted for and that were covered by the governor's certificate, when the electoral college met they were not in attendance; that the statute prescribed that their attendance should be waited for until four o'clock in the afternoon of the day, and that for non-attendance by itself and of itself alone on the part of any person chosen or accredited by the action of the State authorities, the vacancy thus created should be filled by the acting electors; that at that moment, on that fact, the college of electors proceeded and chose these same men, who thereafter on that title took their seats in the electoral college and voted, and are to be counted or disparaged on that showing, to wit, the entire showing of this certificate opened by the President of the Senate.

Beyond that there is not in this argument about evidence any particular circumstance that I care to call attention to in regard to that first certificate; nor do I need certainly to make any addition to the observations already made to discuss the second certificate at all.

What proof, then, is offered? I now proceed to discuss it as matter of proof as to its application and where its effect, if at all, is to be expected.

In the first place, the offers of proof do not seek, any of them, to disparage the truth of that certificate; I mean its truth as made up of the elements of the governor's certification of the fact in the State's action that he is to certify, nor any impeachment of the transaction which by the certificate is shown to have taken place in the election. No proof offered touches that space in the transaction or questions the governor's right to certify, his right by being governor to certify, or that the fact in the culminating and recorded result of the election in the State comports with the fact that he did so, nor on the point that Brewster and Levissee came into the electoral college on the transaction preserved in the minutes of the electoral college as presented here. If we look at the offers of proof, we see that at once. So far from introducing, therefore, any element of proof that is to separate the governor's certificate from the thing certified, or that is to disparage the governor's right under the Constitution of the United States, these offers of proof expressly concede that condition of things, and plant themselves wholly upon something antecedent in the State's transaction to this action of the governor, and which is the occasion of this action of the governor, to wit, the action in the State which produces the recorded result on which the governor must certify.

In the first place, we are saved any question, and I think we might have been saved any argument, about Governor Kellogg's being a *de facto* governor, filling the office and performing its duties, for they offer under their first head to prove "that said Kellogg was governor *de facto* of said State during the months of November and December, A. D. 1876." Then, when you come to other offers concerning the disqualification of Levissee and of Brewster, found on the seventeenth page, you will observe that there is not the least proposition that on the 6th day of December, when these two men came into the office of elector by the choice of the electoral college filling the vacancies, they were under any disqualification whatever. The proposition is—I read now from what is called the fourth proposition—

That on the 7th day of November, A. D. 1876, A. B. Levissee, who was one of the pretended college of electors of the State of Louisiana, * * * was at the time of such election a court commissioner of the circuit court of the United States for the district of Louisiana.

And for Brewster in the same way. The offer of proof, then, falls entirely short of disparaging their capacity to receive an election on the 6th day of December, and the proof does not offer to contradict the transaction by which they came in through the vote of the electoral college as displayed in the certificate.

Now, in regard to the substantive matters of proof, so far from being obliged to rest upon the proposition that there is no offer to intervene with proof between the recorded result of the election and the governor's certificate to that result, as producing these electors and no others, the offers of proof are affirmative in their propositions that that state of facts does exist, and is part of the things that they are able and ready to prove. I ask attention to this principal offer of proof, which is, I suppose, the one on page 13, the last paragraph but one on the page.

And that said returning-board, in further pursuance and execution of said unlawful combination and conspiracy, knowingly, willfully, falsely, and fraudulently did make a certificate and return to the secretary of state that said Kellogg, Burch, Joseph, Sheldon, Marks, Levissee, Brewster, and Joffrion had received majorities of all the legal votes cast at said election of November 7, 1876, for presidential electors, they then and there well knowing that the said McEnery, Wickliffe, St. Martin, Poché, De Blanc, Seay, Cobb, and Cross had received majorities of all the votes cast at said election for presidential electors, and were duly elected as the presidential electors of said State. And that the said returning-board, in making said statement, certificate, and return to the secretary of state, were not deceived nor mistaken in the premises, but knowingly, willfully, and fraudulently made what they well knew when they made it was a false and fraudulent statement, certificate, and return; and that the said false and fraudulent statement, certificate, and return, made by said returning-board to the secretary of state in that behalf, was made by the members of said returning-board in pursuance and execution of, and only in pursuance and execution of, said unlawful combination and conspiracy.

We have, then, in the offers of proof a recognition of the fact that the governor's certificate in No. 1 is by the acting governor of the State; that it is of a fact which has been deliberately produced and made of record in the proper office of that State; that by the authority intrusted with that final act of canvass and certification these electors did receive a majority of the legal votes in the State of Louisiana; that that was done *mala fide* and fraudulently. It was then done. The act was consummated. You are relieved, therefore, from any disturbance of this definite and limited proposition of whether it is competent for the two Houses of Congress to penetrate the action of the State and determine, first, whether it conforms to the real facts of the election as deducible through successive steps from the deposit of the votes in the ballot-box; and secondly, whether, though conforming to legal authority, it has been a corrupt, *mala fide* transaction.

It is necessary for us, then, before we can approach definitely the consideration of whether any of this proof can be offered, to understand at least what the laws of Louisiana are; not that it will follow that we have any right here to consider the conformity of the action of the canvassers or any of the subordinate functionaries in the election or of the voters themselves to that law, but that we may see at least upon what state of statutory enactments these objectors seek to base their question of the action had in these subordinate departments of the transaction.

I confess to an inability to understand that there should really exist any confusion on this subject as to what the statutory enactments in force—I mean on their face—were. This election, as it took place on the 7th of November, in the primary deposit of the votes, was concluded later in the year by the final result of the canvass certified and recorded. Some confusion, I am afraid, has been made out of the attempt to shorten a little the reprint, so useful in all particulars, made under the direction of the Commission. I have before me the session laws of 1868. In the acts of that session are found two independent acts on independent subjects, both of which were in force until either or both of them were repealed. They were not inconsistent; and they were not *in pari materia*, unless so far as that some portion of an enactment that might have been included in a general law, and was not, was included in the special or particular law to which I shall call attention. The first of these acts is found at page 218 of the session laws and is numbered 164. Its title is, " Relative to elections in the State of Louisiana and to enforce article 103 of the constitution of the State."

Mr. Commissioner THURMAN. Where is that in this pamphlet which has been printed for us?

Mr. EVARTS. I do not think it is there. Subsequent laws that are supposed to have taken its place have been printed, but this has not been printed at all. A portion of the revised statutes is printed, and somebody has put at the top of it "laws of 1868." It is not a print of any part of the law of 1868. It is a reproduction of certain sections of the revised statutes which were passed in 1870.

Mr. Commissioner ABBOTT. It was stated to us that this revision and the law of 1868 were precisely the same.

Mr. EVARTS. I will proceed with my argument, if you please, because my object is to show exactly how the thing does run. That law printed on that page is not any part of the law that I have asked your attention to thus far; it is not a reproduction of that; it has nothing to do with it. There is another law of 1868.

Mr. Commissioner BRADLEY. That law is a general election law.

Mr. EVARTS. A general election law to enforce article 103 of the constitution. On page 245, No. 193, is another law, of which I will read the title, to wit: " Relative to presidential electors." That is a short act. It contains in its first section an attribution of the conduct of *their* election to the provisions of the general election law:

And such election shall be held and conducted in the manner and form provided by law for general State elections.

Mr. Commissioner BRADLEY. Mr. Evarts, while you are on that, I wish to ask a question for information. I have tried to get hold of those acts of 1868 for about twenty-four hours, but have been unable to do so. Does that first section commence in this way: "In every year in which," &c.?

Mr. EVARTS. It does.

Mr. Commissioner BRADLEY. And the thirty-fifth section of the act of 1868 is in the same terms exactly. These two are copies of one another, are they not? I wish to ascertain that fact.

Mr. EVARTS. I will look. The thirty-fifth section of the act of 1868?

Mr. Commissioner BRADLEY. Yes.

Mr. EVARTS. No; that comes into the act of 1870, if at all. There is nothing of the kind in the act of 1868. There is section 32 of the act of 1868, which I will read. I will read not section 35, but section 32, which relates to the subject.

Mr. Commissioner EDMUNDS. Which of these two acts do you read from?

Mr. EVARTS. The general election law of 1868, which begins on page 218 of the session laws of that year.

Mr. Commissioner THURMAN. What is the date of it?

Mr. EVARTS. It is the 19th of October, 1868. This is section 32, which is probably the section to which Mr. Justice Bradley had reference.

That in every year in which an election shall be held for electors of President and Vice-President of the United States, such election shall be held on the Tuesday next after the first Monday in the month of November, in accordance with the act of the Congress of the United States approved January 23, 1845, and such election shall be held and conducted in the manner and form provided by law for general State elections.

Which is, I believe, an accurate statement.

Mr. Commissioner BRADLEY. An exact copy.

Mr. EVARTS. It is identical with the first section of the presidential-electors statute. Now, in this presidential-electors act there are two provisions which do bear on the questions which we are to discuss as to the proper method of carrying on, certifying, and canvassing the election held last November. There is no doubt about that, if they were in force, and I will ask attention to them. The first is section 4 on page 245 of the session laws of 1868:

Immediately after the receipt of a return from each parish, or on the fourth Monday of November, if the returns should not sooner arrive, the governor, in the presence of the secretary of state, the attorney-general, a district judge of the district in which the seat of government may be established, or any two of them, shall examine the returns and ascertain therefrom the seven persons who have been duly elected electors.

Then there are certain administrative provisions which are not important. Then section 8 on the same page.

Mr. Commissioner BRADLEY. It speaks of "seven persons" there.

Mr. EVARTS. That word is there; the State then was entitled to seven electors. The eighth section is:

If any one or more of the electors chosen by the people shall fail from any cause whatever to attend at the appointed place at the hour of four p. m. of the day prescribed for their meeting, it shall be the duty of the other electors immediately to proceed to ballot to supply such vacancy or vacancies.

Our learned and ingenious friend, Mr. Carpenter, brought your honors to this result from his discussion, that it was wholly immaterial to the practical result in this case whether you hold that the law was repealed or whether you hold that it was in force; he contending that, if it was repealed so as to carry down the canvassing section, and therefore make the canvass proper by this canvassing-board—I mean in respect to its authority—then section 8, being carried down, the power to fill vacancies did not exist, and two vacancies were therefore left in the college of electors, which, as he said, would be enough for his purpose, and which is true; two vacancies are enough, perhaps one. But we are under no such alternative as that. By the subsequent laws, the canvassing section was repealed, and by no subsequent laws was the rest of the electoral act affected. That is a proposition which at once liberates us and this Commission from any confusion or from any resort to either of the horns of the dilemma.

On what does our proposition rest?—for it needs but to be stated to be understood, and the laws need but to be pointed out to carry the evidence of what the existing state of law was in Louisiana in 1876. There came about in 1870 a revision of the statutes of the State of Louisiana, not a repeal, not a re-enactment, but a revision of the laws that were or were understood to be in force, in regard to which the *fiat* of the legislature was to be impressed upon them that they were the laws in force, a transaction entirely similar to that which took place in Congress in the production of the Revised Statutes of the United States, under which we now are. In this revision which I read from, a book published in 1876——

Mr. Commissioner BRADLEY. I have the original.

Mr. EVARTS. We shall be greatly obliged to you if we can get the pages from that. My friend who provided this book could not find the other in the Library; we were obliged to resort to this; but the sections, as I understand, are the same. I shall be very glad to refer to that volume instead of this for those two laws, and I will give the citations as they shall be determined; but for the purpose of my present argument, without giving pages, I can now say how the matter stood on these revised statutes. In the first place, there was a statute entitled "Elections," and it was, we will assume, the statute of 1868. So far as I know, there is nothing to be said on this subject.

Mr. Commissioner EDMUNDS. You mean by that, that there is a head in the revised statutes "Elections"?

Mr. EVARTS. A head in the revised statutes called "Elections." I will now give the page, to avoid confusion, that is found in this edition of the revised statutes of Louisiana printed in the year they were passed; in 1870. It is page 272, and it is headed in the margin by these figures, "1868, 218," which means this law that I have read.

Mr. Commissioner GARFIELD. The same reference that you made to the session acts of 1868.

Mr. EVARTS. The same reference. Then there comes, after exhausting, I believe, the general provisions about elections, grouped under this general title of "Elections," a statute concerning contested elections, which in the same manner is referred to as a statute of 1865, page 408.

Mr. Commissioner EDMUNDS. Is that in the same title?

Mr. EVARTS. The same title.

Mr. Commissioner BRADLEY. Under the same title, but at the end.

Mr. EVARTS. Exhausting the general election law, you then come into an independent subject, and that is "Contested Elections," and there is reprinted another law not material for us to consider, but it is reprinted and referred to as a law already in existence.

Mr. Commissioner THURMAN. Are you reading from the revised statutes of 1870?

Mr. EVARTS. I am; and the edition of 1870, which is the proper one to refer to.

Mr. Commissioner THURMAN. Was that passed as one act?

Mr. EVARTS. Passed as one act. Then we have another title in these revised statutes separated by one hundred pages, and indeed the arrangement is, I think, alphabetical, and the title of this section of the revised statutes is "Presidential Electors." That is at page 550. It begins by reciting the acts of Congress, and then it proceeds in ten sections, numbered from 2823 to 2832, which contain the election law, and the heading in the margin of this is "1868, 245." Nine of the sections, to 2831 inclusive, are embraced in that notation, and in fact in the act of 1868 section 2832 is noted as a section proceeding from the act of 1855, 481, and is simply, "when a new parish shall be established, it shall form a part of the district to which it belonged previous to its change of organization."

Those two laws being for our purposes as the two laws of 1868, were in force when these revised statutes came into operation, unless by actual repeal, or by the methods of legislation which operate repeal, before these revised statutes went into operation, a repeal of one or the other of them in some part had taken place. These were passed on the 14th day of March, 1870; and on the 16th day of March, 1870, a law was passed, which was printed and is to be found in the first edition of this compilation which is without a cover, and I will refer to the act of 1870 itself in pursuance of my previous intention.

Mr. Commissioner EDMUNDS. Is there any law or provision of the constitution in Louisiana which provides generally at what time acts passed at a session shall take effect?

Mr. EVARTS. I do not know whether there is or not.

Mr. Commissioner BRADLEY. These acts that we refer to, all declare the time when they shall take effect.

Mr. EVARTS. I do not understand that there is any general provision, and as a matter of fact the general declaration of the acts is that they shall take effect from and after their passage. There was passed in 1870, on the 16th day of March, an act which is found in the session laws of 1870, at page 145; it is numbered 100. I will read the title of this act:

To regulate the conduct and to maintain the freedom and purity of election; to prescribe the mode of making and designate the officers who shall make the returns thereof; to prevent fraud, violence, intimidation, &c.; limiting the powers and duties of sheriffs; and to enforce article 103 of the constitution.

The title of this act is the same as that of the election act of 1868 in its general purpose to regulate elections and enforce article 103 of the Constitution. This act provides, at section 54:

That the governor, the lieutenant-governor, the secretary of state, and John Lynch, and T. C. Anderson, or a majority of them, shall be the returning-officers for all elections in this State.

There is no other description and no limitation; they are "the returning-officers for all elections in this State;" and there is at section 85, the final section of the act, this repealing clause:

That all laws or parts of laws contrary to the provisions of this act, and all laws relating to the same subject-matter, are hereby repealed; and this act shall take effect from and after its passage.

What went down under that repeal? In the first place, upon general principles, all of the revised statutes that was on the title of "Elections" and enforcing this article of the constitution, No. 103, and all parts of other laws that were within the purview of the conduct of elections, any election held in that State, and no other parts of such laws, were repealed by that section. You have, then, in the general start of the first section of the act, a provision "that all elections for State, parish, and

judicial officers, members of the general assembly, and for members of
Congress, shall be held on the first Monday in November; and said
elections shall be styled the general elections. They shall be held in
the manner and form, and subject to the regulations hereinafter prescribed, and in no other."

Then the provisions go on. Section 35 of this act, which is the number which was in Mr. Justice Bradley's mind, is the equivalent of
section 32 in the general election act of 1868, and is identical with section 1 of the electoral act of 1868. It is reproduced here as section 35;
so that we have a provision that all general elections so called shall
take place on the first Monday of November; that an election for
electors shall take place on the first Tuesday after the first Monday in
November, according to the provision of the act of Congress, and then,
in a section coming after the description of general elections, and after
the section that has relation to presidential electors, you have the fifty-
fourth section, which provides that the canvassing-board there provided
"shall be the returning-officers," not for all general elections, but "for
all elections held in this State," covering by necessary statutory construction the elections that had been mentioned preceding, some of which
were called elections of State officers, members of Congress, &c., and
called general elections, and one which was called a presidential election.

The election of 1872 was held under that law. Did anybody in the
State of Louisiana conceive that the governor was to canvass? Some
question was raised about whether the act of 1872, which was passed on
the 20th of November, providing another returning-board, was in operation; but the courts of the State, in the authorities that have been proposed for your honors' consideration by my learned associates, disposed
of this question as to who were the returning-board and the canvassing-
board, being one and the same thing, on November, 1872, prior to the
20th of November of that year. Therefore the whole operation of this
act of 1870, in repeal of this or that portion of the independent acts—
the general-election act and the presidential-electors' act—was not an
act concerning their election, but concerning their discharge of their
duties; giving them nothing but the State apparatus, unvaried except
in a canvassing-board. Now what the canvassing-board of 1868 for
general elections was, I have not stopped to inquire; whether it was
the same governor or not, it is not material here. Now comes the act of
1872, which is reproduced.

Mr. Commissioner BRADLEY. Right here is a matter which I wish
to understand. The digest of the statutes, made immediately after the
revision and published in January, 1871, contains these two titles which
the revision does, the title "Elections" and the title "Presidential
Electors." The digest was made by John Ray, under the direction of
the committee of revision; and in that digest, under the head of "Elections," he inserts the act of 1870 instead of the act of 1868, and under
the head of "Presidential Electors" inserts the same title that the revision contained, with the exception that the section establishing the
returning-board replaces the original canvass. This seems to indicate
the opinion of the profession at that time as to the state of the law.
What effect it would have, I do not know.

Mr. EVARTS. In other words, what we now contend for, that the
section which gave a special canvassing-board for presidential electors
was repealed by the act of 1870, and the rest of the statute, and which
had nothing to do with their election but only with their conduct as
electors after they were elected, was left standing; and Mr. Justice
Bradley enables me to refer to a digest of the statutes of Louisiana.

In volume 2 of that digest, at page 356, is found the electoral law, and it is attributed under its various sections to the acts on which it is supposed to rest. The first section is attributed to the act of 1870, page 145. This is substantially the same section as is found in the act of 1868. Then the second section is attributed to the act of 1868, page 245; the third the same. The fourth, which is the provision of a returning-board, takes the section that makes the governor, the lieutenant-governor, the secretary of state, John Lynch, and T. C. Anderson, the returning-board, and attributes that to the act of 1870, page 145. And then it goes on, resuming at the fifth section its attribution to the act of 1868, page 245, and in the sixth section is reproduced the provision about electors filling their vacancies. This act is found on page 355 and page 358 of the second volume of this digest, published under the authority of the State in 1870.

Mr. Commissioner BAYARD. Does it contain no memorandum of the date when it was passed?

Mr. EVARTS. I have stated that these sections which are thus digested are each referred to their appropriate originating statute.

Mr. Commissioner BRADLEY. Here is the act under which the digest was made, Mr. Evarts, showing that it had a quasi authority.

Mr. EVARTS. It is very apparent that this is no new construction that we are putting upon the force of the repealing act. It is the published construction, in the authorized publication of the statutes in the form of 'a digest, followed by the courts, and accepted by the profession. The novelty is in the stress that now here for the first time seeks to produce a collapse of statutory law in order to destroy an election. Did any of those eminent lawyers that attended in New Orleans through the month of November suggest to Governor Kellogg to canvass these votes for presidential electors? And now the vice, the fault, the irremediable wound of this election is that Governor Kellogg did not canvass them!

The act of 1872 takes up this whole subject and substitutes itself for the act of 1870 and repeals all existing regulations that properly are in the very matter of conduct and regulation of elections in general, and all special provisions found in any other act that are at variance with the imposition of its form, its methods, and its agents on all elections held in the State. But the act of 1870 had already excluded the section of the electoral law that related to canvass, and excluded that alone, and left standing the clause that relates to the conduct of the electoral college, among other things, in filling vacancies.

Now, I have satisfied your honors that not only was it wholly immaterial which of Mr. Carpenter's views you adopted, but it was immaterial that you adopted them both, for the subsequent legislation had left the matter in this shape, that the canvassing-board for all elections had been applied to presidential elections, and the conduct of the electoral college, after it was elected, in its transaction under the laws of the State and of the United States, was left wholly untouched, as it well might be. What change could you have made, what change was needed? That is not the point; but the point is that the legislature had suppressed presidential elections by having no law under which they could be conducted. Well, if there is any State that in the election of 1872 or in anticipation of the election of 1876 has had the attention of all its citizens, all its lawyers, all its judges, all its politicians, all its honest men attracted to it, it is the State of Louisiana; and they all thought that they could elect presidential electors, and one political party was perfectly convinced that it had, and the other political party was perfectly convinced that it had, and the only question was which of the two sets produced by this birth was the genuine child.

Mr. Commissioner FRELINGHUYSEN. Mr. Evarts, did you refer to the act authorizing the revision?

Mr. EVARTS. I beg pardon. That is in the first volume of the digest. It is an act passed on the 16th of March, 1870, the very day this act was passed:

That John Ray be, and is hereby, appointed and authorized to compile a digest of the statutes of the State of general character from the acts passed at the present session of the general assembly, including the act of revision, and to superintend the printing, and that such digests and codes be stereotyped and printed as required, &c.

Mr. Commissioner MORTON. Was there a provision requiring that digest to be subsequently submitted to the legislature before it went into force?

Mr. EVARTS. I think not.

Mr. Commissioner BRADLEY. There was not.

Mr. EVARTS. I cannot say without looking at the act, because this is only one section of the act that answers the purpose of advertising the book.

Mr. Commissioner BRADLEY. It was submitted to the committee of revision. The act required that, and that was all.

Mr. EVARTS. It was to be submitted to the committee of revision, Mr. Justice Bradley suggests, of that session which conducted this whole matter. Here is a little act, which is at page 80 of the session laws of 1870, "An act giving precedence in authority to all the other acts and joint resolutions passed by the general assembly at this session over the acts known as 'the revision of the statutes, and of the civil code and code of practice,' when there exists any conflict in the provisions of said acts and revisions."

I think nothing could be made clearer than that. We have, then, the proposition that our act of 1870 was passed two days after the revision—enough of itself to amend it. They did not pass an unamendable revision. They passed a revision that when it came into force had all the dilapidation which has been accomplished in its frame by all the legislation of that session of 1870. Such provisions are necessary. Something similar to that was the arrangement in which your recent great work of revision was carried on.

This law, then, as to what its text is, is understood: Whatever there is in the election law of Louisiana that governs, gives authority in, prescribes methods of, the election of others in that State, applies to the presidential electors' elections, and nothing that reaches the conduct of the electors after their election is different from the act as it stood in 1868.

In the act of 1872, which governed, of course, the election of 1876, there are provisions, mainly of sections 3 and 26, which include the powers, and prescribe the methods of their execution, accorded to this returning-board; and those powers were exercisable according to the law of Louisiana and exercisable in reference to the election of electors just as well as in regard to any other officers of the State; and in regard to their exercise in respect to the election of presidential electors the Government of the United States had no more power and authority than it had in regard to any other election in that State. Why should it? It would have been very easy to have inserted in the Constitution of the United States a provision which, while it fixed in the frame of the government the power of election in the States, had made Congress the judges of the elections, of the returns, and of the certificates of electors. That might have been done; but if it had been done, all that had been done by the convention up to that time would have been annulled, for the independence of the State's transaction would have been subjected to the political authority of the United States, ungoverned by any paramount dominion over it; and our ancestors that would not let the little finger of Federal influence be inserted into the State election by having a Federal officer voted for by it, is now laying the thickness of a hand on the State election by judging of the election, the qualifications, and the returns.

I ask the eminent lawyers who are to stand by their proposition, if there is one particle of power possessed by the Houses of Congress, or that was ever exercised by them in the experience of this Government, in searching the elections, the returns, and the qualifications of members of Congress, that falls within the whole range of this proposition of proof? Is it not offered to you as the measure and the means and the resort of your inspection of the Louisiana election of electors? Could you do anything more? Where do you get the right to do what you do about members of Congress? You could not get it by mere parliamentary law; and the framers of the Constitution put it in that there might be no doubt about it; for the jurisdiction of Parliament to judge of the qualifications of its members is a resident and remaining part of its authority as the great court of the realm. For, according to the principles of the common law, the execution of a writ is to be determined by the court where it is returnable; and when the Crown issues its writ to the burgesses and shires it is returnable in Parliament, and Parliament judges of the return. But when you are making a complex frame of government and distributing authority between the States and the General Government, you must determine exactly how far the States are to have authority on the subject of this election of members of Congress and how much is to belong to the Federal Government. In other words, while the States are allowed to provide for the election of Congressmen and while the suffrage is measured out by the Constitution to be the same that they accord to the lower house of representatives in the States, yet there is secured to Congress the power of making and altering those regulations; and this final political power acts, irresponsible for the exercise of its will; will governed by duty, if you please, but will not controlled by any authority of law. And now it is gravely pretended here, not in terms—for the effrontery of the proposition would affright the lawyer that made it; but on the basis of that offer of proof they ask you to ascribe to the two Houses of Congress, when met to count the vote, with the President of the Senate in the chair, precisely the same power in extent, in measure, in uncontrolled execution, that is attributed to the election of members of Congress.

Why did not the wise framers of the Constitution say so if they meant that? And how could they anticipate that the whole spirit and purpose of excluding Federal authority in the choice and the election and the certification of the choice of electors should be perverted into the monstrous claim that an uncontrolled political authority rests in the two Houses of Congress to sift and sift, discard, discount, destroy the election, and make such men as it chooses, or annul the vote of a State when it will answer the purpose, as it will here upon this pretension of authority?

If any further elucidation of my general views is needed, I must respectfully ask attention to the reported arguments of Mr. Matthews and myself in the Florida case.

I now come to consider the very matter of the proof offered. How about these Federal disqualifications? We talked about that subject in the Florida case. It so happened that the proofs which were allowed provisionally did not raise the question there; but our propositions are unchanged. In the absence of congressional regulation furnishing the appropriate, adequate, seasonable means to purge the lists that the governor has certified, on the Federal disqualifications that should discard an electer, the two Houses, met in the presence of the President of the Senate, cannot execute the Constitution; and you can do no more. They are elected; they are acting; they are certifying, for there is nothing in that idea of the subject at all that a man made ineligible cannot be elected. You might as well say that the forbidden fruit could not be eaten because it was forbidden. I ask attention to an authority of great weight, the supreme court of Pennsylvania, where Gibson, justice, gives the opinion before he was chief-justice in 11 Sergeant & Rawle's Reports, page 411. I cannot detail the particular circumstances of the case; but these observations are in point in that case and are important here. It is the case of Baird vs. The Bank of Washington:

The bank was governed by thirteen directors, five of whom were competent to the business of ordinary discounts, but nothing less than a majority of the whole number constituted a quorum for transacting any other business. At the meeting of the 11th of August, just spoken of, only seven members, including George Baird, were present when the vote was taken; so that if he were not a director, either de facto or de jure, there was at that moment not a quorum present, and hence a question as to the validity of his appointment is thought to be material. As has been just said, to constitute a quorum competent to fill vacancies or transact any other business than that of ordinary discounts required a majority of the whole number of the directors; and this gentleman was elected at a meeting at which only five were present, so that originally his election was unquestionably invalid. And this brings us to the first question, whether he is to be considered as an officer de facto, or as an usurper. The judge who tried the cause was of opinion that his election was not merely irregular as to time, place, or notice of it, and therefore voidable, but that it was absolutely void; and that he was an unauthorized agent, who could do no act to bind the bank; in other words, that he was an usurper.

In analogy to the distinction between judicial proceedings that are absolutely void for want of jurisdiction and those that are only voidable for irregularity, there is something extremely plausible in this opinion. Still, however, it will be found that the question does not depend on whether the appointment is void or only voidable, or whether it emanated from an authority which had full power to make it; but whether the officer has come in under color of right or in open contempt of all right whatever. (The King vs. Leslie, Ans. Rep., 163; S. C., 2 Stra., 190.) This distinction runs through all the cases. Where an abbot or parson, inducted erroneously, and having made a grant or obligation, is afterward deprived of his benefice, this shall bind; but the deed of one who usurps before installation or induction, or who enters and occupies in the time of vacation without election or presentation, is void. So, if one occupies as abbot of his own head, without installation or induction, his deed shall not bind the house.

McEnery acted "of his own head;" doubtless a very good head, but "of his own head" and nothing else, and the electors named on the second certificate were hurried to execute on the 6th of December an office into which they had not been inducted, into which they had not been installed, did it "of their own head;" but they might have been prompted. You can put ideas into one's head; nevertheless it is his own head that he acts upon.

In the case at bar, the court put the matter on the ground that five directors did not constitute a board for any other business than that of ordinary discounts; and that, having no right to go into an election at all, their act could not give color of right. But in Harris vs. Jays, Cro. Eliz., 609, it was conceded that the Queen's auditor and surveyor had not the right to appoint the steward for the manor in question; yet it was resolved that a steward appointed by him was an officer de facto, and that his acts were good. This is exactly in point. The inquiry then is, was there the color of an election in Mr. Baird's case? He was elected by the very body in which the right to elect was vested, the only thing wanting to the perfect validity of the act being the presence of two or more electors. But the presence of these would not have changed the board to another and a distinct body; it would still have been the president and directors of the Bank of Washington. It is impossible, therefore, to say that Mr. Baird usurped the office without the semblance of right.

Now this clause in the judge's opinion I ask particular attention to:

This principle of colorable election holds not only in regard to the right of electing, but also of being elected. A person indisputably ineligible may be an officer *de facto* by color of election, (Knight *vs.* The Corporation of Wells, Lutw., 508.) So, even where the office was not vacant, but there was an existing officer *de jure* at the time.

Perhaps this is the only authority on this subject that I shall need to add to those that were adduced in the argument on the Florida case and that have been presented by my learned associate in this.

Now suppose that Levissee and Brewster were each of them ineligible. They are elected; they are inducted; they are in execution of the office, and the State is not to be stripped in an execution that is satisfactory to itself by extraneous evidence adduced at the moment of counting the votes, that a man was ineligible. Congress must give that consequence by some legislation and some mode of determination, or it cannot arise.

But here these men are in by the election to fill vacancies. Well, the Oregon brief, contrived not only a double but a treble debt to pay, comes up again to prove that when an ineligible person is elected there has been no election, and from that it is argued that when one out of eight fails to be elected, then there has failed to be an election within the sense that a legislature may fill the place; and then, to make all this applicable to the existing state of law in Louisiana, you are asked to believe, you are asked to hold, against all the authorities, that an elector ineligible is not elected, and that if he has not been elected there is not a vacancy in the college; when one State has said, "Our method of filling any vacancy that shall happen for any cause, any defect of full numbers that shall show itself at 4 o'clock for any reason, is that it shall be filled by the State of Louisiana in this way, that those who have been chosen and attend shall fill the place," this cannot avail. What more do we need to say? We arrive at the same result. Our learned friends, so precise in language, hold that there not being a vacancy, that an office not being vacant, that there being no vacancy in an office, is equivalent to the office not having been filled; that if it has not been filled it is not vacant. That is the proposition: if it has not been filled, it is not vacant.

Now, an office is either vacant or full. There are no terms in law between those two qualifications of being vacant or full. It is not half full; it is not full with an embryo that may grow; it is full or it is vacant. The Constitution of the United States provides that in the case of a vacancy in the representative force of a State in Congress the governor shall issue writs to fill the vacancy. That phrase is used. In 1837, at a special session called of Congress, commencing I think in September, some States had no Representatives elected for that Congress. Congress began usually in December. There was time enough to elect them to send them in season, and have the freshest choice of the people. The governor of Mississippi, not desiring that State to be unrepresented in that important special session, issued his writs for a special election to fill the vacancy. Was there a vacancy or not? Certainly our learned friends would have found out a void vacancy in that case. Nobody had perceived it. Messrs. Gholson and Claiborne were returned, and the question came up on their qualifications, on the validity of the election, within the power doubtless of Congress; and the House held that they were duly elected, and gave them seats for the full term.

They concluded in Mississippi that they would have another election for
the rest of the term, and they sent up other persons chosen in November
at the regular election. So in December we had a new choice of Congressmen, and it was concluded I think then that the admission of
them for the whole Congress was erroneous.

Mr. MATTHEWS. The House rescinded the former resolution, and
refused to allow the newly-elected members to come in, on the ground
that the people had been misled as to the time of the election.

Mr. EVARTS. They held them only to be entitled to fill the vacancy,
and they did not admit the new people, because they were judges of the
whole matter, and concluded that it was better to have another election.
What happened then is unimportant; but you can have no better case
than that. This is to be found, I think, in the volume of Contested
Elections of 1834 to 1865, page 9, and in the fifth volume of the Congressional Globe, pages 80 to 96, and Appendix, page 85.

Now, then, we say in regard to the Federal disqualification, no proof
can reach the point, none is offered that touches the point, none would
be admissible if it did touch the point, because of the want of legislation
or of means of ascertaining it.

I now come to the question of State disqualification. The constitution
of this State of Louisiana has a provision:

No person shall hold or exercise at the same time more than one office of trust or
profit except that of justice of the peace or notary public.

Governor Kellogg was governor; Governor Kellogg was elector.
Some of these other electors held minor offices, it is said. Proof of
this fact is offered in regard to the others in order that State disqualification may now be inquired into and verified in the counting of the
vote here. There are sufficient answers to this. Let us look at another
clause of this constitution which provides some other disqualifications:

ART. 99. The following persons shall be prohibited from voting and holding any
office: All persons who shall have been convicted of treason, perjury, forgery, bribery,
or other crime punishable in the penitentiary, and persons under interdiction; all
persons who are estopped from claiming the right of suffrage by abjuring their allegiance to the United States Government, or by notoriously levying war against it, or
adhering to its enemies, giving them aid or comfort, but who have not expatriated
themselves nor have been convicted.

So on with a numerous list of disqualifications for holding any office
in the State. Suppose an imputation were made against an elector,
in the certified forwarded lists by the electoral college and authenticated
by the governor, of any of these disqualifications, could you try it? Certainly not. It is a judicial inquiry.

But this office of elector, say Mr. Trumbull and Mr. Carpenter, is not
a State office. It is not a State office; he is an elector, a representative
elector. When he comes into office he holds the office under the Constitution of the United States, and he acquires the office by the action
of the State, the function, the right to vote. He is a representative
elector. This clause of the Constitution does not say that no officer
under that State shall hold a Federal office. The courts of that State
have settled the question that it not only means State officers, but it
means constitutional officers. They have not hampered all future legislation of that State with the inconvenience of never having a man a
member of two charitable boards, as one of these electors is charged to
have been. They have not hampered the future legislation of that
State in the trammels of providing that a citizen shall be made useful
in no two occupations, employments, or commissions; but it is constitutional officers that it applies to; and I ask attention to the cases in 5

Louisiana Annual Reports, 155; 6 Louisiana Annual Reports, 175. The case in 25 Louisiana Annual Reports, 138, I think was referred to by Mr. Shellabarger.

Mr. Commissioner THURMAN. Do you mean to be understood as admitting that an elector is an officer at all, either Federal or State?

Mr. EVARTS. I do not think he is. Certainly he is not a State officer. I do not think he is an officer. I think he is a voter, having qualifications, and his office is of the same kind with the office of a citizen who is an elector, so called in the constitutions of most of the States, but whose qualifications are primary. This is a representative elector, and the moment the representative credentials are closed and accorded to him, he is then an elector. In other words, he is not a State officer.

Therefore there seems to be nothing in that proposition which should produce proof, because proof would be entirely ineffectual, first, for the reason that the inhibition does not prevail; secondly, for the reason, which would apply to the supervisor as well, that there is no provision by any legislation of Congress that can give this action of the two Houses, either in their joint assembly or in this Commission with the rights accorded to it, jurisdiction over the question of fact involved in abuses or violations of the State constitution; and, further, for the reason, insisted on already, that these provisions of the State constitution do not touch the Constitution of the United States, which, while it was careful to exclude Federal intervention of office-holders, was not guilty of the folly of saying that no State should accredit as its elector an honored citizen who filled in the affections of the people and the authority of the State a place of trust. If anything, it was desired that these electors should be State notables, men who had the adhesion of their fellow-citizens; and to say that we must take the residuum of public character and of public interest and of public repute after all the State's offices are filled, from constable to governor, from whence we cannot have an elector, is imputing a folly to the framers of our Constitution that they are not open to and which cannot be forced upon them by State legislation.

Governor Ingersoll, of Connecticut, heads the electoral choice of that State. Every man honors him as a representative of his State. He is governor. He certifies to himself. He discharges a governor's duty to certify to whomsoever the people choose. He does not make himself an elector. He certifies upon the recorded evidence, as John Adams declared that he was President of the United States by the count of the votes.

This being so, we come to the primary question of interest to the public, of interest to all citizens, of interest to every man who loves his country, every man who loves its Constitution in its spirit of being popular government, obedient to law; and I am at a loss to see that anything that I have to say on this subject should approve itself to one portion of this Commission and be unpalatable to another by reason of any political adhesions of one side or the other. I shall say nothing that I would not say as a citizen holding the common ground with all of you who are citizens first and partisans afterward.

When I talk of the mischiefs in the State of Louisiana which are attempted to be curbed and robbed of their rapine by the energetic laws of that State, I do not understand that to any man, because his inclinations or his convictions incline him in favor of the elevation of Governor Tilden, I am to impute that he looks with less horror upon that subjugation of the suffrage, that degradation of citizenship, that confusion of society, that subversion of the Constitution than I do. He only wishes that it should be curbed and redressed by law. And when I speak of the frauds as charged—for I must speak of them as charged at this stage of the business, for they have not been proved at all—when I speak of them as charged, involving falsification, oppression, false counting, forgery, conspiracy, every shade of the *crimen falsi*, am I to be charged in this presence or any other with having less complacency even in the lowest grade of this vice than those who uphold their correction and desire that they shall be frustrated, when I demand that it shall be done by law ?

That is my demand. Is it a partisan demand? It is the same demand that is made in respect to the gross afflictions which every citizen feels as beaten by the same stripes that were inflicted on the backs of those poor, unbefriended negroes. That is citizenship; it is not partisanship. And when this other vice is added to violence, together ruling the evil in the world—violence and fraud—when that other form is corrupting and afflicting our citizenship, I feel it as bearing a full share of the common shame, whether it be inflicted by the relentless and shameless tyranny of the New York dynasty or by the alleged frauds of the Louisiana dynasty. But why is it that fraud is so detestable? Why is it that the law searches for it as with candles and condemns it when it is brought into judgment ? Because it is but another form of violence— *Fraus æquiparatur vi.* That is the reason why the violence that ravishes is more heinous than the fraud that secretly purloins the virtue and the fame of American citizenship.

We do not wish to be told that fraud is *worse* than violence. Its vice is that it robs the act of that *consent* on which its freedom depends, to the same effect as violence does. Fraud is compared, as in a simile, to the principal evil, itself described as *violence.* Here all agree that under the great national transactions that closed the war and under the experience of the condition of society in Louisiana thereafter there was exhibited, not indeed a continuation of armed revolt against the Government, but far from the repose that belongs to peace. There were these outbreaks of a bastard and seditious soldiery, the authors of which, by the laws of war, while flagrant, would all be hanged in either camp. What was the scene ? Was it revolt? Was it peace? It was that more dangerous condition of the body-politic which, unprobed and uncured, must breed a conflagration both of civil and domestic war. " *Nec tumultus nec quies; quale magni metus et magnæ iræ silentium est.*"

It is that brooding silence of preparation which is to determine whether outbreak shall assert, or whether fear reduced to despair shall surrender, liberty; and to that state of things the independent action of the State of Louisiana was directed. It was to them a real state of things. It was not a state of things to be smiled at at a distance, whichever side the smile came from. It was the brooding of great fear and great wrong over a whole population, and they undertook to put it into the frame-work of their constitution that—

The privilege of free suffrage shall be supported by laws regulating elections and prohibiting under adequate penalties all undue influence thereon from power, bribery, tumult, or other improper practice.

In pursuance of that duty, imposed upon the legislature by the same independent right, dealing with an actual situation, the legislature undertook to support the free suffrage, and in their judgment, in the choice they made, who can control them ? Shall the proud purity of New York City judge of the means to be used in Louisiana ? Shall the saint-protected postures of Senators and Representatives and judges and advocates judge in the silence of this court-room of the means? No. There is but one limit to the means; I mean one limit to be imposed outside that State; under that clause of the Constitution, none in the State, except that these means should be adequate, appropriate, and seasonable, and they might be used.

Now, eminent statesmen and lawyers say that, when these methods in this law prescribed are resorted to by a State to save itself from the ruin of civil and domestic war, it prevents the State from being considered republican; and the demonstration and the proof of what was republican government advanced by the learned counsel, Judge Trumbull, was that if a government needed to be supported by arms, it was not republican. Well, was our Government a monarchy because we had to support it by arms through four years of civil war? What else did support it? What else prevented the pillars of this court-room crushing the judges in their office? What but armed men, servants of the civil power, citizens in arms supporting their Government because they loved it; and they loved it because it was republican. I think that the *quod erat demonstrandum* does not come by that process.

What is the proof offered; what in principle, what in nature? How far is it within the disposition of the offers made in the Florida case? The offer there was to show that, though the governor's certificate was conformed to the recorded canvass of the final State authority, and there was no room for intervening proof between them, yet behind the canvass a resort to simple and record facts would show that the returning-officers acted without jurisdiction. That was the principle of the offer. Will any one say that the act of officers without jurisdiction is a mild and moderate form of defective authority, compared with which fraud was a more evident and a more palpable defeat of such action? By no means. When, therefore, you had an offer to produce by proof the county returns in Florida, in order to base on that fact an argument that the action of the canvassing-board on those returns, wherein it assumed to redress or re-arrange them, was without jurisdiction, it carried every possible legal and constitutional ground of proof that can be conceived. Let me show that I speak by the card, when I refer to the very accurate statement of his proposed proof by Mr. O'Conor, found on page 44 of the Congressional Record of February 4:

In so doing—

That is, stating what they did in respect to the manipulations of the county returns—

In so doing the said State board acted without jurisdiction, as the circuit and supreme courts of Florida decided. It was by overruling and setting aside as not warranted by law these rejections that the courts of Florida reached their respective conclusions that Mr. Drew was elected governor, that the Hayes electors were usurpers, and that the Tilden electors were duly chosen. No evidence that in any view could be called extrinsic is believed to be needful in order to establish the conclusions relied upon by the Tilden electors, except duly authenticated copies of the State canvass—

That is, "the erroneous canvass," as Mr. O'Conor considered it—

and of the returns from the above-named four counties, one wholly and others in part rejected by said State canvassers.

In order to show that their return rested on action behind it that was without jurisdiction. Well, one ground covers all. *Extra vires*, without law, without authority, is as much a condemnation, if the proof will sustain it, as it is possible to suggest.

Mr. Commissioner THURMAN. Mr. Evarts, allow me to suggest to you that, if a majority of the Commission thought the Florida statute

authorized what was done, then the introduction of proof would have
been improper; and therefore it does not follow, because an argument
was made that the board exceeded its jurisdiction in throwing out votes,
that this Commission so held, for a decision that the true interpretation
of the statute would justify what they did made it immaterial to inquire what the motive was.

Mr. EVARTS. I can only say that the offer of proof was offered only
on that ground, only on the single ground, and the grounds here are of
that nature and of the nature of fraud or *mala fides* in the transaction
itself, which last I shall consider.

Mr. O'Conor, as was to be expected from his clear relish of legal propositions, understood that that involved in principle going behind the returns at the polls, and he argued that our objections to that were of that
somewhat disfavored complexion of its being inconvenient to go into
those proofs. He did not, as I think, correctly appreciate our position;
but he did not deny that if he were allowed to adduce that proof, we
had a right, on the principles on which he was allowed to introduce it,
to go to the bottom of every precinct poll, and he met the difficulty of
time and resources for it by saying that the Commission here might temper that jurisdiction by going as far as they found it convenient, and
then stopping; that, I suppose, if they found themselves getting beyond their depth they might swim ashore, and leave to drown the candidate that at that stage of the water found it over his head. But here
our friend, Mr. Carpenter, proposes another solution, that the fact
that they have not time to do the thing is not a reason for concluding
that perhaps it is not one of the duties assigned to you, but simply affords a reason for peremptory adjournment; that the thing had better
be undone than done; and there is no choice but one way or the other;
for, if anything, these proffers go into the whole untraversed sea of
action, jurisdiction based on the action of subordinate officers in the conduct of the election on days, on forms, on the facts that must appear,
and the proofs that must show the facts to give jurisdiction, and you are
turned into a supervising court that takes up the transactions of a
special jurisdiction by *certiorari* to search it, and see whether the jurisdictional facts existed; whether they existed in throwing out this poll, that
poll, the other poll; and whether, when it is rectified, the object being
to produce only then a *prima facie* officer, you have been discharging
the duty that the Constitution imposed upon you, or whether it rested
on the governor and the canvassing-board to determine.

Well, now, the fraud, in the sense of *mala fides*, of returning-officers
or canvassing-boards is extraneous fact, is fact that does not vitiate as
much as being *ultra vires* does or can. It is more opprobrious in epi-
thet; it is more damnable in its morality; but in its legality it is a step
lower than *ultra vires*.

Now let us look at once and briefly at the very proposition as to the
right to trouble the State's elections, whether they have been honest,
whether they have been wise, whether they have been careful, whether
they have been prosperous. Supposing that the Constitution had given
the casting of the electoral votes of a State to the governor of that
State; he should be the representative elector; he should throw the
votes that were distributed to the population of that State; what right
would you have had to inquire beyond the single point who is governor,
who is governor *de facto*, who is the governor governing the State at
the time that he enters upon that transaction? Could you inquire
whether he had been fraudulently elected, whether in his election the
liberties of the people had been suppressed, whether he was in by a

fraudulent conspiracy by which he bought his office, whether he had taken part in the plots that had subverted the suffrage and falsified the action of the people? You could not. It is enough for you that the governor who governs is the man who is to represent the electoral votes of that State. What other right have you in regard to *electors* in inquiring into the facts by which the State has transacted the business of bringing into existence electors *de facto?* I submit, on principle none whatever. And on this question of fraud or *mala fides* or oppression, upon what possible principle can you enter into that inquiry? Who does not see that if you give the great power of the Federal Union a judgment in the matter of how the State has performed its duty you give the judgment that the wolf had over the conduct of the lamb, and can trace the vice in that conduct to any remoteness of relation that you choose?

I apprehend that nothing is sounder and safer than this, that we are to redress these mischiefs by law and the Constitution, although fraud may make us recoil from its touch, and although violence may make us shudder at its degradation of the American name. I have heard that fraud vitiates everything, and it is spoken of here as if it did it of its own force; that every *factum* in which an ingredient of fraud entered thereby became *infectum*, and so the bane always bred its antidote. Fraud would not be so dangerous an element if that were so. I have heard that the liberties of the people are to be paramount in every particular juncture, and that laws, and constitutions, and courts, and the permanence of the system of justice, and the truth that will endure, are all to be thrown aside upon the mere intrusion of this afflictive element of fraud, and that this course alone will secure their liberties to the United States and their people. We have a maxim of the law, and of social ethics and philosophy, that goes behind all this: *Misera est servitus, ubi jus vagum aut incertum.* There is no condition of a people so abject as where the law does not rest upon firm foundation, and its lines are not certainly drawn.

In the pressure of particular considerations that affect the sympathies and the conscience, this is always the appeal. What, it is said, is a constitution compared with human interests and human liberty? Nothing, to be sure, except that *all* our social interests and *all* our liberties rest on law and the Constitution. These are not the deity, but they are the shrine, without whose shelter no human worshiper can detain the goddess from the skies.

Now, for these poor people of Louisiana, if the Federal power now undertakes to thwart, to uproot this scheme of energetic law to preserve society there from destruction, and leaves these unbefriended, uneducated, simple black people to the fate from which the State strove hard to save them—I say that you will have made them, by that action, the *victims* of your Constitution, for your Constitution gave them the suffrage, and they are to be slaughtered for having the gift found in their hands. I say that you make them the sacrifices to the triumph of the Government over the rebellion. I say that such self-abasement of the powers of this Government is beyond all cure. It teaches the sad lesson that the American people, in the attempt to make good the largeness of its promise and to work out the glory of its proud manifesto of freedom and equality before the law, finds itself thwarted by the exhibition of violence in this turbulent population, and forced, with its own hand, to crush the methods of law by which the State has sought, alas! how vainly, to curb and redress this menace and this mischief to its honor and its peace.

Mr. Commissioner THURMAN. I move that the Commission take a recess until a quarter to two o'clock.

The PRESIDENT. A recess for half an hour?

Mr. Commissioner THURMAN. Thirty-two minutes.

The PRESIDENT. Mr. Commissioner Thurman moves that the Commission take a recess until a quarter before two o'clock.

The motion was agreed to.

The Commission re-assembled at one o'clock and forty-five minutes p. m.

The PRESIDENT. Before proceeding to business I will read a copy of a resolve sent to me by the Secretary of the Senate.

IN THE SENATE OF THE UNITED STATES,
February 15, 1877.

Resolved, That the Electoral Commission have leave to occupy the Senate chamber for its sittings in the evening after the Senate shall have taken a recess for the day.

Attest:

GEORGE C. GORHAM,
Secretary.

I suppose this will lie on the table for the present. That course will be pursued if there be no objection.

Mr. CAMPBELL. What is the length of time that will be allowed to me?

The PRESIDENT. The time on your side, under the order passed on motion of Justice Strong, has expired. You have, however, two hours and thirty minutes of the other time left.

Mr. CAMPBELL. Mr. President and gentlemen of the Commission, I differ so fundamentally with the learned counsel who preceded me upon the principle of the generative process by which the electors of President and Vice-President came into the Constitution that I shall alter the arrangement of my argument as I had prepared it and follow the arrangement pursued by the learned counsel who last addressed the court. I do not understand that the election of President had its origin in any State constitution or that it derived its existence from any reserved fund of power belonging to the States. My impression of that office, my impression of the means by which that office is to be filled, is that it is from the first to the last a power derived from the people of the United States, the people of the States united; that it owes its birth to no State constitution; it derives the power from no State law or State will. I do not assert that the Government of the United States came into being only with this Constitution, or that the United States themselves came into being by the ratification of this Constitution. The Constitution came into being by the ratification and acceptance of the States; but if the States had rejected this Constitution there would have been still a United States. The United States came into existence with the Declaration of Independence.

We are told by Mr. Justice Chase, in one of the most interesting opinions that ever came from the Supreme Court, in the case of Ware *vs.* Hilton, that during the war of the Revolution the United States exercised all the powers of a sovereign government without much inquiry as to where the source of their authority came from. During the period of the Confederation they were still the United States under confederate articles; but the people of the United States constituted some sort of a Union, a historical Union, stronger than the Union formed by the confederate compact; and so, when they sent delegates to Philadelphia who formed and organized the articles which compose the Federal Constitution, it was a proposition to the States to accept those articles and to form a Union, not for the first time, but, as declared in the very face of the Constitution itself, "a more perfect Union." When they spoke again in the language of this Constitution, and which language became "the supreme law of the land" on the adoption of this Constitution, it was no language that they spoke to the States on this subject such as has been represented to the Commission. The people of the United States on the face of this Constitution speak with power, with sovereign power: "We, the people of the United States, do ordain and establish this Constitution." When they came to the subject of the Presidency they said, "The executive power shall be vested in a President of the United States of America;" and when those words were accepted as law, he was the President of the United States of America; and when they came to speak of the manner of his appointment, it is said "each State shall appoint electors." Each State is permitted to appoint, each State is charged to appoint, each State is required to appoint, each State is commanded to appoint "in such manner as the legislature thereof may direct." It is not the State saying "We allow you to make a President of the United States, provided you will allow us and our legislature to show the manner and means by which that election shall be made." The language of the Constitution is imperative; it is the absolute "shall appoint."

Coming now to the conclusion of it, what are the powers that the two Houses of Congress have exercised in relation to the exercise of this power? Do the States come before you in the shape of sovereigns, claiming of you by any title superior to that of the Constitution that their votes shall be counted? Do they come here and tell your President of the Senate, "Lay these votes before these Houses and tell that Senate and tell that House of Representatives to count them at the peril of our displeasure"? Has that been the soul and the temper with which the States have come to the two Houses of Congress; and has their reception been with any submissive tone and temper on the part of the two Houses in joint convention? Why, sir, there is one instance, the like of which I trust will never appear again, when these two Houses of Congress said to four of the original States, to that one of the original States to which more than any other may be ascribed the production of this Constitution, and said to six others in company with the four original members, "We will not count any votes that may come from those States;" said it in advance of the reception of any votes, without the expectation of receiving any votes, but in the vindication of their own authority, expressing the will of a proud and powerful people carrying on hostilities with those States. Seeing here an apparent title on this Constitution which might allow them to present the votes of electors for President and Vice-President, in advance of any presentation of votes Congress passed a resolution that such votes should not be received.

There were some chimerical governments, so called, existing in those States that did pretend to send electoral lists to the two Houses; but they were regarded as being unworthy of any consideration. The two Houses knew perfectly well that the ten States they excluded were not in any manner represented by those caricatures of governments; and dealing with the principals, dealing with the States themselves, they declared to them that they could not employ the power granted in this Constitution. Now, I can suppose a case. Suppose that the legislature of Virginia had sent here electoral lists in 1865 to vote for the incumbent of the office at that time; suppose that she had demanded her right under this Constitution; suppose she had told you, "It was our

Washington who signed that document; it was our Madison who furnished the eloquence that enabled it to succeed; it was the profound wisdom of George Mason that appears in the lines of it; we come here by that title; here are the votes of our electors, appointed by our legislature; count them;" what would have been the answer? It would have been as haughty and as proud as the demand: "You are no longer entitled to the benefits of this Constitution, because you have attempted to abrogate it; and we will not count your votes or allow you even to come so far as our Houses to present them;" and this Government, these two Houses speaking in that voice of authority for the whole people of the United States, which was vested in them for that purpose, is now the poor, feeble, paltry imbecile thing that cannot deal with a certificate of a fraudulent returning-board!

But I am told that the action of the legislature of the State is conclusive; no examination can be made into their authority, no inquiry into the force of their acts; they have the supreme authority to direct on this subject; it is their reserved right; you cannot touch it; you cannot impair it; it belonged to them before you existed; while those States were living you were unborn, and all that you have has been given from them to you; this they never gave, and here is a gross usurpation if you venture to inquire into the act of that legislature. Is that true? The State has the power to appoint; the legislature the manner and means of that appointment. But is it not a trust power? Is that power given to it for the benefit of the State or any gratification of the State, or as a bauble for the State to play with? This joint convention has the power to look into every act of that legislature; and if that legislature offends the spirit of the Union, if it contravenes the fundamental principles that lie at the foundation of American liberty, it can reject the votes. While the learned gentleman was speaking I drew up the form of an act of the legislature of Louisiana to enable me to put the case fairly before you:

Be it enacted, &c., That William Pitt Kellogg and J. Madison Wells, and their associates, are made a body corporate, and with all the powers of a corporation under the civil code of Louisiana; and that there is granted to them the sole and exclusive power and privilege to nominate and appoint, in all the forms and at the times that may be designated in the acts and statutes of the United States, electors for President and Vice-President of the United States, at each presidential election under the Constitution of the United States, which may be apportioned and allotted to the State of Louisiana, or which the State of Louisiana may be entitled to appoint; and from time to time the legislature contracts to make such directions as may be necessary to make this grant effective; and the governor shall grant all such certificates and commissions, and do all other acts in furtherance thereto.

It is not very far from the case before the court. But if electoral votes were presented by that corporation with the seals and the signatures that the laws of United States have provided, is there a member, either of the House of Representatives or of the Senate, not being a stockholder in that corporation, who would hesitate for a moment to reject it with contumelious scorn? The answer would be clear; it would be unequivocal, and the judgment would be a just judgment.

It is the United States, now thirty-eight in number, who are interested in the exercise of this power. The subject of the exercise is the appointment of the Executive Chief Magistrate of this Union. He commands our armies; he commands our navies. The might of the nation is under his command. He represents us, through embassadors commissioned by him, in all foreign nations, and he receives embassadors and ministers from foreign nations; he conducts intercourse with them, negotiates treaties. He comes down with a veto upon the acts of our Congress, the legislative department of the Government, and an enlarged majority must be given to overcome that veto. The judges of the Supreme Court and other courts are nominated and commissioned by him. He is the head, the most distinct representative of the nation abroad and of the nation at home; and we cannot consent to receive appointments of electors who elect him, from William Pitt Kellogg and James Madison Wells, although sanctioned by legislative enactment. You may treat it with sorrow and you may treat it with rebuke, but you will be obliged, by your oath to support the Constitution, not to permit it to interfere in the election of that officer.

The State must appoint, that corporate being composed of persons; and if it had not a person on it, still having rights under the Constitution as a territorial corporate being; and unless the voice that comes to the two Houses be the voice of that State, whether expressed by its legislature or expressed by its people, that voice must come before the electoral lists can be received. You must have assurance that it is the State, the member of the Union, the equal of all the other States of the Union. Its voice must be heard in that vote; no voice other will be accepted.

Such being the fact, let us go one step further. The legislature may direct the manner. I have put a case in which I have not a question every member of this Commission would concur with me that that voice could not be given by a corporation. If this presidential appointment cannot go into the market as stock to be bought and sold, although there may be "millions in" a presidential election, it must speak the present voice of the State; it ought, if it is to represent its best feelings, its best intelligence, its highest honor; and if you see certainly that none of these can possibly be represented in the directions of the legislature, you will discard the directions.

Having shown, I think, that the legislative directions must be conformable to the spirit of the Constitution and in harmony with the general purpose to be accomplished, it follows inevitably that these two Houses of Congress must look into the nature and character of those directions. I do not claim for these two Houses any nice critical or captious spirit; but a broad and generous interpretation is to be given to the action of the legislature. It is not an absolute or an arbitrary power that is conferred upon the legislature. They do not possess it in full sovereignty, as the argument would seem to imply. They are responsible, and responsible to the people of the United States, quite as much as the legislature is responsible to the people of its own State. Then, looking at those directions and finding those directions to comport with the terms and spirit of the Constitution, what next is it that these Houses can do?

The next thing for them to see is that those directions have been conformed to; and precisely here another exercise of power by the two Houses of Congress, in my judgment a perfectly justifiable and proper exercise of power, was made in the case of Louisiana in 1873, as her vote was rejected in 1865 by the two Houses. The case there was a quarrel in Louisiana between two returning-boards. The one returning-board under which the election was made, some ten days after the election was made, was annulled by the act of the governor of the State. Your honors ought to know that a most pernicious practice or privilege allowed to a governor, who receives a bill within five days of the adjournment of the legislature, is to hold it until the next legislature. You will notice to nearly all these laws the signature and approval of the governor were given in what may be termed ordinarily the vacation, in the time between one legislature and another. The governor of that

State at that time had procured, a year or two before, the act of 1870; and possibly—for there is no other material difference between the laws—possibly doubting his returning-board under that act, which consisted of the governor, lieutenant-governor, and two other persons, another act was passed appointing another returning-board, constituted differently and selected differently.   He held up that act until a bill was filed for the purpose of causing the returns that were in his hands as the president of the first board to be produced.   Proceedings were begun to cause him to recognize that board and to put these returns in their hands.   There had been two boards constituted.   In order to put an end to all discussion on that subject, within a few days—four or five days—after the service of the bill, he signed and promulgated that act of 1872 which repealed all acts and parts of acts in conflict with or relating in any manner to it.

He had not, in my judgment, the slightest title to appoint the second board, because that board was to be appointed by the State senate; but the other board was certainly extinguished, because that act repealed the act in which it had its existence and which gave it any power.   The committee of the Senate of the United States which investigated the subject, apparently recognized his power to fill the board under the second act.   The first board was certainly annihilated; and it was held that he might fill the vacancy, as it was called, that the act had appointed the senate to fill.   They examined it.   Regular certificates and regular votes were sent to the Senate; but it appeared in proof that Warmoth's clerks had done all the canvassing that was done and furnished all the estimates that were made; that the returning-board then, if it were a good returning-board, had nothing to do with the canvassing and compilation of votes according to the statute.   Thereupon the Senate, in a very clear opinion, and with perfect logic in its conclusions, said that it would not receive a return computed and collected in that manner, even though the office had been accepted by the electors claiming to have been chosen and their votes had been regularly returned.

That case is parallel with the case we make before the Commission. The case we make before you is that the returning-board appointed by that act, and required by their oath of office, which defined their powers with perfect precision, to canvass and compile the original returns, never made such a canvass; we say that that compilation never took place; that those original returns were thrown aside and another paper, called by some of the witnesses a "contabulated statement," substituted.   It was so called by a member of that board before a committee of Congress.   He said they never examined any paper but the "contabulated statement" of the supervisors; and all of them concur in the fact that a compilation and canvass of the commissioners' returns was never made.   If the opinions contained in the report to which I have alluded, clearly and distinctly expressed and adopted by a very large majority of the Senate, have any weight as authority, the whole weight of that authority is in favor of the proposition I maintain.

Proceeding with the constitutional clause, the State appoints electors in such manner as the legislature may direct.   Of course that comprehends all the directions of the legislature.   "The manner" of an election includes all the regulations leading to and proceeding to carry out an election; and those, I say, are all examinable here.   Then the twelfth amendment becomes a part of it.

The learned counsel who argued last is unable to tell what sort of a creature an elector is.   I am not sure that in his conception he is a human being.   He need not be a citizen of the United States or of the

State; he is not an officer of the United States; he is not an officer of the State; but whatever he be, the Constitution of the United States, having obtained his appointment, not according to any State power, not according to any State direction, the State getting the power to appoint from the Constitution, the legislature getting the power to direct from the Constitution, those directions become a part of this Constitution; and the power to direct being so derived is examinable by the superior authority, and if conformable to the Constitution the directions are as if they had been written in the Constitution.

He then becomes an elector in the manner and by the process directed by the Constitution of the United States, and he comes to perform his duty, and he is to perform his duty by giving votes and sending lists to this body, and at a certain day this body meets, opens the votes, and is to count the voices. If those voices have any uncertain sound; if they are not the clear, full, sonorous voice of a State coming to the assembly of the States on the one hand and the assembly of the people on the other, they will not hearken, they will not accept the treble voice of Jacob if it comes in subtle guise clothed in a garment not suitable. It must be a lawful, legitimate voice before they will give any hearkening to it. This being so, if it be doubtful, if it be uncertain, then the power and the duty and the obligation rest upon them to do it, for how else can it be done? Would the people of the United States agree that the capacity of the persons chosen for electors should be determined by thirty-eight different supreme courts or the circuit courts that exist through thirty-eight States? Would the judgment of any State court be accepted as such a judgment ought to be accepted; that is, in the fullness of its cordial reception—would it be accepted as irrefutable proof by the people of the United States? Would they consent that the gentlemen of this Commission or the two Houses should look to the transcript of a record certified from a circuit court in Florida or Colorado as determining the result of an election and according to the result of their election receive the votes of such parties? It is perfectly evident that no such acceptance could possibly be given.

Seventy-five or eighty years ago, in the infancy of the Republic, when the history of every State and the name of every prominent man was known to the whole country, the character of its tribunals was ascertained, and there was entire confidence among the bar; then, possibly, a State tribunal might have commanded some degree of respect for its decision. But now when the breadth of a continent separates one State from another; when it is very hard to carry in your minds the names of the States, and very few of us can state exactly where they are; under such circumstances it is impossible for the States to exercise such a power. Where, then, is it proper that such a power should be placed? I know the enormous difficulty that arises out of its deposit here, because of the force of partisanship, the diversity of interest, the jealousy of the various parts of the country, and various other considerations. There are objections to it; but where else can you place it? If the assemblies of the States and the representatives of the people be entirely unfit and incapable, where else are you to look for fitness and capacity, coupled also with power? Where else will every man in the United States be represented in the final decision? In the two Houses every man in the United States has some measure of representation; in the Senate every State stands on an equality; and if bodies thus composed be unfit and incapable, where else can you find a body to make the depository of this vast power?

We learn a great deal, Mr. President and gentlemen, from the experience of our mother-country. Her institutions have been growing up for hundreds of years, and the vicissitudes and changes in them have been the result of the vicissitudes and changes in the condition of the people. The learned counsel in speaking of a member of Parliament said the returns were made into Parliament; that the writs came there; that had they been made elsewhere the returns would have been examinable where the writ was returned. That was precisely what James I said in a famous incident in history, reported in 2 State Trials. James I in his proclamation for the convention of his first Parliament lectured the people as to what sort of Parliament he wanted. He did not want any outlaws or bankrupts, among other proscribed classes. In a sharply contested election Sir Francis Goodwin was elected, and he was under a civil sentence of outlawry. The king took that to be a base affront on his proclamation. The Lords sent down to the Commons a message that they desired to have a conference on the subject; and in the committee of the Lords were nine earls, one viscount, six bishops, and thirteen barons, who were attended by two lord chief-justices, four judges, Mr. Sergeant Crook, and Mr. Attorney-General, the attorney-general being Coke. They sent for the Commons to meet them, and the Commons said they had no business with them on that subject; that it was the privilege of the House of Commons to examine its own returns. Then the King directly interfered. They sent a committee of sixty to wait upon the King, and the King told them:

His Majesty answered: He was loath he should be forced to alter his tune; and that he should now change it into matter of grief by way of contestation. He did sample it to the murmur and contradiction of the people of Israel. He did not attribute the cause of his grief to any purpose in the house to offend him; but only to a mistaking of the law. For matters of fact, he answered them all particularly. That, for his part, he was indifferent which of them were chosen, Sir John or Sir Francis; that they could suspect no special affection in him, because this was a counselor not brought in by himself. That he had no purpose to impeach their privilege; but since they derived all matters of privilege from him, and by his grant, he expected they should not be turned against. That there was no precedent did suit this case fully: Precedents in the time of minors, of tyrants, of women, of simple kings, not to be credited, because for some private ends. By the law this house ought not to meddle with returns, being all made into the chancery, and are to be corrected or reformed by that court only into which they are returned. (35 Hen., 6.) It was the resolution of all the judges that matter of outlawry was a sufficient cause of dismission of any member out of the house.

The Commons made answer, and finally they went to their house and reduced their reasons to writing:

The reasons of the proceeding of the house in Sir Francis Goodwin's case, penned by the committee, were, according to former order, brought in by Mr. Francis Moore and read by the clerk, directed in form of a petition.

In the petition, they said that every Parliament writ contained this clause:

Et electionem tuam, in pleno comitatu factum distincte et aperte, sub sigillo tuo et sigillis eorum qui electioni illi interfuerint, nobis in cancellarium nostram ad diem et locum in brevi content certifices indilate.

That they should return the writ to the chancellor. The Commons said that there was a period when that was the case:

And also the Commons, in the beginning of every Parliament, have ever used to appoint special committees, all the Parliament time, for examining controversies concerning elections and returns of knights and burgesses, during which time the writs and indentures remain with the clerk of the Crown, and after the Parliament ended, and not before, are delivered to the clerk of the petty-bag in chancery, to be kept there; which is warranted by reason and precedents: Reason, for that it is fit that the returns should be in that place examined, where the appearance and service of the writ is appointed. The appearance and service is in Parliament, therefore the return examinable in Parliament.

From that time forth the Commons have been in the possession of that privilege, and for a long time the privilege was greatly abused; but in 1774 a law placed it in the hands of special committees organized for the purpose of giving judicial decisions upon those returns. De Lolme says of that law of Mr. Granville, that it was "one of those victories which the Parliament from time to time gains over itself, in which the members, forgetting all views of private ambition, only thought of their interest as subjects."

Now, I say that the Constitution of the United States obviously intended when these returns were brought to the two Houses of Congress, representing as they did the legislative department of the Government, and their business being to furnish an executive head, without which no law could be passed and no administration conducted—that these two Houses should examine fully and entirely, and just so far as it was necessary to ascertain that there was a concurring will in the appointment of a majority of the electors. That was the question to be submitted to and determined by them, and until that decision was made by the two Houses there could be no President appointed by electors, no President could have any commission from any source. He became the President of the United States of America solely, exclusively by the count made by the two Houses and their certificate that he had received a majority of all the electors; and before they can be possibly required to make any such judgment, they are, in the necessity of the case, bound to find all the just and proper grounds on which such a judgment shall be based. Hearn gives a very interesting account of the struggle, lasting more than a century, of the Commons to get into the position which they now occupy, and in the work called Hearn's Government of England, discoursing on this case, he says:

Such a power as that claimed by the Crown was manifestly fatal to the intelligent action of the House of Commons. This truth seems to have been fully recognized by all parties.

I return to the point where I commenced, to the inquiry in respect to the directions made by the State of Louisiana in reference to the election of President and Vice-President. I shall not follow the discussion in respect to the acts of the legislature and whether the act of the legislature of 1868 has been repealed or not. I will come directly to the question, assuming it to be true for the present that the act of 1872 fully provides for the election of electors for President and Vice-President.

I call your attention to the oath of office that the members of the returning-board are to take, found on page 96 of the compilation printed by order of the Commission, the latter part of section 2 of the act of 1872:

I, A B, do solemnly swear (or affirm) that I will faithfully and diligently perform the duties of a returning-officer as prescribed by law; that I will carefully and honestly canvass and compile the statements of the votes, and make a true and correct return of the election: So help me God.

What statements of votes? That is prescribed in the succeeding sentence:

Within ten days after the closing of the election said returning-officers shall meet in New Orleans to canvass and compile the statements of votes made by the commissioners of election, and make returns of the election to the secretary of state. They shall continue in session until such returns have been compiled.

Therefore it is defined in the following sentence that the statements of votes made by the commissioners of election are the statements that the members of the board have sworn to compile, and they are the only papers that are referred to or mentioned in that oath of office. They swear to "carefully and honestly canvass and compile the statements of the votes and make a true and correct return." It is offered on our part to prove that they never canvassed and compiled a single return made by the commissioners of election. As I mentioned before, they had a "contabulated statement" of the supervisors, which was a secondary paper; and here it may be proper, and perhaps in answer to a good deal of the tirade that has been spoken on the other side in reference to affairs in Louisiana, it would be right, for me to tell you precisely how this election came about, and who were the persons that were watching the precincts and controlling the election.

You will perceive that there is a supervising registrar appointed by the governor of the State, that governor being then a candidate for elector, and eventually a candidate for Senator to the Congress of the United States, which since this election he has, in some manner or other, got some sort of election for or title to. Fifty-seven parishes in the State and eighteen or twenty wards in the city of New Orleans each have a supervising registrar. The supervising registrar has the absolute power to reject or admit any voter on the list. The law, as you will perceive, prohibits mandamus, injunction, or any interference of the courts with his function, and prescribes that his judgment shall be absolutely conclusive upon the capacity of giving a vote. That supervisor of registration in each parish appoints three commissioners at each poll. He is required to take men of fair standing in their parties, so as to make something like a fair representation. I will assume that he takes two from his own party and one from the other. There are over seven hundred polling-places in the State, in round numbers. There are, then, twenty-one hundred persons in all, fourteen hundred of them of one party, and those men are to take the vote from the hands of the voter, and it is a criminal offense for anybody else to touch the vote in its passage from the voter's hand into the box. There are fourteen hundred, then, members of the supervisor's party distributed over the different polls of the State. In addition to that, he has the power to appoint a special constable to attend the polls and to perform all the duties that are required of him by the commissioners; he may appoint just as many as he pleases—"one or more" is the language of the law—say eight hundred. That makes twenty-nine hundred persons.

In addition to this, the United States court in New Orleans appointed sixteen hundred supervisors, two for each poll. In addition to that, the marshal of the district appointed eight hundred deputies for New Orleans and fifteen hundred deputies for the country, to attend the polls in the country. In addition to that, under the opinion of the Attorney-General of the United States, large detachments of the Army were placed in various parts of the States, so that they might be "bystanders," I think was the language of the opinion, to serve as a sort of *posse comitatus* in the event that the marshal should find any use for that sort of assistance.

Taking out the Army, there were about seventy-five hundred persons who were employed, lawfully or unlawfully, but still with a show of authority, all coming either from the governor or his friends. They were there engaged in watching the polls. Now, is this Commission astonished, under that sort of array, that there was not from a single poll, unless perhaps one, a protest or report by any commissioner of election that there was riot, tumult, intimidation, confusion, or anything else that the statute speaks of at his box ? Nor was there, so far as I have been informed, a single report from any supervisor of registration that there was tumult, riot, or interference, or obstruction in the performance of his duty as registrar. On the contrary, on the registration-books there are 225,000 voters registered and the census of the State was 827,855 population. Of the votes appearing on the face of the returns there were 83,000 for one ticket and 75,000 for the other. I undertake to say that two-thirds of the States of this Union that voted at that election have not shown the same quantity of voting population in comparison with the population recorded on the census. I have been informed that there is not a single State.

With these facts standing here upon the face of the law, clearly to be discerned and ascertained, with these votes given, no scene of tumult, no scene of confusion reported by the only authority that could report it, I ask on what foundation, on what show of justice, right, or propriety, have these denunciations of the people and society of Louisiana been ringing in the ears of this Commission and the persons here present ?

I can tell you another fact. I can tell you a fact more startling than any fact which has been reported here and which may serve at the next election for the campaign speeches of that time. On the 30th of October there issued out of the circuit court of the United States at New Orleans ten thousand and upward of warrants of arrest to seize ten thousand different individuals, inhabitants of the city of New Orleans, for having falsely registered themselves in 1874 as competent voters. They embraced some of the most respectable men in the city, my friend and family physician among the number; one of our delegates in Congress among the number of those arrested for fraudulent registration. That is quite equal to the two thousand fights and murders and bloodshed we have heard of. A whole community, comprising its very best citizens, apparently best in standing, in property, in social position, startled by warrants of arrest to seize them and bring them before an officer of the United States court for fraud ! Never was such a picture of any community as that. There were ten thousand lies sworn to in order to procure those warrants. There was not a scintilla of proof nor any desire to have any proof. One thousand three hundred and sixty cases were tried and dismissed on sight; but it served the purpose. The affidavits were made by two men—policemen—all of them. I have read a portion of the affidavits myself, piled up in the court covering a table so high.

Mr. Commissioner THURMAN. Were the whole 10,000 men arrested on those affidavits ?

Mr. CAMPBELL. Yes, sir. Two policemen in each ward made the affidavits, I am advised. On the affidavits of those two policemen a red line was drawn around the names of the citizens on the registration-list, and several thousand voters were unable to restore their names to that list so as to vote. The commissioner who issued those papers brought his account into court for fifteen thousand and odd dollars against the United States for his services, and Judge Billings told him: "On the face of these papers there is a gross fraud, and I will not certify to a cent." That is the character of the proceeding.

I ask if any such thing had happened in the sober, steady States of Vermont or Connecticut, if ten thousand writs had been issued charging men with crimes, what would have been the sentiment and what would have been the act of those people ? Would they have been satisfied to go up and clear themselves of the accusation and return quietly home? I have the opinion that the inhabitants of the State of Ethan Allen would have been rather violent; at all events there would have been ten thousand suits against the officers if there had been any means of making them answer for that sort of dealing. But they were perfectly irresponsible, they were mere tools; I question whether they understood that there was any impropriety in the proceeding at all. But I think that is sufficient to show a perfect answer to those accusations of the wrong that was done some four or five or six years ago, based on newspaper statements.

Of course, neither one of these facts goes in the least toward solving the problem before this tribunal. The problem is whether these commissioners of elections' returns have been examined and whether it is necessary for their examination to take.place before a valid return can be made. I hardly feel that I am doing justice to the Commission and adding anything to that which has been said on this subject, not simply said by my associates, but which has been said in the Congress of the United States in discussing this very election law, which was said with so much force in the report made to the House of Representatives and that has been read here, and said with so much force in the discussion in 1872 and 1873 and so lately as in 1875, and in which there appeared to be no diversity of opinion between the different members of the Senate who composed this Commission or the members of the House who composed this Commission. The discussion both in the House and in the Senate seemed to be concurrent to the same result in reference to the construction of this law.

Why, sir, if a body is charged to do a duty in a particular manner, in a specified manner and none other, if their oath be to do it in that manner and their commission is to do it in that manner and none other, how can any effect be given to the return unless they follow that commission? The whole frame of this act is to lift up into prominence and supremacy the original returns made by the commissioners of election, and none others. Without those returns the returning-board is not allowed to advance a step. "The first thing you are do," says the act to them, "is to ascertain from those returns which are contested and which are not contested;" and in this case neither the contested nor the uncontested returns have been examined and reported upon. In a late case, in 1875, reported in 10 Law Reports, Common Pleas, page 744, Lord Chief-Justice Coleridge says:

As to the second, i. e., that the election was not really conducted under the subsisting election laws at all, we think, though there was an election in the sense of there having been a selection by the will of the constituency, that the question must in like manner be whether the departure from the prescribed method of election is so great that the tribunal is satisfied, as matter of fact, that the election was not an election under the existing law. It is not enough to say that great mistakes were made in carrying out the election under those laws; it is necessary to be able to say that, either willfully or erroneously, the election was not carried out under those laws, but under some other method.

Mr. Commissioner EDMUNDS. In what form did that case arise, Judge Campbell?

Mr. CAMPBELL. It arose on an action for submitting an election under a late act of Victoria to the judgment of the court composed of the Right Honorable Lord Coleridge, chief-justice, and Judges Keating, Brett, Grove, Denman, Archibald, Huddleston, and Lindley.

Mr. Commissioner EDMUNDS. It is under the English statute.

Mr. CAMPBELL. Yes, sir; the ballot act. The language which I have read to the court applies precisely to the act of the returning-officers in this case.

For instance, if, during the time of the old laws, with the consent of a whole constituency, a candidate had been selected by tossing up a coin, or by the result of a horse-race, it might well have been said that the electors had exercised their free will, but it should have been held that they had exercised it under a law of their own invention, and not under the existing election laws, which prescribed an election by voting. So now, when the election is to be an election by ballot, if, either willfully or erroneously, a *whole constituency* were to vote, but *not by ballot at all*, the election would be a free exercise of their will, but it would not be an election by ballot, and therefore not an election under the existing election law. But if, in the opinion of the tribunal, the election was substantially an election by ballot, then no mistakes or misconduct, however great, in the use of the machinery of the ballot act, could justify the tribunal in declaring the election void by the common law of Parliament.

Now, apply that to the case of the returning-board. The returning-board has a prescribed duty to perform under the act of its organization.

Mr. Commissioner BRADLEY. Judge Campbell, was that tribunal a tribunal erected for the trial of elections of members of Parliament?

Mr. CAMPBELL. There is a provision for the election of members of Parliament. This does not arise in the case of an election for Parliament.

Mr. Commissioner BRADLEY. It is for the trial of the election of other officers as well?

Mr. CAMPBELL. Yes, sir. This was a municipal election. They have a jurisdiction over elections for Parliament; and they certify their opinion; but this is not such a case.

Mr. Commissioner BRADLEY. Are the operative words of the section of the act which confers the power on the tribunal in that case, before you?

Mr. CAMPBELL. No, sir. The question was under the ballot act. There were some instructions given to the returning-officers which would give you the information you ask for; I will read them from page 738 of the volume to which I have referred:

The returning-officer will attend at ———, at four o'clock p. m., on the day of election, to receive the ballot-boxes and papers from the officers; when *all* the boxes have been delivered to him, he will then—
1. Open the ballot-boxes.
2. Count the number of ballot-papers in each box separately, and record the number on the inclosed form.
3. Mix all the ballot-papers together, (keeping their faces upward.)
4. Sort into separate packets the votes for each candidate and the doubtful votes.
5. Examine the doubtful votes, and reject for the following reasons only:
1. For want of official mark; 2. Voting for more candidates than entitled to; 3. Writing or mark by which voter could be identified; 4. Unmarked or void for uncertainty.
6. Count the votes for each party. [It is very convenient to arrange them in heaps of twenties.]
7. Seal up in separate packets: 1. The counted ballot-papers; 2. The rejected ballot-papers.
[The packets of tendered ballot-papers, marked copy of ward-list and counter-foils, must not be opened.]
8. Verify the presiding officer's ballot-paper accounts.
9. Fill up and sign return on the printed forms.

I refer to this case for the principle which was announced. There had been an election and there had been a return, and there was a contest as to the election. The principle is:

To render an election void under the ballot act, by reason of a non-observance of or non-compliance with the rule or forms given therein, such non-observance or non-compliance must be so great as to satisfy the tribunal before which the validity of the election is contested that the election has been conducted in a manner contrary to the principle of an election by ballot, and that the irregularities complained of did affect or might have affected the result of the election.

And so I say in regard to the returning-board, that if this returning-board proceeded in a manner which was in contradiction to the letter and the spirit of the act, so as to satisfy the revising tribunal that they did not follow that act, either from error or from fraud, (and we charge in this case both error and fraud,) then the returns of those officers cannot be accepted as valid and proper returns under that act. Let me refer you to Adolphus and Ellis's Reports in Queen's Bench, new series, volume 1, page 892, Caudle *vs.* Seymour; and the object of the citation is to show that there must be a conformity with the directions of the act, that a court or tribunal does not acquire jurisdiction by the mere fact of dealing with a case that has some connection with the subject of the act, but where the act prescribes a mode of proceeding to an inferior court that must be pursued. The syllabus of the case is:

A justice's warrant commanding a constable to apprehend and bring before him the body of A B to answer all such matters and things as on Her Majesty's behalf shall be objected against him on oath by C D, for an assault committed upon C D, on, &c., is bad, as not showing any information on oath upon which the warrant issues.

A deposition on oath, taken by the justice's clerk, the justice not being present, nor at any time seeing, examining, or hearing the deponent, is irregular, and no justification of proceedings founded upon it.

The judgment is this:

An affidavit is a document which is to speak for itself, and to avail or not, merely according to its contents; the court does not examine the party; but, in the case of depositions, the magistrate does; and I am not aware that deputing that office to a clerk has ever been held equivalent to an examination by the magistrate.

*   *   *   *   *   *   *

A magistrate has no jurisdiction in such a case as this, without a charge on oath.

*   *   *   *   *   *   *

The taking of affidavits in this court is quite different; the act is purely ministerial; the party says what he pleases, and the effect of it comes to be considered by the court afterward. But a magistrate taking depositions has a discretion to exercise; he is to examine the witness, hear his answers, and judge of the manner in which they are given.

The act was considered void and an action of trespass was brought against him. In this case I have communicated to the court the terms of the act of 1872 which required these persons to compile and canvass papers of a specific character, and their whole duty is performed when they canvass and compile those papers, and they have no other duty to perform until they make that canvass and that compilation. If in making the canvass and compilation they come across a protest made on the day of the election in the presence of the commissioners and corroborated by three parties, and they find in that a sufficient warrant for further examination and necessity for further examination, then they have an independent and separate duty to perform. And here let me state to the Commission that their duty upon the subject of intimidation and their power upon the inquiry into intimidation is a limited and special power. They do not have the power to go through the country and examine whether there was intimidation which kept persons from the polls, however such intimidation may have affected the election. They have not power to examine into intimidations or tumults or riots occurring at a different place than the place of holding the election, nor at a time other than the election-day. It is the interference on the day of election by tumult, riot, or intimidation, that the commissioners of election have the power to report, and when reported the returning-board have the power to examine.

I do not pretend to say but what at the common law and under the acts of the legislature of the State of Louisiana intimidation and threats and violence in any form, corrupting practices in any form, would invalidate an election. But we are not dealing with any inquiries of that kind. We are dealing with the powers of a returning-board, with a special, limited commission addressed to them, and the manner of performing that commission carefully and rigidly specified. The act of Louisiana is no new act. Here is an entire volume, an Election Manual, and these are the chapters contained in it relative to an election: " acts of agency; bribery; conduct; conveyance; corruption; influence; intimidation; fraud," &c., and the most extensive and ramified inquiries are made there, and rules of the strongest and most rigid character prescribed in order to secure purity in elections. Such unquestionably would be a suitable subject for examination upon a trial where a party had received a certificate of election from any returning-board. In the State of Louisiana, in the decisions contained in the twenty-fifth volume of Annual Reports, made in 1872 and 1873, there has been a perfect abdication or rather abnegation of every sort of jurisdiction over elections in any shape, although our intrusion act is a literal copy from the act of New York, and although the opinions of the courts of New York have extended the operation of the act to every sort of inquiry in elections.

The supreme court in the State of Louisiana held in the decision against Bonner that there was no law authorizing the courts to deal with contested elections, and their decision was to dismiss the case for want of any connection or control over it. That was all that is contained in those decisions. But, unquestionably, in any well-ordered court no such decision could possibly have been made, and when those opinions came before the committee of the Senate (and the report of Mr. Carpenter was submitted several years ago) that committee did not hesitate to say that those opinions were contrary to law and that the law was in the dissenting opinion. In every well-ordered system of jurisprudence, those inquiries, that delegation of power would be co-extensive with the limits ; and any party who had a title to office and wished to establish that title against a party who had been counted in unfairly or who had procured his election unfairly and dishonestly ought to have been heard ; but in the state of the law in Louisiana no such case could have been presented—I mean the state of the law before that supreme court.

Mr. Commissioner STRONG. Mr. Campbell, with regard to a portion of your argument, I should like to ask a question if it will not be interrupting you.

Mr. CAMPBELL. Certainly.

Mr. Commissioner STRONG. What is the position you take in regard to the power of the State over the final action of its returning-board ? To put the question a little more in the concrete, was it in the power of the State of Louisiana to have directed the action of the returning-board or State canvassing-board to have been completed on or before the 20th day of November, and was it in the power of the State to constitute another tribunal to try contests between the two sets of electors which claimed under the election ?

Mr. CAMPBELL. Unquestionably, sir.

Mr. Commissioner STRONG. Then, as I understand you, you contend that the power of judging of the honesty or accuracy of the decision of the returning-board is in the State.

Mr. CAMPBELL. In the case of State officers.

Mr. Commissioner STRONG. I am speaking of electors.

Mr. CAMPBELL. That I will come to after awhile. In reference to that, my own opinion is that the State has no jurisdiction over the elector.

Mr. Commissioner STRONG. Cannot review its own election for electors ?

Mr. CAMPBELL. It cannot review the election for electors, in my judgment. I say that the election is to be reviewed and examined finally by the two Houses of Congress when their certificates of returns come.

Mr. Commissioner STRONG. How then could they constitute a returning-board to make any decision at all?

Mr. CAMPBELL. They make a returning-board with a view of compiling the returns. I am speaking of the final disposition as a final determination on the subject of the right of an elector to cast a vote. Perhaps the question is a doubtful one, and I have not very fully considered it; but my view of these electors under the Constitution is, that the State is the instrument and the agency, and its laws are instrumental for the purpose of communicating to the two Houses of Congress the election of electors, and the two Houses of Congress, in determining who has a majority of all the electors, necessarily can inquire whether those electors were fairly chosen or not.

Mr. Commissioner STRONG. Pardon me, for one question, and that is this: whether you contend that Congress occupies the position of a tribunal for contesting the election of State electors, the same position which a tribunal for the trial of contested elections constituted by a State would have as to any State officer?

Mr. CAMPBELL. That Congress could?

Mr. Commissioner STRONG. Whether Congress occupies that position; in other words, whether Congress is the tribunal for the trial of contested elections of electors?

Mr. CAMPBELL. I have no question that Congress could create a tribunal to inquire into the validity and truthfulness and regularity of any election for electors for the purpose of determining the question whether the votes cast for President and Vice-President are cast by the men competent to do so. It is the only legitimate place where such a tribunal could come from, because the power to be exercised by electors affects every citizen and every interest in the United States; every State in this Union is interested in that decision, and no State would be justified in allowing the determination of such questions finally to rest in a State tribunal.

On the subject of the value of those certificates there is one authority that I ask the attention of the Commission to. It is in 7 Lansing's Reports, page 725, and the same case was affirmed by the court of appeals, page 527 of the fifty-fifth volume New York Reports. I prefer to read from Lansing because it presents the subject very succinctly. We have offered to prove this certificate to be false. In this case it is said:

At common law, where, as in this case, the people are a party, the certificate of the board of inspectors is, first, *prima facie* evidence of the truth of *such* statements as they are permitted or directed to certify. But it is only *prima facie* evidence, it is not conclusive, and like all other merely presumptive evidence, it is subject to be overcome or destroyed by better, higher, or more certain evidence, and may be entirely so overcome or impeached. In this country it is the actual expressed will of the electors, not the certificate of inspectors, that confers the title to an office. It is *truth*, not *form*, that confers the right.

On another page:

When the truth has been so far inquired into and ascertained as to show that the certificate is not true, can it be the duty of the court to hold that, though false and uncertain, it may still be used as evidence? Can such a paradox be introduced into the law as that a thing false in fact may be true as evidence? Or this, that an official certificate proved to be beyond the power of the officer to make certain in what it contains, shall still be held to be certain because it is certified? I think not. If such rules are not found to be established by authority, surely they should not be now first introduced to thwart that inestimable right of a freeman, the right to hold an office when such right is proved by the evidence to be the will of the legal voters.

Mr. Commissioner EDMUNDS. How did that case arise?

Mr. CAMPBELL. It arose on a contest about an election.

Mr. Commissioner BRADLEY. Under the New York intrusion act?

Mr. CAMPBELL. This action " was in the nature of a *quo warranto* to try the title of the defendant to the office of mayor of Albany, to which office the defendant was declared to have been elected on the second Tuesday of April, 1872."

Mr. Commissioner HOAR. If it would not be disagreeable to you, Judge Campbell, I should like to ask a question, as I did not precisely understand your answer to Judge Strong. Suppose, when, in the process of counting, the vote of the State of Oregon was reached, proof should be offered on behalf of one of the candidates that at every polling place in the State of Oregon there had been a different number of votes cast from that certified, so as to change the result in the State, do you claim that it would be the duty of the two Houses to pause in the process of counting the vote until both sides should have put in evidence on that question and the fact should have been ascertained?

Mr. CAMPBELL. That is not the case I have been arguing at all. It is entirely outside of the proffer that we have made in respect to evidence.

Mr. Commissioner HOAR. But I think it would perhaps help us to understand your view of the power and duty of the two Houses, to inquire whether you thought, if such proof were proffered on behalf of one of the candidates as to what the true vote was in that State, it would be the duty of the two Houses to pause in the count until that fact had been settled?

Mr. CAMPBELL. If I was a member of one of the two Houses I would give it all the pause and inquiry that was allowed to me, and then I would decide it according to the result of that conclusion.

I present now the question as to the objections that were raised to some of the alleged electors. The statute law of Louisiana, being the registration act, provides:

That no supervisor of registration, appointed under this act, and no clerk of such supervisor of registration, shall be eligible for any office at any election when said officers officiate.

We charge that another party held several offices, one of them being a senator in the State legislature, and therefore was not eligible; holding one office created under the Constitution, as well as several others under the law, they are disqualified under another article of the State constitution.

It was inquired yesterday by one of the members of the Commission if it were competent for the State to require that an elector should be a citizen of the State. The answer was, I believe, that the State had no right even to put that requisition. The State of Louisiana, in the act of 1868 and in her constitution, has not only required that he should be a citizen of the State but that he should be an inhabitant of one of the congressional districts. It has declared that two of the electors shall be appointed electors at large. As to them no requirement of residence is made except in the State. But six of the eight electors are required to be inhabitants respectively of the various congressional districts.

Mr. Commissioner THURMAN. Are those six chosen by districts?

Mr. CAMPBELL. No, sir; chosen by general ticket. But one of the questions which occur in this case is that in one of the districts the voters concluded they could only vote for the two electors at large and the inhabitant of their own district, and so neglected to vote for any other member on the ticket except the two electors at large and their own district elector. The returning-board, under a general equity juris-diction, concluded that that meant the whole ticket and allotted to the other members of the ticket just as many votes as had been given to the three in that parish.

Mr. Commissioner BRADLEY. What was the number of votes?

Mr. CAMPBELL. Twelve hundred, I think.

The PRESIDENT. Counted 1,200 votes not cast?

Mr. CAMPBELL. The exact figures are 1,362, 1,334, 1,364, 1,364, and 298. They did not allot them impartially, it appears. They allotted some more than others, but that was the excuse that was made.

Mr. Commissioner EDMUNDS. Does that appear in the eleventh point of the offers of proof?

Mr. CAMPBELL. Yes, sir; and that is the point that I am now making.

Mr. Commissioner EDMUNDS. I meant to inquire whether the eleventh offer of proof was directed to that.

Mr. CAMPBELL. Yes, sir; the point I am making now is on the sixteenth, seventeenth, and eighteenth pages of our offers:

We further offer to prove that Oscar Joffrion was, on the 7th day of November, A. D. 1876, supervisor of registration of the parish of Pointe Coupée, and that he acted and officiated as such supervisor of registration for said parish at the said election for presidential electors on that day; and that he is the same person who acted as one of the electors for said State, and on the 6th day of December, A. D. 1876, as an elector cast a vote for Rutherford B. Hayes for President of the United States and for William A. Wheeler for Vice-President of the United States.

And so on the following page is the objection to Morris Marks, one of the pretended electors, who—

Was, ever since has been, *and now is,* holding and exercising the office of district attorney of the fourth judicial district of said State, and receiving the salary by law attached to said office.

Again:

We further offer to prove that on the 7th day of November, A. D. 1876, J. Henri Burch, who was one of the pretended electors who in said pretended electoral college gave a vote for Rutherford B. Hayes for President of the United States and a vote for William A. Wheeler for Vice-President of the United States, was holding the follow-ing offices under the constitution and laws of said State; that is to say: member of the board of control of the State penitentiary, also administrator of deaf and dumb asylum of said State, to both of which offices he had been appointed by the governor with the advice and consent of the senate of said State, both being offices with salaries fixed by law, and also the office of treasurer of the parish school board for the parish of East Baton Rouge; and that said Burch, ever since the said 7th day of November, (and prior thereto,) has exercised and still is exercising the functions of all said offices and receiving the emoluments thereof.

The Constitution of the United States requires the State to appoint eight electors in such manner as the legislature thereof may direct. It has been decided that they might retain the power themselves and appoint the electors, or they might confer it on the people, or they might elect them by general ticket; and the question is presented whether they could as a part of that power designate the class of persons from whom the election was to be made; that is, designate persons from whom the election should not be made. In the exercise of that power they have specifically said that a person who is concerned with the registration, who has the appointment of a commissioner of election of a parish, who is the returning-officer of that parish, shall not be a competent person to be elected. There is an obvious propriety that a supervisor of regisration should not be capable or eligible to any office while conducting the election. Such is the common law, decided very early:

The sheriff of Rutlandshire was chosen, and returned himself, one of the members for that county. Unanimously resolved, that the return was void.

The question arose in Mississippi, and it was there determined under a statute similar to ours that the election of a supervisor of registration to a State office was absolutely null and void:

We entirely concur in so much of this judgment as holds that the appointee was disqualified to take the office. The law prescribes who may vote as well as who may hold office.

The gentlemen on the other side have insisted that on the subject of the appointment of these electors the State has plenary power; that even Congress in determining who shall be President and Vice-President, in the counting of the votes, have no power or authority to go behind the certificate of the State and judge who has been elected. I do not go to that length; but I say that the term "manner of election," "in such manner as the legislature may direct," does include sufficient authority to determine who shall and who shall not be elected. They may say that an infant should not be elected; they may say that an alien should not be elected; they may say that persons convicted of felony should not be elected; they may disqualify from election the persons who have the control and the power to make the returns of the election, and who would be in such condition in respect to the election that fair and impartial action could not reasonably be expected from them; and under that view of the case they have disqualified the whole body of State registrars from acting as returning-officers for themselves, or being in any manner candidates at the place where they are elected.

In the same respect is the governor of the State, a candidate for the office of elector. He has the appointment of every registrar in the State, and is therefore directly interested in having such a registration as would render him a successful candidate; and how potential such an interest is will be sufficiently clear by evidence. Here is a circular that passed to every supervisor of registration; this one is addressed to the supervisor of registration in the parish of Assumption:

HEADQUARTERS REPUBLICAN PARTY OF LOUISIANA,
ROOMS JOINT COMMITTEE ON CANVASSING AND REGISTRATION.
MECHANICS' INSTITUTE, *September* 25, 1876.

DEAR SIR: It is well known to this committee that, from examination of the census of 1875, the republican vote in your parish is 2,200 and the republican majority is 900.

You are expected to register and vote the full strength of the republican party in your parish.

Your recognition by the next State administration will depend upon your doing your full duty in the premises, and you will not be held to have done your full duty unless the republican registration in your parish reaches 2,200 and the republican vote is at least 2,100.

All local candidates and committees are directed to aid you to the utmost in obtaining the result, and every facility is and will be afforded you; but you must obtain the results called for herein without fail. Once obtained, your recognition will be ample and generous.

Very respectfully, your obedient servant,

D. J. M. A. JEWETT,
Secretary.

SUPERVISOR OF REGISTRATION,
Parish of Assumption, Louisiana.

Your honors, therefore, must see that there was an adequate reason for an enlightened legislature to put that restriction upon the appointment of supervisors of registration and also for putting the governor out, having obtained the place of governor, to prevent him from holding any other office, so that he should not contribute to his election to another office to take effect after the expiration of his term as governor. That impartial administration in the matter of elections, that purity o elections which is an object of so much consideration in the constitution and laws of that State, could never be secured if such practices as we bring to your notice should be tolerated. Therefore we think that, if the Commission was to reject all these electors for the reasons set forth, it would be a vindication of the will of the people as manifested in their organic law and in their statutes.

These considerations are as much as the length of time I have will enable me to submit to the court. Upon the whole case, I feel it to be my duty to say that the State of Louisiana is much more concerned in the assertion of her power and of her right to vindicate the purity of elections in the State than she is in the election of any candidate for President or Vice-President. The court must observe, from what I have already exhibited of the laws of the State, that the State is in the possession of an oligarchy of unscrupulous, dishonest, corrupt, overreaching politicians and persons who employ the powers of the State for their own emolument. There is no responsibility on their part to any moral law or constitutional or legal obligation. For years they have usurped the powers of the State by means that have brought upon them the condemnation of the Senate of the United States, of the House of Representatives of the United States, and, I may say, of the whole people of the United States. Those practices have been covered, immunity has been granted to them because of their intercourse and connection with the politics and the parties of the Union; and without that connection they would not stand in that State for a single hour. By their association they have prostrated every material and endangered every moral interest within the limits of the State.

Reading a few days ago a work upon the present state of Turkey, written by a member of the British Parliament who went there to see for himself the situation, I was struck with the way he described the government of Turkey. It was not a government of Mohammedans nor a government of Christians. He said that there was a ring in Constantinople composed of apostates and renegades and adventurers from every state in Europe; that all reform was trampled upon by them because it interfered with their powers and their privileges and their opportunities to enrich themselves; that they inspired and inspirited the massacres of Bulgaria and the oppression of the Servians; that reformation in Turkey was to be accomplished by no other means than the expulsion of that ring. My residence in Louisiana for ten years enables me to fully understand the perils and dangers and miseries under which that empire labors, and which threaten the whole peace of Europe. The rings in Louisiana have affected the peace of this country. The fact that this tribunal is now sitting, and that the whole people of this land look with breathless expectation to see whether their purposes have been accomplished by results, has been brought about mainly by the toleration of misgovernment in that State.

Mr. EVARTS. Mr. President, there are two authorities that I will ask to hand to you: one is the case of Morgan *vs.* Quackenbush, 22 Barbour's Supreme Court Reports, page 73:

That the duty of the common council, in making the first canvass, was purely ministerial, and consisted in a simple matter of arithmetic; they not being at liberty to receive evidence of anything outside of the returns of the inspectors. That in receiving affidavits tending to show fraudulent practices at the polls, and in omitting to canvass the votes of two election districts, on that ground, they acted illegally, and assumed to exercise a judicial power which the legislature had not vested in them. But that, having jurisdiction to make the canvass, their certificate entitled P to the office until the other error should be corrected by legal proceedings.

Mr. HOADLY. Permit me to ask a question. Did the law under

which that case was conducted prescribe the kind of testimony on which the tribunal could act?

Mr. EVARTS.   What tribunal?

Mr. HOADLY.   The tribunal there of which you read.

Mr. EVARTS.   That I do not know.   The statement of their powers is given, and it is said they exceeded them, and that action was illegal. Whatever their powers were they exceeded them, and that action was illegal.

I also refer to the case of Brown *vs.* The City of Lowell, in 8 Metcalf, page 175, as pertinent to the inquiry of what the operation is in respect of an act that is to take effect at a future day as compared with an act passed after the date of the first and between its date and the time it comes into effect.

Mr. Commissioner EDMUNDS.   That question is considered in 3 Dallas, the case of Ware *vs.* Hilton.

Mr. EVARTS.   It is sufficient for me refer to it.

Mr. CAMPBELL.   I understand I have a few minutes more.   There is a point that I omitted to deal with, which was the vacancy in the board not being filled.

The PRESIDENT.   You have ten minutes yet.

Mr. CAMPBELL.   I wish to refer your honors to an authority on that point, Grant on Corporations, page 155:

When a meeting at which a specific thing is to be done is to consist of the different integral parts of a corporation, and each of these integral parts consists of a definite number of corporators, then the meeting will not be properly constituted unless it be attended by a majority of the members of each integral part respectively. Where an act is to be done by a select body consisting of a definite number of corporators, it will not be valid unless a majority of the select body are present at the meeting to do the act. If the act is to be done by an indefinite body, it is valid if passed by a majority of those present at the meeting, however small a fraction they may be of the body at large.

In this case the language of the act is:

That five persons, to be elected by the senate from all political parties, shall be the returning-officers for all elections in the State, a majority of whom shall constitute a quorum, and have power to make the returns of all elections. In case of any vacancy by death, resignation, or otherwise, by either of the board, then the vacancy shall be filled by the residue of the board of returning-officers.

And the word "then" imports time, and when the vacancy occurs that it shall be filled. In this case the vacancy occurred three years ago, in 1874. Repeated requests and demands were made upon this board to fill that vacancy, but that vacancy was not filled, and has not been filled. The reason given for it in the testimony which we shall offer, if permitted, is from the corrupt motive of escaping observation. It was perfectly within their means to have filled it; it was their duty to have filled it; and they acted corruptly in not filling it. It was said yesterday by one of the counsel that they had offered it repeatedly and it had been repeatedly refused. No person to whom the offer was ever made has ever been brought before any committee to testify that the offer had been made to him and that he had refused it. The members of the board themselves, at least one of them, did testify that it was not filled for the reason that they did not wish to be subjected to any sort of observation in the performance of that work. It stood upon that ground. It is such malpractice as to vitiate their subsequent proceedings in the non-performance of that duty, as well as the legal requirement on them to perform it.

Mr. Commissioner EDMUNDS.   Supposing, Judge Campbell, that they were not legally required to perform it in the sense of making their after-acts invalid, then would their failure to perform what the law did not compel them to do, from bad motive, change the validity of their subsequent acts?

Mr. CAMPBELL. They were bound under the terms of the law to have filled the vacancy. Observe the language:

In case of any vacancy by death, resignation, or otherwise, by either of the board, then the vacancy shall be filled by the residue of the board of returning-officers.

Mr. Commissioner EDMUNDS. I do not think you understood my question. Supposing you to be correct, that it was their duty to fill the vacancy, that they had no power to take any step in the performance of their duties until it was filled, then do you claim that their subsequent acts would be invalid, no matter what the motive was? But, supposing on the other hand that it was not a duty to fill it, in the sense of their incapacity to proceed afterward, would the presence of the corrupt motive make any difference in the validity of their subsequent acts? That is the question I should like to have your view upon.

Mr. CAMPBELL. I suppose that the failure to perform any duty enjoined by the law, from a corrupt motive which affects the election, would have the effect. A case in 50 New Hampshire, 140, was this:

It appeared that there were declared as cast at one of the precincts 27 more votes for county commissioner than were marked on the check-list. The court said, " if from the fact of this discrepancy the court ought to find that it was the result of fraud in the managers of the election, the court would hesitate long to count any of the votes cast at an election so tainted, on the ground that, with such proof of fraudulent and corrupt purposes, no confidence could be entertained in coming to any reliable conclusion as to what votes were actually given." And the safe rule probably is, that where an election-board are found to have willfully and deliberately committed a fraud, even though it affect a number too small to change the result, it is sufficient to destroy all confidence in their official acts, and to put the party claiming anything under the election conducted by them to the proof of his votes by evidence other than the return.

I read from the American Law of Elections by McCrary, section 184. I know of no case which is a precise parallel to the one before the Commission, where the fraud has originated in the failure to fill a vacancy; but as the legislature contemplated that there should be five persons and that the board should always be of five, comprising all political parties, the fraudulent refusal to do that would render them incompetent to perform further acts.

The PRESIDENT. The time is exhausted on the side of objectors to certificate No. 1, and an hour and two minutes are left to the other side.

Mr. MERRICK. Mr. President and gentlemen, may I be allowed to file a brief on the subject last referred to by Judge Campbell?*

The PRESIDENT. I think you may submit it to the Commission.

Mr. MERRICK. I beg to call the attention of the Commission to it. It contains some authorities directly in point on the question that this board under the law, while composed of four, did not possess legal authority to act. Among those authorities is an opinion in a case from Mr. Justice Miller. I will state to the Commission with the permission——

The PRESIDENT. It is suggested that I have computed the time wrong; that I have given the objectors to certificate No. 2 too much. I will not stop to revise it now. I shall stand by what I have stated until I see that I was wrong. The journal-clerk thinks I have allowed an hour too much.

Mr. EVARTS. I think you said we had an hour and two minutes left.

* This brief will be found in the Appendix of Briefs, marked " Brief No. 5."

The PRESIDENT. He thinks you have just three minutes left.

Mr. TRUMBULL. I desire to call attention for one moment, by permission of the Commission, to the question of time. It will be recollected that yesterday my time was occupied for at least half an hour with a discussion that occurred between members of the Commission and in reading some incidental papers called for by the Commission. At the time something was said about the propriety of not deducting that from the time used by us, and it seems to me that it is depriving us of some little time that we may want to use, to enforce the rule under such circumstances as against the time that I occupied.

The PRESIDENT. I made no deduction for interruptions. I left that for the Commission to decide. It is proper, therefore, that you should ask the Commission, if you see fit, to make an allowance. I made none.

Mr. TRUMBULL. I do not desire at this moment to make any remarks, but Mr. Merrick does.

Mr. MERRICK. I merely desire, may it please your honors, to make a statement in reply to a statement made by Mr. Evarts, that during the entire progress of the investigation of this subject that took place in Louisiana no protest was made, and no objection intimated, to the power of this board to canvass the electoral vote.

Mr. EVARTS. I did not state it in that form. I stated that no claim was made that Governor Kellogg was to canvass it. I said nothing about a protest.

Mr. MERRICK. Then I misunderstood. A protest was duly filed by those representing the democratic party against the power of the returning-board in Louisiana to canvass the electoral vote on the first day of the session.

Mr. EVARTS. I said nothing on that subject whatever.

The PRESIDENT. I think I am not authorized now to receive any further discussion; the discussion of the pending proposition is concluded. Shall notice be now given that there will be no further public proceedings to-day? [Putting the question.] It is so ordered.

After the doors were closed, at four o'clock and thirty minutes p. m.,

Mr. Commissioner EDMUNDS moved that the Commission take a recess for fifteen minutes; which was agreed to.

On motion of Mr. Commissioner STRONG, the vote on the motion was reconsidered.

Mr. Commissioner EDMUNDS moved that the Commission take a recess for one hour;

And after debate,

The motion was withdrawn.

Mr. Commissioner FIELD moved that the Commission adjourn until to-morrow.

The motion was decided in the negative;

Yeas 7

Nays 8

Those who voted in the affirmative were: Messrs. Abbott, Bayard, Bradley, Field, Hunton, Payne, and Thurman.—7.

Those who voted in the negative were: Messrs. Clifford, Edmunds, Frelinghuysen, Garfield, Hoar, Miller, Morton, and Strong.—8.

So the motion was not agreed to.

Mr. Commissioner HOAR moved that the vote on the question of the admission of testimony in the matter pending be taken at four o'clock p. m. to-morrow;

And after debate,

The motion was withdrawn.

Mr. Commissioner GARFIELD moved that the Commission take a recess until six o'clock and thirty minutes p. m.

Mr. Commissioner HUNTON moved, as a substitute, that the Commission take a recess until seven o'clock p. m.

Pending which,

Mr. Commissioner HUNTON moved that when the Commission adjourn it be until ten o'clock a. m. to-morrow; and that the vote on the question of the admission of testimony in the matter pending be taken to-morrow at four o'clock p. m.

After remarks,

The question being on the adoption of the motion of Mr. Commissioner Hunton,

It was decided in the affirmative.

On motion of Mr. Commissioner HOAR,

Ordered, That the Secretary notify counsel to be present at four o'clock and fifteen minutes p. m. to-morrow to proceed under the direction of the Commission.

Mr. Commissioner HUNTON moved that the Stenographer be allowed to attend the secret sessions of the Commission and take notes thereof.

The question being on its adoption, it was determined in the negative:

Yeas 5
Nays 9

Those who voted in the affirmative were: Messrs. Abbott, Bayard, Field, Hunton, and Payne.—5.

Those who voted in the negative were: Messrs. Bradley, Clifford, Edmunds, Frelinghuysen, Garfield, Hoar, Miller, Strong, and Thurman.—9.

So the motion was not agreed to.

And, on motion of Mr. Commissioner PAYNE, (at five o'clock and twenty-two minutes p. m.,) the Commission adjourned.

FRIDAY, *February* 16, 1877.

The Commission met at ten o'clock a. m., pursuant to adjournment, with closed doors, for the purpose of consultation on the question submitted relative to the offers of proof connected with the objections raised to the certificates of electoral votes from the State of Louisiana.

After debate,

Mr. Commissioner HOAR submitted the following order:

Ordered, That the evidence offered be not received.

Mr. Commissioner ABBOTT offered the following as a substitute for the proposed order:

Resolved, That evidence will be received to show that so much of the act of Louisiana establishing a returning-board for that State is unconstitutional, and the acts of said returning-board are void.

The question being on the adoption of the substitute, it was decided in the negative:

Yeas 7
Nays 8

Those who voted in the affirmative were: Messrs. Abbott, Bayard, Clifford, Field, Hunton, Payne, and Thurman—7.

Those who voted in the negative were: Messrs. Bradley, Edmunds, Frelinghuysen, Garfield, Hoar, Miller, Morton, and Strong—8.

Mr. Commissioner ABBOTT offered the following as a substitute:

Resolved, That evidence will be received to show that the returning-board of Louisiana, at the time of canvassing and compiling the vote of that State at the last election in that State, was not legally constituted under the law establishing it, in this: that it was composed of four persons all of one political party, instead of five persons of different political parties, as required by the law establishing said board.

The question being on the adoption of the substitute, it was decided in the negative:

Yeas 7
Nays 8

Those who voted in the affirmative were: Messrs. Abbott, Bayard, Clifford, Field, Hunton, Payne, and Thurman—7.

Those who voted in the negative were: Messrs. Bradley, Edmunds, Frelinghuysen, Garfield, Hoar, Miller, Morton, and Strong—8.

Mr. Commissioner ABBOTT offered the following as a substitute:

Resolved, That the Commission will receive testimony on the subject of the frauds alleged in the specifications of the counsel for the objectors to certificates numbered 1 and 3.

The question being on the adoption of the substitute, it was decided in the negative:

Yeas 7
Nays 8

Those who voted in the affirmative were: Messrs. Abbott, Bayard, Clifford, Field, Hunton, Payne, and Thurman—7.

Those who voted in the negative were: Messrs. Bradley, Edmunds, Frelinghuysen, Garfield, Hoar, Miller, Morton, and Strong—8.

Mr. Commissioner ABBOTT offered the following as a substitute:

Resolved, That testimony tending to show that the so-called returning-board of Louisiana had no jurisdiction to canvass the votes for electors of President and Vice-President is admissible.

The question being on the adoption of the substitute, it was determined in the negative:

Yeas 7
Nays 8

Those who voted in the affirmative were: Messrs. Abbott, Bayard, Clifford, Field, Hunton, Payne, and Thurman—7.

Those who voted in the negative were: Messrs. Bradley, Edmunds, Frelinghuysen, Garfield, Hoar, Miller, Morton, and Strong—8.

Mr. Commissioner ABBOTT offered the following as a substitute:

Resolved, That evidence is admissible that the statements and affidavits purporting to have been made and forwarded to said returning-board in pursuance of the provisions of section 26 of the election law of 1872, alleging riot, tumult, intimidation, and violence at or near certain polls and in certain parishes, were falsely fabricated and forged by certain disreputable persons under the direction and with the knowledge of said returning-board, and that said returning-board knowing said statements and affidavits to be false and forged, and that none of the said statements or affidavits were made in the manner or form or within the time required by law, did knowingly, willfully, and fraudulently fail and refuse to canvass or compile more than ten thousand votes lawfully cast, as is shown by the statements of votes of the commissioners of election.

The question being on the adoption of the substitute, it was decided in the negative:

Yeas 7
Nays 8

Those who voted in the affirmative were: Messrs. Abbott, Bayard, Clifford, Field, Hunton, Payne, and Thurman—7.

Those who voted in the negative were: Messrs. Bradley, Edmunds, Frelinghuysen, Garfield, Hoar, Miller, Morton, and Strong—8.

Mr. Commissioner HUNTON offered the following as a substitute:

Resolved, That evidence be received to prove that the votes cast and given at said election on the 7th of November last for the election of electors as shown by the returns made by the commissioners of election from the several polls or voting-places in said State have never been compiled or canvassed, and that the said returning-board never even pretended to compile or canvass the returns made by said commissioners of election, but that said returning-board only pretended to canvass the returns made by said supervisors.

The question being on the adoption of the substitute, it was decided in the negative:

Yeas.. 7
Nays.. 8

Those who voted in the affirmative were: Messrs. Abbott, Bayard, Clifford, Field, Hunton, Payne, and Thurman—7.

Those who voted in the negative were: Messrs. Bradley, Edmunds, Frelinghuysen, Garfield, Hoar, Miller, Morton, and Strong—8.

Mr. Commissioner BAYARD offered the following as a substitute:

Resolved, That no person holding an office of trust or profit under the United States is eligible to be appointed an elector, and that this Commission will receive evidence tending to prove such ineligibility as offered by counsel for objectors to certificates 1 and 3.

The question being on the adoption of the substitute, it was decided in the negative:

Yeas.. 7
Nays.. 8

Those who voted in the affirmative were: Messrs. Abbott, Bayard, Clifford, Field, Hunton, Payne, and Thurman—7.

Those who voted in the negative were: Messrs. Bradley, Edmunds, Frelinghuysen, Garfield, Hoar, Miller, Morton, and Strong—8.

Mr. Commissioner FIELD offered the following as a substitute:

Resolved, That in the opinion of the Commission evidence is admissible upon the several matters which counsel for the objectors to certificates numbered 1 and 3 offered to prove.

The question being on the adoption of the substitute, it was decided in the negative:

Yeas.. 7
Nays.. 8

Those who voted in the affirmative were: Messrs. Abbott, Bayard, Clifford, Field, Hunton, Payne, and Thurman—7.

Those who voted in the negative were: Messrs. Bradley, Edmunds, Frelinghuysen, Garfield, Hoar, Miller, Morton, and Strong—8.

The question then recurring on the adoption of the order submitted by Mr. Commissioner Hoar,

Mr. Commissioner PAYNE moved to strike out the word "not."

The question being on the adoption of the amendment, it was determined in the negative:

Yeas.. 7
Nays.. 8

Those who voted in the affirmative were: Messrs. Abbott, Bayard, Clifford, Field, Hunton, Payne, and Thurman—7.

Those who voted in the negative were : Messrs. Bradley, Edmunds, Frelinghuysen, Garfield, Hoar, Miller, Morton, and Strong—8.

The question then recurring on the adoption of the order submitted by Mr. Commissioner Hoar in the following words :

Ordered, That the evidence offered be not received,

It was determined in the affirmative :

Yeas..., 8
Nays... 7

Those who voted in the affirmative were : Messrs. Bradley, Edmunds, Frelinghuysen, Garfield, Hoar, Miller, Morton, and Strong—8.

Those who voted in the negative were : Messrs. Abbott, Bayard, Clifford, Field, Hunton, Payne, and Thurman—7.

On motion of Mr. Commissioner FIELD, it was—

Ordered, That the injunction of secrecy be removed from the proceedings of the Commission.

The order was agreed to.

The doors were thereupon opened at five o'clock and five minutes p. m., and the respective counsel appeared.

The action of the Commission on the various motions and orders submitted was read.

Mr. Commissioner HOAR. Mr. President, I desire to inquire of the Chair whether any of the time that counsel were entitled to under the order of the Commission remains, or whether it has been exhausted. The Chair was not certain yesterday on that point.

The PRESIDENT. The time on the side of the objectors to certificates Nos. 1 and 3 was exhausted. In regard to the time remaining on the part of the objectors to certificate No. 2, I find that I made an error in my announcement yesterday, by the correction of my associate, Judge Miller, and the journal clerk. By these corrections I am advised that ten minutes are left to that side, but, substantially, the time is exhausted.

Mr. Commissioner PAYNE. I move that the time be extended to counsel on each side for one hour on the general question.

Mr. Commissioner GARFIELD. I heard no request for that.

The PRESIDENT. Mr. Payne moves that one hour on each side be allowed to counsel for the discussion of the main question that remains.

Mr. Commissioner GARFIELD. I wish to say that the order under which four hours and a half of time were allowed to each side for the discussion of the whole question was proceeding to be executed when it was intercepted by an offer of testimony, and it was then agreed that two additional hours should be given to each side for the discussion of that question. After that agreement was entered into, it was also agreed that the counsel might draw on their final time on the whole question and use it on that interlocutory question, if they chose to do so.

The PRESIDENT. And they did use it up.

Mr. Commissioner GARFIELD. They did use it up, and they discussed the whole question, together with the interlocutory question. The counsel have not asked for additional time; and if they had, I should myself consider that we ought to stand by our order. I shall vote against the motion of Mr. Payne.

The PRESIDENT. The motion is that an hour on each side be allowed for argument.

Mr. Commissioner MORTON. Unless counsel desire that, I shall certainly vote against it.

Mr. EVARTS. I think that counsel distinctly presented to the Commission, and certainly felt thoroughly, that the discussion thus opened to them covered the whole merits of the case. That was our view.

The PRESIDENT. You are satisfied, then?

Mr. EVARTS. We are satisfied with the discussion as it now stands.

The PRESIDENT. I will put the same inquiry to counsel on the other side.

Mr. CAMPBELL. The time which was granted by the Commission was granted with a view to the discussion of the questions arising on the case presented. We have nothing to add to the case we have submitted to the Commission.

Mr. Commissioner PAYNE. Then I withdraw the motion.

Mr. Commissioner ABBOTT. I understand you to say, Judge Campbell, that the Commission having ruled out all the evidence you offered, you have nothing further to add before the deed is done.

Mr. CAMPBELL. Nothing, sir.

The PRESIDENT. The motion of Mr. Payne is withdrawn.

Mr. Commissioner MORTON. I move that a committee of three members of the Commission be appointed to prepare the report, and that we take an intermission of one hour for that purpose.

Mr. Commissioner THURMAN. What is that motion?

The PRESIDENT. The motion is that a committee of three be appointed——

Mr. Commissioner STRONG. Allow me to suggest that the only question formally passed on is the question of the admissibility of the evidence that was offered. We have not passed on the merits of the case, formally at least. I think we ought first to go into deliberation for that purpose.

Mr. Commissioner MORTON. I withdraw the motion.

Mr. Commissioner STRONG. It is possible that on a discussion of the merits of the case among ourselves we may come to a conclusion which nobody is now authorized to anticipate.

Mr. Commissioner HOAR. I move that the Commission go into consultation.

The motion was agreed to; and (at five o'clock and twenty-five minutes p. m.) the Commission proceeded to consultation with closed doors.

Mr. Commissioner MORTON offered the following resolution:

Resolved, That the persons named as electors in certificate No. 1 were the lawful electors of the State of Louisiana, and that their votes are the votes provided by the Constitution of the United States, and should be counted for President and Vice-President.

Mr. Commissioner THURMAN offered the following as a substitute:

Strike out all after the word "resolved," and insert:

That inasmuch as the votes of the people of Louisiana for electors of President and Vice-President in November last have never been legally canvassed and declared, therefore the votes purporting to be votes of electors of that State for President and Vice-President ought not to be counted, and no electors of President and Vice-President can be regarded as chosen in that State.

The question being on the adoption of the substitute, it was decided in the negative:

Yeas.. 7
Nays.. 8

Those who voted in the affirmative were: Messrs. Abbott, Bayard, Clifford, Field, Hunton, Payne, and Thurman—7.

Those who voted in the negative were: Messrs. Bradley, Edmunds, Frelinghuysen, Garfield, Hoar, Miller, Morton, and Strong—8.

Mr. Commissioner HUNTON moved to amend by striking out all after the word "resolved" and inserting:

That the votes purporting to be the electoral votes of the State of Louisiana be not counted.

The question being on the adoption of the amendment, it was decided in the negative:

Yeas.. 7
Nays.. 8

Those who voted in the affirmative were: Messrs. Abbott, Bayard, Clifford, Field, Hunton, Payne, and Thurman—7.

Those who voted in the negative were: Messrs. Bradley, Edmunds, Frelinghuysen, Garfield, Hoar, Miller, Morton, and Strong—8.

And the question recurring on the adoption of the resolution of Mr. Commissioner Morton, it was decided in the affirmative:

Yeas.. 8
Nays.. 7

Those who voted in the affirmative were: Messrs. Bradley, Edmunds, Frelinghuysen, Garfield, Hoar, Miller, Morton, and Strong—8.

Those who voted in the negative were: Messrs. Abbott, Bayard, Clifford, Field, Hunton, Payne, and Thurman—7.

Mr. Commissioner MILLER moved that Commissioners Strong, Frelinghuysen, and Bradley be a committee to draft a report, as required by law, of the action of the Commission in the matter pending.

Mr. Commissioner GARFIELD moved that said committee consist of Commissioners Edmunds, Bradley, and Miller, the committee appointed to prepare the report of the Commission in the case of the State of Florida.

On motion,

Mr. Commissioner Edmunds was excused from serving on said committee on account of ill-health.

And on motion of Mr. Commissioner FRELINGHUYSEN,

Commissioners Miller, Hoar, and Bradley were appointed as said committee.

On motion of Mr. Commissioner MILLER, (at six o'clock and five minutes p. m.,) the Commission took a recess until seven o'clock p. m.

The recess having expired, on motion of Mr. Commissioner HOAR, the Commission took a further recess until seven o'clock and fifteen minutes p. m.

After the recess,

Mr. Commissioner MILLER, on behalf of the committee to prepare a report of the action of the Commission in the matter of the electoral vote of the State of Louisiana, offered the following:

Ordered, That the following be adopted and signed by those members of the Commission agreeing therein, as the decision of the Commission on the matters submitted to it touching the electoral votes of the State of Louisiana, and the brief grounds of said decision, and be transmitted by the President of the Commission, with all the accompanying papers, to the President of the Senate, to be laid before the two Houses of Congress at the meeting provided for in said act.

ELECTORAL COMMISSION,
Washington, D. C., February 16, A. D. 1877.

To the President of the Senate of the United States, presiding in the meeting of the two Houses of Congress, under the act of Congress entitled "An act to provide for and regulate the counting of votes for President and Vice-President, and the decision of questions arising thereon, for the term commencing March 4, A. D. 1877," approved January 29, A. D. 1877.

The Electoral Commission mentioned in said act having received certain certificates and papers purporting to be certificates, and papers accompanying the same, of the electoral votes from the State of Louisiana, and the objections thereto, submitted to it, under said act, now report, that it has duly considered the same, pursuant to said act, and has, by a majority of votes, decided, and does hereby decide, that the votes of William P. Kellogg, J. Henri Burch, Peter Joseph, Lionel A. Sheldon, Morris Marks, Aaron B. Levissee, Orlando H. Brewster, and Oscar Joffrion, named in the certificate of William P. Kellogg, governor of said State, which votes are certified by said persons, as appears by the certificates submitted to the Commission, as aforesaid, and marked Nos. one (1) and three (3) by said Commission, and herewith returned, are the votes provided for by the Constitution of the United States, and that the same are lawfully to be counted as therein certified, namely: Eight (8) votes for Rutherford B. Hayes, of the State of Ohio, for President, and eight (8) votes for William A. Wheeler, of the State of New York, for Vice-President.

The Commission has, by a majority of votes, also decided, and does hereby decide and report, that the eight persons first above named were duly appointed electors in and by the said State of Louisiana.

The brief ground of this decision is that it appears, upon such evidence as by the Constitution and the law named in said act of Congress is competent and pertinent to the consideration of the subject, that the beforementioned electors appear to have been lawfully appointed such electors of President and Vice-President of the United States for the term beginning March 4, A. D. 1877, of the State of Louisiana, and that they voted as such at the time and in the manner provided for by the Constitution of the United States and the law.

And the Commission has by a majority of votes decided, and does hereby decide, that it is not competent, under the Constitution and the law as it existed at the date of the passage of said act, to go into evidence *aliunde* the papers opened by the President of the Senate in the presence of the two Houses to prove that other persons than those regularly certified to by the governor of the State of Louisiana, on and according to the determination and declaration of their appointment by the returning-officers for elections in the said State prior to the time required for the performance of their duties, had been appointed electors, or by counter-proof to show that they had not, or that the determination of the said returning-officers was not in accordance with the truth and the fact, the Commission by a majority of votes being of opinion that it is not within the jurisdiction of the two Houses of Congress assembled to count the votes for President and Vice-President to enter upon a trial of such question.

The Commission by a majority of votes is also of opinion that it is not competent to prove that any of said persons so appointed electors as aforesaid held an office of trust or profit under the United States at the time when they were appointed, or that they were ineligible under the laws of the State, or any other matter offered to be proved *aliunde* the said certificates and papers.

The Commission is also of opinion by a majority of votes that the returning-officers of elections who canvassed the votes at the election for electors in Louisiana were a legally-constituted body, by virtue of a constitutional law, and that a vacancy in said body did not vitiate its proceedings.

The Commission has also decided, and does hereby decide, by a majority of votes, and report, that as a consequence of the foregoing and upon the grounds before stated, the paper purporting to be a certificate of the electoral vote of said State of Louisiana, objected to by T. O. Howe and others, marked "N. C. No. 2" by the Commission, and herewith returned, is not the certificate of the votes provided for by the Constitution of the United States, and that they ought not to be counted as such.

Done at Washington the day and year first above written.

The question being on the adoption of the report of the committee, it was decided in the affirmative:

YEAS 8
NAYS 7

Those who voted in the affirmative were: Messrs. Bradley, Edmunds, Frelinghuysen, Garfield, Hoar, Miller, Morton, and Strong—8.

Those who voted in the negative were: Messrs. Abbott, Bayard, Clifford, Field, Hunton, Payne, and Thurman—7.

So the report of the committee was adopted; and the decision and report were thereupon signed by the members agreeing therein, as follows:

> SAM. F. MILLER.
> W. STRONG.
> JOSEPH P. BRADLEY.
> GEO. F. EDMUNDS.
> O. P. MORTON.
> FRED'K T. FRELINGHUYSEN.
> JAMES A. GARFIELD.
> GEORGE F. HOAR.

On motion of Mr. Commissioner GARFIELD, it was

Ordered, That when the Commissioners adjourn, it be until to-morrow at four o'clock p. m.

Mr. Commissioner MILLER offered the following :

Ordered, That the President of the Commission sign and transmit to the President of the Senate the following letter, to wit:

"WASHINGTON, D. C., *February* 16, *A. D.* 1877.

"SIR: I am directed by the Electoral Commission to inform the Senate that it has considered and decided upon the matters submitted to it, under the act of Congress concerning the same, touching the electoral votes from the State of Louisiana, and herewith, by direction of said Commission, I transmit to you the said decision, in writing, signed by the members agreeing therein, to be read at the meeting of the two Houses, according to said act. All the certificates and papers sent to the Commission by the President of the Senate are herewith returned.

" Hon. THOMAS W. FERRY,
  " *President of the Senate.*"

The question being on the adoption of the order, it was determined in the affirmative, and the letter was accordingly signed as follows :

"NATHAN CLIFFORD,
" *President of the Commission.*"

Mr. Commissioner MILLER offered the following order :

Ordered, That the President of the Commission sign and transmit to the Speaker of the House of Representatives the following letter:

" WASHINGTON, D. C., *February* 16, 1877.

" SIR: I am directed by the Electoral Commission to inform the House of Representatives that it has considered and decided upon the matters submitted to it, under the act of Congress concerning the same, touching the electoral votes from the State of Louisiana, and has transmitted said decision to the President of the Senate, to be read at the meeting of the two Houses, according to said act."

" Hon. SAMUEL J. RANDALL,
  " *Speaker of the House of Representatives.*"

The question being on the adoption of the order, it was decided in the affirmative ; and the letter was accordingly signed as follows :

"NATHAN CLIFFORD,
" *President of the Commission.*"

On motion of Mr. Commissioner ABBOTT,

Ordered, That the injunction of secrecy imposed on all former consultations of the Commission be removed.

At eight o'clock and fifty-seven minutes p. m. the Commission adjourned.

PROCEEDINGS OF THE TWO HOUSES.

IN SENATE, *Saturday, February* 17, 1877.

The recess taken on the previous day having expired, the Senate resumed its session at ten o'clock a. m. on Saturday, the 17th of February.

The PRESIDENT *pro tempore* laid before the Senate the following communication, which was read :

WASHINGTON, D. C., *February* 17, 1877.

SIR: I am directed by the Electoral Commission to inform the Senate that it has considered and decided upon the matters submitted to it under the act of Congress concerning the same, touching the electoral votes from the State of Louisiana, and herewith, by direction of said Commission, I transmit to you the said decision, in writing, signed by the members agreeing therein, to be read at the meeting of the two Houses, according to said act. All the certificates and papers sent to the Commission by the President of the Senate are herewith returned.

NATHAN CLIFFORD,
President of the Commission.

Hon. THOMAS W. FERRY,
  President of the Senate.

On motion of Mr. Senator HAMLIN, it was

Resolved, That the Secretary be directed to inform the House of Representatives that the President of the Electoral Commission has notified the Senate that the Commission had arrived at a decision of the question submitted to them in relation to the electoral vote of the State of Louisiana, and that the Senate is now ready to meet the House to receive the same and to proceed with the count of the electoral vote for President and Vice-President.

After waiting some time, the following message was received from the House of Representatives, by Mr. George M. Adams, its Clerk:

Mr. President: I am directed to inform the Senate that the House of Representatives will be prepared at 11 o'clock on Monday to receive the Senate in the hall for the purpose of proceeding under the provisions of the act to provide for and regulate the counting of votes for President and Vice-President.

On motion by Mr. Senator WHYTE, at two o'clock and forty-five minutes p. m.,

The Senate took a recess until Monday next, at ten o'clock a. m.

IN THE HOUSE OF REPRESENTATIVES,
Saturday, February 17, 1877.

The recess taken on the previous day having expired, the House of Representatives resumed its session on Saturday, the 17th of February, at ten o'clock a. m., and immediately, on motion of Mr. Representative Clymer, took a further recess until twelve o'clock m.; at which hour the Speaker called the House to order, and, after prayer and the reading of the Journal, laid before the House the following communication, which was read:

WASHINGTON, D. C., *February* 17, 1877.

SIR: I am directed by the Electoral Commission to inform the House of Representatives that it has considered and decided upon the matters submitted to it under the act of Congress concerning the same, touching the electoral votes from the State of Louisiana, and has transmitted said decision to the President of the Senate to be read at the meeting of the two Houses according to said act.
NATHAN CLIFFORD,
President of the Commission.

Hon. SAMUEL J. RANDALL,
Speaker of the House of Representatives.

Mr. Representative LAMAR submitted the following resolution, and demanded the previous question thereon, viz:

Resolved, That the Clerk of the House notify the Senate that the House of Representatives will be prepared at eleven o'clock a. m. on Monday to receive the Senate in the hall for the purpose of proceeding under the provisions of the act to provide for and regulate the counting the votes for President and Vice-President.

Mr. Representative KASSON made the point of order that before action was taken on the pending resolution, a message from the Senate must be received, the Secretary of the Senate being now at the door of the House with a message from that body pertinent to the said communication.

The SPEAKER overruled the point of order, on the ground that the pending resolution was also pertinent to the subject-matter of said communication, and that the previous question had been demanded thereon.

The question then recurring on the demand for the previous question, the same was seconded and the main question ordered; and being put, the resolution was adopted—yeas 152, nays 111.

The following message was received from the Senate by Mr. George C. Gorham, its Secretary, viz:

Mr. Speaker: I am directed by the Senate to inform the House that the president of the Electoral Commission has notified the Senate that the Commission had arrived at a decision on the question submitted to them in relation to the electoral votes of the State of Louisiana, and that the Senate is now ready to meet the House to receive the same and proceed with the count of the electoral vote for President and Vice-President.

On motion of Mr. Representative LAMAR, the House (at one o'clock and twenty minutes p. m.) took a recess until Monday next, at ten o'clock a. m.

ELECTORAL COMMISSION.

SATURDAY, *February* 17, 1877.

The Commission met at four o'clock p. m., pursuant to adjournment; and, on motion of Mr. Commissioner STRONG, the Commission adjourned until Monday, the 19th instant, at four o'clock p. m.

MONDAY, *February* 19, 1877.

The Commission met at four o'clock p. m., pursuant to adjournment; and, on motion of Mr. Commissioner STRONG, the Commission adjourned until Tuesday, the 20th instant, at four o'clock p. m.

PROCEEDINGS OF THE TWO HOUSES.

JOINT MEETING.

MONDAY, *February* 19, 1877.

Each House resumed its session at ten o'clock a. m. At eleven o'clock a. m. the Senate appeared in the hall of the House of Representatives, and was announced by the Doorkeeper of the House.

The Senate entered the hall preceded by its Sergeant-at-Arms, and headed by its President *pro tempore* and its Secretary, the members and officers of the House rising to receive them.

The PRESIDENT *pro tempore* of the Senate took his seat as Presiding Officer of the joint meeting of the two Houses, the Speaker of the House occupying a chair upon his left.

The PRESIDING OFFICER. The joint meeting of Congress for counting the electoral vote resumes its session.

The objections presented to the certificates from the State of Louisiana having been submitted to the Commission, the two Houses have reconvened to receive and consider the decision of that tribunal. The decision, which is in writing, by a majority of the Commission, and signed by the members agreeing therein, will now be read by the Secretary of the Senate, and be entered in the Journal of each House.

The Secretary of the Senate read as follows:

ELECTORAL COMMISSION,
Washington, D. C., February 16, *A. D.* 1877.

To the President of the Senate of the United States, presiding in the meeting of the two Houses of Congress under the act of Congress entitled "An act to provide for and regulate the counting of the votes for President and Vice-President, and the decision of questions arising thereon, for the term commencing March 4, A. D. 1877," approved January 29, A. D. 1877:

The Electoral Commission mentioned in said act, having received certain certificates and papers purporting to be certificates, and papers accompanying the same, of the electoral votes from the State of Louisiana, and the objections thereto submitted to it, under said act, now report, that it has duly considered the same pursuant to said act, and has by a majority of votes decided, and does hereby decide, that the votes of William P. Kellogg, J. Henri Burch, Peter Joseph, Lionel A. Sheldon, Morris Marks, Aaron B. Levissee, Orlando H. Brewster, and Oscar Joffrion, named in the certificate of William P. Kellogg, governor of said State, which votes are certified by said persons, as appears by the certificates submitted to the Commission, as aforesaid, and marked Nos. one (1) and three (3) by said Commission, and herewith returned, are the votes provided for by the Constitution of the United States, and that the same are lawfully to be counted as therein certified, namely:

Eight (8) votes for Rutherford B. Hayes, of the State of Ohio, for President; and Eight (8) votes for William A. Wheeler, of the State of New York, for Vice-President.

The Commission has by a majority of votes also decided, and does hereby decide and report, that the eight persons first above named were duly appointed electors in and by the said State of Louisiana.

The brief ground of this decision is, that it appears, upon such evidence as by the Constitution and the law named in said act of Congress is competent and pertinent to the consideration of the subject, that the before-mentioned electors appear to have been lawfully appointed such electors of President and Vice-President of the United States for the term beginning March 4, A. D. 1877, of the State of Louisiana, and that they voted as such at the time and in the manner provided for by the Constitution of the United States and the law.

And the Commission has by a majority of votes decided, and does hereby decide, that it is not competent under the Constitution and the law as it existed at the date of the passage of said act, to go into evidence *aliunde* the papers opened by the President of the Senate in the presence of the two Houses, to prove that other persons than those regularly certified to by the governor of the State of Louisiana, on and according to the determination and declaration of their appointment by the returning-officers for elections in the said State prior to the time required for the performance of their duties, had been appointed electors, or by counter-proof to show that they had not, or that the determination of the said returning-officers was not in accordance with the truth and the fact; the Commission, by a majority of votes, being of opinion that it is not within the jurisdiction of the two Houses of Congress assembled to count the votes for President and Vice-President to enter upon a trial of such questions.

The Commission, by a majority of votes, is also of opinion that it is not competent to prove that any of said persons so appointed electors as aforesaid held an office of trust or profit under the United States at the time when they were appointed, or that they were ineligible under the laws of the State, or any other matter offered to be proved *aliunde* the said certificates and papers.

The Commission is also of opinion by a majority of votes that the returning-officers of elections who canvassed the votes at the election for electors in Louisiana were a legally constituted body, by virtue of a constitutional law, and that a vacancy in said body did not vitiate its proceedings.

The Commission has also decided, and does hereby decide, by a majority of votes, and report, that as a consequence of the foregoing and upon the grounds before stated the paper purporting to be a certificate of the electoral vote of said State of Louisiana, objected to by T. O. Howe and others, marked " N. C. No. 2" by the Commission, and herewith returned, is not the certificate of the votes provided for by the Constitution of the United States, and that they ought not to be counted as such.

Done at Washington the day and year first above written.

SAM. F. MILLER.
W. STRONG.
JOSEPH P. BRADLEY.
GEO. F. EDMUNDS.
O. P. MORTON.
FRED'K T. FRELINGHUYSEN.
JAMES A. GARFIELD.
GEORGE F. HOAR.

The PRESIDING OFFICER. Are there any objections to the decision of the Commission?

Mr. Representative GIBSON submitted the following objections to the decision and report of the Commission, which were read by the Clerk of the House, viz:

The following objections are interposed by the undersigned, Senators and Representatives, to the decision made by the Commission constituted by the act entitled "An act to provide for and regulate the counting of votes for President and Vice-President and the decision of question arising thereon, for the term commencing March 4,

A. D. 1877,' as to the true and lawful electoral vote of the State of Louisiana, for the following reasons, viz :

First. For that the said Commission as guides to their action adopted and rejected resolutions as follows :

"FRIDAY, *February* 16, 1877.

"The Commission met at 10 o'clock a. m., pursuant to adjournment, with closed doors, for the purpose of consultation on the question submitted relative to the offers of proof connected with the objections raised to the certificates of electoral votes from the State of Louisiana.

"After debate,

"Mr. Commissioner HOAR submitted the following order :

"*Ordered,* That the evidence offered be not received.

"Mr. Commissioner ABBOTT offered the following as a substitute for the proposed order :

"*Resolved,* That evidence will be received to show that so much of the act of Louisiana establishing a returning-board for that State is unconstitutional, and the acts of said returning-board are void.

"The question being on the adoption of the substitute, it was decided in the negative :
Yeas 7
Nays 8

"Those who voted in the affirmative were : Messrs. Abbott, Bayard, Clifford, Field, Hunton, Payne, and Thurman—7.

"Those who voted in the negative were : Messrs. Bradley, Edmunds, Frelinghuysen, Garfield, Hoar, Miller, Morton, and Strong—8.

"Mr. Commissioner ABBOTT offered the following as a substitute :

"*Resolved,* That evidence will be received to show that the returning-board of Louisiana, at the time of canvassing and compiling the vote of that State at the last election in that State, was not legally constituted under the law establishing it, in this : that it was composed of four persons all of one political party, instead of five persons of different political parties, as required by the law establishing said board.

"The question being on the adoption of the substitute, it was decided in the negative :
Yeas 7
Nays 8

"Those who voted in the affirmative were : Messrs. Abbott, Bayard, Clifford, Field, Hunton, Payne, and Thurman—7.

"Those who voted in the negative were : Messrs. Bradley, Edmunds, Frelinghuysen, Garfield, Hoar, Miller, Morton, and Strong—8.

"Mr. Commissioner ABBOTT offered the following as a substitute :

"*Resolved,* That the Commission will receive testimony on the subject of the frauds alleged in the specifications of the counsel for the objectors to certificates Nos. 1 and 3.

"The question being on the adoption of the substitute, it was decided in the negative :
Yeas 7
Nays 8

"Those who voted in the affirmative were : Messrs. Abbott, Bayard, Clifford, Field, Hunton, Payne, and Thurman—7.

"Those who voted in the negative were : Messrs. Bradley, Edmunds, Frelinghuysen, Garfield, Hoar, Miller, Morton, and Strong—8.

"Mr. Commissioner ABBOTT offered the following as a substitute :

"*Resolved,* That testimony tending to show that the so-called returning-board of Louisiana had no jurisdiction to canvass the votes for electors of President and Vice-President is admissible.

"The question being on the adoption of the substitute, it was determined in the negative :
Yeas 7
Nays 8

"Those who voted in the affirmative were : Messrs. Abbott, Bayard, Clifford, Field, Hunton, Payne, and Thurman—7.

"Those who voted in the negative were : Messrs. Bradley, Edmunds, Frelinghuysen, Garfield, Hoar, Miller, Morton, and Strong—8.

"Mr. Commissioner ABBOTT offered the following as a substitute :

"*Resolved,* That evidence is admissible that the statements and affidavits purporting to have been made and forwarded to said returning-board in pursuance of the provisions of section 26 of the election law of 1872, alleging riot, tumult, intimidation, and violence at or near certain polls and in certain parishes, were falsely fabricated and forged by certain disreputable persons under the direction and with the knowledge of said returning-board, and that said returning-board, knowing said statements and affidavits to be false and forged, and that none of the said statements or affidavits were made in the manner or form or within the time required by law, did knowingly, willfully, and fraudulently fail and refuse to canvass or compile more than ten thousand votes lawfully cast, as is shown by the statements of votes of the commissioners of election.

"The question being on the adoption of the substitute, it was decided in the negative:

Yeas ... 7
Nays ... 8

"Those who voted in the affirmative were: Messrs. Abbott, Bayard, Clifford, Field, Hunton, Payne, and Thurman—7.

"Those who voted in the negative were: Messrs. Bradley, Edmunds, Frelinghuysen, Garfield, Hoar, Miller, Morton, and Strong—8.

"Mr. Commissioner HUNTON offered the following as a substitute:

"*Resolved,* That evidence be received to prove that the votes cast and given at said election on the 7th of November last for the election of electors as shown by the returns made by the commissioners of election from the several polls or voting-places in said State have never been compiled or canvassed, and that the said returning-board never even pretended to compile or canvass the returns made by said commissioners of election, but that the said returning-board only pretended to canvass the returns made by said supervisors.

"The question being on the adoption of the substitute, it was decided in the negative:

Yeas ... 7
Nays ... 8

"Those who voted in the affirmative were: Messrs. Abbott, Bayard, Clifford, Field, Hunton, Payne, and Thurman—7.

"Those who voted in the negative were: Messrs. Bradley, Edmunds, Frelinghuysen, Garfield, Hoar, Miller, Morton, and Strong—8.

"Mr. Commissioner BAYARD offered the following as a substitute:

"*Resolved,* That no person holding an office of trust or profit under the United States is eligible to be appointed an elector, and that this Commission will receive evidence tending to prove such ineligibility as offered by counsel for objectors to certificates 1 and 3.

"The question being on the adoption of the substitute, it was decided in the negative:

Yeas ... 7
Nays ... 8

"Those who voted in the affirmative were: Messrs. Abbott, Bayard, Clifford, Field, Hunton, Payne, and Thurman—7.

"Those who voted in the negative were: Messrs. Bradley, Edmunds, Frelinghuysen, Garfield, Hoar, Miller, Morton, and Strong—8.

"Mr. Commissioner FELD offered the following as a substitute:

"*Resolved,* That in the opinion of the Commission evidence is admissible upon the several matters which counsel for the objectors to certificates Nos. 1 and 3 offered to prove.

"The question being on the adoption of the substitute, it was decided in the negative:

Yeas ... 7
Nays ... 8

"Those who voted in the affirmative were: Messrs. Abbott, Bayard, Clifford, Field, Hunton, Payne, and Thurman—7.

"Those who voted in the negative were: Messrs. Bradley, Edmunds, Frelinghuysen, Garfield, Hoar, Miller, Morton, and Strong—8.

"The question then recurring on the adoption of the order submitted by Mr. Commissioner Hoar,

"Mr. Commissioner PAYNE moved to strike out the word 'not.'

"The question being on the adoption of the amendment, it was determined in the negative:

Yeas ... 7
Nays ... 8

"Those who voted in the affirmative were: Messrs. Abbott, Bayard, Clifford, Field, Hunton, Payne, and Thurman—7.

"Those who voted in the negative were: Messrs. Bradley, Edmunds, Frelinghuysen, Garfield, Hoar, Miller, Morton, and Strong—8.

"The question then recurred on the adoption of the order submitted by Mr. Commissioner Hoar in the following words:

"*Ordered,* That the evidence offered be not received.

"The question being on the adoption of the order, it was determined in the affirmative:

Yeas 8
Nays 7

"Those who voted in the affirmative were: Messrs. Bradley, Edmunds, Frelinghuysen, Garfield, Hoar, Miller, Morton, and Strong—8.

"Those who voted in the negative were: Messrs. Abbott, Bayard, Clifford, Field, Hunton, Payne, and Thurman—7.

"On motion of Mr. Commissioner FIELD, it was—

"*Ordered*, That the injunction of secrecy be removed from the proceedings of the Commission.

"The doors were thereupon opened, and the respective counsel appeared.

"The action of the Commission on the various motions and orders submitted was read.

"Mr. Commissioner HOAR. Mr. President, I desire to inquire of the Chair whether any of the time that counsel were entitled to under the order of the Commission remains, or whether it has been exhausted? The Chair was not certain yesterday on that point.

"The PRESIDENT. The time on the side of the objectors to certificates Nos. 1 and 3 was exhausted. In regard to the time remaining on the part of the objectors to certificate No. 2, I find that I made an error in my announcement yesterday, by the correction of my associate, Judge Miller, and the journal clerk. By these corrections I am advised that ten minutes are left to that side, but substantially the time is exhausted.

"Mr. Commissioner PAYNE. I move that the time be extended to counsel on each side for one hour on the general question.

"Mr. Commissioner GARFIELD. I heard no request for that.

"The PRESIDENT. Mr. Payne moves that one hour on each side be allowed to counsel for the discussion of the main question that remains.

"Mr. Commissioner GARFIELD. I wish to say that the order under which four hours and a half of time were allowed to each side for the discussion of the whole question was proceeding to be executed when it was intercepted by an offer of testimony, and it was then agreed that two additional hours should be given to each side for the discussion of that question. After that agreement was entered into, it was also agreed that the counsel might draw on their final time on the whole question, and use it on that interlocutory question if they chose to do so.

"The PRESIDENT. And they did use it up.

"Mr. Commissioner GARFIELD. They did use it up, and they discussed the whole question, together with the interlocutory question. The counsel have not asked for additional time; and if they had, I should myself consider that we ought to stand by our order. I shall vote against the motion of Mr. Payne.

"The PRESIDENT. The motion is that an hour on each side be allowed for argument.

"Mr. Commissioner MORTON. Unless counsel desire that, I shall certainly vote against it.

"Mr. EVARTS. I think that counsel distinctly presented to the Commission and certainly felt thoroughly, that the discussion thus opened to them covered 'the whole merits of the case. That was our view.

"The PRESIDENT. You are satisfied, then?

"Mr. EVARTS. We are satisfied with the discussion as it now stands.

"The PRESIDENT. I will put the same inquiry to counsel on the other side.

"Mr. CAMPBELL. The time which was granted by the Commission was granted with a view to the discussion of the questions arising on the case presented. We have nothing to add to the case we have submitted to the Commission.

"Mr. Commissioner PAYNE. Then I withdraw the motion.

"Mr. Commissioner ABBOTT. I understand you to say, Judge Campbell, that the Commission having ruled out all the evidence you offered, you have nothing further to add before the deed is done.

"Mr. CAMPBELL. Nothing, sir.

"The PRESIDENT. The motion of Mr. Payne is withdrawn.

"Mr. Commissioner MORTON. I move that a committee of three members of the Commission be appointed to prepare the report, and that we take an intermission of one hour for that purpose.

"Mr. Commissioner THURMAN. What is that motion?

"The PRESIDENT. The motion is that a committee of three be appointed——

"Mr. Commissioner STRONG. Allow me to suggest that the question formally passed on, was a question of the admissibility of the evidence that was offered. We have not passed on the merits of the case, formally at least. I think we ought first to go into deliberation for that purpose.

"Mr. Commissioner MORTON. I withdraw the motion.

"Mr. Commissioner STRONG. It is possible that on a discussion of the merits of the case among ourselves we may come to a conclusion which nobody is now authorized to anticipate.

"Mr. Commissioner HOAR. I move that the Commission go into consultation.

"The motion was agreed to; and (at 5 o'clock and 25 minutes p. m.) the Commission proceeded to consultation with closed doors.

"Mr. Commissioner MORTON offered the following:

"Resolved, That the persons named as electors in certificate No. 1 were the lawful electors of the State of Louisiana, and that their votes are the votes provided by the Constitution of the United States, and should be counted for President and Vice-President.

"Mr. Commissioner THURMAN offered the following as a substitute:

"Strike out all after the word 'Resolved,' and insert:

"'That inasmuch as the votes of the people of Louisiana for electors of President and Vice-President in November last have never been legally canvassed and declared, therefore the votes purporting to be votes of electors of that State for President and Vice-President ought not to be counted, and no electors of President and Vice-President can be regarded as chosen in that State.'

"The question being on the adoption of the substitute, it was decided in the negative:

Yeas.. 7
Nays.. 8

"Those who voted in the affirmative were: Messrs. Abbott, Bayard, Clifford, Field, Hunton, Payne, and Thurman—7.

"Those who voted in the negative were: Messrs. Bradley, Edmunds, Frelinghuysen, Garfield, Hoar, Miller, Morton, and Strong—8.

"Mr. Commissioner HUNTON moved to amend by striking out all after the word 'Resolved' and inserting—

"'That the votes purporting to be the electoral votes of the State of Louisiana be not counted.'

"The question being on the adoption of the amendment, it was decided in the negative:

Yeas.. 7
Nays.. 8

"Those who voted in the affirmative were: Messrs. Abbott, Bayard, Clifford, Field, Hunton, Payne, and Thurman—7.

"Those who voted in the negative were: Messrs. Bradley, Edmunds, Frelinghuysen, Garfield, Hoar, Miller, Morton, and Strong—8.

"And the question recurring on the adoption of the resolution of Mr. Commissioner Morton, it was decided in the affirmative:

Yeas.. 8
Nays.. 7

"Those who voted in the affirmative were: Messrs. Bradley, Edmunds, Frelinghuysen, Garfield, Hoar, Miller, Morton, and Strong—8.

"Those who voted in the negative were: Messrs. Abbott, Bayard, Clifford, Field, Hunton, Payne, and Thurman—7."

Second. For that the said Commission refused to receive evidence offered, as in the annexed paper stated, or any part of said evidence, and decided that the votes mentioned in the certificates numbered 1 and 3 shall be counted for Hayes and Wheeler, said evidence to the contrary notwithstanding.

W. H. BARNUM, Conn.,	WM. W. EATON, Conn.,	GEO. R. DENNIS, Md.
CHAS. W. JONES, Fla.,	S. B. MAXEY, Tex.,	G. GOLDTHWAITE, Ala.,
FRANCIS KERNAN, N. Y.,	T. F. RANDOLPH, N. J.,	A. S. MERRIMON, N. C.,
FRANK HEREFORD, W. Va.,	R. E. WITHERS, Va.,	T. M. NORWOOD, Ga.,
HENRY COOPER, Tenn.,	J. E. BAILEY, Tenn.,	T. C. McCREERY, Ky.,
LEWIS V. BOGY, Mo.,	H. G. DAVIS, W. Va.,	J. E. McDONALD, Ind.,

Senators.

LUCIEN L. AINSWORTH,	AYLETT H. BUCKNER,	ALEX. G. COCHRANE,
JOHN D. C. ATKINS,	GEORGE C. CABELL,	FRANCIS D. COLLINS,
JOHN C. BAGBY,	JOHN H. CALDWELL,	PHILIP COOK,
HENRY B. BANNING,	WILLIAM P. CALDWELL,	JACOB P. COWAN,
GEORGE M. BEEBE,	MILTON A. CANDLER,	SAMUEL S. COX,
RICHARD P. BLAND,	GEORGE W. CATE,	DAVID B. CULBERSON,
JAMES H. BLOUNT,	BERNARD G. CAULFIELD,	JOSEPH J. DAVIS,
ANDREW R. BOONE,	CHESTER W. CHAPIN,	REZIN A. DE BOLT,
TAUL BRADFORD,	JOHN B. CLARKE,	GEORGE G. DIBRELL,
JOHN M. BRIGHT,	JOHN B. CLARK, Jr.,	MILTON J. DURHAM,
JOHN YOUNG BROWN,	HIESTER CLYMER,	JOHN R. EDEN,

ALBERT G. EGBERT,
E. JOHN ELLIS,
CHARLES J. FAULKNER,
WILLIAM H. FELTON,
DAVID DUDLEY FIELD,
JESSE J. FINLEY,
WILLIAM H. FORNEY,
BENJAMIN J. FRANKLIN,
BENONI S. FULLER,
LUCIEN C. GAUSE,
RANDALL L. GIBSON,
JOHN M. GLOVER,
JOHN GOODE, JR.,
JOHN R. GOODIN,
THOMAS M. GUNTER,
ANDREW H. HAMILTON,
ROBERT HAMILTON,
AUG. A. HARDENBERGH,
HENRY R. HARRIS,
JOHN T. HARRIS,
CARTER H. HARRISON,
JULIAN HARTRIDGE,
WILLIAM HARTZELL,
ROBERT A. HATCHER,
ELI J. HENKLE,
ABRAM S. HEWITT,
GOLDSMITH W. HEWITT,
BENJAMIN H. HILL,
WILLIAM S. HOLMAN,
CHARLES E. HOOKER,
JAMES H. HOPKINS,
JOHN F. HOUSE,
ANDREW HUMPHREYS,
FRANK H. HURD,
GEORGE A. JENKS,
FRANK JONES,
THOMAS L. JONES,
EDWARD C. KEHR,
J. PROCTOR KNOTT,

LUCIUS Q. C. LAMAR,
FRANKLIN LANDERS,
GEORGE M. LANDERS,
LAFAYETTE LANE,
WILLIAM M. LEVY,
BURWELL B. LEWIS,
JOHN K. LUTTRELL,
WILLIAM P. LYNDE,
L. A. MACKEY,
LEVI MAISH,
WILLIAM McFARLAND,
JOHN A. McMAHON,
HENRY B. METCALFE,
CHARLES W. MILLIKEN,
ROGER Q. MILLS,
HERNANDO D. MONEY,
CHARLES H. MORGAN,
WILLIAM R. MORRISON,
WILLIAM MUTCHLER,
LAWRENCE T. NEAL,
JEPTHA D. NEW,
JOHN F. PHILIPS,
EARLEY F. POPPLETON,
JOSEPH POWELL,
SAMUEL J. RANDALL,
DAVID REA,
JOHN H. REAGAN,
JOHN REILLY,
JAMES B. REILLY,
AMERICUS V. RICE,
HAYWOOD Y. RIDDLE,
JOHN ROBBINS,
WILLIAM M. ROBBINS,
MILES ROSS,
JOHN S. SAVAGE,
MILTON SAYLER,
ALFRED M. SCALES,
JOHN G. SCHUMAKER,
JAMES SHEAKLEY,

OTHO R. SINGLETON,
WILLIAM F. SLEMONS,
MILTON I. SOUTHARD,
WILLIAM A. J. SPARKS,
WILLIAM M. SPRINGER,
WILLIAM H. STANTON,
WILLIAM S. STENGER,
ADLAI E. STEVENSON,
WILLIAM H. STONE,
THOMAS SWANN,
JOHN K. TARBOX,
FREDERICK H. TEESE,
WILLIAM TERRY,
CHARLES P. THOMPSON,
PHILIP F. THOMAS,
J. W. THROCKMORTON,
JOHN R. TUCKER,
JACOB TURNEY,
JOHN L. VANCE,
ROBERT B. VANCE,
ALFRED M. WADDELL,
ANSEL T. WALLING,
ELIJAH WARD,
LEVI WARNER,
WILLIAM W. WARREN,
HENRY WATTERSON,
ERASTUS WELLS,
WASH. C. WHITTHORNE,
PETER D. WIGGINTON,
ALPHEUS S. WILLIAMS,
JAMES WILLIAMS,
JERE N. WILLIAMS,
BENJAMIN A. WILLIS,
WILLIAM W. WILSHIRE,
BENJAMIN WILSON,
FERNANDO WOOD,
JESSE J. YEATES,
CASEY YOUNG,
Representatives.

The "annexed paper" referred to in the foregoing is as follows:

I.

We offer to prove that William P. Kellogg, who certifies as governor of the State of Louisiana to the appointment of electors of that State, which certificate is now before this Commission, is the same William P. Kellogg who, by said certificate, was certified to have been appointed one of said electors. In other words, that Kellogg certified his own appointment as such elector.

That said Kellogg was governor *de facto* of said State during all the months of November and December, A. D. 1876.

CONSTITUTION OF LOUISIANA.

ART. 117. No person shall hold or exercise at the same time more than one office of trust or profit, except that of justice of the peace or notary public."

II.

We offer to prove that said William P. Kellogg was not duly appointed one of the electors of said State in A. D. 1876, and that the certificate is untrue in fact.

To show this we offer to prove—

(1) By certified copies of the lists made out, signed, and sworn to by the commissioners of election in each poll and voting-place in the State, and delivered by said commissioners to the clerk of the district court wherein said polls were established, except in the parish of Orleans, and in that parish delivered to the secretary of state, that at the election for electors in the State of Louisiana, on the 7th day of November last, the said William P. Kellogg received for elector 6,300 votes less than were at said election cast for each and every of the following-named persons, that is to say: John McEnery, R. C. Wickliffe, L. St. Martin, E. P. Poché, A. De Blanc; W. A. Seay, R. G. Cobb, K. A. Cross. (Sec. 43, act 1872.)

(2) In connection with the certified copies of said lists we offer to prove that the

returning-board, which pretended to canvass the said election under the act approved November 20, 1872, did not receive from any poll, voting-place, or parish in said State, nor have before them, any statement of any supervisor of registration or commissioner of election in form as required by section 26 of said act, on affidavit of three or more citizens, of any riot, tumult, acts of violence, intimidation, armed disturbance, bribery, or corrupt influences which prevented or tended to prevent a fair, free, and peaceable vote of all qualified electors entitled to vote at such poll or voting-place.

(3) We further offer to show that in many instances the supervisors of registration of the several parishes willfully and fraudulently omitted from their consolidated statement, returned by them to the State returning-board, the result and all mention of the votes given at certain polls or voting-places within their respective parishes, as shown to them by the returns and papers returned to said supervisors by the commissioners of election, as required by law; and that in consequence of this omission the said consolidated statements, on their face, omitted of majorities against the said Kellogg, and in favor of each and every the said McEnery, Wickliffe, St. Martin, Poché, De Blanc, Seay, Cobb, and Cross, amounting to 2,267, but that said supervisors of registration did, as by law required, return to the said returning-board, with their consolidated statements, the lists, papers, and returns received by them according to law from the commissioners of election at the several polls and voting-places omitted as aforesaid from said consolidated statements of said supervisors.

And that the said returning-board willfully and fraudulently neglected and refused to make any canvass of the majorities so omitted, or estimate them in any way in their pretended determination that the said Kellogg was duly elected an elector at the election aforesaid.

(4) We offer to show that by the consolidated statements returned to said returning-board by the supervisors of registration of the several parishes of the State of the result of the voting at the several polls or voting-places within their parishes respectively, it appeared that said Kellogg received at said election 3,459 less votes for elector than said McEnery, Wickliffe, St. Martin, Poché, De Blanc, Seay, Cobb, and Cross, and each and every of them.

(5) We further offer to show that the said returning-board willfully and fraudulently estimated and counted as votes in favor of said Kellogg 234 votes which were not shown to have been given at any poll or voting-place in said State, either by any consolidated statement returned to said returning-board by any of the said supervisors, nor by the statements, lists, tally-sheets, or returns made by any commissioners of election to any of said supervisors, or which were before said returning-board.

(6) We offer to prove that the votes cast and given at said election on the 7th of November last for the election of electors, as shown by the return made by the commissioners of election from the several polls or voting-places in said State, have never been compiled nor canvassed; and that the said returning-board never even pretended to compile or canvass the returns made by said commissioners of election, but that said returning-board only pretended to canvass the returns made by the said supervisor.

Act of 1872, section 43: "Supervisor must forward." Act of 1872, section 2: "Board must canvass."

(7) We offer to prove that the votes given for electors at the election of November 7 last at the several voting-places or polls in said State have never been opened by the governor of the said State in presence of the secretary of state, the attorney-general, and a district judge of the district in which the seat of government was established, nor in the presence of any of them; nor has the governor of said State ever, in presence as aforesaid, examined the returns of the commissioners of election for said election to ascertain therefrom, nor has he ever, in such presence, ascertained therefrom, the persons who were, or whether any one was, duly elected electors or elector at said election; nor has he ever pretended so to do. (Revised Statutes, section 2826.)

(8) We further offer to prove—

That the said William P. Kellogg, governor as aforesaid, when he made, executed, and delivered the said certificate, by which he certified that himself and others had been duly appointed electors as aforesaid, well knew that said certificate was untrue in fact in that behalf, and that he, the said Kellogg, then well knew that he, the said Kellogg, had not received, of the legal votes cast at the election of November 7, 1876, for electors, within five thousand of as many of such votes as had at said election been cast and given for each and every of the said McEnery, Wickliffe, St. Martin, Poché, De Blanc, Seay, Cobb, and Cross; and that he, the said Kellogg, when he made and executed the aforesaid certificate, well knew that of the legal votes cast at the popular election held in the State of Louisiana on the 7th day of November last, for the election of electors in said State, as shown by the lists, returns, and papers sent, according to law, by the commissioners of election, who presided over and conducted the said election at the several polls and voting-places in said State, to the supervisors of registration, and as shown by the said lists, returns, papers, and ballots deposited by said commissioners of elections in the office of the clerks of the district courts, except the parish of Orleans, and deposited for the parish of Orleans in the office of secretary of state, according to law, that each and every the said McEnery, Wickliffe, St. Martin, Poché, De Blanc, Seay, Cobb, and Cross had received more than five thousand of the legal votes cast at said election for electors more than had been cast and given at said election for the said Kellogg as elector, and that the said McEnery, Wickliffe, St. Martin, Poché, De Blanc, Seay, Cobb, and Cross had been thus and thereby duly appointed electors for said State in the manner directed by the legislature of said State..

(9) We further offer to prove—

That at the city of New Orleans, in the State of Louisiana, in the month of October, A. D. 1876, the said William P. Kellogg, J. H. Burch, Peter Joseph, L. A. Sheldon, Morris Marks, A. B. Levissee, O. H. Brewster, Oscar Joffrion, S. B. Packard, John Ray, Frank Morey, Hugh J. Campbell, D. J. M. A. Jewett, H. C. Dibble, Michael Hahn, B. P. Blanchard, J. R. G. Pitkin, J. Madison Wells, Thomas C. Anderson, G. Casanave, L. M. Kenner, George P. Davis, W. L. Catlin, C. C. Nash, George L. Smith, Isadore McCormick, and others entered into an unlawful and criminal combination and conspiracy to and with each other, and each to and with each of the others, to cause it to be certified and returned to the secretary of state by the returning-board of said State, upon their pretended compilation and canvass of the election for electors, to be thereafter held on the 7th day of November, A. D. 1876, that the said Kellogg, Burch, Joseph, Sheldon, Marks, Levissee, Brewster, and Joffrion had received a majority of all votes given and cast at said election for electors, whether such should be the fact or not; and

That afterward, to wit, on the 17th day of November, A. D. 1876, after said election had been held and it was well known to all of said conspirators that said Kellogg and others had not been elected at said election, but had been defeated, and their opponents had been elected at said election, the said returning-board assembled at the city of New Orleans, the seat of government of said State, to pretend to compile and canvass the statements of votes made by the commissioners of election from the several polls and voting-places in said State for presidential electors, and make returns of said election to the secretary of state, as required by an act of the legislature of that State, approved November 20, 1872; that, when said returning-board so assembled, said Wells, said Anderson, said Kenner, and said Casanave, who were all members of one political party, to wit, the republican party, were the only members of said board, there being one vacancy in said board, which vacancy it was the duty of said Wells, said Anderson, said Kenner, and said Casanave, as members of said board, to fill, then and there, by the election or appointment of some person belonging to some other political party than the republican party; but that the said Wells, Anderson, Kenner, and Casanave, then and there, in pursuance of said unlawful and criminal combination aforesaid, then and there neglected and refused to fill said vacancy, for the reason, as assigned by them, that they did not wish to have a democrat to watch the proceedings of said board; and that although frequently during the session of said board, assembled for the purpose aforesaid, they, the said Wells, Anderson, Kenner, and Casanave, were duly, and in writing, requested by said McEnery, Wickliffe, St. Martin, Poché, De Blanc, Seay, Cobb, and Cross to fill said vacancy, they refused to do so, and never did fill the same, but proceeded as such board, in pursuance of said combination and conspiracy, to make a pretended compilation and canvass of said election without filling the vacancy in said returning-board; and

That said Wells, Anderson, Kenner, and Casanave, while pretending to be in session as a returning-board for the purpose of compiling and canvassing the said election, and in pursuance of said combination and conspiracy, employed persons of notoriously bad character to act as their clerks and assistants, to wit, one Davis, a man of notoriously bad character, who was then under indictment in the criminal courts of Louisiana, and said Catlin, said Blanchard, and said Jewett, three of said conspirators who were then under indictment for subornation of perjury in the criminal courts of Louisiana; the said Jewett being also under indictment in one of the criminal courts of Louisiana for obtaining money under false pretenses; and Isadore McCormick, who was then under indictment in a criminal court of said State charged with murder.

And that, in pursuance of said unlawful combination and conspiracy aforesaid, the said Wells, Anderson, Kenner, and Casanave, acting in said returning-board, confided to their said clerks and employés, said co-conspirators, the duty of compiling and canvassing all returns which were by said returning-board ordered to be canvassed and compiled; and, although thereto particularly requested by a communication, as follows—

" *To the honorable returning-board of the State of Louisiana :*

"GENTLEMEN: The undersigned, acting as counsel for the various candidates upon the democratic-conservative ticket, State, national, and municipal, with respect show:

"That the returns from various polls and parishes are inspected by this board and the vote announced by it is merely that for governor and electors;

"That the tabulation of all other votes is turned over to a corps of clerks, to be done outside of the presence of this board;

"That all of said clerks are republicans, and that the democratic-conservative candidates have no check upon them, and no means to detect errors and fraudulent tabulations, or to call the attention of this board to any such wrongs, if any exist;

"That by this system the fate of all other candidates but governor and electors is placed in the hands of a body of republican clerks, with no check against erroneous or dishonest action on their part;

"That fair play requires that some check should be placed upon said clerks and some protection afforded to the said candidates against error or dishonest action on the part of said clerks;

"Wherefore they respectfully ask that they be permitted to name three respectable persons, and that to such parties be accorded the privilege of being present in the room or rooms where said tabulation is progressing, and of inspecting the tabulation and comparing the same with the returns, and also of fully inspecting the returns, and previous to the adoption by this board of said tabulation, with a view to satisfy all parties that there has been no tampering or unfair practice in connection therewith.

"Very respectfully,

"F. C. ZACHARIE.
"CHARLES CAVANAC.
"E. A. BURKE.
"J. R. ALCÉE GAUTHREAUX.
"HENRY C. BROWN.
"FRANK McGLOIN.

"I concur herein.

"H. M. SPOFFORD,
"*Of Counsel*"—

they, the said Wells, Anderson, Kenner, and Casanave, acting as said board, expressly refused to permit any democrat, or any person selected by democrats, to be present with said clerks and assistants while they were engaged in the compilation and canvass aforesaid, or to examine into the correctness of the compilation and canvass made by said clerks and assistants as aforesaid.

And that said returning-board, in pursuance of said unlawful combination and conspiracy aforesaid, and for the purpose of concealing the animus of said board and inspiring confidence in the public mind in the integrity of their proceedings, on the 18th day of November, A. D. 1876, adopted and passed a preamble and resolution, as follows:

"Whereas this board has learned with satisfaction that distinguished gentlemen of national reputation from other States, some at the request of the President of the United States and some at the request of the national executive committee of the democratic party, are present in the city, with the view to witness the proceedings of this board in canvassing and compiling the returns of the recent election in this State for presidential electors, in order that the public opinion of the country may be satisfied as to the truth of the result and the fairness of the means by which it may have been attained; and

"Whereas this board recognizes the importance which may attach to the result of their proceedings, and that the public mind should be convinced of its justice by a knowledge of the facts on which it may be based: Therefore,

"*Be it resolved*, That this board does hereby cordially invite and request five gentlemen from each of the two bodies named, to be selected by themselves respectively, to attend and be present at the meetings of this board while engaged in the discharge of its duties under the law in canvassing and compiling the returns and ascertaining and declaring the result of said election for presidential electors, in their capacity as private citizens of eminent reputation and high character, and as spectators and witnesses of the proceedings, in that behalf, of this board."

But that said returning-board, being convinced that a compilation and canvass of votes given at said election for presidential electors, made fairly and openly, would result in defeating the object of said conspiracy, and compelling said returning-board to certify that said McEnery, Wickliffe, St. Martin, Poché, De Blanc, Seay, Cobb, and Cross had been at said election duly chosen, elected, and appointed electors by the said State of Louisiana; and, in pursuance of said unlawful combination and conspiracy, did afterward, to wit, on the 20th day of November, A. D. 1876, adopt and pass the following rules for the better execution and carrying into effect said combination and conspiracy; that is to say:

(7)

"The returning-officers, if they think it advisable, may go into secret session to consider any motion, argument, or proposition which may be presented to them; any member shall have the right to call for secret session for the above purpose."

(10)

"That the evidence for each contested poll in any parish, when concluded, shall be laid aside until all the evidence is in from all the contested polls in the several parishes where there may be contests, and after the evidence is all in the returning-officers will decide the several contests in secret session; the parties or their attorneys to be allowed to submit briefs or written arguments up to the time fixed for the returning-officers going into secret session, after which no additional argument to be received, unless by special consent."

That the proceedings thus directed to be had in secret were protested against by the said McEnery, Wickliffe, St. Martin, Poché, De Blanc, Seay, Cobb, and Cross; but said board thereafter proceeded and pretended to complete their duties as such returning-board, and did perform, execute, and carry out the most important duties devolving upon said board in secret, with closed doors, and in the absence of any member of their board belonging to the democratic party or any person whatever not a member of said board not belonging to the republican party.

That the said Wells, Anderson, Kenner, and Casanave, acting as said returning-board, while engaged in the compilation and canvass aforesaid, were applied to to permit the United States supervisors of elections, duly appointed and qualified as such, to be present at and witness such compilation or canvass.

That application was made to said returning-board in that behalf, as follows:

" *To the president and members of the returning-board of the State of Louisiana:*

"GENTLEMEN: The undersigned, of counsel for United States supervisors of election, duly appointed and qualified as such, do hereby except, protest, and object to any ruling made this 20th day of November, 1876, or that hereafter may be made, whereby they are deprived of the right of being present during the entire canvass and compilation of the results of the election lately held in the State of Louisiana, wherein electors for President and Vice-President and members of the Forty-fifth Congress were balloted for, and the result of which said board are now canvassing.

" That under the fifth section of the United States act of February 28, 1871, they are to be and remain where the ballot-boxes are kept, at all times after the polls are open, until each and every vote cast at said time and place shall be counted, and the canvass of all votes polled to be wholly completed, and the proper and requisite certificate or returns made, whether said certificate or returns be required under any law of the United States, or any State, territorial, or municipal law.

" That under said law of the United States, District Attorney J. R. Beckwith, under date of October 30, 1872, gave his written official opinion for the instruction and guidance of persons holding the office now held by protestants, wherein said United States district attorney said:

" ' It cannot be doubted that the duty of the supervisors extends to the inspection of the entire election from its commencement until the decision of its result. If the United States statutes were less explicit, there still could be no doubt of the duty and authority of the supervisors to inspect and canvass every vote cast for each and every candidate, State, parochial, and Federal, as the law of the State neither provides nor allows any separation of the election for Representatives in Congress, &c., from the election of State and parish officers. The election is in law a single election, and the power of inspection vested in law in the supervisors appointed by the court extends to the entire election, a full knowledge of which may well become necessary to defeat fraud.'

" In which opinion the attorney-general of the State of Louisiana coincided. Whereupon protestants claim admittance to all sessions of the returning-board, and protest against their exclusion as unwarranted by law, as informed by their attorneys has been done and is contemplated to be done hereafter in said proceedings of said board.

" F. C. ZACHARIE,
" E. A. BURKE,
" CHAS. CAVANAC,
" FRANK McGLOIN,
" J. R. A. GAUTHREAUX,
" H. C. BROWN,
" Of Counsel."

But that said Wells, Anderson, Kenner, and Casanave, acting as such returning-board, in further pursuance and execution of said unlawful combination and conspiracy, then and there refused to permit said United States commissioners of election to be present for the purpose aforesaid, but proceeded in their absence to the pretended compilation and canvass aforesaid.

That the said returning-board, while in session as aforesaid, for the purpose aforesaid, to wit, on the 20th day of November, 1876, adopted the following rule to govern their proceedings; that is to say:

(9)

" No *ex parte* affidavits or statements shall be received in evidence, except as a basis to show that such fraud, intimidation, or other illegal practice had at some poll requires investigation; but the returns and affidavits authorized by law, made by officers of election, or in verification of statements as required by law, shall be received in evidence as *prima facie*."

But that said board subsequently, while sitting as aforesaid, for the purposes aforesaid, having become convinced that they could not, upon other than *ex parte* testimony, so manipulate the said compilation and canvass as to declare that said Kellogg, Burch, Joseph, Sheldon, Marks, Levissee, Brewster, and Joffrion were elected electors at said election, and in further pursuance of said unlawful combination and conspiracy did subsequently modify said rule, and declare and decide that, as such returning-board, they would receive *ex parte* affidavits, under which last decision of said board over two hundred pages of *ex parte* testimony was received by said board in favor of said Kellogg and others ; and afterward, when the said McEnery and others offered *ex parte* evidence to contradict the *ex parte* evidence aforesaid, the said returning-board reversed its last decision, and refused to receive *ex parte* affidavits in contradiction as aforesaid.

And that in pursuance of said unlawful combination and conspiracy the said returning-board, in violation of a law of said State, approved November 20, 1872, neglected and refused to compile and canvass the statements of votes made by the commissioners of election which were before them according to law for canvass and compilation as aforesaid in regard to the election of presidential electors, but that said board did, in pursuance and further execution of said combination and conspiracy, canvass and compile only the consolidated statements and returns made to them by the supervisors of registration of the several parishes of said State.

And that said returning-board, in pursuance and further execution of said unlawful combination and conspiracy, did knowingly, willfully, and fraudulently refuse to compile and canvass the votes given for electors at said election in more than twenty parishes of said State, as was shown and appeared by and upon the consolidated statement and return made to them by said supervisors of said parishes.

And that said returning board did, in said canvass and compilation, count and estimate, as a foundation for their determination in the premises, hundreds of votes which had not been returned and certified to them either by the commissioners of election in said State or by the supervisors of registration in said State, they, the said members of said board, then and there well knowing that they had no right or authority to estimate the same for the purpose aforesaid.

And that said returning-board, in further pursuance and execution of said unlawful combination and conspiracy, knowingly, willfully, falsely, and fradulently did make a certificate and return to the secretary of state that said Kellogg, Burch, Joseph, Sheldon, Marks, Levissee, Brewster, and Joffrion had received majorities of all the legal votes cast at said election of November 7, 1876, for presidential electors, they then and there well knowing that the said McEnery, Wickliffe, St. Martin, Poché, De Blanc, Seay, Cobb, and Cross had received majorities of all the votes cast at said election for presidential electors, and were duly elected as the presidential electors of said State.

And that the said returning-board, in making said statement, certificate, and return to the secretary of state were not deceived or mistaken in the premises, but knowingly, willfully, and fraudulently made what they well knew when they made it was a false and fraudulent statement, certificate, and return ; and that the said false and fraudulent statement, certificate, and return, made by said returning-board to the secretary of state in that behalf, was made by the members of said returning-board in pursuance and execution of, and only in pursuance and execution of, said unlawful combination and conspiracy.

And that said returning-board, while in session as aforesaid for the purpose aforesaid, in further pursuance and execution of said unlawful combination and conspiracy, did alter, change, and forge, or cause to be altered, changed, and forged, the consolidated statement and return of the supervisor of registration for the parish of Vernon, in said State, in the manner following, to wit: The said consolidated statement, as made and returned to said board, showed that of the legal votes given in said parish for electors at said election of November 7, 1876, said McEnery received 647, said Wickliffe received 647, said St. Martin received 647, said Poché received 647, said De Blanc received 647, said Seay received 647, said Cobb received 647, said Cross received 647 ; and that said Kellogg received none, said Burch received none, said Joseph received 2, said Brewster received 2, said Marks received 2, said Levissee received 2, said Joffrion received 2, said Sheldon received 2 ; and said board altered, changed, and forged, or caused to be altered, changed, and forged, said consolidated statement so as to make the same falsely and fraudulently show that the said McEnery received 469, said Wickliffe received 469, said St. Martin received 469, said Poché received 469, said De Blanc received 469, said Seay received 469, said Cobb received 469, said Cross received 469 ; and that said Kellogg received 178, said Burch received 178, said Joseph received 178, said Sheldon received 180, said Marks received 180, said Levissee received 180, said Brewster received 180, said Joffrion received 180 ; and that said returning-board, while in session as aforesaid, for the purpose aforesaid, to pretend to justify the alteration and forgery of said consolidated statement, procured and pretended to act upon three forged affidavits, purporting to have been made and sworn to by Samuel Carter, Thomas Brown, and Samuel Collins, they, the said members of said returning-board, then and there well knowing that said pretended affidavits were false and forged, and that no such persons were in existence as purported to make said affidavits. And that said members of said return-ing-board, acting as said board, in pursuance and execution of said unlawful combina-tion and conspiracy, did, in their pretended canvass and compilation of the legal votes given at said election on the 7th day of November, A. D. 1876, for presidential electors in said State of Louisiana, as shown to them by the statements, papers, and returns made according to law by the commissioners of election presiding over and conducting said election at the several polls and voting-places in said State, all of which votes were legally cast by legal voters in said State at said election, knowingly, willfully, and fraudulently, and without any authority of law whatever, excluded and refused to count and estimate or compile or canvass votes given at said election for electors, as follows, which papers, statements, and returns were before them, and which it was their duty by law to compile and canvass, that is to say : for said John McEnery, 10,280 ; for said R. C. Wickliffe, 10,293; for said L. St. Martin, 10,291 ; for said F. P. Poché, 10,280 ; for said A. De Blanc, 10,289; for said W. A. Seay, 10,291 ; for said R. A. Cobb, 10,261; for said K. A. Cross, 10,288 ; they, the said members of said returning-board, then and there well knowing that all of said votes which they neglected and refused to canvass and compile had been duly and legally cast at said election for presidential electors by legal voters of said State ; and then and there, well knowing that had they considered, estimated, and counted, compiled, and canvassed said votes as they then and there well knew it was their duty to do, it would have appeared, and they would have been com-pelled to certify and return to the secretary of state, that said Kellogg had not been duly elected or appointed an elector for said State; but that at said election the said McEnery, the said Wickliffe, the said St. Martin, the said Poché, the said De Blanc, the said Seay, the said Cobb, and the said Cross had been duly elected and appointed presi-dential electors in said State.

And that by false, fraudulent, willful, and corrupt acts and omissions to act by said returning-board as aforesaid in the matter aforesaid, and by said nonfeasance, mis-feasance, and malfeasance of said returning-board, as hereinbefore mentioned, the said returning-board made to the secretary of state of said State the statement, certificate, and return upon which the said Kellogg, as *de facto* governor of said State, pretended to make his said false certificate, certifying that himself and others had been duly ap-pointed electors for said State, as hereinbefore mentioned ; and that said statement, certificate, and return made by said returning-board, and that the said certificate made by the said Kellogg as *de facto* governor, each, every, and all were made in pursuance and execution of said unlawful and criminal combination and conspiracy, as was well known to and intended by each and every of the members of said returning-board when they made their said false statement, certificate, and return to the secretary of state of said State, and by the said Kellogg when, as governor *de facto* of said State, he made his said false certificate hereinbefore mentioned.

III.

We further offer to prove—
That Oscar Joffrion was on the 7th day of November, A. D. 1876, supervisor of reg-istration of the parish of Point Coupee, and that he acted and officiated as such super-visor of registration for said parish at the said election for presidential electors on that day ; and that he is the same person who acted as one of the electors for said State, and on the 6th day of December, A. D. 1876, as an elector cast a vote for Rutherford B. Hayes for President of the United States, and for William A. Wheeler for Vice-President of the United States.

IV.

We further offer to prove—
That on the 7th day of November, A. D. 1876, A. B. Levissee, who was one of the pretended college of electors of the State of Louisiana, and who in said college gave a vote for Rutherford B. Hayes for President of the United States and for William A. Wheeler for Vice-President of the United States, was at the time of such election a court commissioner of the circuit court of the United States for the district of Louisi-ana, which is an office of honor, profit, and trust under the Government of the United States.

V.

We further offer to prove—
That on the 7th day of November, A. D. 1876, O. H. Brewster, who was one of the pretended electors in the pretended college of electors of the State of Louisiana, and

who in said college gave a vote for Rutherford B. Hayes for President of the United States and for William A. Wheeler for Vice-President of the United States, was at the time of such election as aforesaid holding an office of honor, profit, and trust under the Government of the United States, to wit, the office of surveyor-general of the land-office for the district of Louisiana.

VI.

We further offer to prove—
That on the 7th day of November, 1876, Morris Marks, one of the pretended electors who, in said college of electors, cast a vote for Rutherford B. Hayes for President of the United States and a vote for William A. Wheeler for Vice-President of the United States, was, ever since has been, and now is holding and exercising the office of district attorney of the fourth judicial district of said State and receiving the salary by law attached to said office.

VII.

We further offer to prove—
That on the 7th day of November, A. D. 1876, J. Henri Burch, who was one of the pretended electors, who in said pretended electoral college gave a vote for Rutherford B. Hayes for President of the United States and a vote for William A. Wheeler for Vice-President of the United States was holding the following offices under the constitution and laws of said State; that is to say: member of the board of control of the State penitentiary, also administrator of deaf and dumb asylum of said State, to both of which offices he had been appointed by the governor, with the advice and consent of the senate of said State, both being offices with salaries fixed by law, and also the office of treasurer of the parish school-board for the parish of East Baton Rouge; and that said Burch, ever since the said 7th day of November, (and prior thereto,) has exercised and still is exercising the functions of all said offices and receiving the emoluments thereof.

VIII.

We further offer to prove the canvass and compilation actually made by said return_ing-board, showing what parishes and voting-places and polls were compiled and canvassed, and what polls or voting-places were excluded by said returning-board from their canvass and compilation of votes given for presidential electors; and we also offer to show what statements and returns of the commissioners of election and of the supervisors of registration were duly before said returning-board.

IX.

We further offer to prove that a member of said returning-board offered to receive a bribe, in consideration of which the board would certify the election of the Tilden electors.

X.

We offer to prove that the statements and affidavits purporting to have been made and forwarded to said returning-board, in pursuance of the provisions of section 26 of the election-law of 1872, alleging riot, tumult, intimidation, and violence at or near certain polls and in certain parishes, were falsely fabricated and forged by certain disreputable persons under the direction and with the knowledge of said returning-board, and that said returning-board, knowing said statements and affidavits to be false and forged, and that none of said statements or affidavits were made in the manner or form required by law, did knowingly, willfully, and fraudulently fail and refuse to canvass or compile more than 10,000 votes lawfully cast, as is shown by the statements of votes of the commissioners of election.

XI.

We further offer to prove—
That said returning-board did willfully and fraudulently pretend to canvass and compile, and did promulgate as having been canvassed and compiled, certain votes for the following-named candidates for electors which were never cast, and which did not appear upon any tally-sheet, statement of votes, or consolidated statement or other return before said board, namely: J. H. Burch, 241; Peter Joseph, 1,362; L. A. Sheldon, 1,364; Morris Marks, 1,334; A. B. Levissee, 829; O. H. Brewster, 776; Oscar Joffrion 1,364.

The PRESIDING OFFICER. Are there further objections to the decision of the Commission ?

Mr. Senator WALLACE. I offer the objection which I send to the desk, signed by Senators and Representatives.

The PRESIDING OFFICER. The objection will be read by the Secretary of the Senate.

The Secretary of the Senate read as follows :

The undersigned, Senators and members of the House of Representatives, object to the decision of the Electoral Commission as to the electoral votes of the State of Louisiana, because—

First. The said decision was made in violation of the law under which said Commission acts, in this, that by said act the said Commission is required to decide whether any and what votes from such State are the votes provided for by the Constitution of the United States, and how many and what persons were duly appointed electors in said State; yet said Commission refused to examine and ascertain who were duly appointed electors in and by the State of Louisiana, and what votes from such State are within the provisions of the Constitution of the United States.

Second. Because the act creating said Commission was passed to the end that the Commission would hear and examine evidence and honestly decide which electors in any disputed State were fairly and legally chosen; whereas the said Commission refused to hear and consider evidence offered to show that the electors whose votes the said Commission has decided shall be counted were not duly chosen, but falsely and fraudulently acted as such electors, as well as the evidence offered to show that the pretended certificates of election of said electors were produced by corruption and were wholly untrue.

Third. Because the said decision is in disregard of truth, justice, and law, and establishes the demoralizing and ominous doctrine that fraud, forgery, bribery, and perjury can lawfully be used as a means to make a President of the United States against the well-known or easily ascertained will of the people and of the States.

> JNO. W. JOHNSTON,
> WM. A. WALLACE,
> J. E. BAILEY,
> GEO. R. DENNIS,
> FRANCIS KERNAN,
> JAMES K. KELLY,
> ELI SAULSBURY,
> *Senators.*
> JAMES H. HOPKINS,
> ANDREW R. BOONE,
> CHAS. B. ROBERTS,
> THOS. S. ASHE,
> H. D. MONEY,
> HIESTER CLYMER,
> *Representatives.*

The PRESIDING OFFICER. Are there further objections to the decision of the Commission?

Mr. Representative COCHRANE. I desire to offer a further objection to the decision.

The PRESIDING OFFICER. The Clerk of the House will read the objection.

The Clerk of the House read as follows:

The undersigned, Senators and Representatives, do object to the counting of the votes as recommended by eight members of the Joint Commission, and do protest against counting the electoral vote of the State of Louisiana, for the reasons following, to wit:

First. It was not denied before the Commission that the Tilden electors received a large majority of the votes cast.

Second. It was not denied before the Commission that Wells and his associates, who style themselves a returning-board, were guilty of gross fraud ; that their certificate given to the Hayes electors was false and fraudulent; and that their action in canvassing the votes was in violation of the constitution and laws of the State of Louisiana.

Third. The action of the eight members of said joint commission in declining to hear evidence of the above and other facts was a violation of the letter and spirit of the act under which said Commission was created and of the spirit of the Constitution of the United States.

R. E. WITHERS,
JOHN W. JOHNSTON,
GEORGE R. DENNIS,
HENRY COOPER,
S. B. MAXEY,
Senators.

M. I. SOUTHARD,
ALEXANDER G. COCHRANE,
JOHN H. CALDWELL,
JAMES SHEAKLEY,
A. H. BUCKNER,
WM. MUTCHLER,
BENJAMIN WILSON,
Representatives.

The PRESIDING OFFICER. Are there further objections to the decision of the Commission? [A pause.] There are none. Objections to the decision of the Commission having been submitted and read, the Senate will now withdraw to its chamber, that the two Houses separately may consider and decide upon the objections.

Accordingly (at twelve o'clock and fifty-three minutes p. m.) the Senate withdrew.

IN SENATE, *Monday, February* 19, 1877.

The Senate having returned to its chamber from the joint meeting at twelve o'clock and fifty-five minutes p. m., the President *pro tempore* took the chair and called the body to order.

The decision of the Commission and the various objections thereto presented in joint meeting having been read,

Mr. Senator SHERMAN submitted the following resolution; which (after debate and the rejection of an amendment proposed to it) was agreed to by a vote of yeas 41, nays 28, viz:

Resolved, That the decision of the Commission upon the electoral vote of the State of Louisiana stand as the judgment of the Senate, the objections made thereto to the contrary notwithstanding.

On motion of Mr. Senator HAMLIN, it was

Ordered, That the Secretary notify the House of Representatives thereof, and that the Senate is now ready to receive the House to proceed with the count of the electoral votes for President and Vice-President.

On motion of Mr. Senator WHYTE, (at three o'clock and thirty-five minutes p. m.,) it being stated that the House of Representatives had taken a recess, the Senate took a recess until Tuesday, February 20, at ten o'clock a. m.

IN THE HOUSE OF REPRESENTATIVES,
Monday, February 19, 1877.

The Senate withdrew from the hall of the House at twelve o'clock and fifty-three minutes p. m., whereupon the House of Representatives was called to order by the Speaker and resumed its session.

On motion of Mr. Representative WOOD, of New York, the House, (at one o'clock and twenty-five minutes p. m.,) by a vote of yeas 140, nays 130, took a recess until Tuesday, February 20, at ten o'clock a. m.

IN SENATE, *Tuesday, February* 20, 1877.

The Senate resumed its session at ten o'clock a. m., transacting no business; and at one o'clock and thirty minutes p. m. it was advised of the resolution of the House of Representatives on the decision of the Electoral Commission relative to the electoral vote of Louisiana, whereupon the Senate proceeded to the hall of the House of Representatives.

IN THE HOUSE OF REPRESENTATIVES,

Tuesday, February 20, 1877.

The House of Representatives resumed its session at ten o'clock a. m. A quorum not being present, a call of the House was ordered, which resulted in securing the presence of a quorum.

A message was received from the Senate announcing its action on the objections to the decision of the Electoral Commission relative to the electoral vote of Louisiana.

Mr. Representative GIBSON submitted the following resolution; which, after debate, was agreed to by a vote of yeas 173, nays 99, viz:

Ordered, That the votes purporting to be electoral votes for President and Vice-President which were given by William P. Kellogg, J. Henri Burch, Peter Joseph, Lionel A. Sheldon, Morris Marks, Aaron B. Levissee, Orlando H. Brewster, and Oscar Joffrion, claiming to be electors for the State of Louisiana, be not counted.

It was further

Ordered, That the Clerk inform the Senate of the action of this House, and that the House is now ready to meet the Senate in this hall to proceed with the counting of the electoral votes for President and Vice-President.

JOINT MEETING.

TUESDAY, *February* 20, 1877.

At one o'clock and thirty-five minutes p. m. the Senate entered the hall of the House of Representatives, preceded by its Sergeant at Arms and headed by its President *pro tempore* and its Secretary, the members and officers of the House rising to receive them.

The PRESIDENT *pro tempore* of the Senate took his seat as Presiding Officer of the joint meeting of the two Houses, the Speaker of the House occupying a chair upon his left.

The PRESIDING OFFICER. The joint meeting of Congress for counting the electoral vote resumes its session. The two Houses acting separately have considered and decided upon the objections to the decision of the Commission upon the certificates from the State of Louisiana. The Secretary of the Senate will read the resolution of the Senate.

The Secretary of the Senate read as follows:

Resolved, That the decision of the Commission upon the electoral vote of the State of Louisiana stand as the judgment of the Senate, the objections made thereto to the contrary notwithstanding.

The PRESIDING OFFICER. The Clerk of the House will now read the action of the House of Representatives.

The Clerk of the House read as follows:

Ordered, That the votes purporting to be electoral votes for President and Vice-President which were given by William P. Kellogg, J. Henri Burch, Peter Joseph, Lionel A. Sheldon, Morris Marks, Aaron B. Levissee, Orlando H. Brewster, and Oscar Joffrion, claiming to be electors for the State of Louisiana, be not counted.

The PRESIDING OFFICER. The two Houses not concurring in a contrary opinion, the decision of the Commission stands, and the counting will now proceed in conformity therewith. The tellers will announce the vote of the State of Louisiana.

Mr. Senator ALLISON, (one of the tellers.) The State of Louisiana casts 8 votes for Rutherford B. Hayes, of Ohio, for President, and 8 votes for William A. Wheeler, of New York, for Vice-President.

UNDISPUTED STATES.

The count then proceeded, the certificates from the States of—
Maine, casting 7 votes for Hayes and Wheeler;
Maryland, casting 8 votes for Tilden and Hendricks; and
Massachusetts, casting 13 votes for Hayes and Wheeler—
being opened by the Presiding Officer and read by the tellers, and the votes thereof counted without objection.

MICHIGAN.

The PRESIDING OFFICER. The Chair hands to the tellers the certificate of the electoral vote of the State of Michigan, received by messenger, and the corresponding one received by mail.

Mr. Senator ALLISON (one of the tellers) read the certificate *in extenso.*

Mr. Representative TUCKER. I offer objections, signed by Senators and Representatives according to law, to the electoral vote of Daniel L. Crossman, of the State of Michigan, and also send up a duplicate.

The PRESIDING OFFICER. The objection presented by the Representative from Virginia will be read by the Clerk of the House.

The Clerk of the House of Representatives read as follows:

The undersigned, Senators and Representatives, object to the vote of Daniel L. Crossman as an elector for the State of Michigan upon the grounds following, to wit: That a certain Benton Hanchett, of Saginaw, Michigan, was voted for and certified to have been elected and appointed an elector for the State of Michigan; that the said Benton Hanchett was on the 7th day of November, 1876, the day of the presidential election, and for a long period prior thereto had been, and up to and after the 6th day of December, 1876, the day on which the electors voted according to law, continued to be an officer of the United States, and held the office of United States commissioner under and by appointment of the United States court for Michigan, which was an office of trust and profit under the United States, and that as such officer he could not be constitutionally appointed an elector under the Constitution of the United States.

And further, that by the laws of the State of Michigan there is power to fill vacancies in the office of electors under and by virtue of the following statute, and not otherwise:

"The electors of President and Vice-President shall convene at the capital of the State on the first Wednesday of December; and if there shall be any vacancy in the office of an elector, occasioned by death, refusal to act, neglect to attend, by the hour of twelve o'clock at noon of that day, or on account of any two of such electors having received an equal and the same number of votes, the electors present shall proceed to fill such vacancy by ballot and plurality of votes, and when all the electors shall appear or vacancies shall be filled as above provided, they shall proceed to perform the duties of such electors, as required by the Constitution and laws of the United States."—*Compiled Laws of 1871*; compiler's section, 115.

And the undersigned further state that there was no vacancy in the office of elector for which said Hanchett was voted and to which he was not appointed by reason of the disqualification aforesaid; nor was any vacancy therein occasioned by the death, refusal to act, or neglect to attend of any elector at the hour of twelve o'clock at noon of the 6th day of December, 1876, nor on account of any two electors having an equal vote, nor in any manner provided for by the statute aforesaid. And the undersigned therefore object that the election of Daniel L. Crossman by the electors present at Lansing, the capital of Michigan, on the 6th day of December, 1876, was wholly without authority of law, and was void, and he was not appointed an elector in such manner as the legislature of Michigan directed.

Wherefore they say that said Daniel L. Crossman was not a duly-appointed elector for the State of Michigan, and that his vote as an elector should not be counted.

And the undersigned hereunto annex the evidence taken before the committee of the

House of Representatives on the powers, privileges, and duties of the House, to sustain said objection.

> T. M. NORWOOD, Georgia;
> WILLIAM A. WALLACE, Pennsylvania;
> W. H. BARNUM, Connecticut;
> FRANK HEREFORD, West Virginia;
> Senators.
>
> A. S. WILLIAMS, Michigan;
> J. R. TUCKER, Virginia;
> JOHN L. VANCE, Ohio;
> J. A. McMAHON,
> A. V. RICE,
> WILLIAM A. J. SPARKS,
> JOHN S. SAVAGE,
> LEVI MAISH,
> FRANK H. HURD,
> Representatives.

COMMITTEE ON PRIVILEGES, *January* 30, 1877.

BENTON HANCHETT sworn and examined.

By Mr. TUCKER:

Question. Where is your residence ?—Answer. Saginaw, Michigan.

Q. Were you a candidate for the position of presidential elector in Michigan at the late election ?—A. I was.

Q. On what ticket ?—A. On the republican ticket.

Q. Were you elected ?—A. I was.

Q. Did you vote in the college of electors?—A. I did not.

Q. Were you present ?—A. No, sir ; I was not present.

Q. Did you absent yourself ?—A. I remained away ; I did not attend.

Q. For what reason did you remain away ?—A. The facts are these: In the spring of 1863, when I was living at Owassee, in the county of Shiawasse, Michigan, some statements were made to me in reference to a man living in an adjoining town, who, I think, sold liquor and paid no taxes under the revenue law. The parties desired me to write to the district attorney, living in Detroit, in reference to the matter. I did so. I received a reply from the district attorney saying that he would have me appointed a commissioner by the United States court, and he inclosed to me instructions what to do in the case. About the same time that I received that, I received a letter from the clerk of the court saying that I had been appointed, and, I believe, inclosing the form of oath for me to take as commissioner, and, I believe, I took it and returned it to him. I have no recollection on the subject, but I suppose I did of course. I forwarded instructions to the district attorney in reference to the matter and issued a warrant for the man. He came in and paid it, the matter dropped, and there my services as commissioner ended, to the best of my recollection. It was not an office which I wanted to hold, but I performed that duty. In the fall of 1865 I went from that county to where I now reside, in Saginaw. The matter had entirely passed out of my mind. I have never acted since. Two or three days before the time appointed for the meeting of the electors, my attention was called to the subject in two ways. One was that some person spoke to me and said, " You are a United States commissioner," and the other was that I had noticed that an objection had been made to one of the electors in New Jersey on that ground. This called my mind to the circumstances which I have related to you, and in order to avoid any doubt that might arise on the subject, I determined not to meet with the electors and did not.

Q. You were, then, duly appointed United States commissioner in 1863, and acted under the appointment by issuing a warrant against a party. Have you ever resigned it ?—A. No, sir, I never made any resignation. I declined to act, and that was all there was to it.

Q. How did you decline to act ?—A. Some persons applied to me to do further duties as commissioner, and I stated that I would not act.

Q. And you never resigned your position ?—A. I never resigned my position formally.

Q. Then you failed to perform the duties of the office after the particular case mentioned ?—A. Yes, sir.

Q. But you never resigned the position ?—A. I never resigned the position.

Q. Do you know who was appointed in your place in the college of electors ?—A. I know by hearsay.

Q. Who was he ?—A. Mr. Daniel L. Crossman, of Williamstown.

By Mr. LAWRENCE:

Q. Did you resign the office of elector ?—A. No, sir.

Q. You just failed to attend ?—A. I just failed to attend.

The PRESIDING OFFICER. Are there further objections to the certificate from the State of Michigan ?

There was no further objection.

The PRESIDING OFFICER. An objection having been submitted by the member from Virginia, the Senate will now withdraw to its chamber, that the two chambers may separately consider and decide upon the objection.

The Senate accordingly withdrew to its chamber at two o'clock and twenty-five minutes p. m.

IN SENATE, *Tuesday, February* 20, 1877.

The Senate returned to its chamber from the joint meeting at two o'clock and twenty-eight minutes p. m., when the President *pro tempore* took the chair and caused the objection to the vote of D. L. Crossman, as one of the electors for the State of Michigan, to be read ;

Whereupon

Mr. Senator ALLISON submitted the following resolutions :

Resolved, That the objection made to the vote of Daniel L. Crossman, one of the electors of Michigan, is not good in law, and is not sustained by any lawful evidence.

Resolved, That said vote be counted with the other votes of the electors of said State, notwithstanding the objections made thereto.

After debate,

Mr. Senator WHYTE moved an amendment to strike out all after the first word " Resolved," and insert :

That while it is the sense of the Senate that no Senator or Representative or person holding an office of trust and profit under the United States shall be appointed an elector, and that this provision of the Constitution shall be carried in its whole spirit into rigid execution, yet that the proof is not such as to justify the exclusion of the vote of Daniel L. Crossman as one of the electors of the State of Michigan, and that his vote should be counted.

The amendment was rejected by a vote of 27 yeas, 39 nays.

Mr. Senator McDONALD moved to amend the first resolution by striking out the words " is not good in law, and."

The amendment was rejected by a vote of 26 yeas, 38 nays.

The question recurring on the resolutions submitted by Mr. Senator Allison,

A division of the question was called for by Mr. Senator Cooper.

The first resolution was agreed to by a vote of 40 yeas, 19 nays.

The second resolution was unanimously agreed to—63 yeas, 0 nay.

A message was directed to be sent to the House of Representatives, announcing the action of the Senate and its readiness to meet that House in order to proceed with the count.

At five o'clock and thirteen minutes p. m., the Senate was advised of the action of the House of Representatives, and immediately proceeded to the House hall to resume the joint meeting.

IN THE HOUSE OF REPRESENTATIVES,
Tuesday, February 20, 1877.

The Senate having withdrawn from the hall of the House of Representatives at two o'clock and twenty-five minutes p. m., the House resumed its session.

Mr. Representative SOUTHARD moved that the House take a recess until Wednesday, February 21, at ten o'clock a. m.

Mr. Representative HALE made the point of order that the motion was not in order under section 4 of the electoral act, approved January 29, 1877.

The Speaker overruled the point of order, holding that nothing in the section referred to, or in any part of the act, prohibited the taking of a recess at this stage of the proceedings.

The motion for a recess was then rejected by a vote of 57 yeas, 192 nays.

A message from the Senate was received announcing its action in the case of Daniel L. Crossman, whose vote as an elector of the State of Michigan had been objected to.

Mr. Representative TUCKER submitted the following resolution:

Resolved by the House of Representatives, That Daniel L. Crossman was not appointed an elector by the State of Michigan, as its legislature directed, and that the vote of said Daniel L. Crossman, as an elector of said State, be not counted.

After debate,

Mr. Representative JENKS offered the following as a substitute for the resolution:

Whereas the fact being established that it is about twelve years since the alleged ineligible elector exercised any of the functions of a United States commissioner, it is not sufficiently proven that at the time of his appointment he was an officer of the United States: Therefore,

Resolved, That the vote objected to be counted.

The substitute was agreed to without a division; and the resolution as amended was agreed to without a division.

A message was directed to be sent to the Senate informing it of the action of the House, and that the House was ready to receive the Senate to proceed with the count.

JOINT MEETING.

TUESDAY, *February* 20, 1877.

At 5 o'clock and 16 minutes p. m., the Senate entered the hall of the House of Representatives, preceded by the Sergeant-at-Arms and headed by its President *pro tempore* and its Secretary, the members and officers of the House rising to receive them.

The President *pro tempore* of the Senate took his seat as Presiding Officer of the joint meeting of the two Houses, the Speaker of the House occupying a chair upon his left.

The PRESIDING OFFICER. The joint meeting of Congress for counting the electoral vote resumes it session. The two Houses retired to consult separately and decide upon the vote of the State of Michigan. The Secretary of the Senate will read the resolutions adopted by the Senate.

The Secretary of the Senate read as follows:

Resolved, That the objection made to the vote of Daniel L. Crossman, one of the electors of Michigan, is not good in law, and is not sustained by any lawful evidence.

Resolved, That said vote be counted with the other votes of the electors of said State, notwithstanding the objections made thereto.

The PRESIDING OFFICER. The Clerk of the House of Representatives will now read the resolution adopted by the House of Representatives.

The Clerk of the House read as follows:

Whereas the fact being established that it is about twelve years since the alleged ineligible elector exercised any of the functions of a United States commissioner, it is not sufficiently proven that at the time of his appointment he was an officer of the United States: Therefore,

Resolved, That the vote objected to be counted.

The PRESIDING OFFICER. Neither House having concurred in a mere affirmative vote to reject the vote of the State of Michigan, the entire vote of that State will be counted as cast.

Mr. Senator ALLISON, (one of the tellers.) In the State of Michigan 11 votes were cast for Rutherford B. Hayes, of Ohio, for President, and 11 votes for William A. Wheeler, of New York, for Vice-President.

UNDISPUTED STATES.

The count then proceeded, the certificates from the States of—
Minnesota, casting 5 votes for Hayes and Wheeler;
Mississippi, casting 8 votes for Tilden and Hendricks;
Missouri, casting 15 votes for Tilden and Hendricks; and
Nebraska, casting 3 votes for Hayes and Wheeler—
being opened by the Presiding Officer and read by the tellers, and the votes thereof counted without objection.

NEVADA.

The PRESIDING OFFICER. Having opened the certificate from the State of Nevada, the Chair hands it to the tellers, who will announce the vote of that State. Is there objection to the counting of the vote of that State?

Mr. Representative SPRINGER. I submit the following objections to the counting of the vote of one of the electors of the State of Nevada.

The Clerk of the House read the objection, as follows:

The undersigned Senators and Representatives object to the vote of R. M. Daggett as an elector from the State of Nevada, upon the grounds following, namely:

That the said R. M. Daggett was, on the 7th day of November, 1876, and had been for a long period prior thereto, and thereafter continued to be, a United States commissioner for the circuit and district courts of the United States for the said State, and held therefore an office of trust and profit under the United States, and as such could not be constitutionally appointed an elector under the Constitution of the United States:

Wherefore the undersigned say that the said R. M. Daggett was not a duly-appointed elector, and that his vote as an elector should not be counted.

And the undersigned hereto annex the evidence taken before the Committee of the House of Representatives on the Powers, Privileges, and Duties of the House to sustain said objection.

                        W. H. BARNUM, Connecticut,
                        WILLIAM A. WALLACE, Pennsylvania,
                        FRANK HEREFORD, West Virginia,
                                          Senators.

                        J. R. TUCKER, Virginia,
                        JOHN L. VANCE, Ohio,
                        WM. A. J. SPARKS,
                        JNO. S. SAVAGE,
                        LEVI MAISH,
                        G. A. JENKS,
                        WILLIAM M. SPRINGER,
                                          Representatives.

                              COMMITTEE ON PRIVILEGES,
                                  Washington, February 9, 1877.

R. M. DAGGETT sworn and examined.

    By Mr. TUCKER:

Question. Were you a candidate for the office of presidential elector in the State of Nevada at the presidential election in November, 1876?—Answer. I was.

Q. Were you present in the college at the time of the vote for President and Vice-President?—A. Yes.

Q. Did you cast a vote for President and Vice-President ?—A. I did.

Q. For whom did you vote ?—A. I voted for Hayes and Wheeler.

Q. Mr. Hayes for President and Mr. Wheeler for Vice-President ?—A. Yes, sir.

Q. Are you the messenger who brought the vote to Washington by the appointment of the college ?—A. I am.

Q. Did you hold any office under the United States prior to the election ?—A. Yes.

Q. What office was that ?—A. I was clerk of the Federal courts; the district and circuit courts of the State of Nevada.

Q. When were you appointed ?—A. I think in 1868.

Q. Was that under the State government ?—A. Yes; Nevada became a State in 1864, I believe.

Q. Do you hold that office now ?—A. I do not.

Q. Who holds that office?—A. I think it is a man named McLean.

Q. When was he appointed ?—A. I don't know exactly when he was appointed.

Q. By whom were you appointed ?—A. I was appointed first by Associate Justice Field of the circuit court, and subsequently by Judge Sawyer of the circuit court and by Judge Hillyer for the district.

Q. The appointment was made not by the judge but by the court, was it not ?—A. Made by the judge.

Q. In court?—A. No, I believe not; it may have been.

Q. Where were you when you received the appointment?—A. I was in Virginia City; for the circuit court.

Q. How was the appointment notified to you ?—A. It was sent to me by mail.

Q. Did you appear in court and take the oath and give the bond required by law ?—A. Yes, sir; subsequently.

Q. You were the keeper of the records of the court. Was not your appointment made a matter of record in that court ?—A. I presume so.

Q. And your qualification was also entered upon the record ?—A. Yes, sir.

Q. When did you cease to be the clerk of the court, or cease to perform its duties ?—A. I ceased on the 6th day of November, the day before the election.

Q. What made you cease to perform its duties ?—A. Because it was a question in my mind whether I would be eligible as an elector if I continued to hold the office, and I therefore resigned.

Q. How did you resign ?—A. I resigned by telegraph.

Q. A telegram to whom ?—A. To Judge Sawyer in San Francisco, and also to Judge Hillyer in Carson. I was then living in Virginia City.

Q. Where is Virginia City ?—A. It is about twelve miles from Carson.

Q. Carson is the capital, where the Federal court holds its sessions ?—A. Yes, sir.

Q. Where is the telegram which you sent to either of those judges ?—A. I do not know. It is not with me. I did not bring it.

Q. Have you got a copy of the telegram ?—A. I think not.

Q. Who has ? To whom did you send it ?—A. I sent it to Judge Sawyer.

Q. Directed to what point ?—A. To San Francisco.

Q. Does he live in San Francisco ?—A. Well, he is judge of the district comprising those three States, California, Nevada, and Oregon.

Q. Does he reside in San Francisco ?—A. Most of the time.

Q. You say you sent a telegram to another judge; whom ?—A. Judge Hillyer, of Carson, the district judge.

Q. And you have no copy of that telegram ?—A. I have not. I did not think of saving it.

Q. Did you ever receive an answer to that telegram ?—A. I received an answer from Judge Sawyer the same day, about an hour afterward.

Q. Where is that telegram ?—A. I left it in Virginia City; I did not think of bringing it. I believe I have it.

Q. Why did not you bring it ?—A. Well, I did not know that there would be any question about it.

Q. Did not you know what you were sent for ?—A. I was only subpœnaed here two or three days ago.

By Mr. FIELD :

Q. You telegraphed Judge Sawyer on the 6th of November ?—A. Yes, sir.

Q. Can you not give the exact words of the telegram ?—A. I think I can.

Q. Give the exact words, then.—A. I think the telegram read this way : " Honorable Alonzo Sawyer, San Francisco : I have this day filed my resignation as clerk of the circuit court of the ninth circuit, and request the acceptance of my resignation." I, at the same time that I sent that telegram to Judge Sawyer, sent to Carson my resignation.

Q. No ; do not say you sent your *resignation*. I am only asking about the telegram to Judge Sawyer. Have you given the whole of that ?—A. Yes, sir ; I think that is about the substance of it, and I think pretty nearly the words.

Q. You received from him an answer ?—A. Yes, sir.

Q. On the same day, about an hour afterward ?—A. An hour or two afterward.

Q. That you have got, I suppose ?—A. I think it is among my papers in Virginia City.

Q. Do you remember the exact words of that ?—A. Pretty nearly.

Q. Give them.—-A. "Your resignation as clerk of the circuit court is accepted. Alonzo Sawyer."

Q. Have you ever had any other communication with Judge Sawyer on the subject ?—A. I have not.

Q. You have never written him ?—A. I never have.

Q. Nor received a letter from him ?—A. Never.

Q. You did not send to him a copy of your written resignation ?—A. By telegraph ?

Q. No. You say you wrote something; you did not send him a copy of that ?—A. No; do you mean, sent it by mail ?

Q. Yes; or any way.—A. I did send it.

Q. How ?—A. I sent it.to Carson the same day.

Q. I am talking about Judge Sawyer. Did you send to Judge Sawyer any copy or any paper ?—A. Yes.

Q. What did you send him ?—A. My resignation.

Q. In what form ?—A. In the usual form of resignations.

Q. You sent him a copy of your written paper ?—A. My written paper; my resignation, you mean ?

Q. Yes; do not you understand me ? Did you send Judge Sawyer anything in the world but the telegram ?—A. Yes.

Q. What else ?—A. I sent him my resignation.

Q. You mean a written paper ?—A. Yes, sir.

Q. Did you send him the original that was filed or a copy ?—A. I sent him the original. I only made one.

Q. You made one; then you did not file it ?—A. I sent it down to be filed.

Q. You sent it to him to file by mail ?—A. I did not send it to San Francisco.

Q. Where did you send it ?—A. I sent it to Carson.

Q. Now I think I get an answer. Did you send anything to Judge Sawyer ?—A. Yes.

Q. What ?—A. I sent that resignation.

Q. That paper ?—A. Yes.

Q. To Judge Sawyer, at San Francisco ?—A. I did not say that I did send it to San Francisco.

Q. Well, he was there, was he not ?—A. He was there that day, I think.

Q. Then that day you did not send it. Did you send it to San Francisco the next day ?—A. I did not send it to San Francisco.

Q. At all ?—A. Not at all.

Q. Did you ever send the original paper anywhere ?—A. Yes.

Q. Where did that go ?—A. To Carson.

Q. How did you send that ?—A. I sent it by mail.

Q. You mailed it in Virginia City direct to Carson, did you ?—A. Yes, sir.

Q. When did you mail it in Virginia City ?—A. I mailed it on the 6th.

Q. What time or hour on the 6th ?—A. Along about eleven o'clock in the day.

Q. When did the next post leave Virginia City for Carson ?—A. At about half-past two in the afternoon.

Q. You say you telegraphed to Judge Hillyer ?—A. Yes, sir.

Q. Have you that telegram ?—A. They were very much alike, except the change of name.

Q. As near as you can remember, were they exactly the same ?—A. Yes, sir; precisely the same, with such changes as there would necessarily be in telegraphing to a different person.

Q. Did you receive an answer from him ?—A. I did not.

Q. He never answered you at all ?—A. No.

Q. By letter or telegraph ?—A. No.

Q. Has the circuit court ever been in session since that time ?—A. Yes.

Q. When ?—A. On the 6th of November.

Q. In session where ?—A. In Carson City.

Q. Were you there ?—A. I was not.

Q. When were you, next after the 6th of November, in the court ?—A. I have not been there since.

Q. Personally, therefore, you do not know who transacted the business, as clerk, in the circuit court on the 7th day of November ?—A. I do not.

Q. Did you yourself give any directions about the business of the court to be transacted on that next day ?—A. I did not.

Q. Have you ever since ?—A. I have not.

Q. Who is doing the business of the clerk ?—A. There is a clerk there—Mr. McLean ; I have forgotten his first name.

Q. Do you know whether he has been appointed by the circuit court?—A. Yes; I am certain he has.

Q. Well, you understand that he has?—A. Yes, sir.

Q. When was he appointed?—A. That I do not know exactly.

Q. What month?—A. O, he was appointed in November.

Q. Do you know that?—A. Yes.

Q. You know that?—A. Well, I do not *know* it, because I never saw the appointment.

Q. And you have never seen any record of his appointment?—A. No; I never have.

Q. Was Mr. McLean your deputy?—A. No, he was not.

Q. Did your deputy make the entries and keep the minutes of the court until Mr. McLean took possession of the office?—A. I presume he did. I do not know. I never was there afterward.

Q. Did you make any communications to him?—A. I did not.

Q. Where is the paper that you call your written resignation?—A. It must be on file in Carson, in the clerk's office.

Q. That is to say, as far as you know?—A. So far as I know.

Q. Give the language, as near as you can, of that written paper which you call your resignation.—A. I think it was addressed to Judge Sawyer, and ran about in this style: "Having been nominated as presidential elector, I hereby tender my resignation as clerk of the circuit court, ninth circuit, and trust the resignation may be immediately accepted." I think that is about the purport of it.

Q. You inclosed that in an envelope, did you?—A. Yes.

Q. Directed to whom?—A. To Judge Sawyer.

Q. At Carson City?—A. At Carson City.

Q. It was sealed up, directed to Judge Sawyer, and put into the mail?—A. Yes.

Q. Judge Sawyer was then in San Francisco?—A. Yes; he was then in San Francisco.

Q. Do you know of your own knowledge that Judge Sawyer has ever been in Carson City since?—A. Yes.

Q. Were you there?—A. I was not.

Q. Do not you know what I mean by your own knowledge? Did you see him?—A. No, I did not see him,

Q. Very well; you do not know of your own knowledge that he has ever been there since?—A. Not by seeing him.

Q. That is your knowledge. You do not know, then, of your own knowledge that Judge Sawyer ever saw that package or letter?—A. I do not.

Q. You do not know of your own knowledge that it is not now in the post-office? A. I do not.

Q. Have your accounts as clerk ever been settled?—A. Yes; I think so.

Q. You think so; do you know?—A. I did not attend to the business much; my deputy always did it.

Q. What deputy?—A. Mr. Edwards.

Q. Is he still there?—A. He is in Carson.

Q. Is he still in the office of the clerk?—A. I do not know.

Q. Do you know whether he has ever been out of it?—A. I do not know; I presume he was out of it after I resigned.

Q. Do you know that he was ever out of it? Were you there? Do you know whether he did not attend in court every day and transact business?—A. I do not, of my own knowledge.

Q. Did not you as clerk receive money to be deposited to your credit in bank?—A. Frequently.

Q. In what bank?—A. I have forgotten where the deposits were made. We shifted them around quite often.

Q. In different banks?—A. Yes, sir.

Q. Give us the names of some of them?—A. The Bank of California, and Wells, Fargo & Co.

Q. What amount of money had you standing in your name or to your credit as clerk of the circuit court of the United States?—A. I think not a dollar.

Q. It had all been previously paid out?—A. Yes.

Q. Paid out for what purposes?—A. Paid out in the regular course of business.

Q. You think there were no moneys on deposit to your credit as clerk at that time?—A. I think not; I am not positive.

Q. Has your bond ever been discharged?—A. Not that I know of.

Q. I repeat now what I asked you before: Have your accounts as clerk to your knowledge ever been settled?—A. We made our quarterly settlements.

Q. That is not an answer to my question.—A. You mean since that time?

Q. Have your accounts ever been finally settled?—A. Well, I do not know that there was any accounts to settle.

Q. You received fees?—A. I received fees.

Q. And you were paid through fees?—A. Paid through fees.

Q. Up to a certain amount, or all the fees ?—A. Up to a certain amount.

Q. Very well, then, there must have been, of course, an account to be kept of the amount of fees received, and so far as they exceeded the limit you paid them over to the Treasury, did you not ?—A. I should have done so had they ever exceeded the amount.

Q. When were your periodical accounts regularly settled ?—A. They were settled semi-annually.

Q.· In what months ?—A. In June and December, the 31st.

Q. Then you settled an account on the 31st of June, 1876 ?—A. Yes.

Q. Have you ever settled an account since ?—A. I have not.

Q. Could you state, if you were asked, the items on different sides of the account ?—A. O, no ; I could not.

Q. Have you ever had any communication with Mr. Edwards since the 6th of November ?—A. I have not; I have never been in Carson since but once; that was at the meeting of the college, and I did not see him.

Q. Did you have any communication with him on the 6th of November ?—A. No, sir ; I was in Virginia City.

Q. When first after the 6th of November did you visit Carson City ?—A. Not until the meeting of the college.

Q. That was on the 6th of December ?—A. I think so.

Q. In what business have you been engaged since ?—A. Well, I am in the mining business principally, and always have been.

Q. Do you say that the circuit court has been in session since the 6th of November ?—A. Yes.

Q. Was it not the district court ?—A. The circuit court was in session also.

Q. Are you sure ?—A. I am pretty positive.

Q. What are the times for the meeting of the circuit court in Nevada ?—A. I don't remember just now ; they made some changes, I think, in the last Congress.

Q. As the law stood on the first of November, what was the time for the meeting of the court ; not the district, but the circuit court ?—A. My opinion is that the circuit court was to meet on the 6th of November. That is my impression now, and that is what I thought at the time.

Q. Your impression from what ?—A. From the law. The first Monday, I think, in November.

Q. You can easily tell, cannot you, by looking at the law ?—A. Yes, I can tell.

Q. I wish you would tell us, then, before you leave the city.—A. I will do so.

By Mr. TUCKER :

Q. You did not file the paper that you call your resignation, in the clerk's office on the 6th of November ?—A. I transmitted it for filing, or rather to the judge.

Q. To Judge Sawyer, at Carson ?—A. Yes.

Q. He was that day at San Francisco ?—A. I understood that he was.

Q. Well, you got a telegram from him from there ?—A. Yes.

Q. How long would it take Judge Sawyer to come by the quickest route from San Francisco to Carson ?—A. Twenty hours, I believe.

Q. Coming by steamer ?—A. No ; by rail.

Q. You do not know when he did come ?—A. I do not.

Q. Then, if he had left San Francisco on the 6th, he would not get to Carson until what time ?—A. He could have got there on the 7th.

Q. What time on the 7th ?—A. It would have been along in the evening.

Q. When you communicated with the judges, as you say, on the 6th, did you communicate to your deputy, Edwards, that you were no longer clerk of the court ?—A. I did not.

By Mr. BURCHARD :

Q. You did not exercise the duties of the clerk since the time of your telegram ?—A. I have not.

Q. And they have been performed, as I understand, by a successor appointed by the court ?—A. Yes, sir.

Q. Your recollection is that the district and circuit court were then in session that day in Carson City ?—A. I believe that was the day fixed for it.

Q. Where do I understand you to say Judge Hillyer was ?—A. He was in Carson.

Q. Is there a railroad from Virginia City to Carson ?—A. Yes.

Q. How far is it, in time, by rail ?—A. Well, the railroad is a little long and pretty crooked, about twenty-four miles ; they make it generally in about two hours and a half, sometimes a little less.

Q. The telegram was sent at what time to Judge Hillyer ?—A. I think along about noon some time.

Q. You put your resignation in the mail before the hour of sending the mail from Virginia City to Carson ?—A. Yes ; in order that it might reach there on that day, the 6th.

Q. Do you remember whether the envelope was addressed 'to your deputy, or a clerk, or to the judge himself ?—A. It was addressed to the judge himself.

Q. And you sent a resignation to each judge, if I understand ?—A. To each.

By Mr. FIELD :

Q. Not a written paper to each ?—A. Yes, I sent a resignation to each.

Q. The telegram, you said, you sent to each ?—A. I sent the resignation also.

By Mr. BURCHARD :

Q. Then you sent a resignation to each of the judges, through the mail, on the 6th ?— A. Yes, and at the same time I telegraphed them that I had so sent it.

Q. And Judge Hillyer was then, as I understand, holding court at Carson City ?—A. The circuit court, I think, was to meet.

By Mr. MAISH :

Q. He was the district judge ?—A. Yes, sir ; but I had understood that Judge Sawyer was in San Francisco. I had learned it from some source, and therefore telegraphed to him there.

By Mr. FIELD :

Q. Let me see if I understand you about this resignation directed to the district judge. Did you send exactly the same paper to the district judge that you had sent the circuit judge ?—A. Not the same paper.

Q. Was it a copy of the same paper ?—A. Pretty nearly.

Q. Can you give the contents of the paper ?—A. A moment ago I gave it, and the other was pretty nearly a copy of it, with the exception of such changes as would necessarily be made.

Q. Did you put that in an envelope directed to somebody ?—A. I did.

Q. How was it directed ?—A. To Judge Hillyer.

Q. Give the direction all together.—A. " Hon. E. W. Hillyer, U. S. District Judge, Carson City."

Q. Was the inside also directed in the same way to Judge Hillyer ?—A. Yes.

Q. With the same designation of office and everything else as in the other ?—A. Yes.

Q. You do not know whether he ever received that letter or not ?—A. I think he told me he had received it.

Q. That is not evidence. Do you *know* it in any way ?—A. O, no.

Q. You think that he afterward told you he had received it ?—A. Yes, in Virginia City.

Q. When do you think he told you ?—A. Well, probably a week after, or possibly two weeks.

Q. You do not know that Judge Hillyer was in Carson City on the 6th or 7th of November, do you ? *Knowledge* is what I ask for.—A. I was not there.

Q. Well, you do not *know*, then, in any way, that they were received, either of them ?—A. That seems to be the kind of information you want. I do not.

Q. And if he did receive that letter to him, you do not know when he received it ?— A. Of course not ; I don't know that he received it at all, unless I take his word for it.

Q. And you have no information of his having received it within two weeks ?—A. What kind of information ?

Q. From him ?—A. I tell you I think he told me so.

Q. Within two weeks he told you that he had received it ; that was the information, was it not ?—A. Yes, sir. He talked about sending the bankruptcy letters down— they were in Virginia City ; that is the reason I happened to be there. He said he would send Mr. McLean up and remove the bankruptcy records. They had been in Virginia City for seven years, and I had been attending to that branch of the business.

By Mr. TUCKER :

Q. In your possession ?—A. In my possession.

By Mr. FIELD :

Q. And remained in your possession until when ?—A. They were locked up until Mr. McLean came up, some two or three days afterward.

Q. They remained in your possession until two or three weeks after ?—A. No ; not so long.

Q. For how long ?—A. Well, some days.

Q. Some days after the 7th of November they remained in your possession ?—A. Yes, sir.

Q. And then you gave them up ?—A. Yes.

Q. Were those records locked up on the 6th of November ?—A. Yes ; they were always locked up.

Q. Did they remain locked ; had they been touched ?—A. Not that I know of.

Q. Who had charge of them ?—A. I had.

Q. Nobody else under you?—A. Mr. Strother, the register in bankruptcy, had an office in the same place, and sometimes he had access to the documents.

Q. Was that bankruptcy business going on all the time from the 6th of November to the 6th of December?—A. It was not. There was no work done in the office, or in any part of the office.

Q. Where was that bankruptcy business going on?—A. It was not going on at all.

Q. There was none?—A. There was none.

Q. But Mr. Strother remained there, did he not?—A. He was a register in bankruptcy in the same office.

Q. And he was there all the time?—A. Not all the time.

Q. Well, he was off and on?—A. Off and on.

Q. From the 6th until the present time?—A. Yes, sir.

Q. Was he kept in office by Mr. McLean?—A. He is a register in bankruptcy, appointed by the judge.

By Mr. TUCKER :

Q. When did you mail your letter to Judge Hillyer?—A. I mailed it about the time I sent the dispatch, or pretty soon afterward.

Q. What time did you send the dispatch?—A. Some time about twelve o'clock; between eleven and one, sometime.

Q. When did the mail leave Virginia City for Carson?—A. I think there are two mails; one in the morning, and one at 2.30 p. m., or at 1.30; I am not sure which—along in the afternoon.

By Mr. BURCHARD :

Q. Is there any special provision of law in regard to the appointment of district or circuit clerks in Nevada?—A. No.

Q. Nothing but the general provision that the clerk shall be appointed for each district court by the judge thereof, and that the clerk shall be appointed for the circuit court by the circuit judge of the same?—A. Yes.

Q. Your appointment was made by the judge?—A. Yes.

By Mr. LAWRENCE :

Q. Did you put on to the two letters that you sent to Carson City the proper postage-stamps?—A. Yes.

Q. What time would these letters reach Carson in the ordinary course of the mail?—A. They ought to have reached there along in the evening of the 6th, about five or six o'clock.

Q. Did the fees of the office, or either of your offices, ever exceed the limits fixed by law?—A. No. I lost $500 a year running the office for eight years.

Q. At the time you resigned, was there any excess of fees above the limit prescribed by law?—A. O, no.

Q. You would owe the Government nothing, then?—A. O, no.

By Mr. BURCHARD :

Q. What do you mean?—A. Well, there was nothing in the office. I had to pay the rent; the Government did not; that is what was the matter, and I kept it on to accommodate a deputy.

By Mr. TUCKER :

Q. You have spoken of the time of mailing these letters; are you certain you mailed them in time for the evening mail on the 6th?—A. That was my purpose in putting them in; I presumed so at the time; I did not doubt it at the time; exactly at what time the cars went I am now unable to say, but I put them in the office on the supposition that I would get them there in time.

By Mr. LAWRENCE :

Q. You signed your name to both resignations?—A. I did.

By Mr. TUCKER :

Q. How many hours does it take the mail to go from Virginia City to Carson?—A. About two hours and a half, sometimes a little less; it is twenty-four miles by rail.

The PRESIDING OFFICER. Are there any further objections to the certificate of the State of Nevada? The Chair hears none. The Senate will now withdraw to its chamber that the two Houses may separately consider and decide upon this objection.

The Senate accordingly (at 5 o'clock and 45 minutes p. m.) withdrew.

IN SENATE, *Tuesday, February* 20, 1877.

The Senate returned from the joint meeting to its chamber at 5 o'clock and 47 minutes p. m., when the President *pro tempore* took the chair and caused the objection to the vote of R. M. Daggett, as one of the electors from the State of Nevada, to be read.

Whereupon,

Mr. Senator JONES, of Nevada, offered the following resolution, which was agreed to without debate and without a division, viz:

Resolved, That the vote of R. M. Daggett be counted with the other votes of the electors of Nevada, notwithstanding the objections made thereto.

On motion of Mr. Senator HAMLIN it was

Ordered, That the Secretary notify the House of Representatives thereof, and that the Senate is now ready to meet the House to continue the count of the electoral votes for President and Vice-President.

The Senate (being advised that a recess had been taken by the House of Representatives) took a recess at 6 o'clock and 15 minutes p. m. until Wednesday, February 21, at 10 o'clock a. m.

IN THE HOUSE OF REPRESENTATIVES,
Tuesday, February 20, 1877.

The Senate having withdrawn from the hall of the House at 5 o'clock and 45 minutes p. m., the House of Representatives was called to order by the Speaker, and resumed its session.

Mr. Representative WOOD, of New York, moved that the House take a recess till to-morrow morning at 10 o'clock.

The yeas and nays being called for, the motion was agreed to by a vote of 97 yeas, 88 nays; and (at 6 o'clock and 10 minutes p. m.) the House took a recess until Wednesday, February 21, at 10 o'clock a. m.

ELECTORAL COMMISSION.

TUESDAY, *February* 20, 1877.

The Commission met at 4 o'clock p. m., pursuant to adjournment.

The Journal of the 16th, 17th, and 19th instant, respectively, was read and approved.

Mr. Commissioner ABBOTT moved that each Commissioner have leave until March 10, proximo, in which to file for publication in the Record an opinion respecting the cases that have at present been acted on by the Commission.

After debate,

The motion was withdrawn.

On motion of Mr. Commissioner GARFIELD, the Commission took a recess until 6 o'clock and 30 minutes.

And before the expiration of the recess,

On motion of Mr. Commissioner STRONG, (at 6 o'clock and 15 minutes p. m.) the Commission adjourned until to-morrow at 11 o'clock a. m.

PROCEEDINGS OF THE TWO HOUSES.

IN SENATE, *Wednesday, February* 21, 1877.

The Senate resumed its session at 10 o'clock a. m., transacting no business. Being notified at 11 o'clock and 38 minutes of the action of the House of Representatives on the objection to the vote of R. M. Daggett, as an elector for the State of Nevada, and of its readiness to receive the Senate to proceed with the count, the Senate proceeded to the hall of the House of Representatives.

IN THE HOUSE OF REPRESENTATIVES,
Wednesday, February 21, 1877.

The House of Representatives resumed its session at 10 o'clock a. m.

The objection made to the counting of the vote of R. M. Daggett as one of the electors for the State of Nevada, with the evidence in support thereof, was read.

Whereupon,

Mr. Representative SPRINGER offered the following resolution; which, after debate, was adopted without a division, viz:

Resolved, That the vote of R. M. Daggett, one of the electors of the State of Nevada, be counted, the objections to the contrary notwithstanding.

A message was ordered to be sent to the Senate announcing this action, and the readiness of the House to receive the Senate to proceed with the count.

JOINT MEETING.

WEDNESDAY, *February* 21, 1877.

At 11 o'clock and 40 minutes a. m. the Senate entered the hall of the House of Representatives, preceded by its Sergeant-at-Arms and headed by its President *pro tempore* and Secretary, the members and officers of the House rising to receive them.

The PRESIDENT *pro tempore* of the Senate took his seat as Presiding Officer of the joint meeting of the two Houses, the Speaker of the House occupying a chair upon his left.

The PRESIDING OFFICER. The joint meeting of Congress for counting the electoral vote resumes its session. The two Houses acting separately having determined on the objection submitted to the certificate from the State of Nevada, the Secretary of the Senate will report the resolution of the Senate.

The Secretary of the Senate read as follows:

Resolved, That the vote of R. M. Daggett be counted with the other votes of the electors of Nevada, notwithstanding the objections made thereto.

The PRESIDING OFFICER. The Clerk of the House will now report the resolution of the House.

The Clerk of the House read as follows:

Resolved, That the vote of R. M. Daggett, one of the electors of the State of Nevada, be counted, the objections to the contrary notwithstanding.

The PRESIDING OFFICER. Neither House having decided to reject the vote objected to from the State of Nevada, the full vote of that State will be counted. The tellers will announce the vote of the State of Nevada.

Mr. Representative STONE, (one of the tellers.) The State of Nevada casts 3 votes for Rutherford B. Hayes, of Ohio, for President of the United States, and 3 votes for William A. Wheeler, of New York, for Vice-President.

UNDISPUTED STATES.

The count then proceeded, the certificates from the States of—

New Hampshire, casting 5 votes for Hayes and Wheeler;

New Jersey, casting 9 votes for Tilden and Hendricks;

New York, casting 35 votes for Tilden and Hendricks;

North Carolina, casting 10 votes for Tilden and Hendricks; and

Ohio, casting 22 votes for Hayes and Wheeler,—

being opened by the Presiding Officer and read by the tellers, and the votes thereof counted without objection.

OREGON.

The PRESIDING OFFICER. Having opened a certificate received by messenger from the State of Oregon, the Chair hands the same to the tellers, to be read in the presence and hearing of the two Houses, with the corresponding one received by mail.

Mr. Senator MITCHELL. I ask that all the papers in this case be read in full.

The PRESIDING OFFICER. They will be so read.

Mr. Representative STONE (one of the tellers) read the certificate and accompanying papers, as follows:

CERTIFICATE No. 1.

UNITED STATES OF AMERICA,
    State of Oregon, County of Multnomah, ss :

We, J. C. Cartwright, W. H. Odell, and J. W. Watts, being each duly and severally sworn, say that, at the hour of 12 o'clock m. of the (6th) sixth day of December, A. D. 1876, we duly assembled at the State capitol, in a room in the capitol building at Salem, Oregon, which was assigned to us by the secretary of state of the State of Oregon. That we duly, on said day and hour, demanded of the governor of the State of Oregon and of the secretary of state of the State of Oregon certified lists of the electors for President and Vice-President of the United States for the State of Oregon, as provided by the laws of the United States and of the State of Oregon, but both L. F. Grover, governor of the State of Oregon, and S. F. Chadwick, secretary of state of said State, then and there refused to deliver to us, or either of us, any such certified lists or any certificate of election whatever. And being informed that such lists had been delivered to one E. A. Cronin by said secretary of state, we each and all demanded such certified lists of said E. A. Cronin, but he then and there refused to deliver or to exhibit such certified lists to us, or either of us. Whereupon we have procured from the secretary of state certified copies of the abstract of the vote of the State of Oregon for electors of President and Vice-President at the presidential election held in said State November 7, A. D. 1876, and have attached them to the certified list of the persons voted for by us and of the votes cast by us for President and Vice-President of the United States, in lieu of a more formal certificate.

W. H. ODELL.
J. W. WATTS.
JOHN C. CARTWRIGHT.

Sworn and subscribed to before me this 6th day of December, A. D. 1876.
    [SEAL.]   THOS. H. CANN,
                                Notary Public for State of Oregon.

UNITED STATES OF AMERICA, STATE OF OREGON,
    Secretary's Office, Salem, December 6, 1876.

I, S. F. Chadwick, do hereby certify that I am the secretary of the State of Oregon and the custodian of the great seal thereof; that T. H. Cann, esq., resident of Marion County, in said State of Oregon, was on the 6th day of December, A. D. 1876, a notary public within and for said State, and duly commissioned such by the governor of the State of Oregon under its great seal, and was duly qualified to act as such notary public by the laws of this State, as it fully appears by the records of this office; that as said notary public the said T. H. Cann had, on the day aforesaid, to wit, December 6, A. D. 1876, full power and authority, by the laws of the State of Oregon, to take acknowledgments of all instruments in writing and administer oaths; that the annexed certificate is made in conformity with the laws of this State; that the signature thereto of T. H. Cann is the genuine signature of T. H. Cann, notary public; that the seal affixed to said acknowledgment is the official seal of said T. H. Cann, notary public; and that full faith and credit should be given to his official acts as notary public aforesaid.

In witness whereof I have hereto set my hand and affixed the great seal of the State of Oregon the day and year first above written.

    [SEAL.]   S. F. CHADWICK,
                                Secretary of the State of Oregon.

Abstract of votes cast at the presidential election held in the State of Oregon, November 7, 1876, for presidential electors.

Counties.	W. H. Odell.	J. W. Watts.	J. C. Cartwright.	Henry Klippel.	E. A. Cronin.	W. B. Laswell.	D. Clark.	F. Sutherland.	B. Carl.
Baker	318	319	319	549	550	549	1	1	1
Benton	615	615	615	567	567	567	77	77	77
Clackamas	949	950	950	724	724	724	17	17	17
Clatsop	432	432	432	386	385	386	......	......	..
Columbia	157	156	157	179	179	179	22	22	22
Coos	571	571	571	512	516	515	......	......	......
Curry	131	131	131	124	124	124	3	3	3
Douglas	1,002	1,002	1,003	847	847	847	43	43	43
Grant	315	314	316	279	279	277	3	3	3
Jackson	585	585	586	827	840	840	5	5	5
Josephine	209	209	209	252	252	252	4	4	4
Lane	949	949	949	946	946	946	33	33	33
Lake	173	173	173	258	258	258	......	......	......
Linn	1,323	1,324	1,323	1,404	1,404	1,404	140	141	140
Marion	1,780	1,782	1,781	1,154	1,154	1,155	21	23	22
Multnomah	2,124	2,122	2,122	1,525	1,528	1,525	2	2	2
Polk	607	608	608	542	542	542	54	55	54
Tillamook	119	119	119	76	76	76	1	1	1
Umatilla	486	486	486	742	742	742	42	42	42
Union	366	366	366	525	525	525	32	32	32
Wasco	491	491	493	621	621	619	......	......	......
Washington	693	692	693	423	424	423	......	......	......
Yamhill	811	810	812	674	674	674	6	6	6
Total	15,206	15,206	15,214	14,136	14,157	14,149	509	510	507

Simpson, 1; Gray, 1; Salisbury, 1; McDowell, 1.

SALEM, STATE OF OREGON:

I hereby certify that the foregoing tabulated statement is the result of the vote cast for presidential electors at a general election held in and for the State of Oregon on the 7th day of November, A. D. 1876, as opened and canvassed in the presence of his excellency L. F. Grover, governor of said State, according to law, on the 4th day of December, A. D. 1876, at 2 o'clock p. m. of that day, by the secretary of state.

[SEAL.]

S. F. CHADWICK,
Secretary of State of Oregon.

UNITED STATES OF AMERICA,
STATE OF OREGON, SECRETARY'S OFFICE,
Salem, December 6, 1876.

I, S. F. Chadwick, secretary of the State of Oregon, do hereby certify that I am the custodian of the great seal of the State of Oregon. That the foregoing copy of the abstract of votes cast at the presidential election held in the State of Oregon, November 7, 1876, for presidential electors, has been by me compared with the original abstract of votes cast for presidential electors aforesaid on file in this office, and said copy is a correct transcript therefrom and of the whole of the said original abstract of votes cast for presidential electors.

In witness whereof I have hereto set my hand and affixed the great seal of the State of Oregon the day and year above written.

[SEAL.]

S. F. CHADWICK,
Secretary of the State of Oregon.

List of votes cast at an election for electors of President and Vice-President of the United States in the State of Oregon held on the 7th day of November, 1876.

FOR PRESIDENTIAL ELECTORS.

W. H. Odell received fifteen thousand two hundred and six (15,206) votes.
J. W. Watts received fifteen thousand two hundred and six (15,206) votes.
J. C. Cartwright received fifteen thousand two hundred and fourteen (15,214) votes.

E. A. Cronin received fourteen thousand one hundred and fifty-seven (14,157) votes.
H. Klippel received fourteen thousand one hundred and thirty-six (14,136) votes.
W. B. Laswell received fourteen thousand one hundred and forty-nine' (14,149) votes.
Daniel Clark received five hundred and nine (509) votes.
F. Sutherland received five hundred and ten (510) votes.
Bart Curl received five hundred and seven (507) votes.

S. W. McDowell received three, (3,) Gray one, (1,) Simpson one, (1,) and Salisbury one (1) vote.

I, S. F. Chadwick, secretary of state in and for the State of Oregon, do hereby certify that the within and foregoing is a full, true, and correct statement of the entire vote cast for each and all persons for the office of electors of President and Vice-President of the United States for the State of Oregon at the general election held in said State on the 7th day of November, A. D. 1876, as appears by the returns of said election now on file in my office.

[SEAL.]

                                        S. F. CHADWICK,
                                    Secretary of State of Oregon.

UNITED STATES OF AMERICA,
    State of Oregon, County of Marion, ss :

We, W. H. Odell, J. C. Cartwright, and J. W. Watts, electors of President and Vice-President of the United States for the State of Oregon, duly elected and appointed in the year A. D. 1876, pursuant to the laws of the United States and in the manner directed by the laws of the State of Oregon, do hereby certify that at a meeting held by us at Salem, the seat of government in and for the State of Oregon, on Wednesday, the 6th day of December, A. D. 1876, for the purpose of casting our votes for President and Vice-President of the United States—

A vote was duly taken, by ballot, for President of the United States, in distinct ballots for President only, with the following result:

The whole number of votes cast for President of the United States was three (3) votes.

That the only person voted for for President of the United States was Rutherford B. Hayes, of Ohio.

That for President of the United States Rutherford B. Hayes, of Ohio, received three (3) votes.

In testimony whereof we have hereunto set our hands on the first Wednesday of December, in the year of our Lord one thousand eight hundred and seventy-six.

                                        W. H. ODELL.
                                        J. C. CARTWRIGHT.
                                        J. W. WATTS.

UNITED STATES OF AMERICA,
    State of Oregon, County of Marion, ss:

We, W. H. Odell, J. C. Cartwright, and J. W. Watts, electors of President and Vice-President of the United States for the State of Oregon, duly elected and appointed, in the year A. D. 1876, pursuant to the laws of the United States, and in the manner directed by the laws of the State of Oregon, do hereby certify that at a meeting held by us at Salem, the seat of government in and for the State of Oregon, on Wednesday, the 6th day of December, A. D. 1876, for the purpose of casting our votes for President and Vice-President of the United States—

A vote was duly taken, by ballot, for Vice-President of the United States, in distinct ballots for Vice-President only, with the following result:

The whole number of votes cast for Vice-President of the United States was three (3) votes.

That the only person voted for for Vice-President of the United States was William A. Wheeler, of New York.

That for Vice-President of the United States William A. Wheeler, of New York, received three (3) votes.

In testimony whereof we have hereunto set our hands on the first Wednesday of December, in the year of our Lord one thousand eight hundred and seventy-six.

                                        W. H. ODELL.
                                        J. C. CARTWRIGHT.
                                        J. W. WATTS.

SALEM, OREGON, *December 6, 1876—12 o'clock m.*

This being the day and hour fixed by the statutes of the United States and of the State of Oregon for the meeting of the electors of President and Vice-President of the United States for the State of Oregon, the electors for President and Vice-President of the United States for the State of Oregon met at Salem, the seat of government of said State of Oregon, at twelve o'clock noon of the 6th day of December, A. D. 1876, said day being the first Wednesday in December.

Present, W. H. Odell and J. C. Cartwright.

The meeting was duly organized by electing W. H. Odell chairman and J. C. Cartwright secretary.

The resignation of J. W. Watts, who was on November 7, A. D. 1876, duly elected an elector of President and Vice-President of the United States for the State of Oregon, was presented by W. H. Odell, and, after being duly read, was unanimously accepted.

There being but two electors present, to wit, W. H. Odell and J. C. Cartwright, and the State of Oregon being entitled to three electors, the electors present proceeded to and did declare that a vacancy existed in the electoral college, and then and there, under and by virtue of the provisions of section fifty-nine, (59,) title nine, (9,) chapter fourteen, (14,) of the General Laws of Oregon, (Deady and Lane's Compilation,) the said electors, W. H. Odell and J. C. Cartwright, immediately, by *viva voce* vote, proceeded to fill said vacancy in the electoral college.

J. W. Watts received the unanimous vote of all the electors present, and was thereupon declared duly elected to the office of elector of President and Vice-President of the United States for the State of Oregon.

Whereupon the said electors, on motion, proceeded to vote by ballot for President of the United States.

The whole number of votes cast for President of the United States was three (3) votes.

The only person voted for for President of the United States was Rutherford B. Hayes, of Ohio.

For President of the United States Rutherford B. Hayes, of Ohio, received three (3) votes.

The said electors then, on motion, proceeded to vote by ballot for Vice-President of the United States.

The whole number of votes cast for Vice-President of the United States was three (3) votes.

The only person voted for for Vice-President of the United States was William A. Wheeler, of New York.

For Vice-President of the United States, William A. Wheeler, of New York, received three (3) votes.

The electors, on motion, then unanimously, by writing under their hands, appointed W. H. Odell to take charge of and deliver to the President of the Senate, at the seat of Government, Washington, D. C., one of the certificates containing the lists of the votes of said electors for President and Vice-President.

On motion, it was ordered that one of the certified copies of the abstract and canvass of the entire vote of the State of Oregon, cast at the presidential election held November 7, A. D. 1876, for electors of President and Vice-President of the United States for Oregon, as certified and delivered to the electors by S. F. Chadwick, secretary of state of the State of Oregon, be attached to each certificate and return of the list of persons voted for by the electors here present for President and Vice-President of the United States.

The electors then adjourned.

> W. H. ODELL,
> *Chairman.*
> JOHN C. CARTWRIGHT,
> *Secretary.*

We hereby certify that the within and foregoing is a true, full, and correct statement of all the acts and proceedings of the electors of President and Vice-President for the State of Oregon at a meeting of said electors held at Salem, in the State of Oregon, on the 6th day of December, A. D. 1876, at 12 o'clock noon of said day.

> W. H. ODELL, *Elector.*
> JOHN W. WATTS, *Elector.*
> JOHN C. CARTWRIGHT, *Elector.*

SALEM, OREGON, *December 6th*, 1876.

We, the duly appointed and elected electors of President and Vice-President of the United States for the State of Oregon, do hereby designate and appoint W. H. Odell to take charge of and deliver to the President of the Senate of the United States, at the seat of Government, to wit, at Washington, District of Columbia, before the first Wednesday in January, A. D. 1877, the certificates and papers relating to the vote for President and Vice-President of the United States, cast by us at Salem, in the State of Oregon, on the 6th day of December, A. D. 1876.

> W. H. ODELL.
> J. C. CARTWRIGHT.
> J. W. WATTS.

For President of the United States, Rutherford B. Hayes, of Ohio.
(Indorsed)   W. H. ODELL.
For President of the United States, Rutherford B. Hayes, of Ohio.
(Indorsed)   •   JNO. C. CARTWRIGHT.
For President of the United States, Rutherford B. Hayes, of Ohio.
(Indorsed)   J. W. WATTS.
For Vice-President of the United States, William A. Wheeler, of New York.
(Indorsed)   W. H. ODELL.
For Vice-President of the United States, William A. Wheeler, of New York.
(Indorsed)   JOHN C. CARTWRIGHT.
For Vice-President of the United States, William A. Wheeler, of New York.
(Indorsed)   J. W. WATTS.

To the honorable Electoral College in and for the State of Oregon for President and Vice-President of the United States:

Whereas I, J. W. Watts, did receive a majority of the legal votes cast for presidential electors at an election held for President and Vice-President of the United States on the 7th day of November, A. D. 1876, as appears from the official returns on file in the secretary of state's office in and for said State; and whereas there has arisen some doubts touching my eligibility at the time of such election: Therefore, I hereby tender my resignation of the office of presidential elector.

Very respectfully,

J. W. WATTS.

SALEM, OR., *December 6th,* 1876.

During the reading,

The PRESIDING OFFICER. Does the Senator from Oregon desire the reading of the tabular statement accompanying the papers?

Mr. Senator MITCHELL. I do not think it will be necessary to read all the figures, but simply the results. I presume the whole will go into the Record.

Mr. Representative LANE. I object to any portion being omitted.

The reading was concluded.

The PRESIDING OFFICER. Having opened another certificate received by messenger from the State of Oregon, the Chair hands it to the tellers to be read in the presence and hearing of the two Houses, handing also the corresponding one received by mail.

Mr. Senator INGALLS (one of the tellers) read as follows:

CERTIFICATE No. 2.

STATE OF OREGON, EXECUTIVE OFFICE,
Salem, December 6th, 1876.

I, L. F. Grover, governor of the State of Oregon, do hereby certify that, at a general election held in said State on the seventh day of November, A. D. 1876, William H. Odell received 15,206 votes, John C. Cartwright received 15,214 votes, E. A. Cronin received 14,157 votes for electors of President and Vice-President of the United States; being the highest number of votes cast at said election for persons eligible, under the Constitution of the United States, to be appointed electors of President and Vice-President of the United States, they are hereby declared duly-elected electors as aforesaid for the State of Oregon.

In testimony whereof I have hereunto set my hand and caused the seal of the State of Oregon to be affixed this the day and year first above written.

LA FAYETTE GROVER,
Gov. of Oregon.

Attest:
[SEAL.]   S. F. CHADWICK,
              Secretary of State of Oregon.

This is to certify that on the 6th day of December, A. D. 1876, E. A. Cronin, one of the undersigned, and John C. Cartwright and William H. Odell, electors, duly appointed on the 7th day of November, A. D. 1876, as appears by the annexed certificate to cast the vote of the State of Oregon for President and Vice-President of the United States, convened at the seat of government of said State, and for the purpose of discharging their duties as such electors; that thereupon said John C. Cartwright and William H. Odell refused to act as such electors; that upon such refusal the undersigned, J. N. T. Miller and John Parker, were duly appointed electors, as by the laws of Oregon in such cases made and provided, to fill the vacancies caused by the said refusal; that thereupon the said electors, E. A. Cronin, J. N. T. Miller, and John Parker proceeded to vote by ballot, as by law provided, for President and Vice-President of the United States, they being duly qualified to act as such electors, and the electoral college of said State having been duly organized; that upon the ballots so taken Rutherford B. Hayes, of the State of Ohio, received two (2) votes for President, and Samuel J. Tilden, of the State of New York, received one (1) vote for President, and that William A. Wheeler, of the State of New York, received two (2) votes for Vice-President, and Thomas A. Hendricks, of the State of Indiana, received one (1) vote for Vice-President; that the said votes were all the votes cast and the said persons were all the persons voted for. And we further certify that the lists hereto attached are true and correct lists of all the votes given for each of the persons so voted for for President and Vice-President of the United States.

Done at the city of Salem, county of Marion, and State of Oregon, this 6th day of December, A. D. 1876.

E. A. CRONIN,
J. N. T. MILLER,
JOHN PARKER,
Electors for the State of Oregon to cast the vote of said State
for President and Vice-President of the United States.

List of all the persons voted for by the electoral college of the State of Oregon, and of the number of votes cast for each person, at the city of Salem, the seat of government of said State, on Wednesday, the 6th day of December, A. D. 1876, as provided by law, for President of the United States:

Rutherford B. Hayes, of Ohio, received two (2) votes............................... 2
Samuel J. Tilden, of New York, received one (1) vote............................. 1
Attest:

E. A. CRONIN,
J. N. T. MILLER,
JOHN PARKER,
Electors.

List of all the persons voted for by the electoral college of the State of Oregon, and of the number of votes cast for each person, at the city of Salem, the seat of government of said State, on Wednesday, the 6th day of December, A. D. 1876, as provided by law, for Vice-President of the United States:

William A. Wheeler, of New York, received two (2) votes.......................... 2
Thomas A. Hendricks, of Indiana, received one (1) vote............................. 1
Attest:

E. A. CRONIN,
J. N. T. MILLER,
JOHN PARKER,
Electors.

We, the undersigned, duly appointed electors to cast the votes of the State of Oregon for President and Vice-President of the United States, hereby certify that the lists of all the electoral votes of the said State of Oregon given for President of the United States, and of all the votes given for Vice-President of the United States, are contained herein.

E. A. CRONIN,
J. N. T. MILLER,
JOHN PARKER,
Electors.

The PRESIDING OFFICER. Are there any objections to the certificates from the State of Oregon?

Mr. Senator MITCHELL. On behalf of the Senators and Representatives whose names are signed thereto, I present an objection to the lists and certificates signed by E. A. Cronin, J. N. T. Miller, and John Parker, claiming to be electors for the State of Oregon, and to the votes cast by them respectively for President and Vice-President.

The PRESIDING OFFICER.   The Secretary of the Senate will read the objection submitted by the Senator from Oregon.

The Secretary of the Senate read as follows:

OBJECTION NO. 1.

The undersigned Senators and members of the House of Representatives of the United States object to the list of names of the electors E. A. Cronin, J. N. T. Miller, and John Parker, one of whom, E. A. Cronin, is included in the certificate of La Fayette Grover, governor of Oregon; and to the electoral votes of said State signed by E. A. Cronin, J. N. T. Miller, and John Parker; being the certificate second presented by the President of the Senate to the two Houses of Congress in joint convention, for the reasons following:

1. Because neither of said persons, E. A. Cronin, J. N. T. Miller, nor John Parker, was ever appointed elector of President or Vice-President by the State of Oregon, either in the manner directed by the legislature of such State or in any other manner whatsoever.

2. Because it appears from the records and papers contained in and attached to the certificate of W. H. Odell, John C. Cartwright, and John W. Watts, as presented by the President of the Senate to the two Houses of Congress in joint convention, that said W. H. Odell, John C. Cartwright, and John W. Watts were duly and legally appointed electors for President and Vice-President by the State of Oregon, in the manner directed by the legislature thereof, and duly cast their votes as such.

3. Because it does not appear from the face of the certificate of La Fayette Grover, governor of the State of Oregon, attached to and made a part of the returns of the votes cast by E. A. Cronin, J. N. T. Miller, and John Parker, that such certificate was issued by the governor to the three persons having the highest number of votes for electors for the State of Oregon, and were duly chosen and appointed by said State, according to the laws thereof; but was issued by him to the persons whom he *deemed to be eligible* to said appointment, although one of such persons, E. A. Cronin, was not appointed thereto according to the laws of said State.

4. Because it appears from the certificate of S. F. Chadwick, secretary of state, under the seal of the State, attached to and made a part of the returns and certificate of W. H. Odell, John C. Cartwright, and John W. Watts, that said persons, W. H. Odell, John C. Cartwright, and John W. Watts, received the highest number of votes at the election on the 7th day of November, 1876, for the office of electors of President and Vice-President; and that the secretary of state on the 4th day of December following, officially declared in pursuance of law that they, Odell, Cartwright, and Watts, had received the highest number of votes; and that therefore the certificate of the governor, in so far as it omitted to certify the name of John W. Watts as one of the electors appointed, and in so far as such certificate contained the name of E. A. Cronin as one of the electors appointed, fails to conform to the act of Congress in such case made and provided and the laws of Oregon in that behalf, and that such certificate is, as to said Cronin, without authority and of no effect.

5. Because it appears from both certificates that W. H. Odell and John C. Cartwright, a majority of the electoral college, were duly appointed electors by the State of Oregon in the manner directed by the legislature thereof; that their record presented to the President of the Senate, and by him to the two Houses of Congress, shows that a vacancy in the office of elector existed on the day fixed by law for the meeting of the electors, and that such vacancy was filled by the appointment of John W. Watts.

JOHN H. MITCHELL,
A. A. SARGENT,
United States Senators.
WILLIAM LAWRENCE,
HORATIO C. BURCHARD,
JAMES W. McDILL,
Members House of Representatives.

The PRESIDING OFFICER.   Are there further objections to the certificates from the State of Oregon?

Mr. Senator KELLY.   I present objections to the electoral vote for President and Vice-President as cast by J. C. Cartwright, W. H. Odell, and J. W. Watts.

The PRESIDING OFFICER.   The objections will be read by the Clerk of the House.

The Clerk of the House read as follows:

OBJECTION NO. 2.

In the matter of the electoral vote of the State of Oregon for President and Vice-

President of the United States, the undersigned, United States Senators and members of the House of Representatives, make the following objections to the papers, purporting to be the certificates of the electoral votes of the State of Oregon, signed by John C. Cartwright, William H. Odell, and John W. Watts:

I. The said papers have not annexed to them a certificate of the governor of Oregon, as required to be made and annexed by sections 136 and 138 of the Revised Statutes of the United States.

II. The said papers have not annexed to them a list of the names of the said Cartwright, Odell, and Watts as electors, to which the seal of the State of Oregon was affixed by the secretary of state and signed by the governor and secretary, as required by section 60 of chapter xiv, title 9, of the general laws of Oregon.

III. The said J. W. Watts, therein claimed to be one of the said electors, was, in the month of February, 1873, appointed a postmaster at La Fayette, in the State of Oregon, and was duly commissioned and qualified as such postmaster, that being an office of trust and profit under the laws of the United States, and continued to be and act as such postmaster from February, 1873, until after the 13th day of November, 1876, and was acting as such postmaster on the 7th day of November, 1876, when presidential electors were appointed by the State of Oregon; and that he, the said John W. Watts, was ineligible to be appointed as one of the said presidential electors.

IV. When the governor of Oregon caused the lists of the names of the electors of said State to be made and certified, such lists did not contain the name of the said John W. Watts, but did contain the names of John C. Cartwright, William H. Odell, and E. A. Cronin, who were duly appointed electors of President and Vice-President of the United States in the State of Oregon on the 7th day of November, 1876.

V. It was the right and duty of the governor of Oregon, under the laws of that State, to give a certificate of election or appointment as electors to John C. Cartwright, William H. Odell, and E. A. Cronin, they being the three persons capable of being appointed presidential electors who received the highest number of votes at the election held in Oregon on the 7th day of November, 1876.

VI. The said John C. Cartwright and William H. Odell had no right or authority in law to appoint the said John W. Watts to be an elector on the 6th day of December, 1876, as there was no vacancy in the office of presidential elector on that day.

VII. The said John C. Cartwright and William H. Odell had no right or authority in law to appoint the said John W. Watts to be an elector on the 6th day of December, 1876, inasmuch as they did not on that day compose or form any part of the electoral college of the State of Oregon as by law constituted.

VIII. The said John C. Cartwright and William H. Odell had no authority to appoint the said John W. Watts to be an elector on the 6th day of December, 1876, because the said Watts was still on that day the postmaster at La Fayette, in the State of Oregon, and was still on that day holding the said office of profit and trust.

JAMES K. KELLY,
United States Senator, Oregon.
HENRY COOPER,
United States Senator, Tennessee.
LEWIS V. BOGY,
United States Senator, Missouri.
J. E. McDONALD,
United States Senator, Indiana.
J. W. STEVENSON,
United States Senator, Kentucky.
DAVID DUDLEY FIELD, of New York.
J. R. TUCKER, of Virginia.
LAFAYETTE LANE, of Oregon.
G. A. JENKS, of Pennsylvania.
ANSEL T. WALLING, of Ohio.
HIESTER CLYMER, of Pennsylvania.
P. D. WIGGINTON, of California.
E. F. POPPLETON, of Ohio.
JOHN L. VANCE, of Ohio.
FRANK H. HURD, of Ohio.
J. K. LUTTRELL, of California.

The PRESIDING OFFICER. Are there further objections to the certificates from the State of Oregon?

Mr. Representative LAWRENCE. I present additional objections to the certificates and papers purporting to be certificates of the electoral vote of the State of Oregon cast by E. A. Cronin, J. N. T. Miller, and John Parker.

The PRESIDING OFFICER. The Secretary of the Senate will read the objections.

The Secretary of the Senate read as follows:

OBJECTION NO. 3.

The undersigned Senators and members of the House of Representatives of the United States object to the certificates and papers purporting to be certificates of the electoral votes of the State of Oregon cast by E. A. Cronin, J. N. T. Miller, and John Parker, and by each of them, and to the list of votes by them and each of them signed and certified as given for President of the United States and for Vice-President of the United States, for the following reasons:

1. The said E. A. Cronin, J. N. T. Miller, and John Parker were not, nor was either of them, appointed an elector of President and Vice-President of the United States for the State of Oregon.

2. For that W. H. Odell, J. C. Cartwright, and J. W. Watts were duly appointed electors of President and Vice-President of the United States for the State of Oregon, and as such electors, at the time and place prescribed by law, cast their votes for Rutherford B. Hayes for President of the United States and for William A. Wheeler for Vice-President of the United States; and the list of votes signed, certified, and transmitted by such electors to the President of the Senate are the only true and lawful lists of votes for President and Vice-President of the United States.

3. That the said W. H. Odell, J. C. Cartwright, and J. W. Watts received the highest number of all the votes cast for electors of President and Vice-President of the United States by the qualified voters of the State of Oregon at the election held in said State on the 7th day of November, A. D. 1876, and the secretary of state of Oregon duly canvassed said votes and made and certified under his hand and the great seal of the State of Oregon and delivered to said W. H. Odell, J. C. Cartwright, and J. W. Watts two lists of the electors of President and Vice-President of the United States elected by the qualified voters of said State at said election, and showing that said W. H. Odell, J. C. Cartwright, and J. W. Watts were the persons having the highest number of votes of said qualified voters at such election, and were elected, which certificate is dated the 6th day of December, A. D. 1876, and which has been read before the two Houses of Congress; by reason of all which said Odell, Cartwright, and Watts were the lawful electors of President and Vice-President of the United States for the State of Oregon.

JOHN H. MITCHELL,
A. A. SARGENT,
Senators.
WILLIAM LAWRENCE,
GEO. W. McCRARY,
EUGENE HALE,
N. P. BANKS,
Members of the House of Representatives.

The PRESIDING OFFICER. Are there further objections to the certificates from the State of Oregon? If there be no further objections, the certificates objected to, with the accompanying papers, together with the objections, will be submitted to the Commission for its judgment and decision. The Senate will now retire to its chamber.

At twelve o'clock and fifty minutes p. m. the Senate withdrew.

ELECTORAL COMMISSION.

WEDNESDAY, February 21, 1877.

The Commission met at 11 o'clock a. m., pursuant to adjournment, all the members being present.

On motion, the Commission took a recess until 1 o'clock p. m.

The Commission re-assembled at 1 o'clock p. m.

The Journal of yesterday was read and approved.

OREGON.

Mr. George C. Gorham, Secretary of the Senate, appeared and presented the following communication; which was read:

HALL OF THE HOUSE OF REPRESENTATIVES,
February 21, 1877.

To the President of the Commission:

More than one return or paper purporting to be a return or certificate of the electoral votes of the State of Oregon having been received and this day opened in the presence of the two Houses of Congress, and objections thereto having been made, the said returns, with all accompanying papers, and also the objections thereto, are herewith submitted to the judgment and decision of the Commission, as provided by law.

T. W. FERRY,
President of the Senate.

Mr. Commissioner ABBOTT. I move, Mr. President, that all the papers received be printed.

Mr. Commissioner EDMUNDS. I hope that order will not be entered, because I trust we shall be able to use the papers here, as they are evidently tolerably brief, and no doubt both sides understand exactly what are the points. I hope the papers will be here for the mere purpose of examining them; and upon them it is understood a question of law arises. The only doubt about the printing is that it may involve a delay until to-morrow.

The PRESIDENT. The question is on the motion to print.

Mr. Commissioner ABBOTT. I think they ought to be printed.

The PRESIDENT. One of the assistant secretaries has suggested to me that they are pretty long.

Mr Commissioner MILLER. If by printing is meant that they shall be printed when it is convenient to send them out, I see no objection; but if it is meant that they shall be sent out at once to be printed, I for one object to it. I think we ought to get along with this case; but if we can have them printed by to-night or to-morrow morning, very well, we going on in the mean time.

Mr. Commissioner ABBOTT. I want to get along with this case as fast as anybody else. Nobody is more desirous of getting on fast than I am, and I believe I have given evidence of it generally; but I do not think with the bundle of papers here submitted, which we are to pass on, that we ought to pass on them without seeing them in print. I think it is better to get along rightly than to get along too fast and not get along rightly.

Mr. Commissioner EDMUNDS. May I ask if there are not duplicates of each set? I have no doubt there are. Now, Mr. President, if I can have the attention of my brother, Judge Abbott, I understand, as undoubtedly the fact is, that there are duplicates of each of the conflicting certificates; and, that being the case, I have no objection to the order to print, because only one set need go away, reserving the question of what shall be done if the printing is not completed in time.

The PRESIDENT. The question is on the motion to print.

The motion was agreed to.

Mr. Commissioner EDMUNDS. Now, Mr. President, I ask that the papers be read, that we may see what we have before us.

The PRESIDENT. Mr. Commissioner Edmunds moves that one set of the papers, as he understands there are two, be read.

Mr. Commissioner EDMUNDS. By that I mean one copy of each set.

The PRESIDENT. The question is on the motion of Mr. Commissioner Edmunds.

The motion was agreed to.

The PRESIDENT. The Secretary will read the papers.

The Secretary read the various certificates and objections.

The PRESIDENT. Two objectors to certificate No. 1 are entitled to be heard. Who represent the objectors?

Mr. Senator KELLY. Mr. President and gentlemen of the Commission, I will open the case on the part of the objectors to the first certificate. I should like, however, a few minutes.

Mr. Commissioner EDMUNDS. What other objector appears to certificate No. 1?

Mr. Senator KELLY. Mr. Jenks, of the House of Representatives.

The PRESIDENT. Who appear for the objectors to certificate No. 2?

Mr. Senator SARGENT. Senator Mitchell of Oregon, and Mr. Lawrence of Ohio, of the House of Representatives.

Mr. Representative JENKS. Mr. President and gentlemen, before proceeding with the hearing of the cause, it may be necessary to have certain testimony obtained—the certificate of appointment and the commission of J. W. Watts as postmaster from the Post-Office Department, and also the certificate of appointment and commission of his successor. I applied personally to that Department for those papers, and they declined to give them unless ordered by the Commission. We would ask that an order be made that they may be produced. We also desire a subpœna for two witnesses, Mr. Watts and Senator Mitchell. Senator Mitchell, however, is here, and I suppose will readily respond.

Mr. Commissioner HOAR. Mr. Jenks, is it not possible for you to agree with the other side as to the facts?

The PRESIDENT. Please wait a moment, Mr. Hoar. Let me suggest that the application had better be made by counsel.

Mr. Representative JENKS. I apprehend that it is not important from whom the application comes. Those who make the objection have a right to be heard personally. It is only to save time that we make the application now, so that the witnesses may be here when wanted.

Mr. MERRICK. It is done at the suggestion of counsel.

The PRESIDENT. The request is before the Commission. What order shall be taken?

Mr. Commissioner EDMUNDS. I move that the Commission issue the subpœna as requested and ask for certified copies of the papers wanted, to be furnished by the Post-Office Department. Whether the evidence will be competent is another question.

The PRESIDENT. Mr. Commissioner Edmunds moves that the Commission grant subpœnas for the witnesses named and also an order for the papers called for from the Post-Office Department.

Mr. Commissioner EDMUNDS. Are the witnesses within reach?

Mr. Senator MITCHELL. I will say in reference to the witnesses Mr. Jenks desires, that they are here in the court-room and will respond at any time whenever the Commission determines that it is proper that they should be called.

The PRESIDENT. The question is on the motion of Mr. Commissioner Edmunds.

The motion was agreed to.

Mr. Senator KELLY. I should like a few minutes' time to gather together some books before proceeding.

The PRESIDENT. How much time do you wish?

Mr. Senator KELLY. Half an hour, or any time that will suit the Commission.

Mr. Commissioner EDMUNDS. Mr. President, I move that the Commission take a recess for half an hour.

The motion was agreed to; and (at one o'clock and forty minutes p. m.) the Commission took a recess for half an hour.

At two o'clock and ten minutes p. m. the Commission re-assembled, all the members being present.

The objectors were also present, and the following counsel:

Richard T. Merrick, esq.,
George Hoadly, esq.,
Ashbel Green, esq.,
Alexander Porter Morse, esq., } In opposition to certificate No. 1.

Hon. William M. Evarts,
Hon. E. W. Stoughton,
Hon. Stanley Matthews,
Hon. Samuel Shellabarger, } In opposition to certificate No. 2.

The PRESIDENT. The objectors to certificate No. 1 may proceed under Rule 4, two hours to a side.

Mr. Senator MITCHELL. I desire to know whether the objectors on that side both proceed before the objectors on the other side?

The PRESIDENT. They both speak first. Counsel alternate, but objectors do not in this proceeding.

Mr. Senator KELLY. Mr. President and gentlemen of the Commission, the first objection to certificate No. 1 on which I shall dwell is this:

The said J. W. Watts, therein claimed to be one of the said electors, was in the month of February, 1873, appointed a postmaster at La Fayette, in the State of Oregon, and was duly commissioned and qualified as such postmaster, that being an office of trust and profit under the laws of the United States, and continued to be and act as such postmaster from February, 1873, until after the 13th day of November, 1876, and was acting as such postmaster on the 7th day of November, 1876, when presidential electors were appointed by the State of Oregon, and that he, the said John W. Watts, was ineligible to be appointed as one of the said presidential electors.

There will be no dispute, I presume, of the facts averred here. It is true beyond doubt that this Mr. Watts was a postmaster, and I do not think it is necessary for us under the circumstances to offer any proof of that, because the view we take of it is that that matter was found by the returning-board, and the returning-board really decided that he had no part in that election. I think, therefore, it will be unnecessary for us to produce proof of that fact. But be that as it may, if it become necessary we shall establish the point.

Now what is the result of these facts? I refer to the Constitution of the United States:

Each State shall appoint, in such manner as the legislature thereof may direct, a number of electors, equal to the whole number of Senators and Representatives to which the State may be entitled in the Congress: but no Senator or Representative, or person holding an office of trust or profit under the United States, shall be appointed an elector.

The question occurs, is this an office of profit or trust? If so, the constitutional inhibition is as clear as the English language can make it. No person shall be appointed an elector who holds an office of trust or profit. On the first point, whether it is an office of trust or profit, I will refer in the first place to the fifteenth volume of California Reports, the case of Searcy vs. Grow, reported on pages 120 and 121. I will read only so far as may be necessary and no further, because I do not wish my time to be consumed in reading unnecessary matter:

This case was before us at the last term, and was decided upon a point not now presented. The proceeding is a contest for the office of sheriff of Siskiyou County. Grow, the appellant, was returned as elected to the office at the September election, 1859. The ground of contest is that, at the time of the election, he was postmaster in the town of Yreka, and that the compensation of the office exceeded $500 per annum. The court below found for the contestant, and Grow appeals.

I call attention to this:

The court below found for the contestant.

That is, for the person next highest. I shall dwell upon that in an after portion of the argument, to show that the person next highest to the ineligible candidate received the office.

The constitution, in the twenty-first section of the fourth article, provides: "No person holding any lucrative office under the United States, or any other power, shall be eligible to any civil office of profit under this State: *Provided,* That offices in the militia to which there is attached no annual salary, or local officers and postmasters whose compensation does not exceed $500 per annum shall not be deemed lucrative." The act of the legislature prescribing the mode of contesting elections and the grounds of contest makes the fact that the returned candidate was ineligible at the time of the election one of those grounds. Grow was postmaster at the time of the election, but had resigned at the time of his qualification. It is in proof, and so found, that the income of the office of postmaster was some $1,400, but that the expenses of assistant, rent, &c., were some $1,000 per annum, so that the net sum received or enjoyed by Grow was less than $500.

The counsel for the appellant contends that the true meaning of the constitution is that the person holding the Federal office described in the twenty-first section is forbidden to take a civil State office while so holding the other; but that he is capable of receiving votes cast for him, so as to give him a right to take the State office upon or after resigning the Federal office. But we think the plain meaning of the words quoted is the opposite of this construction. The language is not that the Federal officer shall *hold* a State office while he is such Federal officer, but that he shall not while in such Federal office be *eligible* to the State office. We understand the word "eligible" to mean capable of being chosen, the subject of selection or choice. The people in this case were clothed with this power of choice; their selection of the candidate gave him all the claim to the office which he has; his title to the office comes from *their* designation of him as sheriff. But they could not designate or choose a man not eligible; *i. e.,* not capable of being selected. They might select any man they chose, subject only to this exception, that the man they selected was capable of taking what they had the power to give.

We do not see how the fact that he became capable of taking office after they had exhausted their power can avail the appellant. If he was not eligible at the time the votes were cast for him, the election failed. We do not see how it can be argued that, by the act of the candidate, the votes which, when cast, were ineffectual, because not given for a qualified candidate, became effectual to elect him to office.

Can it be contended that, if Grow had not been a citizen of the county or of the State at the time of the election, or had been an alien at that time, the bare fact that he did so become a citizen at the time he qualified would entitle him to the office? Or suppose a man, when elected, under sentence and conviction for crime—if such a case can be supposed—would a pardon before qualification give him a right to hold the office?

When the words of the constitution are plain, we cannot go into curious speculation of the policy they were meant to declare. It may, however, have been a part of the policy of the provision quoted to prevent the employment of Federal patronage in a State election.

I refer to that case as conclusive if the law stated be sound. And here I may just as well as at any other time call attention to the marked distinction that exists between a person who is ineligible or incapable of being appointed and one who may hold the office. If a person may hold the office he may be elected while he is under disqualifications, and if he becomes qualified at the time of holding, it is sufficient. For instance, let us refer to the provisions of the Constitution of the United States as to the election of Senators and Members of the House of Representatives:

No person shall be a Senator who shall not have attained to the age of thirty years.

No person shall be a Representative who shall not have attained a certain number of years and have certain other qualifications. "No person shall be a Senator;" that is, while he may be disqualified before, yet if the disqualification is removed when he becomes a Senator or Representative, he can hold the office. For instance, a man is holding the office of governor this day, a State office; he has been elected Senator while so holding the office. It is no bar to him taking his seat on the 4th of March next if on that day he does not hold the office of governor. That, however, is a very different case from this, which strikes at the beginning of the matter; that is, where the prohibition is to the election, or, in this instance, to the appointment.

Now, when does the appointment begin? What is the day of appointment? It is contended, or at least was by other gentlemen in Oregon—it was contended by Mr. Watts that he could hold the office of elector if he was eligible at the time the vote was cast; that the appointment was not complete until the certificate was given; and I here say, if it was not complete until the certificate was given, it was never completed at all, because he never got one. But he contends that the appointment was not perfect by the election of the 7th of November, but was perfected when the canvass of votes was made. That is a fallacious position. It cannot be maintained, because the returns of a canvass are merely evidence of appointment; they are not the appointment itself. The Constitution gives the right to Congress to appoint the time of holding the election, and section 131 of the Revised Statutes provides:

The electors of President and Vice-President shall be appointed, in each State, on the Tuesday next after the first Monday in November in every fourth year succeeding every election of a President and Vice-President.

They must be appointed on that day; if they are not appointed on that day they are not appointed at all. I contend, therefore, that the appointment of Mr. Watts, if it was not made on the 7th day of November, could not be made at any other time by a canvass of the votes. The mere evidence of a fact is not the fact itself. That I am correct in that position I think there can be no doubt. So it was held by the court in California.

I refer now to the election in the State of Vermont. Of course I do not know all the facts attending it except those which were current at the time or shortly after the election; but as nearly as I can recollect them they are these: A man by the name of Sollace was a postmaster at the time of the election on the 7th of November; he resigned a few days afterward; he was a candidate for elector. The legislature of Vermont convened, I do not know whether by proclamation, but I think the honorable Senator from Vermont [Mr. Edmunds] stated sometime ago that it was by virtue of some law in that State, without proclamation of the governor. At all events the legislature of that State convened. They took this matter into consideration; they declared virtually, I do not know whether by resolution or otherwise, that Sollace was not appointed on that day, and proceeded by legislative enactment, as prescribed by the Constitution, to fill that vacancy occasioned by a failure to elect. It was under this section of the Revised Statutes, I presume:

SEC. 134. Whenever any State has held an election for the purpose of choosing electors, and has failed to make a choice on the day prescribed by law, the electors may be appointed on a subsequent day, in such a manner as the legislature of such State may direct.

So the State of Vermont in its sovereign capacity declared that a postmaster was an officer holding an office of trust and profit under the United States, and that there was a failure to elect, and they proceeded to provide for the case. So in Rhode Island: Mr. Corliss was a centennial commissioner under the United States. Under the peculiar provisions of many of the New England States the governor has the right to submit questions of law to the courts. The governor of Rhode Island did submit the question to the supreme court of Rhode Island. There was one dissenting voice as to whether the position of centennial commissioner was an office of trust or profit. The majority of the court held that it was, and the unanimous voice of the court was that, if it was an office of trust or profit, the person holding it who had been voted for was not elected, and that, not being elected, there was a failure to elect; and the legislature proceeded to provide for the case.

There are two legislatures who have established this fact clearly beyond doubt, that a person holding an office of profit or trust under the United States could not be an elector, and that a resignation of the office after the election did not make him qualified.

In addition to that, let me refer to what was said by a committee appointed by the Senate and House of Representatives in 1837, of which Mr. Grundy was chairman. It was composed on the part of the Senate of Felix Grundy, Henry Clay, and Silas Wright, certainly three persons who ought to carry weight. Wherever they signed their names to any document of a political character, it ought to carry conclusive weight as to its integrity and its worth. I do not care about reading it all, but I will read a portion of it. Certain postmasters had been elected electors in North Carolina, Connecticut, and New Hampshire; but it made no difference at that time whether their votes were disallowed or not, as it would not change the result of the election; so there was nothing done in the matter, but the committee gave this opinion in their report:

The committee are of opinion that the first section of the second article of the Constitution, which declares that " no Senator or Representative, or person holding an office of trust or profit under the United States, shall be appointed an elector," ought to be carried in its whole spirit into rigid execution, in order to prevent officers of the General Government from bringing their official power to influence the elections of President and Vice-President of the United States. This provision of the Constitution, it is believed, excludes and disqualifies deputy postmasters from the appointment of electors; and the disqualification relates to the time of the appointments, and that a resignation of the office of deputy postmaster after his appointment as elector would not entitle him to vote as elector under the Constitution.

In the debate ensuing in the House of Representatives upon the report of this joint committee, Mr. Francis Thomas, chairman of the House committee, said that—

The committee came unanimously to the conclusion that they (the postmasters in question) were not eligible at the time they were elected, and therefore the whole proceeding was vitiated *ab initio*.

Mr. Representative LAWRENCE. Those postmasters voted.

Mr. Senator KELLY. I suppose they did vote, but I do not know; their votes, however, made no difference in the result. Here I will call attention to this fact—it is a little out of the way, but it is an answer to a suggestion—I contend that a State has the power to enforce the Constitution if the Federal Government does not. I contend that every State has a right to exclude Federal officers. Here the mandate of the Constitution is clear. If other States have permitted it to be violated, the State of Oregon has not. If other States have failed to take advantage of the provision, the State of Oregon has decided that the Constitution shall be obeyed; and I contend that whatever may have been done in 1837 has no application now. The mandate is clear that these persons shall not be appointed electors, and each State has a right to appoint presidential electors in its own way, and if the law of the State excludes these men from that office, the State has a perfect right to exclude them, and the decision in this case has done it. I do not see how anything can be plainer than this, and as I have dwelt long enough on the point I will leave it.

The next question presented is, if Mr. Watts was not eligible, then was Mr. Cronin, who received the next highest number of votes, elected? It is impossible for me to refer to all the decisions in the brief space of one hour; I must necessarily be hurried; and I will, therefore, only cite a few to show that where a person who is ineligible has received the highest number of votes, the next highest takes the election. It has been so decided in Indiana, in Maryland, and in Maine, and it was confirmed by legislative enactment in the latter State, and I contend that in California this is the rule. I shall refer to decisions in support of that position. On account of the rapidity with which my time is going, I will refer to the brief more than I will to the law-books. Here is what is said in Gulick *vs.* New, 14 Indiana Reports, page 93:

The governor may determine, even against the decision of a board of canvassers, whether an applicant is entitled to receive a commission or not, where the objection to his right to receive it rests upon the ground that the constitutional prohibition is interposed. If the governor should ascertain that he has commissioned a person who is ineligible to the office, he may issue another commission to the person legally entitled thereto. Where a majority of the ballots at an election were for a person not eligible to the office under the Constitution, it was held that the ballots cast for such ineligible person were ineffectual, and that the person receiving the greatest number of legal votes, though not a majority of the ballots, was duly elected and entitled to the office. The mayor of a city, under the general law, has jurisdiction as a judicial officer throughout the county, and the voters of the county are therefore chargeable with notice of his ineligibility under the Constitution to any office other than a judicial one during the term for which he was elected.

To the same effect are the cases in 41 Indiana, 572, and 15 Indiana, 327. It is the doctrine in Maine, so adjudged by the supreme court upon a question submitted by the legislature to the court. I have referred already to the case of Searcy *vs.* Grow, in 15 California. In that case—

The ground of contest is that at the time of the election he was postmaster in the town of Yreka, and that the compensation of the office exceeded $500 per annum. The court below found for the contestant, and Grow appeals.

Grow was the postmaster. The office was adjudged to the contestant in that case.

Now, there are facts that we cannot produce here, I suppose, though taken before a committee of the Senate, showing that notice of the disqualification was given to a great many voters in this case; that Mr. Watts had proclaimed at a meeting in Portland, one of the largest meetings held there, that he was postmaster; the fact that he was postmaster was declared at Oregon City; it was published in a newspaper published in his own town, and also in a paper published in Portland; but these facts I cannot, I suppose, bring before this tribunal. I contend, however, as matter of law and upon principle, that in Oregon the next highest person to an ineligible candidate takes the place. We have in our constitution this clause:

In all elections held by the people under this constitution the person or persons who shall receive the highest number of votes shall be declared duly elected.

There are certain prohibitions in our constitution, among others that a person who is a defaulter shall not be elected; a person who has sent a challenge to fight a duel shall not be elected; a man who has been convicted of an infamous crime shall not be elected. Now, can it be contended, taking these clauses together, that when the constitution says the person who receives the highest number of votes shall be declared duly elected, the people can elect a person who has been convicted of felony, a defaulter, one who has fought a duel or sent a challenge? No, they must be construed together; and they mean this, that the person who is qualified to receive the votes shall be elected if he receives the highest number of votes, and if the person having the most votes is ineligible, the qualified person receiving the next highest number shall be declared elected.

Again, the Constitution of the United States says that persons shall be elected electors on the day prescribed by Congress; Congress has fixed the day; and the law of Oregon provides:

On the Tuesday next after the first Monday in November, 1864, and every four years thereafter there shall be elected by the qualified electors of this State as many electors of President and Vice-President as this State may be entitled to elect of Senators and Representatives in Congress.

There is a positive injunction that they shall be elected on that day; there is no authority to hold an election after that time; and I contend according to principle that the first election should decide the whole matter, because it is impossible to convene the electors at a subsequent time and hold a new election to supply a vacancy. In all those cases where it is held that the next highest to the ineligible candidate is not elected, it is because it may be referred to the people to vote again upon the question; but here they cannot do that. The power of the people having been exhausted, they cannot vote a second time. They have not time to do it, because the presidential electors vote within thirty days after the State election, so that it is impossible to hold a second election, and necessarily the first one must decide the matter. The three highest eligible candidates must be chosen then, or the State will have no representation; there will be a failure to elect one person, and the State will lose its rights. The position I take here is that there is a positive injunction that the State must do that. The law is mandatory. It says the election must take place on that day; three electors must be chosen on that day.

A State cannot elect a man that the Constitution says cannot be elected; and therefore if three must be elected on that day, it must be the three highest qualified persons. It is different, I contend, from ordinary cases of office where a majority not being had, the matter is referred back to the people. A plurality elects in the State of Oregon. And I may as well here state the difference between the case of Abbott, which was before the Senate of the United States a few years ago, and this case. Mr. Abbott claimed that he was elected Senator from North Carolina because Mr. Vance, his competitor, was ineligible. He received but a few votes. The Senate rejected him and for a very good reason; not because Mr. Vance was not ineligible, but because the law regulating the election of Senators says that the person receiving the highest number of votes, provided it shall be a majority of all the senators and representatives of the legislature present, shall be elected, and he must have that majority. No person contended that Abbott had such a majority. In this case it is not required that a man shall have a majority, but a plurality or the highest number of votes; that is, as I contend, the highest number of votes if he be eligible to be elected.

The next point which I shall discuss is the one which will probably be most strenuously contested, and therefore I shall refer to it at greater length. It is said that the governor had no right to decide this matter; that it was a judicial question and not a question for the executive. There is nothing more fallacious. In every department of the Government of the United States, as well as in the government of the States, every officer, whether legislative, executive, or judicial, is compelled to exercise judgment in certain cases. Take for instance the Executive of the United States. When the disposition of land has to be made between two persons, rival claimants, is it referred to the courts to settle that matter? Not at all. The Land-Office adjudicates it. They settle the case where two rival claimants, two settlers holding adversely to each other, present themselves before the Land-Office. The Land Department decides the case preliminary to a final adjudication according to law in the courts. It is a preliminary decision that must be made.

So there must be a preliminary decision made in regard to many other matters that it is needless for me to call to your attention. So it is in the State governments. The executive is called upon to exercise certain duties and rights. He must decide. For instance, an office-holder has ceased to be a resident of the State, or he has died. The executive must take cognizance of the fact of the death of an incumbent without having a court decide that fact. He takes cognizance of an abandonment where a person leaves the State, and makes an appointment to fill the vacancy. Here let me refer to decisions in support of this position which I take——

Mr. Commissioner GARFIELD. Are these cases cited in your brief?

Mr. Senator KELLY. Yes, sir. I will only read the syllabus of the case in 1 Arkansas Reports, page 21:

The Supreme Court has the power to issue writs of mandamus. The party applying for this writ must show that he has a specific legal right, and no other adequate specific legal remedy.

A collector or holder of public moneys who was in default for moneys collected at the time of the adoption of the Constitution, at the time of his election to another or the same office, and at the time of his application for his commission, is not entitled to his commission.

I will now read a part of the opinion of the court:

He is, then, clearly within the meaning of the Constitution, and consequently ineligible to any office of profit or trust. So far as the rights and interests of the present applicant are concerned, the Executive has done nothing that the law forbids; and whether his subsequent acts in relation to the same matter are inconsistent with his constitutional obligations to the country, or in violation of private rights, this court will not take upon themselves to determine; for that question is not properly before them. The Executive, in common with every other officer, is bound by oath to support the Constitution, and whenever an effort is made to evade or violate it, it is not only his privilege but his duty to interpose and prevent it.

So in 14 Indiana Reports, Gulick vs. New. This was a case of mandamus to compel the governor to issue a commission. The court say:

The governor may determine, even against the decision of a board of canvassers, whether an applicant is entitled to receive a commission or not, where the objection to his right to receive it rests upon the ground that the constitutional prohibition is interposed.

If the governor should ascertain that he has commissioned a person who is ineligible to the office, he may issue another commission to the person legally entitled thereto.

So in 39 Missouri Reports, a mandamus was asked against the governor to compel him to give a certificate to a person who was ineligible. The court took this position:

The governor is bound to see that the laws are faithfully executed, and he has taken an oath to support the constitution. In the correct and legitimate performance of his duty, he must inevitably have a discretion in regard to granting commissions; for, should a person be elected or appointed who was constitutionally ineligible to hold any office of profit or trust, would the executive be bound to commission him when his ineligibility was clearly and positively proven? If he is denied the exercise of any discretion in such case, he is made the violator of the constitution, not its guardian. Of what avail, then, is his oath of office? Or, if he has positive and satisfactory evidence that no election has been held in a county, shall he be required to violate the law and issue a commission to a person not elected because a clerk has certified to the election? In granting a commission, the governor may go behind the certificate to determine whether an applicant is entitled to receive a commission or not, where the objection to the right of the applicant to receive it rests upon the ground that a constitutional prohibition is interposed—(Gulick vs. New, 14 Indiana 93.) The issuing of a commission is an act by the executive in his political capacity—

Not his judicial.—

The issuing of a commission is an act by the executive in his political capacity, and is one of the means employed to enable him to execute the laws and carry on the appropriate functions of the State, and for the manner in which he executes this duty he is in no wise amenable to the judiciary. The court can no more interfere with executive discretion than the legislature or executive can with judicial discretion. The granting of a commission by the executive is not a mere ministerial duty, but an official act imposed by the constitution, and is an investiture of authority in the person receiving it. We are of the opinion, therefore, that mandamus will not lie against the governor in a case like this.

I will now turn to 1 Arkansas, page 595:

In all of these cases he certainly possesses a political discretion, for the use of which he is alone answerable to his country. Why, then, is his discretion taken, away or destroyed when his duty concerns the issuing of a commission? It certainly is not. His duty is as clearly political in that case as in any of the other enumerations, and if the courts have jurisdiction in that instance to prescribe the rule of his conduct, by a parity of reasoning they certainly possess it in regard to all the other cases. This would make the judges the interpreters not only of the will of the executive, but of his conscience and reason; and his oath of office, upon such a supposition, would then be both a mockery and a delusion.

Again, the executive is bound to see that the laws are faithfully executed, and he has taken an oath of office to support the constitution. How can he perform this duty if he has no discretion left him in regard to granting commissions? For should the legislature appoint a person constitutionally ineligible to hold any office of profit or trust, would the executive be bound to commission him? and that, too, when his ineligibility was clearly and positively proven? In such a case, the exercise of his discretion must be admitted, or you make him not the guardian but the violator of the constitution. What, then, becomes of his oath of office?

Not only that, but the State of Oregon itself has decided this matter. I will call the attention of the Commission now to not a reported case, but to a matter familiar to my colleague and to myself. In the election of 1870 Ex-Governor Gibbs was elected district attorney for the State—prosecuting attorney, as we call it there. After entering upon the discharge of the duties, in March, 1872, he received from the President of the United States an appointment to the office of United States district attorney, and he was holding both offices at the same time. The governor knowing that fact, knowing too that the constitution of the State of Oregon prohibited any person who was holding an office under the Federal Government to hold a State office, this very Governor Grover appointed C. B. Bellinger prosecuting attorney for the State. Ex-Governor Gibbs refused to recognize that appointment; he claimed the right to prosecute the criminals in the State courts and in the Federal courts. Mr. Bellinger presented his certificate of appointment from the governor to Judge Upton, chief-justice then of the State, who refused to recognize him because he said the governor had no right to ascertain that matter; it was a question for the judiciary to ascertain. On the other hand, Mr. Bellinger, believing himself right, brought a writ of *quo warranto* to ascertain that fact, whether he was not entitled to hold the office. He brought it in the court where Judge Upton presided, who was chief-justice of the State. He decided adversely to him on the same ground, that it was a matter of judicial inquiry and the governor had no right to act. An appeal was taken to the supreme court, and by a unanimous court it was decided that the governor had that right. The case is not yet reported, for reasons which are given by the present chief justice of Oregon in this letter to the governor:

SUPREME COURT ROOM,
Salem, Oregon, December 20, 1876.

SIR: Your communication of the 18th instant was duly received, and, in reply thereto, I beg leave to submit the following:

The case of the State of Oregon ex rel. C. B. Bellinger, appellant, *vs.* A. C. Gibbs, respondent, was heard and determined at the January term, 1873, of the supreme court. The action was instituted in the circuit court of the State of Oregon for the county of Multnomah, and was determined at the March term, 1872, of said court. The complaint alleged in effect that the respondent had been elected to the office of prosecuting attorney in the fourth judicial district in June, 1870, for the term of two years; that he entered upon, held, and exercised the office; that thereafter, and while so holding, he was appointed to the office of United States district attorney for the district of Oregon, and that he qualified and entered upon said office on March 2, 1872. Allegations showing that both offices were lucrative were duly made, and it was further alleged that on March 6, 1872, the governor of Oregon duly appointed the relator to the office of prosecuting attorney for the said fourth judicial district, and that said relator duly qualified on March 8, 1872, and thereupon made demand upon the respondent for the office, which demand was refused.

Respondent demurred to the complaint in the court below upon the ground, among others, that the complaint did not state facts sufficient to constitute a cause of action.

The court below (Upton, J.) sustained the demurrer and entered a judgment against the relator for costs, &c.

An appeal was thereupon taken to the supreme court at the term mentioned. Upon the argument in the supreme court the respondent, in support of his demurrer, contended "that the governor could not determine for himself that a vacancy existed in the office of prosecuting attorney in the fourth judicial district so as to authorize the appointment of the relator, for the reason that the determination of that fact involved the exercise of judicial functions by the executive."

This was the principal legal question in the case, and the court unanimously declared that the governor was invested with authority, in cases of the kind, to look into the facts and pass upon the same without awaiting the action of the courts.

The justices of the supreme court were, at the time, Hon. W. W. Upton, chief-justice; Hon. A. J. Thayer, P. P. Prim, B. F. Bonham, and L. L. McArthur, associate justices. As the case was from the fourth district, Upton, chief-justice, did not participate in the hearing and decision in the supreme court. The writing of the opinion was assigned to Hon. A. J. Thayer, who died shortly after the adjournment of the term, leaving the duty unperformed. Ex-Chief-Justice Bonham and Justice McArthur authorize me to say that their recollection of the case and the point decided comports with my own.

I have the honor to be, your excellency's obedient servant,

> P. P. PRIM,
> *Chief-Justice of Oregon.*

His Excellency L. F. GROVER,
Governor of Oregon.

There is the very point decided that the governor has a right to inquire into these facts; has a right to inquire into ineligibility and to issue a commission when there is any infraction of the constitution. In the very words of the constitution of the State, he is to see that the laws are faithfully executed, and he is to take an oath prescribed there that he will support the Constitution of the United States and of the State. Shall it be held that the governor of the State of Oregon is all-powerless when the Constitution of the United States is to be invaded and he is to certify that a man has been elected who cannot be elected without a violation of that Constitution? Is he to sit quietly by when the fact is presented to him, as it was by affidavits at the time of the canvass of these votes, that this man was a postmaster, that he was holding an office of profit and trust under the United States? And I again ask, in the language of the courts of Missouri and other States, is he, when he has sworn to support the Constitution of the United States and of the State of Oregon, to see both trampled under foot by giving a certificate to a man who is ineligible? No, it is not so. They say, Why not go to the courts? The executive has the right, as I have shown you, to decide questions of this kind.

It is impossible for me to elaborate on these points in the limited time allowed me; but I call attention to this law of Oregon:

The votes for electors shall be given, received, returned, and canvassed as the same are given, returned, and canvassed for members of Congress.

Another duty, in addition to that, is imposed upon the secretary of state:

The secretary of state shall prepare two lists of the names of the electors elected, and affix the seal of the State to the same. Such lists shall be signed by the governor and secretary, and by the latter delivered to the college of electors at the hour of their meeting.

This is the evidence of their appointment; this is their right to act, from what has appeared from the reading of the certificates. There is no canvass mentioned; there is simply a list of the votes given. I contend that the governor of Oregon and the secretary of state are the persons to canvass these votes. There is no evidence that there was any canvass by any other person. They must decide upon that question; it is for them and them only, and they have decided and they have given their certificate that these three gentlemen are eligible, including Mr. Cronin. It matters not how they came to that conclusion; the presumption of law will always be that it was upon sufficient evidence. They had evidence of the ineligibility of one of the candidates, and they decided upon that point. They decided that that was sufficient to exclude him, and therefore a certificate was given in the language that was read here, that the highest eligible candidates were Cartwright, Odell, and Cronin.

Mr. Senator MITCHELL. Mr. President——

Mr. Senator KELLY. I cannot yield any part of my time, it is so short.

Mr. Senator MITCHELL. I simply want to say, if my colleague will permit me——

Mr. Senator KELLY. You can answer me in your own time. I say it is clear that these two officers had the right to decide and did decide that matter. They are the only medium of communication between the State and the Federal Government. What authority had Cartwright, Odell, and Watts by going to the secretary of state and getting a list of the votes of the people?—what right have they to say that they are electors simply by getting that? Any person can go and get that certificate by paying the fees. Suppose three or four persons who did not care anything about their obligations as good citizens of the United States had gone and got a certificate of the same kind, as they could get it from the secretary of state by paying for it, and signed the names of Watts, Odell, and Cartwright, and given their votes for Tilden, how would you know the difference? You cannot tell by it; you cannot tell whether their signatures are genuine or not, excepting from the fact that they have the certificate of the governor, which attests them and which is required by the law of the United States. I contend that the United States have the right to prescribe how those votes shall be certified. The legislatures of the States have the right to regulate the manner of election, the exclusive right. That I admit; but when the election was completed, when the electors were chosen, and the votes were to be certified from the State to the President of the Senate, it must be done under United States laws. They regulate that in the State itself, and the State laws of Oregon demand that this certificate shall be signed by the governor and attested by the secretary of state.

Mr. Commissioner THURMAN. Mr. Kelly, I should like to ask one question. Does the law of Oregon require the secretary of state to give any decision at all, or does it require the governor to give the evidence of the decision?

Mr. Senator KELLY. I will read the law:

The votes for electors shall be given, received, returned, and canvassed as the same are given, returned, and canvassed for members of Congress.

That is, so far as the mere counting and tabulation go, it is given to the secretary, the governor being present. Then in addition:

The secretary of state shall prepare two lists of the names of the electors elected—

So that they have a right to judge of the qualifications—

The secretary of state shall prepare two lists of the names of the electors elected, and affix the seal of the State to the same. Such lists shall be signed by the governor and secretary, and by the latter delivered to the college of electors at the hour of their meeting on such first Wednesday of December.

Mr. Commissioner THURMAN. Now I want to ask a question of fact; did the secretary of state make out that list including the name of Watts?

Mr. Senator KELLY. No, sir; he did not include the name of Watts. Upon the facts and upon the law—the interposition of a protest by a number of gentlemen to the counting of the vote of Watts, an affidavit being made that the identical man was a postmaster—the governor undertook to decide that matter, as he had a right to decide it under the decisions I have cited, and under the laws of Oregon. He did so in pursuance of his right as chief executive of the State and by authority of law, and the secretary of state attested his act; and that decision is in evidence here, and is the only evidence of who had a right to cast the electoral votes, and that was given to Mr. Cronin as well as the other two.

Mr. Senator MITCHELL. Will my colleague allow me to interrupt him a moment?

Mr. Senator KELLY. I will not allow you a moment; you have an hour.

The PRESIDENT. The speaker has the floor unless he yields.

Mr. Senator MITCHELL. Certainly; I understand that, Mr. President.

Mr. Senator KELLY. Mr. President——

Mr. Commissioner MILLER. Perhaps you will answer me a question.

Mr. Senator KELLY. Certainly.

Mr. Commissioner MILLER. "The votes for electors shall be given, received, returned, and canvassed as the same are given, returned, and canvassed for members of Congress." How do we find out how that is done?

Mr. Commissioner EDMUNDS. Section 37 of the general laws seems to provide for it.

Mr. Senator·MITCHELL. Found at page 139 of your compilation.

Mr. Commissioner ABBOTT. I wish to ask a single question of fact, whether the certificate No. 2 which we have here is not in exact accordance with that provision of the law of Oregon which you have read; that is, that a certificate should be given signed by the secretary of state and the governor?

Mr. Senator KELLY. It is in exact accordance with the requirements of the law of Oregon and the law of the United States.

Mr. Commissioner ABBOTT. Have you any other board in Oregon to certify to the election of the electors but that board?

Mr. Senator KELLY. None.

Mr. Commissioner ABBOTT. That is what I wanted to get at.

Mr. Senator KELLY. I find I have but five minutes left, and I will give that to my associate objector.

Mr. Representative JENKS. Mr. President and gentlemen of the Commission, we propose to plead the cause of truth and justice, the cause of thirty-five millions out of forty of the free people of the United States; a cause whose justice is attested by a clear majority of 250,000 of the popular vote; a cause whose justice is corroborated by a clear majority of 25 in the electoral college of the United States. With these facts behind us, and with the questions of law and fact involved in this case, we shall ask at your hands that it shall be decided according to them. We ask no technical advantage, but recognizing that the law of the land is truth in law as facts may be truth in fact, we ask that you shall give them their true weight; and regarding the Constitution of the United States as the primordial law, the all-controlling fact in this case, we ask, all having sworn to its support, that that support, without abatement, shall be fully accorded to it.

The first question, necessarily, is a question of evidence. What evidence is there before this tribunal, or what evidence can or will be received by it, are the first questions; and in answer to them, if we are to judge by the precedents established by this tribunal in the past, we would infer that there is to be no evidence except those papers which come, with the several returns, from the President of the Senate. That would narrow the inquiry to a very small space, and that space first we propose to discuss; not that we say differently from what we said before, that we would ask you finally to a frugal feast; we would invite you, as before, to go down to the bottom facts, for if our case be not founded upon the merits of truth and justice I would not have it.

But inquiring in the light in which this tribunal must first inquire, we will consider it on the narrow ground of the papers submitted by the President of the Senate. With reference to these, the inquiry would arise, which of these, if any, is legal evidence? If either one be legal evidence and the other be not, if you are guided by the law of the land, you must find in accordance with the legal evidence. The evidence as offered with the returns by the President of the Senate is, first, the certificate of the governor of Oregon, in the following words, also attested by the secretary of state, under the great seal thereof:

STATE OF OREGON, EXECUTIVE OFFICE,
Salem, December 6, 1876.

I, L. F. Grover, governor of the State of Oregon, do hereby certify that, at a general election held in said State on the 7th day of November, A. D. 1876, William H. Odell received 15,206 votes, John C. Cartwright received 15,214 votes, E. A. Cronin received 14,157 votes for electors of President and Vice-President of the United States. Being the highest number of votes cast at said election for persons eligible, under the Constitution of the United States, to be appointed electors of President and Vice-President of the United States, they are hereby declared duly elected electors as aforesaid for the State of Oregon.

And there is the usual clause of attestation, with the seal of the State, the signature of the governor, and the countersigning of the secretary of state. That is the evidence on the part of certificate No. 2. The evidence on the part of certificate No. 1 consists of an affidavit of three persons whom we know not, because there is no evidence to identify them as having been any of the persons voted for at that election, swearing that they had gone to the governor and asked for a certificate. Is it not his duty to judge to whom he will deliver certificates? May there not be two John Smiths in this world? And what right have these men to come in and by their oath attempt to supply that which is fixed by statute as the only legal evidence of a given transaction?

There, then, is the oath of three men, whom you know not and who have no indentification before this tribunal of any character recognized by the law, that they have gone and asked for a certificate, and that the governor would not give it to them. That is the first paper; and if that be legal evidence before this tribunal, what would not be? The affidavit of any other three men in the United States would be received with the same weight as theirs; and if this tribunal acts on the same theory it has heretofore promulgated, that is a simple nullity.

Then the next evidence of authentication which they attempt to originate is a statement of votes in that State, with the certificate of the secretary of state that it is a true statement of the votes as cast, with the electoral vote of the persons therein claiming to be electors thereto attached.

Now, we stand on the legal proposition that where there is a statutory mode of authentication, no other mode of authentication can be received as legal evidence in a court of justice. Then the inquiry would be, what is the statutory authentication required by the law? In support of this proposition we will give your honors an authority. We will cite you to the case of Bleecker *vs.* Bond, 3 Washington's Circuit Court Reports, page 531. There the offer made before Judge Washington was:

> The certificate of Joseph Nourse, the Register of the Treasury Department, under his hand, that certain receipts, of which copies are annexed, are on file in his office, with a certificate of the Secretary of the Treasury, under the seal of the Department, that Joseph Nourse is Register, was offered in evidence, and objected to.
>
> The court overruled the evidence upon the ground that it is not sufficient that the officer who gives this certificate has the custody of the papers, unless it also appeared that he is authorized by law to certify such papers, which this officer is not. A sworn copy ought to have been produced.

Then as a *sequitur* from that we would cite your honors to the case of Pendleton *vs.* The United States, 2 Brockenborough's Reports, page 75, in which the principle announced is that "the certificate must be in the form prescribed by law."

Then if the officer has not power to certify, or if the certificate be not in the form prescribed by law, it is not evidence before any tribunal. Now is there a form prescribed by law that this certificate shall have; and, if there is, will you, in the face of clearly-established law, rule that this is any evidence, for any purpose whatever, as against a certificate that fully, in all particulars, conforms to the law of the land? What is the law of the land in reference to that? First, with reference to the law of Oregon, what does it require? It says:

> The secretary of state shall prepare two lists of the names of the electors elected, and affix the seal of the State to the same. Such lists shall be signed by the governor and secretary, and by the latter delivered to the college of electors at the hour of their meeting on such first Wednesday of December.

Then, by the law of Oregon, it is necessary that the certificate shall have, first, the attestation of the secretary of state; second, it shall have the signature of the governor. Our certificate has this; the other has not. If the law of Oregon, then, is to be your rule as to evidence, no other can be received in the face of that statute. But is there any other law beside that of Oregon that can be used as a guide in this tribunal? We will give you the law of the United States, in which it is provided that—

> It shall be the duty of the executive of each State to cause three lists of the names of the electors of such State to be made and certified, and to be delivered to the electors on or before the day on which they are required by the preceding section to meet.—*Section 136, Revised Statutes United States.*

Here, then, is the statute of Oregon and here is the statute of the United States, each of which prescribes the mode of testifying to a given fact. There is a conformity to that, in all particulars, in the one, and there is not even the semblance of a conformance in the other; and which shall be received?

We say, then, that this evidence, in the absence of fraud, intentional fraud, should be received and held conclusive. If the allegation were, and it were proven, that the governor fraudulently refused to do a duty, it would be your duty, I should say, to inquire concerning that, and never give vitality to infamy; but, in the absence of the allegation of fraud, the certificate of the governor and the secretary of state must be taken as complete and conclusive evidence of the fact therein contained; and that fact is that this man Cronin, with two others, was elected.

Then as to the question of evidence: one side offers you the evidence required by law; the other gives you no evidence authorized by law. This certificate and its delivery by the governor and the secretary of state are not altogether purposeless either. The object of that and the requirement of the statute of the United States, which says that it shall accompany their votes, is to identify the persons who do the voting with the persons who were voted for. If a man came without a certificate, how do you know, in a large State like New York, that there might not be a dozen men of identically the same name as his who recorded the vote? Hence, the statute of the United States has wisely said, in order that we may judge as to whether the person who has cast the vote is the identical person voted for and commissioned, that the presence of the certificate is required with the vote, and it must attend it. So this is not to be neglected either.

But the question of evidence being the narrow plank of this platform, let us go beyond it. The next question is, what would be the effect of that evidence even in the case of error or mistake? If that error were willful and fraudulent, we assert now, as we have ever asserted, that fraud vitiates all things into which it enters as a constituent element; but if it were merely a mistake or error in the integrity of the person whose duty it was to give it, it must be received as a verity; and to sustain this we first assert the proposition that granting the commission is a political act, and as such cannot, except for willful fraud, be inquired into by any other tribunal than that whose duty it is to exercise the political function. In support of that we would call your honors' attention to Gulick vs. New, 14 Indiana Reports, page 96:

As to the second branch of the objection. It is made the duty of the governor to issue commissions in certain cases and to certain officers. The sheriff is one of the officers that thus receives a commission upon his election; and we have no doubt that if the governor should ascertain that he had, through mistake or otherwise, improperly issued a commission to one person to fill that office, when in truth it ought to have been issued to another, he may correct the error by issuing one to the person legally entitled thereto.

Again, I cite High on Extraordinary Legal Remedies, page 98, speaking of political duties:

The doctrine as thus stated has been most frequently applied in cases where it has been sought by mandamus to compel the governor of a State to issue commissions to persons claiming to be rightfully elected to public offices. And the courts have held the duty of issuing such commissions to be of a political nature, requiring the exercise of the political powers of the governor, and none the less an executive act because it is positively required of the governor by law. The mere fact that no discretion is left with the executive as to the manner of its performance, does not render it a ministerial duty in the sense that mandamus will lie to compel its performance, and whatever constitutional powers are conferred upon the executive are regarded as political powers, and all duties enjoined upon him as political duties.

Then if the governor issues this, even to the wrong person, it is a political duty imposed upon him by the law of the land and by the constitution of the State, and when he is acting under the obligation of his oath to support the Constitution of the United States his act, if exercised bona fide, cannot be inquired into elsewhere, and in the absence of the allegation of fraud that certificate, no matter how groundless it might be, is entirely conclusive on this tribunal and every other.

But the evidence is attested, as I might have stated before, by the very canvassing-board itself. The secretary of state and the governor, the canvassing-board, declare that as the result of the election; and the governor in pursuance thereof having exercised a political function, you have no legal right to go back of that in the absence of the allegation of fraud and inquire into its issues.

But having considered it in the light of an evidential question, we do not propose to limit ourselves to that narrow sphere, for a President of the United States ought not to be elected upon a mere technicality. The ruler of a great people needs some title broader than a hair-splitting distinction on which to rest his title, and we ask to go to the merits and the truth of the case. Assuming now for the sake of the argument that Mr. Watts received a greater number of votes than Mr. Cronin, and that he was a postmaster of the United States at the time those votes were cast, was he elected? We propose to demonstrate that he was not elected, even if he received a majority of the votes cast; and in support of that, of course, the fundamental proposition would be the Constitution of the United States, and I will refer to it in order to call your honors' attention to a distinction which exists between cases which must be distinguished or cause utter confusion in the law as administered and announced in the different States. On this subject the Constitution of the United States says:

No * * person holding an office of trust or profit under the United States shall be appointed an elector.

It does not say no person holding an office of trust or profit shall hold the privilege of an elector; nor does it say he shall not be an elector; but it says he shall not be "appointed an elector." The time of appointment is the all-important time with reference to this. The very object in putting this provision in the Constitution doubtless was that the Federal Government should never exercise its influence in the election of electors to perpetuate itself in power. The influence in the election was what was wished to be excluded; and hence the appointment was the vital moment intended to be taken into consideration. You will notice the language is, that they shall not be "appointed." It is not that they shall not hold, or, that they shall not exercise the functions; or, that they shall be incompatible, as many of the statutes of the States are; but, he shall not be appointed at all.

While noticing that distinction, allow me to call the attention of the Commission to what will explain consistently all the decisions throughout the United States. We find in one of the Pennsylvania reports an opinion delivered by his honor Mr. Justice Strong, in Commonwealth *vs.* Cluly, 56 Pennsylvania State Reports, in which the expression is made that he knows no judicial authority to support the proposition that a man who does not receive a majority of votes can be elected, and he cites congressional authority against it, ruling on what has been done in Congress and in the Senate of the United States in reference to determining the law as to contested appointments. In reference to Representatives of the United States, the language is:

No person shall be a Representative who shall not have attained to the age of twenty-five years and been seven years a citizen of the United States.

It does not say no person shall be elected to Congress or nobody shall be appointed a Congressman, but it says he shall not be a Congressman. The same language holds with reference to the Senate:

No person shall be a Senator who shall not have attained to the age of thirty years.

Showing that the time of holding is what is referred to in these several sections. This is also corroborated by the next clause:

No person shall be a Representative who shall not have attained to the age of twenty-five years and been seven years a citizen of the United States, and who shall not, *when elected,* be an inhabitant of that State in which he shall be chosen.

There are three qualifications: he shall not be a Representative unless he is twenty-five years of age; he shall not be a Representative unless he shall have been seven years a citizen of the United States, and then there is another qualification of a different class, the distinction being made in the same section, "and who shall not, when elected"—going back from the time of holding to another period—" be an inhabitant of that State in which he shall be chosen." He must at the time of the election be an inhabitant of the State in which he is chosen ; but at the time of being a Representative he must be seven years a citizen of the United States and he must be twenty-five years of age. The same distinction is made between the time of election and the time of holding with reference to Senators, because—

And who shall not, when elected, be an inhabitant of that State for which he shall be chosen.

Making the very distinction that is necessary to render consistent with each other all the well-considered authorities on this subject. The time of the appointment is what is here spoken of by the Constitution of the United States as to electors. When it says no person of this class shall be appointed an elector, it is an utter denial of power in the voter to vote for him. The citizen is just as much bound by the Constitution as is the officer. He has taken the oath either directly himself or inherited it, and when he swears "I will not appoint one who is holding an office of trust or profit under the United States," and he violates that oath, are you entitled to give validity to that violation, or are you to consider it as a nullity? It is to be treated as though it was not done.

It is true that, on the theory announced by learned counsel (Mr. Evarts) in a former case, that may be gotten over. It is not utterly conclusive, provided you resort to the grounds taken by the learned counsel in a former case, who said this:

They are elected; they are acting; they are certifying; for there is nothing in that idea of the subject at all that a man made ineligible cannot be elected. You might as well say that the forbidden fruit could not be eaten because it was forbidden.

That is true; you can violate and defy law. The forbidden fruit could be eaten notwithstanding it was forbidden, but it could be eaten in defiance of the laws of God, and that defiance brought upon the world "death and all our woe."

And will you adopt the same theory that a man can do that which is forbidden and sustain argument upon it; that when it is forbidden he may do it and you will approve and give validity and vitality to that act? Can you, on the line announced by the learned counsel in one of the former cases, say that when a man swears he will not do a thing he may do it; when he swears that he will not do it he can do it? It can be done only on the principle that the Constitution has become obsolete literature, merely for the study of the antiquary.

So we say there can be no power to appoint an ineligible person. But it is not mere reasoning on which this rests. We will furnish authority to corroborate it. The first case that we call your attention to is the case of Gulick *vs.* New, (14 Indiana Reports, page 93,) in which the following language occurs:

True, by the constitution and laws of this State the voice of a majority controls our elections, but that voice must be constitutionally and legally expressed. Even a majority should not nullify a provision of the constitution or be permitted at will to disregard the law. In this is the strength and beauty of our institutions. * * * Suppose that eight years ago, at the first election under our new constitution, when nearly all the offices in the State were to be filled, a majority of the voters in the State, and in the several districts and counties, had voted for persons wholly ineligible to fill the several offices, would those offices have thereby remained vacant? Could that majority, by pursuing that course, have continued the anarchy that might have resulted from such action? Or, rather, is it not the true theory that those who act in accordance with the constitution and the law should control even a majority who may fail so to act?

We also find that principle corroborated in 41 Indiana Reports, 577, Price *vs.* Baker, in which the following language is held:

> It is a principle of law, well settled in this State, that where a majority of the ballots at an election are given to a candidate who is not eligible to the office, the ballots so cast are not to be counted for any purpose. They cannot be counted to elect the ineligible candidate or to defeat the election of an opposing candidate, by showing that he did not receive a majority of the votes cast at such election. They are regarded as illegal, and as having no effect upon the election for any purpose. As a consequence, it follows that the candidate who is eligible, having the highest number of legal votes, though that number may be less than the number of votes cast for the ineligible candidate, and less than a majority of all the votes cast at such election, is entitled to the office.

So that the legal votes are to control those that are illegal.

Mr. Commissioner EDMUNDS. Does that case put the question independently of the knowledge of the voter?

Mr. Representative JENKS. It puts it independently of the knowledge of the voter. We shall consider that further on.

Mr. Commissioner EDMUNDS. I simply wish to know how the court held.

Mr. Senator MITCHELL. The court there held that there was constructive knowledge.

Mr. Representative JENKS. I have read what the court said. The next case we cite is on the same subject, the case of Hutchenson *vs.* Tilden and Boardley, 4 Harris and McHenry, page 280, in which the following occurs; this is a Maryland case:

> All votes given for a candidate not having such qualification are to be thrown away and rejected as having no force or operation in law.

The same as if not cast at all. We may also say that Chief-Justice Thompson, in the case of Commonwealth *vs.* Cluly, asserts the same principle in Pennsylvania, the court resting its decision upon the decisions of the Houses of Congress. I will read from that case in 56 Pennsylvania State Reports, page 273. The decision of the court was that an illegal person voted for was not elected and his competitor was not. That was the conclusion of the court; but that was founded on the false hypothesis that the decisions of legislative assemblies settled the question by acting on the language of the Constitution, which spoke of a person not being a Senator or a Congressman, under which those who were disqualified at the time of the election, but became qualified before the time of their admission, were admitted.

Mr. Commissioner STRONG. I do not so recollect the case.

Mr. Representative JENKS. I will read to your honor, and then perhaps it will call back your honor's recollection.

Mr. Commissioner STRONG. My recollection is that the political cases were referred to as a mere illustration, not as the basis of the decision.

Mr. Representative JENKS. Your honor there said that here there were no judicial cases on record.

Mr. Commissioner STRONG. In this country.

Mr. Representative JENKS. After announcing that the person who received the minority vote is not elected, the court, through his honor Judge Strong, say in that case:

> We are not informed that there has been any decision strictly judicial upon the subject; but in our legislative bodies the question has been determined.

We think we have shown the true difference between those two. In the present case it would be baseless founded on that kind of decision. Then his honor goes further, and says :

Besides, a man who votes for a person with knowledge that the person is incompetent to hold the office, and that his vote cannot therefore be effective, that it will be thrown away, may very properly be considered as intending to vote a blank or throw away his vote.
But the present relator—.

Applying it to the facts of the case—

But the present relator suggests no such case. He does not even aver that, if the votes given for Cluly were thrown out, he received a majority, though doubtless such was the truth. He has, therefore, exhibited no such interest as entitles him to be heard.

Now I refer to 7 Maine Reports, pages 497 and 501, which to me seems to be very pertinent in this case. That arose under the authority of the governor and council to submit certain propositions to the supreme court for their opinion. This is the question asked by the governor and council :

Can ballots having the names of persons on them who do not possess the constitutional qualifications of a representative be counted as votes under the fifth section of fourth article, part first, of the constitution of Maine, so as to prevent a majority of the votes given for eligible persons constituting a choice?

That is a question covering this whole case. The answer is:

To the fourth question proposed, without a particular statement of reasons, we merely answer in the negative

This occurred in 1831. In 1833 an act was passed in Maine conforming to the theory or doctrine laid down by these judges in this opinion ; so that it has been authoritatively announced in many States. The English cases assume this doctrine, that if the person who votes knows that the person for whom he votes is disqualified, in that event his vote is thrown away. If that were the doctrine in this country, where the people are principals and the officers their agents, still the case would be covered by the fact. Suppose we now assume that the English doctrine is the true doctrine, that the voter must know that a disqualified person is disqualified. What is the theory of our Government? The people are the principals; the officers are their agents. The principal knows who his agents are. Hence when he votes for a public officer he votes knowing that he is voting for his own agent. He cannot have an agent, is not to be presumed to have any agent, that he does not know of. The theory would not hold good in the British government, where the source of power is the Crown and the people are not constructively notified of who the agent is; but here when we appoint an agent ou - selves, either directly or indirectly, can any man say in law "I did not know who he was?" So, in consequence of the construction of our Government, in opposition to that of the British government, constructive notice exists to every individual of every officer in the United States, and the doctrine of constructive notice, that the principal knows who his agents are, would bring this within the doctrine of the judicial decisions that no one disputes, either English or American, that where the provision is that a man shall not be voted for, a vote for him, so far as the power of being elected is concerned, does not have that power. So Watts was not elected, even if he received a majority of the votes.

Mr. Commissioner THURMAN. Your proposition is that where the man cannot be voted for, then knowledge on the part of the voter is of no consequence.

Mr. Representative JENKS. It is of no consequence at all. The

English authorities do not pretend to allege that it was necessary that the voter should know that he was voting for a disqualified candidate. The only question was whether the result was to elect the next highest where this knowledge did not exist. In any event the man was not elected who received the highest number of votes, but the question was whether the other was elected; but I say under the theory of our Government that the people are the principals and the officers are the agents, there is notice *per se* to every principal of every agent he has got, constructively, and we know who our agents are.

We first will assume, then, that Watts was not elected. If he was not elected, the next question would be, was Cronin elected? We have already cited authorities on that point sufficient to call your attention to the principle, and as time is short I will pass to the next point. The question whether Cronin was elected or not will be elaborated by counsel.

Then the next question that would arise would be, if Watts was not elected and Cronin was not elected, what would be the effect? Would there be a vacancy? We assume there would not be a vacancy. If Watts was not elected, and if Cronin was not elected by the smaller number of votes, then there was no vacancy.

Before entering upon the discussion of this on principle and authority, it may be well to respond to the argument made by the very learned counsel on the part of the opposite party in a former case, that there must be a vacancy where there is not an incumbent. The proposition was stated something like this: If there is not some person in possession, there must be no person in possession; and if there is no person in possession, there must be a vacancy. That was about the form of the syllogism. Let us inquire concerning that. We start with the proposition, which seemed to be conceded by the same learned counsel the other day, that the electors for President of the United States are qualified persons, not officers, but citizens of a given qualification, voters for President of the United States, not having a public employment or private employment, (whatever is the definition of office,) but the privilege of performing a given act. Now, if a man does not exercise a privilege, does it necessarily become vacant at all? Take the common case of the elective franchise. Suppose there be a township with a hundred voters, and one of them—a privileged voter—does not attend the election. Does that make a vacancy, or does it not? Is there a vacancy in that election? Where there is a privilege that a man may use or may not, and he does not exercise it, that failure does not constitute any vacancy whatsoever. A neighbor may grant me the privilege of walking in his garden. I may exercise that privilege or I may not, depending upon my own volition; but whether I do or do not, there is no vacancy either in the privilege or the right to it. It does not exist at all except at the option of the person to whom that privilege belongs. Hence it is not a *sequitur* at all that, if a man having a privilege does not exercise it, there is necessarily a vacancy in anything.

Then starting with that proposition, is there a vacancy? On this subject I call your honors' attention, first, to a very recent case decided during this presidential election, that of George H. Corliss, of Rhode Island, which I find in the American Law Register of January, 1877, on page 19. The inquiry was made by the governor of Rhode Island, as in the case in Maine, of the supreme court of the State. The second proposition is:

We think a centennial commissioner, who was a candidate for the office of elector and received a plurality of the votes, does not by declining the office create such a vacancy as is provided for in general statutes.

And now comes the quotation from the statute:

If any electors, chosen as aforesaid, shall, after their said election, decline the said office, or be prevented by any cause from serving therein, the other electors, when met in Bristol, in pursuance of this chapter, shall fill such vacancies, and shall file a certificate in the secretary's office of the person or persons by them appointed.

When they decline the office or are "prevented by any cause," full and comprehensive words, so that if there be a vacancy it can be filled. Then the court proceed:

Before any person can decline under this section he must first be elected, and no person can be elected who is ineligible, or, in other words, incapable of being elected. "Resignation," said Lord Cockburn, C. J., in The Queen vs. Blizzard, Law Report 2 Q. B., 55, "implies that the person resigning has been elected unto the office he resigns. A man cannot resign that which he is not entitled to and which he has no right to occupy."

Hence there is no vacancy where there is nothing to resign. It is a privilege in the first instance; and this man's declining would not authorize the filling of the place as a vacancy. I call your attention to another case in order to show more especially the comprehensiveness of the language of the statute under which they acted: that is the Lanman case in Connecticut, which is found in Clarke & Hall's Contested Elections, page 872. Lanman had been a Senator up to the 3d of March, 1825. There was no meeting of the legislature of Connecticut between the 3d of March, 1825, and the fall of the year. There was an *interim* there when the State had no Senator. A meeting of the Senate was called. The governor appointed Lanman to fill the vacancy from the time of his last incumbency up to the meeting of the next legislature, and for warrant therefor this was the statute of Connecticut:

Whenever any vacancy shall happen in the representation of this State in the Senate of the United States, by the expiration of the term of service of a Senator, or by resignation or otherwise, the general assembly, if then in session, shall, by a concurrent vote of the senate and house of representatives, proceed to fill said vacancy by a new election; and in case such vacancy shall happen in the recess of the general assembly, the governor shall appoint some person to fill the same until the next meeting of the general assembly.

The appointing power of the governor was co-extensive as to vacancies with that of the legislature, and the language in reference to the legislature was that "if the term of service of the Senator expired, or by resignation or otherwise," a vacancy happened. The decision then was that there was no vacancy as prescribed by that statute. There must be an incumbent, in other words, to constitute a vacancy; there must be some person in the enjoyment to constitute such a vacancy as came within the terms of the broadest statute.

I cite next the case of Broom vs. Hanley, 9 Pennsylvania State Reports, page 513, which decided substantially—

That even death, after a lawful election and before qualification, does not create an incumbent of the office; nor does it create a vacancy which can be filled by appointment, where the law authorizes vacancies to be so filled.

In corroboration of that we also cite the cases of People vs. Tilton, 37 Cal., 614; People vs. Parker, 37 Cal., 639; Stratton vs. Oulton, 28 Cal., 51; People vs. Stratton, 28 Cal., 382; Battle vs. McIver, 68 N. C. R., 469; Dodd ex parte, 6 English, (Ark.) 152; State vs. Jenkins, 43 Mo., 261.

Then let us look to the statutes of Oregon to see if there be no provision to fill any given vacancy, even if there were a vacancy to be filled, which we deny, because an incumbent signifies one in possession of an office; and where there has been no incumbent it has been decided all the time that there is no vacancy, and if there is no vacancy there can be nothing to fill. But the statutes of Oregon have defined what shall constitute a vacancy, and confined it to an office; and this, as conceded by the learned counsel, is not an office. That definition is as follows:

SEC. 48. Every office shall become vacant on the occurring of either of the following events before the expiration of the term of such office:

1. The death of the incumbent;

There must be an incumbent; that is, one in possession.

2. His resignation;

That is, the resignation of an incumbent.

3. His removal;

The removal of an incumbent.

4. His ceasing to be an inhabitant of the district, county, town, or village;

"His" referring to the incumbent's ceasing, &c.

5. His conviction of an infamous crime;

The incumbent's conviction of an infamous crime.

6. His refusal or neglect to take his oath of office;

The incumbent's refusal.

7. The decision of a competent tribunal, declaring void his election or appointment.

The only instance in which a vacancy can occur under that statute is when the decision of a competent tribunal declares his election or appointment void; and that was not done in this case.

Mr. Commissioner EDMUNDS. How would that apply to this action of the governor in declaring the election void?

Mr. Representative JENKS. The act of the governor was an act in pursuance of a duty conferred by the Constitution upon that governor, on which he was to exercise that discretion with which God and nature had endowed him; and if honestly exercised, that was conclusive, because it was a political duty. He having sworn that he would not commission one who was disqualified, he could not commission one who was disqualified, and he had a right to decide the question as to whether there was an election or not.

Mr. Commissioner EDMUNDS. If I understand you, then, had this been an ordinary State office, with a term for a year, for instance, and the governor had done exactly the same thing, it would not have been competent for the courts to have reversed the judgment and to have decided the other way?

Mr. Representative JENKS. In conformity to the law of the land it would. Without that conformity, by express statutory authority, it would not, because the governor is limited by the same law as the others are in the exercise of their duties. But if, in the first instance, we are to be controlled by an express statutory provision, this action of his would be conclusive; and there is no statutory provision of that kind, as I understand.

Mr. Commissioner MORTON. I should like to ask the gentleman a question. I ask whether, in his opinion, it is competent for a State, by the State constitution, in any way to regulate the appointment of electors.

Mr. Representative JENKS. The Constitution of the United States confers that power, in some instances, upon the legislature of the State.

Mr. Commissioner MORTON. You spoke about the governor being

empowered by the Constitution to do thus and so. My inquiry [is whether it is competent for a State, by its constitution, to regulate in any way the appointment of electors.

Mr. Representative LAWRENCE. By the constitution as distinguished from the legislature?

Mr. Representative JENKS. By the Constitution of the United States, which becomes a part of and incorporates itself into that of every State, the two constituting one, he is authorized to so do. The constitution of each State and the United States Constitution are equally binding upon legislature and governor. At least this position stands always the same, that the governor's functions in commissioning are political, and as such, when not in contravention of well-ascertained law, they are conclusive. If it be a discretion which must be exercised politically, that discretion, unless done *mala fide*, is conclusive.

Then the propositions we have attempted to establish are these:

First. That with reference to evidence, the only evidence before you which conforms to the law of the land is the evidence as required by the law of Oregon and the law of the United States, being that which is certified to by the governor of the State of Oregon.

Second. That the act of that governor, if discharged in good faith, is conclusive upon this tribunal in this inquiry.

Third. That Watts could not be elected even if he had a majority of the votes.

Fourth. That if Cronin was the next highest, and those votes were cast for one who could not be appointed, the next highest, Cronin, was elected.

Fifth. That even if Cronin was not elected there was no vacancy, and being no vacancy, there could be no filling by any college whatever.

Then, as a consequence, how does the case stand? Cronin came up and voted; two others came and voted. You do not know whether they are the persons voted for or not, because they do not come identified as the law says they shall come. But, assuming that they were the same persons who were voted for, and are properly identified, each of these voters being one, that which is evidenced according to the law of the land, would have to be counted as the true vote. Cronin's vote must be counted as cast, the other two as they are cast. This would be the conclusion I would come to from these several propositions. We believe this to be a correct exposition of the law and the truth of the case, because the constitutional language of this qualification is not one that is to be forgotten or repudiated. It is, perhaps, too common now to regard the provisions of the Constitution as directory, to be obeyed or disobeyed at the option of the person who may have the administering thereof, but the constitutional truth remains that an office-holder should not be appointed an elector. We ask you to give to this truth its proper weight in this decision, and giving it its proper weight, the result would be, as we maintain, as stated before.

This tribunal is such a one as the world has never known before. Questions of this kind have heretofore been decided on the field of battle, decided amid smoking hamlets, decided amid the clash of arms. Successions have not heretofore been settled peaceably. Standing, then, as the last arbiter instead of the last resort to arms, I would ask that you do your duty impartially and in full view of the whole facts and truth of the case.

Then further, as this is such a tribunal as was never constituted before, and the first of the kind known on earth, it can either give character or discredit to its kind. If this tribunal forgets its high obligations and guides itself by aught else than simple truth and simple justice, it will again throw back mankind to the place from which they started, leaving the question of succession to be decided by the wager of battle, as lawsuits often were in barbarous ages. We ask you not to turn back this hand on the dial of time. Let it go on. Let peace be the rule, and not war. It is true many would have preferred war. The corrupt, the deformed, would have preferred war, just as when the mighty deep is disturbed from its slimy abysses the crude monsters come to the surface and there disport themselves; so in the ruin of a country, so in the turmoils of internecine war, these crude monsters now in the abyss might rise to the surface and once again disport themselves. From this deliver us. Give to mankind confidence in their fellow-men that they can be trusted to decide impartially according to the truth and verity of the case.

We leave this in your hands, asking that you give it a candid consideration, deciding upon principles of right and truth, bearing in mind that in the case of Florida a certain list came from the secretary of state, a compilation of votes canvassed by a returning-board came from the State, and this was overruled by the governor's certificate; that in Louisiana evidence was offered you to show what was the true state of the votes, and that was declined. Now we ask that in this case the principles of law and the principles of truth be recognized and the vote be cast as in truth and justice it should.

The PRESIDENT. We will now hear the objectors on the other side.

Mr. Senator MITCHELL. Mr. President and gentlemen of the Commission, I desire that the words I shall employ in this important cause shall be measured, and the principles I announce and upon which I claim your decision shall be well considered. The limited time prescribed by the rules of your honorable body for the presentation of cases upon the part of objectors admonishes me that I must advance directly and without prefatory remark to a discussion of the issues involved. So momentous are these in the effect of their decision, though not in point of solution, that to their final determination by this high tribunal the whole people of this nation, and may I not say of all Christendom, are with bated breath looking forward with ever-increasing and intense anxiety. The hopes, the fears, the aspirations of two great political parties, each struggling for the control of the administration of a great government, have, on the faith of the right, the justice, and the law upon which each bases its claim to the votes of certain disputed States, by common consent, by solemn legislative enactment, in which leading members of both political parties have voluntarily and earnestly joined, been submitted to the arbitrament of this dignified and honorable Commission.

The Constitution of the United States declares that—

The President of the Senate shall, in the presence of the Senate and House of Representatives, open all the certificates, and the votes shall then be counted.

The law of your creation provides in substance and effect that if more than one return, or paper purporting to be a return, from a State shall have been received by the President of the Senate, purporting to be the certificate of electoral votes given for President and Vice-President in any State, all such returns, after having been opened by the President of the Senate in the presence of the two Houses and read by the tellers, shall thereupon be submitted to the judgment and decision of your honorable Commission as to which is the true and lawful electoral vote of such State.

The State of Oregon sends two returns; hence your jurisdiction under the Constitution and the law to determine which of these is the true one and which the false, which comes from the electoral college of that State, which of the six persons claiming to have been appointed electors by that State in the manner directed by the legislature thereof, if any, were so appointed, and which votes cast for President and Vice-President by the six persons claiming to have been appointed electors should of right be counted. A perfect understanding of the facts presented by the two returns is important. From these, taken together, it appears that, at the recent election in Oregon, the three republican candidates, W. H. Odell, John C. Cartwright, and John W. Watts, received respectively 15,206, 15,214, and 15,206 votes. The three democratic candidates, E. A. Cronin, Henry Klippel, and W. B. Laswell, received respectively 14,157, 14,136, and 14,149 votes. That John W. Watts, who received the lowest republican vote, had a majority of 1,049 votes over E. A. Cronin, who received the highest democratic vote. That on the 4th day of December, 1876, that being the day on which it was his duty under the law to canvass the votes and determine who had received the highest number, the secretary of state did, in the presence of the governor, canvass the votes, and did officially declare that Odell, Cartwright, and Watts had received the highest number of votes. That the governor, notwithstanding this official declaration of the secretary of state, issued his certificate not to Odell, Cartwright, and Watts, but to Odell, Cartwright, and Cronin. That these three persons, so certified by the governor, did not, in the organization and proceedings of the electoral college, act together; but that Odell, Cartwright, and Watts, the persons whom the State had appointed at the election, acted together, organized as an electoral college, and cast three votes for Rutherford B. Hayes, of Ohio, for President, and three votes for William A. Wheeler, of New York, for Vice-President. That Cronin, acting alone, organized or attempted to organize a college of his own; declared or attempted to declare two vacancies; and appointed or attempted to appoint, to fill such alleged vacancies, J. N. T. Miller and John Parker, neither of whom had received any votes from the people. That these three persons, so claiming to be an electoral college, cast 2 votes for Hayes and Wheeler and 1 vote for Tilden and Hendricks. That the return of Cronin, Miller, and Parker contains the certificate of the governor to Cronin, Odell, and Cartwright. That the return of Odell, Cartwright, and Watts has no certificate of the governor attached, but has the certificate of the secretary of state under the great seal thereof, showing that these three persons constituting this college received the highest number of votes at the election, and that this was so officially declared by the sole canvassing-officer, the secretary of state, at the time and place and in the manner designated by law.

It is claimed, and the papers show, that Watts, at the time of the election, was a postmaster, and therefore ineligible, as it is claimed, to be appointed an elector. The evidence establishes the facts in reference to this postmastership to be these: Watts, at the time of the election, was a deputy postmaster at the town of La Fayette, Yam Hill County. His compensation was about $268 per annum. The whole number of votes in the county of Yam Hill was 1,484. Of these, 810 were cast for the republican candidates for electors, and 674 for the democratic candidates. There were at the time of the election eleven other post-offices in that county. The total vote of La Fayette precinct, in which Watts was postmaster, was:

For Hayes electors 106
For Tilden electors 83

Total votes... 189

This precinct includes considerable scope of territory outside of the town of La Fayette, and which is nearer to other post-offices, and not more than one hundred voters of both political parties receive or transmit their mail through the La Fayette post-office. It is further shown that the fact that Watts was postmaster was not generally or publicly known throughout the State or in any part of the State prior to the election, except in his own immediate town; that neither the democratic nor republican leaders, nor the masses of the voters of either political party in the State, nor any considerable portion of them, knew that he was postmaster until several days after the election; nor was the fact that he was postmaster or the question of his ineligibility publicly discussed during the campaign.

It is insisted that these facts made Watts ineligible to appointment as an elector; that the governor of the State for this reason had the jurisdiction, and rightfully exercised it, to refuse to issue his certificate to Watts and to issue it to Cronin, the candidate having the next highest vote.

Had Governor Grover the right to refuse Watts a certificate, and, if so, had he any jurisdiction to issue it to Cronin, and what effect is to be accorded such certificate?

I contend with perfect confidence in the integrity of our position that the governor of Oregon had no jurisdiction whatever to entertain or adjudicate upon the question of the alleged ineligibility of Watts, and that all his proceedings in that regard were *ultra vires*, void *ab initio*, affecting no interest, attaching to no subject-matter, and binding no one. If Governor Grover possessed any such power he must derive it from one of four sources: the Constitution of the United States, the laws of Congress, the constitution of Oregon, or the statutes of that State. So far as the Constitution of the United States is concerned, it confers no power whatever on the governor of a State to pass upon the eligibility of any person elected to office under either national or State authority. It prescribes qualifications for office and imposes disqualifications. It nowhere vests the appointment to any office, Federal or State, in the executive of a State, save in the case of a vacancy in the office of Senator of the United States when the legislature is not in session. It nowhere, directly or by implication, constitutes him a tribunal to act as the conservator of the constitution in the matter of the eligibility of persons elected or appointed to office. Were the appointment of electors vested by the Constitution in the executive of a State instead of in the State itself, then there might attach to him by reasonable, if not necessary, implication the power to pass upon the constitutional qualifications of any person by him appointed. Or had the legislature of the State, under the clause of the Constitution authorizing the State to appoint electors in such manner as the legislature thereof may direct, provided by statute that such electors should be appointed not by the people but by the governor, then it might with some propriety and claim of support in law be held that he could pass upon the question of the constitutional qualifications of those appointed. The Constitution of the United States in one clause says:

No Senator or Representative or person holding an office of trust or profit under the United States shall be appointed an elector.

And in another clause that—

No person shall be a Representative who shall not have attained to the age of twenty-five years and been seven years a citizen of the United States, and who shall not, when elected, be an inhabitant of the State in which he shall be chosen.

And in still another that—

No person holding any office under the United States shall be a member of either House during his continuance in office.

Here, then, are several constitutional disqualifications in reference to members of Congress and presidential electors. If it is the duty of the governor to pass upon the question of ineligibility of an elector before issuing his certificate, then it is also his duty to pass upon the question of the ineligibility of a member of Congress before granting his certificate, as his duty in reference to each is under the law precisely the same, namely, that he shall issue his certificate to the person having the highest number of votes; and if he can pass upon the question of fact as to whether the person receiving the highest number of votes for elector was at the time of the election a postmaster, and also upon the question of law as to whether such fact when found disqualifies him from being appointed as an elector, and in such event to withhold from him his certificates, then he also has the power to adjudicate upon the question in the case of a person elected to Congress as to whether he is twenty-five years of age, has been seven years a citizen of the United States, and an inhabitant of the State at the time of his election; and also upon the further question as to whether any person elected to the lower House of Congress is holding any office under the United States. The extent to which the position would lead shows the absurdity of the position assumed. It will not do for my friend, Mr. Jenks, to say that this disability in the case of a member of Congress applies only to his acting as a member of Congress, and not to his appointment; for, as I maintain, he claims his right to his seat in Congress *prima facie*, by virtue of the commission issued by the governor.

Again, if the governor has the power to adjudicate upon the question and refuse a certificate upon a *conceded* state of facts as to ineligibility, then he also has the right to determine the question of both fact and law in a case wherein both are *contested ;* and this too without the power to issue process for, or to compel the attendance of a solitary witness, and barren of all right or authority to administer an oath to any that might voluntarily attend.

In a case, therefore, wherein the facts and the law were controverted—for instance, as to whether or not a person appointed an elector held a particular Federal office, and, if so, whether such office was one of trust or profit within the meaning of the Constitution of the United States—a trial before the executive would be little else than a farce. That the framers of the Constitution, either national or State, or Congress, or the legislatures of States, ever contemplated lodging such a power in the hands of the governor of a State is conclusively negatived by the results that would flow from its assumption and exercise.

Mr. Commissioner HOAR. I should like to ask you, for my own understanding of your position, who you understand has this right to adjudicate under the laws of Oregon.

Mr. Senator MITCHELL. I understand that it is the duty of the secretary of state, and him alone, under the laws of Oregon, to declare who is elected ; in other words, to declare who has received the highest number of votes; and when that declaration is made, then the electors are appointed by the State in the manner directed by the legislature

thereof, and that beyond that this tribunal cannot go. I shall, as I
proceed, state my views as to the tribunal that may adjudicate upon
the question of alleged ineligibility, and the time when this may properly be done.

But it is said the clause in article 6 of the Constitution of the United
States declares that—

All executive and judicial officers, both of the United States and of the several
States, shall be bound by oath to support this Constitution.

And, furthermore, that the constitution of the State of Oregon requires the governor to take an oath to support the Constitution of the
United States, and, inasmuch as the Constitution of the United States
provides that no person holding an office of trust or profit under the
United States shall be appointed an elector, therefore the governor, in
order to conform to the letter and spirit of his oath of office, *must*, before issuing a certificate to any person appointed an elector, determine
the question as to his constitutional eligibility, and, if in his judgment
such person is laboring under such constitutional disability, then to not
only refuse to issue to him his certificate but to issue it to somebody else.
In other words, that by virtue of these provisions the governor becomes
the conservator of the constitution and to the extent that authorizes
him to determine grave questions of law and fact, whether controverted
or conceded, relating to the eligibility of persons elected to office; questions, too, that in many instances not only touch the question of eligibility to office but affect the person concerned criminally, and in reference to which such person has under the Constitution of the United
States the right of trial by jury; because it must be borne in mind that
several causes of ineligibility to office under the constitution of Oregon—
and I contend that the duties of the governor are the same in either case—
are by the laws of Oregon declared to be felonies. No such claim can
be successfully maintained for a moment. It is untenable, illogical, and
baseless as the fabric of a dream. It is unsupported in law and unaided
by any rule of ethics.

The Constitution of the United States says:

No * * person holding an office of trust or profit under the United States shall
be appointed an elector.

Does the governor appoint electors? By no manner of means. It is
the *State* that appoints electors, in such manner as its legislature has
directed. *It* has directed that the manner in which they shall be appointed is by a plurality of the votes of the people; and, furthermore,
that the person receiving the highest number of votes shall, in the language of the statute, *be deemed elected.* The governor has nothing
whatever to do with the appointment of electors, nor yet with the question of determining who have been appointed. The appointment is by
the people—the legal voters. The question as to whom they have appointed is, under the law, to be determined by the secretary of state,
and in that determination but one ingredient can enter, and that is, *who
had the highest number of votes?* and, *after* this has all been done, *after*
the people have appointed and the secretary of state has determined
and officially declared whom they have appointed, then, and not till
then, has the governor anything to do in connection with it. Until all
this has taken place, he has no jurisdiction whatever to do any act or
thing, ministerially or otherwise, save and except to be present when
the secretary of state canvasses the votes. And even after all this has
been done, his *only* authority in connection with the whole matter is, if
he follow the State statute, to sign the certificates made out by the

secretary of state to the persons having the highest number of votes, or, if the act of Congress, to cause three lists of the names of the electors to be made and certified and to be delivered to the electors on or before the day of meeting. No act of his can undo what has necessarily been done by the State and passed into history before his right to act at all could, under the Constitution or the laws, *possibly* attach, namely, the appointment of electors and the determination by the secretary of state as to the persons appointed. Can it be said therefore that the oath of the governor to support the Constitution of the United States would call upon him, either in law or morals, much less empower him, to undo not only the appointment made by the people, but also the official determination of the secretary of state as to the persons appointed, and usurp the functions of State, people, and secretary of state, and make an appointment himself, and that too of a person rejected by the people? The absurdity of any such claim is the conclusive answer to the proposition.

So far then as the Constitution of the United States is concerned, the governor of the State has no connection whatever with electors or the electoral college.

Let us examine, then, as to his power and duties under the act of Congress under which he claims to have acted in issuing his certificate; and in this connection I desire to speak also as to the effect of a certificate issued by the executive of a State in pursuance of the act of Congress of 1792. The third section of the act of Congress of 1792, section 136 of the Revised Statutes, provides that—

It shall be the duty of the executive of each State to cause three lists of the names of the electors of such State to be made and certified and to be delivered to the electors on or before the day on which they are required by the preceding section to meet.

By the preceding section, 135, of the Revised Statutes, the electors are to meet on the first Wednesday in December in the year in which they are appointed.

By this act the executive authority is required to make and certify three lists of the names of the persons who have been appointed electors, which are to be delivered to the electors on or before the first Wednesday in December. These lists certified by the executive authority are simply evidence to the persons that they have been appointed electors. The governor's certificate is no part of the appointment of an elector. The appointment is to be made by the State, and can only be made in such manner as the legislature has directed. The manner in which the several legislatures have declared these appointments shall be made is through an election by the qualified voters of the States; and the governor's certificate is intended only to furnish evidence of the result of the election. The statute in regard to the governor is merely directory, and is no part of the appointment of an elector, which is left *exclusively* by the Constitution to the several States. Should the governor of a State choose for any reason to withhold his certificate, he could not thereby defeat the appointment of electors by the State, nor could he do so by giving a false certificate of the appointment of persons as electors who were not appointed; nor by giving a true certificate to persons who were not electors and withholding the same from the persons entitled. In any of these cases the title of the electors appointed by the State in the manner directed by the legislature thereof would not be affected; but such electors, or those claiming rights under and by virtue of their action, would have a right to resort to the next best evidence of their appointment, which would in the case of Oregon be a certificate of the secretary of state, (the secretary of state being the canvassing-board,) under the seal of the State, showing the result of the election and who had been appointed electors and declared such by the canvassing-officer. The part to be performed by the governor is merely ministerial, and constitutes simply a form of evidence as to who have been appointed electors. Such certificate cannot confer title, neither can it take away title. It is no part of or ingredient in title; it is merely a prescribed form of evidence of title, but not by any means a *conclusive* one. It cannot be converted into an instrument of fraud, or made the means of defeating the vote of the State, or falsely giving the election of President or Vice-President to persons who were not appointed by the State.

If the governor's certificate be any part of the manner of appointment, then the form and character of the certificate are solely a matter within the power of the State legislature, and in such event sections 136 and 138 of the Revised Statutes of the United States are unconstitutional and void, for it must be conceded that the Constitution of the United States grants to the States the exclusive power of appointing electors in such manner as the legislatures may direct. No power on earth can prescribe the *manner* of appointment except the legislature of the State. If, therefore, the certificate of the governor is a part, one ingredient in the *manner* of appointment, then Congress, in attempting to prescribe the form and character of the certificate, has transcended its constitutional limit by undertaking to regulate the *manner* of appointment, thus encroaching upon a jurisdiction which under the Constitution belongs exclusively to the legislatures of the States. But the certificate of the governor, as prescribed by Congress, is no *part* of the *manner* of appointment. Congress has not in prescribing the character of the governor's certificate undertaken to interfere with the manner of appointment, but simply to prescribe a convenient form of evidence of the appointment. Any certificate that Congress has provided for or could prescribe could rightfully confer no power upon the governor to do anything except certify the ultimate result of the vote as declared by the canvassing-officers of the State. He must take what the State has done in the manner prescribed by its legislature. He cannot in the slightest degree interfere with or change the appointment made by the State.

In Oregon there was no law authorizing the governor to certify a minority candidate elected. The legislature of Oregon might have provided that the electors should be appointed by the governor, the supreme court, or the secretary of state, but it did not; it did direct that the people, the qualified electors, shall by a plurality of votes to be cast in the different precincts choose electors, but the result of this vote cannot be ascertained unless the manner prescribes more. The manner of appointment necessarily includes, not merely the way in which the votes shall be cast, but also a means of determining what votes were cast, and the result of such vote; hence the legislature of the State has provided, as a part of the means necessary to an appointment, the mode of determining and declaring the result of the vote. This in Oregon prescribes returns from precincts to county boards, from county boards to the secretary of state, whose final duty it is to canvass the votes and ascertain who has the greatest number of votes. This is the last act in the process of the appointment of a presidential elector by the State, the closing scene in the manner of appointment. This done and officially declared, and the electors *are appointed*. What follows is no part of the appointment, but simply matter of evidence of the fact. All that precedes enters into and constitutes a part of *the manner of appointment.*

Governor Grover in the matter of issuing his certificates, he tells us, ignored the State statute and followed that of Congress. If Congress had the power to prescribe the form of a certificate, and I believe it had, then such certificate is no part of the manner of appointment, and in issuing it the governor could not change the appointment as made by the State and officially determined by the secretary of state as the *final* and *conclusive* act in the process of appointment. Behind this ultimate determination of the canvassing-board, neither the governor of the State nor the tribunal whose final duty it is to count the votes for President and Vice-President, whether it be the President of the Senate, the two Houses of Congress, or the electoral tribunal, can rightfully go. The determination of the canvassing-board is *final* and *conclusive* on *all departments and on all persons, concluding voter and candidate, State and nation.* Not so, however, with the certificate of the governor, which, whether issued under the State statutes or the Revised Statutes of the United States, is in no respect a part of the *manner of appointment,* but simply a species of evidence of such appointment, which, if *false* or *fraudulent* or issued through *mistake,* is *not* conclusive upon the tribunal whose duty it is to count the votes of the electors appointed, and which cannot count the votes of persons whom the State *never* appointed but who through *mistake, fraud,* or *corruption* may have succeeded in obtaining a certificate from the governor. The electoral tribunal can question this or any other proceeding down to the boundary-line where they touch the *manner of appointment;* there the jurisdiction ends—the decision of the State through its canvassing officer being final and conclusive.

Mr. Commissioner GARFIELD. Allow me to ask whether the language of the thirty-seventh section of the law of Oregon, that requires the governor to issue a proclamation declaring the election of the officers, applies to the election of electors?

Mr. Senator MITCHELL. It does not.

Mr. Commissioner GARFIELD. And whether as a matter of fact the governor does issue a proclamation of election to the electors?

Mr. Senator MITCHELL. He does not. I do not understand that the language applies. My own opinion is that it does not apply.

Mr. Commissioner GARFIELD. Does he issue a proclamation to that effect?

Mr. Senator MITCHELL. Not as a matter of fact. It does not apply at all, I claim.

Mr. Commissioner ABBOTT. Is there any other law on this subject of canvassing the votes except the thirty-seventh section?

Mr. Senator MITCHELL. That is all; and that prescribes that it shall be done in the manner prescribed in reference to members of Congress and set out in the foregoing section.

Mr. Commissioner ABBOTT. I see there is no provision that the secretary shall certify who has been elected, but simply that he shall canvass the votes and the governor give the certificate.

Mr. Senator MITCHELL. It prescribes that the secretary of state shall canvass the votes and declare who has received the highest number of votes, and that he shall prepare lists to that effect, that he shall sign his name to those lists, and that it shall be the duty of the governor to certify to those lists.

Mr. Commissioner ABBOTT. I do not see here—will you please point it out to me—where the secretary of state is to ascertain that?

The PRESIDENT. The floor is yours, Mr. Mitchell.

Mr. Senator MITCHELL. I have no objection to yielding, but I do not desire that it shall be taken out of my time.

The PRESIDENT. The Commissioners would object if I did not take it out of your time. I have therefore admonished you that you have the floor.

Mr. Senator MITCHELL. I have no objection to yielding except that it shall not be taken out of my time.

I pass now to consider the question as to the power and duty of the governor in this regard under the constitution of the State of Oregon.

Should it be held that the determination by the governor of a State of a question as to the ineligibility of an elector is the exercise of judicial power, then clearly neither the constitution of the State nor the statutes confer such power. If, upon the contrary, it is the exercise of administrative or political power, then it can only be exercised in pursuance of some warrant contained in the statutes of the State. Without stopping to inquire what it is, I will proceed to show that there is no authority for the one or the other either in the constitution or the statutes.

The jurisdiction of the different departments is clearly defined in the constitution of the State of Oregon, and under the distribution of powers therein contained the governor can exercise no judicial functions whatever, while all the judicial power is expressly conferred upon other departments and officers. Article 3 of the constitution of the State provides as follows, under the head of—

DISTRIBUTION OF POWERS.

SECTION 1. The powers of the government shall be divided into three separate departments, the legislative, the executive, (including the administrative,) and the judicial; and no person charged with official duties under one of these departments shall exercise any of the functions of another, except as in this constitution expressly provided.

Section 1 of article 7 reads as follows:

The judicial power of the State shall be vested in a supreme court, circuit courts, and county courts, which shall be courts of record having general jurisdiction, to be defined, limited, and regulated by law in accordance with this constitution. Justices of the peace may also be invested with limited judicial powers, and municipal courts may be created to administer the regulations of incorporated towns and cities:

While section 9 of article 7 is in these words:

All judicial power, authority, and jurisdiction not vested by this constitution or by laws consistent therewith exclusively in some other courts; and they shall have appellate jurisdiction and supervisory control over the county courts, and all other inferior courts, officers, and tribunals.

From these several provisions it is clear that the governor of Oregon cannot rightfully exercise any judicial power; that any attempt to do so is an usurpation of power, and his action would be not merely *voidable*, but *absolutely void* for want of jurisdiction. And these several provisions of the constitution are in full consonance with the well-recognized division of the powers of a free republican government, as stated by elementary writers.

Story on the Constitution, page 520, in speaking on the subject, says:

In the establishment of a free government, the division of the three great powers of government, the executive, the legislative, and the judicial, among different functionaries, has been a favorite policy with patriots and statesmen.

It has by many been deemed a maxim of vital importance that these powers should forever be kept separate and distinct. And, accordingly, we find it laid down with emphatic care in the bill of rights of several of the State constitutions. In the constitution of Massachusetts, for example, it is declared that " in the goverment of this Commonwealth, the legislative department shall never exercise the executive and judicial powers, or either of them; the executive shall never exercise the legislative or judicial powers, or either of them; the judicial shall never exercise the legislative and executive powers, or either of them; to the end it may be a government of laws and not of men."

Again, a writer in the Federalist, in adverting to the great danger of an accumulation of legislative, executive, and judicial powers in the same hands, and of the importance of keeping them separate, says:

The accumulation of all powers, legislative, executive, and judicial, in the same hands, whether of one, a few, or many, and whether hereditary, self-appointed, or elective, may be justly pronounced *the very definition of tyranny.*

We inquire further, moreover, as to the startling magnitude of the power claimed by Governor Grover in assuming to pass upon and determine the question as to the ineligibility of persons elected to office under the constitution and laws of Oregon, whether it be called judicial, administrative, or political. As has been said, if he has the power in *one* case of alleged disability he has it in *all* cases, and it is his duty to exercise it in all cases coming before him. The statute of Oregon provides that—

The votes for the electors shall be given, received, returned, and canvassed as the same are given, returned, and canvassed for members of Congress.

On a reference to how votes for members of Congress are given, received, returned, and canvassed, we find that the votes for secretary of state, State treasurer, State printer, justices of the supreme court, and district attorneys are given, received, returned, and canvassed in precisely the same manner. In any and all these cases the certificate of the governor is to be given to the person receiving the highest number of votes. This being so, we turn again to the constitution of the State of Oregon for the purpose of inquiring as to the constitutional causes of ineligibility of persons to be elected to any of these offices under such constitution, and to the character of the inquiry the governor would necessarily be compelled to make in case of a contest in determining these several questions of ineligibility; all of which will show conclusively that to act on any such assumption is the exercise of judicial power of the very gravest character. For instance, section 7 of article 2 of the constitution of the State of Oregon, under the head of " suffrage and elections," reads as follows:

Every person shall be disqualified from holding office during the term for which he may have been elected, who shall have given or offered a bribe, threat, or reward to procure his election.

Here, then, is a constitutional disqualification. Under the position assumed by Governor Grover, if it is suggested to him by some *ex parte* affidavit or otherwise that a person who has received the highest number of votes for State treasurer, secretary of state, State printer, or any of the officers named had given or offered a bribe, threat, or reward to procure his election, and the person accused denies it, he must enter upon an investigation of the charge, which under the statutes of the State is a criminal one, and, because he has taken an oath to support the Constitution of the State and of the United States, he must determine this question as to the *eligibility* of the person elected. And so in reference to section 9 of article 2, which provides that—

Every person who shall give or accept a challenge to fight a duel, or shall knowingly carry to another such challenge, or who shall agree to go out of the State to fight a duel, shall be ineligible to any office of trust or profit.

Section 10 of the same article reads as follows :

No person holding a lucrative office or appointment under the United States or under this State shall be eligible to a seat in the legislative assembly ; nor shall any person hold more than one lucrative office at the same time, except as in this constitution expressly permitted : *Provided,* That offices in the militia, to which there is attached no annual salary, and the office of the postmaster, where the compensation does not exceed $100 per annum, shall not be deemed lucrative.

And section 11 reads as follows :

No person who may hereafter be a collector or holder of public money shall be eligible to any office of trust or profit until he shall have accounted for and paid over, according to law, all sums for which he may be liable.

Passing then from a consideration of the powers of the executive of Oregon as prescribed by the provisions of the constitution of the State, we next inquire what are his powers and duties as prescribed in the statutes of the State in so far as they relate to the electoral college. And here we find that in all legislation on the subject the limitations in the constitution on executive power have been carefully borne in mind and jealously guarded by the law-making power of the State, the duties prescribed for and imposed upon the governor being of a *purely ministerial character.* Before proceeding, however, to introduce the statutes of the State, it may be well to attract attention to section 16 of article 2 of the constitution of the State, for the purpose of showing that in all elections by the people, which of course includes the election of presidential electors, the person or persons receiving the highest number of votes shall be declared duly elected. The section reads as follows :

In all elections held by the people under this constitution the person or persons who shall receive the highest number of votes *shall be declared duly elected.—Section 16, article 2 of State constitution.*

Here is a constitutional mandamus to the secretary of state directing him to declare the person who has received the highest number of votes duly elected ; and neither the secretary of state as the canvassing-officer, nor the governor as the ministerial officer, whose sole duty it is to place his signature to the lists made by the secretary of state, and which the secretary alone has the power to make, has any power whatever to adjudicate the question as to whether such person so receiving the highest number of votes was ineligible *or* for any other cause not duly elected. *That* belongs to another department and another tribunal.

I now pass to a consideration of the powers and duties of the governor under the statutes of Oregon.

Section 10 of the election laws of Oregon provides that—

The county clerk, immediately after making the abstracts of the votes given in his county, shall make a copy of each of said abstracts and transmit it by mail to the secretary of state at the seat of government, and it shall the duty of the secretary of state, in the presence of the governor, to proceed within thirty days after the election, and sooner if the returns be all received, to canvass the votes given for secretary and treasurer of state, State printer, justices of the supreme court, member of Congress, and district attorneys ; and the governor shall grant a certificate of election to the person having the highest number of votes, and shall also issue a proclamation declaring the election of such person. In case there shall be no choice, by reason of any two or more persons having an equal and the highest number of votes for either of such offices, the governor shall by proclamation order a new election to fill said offices.

It will be observed that the secretary of state is made the canvassing or returning officer of the State to count the votes and determine who have been elected to the offices named therein, which is to be done in the presence of the governor. The governor takes no part in the canvass or determination of the result, but is simply required to be present as a witness, and then he is required to grant a certificate of election to the person having the highest number of votes, and is thus precluded by express provision from passing upon questions as to the eligibility of candidates, his duty being peremptorily prescribed by the statute to grant a certificate to the person having the highest number of votes.

Section 3 of the act providing for the election of presidential electors provides that—

> The votes for the electors shall be given, received, returned, and canvassed as the same are given, returned, and canvassed for members of Congress. The secretary of state shall prepare two lists of the names of the electors elected, and affix the seal of the State to the same. Such lists shall be signed by the governor and secretary, and by the latter delivered to the college of electors at the hour of their meeting on such first Wednesday of December.

By the section of the statute first quoted, it is made the absolute duty of the governor to give a certificate of election to the candidate for Congress having the highest number of votes; and the section relating to presidential electors provides that the votes for electors shall be given, received, returned, and canvassed as the same are for members of Congress. Thus it is made the absolute duty of the governor to give a certificate to the candidate for elector having the highest number of votes. The statute leaves him no discretion whatever. The secretary of state is, as in the other case, made the returning-officer, and he is to prepare the lists of the names of the electors elected, and affix the seal of the State to the same.

The secretary of state, as in the case of members of Congress, is to certify the "names of the electors elected, and affix the seal of the State to the same." The lists thus prepared by the secretary of state the governor is required to sign, and by the secretary of state they are to be "delivered to the college of electors at the hour of their meeting on such first Wednesday of December." It is made the peremptory duty of the governor to sign the lists as prepared by the secretary of state. The secretary of state is positively required by law to give the certificate to the person having the highest number of votes. For the governor to assume to exercise the judicial or discretionary power in regard to the eligibility of candidates for Congress, supreme judge, treasurer of the State, secretary of state, State printer, prosecuting attorneys, or electors, would be to act in the face of a direct provision of the statute of the State. With the effect of the certificate the governor has nothing to do. His duties are purely ministerial, and are prescribed in plain, direct terms by the statute, and about them there can be no possible room for controversy.

Governor Grover assumes that there is a conflict between the act of Congress of 1792 and the statute of Oregon, and bases his justification for a violation of the statute of Oregon upon his duty to execute the act of Congress. There is no possible conflict between the act of Congress and the statute of Oregon, except in the one immaterial particular, namely, that the act of Congress requires *three* lists of the names of electors to be made out, while the statute of Oregon prescribes only *two*. The third section of the act of Congress touching this question reads thus:

> That the executive authority of each State shall cause three lists of the names of the electors of such State to be made and certified, to be delivered to the electors on or before the said first Wednesday in December, and the said electors shall annex one of the said lists to each of the lists of their votes.

The governor is required to make three lists or certificates of the elect-

ors of the State. How is he to know that they are electors? By an
inquiry inaugurated on his own account upon an issue raised by *ex
parte* petitions or affidavits coming from unofficial sources or irresponsible parties? Certainly not. But simply because they have been
certified to him as having been appointed electors in the mode prescribed
by the legislature of the State, the legislature being expressly authorized by the Constitution of the United States to prescribe the mode of
appointment. Whoever, then, are officially declared or certified to
have received the highest number of votes in the mode prescribed by
the legislature are the persons to whom the act of Congress requires he
shall give the lists or certificates. With the appointment of these electors he has nothing to do and can have nothing to do, for that by the
Constitution is expressly left to the State, to be done in the manner
prescribed by its legislature, and when their appointment has been
declared by the officer or officers of the State appointed by the laws of
the State for that purpose, which under the laws of Oregon is the secretary of state, and him alone, they are the *electors* to whom the act of
Congress requires that he shall give the certificates. The assumption
upon his part of the right to decide that the persons who have been
appointed electors in the method prescribed by the legislature are ineligible is wholly without warrant in law. The act of Congress simply
provided a form of evidence as to who had been appointed electors by
the State, and the executive authority of the State is introduced simply
for the purpose of making the certificates or lists. The statute of the
State requires the secretary of state to canvass and return the votes for
electors as it is done for members of Congress; and as he is required in
the case of members of Congress to certify to the candidate having the
highest number of votes, so he is required in the case of electors to certify to the candidate having the highest number of votes; and as the
governor is required in the case of a candidate for Congress to give a
certificate to the person having the highest number of votes, so he is
required in the case of an elector to give a certificate to the person
having the highest number of votes; and he has just as much right, and
no more, no less, to pass upon the eligibility or qualifications of a candidate for Congress as he has upon those of a candidate for elector. And
to illustrate the absurdity of the position assumed by the governor, he,
in his evidence before the committee, said that he considered it his duty
to pass upon the qualifications of a candidate for Congress in giving his
certificate, and that he would refuse a certificate to a candidate whom
he believed to be ineligible. The idea that the governor of a State may
refuse to grant a certificate of election to a candidate for Congress who
has received the highest number of votes because in his opinion the
candidate is ineligible under the Constitution or law, and that he may
exercise a like judicial power in regard to candidates for electors, seems
to be supremely ridiculous, entirely destitute of support in law, and at
irreconcilable variance with reason and common sense.

Mr. Commissioner FRELINGHUYSEN. May I ask one question?

Mr. Senator MITCHELL. Certainly.

Mr. Commissioner FRELINGHUYSEN. Does this act, which provides for canvassing the votes for electors, provide for any declaration
or proclamation being made by the governor?

Mr. Senator MITCHELL. It does not. It simply provides that the
secretary of state shall canvass the votes and issue the certificate to the
person having the highest number of votes, and the law makes it the
imperative duty of the executive of the State to sign that list. No
power whatever is given him, ministerially, politically, judicially, or any

other wise, to pass on the question whether the person receiving the highest number of votes was eligible or ineligible.

I now pass to a consideration of the question, could Cronin, being a minority candidate, be elected?

Admitting, for the sake of the argument, that the governor of Oregon had jurisdiction to pass upon the question of the ineligibility of Watts— an assumption I have tried to show is wholly destitute of support in law—the next inquiry is as to whether it was his right, under the law, to issue the certificate of election to a minority candidate, or, in other words, whether a minority candidate was elected if the majority candidate were ineligible to receive the office.

It may be stated, without fear of successful contradiction, that no decision can be found in the English or American reports which would give the election to a minority candidate under the circumstances of this case. It has been held in England that the minority candidate is elected where the electors have *personal* and *direct* knowledge of the ineligibility of the majority candidate. It is believed that no case can be found in England where it was held that *constructive knowledge* of the ineligibility of the majority candidate would be sufficient to give the election to the minority candidate. All the cases in which the minority candidates have been held to be elected were where there were very small constituencies, generally corporations, and where the knowledge of the ineligibility was brought home to every voter. More than that, it is the well-settled law in England that the voter is not in such a case presumed or required to know the law, and that it is not to be presumed that he knows either what the law is creating the ineligibility, or even if he knows the law that he knows the effect of it to be such as to make the candidate ineligible. It must, therefore, not only be shown that he knows the disqualifying provision of the law or the decision of the courts which, in fact, made the candidate ineligible, but that he also knew the *legal effect* of the law or of the decision, and that it had the effect to disqualify the candidate from being elected to the office.

The doctrine of the law in England on this subject cannot be better, more ably, or clearly stated than by quoting from the able speech made by Senator Thurman, of Ohio, in the United States Senate in the Forty-first Congress, in the contested case of Abbott *vs.* Vance. The Senator in that case used the following language:

Again, in the English cases the intention of the voter to throw away his vote might well enough be imputed to him, because, as I said, it belonged to him; and if he knowingly and willfully voted for a man whom he knew would never be allowed to hold the office, the natural presumption was that he intended to throw away his vote; and it is upon this ground, that he did willfully throw away his vote, that his vote is rejected from the count. This can be proved in a sentence almost. If the English voter voted for a disqualified man, not knowing of the disqualification, then the minority man is *not* elected. We all agree to that. Every case says that. The bare fact, then, of disqualification or disability on the part of the man receiving a majority does not elect the minority man. It is necessary not only that the majority man shall be disqualified, but that the voters shall have had clear, positive, certain knowledge of this disqualification, and yet contumaciously, willfully, and knowingly cast their votes for him; and when that is the case they may well enough be presumed to have intended the natural result of their act, intended to throw away their votes.

*　　　　*　　　　*　　　　*　　　　*

I proceed to show further differences between the English cases and the case before us. In the English cases the voter knew, to a moral certainty, that the person for whom he voted would never be permitted to hold the office. There was nothing in the British constitution, nothing in any act of Parliament, nothing in any judicial or parliamentary decision that held out the least idea or hope that the disqualification of the person voted-for would be removed, and he permitted to take and hold the office.

*　　　　*　　　　*　　　　*　　　　*

Again, in England numerous decisions had settled the law. The Senator from Wisconsin said it had been settled for three hundred years. I do not care about going into the chronology to know whether that statement was perfectly exact or not; but it was well settled in England that in the elections of the kind that have been referred to, if the voter knowingly cast his vote for a disqualified man that vote would be rejected. Every voter, therefore, casting his vote for a disqualified man, knowing him to be so, knew that the minority man would be seated, and therefore he might be held to have assented to the seating of that minority man. But no such thing was known to the general assembly of North Carolina. They had no right to think any such thing; *for from the very foundation of this Government down to this day, at least from 1798 down to this day, there is an unbroken chain of cases in both Houses of Congress against the idea of seating a minority man, while there is not one single instance from the foundation of the Government to this day in which a minority man has been seated in either branch of Congress on the ground that the man who received a majority of the votes was a disqualified person.*

Again, further on in the same speech, the distinguished Senator said:

Again, here is another thing that the legislature of North Carolina had a right to know, and that distinguishes this case from the English cases, and that is, *that the weight of judicial decision in the United States is decidedly against the claim of a minority man to an election.* That is an element wholly wanting in the English cases. In England the entire current of decisions was that the minority man could have the seat. *In America the decided weight of judicial, in fact every case but one decided by a supreme court, is against the pretensions of the minority candidate;* and *that* the legislature of North Carolina had a right to look at and to build their expectations upon when they voted for Mr. Vance.

Here, then, are no less than six or seven important, nay almost every one of them conclusive, elements in this case, not one of which was in the English cases; and yet it is contended *that the Senate of the United States is to disregard the first principles of republican government and seat a man who did not receive one-third of the votes of the legislature upon the doctrine of the English cases, when those cases and the case before us stand on wholly different foundations.*

The Senator in the above quotation stated the case broadly and strongly as to the rule in England. He did not, however, mention one ingredient of importance in the rule as laid down by the decisions in the English courts and in Parliament, namely, that this knowledge upon the part of a voter referred to by him must apply as well to the disqualifying *law* as to the disqualifying *fact.* And under the English law a knowledge of the disqualifying *fact* alone was *not* sufficient to elect a minority candidate, but he must have *actual* knowledge of the disqualification in law arising from the existence of such fact. In other words, the doctrine that all men are presumed to know the law does not apply in this class of cases; while, as a general rule, ignorance of the law excuses no one, in this case it does. He must have *actual* knowledge both of the existence of the disqualifying fact and the disqualifying law.

In the case of The Queen *vs.* The Mayor, Aldermen, and Burgesses of Tewksbury, reported in English Law Reports in 1868, the court held "*that the mere knowledge on the part of the electors who voted for B. that he was mayor and returning-officer did not amount to knowledge that he was disqualified in a point of law as a candidate; and therefore their votes were not thrown away so as to make the election fall on the fifth candidate.*"

The reason of the rule as held formerly in England is given in a few words in Southwark on Elections, page 259, as follows:

That it is willful obstinacy and misconduct in a voter to give his vote for a person laboring under a known incompetency.

Clarke on Election Committees, page 156, in referring to the English rule, says:

Whenever a candidate is disqualified from sitting in Parliament, *and notice thereof is publicly given to the electors,* all votes given to such disqualified candidate will be considered as thrown away.

In King *vs.* Hawkins, 10 East, 210, Lord Ellenborough said the election of a person ineligible was void when the votes were cast *after notice of ineligibility.*

Heywood on County Elections says, page 535:

If before the election comes on or a majority has polled, *sufficient notice has been publicly given of his disability*, the unsuccessful candidate next to him on the poll must ultimately be the sitting member.

Male on Elections, page 336, states the English rule thus:

If an election is made of a person or persons *ineligible*, such election is void *where that ineligibility is clear and pointed out to the electors at the poll.*

The English rule, as above stated, is the one laid down in the celebrated case of Wilkes *vs.* Luttrell. It is believed, however, that during late years the rule in England, as above stated, has undergone a change in the direction of the American doctrine. In a recent case decided in England, The Queen *vs.* Mayor, 3 Law Reports, Queen's Bench, 629, the rule as to knowledge of the disqualifying law being necessary in England, was stated strongly, as follows: After holding that though the elector had actual notice of the fact which had been adjudged by the courts to disqualify, yet knowledge or notice in the elector of the adjudication *could not be presumed,* it further said:

It is not enough to show that the voter knew the fact only; but it is necessary to show sufficient to raise a reasonable inference that he knew that the fact amounted to a disqualification.

In the United States the general current of authorities sustains the doctrine that the ineligibility of the majority candidate does not elect the minority candidate, and this without reference to the question as to whether voters knew of the ineligibility of the candidate for whom they voted, and herein is the distinction between the English and American authorities. In England *actual* knowledge of the existence of a fact and actual knowledge of the disqualifying consequence following from the existence of such fact, it has been held in certain cases, elect the minority candidate. In America the doctrine is that the minority candidate is *not* elected *under any state of circumstances.*

This doctrine has been fully declared by the Senate of the United States in several adjudications and by the House of Representatives, as well as by the decision of the supreme courts of many of the States. The only case that has been produced which would give even a shadow of excuse or pretense for the claim of Cronin, the minority candidate in Oregon, to have been elected, is the case of Gulick *vs.* New, 14 Indiana Reports. That case has been expressly referred to and overruled in argument in the Senate and House of Representatives, as well as by the decisions of the courts of some of the States. By the law of Indiana the mayor of the city of Indianapolis had judicial power in certain classes of criminal cases co-extensive with the county in which the city is situated, and by the constitution of the State he was not eligible to be elected to any other office during the period for which he was elected mayor. Before the expiration of this period, Gulick, the mayor, was elected sheriff of the county of Marion, and the question arose as to his eligibility. The supreme court of Indiana held that the voters in the county, inasmuch as the criminal jurisdiction of the mayor extended all over the county, must take *constructive* notice of his ineligibility.

The decision was unsupported by any authority whatever, and applying it in this case in its full length and breadth it would furnish no excuse for the action of Governor Grover.

Dr. Watts, the candidate for elector on the republican ticket, was postmaster at a little town, La Fayette, in Yam Hill County. There were eleven other post-offices in the county and one within two miles of La Fayette, and the testimony shows that the whole number of voters receiving their mail-matter at La Fayette did not exceed one hundred, while the entire majority of Dr. Watts in the State was 1,049. If it should be held that the voters within the mail-delivery of Dr. Watts must not only have taken notice of the fact that he was postmaster, but also of his consequent ineligibility under the Constitution, and the votes of such persons should be deducted from his majority, it would still leave him over nine hundred majority among the voters who could not be presumed to have even *constructive* knowledge of his character as a postmaster and of his consequent ineligibility.

In America the settled doctrine of the law as established not only by the judicial tribunals but by both Houses of Congress is that voting for an ineligible candidate, even with full knowledge of the disqualifying fact and its legal consequences, does *not* elect the minority candidate where either a majority or plurality of votes is required to elect.

In McCrary's American Law of Elections, page 167, the following is stated on this subject:

We come now to a question which has been much discussed and upon which the authorities are somewhat conflicting; it is this: Suppose the candidate who has received the highest number of votes for an office is ineligible, and that his ineligibility was known to those who voted for him before they cast their votes, are the votes thus cast for him to be thrown out of the count and treated as never cast, and should the minority candidate, if eligible, be declared elected in such a case? No doubt the English rule is that where the majority candidate is ineligible, and sufficient notice of his ineligibility has been given, the person receiving the next highest number of votes being eligible must be declared elected. Great stress is laid upon the fact of notice having been given, and the reason of the English rule is said to be "that it is willful obstinacy and misconduct in a voter to give his vote for a person laboring under a *known* incompetency." (Southwark on Elections, page 259.) An examination of the English cases will show that in some of them the election was declared void and sent back to the people on the ground that there was not sufficient notice of the incapacity of the successful candidate; while in others the minority candidate was declared elected on the ground that due notice of the ineligibility of the person receiving the majority was given. The following are some of the principal English authorities upon the subject: Rex vs. Monday, Cowp., 537; Rex vs. Coe, Heywood, 361; Rex vs. Bissell, *ibid.*, 360; Rex vs. Parry, 14 East., 549; Regina vs. Cookes, 28 Eng. L. and Eq., 304, Q. B., 406; Heywood on County Elections, 535; Male on Elections, 536; King vs. Hawkins, 10 East., 210; Claridge vs. Evelyn, 5 B. and A. 8; Clarke on Election Committees, page 156; Southwark on Elections, page 259.

Mr. McCrary then cites numerous authorities in support of the position assumed by him to be the rule in this country, in the following language:

Thus, in Commonwealth vs. Cluly, 56 Pa. St., 270, the supreme court of Pennsylvania held that where in an election for sheriff a majority of the votes are cast for a disqualified person, the next in vote is not to be returned as elected; and the supreme court of California, in Saunders vs. Haynes, 13 Cal., 145, holds the same doctrine, and enforces it by cogent reasoning. And in Wisconsin we have the same ruling in State vs. Giles, 1 Chand., 112, and in State vs. Smith, 14 Wis., 497, and see opinion of judges, 38 Maine, 597; State vs. Boal, 46 Mo., 528; Cushing Election Cas., 496, 576, and see State vs. Anderson, 1 Cox, N. J., 318; People vs. Clute, 50 N. Y. But in Indiana the doctrine of the English authorities has been followed. (Gulick vs. New, 14 Ind., 93.)

And then in section 234 the whole matter is summed up by Mr. McCrary as follows:

Thus it will be seen that the weight of authority in this country is decidedly against the adoption here of the English doctrine. And we think that sound policy, as well as reason and authority, forbids the adoption of that doctrine in this country. It is a fundamental idea with us that the majority shall rule, and that a majority or at least a plurality shall be required to elect a person to office by popular vote. An election with us is the deliberate choice of a majority or plurality of the electors. Any doctrine which opens the way for the minority rule, in any case, is anti-republican and anti-American. The English rule, if adhered to, would in many cases result in compelling very large majorities to submit to very small minorities, as an ineligible person may receive, and in many cases has received, a great majority of the votes.

In the case of the Commonwealth vs. Cluly, 56 Pennsylvania State

Reports, which was a case wherein at an election for sheriff in a certain county of Pennsylvania a person receiving the majority of votes was ineligible under the constitution of that State, Justice Strong, now of the Supreme Court of the United States and present member of this Commission, then on the supreme bench of Pennsylvania, in delivering the opinion of the court, said:

Now, on this showing, what interest has the relator in the question he attempts to raise? What more than any inhabitant of Allegheny County, or of the Commonwealth? He was a rival candidate at the election for the office, but he was defeated, with a majority against him of six thousand nine hundred and ninety. Doubtless, if his successful rival is incapable of holding the office on account of the constitutional provisions "that no person shall be twice chosen or appointed sheriff in any term of six years," or for any other reason, and that incapacity entitles him, the relator, to the office, he has an interest. He certainly can have none if a judgment of ouster against Cluly would not give the sheriffalty to him. But surely it cannot be maintained that in any possible contingency the office can be given to him. The votes cast at an election for a person who is disqualified from holding an office are not nullities. They cannot be rejected by the inspectors, or thrown out of the count by the return-judges. The disqualified person is a person still, and every vote thrown for him is formal. Even in England it has been held that votes for a disqualified person are not lost or thrown away so as to justify the presiding officers in returning as elected another candidate having a less number of votes, and if they do so a *quo-warranto* information will be granted against the person so declared to be elected, on his accepting the office. (See Cole on Quo Warranto Informations, 141, 142; Regina *vs.* Hiorns, 7 Ad. & E., 960; 3 Nev. & Perry, 184; Rex *vs.* Bridge, 1 M. & S., 76.)

Under institutions such as ours are there is even greater reason for holding that a minority candidate is not entitled to the office if he who received the largest number of votes is disqualified. We are not informed that there has been any decision strictly judicial upon the subject, but in our legislative bodies the question has been determined. It was determined against a minority candidate in the legislature of Kentucky, in a case in which Mr. Clay made an elaborate report, and was sustained. In 1793, Albert Gallatin, elected a Senator from this State, was declared by the Senate of the United States disqualified because he had not been a citizen of the United States nine years, and his election was declared void for that reason, but the seat was not given to his competitor. Nobody supposed the minority candidate was elected. There have been several other cases of contested elections in which the successful candidates were decided to have been disqualified, and denied their offices.

John Bailey's case is one of them. He was elected to Congress from Massachusetts and refused his seat in 1824. But neither in his case, nor in any other with which we are acquainted, were the votes given to the successful candidate treated as nullities, so as to entitle one who had received a less number of votes to the office. There is a class of cases in England apparently, but not really, asserting otherwise. The earliest of them are referred to by Mr. Butler in his argument in Rex *vs.* Monday, Cowper, 530. They were followed by Rex *vs.* Hawkins, 10 East., 211, and Rex *vs.* Parry, 14 Id., 549. In these cases it is said that if sufficient notice is given of a candidate's disqualification, and notice that votes given for him will be thrown away, votes subsequently cast for him are lost, and another candidate may be returned as elected if he has a majority of good votes after those so lost are deducted. There is more reason for this in England, where the vote is *viva voce* and the elective franchise belongs to but few, than here, where the vote is by ballot and the franchise well nigh universal. In those cases the notice was brought home to almost every voter, and the number of electors were never greater than three hundred, and generally not more than two dozen. Besides, a man who votes for a person with knowledge that the person is incompetent to hold the office, and that his vote cannot therefore be effective, that it will be thrown away, may very properly be considered as intending to vote a blank, or throw away his vote.

In the supreme court of the State of California, in the case of Saunders *vs.* Haynes, 13 California Reports, Justice Baldwin, in announcing the opinion of the court, said:

It will be observed that the point of this defense is, that the votes cast for treasurer, supposing he received the highest number, were nullities, because of his assumed ineligibility. But we do not so consider. Although some old cases may be found affirming this doctrine, we think that the better opinion at this day is that it is not correct.

The celebrated controversy in the British Parliament between Wilkes and Luttrell has given rise to much discussion, and the opinions of jurists and statesmen have been somewhat divided. But the prevailing opinion, English and American, of modern times, seems to be against the precedent established in that case. In the case of Whitman and Maloney, (10 Cal.,) Mr. Justice FIELD clearly intimates his opinion in favor of the principle that the votes given for an ineligible candidate are not to be counted for the next highest candidate on the poll. In the State of Wisconsin *vs.* Giles, (1 Chandler, page 117,) the same doctrine is held, and it is enforced by the judges of the supreme court of Maine in their opinion, to be found in 38 Maine Reports, page 597.

Our legislative precedents seem to be the same way. Upon principle we think the law should so be ruled. An election is the deliberate choice of a majority or plurality of the electoral body. This is evidenced by the votes of the electors. But if a majority of those voting, by mistake of law or fact, happen to cast their votes upon an ineligible candidate, it by no means follows that the next to him on the poll should receive the office. If this be so, a candidate might be elected who received only a small portion of the votes, and who never could have been elected at all but for this mistake. The votes are not less legal votes because given to a person they cannot be counted for; and the person who is the next to him on the list of candidates does not receive a plurality of votes because his competitor was ineligible. The votes cast for the latter, it is true, cannot be counted for him; but that is no reason why they should, in effect, be counted for the former, who possibly could never have received them. It is fairer, more just, and more consistent with the theory of our institutions to hold the votes so cast as merely ineffectual for the purpose of an election, than to give them *the effect of disappointing the popular will and electing to office a man whose pretensions the people had designed to reject.*

The supreme court of California, with a democratic chief-justice, (Mr. Wallace,) no longer ago than the 13th of last November, in the case of Crawford *vs.* Dunbar, held to the same doctrine. The chief-justice, in announcing the opinion of the court, refers with unqualified approval to the doctrine laid down in 13 California, that the ineligibility of the person receiving the highest number of votes cannot operate to elect the minority candidate. The facts and conclusions of law in this recent case, as found and enunciated by the supreme court of California in their opinion, are as follows:

1. The office of inspector of customs at Stockton, in the San Francisco collection district, to which there is annexed a salary of $1,000 per annum, is a lucrative office within the meaning of section 21, article 4 of the constitution of the State, and if the defendant, Dunbar, held that office in September, 1875, then he was ineligible to the office of school superintendent in the county of San Joaquin, which is a "civil office of profit under the State," the salary thereof being $1,500 per annum.

2. It is settled here that a mere *de facto* incumbency of the inspectorship of customs would not render Dunbar ineligible to the office of school superintendent under the disqualifying clause of the constitution referred to. He must have been inspector *de jure* in order to work that result. (People *ex rel.* Attorney-General *vs.* Turner, 20 Cal., 142.)

3. The case made upon the part of the contestant established that Dunbar, on the first Wednesday of September, 1875, was *de jure* as well as *de facto* inspector of customs at Stockton. It appeared from the evidence adduced by the contestants that upon the nomination of the collector of customs, and with the approval of the secretary of the treasury, Dunbar had been appointed such inspector of customs, and had taken the oaths, two in number, prescribed by law, and had entered upon the discharge of his official duties, pursuant to his appointment. His appointment and the taking by him of the prescribed oaths of office, the last of them on the 6th day of April, 1875, was established by the records thereof in due form, which, or copies of which, duly certified, were produced from their proper custodian, and it was proven and found by the court below to be the fact, that, pursuant to his appointment, Dunbar, thereafter and on or about the 10th day of April, 1875, took possession of all the public property belonging to the office of inspector of customs of Stockton, theretofore under the control of his predecessor, and then and there entered upon the discharge of the duties pertaining to said office, and that he had not resigned nor been removed therefrom.

4. It further appears by the findings that at the regular election in question, the respondent, Dunbar, received 1,702 votes, the contestant, Crawford, (the next highest vote,) 1,182 votes, and Jenny Phelps 830 votes.

Upon these facts the contestant claims that he is entitled to the office, and should have judgment here to that effect. This claim is in argument put upon the ground that Dunbar, being ineligible, the votes cast for him, though amounting in number to a plurality, were mere nullities, and that the respondent received a majority of the votes over Jenny Phelps, the only other eligible candidate for the office. But this position cannot be maintained. This was directly ruled here, and adhered to upon a petition for a rehearing, in Saunders *vs.* Haynes, (13 California Reports, 145.) In that case the court said—

And then they go on and quote the portion which has been read from their opinion, and conclude by saying:

It results from this view that the judgment of the court below must be reversed, and the cause remanded with directions to render judgment vacating the office.

In the case of The People *ex rel.* Furman *et al. vs.* Clute, 50 New York Reports, the authorities, English and American, are reviewed, and the doctrine clearly and forcibly stated in the following extract from the opinion:

In the multitude of cases in which the question has arisen, we think that up to this point there is no essential difference of result. All agree that there must be prior notice to or knowledge in the elector of fact and law, to make his vote so ineffectual as that it is thrown away. But some say that if there be a public law declaratory that the existence of a certain fact creates ineligibility in the candidate, the elector having notice of the fact is conclusively presumed in law to have knowledge of the legal rule and to be deemed to have voted in persistent disregard of it. Others deny that the maxim *"Inorantia juris excusat neminem"* (even with the clause of it, *"quod quisque scire tenetur,"* not often quoted, and of which we are reminded by the very thorough brief of the learned counsel for the relator) can be carried to that length, and insist that there does not apply to this question the rule that all citizens must be held to know the general laws of the land and the special law affecting their own locality.

That maxim, in its proper application, goes to the length of denying to the offender against the criminal law a justification in his ignorance thereof; or to one liable for a breach of contract or for civil tort, the excuse that he did not know of the rule which fixes his liability. It finds its proper application when it says to the elector, who, ignorant of the law which disqualifies, has voted for a candidate ineligible, "Your ignorance will not excuse you and save your vote; the law must stand and your vote in conflict with it must be lost to you." But it does not have a proper application when it is carried further, and charges upon the elector such a presumption of knowledge of fact and of law as finds him full of the intent to vote in the face of knowledge, and to so persist in casting his vote for one for whom he knows that it cannot be counted, as to manifest a purpose to waste it. The maxim itself concedes that there may be a lack of actual knowledge of the law. For it is ignorance of it which shall not excuse. Then the knowledge of the law to which each one is held is a theoretical knowledge; and the doctrine urged upon us would carry a theoretical knowledge of the statute further than goes the statute iself. The statute but makes ineffectual to elect the votes given for one disqualified. The doctrine would make knowledge not actual, of that statute thus limited, waste the votes of the majority and bring about the choice to office by the votes of a minority. We are not cited to, nor do we find, any decision to that extent of any court in this State. The industrious research of the learned counsel for the relator has found some from courts in sister States. Gulick *vs.* New (14 Indiana, 97) is to that effect. Carson *vs.* McPhetridge (15 *id.*, 331) follows the last-cited case. Hatcheson *vs.* Tilden (4 Har. and McH., 270) was a case at *nisi prius*, and is to that effect. With respect for these authorities, we are obliged to say that they are not sustained by reasoning which draws with it our judgment. Commonwealth *vs.* Read (2 Ashmead, 261) is also cited. But that was a case of a board of twenty assembling in a room to elect a county treasurer. On motion being made to elect *viva voce*, a protest was made that the law under which they were acting prescribed a vote by ballot. Thus, *actual notice* of law and fact was brought directly to each elector before voting. Nineteen persisted in voting *viva voce*. These were held to be wasted votes. One voted by ballot; and his vote was held to prevail, and the person he voted for to be elected. Commonwealth *vs.* Cluly (56 Pennsylvania State Reports, 270) is also cited. But the language of the court there is: "The votes cast at an election for a person who is disqualified from holding an office are not nullities. They cannot be rejected by the inspectors or thrown out of the count by the return judges. The disqualified person is a person still, and every vote thrown for him is formal." And that was the case of one who was ineligible by reason of having held the office of sheriff of a county, and became a candidate in the same county for the same office before the lapse of time prescribed by the constitution; a case in its facts quite like this in hand.

The relator also cites many instances of the action of legislative bodies and their committees. As to these, a respectable authority on these questions has remarked "that they cannot be said to afford any precise or useful principle," (1 Peckwell, 500;) and learned counsel, arguing in support of the principle now claimed by the relator, has conceded that "no fixed principle is established by the decision of committees," (Galway Election Cases, 2 Moak English Cases, 714;) and it may safely be said that they are not so conclusive and satisfactory as judicial determinations, as it is difficult to arrive at the exact principle upon which the votes of so many as constitute a legislative body are put. Besides that, they are not uniform, but quite diverse in their results, as appears from the citations of the counsel of the relator, and the instances noted in 56 Pennsylvania State Reports, (*supra*.)

We have consulted many of the authorities cited to us from the English books, and in them it will be found, we think, that where it was held that votes for an ineligible person would be treated as thrown away, it was not extended beyond cases in which there was actual notice of fact and of law to the voters before their votes were cast.

And there are American authorities which hold that if a majority of those voting, by mistake of law or fact, happen to cast their votes upon an ineligible candidate, it by no means follows that the next to him in poll shall receive the office. (Saunders *vs.* Haynes, 13 California, 145; State *vs.* Giles, 1 Chandler, [Wisconsin,] 112; State *vs.* Smith, 14 Wisconsin, 497.) And in Dillon on Municipal Corporations (page 176 section 135,) it is stated that unless the votes for an ineligible person are expressly declared to be void, the effect of such person receiving a majority of the votes cast is, according to the weight of American authority and the reason of the matter, (in view of our mode of election, without previous binding nominations, by secret ballot, leaving each elector to vote for whomsoever he pleases,) that a new election must be had, and not to give the office to the qualified person having the next highest number of votes. And this view is sustained by a preponderance of the authorities cited by the author in the foot-note, some of which are cited above.

We think that the rule is this: The existence of the fact which disqualifies and of the law which makes that fact operate to disqualify must be brought home so closely and so clearly to the knowledge or notice of the elector as that to give his vote therewith indicates an intent to waste it.

The following letter, read during the debate in the Senate over the Oregon electoral controversy, will indicate the opinion of the Hon. Jeremiah S. Black, late Attorney-General under President Buchanan, and present counsel of the democracy of the nation upon this question. It reads as follows:

HOLLIDAYSBURGH, PENNSYLVANIA, *December* 9, 1876.

DEAR SIR: At the October election of 1846, Ephraim Galbreath was the whig candidate for the office of recorder of Blair County, and died on the morning of the election before the opening of the polls. It was found by the return judges that a majority of the votes for recorder were cast for Galbreath, and at the October term of the court of common pleas, held by Hon. Jeremiah S. Black, then president judge, the democratic candidate, Samuel Smith, appeared and asked to be qualified as recorder, on the ground that the votes cast for Galbreath, having been given for a dead man, should be disregarded, and the votes given for the claimant only should be counted.

Judge Black referred to the case of Mr. Wilkes, in the British Parliament, and denounced the seating of Luttrell as a high-handed outrage. He followed the line of argument of those who opposed the seating of Luttrell and declared emphatically that two things were settled by the election in question: first, that the *people did want Galbreath;* secondly, that they *did not want Smith.*

The result was that the democratic governor, Shunk, I think, filled the vacancy by the appointment of John M. Gibbony.

Truly yours,

SAM'L S. BLAIR.

Hon. SIMON CAMERON.

But the rule upon this subject established by the judicial tribunals of this country has also received the sanction of the National House of Representatives, and of the Senate of the United States as well. In the case of Samuel E. Smith *vs.* John Young Brown, contestant for a seat in the House of Representatives in 1868, from the second district of Kentucky, the doctrine that the minority candidate is elected when the person receiving the majority of the votes was disqualified was repudiated. In that case Brown received 8,922 votes; Smith, 2,816. Brown was ineligible, and Smith claimed that he for that reason, although receiving a minority of the votes, was elected. In the able report made in that case by Mr. Dawes of the Election Committee, after referring to the English doctrine, as above stated, the following language occurs, 2 Bartlett's Digest of Election Cases, pages 402 and 403:

But the committee do not find any such law regulating elections in this country in either branch of Congress, or in any State legislature, as far as they have been able to examine. Their attention has been called to no case, and it was not claimed before the committee that, as yet, this rule by which one receiving only a minority of the votes actually cast had been adjudged elected, had ever been applied in this country.

On the other hand, there have been many cases of alleged ineligibility in both branches of Congress since the formation of the Government, in some of which seats have been declared vacant on that ground, and in which, had there existed in this country any such rule, it certainly would have been resorted to. The very first contested election, at the first session of the First Congress, in 1789, Ramsey *vs.* Smith, (1 Contested Elections, 23,) was based on alleged ineligibility. The case was very ably and elaborately debated by Mr. Madison and others, and neither Ramsey nor any one in his behalf claimed for a moment that the ineligibility of Smith, who had received a majority of the votes, elected Ramsey, the minority candidate.

In 1793, Albert Gallatin was elected a Senator from Pennsylvania before he had been nine years a citizen of the United States. After a very lengthy discussion, (1 Contested Elections, 851,) his seat was declared vacant. In 1807, (1 Contested Elections, 224,) sundry electors of Maryland memorialized Congress to declare vacant the seat of Philip Barton Key, one of the Representatives from that State, because of alleged ineligibility arising from non-residence. Much time of the House was occupied in deciding the case, but no one appeared or found an advocate as a minority candidate. In 1824, on a like memorial, the seat of John Bailey, of Massachusetts, was for a like ineligibility declared vacant and a new election ordered, without a claim on the part of or in behalf of a minority candidate. In 1849, the seat of James Shields, a Senator from Illinois, was declared vacant because of ineligibility, and the right of a minority candidate was not even raised; and Mr. Brown himself was elected to the Thirty-sixth Congress before he had reached the age of twenty-five years, and therefore when he was ineligible and could not take the oath of office. At the opening of that Congress there was a protracted struggle for power, and the organization of the House was not effected for several months, after failing for lack of a single vote. There was a very strong temptation in every quarter to secure every possible vote; yet not only did no one appear to claim, or was the claim made, in behalf of any one as a minority candidate, that votes cast for Mr. Brown were to be thrown away and himself seated in his place; but at the second session Mr. Brown, having become of age, took his seat unchallenged, by force of the very votes cast for him when he was, in fact, ineligible. In very many other cases ineligibility has been discussed and passed upon without ever mooting the question now under consideration.

If any such rule as is now claimed, by which a candidate with a minority of the votes is put in a seat vacated for ineligibility, had ever obtained foothold in this country, this uniform current of decisions could not have run undisturbed through all Congresses from 1789 till the present time.

*   *   *   *   *   *   *

The committee are of opinion that a recurrence to the origin and history of this rule in the British Parliament will show the impossibility of its application to a case in the American House of Representatives. Parliament has no limitation of written constitution upon its powers. Sir Edward Coke says that " its power and jurisdiction are so transcendent and absolute that it cannot be confined, either for causes or persons, within any bounds."

Blackstone says "it hath sovereign and uncontrollable authority in making, conforming, enlarging, restraining, abrogating, repealing, reviewing, and expounding of laws concerning matters of all possible denominations, ecclesiastical or temporal, civil, military, maritime, or criminal—this being the place where that absolute despotic power which must in all governments reside somewhere is intrusted by the constitution of these kingdoms."

And either house of Parliament may, upon proof of any crime, adjudge any member disabled and incapable to sit as a member.—1 *Black. Com.*, page 163.

With this power, called by some *omnipotent*, Parliament grants and takes away the right to vote at its pleasure, erects and destroys constituencies when and where it pleases.

If there has been bribery at an election, it sometimes fines and sometimes disfranchises a whole constituency.

Indeed, it is not the theory of the British government that power originates with the people. In theory the right of the monarch is a divine right, and he has graciously *conceded* from time to time to the people whatever share in the government they possess.

It matters not to the theory that the people, in point of fact, wrenched all this power out of the hands of the monarch; the conclusion is very easy, that what has been conceded *to* the people can, at pleasure, be modified, limited, or even taken away.

Parliament has, therefore, exercised its *omnipotence* with an exceedingly lavish hand in the matter of elections to its own body, declaring by statute, George II, chapter 24, that " the right of voting for the future shall be allowed according to the last determination of the House of Commons concerning it," and, 34 George III, chapter 83, " that all decisions of committees of the House of Commons with respect to the right of election, or of choosing or appointing the returning-officer, shall be final and conclusive upon the subject forever." Thus they have made the rule here contended for a statute of the realm.

There certainly can be no need of argument to show that such law can find no place in our system.

In concluding this report, which received the sanction of the House of Representatives by a very large majority, Mr. Dawes employed the following language:

The committee are therefore of opinion that the case does not come within the law of the British Parliament, for want of a sufficient notice to the electors at the polls of an ineligibility known and fixed by law; that the law of the British Parliament in this particular has never been adopted in this country, and is wholly inapplicable to the system of government under which we live.

The will of the majority, expressed in conformity with established law, is the very basis on which rest the foundations of our institutions, and any attempt to substitute therefor the will of a minority is an attack upon the fundamental principles of the government, and if successful will prove their overthrow.

In the case of Abbott *vs.* Vance, of North Carolina, for a seat in the Senate of the United States, the question was elaborately and ably discussed, as has been already shown, and the decision of the Senate was against the doctrine that the minority candidate is elected where the person receiving a majority of the votes is ineligible, and in the report of the committee in that case, which received the able advocacy of Senator Thurman and others, and which was adopted by the Senate, it was distinctly stated that the fact that the voters have notice of the ineligibility of the candidate at the time they cast their votes for him makes no difference.

The concurrent authority, therefore, of the judicial and legislative tribunals of this country is in direct contravention of the position assumed by Governor Grover in holding that Cronin, the minority candidate, was elected and in issuing him a certificate, and not only so, but even were the rule as formerly held in England as above stated to obtain, as it does not, it would not furnish the executive authority the slightest vindication for his action in this regard under the clearly established circumstances of this case.

I now pass to the question as to whether a person who is ineligible under the Constitution to be appointed an elector, and who is a candidate before the people, receives a majority of all the votes cast, and is so officially declared by the proper canvassing officer, and who takes his seat in the college of electors, participates in its proceedings and casts his vote for President and Vice-President, the question of his ineligibility not having prior to that time been passed upon by any competent tribunal, is a mere usurper or an officer *de facto* acting under color of title. If the former, it must be conceded that all his acts are absolutely void. If the latter, as I insist he clearly is, then his acts are not void; and while his right to act *might* have been questioned in a competent tribunal *prior* to the meeting of the college of electors, it *cannot now* be questioned *by any power on earth.*

It is true the Constitution of the United States declares that no person holding an office of trust or profit under the United States shall be appointed an elector; but suppose the people of a State, in ignorance of both the disqualifying fact and the consequences attaching to it, by their unanimous votes or by a plurality, as they may in Oregon, appoint such a person as an elector, and his right to be appointed is never questioned or adjudicated upon by any tribunal having authority, and he takes his seat in the electoral college unchallenged and participates in its proceedings and casts the vote of his people and party for President and Vice-President, the record of the fact is made up and transmitted to the President of the Senate, and the college of electors, having lived its time, its existence expiring by limitation of law, dissolves and is an electoral college no more forever, nor are its individual members any longer presidential electors, they being *functus officio*. Can it be said in such a case that the vote given by such ineligible person is *void* as to *third persons* and the *public;* that the *people,* upon the one hand, who have acted in perfect good faith and in entire ignorance of the ineligibility of the elector, are to be deprived of their voice in the selection of a President and Vice-President, and the candidates for President and Vice-President, on the other hand, for whom such vote was cast, to be deprived of the benefit of it?

It would seem that such a doctrine would be at variance with the well-settled principles of law applicable to the acts of *de facto* officers acting under color of title in their relation to and effect upon third persons and the public. McCrary, in his American Law of Elections, in speaking of the acts of officers *de facto* acting under color of title, after referring to several authorities, in section 77 of that work uses the following language:

But in the case of Barnes *vs.* Adams, which arose in the Forty-first Congress, (2 Bartlett, 760,) the question was reviewed at length, and most of the cases arising both in Congress and the courts were cited and examined, and the conclusion was reached both by the committee and by the House that in order to give validity to the official acts of an officer of an election, so far as they affect third parties and the public, and in the absence of fraud, it is only necessary that such officer shall have color of authority. It is sufficient if he be an officer *de facto*, and not a mere usurper.

The report in this case, after quoting from numerous decisions, both in the House and in the courts of this country, continues as follows.

Here Mr. McCrary quotes from the report of the committee of the House of Representatives in the case of Barnes *vs.* Adams, which quotation is as follows:

The question, therefore, regarded in the light of precedent or authority alone, would stand about as follows:

The judicial decisions are all to the effect that the acts of officers *de facto* so far as they affect third parties or the public, in the absence of fraud, are as valid as those of an officer *de jure*.

The decisions of this House are to some extent conflicting; the point has seldom been presented upon its own merits, separated from questions of fraud; and in the few cases where this seems to have been the case the rulings are not harmonious.

In one of the most recent and important cases, (Blair *vs.* Barrett,) in which there was an exceedingly able report, the doctrine of the courts as above stated is recognized and indorsed.

The question is therefore a settled question in the courts of the country, and is, so far as this House is concerned, to say the least, an open one.

Your committee feel constrained to adhere to the law as it exists, and is administered in all the courts of the country, not only because of the very great authority by which it is supported, but for the further reason, as stated in the outset, that we believe the rule to be most wise and salutary. The officers of election are chosen of necessity from among all classes of the people; they are numbered in every State by thousands; they are often men unaccustomed to the formalities of legal proceedings. Omissions and mistakes in the discharge of their ministerial duties are almost inevitable. If this House shall establish the doctrine that an election is void because an officer thereof is not in all respects duly qualified or because the same is not conducted strictly according to law, notwithstanding it may have been a fair and free election, the result will be very many contests, and, what is worse, injustice will be done in many cases. It will enable those who are so disposed to seize upon mere technicality, in order to defeat the will of the majority.

Mr. McCrary concludes his reference to this case by saying:

The report of the committee in this case was adopted by the House *nem. con.*, after a full discussion, (Congressional Globe, July, 1870, pages 5179 to 5193,) and the doctrine there asserted may now be regarded as the settled law of the House.

Again, in section 79 of the same work, American Law of Elections, the following statement of the rule as established by the judicial courts is made :

In the courts of the country the ruling has been uniform, and the validity of the acts of officers of election who are such *de facto* only, so far as they affect third persons and the public, is nowhere questioned. The doctrine that whole communities of electors may be disfranchised for the time being and a minority candidate forced into an office because one or more of the judges of election have not been duly sworn, or were not duly chosen, or do not possess all the qualifications requisite for the office, finds no support in the decisions of our judicial tribunals.

In the case of The People *vs.* Cook, 4 Selden New York Reports, the court says :

The neglect of the officers of the election to take any oath would not have vitiated the election. It might have subjected those officers to an indictment if the neglect was willful. The acts of public officers being in by color of an election or appointment are valid, so far as the public is concerned.

Again :

An officer *de facto* is one who comes into office by color of a legal appointment or election. His acts in that capacity are as valid, so far as the public is concerned, as the acts of an officer *de jure.* His acts in that capacity cannot be inquired into collaterally.

In the case of Baird *vs.* Bank of Washington, in the supreme court of Pennsylvania, 11 S. & R., 414, the court said :

The principle of colorable election holds not only in regard to the right of electing, but of being elected. A person *indisputably ineligible* may be an officer *de facto* by color of election.

This case, it will be observed, is directly in point upon the proposition that a person " indisputably ineligible" may become an officer *de facto* by color of election, and, such being the case, it follows, under the rule as it exists in this country, as before stated, that his acts as such officer *de facto* are valid as to third persons and the public. Again, in the case of Pritchell *et al. vs.* The People, in the supreme court of the State of Illinois, 1 Gilmer's Reports, 529, the same doctrine was held. The court, in their opinion in that case, use the following language :

It is a general principle of the law that ministerial acts of an officer *de facto* are valid and effectual when they concern the public and the rights of third persons, although it may appear that he has no *legal or constitutional right to the office.* The interests of the community imperatively require the adoption of such a rule.

The same court, in the case of The People *vs.* Ammons, 5 Gilmer, 107, enunciated the same doctrine and used this language :

The proof offered would have shown that he was an officer *de facto,* and as such his acts were as binding and valid when the interests of third persons or the public were concerned, as if he had been an officer *de jure.*

The supreme court of the State of Missouri, in the case of Saint Louis County *vs.* Sparks, 10 Missouri, 121, say :

When the appointing power has made an appointment, *and a person is appointed who has not the qualifications required by law, the appointment is not therefore void.* The person appointed is *de facto* an officer ; his acts in the discharge of his duties are valid and binding. * * * A statute prescribing qualifications to an office is merely directory, and, *although an appointee does not possess the requisite qualifications his appointment is not therefore void, unless it is so expressly enacted.*

The supreme court of the State of New York, in the case of The People *vs.* Cook, 14 Barbour, 259, in discussing this question, says that the principle is so well established as to have become elementary, and uses the following language :

The rule is well settled by long series of adjudications, both in England and this country, that acts done by those who are officers *de facto* are good and valid as regards the public and third persons who have an interest in their acts, and the rule has been applied to acts judicial as well as to those ministerial in their character. This doctrine has been held and applied to almost every conceivable case. It cannot be profitable to enter into any extended discussion of the cases. The principle has become elementary, and the cases are almost endless in which the rule has been applied.

In the case of McGregor *vs.* Balch, 14 Vermont, 428, it was held that, *although a person cannot legally hold the office of justice of the peace at all* while holding the office of assistant postmaster under the United States, yet *having entered the former office under the forms of law* he was a justice of the peace *de facto*, and his acts as such were valid as to third persons and the public.

These cases go to the extent, therefore, of holding that if a person who is *ineligible to be elected or appointed* to office is voted for by the people, and receives the requisite number of votes to elect or appoint in case he had been eligible, and enters upon the duties of the office, he is not a mere usurper but an officer *de facto* acting under color of title, and that his acts as such officer, in the absence of fraud, are binding upon third persons and the public. In all these cases and in others that might be cited, distinction is clearly drawn between the case of a person who is a mere usurper, and whose acts are absolutely void, and that of a person who, although ineligible or disqualified, acts under color of right, and is therefore an officer *de facto*, whose acts are *not* void, but binding upon third persons and the public.

But it is said that the clause in the Constitution of the United States, conferring upon the States the power to appoint electors, not only imposes a *personal disqualification* on a certain *class of persons*, rendering them ineligible to be appointed electors, but limits and circumscribes the power of the States in the matter of appointment as to such persons by the very terms of the grant, and that therefore, if the State appoint a person falling within this class, in reference to which it is claimed no grant of power is given to the State to appoint, such appointment is void and the person so appointed would not be an officer either *de jure* or *de facto*, but a mere usurper. But the answer to this is twofold. In the first place, even admitting that the true construction of the constitutional provisions is that the grant is circumscribed and confers no power on the State to appoint except from a certain class of persons, or rather that no power is conferred upon the State to appoint *from* a certain class, is there any greater or weightier reason for holding that a person actually appointed by a State from among the prohibited class, and who, clothed with all the insignia of office, entered upon and discharged the duties of the same, should not be considered an officer *de facto* acting under color of title, than a person who might be appointed, but who was laboring under a constitutional disability preventing him from exercising the duties of an office? It seems to me not. In either event, the person is constitutionally prohibited from holding the office. In either event, he comes into possession of it under color of legal authority, surrounded by all the insignia attaching to office.

But again, suppose there is a grant of power to the State to appoint electors, but that this grant is limited as to persons, excepting from its scope a certain class of persons—Federal office-holders for instance; who must determine this question of fact in the first instance as to whether a person about to be appointed comes within the prohibited class? Clearly the State. It has jurisdiction to appoint, and jurisdiction necessary to pass upon and determine the question in the first instance as to whether a person is or is not within the class to which the power of the State attaches; and having jurisdiction to pass upon this question, a *mistake* in the matter by appointing a person really within the prohibited class, would not be a *void* act upon the part of the State, but simply *voidable* by the decision of a *competent tribunal* made at any time *before* the act, which the elector was appointed to perform, was accomplished; and if no such decision is made, his act is the act of an officer *de facto* and cannot afterward be questioned.

In such a case rights have vested, by virtue of the act of a person, acting in the capacity of an elector under an appointment from the only power authorized to appoint electors, and such a person is no *usurper;* his acts are *not void.*

But another, and it seems a conclusive answer, is that this provision of the Constitution is not self-executing, that it requires legislation to enforce it, and no such legislation has ever been enacted.

In the present case, therefore, conceding for the argument that Watts was ineligible at the time of election, that he was not within the class from which the State was authorized to appoint, and admitting that the fact of his ineligibility was not questioned or adjudicated upon by any competent tribunal, (and I will speak of that hereafter,) having, as is conceded, received 1,049 more votes than his competitor, and having acted as an elector in the electoral college and voted for President and Vice-President, such vote cannot now be questioned either by the judicial courts, by Congress, by the electoral tribunal, or any other power on earth, so as to invalidate the vote thus cast by him as an elector for President and Vice-President.

The legislature of Oregon in its legislation upon the subject of vacancies in office treats the election or appointment of an ineligible person to office in that State as merely *voidable* and not *void*, and provides that a vacancy shall occur in the office to which he was elected upon the decision of a competent tribunal declaring void such election or appointment.

Section 45 of the election laws of Oregon, relating to vacancies in office, reads as follows:

Every office shall become vacant on the happening of either of the following events before the expiration of the term of such office:
1. The death of the incumbent.
2. His resignation.
3. His removal.
4. His ceasing to be an inhabitant of the district, county, town, or village for which he shall have been elected or appointed, or within which the duties of his office are required to be discharged.
5. His conviction of an infamous crime, or of any offense involving a violation of his oath.
6. His refusal or neglect to take his oath of office or to give or renew his official bond, or to deposit such oath or bond within the time prescribed by law.
7. *The decision of a competent tribunal declaring void his election or appointment.*

From the provisions contained in this last subdivision of the section relating to vacancies, it would seem conclusive that the legislature contemplated that an office might be filled by a person whose election or appointment was really void by reason of *ineligibility or any other cause,* until the decision of a *competent tribunal* was had declaring such election or appointment *void.* The legislature does not state what the competent tribunal is. Unquestionably, however, under the constitution of the State of Oregon the only *competent tribunal* would be a *judicial tribunal.*

I come now to the question as to the powers and duties of the electors present, under the statutes of Oregon, to supply by appointment any deficiency in the number of electors that may exist on the day fixed for the meeting of the college.

And first, admitting Watts to have been ineligible to be appointed an elector, and that the election is the appointment within the meaning of that term as employed in the Constitution, did his resignation as such elector, tendered by him to the electors present on the day of the meeting of the electoral college, create *such* a vacancy as could, under the statutes of Oregon, be filled by the electors present? I submit with all confidence that it did create such vacancy, and that the same was lawfully filled by the electors present in the election of Watts.

The statute of Oregon, section 2 of the act of 1864, is as follows:

> The electors of President and Vice-President shall convene at the seat of government on the first Wednesday of December next after their election, at the hour of twelve of the clock at noon of that day; and if there shall be *any vacancy* in the office of an elector occasioned *by death, refusal to act, neglect to attend, or otherwise*, the electors present shall immediately proceed to fill by *viva voce* and plurality of votes *such vacancy* in the electoral college; and when all the electors shall appear or the vacancies, if any, shall have been filled as above provided, such electors shall perform the duties required of them by the Constitution and laws of the United States.

In title 7, section 45, general laws of Oregon, page 709, it is provided that—

> Every office shall become vacant on the happening of either of the following events before the expiration of the term of such office:
>
> 1. The death of the incumbent.
> 2. His resignation.
> 3. His removal.
> 4. His ceasing to be an inhabitant of the district, county, town, or village for which he shall have been elected or appointed, or within which the duties of his office are required to be discharged.
> 5. His conviction of an infamous crime or of any offense involving a violation of his oath.
> 6. His refusal or neglect to take his oath of office or to give or renew his official bond, or to deposit such oath or bond within the time prescribed by law.
> 7. *The decision of a competent tribunal declaring void his election or appointment.*

It is contended in justification of the action of Governor Grover that under the circumstances of this case there was no vacancy in the office of elector that could be filled by the electors present under the provisions of the statute quoted; in other words, that Watts being, as claimed, ineligible to be appointed, and the election being the appointment, there was in this case no election; and there being a failure to elect there was no vacancy created within the legal definition of that term as employed in the statute. Doubtless, the very strongest possible presentation of argument in favor of such a position is made by Governor Grover himself, in a printed pamphlet entitled "Executive decision by the Governor of Oregon in the matter of eligibility of electors of President and Vice-President of the United States for 1876; printed at Salem, Oregon: Mart. V. Brown, State printer, 1876." If the position assumed by Governor Grover cannot be maintained by the arguments presented in this "executive decision," it is fair to presume that it cannot be maintained at all.

What, then, is the result in the way of argument upon the part of the governor in defense of the position assumed by him? It is this and this only: There can be no vacancy in the office of presidential elector in Oregon, "occasioned by death, refusal to act, neglect to attend, or otherwise," unless there has been an *incumbent;* and, as Watts never was, as argued, an *incumbent,* therefore no vacancy can be created in the office either by his death,.refusal to act, neglect to attend, or otherwise. I quote the argument in the governor's own words, copied from the executive decision referred to:

> Watts being ineligible to be elected, is there a vacancy in the electoral college to be filled by the other electors? What constitutes a vacancy in office in this State?
>
> In title 6, section 48, General Laws of Oregon, page 576, of vacancies, we have the following provisions:
>
> "SEC. 48. Every office shall become vacant on the occurring of either of the following events before the expiration of the term of such office:

"1. The death of the incumbent;

"2. His (the incumbent's) resignation;

"3. His (the incumbent's) removal;

"4. His (the incumbent's) ceasing to be an inhabitant of the district, county, town, or village for which he shall have been elected or appointed, or within which the duties of his office are required to be discharged;

"5. His (the incumbent's) conviction of an infamous crime or of any offense involving a violation of his oath;

"6. His (the incumbent's) refusal or neglect to take his oath of office or give or renew his official bond, or to deposit such oath or bond within the time prescribed by law;

"7. The decision of a competent tribunal declaring void his (the incumbent's) election or appointment."

The word "*incumbent's*" placed in parentheses in this quotation from the code of Oregon is placed there by me to indicate clearly the construction which is given the law.

There can be no vacancy in office in this State unless there has been an incumbent and that incumbent has gone out of office.

An "*incumbent*," says Webster, is a person who is in the *present possession* of a benefice or any office.

Bouvier says: "It signifies one who is in *possession* of an office;" and Sawyer, C. J., in the case of The People *vs.* Tilton, 37 Cal., 617, defines a vacancy as follows: "A vacancy, in the statutory sense, is when the party enters upon the duties of the office and afterward dies, resigns, or in any manner ceases to be an incumbent of the office before the expiration of the term."

In Comm. *vs.* Harley, 9 Penn., 513, it is decided that even death, after a lawful election and before qualification, does not create an incumbent of the office, nor does it create a vacancy which can be filled by appointment where the law authorizes vacancies to be so filled. In this case Watts was never an incumbent of the office of elector. His approach to it was absolutely barred by the Constitution. * * * On the subject of filling vacancies in the college of electors in this State the statute (Code, page 598, section 59) provides that—

"If there should be a vacancy in the office of elector occasioned by death, refusal to act, neglect to attend, or otherwise, the electors present shall immediately proceed to fill, by *viva voce* and plurality of votes, such vacancy in the electoral college."

As far as Watts is concerned, there has been no "death," no "refusal to act," no "neglect to attend," and there has been no vacancy "otherwise," for the vital reason that he has never been an incumbent of office. It is, then, clear that there has occurred no vacancy that can be filled by the other electors under the authority of the statutes of Oregon.

It will be observed that it is contended by Governor Grover that no person is an *incumbent* of an office until he is not only elected to such office, even where there is no question as to his eligibility, but has also qualified and taken possession of the same, until he has *entered upon the duties of his office*. In other words, even admitting him to have been eligible to be appointed an elector and to have been duly elected, still, unless he had first actually taken possession of the office, in the language of one of the opinions quoted "*entered upon the duties of the same*," no vacancy could have been created by his "death, refusal to act, neglect to attend, or otherwise."

That the authorities quoted by the governor have no sort of reference to a case like the one before us, and can possibly have no bearing whatever upon the construction of the Oregon statute, is so transparent as to meet with the instantaneous comprehension of the most casual observer, either lawyer or layman, and to scarcely need more than a passing notice. The argument of the governor proves too much, and its application ingulfs him in inextricable confusion. His argument would prevent a vacancy, such as could be filled by the electors present, in a case where a person who was clearly eligible and who had been legally elected should, before the meeting of the electoral college and before he had entered upon the duties of his office, either have died, or for any cause refused to act, resigned, or neglected to attend. Not having been an *incumbent*, says the governor, which as construed by him and his authorities—and I do not question the construction, but simply its application to the case—means a person in possession of an office, one who has entered upon the duties of an office, no vacancy therefore, it is claimed, within the meaning of the Oregon statute, could be created that could be filled by the electors present.

The clause in the Oregon statute as to vacancies in the office of elector and the manner in which they shall be filled, is evidently different from most of the clauses in constitutions, Federal and State, and in statutes generally. It is broad and comprehensive, including every possible vacancy that may occur, and not merely those that happen when an incumbent in possession of the office and exercising its duties, for any reason refuses to act or is disabled from acting further, but those occasioned by the "death, resignation, and refusal to act, or otherwise," which includes the case of a failure to appoint. Hence the technical, legal construction as given by courts to the term "vacancy," where standing alone in constitutions and statutes without words of definition or construction as to what it means and is intended to include, could have no kind of application to the case under consideration.

It has been said that the words "occasioned by death, refusal to act, neglect to attend, or otherwise" in the Oregon statute are words of limitation, contracting rather than enlarging the definition of the term "vacancy." This is not so. They are words of *definition* and not of *limitation*. The terms "vacancy" and "all vacancies," as used in constitutions and statutes, had by some judicial tribunals (although such does not appear to be the weight of authority) been construed to mean only such as were created in a case where an *incumbent* in the *actual possession of an office, exercising its duties*, had either died, resigned, or become legally disabled. And it was to obviate the application of any such construction of the terms "vacancy" and "all vacancies" that the legislature of the State of Oregon gave definition to the word "vacancy" in the electoral statute, and to the end that it might not be limited merely to cases where there had been an incumbent, an elector actually in possession of the office, exercising its duties as such incumbent, who had either died, resigned, or become legally disabled.

The reason why a different rule should have been established in reference to filling vacancies in the office of presidential elector from that relating to many if not all other offices, is apparent. While the office of presidential elector is one of the most important created by the Constitution of our country, it is the shortest lived. The term of office is confined to less than a single day. He enters upon its duties, takes possession of it, becomes an *incumbent in it* at twelve o'clock meridian on a certain day, and with the performance of his duty (which usually does not require more than an hour) his term by operation of law ceases; his official robes drop. He is *functus officio* and a private citizen. To hold, therefore, that, under the Oregon statute, the electors present could only fill such vacancies as might by "death, resignation, refusal to act, neglect to attend, or otherwise," occur *after* twelve, meridian, on the day of meeting, *after* they had entered upon their duties and become *incumbents*, would be to insist upon an absurdity so glaring on the very face of the proposition as to put to shame and confusion the lawyer that would seriously insist upon it. If there can, as contended by Governor Grover, be no vacancy such as the electors present could fill unless there had first been an attendance of the elector who had entered upon the duties of his office and become an *incumbent* of the office, then why, I would inquire, did the legislature of Oregon provide that the "electors present should immediately proceed to fill by *viva voce* and plurality of votes any vacancy caused," among other things, by *neglect to attend or otherwise?* Are these words meaningless? Are they to be eliminated from the statute, and their force obscured and buried under a legal interpretation of the term "vacancy," when standing alone?

But again, the governor in his *decision* assumes that no person but one who is eligible to be appointed can become an incumbent. And yet the *very statute he quotes*, subdivision seven relating to vacancies, contemplates that a person whose election *is void* may become an incumbent and exercise the duties of an office. And although his election is *void*, no vacancy occurs until by the decision of a *competent tribunal* such election is *declared to be void*. But not only so, says Governor Grover in his "executive decision," but "no vacancy could be created in the office of presidential elector which the electors present could fill, unless there had been an *incumbent.*" If this is true, then, although Watts had been clearly eligible, there had been no question about the legality of his election, yet, if before he had entered upon the duties of his office as elector and become an incumbent, which he could not do before the 6th day of December, he had died, resigned, *neglected to attend*, or refused to act, no vacancy, according to the law and logic of the governor, would have been created which the electors present could fill.

Should it be held, therefore, that the appointment of Watts was not merely voidable but absolutely void—and I insist in any possible view of the case it was but voidable—and that there was, as to him, a failure to elect, still under the statute of Oregon, broad and comprehensive as it is, the electors present had the right, and it was their duty, to fill the vacancy occasioned by such failure to elect. If his appointment was merely voidable and might have been declared void under the statute by a competent tribunal, but was *not* so declared, then he could rightfully act in the college of electors either under his original appointment by the people as an elector or by virtue of his appointment by the electors present when they accepted his resignation.

Or, again, should it, for the sake of argument, be conceded that Watts was *not* appointed and that Cronin was—and it is also conceded, as it must be as a matter of fact, that Odell, Cartwright, and Cronin did not act together as an electoral college, but that Odell and Cartwright, a majority of the college, acted together with Watts, whom they elected to fill the vacancy; and Cronin, a minority of one, acting by himself, and declaring or attempting to declare, and filling or attempting to fill two vacancies—*which*, in such case, is the legally constituted college? There can be but one college of electors in a State, and under these circumstances the former must be held to be that one. The only record the law contemplates as to vacancies in the electoral college is the record made by the electors themselves: the certificate of the organized tribunal, the electoral college. This is not merely the only record, but it is, as I confidently insist, *conclusive* upon that subject; and Odell and Cartwright being a majority of the electors constituting the electoral college in Oregon, whose title is indisputable, questioned by no one, not even by the governor in his certificate, but by it approved, their certificate as to the fact that there was a vacancy, and that such vacancy was filled by them, is *conclusive*, not only against Cronin, but all other persons, the State, the General Government, Congress, and the electoral tribunal as well.

This appointment to fill a vacancy is an appointment by the State, in the *manner directed by the legislature*, and in pursuance also of the Constitution of the United States and the act of Congress; and as the canvass of the secretary of state is *conclusive* as to those appointed by the people, so the certificate of the electoral college is *conclusive* as to the *fact of vacancy* as well as *to the person appointed to fill it.* And it is immaterial to inquire or know whether such vacancy was occasioned because Cronin did not act with the majority or because Watts resigned. And the fact that Cronin set up or attempted to organize a college of his own, filled or attempted to fill two vacancies, and voted for President and Vice-President in connection with the persons brought to his assistance, must be held to be *conclusive against Cronin* that he did not act or attempt to act with Odell and Cartwright; and in that event, conceding that Cronin was elected, there was a vacancy which was legally filled by Odell and Cartwright, and the record made by them is the record of the *real electoral college.* If Cronin was appointed an elector, then it was his duty to act with the majority, and that he did *not* act is conclusively shown in the fact that he organized a college of his own. It will not do for Cronin to say that Odell and Cartwright refused to act with him or to permit him to act with them. He is in no position to make any such claim, nor is his party. If such had been the fact—and it clearly was not—Cronin instead of attempting to set up a college of his own should have contented himself with insisting upon his right to act with Odell and Cartwright; and, had they refused to act with him, then presented and filed his protest and cast his vote for President and Vice-President, and stood upon his rights as a member of *that,* the only electoral college in the State. It is clear, however, as before stated, that all the acts of Cronin at the meeting of the electoral college were inconsistent with any claim that may be made that Odell and Cartwright refused to recognize him or to act with him. They demanded an exhibition of his credentials to act as an elector, that they might determine as to their validity and as to his right to act as an elector. This he peremptorily refused to do; and it is no excuse to say that the reason he refused to produce or exhibit his credentials was from a fear, imaginary or otherwise, that he would not be treated fairly by the majority of the electors. He had no right in law or, so far as the testimony shows, in fact, to act upon any such presumption, although he held in his hands three certificates from the governor, each one containing the three names of Odell, Cartwright, and Cronin, yet, against the repeated requests of Cartwright and Odell to produce them or exhibit them for the guidance of the college, and that they might determine as to his right to a seat in the college, he kept them in his pocket, only reading one of them in part, as testified to by the republican electors, and in full as testified to by democrats present who were not electors, and who had no right to be present, and peremptorily refused to deliver any of them to either Cartwright or Odell. He might have delivered one to each, and had they then refused to act with him or treat him fairly, he would have had in his possession the third certificate from the governor showing the fact that he had been certified to as one of the electors for whatever it might have been worth. Such a course, however, upon his part would have been inconsistent with the harmony of the conspiracy planned in New York and executed in Oregon, conceived in corruption and brought forth in shameless, unblushing fraud, with a view of robbing the majority of the people of the State of their choice, as expressed at the ballot-box, for President and Vice-President of these United States.

Upon this point, that Cronin's own version may be seen, I quote from his testimony. After describing the situation of the parties in the room of the electoral college, those present, &c., Mr. Cronin said:

After we had taken seats as I have described, Mr. Cartwright demanded those certificates of me. I told him he should not have them. He remarked, " We have as much right to those as you have, and there are two of us, and we have a right to those certificates, and we want them." I repeated again that he should not have them; that the certificates were of no use any way except to attach to our return. He replied to that, as near as I can recollect, "We want those certificates, and why don't you give them to us?" I replied by saying, "I don't think you intend to treat me fairly. In the first place here is a United States marshal who takes possession of the college; then Mr. Odell takes the key; and you might as well understand first as last that you shall not have those certificates." About that time, I think, Dr. Watts got up and read his resignation, and his resignation was accepted, and he was elected to fill that vacancy, as they called it. I then remarked, "Gentlemen, you refuse to act with me?" I am quite positive that Mr. Odell said, "You give us those certificates; we have got nothing to act on; we want those certificates," or words to that effect. I suppose I might as well say here that I did not hear Mr. Cartwright or Mr. Odell in terms refuse to act with me.

    *   *   *   *   *   *   *

Q. Why did you not produce the certificates and put them on the table?
A. Because I did not propose that Mr. Cartwright, Mr. Odell, or Mr. Watts should get those certificates.
Q. Did you not consider that Mr. Cartwright and Mr. Odell had as much right to them as you had?
A. Certainly.
Q. Why did you not put them on the table before them?
A. Because if I had put those certificates on the table or had given those certificates either to Mr. Odell or Mr. Cartwright or Dr. Watts, I suspected they would do just what they did do, and I should be left without a certificate. The certificates made out in proper order would have been returned to President Ferry with their proceedings, and that would have been recognized in preference to any other.
Q. Still I ask you if you did not feel bound to obey the majority of the electors known to be elected, when they asked you to put the certificates on the table?
A. No, sir.
Q. Did you think you had a right to take them away from the majority?
A. The question of right did not enter into that as much as the question of expediency.

From this it would seem that Mr. Cronin was not acting from a *sense of right or duty*, but solely from *considerations of expediency*.

By the statutes of all the States the electors are authorized to fill vacancies in the college. The certificate that goes to the President of the Senate is from the electors themselves, and not from the governors of the States. The only way the President of the Senate has knowledge of the certificate of the governor is through the certificate of the college of electors. To that body, the college of electors, is referred the determination of all questions of vacancy. If its journal recites that there was a vacancy which had been filled by the body, it is not competent to go behind that certificate and inquire whether there was such a vacancy. If there are two or more certificates from the same State, the first duty of the counting officer or tribunal is to find out which came from the electoral college, and when that certificate which contains the names and the action of a majority of the electors, conceded by all to be such, is found, we may be sure we have the record of the electoral college; and when the true college is found, the counting officer or tribunal may look to its action with entire certainty as that by which the count must be governed. For example, if a certificate made by two of the known and conceded electors in Oregon is found, the counting officer or tribunal may know that those two constitute the electoral college of that State, and their decision must govern in determining the question whether there was a vacancy, and how it was filled, and by whom.

In the case under consideration two certificates have been opened, one made by two of the known and recognized electors about whose election there is no dispute; hence this tribunal is bound to receive *that* as the certificate of the college of electors and to be governed by its determination in regard to any question of vacancy, although the other certificate contains the name of one man who was certified by the governor as having been appointed, and who has assumed to act as the college of electors, and who had attempted to appoint two substitutes in the place of the other electors who are known to have been appointed and who executed the former certificate. The latter certificate amounts to nothing, and should be utterly disregarded, except in so far as it contains the certificate of the governor of the appointment of the two electors who executed the former certificate. To that extent and that only can the certificate of the governor be accorded recognition, for the reason that only to that extent is it true to the purpose of its creation, which is to chronicle a pre-existing fact; only so far is it a faithful record of the *fact* of appointment *by the State;* and being no part of the manner of appointment but merely a form of evidence, but *not a conclusive* one, of the *fact* of appointment, it should only be received in so far as it is a true and faithful chronicler of the facts as to the persons appointed by the State; and in so far as it *falsifies the fact* it should be *repudiated and disregarded.* In so far, then, as the governor's certificate bears evidence that Odell and Cartwright were appointed by the State it is a faithful and true certificate of the fact, and should be accorded full faith and credit by the counting tribunal; but in so far as it certifies Cronin to have been appointed it is a *falsifier of history,* a *misrepresenter of a great fact, a contradiction of the record* made by the canvassing officers, *the product of usurpation, fraud, or mistake,* and entitled to no recognition or credence upon the part of either this high tribunal or any other officer or department of government.

It has been said that the supreme court of the State of Rhode Island has recently decided that the resignation of a person who was ineligible to be appointed an elector, and who had received a majority of the votes, did not, under the statutes of that State, create such a vacancy as the other electors could fill. This may all be true, and still it does not affect the Oregon case. The State, having the sole power to appoint, may prescribe for filling vacancies in the electoral college, whether arising from death, resignation, neglect to attend, refusal to act, or any other cause, including that of a *failure to elect.* The legislature may direct that a vacancy occurring from a failure of the elector to attend, or from a failure of the people to elect, shall be filled by a new election by the people, or it may direct that the other electors, or the electors present, shall appoint persons to supply such vacancies, and upon this point the statutes of the several States are different, and the statute of the State of Rhode Island is, in this respect, widely different from that of Oregon. The Oregon statute, as we have seen, provides that " If there shall be *any vacancy* in the office of elector occasioned by death, refusal to act, neglect to attend, *or otherwise,* the electors present shall immediately proceed to fill by *viva voce* and plurality of votes such vacancy in the electoral college"—evidently intended to cover all cases where the requisite number of electors was not present, whether such number was diminished by death, refusal to act, neglect to attend, or failure to elect, whereas the statute of Rhode Island provided as follows :

If any electors chosen as aforesaid shall after their said election decline the said office, or be prevented by any cause from serving therein, the other electors * * * shal fill such vacancies.

It may well be said that under the Rhode Island statute the electors present, or, as the statute has it, the " *other electors,*" have no right to fill a vacancy occasioned by a failure to elect; but such cannot be claimed under the statute of Oregon, as there the statute clearly authorizes the electors present to fill any vacancy, whether occasioned by death, resignation, refusal to act, neglect to attend, or, under the "*otherwise*" clause, *failure to elect.*

The statutes of the several States upon this subject are very dissimilar, and the power of the electors present in each State to fill vacancies must be determined in each State by reference to and construction of the statute of such State.

The statutes of California, for instance, provide that—

In case of the death or absence of any elector so chosen, or in case the number of electors shall, *from any cause, be deficient,* the electors then present shall forthwith elect from the citizens of the State so many persons as shall supply the deficiency.

Under this statute, therefore, the electors present clearly have the right to fill *any vacancy,* whether occasioned by death, resignation, refusal to act, neglect to attend, or failure to elect.

Mr. President and gentlemen of the Commission: I submit this case upon the papers before you. Were I authorized to invoke your judgment upon facts *aliunde* the record, then would I feel justified in directing your attention to acts of intrigue, corruption, and fraud in connection with the Oregon electoral vote that will stand forever in history as the crowning infamy of an unrestrained and insane personal and political ambition. While the charge of perjury and fraud against the returning-boards of Louisiana and Florida is by disappointed and maddened partisans echoed throughout the land, I might, were it proper, point you to a conspiracy that had its origin at No. 15 Gramercy Park, New York City, at the home and by the fireside of Samuel J. Tilden, the democratic candidate for President, that had for its purpose the purchase of an electoral vote, upon the faith of which his title to the Chief Magistracy of the nation might be established.

Mr. Commisioner STRONG. I would rather not hear anything on that subject. There is no such evidence before us.

Mr. Senator MITCHELL. I submit to the intimation, and though the law of your creation may not authorize you to look into or consider this record of intrigue, corruption, and fraud, it will stand nevertheless as a part of the history of the times, a changeless, palsied plague-spot upon the record of the democratic party, that time cannot obscure or repentance obliterate.

Mr. President, I have faith in this Commission and in the justice of its final judgment. I feel that when the arduous and responsible labors of you and your honorable associates have ended, forty-five millions of people can raise their eyes to heaven and exclaim in the language of the gifted bard—

> Great God! we thank thee for this home,
> This bounteous birth-land of the free,
> Where wanderers from afar may come
> And breathe the air of liberty.
> *Still* may her flowers untrampled spring,
> Her harvests wave, her cities rise,
> And yet, till Time shall fold his wing,
> Remain earth's loveliest paradise.

Mr. Representative LAWRENCE. Mr. President and gentlemen of the Commission, so much time has already been consumed continuously in this debate that I know very well that any words I may utter must fall upon weary ears. In a matter of so much consequence as this, I can only invoke the indulgence and patient attention of the Commission.

Mr. Commissioner THURMAN. Allow me to interrupt you, Mr. Lawrence. I beg leave to make a suggestion. There are five hours more of argument, one by Mr. Lawrence and four by counsel. I do not think it is possible for us to sit here for those five hours to-night, and I suggest that it would be more convenient to proceed to-morrow, and unless Judge Lawrence prefers to proceed to-day I move that we adjourn until ten o'clock to-morrow. If he wishes to proceed now, I have not a word to say.

Mr. Representative LAWRENCE. It will suit my convenience in any way that meets the approbation of the Commission.

Mr. Commissioner THURMAN. If we could get through to-day I should prefer to do so.

Mr. Commissioner GARFIELD. It seems to me it will be convenient to the Commission if we can at least have the authorities that have been cited and are to be cited by the objectors. If we can have to-morrow morning in print before us the argument of the objectors, I think it would make a complete exhibit of the objectors' case on both sides, and I would prefer that the objectors should finish to-night.

Mr. Representative LAWRENCE. I have authorities which I think may be of some value and weight in the way of aiding the Commission.

Mr. Commissioner EDMUNDS. Had we not better take a recess and get on with part of the argument to-night?

Mr. HOADLY. I desire to make a suggestion to the Commission. On our side we shall desire an extension of time. We do not think that we can present the very great number of questions of law and authorities within the time allowed by the Commission. We are willing to sacrifice our own convenience in order to arrive at a speedy result. I am authorized by my associates to say that we would prefer very much, in order that the decision of the Commission may be hastened, to sit this evening to any hour rather than not to have our request for additional time granted.

Mr. Commissioner HOAR. Will Judge Hoadly be kind enough to state, if he has considered, what additional time he proposes to ask for?

Mr. HOADLY. We desire that our time be extended to double the amount which the Commission allows by its rules; and as I said, we are willing to take it out of the hours of the night rather than not have the extension.

Mr. Commissioner EDMUNDS. I venture to submit this motion for the decision of the Commission, that we now take a recess until half past six o'clock, to meet in the Senate Chamber, which is at our disposal.

Mr. Commissioner HUNTON. I should rather hear the objectors.

Mr. Commissioner PAYNE. I think we had better hear the objectors.

Mr. Commissioner EDMUNDS. Very well, I withdraw the motion.

The PRESIDENT. The motion is withdrawn.

Mr. Representative LAWRENCE. Mr. President and gentlemen, the Commission before which I have the honor now to appear is charged with the momentous and solemn duty of considering "the certificates and papers purporting to be certificates of the electoral votes" of the State of Oregon, with the "objections" thereto, and with the further duty to "decide whether any, and what, votes from" that "State are *the* votes provided for by the Constitution of the United States, and how many, and what, persons were duly appointed electors in" the State.

There are before the Commission duplicate papers purporting to be certificates of the electoral votes cast by two different sets of persons each claiming to be the electoral college. It is my purpose to maintain that W. H. Odell, J. C. Cartwright, and J. W. Watts, whom I will for brevity designate " the Hayes electors," were duly appointed ; that they present the proper evidence of this fact, and that the votes by them given for Rutherford B. Hayes for President and for William A. Wheeler for Vice-President are the votes provided for by the Constitution; and that E. A. Cronin, J. N. T. Miller, and John Parker, the so-called " Tilden electors," were not duly appointed ; that they are without sufficient evidence of title to office, and that the votes they gave for Samuel J. Tilden for President and for Thomas A. Hendricks for Vice-President are not the votes provided for by the Constitution.

In conducting the inquiries which are to be answered by this Commission I will first ask attention to the constitutional and statutory provisions which create the office of elector, provide for filling it, and prescribe the appropriate evidence of title to it.

The Constitution of the United States provides that—

The executive power shall be vested in a President of the United States of America. He shall hold his office during the term of four years, and together with the Vice-President, chosen for the same term, be elected as follows :

Each State shall appoint, in such manner as the legislature thereof may direct, a number of electors, equal to the whole number of Senators and Representatives to which the State may be entitled in the Congress ; but no Senator or Representative, or person holding an office of trust or profit under the United States, shall be appointed an elector.—*Article 2, section 1.*

The electors shall meet in their respective States, and vote by ballot for President and Vice-President, one of whom, at least, shall not be an inhabitant of the same State with themselves ; they shall name in their ballots the person voted for as President, and in distinct ballots the person voted for as Vice-President, and they shall make distinct lists of all persons voted for as President, and of all persons voted for as Vice-President, and of the number of votes for each ; which lists they shall sign and certify, and transmit sealed to the seat of government of the United States, directed to the President of the Senate. The President of the Senate shall, in the presence of the Senate and House of Representatives, open all the certificates, and the votes shall then be counted ; the person having the greatest number of votes for President shall be the President, if such number be a majority of the whole number of electors appointed ; and if no person have such majority, then from the persons having the highest numbers not exceeding three on the list of those voted for as President, the House of Representatives shall choose immediately, by ballot, the President. But in choosing the President, the vote shall be taken by States, the representation from each State having one vote; a quorum for this purpose shall consist of a member or members from two-thirds of the States, and a majority of all the States shall be necessary to a choice. And if the House of Representatives shall not choose a President whenever the right of choice shall devolve upon them, before the fourth day of March next following, then the Vice-President shall act as President, as in the case of the death or other constitutional disability of the President.

The person having the greatest number of votes as Vice-President shall be the Vice-President, if such number be a majority of the whole number of electors appointed ; and if no person have a majority, then from the two highest numbers on the list the Senate shall choose the Vice-President.—*Article 12, Amendments.*

No person except a natural-born citizen, or a citizen of the United States at the time of the adoption of this Constitution, shall be eligible to the office of President ; neither shall any person be eligible to that office who shall not have attained to the age of thirty-five years, and been fourteen years a resident within the United States.—*Article 2, section 1.*

The Congress may determine the time of choosing the electors and the day on which they shall give their votes; which day shall be the same throughout the United States.—*Article 2, section 1.*

The Congress shall have power * * * to make all laws which shall be necessary and proper for carrying into execution the foregoing powers and all other powers vested by this Constitution in the Government of the United States, or in any department or officer thereof.—*Article 1, section 8.*

Congress has legislated upon the subject of electoral votes by repeated laws, and among other provisions has enacted that—

The electors of President and Vice-President shall be appointed, in each State, on the Tuesday next after the first Monday in November, in every fourth year succeeding every election of a President and Vice-President.—*March 1, 1792, ch. 8, sec. 1, vol. 1, p. 239 ; January 23, 1845, ch. 1, vol. 5, p. 721, Revised Statutes, section 131.*

It shall be the duty of the executive of each State to cause three lists of the names of the electors of such State to be made and certified, and to be delivered to the electors on or before the day on which they are required to meet.—*Act March 1, 1792, ch. 8, sec. 3, vol. 1, p. 240, Revised Statutes, section 136.*

Each State may, by law, provide for the filling of any vacancies which may occur in its college of electors when such college meets to give its electoral vote.—*Act January 23, 1845, Revised Statutes, section 133.*

Whenever any State has held an election for the purpose of choosing electors and has failed to make a choice on the day prescribed by law, the electors may be appointed on a subsequent day in such a manner as the legislature of such State may direct.—*Revised Statutes, section 134.*

The electors for each State shall meet and give their votes upon the first Wednesday in December in the year in which they are appointed, at such place, in each State, as the legislature of such State shall direct.—*Act March 1, 1792, Revised Statutes, section 135.*

Congress shall be in session on the second Wednesday in February succeeding every meeting of the electors, and the certificates, or so many of them as have been received, shall then be opened, the votes counted, and the persons to fill the offices of President and Vice-President ascertained and declared, agreeably to the Constitution.—*Act March 1, 1792, Revised Statutes, section 142.*

The electors shall vote for President and Vice-President, respectively, in the manner directed by the Constitution.—*Revised Statutes, section 134.*

The electors shall make and sign three certificates of all the votes given by them, each of which certificates shall contain two distinct lists, one of the votes for President and the other of the votes for Vice-President, and shall annex to each of the certificates one of the lists of the electors which shall have been furnished to them by direction of the executive of the State.—*Revised Statutes, section 138.*

The electors shall seal up the certificates so made by them, and certify upon each that the lists of all the votes of such State given for President, and of all the votes given for Vice-President, are contained therein.—*Revised Statutes, section 139.*

The electors shall dispose of the certificates thus made by them in the following manner:

One. They shall, by writing under their hands, or under the *hands of a majority of them,* appoint a person to take charge of and deliver to the President of the Senate, at the seat of government, before the first Wednesday in January then next ensuing, one of the certificates.

Two. They shall forthwith forward by the post-office to the President of the Senate, at the seat of government, one other of the certificates.

Three. They shall forthwith cause the other of the certificates to be delivered to the judge of that district in which the electors shall assemble.—*Revised Statutes, section 140.*

The constitution of Oregon provides:

In all elections held by the people under this constitution, the person or persons who shall receive the highest number of votes shall be declared duly elected.—*Article 2, section 16.*

And again:

The powers of the government shall be divided into three separate departments: the legislative, the executive, (including the administrative,) and the judicial; and no person charged with official duties under one of these departments shall exercise any of the functions of another, except as in this constitution expressly provided.

The legislature of Oregon has also provided by statute that—

In all elections in this State the person having the highest number of votes for any office shall be deemed elected.—*General Laws, section 40, page 574.*

On the Tuesday next after the first Monday in November, 1864, and every four years thereafter, there shall be elected by the qualified electors of this State as many electors of President and Vice-President as this State may be entitled to elect of Senators and Representatives in Congress.—*General Laws, section 58, page 578.*

The statute provides that abstracts of votes shall be sent to the secretary of state. And then the mode of canvassing the votes and certifying the appointment of electors is provided for as follows:

The votes for the electors shall be given, received, returned, and canvassed as the same are given, returned, and canvassed for members of Congress. The secretary of state shall prepare two lists of the electors elected and affix the seal of the State to the same. Such lists shall be signed by the governor and secretary, and by the latter delivered to the college of electors at the hour of their meeting on such first Wednesday of December.—*General Statutes, section 60, page 578.*

The canvass of votes for members of Congress is provided for as follows :

And it shall be the duty of the secretary of state, in the presence of the governor, to proceed within thirty days after the election, and sooner if the returns be all received, to canvass the votes for   *   *   * member of Congress; *   *   * and the governor shall grant a certificate to the person having the highest number of votes ; and shall also issue a proclamation declaring the election of such persons.—*General Statutes, section 37, page* 574.

This proclamation is not required as to electors.

In another portion of the general statutes relating to the governor it is provided that—

He [the governor] shall grant certificates to members duly elected to the Senate of the United States, and also to members of Congress, which shall be signed by him and countersigned by the secretary of state under the seal of the State.—*General Laws, section 3, page* 489.

But this does not apply to electors.

The statute of Oregon, in a title relating only to State officers, shows what shall be deemed a *vacancy* in a State office. It provides :

Any person who shall receive a certificate of his election as a member of the legislative assembly, coroner, or commissioner of the county court, shall be at liberty to resign such office, though he may not have entered upon the execution of its duties or taken the requisite oath of office.—*General Statutes, section 46, page* 575.

Every office shall become vacant on the occurrence of either of the following events before the expiration of the term of such office :

1. The death of the incumbent.
2. His resignation.
3. His removal.
4. His ceasing to be an inhabitant of the district, county, town, or village for which he shall have been elected or appointed or within which the duties of his office are required to be discharged.
5. His conviction of an infamous crime or of any offense involving a violation of his oath.
6. His refusal or neglect to take his oath of office, or to give or renew his official bond, or to deposit such oath or bond within the time prescribed by law.
7. The decision of a competent tribunal declaring void his election or appointment.—*General Statutes, section* 48, *page* 576.

But the Oregon statute, when providing for vacancies in the electoral college, does not limit vacancies to those arising from specific causes, but declares that—

The electors of President and Vice-President shall convene at the seat of government on the first Wednesday of December next after their election, at the hour of twelve of the clock at noon of that day, and if there shall be any vacancy in the office of an elector, occasioned by death, refusal to act, neglect to attend, or otherwise, the electors present shall immediately proceed to fill by *viva voce* and plurality of votes such vacancy in the electoral college, and when all the electors shall appear, or the vacancies, if any, shall have been filled as above provided, such electors shall proceed to perform the duties required of them by the Constitution and laws of the United States.—*General Laws, section* 59, *page* 578.

Here, then, are all the *constitutional* and *statutory* provisions *creating the office* of elector, the material provisions for *filling it* and for furnishing evidence of *title* to the office.

That the *office* is *created* by the Constitution of the United States, admits of no doubt, and is not disputed.

That the electors are to be appointed in each State "in such manner as the legislature thereof may direct," is equally certain and undisputed.

That the legislature of Oregon has provided for the original appointment of electors by popular vote is conceded on all hands.

That it has provided for filling vacancies " occasioned by death, refusal to act, neglect to attend, or otherwise," is declared by the statute, and is not disputed.

The Hayes electors present as evidence of title to the electoral office the following:

1. A "list of the electors elected" for Oregon, duly certified and signed by the secretary of state, with the seal of the State by him affixed thereto. This has every formality required by law except only that the governor has failed to comply with a directory and immaterial provision of the statute requiring that it "shall be signed by the governor."

Mr. Commissioner EDMUNDS. What is the date of that?

Mr. Representative LAWRENCE. It is without date. Next:

2. A certified abstract of the popular vote for electors as canvassed according to law by the secretary of state, dated December 6, 1876, showing that the Hayes electors are "the persons having the highest number of votes," on which fact the statute says "they shall be *deemed elected*."

Mr. Commissioner EDMUNDS. Is that the certificate of the secretary of state as to the number of votes for electors?

Mr. Representative LAWRENCE. That is the abstract of votes—a different paper.. The paper I first referred to is the certificate of the secretary of state.

Mr. HOADLY. There is no such certificate.

Mr. Representative LAWRENCE. There is such a paper, unless I am greatly mistaken.

Mr. HOADLY. I heard the papers read, and there is no such paper.

Mr. Representative LAWRENCE. I have copies of what purport to be the papers. It is a full list of electors, showing the number of votes given for each.

Mr. Commissioner ABBOTT. Is it anything more than this: a certificate of the names of the persons voted for, showing the votes given to each?

Mr. Representative LAWRENCE. Yes; but it is different from the tabulated result.

Mr. Commissioner ABBOTT. But no certificate.

Mr. Representative LAWRENCE. That is a certificate. I shall claim to this honorable Commission that that is a certificate within the meaning of the statute of Oregon. That is what I call a certificate in complete compliance with the statute of Oregon, lacking only the unimportant signature of the governor, the lack of which cannot invalidate a paper made in pursuance of law.

Mr. Commissioner THURMAN. Judge Lawrence, may I ask you if you have examined the statute of Oregon to see whether any one has a right to demand an exemplification of any paper on the files of that office?

Mr. Representative LAWRENCE. I have not, nor do I deem it material. The question is not, as I respectfully submit, whether any one has a right to demand it, but does any one come with that as evidence of title? We have it; it is made in pursuance of law; it is made in pursuance of the statute of Oregon, which authorizes and requires the secretary of state to make these lists of electors. Then we have—

3. The certificate under the seal of the State, signed by the governor and secretary of state, dated December 6, 1876, by which the governor of Oregon certifies that W. H. Odell, J. C. Cartwright, and E. A. Cronin received each a given number of votes at the election, November 7,

which " being the highest number of votes cast for persons eligible," they " are hereby declared duly elected electors."

4. The record of the proceedings of Odell, Cartwright, and Watts, as electors, dated December 6, shows that Odell and Cartwright met, accepted the resignation of Watts, and they two only being present, they re-appointed Watts, who accepted, and all three voted for Hayes and Wheeler for President and Vice-President and made the proper return.

This, as the Constitution requires, is *certified* by the electors—made *absolutely certain*—beyond contradiction by any other evidence.

For the so-called " Tilden electors" the entire record shows as their evidence of title to office—

1. The certificate of the governor, attested by the secretary of state, for Odell, Cartwright, and Cronin, already referred to, showing *not* that Cronin, as the law requires, " received the highest number of votes," but only that " Cronin received 14,157 votes, being the highest number of votes cast at said election (November 7) for persons eligible," and he, with Odell and Cartwright, is " declared duly elected."

2. The record of proceedings of the so-called Tilden electors shows that Cronin assembled on the 6th of December, " solitary and alone in his glory" or shame, declared that Odell and Cartwright "refused to act," whereupon Cronin appointed Miller an elector, and these two then appointed Parker, when all voted, one vote for Tilden for President and Hendricks for Vice-President, and two for Hayes and Wheeler for the same offices.

Here, then, are the two sets of electors; here the whole evidence of title to office; here the votes cast by each for President and Vice-President.

From this it will be seen the Hayes electors all claim title to office by original appointment or election by the people of Oregon, and as to one of them a title after a resignation by appointment of the remaining electors.

One of the Tilden electors, Cronin, claims title by original appointment or election by the people and the remaining two by appointment to fill vacancies.

The one important and indisputable fact to be noticed so far in these proceedings is that the title of Odell and Cartwright, two of the Hayes electors, is clear beyond question and is not disputed. As to these, elected by the people, there are just five provisions of law relating to the evidence of title. They are these:

1. The act of Congress declares that—

It shall be the duty of the executive of each State to cause three lists of the names of the electors of such State to be made and certified and to be delivered to the electors.

It does not say in terms that the governor shall certify or sign the lists. When it says the governor shall "*cause*" the lists to be made, this means that he, as the officer charged with the duty of executing the State laws, shall cause the proper State officer to make the lists, whether he be the officer designated by the State law or some other; or if no State law direct the mode, then the governor shall certify.

2. The constitution of Oregon provides that—

In all elections * * * the person or persons who shall receive the highest number of votes shall be declared elected.

3. The statute of Oregon provides that—

In all elections * * * the person having the highest number of votes * * * shall be deemed elected.

4. The statute again provides that a return of votes shall be sent from the several counties to the secretary of state, and then—

It shall be the duty of the secretary of state, in the presence of the governor,—

But the governor is a mere witness with no power—

* * * to canvass the votes.

5. And again the statute says:

The secretary of state shall prepare two lists of the electors elected, and affix the seal of the State to the same. Such lists shall be signed by the governor and secretary, and by the latter delivered to the college of electors.

This is the mode in which *Oregon* executes the act of Congress. The governor has no power over the canvass or the result, except to attest what the secretary of state certifies as mere matter of authentication.

Now, Odell and Cartwright come with the evidence of title which satisfies all these provisions. The secretary of state canvassed the votes of the people, as shown by his certified abstract. Odell and Cartwright had the highest number of votes, and must, as the constitution and statute say, "be declared and deemed elected," and they have the properly certified lists of election "signed by the governor and secretary" under the seal of State.

I say they have these lists of electors because they *are here*, and it matters not how they came. No law requires that all the evidence of title shall be transmitted in one envelope, nor that it shall come with the votes for President, nor even that it shall be transmitted by the electors. The mode of transmitting at most could be only *directory*, and the manner is not material.

All the records, so far as they contain lawful evidence, may be considered. (Switzler *vs.* Anderson, 2 Bartlett, 374; McCrary, section 104.)

Mr. Commissioner HOAR. I am sorry to interrupt you——

Mr. Representative LAWRENCE. Nothing interrupts me.

Mr. Commissioner HOAR. I want to ask you whether that paper which you said was without date, appears to have been sealed up with the other papers which were sealed on the 6th of December.

Mr. Representative LAWRENCE. Undoubtedly. It comes with the papers. But even that would not be material. The provision which requires papers to be transmitted by the electors is directory, and no matter how they come they are evidence.

Mr. Commissioner HOAR. The point of my inquiry was that at least it must have been made as early as the 6th of December.

Mr. Representative LAWRENCE. O, yes; it must have been made as early as the 6th of December; but its date cannot be material. I repeat that the one important fact to which I desire first to call attention is that the title of two of the Hayes electors is undisputed.

Mr. Commissioner ABBOTT. Permit me to ask whether the certificate you refer to states that the secretary of state had ever canvassed any votes and determined who had been elected.

Mr. Representative LAWRENCE. It is not necessary that he should.

Mr. Commissioner ABBOTT. I only ask whether the fact is so.

Mr. Representative LAWRENCE. The certified abstract of votes, by inference, if not directly, shows that he did canvass the votes, and there is that certificate which satisfied the statute, the list of electors made by the secretary of state, the only officer who has power to make any paper. The governor has a duty, but not a power, to witness a paper, although made by another officer.

Upon these facts, and upon the law, this whole controversy may be disposed of in favor of the Hayes electors by a single proposition, which is:

That, if the monstrous position could be maintained that Cronin was legally appointed, yet he "refused to act," "neglected to attend" with Odell and Cartwright, his place became vacant, and Watts was duly appointed to fill it.

This leaves no question of eligibility to be considered, and no controversy over any question of vacancy by non-election. If this position is supported by law, it is conclusive, and it is unnecessary to go beyond it to show, as the fact is, that Cronin was not elected, and on the whole record is without evidence of title.

The electoral college is charged with three duties: (1) to fill all vacancies, (2) to vote for President and Vice-President, and (3) to make and transmit to the President of the Senate "distinct lists of all persons voted for as President and Vice-President, which lists they shall sign and *certify*." Here are duties to do certain acts and to furnish evidence of them.

The statute of Oregon provides that—

If there be any vacancy in the office of an elector occasioned by death, refusal to act, neglect to attend, or otherwise, the electors present shall fill such vacancy.

The electoral college is a deliberative body, as much so as Congress; the single individual members, acting separately and apart from all others, can do no official act, no more so than individual members of Congress, or of a court, or of this Commission; and the record of what the college or a majority of its members does is conclusive evidence, and can no more be impeached *aliunde* than the record of Congress, or of a court, or of this Commission.

The major part of the electors present is a quorum; the acts of a quorum are valid to decide when a vacancy has arisen, and to fill it.

All this I propose to show from the Constitution and laws, from their manifest purpose, from the authority of the courts, and from the necessities of the case.

1. *The electoral college is a deliberative body.* The Constitution says:

The electors shall *meet* and vote by ballot for President.
They shall make distinct lists of all persons voted for as President.
They shall sign and certify and transmit, sealed, to the President of the Senate [these lists.]

The statute of Oregon says:

The electors shall *convene* at the seat of government. * * * If there be any vacancy the electors *present* shall *immediately* proceed to fill by *viva voce* and plurality of votes such vacancy. * * * Such electors shall proceed to perform the duties required of them.

The electors when convened are declared to be the "electoral college."

All these acts require deliberation, united action, collective wisdom.

The original purpose of the Constitution was that the electors should themselves deliberate on and select the candidates for President of their own judgment, without party nominations or previous pledges.

From all this it is certain that *the electors must act as a deliberative body, not as members acting separately and apart.*

2. The *major part* of the electors who convene are a quorum to fill vacancies and vote. As against them the minority can do nothing.

The act of Congress expressly so provides:

If there be a vacancy the electors present shall fill it.

They are made the sole judges to decide when an elector has "refused to act," "neglected to attend," or when a vacancy has arisen "otherwise."

This is so on authority. By *general* parliamentary law, in all deliberative bodies of a fixed number, unless otherwise expressly provided, a majority is a quorum, and a majority of the quorum decides all questions. This has been the settled doctrine of the courts from our earliest history. The supreme court of South Carolina as early as 1821, in an elaborate opinion on this subject, so determined. The court, after reviewing authorities, said:

The conclusion then follows that a majority must constitute a quorum; * * * for, according to the principle of all the cases referred to, a quorum possesses all the powers of the whole body, a majority of which quorum must, of course, govern. * * * Thus, Grotius says, "Though there were no contracts or laws that regulate the manner of determining affairs, the majority would naturally have the right and authority of the whole." (Sec. 2, Rutherford, b. 2, c. 195; State *vs.* Deliesseline, McCord's South Carolina sep., 62.)

Dillon, in his work on Municipal Corporations, in discussing the constitution and powers of select governing bodies of a fixed number, says:

In the absence of special provision, the major part of those present at a meeting of a select body must concur in order to do any valid act. * * *

And as a general rule it may be stated that * * * where the corporate power resides in a select body, in the absence of special provision otherwise, a minority of the select body are powerless to bind the majority or do any valid act. (Vol. 1, pp. 333-4, sec. 220, 221.)

And again:

If the major part withdraw so as to leave no quorum, the power of the minority to act is in general considered to cease. (Idem, p. 334, sec. 221.)

This sufficiently appears in Downing *vs.* Ruger, 21 Wendell, 181, where it is said:

The rule seems to be well established that in the exercise of a public as well as private authority, whether it be ministerial or judicial, all the persons to whom it is committed must confer and act together, unless there be a provision—

As there is in case of electors—

that a less number may proceed—

As Odell and Cartwright did.

Where the authority is public, and the number is such as to admit ot a majority—

And Odell and Cartwright were a majority—

that will bind the minority.

And Cronin was a minority, and so is concluded by the act of the majority.

This must be so on *reason* and *public policy.* Oregon is entitled to three electors only. If a controversy exists as to who assembled at the proper time and place, as to who acted or refused to act, it is much more reasonable to take the official certificate of two than of one. If a State has twenty electors, it is more reasonable that eighteen should certify two as absent than that two should certify eighteen absent.

3. *The electors present are authorized to furnish evidence conclusive of a vacancy and of their appointment to fill it.*

(*a*) This is made so by the Constitution. It declares that the electors—

Shall sign, and certify, and transmit sealed * * * to the President of the Senate * * * distinct lists of all persons voted for as President.

To certify is to *make certain.* When the electors certify their list of votes, it is certain that they are the votes, and it must be equally certain that they have properly filled vacancies.

If this can be contradicted by some one elector or other evidence, then it is not *certain*, it is not certified; the electors cannot say, *faciemus certum*—we certify.

This rests upon the broad principle so well understood, that it must be presumed that officers will do and have done their duty.

Mr. Commissioner THURMAN. May I interrupt you, without disturbing your argument? Do I understand your argument to go to this point: that a majority of the electoral college may try the title of a member to a seat in that college?

Mr. Representative LAWRENCE. No, not by any manner of means; but when the majority say that electors are absent, are not present, fail to attend, the decision of the majority on that question is conclusive and cannot be inquired into. Like any other election return, it is absolutely conclusive.

Mr. Commissioner THURMAN. Why, then, might they not say that a man claiming to sit there had no title?

Mr. Representative LAWRENCE. In this case no such question arises, because they have not said so. They have only said there were but two electors present; the other, Cronin, failed to attend; he was not there; he did not go at the right time of day; he was not in the right building; he made a mistake and got into the wrong box. That is what they say, and what they say is evidence, and it is conclusive evidence.

Mr. MERRICK. O, they do not say that.

Mr. Representative LAWRENCE. They say that in effect; they say they were the only ones present, and Cronin himself says he was not present with them.

(*b*) *This must be so on principle and authority.*

It is an *incident* of the authority to appoint. (Broom, Legal Max., 465; Martin *vs.* Mott, 12 Wheat., 19; Allen *vs.* Blunt, 3 Story C. C., 742; Gould *vs.* Hammond, 1 McAll., 235; Noble *vs.* U. S., Dev., 84.) The electors are clothed with the power to fill vacancies. It is within the scope and purpose of their powers to make evidence of the appointment.

It is said in a work of high authority:

No particular form of credentials is required. It is sufficient if the claimant to an office presents a certificate signed by the officer or officers authorized by law to issue credentials. * * * If several officers or persons are by law required to join in such certificate, it is generally sufficient if a majority have signed it.—*McCrary*, chap. 4, p. 149.

Where a duty is imposed by law upon officers there is given them as an *incident* of their duty the power to do all things necessary to make it effectual, including the authority to furnish evidence of their acts, and especially when, as in this case, no other evidence is provided for.

Broom says:

When the Crown creates a corporation it grants to it by implication all powers that are necessary for carrying into effect the objects for which it is created.—*Legal Maxims*, 435.

Abbott, in his Digest, collects authorities on the subject, and says:

Whenever a statute gives a discretionary power to any person to be exercised by him upon his own opinion of certain facts, it is a sound rule of construction that the statute constitutes him the sole and exclusive judge of the existence of those facts. (Martin *vs.* Mott, 12 Wheat., 19; Allen *vs.* Blunt, 3 Story C. C., 742; Gould *vs.* Hammond, 1 McAll., 235; Noble *vs.* United States, Dev., 84.)

But if the evidence furnished by the electors is not *conclusive*, then they are not, as the law says, "the sole and exclusive judges."

(*c*) *Usage has made this the law.*

The practice of nearly a century has so determined. In no instance has the evidence been contradicted.

(*d*) *It is conclusive because it is part of the election-return.*

This Commission and the Houses of Congress are merely canvassing-officers; their sole power is to "count" the votes.

Canvassing-officers cannot controvert returns which come with all the formalities of law. This is settled by authority, settled by this tribunal.

All this must be so on grounds of public policy.

Then upon the law, upon the evidence, it is shown that Odell and Cartwright met at the proper time and place; that Cronin "neglected to attend, refused to act" with them; that they filled the vacancy thereby created by appointing Watts; that Odell, Cartwright, and Watts voted for Hayes and Wheeler, and these votes must be counted.

Here I might rest this controversy.

But the contest before this Commission is of too much importance to leave unconsidered *any question* that may possibly arise, and for that reason alone I proceed to show, as a second proposition, *that Cronin was not elected, and on the whole record presents no sufficient evidence of title to the electoral office.*

1. *His ambiguous evidence of title is disproved by evidence of equal dignity, free from ambiguity.*

If it should be conceded that the "governor's certificate of election" unexplained could give a *prima facie* title to office, yet it is not conclusive.

It does not certify that Cronin, as the law requires, received "the highest number of votes," or that he is duly appointed, but only that he "received 14,157 votes, * * * being the highest number for persons eligible."

The averment as to ineligibility is a stamp of suspicion, an admission of doubt; it opens the door for inquiry. The certificate is not, and does not profess to be, conclusive of the essential fact; it equivocates in a manner equivalent to "a negative pregnant;" it is pregnant with fraud.

The effect of a certificate of election is well understood.

When it is necessary, as in this case, to the canvass of votes for President, the canvassing-board must decide if it is a certificate.—*McCrary's Law of Elections*, section 82.

In a note to page 319 of Brightly's Leading Cases on Elections t is said of a certificate of election:

If, however, the certificate *upon its face* recite facts upon which the canvassers rely as their justification and authority for giving it, and *these facts* show that the holder was not duly-elected, it may be disregarded. (Hartt *vs.* Harvey, 32 Barb., 61.)

To this I think I may safely add that if there be two certificates of election, as in this case, to two different persons for the one same office, and one is sufficient in form and free from suspicion, it must take effect as against one which on its face carries doubt as to the fact it certifies. And that is precisely the case before us. Watts has a certificate of election sufficient in form, the list of electors certified to be elected by the secretary of state, under the seal of the State, irregular in a single particular—the attestation of the governor is wanting. The statute makes the secretary of state the sole canvassing officer to ascertain what person has the "highest number of votes." And then it provides that—

The secretary of state shall prepare two lists of the electors elected, and affix the seal of the State to the same. Such lists shall be signed by the governor and secretary, and by the latter delivered to the college of electors.

The governor is intrusted with no power. He has a duty, and the whole of this is contained in eight words:

Such lists shall be signed by the governor.

The governor has not signed the lists. But what matter is that? The provision requiring him to do so is *directory*. It is not of the *essence* of the lists or the election they evidence. There is a substantial compliance with the law without his signature, and all the authorities say this is sufficient. The want of his name is a mere irregularity. It is not *the evidence*, but a mere *attestation* of the *real evidence* of election made and furnished by the secretary of state. This irregularity cannot affect the evidence or defeat the will of the people. McCrary says:

The principle is that irregularities which do not tend to affect results are not to defeat the will of the majority; the will of the majority is to be respected even when irregularly expressed.—*Law of Elections*, sections 127, 128.

He cites Juker *vs.* Comm., 20 Pa. State, 493; Carpenter's Case, 2 Pars., 540; Pratt *vs.* People, 29 Ill., 72; Brightly's Election Cases, 448–450; Keller *vs.* Chapman, 34 Cal., 635; Sprague *vs.* Norway, 31 Cal., 173; Gorham *vs.* Campbell, 2 Cal., 135; Hardenburgh *vs.* Farmers' Bank, 2 Green., (N. J.,) 68; Day *vs.* Kent, 1 Oregon, 123; Taylor *vs.* Taylor, 20 Minn., 107; People *vs.* Bates, 11 Mich., 363; McKinney *vs.* O'Connor, 26 Texas, 5; Jones *vs.* State, 1 Kansas, 270; Arnold *vs.* Lea, Clarke & Hall, 601.

The whole is summed up in a few words by Brightly, who says:

That a mere irregularity on the part of the election officers or their omission to observe some merely directory provision of the law will not vitiate the poll, is a point sustained by the whole current of authorities. * * * The conduct of the election officers in the performance of the duties enjoined by law, and their observance of the provisions of the statutes in regard to the recording and return of the legal votes received by them, would seem to fall within the description of directory provisions, and any departure on their part from a strict observance of such portions of the election law to be regarded as irregularities which do not vitiate. (People *vs.* Schermerhorn, 19 Barb., 540; Comm. *vs.* Meeser, 44 Pa. St., 343; Lancaster election, 4 Votes of Assembly, 127; Thompson *vs.* Ewing, 1 Brewst., 107; Mann *vs.* Cassidy, 1 Brewst., 60; Weaver *vs.* Given, *idem.*, 157; Gibbons *vs.* Shepherd, 2 Brewst., 74; Doughty *vs.* Hope, 3 Denio, 249; Elmendorf *vs.* Mayor, 25 Wend., 696; *Ex parte* Heath, 3 Hill, 43; Jackson *vs.* Young, 5 Cow., 269; Stryker *vs.* Kelly, 7 Hill, 9; People *vs.* Peck, 11 Wend., 604; 19 Wend., 143; Smith on Statutes, 782, 789.)

These provisions of law make the lists of electors certified by the secretary of state *evidence—sufficient evidence*. We are not seeking to use evidence unauthorized by law to defeat that *which is*, but we are asking to defeat that *which is in violation of law* by that which is *in pursuance of law*. Watts then comes with *sufficient* evidence of title.

In examining the evidence of title to office, the question is not so much what a certificate may in mere words say, but what is the legal effect of the facts lawfully shown by it.

Let me illustrate: Suppose a certificate of election shows the vote given for two eligible candidates to be 10,000 for one and 20,000 for another, and then declares the minority candidate elected, when the statute provides that the candidate having the highest number of votes shall be deemed elected; can it be doubted that such certificate would give a title to the majority candidate?

It says in mere words the minority candidate is elected, but in *legal effect* it says the majority candidate is elected. To hold the minority candidate as having the title to the office, would be to stick in the bark: *Qui hæret in litera, hæret in cortice.*

Here, then, without going back to the abstract of votes, the Cronin certificate of election is shown by sufficient evidence to be untrue, and so must be rejected.

2. *Cronin's certificate is contradicted by the certified abstract of votes, and is therefore invalid as to him.*

It is well settled that it is the election which gives the right to an office, and not the commission or certificate of election.

In People *vs*. Pease, 27 New York, 55, it was said:

It is not the canvass or estimate or certificate which determines the right. These are only evidences of the right.

In Mansfield *vs*. Moor, 53 Illinois, 428, it was said:

The commission was evidence of the title, but not the title. The title was conferred by the people, and the evidence of the right by the law.

Whatever may be the rule in other States, the constitution and statute of Oregon have limited the power of the secretary of state in declaring the result of a canvass and the governor in attesting it, so that they cannot, for any cause, certify the election of a minority candidate. They give an effect to the result of the canvass which is prescribed by law, and this cannot be defeated by a certificate in violation of law. The final canvass is the substance, the certificate based on it is the shadow—the mere legal result. The fountain can rise no higher than its source; the structure can only stand on its foundation. The abstract of votes is higher in authority and greater in effect than any certificate founded on it. If the secretary of state should, by his certificate, give it a construction contrary to law, his error may be corrected by the law.

This is the result which on the facts arises from the constitution and statute of Oregon.

The Oregon statute requires the votes in each county for electors to be returned duly certified to the secretary of state. It then provides that—

It shall be the duty of the secretary of state, in the presence of the governor, to canvass the votes.

Then the constitution says:

That person or persons who shall receive the highest number of votes shall be *declared* duly elected.

And the statute provides that—

The person having the highest number of votes shall be *deemed* elected.

The constitution says the plurality candidate shall be *declared* duly elected. This is a direction to the secretary of state in his canvass. But it was foreseen that his certificate might not conform to the actual result of the canvass, and the statute goes further and says "the person having the highest number of votes shall be *deemed* elected." Where so deemed? Everywhere. By whom? Not merely by the canvasser, but by the entire public. This authorizes the officer to assert his title on the highest and best evidence which shows who is "the person having the highest number of votes." This provision is a remedy for such stupendous frauds as that attempted by the governor of Oregon. The same question had been made in the legislature of Ohio in December, 1848, and the statute of Oregon intended to avoid it. The certificate of Cronin, then, is unauthorized, because disproved by the certified abstract of votes.

The result arises on the record. A conclusion declared by law on facts certified according to law cannot be annulled by a certificate in conflict with law, made by an officer whose duty it is to act in obedience to law. If the canvass of votes and lists of electors, certified by the secretary of state, should show that there were three sets of candidates, and should certify the vote or show which candidates "received the highest number of votes," and these officers should certify in the same paper that those receiving the lowest number of votes were elected, could this be claimed as evidence of title to office in the candidates having the lowest number of votes? Such certificate would be valid as to the authorized facts it recites; it would be void in stating a conclusion which the law does not permit to be drawn. The statute is mandatory as to the person elected. It is a universal rule of law that any act done in violation of a mandatory law is void.

Mr. Commissioner THURMAN. Do I understand you to say that the certificate of the governor must show the number of votes given to the electors?

Mr. Representative LAWRENCE. I say that a certificate which has within it an allegation which is equivalent in effect to a negative pregnant is equivocal, doubtful on its face, and, when contradicted by evidence of equal dignity, it falls. Besides that, I say that Cronin does not come with the certificate required by law, with separate lists prepared and certified by the secretary of the State, and that the governor's paper is not a certificate of the secretary at all. "I, Grover, the governor, do certify;" not "I, the secretary of state." The governor should have attested the lists which were given to the Hayes electors. Instead of that, he has undertaken to certify, when the law does not authorize him to certify anything. He is merely to attest the lists of electors, and Cronin is absolutely without title.

The certificates then show the election of Watts. The utmost that could be claimed for all the certificates taken together is that they show the election of Odell, Cartwright, and Watts by a majority of the popular vote, but that the governor decided Watts *ineligible*, and so declared Cronin, an opposing minority candidate, elected. It amounts to no more than the expression of a *legal opinion* by the governor that on *the facts* Cronin is elected. But if his legal opinion is wrong, if it assigns to the facts an effect they cannot in law have, then the certificates show Watts elected or, at least, Cronin not elected. The *legal opinion* that he was is disproved by other facts stated, and effect must be given according to the real law, not the governor's erroneous opinion of the law. His legal opinion may be rejected as surplusage; the law rejects it on the facts.

The certificates all taken together show that Watts was duly elected. To illustrate this, let me suppose that a certificate had been made in the form following:

"The undersigned, secretary of state and governor of Oregon, certify as follows:

"The said secretary certifies that at the election of November 7, for presidential electors—

"W. H. Odell received 15,206 votes.

"J. W. Watts received 15,206 votes.

"J. C. Cartwright received 15,214 votes.

"Henry Klippel received 14,136 votes.

"E. A. Cronin received 14,157 votes.

"W. B. Laswell received 14,149 votes.

"That the foregoing votes were, December 4, 1876, opened and canvassed by the secretary, in the presence of the governor, according to law, and that the foregoing is the result of the votes cast.

"The said governor also certifies that of said persons voted for, J. W. Watts was ineligible; and the said governor therefore hereby declares—

"William H. Odell,

"John C. Cartwright, and

" E. A. Cronin to be duly elected electors of said State.
Dated December 6, 1876.

" LA FAYETTE GROVER,
" *Governor.*

[L. S.]

" S. F. CHADWICK,
" *Secretary of State.*"

Can it be doubted that the *legal effect* of such a certificate would be to vest in Watts the title to the electoral office? Clearly this must be so. Now all the certificates before the Commission show no more than this, and therefore they show Watts to be legally elected, without going back of the returns into evidence *aliunde.*

To summarize this : the objections to the votes given by the " Tilden electors," all resting on Cronin's assumed evidence of title to the electoral office, are these :

1. Cronin " refused to act" with the other electors duly appointed, or " neglected to attend," and if he was an elector his office became *vacant.*

2. The governor's certificate of appointment is, as to Cronin, shown to be unauthorized and untrue, by evidence of equal dignity and legal value : first, the list of electors certified by the secretary of state; and, second, the abstract of the popular vote.

3. While the governor's certificate shows two of the Hayes electors, Odell and Cartwright, duly appointed, and the certified abstract of votes proves the certificate as to them to be legal and authorized, it is shown from the same evidence that as to Cronin the governor's certificate on its face gives no title to office, because it does not certify, as the law requires, that he " received the highest number of votes," but only that he received the highest 'number " for persons eligible." As to Cronin, it is no better than if it should certify that he received the " highest number of votes given for persons of color," or the " highest number for persons of Chinese origin," or " the highest number for native-born citizens of Oregon."

4. Cronin fails to produce any certificate from the secretary of state showing a list of the electors duly elected. In the governor's certificate the secretary of state certifies nothing. He merely, as a subscribing witness, attests the act of the governor. There is no escape from this conclusion unless two principles be resolved in the affirmative :

First, That the governor had power to ascertain and declare the alleged ineligibility; and,

Second, That this would render the election of Watts void, and elect Cronin, a minority candidate.

Neither one of these positions can be maintained. This I proceed to show.

1. *Neither the governor, nor secretary of state, nor both combined have any power to inquire or decide whether Watts held an office which rendered him ineligible as an elector.*

(*a*) *The governor is not a canvassing-officer, and hence has no power to make any inquiry.*

It is by law made the duty of the secretary of state to canvass the votes and make two lists of the electors having " the highest number of votes." The governor canvasses nothing; he makes no certificate. His *whole power* as to the election and the lists made by the secretary of state is given in eight words:

Such lists shall be signed by the governor.

It is not a power at all, it is a naked duty, *to sign his name.*

(*b*) *The secretary of state as a canvassing officer has no such power.* The secretary of state is the canvassing-officer. His whole power is given in these words:

> It shall be the duty of the secretary of state   *   *   *   to canvass the votes, *   *   *   prepare two lists of the electors elected,   *   *   *   affix the seal of the State, *   *   *   and sign and deliver them to the electors.

The power to canvass is merely a power to count. It was said in Morgan *vs.* Quackenbush, 22 Barb., 77, that canvassing-officers " are not at liberty to receive evidence of anything outside of the returns themselves."

The whole law is clearly stated by McCrary, who says of canvassing-officers:

> The true rule is this. They must receive and count the votes as shown by the returns, *and they cannot go behind the returns for any purpose;* and this necessarily implies that if a paper is presented as a return, and there is a question as to whether it is a return or not, they must decide that question from what appears upon the face of the paper itself.—*Law of Election,* sec. 82.

He has collected the numerous authorities upon the subject, and, among them all, there is not one to controvert this rule, except only the one case in Indiana, of Gulick *vs.* New. The cases in England and New York concede no such power to any canvassing or executive officer.

The direct question now before the Commission has been decided. In State *vs.* Vail, 53 Missouri, 97, the facts were these: Dining received a majority of the votes for judge, as shown by the election returns, over Vail. The secretary of state certified the vote as given to the governor. He undertook to inquire as to the eligibility of Dining, and decided that he was ineligible as under age and otherwise, and issued a commission to Vail. The court on *quo warranto* decided that—

> In opening and casting up the votes at an election   *   *   *   the secretary of state [as a canvassing-officer] has no discretion and cannot determine upon the legality of the votes, and it is the duty of the governor to issue the commission in accordance with the result so ascertained. All of these officers act ministerially and not judicially.

The court say:

> To allow a ministerial officer arbitrarily to reject returns   *   *   *   is to infringe or destroy the rights of parties without notice or opportunity to be heard; a thing which the law abhors and prohibts.   *   *   *   The law has provided [judicial] tribunals with ample power to hear and determine all questions,   *   *   *   where the parties can have a fair trial.
>
> The governor,   *   *   *   where he issues a commission,   *   *   *   is simply performing a ministerial duty, in which he must necessarily be governed by the returns. *   *   *   He has no means of ascertaining   *   *   *   whether opposing candidates are disqualified. These matters   *   *   *   may be inquired into elsewhere, [in the courts.]

This doctrine was affirmed in State *vs.* Townsley, 56 Missouri, 107; where it was held that—

> In counting the votes for a circuit judge, neither the governor nor secretary of state has any authority to go behind the returns.

In Commonwealth *vs.* Cluly, 56 Pa. State, 270, it is said by his honor Judge Strong that votes given for an ineligible candidate "cannot be rejected by the inspectors nor thrown out of the count by the return judges."

The reason is, the *want of power* to *judge* of *ineligibility*. Where votes are so thrown out, where an act is done beyond lawful power, it is *ultra vires* and void. Bouvier defines *ultra vires*, as applied to corporations, "acts beyond the scope of their powers," and says, "Such acts are void."

(*c*) It is not pretended that any power is given in express terms to the governor or secretary of state to pass upon the question of eligibility. But the governor of Oregon, in defending his exercise of power, claims that it exists as incidental to his office, and he quotes from Judge Cooley, in his work on Constitutional Limitations, pages 39, 41, as follows:

> Whenever any one is called upon to perform any constitutional duty, or to do any act in respect to which it can be supposed that the Constitution has spoken, it is obvious that a question of construction may at once arise, upon which some one must decide before the duty is performed or the act done. From the very nature of the case this decision must commonly be made by the person, body, or department upon whom the duty is devolved, or from whom the act is required. * * * It follows, therefore, that every department of the Government, and every official of every department, may at any time when a duty is to be performed be required to pass upon a question of constitutional construction.

He then assumes that the statute says he "shall grant certificates to the members *duly* elected," and that hence he must judge who is elected. But there is no such statute as to electors. There is as to Senators and Representatives in Congress. But even as to these he has no power to judge of ineligibility. If he had, it would not enlarge his power as to electors, but rather would show that as to them it did not exist.

The *incidental* power which Cooley asserts to exist as applied to governor must be limited to *executive power*, and cannot be enlarged by construction to *include judicial power*.

In Commonwealth *vs.* Jones, 10 Bush. Kentucky Reports, 726, it is sufficiently shown that the governor, as a canvassing-officer, cannot pass upon any question of ineligibility. The court held that—

> Where the inquiry to be made involves questions of law as well as fact, where it affects a legal right, and the decision may result in terminating or destroying that right, the power to be exercised and the duties to be discharged are essentially judicial, and such as cannot be constitutionally delegated to or imposed upon executive officers.

That was in a case, too, where the canvassing-officers had authority to try contested questions.

The same question in effect was decided in Cæsar Griffin's case, reported in Chief-Justice Chase's Decisions, by Johnson.

(*d.*) The power to judge of ineligibility is *judicial power* and therefore cannot be exercised by the governor or secretary of state, for they have no judicial authority.

This results from the inherent character of the office of governor and secretary of state. The constitution of Oregon creates three separate, distinct, co-ordinate branches of government, legislative, executive, and judicial. It does more; it expressly prohibits the executive officers from assuming to decide a question of eligibility by declaring that—

> No person charged with official duties under one of these departments shall exercise any of the functions of another.

The construction which would give to the governor as incidental to his office authority to judge of the eligibility of candidates would enable him to swallow up the duties of all other departments. It is made the duty of the governor to execute the laws. The laws require the punishment of those who are guilty of crime. But the governor cannot inquire as to the guilt of the smallest offender, though the law would not otherwise be executed as to him, because the inquiry is *judicial.*

1. *The governor had no power to appoint an elector.* This is not pretended. As he was utterly destitute of power, Cronin cannot claim any right as an officer *de facto* by virtue of any unsupported act of the governor.

An attempted appointment would be *ultra vires* and void. It would confer no color of right. If Cronin claimed under such appointment he would be a mere *usurper*, and his acts would be void.

"A mere usurper in office," says McCrary, "can have no authority and can perform no valid official act." (Daily *vs.* Estabrook, 1 Purtlett, sections 80, 299.)

And now, to recapitulate on this point, the governor and secretary of state cannot judge of ineligibility:

1. Because the power to canvass votes, as determined by every respectable authority, does not reach back of the returns.

2. The direct question as to eligibility has been decided by courts whose reasoning is unanswerable.

3. The power is judicial, and executive officers can exercise no judicial power.

4. The constitution of Oregon expressly prohibits it by declaring that—

The persons who shall receive the highest number of votes *shall be declared* duly elected,

without regard to eligibility, which, being a judicial inquiry, is left to the courts.

5. The statute of Oregon expressly prohibits it by declaring that—

The person having the highest number of votes for any office shall be *deemed* elected,

no matter what the governor may, without authority, declare.

2. *The ineligibility of Watts would not give the election to Cronin, a minority candidate.*

The Constitution of the United States provides that—

Each State shall appoint * * * electors, * * * but no Senator or Representative, or person holding an office of trust or profit under the United States, shall be appointed an elector.

It is a general rule that if an ineligible person should be elected, he can, by a judicial proceeding by *quo warranto*, be ousted from office. The fact that *quo warranto* will lie, shows that the election is not absolutely void. (State *vs.* Boal, 46 Missouri, 528.)

The election is not void, but at most only voidable.

The authorities are so abundant to prove that a minority candidate is not elected by the ineligibility of an opposing candidate, the reasoning so logical and conclusive, the consequences of so holding, so unjust, pernicious, and against the policy of our republican institutions, that I will content myself with a reference to some of the authorities without commenting on the cases at large. They hold the doctrine that the minority candidate is not elected. This has been decided in Georgia, Wisconsin, Louisiana, Pennsylvania, Mississippi, and California, and it has been well said that these decisions have the stamp of unqualified approval from such distinguished jurists as Cooley and Dillon. Cooley, on Constitutional Limitations, page 620, says:

If the person receiving the highest number of votes was ineligible, the votes cast for him will still be effectual so far as to prevent the opposing candidate being chosen.

Dillon, on Municipal Corporations, volume 1, page 258, section 135, observes:

That when the statute fails to declare that votes cast for an ineligible person are void, (and there is no such statute in Oregon,) the effect of such person receiving a majority of the votes cast is, according to the weight of American authority and the reason of the matter, that a new election must be held, and not to give the office to the qualified person having the next highest number of votes.

He cites the following cases: The State *vs.* Swearingen, (12 Georgia,

23;) State *vs.* Giles, (1 Chandler, Wisconsin, 112;) State *vs.* Gartwell, (20 Louisiana, 114;) Cooley on Limitations, 620; McLaughlin *vs.* Sheriff of Pittsburgh, (Legal Journal, July, 1868;) opinion of the judges of Maine, appendix to volume 38 of Reports; Saunders *vs.* Haynes, (13 Cal., 145;) State *vs.* Smith, (14 Wisconsin, 497.)

Since Dillon wrote, in the State of Mississippi, in the case of Sublett *vs.* Bidwell, (47 Miss., 266,) it was held:

> If the majority candidate is disqualified it does not follow that he who has received the next highest vote, and is qualified, shall take the office.

In Fish *vs.* Collins, (21 Louisiana, 289,) it was said:

> If a competitor received a greater number of lawful votes than the claimant, the latter does not establish a right to the office by showing that his competitor was ineligible.

In California, in 1859, when the justices of the supreme court were Field, Baldwin, and Terry, in Saunders *vs.* Haynes (13 Cal., 155) the exact question was decided. The court said:

> It will be observed that the point of this defense is, that the votes cast for Turner supposing he received the highest number, were nullities, because of his assumed ineligibility. But we do not so consider, although some old cases may be found affirming this doctrine. We think that the better opinion at this day is that it is not correct.
>
> Our legislative precedents seem to be the same way. Upon principle, we think the law should be so ruled. An election is the deliberate choice of a majority or a plurality of the electoral body. This is evidenced by the votes of the electors. But if a majority of those voting, by mistake of law or fact, happen to cast their votes upon an ineligible candidate, it by no means follows that the next to him on the poll should receive the office. If this be so, a candidate might be elected who received only a small portion of the votes, and who never could have been elected at all but for this mistake. * * * It is fairer, more just, and more consistent with the theory of our institutions to hold the votes so cast as merely ineffectual for the purposes of an election than to give them the effect of disappointing the popular will and electing to office a man whose pretensions the people had designed to reject.

And from an eminent lawyer of that State, Hon. George Cadwalader, I learn that " after the lapse of seventeen years the same question again came up before the present supreme bench, and was decided by it in the same way, on the 13th day of November, 1876, in the case of Crawford *vs.* Dunbar. The court, in its opinion, after stating that Dunbar, receiving the highest number of votes, was not elected because ineligible, in regard to the claim of Crawford, that he should have the office because he had received the next highest number of votes, said emphatically: ' This position cannot be maintained;' and then goes on to approve and adopt the views expressed in Saunders *vs.* Haynes, seventeen years before."

There are still other American cases against the doctrine that a minority candidate is elected: (Comm. *vs.* Cluly, 56 Pa. St., 270; Corliss's Case, 16 American Law Register, N. S., 15; Whitman *vs.* Malony, 10 Cal., 47; People *vs.* Moliter, 23 Mich., 341; State *vs.* Vail, 53 Missouri, 97; State *vs.* Gastinel, 18 La. An., 517; Cochran *vs.* Jones, 14 American Law Register, N. S., 222; McCrary, Law of Elections, chapter 5, sec. 231–235.)

The legislative precedents generally hold the same doctrine. (McCrary, Law of Elections, sec. 232; Smith *vs.* Brown, 2 Bartlett, 395.)

The English rule, as stated by Cushing, by Grant, by Angell and Ames, and as shown by the decided cases, is that the ineligibility of the plurality candidate does not secure the election of the minority candidate unless the ineligibility is proved to be known, for it is never presumed unless patent and notorious; and in Queen *vs.* Mayor, 3 Law Reports Q. B., 629, it was said:

It is not enough to show that the voter knew the fact only, but it is necessary to show sufficient to raise a reasonable inference that he knew that the fact amounted to a disqualification. (King *vs.* Monday, Cowper, 537; Rex *vs.* Hawkins, 10 East, 211; Hawkins *vs.* Rex, 2 Dow, 124; Gosling *vs.* Veley, 7 Adol. and Ellis, 406; Cleridge *vs.* Snyder, 5 Barn. and Adol., 81; Douglas, 398, n. 22; Rex *vs.* Bridge, 1 Maule and Selwyn, 76.)

The Indiana cases follow substantially the English rule. (Gulick *vs.* New, 14 Ind., 93; Carson *vs.* McPhetridge, 15 Ind., 327; Price *vs.* Baker, 41 Ind., 572.)

The rule in New York is stated in People *vs.* Clute, 50 New York, 451, by the court as follows:

The existence of the fact which disqualifies, and of the law which makes that fact operate to disqualify, must be brought home so closely and so clearly to the knowledge or notice of the elector as that to give his vote therewith indicates an intention to waste it. The knowledge must be such, or the notice so brought home, as to imply a willfulness in acting when action is in opposition to the natural impulse to save the vote and make it effectual. He must so act in defiance of both the law and the fact, and so in opposition to his own better knowledge, that he has no right to complain of the loss of the franchise, the exercise of which he has wantonly misapplied.

The alleged ineligibility of Watts was utterly unknown to the voters of Oregon. There is not one case in any court in any country which supports Cronin in his claim to office. Solitary and alone it stands out in the naked deformity of a huge iniquity which no mantle of charity can cover.

Cronin, then, had no title to the office of elector.

I now proceed to a third proposition material to the inquiry before the Commission, which is:

That upon the law and the evidence Watts was duly appointed an elector.

His appointment by Odell and Cartwright is regular in form. It is attacked upon the ground that there was no vacancy to fill; that the ineligibility of Watts rendered his election void; that he was not an *incumbent* of the office, and therefore there was no *vacancy*, but only a case of non-election, and that the statute of Oregon does not provide for filling such place by appointment.

I will maintain—

First, that the Oregon statute does provide for the case of a non-election; and,

Second, that in law and fact no such case has arisen, but that Watts was duly elected.

These positions I will discuss in the order I have stated.

1. *The Oregon statute provides for filling a vacancy by non-election.*

The act of Congress of January 23, 1845, passed before Oregon was a State, declares—

First. That each State may by law provide for the filling of any vacancies which may occur in its college of electors when such college meets to give its electoral vote;

And,

Second. When any State has held an election * * * and failed to make a choice, the electors may be appointed on a subsequent day in such manner as the legislature of such State may direct.

This word "may" in each of these provisions is by all the authorities to be construed imperative—*shall.* (Supervisors *vs.* United States, 4 Wallace, 435.)

These provisions can give no *new power* to the legislature. The Constitution had already given the power. But as Congress had *fixed a day* for the appointment of electors, "the Tuesday next after the first Monday in November," it was necessary to provide for a *vacancy* by a *failure to elect* on that day, and for a vacancy occurring thereafter.

The legislature of Oregon knew these contingencies, and with this law of Congress before it provided for a popular election of electors on the proper day, and, to meet both the contingencies I have stated, provided by law as follows:

> The electors of President and Vice-President shall convene at the seat of government on the first Wednesday of December, * * * and if there shall be any vacancy in the office of an elector occasioned by (1) death, (2) refusal to act, (3) neglect to attend, or (4) otherwise, the electors present shall immediately proceed to fill * * * such vacancy.

This authorizes an appointment in a case of non-election ; there is in such case a *vacancy.*

I will present some of the reasons why this must be so.

(1.) *This is a statute to be liberally construed.*

(*a*) If it does not provide for a vacancy in case of non-election, no provision is made, and the legislature of Oregon *intended* to disregard a duty required by the Constitution of the United States ; intended to deprive Oregon of an electoral vote; intended to deprive all the States of their claim that Oregon should act with her whole political power. Sedgwick says:

> It is a safe and wholesome rule to adopt the restricted construction when a more liberal one will bring us in conflict with the fundamental law, the Constitution. (People *vs.* Board of Education, 13 Barb., 409.)

E converso, when a liberal construction will avoid a conflict with the Constitution and execute a duty required, it must be adopted.

(*b*) *It is a remedial statute, to be liberally construed.* It provides a remedy for the accident of non-election, death, and all other cases of vacancy.

> There can be no question—

Says Dwarris—

> that the words of a remedial statute are to be construed largely and beneficially, so as to suppress the mischief and advance the remedy.—*Dwarris*, page 632.

This is indorsed by Sedgwick, page 359. Broom says this rule is adopted " to add force and life to the cure and remedy according to the true intent of the makers of the act *pro bono publico.*" Here this rule is emphatically invoked *pro bono publico.* Its words are fairly capable of a construction which will secure the public good. (State *vs.* Newhall, 3 Dutcher, 197; 14 Opinions Attorneys-General, 265.)

2. *The rule that statutes in pari materia are to be considered together, leads to the same result.*

"All acts *in pari materia*," said Lord Mansfield, " are to be taken together." This rule is well known and recognized in this country. (Sedgwick, 247.) It enables courts to judge what one provision of a law means, by reference to another. The Oregon statute, in providing for some vacancies in local offices to be filled by the governor and the courts, limits the vacancies by enumerating those which arise from (1) death, (2) resignation, (3) removal, (4) non-residence, (5) conviction of crime, (6) refusal to qualify, and (7) judgment of ouster ; vacancies in all other cases are to be filled by popular vote. The appointing power is limited, because in derogation of popular suffrage. But when the legislature provided for electors these limitations are dropped, and it is declared that a vacancy shall be filled, if there be any, "occasioned by death, refusal to act, neglect to attend, *or otherwise.*"

Here is the broad, unlimited, comprehensive term "*or otherwise.*" It cannot be said that this is only a provision for vacancies arising from death, refusal to act, neglect to attend, and other *like* cases. Here is no case for the application of the maxim *noscitur a sociis*, because this cannot limit the rules of construction to which I have already referred. *They* apply to *this* case, and, if so, no other rule can overrule them. But here is clearly no case for the application of the maxim *noscitur a sociis*. The statute does not say that vacancies may be filled in cases of " death, refusal to act, neglect to attend, and other *like* cases," but it says " or *otherwise*."

" Otherwise" cannot be in similar cases, but in dissimilar cases. There can be no similar cases. There is nothing *like* death, or refusal to act, or refusal to attend, which could create a vacancy.

The statute regulating electors is special and applicable to that particular subject. By a well-known rule of construction it would control any general statute as to vacancies. And it employs words other and different from the general statute to give it a broader, wider, unlimited scope.

3. *The rule that statutes are to be construed according to the intention of the legislature, leads to the same results.*

It must be presumed the legislature intended to provide for every contingency. A want of skill is not to be presumed. To admit a *casus omissus* is to impute to the legislature ignorance, or neglect of duty, or both. This cannot be justified. A *casus omissus* is odious. Attorney-General Stanbery, in discussing the power of the President to fill vacancies, said the *policy* of the Constitution was clear that " there shall be no cessation, no interval of time when there may be an incapacity of action." (12 Opinions, 36.) The same policy was understood by the legislature of Oregon, and the same policy requires a construction now which shall not leave the office of elector incapable of action at the appointed time.

4. *The language employed gives the most plenary power to appoint in case of vacancy by non-election.*

The power to appoint is given " if there shall be *any vacancy* by death, refusal to act, neglect to attend, or *otherwise*." Worcester defines " *vacancy* " for legal purposes :

The state of a post, office, or employment, *when destitute of and wanting an incumbent;* a place or office which is empty or not filled.

Johnson :

State of a post or employment when it is *unsupplied.*

Bouvier :

A place which is *empty.*

When the Constitution creates the office of elector and fixes the number three for Oregon, and only two are elected, and the law requires one more, is not this one " wanting an incumbent," " empty," " not filled ?" If so, there *is* a vacancy, or these philologists are mistaken. The law says :

If there shall be a vacancy by death, refusal to act, neglect to attend, or otherwise

Webster defines " otherwise," " in a different manner," " by other causes," " in other respects." The statute may be read, then, as if it said :

If there shall be a vacancy by death, refusal to act, neglect to attend, or " in a different manner," " by other causes," " in other respects."

This would cover a case of non-election.

Philology is with us, reason is with us, justice is with us, common sense is with us.

5. *The authority of the courts is conclusive in favor of this result.*

The case of The State *vs.* Adams, 2 Stewart's Alabama Reports, 231, by reason of its ability, research, and sound law, is placed by Brightly in his Leading Cases on Elections, page 286. A part of the syllabus is this:

A failure to elect creates a vacancy, which can be filled by executive appointment.

Two candidates for sheriff received an equal number of votes, and the governor filled the vacancy. The authority of the governor is found in these words of the constitution:

Should a vacancy occur subsequent to an election, it shall be filled by the governor, as in other cases.

The court say:

The whole object of the section—

Of the constitution quoted—

is to secure the means by which offices of this description throughout the State shall be filled.

   *   *   *   *   *   *   *

The convention could make no provision by which the office would be at all times filled by the people; there might be vacancies, and as it would require time to fill such offices by the people, it was necessary that the duties of the office should be discharged in the mean time.

The convention therefore intended to provide for filling the office by an election in the first instance, and a vacancy by executive appointment when it occurred. They took it for granted that elections would always be held * * * and they proceeded to provide a mode of appointment in the event of the election by the people not effecting the object of providing a sheriff. * * * This construction, and no other, completely fulfills the intention of the constitution. Should they fail to elect a sheriff by being divided as to their choice, the general election terminates, and a vacancy in the office of sheriff takes place.

In State *vs.* City of Newark, 3 Dutcher, 185, it was held that—

A law which confers power to supply by appointment a place vacated by death or disability, authorizes an appointment to be made where the vacancy is occasioned by resignation.

The Attorney-General has decided that—

In the event of the disability or death of a surveyor, where there is a power to fill a vacancy, a resignation creates a vacancy.—14 *Opinions,* 264.

The same doctrine was held in State *ex rel.* Attorney-General *vs.* Irwin, 5 Nevada, 111. The constitution of Nevada provides that—

When any office shall, from any cause, become vacant, and no mode is provided by the constitution and laws for filling such vacancy, the governor shall have power to fill such vacancy.

The legislature by act of February 23, 1869, which took effect April 1, 1869, created a new county, requiring county officers. The governor appointed a sheriff for the county, and his right to the office was inquired of by *quo warranto,* upon the ground that there was no vacancy which the governor could fill. The supreme court held there was a vacancy, which was properly filled, and quoted with approval the language of the supreme court of Indiana in Stocking *vs.* State, 7 Indiana, 329:

There is no technical nor peculiar meaning to the word "vacant" as used in the constitution. It means *empty, unoccupied.* As applied to an office without an incumbent, there is no basis for the distinction urged, that it applies only to offices vacant by death, resignation, or otherwise. An existing office without an incumbent is vacant, whether it be a new or an old one. A new house is as vacant as one tenanted for years, which was abandoned yesterday.

In Stocking *vs.* State, 7 Indiana, 326, it was shown that the legislature created a new judicial circuit for which the governor appointed a judge under section 18, article 5, of the constitution, which provides that the governor shall by appointment fill a vacancy in the office of judge of any court; and it was held that it was competent for the governor to appoint a judge "to hold his office until a judge" should be elected.

In People *vs.* Parker, 37 California, 650, it was said by Sprague, justice, in his opinion defining the term "vacancy :"

It not only includes vacancies in terms of office which have been partially filled by an incumbent, but includes all offices and terms of office, constitutional and statutory, having no *de jure* incumbent, either by reason of a statutory vacancy or by reason of the existence of an office or term of office for the incumbency of which no person has been legitimately designated.

Crockett, justice, remarked :

A vacancy in an office begins when there ceases to be an incumbent to fill it, and it continues as long as there is no incumbent.

The California cases hold that the power to fill a " vacancy occurring from any cause gives authority to fill vacancies caused by the failure of the people to elect." Chief-Justice Field, now of this Commission, in his learned opinion in The People *vs.* Whitman, 10 California Reports, 48, denied that an officer holding beyond a term " until his successor was elected and qualified" prevented a "vacancy." He said :

For many of the most responsible and important offices in the State there can be no election except to fill a vacancy or for a full term, and if a vacancy cannot exist by a failure of a person to qualify, whether such failure arises from death, acceptance of an appointment under the Federal Government, or resignation in advance of the right to the office—and the reasons assigned in the present case will apply to any of those causes—it would often happen that weak and incompetent men, for whom not a vote could be obtained from the people, would retain for long terms positions of great trust and power, to the serious detriment of the public interests.

But it is said that the supreme court of Rhode Island decided in November last that ineligibility avoids an election, and that in such case, with or without resignation, there is no vacancy. (16 American Law Register, N. S., 15.) But the court decided no such general question. The court held that these facts did not create *such* a vacancy as is provided for in the peculiar statute of that State. Its language is :

If any electors *chosen as aforesaid* shall, after their said election, (1) decline the said office or (2) be prevented by any cause from serving thereon, the other electors, when met, * * * shall fill *such vacancies.*

Here the power is not to fill *all* vacancies, but *such* vacancies : vacancies of electors who had been *actually chosen*, vacancies only in two specified cases: (1) when a duly-appointed elector *declines* to act, and (2) when *such* elector is prevented from serving by sickness or other causes. The Oregon statute gives a broader power, a power to fill vacancies arising *in any manner ;* not in two specified cases, but in *all cases.*

There is a class of cases in which some courts have held that, when an officer is elected for a given term, "and *until a successor is elected and qualified*," in case of a non-election at the expiration of the term, there is no *vacancy*, because, by force of express provision, the *incumbent continues.* (Brightly, 670; Comm. *vs.* Hanley, 9 Pa., St., 513; Comm. *vs.* Baxter, 27 Pa. St., 444; State *vs.* Cobb, 2 Kansas, 32 ; State *vs.* Jenkins, 43 Mo., 261; State *vs.* Robinson, 1 Kansas, 17; State *vs.* Benedict, 15 Minn., 199 ; McCrary on Elections, page 170, section 236; Stratton *vs.* Oatland, 28 Cal., 51; People *vs.* Stratton, 28 Cal., 382 ; People *vs.* Tilton, 37 Cal, 614; *Contra.* People *vs.* Reed, 6 Cal., 288; People *vs.* Mizner, 7 Cal., 524 ; People *vs.* Parker, 37 Cal., 639.) These cannot affect the question I am now discussing.

The Constitution of the United States provides as to Senators that—

If vacancies *happen* by resignation or otherwise during the recess of the legislature any State, the executive thereof may make temporary appointments until the next meeting of the legislature.—*Art.* 1, *sec.* 3.

It has been held that this does not authorize an appointment in a case where the legislature has failed to elect. But this rests on two grounds not applicable to the case of electors: First, that the word "*happen*" limits the power to cases where there has been an *incumbent*, and that a restrictive rule of interpretation applies, because the legislature can always be convened, and the governor should, on grounds of public policy, have no occasion for refusing to call a session, thereby to magnify his own power. (Story, Const., sec. 1559; McCrary, 171, sec. 237; Clarke & Hall, 871.)

I submit, then, to this honorable Commission, that *if there was a case of non-election there was a "vacancy"* which Odell and Cartwright could and did lawfully fill.

I now proceed to show—

Second, that Watts was elected; that he became *de facto* an elector, if not *de jure;* that the acts of such an officer are valid, and that his resignation created a *vacancy* which was properly filled by his re-appointment.

It has already been shown that Watts received a majority of the popular vote and that he presents sufficient evidence of title to the office. On these facts he was lawfully elected, for reasons some of which I will state:

1. The constitution and statute of Oregon in express terms declare that he "having the highest number of votes shall be declared and deemed elected." The policy of the statute is to secure officers without an interregnum.

2. The disqualifying clause of the Constitution is *directory,* not *mandatory.*

The Constitution does not say that "a person holding an office of trust or profit" shall not hold the office of elector, but it *directs* the people who vote in the exercise of their duties. It prescribes a *rule of public policy,* but not a *mandatory prohibition* on *the person* appointed.

Lord Mansfield declared that those provisions are *mandatory* which relate to "circumstances which are of the *essence* of a thing required to be done," while others are directory. (Rex *vs.* Loxdale, 1 Burr., 447.) The *appointment* is the essence of the thing required to be done; the qualifications of the candidate are non-essentials, or at least are not the essence of what is to be done.

3. *This question is determined by the authorities.* In Saint Louis County *vs.* Sparks, 10 Missouri, 121, the court say:

A statute prescribing qualification to an office is merely *directory,* and although an appointee does not possess the requisite qualification his appointment is not therefore void, unless it is so expressly enacted. (20 Louisiana An., 114; People *vs.* Cook, 14 Barb., 259; Greenleaf *vs.* Low, 4 Denio, 168; Weeks *vs.* Ellis, 2 Barb., 324; Keeser *vs.* McKisson, 2 Rawle, 139; McCrary on Elections, sec. 78.)

In Commonwealth *vs.* Cluly, 56 Pa. State Reports, 270, it was shown that Cluly received a majority of votes as a candidate for sheriff against McLaughlin, the minority candidate. McLaughlin instituted *quo warranto* proceedings to oust Cluly, on the ground that he was ineligible by reason of having held the office previous to this election as long as the constitution permitted. His honor Judge Strong, now of this Commission, in deciding the case, said:

The votes cast at an election for a person who is disqualified from holding an office are not nullities; they cannot be rejected by the inspectors, nor thrown out of the count by the return-judges; the disqualified person is a person still and every vote thrown for him is formal.

In Saunders *vs.* Haynes, 13 California, page 153, the court say:

It will be observed that the point of this defense is that the votes cast for Turner

supposing he received the highest number, were nullities because of his assumed ineligibility; but we do not so consider. Although some old cases may be found affirming
this doctrine, we think that the better opinion at this day is that it is not correct.

4. If Watts was ineligible his election and induction into office made
him an officer *de facto*, and his acts as such are valid.

The courts have met directly the question whether the acts of officers
can be declared invalid because not duly elected, and it is now undisputed law that, if a person comes into office by color of legal appointment or election, he is an officer *de facto*, his acts in that capacity are
valid and effectual when they concern the public and third persons,
although it may finally appear that he has no legal or constitutional
right to the office. His official acts are as valid as those of an officer
de jure, and they cannot be invalidated by any inquiry or evidence back
of his certificate of election.

This doctrine has been deemed so essential to the public interest that
persons declared ineligible by law have nevertheless been regarded as
officers *de facto* and their official acts valid when done under color of
legal appointment. The law is so well settled upon this subject that I
will content myself with a reference to authorities without reading them.
In McGregor *vs.* Balch, 14 Vermont, 428, it was held that although a
postmaster was ineligible to be elected justice of the peace, yet having
been elected and acting under color of office he was a justice of the peace
de facto, and his acts were valid as to the public and third persons. In
Baird *vs.* Bank of Washington, 11 Serg. and R., (Pa.) 414, the court say:

> The principle of colorable election holds not only in regard to the right of electing,
> but of being elected. A person *indisputably ineligible* may be an officer *de facto* by color
> of election. (Pritchett *vs.* People, 1 Gilmer, 529; People *vs.* Ammons, 5 Gilmer, 107;
> cases collected in Chase's Decisions by Johnson, 462, where see Cæsar Griffin's case.)

In Saint Louis County *vs.* Sparks, 10 Missouri, 121, the court say:

> When the appointing power has made an appointment and a person is appointed
> who has not the qualifications required by law, the appointment is not therefore void.
> The person appointed is *de facto* an officer. His acts * * * are valid and binding.

To the same effect is Knight *vs.* Wells, Luftwych, 508; 16 Viner's
Abridgment, 114; Bean *vs.* Thompson, 19 New Hampshire, 115; Mc-
Crary on Elections, sec. 79.

The postmasters who were appointed as electors in 1836, although
ineligible, voted for President, and their right to do so was so far conceded that no complete inquiry was made of the facts. (House Miscellaneous Document 13, second session Twenty-fourth Congress, p. 71.)

The Houses of Congress have determined that the acts of officers
de facto are valid for all purposes of an election. (Barnes *vs.* Adams,
2 Bartlett, 760; McCrary, sec. 79.)

Many laws have been passed in Congress by the casting votes of
members who were subsequently declared not legally elected. But the
laws they made by their votes have always been held valid. The
same may be said of the laws in almost every State in the Union. Judgments have been rendered in the courts by judges who were subsequently ousted from office on *quo warranto* as not legally elected, but
their judgments still stood as valid and unquestioned. A large part of
the land-titles in many of the States depends on official acts of persons
ousted from office as not legally elected, but the titles are not thereby
disturbed.

To overturn all this law is to destroy the foundations of society, the
title to property, the obligations of the domestic relations, and convert
the land into a pandemonium.

The ineligibility of Watts, then, did not render his election void. He was an elector *de facto* when he did any official act. As there was then no vacancy, it was impossible that Cronin could be at the same time an elector *de jure* or *de facto*. Watts *did act* under his election. He *resigned*, and that was an official act. He must have entered on the office in order that he might resign. The record shows sufficiently that he acted in the organization of the electors, and after that absented himself, resigned, was re-appointed, again appeared, and acted.

His title to office is twofold : an appointment by the people, shown in evidence by the lists of electors certified by the secretary of state, and an appointment by the remaining two electors, whose title to office is clear and unquestionable.

From all this it is shown that Watts was duly appointed an elector and that the votes cast by Odell, Cartwright, and Watts for President and Vice-President are *the* votes provided for by the Constitution. This result is not only sanctioned and sanctified by law, but it is still further sanctified by the gratifying fact that it carries out the purpose of our republican institutions by giving effect to the will of the people of Oregon.

If the vote of Cronin could be counted for President and Vice-President, it would rob the people of Oregon of the highest political right they have ; it would rob the people of the whole republic of their lawful choice of President and Vice-President, and bring shame and dishonor upon our institutions. It needs no *exposé* of any attempted bribery to render this purpose effectual, to secure for it the detestation of mankind and the execration of history.

Mr. Commissioner EDMUNDS. Mr. President, I move that the Commission take a recess until seven o'clock, to meet in the Senate chamber.

Mr. Commissioner ABBOTT. I move that we now adjourn until ten o'clock to-morrow morning.

Mr. Commissioner THURMAN. I hope the motion will be withdrawn for a moment until we decide whether we shall extend the time for the argument by counsel.

Mr. Commissioner ABBOTT. I withdraw the motion if Judge Thurman desires.

Mr. Commissioner EDMUNDS. I withdraw my motion.

Mr. Commissioner THURMAN. If we are not to extend the time allowed for argument I should be in favor of adjourning until to-morrow, and then the four hours of argument may be heard and concluded by two o'clock and we shall have time to deliberate ; but if the time is to be extended, then I might be quite willing, unwell as I am, to stay to-night.

The PRESIDENT. I understood that counsel asked for an extension.

Mr. Commissioner THURMAN. If counsel insist upon that request, I hope that will be decided first.

The PRESIDENT. What was the request ?

Mr. HOADLY. We did request an extension of time for two hours additional.

Mr. EVARTS. On our part we do not desire any additional time, as we suppose the discussion is mainly one of law.

Mr. Commissioner HOAR. I should like to have the counsel state whether they propose to offer any testimony and whether they have that offer of testimony now prepared.

The PRESIDENT. I will allow that question to be answered before I put the motion.

Mr. HOADLY. We expect to offer testimony. We have asked the Commisson to make an order for the production of certain testimony which we desire to use.

The PRESIDENT. It has been made. The subpœna has been signed.

Mr. Commissioner HOAR. I should like, Mr. President, before determining the question of the extension of time, to have the offer of testimony made in form, made now.

Mr. Commissioner BRADLEY. So as not to occupy time to-morrow?

Mr. Commissioner HOAR. I do not mean by that that I desire the counsel to offer their witnesses now, but I desire to have the offer (which has been made in all the other cases) before the tribunal as to the substance of the fact that is proposed to be proven before voting on the question of the extension of time.

The PRESIDENT. I will inquire, are counsel ready to make the offer?

Mr. HOADLY. We are.

The PRESIDENT. Make it.

Mr. HOADLY. I say "ready." I suppose it is in the next room. We have prepared the offer and caused it to be printed, and I suppose it can be had in a moment.

Mr. MERRICK. It is very brief.

Mr. HOADLY. There is not a copy in the room now.

Mr. Commissioner HOAR. I move that counsel be permitted to offer that before the other question is decided.

Mr. Commissioner EDMUNDS. To occupy the time while this paper is being sent for, I wish to say on the question of the extension of time that it is now Wednesday night; Saturday week will be the 3d day of March, and there are several States yet to be gone through, and one which, according to the general rumor, will be one that we shall be obliged ourselves to act upon. Now it does seem to me that we ought all to submit to much personal inconvenience, as I do, and as I know Judge Thurman does, in order to get on. The Senate Chamber is at our disposal, where we can be as comfortable at night as we can be here in the day-time, except from the weariness of long sitting. So I should hope that on all hands we should be willing now, with all these questions as to what are the offers and how much time may be needed, which perhaps we cannot tell—I should be very glad to give all that is necessary and that is possible—but I think it better that we should take a recess now and meet at seven o'clock, and then, in an hour or two, we can ascertain exactly where we are and what we ought to do.

The PRESIDENT. I think we ought to receive the offer before any motion.

Mr. Commissioner EDMUNDS. I did not make a motion, only a suggestion.

Mr. Commissioner MORTON. Mr. President, I desire to say that considering the critical condition of public business, and the exigency now before the country, we ought not to extend the time. I would always be willing to gratify and accommodate counsel; but I believe that every idea they have to advance, every authority to refer to, can be produced satisfactorily in two hours on each side. I do not believe there is the slightest advantage to be gained by anybody by the extension of time.

The PRESIDENT, (to counsel.) Are you ready to make the offer of proof?

Mr. HOADLY. Not at this moment. Mr. Green has gone for it.

Mr. MERRICK. The papers were here, but accidentally have been mislaid.

The PRESIDENT. Mr. Commissioner Miller suggests that we had better take the question upon the motion for the extension of time without waiting for the offer.

Mr. MERRICK. I have a copy here now.

The PRESIDENT. You can read that. The Commission desire that the offer should be read in their hearing audibly.

Mr. HOADLY—

First. The undersigned, of counsel for objectors to certificate No. 1, offer in evidence a duly-certified copy of the commission of John W. Watts as postmaster at Yam Hill, in the county of La Fayette, State of Oregon, which said commission was issued in the year 1873, and they also offer to prove that said Watts duly qualified and entered upon said office, being an office of profit and trust under the United States, and that he was the incumbent thereof on the 7th day of November, 1876, and up to and after the 6th day of December, 1876, and until his successor was thereafter appointed and qualified; and they further offer to prove that said John W. Watts is the same person whose name appears in said certificate No. 1 as having voted for President and Vice-President of the United States as a member of the electoral college of the State of Oregon.

Second. The undersigned further offer to prove that more than eleven hundred voters of the State of Oregon who cast their ballots in favor of said Watts as elector for President and Vice-President of the United States, at the election held on the 7th day of November, 1876, had notice that said Watts was a postmaster in the service of the United States, and that he was thereby disqualified from becoming an elector for President and Vice-President of the United States.

This is signed:

R. T. MERRICK.
GEORGE HOADLY.

The PRESIDENT. Now I will put the question on the extension of time. The request is to extend the time two hours on the side of the objectors to certificate No. 1.

Mr. Commissioner BRADLEY. Mr. President, I should be very reluctant to curtail the time of counsel in the discussion of the questions before us, so important as they are, and I always have been disposed to extend time when it has been asked; but it seems to me that after the question has already been discussed in many of its leading aspects, two hours on each side already occupied, with two hours more, will be as much as can be reasonably asked in the present exigency of public affairs. I would much prefer that counsel should confine themselves to the time we have laid down in our rules, and that we should adjourn until to-morrow, instead of extending the time and sitting to-night.

Mr. Commissioner HUNTON. Mr. President, I understand that the two hours proposed to be devoted to the argument of this case on either side embrace also the argument on the offer of testimony and upon the whole case. Now, under the rules of this Commission counsel have a right to debate each offer of evidence for fifteen minutes on each side; and it was understood in the last case, as I believe, that in lieu of those fifteen minutes on the offering of each piece of testimony we should extend the time for the main argument and let all the offers be made at once. I think that rule ought to be pursued in this case; in lieu of the fifteen minutes that the counsel would have a right to debate each offer of testimony under the rule, I think we should extend the time so as to cover that fifteen minutes' debate on each point of testimony. I think, therefore, it is reasonable that the time of the argument should be extended.

The PRESIDENT. I desire to add one remark in explanation of the vote I shall give. I shall vote to extend the time. I do it very largely on the ground that, after the argument closes, there is no opportunity for the examination of authorities. We depend chiefly upon the bar, during the arguments, for our information in respect to the authorities, and with that view I shall vote to extend the time.

Mr. Commissioner EDMUNDS. Mr. President, I make this motion on the subject of the application for the extension of time:

That we proceed with the case at seven o'clock in the Senate Chamber, and that counsel have three and a half hours.

There are two objections here which would cover half an hour's argument. I want to give all the time possible. I move that they have three and a half hours on a side for the argument of objections, and merits, and everything.

Mr. EVARTS. The offers of testimony?

Mr. Commissioner EDMUNDS. Yes, including the offers of testimony.

Mr. MERRICK. That will be satisfactory.

Mr. Commissioner BAYARD. Is the extension of time desired on both sides?

Mr. Commissioner EDMUNDS. No; the opposite side say not; but of course in making the order we ought to extend it to both sides. If we can spend two hours this evening, it will be about fair.

The PRESIDENT. I will treat that as the original motion. Please reduce it to writing.

Mr. Commissioner EDMUNDS. My motion is that the hearing proceed in the Senate Chamber at seven o'clock and thirty minutes p. m., and that counsel have three hours and a half on each side for the whole case, covering offers of proof, &c.

Mr. Commissioner THURMAN. Mr. President, as that order is drawn up, it does not include the time that might be occupied in hearing the testimony in case any shall be admitted.

Mr. Commissioner EDMUNDS. I do not intend to have the testimony of witnesses come out of the three hours and a half, because it is obvious that we could not hear the testimony of eleven hundred witnesses, to prove that they knew the disqualification, in that time.

Mr. Commissioner THURMAN. Then the proposition is that the argument shall proceed before any testimony is offered.

Mr. Commissioner EDMUNDS. That depends. In whatever order they go, they have so much time for speaking.

Mr. Commissioner THURMAN. I have never been able to understand since this Commission had its first sitting why facts that are indisputable have not been admitted and thereby the time of the Commission saved. The first offer of proof in this case is that Watts was postmaster at Yam Hill, in the county of La Fayette, Oregon, on the 7th of November, 1876, and up to and after the 6th of December, 1876. That he was postmaster on the 7th of November, 1876, I have supposed was not a disputed fact. Why that should not be admitted, and proof in regard to that and the time that would be occupied in making the proof should not be saved, I am not at all able to understand. Whether he was postmaster on the 6th of December, 1876, I do not understand to be an undisputed question, and upon that, testimony might well be taken.

So as to the second proposition, as to whether more than eleven hundred voters of the State of Oregon who cast their votes for him knew of his ineligibility; that is a statement, of course, which no one could be asked to admit. But so far as time can be saved by admitting what is indisputable, I have thought from the very first that the admission ought to have been made on both sides.

Now, in respect to this testimony, until the Commission decides whether it shall be received or not, I do not know how counsel can proceed. We propose to give three hours and a half. I think that is ample for the discussion, both of the question of admissibility and of the merits, but until you decide whether the testimony shall be admitted at all I really do not see how counsel are to know how to conduct their case.

Mr. Commissioner HOAR. Mr. President, if this motion should be adopted, a motion will be made that the counsel, in discussing the admissibility of their testimony on either side, may draw at their pleasure on the time allowed for their final argument, as was done in the Louisiana case. That answers Judge Thurman's question.

The PRESIDENT. I do not quite understand you, Mr. Hoar.

Mr. Commissioner HOAR. I say, if this proposition of Mr. Edmunds shall be adopted, a further motion will be made, that counsel, in discussing the question of the admissibility of testimony, shall be permitted to add to the fifteen minutes as much of their final time as they see fit to take, as they did in the Louisiana case; that is, counsel having three and a half hours in all, if they choose, instead of spending fifteen minutes only on their first offer of testimony, may spend three and a half hours on it.

The PRESIDENT. I do not consider any motion before the Commission except the one submitted by Mr. Edmunds, that the Commission proceed in the Senate Chamber at seven and a half o'clock this evening, and that the counsel have three and a half hours on each side for the discussion of the whole case.

Mr. Commissioner GARFIELD. Mr. President, I have no objection to that proposition if it can be executed in accordance with the manifest intention of the mover; that is, if we can go forward to-night and hold a session which will hear a large part of the argument that we expect to hear. But we did precisely this sort of thing a week ago, extended the time to four hours and a half on a side, with an understanding that we were to have a night session, and before we had started over twenty minutes on that night's session, or a little longer, perhaps, we adjourned over, and then we had the whole accumulated time on our hands and nothing gained.

Mr. Commissioner MILLER. That was on account of counsel who said they could not go on.

Mr. Commissioner GARFIELD. I was out at the moment that was done. But if it can be that we shall have a session to-night and hear the major part of this argument, I shall cheerfully vote for the resolution.

Mr. Commissioner THURMAN. I want to say one word in reply to the suggestion of brother Hoar. He says that if this rule be adopted, then the counsel may take out of their time allowed for the argument upon the merits as much time as they please and occupy that time in arguing the question of the admissibility of the testimony, as was done in the Louisiana case. But the cases are very different. In the Louisiana case the Commission directed them to argue the question of the admissibility of the testimony, and the Commission decided that question before they were called upon to make any argument on the merits. It is very true that they occupied all their time, so that they had no time left for argument upon the merits. But if this order be adopted, then, without knowing whether they are to give their evidence or not, they are to go on upon each side and occupy the three hours and a half, and they will not know what will be the decision of the Commission as to the admissibility of the testimony. I do not think that is the way to try a case. It seems to me it would be very much better to stick to our rule and allow fifteen minutes upon an offer of testimony which would give half an hour on a side, and then allow the three hours for the argument upon the merits, which would amount to the same thing as the order offered by the Senator from Vermont.

Mr. Commissioner HOAR. The suggestion I made does not require counsel to take more than fifteen minutes. It leaves the whole matter to the discretion of counsel. Counsel make these two offers of testimony. If they choose to present that point of their case in a fifteen minutes' argument, or without argument, they can do so. If they wish to draw fifteen minutes or an hour out of their final time, as it has been extended, they can do so. The order does not require them; it only permits them in their discretion, to which the case certainly can be intrusted.

Mr. Commissioner THURMAN. But the question which troubles me is, when will the Commission decide on the admissibility of the testimony?

Mr. Commissioner HOAR. After it is argued.

Mr. Commissioner MILLER. When the court get through hearing argument, they decide whether the testimony shall be admitted or not.

The PRESIDENT. The only question before the Commission is on the motion of Senator Edmunds.

Mr. Commissioner ABBOTT. I desire to ask Senator Edmunds how long it is proposed that we shall hold a session this evening?

Mr. Commissioner EDMUNDS. I think we ought to sit two full hours.

Mr. Commissioner ABBOTT. I agree to that.

The PRESIDENT. Are you ready for the question on the motion?

Mr. Commissioner MORTON. What is the motion?

The PRESIDENT. That the hearing of the case proceed in the Senate Chamber at half past seven o'clock; and that the parties have three and a half hours on each side for argument.

Mr. Commissioner MORTON. I suggest that that motion is divisible. The question about going to the Senate Chamber is one thing. I should like to have the question separated.

The PRESIDENT. I will regard the question as divisible. The first question is whether the Commission will proceed with the hearing in the Senate Chamber at half past seven o'clock.

This branch of the motion was agreed to.

The PRESIDENT. The other division of the motion is that the parties be allowed three hours and a half on a side for the discussion of the whole question.

This branch of the motion was agreed to.

Mr. Commissioner HOAR. I move that in arguing the question of admissibility of evidence, counsel be permitted to take, in addition to the fifteen minutes allowed by the rule, as much of the time remaining to them as they see fit.

Mr. Commissioner EDMUNDS. That is unnecessary. This is a substitute for the whole thing. They proceed under this order alone.

Mr. Commissioner HOAR. If that is the understanding, all right.

The PRESIDENT, (at six o'clock and forty-four minutes p. m.) The Commission will now take a recess until half past seven o'clock.

The Commission re-assembled in the Senate Chamber at seven o'clock and thirty minutes p. m.

Mr. HOADLY. Mr. President and gentlemen of the Commission, the first proposition to which I address myself is that the decisions made by the Commission in the cases of Florida and Louisiana, applied to this case, require the Commission to sustain the electoral votes cast by Cronin, Miller, and Parker, namely, one for Tilden and Hendricks, and two for Hayes and Wheeler. Without retracing its steps and withdrawing the conclusions the Commission has announced in the cases of Florida and Louisiana, the result cannot be reached which is desired by our learned antagonists.

In order that we may in the briefest possible manner ascertain the point of contention, I will read from the decision of this Commission in the case of Louisiana:

> And the Commission has by a majority of votes decided, and does hereby decide, that it is not competent, under the Constitution and the law as it existed at the date of the passage of said act, to go into evidence *aliunde* the papers opened by the President of the Senate in the presence of the two Houses to prove that other persons than those regularly certified to by the governor of the State of Louisiana, on and according to the determination and declaration of their appointment by the returning-officers for elections in the said State prior to the time required for the performance of their duties, had been appointed electors, or by counter-proof to show that they had not, or that the determination of the said returning-officers was not in accordance with the truth and the fact; the Commission by a majority of votes being of opinion that it is not within the jurisdiction of the two Houses of Congress assembled to count the votes for President and Vice-President to enter upon a trial of such questions.

I do not understand that this is a ruling upon a mere question of proof, but that is a ruling upon a high proposition of jurisdiction. Nor do I understand that by this decision is meant that anything and everything which any person claiming to be an elector may inclose in an envelope and address to the President of the Senate has the force of testimony before this honorable Commission, but only that those documents and papers which if offered *aliunde* would be competent, may be considered when found within the envelopes, and that the determination and decision of the returning-board of a State, acted upon by the governor of the State in the manner provided in the one hundred and thirty-sixth section of the Revised Statutes, is final and conclusive, and that the names therein contained are the names of the true and valid electors of the State.

That I am right in this construction of this decision is confirmed by the views of one for whom long knowledge has impressed me with great respect. I am not personally intimate with him, but intimate in the sense in which any citizen may be said to be intimate with the judgment, the opinions, and the. habits of accuracy of statement of a statesman. I say, that I am right in this conclusion is confirmed by a statement of reasons for this conclusion given in the Senate of the United States on the 20th of February by a member of this Commission, the honored Senator from Indiana, [Mr. Morton.] He said:

> The Constitution says the certificates shall be opened by the President of the Senate in the presence of the two Houses. Whether he is to count the votes or whether the two Houses are to count the votes, and I assume under this law the two Houses are to do it, or in certain cases this Electoral Commission, what can they do? They have but one duty to perform, and that is to ascertain that these certificates came from the electors of the State. When that is done, "the votes shall then be counted." They must ascertain the fact whether they came from the electors of the State; and when they have ascertained that, their duty is at an end. There is no time, there is no place to try any question of ineligibility or of election when the votes are to be counted. And how are we to know that the certificates came from the electors of the State? In the first place the act of Congress provides *prima-facie* evidence, the governor's certificate, but that is not conclusive. That is the result of an act of Congress. Congress may repeal that act, or it may provide by another to go behind it, but when you go behind that and come to the action of the officers of the State, there your inquiry is

at an end. Whenever the officers appointed by a State to declare who have been chosen electors have acted and made that declaration, it is final so far as Congress is concerned. The action of the State officers is the act of the State.

With this statement of principle I am content. My proposition is that the State of Oregon, through her State officers, through her governor, supported by her canvassing-board, has spoken, and the result of her speech is here in the certificates of E. A. Cronin, William H. Odell, and John C. Cartwright, which certificates are attached to the votes of Cronin, Miller, and Parker, and are the only legitimate, lawful evidence of the act of Oregon, without which the pretended votes of Odell, Cartwright, and Watts fail to have any legal effect whatever.

The views expressed by Senator Morton find confirmation in the case of Dennett, petitioner, in volume 32 of the Reports of the State of Maine, page 508. The opinion was pronounced by Shepley, chief-justice, and there was no dissenting opinion:

The act of opening and comparing the votes returned for county commissioners cannot be performed by the persons holding the offices of governor and of councilors unless they act in their official capacities, for it is only in that capacity that the power is conferred upon them. The duty is to be performed upon the responsibility of their official stations and under the sanctity of their official oaths. The governor and council, and not certain persons that may be ascertained to hold those offices, must determine the number of votes returned for each person as county commissioner, and ascertain that some one has or has not a sufficient number to elect him.

It is, then, the State of Oregon which speaks when the governor, under section 136 of the Revised Statutes of the United States, in obedience to the return and canvass of the returning-officers, to the declaration and determination of the result of the canvass by the returning-officers, issues that certificate.

It shall be the duty of the executive of each State—

Says the statute—

to cause three lists of the names of the electors of such State to be made and certified, and to be delivered to the electors on or before the day on which they are required by the preceding section to meet.

Again, section 138:

The electors shall make and sign three certificates of all the votes given by them, each of which certificates shall contain two distinct lists, &c.

And so the next section, that the certificates shall be sealed and delivered, one to the Federal district judge, one sent by mail to the President of the Senate, and one sent by messenger to the President of the Senate.

Now, I ask your honors' attention to the question, Who were the electors ascertained to be appointed by the official decision and determination (that I believe to have been the language used in the Florida case) of the board of State canvassers of the State of Oregon? Or, to use the language adopted in the Louisiana case, Who were the returning-officers upon and according to whose determination of their appointment the governor acted or failed to act, as the case may be, in the issue of the certificates of the State of Oregon?

This leads us to an examination and comparison of the statutes of the State of Oregon in connection with the statutes of the States of Florida and Louisiana, for I refer to Florida and Louisiana in order that we who are of counsel may have a guide to the real effect of the opinions already pronounced by this Commission; I mean, of course, in applying to the case of Oregon the decisions made by this Commission in the matter of Florida and Louisiana.

In Florida certain persons are to

form a board of State canvassers, and proceed to canvass the returns of said election, and determine and declare who shall have been elected to any such office or as such member, as shown by such returns.

Here the office of determination and declaration is superadded to the office of canvassing; and by a later provision in the same section the board are required to

make and sign a certificate containing in words written at full length the whole number of votes, &c.

And—

When any person shall be elected to the office of elector, * * * the governor shall make out, sign, and cause to be sealed with the seal of the State, and transmit to such person, a certificate of his election.

The point to which I desire particularly your attention is that under the laws of Florida the determination and decision are separated in legal thought, and thus, in legal act, from the canvass itself; and so we find it in Louisiana, as is made manifest in the oath that—

I will carefully and honestly canvass and compile the statements of the votes.

Again—

Within ten days after the closing of the election said returning-officers shall meet in New Orleans to canvass and compile the statements of votes made by the commissioners of election, and make returns of the election to the secretary of state. They shall continue in session until such returns have been compiled. The presiding officer shall, at such meeting, open in the presence of the said returning-officers the statements of the commissioners of election, and the said returning-officers shall, from said statements, canvass and compile the returns of the election in duplicate; one copy of such returns they shall file in the office of the secretary of state, and of one copy they shall make public proclamation, by printing in the official journal and such other newspapers as they may deem proper, declaring the names of all persons and officers voted for, the number of votes for each person, and the names of the persons who have been duly and lawfully elected. The returns of the election thus made and promulgated shall be *prima facie* evidence in all courts of justice and before all civil officers, until set aside after contest according to law, of the right of any person named therein to hold and exercise the office to which he shall by such return be declared elected. The governor shall, within thirty days thereafter, issue commissions to all officers thus declared elected, who are required by law to be commissioned.

Now, in Oregon the language of the sixtieth section is this:

The votes for the electors shall be given, received, returned, and canvassed as the same are given, returned, and canvassed for members of Congress. The secretary of state shall prepare two lists of the names of the electors elected, and affix the seal of the State to the same, &c.

I will come back to that presently. Let us now see how votes are given, received, returned, and canvassed for members of Congress. Section 37 is:

The county clerk, immediately after making the abstract of the votes given in his county, shall make a copy of each of said abstracts, and transmit it by mail to the secretary of state, at the seat of government; and it shall be the duty of the secretary of state, in the presence of the governor, to proceed, within thirty days after the election, and sooner if the returns be all received, to canvass the votes given for secretary and treasurer of state, state printer, justices of the supreme court, members of Congress, and district attorneys.

If this were all the statute, an argument by implication might be made, to the effect that the duty to canvass involves the duty to determine the results of the canvass. But this is not all, for the governor, who is required to be present, is not an idle spectator, as is claimed by the objectors to certificate No. 2:

And the governor shall grant a certificate of election to the person having the highest number of votes, and shall also issue a proclamation declaring the election of such person.

And this is made perfectly plain by the next sentence:

> In case there shall be no choice by reason of any two or more persons having an equal and the highest number of votes for either of such offices, the governor shall, by proclamation, order a new election to fill said offices.

For what purpose is the governor present? He is to witness the canvass and declare its result, and his declaration of its result is the certificate he gives, and his proclamation declaring the election of such person. He is not there by way of idle ceremony any more than the two Houses of Congress are present at the opening of the envelopes as a mere idle ceremony. He is there to do what is required of him to do—to witness the canvass and to declare its result. But if this be not so in the matter of members of Congress of Oregon, it is unquestionably so with regard to the final determination, decision, and declaration of the result of the election of electors. The secretary of state is to canvass. No duty is imposed on him to declare any result whatever. He is to canvass, and what is that canvass? I copied—perhaps it was an idle thing—from the approved lexicographers the definition of the word. Worcester says:

> 1. To sift; to examine; to scrutinize.
> I have made careful search, and *canvassed* the matter with all possible diligence.—*Woodward.*
> 2. To debate; to discuss; to agitate.
> They *canvassed* the matter one way and t'other.—*L'Estrange.*
> To solicit votes from; to bespeak.

And Webster traces the origin of the word to the old French word *canebasser*, and defines it thus:

> To examine curiously; to search or sift out, as canvass in Old English, and probably in Old French, signified also a sieve, a straining-cloth.
> 1. To sift; to strain; to examine thoroughly; to search or scrutinize; as, to *canvass* the votes for senators.
> 2. To take up for discussion; to debate.
> An opinion that we are likely soon to *canvass.*—*Sir W. Hamilton.*
> 3. To go through in the way of solicitation; as, to *canvass* a district for votes.

Here is no necessary implication that the word means "to determine the result." It is to examine, scrutinize, tabulate, and formulate, but not necessarily to ascertain and determine results, and so the word is used in Florida, and so the word is used in Louisiana, and so the corresponding word "examine," as I shall presently show you, is used in Massachusetts, and so the word is used in Oregon. When we come to the sixtieth section of the statute we find that this view is confirmed. Let us now return to the sixtieth section:

> The votes for the electors shall be given, received, returned, and canvassed as the same are given, returned, and canvassed for members of Congress.

It does not say "given, received, returned, canvassed, and declared," or "given, received, returned, canvassed, and certified." It says, "given, received, returned, and canvassed," and the provision with regard to the final determination and decision is contained in the next clause of the section:

> The secretary of state shall prepare two lists of the names of the electors *elected,* and affix the seal of the State to the same.

Two lists, not three; the secretary of state, not the governor. It is not under the act of Congress that this is required, for the act of Congress calls for no great seal of Oregon, and calls for no certificate of the secretary of state of Oregon. The act of Congress calls for a certificate which may be without a seal, which may be without the attestation of a secretary. The act of Congress simply provides that it shall be the duty of the executive of each State to cause three lists of the names of the electors of such State to be made and certified. But Oregon says :

> The secretary of state shall prepare two lists of the names of the electors *elected*, and affix the seal of the State to the same. Such lists shall be signed by the governor and secretary, and by the latter delivered to the college of electors at the hour of their meeting on such first Wednesday of December.

And here are the lists prepared under this section, to which are signed the names of the governor and secretary, under the great seal of the State, declaring that William H. Odell, John C. Cartwright, and E. A. Cronin are the electors elected:

> I, L. F. Grover, governor of the State of Oregon, do hereby certify that at a general election held in said State on the 7th day of November, A. D. 1876, William H. Odell received 15,206 votes, John C. Cartwright received 15,214 votes, E. A. Cronin received 14,157 votes, for electors of President and Vice-President of the United States ; being the highest number of votes cast at said election for persons eligible, under the Constitution of the United States, to be appointed electors of President and Vice-President of the United States, they are hereby declared duly elected electors as aforesaid for the State of Oregon.

This is the voice of Oregon, according to the judgment of this Commission in the cases of Florida and Louisiana. Its truthfulness has been impeached; but one thing I am certain I may say in this presence: it is as true as the certificates which have received the approval of this Commission coming from Florida and Louisiana.

They are duly elected. They are hereby declared—

duly elected electors as aforesaid for the State of Oregon.

LA FAYETTE GROVER,
Governor of Oregon.

Attest:

S. F. CHADWICK,
 Secretary of State of Oregon.

But, says my learned friend, the secretary of state has simply signed it as a witness. Not so. He signed it in attestation of the truth of the fact. He is a participant in the declaration thereby. He has attached the great seal of the State. It is the act of the governor and the act of the secretary in the ordinary form, and being such, it is in compliance with the sixtieth section of the statute of Oregon, and at the same time with the one hundred and thirty-sixth section of the Revised Statutes of the United States, and thus constitutes the final and conclusive decision and determination of the vote of the State of Oregon, according to the only evidence provided by law by which this tribunal can communicate with the State of Oregon. The laws of the United States have provided but a single method by which this tribunal can communicate with Oregon. It is in the one hundred and thirty-sixth section of the Revised Statutes of the United States. There is the method pointed out by law by which the voice of Oregon may speak to this tribunal, to the two Houses of Congress, and which this tribunal, standing in the place of the two Houses of Congress, may hear as the voice of Oregon, as has been decided in the cases of Florida and Louisiana.

I submit this proposition in connection, however, with a decision in the State of Massachusetts.

Mr. Commissioner THURMAN. Who, by the laws of Oregon, had the custody of the great seal of the State ?

Mr. HOADLY. I am unable to answer the question.

Mr. MATTHEWS. The secretary of state, by the constitution.

Mr. HOADLY. It has been answered probably correctly. I do not mean by "probably correctly" to impeach my learned friend; I mean——

Mr. MATTHEWS. The constitution says so.

Mr. HOADLY. I have not looked at it; but I say there is nothing in the laws of Oregon which requires any such certificate or exemplification as is presented by the supporters of certificate No. 1. It cannot be found there. There is the provision of Oregon, section sixty, and the abstract, which is simply a certified statement of the number of votes received at the election, is a provision *aliunde* the laws of Oregon, although it was within the envelope opened by the President of the Senate.

Mr. Representative LAWRENCE. The secretary of state can certify at common law.

Mr. HOADLY. But the laws of Oregon have determined and prescribed who shall certify to this tribunal. That certificate we present.

Now I call your honors' attention to the opinion of the judges of the supreme judicial court of Massachusetts, signed by them all—Horace Gray, John Wells, James D. Colt, Seth Ames, Marcus Morton, William C. Endicott, and Charles Devens, jr., Boston, March 5, 1875—to be found on page 600 of the one hundred and seventeenth volume of Massachusetts Reports:

> The seventh chapter of the general statutes has constituted the governor and council a board to *examine*, as soon as may be after receiving them, the returns of votes from the various cities and towns for district attorneys and other officers named in this article of the constitution, and requires the governor forthwith to transmit to such persons as appear to be chosen to such offices a certificate of such choice, signed by the governor and countersigned by the secretary of the commonwealth.

Notice, the governor and council are obliged to examine the returns; it does not say " to examine and declare the result," but " to examine:"

> The nature of the duties thus imposed and the very terms of the statute show that they are to be performed without unnecessary delay, and that the certificate issued by the governor to any person appearing upon such examination to be elected is the final and conclusive evidence of the determination of the governor and council as to his election.

I submit that by parity of reasoning the certificate or list signed by the governor and secretary of state of Oregon, under the great seal of the State, and by the latter delivered to the college of electors at the hour of their meeting on the first Wednesday of December, is the final and conclusive evidence of the determination of the governor and secretary as to their election. Why are the governor and secretary required to sign these lists ? It is that the chief executive of the State and the canvassing-officer shall unite in declaring who are elected. The secretary, the canvassing-officer, is required to prepare two lists of the names of electors elected, and to affix the great seal of the State to the same; and the governor, in whose presence the canvass is made, must also sign, and together their signatures, with the great seal of the State, constitute the final and conclusive, irrefragable evidence who are the electors of the State of Oregon.

I pass from this proposition to consider another. It is a familiar proposition of law that when a commission or certificate of election has been delivered to an officer, and he accepts it, and enters upon the performance of the duties of that office, he becomes an officer *de jure et de facto*, and is to be so treated in all courts, in all places, under all circumstances, except when his title may be impeached by *quo warranto*, *certiorari*, or proceeding under a statute for contest. This evidence is here presented by E. A. Cronin, J. N. T. Miller, and John Parker. They come here, Cronin, as a certificated elector, having vouched in Miller and Parker to vote with him in consequence of the refusal of Cartwright and Odell to act with him. I will stop a moment simply to say that in my judgment the statements contained in the record in connection with certificate No. 2 are confirmed and placed beyond the possibility of a doubt by the statements contained in certificate No. 1. Mr. Cronin says (and he presents the authentic, official advice to this Commission of his election and the election of Odell and Cartwright) that they refused to act with him, and they say that they were elected with Watts, and that they organized with Watts by accepting the resignation of Watts and electing into the place, thus made vacant by the declination of Watts, Mr. Watts himself.

I respectfully submit, Mr. President and gentlemen of the Commission, that there is no contradiction between these certificates. Mr. Cronin was in possession of the official decision and determination of the canvassers of Oregon. He proposed to act. Mr. Watts's name is not in the official decision and determination of the canvassers of Oregon, but was excluded by them. Mr. Watts proceeded to act with Odell and Cartwright. They did not say, as my learned friend who closed the argument for the objectors would have this Commission to understand, that they (Odell and Cartwright with Cronin) made the board, and that Cronin refused to act with them. There can be no refusal without an opportunity. They proceeded to exclude Cronin by accepting Watts's resignation.

Mr. Commissioner ABBOTT. Is there any allegation anywhere on that certificate that they refused to act with Cronin or that Cronin refused to act with them?

Mr. HOADLY. Cronin's name is not in that certificate. He is ignored utterly and entirely. Odell and Cartwright state that they acted with Watts, that they accepted Watts's resignation, and elected Watts to take the place of Watts, all the while it being shown by the official decision and determination that Cronin was ready to act, Cronin alleging, with Miller and Parker, that they refused to act with him, and they alleging, without naming him, that they refused to act with him by alleging that they did act without him and with Watts.

I was wrong in saying that their record does not name Cronin. It does name him, but it names him to confirm the statement I have just made. Certificate No. 1 says that Odell and Cartwright required of the governor and the secretary of state certified lists, which both those officers refused to give them, thus adding to their official decision and determination a refusal to give such evidence to anybody else.

And so far as evidence *aliunde* the lists may be considered (a question which this Commission may yet be called upon to decide) they do say:

And being informed that such lists had been delivered to one E. A. Cronin, by said secretary of state, we, each and all—

That is, Watts, Odell, and Cartwright, each and all—

demanded such certified lists of said E. A. Cronin; but he then and there refused to deliver or to exhibit such certified lists to us or either of us.

And, therefore, Mr. Cronin produces the lists which do not contain the name of Watts.

I was going on to say that a certificated or commissioned officer who enters upon the discharge of duty is an officer *de jure et de facto* in all tribunals, in all places, with reference to any action of his in his office, until challenged by writ of *quo warranto*, or contest of election, or writ of *certiorari*. The lists provided for by the one hundred and thirty-sixth section of the Revised Statutes and the sixtieth section of the statutes of Oregon being held by E. A. Cronin did make him an elector *de jure et de facto* as to all persons, except the State challenging upon *quo warranto*, or except upon *certiorari*, or except upon contest of election; and to that proposition I desire to direct a few remarks, which will be mainly by way of referring to authority.

I will read first from the case of the People *v.* Miller, 16 Michigan Reports, page 56. It is the opinion of his honor Mr. Justice Christiancy, concurred in by Judge Cooley and Judge Campbell, and I am sure I need not say in this hall that an opinion from such a source, with such confirmation, cannot be challenged with safety in any court of justice in the land.

The certificate of election, whether rightfully or wrongfully given, confers upon the person holding it the *prima-facie* right of holding it for the term, and this *prima-facie* right is subject to be defeated only by his voluntary surrender of the office, or by a judicial determination of the right. We do not mean to say that if the respondent had abandoned or should abandon his claim to the office under the election, witnessed by the certificate admitting the relator's right, that the board might not have received and approved the relator's bond, but they certainly had no jurisdiction to try the validity of the election as between the relator and the respondent, and in such a contest the certificate of election was conclusive upon them until the right should be judicially tried.

The head-note or syllabus of the case is:

The certificate of election, whether rightfully or wrongfully given by the board of canvassers, confers upon the person holding it the *prima-facie* right to the office until his right is rejected by a voluntary surrender or by a judicial determination against him.

This proposition has been three times decided in the State of Pennsylvania, in cases to which I will direct your honors, beginning with the case of Commonwealth *ex relatione* Ross *v.* Baxter, 35 Pennsylvania State Reports, p. 263:

A return by the election-officers that A B received a majority of the votes for a township office is legal and *prima-facie* evidence of his title to the office; and it can only be set aside by proceedings for a false return under the act of July 2, 1839. It cannot be inquired into by *quo warranto*.

So in the forty-first volume Pennsylvania State Reports, Hulseman and Brinkworth *v.* Rems and Siner, page 401, a case of great interest in many respects. I read from pages 400 and 401. It was an action in equity for an injunction, for in Pennsylvania it is held that a conflict between two officers claiming in conflicting rights may be decided under certain circumstances by injunction in equity.

We have, therefore, no ground left for our interference but the single one that the return judges included in their enumeration returns purporting to be from three companies of volunteers, which were forgeries. We admit, therefore, that the evidence proves that these certificates of the election of the defendants are founded in manifest fraud, the forgery of some unknown person, but we do not find that the defendants had any hand in it; and we trust they had not. Can we on this account interfere and declare the certificates void?

Mr. Commissioner HOAR. Who were the defendants in that case?

Mr. HOADLY. It was a proceeding in equity by John Hulseman and George Brinkworth, citizens and qualified voters, against James Rems and Charles B. Siner.

Mr. Commissioner HOAR. Were they the persons claiming the office?

Mr. HOADLY. They were the persons claiming the office and holding the certificates of election.

According to our laws the election has passed completely through all its forms, the result has been in due form declared and certified, and the defendants have received their certificates of election, and are entitled to their seats as members of the common council. The title-papers of their offices are complete, and have the signatures of the proper officers of the law; and if they are vitiated by any mistake or fraud in the process that has produced them, this raises a case to be tried by the forms of "a contested election" before the tribunal appointed by law to try such questions, and not by the ordinary forms of legal or equitable process before the usual judicial tribunals.

In Kerr and others *vs.* Trego and others, 47 Pennsylvania State Reports, page 292, the syllabus is:

In all bodies that are under law, where there has been an authorized election for the office in controversy, the certificate of election which is sanctioned by law or usage is the *prima facie* written title to the office, and can only be set aside by a contest in the forms prescribed by law.

To the same effect the case of The People *vs.* Cook, in 4 Selden's Reports, page 68:

The certificate of the board of canvassers may be conclusive of the election of an officer in a controversy arising collaterally, or between the party holding it and a stranger. But between the people and the party in an action to impeach it, it is only *prima facie* evidence of the right. It is the will of the electors and not the certificate which gives the right to the office.

So again in 33 New York Reports; I will read from page 606, the case of Hadley *vs.* The Mayor. It was a case of a policeman suing for salary. In other words, it was an action in which the question arose, as it arises here, collaterally; it did not arise by *quo warranto;* it did not arise by *certiorari;* it did not arise by contest; it arose as here:

The second exception was to the decision by which the court excluded the inspector's returns. The object, I suppose, was to show that the returns elected Mr. Quackenbush and not Mr. Perry. But the law having committed to the common council the duty of canvassing the returns and determining the result of the election from them, and the council having performed that duty and made a determination, the question as to the effect of the returns was not open for a determination by a jury in an action in which the title of the officer came up collaterally. If the question had arisen upon an action in the nature of a *quo warranto* information, the evidence would have been competent. But it would be intolerable to allow a party affected by the acts of a person claiming to be an officer to go behind the official determination to prove that such official determination arose out of mistake or fraud.

So also in Dutcher's Reports, New Jersey, page 355, the case of The State *vs.* The Clerk of the County of Passaic:

A *quo warranto* is the legal and usual mode in which title to office may be tried and finally adjudicated.

The determination of the board of county canvassers has no such final effect as to interfere with a full investigation of the result of an election upon a writ of *quo warranto.*

Again, on page 356:

In the present instance, the writ appears to have been designed as ancillary to the application for a mandamus, in order to bring before the court the decision of the board of county canvassers and the evidence upon which it was founded. That application having been denied, and the office having been filled, a decision upon the validity of the proceedings of the board would be nugatory. It would neither vacate the commission which has been issued nor avail the plaintiff in any subsequent proceedings which may be instituted to determine his rights. If the determination of the board of county canvassers partakes at all of the character of a judicial act, it certainly has no such final or conclusive effect as to interfere with the full and free investigation of the legal result of the election upon a writ of *quo warranto.*

So in Minnesota, in the fifteenth volume of Minnesota Reports, page 455, the decision of a court, one of the judges of which is now a member of the United States Senate, (Mr. McMillan,) State of Minnesota *ex rel.* R. A. Briggs *vs.* O. A. Churchill, auditor, &c.:

Under the laws of this State the result of the canvass by a board of county canvassers is a decision and determination of the election of the persons whom they declare to be elected.

The abstract of the canvass of the votes in the form prescribed in the statute is the authentic and official evidence of the canvass by the board by which the county auditor is to be governed in issuing the certificates of election.

When a certificate of election is issued and delivered by the auditor to a person declared to be elected to a county office, in accordance with the official canvass, regular upon its face, the certificate is conclusive evidence of the right of the person holding it to the office to which it shows him to have been elected, *except* in a proceeding where this right is directly in issue. To go behind a certificate thus issued and determine the correctness of the canvass involves the determination of the right of the holder of the certificate to the office ; this cannot be done upon mandamus.

And so in three cases in the twenty-fifth volume of the Louisiana Reports. Certainly whatever authority this volume may have, whatever respect or want of respect may be shown to it, it is not for those who have sustained before this tribunal the acts of the State government of which the authors of this volume are part and parcel, to challenge the decision made by the court of which Mr. Ludeling was chief-justice. In The State *vs.* Wharton, page 3, they say :

Where two sets of officers claim to be the legal board of returning-officers, it is difficult to conceive why this is not a judicial question.

In Collins *vs.* Knoblock and others, page 263, they say :

The adjustment and compilation of election-returns, determining the number of legal and illegal votes cast for each candidate, declaring the result of an election and furnishing the successful candidate with the proper certificate, in short superintending and controlling all the details of an election, belong properly to the political department of the government.

In The State on the relation of Bonner *vs.* Lynch, page 267, they say :

The defendant having been returned by the legal returning-board of the State as elected judge of the fourth district court of New Orleans, and upon that return the acting governor having issued a commission to him according to law, it cannot be said that one holding an office under such a commission has intruded into or unlawfully holds the office.

In the twentieth volume of Vermont Reports, page 473, in the case of Overseer of the poor of Norwich *vs.* Halsey J. Yarrington, the court say :

When a person acting as justice of the peace holds a commission for that office from the governor, under the seal of the State, the court will not go behind that commission to inquire whether he had been duly appointed to that office by the general assembly of the State or not.

So in three cases in the State of Ohio.

Mr. Commissioner MILLER. That was not in a proceeding directly against him to invalidate the act.

Mr. HOADLY. Of course if it had been a *quo warranto*, a *certiorari*, or a contest, the question would have arisen judicially and properly ; but it was not. It was a complaint in bastardy, where the woman for the space of thirty days had neglected to charge the putative father, and a controversy thereupon arose.

So in three cases in the State of Ohio, in which it was decided by the supreme court of that State each time that a proceeding to try a title to an office was a judicial proceeding. In one of these cases the supreme judicial court of the State of Ohio were called upon to pass upon one of the most important questions that ever arose in the State. It had been held in the county of Wayne that John K. McBride was elected probate judge of the county of Wayne by reason of the decision that the law allowing the soldiers in the field, out of the State of Ohio, to vote, was not in conformity with the constitution of the State of Ohio ; and the cause was taken by writ of error to the supreme court of Ohio. The first question that court was called upon to decide was whether this was a judicial question which could be removed by petition

in error, in accordance with our forms of practice, to that court; and
the court decided that it was—that a proceeding to contest the election
of John K. McBride was a judicial proceeding, and the commission
having been delivered to him, the decision and ascertainment of who
was the duly-elected probate judge of the county of Wayne was a judicial determination and decision in that cause.   To the same effect is the
case of The State *vs.* The Commissioners of Marion County, (14 Ohio State
Reports, 578,) and the case of Powers *vs.* Reed and others, (19 Ohio State
Reports, 205, 206,) in which the question that arose was whether the
declaration of the result of an election, upon which depended the change
of the county-seat of Wood County from Bowling Green to Perrysburgh,
or from Perrysburgh to Bowling Green, was a judicial determination,
and it was argued before the supreme court of Ohio, as your honors will
find by reference to that case, by one of the first lawyers in the Western
States, a gentleman who had filled the highest places in the judicial
department of the State of Ohio—I mean Judge Ranney—and whose
abilities are equal to the positions he has held, that that question was a
political question and not a judicial question.   But his argument was
overruled by the unanimous opinion of the court.

So in the case of Morgan *vs.* Quackenbush, which was cited to us the
other day—I will read a passage or two—decided by Mr. Justice Ira
Harris.   I will read from page 72 of 22 Barbour:

> The certificate of a board of canvassers is evidence of the person upon whom the
> office has been conferred.   Upon all questions arising collaterally, or between a party
> holding a certificate and a stranger, it is conclusive evidence ; but in a proceeding to
> try the right to office, it is only *prima facie* evidence.

Again, on page 79—

> If the certificate of the canvassers declaring Mr. Perry elected vested him with *color-*
> *able* title to the office, as I think it did, so that he had a right to enter upon the dis-
> charge of its duties, another effect of that decision was to exclude the defendant,
> Quackenbush, as well as everybody else, from the office.   They could not hold as ten-
> ants in common, each having a legal right to perform its functions.   If Mr. Perry be-
> came mayor *de facto*, the defendant Quackenbush, whatever his right, could not be
> mayor in fact at the same time.

My proposition is that E. A. Cronin became vested with the title and
the office, if it may be called an office, at least with the right to discharge
the trusts and functions of an elector, by the certificate of the governor
of Oregon, attested by the secretary of state under the great seal of the
State, and that this made him *de facto* elector, so that the office could
not be held at the same time as tenant in common or otherwise by John
W. Watts.   He was the incumbent ; and the only reply that I care to
make to the argument which is founded on the statute of Oregon with
regard to vacancies is, that the statute relates to and authorizes an
incumbent to resign and does not authorize a claimant to resign, even
though he be claiming *de jure* against an incumbent *de facto* holding.   I
am not now alluding to the statute of Oregon with regard to the election
of electors, but to the statute in regard to filling vacancies in State offices.
That I do not think your honors will find has any reference to this case
at all under any circumstances.

Again, in Coolidge *vs.* Brigham, 1 Allen, 335, Chief-Justice Bigelow,
pronouncing the opinion of the whole court, said:

> The magistrate before whom the action was originally brought was an officer *de*
> *facto*.   He was not a mere usurper, undertaking to exercise the duties of an office to
> which he had no color of title.   He had an apparent right to the office.   He had a com-
> mission under the great seal of the State, bearing the signature of the governor, with
> his certificate thereon, that the oaths of office had been duly administered, and in all
> respects appearing to have been issued with the formalities required by the constitu-

tion and laws of the commonwealth. He was thus invested with the apparent muniments of full title to the office. Although he might not have been an officer *de jure*, that is, legally appointed and entitled to hold and enjoy the office by a right which could not on due proceedings being had be impeached or invalidated, he was nevertheless in possession, under a commission *prima facie* regular and legal, and performing the functions of the office under a color and show of right. This made him a justice of the peace *de facto*.

So your honors will find, unless something can be discovered by more diligent search than I have made, and I have been very diligent, that when a man holds a certificate or a commission, whichever may be the ordinary evidence of title, and enters upon the possession of the office, he is an officer *de facto*, the office is full, there can be no other officer *de facto*. His title can only be impeached judicially. It may be taken from him by *quo warranto ;* it may be taken by *certiorari ;* it may be taken from him by proceedings to contest his election; but in the absence of these three methods of proceeding his title is perfect against all the world. Where is the *quo warranto* against E. A. Cronin? It may be said that there was a very short time in which to try it. No shorter, your honors, than was given in the case of Florida. Where is the *certiorari ?* Where was the proceeding to contest? Here comes E. A. Cronin with the certificate of election under the great seal of Oregon, signed by the secretary of state, signed by the governor, and no judicial proceeding to impeach it. Is this tribunal a judicial tribunal? And were it a judicial tribunal, long ago the frauds that were offered to be proven to your honors in the case of Louisiana would have been heard and redressed. Were this a judicial tribunal, long ago the wrongs that were done in Florida would have been heard and redressed. But this is a legislative body, or part of a legislative body—delegates from the legislative body of the United States— without power to exercise any judicial function whatever. You cannot try upon *quo warranto;* you cannot try upon *certiorari;* you cannot consider as upon proceedings to contest elections. The judicial power of the United States has been confided to the judges of the Supreme Court of the United States and of the inferior courts ; and this is not the Supreme Court of the United States nor any other court, inferior or otherwise.

If it be thought that my argument is inconsistent with what has been argued by others in the cases of Florida and Louisiana, I have to reply that it is consistent with perfect respect to the decisions of this tribunal. It is not for counsel to exhibit such disrespect to this tribunal as to attempt to overrule or overthrow its decisions. The object of this argument is to enforce the decisions of this tribunal and cause their application to the State of Oregon in such way that the decisions made in Florida and Louisiana shall not have the effect to reverse the judgment which the people of the United States on the 7th of November last pronounced. Your determination, which I have the right to cite as authority, written in your decisions, pronounced as the result of your conscientious examination, is here higher authority than any expression of persuasive opinion, however cogent, that I might quote from the decisions of courts, however respectable; and therefore I commend it to this tribunal as final and conclusive evidence of the principles and rules of action which this tribunal ought to adhere to and apply in this case.

But, if otherwise, I submit that, upon the merits of this controversy, waiving for the present the propositions I have made, your honors are required to decide in favor of the Cronin vote. Here I desire to call your honors' attention to two propositions: First, that the papers inclosed with the certificate No. 1 are of no value as evidence by being in that certificate or otherwise unless they are shown to be duly authenticated in conformity with the laws of Oregon. I read from section 78 of Freeman on Judgments:

Nothing can be made a matter of record by calling it by that name, nor by inserting it among the proper matters of record.

And from 27 Connecticut Reports, Nichols *vs.* City of Bridgeport. This is not on my brief. The question was only called to my attention by hearing the debate of the objectors to certificate No. 2.

Mr. Commissioner GARFIELD. The point you are making now is on your brief?

Mr. HOADLY. It is not. I did not know what was contained in certificate No. 1 until this afternoon. I read from 27 Connecticut, page 465:

Between the reservation of the case and the term to which it had been continued to await our advice, it is obvious that there were no proceedings in the superior court, and that whatever proceedings took place in the case were in this court, and consequently that there were no proceedings, excepting the continuance of it, which it was the duty or province of the clerk of the superior court, or which it would have been proper for him to record as a part of the doings of that court; and, plainly, it is only of the doings of that court that the plaintiff in error can complain on this writ of error. Such being the case, the reservation by that court cannot properly be regarded as a part of its record, notwithstanding it has been inserted, as if it were a part of it, by the clerk, or certified by him to be such; for if it is not, in its nature, a proper method of record in the case, it cannot be made such by the mere circumstance that it has been so inserted or attested. He cannot make it a record, if, from its qualities, it is not so, either by treating it as such or calling it by that name.

And, secondly, a canvass is not even *prima facie* evidence of eligibility, as held by the court of appeals of Kentucky in Patterson *vs.* Miller, &c., 2 Metc., Ky., 497:

The certificate which the examining-board issues to a candidate that he is elected to the office of sheriff—although conclusive evidence that he was elected thereto, unless his election be contested before the proper board—is not even *prima facie* evidence that he was eligible to the office.

In the next place, the question arises, going behind these matters and going to what, if evidence were received, might be called the merits of the controversy, the question arises, what is the law of Oregon—not the general American public law, but the law of Oregon with regard to the election of electors under circumstances like the present? It has been argued and seriously claimed that the governor of Oregon had no right to pass upon the eligibility of electors; that he was bound to see the Constitution of the United States violated; that he was imbecile, without power. My friends seem to deal, as their stock in trade, in want of power, imbecility. It was the imbecility of this tribunal, according to their argument, which prevented the examination of the truth of the fact with regard to Florida and Louisiana, and now it is the imbecility of the governor of Oregon which will enable this tribunal to lend its aid to a violation of the Constitution of the United States, although the governor refused to be a partaker in that wrong. Let us see.

It is admitted that the law of Indiana is that where there is an ineligible elector, the governor not only may but must take cognizance of the fact and refuse the commission. It is admitted that this is the law of Indiana; that the governor not only may but must recall a commission once issued when the evidence of ineligibility growing out of a constitutional disqualification is presented. If it be law in Indiana, why is it not law in Oregon? It is law in Arkansas; it is law in Missouri; it is law in Rhode Island; it is law in Massachusetts; it is law in Oregon;

and the authority for the statement is the solemn adjudication of the supreme court of each one of these States ; in all but two, of the court, judicially speaking, in a controversy between parties ; in two, speaking in obedience to the constitution and laws of the State in answer to a demand by the governor for judicial information. It is the law of Arkansas ; so held in two cases in the first volume of Arkansas reports, (Pike's Reports,) and one of those cases is that which Senator Kelly began to read this afternoon, page 21, Taylor *vs.* The Governor, which was a case where, by the law of Arkansas, a defaulter in office was disqualified. There it was held by the supreme court of that State that the governor had a right to take notice of the disqualification and withhold the commission, and not only that he had the right to do it, but that it was his duty to do it. In the same volume, in a later case, the exact proposition now under discussion was at great length considered. I refer to the case of Hawkins *vs.* The Governor, pages 570 to 595. There it is said :

Again, the executive is bound to see that the laws are faithfully executed; and he has taken an oath of office to support the constitution. How can he perform this duty if he has no discretion left him in regard to granting commissions ? For should the legislature appoint a person constitutionally ineligible to hold any office of profit or trust, would the executive be bound to commission him ? and that, too, when his ineligibility was clearly and positively proven ? In such case the exercise of his discretion must be admitted, or you make him, not the guardian, but the violator of the Constitution. What, then, becomes of his oath of office ?

Your honors, long, long ago, and by one of the greatest men who ever sat in judgment in the United States of America, a man whose word is law to-day, though the grass has been growing over his grave now for more than half a century, the law was thus laid down :

It is argued—

Said Chief-Justice Parsons, in 5 Massachusetts, 533—

that the legislature can not give a construction to the constitution, cannot make laws repugnant to it. But every department of Government invested with certain constitutional powers must, in the first instance, but not exclusively, be the judge of its powers, or it could not act.

In accordance with the same principle, in the great case of Martin *vs.* Mott, 12 Wheaton, 29, the President of the United States was declared to be the final and conclusive judge whether a case of insurrection existed calling for the use of the military and naval forces of the United States for its suppression. So it will be found in the case of The State *ex relatione* Bartley *vs.* Fletcher, 39 Missouri, 388 ; and if your honors will refer to the case of The State *vs.* Vail, 53 Missouri, 97, which was cited this afternoon by Mr. Lawrence, you will find that the two cases can stand together. The case of The State *vs.* Vail does not overrule the Indiana case of Gulick *vs.* New, but cites it and distinguishes it. But let me read a passage from 53 Missouri to show that the case in Indiana is there cited and not disapproved :

But in the case in Indiana, it is conceded that where the candidate receiving the highest number of votes is ineligible by reason of a cause which the voters were not bound to know, such as nonage, want of naturalization, etc, the result is a failure to elect. * * * * * *It is unnecessary to determine whether it would be the rule, in any case of disqualifications, whether patent or latent.*

Now come back to the case of The State on the relation of Bartley *vs.* Fletcher, 39 Mo., 388. The opinion was pronounced by Mr. Justice Wagner. After reciting that it is by the constitution of the State made the duty of the governor to commission all officers not otherwise provided by law, that this is clearly an exercise of political power of a ministerial character, the court say :

The governor is bound to see that the laws are faithfully executed, and he has taken.

an oath to support the constitution. In the correct and legitimate performance of his duty he must inevitably have a discretion in regard to granting commissions; for should a person be elected or appointed who was constitutionally ineligible to hold any office of profit or trust, would the executive be bound to commission him when his ineligibility was clearly and positively proven? If he is denied the exercise of any discretion in such case, he is made the violator of the Constitution, not its guardian. Of what avail, then, is his oath of office? Or if he has positive and satisfactory evidence that no election has been held in a county, shall he be required to violate the law and issue a commission to a person not elected, because a clerk has certified to the election? In granting a commission the governor may go behind the commission to determine whether an applicant is entitled to receive a commission or not where the objection to the right of the applicant to receive it rests upon the ground that a constitutional prohibition is interposed. (Gulick *vs.* New, 14 Ind., 93.)

The issuing of a commission is an act by the executive in his political capacity, and is one of the means employed to enable him to execute the laws and carry on the appropriate functions of the State; and for the manner in which he executes this duty he is in nowise amenable to the judiciary. The court can no more interfere with executive discretion than the legislature or executive can with judicial discretion.

The granting of a commission by the executive is not a mere ministerial duty, but an official act imposed by the constitution, and is an investiture of authority in the person receiving it. We are of the opinion, therefore, that mandamus will not lie against the governor in a case like this.

So in the case in Maine, 7 Greenl., 497. In Maine, the language of the constitution is that a *majority* of the votes shall elect, and yet to the opinion which was read by Senator Kelly this afternoon declaring that by that constitutional provision a majority of votes for *eligible* candidates is meant are signed the honored names of Prentiss Mellen and Nathan Weston, with their associate, Albion K. Parris. Tell me that the opinion that votes for ineligible candidates are void stands upon no authority in America, when the name of one of the greatest judicial lights that ever illumined the sky of legal jurisprudence in New England and of another second only to him are signed to that opinion!

This opinion comes first to us from one of the signers of the Declaration of American Independence. The first judgment ever pronounced in the United States to the effect that a million of people voting for an ineligible candidate cannot defeat the mandate of the Constitution to elect, came from Samuel Chase, who long presided at the head of the judiciary of Maryland, and as a member of the Supreme Court of the United States, against whose temper much was said, but of whose judicial judgments there has passed into history no sound criticism whatever.

It has been said here this afternoon that a few insignificant opinions are to that effect. Yes, they are the insignificant opinions of Samuel Chase, and Prentiss Mellen, and Nathan Weston, and Albion K. Parris, and Samuel E. Perkins, who, for a score of years, has been a judge of the supreme court of Indiana, and now by the vote of the people last October has entered upon another term of six years. The judicial opinions of these men are those upon which this doctrine rests. The time may come when Justice, blind, deaf, and robbed of the rest of her powers, may be wafted into that Nirvana of intellectual inanition which the majority of the human race believe is reserved for that which is absolutely perfect when its earthly work is done. On that day the names of these great jurists and the recollection of the wise counsels they have left us will be forgotten among those who walk in the ways of American jurisprudence according to the traditions of the fathers, because on that day, but not sooner, a violation of the Constitution will become a muniment of office.

But I was considering the question whether the governor had not furnished to us the final and conclusive evidence of the law of Oregon.

and I had cited the case in Arkansas, the case in Missouri; I had not cited, but I do now refer your honors to the opinion of Mr. Justice Cooley, as stated in his work on Constitutional Limitations, page 41. I had cited the opinions of the judges of Maine, in the seventh volume of Greenleaf's Reports. I now ask your attention to the very recent action of the judges and executive of the State of Rhode Island, in the case of Corliss, which is precisely the action which was taken in the case of Cronin by the governor of Oregon. Had the governor of Oregon been invested by the constitution of Oregon with the right to call for the opinions of the judges, and upon that call received them, the action of Rhode Island and the action of Oregon would have been precisely parallel. In Rhode Island the governor was confronted by the fact that George H. Corliss was a centennial commissioner and that his name was on the roll of those receiving the highest number of votes for electors. Did he give him the certificate? Did he refuse the certificate? He refused. He called upon the judges of Rhode Island for their judgment and advice. I have furnished the law on this subject in my brief, and you will find, by reference to it, that the advice was given to him not as a judicial judgment, but as advice for the guidance of his executive action, and he acted. He called the legislature together. He did not give the certificate to Corliss; he withheld it from Corliss. He called the legislature together, and they elected Slater, who received the certificate by force of the election by the legislature. So in Oregon; Senator Kelly read you this afternoon the letter from the chief-justice of Oregon, from which it appears that in the State of Oregon it has been judicially determined that the governor has a right, although a district attorney may be in office exercising the powers and discharging the duties of the office, to declare the office vacant, and, where the constitution has worked a vacation of the office by reason of the incompatibility of the two officers, to appoint a successor, and this action of the governor in Oregon, in the case of Gibbs *vs.* Bellinger, was sustained by the supreme court of Oregon. The opinion would have been pronounced and published in the reports long ago but for the death of the lamented Judge Thayer, by whom it was expected to be written.

So, I say that in Oregon as well as in Rhode Island, in Maine, in Arkansas, in Missouri, we are fortified in the opinion that the action of the governor in this case was proper, and that it was and is the action of the executive, conclusive and final as evidence to this court of what the law of Oregon is. Why, consider for one moment. Suppose the governor had given a certificate to Mr. Watts, notwithstanding his disqualification, would not that have been evidence that Mr. Watts was the elector? Would it not have been cited as evidence that the law of Oregon was that, notwithstanding the disqualification, Mr. Watts had a right to the certificate? Was not the governor called upon, compelled, to elect which horn of the dilemma, if it were such, he would choose; which view of the law at least he would take? Could he avoid it? He must say, by giving the certificate to Watts, "Notwithstanding the Constitution of the United States, and although the constitution of Oregon says that I am to maintain the laws, notwithstanding this man is disqualified by law, he shall have the certificate." What is the constitution of Oregon in this particular? Let me read the passage. Section 10, article 5, of the executive department, says, that "he" (the governor) "shall take care that the laws be faithfully executed." And he is sworn to support the Constitution of the United States and of Oregon; yet it is said that he, bound to see that the laws were faithfully executed and to maintain the Constitution of the United States, violated his duty in not giving to one disqualified by the Constitution of the United States a certificate of election!

In the next place there was no vacancy into which Watts could be elected. First, there was an officer, if it may be called such, an elector holding office *de facto*, and I refer to the case read the other day by the learned senior counsel on the other side from the eleventh volume of Sergeant and Rawle. I refer to the passages which were read by him to show that when there is in office an officer *de facto* he completes the whole circumference of the office and occupies it all, and that there can be no vacancy and can be no intrusion upon him while he occupies, otherwise than by the action of a court of justice acting judicially.

Also, there was no vacancy, for the reason that by the laws of the United States contemplation is made of two contingencies, namely, a failure to elect, and a vacancy when the electors meet; and this was the first of these two cases. Upon this subject I have already been heard in the Florida case by the Commission.

My learned friend, if he will allow me to call him such, [Mr. Evarts,] informed us the other day that there is no choice; we have to say office filled or office vacant; there is no *tertium quid*, no *via media* in which our footsteps may be safely directed. But such is not the law of the Senate of the United States as held in this chamber. I say that the Senate of the United States, from the foundation of the Government, has never deviated from the rule that the office of Senator cannot be filled by the appointment of the governor of a State when the legislature has failed to elect an incumbent during its session, as is shown by Lanman's case. Clarke & Hall, 871.

But I am told that the House decided otherwise. Ay, the House did decide, and if my friend [Mr. Matthews] had not stopped with his reading of history just where he did, you would have learned all that the House decided in the case to which he referred. I do not consider the decision of a partisan House in times of hot party politics as of much value, and I certainly do not count the decision which was reached by 118 yeas against 101 nays on the 3d day of October, 1837, giving to Claiborne and Gholson their seats as Representatives from the State of Mississippi, as authority when I find that in the list of negative votes are inscribed the names of John Quincy Adams and Millard Fillmore, of John Sergeant and Richard Fletcher, of John Bell and Thomas Corwin, of Caleb Cushing and R. M. T. Hunter, of Henry A. Wise and George Evans, of Elisha Whittlesey and James Harlan and Thomas M. T. McKennan. That is a roll of names before which I bow as possessing greater authority than the whole list of the 118 who voted in the affirmative. But the record of the House does not stop there. On Monday, the 5th day of February, 1838, (page 160 of the sixth volume of the Congressional Globe,) on motion of John Bell, of Tennessee, by a vote of 121 yeas to 113 nays, the following resolution was adopted:

Resolved, That the resolution of this House of the 3d of October last declaring that Samuel J. Gholson and John F. H. Claiborne were duly elected members of the Twenty-fifth Congress be rescinded, and that Messrs. Gholson and Claiborne are not duly elected members of the Twenty-fifth Congress.

First, on adopting this as an amendment, the yeas were 119, the nays 112, and, secondly, on adopting the resolution as thus amended, the yeas were 121, the nays 113. And this is " the sober second thought" of the House of Representatives of 1837 and 1838 on this question.

Mr. Commissioner EDMUNDS. Is there not something peculiar in the conclusion respecting the filling of the office of a Senator by a governor, growing out of the language of the Constitution, that where a vacancy shall happen during the recess of the legislature the governor may fill it by a commission, which shall hold until the next meeting of the legislature? Does not that have some bearing upon the subject?

Mr. HOADLY. No doubt. I do not claim that all the cases are *precisely* parallel.

Mr. Commissioner HOAR. What was the point decided in that case? Be good enough to state it.

Mr. HOADLY. The point was that neither Claiborne and Gholson nor Prentiss and Ward were duly elected Representatives in the Twenty-fifth Congress.

Mr. Commissioner HOAR. That was not the point decided; that was the fact.

Mr. HOADLY. The point decided was that the resolution adopted on the 3d of October, to which reference was made the other day, awarding to Claiborne and Gholson their seats as members of the Twenty-fifth Congress, should be *rescinded*.

Mr. Commissioner HOAR. My question was, what was the principle of law which was decided and for which you cited that case?

Mr. HOADLY. It is extremely difficult to answer that question. There may have been differences of opinion among those voting. I do not cite this case as authority, but it having been cited in authority against me the other day, I state the whole of the facts of the case in order that it shall not be vouched in any longer as authority upon the other side. Of course, there was a political controversy, and my own opinion is, if I may be allowed to state it, that the party feeling of the supporters of Mr. Van Buren and the antagonists of his administration had much more to do with the result than any judicial considerations whatever.

Mr. Commissioner HOAR. Was it not a case where an extra session was called and gentlemen from Mississippi were chosen before the general law permitted them to be chosen, on proclamation of the governor?

Mr. HOADLY. That was the case.

Mr. MATTHEWS. Allow me to interrupt a moment. I would ask you whether or not the resolution of the House of Representatives admitting Claiborne and Gholson to the extra session was not that there was a vacancy in the representation of Mississippi in the House of Representatives in consequence of the expiration of the terms of the previous members of Congress, and the fact that the election for the members of the next Congress did not occur until the following November, and did not the governor of Mississippi cause that vacancy to be filled by a proclamation, in which he called upon the electors to elect Representatives to fill that vacancy? Was not the resolution admitting them as members of the Congress rescinded at the regular session because they were elected only to fill a vacancy?

Mr. HOADLY. I will answer by saying that the whole statement is correct except the "because." It was rescinded. Now, rescinding means withdrawing the original proposition, and that is the language used. It was not by virtue of a vote that, the vacancy having expired or the time having expired, therefore they were no longer members. But Mr. Bell's amendment was that the original resolution should be rescinded.

This reminds me of another matter which I had almost forgotten, and that is that my friends may possibly cite against me the decision of the United States House of Representatives in what is known as the "broad-seal case" from New Jersey, a debate in which the learned President of this Commission participated as a member of the House. My answer to that, if it be cited against me, will be that it was before a House who were the judges of the returns and qualifications of their own members; and a reference to Cooley, page 133, will show that this is a judicial power expressly conferred upon the House.

This reminds me also of a case famous in the annals of Ohio, and which ought to be famous in the annals of the Federal Union, where a question once arose between the certificate of the returning-officer and the abstract of the votes, in which the judgment arrived at was most conspicuous and most beneficent. In the year 1848 the clerk of the court of common pleas of the county in which I live, who, by law, was the returning-officer, certified under the seal of the county that George E. Pugh, Alexander Long, and their associates were elected representatives to the legislature of Ohio; and the abstract of votes, of which a certified copy was taken, by Oliver M. Spencer and George W. Runyan, showed that they had a majority of the votes cast. The question was upon the constitutionality of the act of the legislature of Ohio dividing the county of Hamilton for the purposes of representation in the State legislature. For thirty days the State of Ohio was without a legislature, in anarchy and confusion, with two conflicting parties contending for pre-eminence; and at the end of thirty days, two gentlemen, still living, honored citizens of Ohio, men of neither the whig nor the democratic party, took the responsibility of judging that the certificate of the clerk was the official evidence of the title, and upon it organized that legislature.

Mr. MATTHEWS. Let me ask you there whether or not both sides were not excluded until after the organization?

Mr. HOADLY. That may be; but the organization——

Mr. MATTHEWS. Mr. Commissioner Payne can answer, probably.

Mr. HOADLY. I accept your statement, as you were one of the authors of the illustrious act to which I allude, a partaker of its honors and of its responsibilities; and among the many reasons for which the people of Ohio have to be thankful that you have lived, this is the most conspicuous.

Mr. MATTHEWS. I hope not.

Mr. HOADLY. I will take your statement. At least the abstract did not secure the seats. What did that act result in? As its first result it made it possible for the black man, who before that time had been an alien and a vagabond in Ohio, to live on its soil a citizen of the State. It made it, in the second place, possible for him to be heard in a court of justice as a witness against a white man. In the third place, it made Salmon P. Chase Senator of the United States from the State of Ohio, to begin that illustrious career which ended in the chief-justiceship of the Supreme Court of the United States, in which he died. Every man in Ohio who joined in this act has been honored by the people of the State. George E. Pugh became attorney-general and senator; Salmon P. Chase twice governor by the votes of his then opponents. I think, as a citizen of Ohio, I have no reason to be ashamed of the doctrine that the broad seal of the county of Hamilton is better evidence of title to office, even though the clerk in issuing it determine against the constitutionality of a statute, than the abstract of votes copied and certified to by him.

There was no vacancy in the office in Oregon; I come back to that. A vacancy may exist in Oregon when "*occasioned* by death, refusal to act, neglect to attend, or otherwise." My learned friend, Mr. Lawrence, says the word "otherwise" means every other possible manner whatsoever. It is a cardinal rule in the interpretation of statutes that every word must have its force, and that words will not be treated as super-fluous; and yet, by this argument, the learned gentleman has elimin-ated all these words, including the word "otherwise," from the statute. He defines the word "otherwise" so that it might as well be obliterated in fact from the law in which it is written.

And if there shall be any vacancy in the office of elector occasioned by death, refusal to act, neglect to attend, or otherwise—

This means that there are some vacancies which the electors present may not proceed to fill. It is not "if there shall be *any* vacancy in the office of elector, the electors present shall immediately proceed to fill it," but it is "if there shall be any vacancy *occasioned* by death, refusal to act, neglect to attend, or otherwise." This is the class of vacancies they may fill; not every vacancy. If it had been every vacancy they might fill, then the words, "occasioned by death, refusal to act, neglect to attend, or otherwise," would have been omitted. In order that these words may have their proper force, the word "otherwise" must be con-strued in its ordinary and normal legal signification, "of other like manner;" *noscitur a sociis* is the rule. General words are restrained by the fitness of things. We have in the statutes of Ohio a law by which a railroad company may acquire and convey at pleasure all real or personal estate necessary or proper; and yet the supreme court of Ohio, in 10 Ohio State Reports, the case of Coe *vs.* The Columbus, Piqua and Indiana Railroad Company, have said that although the language of the statute is general, and they may convey any real estate necessary and proper to be acquired by them, yet they cannot convey one foot of the land which is pledged to the maintenance of the public uses for which they are established. They cannot convey the track; they cannot convey the right of way except by mortgage; and that is because the general words are restrained by the fitness of the subject-matter.

"Occasioned by death, refusal to act, neglect to attend, or otherwise," does not mean "occasioned by every possible circumstance on earth." If it did the law would have said so. It means "occasioned by these methods," and not occasioned otherwise except by these methods or the like unto them, in like manner; death——

Mr. Representative LAWRENCE. Death or something like death.

Mr. HOADLY. Death, or something which comes within the chain of thought which connects these three enumerated classes, consisting of occurrences happening after election. The act of Congress makes the distinction. It says if there is a failure to elect, the legislature may decide what provision shall be made. If there is a vacancy when the college meets, the legislature may provide for it. These are all cases of vacancy occurring after the event of the election, and do not contem-plate a vacancy which occurs by reason of what I should call the non-filling of the office occasioned by reason of there being a non-election.

Suppose there had been a tie vote. Is that "otherwise"? Does non-election by a tie vote create a vacancy within the meaning of that statute? That tests the question. I say not. Why not? Because "occasioned by death, refusal to act, neglect to attend, or otherwise" are words that cannot be dispensed with, and necessarily involve the conclusion that there are some methods of occasioning vacancy which are not within the statute. It would have said "if there be any vacancy the electors present may fill it" had it been supposed these words would be interpreted as now claimed. A tie vote involves a vacancy or what may be called by way of courtesy a vacancy. It is a failure to elect, which is not contemplated by this statute, and not provided for by this statute, and that was the case in the State of Rhode Island of Corliss or might have been. It was alluded to in the decision of the State of Rhode Island. Your honors will find, by referring to the brief which we have on file, a large number of cases in which the same principle is upheld.

Mr. Commissioner MILLER. What do you make of the words "refusal to act"?

Mr. HOADLY. An elector who has been elected and refuses to act creates a vacancy. I consider the word "otherwise" to refer to cases which occur after there has been a complete election, just as section 133 of the Revised Statutes of the United States provides. These are all cases coming within this section.

Mr. Commissioner MILLER. You do not think it necessary that he should have accepted or entered on the duties of the office?

Mr. HOADLY. The words "refusal to act" avoid that difficulty. If it were not for those words and the power of the legislature to provide in that way, I think the rule would have been otherwise. But where there is an elector in office *de facto*, as Cronin was, another party cannot make a vacancy by refusing to act. The ordinary rule is that in order that a party may resign he must be an incumbent. So Cockburn, chief-justice, in The Queen *vs.* Blizzard, Law Reports, 2 Q. B., 55, held; so Sawyer, chief-justice, now judge of the United States circuit court, held, in People *vs.* Tilton, 37 California, 617; so it was held in Miller *vs.* The Supervisor of Sacramento County, 25 California, 93; so in Commonwealth *ex. rel.* Broom *v.* Hanley, 9 Pennsylvania State Reports, 513. And it is held in an opinion, which I will hand to your honors, received to-day by mail, of the supreme court of Missouri, a case printed in the Central Law Journal of Saint Louis, vol. 4, No. 7, on Friday last, page 156, (in accord with the views to which I have alluded,) that the office had been once filled, and therefore there was a vacancy; as they cite with approval the case of The State *vs.* Lusk, 18 Missouri, 333, to the effect that if the office had not been filled by the qualification of the officer before his death, there would have been no vacancy.

I come to consider the remaining question in the case: I say that by Oregon law, as shown by the certificate of the governor who was obliged to act, as well as by the better opinion, the weight of authority, if not the number of cases in the United States, the mandate to elect is of such paramount authority that the people may not disobey it by voting for a disqualified candidate. My friends on the other side, in order to maintain their proposition, must not only stand upon a violation of the Constitution of the United States by the election of a disqualified person; they must also contend that a plurality may violate the Constitution and prevent an election. That is their proposition; and by making their candidate, Watts, an officer *de facto* who did not hold the certificate *de facto*, they thus manufacture this violation of the Constitution of the United States by a plurality into a muniment of title to office.

We have several things to consider here: First, the Constitution of the United States says, "thou shalt elect," to the people of Oregon. If I may, without irreverence, borrow the simile, the first great commandment of the gospel of American liberty is, "thou shalt elect," and the second is, "thou shalt not elect a disqualified candidate." The plurality may elect; and if the plurality may elect, and electing a disqualified candidate defeats an election, then the plurality may defeat an election. What is more than this, it is perfectly easy for more than three candidates each to receive a majority of votes in the State of Oregon. I will take the liberty to ask your honors' attention to a supposition which fairly illustrates the principle we are considering. Thus we may suppose that in the State of Oregon, where there were three electors to be chosen, 20,000 votes may be cast, divided among six candidates: A, B, and C receive each 9,800 votes; D, E, and F receive 9,700 votes. The remaining 500 votes may be thus distributed: To A, B, and D, 200 votes; to A, C, and D, 200 votes; to B, C, and D, 100 votes. The result will be: For A, 10,200; for B, 10,100; for C, 10,100; and for D, 10,200. Supposing, now, that A were disqualified by holding a Federal office, who would be elected, and which rule ought to be adopted? That which rejects A as disqualified, and B and C as not elected, by reason of the votes for them having resulted in a tie, and only D elected; or that which rejects A as disqualified and returns B, C, and D as elected?

This is not very likely to happen at this time, when electors are mere automata to register the wishes of their constituents; but when there shall be three parties again, if that may ever be, and that shall happen which happened in Pennsylvania, that two of them coalesce on the same list of electors, with the intention of dividing the votes of the electors according to the heads of the tickets, as was proposed to be done in Pennsylvania in 1856, this might very easily happen; and yet, according to the proposition of my friends on the other side, the result would be that the man having the highest number of votes was elected though disqualified. Now, the principle, to govern us, must be consistent: First, with the constitutional mandate that the State shall appoint. That is the mandate of the Federal Constitution; it is the mandate of the Revised Statutes; it is the mandate of Oregon. Secondly, with the constitutional inhibition that no person holding an office of trust or profit under the United States shall be appointed. Thirdly, with the rule that a majority vote is not necessary, but a plurality suffices for election. Fourthly, with the possibility to which I have just addressed my attention. And, fifthly, with the fact that upon the views of their work entertained by those who made the Constitution, the candidates for electors do not run, like rivals for the office of sheriff, against each other, but the choice is made by selection of the successful candidates out of the whole list of those named in that connection.

I have referred your honors to the decision in Maine. It so happens that in the State of Maine that opinion of Chief-Justice Mellen, Chief-Justice Weston, and Judge Parris became crystallized by the legislative department of the State as one of the laws of the State as early as 1840, and has remained the law of the State of Maine until now, and my brief refers your honors to this law of the State of Maine by which ballots cast for ineligible persons are not to be counted. It is only in igno-rance of this opinion and this legislation that Spear *vs.* Robinson, 29 Maine, 531, (a decision really directly in favor of my proposition,) and the opinion of the judges, 38 Maine, 597, (which does not touch the point,) have ever been cited against it.

It is the law of the State of Massachusetts, God bless her. I have here a book printed by the authority of the State of Massachusetts, being reports of election cases in Massachusetts. This book came from the legislature of Massachusetts, and in it is a decision in 1849 by a committee, approved by the vote of her legislature. This book was compiled by Judge Luther S. Cushing and his associates, by direction of the legislature, and printed by the State for the information of her people and people beyond her borders, in which it is stated as the law of Massachusetts that—

There is no reason why a person who votes for an ineligible candidate should not be put upon the same footing with one who does not vote at all as in both cases the parties show a disposition to prevent an election, and both of them show an unwillingness to perform their duty by aiding to promote those elections which are absolutely essential to the existence of the government; for if every voter refrained wholly from voting, or voted for an ineligible candidate, the result would be the same, no choice; and although it is true that no penalty is attached by law to a neglect of this obligation of voting, yet the obligation is not the less plain for that, and the committee believe it to be a duty too important to be neglected and too sacred to be trifled with by voting for fictitious persons or ineligible candidates.

Maryland spoke in 1794, in the case of Hatcheson *vs.* Tilden & Bordley, 4 Harris & McHenry, 279; and in 1865 and 1866 the legislature of Maryland, acting once in their legislative capacity, and acting once in their judicial capacity, followed, in the cause of loyalty and of reconstruction upon loyal principles, the rule which Chief-Justice Samuel Chase laid down for their government. I have the house journal and documents of the State of Maryland for 1865, which have been kindly furnished me by a friend in Baltimore in order that I might present the original authorities to your honors. In the constitution of Maryland, as it was in 1865, was the following provision:

If any person has given any aid, comfort, countenance, or support to those engaged in armed hostility to the United States, or has, by any open deed or word, declared his adhesion to the cause of the enemies of the United States, or his desire for the triumph of said enemies of the United States, he is disqualified from holding any office of honor, profit, or trust, under the laws of this State.

Hart B. Holton, who had not a majority or plurality of the votes cast for senator of Howard County in 1865, contested the seat of Littleton Maclin, who had the majority of the legal votes of the voters of Howard County, and on the principles enunciated by Chief-Justice Chase, because of the disloyalty of Littleton Maclin, Hart B. Holton gained the seat and sat as a senator from that county. In 1866, before the house of delegates, acting judicially, George E. Gambrill contested the office of Sprigg Harwood, as clerk of the circuit court of Anne Arundel County, on the ground of constitutional ineligibility, caused by an increase in the profits of this clerkship, while Harwood was a senator from Anne Arundel County in 1865. The committee said that Harwood was ineligible, that it "must be presumed to have been known by every voter," that in a case like this it would be highly inexpedient to submit this matter to another election, and on their report the incumbent of the office was ousted and the contestant inducted into the office of clerk of Anne Arundel County.

So in the States of Missouri and Mississippi, by constitutional amendments, introduced and adopted for the purpose of securing the reconstruction of those States in accordance with the loyal sentiment which demanded the maintenance of the Federal Union at all hazards, it was provided that disloyalty should cause such disqualification that votes given for disloyal persons in Mississippi and Missouri should not be cast up or counted as ballots. This principle, springing from our revolutionary fathers and helping the great work of reconstruction, helping to secure the maintenance of the Federal Union and the principles of loyalty to the Federal Union, has so soon as this become so odious to those who maintained and espoused it so recently that by its rejection is to be elected a President of the United States! What is there to the contrary? Six, or eight, or ten *obiter dicta*, and that is the whole of it, and not one of them in conflict with the principle for which we contend. Why, your honors, the presumption *omnia bene et rite esse præsumuntur donec probetur in contrarium*, sustains the action of the governor of Oregon until there shall be produced in evidence something to show that the governor of Oregon was not justified in the course which he took.

We are justified, then, in presuming—we need not the evidence which we offer—that the fact of disqualification existed, and was so notorious as to work the law of disqualification. Therefore, we are within the rule of Furman *vs.* Clute, in 50 New York, 451 ; therefore we are within the rule which has been adopted in the case of Commonwealth *vs.* Cluly in 56 Pennsylvania State Reports, 277 ; so that we are within the rule which was adopted in the *obiter dicta* to which I shall refer.

Mr. Commissioner EDMUNDS. Did not the court in 50 New York hold also that every voter must know what the law was ?

Mr. HOADLY. Precisely so ; and it would be a fitting commentary upon the serious character of the suggestions which have been made in disparagement of the course taken by the governor of the State of Oregon if it should be held that his course was improper in consequence of the fact that the 15,000 people who voted for John W. Watts were presumably ignorant of the Constitution of the United States. Of a lurking statute hidden in the corners of a statute-book, like the statute that governed the disqualification of the supervisor of Schenectady, it may well be that the voters might be ignorant, but of a disqualification inherent in a constitutional provision which enables the State to appoint electors no man ought to say that he is ignorant. No man can be heard in any court of law in any such case to say, I submit, that he is " ignorant."

Three times Indiana has promulgated the principle which I have suggested. It has been espoused by Judge Cushing in his book, sections 177, *et seq.;* it is espoused by Grant on Corporations, 208 ; it is the law of the English and Irish cases, all of which are referred to in the brief, that a man might as well vote for the man in the moon, or, as Governor Grover in his decision says, for Mount Hood, as to vote for a disqualified candidate knowingly ; and what is there to the contrary ? As I said, the Pennsylvania case concedes that a vote given with knowledge for an ineligible candidate cannot be counted. In the cases in California, in the first one, Malony *vs.* Whitman, 10 Cal., 38, the question did not require or receive decision, for the majority of the court found that the officer was not ineligible. In Saunders *vs.* Haynes, 13 Cal., 145, the other case, it is assumed that a majority of those voting by mistake of law or fact happened so to cast their vote. The case in Wisconsin (State *vs.* Giles, 1 Chandl., 112,) which has been considered the leading case on the other side, is as pure a piece of *gratis dictum* as ever was pronounced in a court in this country. After stating that the officer was not ineligible, the court go on to say :

Such being the opinion of the court, it is unnecessary to pass on the second question whether in the event of the person receiving the highest number of votes being ineligible, the person having the next highest number is elected.

Then, I will not say by the same force with which I address the pupils in my law school, but by the same judicial authority that I have the right to express when I address students in a law-school, the court go on, having decided that it was not their duty to say anything about it, to expound the law, in order that on future occasions their succesors may have the benefit of it, and in State *vs.* Smith, 14 Wisconsin, 497, their successors get the benefit of it, and adopt it without giving any reasons. Judge Lumpkin, in Georgia, State *vs.* Swearingen, 12 Geo., 23, followed the same wise example, deciding that no restriction of residence " was imposed on the voters of the young but rapidly growing town of Oglethorpe in their selection of a suitable person to fill the office of clerk and treasurer." Having decided that there was no such ineligibility, he proceeded to lay down the law of the court *obiter* in these words:

> Under no circumstances could we permit the informant to be installed into these appointments.

In Missouri the first case, State *vs.* Boal, in 46 Missouri, 528, is in accordance.with the views which we maintain.

> As regards the votes cast for the defendant, they were nugatory. It was as though no such votes had been cast at the election.

And the case of The State *vs.* Vail, 53 Mo., 97, does not withdraw this limitation, but simply confines it to cases of latent disqualification, saying:

> It is unnecessary to determine whether it would be the rule in any case of qualifications, whether patent or latent.

The case in Tennessee, Pearce *vs.* Hawkins, 2 Swan, 87, decides that the votes are illegal and void, which is a case, as far as it goes, in our favor. The case in Michigan, People *vs.* Molitor, 23 Mich., 341, is disposed of by an admission in pleading; the court say the party admitted his case away in pleading. The case in 21 Louisiana Annual Reports, 289, Fish *vs.* Collins, decides, with modesty, I suppose, if there be such an article in the supreme court of that State, that it was unnecessary to express an opinion whether the votes cast for a person notoriously known to be ineligible should be rejected or not, as no such allegations were made in the petition. The cases in 18 and 20 Louisiana Annual Reports, 114, State *vs.* Gastinel, are to the same effect.

> Whatever might have been his rights had he contested the election of the defendant in accordance with law, we are not called upon to say.

The case in Mississippi, Sublett *vs.* Bidwell, 47 Miss., 273, is nearest to a case in opposition to the principle for which I contend, of any in the United States. There it is said:

> If the majority make choice of a candidate under some personal disability disqualifying him from taking and enjoying the office, the utmost that can be said of it is that there has been no election.

"Personal disability," not the disability of the State to appoint, but personal disability applicable to the candidate.

In Rhode Island, as is shown by a letter from William Beach Lawrence, of which I have reprinted a large portion in my brief, the opinion on this proposition is purely *obiter dictum*, there having been a tie between the three highest democratic candidates for elector, and, therefore, the result which was reached by the governor, that there was no vacancy, a failure to elect being the necessary result, and not the result produced by the reasons given by the supreme court.

These are all the cases in the United States. I believe I have referred in my brief to every case within the borders of this land and of Great Britain, except one case in Coxe's Reports, page 318, The State *vs.* Anderson, which went off on the proposition that in *certiorari* there was a discretion, but the court would not exercise that discretion to displace a man who was disqualified, because it would leave the office vacant, and did not allude at all to the question whether there was any antagonist or whether his antagonist received any votes.

And if we look beyond the United States, and assume that the common law of England prevails in Oregon, there is nothing to the contrary of our view.

Now, testing by principle, I say Cronin was elected. Testing by method, would a *quo warranto* have run in favor of Watts? Would not the disqualification have killed his title? Could he by *quo warranto* or *certiorari* or contest have obtained the place? Cronin held it *de facto;* Watts was a postmaster disqualified. Test it now by the rules of method under laws similar to that which we have in Ohio and many of the States in which a *quo warranto* may be supported at the instance of the competing candidate, and pursued, not merely to the ousting of the incumbent, but to the induction of the man who ought to have been successful; and on what principle of law could John W. Watts, who did not hold this commission, have got from any court of justice in this land the title to which he now lays claim? Cronin held the title; Cronin cast the vote; Watts was not elector *de facto*, and it is a question whether he was *de jure.* Ask yourselves, learned judges, whether any one of you sitting in *quo warranto* would have awarded, as against the officer *de facto*, possession of the office to a man whom the Constitution of the country said should not hold it? On principle the mandate to elect was fulfilled by the election of Cronin. If Watts be called elected, the mandate to elect was disobeyed. If Watts be called elected, the mandate not to elect a disqualified person was disobeyed. Tested by method and by the rules which apply in courts of justice, tell me how any lawyer can say that a disqualified candidate can seize an office by any process known to the laws of our country out of the hands of one who holds it *de facto*, even although that one be not elected? He may have a judgment that the office is vacant; that is all he can have, and that is the end of the whole thing as far as he is concerned.

Mr. President and gentlemen of the commission: Into your hands, assisted by the enlightened labors of those who are to follow me in argument, I commit this cause. No cause was ever submitted more momentous in its issues or its consequences. It involves the question whether government of the people, by the people, for the people, shall be suspended in the Executive department of these United States for the next four years.

At the election in November last, Samuel J. Tilden and Thomas A. Hendricks received for President and Vice-President of the United States a vast majority of the total popular vote, a majority of the legal popular vote in the States of Louisiana and Florida, and one certificated electoral vote in the State of Oregon. Your sense of duty has prevented your listening to the testimony which would have established their title to the electoral votes of Louisiana and Florida. This was because you possessed no judicial power whatever. Had you been endowed with any portion of the judicial power of the United States, there is no doubt, that, before this time, its exercise would have relieved the people of the United States from the serious apprehension of great danger, of danger that, for four weary years, the choice of the American people shall be frustrated, and a usurper sit in the seat of Washington and Jefferson, of Jackson and of Lincoln.

If you adhere to the principle which has thus far guided your action, this danger will be averted. Without the exercise of judicial power, you cannot deprive Tilden and Hendricks of their Oregon vote, or award it to Hayes and Wheeler.

You have been likened unto judges in Israel, and warned not to make your proceedings so intolerably inconvenient that the people should desire a king. The people, whose cause I represent, will never, never, never wish for a king; but I may remind the counsel that it was not because the action of their judges was inconvenient that the people of Israel desired a king, but because their judges "*perverted* judgment."

Conscript fathers of the American Republic, the flower and crown of the enlightened jurisprudence of pagan Rome were the two maxims, "*Ubi jus, ibi remedium*," "*Suum cuique tribuito*." May it be the happy fortune of our nation and of yourselves, as the expounders of its constitutional powers, not to lessen the force or diminish the universality of their application.

So shall Time, the corroder and consumer of all finite things, pass your work by untouched, and after generations, as they may meet with questions of disputed succession, shall point to and follow it, saying " Behold the great example of our fathers. In their ways will we walk, for they are the ways of righteous judgment and of peace ; " and the arms of them who serve liberty in all the lands shall be strengthened, for they shall know that in monarchies questions of succession are resolved by the sword, in republics by justice.

So shall Art, which keeps in eternal remembrance the realities of things, still delineate Justice with bandaged eyes and open ears, and History shall not record that Justice here, at the expense of her hearing, regained her sight.

Mr. Commissioner ABBOTT. I move that the Commission adjourn to meet at ten o'clock to-morrow morning in the Supreme Court room.

The motion was agreed to ; and (at nine o'clock and fifty-five minutes p. m.) the Commission adjourned.

THURSDAY, *February* 22, 1877.

The Commission met at ten o'clock a. m., in the Supreme Court room, pursuant to adjournment, all the members being present.

The counsel representing the objections to the various Oregon certificates were present.

The Journal of yesterday was read and approved.

The PRESIDENT. Counsel in opposition to certificate No. 2 will now be heard.

Mr. MATTHEWS. Mr. President and gentlemen of the Commission, life is a series of surprises, and the succession of the arguments which has taken place before this Commission is no exception to, but rather an illustration of, that truth. When the case of Florida was opened by the learned counsel who is to conclude the argument in this, [Mr. Merrick,] he assumed and attacked as our position that the certificate of the governor of a State accompanying the list of electors was conclusive and could not be impeached, could not be set aside, could not be contradicted. And among the first words which I had the honor in reply to say in the presence of this honorable Commission, I was compelled to remove that misapprehension on the part of the adverse counsel, and to say that we held to no such doctrine; and in the course of argument I stated our proposition in this way :

But, Mr. President and gentlemen, if you go behind the certificate, what are you limited to by the necessity of the thing ? In my judgment, you are limited to this: to an inquiry into what are the facts *to which he should have certified and did not ;* not what are or may be the ultimate and final facts and right of the case. The facts to be certified by the governor in this or in any case are the public facts which by law remain and constitute a part of the record in the public offices and archives of the State, and of which, being governor for the time being, he has official knowledge.

We undertook to draw a line of demarkation in that instance, first, between the constitutional authority of the State in the making of the appointment, in the doing of all those things which constitute and verify the appointment, which complete it, which constitute a *factum* to be enrolled in the public offices of the State in perpetual memorial of the fact; and, on the other hand, the Federal authority which took the matter up from the point where the State left it, after it had been transferred by the State into the custody of Federal authority.

We undertook, also, to draw a line of distinction in another place; and that was between things and proofs, between the thing to be certified and the certificate which certified it; and we claimed then, as we have consistently done throughout, that the certificate of a thing was matter of form; the thing certified was the matter of substance; and that in every case where it could be alleged that the certificate was false, in that it did not conform to the thing to be certified, you might correct the certificate by showing the fact to be certified.

The statement of these propositions was made in the opening of the argument in the Florida case on our side. It was enlarged and amplified and demonstrated and applied by the learning and the eloquence of my colleagues who continued the further argument in that and the succeeding case of Louisiana; and under the guidance of their skillful and experienced hands in applying the sound constitutional principle out of which those manifest distinctions sprung, we were guided by a pilot as wise and successful as Palinurus himself between Scylla and Charybdis. It was therefore, Mr. President, somewhat of a surprise to find that the position which we had taken so much pains to make clear and to prove, now not only has been adopted by the gentlemen on the other side, but that, going beyond that, they have adopted the dogma which originally they improperly ascribed to us; and we hear for the first time in this continuous, although interrupted debate, the cry from our adversaries of the sanctity and impenetrability of the formal certificate of the governor. It is now claimed by the learned gentleman who spoke with so much ability in the Senate chamber last night [Mr. Hoadly] that the idea on which he founded the whole structure of his argument has passed into adjudication by the decision of this tribunal in the Louisiana case. The language of this tribunal upon that point is this:

And the Commission has by a majority of votes decided, and does hereby decide, that it is not competent, under the Constitution and the law as it existed at the date of the passage of said act, to go into evidence *aliunde* the papers opened by the President of the Senate in the presence of the two Houses, to prove that other persons than those regularly certified to by the governor of the State of Louisiana on and according to the determination and declaration of their appointment by the returning-officers for elections in said State prior to the time required for the performance of their duties had been appointed electors, or by counter-proof to show that they had not.

So that the very ground on which we stood at the beginning is the ground which has been hallowed by this tribunal and is the ground on which we stand to-day; and that is, that it is the certificate of the governor which is based on and according to the determination and declaration of the appointment of electors by the returning-officers for elections in the said State prior to the time required for the performance of their duties, which is under the Constitution and laws of the United States the conclusive evidence of the persons who are entitled to cast the electoral vote of the State.

Mr. President, that is not the only surprise. In the case of Florida the attempt was made by the show and offer of proof to go behind the final action of the State in the appointment of electors by showing that the process had been erroneous, illegal, without jurisdiction, involving transgressions of law, and tainted by fraud. The same offer, though greatly exaggerated and enlarged, was made in the case of Louisiana; and it seemed as if the offers of their proof proposed by the gentlemen on the other side grew the stronger and larger just in proportion to the certainty which they had attained that they would not be put to the test of an attempt to make them good; and we were treated

at the same time with exhibitions of virtuous indignation, which for
one at least I was not expecting or prepared to witness in that quarter,
of the enormity of sanctifying wrong and fraud; and the tribunal and
the counsel and all who were engaged in the transaction were involved
in one universal sentence of condemnation, as if, by establishing some
legal principles in the course of a transaction which at least has the
form of a judicial inquiry and professes to be governed by constitutional
and legal principles, we were confessing the wrongs which we alleged
it was incompetent for this tribunal to investigate.

I was reminded, Mr. President, by that of some remarks which bear
the authority of the Supreme Court of the United States, and were delivered by Mr. Justice Field, in the case of Bradley *vs.* Fisher, in 13
Wallace, 348; where it was decided by the Supreme Court of the United
States that a civil action for damages would not lie against the judge
of a superior court for anything done by him in his official capacity,
although it was alleged in the petition to have been done corruptly,
wantonly, and maliciously, to the injury of the plaintiff; and that
learned judge, who delivered the opinion of the court, made these general remarks, which apply in the present controversy, wherein (quoting
from an old authority in Coke as to the ground of that public policy,
that it would tend to the scandal and subversion of all justice, and those
who are the most sincere would not be free from continual calumniation)
he says:

The truth of this latter observation is manifest to all persons having much experience with judicial proceedings in the superior courts. Controversies involving not
merely great pecuniary interests, but the liberty and character of the parties, and consequently exciting the deepest feelings, are being constantly determined in those
courts, in which there is great conflict in the evidence and great doubt as to the law
which should govern their decision. It is this class of cases which impose upon the
judge the severest labor, and often create in his mind a painful sense of responsibility.
Yet it is precisely in this class of cases that the losing party feels most keenly the decision against him, and most readily accepts anything but the soundness of the decision
in explanation of the action of the judge. Just in proportion to the strength of his
convictions of the correctness of his own view of the case is he apt to complain of the
judgment against him, and from complaints of the judgment to pass to the ascription
of improper motives to the judge. When the controversy involves questions affecting
large amounts of property or relates to a matter of general public concern, or touches
the interests of numerous parties, the disappointment occasioned by an adverse decision often finds vent in imputations of this character, and from the imperfection of
human nature this is hardly a subject of wonder. If civil actions could be maintained
in such cases against the judge, because the losing party should see fit to allege in his
complaint that the acts of the judge were done with partiality or maliciously or corruptly, the protection essential to judicial independence would be entirely swept away.
Few persons sufficiently irritated to institute an action against a judge for his judicial
acts would hesitate to ascribe any character to the acts which would be essential to the
maintenance of the action.

In those cases the offer of proof, even in the form in which it was most
offensive, went only to a certain point, to prove, it was alleged, fraud in
that return and result which had been declared by the returning-board
of the State, in order to penetrate below that, to the primary returns.
But when, on the other hand, it was urged that when they were reached
we should have occasion to retort with charges of fraud and oppression,
and intimidation and cruelty, and arts and stratagems, the effect of
which had been to falsify those primary election returns, there we were
met with the *argumentum ab inconvenienti*, and no less a personage and
lawyer than the distinguished advocate at that time in the case, from
New York, Mr. O'Conor, in answer to the objection, said that when the
inquiry took that range—when it came to involve questions of fraud on
both sides—this tribunal, by virtue either of some judicial or parliamentary discretion, could stop the inquiry at the most convenient point;

could stop the inquiry, I suppose, when they had heard one side, and refuse to hear the other.

No, Mr. President, I am not willing to let this last opportunity in all probability which I shall have to address this tribunal, pass without entering my solemn protest against the pretension to morality which by ascription has been made the foundation and substratum of this complaint. It is a morality which does not go very deep. It is, to say the most of it, not more than skin deep; for when the proposition is made to probe the wound to the bone, then it is said that you cannot go behind the record of the votes actually cast. It is a morality based upon the sanctity of votes actually cast, without reference to who cast them, how they were cast, whether the same man cast more than one, whether or not thousands upon thousands of honest and legitimate votes were not kept out and prevented from being actually cast by the frauds and violence of those who want their votes to be counted because they are cast and exclude those who wanted to cast them and were deprived of the opportunity.

Now, one of the things which are not a surprise is that, in spite of the changed circumstances of the case, we have an exhibition in this of precisely the same standard and gauge of morals. We have Cronin elevated upon a pedestal for public adoration by his inventor as the new statue of popular rights, freedom of elections, purity of the ballot-box, honest ballots, fair voting, and we are all called to fall down and worship him!

We have no offers in this case to prove any bribery, to show that he was paid $3,000, under pretense of his expenses to Washington City as mesenger, made by contract notoriously before he flocked altogether by himself to make a college of himself. We have no offer to prove the various tricks, and devices, and stratagems, and the correspondence locked in what were supposed to be undecipherable hieroglyphics, to show that, so far from this being an attempt on the part of any of the parties implicated in it as actors or advisers to maintain constitutional doctrines and constitutional rights, it was a deep-laid and deliberate scheme to defraud and rob the people of Oregon of their just influence in the electoral college.

I wonder that my friend who spoke last night, when he was undertaking to cite to this tribunal the definition of what constituted a vacancy from Worcester and from Webster, did not disclose the little pocket dictionary which was made use of as the means of transmitting unintelligible hypocrisy between Gramercy Park and Salem, and let us see by the application of that cipher what it was he wished to have understood.

Mr. President, the argument made last evening in support of what for convenience sake may be called the Cronin certificate by my learned friend Judge Hoadly is founded, in my judgment, upon two false assumptions, the proper understanding and recognition of which at once put an end to the whole mountain both of authority and reasoning by which he undertook to support his conclusions. The first of these false assumptions is this: that the Cronin certificate, the certificate of the governor of Oregon appended to the list of electors of which Cronin is one, was and is the authorized declaration of the result of the election by the proper legal canvassing officer of the State of Oregon. He could not claim less than that, for otherwise he was unable to bring his argument within the scope of the decision of this tribunal in the Louisiana case. He was therefore compelled to assume and argue that by the statutes of Oregon the governor of that State was authorized to make such a certificate as he has made, and that in law that document in its form and substance is the canvass of the election for electors, behind which this tribunal has decided that it constitutionally cannot go.

The next false assumption on which his argument is based is that this certificate is in the nature of a commission lawfully issued by the governor to an officer, and which it is necessary that he should have in order to be a warrant in law for the execution of the duties of his office. It is in respect to this second proposition that a large number of authorities was cited to show that, in cases where a governor has, by law or under the constitution of his State, an executive discretion in respect to the appointment and commissioning of officers, that discretion may be exercised by him in granting or withholding that commission for sufficient legal reasons, in which he cannot be controlled by the action of the judicial tribunals of the country by *mandamus* or *quo warranto;* and that therefore, in such cases, he is made the judge of the facts in respect to eligibility or otherwise, on which he may proceed in the execution and exercise of his official discretion, the whole of which immediately and peremptorily falls to the .ground when it is once known and ascertained and declared, as the law is, that this certificate, even if it had been made in conformity with some law, which it is not, either of Congress or of the State of Oregon, was not intended and does not have the effect of constituting the warrant of these officers for the exercise of their official duties.

Now, let me examine the first of these two propositions in the light of the statutes and constitution of the State of Oregon, in order to ascertain what mode has been adopted by the legislature of the State of Oregon for the appointment of electors for that State. By section 58 (page 141 of the printed pamphlet) it is provided that—

On the Tuesday next after the first Monday in November, 1864, and every four years thereafter, there shall be elected by the qualified electors of this State as many electors of President and Vice-President as this State may be entitled to elect of Senators and Representatives in Congress.

They are to be elected by the qualified electors of the State, by a popular election. Now, by the sixtieth section it is provided that—

The votes for the electors shall be given, received, returned, and canvassed as the same are given, returned, and canvassed for members of Congress.

There that proposition ends. We are to ascertain what constitutes the legal canvass for electors of Oregon, and in order to do that we are referred by this section to those steps which by law are provided to be taken in the canvass for the election of members of Congress. Now, we shall ascertain that by turning to the thirty-seventh section, on page 139, wherein it is provided:

The county clerk, immediately after making the abstract of the votes given in his county, shall make a copy of each of said abstracts, and transmit it by mail to the secretary of state, at the seat of government; and it shall be the duty of the secretary of state, in the presence of the governor, to proceed within thirty days after the election, and sooner if the returns be all received, to canvass the votes given for secretary and treasurer of state, State printer, justices of the supreme court, member of Congress, and district attorneys.

And there that proceeding ends, and there ends the declaration of the statute in reference to all the steps which are included in the canvass for members of Congress. When a canvass takes place, however, for member of Congress, after the canvass is concluded, it is then provided that—

The governor shall grant a certificate of election to the person having the highest number of votes, and shall also issue a proclamation declaring the election of such person.

But inasmuch as that constitutes no part of the canvass for members of Congress, it is not any part of the canvass for electors of the State. On the other hand, the original section, 60, to which I now recur, provides, instead of that:

> The secretary of state shall prepare two lists of the names of the electors elected, and affix the seal of the State to the same.

But, mark you, that is no part of the canvass; it is a certification merely of the result of that canvass. The canvass is something distinct; the canvass is the determination, the declaration, the record of the facts of the election as they have been transmitted by the clerks of the various counties to the secretary of state, and by him are put into that form which shows who had the highest number of votes, and there entered of record in his office as a part of the public archives of the State for the benefit of whom it may concern; and, as was remarked, any man in the State, any citizen, has a right by law to go to the secretary of state, and, upon the tender of the payment of the lawful fees, demand from him a certificate of that record as of any other.

Now, then, we have arrived at the two things which are separate and distinct: the substantial thing, which consists of the showing made of record of the number of votes cast for each of the electors, showing who had the greatest number of votes, and that is the canvass; and it is not essential, it is no necessary part of that canvass, it is not made so by any law, that the secretary of state or anybody else should by any formal declaration or publication make manifest, more than it is by the inspection of the record, who has been in point of fact elected. There is no discretion in that matter; there is no room for any doubt; there is no possible uncertainty. The law and the constitution of the State of Oregon both unite in stamping upon that document and that record as it remains in the office of the secretary of state the legal, constitutional, and only possible result, namely, that the man appearing from that record to have the highest number of votes shall be deemed to be elected.

Then what have we here? On page 2, certificate No. 1, we have the very thing. It is not proof of the thing; it is an exhibition of the thing; and it is a production of it in court. We have made profert of the identical, substantial, and only real thing; and that is the canvass of the election. The secretary of state of Oregon, who is the custodian of the great seal of the State by virtue of his office, certifies:

> That the foregoing tabulated statement is the result of the vote cast for presidential electors at a general election held in and for the State of Oregon on the 7th day of November, A. D. 1876, as opened and canvassed in the presence of his excellency L. F. Grover, governor of the said State, according to law, on the 4th day of December, A. D. 1876, at two o'clock p. m. of that day, by the secretary of state.

That is the *res gestæ;* that is the appointment by the State in the manner prescribed by the legislature thereof; that is the muniment of title; that is the constitutional and legal foundation of right. That it is which constitutes the investiture by the State upon the party of his official title, rank, and character. All else is mere certification; all else is mere proof, *prima facie* or conclusive as the law makes it in express terms, and not otherwise; and no scrap of law, no iota of a statute, no word has been quoted to give effect to any certification other than that which according to the principles of the common law belong to it. It is *prima facie* evidence; it is to be taken as true until, confronted with the fact, it is shown to be false, just as the exemplification of a recorded judgment is to be taken as true until on allegation of diminution or error or mistake, on *certiorari*, the court may order up the original and compare it with the alleged copy.

"That this certificate provided in section 60 to be made by the secretary of state, containing lists of the names of the electors elected, has no other or greater effect than that I have ascribed to it, and is not in the nature of a warrant required by law to enable the parties named therein to proceed in the execution of their office, is apparent from the language of the statute and from the whole purview and meaning of the constitution and the laws.

Now, Mr. President, leaving the parties to stand upon that document, proven in that way, making manifest that fact, which by the constitution and laws of Oregon constitutes their appointment, is the very appointment to their office of electors, let us examine for a while its rival.

The certificate of the governor, No. 2, is a document which is intruded here in argument as a substitute for that canvass, under pretense of being that canvass. This certificate is a certificate of the governor. It is attested, to be sure, by the secretary of state, but only as a witness. It is not the certificate of the secretary of state; it is not the declaration of the canvassing officer. It conforms in no particular with any statutory requirements affecting the declaration of the result of the election. It, to be sure, purports to give the names of three persons with the number of votes received by each; but it does not state that they are the persons who had the highest number of votes cast at that election, and it interpolates a conclusion of law—at least that is an admissible inference from its face—incorporating the judgment of the governor upon a question of law, when, according to these statutes, if he did anything at all, he could only certify to the fact. And as to the functions of canvassing boards upon that matter, I beg to call the attention of the tribunal to a decision in the case of Newcum vs. Kirtley, in 13 Ben Monroe. I read from page 524, from a decision of Judge T. A. Marshall, of Kentucky, the point of which was that a canvass after an election had been made by the proper canvassing board wherein the facts shown were contradicted by the result declared, and the court held that the facts shown were to be taken as the authority, rejecting the incompetent and unwarranted and unauthorized declaration made by the canvassing officer inconsistent with the facts which he had certified to, saying:

And if the consequence stated be regarded as a decision—

That is, consequently entitling him to the certificate of election—

or a certificate that Kirtley is, on the ground of the majority stated, entitled to the office, it is unauthorized and illegal, because upon the facts found and stated by the board Kirtley had not a majority of the legal votes given, and his title could not be made out either by adding to his votes others not given or by taking from Newcum votes admitted to be legal and actually given for him. If the board had a right to do anything with the 2 votes not given, surely it was to have added them to the poll of Kirtley. But although this would have made a majority, it would not, as we have seen, have entitled Kirtley to the office. And they might just as well and with equal effect have made the majority in correcting the vote improperly set down for Newcum when it was given for Kirtley, by taking 2 from Newcum and adding 2 to Kirtley on that account, as to have made it as they have done, by subtracting 11 instead of 9 votes from Newcum, when from their own showing 9 only should have been subtracted. Or they might as well, after finding that Newcum had a majority of 1 of the legal votes given, have gone on to say, "and subtracting 2 legal votes from Newcum gives Kirtley a majority of 1 vote, consequently entitling him to the certificate of election." The subtraction of the 2 votes, for a reason not only insufficient but actually excluded by statute from all influence in the calculation, is just as illegal as the subtraction of them without any reason at all.

The case, then, as appearing upon the face of the document exhibited by Kirtley to establish his right to the office, is substantially this: that the board, finding that Newcum has a majority of 1 of all the legal votes given, illegally subtract from his poll 2 of the legal votes given for him, and thus produce an apparent majority of 1 vote for Kirtley; consequently, as they say, entitling him to the certificate. And the question is whether the court to which this document was presented as evidence of Kirtley's right to be sworn in as its clerk was bound by this argumentative conclusion, contradicted by the facts established by the document itself, and manifestly based upon an illegal and arbitrary calculation. We say that this conclusion is no more authoritative when based upon a palpable violation of the law of the land directly applicable to the subject, and about which there can be no mistake or difference of opinion, than if it had been based upon a palpable violation of the plainest rules of vulgar arithmetic; that, the document being offered to the court as evidence of the right involved in the motion and for its consideration in determining the right, it was the right and duty of the court to consider the whole document and to determine the right as upon the whole document and the law arising thereon, as it appeared to be for one or the other party; and that if the conclusion had been expressed in the most formal terms, that "consequently," (that is, in consequence of the majority assumed or produced in the mode actually pursued,) "it was adjudged by the board that Kirtley was duly elected and was entitled to the office of clerk," still, as the same document disclosed the process by which this conclusion was arrived at and showed conclusively that it was in direct contradiction of the facts found and a palpable violation of the law applicable to them, it was the right and duty of the court to disregard the concluding judgment as illegal and void, and consequently insufficient to entitle Kirtley to the office.

Now, with respect to the office of this certificate, without reading what nevertheless if there were more time I should think very profitable reading, I ask your honors to remember what you are all familiar with, and that is the language and reasoning of Chief-Justice Marshall in the case in 1 Cranch, of Marbury vs. Madison, wherein he draws the distinc-. tion between the appointment and the evidence of that appointment and points out the cases where the commission itself is the appointment and where the delivery is not essential; and I refer also to the case in 19 Howard, of The United States vs. Le Baron, from which I shall read a paragraph on page 78:

The transmission of the commission to the officer is not essential to his investiture of the office. If, by any inadvertence or accident, it should fail to reach him, his possession of the office is as lawful as if it were in his custody. It is but evidence of those acts of appointment and qualification which constitute his title and which may be proved by other evidence, where the rule of law requiring the best evidence does not prevent.

Upon the authority of an officer whose sole duty it is to certify to the facts which constitute a result without inquiry into the right of the party, or into his qualification, or into his eligibility, I ask attention also to a case in 3 Wendell, on page 437:

The relator has been appointed since the 1st day of January, instant, a commissioner of deeds in the city of New York. On presenting himself before the clerk of the common pleas of New York to take the oath of office, the clerk refused to administer the oath, on the ground that the relator was a minor within the age of twenty-one, and therefore incompetent to hold the office. The relator applies for a mandamus directing the clerk to administer the oath.

Chief-Justice Savage says:

A minor and an alien are incapable of holding a civil office within this State, (1 Revised Statutes, 116, sec. 1;) but it is not the province of the officer to whom application is made to administer the oath of office to determine whether the person presenting himself is or is not capable of holding an office. It is the duty of such officer, on the production of the commission, to administer the oath. If an appointment has been improvidently made, there is a legal mode in which it may be declared void. Let an alternative mandamus issue.—3 Wendell's Reports, 437, 438.

And yet why should not the clerk of the court of common pleas in the State of New York, who, I presume, takes the oath to support the constitution of the State of New York and the Constitution of the United States, whenever an incompetent person applies to him to be inducted into an office, and he is required to clothe him with that without which he cannot act—why should he not, in imitation of the example of La Fayette Grover, the governor of Oregon, constitute himself the guardian of the Constitution of the country? Why should he not assume also the same right, the same duty to undertake to exercise a discretion which, if not given to him by statute, yet belongs to him as the natural protector and guardian of the constitutional liberties of the country, and so refuse to do any act which he may be called upon to perform, and which may be necessary to put into office an incompetent, ineligible, and incapable person?

Why, Mr. President, in no particular does this certificate of the governor of Oregon conform in any respect either to the statutes of the United States or to the statutes of Oregon. It is no declaration of the canvass; it does not profess to be. It is not a list of the electors; it does not profess to be. It is not a declaration of the canvassing officer, because he is not that officer, but the secretary of state is; and it might as well be claimed that the attesting witness to a deed is a party to its covenants, and that Mr. Chadwick by attesting this certificate has in that contradicted that which he had no right to contradict, and which he has certified to under the great seal of the State, and which constitutes the valid, sole, and only binding result of that canvass.

But, Mr. President, let us suppose for a moment that this certificate No. 2 is sufficient and proper and conformable to law; and let us see what legal consequences follow. It declares that William H. Odell, John C. Cartwright, and E. A. Cronin were "duly elected electors as aforesaid for the State of Oregon." Suppose now for a moment that the governor had a right to make that declaration, and that he had a right to make it in this form; let us see what the result is. Then Odell, Cartwright, and Cronin constituted the college of electors. As has been said forcibly by one of the contestors on our side, that is a body composed of these individuals who are required to meet to consult, to deliberate, to act in conjunction. They cannot each go off by himself and act as an elector individually; it is a college; and a college, even according to the maxim of the civil law, can only be constituted by three persons, not less; and by the Constitution of the United States no college of electors can be composed of any less number, because they must be equal to each State's Senators and Representatives, and as each State is entitled to one Representative without respect to population, the minimum of a college of electors is at least three persons meeting together, consulting together, deliberating together, voting together. There seems to have prevailed a contrary impression in Oregon, and that is that one of them might meet by himself. I beg upon that point, as the only case that I have heard of at all in analogy, to call the attention of the tribunal to the case of Sharp *vs.* Dawes, decided in the court of appeals of England, reported in the January number of the Law Reports of this year, in the Queen's Bench division, on page 26. It was an—

Appeal from an order of the Queen's Bench division making absolute an order to increase the amount of a verdict for the plaintiff.

At the trial it appeared that the Great Caradon mine was a mining company in Cornwall, carrying on business on the cost-book system. The company had offices in London, and on the 22d of December, 1874, a notice was duly given that a general quarterly meeting of the shareholders would be held on the 30th of December, at the London offices, for the purpose of passing the accounts, making a call, receiving a report from the agent, and transacting any ordinary business of the company.

The only persons who attended at the time appointed for the meeting were the secretary, G. Sharp, and one shareholder, R. H. Silversides—

The secretary not being a member of the corporation—

who held twenty-five shares. A circular was then sent to the shareholders, with the accounts and the following notice:

"At a general meeting of the shareholders, held at 2 Gresham buildings, Basinghall street, London, E. C., on Wednesday, the 30th day of December, 1874, pursuant to notice, R. H. Silversides in the chair. The notice convening the meeting having been read, the minutes of the last meeting were confirmed.

"The financial statement ending the 28th of November, showing a balance of £83 11s. 6d. against the shareholders, having been read, it was

"*Resolved*, That the same be received and passed.

"Captain William Taylor's report having been read, it was

"*Resolved*, That the same be received and passed, and, together with the financial statement, be printed and circulated among the shareholders.

"*Resolved*, That a call of 4s. 6d. per share be now, and is hereby, made, payable to the secretary, and that a discount of 5 per cent. be allowed if paid by the 25th of January, 1875.

"*Resolved*, In consequence of the death of Lieutenant-Colonel W. T. Nicolls, and until the appointment of a shareholder to act in his stead, that all checks be signed by Mr. R. H. Silversides and Mr. Granville Sharp jointly.

"R. H. SILVERSIDES,
"*Chairman.*

"*Resolved*, That a vote of thanks be given to the chairman.

"GRANVILLE SHARP,
"*Secretary.*"

There was no rule of the company varying the requirements of the Stannaries act, (32 and 33 Vict., c. 19.) By rule 4 :

"The secretary shall call a general meeting of the shareholders once in every three calendar months, to be held at such time and place as shall be appointed by the committee of management."

The defendant, one of the shareholders, refused to pay this call, and the action was brought against him in the name of the secretary for the amounts due on a previous call and on this call.

Judgment was given for the plaintiff for the amount due on the previous call, with leave to move to increase it by the amount due on the second call.

*   *   *.   *   *   *   *

Lord COLERIDGE, chief-justice. This is an attempt to enforce against the defendant a call purporting to have been made under § 10 of the Stannaries act, 1869. Of course it cannot be enforced unless it was duly made within the act. Now, the act says that a call may be made at a meeting of a company with special notice, and we must ascertain what, within the meaning of the act, is a meeting, and whether one person alone can constitute such a meeting. It is said that the requirements of the act are satisfied by a single shareholder going to the place appointed and professing to pass resolutions. The sixth and seventh sections of the act show conclusively that there must be more than one person present ; and the word "meeting" *prima facie* means a coming together of more than one person. It is, of course, possible to show that the word "meeting" has a meaning different from the ordinary meaning, but there is nothing here to show this to be the case. It appears, therefore, to me that this call was not made at a meeting of the company within the meaning of the act. The order of the court below must be reversed.

MELLISH, L. J. In this case, no doubt, a meeting was duly summoned, but only one shareholder attended. It is clear that, according to the ordinary use of the English language, a meeting could no more be constituted by one person than a meeting could have been constituted if no shareholder at all had attended. No business could be done at such a meeting, and the call is invalid.

Mr. MERRICK. Permit me to ask a question. Suppose there had been no dispute about the regularity of the appointment of electors and two of them had died ?

Mr. MATTHEWS. I suppose the vacancy would have to be filled in some mode to be provided by the legislature. They did not die; they were there in their places. But this gentleman, Mr. Cronin, according to his own statement of what occurred at that time, did not act with the others and went on and appointed two more himself.

Mr. Commissioner EDMUNDS. He says in his certificate that they refused to act with him.

Mr. MATTHEWS. And he thereupon appointed two others in their stead. Now, Mr. President and gentlemen, I take it that one in a college which necessarily consists of three is not capable by himself of instituting any action, and that the action of a quorum or majority of the body, the record of whose action is before us, who certify that they, having ascertained the existence of a vacancy, went on to fill it, is to be taken as the conclusive and legitimate account of the proceedings of the body. In support of the conclusion to be based upon this argument, I refer with satisfaction to the decision of the supreme court of the State of Oregon, cited by my learned friend Judge Hoadly last evening. That was a case where the prosecuting attorney having accepted an office under the Government of the United States, which was incompatible according to the laws of Oregon with the office which he had previously exercised under the laws of Oregon, the governor of Oregon commissioned another person as district attorney, upon the ground that he had ascertained and declared a vacancy in consequence of the ineligibility of the occupant, on account of his incompetency to continue to hold the office. In that case, by the law of Oregon, the governor is authorized to fill vacancies, and upon the argument that the person authorized to fill a vacancy has the power to ascertain and determine and declare the existence of the facts which constitute a vacancy, by that judgment these two electors, who by the terms of the statute of Oregon were the only persons who had power to fill vacancies, had the right also to ascertain and declare the existence of those facts which constituted in law a vacancy.

And that brings me to a consideration of the question as to what under the laws of Oregon constitutes a vacancy in the electoral college. My friend on the other side who addressed the tribunal last evening expended some time and strength in undertaking to demonstrate by the application of the maxim *noscitur a sociis*, that the enumeration of the particular instances of a vacancy in that section of the statute which authorizes the body to fill the vacancy excludes the idea of the words "or otherwise" expressing any other than those of a like class. He limits, therefore, what constitutes a vacancy to the occurrence of facts transpiring since the date of the popular election. I think that in such a statute, where the object is to see to it that the substantial rights of the State are preserved in keeping up the full number to which it is entitled in its electoral college, in order that its just influence in public affairs may not be diminished by any of the accidents and casualties of life, no such rule, no such maxim, no such limit can be applied to its interpretation; that it is, on the other hand, to be interpreted in a large and liberal sense for the promotion of the object which the statute had in view, and that is the furnishing to the body of the electoral college the means, the opportunity, the power to fill vacancies in their body which at the day when they meet are ascertained to have occurred, as fully and completely as the legislature itself by any means could supply. Certainly there is no reason why, in its application to such a state of things, the ordinary, plain, and common-sense meaning of the terms should be wrested by the application of any artificial maxim.

But without dwelling on that, I beg to call the attention of yourself, Mr. President, and the tribunal, to one or two authorities on the point that a vacancy such as we claim to have existed in this case may be and be declared. I refer to the case of Stevens *vs.* Wyatt, 16 Ben. Monroe, 542, where it was expressly held that the election of an ineligible candidate, (the very point made here,) so far from electing a minority candidate, created a vacancy, a vacancy *ab initio*, from the commencement of the term; and with reference to the case of The Commonwealth *vs.* Hanley, in 9 Pennsylvania State Reports, 513, and a large number of similar cases, it is only necessary to point out this fact to show their want of application to this argument; and that is, that in these cases, notably in the case in 9 Pennsylvania State Reports, the facts were that there was an incumbent of the office by virtue of a previous election holding over, under a statute to that effect, until his successor should be elected and qualified. The successor was elected, but died before he was qualified and before the commencement of the term of office, and because by express statute the officer already in held over, it was adjudged that there was no vacancy because there was an existing incumbent.

Mr. Commissioner EDMUNDS. Under the statute he would hold until his successor was qualified.

Mr. MATTHEWS. Until elected and qualified. In the opinion of the judges *in re* Dinslow, 38 Maine, 597, the judges of the supreme court of Maine certified to the governor the exact state of the case as furnishing the ground for the opinion which I maintain; a majority of the votes at an election having been canvassed for a man already dead, the judges held that there was a vacancy in the office beginning with its term and entitling the governor to appoint.

I have already referred last evening, in a colloquy which took place, between my brother Hoadly and myself, to the Claiborne and Gholson case, which is a valid precedent on the point. What was that? In the *interim* between the expiration of the term of a member of Congress by the expiration of the Congress itself on the 4th of March and the period provided by the laws of the State for the regular election biennially, in the case of an extra session being called, there is a vacancy in the representation of that State in the House of Representatives, which, under the Constitution of the United States, is to be filled, and it was filled in that case by an election held under a proclamation of the governor calling for an election to fill a vacancy. The two members sent were admitted in the extra session to the whole Twenty-fifth Congress; and afterward the resolution was only rescinded so far as to adjudge that they ought not to have been admitted as members for the entire term, but only to fill that vacancy until by regular election under the statutes of the State the full term could be filled.

Now I call attention to another congressional precedent *in re* Flanders and Hahn, Thirty-seventh Congress, third session, in which there was a report by Mr. Dawes, chairman of the Committee of Elections. Flanders and Hahn claimed to have been elected members of the House of Representatives from Louisiana. The law of that State, entitled "An act relative to elections," approved March 15, 1855, provided:

SEC. 33. *Be it further enacted, &c.,* That in case of vacancy, by death or otherwise, in the said office of Representative, between the general elections, it shall be the duty of the governor, by proclamation, to cause an election to be held according to law to fill the vacancy.

General Shepley, having been appointed military governor of the State, on the 14th of November, 1862, issued his proclamation ordering an election for members of Congress in the first and second congressional districts, to be held on the 3d of December, 1862. The objection was made in debate that the election was void, because, the time for the regular election having passed without one being held, there was no vacancy occasioned by death or otherwise which could be filled by a special election under the governor's proclamation. Mr. Dawes, in reply, said:

Where the time prescribed by the regular law for the election of a Representative to

Congress passes, for any reason whatever, and there is nobody in office, there is a vacancy which the governor of a State is required to fill. I think the office is quite as empty with nobody in it as if somebody had been in it a part of the term and then died. The House has passed upon that question heretofore. The question was up for discussion in this hall in one of the Virginia cases, and the point was taken by the claimant in the House that there could not be a vacancy unless the office had been once filled ; but the House thought otherwise, and I think the House was right.

The claimants were admitted. But, Mr. President and gentlemen of the Commission, it is hardly worth while to hunt for authority on this point when it is so near at hand in the State of Oregon itself, for that State has undertaken to define by statute what shall constitute a vacancy. The very text of the statute which prescribes the mode for the election of presidential electors, title 6, section 48, enumerates the instances which shall constitute vacancies. They are:

1. The death of the incumbent.
2. His resignation.
3. His removal.
4. His ceasing to be an inhabitant of the district, county, town, or village for which he shall have been elected or appointed, or within which the duties of his office are required to be discharged.
5. His conviction of an infamous crime, or of any offense involving a violation of his oath.
6. His refusal or neglect to take his oath of office, or to give or renew his official bond, or to deposit such oath or bond within the time prescribed by law.
7. The decision of a competent tribunal, declaring void his election or appointment.

Now, it is argued on the other side that this cannot apply, because, in the case of Watts, on the supposition that he was ineligible at the time of his original appointment, there was no decision by a competent tribunal declaring void his election or appointment; and yet the other side have argued that the governor had the right to declare his election void, and that that was the decision of a competent tribunal. If so, then I ask whether the consequence does not flow from this statute that, instead of electing the minority candidate, it merely created a vacancy.

But, Mr. President and gentlemen of the Commission, there is another view to take, much stronger and entirely conclusive. It has been argued—it must be argued in order to sustain the claim made here; without it there is no standing ground—that the election of an ineligible candidate under the Constitution is void, void *ab initio*, void by virtue of the constitutional provision. On that they base the right of the minority candidate, because they say that a man ineligible to hold an office, or a man ineligible to be appointed to an office cannot take it, cannot hold it; that the attempt is abortive ; that it is null and void ; in other words, that an ineligible candidate actually elected cannot become an incumbent; and the gentlemen interpret this statute by interpolating the word "incumbent" throughout all of its provisions. Be it so; it establishes my proposition. What is it, then ? "The decision of a competent tribunal declaring void his," that is, the incumbent's, "election or appointment." *Then a man can be an incumbent, although his election or appointment is void!* In other words, this statute recognizes the law and the fact that prohibitions establishing incapacities for office do not necessarily execute themselves otherwise than through the judgments of competent tribunals ; that a man, notwithstanding the incapacity, may in fact hold the office, and if his holding of that office is not legal and valid he fills it with his natural person and capacity as completely as if he was invested with all lawful power, until it becomes vacant either by the decision of a competent tribunal declaring the nullity of his original appointment, or by his getting out of the way in some other mode. Now if, notwithstanding the election is void, an ineligible candidate may actually be put into occupation of the office until a decision of a competent tribunal declaring the invalidity of his election creates a vacancy under that statute, I ask in all reason and common sense whether he cannot voluntarily create a vacancy by doing that which he might be compelled to do by a decision of a competent tribunal.

But it is said that this title only applies to vacancies occurring in State offices and cannot be held to apply to the case of the office of elector. But, Mr. President and gentlemen, even on the supposition that it refers primarily to elections to offices held under the State constitution and the authority of the State, nevertheless the reference in the other title, which has express directions concerning vacancies in the electoral body and a mode of filling them, must be construed, because *in pari materia*, by the context; so that when you come to understand what the legislature meant by a vacancy occurring "otherwise" in the electoral body, it means a vacancy occurring in any one of the ways in which by law a vacancy may be created in reference to State offices.

So, then, there is no flaw in the argument; it is conclusive; it is irrefragable. There it stands on the express terms and letter of the very statutes of the State, showing that, admitting Watts to have been an ineligible candidate, admitting his election to have been utterly void, still he was the person declared duly elected because he had the highest number of votes; and notwithstanding his ineligibility and notwithstanding the voidness of his election, he was capable under the constitution and laws of Oregon of being inducted into the office, of holding it until by resignation or the decision of a competent tribunal ousting him from it a vacancy should be declared; and then a majority of the electoral college by a plurality of votes, and not by the solitary voice of Cronin, were called into being and into efficacy, and had power to fill up to the full measure of constitutional right the number of votes to which the State of Oregon was entitled.

I must confess, Mr. President and gentlemen, that I was not a little surprised at the view which my learned friend [Mr. Hoadly] took about the condition of the law of England and this country on the subject of the effect of votes cast for an ineligible candidate. I know that he has given far more industriously his attention to the collection of cases on that subject than I have, for I confess that I never regarded it as quite worth my while to trace out in detail the history of judicial decisions on that subject. I was satisfied with a general knowledge derived from an examination of a few cases and from the tendency of the reasonings which lie at the foundation of the true doctrine on the subject.

The PRESIDENT. Is there any difference between a vote cast for an ineligible candidate and a blank?

Mr. MATTHEWS. Yes, sir; just as much as there is between a man and a mouse, between a live man capable, by the natural exercise of his functions, of doing the thing which the law puts upon him, and a mere nothing.

A man's a man for a' that.

And though incapable by law of holding an office, he nevertheless may be put into an office, and if nobody objects he can exercise the functions of the office and discharge its duties, and every single act has just as much vitality and validity as if he was the most thoroughly-furnished man by the law for the performance of all its duties. Allow me on that point to refer for a moment to a case that I intended to refer to, a decision and an opinion of Chief-Justice Chase in the Cæsar Griffin case, for the purpose of enforcing what I believe to be the true doctrine on this subject; and that is, that without legislation declaring the consequences of the casting of votes for an ineligible man, under such circumstances there is no power in the Constitution or out of it to put it in force.

By the fourteenth amendment to the Constitution certain persons were declared to be disqualified to hold certain offices, and a judge in the State of Virginia came within the prohibition, the actual incumbent of an office. If the prohibition has that blighting and paralyzing effect which seems to be attributed to it by some, it executes itself at the moment it comes into force upon the state of things just as they are, and it deprives the officer, if he be in office, of the power to continue in office just as much as it deprives the elected man from taking office. And if the doctrine be true, every act done by this judge after the adoption of that fourteenth amendment became utterly null and void, provided always it be, as is claimed, the legal consequence from the doctrine that an incapable person holding an office makes all his acts invalid. In this case it was said to invalidate the sentence of punishment of a criminal who had been adjudged to the penitentiary by this judge while in office, Judge Sheffey. What I call special attention to is that Chief-Justice Chase, not content with referring to the general principle and to the decided cases—which are just as numerous as all the disqualifying acts and statutes of Parliament in Great Britain passed during the time of civil war—but arguing upon our own Constitution, goes on to show by illustrations what his opinion is.

Mr. Commissioner THURMAN. From what do you read?

Mr. MATTHEWS. This is Johnson's Reports, so called, of Chase's Decisions, page 425.

Mr. Commissioner GARFIELD. Circuit Court Reports?

Mr. MATTHEWS. Of the circuit court in Virginia.

Instructive argument and illustration of this branch of the case might be derived from an examination of those provisions of the Constitution ordaining that no person shall be a Representative or Senator or President or Vice-President unless having certain pre-prescribed qualifications. These provisions, as well as those which ordain that no Senator or Representative shall, during his term of service, be appointed to any office under the United States under certain circumstances, and that no person holding any such office shall, while holding such office, be a member of either House, operate on the capacity to take office. The election or appointment itself is prohibited and invalidated; and yet no instance is believed to exist where a person has been actually elected, and has actually taken the office notwithstanding the prohibition, and his acts while exercising its functions have been held invalid.

*   *   *   *

It results from the examination that persons in office by lawful appointment or election before the promulgation of the fourteenth amendment are not removed therefrom by the direct and immediate effect of the prohibition to hold office contained in the third section, but that legislation by Congress is necessary to give effect to the prohibition, by providing for such removal. And it results further that the exercise of their several functions by these officers, until removed in pursuance of such legislation, is not unlawful.

On page 421—

In the judgment of the court there is another, not only reasonable, but very clearly warranted by the terms of the amendment, and recognized by the legislation of Congress. The object of the amendment is to exclude from certain offices a certain class of persons. Now, it is obviously impossible to do this by a simple declaration, whether in the Constitution or in an act of Congress, that all persons included within a particular description shall not hold office, for, in the very nature of things, it must be ascertained what particular individuals are embraced by the definition before any sentence of exclusion can be made to operate. To accomplish this ascertainment and insure effective results, proceedings, evidence, decisions, and enforcements of decisions, more or less formal, are indispensable, and these can only be provided for by Congress.

Mr. President and gentlemen, certainly it is reasonable to suppose that such ought to be the construction.

Mr. Commissioner MORTON. I wish to ask a question. Where an office is filled by an ineligible person serving as officer *de facto* and his acts are held valid as to third persons, could the office at the same time be held to be vacant?

Mr. MATTHEWS. No, sir, it is not vacant. He is in office, acting in office. He can vacate it by resignation; but if there is an officer *de facto* the office is not vacant.

Mr. Commissioner MORTON. My question is whether, holding the office to be vacant, would not the effect be to hold his acts to be void as to third persons?

Mr. MATTHEWS. Yes, sir, if the office was vacant, certainly. Then there is no officer there. But the very point of this decision is that although ineligible to hold, though incapable to take, though prohibited by the constitution from continuing in office, nevertheless he was in office, and there was no vacancy. Such is the case in 11 Sergeant and Rawle, which was read to the court in the Louisiana argument, the case of the director of the Bank of Washington.

Mr. Commissioner GARFIELD. What was the decision of Chief-Justice Chase in regard to the judgment against Griffin?

Mr. MATTHEWS. He upheld the judgment and remanded the prisoner, it being an application for a *habeas corpus* to discharge him on the ground of the invalidity of the sentence. The case in 11 Sergeant and Rawle, 413, of Baird *vs.* The Bank of Washington, which argues the question at length, states that—

This principle of colorable election holds not only in regard to the right of election but also of being elected. A person indisputably ineligible may be an officer *de facto* by color of election.

I was on the point, however, of referring a little more at large to the question about the self-executing power of the Constitution in reference to these prohibitions. It was urged in argument on another occasion that no such legislation was needed in the case of these prohibitions, as was shown by the analogy of certain other prohibitions, as, for instance, it was said that there was a prohibition upon the States against emitting bills of credit; the States are prohibited from passing any *ex post facto* laws, or any laws impairing the obligation of contracts; and it was asked with an air of triumph, as if the question itself was its own answer, what legislation was ever needed to execute those provisions of the Constitution? Why, Mr. President and gentlemen, the question proves my proposition, because there has been legislation in execution of those provisions, and without it they could not be executed to-day. For instance, what is the sole example of the execution of that constitutional prohibition against the laws of States impairing the obligation of contracts? It is never executed except when it arises as a judicial question between private persons. A sues B upon a promissory note; B sets up a defense that a statute of the State in which he resides has discharged him from his obligation. A demurs to the defense, and the cause is carried, by virtue of the judiciary act of Congress, to the Supreme Court of the United States from the decision of a State court, in order to determine that question, and they do determine it, because the Supreme Court, having become vested by that act of Congress with jurisdiction and the power to try cases at law and in equity arising under the Constitution and laws of the United States, is bound by the doctrine that the Constitution of the United States is the law of that case to enforce it judicially; but if the court had never been empowered to act by an act of Congress, it could not have executed that provision of the Constitution.

Mr. Commissioner BRADLEY. Could not members of Congress execute it without any act of Congress?

Mr. MATTHEWS. Only by that provision of the Constitution which makes each House the judge of the elections, returns, and qualifications of its own members; and it is not executed in any other way than as dependent on the political will and power of each House, and each House could, in defiance of the Constitution, without any means of preventing it, admit an ineligible member to its body. Where is the power to execute the Constitution against the House if it chooses to admit an incompetent person, an incapable person?

Mr. President, just think of it. It is proposed now in this case, without previous legislation, without any indication of the will of Congress as to what ought to be the consequences, to disfranchise the people of a State because some man holding an insignificant and unknown office of trust or profit under the United States, in violation of the provisions of the Constitution, has been voted for as elector. *Non constat* but that Congress in the execution of its power to legislate to carry into effect those provisions of the Constitution might withhold any such consequence as that; they might by legislation prevent such appointments, anticipate them, impose penalties for the violation; but I take it that the American Congress has yet to come into being that, if deliberately called upon to legislate in that behalf, would impose the penalty of disfranchisement upon a State because an elector had been voted for who was incapable of exercising the office.

Mr. Commissioner BRADLEY. Your position, then, is that no one but the regularly-constituted authorities has jurisdiction and can oust an ineligible person who has been elected?

Mr. MATTHEWS. Yes, sir; because there must be a tribunal to determine the facts. It is a judicial question, a question to be ascertained upon evidence, or at any rate there must be some mode provided by law to go into the question and decide it, whether judicial or otherwise.

Mr. President, I have sufficiently argued all the points arising upon this case that occur to me which require the attention that I ought to give, and I leave the remainder of the argument to be made by the distinguished gentlemen with whom I have the honor to act in this argument. I have endeavored to treat this argument as a judicial argument and as a professional argument. I am aware of the peculiar nature of the question. I am aware of the peculiar constitution of the tribunal. I am perfectly well apprised that this is not an ordinary litigation, that it is a controversy involving party passions, party prejudices, personal interests, and public interests. I have endeavored in the course of what has seemed to me to be considerable provocation, nevertheless to possess my soul in patience. I have not from the beginning until now argued a proposition affirmatively that I did not affirmatively believe to be sound and true. I have not defended any position which I did not sincerely believe not only to be defensible, but worthy of being defended. I do not stand here to-day as counsel for any party or any person. I stand, Mr. President and gentlemen, as I have endeavored to stand from the beginning, in the attitude of a man who stands by great constitutional and legal principles. I care nothing whatever for the popular cry and clamor that it may suit anybody with loud and boisterous trumpets to proclaim to the East and to the West and to the North and to the South. I am satisfied with what I have said or attempted to say, except that I have been able to do it so imperfectly and unsatisfactorily. I am satisfied, and I shall ever remember hereafter with grateful recollections if I shall be able to attribute to any word that I have uttered the safety not only as I believe of our constitutional form of government, but doctrines which lie at the foundation of all possible government.

This idea that any man and every man, whether in his private and individual capacity or in his official character with certain prescribed bounds for his power, has a right to step out of his sphere at any moment when his party interests or his personal prejudices or any other motives may call him to what he considers to be the execution of the high act of conserving and preserving constitutional powers and rights, irrespective merely of his influence morally and politically as a citizen; this idea which has pervaded the action in this case, to ascribe it to the best, to the highest motives—and God knows I only wish it were true that I could ascribe it to any such motives—on the supposition that the governor of a State, limited by law to the performance of certain strictly-defined and well-understood ministerial duties, can upon his own mere motion, on the idea that there is something resting on his conscience on behalf of the great ægis of the Constitution, to take upon himself functions and powers which do not belong to him, which have been denied to him, is simply to confuse all the boundaries and political divisions of government; it is to unite the executive, the judicial, and the legislative powers of society in a single hand; and the wisest statesmen who framed the foundations of our Government warned us at the time of the adoption of our Federal Constitution against that very consummation, and applauded, as they had a right to do, the work of their hands, guided as they were by divine wisdom in the establishment of our present form of government under our model Constitution as the best example the world had ever seen of that deliberate division and entire definition of the boundary between the departments of government. It was the very definition and essence of personal and political freedom.

Mr. Commissioner STRONG. Mr. President, it is very apparent from the course this argument has taken that the whole time allotted to the counsel on each side is likely to be consumed before we come to the question of the admissibility of this evidence. Already, on the part of the objectors to certificate No. 1, two hours and a half have been consumed, and on the other side nearly two hours have been consumed, and yet the question is pending before us whether there is any evidence to be received outside of the certificates and papers submitted to us by the President of the Senate. This is likely to produce a very awkward state of things. I should like to have the evidence in, if it is admissible, before the counsel yet to speak conclude the argument which shall be submitted by them; and I move you, sir, that the evidence described in the first item of the offer which was made last evening be received subject to the decision of the Commission in regard to its legal effect, and if there be any evidence on the other side which is intended to counteract this, that that also be received at this stage of the proceedings, before the two counsel who are to conclude the argument shall commence their arguments.

Mr. Commissioner GARFIELD. You refer to the first offer in the printed offers, Judge Strong?

Mr. Commissioner STRONG. The first offer.

The PRESIDENT. The motion of Judge Strong is that the evidence specified in the first offer of the objectors to certificate No. 1 be now received, subject to all questions as to its legal effect.

Mr. Commissioner EDMUNDS. And any evidence on the same point.

Mr. Commissioner STRONG. Certainly, any evidence on the same point that may be offered on the other side upon the same condition.

The PRESIDENT. The question is on the motion in that form.

The motion was agreed to.

Mr. EVARTS. We may be in a little difficulty, Mr. President and gentlemen. Our witnesses attended all day yesterday, and we were prepared to go on without a moment's delay. I have now inquired whether they are ready, and I find that Mr. Tyner, the Postmaster-General, is not here. He was in attendance last evening and all day yesterday. I have no reason to doubt, however, that he is quite accessible.

Mr. MERRICK. I have not yet learned whether an answer has been returned to our subpœna.

Mr. Commissioner MORTON. The Postmaster-General was here, and told me he could not remain a long time, but would come on being telegraphed for.

Mr. EVARTS. I have no doubt he is quite accessible; only we wished to be excused for any apparent remissness.

The PRESIDENT. Of course we understand that there is a necessary delay. The question is addressed to counsel for objectors to certificate No. 1. Are you ready to offer the proof specified in the first article of your offer?

Mr. MERRICK. I presume we are. We issued yesterday a *subpœna duces tecum*, and I suppose the return is made. It ought to be.

The PRESIDENT. Ascertain that fact and report without delay, if you please.

Mr. Commissioner MILLER, (to Mr. Merrick.) You asked for certain papers, which were ordered to be furnished you.

Mr. MERRICK. Your honors ordered the papers to be furnished, and I presume the papers have been sent here; but I do not know. A request had been previously made, by one of the objectors, of the Department to give certified copies of those public records to be used in this investigation, in the hope that having them on hand any delay might be avoided; but the Department refused to give the papers until required by a subpœna.

Mr. Commissioner THURMAN. Did you not issue a subpœna yesterday?

Mr. MERRICK. There was an order. We asked for a subpœna, and the court gave an order that the papers should be furnished.

Mr. Commissioner THURMAN. Was that served yesterday?

Mr. MERRICK. That I suppose was served, but the Secretary not being in attendance, I am unable to state.

The PRESIDENT. The Secretary will be sent for.

Mr. Commissioner MORTON. Postmaster-General Tyner was here last evening with the papers.

The PRESIDENT. I have sent for the Secretary, and the minute he comes in we shall have the information.

Mr. MERRICK. The papers were placed, by the permission of the court, in the hands of the proper officer of this tribunal to be served on the Postmaster-General; but whether they have been served or not I do not know.

Mr. Commissioner MILLER. Who was the proper officer to serve the papers?

Mr. MERRICK. I presume the marshal.

Mr. Commissioner MILLER. Mr. Reardon is here, and he can state whether he has served them or not. [A pause.] The deputy marshal tells me he served the process on the Postmaster-General last evening in this room.

Mr. MERRICK. It has been served, then.

Mr. EVARTS. He would have been in attendance at the opening of this Commission this morning if it had not been arranged for the business to proceed otherwise.

Mr. Commissioner MILLER. I understand there was no *subpœna duces tecum* asked for or served. These gentlemen asked for an order for the production of a certain paper, which I saw the President sign. I think myself they ought to have seen by this time whether that paper was produced.

Mr. EVARTS. Whenever the Postmaster-General comes I think he will have with him all the papers that are desired on either side.

Mr. Commissioner THURMAN. I move that the Commission take a recess until one o'clock. The papers ought to be here by that time.

Mr. Commissioner MILLER. I think half an hour would be long enough.

Mr. Commissioner GARFIELD. I think the Postmaster-General has been here this morning; and I suppose in twenty or thirty minutes we can have the papers. He may be here sooner than that. I move to amend by making the time half past twelve.

Mr. Commissioner THURMAN. That is only twenty minutes. I will say till quarter of one, then.

Mr. Commissioner GARFIELD. I will accept that.

The PRESIDENT. It is moved that the Commission take a recess until a quarter to one o'clock.

The motion was agreed to at twelve o'clock and ten minutes p. m.

The Commission re-assembled at twelve o'clock and forty-five minutes p. m.

The PRESIDENT. The Commission is ready to receive the evidence specified in the first offer, subject to all questions as to its legal effect.

Mr. MERRICK. Mr. President, we offer a duly-certified copy of the commission of John W. Watts as postmaster at La Fayette, in the county of Yam Hill, State of Oregon, issued on the 7th of February, 1873.

Mr. EVARTS. This paper, if the court please, is satisfactory enough as being a copy, but it does not prove itself as a copy. The Postmaster-General is in attendance here with these papers under a *subpœna duces tecum*, and he can produce them as a witness and also give evidence concerning the facts, if necessary.

The PRESIDENT. Are they not certified?

Mr. EVARTS. They are not certified as copies. Still I do not care. They are no doubt copies, excepting that they should come as a part of the testimony of the Postmaster-General, Mr. Tyner, it seems to me.

Mr. MERRICK. Do counsel on the other side object to the evidence?

Mr. EVARTS. I have stated exactly my position.

The PRESIDENT. I understand the paper is not objected to. It will be therefore received.

Mr. Commissioner THURMAN. Are not these copies exemplified?

Mr. EVARTS. They are not exemplified. As I have said, they do not prove themselves.

The PRESIDENT. The question is, Mr. Evarts, whether you object to the papers.

Mr. EVARTS. I submit this to the Commission, that the Postmaster-

General should produce them here under his subpœna; and he, therefore, should be the witness to produce them. I shall make no objection, however.

Mr. MERRICK. We did not issue a subpœna for him.

The PRESIDENT. The paper will be received. The objection goes to its effect, I understand.

Mr. Commissioner EDMUNDS. I understood Mr. Evarts to make the point that the paper in its present condition is incompetent to prove the fact stated in it, but is willing that it should come in subject to that question.

The PRESIDENT. Subject to that question.

Mr. MERRICK. I take it the objection stated by Mr. Commissioner Edmunds is somewhat different from the character of the objection as stated by the President. Mr. Commissioner Edmunds understands the objection to be to matter of form. The President understood the objection to be waived as to form and go to the substance of the paper, the effect of it. I used inaccurate language in saying that we had issued a *subpœna duces tecum*. We applied for duly-certified copies of these papers, and the Commission ordered the duly-certified copies to be furnished, and these have been placed in my hands.

The PRESIDENT. Under the order?

Mr. MERRICK. Under and in response to the order of the Commission.

Mr. EVARTS. I have no doubt of their authenticity. All I submitted was that their proper production as proof should be through the witness who brought them as copies, they not proving themselves.

Mr. MERRICK. If that is insisted upon as an objection, and the authentication is not sufficiently formal under the statutes of the United States to justify their introduction into the case as testimony, we shall have to ask the indulgence of the Commission to have them authenticated according to law, that there may be a proper return to the order which you have passed in the premises.

The PRESIDENT. I shall rule, in the absence of any instructions, that the papers in their present form are not sufficient, if objected to.

Mr. EVARTS. The Postmaster-General is in attendance, and is ready to verify them as copies from his office.

The PRESIDENT. Pass them to him, then, and have them verified.

Mr. EVARTS. There is not the least occasion for delay or formality. Mr. Tyner is here.

The PRESIDENT, (to Mr. Merrick.) I think you have a right to certified copies, and it is for you to pass them to the Postmaster-General and have them certified; not for the Commission.

Mr. Commissioner MILLER. I concur with the Presiding Officer. I do not think you are compelled to introduce Mr. Tyner as a witness in order to get certified copies of papers from his office. If he has not certified them you can have them certified. I am sorry for the delay.

Mr. MERRICK. I so understand my rights, and with that understanding am endeavoring to discharge my duty.

The PRESIDENT. The Postmaster-General can verify them in five minutes, I suppose.

Mr. EVARTS. If the Commission passes on the question that the Postmaster-General is not the proper party as a witness to produce these papers, then I will waive the certificate. I do not wish to cause delay or trouble. My only point is that the Postmaster-General must have the proper opportunity.

The PRESIDENT. I am of the opinion, Mr. Evarts, that the other side have a right to a certified copy from the Postmaster-General under the order already issued, and Judge Miller concurs with me.

Mr. EVARTS. I am willing that it should be treated as if it were a certified copy.

The PRESIDENT. Very well, then, it will be received. Let the next paper be offered.

Mr. MERRICK. The next paper that we offer in evidence is the commission of Henry W. Hill, as postmaster at La Fayette, in the county of Yam Hill, State of Oregon, issued on the 3d of January in the year 1877, reciting that—

Whereas on the 23d day of November, 1876, Henry W. Hill was appointed postmaster at La Fayette, county of Yam Hill, State of Oregon; and whereas he did, on the 11th day of December, 1876, execute a bond and has taken the oath of office, as required by law, know ye, &c.

Mr. Commissioner HOAR. Is that one of the offices to which the appointment is made by the President or by the Postmaster-General?

Mr. EVARTS. It is a Postmaster-General's appointment. It is not necessary for me to object to this last paper as not being material, for all these objections are reserved.

The PRESIDENT. Under the words "the effect."

Mr. Commissioner THURMAN. Have you any evidence that Hill was the successor of Watts? Nothing appears on this paper to show that he was the successor of Watts.

Mr. MERRICK. Nothing appears on the paper to show that he was the successor of Watts, but taking the two papers together, if they are left to stand alone unexplained by the other side, we respectfully submit that they sufficiently show that Hill was Watts's successor.

The PRESIDENT. Have you any further papers?

Mr. MERRICK. We have no further papers. We rest now.

The PRESIDENT. Is there anything in reply?

Mr. EVARTS. We will call the Postmaster-General.

Hon. JAMES N. TYNER sworn and examined.

By Mr. EVARTS:

Question. You are Postmaster-General of the United States?
Answer. I am.

Q. And have been since what period?
A. About the 12th or 13th of July last.

Q. And in the discharge of the duties of that office during that period?
A. Yes, sir.

Q. Do you know of Mr. Watts having held office as postmaster in Oregon, at Yam Hill?
A. No, sir; John W. Watts held the office of postmaster at La Fayette, in Yam Hill County, Oregon.

Q. Who has the appointment of that class of officers?
A. It is a fourth-class office, the appointments to which are vested in the Postmaster-General. It is not a presidential office.

Q. Did Mr. Watts resign that office?
A. He did.

Q. At what date?

Mr. MERRICK. Wait a moment. Let the resignation be produced.

Mr. EVARTS. I ask what is the date of the resignation?

Mr. GREEN. We submit that the best evidence is the written resignation, if any exists.

The PRESIDENT. Do you object to the question?

Mr. MERRICK and Mr. GREEN. Yes, sir.

The PRESIDENT. I will submit to the Commission the question whether the objection shall be sustained.

Mr. Commissioner GARFIELD. What is the objection?

Mr. Commissioner ABBOTT. I understand the counsel merely desire to know if there was a written resignation, which I suppose they have a right to, upon the question proposed by Mr. Evarts.

The WITNESS. No such question has been put to me.

Mr. EVARTS. I asked at what time the resignation took place.

Mr. Commissioner ABBOTT. I understand, then, that counsel on the other side interpose and ask if that resignation was in writing; because if it was the writing would be the best evidence.

The PRESIDENT. No; they objected generally, as I understand. But that question may be put preliminarily whether it was in writing.

Mr. EVARTS, (to the witness.) Did you receive any resignation from Mr. Watts?

Mr. MERRICK. Was it in writing?

Mr. EVARTS. I first asked whether he received any.

The WITNESS. I did.

Q. (By Mr. EVARTS.) In what form?

A. By telegraph; and afterward in writing.

Q. Have you the telegram?

A. I have.

Q. Produce it.

A. [Producing telegram.] This is it.

Mr. EVARTS. I offer it.

The PRESIDENT. Read it.

Mr. EVARTS. It reads:

PORTLAND, OREGON, November 13, 1876.

Received at Post-Office Department, Washington——

Mr. GREEN. We object to the introduction of that paper. We will let it go, however, for what it is worth.

Mr. Commissioner EDMUNDS. Let us find out exactly what the objection is.

The PRESIDENT. On what ground do you object?

Mr. GREEN. There is no authentication of the signature; there is no proof that Watts sent the paper. It is a mere telegraphic memorandum received by the Postmaster-General at this end of the line.

Mr. EVARTS. We certainly should have to begin with this, I suppose.

The WITNESS. I also stated that there was a resignation in writing. I will submit that also.

Mr. Commissioner EDMUNDS. One thing at a time.

Mr. EVARTS. I propose to read this telegram, if I am allowed.

The PRESIDENT. I must submit the question to the Commission. An objection is made to the admissibility of the telegram, and the question is whether the objection shall be sustained.

Mr. Commissioner HOAR. I do not understand that we are passing finally on the question of its weight, but whether it shall be admitted de bene.

The PRESIDENT. Upon its admissibility at present.

Mr. Commissioner THURMAN. I understand the offer of proof is that the Postmaster-General received a telegram on such a day. That is one step. I do not see why it is not admissible. Whether the whole chain can be established is another thing.

The PRESIDENT. The question is on sustaining the objection.
The question being put, the objection was overruled.
The PRESIDENT. Read the telegram.
Mr. EVARTS. It is—

PORTLAND, OREGON, *November* 13, 1876.

To J. N. TYNER, *Postmaster-General, Washington, D. C.*:

I hereby resign as postmaster at La Fayette, Yam Hill County, Oregon. Answer by telegraph.

JOHN W. WATTS,
Postmaster La Fayette, Oregon.

Q. (By Mr. EVARTS.) Are the stamps as to the Department receipt of the telegram the stamps of the Department?
A. No, sir; that is the stamp of the telegraph company, whose office is located in the building.
Q. Do you know when this was received?
A. It was received on the morning of the 14th of November.
Q. At what hour, do you know?
A. I should think about ten o'clock.
Q. Did you make any answer to this telegram?
A. I did.
Q. Have you a copy of the telegram that you sent?
A. I made answer by telegram, of which this is a copy, [producing paper.]
The PRESIDENT. Do you offer that?
Mr. EVARTS. I do.
The PRESIDENT. Read it if there be no objection.
Mr. EVARTS. It is—

POST-OFFICE DEPARTMENT, OFFICE OF POSTMASTER-GENERAL,
Washington, D. C., November 14, 1876.

To JOHN W. WATTS, *Portland, Oregon* :

Your resignation as postmaster at La Fayette, Yam Hill County, Oregon, bearing date on November 13, 1876, is hereby accepted.

JAMES N. TYNER,
Postmaster-General.

Charge Post-Office Department.

(To the witness.) Did you send that telegram to him on that day?
A. I did; by the Western Union Telegraph Company.
Q. (By Mr. EVARTS.) When did you receive this letter? [Handing a letter to the witness.]
A. This letter was received by the Post-Office Department on the 9th day of December, through J. B. Underwood, special agent of the Post-Office Department.
Mr. EVARTS. It is addressed—

To Hon. J. B. UNDERWOOD, *Special Agent of the Post-Office Department.*

Mr. MERRICK. The signature of that letter is not identified. We object to it on that ground.
The PRESIDENT. On what ground?
Mr. MERRICK. The signature has not been proved.
Mr. EVARTS. I propose to show that this paper was received, and is on file at the Post-Office Department.
Mr. Commissioner THURMAN. What is the date of it?
Mr. EVARTS. November 12, 1876.
The PRESIDENT. The Commission have heard the objection to the admissibility of the paper. Shall the objection be sustained?
The question being put, the objection was overruled.

The PRESIDENT.   Read.
Mr. EVARTS.   It is—

To Hon. J. B. UNDERWOOD,
    Special Agent of the Post-Office Department:
    DEAR SIR: I hereby tender my resignation as postmaster at La Fayette, in Yam Hill
County and State of Oregon, and ask that my resignation be immediately accepted.
                                 J. W. WATTS,
                           Postmaster La Fayette, Oregon.
  NOVEMBER 12, 1876.

(To the witness.) Who is J. B. Underwood, and what was his relation
to the Post-Office Department?
  A. He was a special agent of the Post-Office Department, with official
and personal residence in Oregon at that time.
  Q. (By Mr. EVARTS.) How did this paper come to the Post-Office
Department?
  A. In due course of mail, transmitted by J. B. Underwood, special
agent of the Post-Office Department.
  A. With any communication from him?
  A. Yes, sir.   A communication which referred to another matter, how-
ever.
  Q. Please produce it.
  A. This is it.   [Producing a letter.]
  Q. Upon receiving the telegraphic resignation and accepting it by
telegram, did you make any communication on the subject to Under-
wood?
  A. I did.
  Q. By telegram?
  A. By telegram.
  Q. Have you that telegram?
  A. Yes, sir.   [Producing a telegram.]   This is it.
The PRESIDENT. Let it be read if there is no objection.
Mr. EVARTS.   It is—

    POST-OFFICE DEPARTMENT, OFFICE OF THE POSTMASTER-GENERAL,
                 Washington, D. C., November 14, 1876.
To J. B. UNDERWOOD,
    Special Agent Post-Office Department, Portland, Oregon:
    J. W. Watts, postmaster at La Fayette, Yam Hill County, Oregon, has resigned.
You will take charge of said office and continue in charge thereof until a successor is
appointed. Acknowledge receipt of this telegram.
                      JAMES N. TYNER,
                        Postmaster-General.
Charge Post-Office Department.

(To the witness.)   Did you receive an answer by telegram?
  A. I did.   This is it.   [Producing a telegram.]
The PRESIDENT.   Read, if not objected to.
Mr. EVARTS.   It is—

          PORTLAND, OREGON, *November* 14, 1876.
To JAMES N. TYNER, *Postmaster-General, Washington, D. C.:*
  Your telegram received. Will take charge of office this evening.
                    J. B. UNDERWOOD,
                      Special Agent.

(To the witness.)   Subsequently did you receive any other communi-
cation?
  A. I did in writing, by mail.
  Q. (By Mr. EVARTS.) This is the first?   [Presenting a letter.]
  A. That is the first.
The PRESIDENT.   Read, if not objected to.
Mr. EVARTS.   It is—

EUGENE, OREGON, *November 24, 1876.*

SIR: In accordance with your instructions of the 14th instant, I proceeded at once to take charge of the post-office at La Fayette, in Yam Hill County, Oregon, *vice* J. W. Watts, resigned. I took a full inventory of all property, giving receipts as required by law, and moved the office into another building at once, and got things running in good order the same day. I am now conducting business of the office in my name as special agent and acting postmaster, awaiting the appointment of Henry W. Hill, who is now acting as my assistant under my appointment, it being impossible for me to give my whole attention to the special duties of the office, as just at this time I am crowded with other duties pertaining to the business of the Department. I inclose the oath of my assistant.

I have the honor to be, very respectfully, &c.,

J. B. UNDERWOOD,
Special Agent Post-Office Department.

Hon. J. N. TYNER,
Postmaster-General, Washington, D. C.

(To the witness.) Did you receive that telegram [handing a telegram] and when?

A. I received that telegram on the 22d day of November, 1876.

Q. State when the letter which I have just read was received.

A. It was received at the Post-Office Department December 9, 1876.

Mr. EVARTS. The telegram which is identified is—

EUGENE CITY, OREGON, *November 22, 1876.*

To J. W. MARSHALL,
First Assistant Postmaster, Washington, D. C.:

Appoint Henry W. Hill postmaster, La Fayette, Oregon.

J. B. UNDERWOOD,
Special Agent, Post-Office Department.

(To the witness.) When did you say that was received?

A. On the 22d day of November, 1876.

Q. Did you have any further communications anterior to the issuing of this commission to Mr. Hill?

A. Not any; on that recommendation Mr. Hill was appointed.

Q. You made the appointment at what date?

A. Henry W. Hill was designated for appointment as postmaster at La Fayette, Oregon, on the 23d day of November, 1876.

Q. In what way was he designated?

A. He was designated for appointment in the usual form. That is the original, [producing a paper.]

Q. This is the form?

A. It is.

Q. This is Mr. Marshall's signature, is it?

A. It is.

Mr. EVARTS. I will read it:

November 21, 1876, La Fayette Office, Yam Hill County, Oregon State—John W. Watts postmaster, appointed February 7, 1873; salary, $270; postal bond. $2,000; money-order bond, $3,000. Appoint Henry W. Hill in place of J. W. Watts, resigned. J. W. Marshall, First Assistant Postmaster-General.

(To the witness.) That is the ordinary form?

A. It is the ordinary form.

Q. And after that was any action taken by you otherwise than signing the commission?

A. Yes, sir. A letter designating the appointment was forwarded to the appointee accompanied by a blank bond, which bond on being filled by the appointee is returned to the Post-Office Department, after which and after its approval the commission issues.

Q. At what time did any such letter issue?

A. On the 23d day of November, 1876. This is the bond itself, [producing a paper.]

Q. Was this bond forwarded?

A. That bond was forwarded in blank, filled up by Hill, and returned to the Department.

Q. And then when was the indorsement completed?

A. The bond was executed on the 11th day of December, 1876, as shown by the certificate of the officer. The commission issued on the 3d day of January, 1877, and was transmitted to Henry W. Hill by mail on the 4th day of January, 1877.

Q. When was this bond in blank forwarded with the designation you have spoken of?

A. On the 23d day of November, 1876.

Q. It was sent from your Department on the 23d day of November with the designation and the bond to be filled up?

A. Yes, sir.

Q. Are there any other papers on the subject?

A. None.

Mr. EVARTS. We are through with this witness.

The PRESIDENT. The other side can cross-examine.

Mr. GREEN. We have no questions to ask.

Mr. Commissioner THURMAN. I wish to ask the Postmaster-General a question.

(To the witness.) Is there any law or regulation of the Department which requires the accounts of postmasters to be settled up before their resignation takes effect?

A. No, sir.

By Mr. Commissioner THURMAN:

Q. There is nothing of that kind?

A. Nothing that I am aware of.

Mr. EVARTS. I will call Mr. Watts.

JOHN W. WATTS sworn and examined.

By Mr. EVARTS:

Question. Were you the postmaster at La Fayette, Yam Hill County, Oregon?

Answer. I was.

Q. Did you resign that office?

A. I did.

Q. When?

A. On the 13th day of November, 1876.

Q. By telegram?

A. Yes, sir.

Q. Did you receive any acceptance of your resignation?

A. I did.

Q. When?

A. On the 14th day of November.

Q. Was that by telegram?

A. It was.

Q. Do you know J. B. Underwood, special agent of the Post-Office Department; and did you know him in November last?

A. I did.

Q. What was done in reference to your office after your resignation, by you?

A. On the 14th of November Mr. Underwood showed me a telegram that he said he had received from the Postmaster-General, directing him to take charge of the office, and I immediately delivered it to him, making my settlement with him, and turned everything over to him.

Q. Did you have a settlement with him?

A. Yes, sir; I settled the accounts of my office with him.

Q. Was the post-office kept by you, in what building, or in what relation to any other business?

A. It was in my drug-store.

Q. Did it continue in that store?

A. It did not.

Q. Where was it removed to, and when?

A. It was removed about a block away from my store to the drug-store of Littlefield & Hill on the next morning.

Q. That was on the 14th?

A. Yes. It was late in the afternoon when I arrived there by rail, and Mr. Underwood did not move it away that night. It was late in the evening, perhaps eight o'clock. It was locked up there, and the next morning it was taken over to the drug-store of Littlefield & Hill.

Q. Did you act as postmaster at all after the 14th of November, 1876?

A. I did not.

Q. Was the post office kept open there after that?

A. It was not.

Q. Not at your place, but in the town?

A. It was in the town; not at my place.

Q. Who acted as postmaster in charge of the duties there?

A. H. W. Hill, as I understood, was appointed by Mr. Underwood when he arrived. He remained there two or three days opening the new office, and he remained there perhaps the third day.

Q. And thereafter the duties of the office were performed not at all by you but by another person and at another place?

A. It was. I performed no duties as postmaster after that time.

Cross-examined by Mr. GREEN:

Q. Were you a candidate for the office of elector of President of the United States, and Vice-President?

A. I was.

Mr. EVARTS. I object to that inquiry, unless it is for the mere purpose of identification.

Mr. GREEN. That is all.

Mr. EVARTS. I admit that he is the same person.

Q. (By Mr. GREEN.) Where is Eugene, in the State of Oregon?

A. Eugene City you have reference to?

Q. I speak of the place.

A. At the head of the Willamette Valley.

Q. How far is it from La Fayette?

A. I think about seventy-five miles; perhaps a little more.

Q. Have you settled your accounts with the Post-Office Department as postmaster at La Fayette?

A. It is not fully settled, in this way: There is a commission yet coming to me, and I had a few dollars that I did not pay over to Mr. Underwood. There was a commission due to me for part of that quarter and there were a few dollars kept back which would about balance, as we supposed. All the rest I paid to him; every dollar.

Q. Have your accounts been adjusted by the auditing officers of the Post-Office Department?

A. Not that I know of. I went to the Post-Office Department since I came here and inquired, and they said that they had immediately sent a full statement to me, but it had not reached there when I left there. I have not seen it.

Q. When did you leave Oregon?

A. I think I left there about the 15th of December; I think it was on the 15th that I left home.

Mr. GREEN. Has the Commission confined us to testimony under the first offer of proof?

Mr. Commissioner EDMUNDS. We have not passed upon the second offer yet.

The PRESIDENT. It has not been passed upon. If there are no further questions, Mr. Watts can step aside.

Mr. EVARTS. Mr. Watts could identify those papers. They are in his own handwriting, some of them.

The PRESIDENT. Unless there are some further interrogatories, he can retire.

J. M. McGREW sworn and examined.

By Mr. EVARTS:

Question. Does the settlement of postmasters' accounts come under your department?

Answer. It does.

Q. Has the account of Mr. Watts, as postmaster, been settled by the Department?

A. It has.

Q. As of what date are his emoluments and salary fixed by that settlement?

A. To and including the 14th day of November, 1876. This is the last rendered by him.

Mr. EVARTS. I do not care to pursue the details unless it is required. The other side can cross-examine.

Cross-examined by Mr. GREEN:

Q. As the Sixth Auditor, Mr. McGrew, have you charge of the accounts of this postmaster?

A. I have.

Q. When were his accounts audited?

A. They were audited some time during the last of the month—during January.

Q. Fix, as near as your recollection serves, the date when they were audited.

A. His accounts were received in the office on the 11th day of December.

Q. And the action of the auditing department took place some time in the month of January, 1877?

A. It is impossible to give the exact date, as we have 30,000 accounts of that description to settle each quarter. It was settled some time during the last month.

The PRESIDENT. Is the testimony closed?

Mr. EVARTS. I suppose it is.

The PRESIDENT. Anything further on the other side?

Mr. HOADLY. No, sir.

The PRESIDENT. The argument will be resumed.

Mr. EVARTS. Mr. President and gentlemen of the Commission, in assigning at the outset of this discussion the dividing-line between the authority of the Government of the United States, by any legislation that it might think adequate and desirable, or in execution of the constitutional power of counting the votes without any legislation on the subject, and the authority of the respective States—the line that divided what belonged to the State and what might be the subject of inquiry to the Federal Government, observing constitutional limits on the one side and the other—the counsel for the objectors with whom I am associated laid down the proposition that the ultimate fact under the laws of the State in completion of the election by the certification of boards or officers charged with the completion of the final canvass was a point beyond which, in looking into the transactions of the State, the Federal Government could not go. We laid down at the same time the further proposition that this conclusion of the State's action was the principal fact that under the legislation of Congress was made the subject of *any* lawful certification, and that as that principal fact could not be overreached by any previous inquiry into the transaction of the State, so that principal fact could not be disparaged or falsified by any congressional authority exercised in certification of that fact.

The proposition as we then laid it down for Florida, we adhered to in the case of Louisiana; and the proposition as thus laid down we adhere to in the case of Oregon. We find in Oregon, as in Florida or Louisiana, that by its laws there is some final ministerial canvass, which, completed, shows what the election was ; and we need only to look into the laws of this State, as of the other States, to see whether the apparent canvassing-board was one that had such authority under the laws of the State.

We have also asserted and adhered to but one proposition as to the powers and duties of this Commission. From the first and until now we have discarded any notion that you were a court or could exercise the powers of a court in inquiring into the actual facts of an election in the States. Not so, however, with the learned counsel who from time to time in the different stages of this matter have appeared as our opponents. The whole proposition as to Florida, on their part, was based upon the idea that you were a court, with the powers in *quo warranto* of a court, and were controlled in the exercise of those powers by no other consideration than seemed to you just in their exercise and as any other court would be governed in such exercise. The logic of that argument was accepted that if you had not that penetrating and purging power of a court, looking for and producing the very right of the matter as the election itself should disclose it, then our proposition that the evidence upon which we rested as the result of the State's action in producing electors in Florida was the " be-all and the end-all," unless some subsequent movement in that State might have displaced it.

When, then, we came to Louisiana—which differed not at all from Florida in the principles of law applicable to it on this point of the State's authority and the point of inquiry which repelled any further inquisition on your part—the principles then avowed were that the idea of your being a court with powers in *quo warranto* was wholly inadmissible, wholly inadmissible in the nature of the transaction, wholly inadmissible from the impassable barriers interposed by the Constitution. Indeed, these propositions which we had laid down in the Florida case, the support of these propositions in reason and authority, were all adopted and enforced as the doctrine of our opponents in the Louisiana case.

Now when we come to this case, even with more force and earnestness and with a greater reach and exhaustion of argument and authority, every proposition that either in the Florida or in the Louisiana case we contended for, upon this point, is avowed, is defended, is insisted upon by our opponents. Nor will it do for our learned friends to put their acceptance of these propositions upon the mere concession that this Commission has so decided and that further debate is inappropriate and unwarrantable. They have themselves in a prolonged discussion maintained, as matter of law and upon authority, not only the position that we took as to the action of a State bringing an elector into the execution of his power as an elector, but, as I understand the accomplished and experienced lawyer who yesterday presented the argument of our opponents, such a person is, until *quo warranto*, until *certiorari*, until some form of judicial contestation disturbs his position, not only a *de facto* but also a *de jure* representative of the office.

Never having had a doubt that before many weeks had passed the general judgment of the profession of this country would sustain these positions that we espoused, and that have been sanctioned by this Commission, I must yet confess that I did not expect so signal and immediate a confirmation of that expectation as the present and explicit avowal, espousal, and maintenance of these positions by our learned opponents, and I welcome this as a great and valuable aid in furnishing an answer to the irresponsible and rash comments that have been made in various relations, and especially in the public press, upon these controverted points of law, which have formed the material of the forensic discussions before this Commission and of its decisions.

I understand that in securing that unanimity of the profession so desirable in a community accustomed to look upon the *law* as the principal safeguard of the welfare of the state, this adherence of our opponents will go far to check any rising disposition to further public contest on the subject. You have decided questions of constitutional law; you have decided them in the presence of great agitations of the people, and you have decided them in a way that will establish them firm and sure principles in the future, when agitations shall take other complexions and be pushed in the interest of other parties. By what you have done, by what you shall do, the principles of the Constitution and the maintenance of the laws of this country in the great transaction of a presidential election are made certain, intelligible, rational, and sound.

Now in Oregon it is very plain that an election was held and through all its stages was conducted with an entire observance of the requirements of law, with an entire acceptance on the part of the whole population of the election and its result, up to the last stage of it, with every step unquestioned in its integrity, its justice, and its conformity to law. The result reached by the authentic canvass of the votes, by the proper authority, and in the proper presence, showed on each side the vote for electors, according to law, being upon general ticket, that three on the one side ran even with each other, three on the other side even with each other, except by the casual and unimportant disparity of a few votes as between the several candidates on the same ticket. All that has disturbed this result has occurred after the completion of the election and its certification as completed by the proper authority, after the final canvass and its certification by the officer of state charged with the duty of canvassing and certifying. That canvass remains of record now in the secretary of state's office, undisturbed, undisputed, unquestioned. That is the fact upon which the title of the electors for President and Vice-President for the State of Oregon rests. Thereafter there remains nothing to be done on the part of any official of that State, under the terms of the Constitution of the United States nothing whatever, and under the law of Congress there remains but one act to be performed, to wit, the provision by the executive of the State and the delivery to the electoral college that was elected of triple certificates to accompany as a formal authentication the action of the electoral college.

All that our learned friends urge as arguments upon what they consider an improvident, an unsound, and dangerous doctrine on our part, but urged only in anticipation of hearing our views, is that this result of the canvass of an election made matter of record according to the laws of a State might be falsified, might be perverted, might be destroyed by the process of certification, if we should hold that the form was greater than the substance. All those hypothetical suggestions are now brought in play as actual transactions occurring in the State of Oregon; and now the pretension that certification is paramount to the thing certified, not amendable by the thing certified, not amendable by the record which is the thing to be certified—all those propositions proceed from our opponents as their champions. They have not changed places with us, for we never occupied any such position. They have, however, assumed the propositions, from time to time, which were necessary and suitable for the particular occasions on which they used them. It has been convenient, as it seems to us, for this representation of diverse sentiments and opinions at different times, that they have not been presented by the same counsel. We have a change in the advocates attending a change in the propositions.

First, let us understand what is presented, in the shape of evidence, that bears upon the construction of what is contained in the *certificates* which are plenary evidence before you, they having been opened and transmitted by the President of the Senate. It is that Mr. Watts, holding a small post-office of the fourth class in the State of Oregon, appointed years before, was discharging the duties of that office on the 7th of November; that on the 14th of November he resigned his office, and his resignation was accepted; that thereafter the Department accepted the charge of the office and conducted it from that time forward, and that, as matter of fact, the office itself was changed from the place of business of Watts, the postmaster who resigned, to the place of business of the officer designated to take his place, Mr. Hill, having a drug-store, and then becoming immediately assistant postmaster under the special agent, and in due course of time receiving a commission as postmaster in full. Then Mr. Watts, whenever you come to consider, if you do, the question of whether he could be appointed an elector on the 6th of December, on his refusal to act upon his prior appointment, is unmistakably placed before you in the position of a postmaster who had resigned, and who had received from the Post-Office Department the acceptance of the trust that he had laid aside, which thenceforth was conducted by the Department itself under its agents.

I do not think that I need now to re-argue in the least either the question of ineligibility as justifying proof, or the question of whether an ineligible candidate is vested with an office until by some determination he is excluded from it. Whatever we said that received the assent of this Commission in the former arguments needs not to be repeated. Whatever was said that did not receive the assent of this Commission will be of no service in that regard if it be repeated. I shall therefore proceed with the inquiry into the validity of the vote of the three electors in the first certificate, as it rests upon the evidence in your possession proceeding from the State, delivered into the hands of the President of the Senate, and opened before the two Houses of Congress, and now deposited with you as evidence for you to regard.

What, then, does this certificate No. 1 contain? I ask your attention to the parts of it that I shall now designate. I ask attention to the certificate of the electors, commencing at the foot of page 3 of the printed paper. It is their certificate of the votes that they cast:

UNITED STATES OF AMERICA,
 State of Oregon, County of Marion, ss :

We, W. H. Odell, J. C. Cartwright, and J. W. Watts, electors of President and Vice-President of the United States for the State of Oregon, duly elected and appointed in the year A. D. 1876, pursuant to the laws of the United States, and in the manner directed by the laws of the State of Oregon, do hereby certify that at a meeting held by us at Salem, the seat of government in and for the State of Oregon, on Wednesday, the 6th day of December, A. D. 1876, for the purpose of casting our votes for President and Vice-President of the United States—

A vote was duly taken, by ballot, for President of the United States, in distinct ballots for President only, with the following result:

The whole number of votes cast for President of the United States was three (3) votes. That the only person voted for for President of the United States was Rutherford B. Hayes, of Ohio.

That for President of the United States Rutherford B. Hayes, of Ohio, received three (3) votes.

In testimony whereof we have hereunto set our hands on the first Wednesday of December, in the year of our Lord one thousand eight hundred and seventy-six.

W. H. ODELL.
J. C. CARTWRIGHT.
J. W. WATTS.

That is all that the Constitution of the United States requires. The twelfth article of the amendments is:

The electors shall meet in their respective States and vote by ballot for President and Vice-President; * * * they shall name in their ballots the person voted for as President, and in distinct ballots the person voted for as Vice-President, and they shall make distinct lists of all persons voted for as President, and of all persons voted for as Vice-President, and of the number of votes for each; which lists they shall sign and certify, and transmit sealed to the seat of Government of the United States, directed to the President of the Senate. The President of the Senate shall, in the presence of the Senate and House of Representatives, open all the certificates, and the votes shall then be counted.

That, then, is a discharge of the entire constitutional duty, and with the full certification of its discharge that the Constitution requires. What duty has been added by the act of Congress to be performed by the college of electors in this behalf? In the one hundred and thirty-eighth section of your revision this is their duty:

The electors shall make and sign three certificates of all the votes given by them, each of which certificates shall contain two distinct lists, one of the votes for President and the other of the votes for Vice-President, and shall annex to each of the certificates one of the lists of the electors which shall have been furnished to them by direction of the executive of the State.

This paper contains no such list, we will suppose; but is it a failure of duty on the part of the electors? Is there even a presumption that they have received such paper, and have omitted to include it in their return? By no means. If any default, any imperfection in the duty of those electors is to be charged, it must be based on the fact that the executive furnished that college with the list as the act of Congress required the executive to do, and that they have omitted it; and we find as a part of the minutes of this electoral college a statement as to this matter of fact, whether that college was ever furnished with any of the lists that the executive of the State was trusted by the act of Congress to furnish. They make out a sworn statement before a proper magistrate, whose authority to administer the oath is certified by the secretary of state as a proper officer for that purpose:

UNITED STATES OF AMERICA,
 State of Oregon, County of Multnomah, ss :

We, J. C. Cartwright, W. H. Odell, and J. W. Watts, being each duly and severally sworn, say that at the hour of twelve o'clock m. of the (6th) sixth day of December

A. D. 1876, we duly assembled at the State capitol, in a room in the capitol building at Salem, Oregon, which was assigned to us by the secretary of state of the State of Oregon. That we duly, on said day and hour, demanded of the governor of the State of Oregon and of the secretary of state of the State of Oregon certified lists of the electors for President and Vice-President of the United States for the State of Oregon, as provided by the laws of the United States and of the State of Oregon; but both L. F. Grover, governor of the State of Oregon, and S. F. Chadwick, secretary of state of said State, then and there refused to deliver to us, or either of us, any such certified lists or any certificate of election whatever. And being informed that such lists had been delivered to one E. A. Cronin by said secretary of state, we each and all demanded such certified lists of said E. A. Cronin, but he then and there refused to deliver or to exhibit such certified lists to us, or either of us. Whereupon we have procured from the secretary of state certified copies of the abstract of the vote of the State of Oregon for electors of President and Vice-President at the presidential election held in said State November 7, A. D. 1876, and have attached them to the certified list of the persons voted for by us and of the votes cast by us for President and Vice-President of the United States, in lieu of a more formal certificate.

W. H. ODELL.
J. W. WATTS.
JOHN C. CARTWRIGHT.

Sworn and subscribed to before me this 6th day of December, A. D. 1876.
[SEAL.]   THOS. H. CANN,
Notary Public for State of Oregon.

What becomes now of the proposition of a State being defrauded of its vote in the electoral college when its electors, appointed according to the will of the people of the State, have assembled, discharged their constitutional duty, and are deprived by the executive of the State of the certified lists which it becomes a part of their duty, if they receive them from him, and only in such case, to append in verification? Which is it that is to stand, the electors made by the Constitution of the United States sufficient certifiers of their own action, made by the act of Congress only subject to the single duty besides of inclosing the lists that the governor may have given them? Here you have the electors meeting, voting, certifying, and transmitting, and showing that the absence of the governor's list arises from the governor's default and not their own, and that they have supplied the fact on which the governor's list must rest if it be lawful, the fact of the final canvass of the election, produced before you now here just as if you inspected it yourself in the office of secretary of state.

Now my friends are in the face of the proposition whether a fraudulent, or a perverse, or an ignorant governor can subtract or withhold the paper, and the electoral college be destroyed and the presidential vote be lost. If we were to proceed no further, I should ask, the governor's certificate withheld, was there any excuse for that, is there any pretense that it was delivered? Not the slightest. Nobody pretends that the governor of Oregon ever furnished those lists to the electoral college; nobody pretends that any messenger or intermediary of his ever delivered those lists to the electoral college. What is the language of the act of Congress in that behalf?

> It shall be the duty of the executive of each State to cause three lists of the names of the electors of such State to be made and certified, and to be delivered to the electors on or before the day on which they are required by the preceding section to meet.

Is it to the college, to the body, or is it not? It is to the college or body. Did the governor ever deliver them to this college or to this body that was met? Did Mr. Cronin ever deliver them as the agent of the governor to this college or body that was met? Its title to them was complete. The duty and obligation of the governor in this behalf were complete when the college was assembled at the capitol. No

ELECTORAL COUNT OF 1877.

matter who composed it, whether Watts was a member or Cronin was a member, the papers were then to be delivered to the college, and their subtraction, their withholding, needs no description of fraud or contrivance. It was an absolute desertion of duty, and such desertions of duty are never gratuitous. They always have an object, and the result that followed is the object designed.

How is the act of Oregon in this behalf?

The secretary of state shall prepare two lists of the names of the electors elected and affix the seal of the State to the same. Such lists shall be signed by the governor and secretary, and by the latter delivered to the college of electors at the hour of their meeting on such first Wednesday of December.

Was that done? If you employ an agent or messenger, instead of delivering with due formality and openly, as I venture to say has been done in every State in this Union, has been done in Oregon until this election, then you are responsible to see that the messenger or agent makes the delivery. I then say that this certification and action of this college are all that the Constitution and the laws of the United States require, and that on the face of this certificate, the college making its representations, and the knowledge of this college in respect to its majority of attending members being open to any inquiry, you are at once face to face with the proposition whether a subtraction, a suppression by the executive of the State of one of these lists, entitles both Houses of Congress to throw out the vote of the State.

But this certificate contains a great deal more. The occasion for its containing so much more is undoubtedly because of this violation of duty on the part of the executive of the State, but what does it contain? It contains an abstract of votes cast at the presidential election as on file in the secretary of state's office. It is the very canvass itself of every county for every candidate and in every figure that becomes the subject of tabulation.

SALEM, STATE OF OREGON:

I hereby certify that the foregoing tabulated statement is the result of the vote cast for presidential electors at a general election held in and for the State of Oregon on the 7th day of November, A. D. 1876, as opened and canvassed in the presence of his excellency L. F. Grover, governor of said State, according to law, on the 4th day of December, A. D. 1876, at two o'clock p. m. of that day, by the secretary of state.

[SEAL.]   S. F. CHADWICK,
Secretary of State of Oregon.

Besides this there is this certificate, the importance of which will appear from the citation of some of the statutes of Oregon which I shall mention:

UNITED STATES OF AMERICA,
STATE OF OREGON, SECRETARY'S OFFICE,
Salem, December 6, 1876.

I, S. F. Chadwick, secretary of the State of Oregon, do hereby certify that I am the custodian of the great seal of the State of Oregon; that the foregoing copy of the abstract of votes cast at the presidential election held in the State of Oregon November 7, 1876, for presidential electors, has been by me compared with the original abstract of votes cast for presidential electors aforesaid, on file in this office, and said copy is a correct transcript therefrom and of the whole of the said original abstract of votes cast for presidential electors.

That is that transaction which, observed and attended to by the governor in a certificate, would give to his certificate the support in law if he had discharged the duty in fact:

In witness whereof I have hereto set my hand and affixed the great seal of the State of Oregon the day and year above written.

[SEAL.]   S. F. CHADWICK,
Secretary of the State of Oregon.

Besides that there is this:

List of votes cast at an election for electors of President and Vice-President of the United States in the State of Oregon held on the 7th day of November, 1876.

FOR PRESIDENTIAL ELECTORS.

W. H. Odell received fifteen thousand two hundred and six (15,206) votes.
J. W. Watts received fifteen thousand two hundred and six (15,206) votes.
J. C. Cartwright received fifteen thousand two hundred and fourteen (15,214) votes.
E. A. Cronin received fourteen thousand one hundred and fifty-seven (14,157) votes.
H. Klippel received fourteen thousand one hundred and thirty-six (14,136) votes.
W. B. Laswell received fourteen thousand one hundred and forty-nine (14,149) votes.
Daniel Clark received five hundred and nine (509) votes.
F. Sutherland received five hundred and ten (510) votes.
Bart Curl received five hundred and seven (507) votes.
S. W. McDowell received three, (3,) Gray one, (1,) Simpson one, (1,) and Salisbury one (1) vote.

I, S. F. Chadwick, secretary of state in and for the State of Oregon, do hereby certify that the within and foregoing is a full, true, and correct statement of the entire vote cast for each and all persons for the office of electors of President and Vice-President of the United States for the State of Oregon at the general election held in said State on the 7th day of November, A. D. 1876, as appears by the returns of said election now on file in my office.

[SEAL.]

S. F. CHADWICK,
Secretary of State of Oregon.

There is the list by the executive authority of the State of Oregon so far as it was lodged in the office and committed to the secretary of state, so far as the great seal of the State affixed by the executive officer of the State having its custody could make a certification by a State. Who else is there in Oregon that can certify a list? Who has the list? Who has the seal? Who has the office both of record and of certification? The secretary of state. Supposing, then, that to be so for a moment, where do you find any defect of that in being an adequate compliance with the act of Congress and the act of Oregon that gives you a list of the persons appointed? You have nothing to do but to read the laws of Oregon and see that electors are to be appointed by election, and that in every election held in that State the persons that have the highest number of votes shall be declared elected—that is in the Constitution; and in the election laws " that the persons having the highest number of votes shall be deemed elected," and then you discard all the rest as surplusage and unnecessary verification of the thing certified. What does it want under the act of Oregon? The act of Oregon requires a list to be given by the secretary of state under the great seal of the State, and only requires that the governor shall sign it. The governor, in pursuance of the great breach of trust and duty which he had meditated and was performing, refused his name to that certification. Does that cease to be a certification that the Congress of the United States will accept as an adequate observance of the directory duty that the executive authority of a State shall furnish lists of the persons appointed? I think not. We shall see by very brief references that under the laws of Oregon this paper now here before you is to you as matter of evidence precisely the same as if you had before you the original paper in the office of the secretary of state. I ask attention to the laws of Oregon, not printed in the little syllabus, that relate to the subject of evidence of public writings, at pages 253, 256, and 257 of the Oregon code. The constitutional provision is given in this pamphlet, page 137:

There shall be a seal of State, kept by the secretary of state for official purposes, which shall be called " the seal of the State of Oregon."

The secretary of state shall keep a fair record of the official acts of the legislative assembly and executive department of the State.

The secretary of state, by the law of Oregon, is keeper of the action of the executive department of the State—

and shall, when required, lay the same and all matters relative thereto before either branch of the legislative assembly.

The seven hundred and seventh section of the Oregon revision provides:

Every citizen of this State has a right to inspect any public writing of this State, except where otherwise expressed and provided by this code or some other statute. Every public officer having the custody of a public writing which the citizen has a right to inspect, is bound to give him on demand a certified copy of it on payment of the legal fees therefor, and such copy is primary evidence of the original writing.

The documents that are embraced within this duty of the secretary of State are named, so far as pertinent to this inquiry, on page 256, and within this certificate, as provided in section 738:

Whenever a copy of a writing is certified to be used as evidence, the certificate shall state that the copy has been compared by the certifying-officer with the original, and that it is a correct transcript therefrom, and of the whole of such original or of a specified part thereof. The official seal, if there be any, of the certifying-officer shall also be affixed to such certificate, &c.

Looking at this certificate, then, with the act of Congress before you in reference to certified lists that are to be used and employed, can you have any doubt that this contains all that is necessary to make action, the *bona fide* action, the complete lawful action, of the electors and of the State that had chosen them electors—the disparagement of the authentication under the act of Congress by the governor's withholding of his certificate, if unexplained, not affecting the certification by the electors, who have done their duty under the Constitution, and are chargeable with no want of duty under the act of Congress or under the act of Oregon?

We have, besides, the minutes of the college. Now are the electors a body? They are so described in the statutes of the United States; they are so described in the statutes of Oregon. They are necessarily a college under the power confided in them to fill vacancies, which both by the act of Congress and by the statutes of their respective States is confided to them.

Mr. Commissioner BRADLEY. Mr. Evarts, who made this list?

Mr. EVARTS. The original as now on file?

Mr. Commissioner BRADLEY. Yes.

Mr. EVARTS. The secretary of state, as the canvassing-officer, in the presence of the governor, as I understand.

Mr. Commissioner ABBOTT. Permit me to ask if there is any law that you have discovered, Mr. Evarts, which permits the secretary of state to certify to a result drawn from certain figures before him, certain returns? Is it not simply that he can certify to any paper for what it is worth?

Mr. EVARTS. By reason of this general power?

Mr. Commissioner ABBOTT. Yes, sir.

Mr. EVARTS. He has given a certificate of the full paper; that is the canvass. All the rest is a transaction lower down in the election. These are all the counties of the State, all the votes returned, all the candidates voted for, the distribution and the tabulation, and was done by him in the presence of the governor.

Mr. Commissioner ABBOTT. I will call your attention to the certificate on the second page:

I hereby certify that the foregoing tabulated statement is the result of the vote cast for presidential electors, &c.

Mr. EVARTS. Yes.

As opened and canvassed in the presence of his excellency L. F. Grover, governor of said State.

That is canvassing; producing the tabulated vote from the votes forwarded from the precincts and counties is the canvass.

Mr. Commissioner BRADLEY. The next says " copy of abstract."

Mr. EVARTS. Yes.

Mr. Commissioner BRADLEY. " Compared with the original abstract of votes cast for presidential electors aforesaid on file in this office."

Mr. EVARTS. Yes; and the whole of it. Will any one tell me what else there was to canvass? What more can anybody do than take the returns? They cannot alter them; they are all to be opened, all to be canvassed, and the result produced. Whether you call it a result, provided it be a paper formal, complete, recorded, or whether you call it an abstract of the votes according to law, it is the transaction that the law confides to the officer, and it is its execution as he files it after he has performed the duty. You will see by the election laws that section 37 provides :

The county clerk, immediately after making the abstract of the votes given in his county—

The same word is used; that is his return; that is his canvass. The abstract is the canvass set down as the result—

shall make a copy of each of said abstracts, and transmit it by mail to the secretary of state at the seat of government; and it shall be the duty of the secretary of state, in the presence of the governor, to proceed within thirty days after the election, and sooner if the returns be all received, to canvass the votes given for secretary and treasurer of state, state printer, justices of the supreme court, member of Congress, and district attorneys; and the governor shall grant a certificate of election to the person having the highest number of votes, and shall also issue a proclamation declaring the election of such person.

Then for the officers designated in regard to the election of President :

The votes for the electors shall be given, received, returned, and canvassed as the the same are given, returned, and canvassed for members of Congress. The secretary of state shall prepare two lists, &c.

There being no provision for a governor's commission or anything of that kind; but I will not repeat the argument of my learned associate, so effectually, as it seems to me, made, in regard to this operation. What I have to say to your honors is this, that you have included by authentication satisfactory to the laws of Oregon of the very canvass itself as it now appears of record in the department of state. There is no other canvass. The blotter or the slate in which there may have been a tentative addition of numbers is not the transaction of record. This is the very thing. It never existed as a canvass till it stood in that shape, and standing in that shape, it could acquire nothing additional, tolerate nothing additional.

In the minutes this board proceeds with its own transactions. The hour having arrived,

The meeting was duly organized by electing W. H. Odell chairman and J. C. Cartwright secretary.

The resignation of J. W. Watts, who was, on November 7, A. D. 1876, duly elected an elector of President and Vice-President of the United States for the State of Oregon. was presented by W. H. Odell, and, after being duly read, was unanimously accepted,

You have his resignation. It was a transaction in perfect good faith. It was in open day. It was matter of record in this college. It rested upon an uncertain opinion as to whether his having been postmaster destroyed his eligibility, whether it would destroy his vote; he refuses to act under that appointment for fear of that public injury to the State of Oregon. He did his duty in the college of electors. If Cronin was a member of the college and Cronin had attended and Cronin had part in the transactions, whatever was done by Watts was done openly and would be seen and known by Cronin as well as the others, and if there remained further controversy, further action of the college to determine who were the three, that would have been taken, that would have been recorded in the minutes; but of the principal fact, that Watts refused to act under his original appointment on the scruple that his State might thereby lose a vote that it was entitled to, the college proceed (the disability having been removed in their construction, and in yours, as I submit) to recognize the will of the people of Oregon in their selection of the person of Mr. Watts, a man known and trusted by that people, and gave him a title which, trusting to, the State of Oregon would not put in peril one of its votes.

Then the voting proceeds, and the ballots are here. The very ballots themselves, the originals that were deposited are here, each of them bearing the indorsement of the elector who deposited it. Therefore you have the election here, and now I should like to know whether under the Constitution of the United States, under the statute of 1792, under the law of Oregon about presidential elections, these minutes are not plenary proof of the action of that college, if that was a college. Did anybody ever pretend that the certificate named by the act of Congress was any part of the warrant of the electors to act in the college? No. It is to be delivered to the electors acting in the college in order that they may use it as part of their transaction. Who can contradict this? Who can be heard to contradict it? You have then this absolute proof. When this college convened and undertook to act, there were present the two men that without any impeachment had a perfect title to the office. There was present a third man, and there was nobody else present, and then the transaction went on.

I apprehend, therefore, that unless you hold that the want of the governor's certificate, its subtraction by the violation of the governor's duty, is sufficient to suppress the electoral college and the vote of the State, you have here everything that you need under the act of Congress, under the Constitution of the United States, without looking at the certificates which they put in in support of their title, out of abundant caution, in the abundant performance of duty, in order that it may be seen that the absence of any formality is not to be imputed to them from the absence of the principal fact on which and from which the formality derives its sole claim to existence.

We have another certificate, and this contains nothing that contradicts the other, nothing that by itself can stand on its own inspection as an adequate transaction. In the first place, what is the certificate of the governor? Does this comply with the act of Congress?

I, L. F. Grover, governor of the State of Oregon, do hereby certify that at a general election held in said State on the 7th day of November, A. D. 1876, William H. Odell received 15,206 votes, John C. Cartwright received 15,214 votes, E. A. Cronin received 14,157 votes, for electors of President and Vice-President of the United States; —

The syntax arrangement, perhaps, is a little at fault, but we begin after a semicolon thus:

being the highest number of votes cast at said election for persons eligible, under the Constitution of the United States, to be appointed electors of President and Vice-President of the United States, they are hereby declared duly elected electors as aforesaid for the State of Oregon.

That is a negative pregnant. The disparity of votes is shown. The fact of election on a general ticket is matter of law in the State. You have in the other certificate the clear certification of how the fact was as to who had the highest number of votes. Now this governor has undertaken by the insertion of the word "eligible" to cover himself from the condemnation of open and recognized fraud and falsehood, and he has undertaken by giving a reason, instead of obeying the constitution and laws of Oregon, to save himself from having absolutely deserted his duty. If there ever was a State that had taken every precaution to provide that all these suggestions, all these surmises, that by some method of construction, by some usurpation of power, others than the men who received the highest number of votes could be deemed elected anywhere, in that State the constitution and the laws of Oregon had so provided. Why was not the word "eligible" put into the constitution and put into the laws as determining who should be the product of an election, who should be declared the product of an election, who should be treated as the product of an election? The constitution provides, as you have seen, that—

In all elections held by the people under this constitution, the person or persons who shall receive the highest number of votes shall be declared duly elected.

Concede for the moment that electors are not within that clause of the constitution, nevertheless this shows what the constitutional law of Oregon was with respect to what makes an election; and when the legislature has determined that the electors for President and Vice-President of the United States shall be produced by the method of election, and when they have a law which is not limited to anything except the question whether the election is in the State and ascribes the efficacy of the highest number the case is complete and final, as they do in this clause:

In all elections in this State the person having the highest number of votes for any office shall be deemed to have been elected.

That is section 40. But in the election law you will find the strongest provision as to the highest number of votes in the instance when it does prevent an election, because there are two for the same office having the highest number of votes. In section 36:

If the requisite number of county or precinct officers shall not be elected by reason of two or more persons having an equal and the highest number of votes for one and the same office, the clerk whose duty it is to compare the polls shall give notice to the several persons so having the highest and an equal number of votes to attend at the office of the county clerk at a time to be appointed by said clerk, who shall then and there proceed publicly to decide by lot which of the persons so having an equal number of votes shall be declared duly elected; and the said clerk shall make and deliver to the person thus declared elected a certificate of his election as hereinbefore provided.

Had the clerk a right to discharge the duty limited to casting votes and the imperative obligation to declare the one who received the lot—had the clerk the right to substitute for that duty a determination that there were no two persons that had received the highest number of votes, and the lot was not required, because he thought one of them was not eligible? But the clerk has in regard to those officers every power that the governor has in regard to the other officers, (see section 37:)

In case there shall be no choice by reason of any two or more persons having an equal and the highest number of votes for either of such offices—

That is, the larger offices of the State—

the governor shall by proclamation order a new election to fill said offices.

Is not that an imperative duty on the governor when there are two having the highest number of votes? The law of Oregon is that disqualification does not elect the other, and that in that case there must be a new election; and has this governor the authority to determine that, instead of having a new election, he will commission the one, not that has the highest number of votes—for that is inscrutable, they being equal—but the one that he thinks is eligible? What becomes of the right of the people to have a new election? They voted for the men; they have produced that result; and they are entitled to the consequence of the election.

What then is the title? What does it rest upon? It is quite immaterial to you what the Cronin title in the abstract is. The point for you to determine is, which of these colleges is to be counted. There cannot be two colleges. When the civil law lays down the proposition that *tres facit collegium*, it lays it down in the assertion of a principle, not by an arbitrary rule. The principle of a college is that the majority governs, and that principle cannot be applied to a less number than three. One man is not a college; two men are not a college, for there is not a majority there unless it be unanimity. Unanimity is not the essence of a college. So long as people are unanimous they proceed in their natural rights as individuals; but three make a college because the vital principle of a college is that the majority exercise the power of the college; and here what have you before you? A college of three; a college assembled; and what is Cronin's account of it? That all three met, and instead of saying anything short he undertakes to say that they refused to act as electors of President and Vice-President. Will you allow his statement, backed by the certifying names of two men who were not present—for they came in afterward and were chosen electors by Cronin, after the transaction upon which he bases the formation of his college—will you allow Cronin's statement that these two men resigned, declined, remitted, deserted the duty of voting for President of the United States to outweigh their own certificate, their own action, their own return, their own ballots that are here before you? I should think not. And if you are bound to look at the matter upon the legal question whether the majority of the college can fill the vacancy or whether the minority of the college can fill the vacancy, each having assumed to do it, you will have no great trouble in determining that the majority anchors the college to itself, and that the minority is no college at all.

Supposing it to be true that these electors did not recognize Cronin, did not regard him as an elector; they had the right to that judgment. Nobody else, I think, regarded him as such except upon the experimental invention of him to see whether he could be manufactured to stand until after the counting of this vote. But did you ever hear that when a bank director or a member of any corporation or of any board, municipal or civil, under the Government of the United States or under the government of any State, did not recognize the title of one man claiming to be a member of that board, anything happened except that he was excluded, and if he was wrongfully excluded he must right himself by law? Other parties might question whether the action of the board taken after that exclusion was or was not lawful. But did you ever hear that the exclusion of a member of the board, lawful or unlawful, just or unjust, authorized him to go and fill the board and go on with business? I think that is as great a novelty in the law of colleges, of civil boards, of governmental boards, or of private boards, as was ever suggested. If you depart from the proposition that whatever may have happened in respect to Cronin of injustice or exclusion, that did not make him the college, you have this absurd possibility in a State like Oregon, that you would have three colleges, each man preferring to throw the votes his own way and by his own authority. But if you adopt the rule that the majority constitutes the college, you put yourself under the protection of the principle which governs all corporate action, that there can be but one college, one board, because the majority draws to itself all the powers of the board.

Now look at the very peremptory direction of the law of Oregon in respect to the conduct of the board when it meets to discharge its duty —section 59 :

> The electors of President and Vice-President shall convene at the seat of government on the first Wednesday of December next after their election, at the hour of twelve of the clock at noon of that day ; and if there shall be any vacancy in the office of an elector, occasioned by death, refusal to act, neglect to attend, or otherwise, the electors present shall immediately proceed to fill, by *viva voce* and plurality of votes, such vacancy in the electoral college.

Can you have a plurality of votes when only one vote is cast ?

> And when all the electors shall appear or the vacancies, if any, shall have been filled, as above provided, &c.

They are not allowed to go on ; they are not allowed to act for the State of Oregon until they are possessed of the means of casting its whole vote.

Mr. Commissioner ABBOTT. Permit me to ask you, Mr. Evarts, what would be the case if two of the electors had died since the election ? There is but one left in the land of the living; must the State lose its two votes or three ?

Mr. EVARTS. If the whole three have died ?

Mr. Representative ABBOTT. No; if two have died and there is but one left ?

Mr. EVARTS. If two have died and there is one left, the State ought to exercise a power reserved to it to treat the election as having failed, or it may be the votes would be lawful. There is no existing law of Oregon, and no existing law of any State, that in its terms covers the case of there not being a college to proceed to fill vacancies. There can be no college when you are reduced to one. You have an elector, I agree, and it is certainly undesirable that the State should lose its votes. That I agree, and I agree that an honest effort to present the vote to the Congress here acting on the subject should receive every indulgence on the part of the political authority that deals with the question, but I certainly cannot as matter of law admit either under the act of Congress or——

Mr. HOADLY. Will you permit a question ? Does the word " plurality " there refer to plurality of the original number elected, or of those remaining after the vacancy ?

Mr. EVARTS. There is nothing that confines it to the whole number. It is a clear authority to them to choose by the plurality of a quorum.

Mr. HOADLY. To those remaining ?

Mr. EVARTS. Of those remaining ; but that does not touch the question of whether there should or should not be a quorum to act. The ordinary rule of corporations and colleges is that a majority of a quorum is equivalent to a majority of the whole. There must be some statute to the contrary. This college of electors consisted of the two men clearly chosen, that are not blotted out by any evidence before you, except the certificate of Cronin, not that they refused to act with him, but he says they refused to act as electors. Where is his evidence? Where is the record? Where are the minutes? Where is the notice in writing? Where is the absenteeism? That is not certified to; but they refused to act as electors, and he then proceeded to fill their places by his single vote.

Now, whether or not under the laws of some States that faculty could reside in a single elector, it does not reside in a single elector by the act of Oregon. Oregon had, by the provisions of the electoral law of the Union, power to provide for a failure of election. What was that? It was when the election failed, when there was no production of enough electors, if you please, to meet the true exigency of the law in that behalf, if it required a majority to be produced by an election; and it is in that case, and in that case only, that the State is allowed by the United States law to substitute in the place of the regular mode of election some secondary method. But it does not require the State to provide a different mode of filling a vacancy arising from a failure to elect, from the mode that they adopt for filling a vacancy arising in any other manner. Oregon has settled that question for itself, that in *whatever way*, on the very day of casting the electoral vote, a vacancy in the college should exist, it should be filled. Thus, while the Constitution makes it absolutely necessary that there should be a personal attendance to cast a vote, and that a majority cannot cast an absent vote, because the voting is to be by ballot, and the ballots are to be counted, the State determines that by no chance will it lose a vote if there be persons present on that day who can fill the places and save the State its full representation in the electoral college.

The State of Rhode Island, finical as it was in its legislation, instead of making a better arrangement than this of Oregon and the other States, placed itself under a much worse system, according to the judicial opinion given by the supreme court of that State. Suppose that when the legislature of that State undertakes by a new appointment to fill the vacancies originating from a failure of the people to elect, it should be found that the legislature has filled the vacancy by a person who, when he comes to the college, proves himself to be disqualified, what is to happen in that State then? The legislature has not given to the college the plenary power to fill vacancies. The resignation or withdrawal of the disqualified elector will not allow the college to fill his place. The same vice inheres in the choice by the legislature of an unqualified person that would arise from such an election by the people, and the State must lose the vote. To be sure, practically, in a State like Rhode Island, where the governor by blowing his horn at the door of the executive mansion can summon the legislature as the farmer's wife calls to dinner the hands from the hay-field, there would be no difficulty in suddenly supplying the vacancy; but for the great State of Oregon, where there were found insuperable difficulties in getting the legislature together, no such arrangement would be either wise or suitable.

Now, upon an examination of all these certificates I have been quite gratified to find that, although these operators up in Oregon were as harmless as serpents, they were also no wiser than doves. Nothing has been done there that defeats the Constitution of the United States, that defrauds the State of Oregon, that defeats the election of President. All that has resulted from the attempt to perpetrate and consummate a fraud is to exhibit the fraud to public condemnation; but the safety of the State remains unharmed.

Mr. MERRICK. Mr. President and gentlemen of the Commission, it would certainly be extremely grateful to me if I could pass by in acquiescing silence the expressions of satisfaction which the learned counsel who last addressed you was pleased to use at the supposed fact that we of counsel who have been conducting these cases on behalf of the people of the United States had finally, in the vicissitudes to which the cases have been subjected, come to believe in and accept as the law of the land those principles which he and his learned friends had advanced in the beginning of the discussion as the proper and correct rules of law upon which the matters submitted to this Commission should be solved and settled, and which, as he claims, have passed into the judgments of this tribunal. I do not wish to criticise those judgments and shall refrain from any such unpleasant office, but when my personal opinion is challenged or demanded, I should be doing a gross injustice to the profession and to myself if I seemed to acquiesce in the accuracy of the statement made by the counsel. I wish it were different; I lament that the statement is not accurate in every particular, for surely there can be no greater satisfaction to a member of the legal profession than to feel that in the discharge of a conscientious duty he can with all his ability and all his efforts maintain as the law of the land those principles that have passed into solemn adjudication, whether they be the adjudications of courts or the adjudications of tribunals exercising the highest political authority of the country. For myself, as to these principles I occupy now the same position in reference to their conformity to constitutional law and the ordinary rules of justice that I did when I entered upon the office of opening the debate upon the case of the State of Florida; but I must accept, I am compelled to accept, whether I approve or not, the judgment of those tribunals having the authority to pronounce judgment in the premises; and in the argument of cases before the tribunal by which those judgments have been pronounced, and before which they must be respected, it becomes my duty to those I represent and my duty to myself, to conform my arguments and positions to the rules they have laid down and as far as possible adapt my positions to the rulings that have been made; and therefore in the argument of the case of Oregon I shall address myself to this tribunal in an appeal that they shall adhere to what they have already determined and give to Oregon the benefit of the application of the same principles they have applied to Florida and to Louisiana.

It is unquestionably true that if the adjudications referred to had the acceptance and approval of the whole profession of the country, you would have accomplished a result going far to pacify the public mind, and calm the agitations of the public heart, but nothing you can now do will be so effectual in lashing that heart into a higher condition of excitement than to challenge by decisions that are to follow the decisions you have already given.

When we opened the discussion upon the case of Florida, I maintained before this Commission that it was competent for you, in the exercise of the powers vested in you under the organic act, which made you the recipient of all the powers, whether judicial or legislative, in this particular, possessed and capable of being exercised by the two Houses of Congress conjointly or separately, to go behind the certificate of the executive of the State upon charges of mistake or fraud; I speak of the certificate of the executive of the State authorized and directed by the Congress of the United States. In the case of Florida, in addition to claiming for this tribunal the power referred to, we claimed for you the further power to give heed to the voice of the State herself when, after her tones had been simulated by those not authorized to speak for her, she came to the Federal Government through the different departments of her State government, asserting the fact that she had not been truly represented in the electoral college and asking you to hear the voice of her people as testified to by those departments. Her executive, her legislative, and her judicial departments came before you and asked that the opinion of her people might be truly reflected in the estimate to be made of the sentiment of the country upon which was to be founded the title to the succession of the Presidency of the United States.

The learned counsel on the other side took issue upon these positions, and this tribunal determined that there was no authority in this organization to go behind the certificate of the governor authorized by the act of Congress, when founded upon the results of the canvassing-board of the State. But I have always been at a loss to know, I have always been unable to discover, where the tribunal learned that in the case of Florida there ever had been a canvass of the votes of that State by any board other than that which was authenticated in the certificate of the so-called Tilden electors, made under the authority of the act of the 27th of January, 1877, and I therefore infer that whatever may have been in the private opinions of the Commissioners the significance of those words relating to the conformity of the certificate of the governor to the results of the canvassing-board, the true and real meaning of the judgment of the tribunal was that the certificate of the governor was the conclusive fact, the ultimate fact, beyond which you had no power to go.

The learned counsel who opened this case on behalf of the objectors to certificate No. 2, thought proper, in the exercise of a wise and discriminating judgment as to the merits of men, to pay a high compliment to his distinguished associate who has just addressed the Commission. I fully coincide in the high compliment he thought proper to pay to that distinguished gentleman. He spoke of him as the modern pilot in the law; equal in learning and wisdom, upon its vast sea, to guide safely the bark of professional enterprise at whose helm he was placed between Scylla and Charybdis, and challenged in that behalf the fame of old Palinurus. It needed no disclosure from the counsel on the other side to satisfy this Commission that when the bark of the counsel on the other side was tossed against the Scylla of Florida, the pilot looked ahead to the Charybdis that threatened peril in Oregon. It was apparent from the discussion that such was the preconcerted purpose of the voyage, and now it is established from the admission. But adroitly as he may have led on his way, if this Commission adheres to the course to which the helm was set to shun the reefs of Florida, the bark must be wrecked on those of Oregon.

Mr. President and gentlemen of the Commission, looking to the exact words of the decision in the case of Florida, what is it?

The ground of this decision, stated briefly as required by said act, is as follows:

That it is not competent under the Constitution and the law as it existed at the date of the passage of said act, to go into evidence *aliunde* the papers opened by the President of the Senate in the presence of the two Houses to prove that other persons than those regularly certified to by the governor of the State of Florida on, and according to, the determination and declaration of their appointment by the board of State canvassers of said State prior to the time required for the performance of their duties had been appointed electors, or by counter-proof to show that they had not.

In the case of Louisiana the same identical words are repeated in the decision. Now, are we to infer that there is any particular virtue in the decision either of the returning-board of Florida or the returning-board of Louisiana? Is there anything particularly sacred in either of those organizations, and so powerful as to prevent intrusion from the Federal

Government into those States, or to check you in the solemn and serious inquiries you were asked to make? No; the answer has been given by the learned counsel on the other side himself, which was this : that when the United States, in executing the duty confided to the two Houses of Congress of counting the votes for President and Vice-President of the United States, meet with an authentication from a State, under its laws they were thereby arrested and debarred from any further proceeding. You may pass beyond the certificate of the governor, if given in pursuance of the act of Congress, for that certificate is not given in the discharge of a State duty confided to the governor by State law, but that certificate is given in response to what purports to be a mandatory act of Congress, but what in fact is simply a Federal request; and which is given in recognition of such request and under the rules of courtesy rather than from the obligations of law.

But, in this inquiry, how far shall you go, and where shall you stop? You go behind the certificate, as you have decided, until you find some authentication of the fact with reference to which you are inquiring, made under the authority and by virtue of a power in the State herself. When, in the case of Florida and Louisiana, you passed by the certificate of the governor, given in obedience to the act of Congress, and found yourselves confronted with the results arrived at of a returning-board, you said, " Here we must stop, for here the State has challenged Federal power, and bade it take no further step in invading the State and the matters of self-government." It was not the result of the canvass; it was not any virtue in the board; it was not because of any sanctity in Wells or Casanave or their associates, but it was because when you reached them you reached the broad seal of the State, affixed as evidence to a State fact, under State law, and by State authority.

It is needless for me to say that the greatest difficulty the fathers of this Republic encountered in the organization of our complex system was, so to adjust its relations and powers that community independence might be preserved in the States and local self-government perpetuated to those oganizations, and under such limitations and restrictions that while this power was left unimpaired there should be adequate authority given to the central authority of the Union to deal with our foreign affairs, and preserve and perpetuate the combination of States and peoples that was formed and united under the Constitution of the United States. To mark that dividing-line between the States and the Federal Government was the most difficult office those extraordinary men were called on to perform; and they performed it so well, so wisely, and so perfectly that perpetual harmony and perpetual peace would reign in this country, in so far as any internecine strife could ever disturb the one or the other, if each of these great powers, the Federal Government of the Union and the local governments of the States, would move in those respective orbits upon which they were propelled by the fathers of the republic. In regarding the respective rights of these political organizations, the Federal Government, speaking, as I understand your decisions, through the adjudications of this tribunal, has said that as the appointment of the electors is given to the States by special grant of power, as the appointment of the electors is a power in the States, and the States are required to exercise that power, when they have done so, we will go no further into the inquiry as to the propriety of State action than the authentication of the State act by the great seal of the State; and whenever we find that seal affixed to the ultimate fact under the authority of State law, and by the sanction of the State organization, *there we must stop.*

If that is not the meaning ot the decision, then we are here dealing with the smallest matters of technical law, and indulging in something similar to pleas and replications and rejoinders and rebutters and surrebutters and demurrers indefinite, and settling the rights of forty million people upon technicalities and subtleties that any one of the distinguished gentlemen I now address would scout and discard if introduced into his court in any case involving even the smallest and most insignificant right. Your decision must rest, if it rests at all in the confidence of the people, upon the doctrine of State rights in their relation to the rights of the Federal Union. It must rest in the confidence of the people, if it find repose in their confidence at all, upon some broad principle which they can comprehend and understand, and which, comprehending and understanding, they will recognize and accept, and even in the anguish of their disappointment welcome and cherish as wise and judicious, because it comes from wise and judicious men, and is commended by sound and broad reasoning.

But if these questions are to be settled upon any such narrow and technical grounds as my brothers on the other side contend for, the wound which this Commission was organized to heal in the nation they will only make bleed the freer; and for four years to come the American people, while submitting to legitimate authority, will recognize that there is in this country the anomalous condition of two Presidents, one a President *de facto*, and another a President *de jure* though not in office.

I was pleased at first to hear my learned brothers on the other side commend the doctrine of State rights with so much apparent zeal; but I felt their want of earnestness and sincerity, and as I listened to their disquisition upon this subject there was brought vividly to my mind the saddest, grandest, and most transcendent event in the history of the human race: They took him and they clothed him with purple; planted as the insignia of royalty a crown of thorns upon his brow; they put a reed within his hand for a scepter, and fell down before him in the mockery of adoration. When the sacrifice was accomplished, the veil of the temple was rent and darkness was spread upon the face of the earth.

There is a people to-day scattered over the world, inhabitants of every country, but without a home or country of their own.

Mr. President and gentlemen of the Commission, in what particular does the law of Louisiana or the law of Florida, in reference to the ascertainment of the result of the appointment of electors, differ from the law of Oregon? By the law of Florida a board is appointed that is required to canvass the returns and determine the result. Similar language, but hardly so strong, is used in the law of Louisiana. Now, what is the law of Oregon upon this subject? Section 60, which has been frequently read, provides:

The votes for the electors shall be given, received, returned, and canvassed as the same are given, returned, and canvassed for members of Congress.

And, as was very properly remarked by one of the learned counsel, that ends that paragraph and terminates the duty of canvassing.

The secretary of state shall prepare two lists of the names of the electors—

What electors? Not those that have received the highest number of votes, but—

two lists of the names of the electors elected, and affix the seal of the State to the same. Such lists shall be signed by the governor and secretary, and by the latter delivered to the college of electors at the hour of their meeting on such first Wednesday of December.

Here is an executive duty to be performed. The electors that are elected are to receive this certificate. Who is to determine who is elected? Is not that office confided to the parties who are engaged by the mandate of the law in this transaction?

"Prepare two lists of the names of the electors elected." They must determine who are the parties elected. In Florida the returning-board was given the power to determine the result and required to report to the office of the secretary of state of Florida all the votes taken, giving a specific account of those they deemed proper in the exercise of their questionable jurisdiction to throw out, as well as all others. All the votes sent to them were to be returned or lists of all the votes sent to them were to be returned; but this tribunal held that the power of *determination* was in that board. Now, although the word "determine" is not in the section quoted from the law of Oregon, yet the act which the section requires to be performed is an act which cannot be performed unless preceded by a determination. The lists are to be lists of the electors elected. The canvass is to be conducted as is the canvass for members of Congress, and provision is made for certificates. The act as to the canvass for members of Congress is as follows:

And it shall be the duty of the secretary of state, in the presence of the governor, to proceed within thirty days after the election, and sooner if the returns be all received, to canvass the votes given for secretary and treasurer of state, State printer, justices of the supreme court, member of Congress, and district attorneys; and the governor shall grant a certificate of election to the person having the highest number of votes, and shall also issue a proclamation declaring the election of such person.

In the case of members of Congress and certain State officers the provision is that the governor shall grant a certificate or a commission to the person *having the highest number of votes.* The section that relates to electors, though it refers to the section relating to members of Congress, requires the canvass to be conducted in the same manner in which the canvass required by that section is conducted, yet omits—and omitting in the presence of the thing omitted shows that it was before their minds—omits the requirement in the section in reference to members of Congress to the effect that the executive should perform simply the ministerial office of giving the commission to the party who, by the enumeration to be made by the secretary of state, should be shown to have the greatest number of votes.

I submit, in this connection, that to withhold the commission or to withhold the certificate from a party deemed by the governor to be ineligible to the office, is the legitimate performance of a constitutional and proper executive trust. This Commission has told us that the State cannot interfere with an elector, whether he be eligible or ineligible, whether his election be secured by fair means or foul means, after the time when he has cast his vote. You have further told us that he cannot be interfered with except between the time of the conclusion of the returning-board and the time of his voting, which in Florida was, I believe, some six hours, and in Louisiana some four or five. The State of Oregon, seeking to perform her duty, and its much-abused executive seeking to protect that State from the odium of having wantonly violated the Constitution of the United States, when the subject of the election of these electors came before him, entered upon the consideration of the matter which he and he alone could consider and determine, and the State by the only power at her command at that time—the time to which she was limited by your decision—has solemnly determined that one who claimed to be elected an elector was not elected.

I beg to refer you, gentlemen of the Commission, upon the subject of the executive duty in that regard, to the thirty-ninth volume of Missouri

Reports, page 399. I shall not have an opportunity of reading largely from these authorities; but, as the President of the Commission remarked yesterday, the members of the Commission have no opportunity to examine them after the argument, and they must therefore rely upon counsel for whatever information they have in regard to them, I feel compelled to read a few pertinent extracts. The case is that of Bartley *vs.* Fletcher, governor:

> The governor is bound to see that the laws are faithfully executed, and he has taken an oath to support the Constitution.

By the laws of Oregon, which my brother Hoadly hands me to read to the Commission, I find a more careful provision than is to be found in the laws of most of the States of the Union:

> The organic law is the Constitution of the United States and of this State, and is altogether written. Other written laws are denominated statutes. The written law of this State is, therefore, contained in its constitution and statutes and in the Constitution and statutes of the United States.—*Section* 712, page 253.

Oregon, therefore, in her reverence for the supreme law of the United States, has not allowed her obligation to the Constitution of the United States to rest only on its authority as the Constitution of the Federal Government, but she has incorporated it into her own laws and made it a part of her State system of laws; and the governor, having taken his oath to take care that the laws be faithfully executed, as required by her constitution, when a candidate for elector comes before him demanding a certificate of the fact that he is an elector under the broad seal of that State, having due regard to his oath and reverence for the Constitution of the United States, and being satisfactorily informed that such applicant is by the Constitution of the United States inhibited from holding the appointment or being appointed, is compelled to refuse to certify to a statement which would be a falsehood, and therefore in direct violation of both the Constitution of the United States and the constitution of Oregon and his oath as governor of Oregon.

Gentlemen talk about simulated virtue, and the learned counsel went on to speak of our simulating virtue, and severely condemned the governor of Oregon, and, I may remark, went further, and I regretted to hear him as he proceeded. There are few men in the profession for whom I have a higher respect, and it pained me to hear his unbecoming intimations of conspiracies in Gramercy Park, and various telegrams between Oregon and New York. He stated that no such evidence had been offered; but, with significant insinuations, indicated what he might have done if such evidence had been in the case or if he had offered it. Had you offered it, gentlemen, we should have interposed no objection to its introduction. We should have welcomed it and rejoiced at it. We have been seeking for the truth and nothing but the truth, and begged for evidence from the beginning, and you well knew that any offer you might have made would have been met otherwise than by technical objections. A fling at us and those we represent, made under the pretexts of testimony not even offered, hardly reaches the dignified plane of professional honor upon which we supposed we all stood in the conduct of this great debate.

The governor of Oregon could not have given the certificate to an ineligible candidate without violating his oath and being guilty of an infraction of the Federal Constitution. Let me read further from the case in 39 Missouri Reports:

> In the correct and legitimate performance of his duty he must inevitably have a discretion in regard to granting commissions; for should a person be elected or appointed who was constitutionally ineligible to hold any office of profit or trust,

would the executive be bound to commission him when his ineligibility was clearly and positively proven ? If he is denied the exercise of any discretion in such case, he is made the violator of the constitution, not its guardian. Of what avail, then, is his oath of office ?

Need I pursue this inquiry further ? Need I go on to the subsequent decisions of that State and show to this Commission that that opinion stands as the unreversed law of that State to-day ? Although the counsel on the other side referred to an opinion as tending to change and modify the ruling I have read, I would, had I time left me, analyze it and show to the Commission that the case referred to in no way changes the law as pronounced in the opinion read, and that this law is to-day the law of Missouri ; it is the law of Indiana ; it is the law of Massachusetts ; and the governor of that State, in the exercise of his functions, may withhold a certificate and refuse to fix the broad seal of the State when the party claiming it is not capable of being appointed to the office title to which it would evidence.

Now, suppose that the governor issues his certificate, what is the effect of that certificate when issued ? When he has exercised his power, and issued his certificate, and affixed the seal of the State to the certificate, that certificate so accompanied by the seal is conclusive evidence of the title and cannot be questioned except in a regular legal proceeding for the purpose of invalidating the commission. As the counsel on the other side correctly said, when we entered into this inquiry and commenced this investigation, we asked that this tribunal should proceed as though exercising the powers of a court under a *quo warranto*, and search all the facts to the very bottom. But he was in error when he said that the argument of inconvenience came from our side, and that Mr. O'Conor had stated that we could stop at a certain convenient point, and suggested that it would be prudent and wise in your discretion to stop at a certain period of the investigation. The argument of inconvenience, in order that you might thereby be induced not to make the inquiries the people hoped and desired you would make, came from my learned friend who now sits upon my right, [Mr. Evarts,] and was pressed with all his great powers of logic and eloquence ; and to meet that argument we replied that, if you found it so inconvenient that you could not investigate all the facts, there was a discretionary power in the exercise of which you could limit the scope of the inquiry when you had reached a point at which you became satisfied that you had found the *truth*.

This certificate when issued is conclusive evidence of the title, only to be impeached by a judicial proceeding, as I have indicated. Such was the decision of the court of last resort in Massachusetts upon questions submitted to it by the executive department of the government. Other authorities to the same effect will be found in the brief which has been handed to you ; and I am constrained, I regret to say, from the quick passage of my time, to leave that subject thus superficially considered.

Mr. Commissioner HOAR. Mr. Merrick, is there a Massachusetts decision of the supreme court on that question ? Was not that in Maine ?

Mr. MERRICK. There is one in Massachusetts as well as in Maine.

Mr. Commissioner HOAR. I remember now ; there is one in 117 Massachusetts.

Mr. MERRICK. One hundred and seventeen Massachusetts. Shall I pass it to the Commissioner ?

Mr. Commissioner HOAR. I remember it very well. I have read it. I thought you alluded to another one.

Mr. MERRICK. The language is:

The nature of the duties thus imposed and the very terms of the statute show that they are to be performed without unnecessary delay, and the certificate issued by the governor to any person appearing upon such examination to be elected is the final and conclusive evidence of the determination of the governor and council as to his election.

The learned counsel upon the other side, in order to derogate from the effect of the certificate and the seal, refers the Commission to the case of the United States *vs.* Le Baron, in 19 Howard, from which he quoted a single sentence. I looked at the book and found it to be an authority in direct opposition to the point for which it had been referred to:

When a person has been nominated to an office by the President, confirmed by the Senate, and his commission has been signed by the President, and the seal of the United States affixed thereto, his appointment to that office is complete.

The sentence quoted by the counsel on the other side was this:

The transmission of the commission to the officer is not essential to his investiture of the office.

We were left to infer that the word "transmission" included everything that appertained to the execution and the issuing of the commission. The following sentence is:

If by any inadvertence or accident it should fail to reach him, his possession of the office is as lawful as if it were in his custody.

The PRESIDENT. Who gave the opinion?

Mr. MERRICK. Mr. Justice Curtis gave the opinion.

It is but evidence of those acts of appointment and *qualification* which constitute his title, and which may be proved by other evidence, where the rule of law requiring the best evidence does not prevent.

The governor issued his certificate to Cronin and two others, so-called Hayes electors. Cronin held his certificate, and by virtue of that certificate, whether rightfully or wrongfully issued, I respectfully submit that he was an officer *de facto;* and I was gratified to hear the reply of the counsel on the other side to the question submitted by Mr. Commissioner Morton, I think, as to whether or not, if there was an officer *de facto* in the actual possession of the office, there could be a vacancy? Counsel replied promptly there could not. Who, then, was the incumbent of this office? Who had the office on the day that the electors voted, Cronin or Watts? Cronin held the certificate with the broad seal of the State attached to it. He had the muniment of title to the office, that which by the act of Congress is made the muniment of title or evidence and that which is made evidence or a muniment of title by the law of the State. What had Watts? Says the learned counsel on the other side in considering the evidence of title, Watts had a certificate from the secretary of state as to the canvass of the votes. What is it? Concede for a moment that there is in this certificate No. 1 a duly-certified copy of some record in the office of the secretary of state, what does it purport to be? It is headed:

Abstract of votes cast at the presidential election held in the State of Oregon November 7, 1876, for presidential electors.

"Abstract of votes," not the canvass of the votes. The learned counsel, in order to make it appear that "abstract" and "canvass" were synonymous terms, referred back to the statutes of Oregon which required the clerks at the voting-precincts to make out certain abstracts and send them up to the secretary of state. This is the result of those abstracts so sent up by the clerks, and of which abstracts the law of Oregon is speaking when it requires the secretary of state and the governor to canvass. When they have canvassed these abstracts their canvass makes another paper, which should be a paper of record in that office, and which is not here in this certificate.

I hereby certify that the foregoing tabulated statement is the result of the vote cast for presidential electors.

"Is the result of the vote cast." He certifies to results, not that it is a paper on file purporting to reflect the canvass as made, but that it is the result of the vote cast for presidential electors at a general election. Again:

I, S. F. Chadwick, secretary of the State of Oregon, do hereby certify that I am the custodian of the great seal of the State of Oregon; that the foregoing copy of the abstract of votes cast at the presidential election held in the State of Oregon, November 7, 1876, for presidential electors, has been by me compared with the original abstract of votes cast for presidential electors.

What "abstract of votes"? The abstract of votes that my learned brother found called for by a preceding section of the law anterior to that which refers to the secretary of state, namely, the abstract that is to be sent up by the clerks who officiate in that capacity at the election-precincts; not the canvass of the votes which the law requires to be made by the secretary of state in the presence of the governor.

Mr. Commissioner MILLER. Mr. Merrick, let me ask you whether, if that paper contains all the abstracts of votes sent up by the clerk of each county, it is not all that the secretary had before him, and all that he could compare? What other paper could he make?

Mr. MERRICK. May it please your honor, in my experience in these cases I have found that officers discharging duties corresponding to that imposed by the statutes of Oregon upon the secretary of state could make other and very remarkable papers.

Mr. Commissioner HOAR. I should like to ask you one question, if you please, in that connection, Mr. Merrick. When they opened and canvassed the vote, what else would their conclusion be but a result? What would be worked out by the canvass? Then is not the word "result" a correct expression used to express the legal conclusion or determination or whatever the canvass brings them to? When they certify that this is the result, do they not certify that this is the conclusion to which this canvassing-board have come?

Mr. MERRICK. I do not so understand. I understand there is great force in the suggestion of Mr. Commissioner Hoar, as there is force in all that he says, but I do not understand that we can substitute in such papers as these one word for another, and put in some expression that may enable us to give to them an easy and satisfactory construction. I understand that we must take the language as we find it, and that as the statutes of Oregon use the word "canvass" when speaking of the secretary of state, and use the term "abstract of votes" when speaking of clerks officiating at the precinct elections, the "canvass" is something different from the "abstract," and that he ought to certify if he has made a canvass, and you want to use that paper in evidence "that this is the canvass I made," and not say "this is some result I may have reached."

Mr. Commissioner BRADLEY. Is not the canvass an act?

Mr. MERRICK. A canvass is an act.

Mr. Commissioner BRADLEY. You cannot have that certified on paper.

Mr. MERRICK. You cannot have the exact act, but you may have the record of it, the evidence of it.

Mr. Commissioner BRADLEY. Is not that what is meant in this certificate?

Mr. MERRICK. I think not. If it had been what he meant, he would have said " this is the canvass of the votes as made." As Mr. Justice Miller suggests, it is probably true that we have before us here what the secretary had before him; but that is not what this tribunal wants.

Mr. Commissioner MILLER. Mr. Merrick, if there is anything in that idea, I want you to tell me what you mean by a canvass?

Mr. MERRICK. I mean a sifting of the votes.

Mr. Commissioner MILLER. That is the act to be done; but what record on earth ever would be made of it but the putting in of the votes that were canvassed and showing the result? Explain what other thing there could be about it.

Mr. MERRICK. I will explain it if I can. I am required to canvass certain abstracts of votes that you give me. When I have sifted those votes that you have given me, I make a record of what I have done with them. Here are the votes you gave me to canvass, and here is the record of my act.

Mr. Commissioner EDMUNDS. Mr. Merrick, you will notice at the top it is called an abstract and at the foot it is said:

I hereby certify that the foregoing tabulated statement is the result of the vote cast * * * as opened and canvassed in the presence of his excellency L. F. Grover, governor.

Mr. MERRICK. It is " the result of the vote." It is not the canvass.

Mr. Commissioner EDMUNDS. The inquiry I wish to put is this: It is stated at the bottom that the foregoing is a statement. Now what I wish to ask you is, whether you consider that that paper, called at the top an abstract and at the bottom a statement, is a paper that the secretary made, or a paper that came from the county clerks?

Mr. MERRICK. It is the result of the votes, not of the canvass.

Mr. Commissioner EDMUNDS. But who do you understand made that thing? Did the secretary of state make it, or did the county clerks, as you understand?

Mr. MERRICK. I presume the secretary of state reached the result.

Mr. Commissioner THURMAN. Mr. Merrick, let me ask you whether the real question is or is not what by the laws of Oregon is the conclusive evidence of the canvass?

Mr. Commissioner EDMUNDS. That is another question.

Mr. MERRICK. I have dwelt longer with this subject' than I had intended, and have been induced to do so by some inquiries made from the Commission during the progress of the argument on the other side. The real question at issue, as suggested by Senator Thurman, is what is made by the laws of Oregon the conclusive evidence of the canvass. Can you go into the secretary of state's office and get out a paper and have it certified, however solemnly, and set it up against the certificate issued by the governor and secretary of state with the seal of the State attached?

The counsel on the other side have complained that the certificate issued to Cronin and his associates as appears in certificate No. 2 is not the certificate required by the law of Oregon, and I beg to ask the gentlemen of the Commission to look at the law of Oregon as it bears on this certificate.

The secretary of state shall prepare two lists of the names of the electors elected—

Here are the lists—

and affix the seal of the State to the same.

Here is the broad seal of the State.

Such lists shall be signed by the governor and secretary.

Here is the list signed by the governor and by the secretary attesting the fact that the governor signed it. The secretary made it out; the governor signed it; and the secretary affixed the broad seal of the State to it; and I submit to the Commission that this is the final and conclusive evidence of the canvass, or the result of the canvass, or the result of the votes; the final and conclusive evidence as to who was entitled to exercise and perform the office of elector, if you call it an office.

Secondly, I submit that whether rightly done or wrongly done, as Cronin held that certificate with the seal attached, and entered upon that office, as the certificate here shows he did, the office was not vacant, and the act of the *de jure* officer even at the same time, he not having the muniment of title, could not countervail and nullify his act.

But I must pass to another question. It is admitted on the other side that the original title held by Watts was not a valid title. Some suggestions were made a few days since in the argument of a previous case by Mr. Evarts, that this provision of the Constitution of the United States was not self-executing, and some similar suggestions have been made to-day in reference to the same point. I had supposed that all reasonable persons had settled down to the conviction that this provision of the Federal Constitution was self-executing. But as the matter is again brought forward I beg to refer the Commission to the case of Morgan *vs.* Vance, in 4 Bush's (Kentucky) Reports, which is to the following effect:

So far as the Constitution requires of all officers to take the prescribed oath, and so far as it provides disqualifications upon acts, and not upon judgment of conviction, the Constitution, as the supreme law of the land, executes itself without any extraneous aid by way of legislation, nor can its requirements be so defeated.

Mr. Commissioner EDMUNDS. How did the case arise?

Mr. MERRICK. My time presses and I must pass from it; I will hand it to your honor. I will also refer the Commission to Taney's Circuit Court Decisions, published by Mr. Campbell, page 235. There was a provision in the constitution of Maryland that no person should charge more than six per cent. interest upon money, and that the legislature should make appropriate enactments for carrying that provision into effect. Chief-Justice Taney said:

The constitution itself makes the prohibition, and all future legislation must be subordinate and conformable to this provision: "Whoever takes or demands more than six per cent. while this constitution is in force, does an unlawful act; an act forbidden by the constitution of the State."

And without legislation he declared the contract to be void.

Upon the subject of vacancy my time will not allow me the opportunity of much discussion, if any, and I regret it, for this is a subject that I should like to have considered by the Commission with some degree of deliberation, and I intended to address your honors' attention to the various authorities that have reference to it. I respectfully submit that unless an office has been once filled there can be no vacancy, and unless it has been once filled there can be no resignation of the office. The Commission will bear in mind that the vacancy claimed to be filled by these electors was a vacancy created, not by Cronin's absence, but created by Watts's resignation. If they had the power to fill a vacancy at all, they executed that power by filling a vacancy created by a resignation from Watts, and not a vacancy created by the nonaction of Cronin. Now, if Watts never held the office, Cronin having been the party who received the commission, and therefore the officer *de facto*, having received conclusive evidence of his title from the State, the resignation of Watts was unavailing for any purpose. I refer the Commission to The People *vs*. Tilton, 37 California Reports, 617 ; Miller *vs*. The Supervisors of Sacramento, 25 California Reports, 93 ; Broom *vs*. Hanley, 9 Pennsylvania State Reports, and to the authorities upon page 20 of the brief, and to the Corliss case.

The United States statutes, I must remark in this connection, provide for two contingencies : first, the contingency of a vacancy, and second, the contingency of a non-election. And the statutes of Oregon have provided only for the contingency of a vacancy, and not for the contingency of a non-election. But, say the learned counsel on the other side, the word "otherwise" implies all vacancies, and they repudiate the maxim *noscitur a sociis* in reference to the construction of language. Now, what is the language of the statute of Oregon ?

Any vacancy *occasioned* by death, resignation, failure to act, or otherwise.

Vacancy "*occasioned ;*" not *any* vacancy *existing*, but a vacancy "occasioned." What is the meaning of the word "occasioned ?" "To occasion" signifies to produce. Non-filling of an office at the election cannot *occasion* a vacancy if it was vacant before the election took place. That could not be *occasioned* which already existed. But that which already existed could be occasioned. There must have been an existing condition upon which some cause operated to produce the effect before you can say that such effect was *occasioned*. If no change is made in the existing condition, there is no room for the use of the word "occasioned" and nothing to which it can apply. To occasion signifies to produce an effect incidentally. It is even more limited than the word "cause." To cause is to produce an effect in the ordinary operations of human affairs. To occasion is to produce an effect by some incidental circumstance. When the statute of Oregon spoke of a vacancy *occasioned* by certain causes, it meant a vacancy effected by something that had become operative since the day of election, not in the ordinary course of things, and which produced a condition different from that which existed prior to the commencement of its operation.

The PRESIDENT. The time allowed has expired.

Mr. Commissioner GARFIELD. I move, in view of the interruptions, that ten minutes more be granted.

The motion was agreed to.

Mr. MERRICK. I beg to extend my sincere thanks to the gentleman for the courtesy, and it will enable me to refer to one or two authorities which I will do very briefly. An authority was referred to on the other side from the State of Maine, in the thirty-eighth volume of Maine Reports, for the purpose of showing to the Commission that a failure to elect according to the laws of Maine would create a vacancy, and it was either stated or left to be inferred that the statutes of Maine in reference to that subject were similar in their provisions to the statutes of Oregon. The case is in 38 Maine, at page 598 :

The fourth question asked was, in case the second and third questions should be answered in the negative is not there a vacancy in said office.

There had been in that case a failure to elect, and in answering that question propounded the court stated :

The undersigned, therefore, answer the first, second, and third questions in the negative, and the fourth in the affirmative.

The answers declared that there was a vacancy in the office. But when I look back to the statute law of Maine, I find this provision under which that decision was given :

In all cases of election under the act to which this is additional, when no choice shall have been effected or a vacancy shall happen by death, resignation, or otherwise, such vacancy shall be filled by the governor and council.—*Session Laws of* 1844, page 84.

This is the authority upon which the counsel on the other side relied for his position that a non-election created a vacancy and he brought it to his support in this behalf. Looking back to the law it is apparent that the authority is directly adverse to the position which the learned counsel used it to maintain.

My associate suggests that I should give the Commission a reference to the post-office law. It is in the Revised Statutes, section 3836, providing for the supplying of vacancies as they occur in the office of postmaster.

I can enter upon no new point of the case at this late period of the argument, though there are two or three I much desire to elaborate.

Mr. President and gentlemen of the Commission, I must submit the case upon what has already been said. In closing this argument I respectfully submit that I claim, and I claim most earnestly, that you give to Oregon the benefit of your rulings in Louisiana and Florida. I desire that in this case you should adhere to the spirit and principles of the decisions you have rendered in the cases already tried and decided. It is quite unessential, quite immaterial, whether they conform to my opinions on the subject of constitutional law or not, and quite immaterial whether they conform to the opinions of any one else upon those subjects. They have been rendered by this tribunal, recorded upon the journals of both Houses of Congress, passed into the history of the country, and are in operative effect in the process now going on of determining who shall be the Chief Magistrate of the republic.

These opinions will be accepted or rejected by the people of the United States according to their estimate of their wisdom and soundness; but this people will not pass beyond the scrutiny of their character and their merits unless they are first challenged by the men by whom they were pronounced. Consistent adhesion to the solemn conclusions reached by those great men to whom the people have committed the settlement of their rights is essential to the preservation of loyal respect for authority and character; and while mitigating the pangs of disappointment often secure an acquiescence in judgments seemingly the harshest and the most unjust. But when these judgments antagonize one another, and in their very conflict and antagonism are combined in operative effect to accomplish one and the same result, and that result is one with which individual sympathies are closely and warmly connected, unpleasant thoughts will stir within the public mind, and angry emotions will swell the popular heart.

The Supreme Court of the United States is one of the idols of the people. They have in their estimate of its character invested it with a sanctity and a dignity beyond that of any other tribunal on the face of the earth. They believe that all other Departments of the Government are liable to deterioration and possible defilement; but they look to the Supreme Court as lifted above those currents of impure air that float upon the surface of the world, and as still imbued with the virtues and speaking with the wisdom of the fathers of the republic. When this faith is destroyed, the night will have come.

Mr. EVARTS. Will your honors allow me to ask attention to a case in 53 Missouri, page 111, as the cases in that State are so much insisted upon?

Mr. HOADLY. The State *vs.* Vail. That case was cited before.

Mr. MERRICK. It was cited, and I referred to it myself as not in any way reversing—although explaining—the case in Missouri that I read from.

Mr. EVARTS. So I understood the learned counsel.

Mr. MERRICK. If there is to be a reply, very well.

Mr. EVARTS. The one hundred and eleventh page is on this precise question of executive authority to give a certificate to a minority candidate on the ground that the majority candidate is ineligible, and it denies the right.

Mr. HOADLY. Excuse me; it denies the right except in cases which are patent upon which it expressly withholds an opinion in so many words, denies the right in cases of disqualification personal to the candidate, and latent.

Mr. MERRICK. And it refers to the case in 14 Indiana, Gulick *vs.* New, with approval, upon which we rest.

Mr. EVARTS. The section referred to just now in the Revised Statutes is section 3836, page 756.

Mr. Commissioner EDMUNDS. We have a reference to it.

Mr. EVARTS. The tribunal will see that it has no bearing on the question whether the office of postmaster was vacant or not. It expressly provides that if it is vacant the sureties may remain bound for a certain time afterward.

Mr. Commissioner GARFIELD. Mr. President, I move that the public session of the Commission be closed, and that we go into consultation.

The motion was agreed to.

Mr. Commissioner THURMAN. I suggest that, in order to get the room in good condition and purify the air, we had better take a recess. I move a recess for half an hour.

The motion was agreed to at four o'clock and thirty minutes p. m.

The recess having expired, the Commission re-assembled at five o'clock p. m. with closed doors.

After debate,

Mr. Commissioner EDMUNDS offered the following resolution:

Resolved, That the certificate signed by E. A. Cronin, J. N. T. Miller, and John Parker, purporting to cast the electoral votes of the State of Oregon, does not contain or certify the constitutional votes to which said State is entitled.

Pending which,

On motion of Mr. Commissioner ABBOTT, it was

Ordered, That the vote on the matter now pending be taken at four o'clock p. m. to-morrow.

On motion of Mr. Commissioner HUNTON, at seven o'clock and twenty-five minutes, the Commission adjourned until to-morrow at half past ten o'clock a. m.

FRIDAY, *February* 23, 1877.

The Commission met at ten o'clock and thirty minutes a. m., pursuant to adjournment, all the members being present except Mr. Commissioner Thurman.

The Journal of yesterday was read and approved.

The Commission resumed its deliberation on the matter of the electoral vote of the State of Oregon, the question being on the resolution submitted by Mr. Commissioner Edmunds yesterday.

At two o'clock and twenty minutes p. m., Mr. Commissioner Bayard presented the following communication; which was read:

Hon. T. F. BAYARD:

DEAR SIR: Mr. Thurman has been in bed all morning, and is now suffering from such intense pain that it will be impossible for him to meet the Commission to-day.

Respectfully,

M. A. THURMAN.

FRIDAY, *February* 23, 1877.

Mr. Commissioner HOAR submitted the following resolution :

Resolved, That Senators Bayard and Frelinghuysen be a committee to call at once on Mr. Thurman to learn if he will consent that the Commission adjourn to his house for the purpose of receiving his vote on the questions relating to Oregon.

The question being on the adoption of the resolution, it was determined in the affirmative :

Yeas 13
Nays 1

Those who voted in the affirmative were : Messrs. Abbott, Bayard, Bradley, Clifford, Edmunds, Field, Frelinghuysen, Garfield, Hoar, Hunton, Miller, Payne, and Strong—13.

Mr. Morton voted in the negative.

On motion of Mr. Commissioner STRONG, at three o'clock p. m., the Commission took a recess for half an hour.

At three o'clock and forty-seven minutes p. m., the Commission having resumed its session, the committee appointed to wait on Mr. Commissioner Thurman returned, and reported that he would receive the Commission at his house.

Whereupon,

On motion of Mr. Commissioner HOAR, it was

Ordered, That the Commission now proceed to the house of Mr. Commissioner Thurman, there to go on with the case now before it.

The Commission accordingly proceeded to the residence of Mr. Commissioner Thurman, on Fourteenth street, all the members being present.

The Commission was there called to order by the President.

The question being on the resolution of Mr. Commissioner Edmunds, Mr. Commissioner FIELD offered the following as a substitute :

Whereas J. W. Watts, designated in certificate No. 1 as an elector of the State of Oregon for President and Vice-President, on the day of election, namely, the 7th of November, 1876, held an office of trust and profit under the United States: Therefore,

Resolved, That the said J. W. Watts was then ineligible to the office of elector within the express terms of the Constitution.

The question being on the adoption of the substitute, it was determined in the negative:

Yeas 7
Nays 8

Those who voted in the affirmative were : Messrs. Abbott, Bayard, Clifford, Field, Hunton, Payne, and Thurman—7.

Those who voted in the negative were : Messrs. Bradley, Edmunds, Frelinghuysen, Garfield, Hoar, Miller, Morton, and Strong—8.

Mr. Commissioner FIELD offered the following substitute for the resolution :

Whereas at the election held on the 7th of November, 1876, in the State of Oregon, for electors of President and Vice-President, W. H. Odell, J. W. Watts, and John C. Cartwright received the highest number of votes cast for electors, but the said Watts then holding an office of trust and profit under the United States, was ineligible to the office of elector : Therefore,

Resolved, That the said Odell and Cartwright were the only persons duly elected at said election, and there was a failure on the part of the State to appoint a third elector.

The question being on the adoption of this substitute, it was determined in the negative :

Yeas 7
Nays 8

Those who voted in the affirmative were: Messrs. Abbott, Bayard, Clifford, Field, Hunton, Payne, and Thurman—7.

Those who voted in the negative were: Messrs. Bradley, Edmunds, Frelinghuysen, Garfield, Hoar, Miller, Morton, and Strong—8.

Mr. Commissioner FIELD offered the following as a substitute for the resolution:

Whereas the legislature of Oregon has made no provision for the appointment of an elector under the act of Congress where there was a failure to make a choice on the day prescribed by law: Therefore,

Resolved, That the attempted election of a third elector by the two persons chosen was inoperative and void.

The question being on the adoption of this substitute, it was decided in the negative:

Yeas 7
Nays 8

Those who voted in the affirmative were: Messrs. Abbott, Bayard, Clifford, Field, Hunton, Payne, and Thurman—7.

Those who voted in the negative were: Messrs. Bradley, Edmunds, Frelinghuysen, Garfield, Hoar, Miller, Morton, and Strong—8.

Mr. Commissioner BAYARD offered the following as a substitute:

Resolved, That the vote of W. H. Odell and the vote of J. C. Cartwright, cast for Rutherford B. Hayes, of Ohio, for President of the United States, and for William A. Wheeler, of New York, for Vice-President of the United States, are the votes provided for by the Constitution of the United States, and that the aforesaid Odell and Cartwright, and they only, were the persons duly appointed electors in the State of Oregon at the election held November 7, A. D. 1876, there having been a failure at the said election to appoint a third elector in accordance with the Constitution and laws of the United States and the laws of the State of Oregon; and that the two votes aforesaid should be counted, and none other, from the State of Oregon.

The question being on the adoption of this substitute, it was decided in the negative:

Yeas 7
Nays 8

Those who voted in the affirmative were: Messrs. Abbott, Bayard, Clifford, Field, Hunton, Payne, and Thurman—7.

Those who voted in the negative were: Messrs. Bradley, Edmunds, Frelinghuysen, Garfield, Hoar, Miller, Morton, and Strong—8.

The question recurring on the original resolution offered by Mr. Commissioner Edmunds, as follows:

Resolved, That the certificate signed by E. A. Cronin, J. N. T. Miller, and John Parker, purporting to cast the electoral votes of the State of Oregon, does not contain or certify the constitutional votes to which said State is entitled—

It was determined in the affirmative:

Yeas 15
Nays 0

Those who voted in the affirmative were: Messrs. Abbott, Bayard, Bradley, Clifford, Edmunds, Field, Frelinghuysen, Garfield, Hoar, Hunton, Miller, Morton, Payne, Strong, and Thurman.

Mr. Commissioner MORTON offered the following resolution:

Resolved, That W. H. Odell, John C. Cartwright, and John W. Watts, the persons named as electors in certificate No. 1, were the lawful electors of the State of Oregon, and that their votes are the votes provided for by the Constitution of the United States, and should be counted for President and Vice-President of the United States.

Mr. Commissioner HUNTON moved to amend the resolution by striking out the name of John W. Watts; and the question being on this amendment, it was decided in the negative:

Yeas 7
Nays 8

Those who voted in the affirmative were: Messrs. Abbott, Bayard, Clifford, Field, Hunton, Payne, and Thurman—7.

Those who voted in the negative were: Messrs. Bradley, Edmunds, Frelinghuysen, Garfield, Hoar, Miller, Morton, and Strong—8.

The question recurring on the resolution of Mr. Commissioner Morton, it was decided in the affirmative :

Yeas ....,... 8
Nays 7

Those who voted in the affirmative were: Messrs. Bradley, Edmunds, Frelinghuysen, Garfield, Hoar, Miller, Morton, and Strong—8.

Those who voted in the negative were: Messrs. Abbott, Bayard, Clifford, Field, Hunton, Payne, and Thurman—7.

Mr. Commissioner EDMUNDS submitted the following :

Ordered, That the following be adopted as the final decision and report in the matters submitted to the Commission as to the electoral vote of the State of O regon :

ELECTORAL COMMISSION,
Washington, D. C., February 23, A. D. 1877.

To the President of the Senate of the United States, presiding in the meeting of the two Houses of Congress, under the act of Congress entitled "An act to provide for and regulate the counting of votes for President and Vice-President, and the decision of questions arising thereon, for the term commencing March 4, A. D. 1877," approved January 29, A. D. 1877 :

The Electoral Commission mentioned in said act having received certain certificates and papers purporting to be certificates, and papers accompanying the same, of the electoral votes from the State of Oregon, and the objections thereto, submitted to it under said act, now report that it has duly considered the same, pursuant to said act, and has by a majority of votes decided, and does hereby decide, that the votes of W. H. Odell, J. C. Cartwright, and J. W. Watts, named in the certificate of said persons and in the papers accompanying the same, which votes are certified by said persons, as appears by the certificates submitted to the Commission as aforesaid and marked " No. 1, N. C." by said Commission, and herewith returned, are the votes provided for by the Constitution of the United States, and that the same are lawfully to be counted as therein certified, namely : three votes for Rutherford B. Hayes, of the State of Ohio, for President, and three votes for William A. Wheeler, of the State of New York, for Vice-President.

The Commission has by a majority of votes also decided, and does hereby decide, and report, that the three persons first above named were duly appointed electors in and by the State of Oregon.

The brief ground of this decision is that it appears, upon such evidence as by the Constitution and the law named in said act of Congress is competent and pertinent to the consideration of the subject, that the before-mentioned electors appear to have been lawfully appointed such electors of President and Vice-President of the United States for the term beginning March 4, A. D. 1877, of the State of Oregon, and that they voted as such at the time and in the manner provided for by the Constitution of the United States and the law.

And we are further of opinion—

That by the laws of the State of Oregon the duty of canvassing the returns of all the votes given at an election for electors of President and Vice-President was imposed upon the secretary of state, and upon no one else.

That the secretary of state did canvass the returns in the case before us, and thereby ascertained that J. C. Cartwright, W. H. Odell, and J. W. Watts had a majority of all the votes given for electors, and had the highest number of votes for that office, and by the express language of the statute those persons are " deemed elected."

That in obedience to his duty the secretary made a canvass and tabulated statement of the votes showing this result, which, according to law, he placed on file in his office on the 4th day of December, A. D. 1876. All this appears by an official certificate under the seal of the State and signed by him, and delivered by him to the electors and forwarded by them to the President of the Senate with their votes.

That the refusal or failure of the governor of Oregon to sign the certificate of the election of the persons so elected does not have the effect of defeating their appointment as such electors.

That the act of the governor of Oregon in giving to E. A. Cronin a certificate of his election, though he received a thousand votes less than Watts, on the ground that the latter was ineligible, was without authority of law and is therefore void.

That although the evidence shows that Watts was a postmaster at the time of his election, that fact is rendered immaterial by his resignation both as postmaster and elector, and his subsequent appointment, to fill the vacancy so made, by the electoral college.

The Commission has also decided, and does hereby decide, by a majority of votes, and report, that, as a consequence of the foregoing and upon the grounds before stated, the paper purporting to be a certificate of the electoral vote of said State of Oregon, signed by E. A. Cronin, J. N. T. Miller, and John Parker, marked "No. 2, N. C." by the Commission, and herewith returned, is not the certificate of the votes provided for by the Constitution of the United States, and that they ought not to be counted as such.

Done at Washington, D. C., the day and year first above written.

The question being on the adoption of the order, it was decided in the affirmative:

Yeas... 8
Nays... 7

Those who voted in the affirmative were: Messrs. Bradley, Edmunds, Frelinghuysen, Garfield, Hoar, Miller, Morton, and Strong—8.

Those who voted in the negative were: Messrs. Abbott, Bayard, Clifford, Field, Hunton, Payne, and Thurman—7.

So the report of the committee was adopted; and said decision and report were thereupon signed by the members agreeing therein, as follows:

> SAM. F. MILLER.
> W. STRONG.
> JOSEPH P. BRADLEY.
> GEO. F. EDMUNDS.
> O. P. MORTON.
> FRED'K T. FRELINGHUYSEN.
> JAMES A. GARFIELD.
> GEORGE F. HOAR.

Mr. Commissioner EDMUNDS offered the following:

Ordered, That the President of the Commission transmit a letter to the President of the Senate in the following words:

> "WASHINGTON, D. C., *February* 23, *A. D.* 1877.

"SIR: I am directed by the Electoral Commission to inform the Senate that it has considered and decided upon the matters submitted to it under the act of Congress concerning the same, touching the electoral votes from the State of Oregon, and herewith, by direction of said Commission, I transmit to you the said decision, in writing, signed by the members agreeing therein, to be read at the meeting of the two Houses, according to said act. All the certificates and papers sent to the Commission by the President of the Senate are herewith returned.

"Hon. THOMAS W. FERRY,
> "*President of the Senate.*"

The question being on the adoption of the order, it was determined in the affirmative; and the letter was accordingly signed, as follows:

> "NATHAN CLIFFORD,
> "*President of the Commission.*"

Mr. Commissioner EDMUNDS offered the following:

Ordered, That the President of the Commission transmit to the Speaker of the House of Representatives a letter in the following words:

> "WASHINGTON, D. C., *February* 23, 1877.

"SIR: I am directed by the Electoral Commission to inform the House of Representatives that it has considered and decided upon the matters submitted to it under the act of Congress concerning the same, touching the electoral votes from the State of Oregon, and has transmitted said decision to the President of the Senate, to be read at the meeting of the two Houses, according to said act.

"Hon. SAMUEL J. RANDALL,
> "*Speaker of the House of Representatives.*"

The question being on the adoption of the order, it was decided in the affirmative; and the letter was accordingly signed as follows:

> "NATHAN CLIFFORD,
> "*President of the Commission.*"

On motion of Mr. Commissioner MORTON, it was

Ordered, That the injunction of secrecy imposed on the acts and proceedings of the Commission be removed.

On motion of Mr. Commissioner GARFIELD, (at five o'clock p. m.,) the Commission adjourned until twelve o'clock noon to-morrow, to meet in the Supreme Court room.

PROCEEDINGS OF THE TWO HOUSES.

IN SENATE, *Saturday, February 24, 1877.*

The Senate resumed its session, on the expiration of the recess taken from the previous day, at ten o'clock a. m., Saturday, February 24.

The PRESIDENT *pro tempore* laid before the Senate the following communication; which was read:

WASHINGTON, D. C., *February 23, 1877.*

SIR: I am directed by the Electoral Commission to inform the Senate that it has considered and decided upon the matters submitted to it under the act of Congress concerning the same, touching the electoral votes from the State of Oregon, and herewith, by direction of said Commission, I transmit to you the said decision, in writing, signed by the members agreeing therein, to be read at the meeting of the two Houses, according to said act. All the certificates and papers sent to the Commission by the President of the Senate are herewith returned.

NATHAN CLIFFORD,
President of the Commission.

Hon. THOMAS W. FERRY,
President of the Senate.

On motion of Mr. Senator LOGAN, it was

Ordered, That the Secretary be directed to inform the House of Representatives that the President of the Electoral Commission has notified the Senate that the Commission has arrived at a decision of the questions submitted to it in relation to the electoral votes of Oregon, and that the Senate is now ready to meet the House for the purpose of laying before the two Houses the report of the said decision, and to proceed with the count of the electoral votes for President and Vice-President.

The Senate, on being notified, at eleven o'clock and fifty minutes, a. m., that the House of Representatives was prepared to meet it in joint meeting to proceed with the electoral count, repaired to the hall of the House.

IN THE HOUSE OF REPRESENTATIVES,
Saturday, February 24, 1877.

The House resumed its session at ten o'clock a. m., on the expiration of the recess taken from the previous day.

After the transaction of various items of business,

Mr. George C. Gorham, Secretary of the Senate, appeared and delivered the following message:

Mr. Speaker: I am directed by the Senate to inform the House of Representatives that the president of the Electoral Commission has notified the Senate that the Commission has arrived at a decision of the questions submitted to it in relation to the electoral votes of Oregon, and also that the Senate is ready to meet the House for the purpose of laying before the two Houses the report of the Commission, and to proceed with the count of the electoral vote for President and Vice-President.

After the transaction of business, by unanimous consent,

The SPEAKER laid before the House the following communication; which was read:

WASHINGTON, D. C., *February 23, 1877.*

SIR: I am directed by the Electoral Commission to inform the House of Representatives that it has considered and decided upon the matters submitted to it under the act of Congress concerning the same, touching the electoral votes from the State of Oregon, and has transmitted its decision to the President of the Senate, to be read at the meeting of the two Houses, according to said act.

NATHAN CLIFFORD,
President of the Commission

Hon. SAMUEL J. RANDALL,
　　Speaker of the House of Representatives.

Mr. Representative McMAHON thereupon submitted the following resolution, and demanded the previous question thereon:

Resolved, That the Senate be notified that the House of Representatives will be ready to meet the Senate in joint convention at one o'clock p. m. this day, for the purpose of continuing the count of the electoral vote.

Mr. Representative HALE made the point of order that, under the electoral law, nothing was now in order except to inform the Senate that the House was ready to proceed at once with the electoral count; but yielded to—

Mr. Representative WILSON, of Iowa, who submitted the following resolution, and claimed that nothing else was in order under the law, viz:

Resolved, That the Clerk of the House notify the Senate that the House is now ready to meet them in joint meeting of the two Houses to count the vote for President and Vice-President.

The SPEAKER overruled the point of order, and treating the resolution of Mr. Representative Wilson, of Iowa, as an amendment by way of substitute for that offered by Mr. Representative McMahon, the amendment was agreed to by a vote of yeas 146, nays 87, and the resolution as thus amended was agreed to by a vote of yeas 156, nays 89; and the Senate was at once notified accordingly.

JOINT MEETING.

SATURDAY, *February* 24, 1877.

The Senate entered the House hall at eleven o'clock and fifty-five minutes a. m., in the usual manner.

The PRESIDENT *pro tempore* of the Senate took his seat as Presiding Officer of the joint meeting of the two Houses, the Speaker of the House occupying a chair upon his left.

The PRESIDING OFFICER. The joint meeting of Congress for counting the electoral vote resumes its session. The two Houses, having separated pending submission to the Commission of objections to the certificate of the State of Oregon, have re-assembled to receive and to coincide, or otherwise, with the decision of that tribunal. The decision, which is in writing, by a majority of the Commission, and signed by the members agreeing therein, will now be read by the Secretary of the Senate and be entered in the Journal of each House.

The Secretary of the Senate read as follows:

ELECTORAL COMMISSION,
Washington, D. C., February 23, *A. D.* 1877.

To the President of the Senate of the United States, presiding in the meeting of the two Houses of Congress, under the act of Congress entitled "An act to provide for and regulate the counting of votes for President and Vice-President, and the decision of questions arising thereon, for the term commencing March 4, A. D. 1877," approved January 29, A. D. 1877.

The Electoral Commission mentioned in said act having received certain certificates, and papers purporting to be certificates, and papers accompanying the same, of the electoral votes from the State of Oregon, and the objections thereto, submitted to it under said act, now report that it has duly considered the same, pursuant to said act; and has by a majority of votes decided, and does hereby decide, that the votes of W. H. Odell, J. C. Cartwright, and J. W. Watts, named in the certificate of said persons

and in the papers accompanying the same, which votes are certified by said persons, as
appears by the certificates submitted to the Commission as aforesaid, and marked
"No. 1 N. C." by said Commission, and herewith returned, are the votes provided
for by the Constitution of the United States, and that the same are lawfully to be
counted as therein certified, namely :

Three (3) votes for Rutherford B. Hayes, of the State of Ohio, for President; and

Three (3) votes for William A. Wheeler, of the State of New York, for Vice-President.

The Commission has by a majority of votes also decided, and does hereby decide and
report, that the three persons above named were duly appointed electors in and by the
State of Oregon.

The brief ground of this decision is that it appears, upon such evidence as by the
Constitution and the law named in said act of Congress is competent and pertinent to
the consideration of the subject, that the before-mentioned electors appear to have been
lawfully appointed such electors of President and Vice-President of the United States
for the term beginning March 4, A. D. 1877, of the State of Oregon, and that they voted
as such at the time and in the manner provided for by the Constitution of the United
States and the law.

And we are further of opinion—

That by the laws of the State of Oregon the duty of canvassing the returns of all
the votes given at an election for electors of President and Vice-President was imposed
upon the secretary of state, and upon no one else.

That the secretary of state did canvass the returns in the case before us, and thereby
ascertained that J. C. Cartwright, W. H. Odell, and J. W. Watts had a majority of all
the votes given for electors, and had the highest number of votes for that office, and by
the express language of the statute those persons are deemed elected.

That in obedience to his duty the secretary made a canvass and tabulated statement
of the votes showing this result, which, according to law, he placed on file in his office
on the 4th day of December, A. D. 1876. All this appears by an official certificate under
the seal of the State and signed by him, and delivered by him to the electors and forwarded by them to the President of the Senate with their votes.

That the refusal or failure of the governor of Oregon to sign the certificate of the
election of the persons so elected does not have the effect of defeating their appointment as such electors.

That the act of the governor of Oregon in giving to E. A. Cronin a certificate of his
election, though he received a thousand votes less than Watts, on the ground that the
latter was ineligible, was without authority of law and is therefore void.

That although the evidence shows that Watts was a postmaster at the time of his
election, that fact is rendered immaterial by his resignation both as postmaster and
elector, and his subsequent appointment, to fill the vacancy so made, by the electoral
college.

The Commission has also decided, and does hereby decide, by a majority of votes,
and report, that, as a consequence of the foregoing, and upon the grounds before stated,
the paper purporting to be a certificate of the electoral vote of said State of Oregon,
signed by E. A. Cronin, J. N. T. Miller, and John Parker, marked "No. 2, N. C." by the
Commission, and herewith returned, is not the certificate of the votes provided for by
the Constitution of the United States, and that they ought not to be counted as such.

Done at Washington, D. C., the day and year first above written.

SAM. F. MILLER.
W. STRONG.
JOSEPH P. BRADLEY.
GEO. F. EDMUNDS.
O. P. MORTON.
FRED'K T. FRELINGHUYSEN.
JAMES A. GARFIELD.
GEORGE F. HOAR.

The PRESIDING OFFICER. Are there any objections to the decision of the Commission?

Mr. Senator KELLY. I have the honor to file certain objections to
this decision, signed by Senators and Representatives.

The PRESIDING OFFICER. The Senator from Oregon having submitted an objection to this decision, it will be read by the Clerk of the
House.

The Clerk of the House read as follows:

The undersigned, Senators and Members of the House of Representatives of the
United States, object to the decision of the Joint Commission directing the counting
of the vote of John W. Watts, an alleged elector for the State of Oregon, as given for
Rutherford B. Hayes for President of the United States, and for William A. Wheeler, of

New York, for Vice-President, and rejecting the vote of E. A. Cronin as cast for Samuel J. Tilden, of New York, for President, and Thomas A. Hendricks, of Indiana, for Vice-President, on the following grounds:

1. John W. Watts was not elected a presidential elector for Oregon.

2. He (J. W. Watts) was not legally appointed as a presidential elector.

3. He (Watts) was disqualified to receive any appointment as presidential elector or to vote as such, in that he held an office of trust and profit under the United States.

4. E. A. Cronin was elected a presidential elector for the State of Oregon, and in accordance with law, as such, cast a legal vote as an elector for Samuel J. Tilden for President and Thomas A. Hendricks for Vice-President, and the vote so cast should be counted.

> JAMES K. KELLY,
> WM. PINKNEY WHYTE,
> HENRY COOPER,
> J. E. McDONALD,
> T. M. NORWOOD,
> FRANK HEREFORD,
> *Senators.*
> LA FAYETTE LANE,
> E. F. POPPLETON,
> G. A. JENKS,
> JOHN L. VANCE, of Ohio,
> J. W. THROCKMORTON,
> SCOTT WIKE,
> P. D. WIGGINTON,
> J. K. LUTTRELL,
> *Representatives.*

The PRESIDING OFFICER. Are there further objections to the decision of the Commission? [A pause.] There being none, the Senate will withdraw to its chamber, that the Houses separately may consider and determine the objection.

Accordingly, at twelve o'clock and ten minutes p. m., the Senate withdrew.

IN SENATE, *Saturday, February 24, 1877.*

The Senate having returned from the joint meeting at twelve o'clock and twelve minutes p. m., the President *pro tempore* resumed the chair, and laid before the Senate the objection to the decision of the Commission in regard to the electoral votes of the State of Oregon.

Mr. Senator SARGENT submitted the following resoluton, which (after debate and the rejection of an amendment) was adopted by a vote of yeas 41, nays 24, viz:

Resolved, That the decision of the Commission upon the electoral vote of the State of Oregon stand as the judgment of the Senate, the objections made thereto to the contrary notwithstanding.

On motion of Mr. Senator SARGENT it was

Resolved, That the House of Representatives be notified that the Senate has determined upon the objections to the decision of the Commission upon the electoral vote of Oregon, and is prepared to meet the House to proceed with the count of the electoral votes.

At three o'clock and fifty minutes p. m. a message was received announcing the action of the House of Representatives on the objection to the decision, whereupon the Senate at once repaired to the Hall of the House to proceed with the electoral count.

IN THE HOUSE OF REPRESENTATIVES, *Saturday, February 24, 1877.*

The Senate having retired from the joint meeting at twelve o'clock and ten minutes p. m., the House of Representatives resumed its session.

Mr. Representative CLYMER submitted the following resolution :

Resolved, That for the more careful consideration of the objections to the report of the Electoral Commission in the Oregon case, the House now take a recess until ten o'clock on Monday morning.

Mr. Representative HANCOCK made the point of order that, under the fifth section of the electoral act, a recess was not now in order.

The SPEAKER overruled the point of order, on the grounds heretofore stated by him when the same point of order was presented, and held the motion for a recess as made to be in order.

The question being on the resolution offered by Mr. Representative Clymer, it was rejected—yeas, 112 ; nays, 158.

Mr. Representative LANE thereupon moved that the House take a recess until nine o'clock and thirty minutes a. m. Monday, February 26.

Mr. Representative HALE made the point of order that the privilege of the House to take a recess had been exhausted by the vote just taken on a motion for a recess; that the motion of Mr. Representative Lane was a dilatory one; that the regular order was the consideration of the objections to the decision of the Commission in the Oregon case, and that the call for the regular order, which he now made, must bring the said objections before the House for present consideration.

The SPEAKER sustained the point of order, and held the motion to be not in order.

Whereupon,

Mr. Representative HALE submitted the following order :

Ordered, That the count of the electoral vote of the State of Oregon shall proceed in conformity with the decision of the Electoral Commission.

Mr. Representative LANE submitted the following order as an amendment in the nature of a substitute, viz :

Ordered, That the vote purporting to be an electoral vote for President and Vice-President, and which was given by one J. W. Watts, claiming to be an elector for the State of Oregon, be not counted.

After debate,

The amendment was agreed to by a vote of yeas 151, nays 106 ; and the resolution as amended was adopted without a division.

During the roll-call on the amendment, a message was received from the Senate announcing its action on the objection and its readiness to proceed with the count.

On motion of Mr. Representative CLYMER, it was

Ordered, That the Senate be informed of the action of this House on the electoral vote of the State of Oregon, and that the House of Representatives is now ready to meet them in joint convention in its hall.

JOINT MEETING.

SATURDAY, *February* 24, 1877.

At three o'clock and fifty-five minutes p. m. the Senate entered the House hall in the usual manner.

The PRESIDENT *pro tempore* of the Senate took his seat as presiding officer of the joint meeting of the two Houses, the Speaker of the House occupying a chair upon his left.

The PRESIDING OFFICER. The joint meeting of Congress for counting the electoral vote resumes its session. The two Houses having separately determined upon the objections to the decision of the Commission on the certificates from the State of Oregon, the Secretary of the Senate will read the resolution adopted by the Senate.

The Secretary of the Senate read as follows:

Resolved, That the decision of the Commission upon the electoral vote of the State of

Oregon stand as the judgment of the Senate, the objections made thereto to the contrary notwithstanding.

The PRESIDING OFFICER. The Clerk of the House of Representatives will now read the resolution adopted by the House of Representatives.

The Clerk of the House of Representatives read as follows:

Ordered, That the vote purporting to be the electoral vote for President and Vice-President, and which was given by one J. W. Watts, claiming to be an elector for the State of Oregon, be not counted.

The PRESIDING OFFICER. The two Houses not concurring otherwise, the decision of the Commission will stand unreversed, and the counting of the vote will proceed in conformity therewith. The tellers will announce the vote of Oregon.

Mr. Senator INGALLS, (one of the tellers.) Oregon casts 3 votes for Rutherford B. Hayes, of Ohio, for President, and 3 votes for William A. Wheeler, of New York, for Vice-President, of the United States.

PENNSYLVANIA.

The PRESIDING OFFICER. Having opened the certificate from the State of Pennsylvania received by messenger, the Chair hands it to the tellers, and it will be read in the presence and hearing of the two Houses.

Mr. Senator ALLISON (one of the tellers) read the certificate.

The PRESIDING OFFICER. Are there objections to the certificate from the State of Pennsylvania?

Mr. Representative STENGER. I submit on behalf of myself and others the objection which I send to the desk.

The PRESIDING OFFICER. The Clerk of the House will read the objection.

The Clerk of the House read as follows:

The undersigned Senators and Representatives object to the counting of the vote of Henry A. Boggs as an elector for the State of Pennsylvania, on the grounds following, namely:

That a certain Daniel J. Morrell was a candidate for the post of elector for the State of Pennsylvania at the election for electors of President and Vice-President on the 7th day of November, 1876, and was declared by the governor of the State of Pennsylvania to have been duly elected an elector at said election.

And the undersigned aver that the said Daniel J. Morrell was not duly elected an elector for the State of Pennsylvania, because, for a long period before, and on the said 7th day of November, 1876, and for a long period subsequent thereto, the said Morrell held an office of trust and profit under the United States, that is to say, the office of commissioner under the act of Congress, approved March 3, 1871, entitled "An act to provide for celebrating the one hundredth anniversary of American Independence by holding an international exhibition of arts, manufactures, and products of the soil and mine, in the city of Philadelphia and State of Pennsylvania, in the year 1876," to which he was appointed by the President of the United States under the provisions of said act.

Wherefore the undersigned aver that the said Morrell could not be constitutionally appointed an elector for the State of Pennsylvania on the said 7th day of November, 1876, under the Constitution of the United States.

And the undersigned further state that on the 6th day of December, 1876, the said Morrell did not attend the meeting of the electors of the State of Pennsylvania, and that he was not, according to the laws of Pennsylvania and under the Constitution of the United States, duly elected an elector of said State, and could not be constitutionally and legally declared duly elected as such elector, and had no legal right to attend the said meeting of electors.

And the undersigned further state that the college of electors had power under the law of Pennsylvania to fill vacancies in the office of elector under and by virtue of the law of Pennsylvania, which is in the words following, and by none other whatsoever, namely:

"If any such elector shall die, or from any cause fail to attend at the seat of government at the time appointed by law, the electors present shall proceed to choose *viva voce* a person to fill the vacancy occasioned thereby, and immediately after such choice the name of the person so chosen shall be transmitted by the presiding officer of the college to the governor, whose duty it shall be forthwith to cause notice in writing to be given to such person of his election, and the person so elected [and not the person *in whose place* he shall have been chosen] shall be an elector, and shall, with the other electors, perform the duties enjoined on them as aforesaid."

And the undersigned further state that under said law the electors present had no authority to appoint the said Henry A. Boggs to fill the vacancy of the said Daniel J. Morrell or on any other grounds whatever, and that said supposed appointment of said Henry A. Boggs was wholly without authority of law, and was and is null and void.

Wherefore the undersigned aver that the said Henry A. Boggs was not duly appointed by the State of Pennsylvania in the manner that its legislature directed, and that he was not entitled to cast his vote as elector for said State, and that his vote as such should not be, because it cannot be constitutionally, counted.

And the undersigned hereto annex the evidence to sustain the above objections, which has been taken before the committee of the House of Representatives on the powers, privileges, and duties of the House.

WILLIAM A. WALLACE, Pennsylvania,
M. W. RANSOM,
WM. PINKNEY WHITE,
Senators.

W. S. STENGER, Pennsylvania,
J. R. TUCKER, Virginia,
CHARLES B. ROBERTS, Maryland,
F. D. COLLINS, Pennsylvania,
JAC. TURNEY, Pennsylvania,
W. F. SLEMONS, Arkansas,
WM. MUTCHLER, Pennsylvania,
ALEX. G. COCHRANE, Pennsylvania,
JOHN L. VANCE, Ohio,
G. A. JENKS, of Pennsylvania,
Representatives.

UNITED STATES OF AMERICA, DEPARTMENT OF STATE.

To all to whom these presents shall come, greeting :

I certify that the document hereto annexed is a true copy of the original now on file in this Department.

In testimony whereof I, Hamilton Fish, Secretary of State of the United States, have hereunto subscribed my name and caused the seal of the Department of State to be affixed.

Done at the city of Washington this 23d day of February, A. D. 1877, and of the Independence of the United States of America the one hundred and first.

[SEAL.]   HAMILTON FISH.

EXECUTIVE CHAMBER,
Harrisburgh, Pennsylvania, March 10, 1871.

DEAR SIR: I have the honor to inform you that, in conformity with the recent act of Congress "to provide for celebrating the one hundredth anniversary of American Independence," &c., I have made the following appointments, which I submit for your approval:

Hon. Daniel J. Morrell, Johnstown, Cambria County, Pennsylvania, to be United States commissioner for Pennsylvania, in accordance with the provisions of the second section of the act.

Hon. Asa Packer, Mauch Chunk, Carbon County, Pennsylvania, to be the alternate United States commissioner for Pennsylvania, in accordance with the fourth section of the same act.

With assurances of my kindest regards, I am, general, very respectfully and truly, yours,

JNO. W. GEARY.

General U. S. GRANT,
President of the United States, Washington, D. C.

WASHINGTON, D. C., *February* 22, 1877.

JOHN REILLY, a member of the House from the State of Pennsylvania, sworn and examined.

By Mr. FIELD:

Question. Do you know Daniel J. Morrell, of Pennsylvania?—Answer. I do.

Q. How long have you known him ?—A. I suppose fifteen or eighteen years.

Q. Where does he reside ?—A. In Johnstown, Cambria County, Pennsylvania.

Q. Was he one of the centennial commissioners appointed by the President ?—A. Yes, sir.

Q. Is he still such ?—A. I believe he is; he was at the close of the exhibition ; I have not heard of him in connection with it since.

Q. How near to him do you live ?—A. I live within thirty-eight miles of him.

Q. Do. you know him very well ?—A. Yes, sir.

Q. Is he the same gentleman who was appointed one of the presidential electors in the State of Pennsylvania ?—A. Yes, sir.

Q. On the republican ticket ?—A. Yes sir.

By Mr. BURCHARD :

Q. Did you serve with him on the Centennial Commission ?—A. No, sir.

Q. Did you vote for him ?—A. I did not.

Q. You have no personal knowledge as to what you have testified to, have you ?—A. I have seen Mr. Morrell at the Centennial Exhibition in the discharge of his duties.

Q. What duties did you see him perform at the exhibition ?—A. I saw him around there. I don't know that I can state specifically that I saw him perform any particular act.

Q. Did you not see twenty thousand other individuals about there at the same time ?—A. I saw a great many more than that.

Q. One hundred thousand ?—A. Perhaps two hundred thousand.

Q. Walking about the grounds ?—A. Yes, sir.

Q. Can you mention any particular thing you saw Mr. Morrell do at that time ?—A. No, sir; but it is a well-known fact that he was a centennial commissioner.

Q. It is rumor and general information that you have on the subject ?—A. I may state that I had from Mr. Morrell himself, directly, a statement that he had paired with a man on the day of the election for the purpose of attending to his duties as centennial commissioner.

By Mr. FIELD :

Q. You saw him at the Centennial Exhibition in the apparent discharge of his duties ?—A. Yes, sir.

Q. And you heard him speak of his duties as centennial commissioner ?—A. Yes, sir.

Q. Is he universally reported to be a centennial commissioner ?—A. Yes, sir. He was formerly a member of Congress.

Q. Do you know that he was the candidate for presidential elector ?—A. Yes, sir.

Q. Do you know that it was the same person ?—A. Yes, sir.

By Mr. BURCHARD :

Q Do you know that from him ?—A. I do not know that I ever heard him speak of it himself directly.

By Mr. FIELD :

Q. But it was well understood among the people in Pennsylvania that Daniel J. Morrell, who was centennial commissioner, was also a candidate for presidential elector on the republican ticket ?—A. It was generally understood in that district. I cannot speak as to the whole State.

WASHINGTON, D. C., *February* 23, 1877.

JOHN WELSH sworn and examined.

By Mr. TUCKER :

Question. Where do you reside ?—Answer. I reside in Philadelphia, Pennsylvania.

Q. Were you a candidate for the position of presidential elector at the late presidential election, and were you certified as one of the electors for the State of Pennsylvania ?—A. I was, from the first district.

Q. Did you attend the college of electors ?—A. I did.

Q. And cast your vote ?—A. Yes sir.

Q. Do you hold any office of honor, trust, or profit under the United States ?—A. No, sir.

Q. What is your connection with the Centennial Exhibition ?—A. I am a director and also president of the Centennial Board of Finance, which was chartered by the United States on the 1st of June, 1872. It is a stock company. I was elected a director in April, 1873, and every year since then, by the stockholders, and have been chosen president every year by the directors.

Q. Were you president of that corporation on the 7th of November, 1876 ?—A. I was.

Q. And on the 6th of December, 1876 ?—A. Yes, sir; and am still.

Q. You are a stockholder in the corporation ?—A. I am a stockholder in the corporation.

Q. And have been since 1873 ?—A. Yes, sir.

Q. You held no position as centennial commissioner ?—A. No, sir.

Q. Do you know Mr. Daniel J. Morrell ?—A. I do.

Q. Was he a centennial commissioner under appointment of the President ?—A. He was and is.

Q. He was acting as such on the 7th of November, 1876, and on the 6th of December, 1876 ?—A. Yes, sir.

Q. Is he the same gentleman who was elected one of the presidential electors for the State of Pennsylvania ?—A. He is.

Q. Did he appear at the meeting of the electors ?—A. He did not.

Q. Did he assign any reason for not appearing ?—A. He was not present. I cannot say that he ever assigned any reason for his absence.

Q. Did he send a letter ?—A. No. I think he was absent and that his place was supplied.

Q. Who was appointed in his place ?—A. If I recollect right, it was Mr. Boggs, of Cambria County, the same county that Mr. Morrell lives in.

Q. Who appointed Mr. Boggs ?—A. He was appointed by the electoral college.

Q. Did he hold any Federal office ?—A. I think not.

Q. His title as an elector for the State of Pennsylvania was due to an appointment by the college of electors ?—A. Entirely.

Q. To fill the place of Mr. Morrell ?—A. Yes, sir.

By Mr. LAWRENCE:

Q. The corporation was a mere private stock corporation ?—A. Yes, sir.

Q. You had no appointment from the President of the United States ?—A. No, sir.

Q. There is no salary fixed by law to the office of director or president ?—A. The law allows a salary to be paid to the president and the treasurer, but I have never received any salary. I declined to receive it.

Q. The law does not fix any salary ?—A. No, sir.

By Mr. BURCHARD:

Q. The salary would have been paid by the corporation ?—A. Yes; it would have been paid by the corporation.

Q. And your relation to the Centennial Exhibition was simply that of stockholder in this corporation and of an officer elected by the stockholders ?—A. I was elected a director by the stockholders and president by the board of directors.

By Mr. LAWRENCE:

Q. You are no more an officer of the Government of the United States than would be a director of a railroad company incorporated by Congress ?—A. No, sir. I have never held any office under the United States.

By Mr. TUCKER:

Q. Did you give any bond as president of the board of finance to the United States ?—A. Yes, sir; not as president of the board of finance. Congress appropriated $1,500,000, and there was a provision in the appropriation bill that the president and treasurer should give a bond in $500,000. That bond was given by us, signed by one hundred citizens of Philadelphia.

Q. You executed that bond ?—A. Yes, sir.

Q. To whom was the bond given ?—A. I suppose the Secretary of the Treasury. The bond was conditioned on our applying the money to the purpose stated, namely, having the building open on the 10th of May, free of debt. The bond was filed, and vouchers to the amount of $1,727,000 were sent voluntarily by us.

Q. Is this the provision of law on the subject ? [Reading.]—A. Yes, sir; that is it.

Q. You say that you presented vouchers ?—A. Yes, sir.

Q. When ?—A. In the course of the season we sent to the Treasury Department vouchers for $1,727,000. They were sent at various periods during the summer.

Q. Did you send them all to the Treasury before the presidential election ?—A. Long before.

Q. Did you get an acquittance or discharge of the bond ?—A. No, sir; we got no acquittance or discharge.

Q. The bond, therefore, is still outstanding as an obligation ?—A. Yes, sir; I do not know whether the Government ever gives up a bond.

Q. It gave you no acquittance ?—A. No, sir.

Q. Was there any provision for returning this money to the Government ?—A. I have no opinion to offer on that subject. There is a difference of opinion on the subject between gentlemen skilled in the law. My own reading of it is that there is no provision for the return of the money to the Government until after the stockholders shall be paid, unless there be a profit, but I pretend to express no opinion on the subject. It was submitted to the court, and the circuit court has determined that there is no such provision in the law; in other words, that the money which we have on hand belongs to the stockholders; but an appeal has been taken to the Supreme Court of the United States, and it will be argued there.

Q. Then the question was whether there was any money to be paid to the Government in any event?—A. The question was whether any money was to be paid to the Government out of the capital or out of the profits. The construction of the court is that it was to come out of the profits.

Q. Then the court has decided that there is an obligation to refund the money to the Government if there should be a profit sufficient for that purpose?—A. Yes, sir.

Q. Do you hold any fund in your hands now awaiting the decision of that case?— A. We do. We placed before the court a statement that we have about $2,000,000 on hand for which there are two claimants.

Q. Who are the two claimants?—A. The stockholders and the Government. We asked the court to instruct us what to do with the money.

By Mr. BURCHARD:

Q. You were the president of a board of directors, elected by the stockholders under sections 4 and 5 of the act of 1872?—A. Yes, sir.

Q. There has been no change in the law, to your knowledge, in reference to the duration of your term of office or your duties in regard to the Government?—A. No, sir; no change.

Q. That law provides that the president, two vice-presidents, treasurer, and secretary, and such other officers as may be required to carry out the purpose of the corporation, shall hold their respective offices during the pleasure of the board, and the board adopts by-laws for its own government?—A. Yes.

Q. And you are in no way represented as an officer of the United States?—A. No, sir.

Q. You had no power to incur any liability to be charged to the United States?—A. No, sir. Each of the acts of Congress has had specific provisions in that respect—that no debt or responsibility should be incurred on behalf of the United States.

Q. And your relation to this money which was appropriated by Congress was simply that of applying it as the law required?—A. Yes, sir.

Q. But it was appropriated to the corporation?—A. Entirely.

Q. For the purpose of the exposition?—A. Yes.

Q. And the act required the president of the board and the treasurer to give bond to the United States?—A. Yes.

Q. You had no special custody of the funds?—A. The treasurer had custody of the funds, but a bond was required from the president as well as the treasurer.

Q. Your only relation to it was simply that of giving a bond?—A. Yes. The fund was under the control of the board of directors, to be disposed of by them. I was their servant. The funds were all applied in exact accordance with the memorial sent to Congress and signed by me, and it is a very curious fact that the $1,500,000 asked for was precisely the amount that was required.

Q. You hold no office of profit or trust under the United States unless the giving of a bond created you an officer?—A. No, sir. If so, I am an officer of the United States in a great many instances, for I am on a good many custom-house bonds for the last fifty years.

By Mr. TUCKER:

Q. You say that $1,500,000 was just enough?—A. Just enough to enable us to open the exhibition.

Q. How much money have you on hand now interpleaded between the Government of the United States and the stockholders?—A. Something rising $2,000,000. We cannot yet determine definitely the amount, because there are certain large claims which may or may not be allowed. If the Government is to be refunded the $1,500,000, then we shall pay 25 per cent. to the stockholders, and in the other case we shall have probably 85 per cent. to pay to the stockholders.

WASHINGTON, D. C., *February* 24, 1877.

DANIEL J. MORRELL sworn and examined.

By Mr. TUCKER:

Question. Where do you reside?—Answer. Johnstown, Pennsylvania.

Q. Are you or have you been a centennial commissioner by appointment of the President of the United States?—A. Yes, sir.

Q. What was the date of your appointment, and up to what time did you hold the office?—A. I don't remember the exact date, but I think it was in 1871 or 1872.

Q. You were appointed by commission by the President?—A. I was nominated by the governor of Pennsylvania and commissioned by the President of the United States.

Q. Are you still a centennial commissioner?—A. Yes, sir.

Q. And you have continued to be such from the time of your appointment until the present time?—A. Yes, sir.

Q. Were you a candidate for the position of elector at the late presidential election held on November 7, 1876?—A. I was nominated and voted for as an elector.

Q. Was your election certified to you by the governor of the State?—A. Yes, sir.

Q. Did you attend the meeting of the college of electors?—A. No, sir.

Q. Did you resign the position?—A. No, sir; I did not. I was advised that it was not necessary that I should resign, but that I should not attend; that I was not eligible.

Q. Not eligible by reason of your being a centennial commissioner?—A. Yes, sir.

Q. You absented yourself on that account?—A. I did.

Q. Who was appointed in your place?—A. Henry A. Boggs.

Q. Henry, not Harry?—A. I have always understood that his name was Henry; he is called Harry generally, however.

Q. He was appointed in your place?—A. That was my understanding. I was not present at the meeting of the electors.

By Mr. BURCHARD:

Q. Are you paid any compensation out of the Treasury of the United States as centennial commissioner?—A. No compensation whatever from any source.

Q. The position you hold is under the act creating the centennial commissioners?—A. Yes sir.

The PRESIDING OFFICER. Are there further objections to the certificate from the State of Pennsylvania? [A pause.] If there be none, the Senate will now withdraw, that the two Houses separately may consider and determine on the objection.

The Senate then (at four o'clock and twenty minutes p. m.) withdrew.

IN SENATE, *Saturday, February* 24, 1877.

The Senate having returned from the joint meeting at four o'clock and twenty-two minutes p. m. the President *pro tempore* resumed the chair, and laid before the Senate the objection submitted to counting the vote of Henry A. Boggs as an elector for the State of Pennsylvania, which was read.

Mr. Senator CAMERON of Pennsylvania submitted the following resolution; which, after debate, was agreed to without a division:

Resolved, That the vote of Henry A. Boggs be counted with the other votes of the electors of Pennsylvania, notwithstanding the objections made thereto.

On motion of Mr. Senator SARGENT, it was

Ordered, That the Secretary notify the House of Representatives thereof, and that the Senate is now ready to meet the House to proceed with the count of the electoral votes for President and Vice-President.

On motion of Mr. Senator WINDOM, the Senate (at six o'clock p. m.) took a recess until Monday, February 26, at ten o'clock a. m.

IN THE HOUSE OF REPRESENTATIVES,
Saturday, February 24, 1877.

The Senate having retired from the joint meeting, at four o'clock and twenty minutes p. m., the House of Representatives resumed its session.

On motion of Mr. Representative VANCE, of Ohio, the House took a recess (at four o'clock and fifty-two minutes p. m.) until Monday, February 26, at ten o'clock a. m., the vote on the motion being yeas 133, nays 122.

ELECTORAL COMMISSION.

SATURDAY, *February* 24, 1877.

The Commission met at twelve o'clock m., pursuant to adjournment.

Present: The President and Messrs. Commissioners Field, Bradley, Edmunds, Frelinghuysen, Bayard, Payne, Hunton, and Hoar.

The Journal of yesterday was read, corrected, and approved.

There being no business before the Commission, on motion of Mr. Commissioner EDMUNDS, a recess was taken until three o'clock p. m., at which time a further recess was taken till four o'clock p. m., which was again extended till five o'clock p. m.; when, on motion of Mr. Commissioner EDMUNDS, the Commission adjourned till Monday next at ten o'clock a. m.

FILLING OF VACANCY IN COMMISSION.

MONDAY, February 26, 1877.

The Commission met at ten o'clock a. m., and, there being no business before the Commission, it took a recess until one o'clock p. m.

At one o'clock p. m. the Commission re-assembled.

The PRESIDENT laid before the Commission the following communication:

1017 FOURTEENTH STREET, WASHINGTON, D. C.,
February 26, 1877.

Hon NATHAN CLIFFORD,
 President of the Electoral Commission:

SIR: Continued ill-health has confined me to my room, and for several days past to my bed, from which, by order of my physician, I cannot be removed to-day; nor have I any assurance that I will be able to get out for some days to come.

Under these circumstances of physical disability I am compelled to notify the Commission that I am not able to attend its sessions, and ask that the vacancy caused by my absence may be filled as provided by law.

Yours, respectfully,

A. G. THURMAN.

On motion of Mr. Commissioner EDMUNDS, the communication was ordered to be placed on the files of the Commission.

Mr. Commissioner EDMUNDS offered the following resolution:

Whereas Hon. Allen G. Thurman, a member of this Commission on the part of the Senate of the United States, has now communicated to the Commission, by a letter in writing, the fact that he has become physically unable to perform the duties required by the act of Congress establishing said Commission; and whereas the said Thurman has in fact become physically unable to perform the said duties: Therefore,

Resolved, That the President of the Commission forthwith communicate said fact to the Senate of the United States, as required by said act, in order that the vacancy so created in said Commission may be lawfully filled.

The question being on the adoption of the resolution, it was decided in the affirmative.

On motion of Mr. Commissioner EDMUNDS, it was

Ordered, That the President of the Commission transmit a letter to the President of the Senate, in the following words:]

" ELECTORAL COMMISSION,
"Washington, February 26, 1877.

" To the President of the Senate of the United States:

" SIR: I am directed by the Electoral Commission, formed under the act of| Congress approved January 29, A. D. 1877, entitled "An act to provide for and regulate the counting of votes for President and Vice-President, and the decision of questions arising thereon, for the term commencing March 4, A. D. 1877," to communicate to the Senate a copy of a resolution of the Commission, this day adopted, touching a vacancy therein, occasioned by the physical inability of Hon. Allen G. Thurman, a Senator, and member of said Commission, to proceed with its duties.

" Respectfully, yours."

And the communication was thereupon signed accordingly by

" NATHAN CLIFFORD,
" President of the Commission."

On motion of Mr. Commissioner HOAR, the Commission took a recess until four o'clock p. m.

IN SENATE, *Monday, February* 26, 1877.

The recess taken on Saturday, February 24, having expired, the Senate resumed its session on Monday, February 26, at ten o'clock a. m., transacting no business till one o'clock and twenty minutes p. m., when the President *pro tempore* laid before the Senate a communication, which was read, as follows:

ELECTORAL COMMISSION,
Washington, D. C., February 26, 1877.

SIR: I am directed by the Electoral Commission, formed under the act of Congress approved January 29, A. D. 1877, entitled "An act to provide for and regulate the counting of votes for President and Vice-President, and the decision of questions arising thereon, for the term commencing March 4, A. D. 1877," to communicate to the Senate a copy of a resolution of the Commission this day adopted, touching a vacancy therein, occasioned by the physical inability of the Hon. Allen G. Thurman, a Senator, and member of said Commission, to proceed with its duties.

Respectfully, yours,

NATHAN CLIFFORD,
President of the Commission.

To the PRESIDENT
   Of the Senate of the United States.

ELECTORAL COMMISSION,
Washington, D. C., February 26, 1877.

Whereas Hon. Allen G. Thurman, a member of this Commission on the part of the Senate of the United States, has now communicated to the Commission, by a letter in writing, the fact that he has become physically unable to perform the duties required by the act of Congress establishing said Commission; and whereas the said Thurman has in fact become physically unable to perform the said duties: Therefore,

Resolved, That the president of the Commission forthwith communicate said fact to the Senate of the United States, as required by said act, in order that the vacancy so created in said Commission may be lawfully filled.

A true copy.
Attest:

JAS. H. McKENNEY,
Secretary.

The PRESIDENT *pro tempore.* In compliance with the act the Senate will now proceed by *viva voce* vote to elect a Senator to fill the vacancy.

Mr. Senator McDONALD. I offer the following resolution:

Whereas the Electoral Commission created under the act of Congress approved January 29, 1877, entitled "An act to provide for and regulate the counting of votes for President and Vice-President, and the decision of questions arising thereon, for the term commencing March 4, A. D. 1877," has according to said act communicated to the Senate the fact of the physical inability of Senator Allen G. Thurman, a member of said Commission, to perform the duties required by said act: Therefore,

Resolved, That Francis Kernan, a Senator from the State of New York, be, and he hereby is, appointed a member of said Commission, to fill the place so made vacant by said physical inability of said Thurman, as required by said act.

The PRESIDENT *pro tempore.* The Secretary will call the roll of the Senate.

The roll having been called, the vote was yeas 46, nays none.

The PRESIDENT *pro tempore.* The resolution is agreed to, and the Senator from New York (Mr. Kernan) is unanimously elected. The Commission will be notified of the election.

ELECTORAL COMMISSION,
Monday, February 26, 1877—4 p. m.

The recess having expired, the Commission resumed its session at four o'clock p. m.

The PRESIDENT read the following communication:

IN SENATE OF THE UNITED STATES,
February 26, 1877.

SIR: I have the honor to communicate to you, to be laid before the Electoral

Commission, the proceedings of the Senate upon the submission of your communication this day announcing the inability of Hon. Allen G. Thurman, a member of the Commission, to perform the duties required by the act creating the said Commission.

I have the honor to be, sir, respectfully, your obedient servant,

T. W. FERRY,
President pro tempore.

Hon. NATHAN CLIFFORD,
President of the Electoral Commission.

—

IN THE SENATE OF THE UNITED STATES,
February 26, 1877.

The PRESIDENT *pro tempore* laid before the Senate a communication from the President of the Electoral Commission, announcing that Hon. Allen G. Thurman, a member of said Commission on the part of the Senate, had become physically unable to perform the duties required by the act of Congress establishing the said Commission.

The Senate thereupon proceeded, as required by the act of Congress creating the said Commission, to elect, by a *viva voce* vote, a member of the Senate to fill the vacancy in the said Commission created by the inability of Hon. Allen G. Thurman.

And, on counting the votes, it appeared that Hon. Francis Kernan was unanimously elected by the Senate to fill the vacancy in the Commission.

Attest:
GEORGE C. GORHAM,
Secretary.

The oath prescribed by law was administered by the President to Mr. KERNAN, and subscribed by him; whereupon he took his seat as a member of the Commission.

On motion of Mr. Commissioner EDMUNDS, the Commission took a recess until six o'clock, unless sooner called together by direction of the President.

PROCEEDINGS OF THE TWO HOUSES.

PENNSYLVANIA.

IN THE HOUSE OF REPRESENTATIVES,
Monday, February 26, 1877.

The recess taken on Saturday, February 24, having expired, the House resumed its session at ten o'clock a. m. Monday, February 26.

A message from the Senate was received announcing its action on the objection to the vote of Henry A. Boggs as one of the electors for the State of Pennsylvania, and its readiness to meet the House in order to proceed with the counting of the electoral votes.

Mr. Representative CLYMER raised the point of order that there was not a quorum present, and moved a call of the House.

No quorum voting on this motion, the SPEAKER directed the roll to be called.

The calling of the roll developing the presence of a quorum, all further proceedings under the call were dispensed with.

Mr. Representative KELLEY submitted the following resolution:

Resolved, That the vote of Henry A. Boggs be counted as an elector for the State of Pennsylvania, the objections to the contrary notwithstanding.

Mr. Representative STENGER moved to amend the resolution by substituting therefor the following:

Resolved, That the vote of Henry A. Boggs, as an elector for the State of Pennsylvania, should not be counted, because the said Boggs was not appointed an elector for said State in such manner as its legislature directed.

After debate, the amendment was agreed to by a vote of yeas 135, nays 119; and the resolution as amended was agreed to without a division; and the Clerk was directed to inform the Senate of this action and of the readiness of the House to receive the Senate in order to proceed with the count.

IN SENATE, *Monday, February* 26, 1877.

The Senate at three o'clock and thirteen minutes p. m. was notified of the action of the House of Representatives in regard to the vote of Henry A. Boggs as an elector for the State of Pennsylvania, and immediately proceeded to the Hall of the House.

JOINT MEETING.

MONDAY, *February* 26, 1877.

The Senate entered the House-hall at three o'clock and fifteen minutes p. m. in the usual manner.

The PRESIDENT *pro tempore* of the Senate took his seat as presiding officer of the joint meeting of the two Houses, the Speaker of the House occupying a chair upon his left.

The PRESIDING OFFICER. The joint meeting of Congress for counting the electoral vote resumes its session. The two Houses acting separately have considered and determined on the objection to the certificate from the State of Pennsylvania; the Secretary of the Senate will read the resolution of the Senate.

The Secretary of the Senate read as follows:

Resolved, That the vote of Henry A. Boggs be counted with the other votes of the electors of Pennsylvania, notwithstanding the objection thereto.

The PRESIDING OFFICER. The Clerk of the House of Representatives will now read the resolution adopted by the House of Representatives.

The Clerk of the House of Representatives read as follows:

Resolved, That the vote of Henry A. Boggs as an elector for the State of Pennsylvania should not be counted, because said Boggs was not appointed an elector for said State in such manner as its legislature directed.

The PRESIDING OFFICER. The two Houses not concurring in an affirmative vote to reject, the vote of the State of Pennsylvania will be counted. The tellers will announce the vote of the State of Pennsylvania.

Mr. Senator ALLISON, (one of the tellers.) The State of Pennsylvania casts 29 votes for Rutherford B. Hayes, of Ohio, for President, and 29 votes for William A. Wheeler, of New York, for Vice-President.

RHODE ISLAND.

The PRESIDING OFFICER. Having opened the certificate received by messenger from the State of Rhode Island, the Chair hands to the tellers the same to be read in the presence and hearing of the two Houses; also the corresponding certificate by mail is handed to the tellers.

Mr. Representative STONE (one of the tellers) read the certificate from the State of Rhode Island.

The PRESIDING OFFICER. Are there any objections to the certificate from the State of Rhode Island?

Mr. Representative O'BRIEN. On behalf of myself and other signers, Senators and Representatives, I send up objections to one of the votes from the State of Rhode Island.

The PRESIDING OFFICER. The member from Maryland having submitted an objection to the certificate from the State of Rhode Island, the Clerk of the House will read the same.

The Clerk of the House read as follows :

The undersigned, Senators and Representatives, do hereby object to counting the vote of William S. Slater, alleged elector of the State of Rhode Island, and as reasons therefor assign the following:

First. That the said William S. Slater was not duly appointed elector by the State of Rhode Island at the election in said State on the 7th day of November, 1876.

Second. That George H. Corliss, according to the decision of the Electoral Commission rendered in the counting of the vote of John W. Watts, as elector of the State of Oregon, if said decision be law, was duly appointed elector by the State of Rhode Island, and the substitution for him of the said Slater was illegal and unconstitutional.

Third. If in any event it was competent to complete the electoral college of Rhode Island by adding another elector thereto, it could only have been done under the law as announced by the said Electoral Commission, if said decision be law, and pursuant to the laws of said State by act of the majority of the members of said college, and not by the legislature of said State.

JAMES K. KELLY,
J. B. GORDON,
Senators.
WM. J. O'BRIEN,
R. Q. MILLS,
G. A. JENKS,
L. A. MACKEY,
A. V. RICE,
J. L. VANCE,
FRANK H. HURD,
JAMES J. FINLEY,
A. T. WALLING,
E. F. POPPLETON,
M. I. SOUTHARD,
E. J. HENKLE,
JOHN K. LUTTRELL,
A. M. WADDELL,
WM. P. LYNDE,
Representatives.

The PRESIDING OFFICER. Are there further objections to the certificate from the State of Rhode Island? [A pause.] If there be none, the Senate will now withdraw to its Chamber, that the two Houses may separately consider and determine on the objection.

Accordingly (at three o'clock and twenty-eight minutes p. m.) the Senate withdrew.

IN SENATE, *Monday, February 26, 1877.*

The Senate having returned from the joint meeting, at three o'clock thirty minutes p. m. the President *pro tempore* resumed the chair and submitted to the Senate the objection made to counting the vote of William S. Slater as an elector for the State of Rhode Island, which was read.

Mr. Senator BURNSIDE thereupon submitted the following resolution, which, after debate, was agreed to by a vote of yeas 57, nays none, viz :

Resolved, That the vote of William S. Slater be counted with the other votes of the electors of Rhode Island, notwithstanding the objections made thereto.

On motion of Mr. Senator ANTHONY, it was

Ordered, That the Secretary notify the House of Representatives thereof, and that the Senate is now ready to meet the House to continue the count of the electoral votes for President and Vice-President.

At five o'clock and fifty-five minutes p. m. a message was received from the House of Representatives announcing its action on the object on to the vote of William S. Slater as an elector for the State of Rhode Island and its readiness to receive the Senate to proceed with the electoral count; and the Senate immediately proceeded to the Hall of the House.

IN THE HOUSE OF REPRESENTATIVES,
Monday, February 26, 1877.

The Senate having retired from the joint meeting, at three o'clock and twenty-eight minutes p. m. the House of Representatives resumed its session.

Mr. Representative POPPLETON moved that the House take a recess until Tuesday, February 27, at ten o'clock a. m.; which motion was disagreed to—yeas 84, nays 178.

Mr. Representative WOOD, of New York, moved to reconsider the vote just taken refusing a recess, and also moved that the motion to reconsider be laid on the table.

Mr. Representative O'BRIEN raised the point of order that the motions of Mr. Representative Wood, of New York, were not in order.

The SPEAKER overruled the point of order.

The motion to lay on the table the motion to reconsider was agreed to—yeas 182, nays 67.

A message was received from the Senate announcing its action on the objection to the vote of William S. Slater as an elector for the State of Rhode Island and its readiness to proceed with the electoral count.

Mr. Representative O'BRIEN submitted the following resolution:

Resolved, That the vote of William S. Slater as elector for the State of Rhode Island should not be counted because said Slater was not appointed or elected elector for said State in such manner as its legislature had directed.

Mr Representative EAMES moved to amend the resolution by substituting therefor the following:

Resolved, That the vote of William S. Slater as an elector for the State of Rhode Island be counted, the objections thereto to the contrary notwithstanding.

After debate, the amendment was agreed to, and the resolution as amended was agreed to without a division.

Mr. Representative WILSON, of Iowa, moved that the Senate be notified by the Clerk of the action of the House in regard to the electoral vote of Rhode Island, and that the House was ready to meet the Senate at once and continue the counting of the electoral votes for President and Vice-President.

Mr. Representative KNOTT submitted as a substitute for the motion the following:

Ordered, That the Clerk of this House notify the Senate of the decision of the House in the case of the State of Rhode Island, and that the House of Representatives will meet the Senate in this hall at ten o'clock to-morrow morning to proceed with the counting of the electoral vote for President and Vice-President of the United States.

Mr. Representative McCRARY made the point of order that the electoral act (section 1) requires that when the two Houses have voted upon objections, they shall immediately again meet and the presiding officer shall then announce the decision of the question submitted.

The SPEAKER sustained the point of order and ruled out the amendment.

The motion of Mr. Representative WILSON, of Iowa, was adopted; and the Senate was notified.

JOINT MEETING.
MONDAY, <i>February 26,</i> 1877.</div>

The Senate entered the House hall at six o'clock p. m., in the usual manner.

The PRESIDENT *pro tempore* of the Senate took his seat as Presiding Officer of the joint meeting of the two Houses, the Speaker of the House occupying a chair upon his left.

The PRESIDING OFFICER. The joint meeting of Congress for counting the electoral vote resumes its session. The two Houses having separately determined upon the objection to the certificate from the State of Rhode Island, the Secretary of the Senate will read the resolution adopted by the Senate.

The Secretary of the Senate read as follows:

Resolved, That the vote of William S. Slater be counted with the other votes of the electors of Rhode Island, notwithstanding the objections made thereto.

The PRESIDING OFFICER. The Clerk of the House of Representatives will now read the resolution adopted by the House of Representatives.

The Clerk of the House of Representatives read as follows:

Resolved, That the vote of William S. Slater as an elector of the State of Rhode Island be counted, the objections thereto to the contrary notwithstanding.

The PRESIDING OFFICER. The two Houses having concurred in an affirmative vote not to reject the vote of Rhode Island, that vote will be counted. The tellers will announce the vote of Rhode Island.

Mr. Representative STONE, (one of the tellers.) The State of Rhode Island casts four votes for Rutherford B. Hayes, of the State of Ohio, for President, and four votes for William A. Wheeler, of the State of New York, for Vice-President of the United States.

SOUTH CAROLINA.

The PRESIDING OFFICER. Having opened the certificate from the State of South Carolina, received by messenger, the Chair hands it to the tellers to be read in the presence and hearing of the two Houses. The Chair also hands to the tellers the corresponding certificate received by mail.

Mr. Senator ALLISON (one of the tellers) read as follows:

CERTIFICATE No. 1.

STATE OF SOUTH CAROLINA:

Pursuant to the laws of the United States, I, D. H. Chamberlain, governor of the State of South Carolina, do hereby certify that C. C. Bowen, John Winsmith, Thomas B. Johnston, Timothy Hurley, W. B. Nash, Wilson Cook, and W. F. Myers have been chosen electors of President and Vice-President of the United States on the part of this State, agreeably to the provisions of the laws of the said State and in conformity to the Constitution of the United States of America, for the purpose of giving in their votes for President and Vice-President of the United States for the term prescribed by the Constitution of said United States, to begin on the 4th day of March, in the year of our Lord one thousand eight hundred and seventy-seven.

Given under my hand and seal of the State of South Carolina, at Columbia, this twenty-second day of November, A. D. one thousand eight hundred and seventy-six.

D. H. CHAMBERLAIN,
Governor.

By the governor:
[SEAL.]

H. E. HAYNE,
Secretary of State.

List of persons voted for as President of the United States of America for the term prescribed by the Constitution of the United States to begin on the fourth day of March, in the year of our Lord one thousand eight hundred and seventy-seven, by the electoral college of the State of South Carolina, on the first Wednesday in December, in the year of our Lord one thousand eight hundred and seventy-six, at Columbia, the capital of said State of South Carolina, with the number of votes for each, to wit:

Rutherford B. Hayes, of Ohio, received seven (7) votes.

C. C. BOWEN.
J. WINSMITH.
THOMAS B. JOHNSTON.
TIMOTHY HURLEY.
W. B. NASH.
WILSON COOK.
W. F. MYERS.

We, the undersigned, electors of President and Vice-President of the United States of America, appointed by the State of South Carolina at the general election held on the seventh day of November, in the year of our Lord one thousand eight hundred and seventy-six, do certify that the foregoing list is correct.

In witness whereof we have hereunto set our hands this sixth day of December, in the year of our Lord one thousand eight hundred and seventy-six, and in the one hundred and first year of the Independence of the United States of America.

C. C. BOWEN.
J. WINSMITH.
THOMAS B. JOHNSTON.
TIMOTHY HURLEY.
W. B. NASH.
WILSON COOK.
W. F. MYERS.

List of persons voted for as Vice-President of the United States of America for the term prescribed by the Constitution of the United States of America to begin on the fourth day of March, in the year of our Lord one thousand eight hundred and seventy-seven, by the electoral college of the State of South Carolina, on the first Wednesday in December, in the year of our Lord one thousand eight hundred and seventy-six, at Columbia, the capital of said State of South Carolina, with the number of votes for each, to wit:

William A. Wheeler, of New York, received seven (7) votes.

C. C. BOWEN,
J. WINSMITH.
THOMAS B. JOHNSTON.
TIMOTHY HURLEY.
W. B. NASH.
WILSON COOK.
W. F. MYERS.

We, the undersigned, electors of President and Vice-President of the United States of America, appointed by the State of South Carolina at the general election held on the 7th day of November, in the year of our Lord one thousand eight hundred and seventy-six, do certify that the foregoing list is correct.

In witness whereof we have hereunto set our hands this 6th day of December, in the year of our Lord one thousand eight hundred and seventy-six, and in the one hundred and first year of the Independence of the United States of America.

C. C. BOWEN.
J. WINSMITH.
THOMAS B. JOHNSTON.
TIMOTHY HURLEY.
W. B. NASH.
WILSON COOK.
W. F. MYERS.

The PRESIDING OFFICER. Another certificate from the State of South Carolina has been received by messenger, and also by mail. The Chair hands it to the tellers to be read in the presence and hearing of the two Houses.

Mr. Representative STONE (one of the tellers) read as follows:

CERTIFICATE No. 2.

STATE OF SOUTH CAROLINA, *ss:*

We, the undersigned, electors of President and Vice-President of the United States of America for the next ensuing regular term of the respective offices thereof, being electors duly and legally appointed by and for the State of South Carolina, as will hereinafter appear, having met and convened in the city of Columbia, at the capitol of the State, in pursuance of the direction of the legislature of the State of South Carolina, on the first Wednesday, the sixth day, of December, in the year of our Lord one thousand eight hundred and seventy-six, do hereby certify that, being so assembled, duly qualified according to the provisions of said State by taking and subscribing the proper oath of office therein prescribed, and organized, we proceeded to vote by ballot, and balloted first for such President and then for such Vice-President, by distinct ballots.

The list of the names of the electors, signed by the governor, with the seal of the State affixed thereto, as required by law, is not attached, and its absence is explained by the following statement:

First. We claim to have been duly appointed electors by the State of South Carolina in the manner directed by the legislature thereof, and to have been elected by general ticket, and to have received the highest number of votes at the election for President and Vice-President, held on the 7th day of November, A. D. 1876, and that such election will appear by a proper examination of the legal returns of the managers of election for the different precincts in the counties of the State, made to their respective boards of county canvassers, which do not sustain, but are directly opposed to, the statements of votes given for electors in the several counties forwarded and certified to the State board of canvassers by the commissioners of election or boards of canvassers in such counties.

Second. The board of State canvassers, after a pretended canvass of the returns of the election, made an erroneous, imperfect, and false statement of the result of said election, and illegally declare the result to be as follows:

Theodore G. Barker	90,896	C. C. Bowen	91,786
Samuel McGowan	90,737	John Winsmith	91,870
J. W. Harrington	90,895	Thomas B. Johnston	91,852
J. I. Ingram	90,798	Timothy Hurley	91,136
William Wallace	90,905	William B. Nash	91,804
John B. Erwin	90,906	Wilson Cook	91,432
Robert Aldrich	90,860	W. F. Myers	91,830

Third. In this illegal and invalid canvass of the votes given for the electors of President and Vice-President, the board of State canvassers, after canvassing the votes of six of the counties of the State, by comparing the statements of the county boards of canvassers with the returns of the precinct managers in said counties, and after discovering serious discrepancies between such statements and such returns, showing errors in the statements of the county canvassers, refused to continue such comparison and verification as to the remaining twenty-six counties in the State, also refused to allow copies of such returns to be made, and confined their canvass and count to the aggregation of the erroneous returns of county canvassers, and upon such count declared the above erroneous and false result.

Fourth. The undersigned, who claim that they are duly elected electors, filed in the supreme court of South Carolina a suggestion for writ of *mandamus* to require the board of State canvassers to correct the count according to the true vote of the people as cast at said election, but pending that proceeding, of which the board had due notice, the board determined and certified the persons elected upon the above erroneous count, and after making a return to the court, and before the decision thereof, secretly and unlawfully adjourned in defiance and contempt of the authority of the supreme court. The secretary of state, upon such erroneous statement and illegal determination, unlawfully certified to him, caused a copy of the certified determination of the board of State canvassers to be delivered to each of the persons therein declared to be elected, viz, Christopher C. Bowen, John Winsmith, Thomas B. Johnston, Timothy Hurley, William B. Nash, Wilson Cook, and W. F. Myers.

The undersigned thereupon filed in the supreme court of the State their suggestion for a writ of *quo warranto*, disputing the election of said persons and the validity of their legal title to the offices of electors, which proceeding also is now pending in said court.

Fifth. The undersigned, as electors duly appointed, made demand upon the secretrary of state for the lists required by law, and he refused to deliver the same; and we further certify that the following are two distinct lists, one of the votes for President and the other of the votes for Vice-President:

List of all persons voted for as President, with the number of votes for each.

Names of persons voted for.   Number of votes.
Samuel J. Tilden, of the State of New York.. seven (7.)

List of all persons voted for as Vice-President, with the number of votes for each.

Names of persons voted for.   Number of votes
Thomas A. Hendricks, of the State of Indiana .... seven, (7.)

In witness whereof we have hereunto set our hands.

Done at No. 101 Richardson street, in the city of Columbia and State of South Carolina, the 6th day of December, in the year of our Lord 1876, and of the Independence of the United States of America the 101st.

> THEODORE G. BARKER.
> S. McGOWAN.
> JNO. W. HARRINGTON.
> JNO. ISAAC INGRAM.
> WM. WALLACE.
> JOHN B. ERWIN.
> ROBT. ALDRICH.

The PRESIDING OFFICER. Are there objections to the certificates from the State of South Carolina?

Mr. Representative COCHRANE. On behalf of the Senators and Representatives whose names are thereto attached, I submit the following objections to the certificates and papers purporting to be certificates of the electoral votes of the State of South Carolina cast by C. C. Bowen and others.

The PRESIDING OFFICER. The Secretary of the Senate will read the objections.

The Secretary of the Senate read as follows:

OBJECTION No. 1.

The undersigned, Senators of the United States and members of the House of Representatives, object to the certificates and papers purporting to be certificates of the electoral votes of the State of South Carolina cast by C. C. Bowen, D. Winsmith, T. B. Johnson, Timothy Hurley, W. B. Nash, Wilson Cook, and W. F. Myers, on the following grounds:

I.

For that no legal election was held in the State of South Carolina for presidential electors, the general assembly of that State not having provided, as required by article 8, section 3, of the constitution thereof, for the registration of persons entitled to vote, without which registration no valid or legal election could be held.

II.

For that there was not existing in the State of South Carolina on the first day of January, 1876, nor at any time thereafter, up to and including the 10th day of December, 1876, a republican form of government such as is guaranteed by the Constitution to every State in the Union.

III.

For that the Federal Government prior to and during the election on the 7th day of November, 1876, without authority of law, stationed in various parts of the said State of South Carolina, at or near the polling-places, detachments of the Army of the United States, by whose presence the full exercise of the right of suffrage was prevented, and by reason whereof no legal or free election was or could be had.

IV.

For that at the several polling-places in the said State there were stationed deputy marshals of the United States, appointed under the provisions of sections 2021 and 2022 of the Revised Statutes of the United States, which provisions were unconstitutional and void. That the said deputy marshals, exceeding over one thousand in number, by their unlawful and arbitrary action, in obedience to the improper and illegal instructions received by them from the Department of Justice, so interfered with the full and free exercise of the right of suffrage by the duly-qualified voters of the said State of South Carolina that a fair election could not be and was not held in the said State of South Carolina on the said 7th day of November, 1876.

V.

For that there was not from the 1st day of January, 1876, up to and including the 10th day of December, 1876, at any time a State government in the State of South Carolina, except a pretended government set up in violation of law and of the Constitution of the United States by Federal authority, and sustained by Federal troops.

JOHN W. JOHNSTON,	CHARLES B. ROBERTS,
United States Senator, Virginia.	F. D. COLLINS,
W. H. BARNUM,	JAC. TURNEY,
United States Senator, Connecticut.	A. V. RICE, of Ohio,
ALEX. G. COCHRANE, of Pennsylvania,	B. F. FRANKLIN, of Missouri,
M. I. SOUTHARD,	CHARLES P. THOMPSON,
FERNANDO WOOD,	JNO. F. PHILIPS, of Missouri,
J. A. McMAHON,	WM. S. HOLMAN, of Indiana,
W. S. STENGER,	G. A. JENKS, of Pennsylvania,
WM. MUTCHLER, of Pennsylvania,	J. M. BRIGHT, of Tennessee,
GEO. C. CABELL, of Virginia,	S. S. COX, of New York,
JAMES SHEAKLEY,	JNO. B. CLARK, JR.,
LEVI MAISH, of Pennsylvania,	G. C. WALKER,
WM. WALSH,	R. A. DE BOLT,
WM. M. ROBBINS, of North Carolina,	JOHN R. EDEN,
WM. A. J. SPARKS,	J. R. TUCKER, of Virginia,
E. F. POPPLETON,	J. B. CLARKE, of Kentucky,
A. T. WALLING, of Ohio,	THOS. L. JONES, of Kentucky,
THOS. S. ASHE,	J. PROCTOR KNOTT,
A. M. SCALES,	*Representatives.*

The PRESIDING OFFICER. Are there further objections to the certificates from the State of South Carolina?

Mr. Senator PATTERSON. I submit, on behalf of the Senators and Representatives whose names are attached thereto, the following objections to the certificates and papers purporting to be certificates of the electoral votes of South Carolina cast by Theodore G. Barker and others.

The PRESIDING OFFICER. The Clerk of the House will read the objections.

The Clerk of the House read as follows:

OBJECTION No. 2.

The undersigned, Senators and members of the House of Representatives of the United States, object to the certificates and papers purporting to be certificates of the electoral votes of the State of South Carolina cast by Theodore G. Barker, Samuel McGowan, John W. Harrington, John I. Ingram, William Wallace, John B. Erwin, and Robert Aldrich, and by each of them, and to the list of votes by them and each of them signed and certified as given for President of the United States and for Vice-President of the United States, for the following reasons:

I.

The said Theodore G. Barker, Samuel McGowan, John W. Harrington, John I. Ingram, William Wallace, John B. Erwin, and Robert Aldrich were not, nor was either of them, appointed an elector of President and Vice-President of the United States for the State of South Carolina.

II.

The said papers have not annexed to them a certificate of the governor of South Carolina as required to be made and annexed by sections 136 and 138 of the Revised Statutes of the United States.

III.

The said papers have not annexed to them a list of the names of the said Theodore G. Barker, Samuel McGowan, John W. Harrington, John I. Ingram, William Wallace, John B. Erwin, and Robert Aldrich, as electors, to which the seal of the State of South Carolina was affixed by the secretary of state, and signed by the governor and secretary, as required by the general laws of South Carolina.

IV.

For that C. C. Bowen, John Winsmith, Thomas B. Johnston, Timothy Hurley, William B. Nash, Wilson Cook, and William F. Myers were duly appointed electors of President and Vice-President of the United States for the State of South Carolina, and as such electors, at the time and place prescribed by law, cast their votes for Rutherford B. Hayes for President of the United States and for William A. Wheeler for Vice-President of the United States, and the lists of votes signed, certified, and transmitted by such electors to the President of the Senate are the only true and lawful lists of votes for President and Vice-President of the United States.

V.

That the said C. C. Bowen, John Winsmith, Thomas B. Johnston, Timothy Hurley, William B. Nash, Wilson Cook, and William F. Myers received the highest number of all the votes cast for electors of President and Vice-President of the United States by the qualified voters of the State of South Carolina at the election held in said State on the 7th day of November, A. D. 1876, and the proper officers of the State of South Carolina duly canvassed said votes, and made and certified according to law and under the great seal of the State of South Carolina, and delivered to said C. C. Bowen, John Winsmith, Thomas B. Johnston, Timothy Hurley, William B. Nash, Wilson Cook, and William F. Myers lists of the electors of President and Vice-President of the United States elected by the qualified voters of said State at said election, and showing that said C. C. Bowen, John Winsmith, Thomas B. Johnston, Timothy Hurley, William B. Nash, Wilson Cook, and William F. Myers were the persons having the highest number of votes of said qualified voters at such election, and were elected, which certificate is dated the 6th day of December, A. D. 1876, and which has been read before the two Houses of Congress; by reason of all which said Bowen, Winsmith, Johnston, Hurley, Nash, Cook, and Myers were the lawful electors of President and Vice-President of the United States for the State of South Carolina.

VI.

That the lists of votes cast by the said C. C. Bowen, John Winsmith, Thomas B. Johnston, Timothy Hurley, William B. Nash, Wilson Cook, and William F. Myers for President of the United States and for Vice-President of the United States, have annexed to them a certificate of the governor of the State of South Carolina, required to be made by sections 136 and 138 of the Revised Statutes of the United States.

VII.

That said lists of votes have annexed to them a list of the names of the said C. C. Bowen, John Winsmith, Thomas B. Johnston, Timothy Hurley, William B. Nash, Wilson Cook, and William F. Myers as electors, to which the seal of the State of South Carolina was affixed by the secretary of state, and signed by the governor and secretary as required by the general laws of South Carolina.

JNO. J. PATTERSON,
ANGUS CAMERON,
I. P. CHRISTIANCY,
Senators.
WILLIAM LAWRENCE,
E. G. LAPHAM,
N. P. BANKS,
ROBERT SMALLS,
S. L. HOGE,
J. H. RAINEY,
Representatives.

The PRESIDING OFFICER. Are there further objections to the certificates of the State of South Carolina?
There were no further objections.

The PRESIDING OFFICER. The certificates objected to, together with the objections, will be submitted to the Commission for its judgment and decision. The Senate will now retire to its chamber.

The Senate accordingly retired, at six o'clock and thirty minutes p. m

ELECTORAL COMMISSION.

MONDAY, *February* 26, 1877.

Its recess having expired, the Commission re-assembled at six o'clock p. m.

The Journal of Saturday last was read and approved.

At six o'clock and thirty-five minutes p. m., Mr. Gorham, Secretary of the Senate, appeared and presented the following communication; which was read:

HALL OF THE HOUSE OF REPRESENTATIVES,
February 26, 1876.

To the President of the Commission:

More than one return, or paper purporting to be a return, or certificate of the electoral votes of the State of South Carolina having been received and this day opened in the presence of the two Houses of Congress, and objections thereto having been made, the said returns, with all accompanying papers, and also the objections thereto, are herewith submitted to the judgment and decision of the Commission, as provided by law.

T. W. FERRY,
President of the Senate.

Mr. Commissioner EDMUNDS. I think the certificates had better be read, if they are not too long.

The PRESIDENT. The certificates will be read.

Mr. Commissioner PAYNE. Would it not be in order to have them printed?

The PRESIDENT. Certainly; but their reading is asked for. They will be read.

The Secretary read the certificates.

The PRESIDENT. I desire to inquire who represent the objectors to certificate No. 1, under the fourth rule?

Mr. Representative HURD. Mr. Cochrane, a Representative from Pennsylvania, and myself.

The PRESIDENT. Who represent the objectors to certificate No. 2?

Mr. Representative LAWRENCE. I have the honor to represent the objectors on the part of the House, and Senator Christiancy, I understand, represents the objectors on the part of the Senate.

Mr. Senator CHRISTIANCY. Mr. President, I wish to state, on behalf of the objectors on the part of the Senate, that, beyond the interposition of the objections, we do not propose to argue them, but leave them to be argued by counsel, if they see fit, within the time provided by your rules.

Mr. Commissioner HUNTON. I move that the papers referred to the Commission by the joint session, be printed.

Mr. Commissioner EDMUNDS. By that you mean the papers transmitted by the President of the Senate?

Mr. Commissioner HUNTON. Yes, sir.

Mr. Commissioner HOAR. Before we proceed to any other matter, I inquire whether it would not be well to ascertain what counsel represent the two sides?

The PRESIDENT. We have usually made that inquiry after the objectors have been heard; but I can make the inquiry now. Who are the counsel that represent the objectors to certificate No. 1?

Mr. Representative HURD. I am unable to state their names this evening, but I will report to the Commission to-morrow, if that will answer the purpose.

The PRESIDENT. I make the same inquiry now of the other side, if it be convenient for them to answer.

Mr. MATTHEWS. The objections to certificate No. 2 will be represented, so far as counsel are concerned, by Mr. Shellabarger and myself.

The PRESIDENT. The question now is on the motion of Mr. Commissioner Hunton that the papers be printed.

The motion was agreed to.

Mr. Commissioner HUNTON. I move that the Commission adjourn until ten o'clock to-morrow morning.

Mr. Commissioner GARFIELD. I ask the gentleman to withdraw that motion for a moment, to enable me to make a suggestion.

Mr. Commissioner HUNTON. Certainly.

Mr. Commissioner GARFIELD. I do not rise to make a motion; but I wish to suggest that the Commission ought to determine the amount of time to be allowed in this case. It has seemed to me that there might be a reduction of time.

The PRESIDENT. In the absence of any application, the rules determine it.

Mr. Commissioner GARFIELD. I know that; but I am speaking now, not in favor of an extension, but a reduction of time.

Mr. Commissioner EDMUNDS. We had better wait until counsel come in.

Mr. Commissioner GARFIELD. It has already been announced on the part of the Senate that they do not wish to occupy time.

The PRESIDENT. Excuse me, General Garfield. On one side the counsel are not present.

Mr. Commissioner GARFIELD. No; but I am speaking of the whole subject of time, for objectors as well as counsel.

Mr. Commissioner FRELINGHUYSEN. I think that had better go off until to-morrow morning.

Mr. Commissioner GARFIELD. Very well; I will call it up to-morrow morning.

Mr. Commissioner HUNTON. I renew my motion.

The PRESIDENT. It is moved that the Commission adjourn until to-morrow at ten o'clock.

The motion was agreed to; and (at six o'clock and forty-five minutes p. m.) the Commission adjourned.

TUESDAY, *February* 27, 1877.

The Commission met at ten o'clock a. m., pursuant to adjournment. Present: The President and Messrs. Commissioners Miller, Strong, Field, Bradley, Edmunds, Morton, Frelinghuysen, Bayard, Kernan, Payne, Hunton, Abbott, Garfield, and Hoar.

The respective objectors and Messrs. Stanley Matthews and Samuel Shellabarger, counsel representing the objections to the South Carolina certificate No. 2, were also present.

The PRESIDENT. It was said that the counsel on the part of the objectors to certificate No. 1 would be named this morning.

Mr. Representative HURD. No counsel will appear on behalf of the objectors to certificate No. 1, as we are at present advised.

The PRESIDENT. We are ready to hear the objectors to certificate No. 1.

Mr. Representative HURD. Mr. President and gentlemen of the

Commission, I shall as briefly and as rapidly as I can submit to your consideration the reasons which in my judgment require the refusal on your part to count the vote of the State of South Carolina. In the discussion I shall endeavor not to go over any of the ground which has already been traversed. I shall not antagonize any of the propositions which I understand to have already been decided by the Commission. I shall submit, as I regard them, new propositions as to which the opinion of this Commission has not as yet been asked.

The first proposition is that the vote of South Carolina should not be counted, because at the time the election was held there was not a republican form of government in that State. I do not propose in discussing this proposition to refer to the history of the reconstruction measures by which South Carolina was restored to the Federal Union, nor to point out the anti-republican policies by which that result was brought about; nor do I intend to refer to the policies of legislation which have since followed its admission to the Union, policies by which the sovereignty of the State has practically been overthrown and by which the republican nature of its institutions has been destroyed. Nor yet do I intend to refer to the usurpations of those who have held political office in South Carolina, by which more markedly still has the nature of the government of that commonwealth been changed. I simply intend to refer to the condition of things which existed in South Carolina for a few weeks prior to the election, on the day of election, and for a few weeks following it. I apprehend that no person will dispute the proposition that, if in the State of South Carolina there was not a republican form of government at that time, its electoral vote should not be counted.

This seems to follow from two propositions, the first of which is that the Constitution of the United States guarantees to each State a republican form of government. This implies the duty on the part of the State to maintain a republican form of government, and a duty on the part of the United States to make the inquiry, whenever it is necessary, as to whether a republican form of government at that time may exist. The second is that this is a Union of republics, and, if it were permitted that a State without a republican form of government could cast its electoral vote and thus choose a President of the United States, the other republics of the Union would be bound by the act of a State which might be with a government monarchical in its form, or, as in the case of South Carolina, without, in substance, any government at all.

What is meant by "a republican form of government"? This phrase is used in the Constitution of the United States. It does not mean merely the form of a government; it means the essence and substance of the government. It does not mean that the constitution shall be republican in its form, because there is nothing which requires that a State shall have a constitution, and many States have been admitted into the Union without a constitution as that term is ordinarily understood by the American people. It does not mean, either, merely that the legislation shall be of a republican nature; but it does mean that the constitution and the legislation and the administration shall all be republican in their form and in their nature, that they shall together constitute a government based upon republican principles, which gives to the people the right and the opportunity to determine their own rulers freely and without intervention.

In order that it shall be a republican form of government, there must be nothing in the State, at the time that it is objected that there is not a republican form of government, which interferes with a free and fair election, with the free and fair and honest ascertainment of the popular will. Whatever does interfere with that, whatever does thwart the will of the people as it is attempted to be ascertained at the polls, interferes with, and to that extent destroys, a republic and a republican government.

Mr. Commissioner MILLER. If I do not interrupt you may I ask you a question, Mr. Hurd? This constitutional provision has been very much discussed, you know, of late years; and really for my own information I should like to get your views very clearly. What importance do you attach to the word "form" in that phrase? It must have some significance. Is the expression the same as "republican government" without the word "form," or does the word "form" have reference to the division of powers?

Mr. Representative HURD. I regard the phrase as amounting to this, that each State in the Union must be a republic.

Mr. Commissioner MILLER. What is a republic?

Mr. Representative HURD. That is just the proposition I was about to discuss.

Mr. Commissioner HOAR. Allow me to inquire, is not your proposition that it must be a form in force as a government?

Mr. Representative HURD. So I said.

Mr. Commissioner HOAR. I so understood you.

Mr. Representative HURD. As I maintained a moment ago, it must be republican in its constitution, republican in its measures of legislation, republican in its administration; that is, it must be a government actually existing, possessing all the requisites of a republican form of government, whatever they may be; and the essence of that (and that is the only point necessary for me to consider in this discussion) is that the people shall have a free and fair opportunity of expressing their will in the selection of their own rulers and in the management of their own elections.

Mr. Commissioner MILLER. May not the form of the government be essentially republican and its administration be very tyrannical?

Mr. Representative HURD. Possibly it might be. There may be tyranny under a republican form of government, I concede; but when the form of government as administered, when the administration of the government, becomes such as to take out of the form the substance, the essence, and leave there a government not a republic, then that is not such a form of government as is contemplated by the Constitution.

As I was about to remark, whatever prevents a free expression of the popular will at the polls, whatever prevents a fair ascertainment of the wishes of the people in the choice of their rulers, interferes, and, to the extent that it operates, destroys a republican form of government. It is plain that if a monarchy were established in substance, although in form the government might be republican, that is the destruction of a republic, and no republican form of government exists, because a monarchy is the antipodes of the idea of a republic; and it is just as true that anarchy, so far as it may be effective, destroys the republic; for the literal signification of the word is "without government." Anarchy means no form of government at all, either republican or anything else. If lawlessness prevail so that it is impossible that there should be a lawful election; if violence be practiced so that men are not able freely to go to the polls; if intimidation be practiced so that large numbers of men who would otherwise vote do not go near the polls, or if they do go to the polls, are compelled to vote against their will, then an election held under such circumstances is held in a condition of anarchy, in which a republic is a mere myth and a fiction.

In this case, if your honors please, we propose to show by proof which has been taken by the various committees and which we regard as competent for the House of Representatives or the Senate to consider, that in the greater part of South Carolina on the day of the choice of the electors for President and Vice-President, there was a state of anarchy. The proof that was taken by the majority of the House committee shows that in the counties which gave large republican majorities intimidation was practiced by colored men upon their colored friends who desired to vote the democratic ticket; that men in the city of Charleston and in many of the counties outside of Charleston and in the islands near by were whipped and brutally abused at the polls for no other offense than that of proposing to vote the democratic ticket; that men who came to the polls with democratic tickets in their hands had them taken out of their hands and were compelled in the presence of a mob, in the presence of violence and riot and at the peril of their lives, to vote the ticket of the opposing party. We propose to show by the testimony which was taken by the minority of the same committee, that in the counties which gave large democratic majorities the democratic leaders and managers interfered with the freedom of the election by practicing intimidation upon their black employés and those who might happen to live within their districts. We propose to show that rifle-clubs were organized which were not disbanded in accordance with the proclamation of the President of the United States, and that under the effect of these rifle-clubs and of the intimidation that was practiced in that method large numbers of negroes who otherwise would have voted the republican ticket voted the democratic ticket.

These propositions I submit with the testimony which has been taken by the committee of the House of Representatives. The testimony taken by the subcommittee of which my friend Judge Lawrence was the chairman, or taken under his direction, showed very largely the facts as to the democratic intimidation. The testimony which was taken by the majority of the committee showed very largely the facts as to republican intimidation. We propose to put in evidence the proclamation of the President of the United States, which declared weeks before the election that there was a state of insurrection in South Carolina; a state of insurrection which demanded the presence of United States troops, a state of insurrection which could not have been overcome before the day of election; for there were on the day of election more troops in South Carolina than there were at any time before, after the proclamation was issued—thirty-two companies of the United States Army.

With this practice of intimidation as shown by this testimony, with this lawlessness at the polls, with this violence practiced upon the voters, with this practical anarchy everywhere, with this state of insurrection as declared by the President of the United States, with the presence of thirty-two companies of the Army of the United States there at his order, I submit that it was not possible that a fair and free election could be held in which the true announcement of the result could be made. I undertake to say that no person can read the history of the events in South Carolina and can read the testimony which has been taken before these committees and rise from the perusal without the conviction that he cannot tell what is the truth as to the vote of the State.

Will the Commission hear this proof which we tender? The proof goes directly to the question whether there is a republican form of government in the State of South Carolina or not; as to whether anarchy did not in fact exist in this State on the day of the election, destroying the republic. It is not the question that has been submitted to the tribunal before, as to how the officers of the State have discharged their trust; it is not a question of going behind the returns which have been sent to the President of the Senate to be opened; it does not relate to the manner of conducting the State elections; it does not relate to the honesty of State officials; but it goes to the question of whether there is a State government there at all or not. Will anybody dispute that the Congress of the United States has the power to inquire as to the character of the State government when it is said that it is not republican in form and is asked to perform its constitutional obligation of guaranteeing to it a republican form of government? Will anybody dispute that when the proposition is submitted to Congress for its consideration fairly, when the question fairly comes up for its action, it is bound to make inquiry as to the nature and character of the government to determine whether it be republican in form or not?

If it be true, then, that Congress has the right to make this inquiry at any time, it certainly is true that it has the right to make it now, when the question is as to the counting of the vote of a State, for the question then is whether it is a State that has voted; and in determining that question all testimony which tends to show the condition of affairs in the State at that time is competent. It must be competent, else it would be impossible that the two Houses should intelligently determine the question as to whether there was a republican form of government at the time of the election.

This question has been settled, so far as precedents can settle it, by the objections that have been made to counts and by the action of the two Houses heretofore. When Missouri and Indiana came into the Union, and electors had been chosen before the law had been passed by Congress admitting the States, it was objected at the counting that their votes should not be counted, because when given they were not States in the Union. Nobody disputed at that time that that was a perfectly fair ground of objection. It was within the province of the two Houses then counting the vote to determine whether the State had been admitted into the Union or not; and if in that case they had the power to determine whether it had been admitted into the Union or not, whether, in other words, it was a State, have they not the power to determine whether by adopting a government not republican in its form it has gone out of the Union? It is the same question in both cases, whether there is a State there under the Constitution that has cast the vote, the only difference being in the form in which the questions are presented to the two Houses.

When the Southern States were in rebellion it was decided that their votes should not be counted, and during the process of reconstruction it was decided that they should not be counted because there were not governments there republican in form. Congress undertook to decide the question as to the character of the government when it counted the electoral vote, the very question I ask this Commission now to decide by inquiring as to the condition of the government of South Carolina, hearing testimony which we offer to submit to your consideration, in order that you may ascertain whether there is in fact a State in this Union purporting to be the State of South Carolina which has cast an electoral vote.

But admitting that the State of South Carolina is a republic, that it has a republican form of government, I submit that no election has been held as required by the constitution of the State of South Carolina and by the Constitution of the United States. The Constitution of the United States requires that the electors shall be chosen as the legislature of the State may direct. The constitution of the State of South Carolina requires that the legislature shall from time to time adopt laws of registration.

Mr. Commissioner BRADLEY. Can you tell me the date of the adoption of the constitution of South Carolina?

Mr. Representative HURD. The language is:

It shall be the duty of the general assembly to provide from time to time for the registration of all electors.

My friend Mr. Shellabarger will give you the date. I believe it was 1868.

Mr. Commissioner ABBOTT. Before you pass from this other matter, Mr. Hurd, do I understand your claim to be substantially this: that, passing the question whether there is a republican form merely, such was the condition of things in South Carolina, from the interference of the military and the violence on the one side and on the other side, that there was not a free election which should certainly undertake to determine the election of electors?

Mr. Representative HURD. To that point I will address myself directly. I have simply, as far as I have gone, undertaken to say that by reason of the existence of anarchy in the State of South Carolina there was no government at all, and could not, therefore, be a republican form of government, whether in the constitution or in the law a republican form might have been established or not.

This provision of the constitution of South Carolina adopted in 1868, article 8, section 3, I regard as mandatory. I will not refer to the many distinctions made between statutes that are directory and statutes that are imperative, but simply to this, that wherever a statute or a provision of the constitution treats of that which is of the essence of the thing, then it shall be regarded as imperative upon those who are required to obey its provisions. In this case the object was to secure a fair and honest election in the State of South Carolina. Registration was required as a means to that end. It became, therefore, of the essence, in the opinion of the framers of the constitution, that registration should be made in order to secure this fairness of election. Most of the States of the Union have adopted registration laws upon the same theory.

Mr. Commissioner BRADLEY. Has there never been a registration law in South Carolina?

Mr. Representative HURD. There has been no registration-law passed which affects or relates to the choosing of electors, and by which, in the important matter of the representation of the State in the electoral college, this provision of the constitution is to be alone complied with.

I insist, as I was about to remark, that not only have they not passed a law upon this subject with reference to registration, but they have passed a law which defeats the very object in view in the putting of the provision into the constitution. They have enacted a law which has divided the State of South Carolina into four hundred and ninety-two precincts, with only thirty-two counties, a number of precincts in each county, and they have provided that every voter may vote at any precinct in the county that he chooses. The consequence is that not only is there no limitation upon the power of the voter, so far as registration is concerned, but his power to vote, if he be a dishonest man, is limited only by the boundaries of his county and the number of precincts that may be established in it. The consequence is that the object intended to be accomplished by the constitution of the State of South Carolina has entirely been defeated, and a larger vote in proportion to the population is polled this day in the State of South Carolina than in any other State in the Union.

It has been held, over and over again, that where the law requires a registration, and an election is held without a registration, the election is void. I read from McCrary on Elections, page 12 :

It being conceded that the power to enact a registry law is within the power to regulate the exercise of the elective franchise and preserve the purity of the ballot, it follows that an election held in disregard of the provisions of a registry law must be held void.

The authorities cited for the support of the provision are from Missouri and Wisconsin, authorities which fully sustain the text. If that be the effect of a provision of statute, what shall be said of the effect of the provision of the constitution of the State which has been referred to ?

It may be suggested that the legislature has the power under the Constitution of the United States to provide for the choosing of the electors, and that the constitution of the State was not authorized to determine it. But the legislature of the State is organized under the constitution of the State; it has no power excepting that which the constitution confers, and in these matters of election it is determined that there can be no election unless there shall have been a registration. Here then there has been a refusal to regard the fundamental law, a refusal by the legislature to regard the very life of its being, the consequence of which must be to render as void the election as though there had been on the part of the ministerial officers only a disregard of a statutory provision.

But supposing that it shall be held that there was a republican form of government in South Carolina ; supposing that it shall be held that the election was regularly and constitutionally conducted, then I say that the testimony which we propose to offer in this case shows that the intervention of the military authority and the lawlessness at the polls prevented any execution of the ordinary functions of government and destroyed the freedom of election. We propose to show that on the 17th day of October the President of the United States issued his proclamation declaring that a state of insurrection existed in the State of South Carolina, in these words :

A proclamation by the President of the United States of America.

Whereas it has been satisfactorily shown to me that insurrection and domestic violence exist in several counties of the State of South Carolina, and that certain combinations of men against law exist in many counties of said State, known as "rifle-clubs," who ride up and down by day and night in arms, murdering some peaceable citizens and intimidating others, which combinations, though forbidden by the laws of the State, cannot be controlled or suppressed by the ordinary course of justice ;

And whereas it is provided in the Constitution of the United States that the United States shall protect every State in this Union, on application of the legislature, or of the executive when the legislature cannot be convened, against domestic violence ;

And whereas by laws in pursuance of the above it is provided (in the laws of the United States) that, in all cases of insurrection in any State, (or of obstruction to the laws thereof,) it shall be lawful for the President of the United States, on application of the legislature of such State, or of the executive when the legislature cannot be convened, to call forth the militia of any other State or States, or to employ such part of the land and naval forces as shall be judged necessary for the purpose of suppressing such insurrection or causing the laws to be duly executed ;

And whereas the legislature of said State is not now in session and cannot be convened in time to meet the present emergency, and the executive of said State, under section 4 of article 4 of the Constitution of the United States and the laws passed in pursuance thereof, has therefore made due application to me in the premises for such part of the military force of the United States as may be necessary and adequate to protect said State and the citizens thereof against domestic violence and to enforce the due execution of the law;

And whereas it is required that, whenever it may be necessary in the judgment of the President to use the military force for the purpose aforesaid, he shall forthwith, by proclamation, command such insurgents to disperse and retire peaceably to their respective homes within a limited time:

Now, therefore, I, Ulysses S. Grant, President of the United States, do hereby make proclamation and command all persons engaged in said unlawful and insurrectionary proceedings to disperse and retire peaceably to their respective abodes within three days from this date, and hereafter abandon said combinations and submit themselves to the laws and constituted authorities of said State.

And I invoke the aid and co-operation of all good citizens thereof to uphold the laws and preserve the public peace.

In witness whereof I have hereunto set my hand and caused the seal of the United States to be affixed.

Done at the city of Washington, this 17th day of October, in the year of our Lord 1876, and of the Independence of the United States of America the one hundred and first.

[L. S.]   U. S. GRANT.

By the President:
   JOHN L. CADWALADER,
     Acting Secretary of State.

This proclamation evidently was issued in attempted pursuance of a provision of the Constitution, part of which I have already considered. Its language is that—

The United States shall guarantee to every State in this Union a republican form of government, and shall protect each of them against invasion, and on application of the legislature, or of the executive when the legislature cannot be convened, against domestic violence.

The phraseology of this article of the Constitution will be noticed; it is protection against domestic violence; that is, protection against that violence which occurs within the limits of the State and as against State authority, as contradistinguished from such violence as amounts to a rebellion against the authority of the United States; because where it amounts to a rebellion against the authority of the United States the power to suppress it arises from another section of the Constitution. It must be upon the demand of the legislature, excepting in those cases where the legislature cannot be convened. What is the meaning of that provision? It occurs to me that its true sense is that where by reason of domestic violence it is impossible that the legislature of the State can be convened, then the executive may make his demand upon the United States that there be protection given. As suggested already in what I have said, the violence must be directed against the authority of the State. It is the State that is protected against domestic violence; it is not the individuals within the State; it is not the citizens of the State; it must be such domestic violence, therefore, as threatens the existence of the government, as is directed against the government, such domestic violence as amounts to insurrection. In 1795 a law was passed in these words, found in the Revised Statutes as section 5297:

In case of an insurrection in any State against the government thereof, it shall be lawful for the President, on application of the legislature of such State, or of the executive when the legislature cannot be convened, to call forth such number of the militia of any other State or States, which may be applied for, as he deems sufficient to suppress such insurrection; or, on like application, to employ, for the same purposes, such part of the land or naval forces of the United States as he deems necessary.

Section 5298 provides for those cases of insurrection which occur against the Government of the United States, where the President of the United States has the power himself directly to interfere without the request of the State authorities. Section 5299, which was passed in 1871, provides as to power to suppress insurrection in violation of civil rights, and it provides that where insurrection or domestic violence, &c., occurs—

Such facts shall be deemed a denial by such State of the equal protection of the laws to which they are entitled under the Constitution of the United States; and in all such cases, or whenever any such insurrection, violence, unlawful combination, or conspiracy opposes or obstructs the laws of the United States or the due execution thereof, or impedes or obstructs the due course of justice under the same, it shall be lawful for the President, and it shall be his duty, to take such measures, by the employment of the militia or the land and naval forces of the United States, or of either, or by other means, as he may deem necessary, for the suppression of such insurrection, domestic violence, or combinations.

The President was acting evidently under section 5297; because, under section 5298 and section 5299, it would be perfectly competent for him to proceed to issue his proclamation and to call upon the troops without any demand being made on him by the executive of the State or by the legislature of the State. Therefore, it was not an insurrection against the Government of the United States, nor was it an interference with the equal rights or the civil rights of citizens under the law that the President was attempting to suppress; it was an insurrection against the government of the State. Who is to determine whether an insurrection existed in the State at the time this demand was made? The governor of the State in this case made his demand on the President of the United States. But his decision that there was an insurrection in his State was not final, because he was not the final judge. It was the President of the United States who was to determine whether an insurrection existed there or not. Now, let us see what his determination was upon the point. If he had simply said that there was an insurrection in the State, possibly we might not have been permitted to make any inquiry on the subject-matter; but he has stated what the insurrection consisted in, what it was. It was that—

Rifle-clubs ride up and down by day and night in arms, murdering some peaceable citizens and intimidating others, which combinations, though forbidden by the laws of the State, cannot be controlled or suppressed by the ordinary course of justice.

I submit that that did not amount to an insurrection against the government of the State of South Carolina. It was a mere case of violation of law, a case in which the courts, as he said, might be powerless to protect the citizen, but not a case in which there is any evidence that the military authority of the State would not have been sufficient to protect the citizen. The demand was made for troops, merely upon that statement, and it is upon that statement that the proclamation of the President of the United States rests. I say that it does not show a state of insurrection which justified him in issuing the proclamation, and we propose to sustain that proposition by offers of testimony that at the time this proclamation was issued, while there may have been intimidation practiced upon voters, while there may have been excited efforts to carry the election on both sides, there was no such insurrection against the authority of the government of the State as required the intervention of the national authority.

We say with reference to this, therefore, that there was no insurrection which either under the Constitution or the law justified the interference of the President of the United States. We say that the authority of the government of the State of South Carolina was not in danger. We say that the demand that was made by the governor of the State was made when he had abundant power and authority under the constitution to call the legislature together. It was nearly a month until the election, but those troops were kept there for weeks after the election. If they were necessary in the beginning to suppress the insurrection, they were necessary in the end, and in that state of case there was abundant time for the governor of the State of South Carolina to issue his proclamation, bring his legislature together, and make the constitutional demand upon the President for Federal interference.

But I say, in addition to this proposition, that the troops of the United States were in the State of South Carolina unconstitutionally on the day of the election; that, when they were there so unconstitutionally, they violated the laws of the United States which governed them in the performance of their duties as to elections. Sections 2002 and 2003 of the Revised Statutes provide:

No military or naval officer or other person engaged in the civil, military, or naval service of the United States shall order, bring, keep, or have under his authority or control any troops or armed men at the place where any general or special election is held in any State, unless it be necessary to repel the armed enemies of the United States or to keep the peace at the polls.

No officer of the Army or Navy of the United States shall prescribe or fix, or attempt to prescribe or fix, by proclamation, order, or otherwise, the qualifications of voters in any State, or in any manner interfere with the freedom of any election in any State or with the exercise of the free right of suffrage in any State.

These troops in South Carolina, as I have shown, unconstitutionally, on the day of the election, violated the law of the United States. They were at the polls, where there was no trouble at all, not for the purpose of keeping the peace, but for the purpose of interfering with the freedom of the election; and we propose to submit to the consideration of this Commission abundant proof to show that the elections in many precincts of the State of South Carolina were held in the immediate presence of Federal troops; that men were compelled, in some cases, to pass through files of Federal soldiers to deposit their ballots. We propose to show that, without any excuse, the deputy marshals of the United States called upon armed forces to interfere and to aid them in making arrests. We propose to show that, by this military interference, intimidation was practiced directly under the authority of the Federal Government, and that a result was reached which would not have been reached had the military been kept out of the State, or, if in the State, had been kept from violating the duty imposed upon them by the law. Will the Commission hear proof as to this point?

I submit that this question has not been passed upon by this Commission as yet. It is not a question as to how State officers have performed their duty; it is not a question as to the effect of a return which may have been made by a returning-board; it is not a question as to the powers of the judiciary to interfere with the action of the board after it has been done; but it is a question of *vis major* coming to control the ballot-box, take charge of the elections, manage them, and give as the expression of the will of the people that which is not the expression of the people's will at all.

I insist, if your honors please, that if the Federal Government, in violation of the Constitution, in violation of the law, sends its troops to a State and prevents a free election, what is the result is not the true voice of the people any more than if they had been the troops of Great Britain or France that had interfered in the State and prevented the free voice of the people from being expressed. I maintain, therefore, that no decision had been made by this Commission which prevents proof upon this subject. We offer to make the proof that the troops of the Federal Government were there unconstitutionally; that they were there on the day of election in violation of law; and that by their presence they interfered with the freedom of the election and prevented the real, true voice of the State of South Carolina from being expressed.

At the very first session, or nearly the first session, of the Congress of the United States a member sought to take his seat, elected from one of the States of the Union, to whom objection was made upon the ground that he had been chosen when the military power was present at the polls. Our fathers, true to what they had learned from their ancestry, held that the election was absolutely void, and the seat was refused to him. In England, from 1741 until this day, there has never been such an interference with the freedom of elections as has occurred in the State of South Carolina within the last six months. From the time that the three magistrates were compelled to kneel before the Speaker of the Commons and receive the reprimand of the Commons until this day, military interference with elections seems in England to have been unknown. It is reserved for this republic to permit military interference without rebuke and without opposition.

Gentlemen of the Commission, there are two propositions which should never be forgotten in a republic: First, that free and honest elections are essential to its existence; and, second, that the civil power should be superior to the military at every point and free from every suggestion of its influence. These two doctrines are the very soul of free institutions. The one puts the breath into the body-politic and the other preserves the life that that breath imparts. The one declares the will of the people, the other sees to it that that will is expressed in all the majesty of its power, free from all restraint and control from all persons whatsoever, excepting as it may have imposed restraints voluntarily upon itself.

These propositions have been defended with a devotion that never flagged and with a watchfulness that never slumbered, wherever republics have continued. The decay of a republic always begins in the indifference of the people to the maintenance of these doctrines. Indeed, in all history, as the republic has receded and the empire has advanced, the infallible test by which to mark the growth of the one and the decay of the other has been the regard in which the people held the freedom of their elections and military interference.

May this republic be saved from the end to which the unrebuked and successful interference of the United States in South Carolina's elections will inevitably lead!

[During the argument of Mr. Representative Hurd, Hon. J. S. Black and Hon. Montgomery Blair entered the room and took seats at the tables provided for counsel.]

Mr. Representative COCHRANE. Mr. President, I desire to say that Judge Black and Mr. Blair will appear as counsel. The objectors to certificate No. 1 had thought that counsel would not be able to attend, but we find that Judge Black and Mr. Blair can attend, and they are here.

The PRESIDENT. It is very proper to notify us before we proceed further.

Mr. Representative COCHRANE. Before the gentleman objecting to certificate No. 2 is heard, I desire to submit certain offers of evidence.

The PRESIDENT. Will there be any further argument on behalf of the objectors on your side?

Mr. Representative COCHRANE. No, sir, no more argument. Mr. Hurd has covered the ground, and I do not propose to argue it; but

I propose to submit certain offers of evidence which I will read to the Commission and ask the attention of the Commission to them.

"In support of the objections to certificate No. 1 it is proposed to prove by competent evidence the following facts, which said facts are offered separately and as a whole:

"I. That by reason of the failure and refusal of the legislature of South Carolina to provide for a registration of electors, as required by article 8, section 3, of the constitution of said State, and by reason of the acts passed by said legislature in violation of the spirit of such constitution, great frauds were perpetrated by colored republican voters; that at least three thousand illegal votes were cast for the Hayes electors, which said votes being excluded would give a majority to the Tilden electors.

"II. That immediately after the adjournment of Congress, to wit, in the month of August, A. D. 1876, a large number of the United States soldiers, under command of General Ruger, were sent by the President into said State; that on October 16, General Ruger telegraphed to the authorities at Washington that all was quiet, that there was no need for further troops, that if he (Ruger) deemed further force necessary he would call for the same; that he never did call for more troops; but that on October 17 the President issued a proclamation declaring that the people of said State were in a condition of insurrection, and that immediately thereafter large numbers of United States soldiers were sent into said State; that at no time prior to the last-mentioned date was there a condition of violence or insurrection which the authorities of the State were unable to control; that at no time during the year 1876 did such a state of affairs exist in South Carolina as justified the intervention of the Federal Government.

"III. That the troops were sent into said State without any action of the legislature thereof, although the same could have been readily convened.

"IV. That the troops were sent into said State, not for the purpose of quelling insurrection and preserving peace and good order, but for the purpose and with the design of overawing the voters of said State; that said troops were stationed at and near the polls on election day, and that their presence before and at the day of the election did obstruct and interfere with an expression of the popular will and prevent a free election.

"V. That the presence of said troops served to embolden the more desperate of the negroes; being assured by their party leaders that said troops were there for the purpose of protecting them in any act of violence, the blacks throughout the counties of Beaufort and Charleston inaugurated a condition of riot and lawlessness; that the republican officials incited them to the commission of every character of crime; that murder was committed, and the perpetrators allowed to escape punishment; that justices refused to issue warrants for the arrest of criminals charged even with the crime of murder, and sheriffs refused to execute such warrants if issued; that the police force of the city of Charleston, composed almost entirely of republican negroes, employed its time in shooting down upon the public streets quiet and inoffensive white men, members of said force being in many instances leaders in the riots which occurred; that upon election day the negroes assembled at the polls, and with rifles, shot-guns, and other weapons prevented negroes who desired so to do from voting the democratic ticket; that the State militia, composed of the worst element of the negro population and supplied with State arms, was also at the polls aiding and abetting in the violation of law and in the intimidation of voters; that the sheriff of Charleston County, one of the republican electors"—I refer to Mr. C. C. Bowen—"without warrant or authority of law appointed hundreds of so-called deputy sheriffs, all negroes and republicans, investing them with the power to make arrests at their pleasure; that these deputy sheriffs swarmed about the various polls on election-day, and by their threats of violence did hinder and prevent many citizens from voting, and did arrest and imprison without information or warrant many of those who attempted to vote the democratic ticket; that persons styled United States deputy marshals were also stationed at the polls aiding and assisting said deputy sheriffs; that throughout the State the negroes believed that the United States soldiers had been sent to shoot them if they did not vote the republican ticket.

"VI. That such violence and lawlessness existed throughout the counties of Charleston and Beaufort shortly before and on the day of the election, which said lawlessness was primarily attributable to the occupation of the State by United States soldiers, that no free election could be or was held in said counties; but that upon the contrary the popular will found no expression at the polls; that by reason of the lawlessness which existed in the county of Charleston alone the republican electors secured a majority of about 7,000 votes."

Very few, if any, of the republican electors in the State had a majority of more than a thousand in the whole. The majority in the county of Charleston alone, rolled up by means of these terrible frauds and outrages on law and liberty, was 7,000.

In this connection I will call the attention of the Commission to one section in Blackstone which states the principle more tersely than I could. I refer to 1 Blackstone's Commentaries, page 178:

And, as it is essential to the very being of Parliament that elections should be absolutely free, therefore all undue influences upon the electors are illegal and strongly prohibited, for Mr. Locke ranks it among those breaches of trust in the executive magistrate which, according to his notions, amount to a dissolution of the government, "if he employs the force, treasure, and offices of the society to corrupt the representatives, or openly to pre-engage the electors and prescribe what manner of persons shall be chosen. For thus to regulate candidates and electors, and new-model the ways of election, what is it (says he) but to cut up the government by the roots, and poison the very fountain of public security?" As soon, therefore, as the time and place of election, either in counties or boroughs, are fixed, all soldiers quartered in the place are to remove, at least one day before the election, to the distance of two miles or more, and not to return till one day after the poll is ended. Riots likewise have been frequently determined to make an election void.

The PRESIDENT. The Commission will now hear the objectors to certificate No. 2.

Mr. Representative LAWRENCE. Mr. President and gentlemen of the Commission, if the proceedings of this Commission and its decisions were only to be read and judged of by learned lawyers familiar with the truth of history in all that pertains to the electoral vote of South Carolina, I would not deem it necessary to say one word upon the questions which are now submitted for consideration. But they are to be read by others who may not so well understand them, and for this reason it may be proper to submit some remarks. If I had not ceased to be surprised at anything that might be urged on some political questions, however unwarranted, I might confess to astonishment at the objections made to the electoral vote of this State as cast for Rutherford B. Hayes for President and William A. Wheeler for Vice-President.

But when objections are made upon official responsibility they must be met and considered.

Mr. Representative COCHRANE. If the gentleman will excuse me,

I believe it is customary when an offer of proof is made that the objector upon the other side shall determine whether he objects to its reception. I would therefore ask the gentleman to say, before proceeding with his argument, whether he objects to our proving the facts as stated in these offers of proof?

Mr. Representative LAWRENCE. Mr. President and gentlemen, I suppose this Commission would not receive proofs which were clearly incompetent, however much I might undertake to consent.

Mr. Representative COCHRANE. But do you object?

Mr. Commissioner HOAR. Mr. President, I understand that under the rules of the Commission the discretion of objecting to testimony or consenting to its admission is lodged with counsel, on the ground that they are to have the management of the cause, and that question I suppose should properly be addressed to counsel on that side, and not to Judge Lawrence, the objector.

The PRESIDENT. I am inclined to think that is the correct view. It is the office of counsel to object.

Mr. Representative COCHRANE. Very well, sir.

The PRESIDENT. And also for counsel to offer, usually. I will propound the question in due season to counsel.

Mr. Representative LAWRENCE. To this I can only add, that if the counsel who represent the Hayes electors shall deem it proper to offer proof, and if this Commission shall deem it lawful to hear it, we shall by abundant testimony be able to disprove every material allegation made by the objectors on the other side. We shall be able to show that by reason of intimidation and violence practiced by democratic politicians and organized democratic rifle-clubs in the State of South Carolina, many thousands of republican voters were driven away or kept away from the polls, and that but for this intimidation and violence the majority for the so-called Hayes electors would have been many thousands more than it was.

I will first direct the attention of the Commission to the papers purporting to be certificates of electoral votes cast for Samuel J. Tilden for President and for Thomas A. Hendricks for Vice-President, by Theodore G. Barker and others, claiming to be electors for South Carolina.

To these I object—

1. Because they are here without the certificate required by sections 136 and 138 of the Revised Statutes of the United States.

These sections require that there shall be annexed to the certificates of the votes cast by electors a "list of the names of the electors * * made, * * * certified, and * * * furnished to them by direction of the executive of the State."

2. Because they are here without the certificate required by the statute of South Carolina.

By chapter IX of the Revised Statutes of South Carolina of 1873, section 15, it is provided that the secretary of state shall prepare lists—

of the names of the electors, procure to the same the signature of the governor, affix thereto the seal of the State, and deliver them thus signed and sealed to the president of the college of electors.—*Revised Statutes South Carolina*, page 36.

The certificate thus described in the statute is that which is required by the sections of the Revised Statutes to which I have referred. The record of these so-called electors *affirmatively* shows that they never received any certificate, so that there is no room to make inquiry as to any presumption to support their authority.

3. The assumed authority of these so-called electors is overthrown by the fact that C. C. Bowen and others, electors of President and Vice-

President of South Carolina, cast their votes for Hayes and Wheeler, and these are here in proper form and with a certificate under the great seal of the State duly signed by the governor and secretary of state as evidence of the authority of the electors, in the form required by the act of Congress and the statute of South Carolina.

The assumed authority of Barker and his associates as electors is not only without evidence to support it, but it is overthrown by evidence which proves in due form of law the authority of Bowen and his associates who voted for Hayes and Wheeler.

The "Tilden electors," Barker and others, were therefore not "duly appointed electors in" South Carolina, and the votes by them cast are not "*the* votes provided for by the Constitution."

Mr. Commissioner ABBOTT. I do not understand that Mr. Hurd on the other side claimed that this certificate No. 2 should be counted, but the objection was to counting the votes of the electors named in certificate No. 1.

Mr. Representative LAWRENCE. Still this certificate is here and we have made objections to it; and I will in a very few words state the reasons why it should not be counted. It is that certificate that sends the case here.

Mr. Commissioner MILLER. If nobody claims that it ought to be counted, I hardly think that it is worth while to waste time upon it.

Mr. Representative LAWRENCE. Very well. This then brings us to the inquiry as to the legal appointment of the Hayes electors, Bowen and others, and the validity of the votes they gave for President and Vice-President. From the evidence to which I have already referred, it is sufficiently shown that they were duly appointed electors, and that the votes they gave for Hayes for President and for Wheeler for Vice-President are "*the* votes provided for by the Constitution" unless some one of the *five* objections made to them shall be well taken.

These several objections I will proceed very briefly to notice.

The first objection is:

1. That no legal election was held in South Carolina for presidential electors, the general assembly of that State not having provided, as required by article 8, section 3, of the constitution thereof, for the registration of persons entitled to vote, without which registration no valid or legal election could be held.

The constitution of South Carolina provides that—

It shall be the duty of the general assembly to provide from time to time for the registration of all electors.

And it is assumed that a failure to provide for the registration will defeat the title to office of presidential electors chosen by popular vote.

In reply to this, it is proposed now to show—

1. *That clause of the constitution as to registration is* DIRECTORY, *and a failure to comply with it cannot affect the result of an election.*

2. *The State constitution cannot take from the legislature the power given to it by the Constitution of the United States to provide for the appointment of electors without registration,* "*in such manner as the legislature may direct.*"

3. *The legislature* HAS COMPLIED *with the constitutional provision requiring registration.*

To each of these points I will briefly call the attention of the Commission.

1. *This provision of the constitution is* DIRECTORY, *resting for its execution on the conscience of the legislature; and a failure to provide for registration does not invalidate or affect the result of the election.*

This position may be illustrated by a clause in the constitution of Ohio. The constitution of Ohio provides as to the legislature that—

No bill shall contain more than one subject, which shall be clearly expressed in its title.

But the supreme court has said this provision—

is *directory* only, and the supervision of its observance must be left to the general assembly. * * * It is not to be enforced by judicial interposition. * * * It would be most mischievous in practice to make the *validity of every law* to depend upon the judgment of every judicial tribunal as to whether an act or bill contained more than one subject. * * * The only safeguard against the violation of these rules of the houses is their regard for and their oath to support the constitution.—6 *Ohio State Reports*, 176.

Here was a duty imposed by the constitution on the legislature, but a neglect of this duty does not invalidate laws which fail to conform to the constitutional requisition.

The Constitution of the United States, higher than any State constitution, requires the State legislatures to provide for the appointment of electors. A failure of the legislature to follow all the *directions* of the State constitution as to the registration of voters cannot defeat the *duty* imposed on the State by the "higher law" of the supreme national Constitution or *disfranchise* a State in the election of a President.

The *right* of the *National Government* to have each State participate in a presidential election cannot be defeated by the *wrong* of the legislature in not complying with the directions of the State constitution. The *right* of the *entire people* of the United States to have all the States represented in the choice of a President cannot be defeated by the *wrong* stated.

The constitution of South Carolina requires the election of State and county officers by popular vote. To say that an election is void without a registration law, is to affirm that the legislature may dissolve the entire State and local government and produce anarchy. Certainly the convention which made the constitution never intended so disastrous a result to follow the omission to enact a registry law. Yet if this omission defeats the right of the State to representation in the electoral college, it would legalize a fearful anarchy; it would enable a State practically to withdraw from the Union; it would be "secession made easy."

The statute regulating elections in this State provides that—

All bar-rooms, saloons, and other places for the sale of liquors by retail shall be closed at six o'clock of the evening preceding the day of election and remain closed until six o'clock on the morning of the day thereafter; and during the time aforesaid the sale of all intoxicating liquors is prohibited.

And a penalty is provided on conviction. If the State can be deprived of its electoral vote for want of a registration law, it might, with equal propriety, be so deprived by the non-enforcement of this provision, for it is a part of the election machinery prescribed by the legislature for the appointment of electors.

It is the duty of the legislatures in many States to "pass laws to preserve the purity of elections," but a failure to do so could not invalidate the elections held in those States.

The claim now set up would invest Congress with a power to furnish pretexts for disfranchising States and dictate the selection of a President. The legislative power would absorb the executive, and defeat the purpose of the Constitution. This is a danger which the framers of the Constitution never intended to authorize. It has been forcibly said that "if there was no check upon the tyranny of legislative majorities the prospect before us would be gloomy in the extreme." (1 Kent, 450, note, 11th ed.) One of the "checks" provided by the Constitution is that *the* electoral votes forwarded in due form from the States should not be rejected by "the tyranny of legislative majorities," but should, when opened, "*then* be counted."

In the light of authority and reason, it seems certain the omission to enact a registration law cannot affect the appointment of electors. Upon this whole subject, I will refer the Commission to authorities as follows: Pim *vs.* Nicholson, 6 Ohio St. R., 176; Sedgwick on Statutes, 377; 570. To the same effect is Miller *vs.* State, 3 Ohio St., 475; People *vs.* Supervisors, 4 Selden, 317; Washington *vs.* Murray, 4 Cal., 388; Davis *vs.* State, 7 Maryland, 151; Battle *vs.* Howard, 13 Texas, 345. And see Haywood on County Elections, 511; Golden *vs.* Sharp, Clarke & Hall, 410; Van Rensselaer *vs.* Van Allen, Clarke & Hall, 73; Arnold *vs.* Lea, Clarke & Hall, 601; Lyon *vs.* Smith, Clarke & Hall, 101; Orkney & Shetland, Fraser, 360; (see Seaford, Laders III, 3; Case of David Bard, Clarke & Hall, 116; Porterfield *vs.* McCoy, Clarke & Hall, 267; Colchester, Peckwell I, 503–507; Easton *vs.* Scott, Clarke & Hall, 272; Mallary *vs.* Merrill, Clarke & Hall, 328; Draper *vs.* Johnston, Clarke & Hall, 703; Spaulding *vs.* Mead, Clarke & Hall, 157; Standish, Cushing, S. & J., 82; Chatham, Cushing, S. & J. 423; West Boylston, Cushing, S. & J., 394; Limerick, Perry, & Knapp, 355; Cochrane & Rowe, 288; Warwick, Cushing, S. & J., 401; McCrary on Elections, sec. 123–130.

I now proceed to show—

2. *That the State Constitution cannot take from the legislature the right given to it by the Constitution of the United States to appoint electors without a registration of voters " in such manner as the legislature thereof may direct."*

In other words, if the State constitution requires the legislature to enact a registry law for the purpose of choosing electors, it is unconstitutional.

The Constitution of the United States provides that—

Each State shall appoint [electors] in such manner as the legislature thereof may direct.

In every State the legislature has provided by law for the appointment of electors by popular vote. This is done in pursuance of authority given to the legislature by the Constitution of the United States.

Mr. Commissioner ABBOTT. Permit me to ask you a question. Do you mean to say that it is unconstitutional for a State constitution to provide that elections shall take place by a registry law?

Mr. Representative LAWRENCE. I do. I mean to say that the manner of the appointment of electors of President and Vice-President is by the Constitution of the United States intrusted solely to the discretion of the State legislature, and that it is absolutely uncontrollable by any provision of a State constitution. That is precisely what I mean to say.

This legislative authority exists not by force of any State constitution, but the "supreme law" above it. As the power is derived from the Constitution of the United States, and is given in plenary and unlimited terms, the State legislature is made the exclusive judge of the manner in which popular elections shall be authorized, regulated, conducted, and the result declared, subject only to the obligations of the amendments of the Constitution in relation to suffrage and such regulations as Congress may be authorized to make.

A State constitution can no more require a "registration law" against the judgment of the legislature than it can impose restraints on the powers given by the national Constitution to Congress. The provision of the South Carolina constitution requiring a registration law is itself unconstitutional and void so far as it attempts to impose a duty on the legislature to *require* registration of voters authorized to participate in the appointment of electors.

This may be illustrated by other provisions of the Constitution of the United States. This provides that—

> The times, places, and manner of holding elections for Senators and Representatives shall be prescribed in each State by the *legislature* thereof; but the Congress may at any time by law make or alter such regulations, &c.

In discussing the powers of State constitutional conventions, Jameson, a law-writer of acknowledged authority, denies in emphatic terms that *they* can make any regulation affecting "the times, places, or manner of holding elections for Representatives in Congress." He says:

> The rule is general, that it is the *State legislatures* which apportion their several States for congressional electors. (Jameson on Constitutional Conventions. West Virginia contested-election cases, first session Forty-third Congress; Congressional Record, 35, 36, 38, 46, 816–819, 842–849, 875–880, 884–890, 931–937, 958–963; Speer's speech, Appendix, 34.)

And he shows that the exceptional cases in which *constitutional conventions* have provided for the election of Representatives, upon the creation of a *new State*, derive their validity from the action of Congress in ratifying them. His language is, that Congress—

> having the power to "make or alter," Congress doubtless might *ratify* such regulations, however made; or if a State, actual or inchoate, were in such a condition that it had no lawful legislature, Congress might itself, for the sake of convenience, establish them by its direct action.

The great American commentator, whose researches explored every field of legal learning and left their impress on all, whose emphatic words I commend to my learned friend the Commissioner from Massachusetts, [Mr. Abbott,] Mr. Justice Story, in the Massachusetts constitutional convention of 1820, in discussing this subject, said:

> The question then was whether we have a right to insert in our constitution a provision which controls or destroys a discretion which may be, nay *must be*, exercised by the *legislature* in *virtue of powers confided to it by the Constitution of the United States*.
>
> The fourth section of the first article of the Constitution of the United States declares, "That the times, places, and manner of holding elections for Senators and Representatives shall be prescribed in each State by the legislature thereof."
>
> Here an express provision was made for the manner of choosing Representatives by the State legislatures. They have an unlimited discretion on the subject. They may provide for an election in single districts, in districts sending more than one, or by general ticket for the whole State. Here is a general discretion, a power of choice. What is the proposition on the table? It is to limit this discretion, to leave no choice to the legislature, to compel Representatives to be chosen in districts; in other words, to compel them to be chosen in a specific manner, excluding all others. Was not this plainly a violation of the Constitution? Does it not affect to control the legislature in the exercise of its legitimate powers? Does it not interfere with the superintending authority of Congress? * * * * It assumes a control over the legislature which the Constitution of the United States does not justify. It is *bound* to exercise its authority according to its own view of public policy and principle; and yet this proposition compels it to surrender all discretion. In my humble judgment * * * it is a direct and palpable infringement of the constitutional provisions to which I have referred.

There is nothing new in the suggestion that a State constitution may in some of its provisions be unconstitutional and void because in conflict with the higher Constitution of the United States.

But it is not necessary to say that there is any conflict between the national and State constitutions. By a well-known rule of construction, the provisions in relation to registration at most must be deemed as intended only to apply to registration for elections exclusively under State authority. (1 Kent, 460, 11th ed.; State *vs.* Millburn, 9 Gill, 105; 1 Blackst. Com., 261; Comyn's Dig., tit. Parl. R., 8; King *vs.* Allen, 15 East., 33; 6 Term R., 194; 2 Mason, 314; 1 Watts, 54; 4 Cowen, 143; 11 Peters, 598.)

It seems certain, then, that the legislature of South Carolina has been guilty of no omission of duty in relation to registration.

I proceed to show—

3. *That the legislature has complied with the constitutional provision requiring registration.*

The election-law provides as to each voting-precinct that—

Each clerk of the poll shall keep a poll-list, which shall contain one column headed "names of voters," and the name of each elector voting shall be entered by the clerk in such column.

These are public records, which in each county belong to the files of the county commissioners of election. This is a substantial compliance with the constitutional provision requiring a " registration of all electors."

Besides this, the revised statutes of 1873 require a complete census to be taken on or before April 15, 1875, and every tenth year thereafter, and the census for each county is to be deposited with the county auditor. The law, or rather I should say the official instructions under it, require the census returns to show the names of all male persons over twenty-one years of age, and these are voters. This gives a complete registration of all voters, and is a substantial compliance with the constitutional provision requiring registration. This law has been faithfully executed and furnishes the means of detecting illegal voters.

As to municipal elections there is a registry law. The revised statutes of 1873, chapter 11, page 39, require every voter to be " registered in the ward or precinct in which he offers to vote."

The second objection to the " Hayes electoral vote" is :

2. That there was not existing in the State of South Carolina on the 1st of January, 1876, nor at any time thereafter, up to and including the 10th of December, 1876, a republican form of government, such as is guaranteed by the Constitution to every State in the Union.

It is a sufficient answer to this to say that South Carolina was duly represented in the Senate and House of Representatives of the United States during all this time, and this is conclusive evidence in every particular against the objection which has been made. In the case of Luther *vs.* Borden, 7 Howard, 42, Chief-Justice Taney said :

It rests with Congress to decide what government is the established one in a State. For, as the United States guarantee to each State a republican form of government, Congress must necessarily decide what government is established in the State, before it can determine whether it is republican or not; *and when the Senators and Representatives of a State are admitted into the councils of the Union, the authority of the government under which they are appointed, as well as its republican character, is recognized by the proper constitutional authority, and its decision is binding on every other department of the Government, and could not be questioned in a judicial tribunal.*

And see *Ex parte* Coupland, 26 Texas, 434; Federalist No. 21, page 112; Calder *vs.* Bull, 3 Dallas, 386; Wynehamer *vs.* The People, 13 New York, (3 Kernan,) 392.

Mr. Representative HURD. This Commission has the powers of the two Houses of Congress.

Mr. Representative LAWRENCE. The powers of Congress are powers to be exercised by law and with the approval of the President, and this tribunal cannot annul what Congress has done with the approval of the President in the form of law. Greenleaf says:

Courts will judicially take notice of the political constitution or frame of the government of their own country, its essential political agents or officers, and its essential ordinary and regular operations. The great seal of the State and the seals of its judicial tribunals require no proof.

The constitution of South Carolina of 1868 is before the Commission. It is entirely republican in *"form."* The government organized under it is republican in *"form."* It is so in fact. But the Constitution of the United States does not undertake to guarantee at all times a State government strictly republican in its administration or in fact. Its language is: "The United States shall guarantee to every State * * a republican *form* of government."

The guaranty of a republican form of government is to be executed by the United States as an independent sovereign act, and not collaterally or incidentally when the Houses are engaged in counting the electoral vote, and therefore the consideration of the question is not within the jurisdiction of this Commission.

The admission or restoration of the State of South Carolina into the Union under the so-called "reconstruction acts" was the act of the United States, being the act of the two Houses of Congress with the approval of the President, and that act binds all, the two Houses of Congress as well as others, and therefore binds this Commission. That act was a recognition of the government of South Carolina as republican in form, and that act remains in force to the present time.

The third objection is:

That the Federal Government prior to and during the election on the 7th day of November, 1876, without authority of law, stationed in various parts of the said State of South Carolina at or near the polling-places detachments of the Army of the United States, by whose presence the full exercise of the right of suffrage was prevented and by reason whereof no legal or free election was or could be had.

It is a sufficient answer to this to say there is no proof to support it. Still more, it is not competent for this tribunal to hear evidence in support of it or to make the inquiry. This was decided in principle by the determination of this Commission as to the Florida electors, as to whom it was held—

That it is not competent under the Constitution and the law, as it existed at the date of the passage of said act, to go into evidence *aliunde* the papers opened by the President of the Senate in the presence of the two Houses, to prove that other persons than those regularly certified to by the governor of the State of Florida, in and according to the determination and declaration of their appointment by the board of State canvassers of said State prior to the time required for the performance of their duties, had been appointed electors, or by counter-proof to show that they had not, and that all proceedings of the courts, or acts of the legislature, or of the executive of Florida, subsequent to the casting of the votes of the electors on the prescribed day, are inadmissible for any such purpose.

But if the Commission could make the inquiry, the Government of the United States had authority to place troops in South Carolina, and when so placed it must be presumed to have been properly done, on sufficient authority, and for sufficient reasons.

The Constitution and laws have regarded the elective franchise of such inestimable value as to deserve in those extreme cases where necessity requires it military protection from the National Government. This will be clear from a brief statement. Congress, as already shown, has power to make all proper regulations as to the elections of Representatives in Congress, and authorize all acts "necessary and proper for that purpose." The Constitution also declares that the President "shall take care that the laws be faithfully executed." This he can only do by the defensive means placed by law in his hands.

The act of Congress provides that—

No * * * officer or person * * * in the military * * * service * * * shall have * * * any troops * * * at the place where any * * * election is held in any State, *unless it be necessary to repel the armed enemies of the United States or to keep the peace at the polls.* (Revised Statutes, section 2002. For the statute of England on this subject see Congressional Record of January 17, 1877, Johnston's speech.)

From this an unequivocal inference arises, which is positive law, that the President, in executing the Constitution and those laws which give security to the right of voting for Representatives in Congress, may require the presence of troops " at the place where an election is held," in two cases, (1) when "necessary to repel the armed enemies of the United States;" and (2) "to keep the peace at the polls." By statute, also, the President is authorized to employ the military power for the protection of the civil rights of citizens. (Revised Statutes, section 1989.)

Here, then, is AUTHORITY, *under the Constitution and laws of the United States, for the use of troops to protect citizens in exercising the right of suffrage as stated.*

There is also a *duty* to use military power in still other cases.

The Constitution provides that—

The United States shall guarantee to every State in this Union a republican form of government, and shall protect each of them against invasion; and on application of the legislature, or of the executive (when the legislature cannot be convened) against domestic violence.

Here is a covenant for a duty which cannot in good faith be omitted. Whenever there is " domestic violence," within the meaning of the Constitution, and the proper demand is made by the governor of a State on the President.for military aid, it cannot be refused. The character of the violence which justifies military interposition is well understood.

Here, then, is AUTHORITY *under the Constitution for the employment of troops of the United States on certain contingencies in a State.*

Now, I respectfully submit, it must be presumed that the officers of the Government have observed these laws in the performance of their duties, as the truth undoubtedly is, and this is a sufficient answer to the objection taken.

It would be a monstrous proposition to say that a State should be disfranchised in the electoral college because troops were in the State, when their presence did not change the result of the election. It would be equally monstrous to say that if the troops, used in pursuance of law, only gave protection to voters and aided in securing their just rights, a lawful result should be set aside because the Government performed its duty.

The fourth objection is:

That at the several polling places in the said State there were stationed deputy marshals of the United States, appointed under the provisions of sections 2021 and 2022 of the Revised Statutes of the United States, which provisions were unconstitutional and void. That the said deputy marshals, exceeding over one thousand in number, by their unlawful and arbitrary action, in obedience to the improper and illegal instructions received by them from the Department of Justice, so interfered with the full and free exercise of the right of suffrage by the duly-qualified voters of the said State of South Carolina that a fair election could not be and was not held in the said State of South Carolina on the said 7th day of November, 1876.

It is a sufficient answer to this that it is unsupported by evidence, that it is not competent to receive proof in support of it, and the legal presumption is that the deputy United States marshals performed their duties properly. If it were competent to make the inquiry, the evidence would abundantly prove the necessity for these officers and that they did not interfere with the free exercise of the right of suffrage by any qualified voter. But as no such evidence is competent, no question of the constitutionality of the law authorizing deputy marshals arises, and if it could, the power of Congress is ample under the authority "to enforce by appropriate legislation" the Constitution, including the amendments thereto.

Upon this subject I invite especially the attention of the Commission to a report or views which I will submit to the House of Representatives, as a part of House Miscellaneous Document No. 31, part 1, second session Forty-fourth Congress, being evidence, &c., relating to the South Carolina election, and which in a day or two I will submit to the House to go into the Congressional Record.

The fifth and last objection is:

That there was not from the 1st day of January, 1876, up to and including the 10th day of December, 1876, at any time, a State government in the State of South Carolina, except a pretended government set up in violation of law and of the Constitution of the United States by Federal authority and sustained by Federal troops.

It is a sufficient answer to this to say it is unsupported by evidence; it is utterly unfounded in fact; it is contradicted by the truth of history, and is overthrown by the authority of Luther *vs.* Borden, 7 Howard, 42.

The legal validity of the government of South Carolina during the year 1876 is a well-authenticated fact in history. This tribunal, as a question of law, is bound to know and recognize the fact without proof, and it has never been doubted or questioned until now, and the "truth of history" is, that troops of the United States were used only as the Constitution and laws authorize, to suppress "domestic violence" or to "keep the peace at the polls."

Here then I close, and in doing so I indulge the hope that upon the questions submitted to this Commission there may be a decision which will command the unanimous vote of all its members. Let it be such that no State shall ever be disfranchised by the Houses of Congress or practically expelled from the Union of our fathers.

Mr. Commissioner HUNTON. Judge Lawrence, let me call your attention to a point in the case which I have not heard discussed.

Mr. Representative LAWRENCE. Certainly.

Mr. Commissioner HUNTON. The twelfth article of the amendments to the Constitution provides that—

The electors shall meet in their respective States and vote by ballot for President and Vice-President, one of whom, at least, shall not be an inhabitant of the same State with themselves; they shall name in their ballots the person voted for as President, and in distinct ballots the person voted for as Vice-President.

Now in the examination of this certificate No. 1, I find no evidence that this provision of the Constitution has been complied with in voting by ballot.

Mr. Representative LAWRENCE. It will undoubtedly be presumed, in the absence of an allegation to the contrary, that the officers have performed their duty. I think that familiar legal principle, known to every lawyer, is a complete answer to the point suggested by my friend from Virginia. There is no law which requires that the certificate shall state that the electors voted by ballot; but if as a matter of fact the votes were otherwise, *viva voce*, the provision directing that the electors shall vote by ballot, at most, is only directory, and a failure to observe that provision of the Constitution would not affect the validity of the votes.

Mr. Commissioner HUNTON. Has there not been a case before the two Houses of Congress of that character?

Mr. Representative LAWRENCE. Not to my knowledge.

Mr. Commissioner HUNTON. Objections on account of the fact not appearing that the vote was by ballot? I am not distinct in my recollection, but my impression is that there has been a case of that sort before the two Houses of Congress in counting the electoral votes.

Mr. Representative LAWRENCE. I have no recollection of any such case as that, but there may be.

Mr. Commissioner HUNTON. I only desired to call your attention to it so that it might not escape notice in the discussion.

Mr. Representative LAWRENCE. Then the two answers which I have made seem to me entirely to meet the case: First, that in the absence of any allegation in the record to show that the vote was not by ballot, it must be presumed that officers have done their duty and that the votes were by ballot. Second, that if in fact the electors failed to observe the direction of the Constitution in that respect, the provision itself is merely directory, and a failure to comply with it cannot invalidate the vote.

Besides that, as I am reminded by my friend with whom I was associated as a member of the committee of the House of Representatives which investigated the South Carolina election, [Mr. Lapham,] no such objection is made by the objectors to the vote of that State.

The PRESIDENT. Do I understand you to have closed on the part of the objectors?

Mr. Representative LAWRENCE. Yes, sir.

The PRESIDENT. There are no other objectors to be heard?

Mr. Representative LAWRENCE. No other. Senator Christiancy waives the right, as I understand, to argue the objections.

The PRESIDENT. Before calling upon the counsel who support the objections to certificate No. 1, I inquire of the counsel on the other side if they object to the offers of proof?

Mr. MATTHEWS. I was not in at the time the offer was made, but of course we object to any proof being offered.

The PRESIDENT. Counsel in favor of the objections to certificate No. 1 will now be heard. One of the counsel will open and the other will have the close.

Mr. BLAIR. Mr. President——

The PRESIDENT. This question is upon the admissibility of the evidence and its effect.

Mr. BLAIR. Mr. President and gentlemen of the Commission, counsel for the objectors to certificate No. 1 propose to prove, in addition to what has already been offered, that owing to the violence and intimidation existing in South Carolina on the election-day of November, 1876, and then practiced toward voters, and owing to the presence of troops of the United States overawing voters, there was no free election on the part of the people for electors of President and Vice-President. Evidence will also be given to support specifically the third and fourth objections to certificate No. 1, as to the means by which a free and fair election was prevented.

The first ground upon which I shall lay any stress in objecting to the counting of certificate No. 1 is that there was no registration of voters in the State of South Carolina as required by the constitution of that State. The constitution of South Carolina is imperative: "it shall be the duty of the general assembly to provide from time to time for the registration of all electors." It is admitted on the part of the supporters of the Hayes electors that there was in fact no such registration as the constitution requires. All that is contended on their part is that there was a poll-list made at the election by one of the clerks, and that there was a census taken which enumerated the male inhabitants of the different counties in the State, without naming them. That was done in compliance with the constitution.

I am not prepared to show by authorities what a registration is or ought to be. That cannot be necessary. I shall take it for granted that every member of this tribunal knows that neither a poll-list taken by the clerk at the time of voting nor a census is a registration.

I dismiss, therefore, at once and without comment, the attempt to show a compliance with the constitution of the State of South Carolina, and proceed to notice the argument upon which my learned friend [Mr. Lawrence] evidently depends to sustain this certificate; which is, that as the Constitution of the United States provides that each State shall appoint electors in such manner as the legislature thereof shall direct, any provision interfering with the discretion of that body as to the manner of appointment is a violation of the Constitution of the United States. The case of certificate No. 1 rests only upon that proposition. I do not perceive the application of Mr. Justice Story's opinion on the proposed constitutional provisions respecting congressional districts in Massachusetts.

The requirement of a registration of voters does not interfere in any respect with the provision in the Constitution of the United States authorizing the legislature to direct the manner of appointing the electors. There can be no conflict in fact between a requirement and the full exercise of the power by the legislature. For the purpose of appointing an elector the legislature of the State is an agency of the United States; but it is an agency created by the State, and must exercise its agency in accordance with the power which creates it. And, therefore, in the exercise of the authority conferred by the Constitution, it will not be assumed that the Constitution of the United States empowers the legislature to disregard the State constitution, and especially in a matter which is essential to the well-being of society.

The provision in question is indispensable to secure fair elections. The secret-ballot system without registration is simply an unlimited power of repeating, thus invited and facilitated by the laws of South Carolina, whereby multitudes of small electoral precincts have been created in order that the negro voters, many of whom are not easily identified, may repeat their votes indefinitely. How indispensable and necessary to a due ordering of society in such a condition is it that there should be a registration of voters to prevent repeating.

This tribunal will take notice of the constitution and laws of South Carolina, and it therefore is informed of the failure to execute a provision which the constitution itself by the mandatory terms in which it imposes the duty of registration declares to be indispensable to a fair election. Will this tribunal, when the State constitution itself thus pronounces the election fraudulent, permit the irresponsible persons held in power in South Carolina only by the aid of United States soldiers, to decide a great presidential contest?

Mr. Commissioner GARFIELD. I wish to inquire, if the failure on the part of the legislature to pass a registry law in obedience to the constitution has rendered invalid the appointment of electors, has it also rendered invalid the appointment of all their State officers and their State government during the last eight years, during which that neglect has lasted?

Mr. BLAIR. If no question has been made on the subject in the State, the maxim *communis error facit jus* might apply, or acquiescence on the part of the people of the State would make a *de facto*, and as a *de facto* a legal, government; but with respect to the electors the question is one with which the whole country is concerned, and has not been waived or permitted to pass *sub silentio*, but is now here presented for decision, as one arising upon the law. And we insist that the law makes the election void and that the vote of South Carolina ought not to be counted. It is not necessary to prove that the election was fraudulent in fact. The law itself declares it to be so. And this tribunal as a political body knows as a fact in the history of the times that the requirement of the constitution of South Carolina was disregarded to enable the men in charge of its affairs to perpetuate their power and dispose of its electoral vote at their pleasure. You cannot, therefore, shut your eyes to the fact that here is a palpable, gross, persistent violation of law, the only effect of which could be to facilitate fraud.

Every honest and patriotic citizen must feel indignant at the condition to which the criminals who have by military force held South Carolina in thraldom have reduced that State and be inclined to resolve any doubt against them and in favor of the people who hold all the property, possess all the intelligence, and represent the civilization of the State.

And will this tribunal, instead of eagerly availing itself of its violations of law to strike down and crush out the irresponsible power foisted on those people, industriously hunt for quibbles of law and study how to let fraud triumph?

I pass now to the objection founded upon the intrusion of the military power of the United States into the State for the purpose of controlling the election that is claimed, and I think with just reason, to be an all-sufficient ground to invalidate the election; and that also is a matter which does not depend upon proof. It is shown by the proclamation of the President, which is a matter of which all public tribunals can take notice.

This transaction was made known to the public by the proclamations and published orders of the President, to which the attention of this tribunal has been called by the honorable gentleman who opened the case, the obvious purpose of which was to control the election in the interest of the party which here claims the benefit of this illegal and unwarranted interference.

The argument of my learned friend [Mr. Lawrence] is, that inasmuch as these proceedings were by the authority of the President of the United States, we are concluded; that his judgment is final. Is that so? Is that conclusive upon the Congress of the United States that you here represent? Is the judgment of the President of the United States, acting, as he publicly declares, as the representative of a party, decisive against the opposing party? That seems to me to beg the question. We charge that the party organization that possessed itself of power by the war has made use of the power thus obtained to perpetuate it against the will of the people; and when, therefore, you are sitting here in the stead and place of the grand inquest of the nation, must you shut your eyes to the true nature of the transaction and allow an organization to perpetuate its power in defiance of the will of the people because it is done by color of office?

This policy was initiated by what are known as the reconstruction measures adopted on the close of the war. Mr. Stevens, who presented them, admitted in his place that they were outside of the Constitution. In virtue of these confessedly unconstitutional measures electors were openly made by the military power, and the halls of Congress were filled with camp-followers from the transformed States. When these measures produced their natural effect of endangering the hold of the organization upon the great Northern States, it became necessary to fortify themselves then by another amendment of the Constitution spreading negro suffrage all over the United States; and this was done in known defiance of the public will, and after they had expressly disclaimed by resolutions in a national convention that they entertained any such purpose. But, notwithstanding the vast forces thus added, their strength wanes. The tide of intelligent opinion grows steadily against them. Notwithstanding their frantic appeal to sectional hate in the North, they feel that they are losing ground there.

Notwithstanding the indignation that the previous military seizures had aroused, they could not save themselves by again employing the military power to hold the votes of the States when they still held the machinery to call for its interposition. This is the transaction, as seen of all men. It is impossible for any observant man to fail to see it in this light. And I say you will be derelict to your duty if you sanction it and allow its creatures to triumph.

What I have stated is proved by proclamations and orders, all of a public nature, of which you can, as representing Congress, take notice, and by considering which the vote of South Carolina may be rejected without reversing any decision heretofore made. I do not combat what has been decided. I would not waste the time of this tribunal or my own in attempting to get it to reverse its decision. But Congress has itself established a precedent by taking notice of a similar condition of things in these States, and you as the representatives of Congress ought to follow the precedents it has established. Upon just such considerations as now I am addressing to you, Congress excluded the whole southern section of country from participating in the presidential election.

If Congress has refused to allow the votes of States to be counted because they were incapacitated from sharing in the privileges of the Government, is it not equally within the power of this Commission, when it is a matter of general notoriety that a like condition exists, and especially when that condition is produced by the action of a party in power and exercising for the time being, and exercising wrongly, the powers of the Government? It is enough that it appears that such a condition exists as to prevent any legitimate exercise of the franchise, to make the analogy complete.

The general principle is familiar that, where there is disorder in a precinct, where the police have to interfere, where the people are driven from the polls, where there is such oppression as that the polls do not represent fairly the voice of the people, they are excluded.

But here is a grand national case in which you cannot fail to take notice of the proclamation of the President and the governor declaring the State in a state of insurrection, of the march of troops there, of the action of the parties who used the troops and who called them there to put down insurrection. It was because of the insurrectionary character that existed prior to 1865 that the Southern States were not allowed to vote, and here is a proclamation in all respects corresponding with the proclamation declaring an insurrection to exist there. What is the difference in manner or in effect? You would not allow the rebels to vote because they put the States under military duress by force of arms; and now will you allow these people to vote when they are, under military duress, compelled to vote on the other side?

Mr. Commissioner EDMUNDS. That was done by an act of Congress, was it not?

Mr. BLAIR. The exclusion?

Mr. Commissioner EDMUNDS. In 1865, or whatever the time was, when the act passed over the veto of President Johnson.

Mr. BLAIR. If I recollect aright about the rule on that subject, a joint resolution was passed which was presented to Mr. Lincoln for his approval, and he said he had nothing to do with it.

Mr. Commissioner EDMUNDS. But he signed it.

Mr. BLAIR. He signed it, but disclaimed having any authority in the premises, insisting that it belonged to Congress, that is, to the two Houses exclusively.

Mr. Commissioner EDMUNDS. Was there not a later act in President Johnson's time which he vetoed, and which Congress passed over his veto?

Mr. BLAIR. There was a series of acts passed over Mr. Johnson's veto.

Mr. Commissioner EDMUNDS. I mean on that precise point of excluding States from electoral representation.

Mr. BLAIR. There may have been; but the act which was approved by Mr. Lincoln and with his assenting to the power of Congress to throw out votes as they pleased, excluded votes. Mr. Lincoln asserted, and without contradiction from anybody as I remember, that this was a matter entirely with Congress; and the subsequent passage of a law I do not think adds anything to the power of Congress on the subject. That is the view I take of it, and I submit it with great deference to your better judgment.

Mr. Commissioner EDMUNDS. The point was, Mr. Blair, whether there was any distinction between this exercise of political power according to the position the State is in, whether exercised by Congress in the constitutional way, or whether it is also competent to exercise it in the act of counting in the presence of the two Houses. That is the point I should like to hear you upon. You ask us to exercise now this same power and upon the same ground that hitherto has been exercised by acts of legislative will in the form of law.

Mr. BLAIR. Yes, sir; I suppose myself that the act of 1792 itself, as well as all acts subsequent to that, was passed in furtherance of the power of Congress to count. I do not know any other clause in the Constitution that gives them any power over the subject. They have the power to count; and in pursuance of that power, and to facilitate it, they required that the executive officers of the several States should send them certificates as evidence by which they were *prima facie*, as I always understood until the late decisions here, to determine who were the proper names to count in the electoral college. That was an exercise of power by Congress. There is no other clause in the Constitution which gives it to them that my attention has ever been called to.

But that did not exhaust the power of Congress, because Congress in the exercise of the same power has subsequently thrown out votes, as Mr. Lincoln said rightly as I always understood, and as the joint resolution of 1865 and as all the resolutions and acts of Congress taking place since have been, as Louisiana has been excluded up to this time; for her vote has never been counted since the war until the other day. All this was simply by virtue of the power of the two Houses, done without any law, but looking at the condition of the State, purely and simply, Congress excluded her as being not in that condition which made it proper to allow her to participate in the privileges of a presidential election. That was done by the same power, the whole of which is vested in this Commission, the power to look into the state of affairs there to see for yourselves that they are not exercising a perfectly free will.

A Senator of the very highest authority reported in regard to Mississippi last year that it was competent for Congress to decide whether the vote of that State should be excluded because of the exercise of illegal and improper power there in the control of elections. It was deemed perfectly competent by gentlemen of the party with whom I am not now acting, and seemed to be a general expression of feeling upon that subject, that it was perfectly competent to exclude States where there was no interference of the military, no call by the legislature or governor, but in the discretion of the two Houses to exclude States from their own knowledge as legislative bodies that the condition of affairs there was not such as to authorize the votes to be counted.

But in this case evidence is such as must be taken notice of upon the very strictest rules. The proclamation declaring an insurrection to exist in South Carolina puts the case strictly in the category of the States which were excluded by Congress.

My learned friend [Mr. Lawrence] referred to the deputy marshals and the troops that were sent there and the Attorney-General's circular. That strongly enforces our argument. Can it possibly be a free State authorized to vote and decide a presidential election when the State is covered with deputy marshals and troops, and voters have to pass through files of armed men to the polls? Now I assert that we shall be able to show you they had a deputy marshal for every ten negroes, with labels on their shoulders, and marched their squads of ten up before the soldiery and swore them to vote the whole republican ticket, then marched them to the polls and stood by them till they voted. The instructions to these deputy marshals were in the public press.

When such means are resorted to to carry a State, and it is carried by less than a thousand majority, can you justify yourselves in counting that vote? Is there any essential difference in such a case more than if the rebels in South Carolina had carried the State by 1,100 votes, and had asked to cast them against Mr. Lincoln in 1864? Could there possibly have been an election in any proper sense of the word, with all this paraphernalia of United States troops, United States deputy marshals, and armed negro militia, a proclamation of insurrection, and disorder existing everywhere?

You can legally take notice of all this, and if you will let us we will show it all up *in limine*. But that is not required. You cannot refuse to see what Congress has seen in similar cases, and has acted upon. You cannot shut your eyes to these public documents, which I need not read because they are a part of the statute-book, and every judicial functionary and every legislative functionary is obliged to take notice of them.

I omitted in the consideration of the first point to call the attention of the tribunal to an authority on the subject of the registration question. You will find in the ninth section of the American "Law of Elections," by McCrary, a citation which he adopts as the law. I have the original case here, but will not read it, contenting myself with calling the attention of the tribunal to the ninth section of the book:

It being conceded that the power to enact a registry law is within the power to regulate the exercise of the elective franchise and preserve the purity of the ballot, it follows that an election held in disregard of the provisions of a registry law must be held void. In Ensworth *vs.* Albin *et al.*, 44 Missouri, 347, an election was set aside upon the ground that there was no registration whatever, although the statute required registration as an indispensable prerequisite to an election. It has been suggested that this doctrine puts it in the power of the board of registration to defeat an election by failing to meet and refusing altogether to discharge their official duties. But it is hardly safe to attempt to test the validity of a statute by presupposing a case so extreme and so improbable as the refusal of a sworn officer of the law to act.

Contrary to the author's supposition of what was possible, we have here the extreme case. The case referred in the text occurred in Missouri, where the officers of the county which was there in question did refuse to make the registry required by the statute, which was not a particle more mandatory than the constitution of South Carolina.

Mr. Commissioner EDMUNDS. You cite that, then, as authority to prove that this election was void because the legislature had made no law providing for any registration.

Mr. BLAIR. Exactly.

Mr. Commissioner EDMUNDS. The constitution making a general requirement that the legislature should enact such a law?

Mr. BLAIR. Making the positive requirement, just as the statute law of Missouri did.

Mr. Commissioner EDMUNDS. On the same principle would you hold on another section of the constitution of South Carolina, which says that the legislature shall make laws for preserving the purity of elections, that, if the legislature had not made any law punishing false voting, therefore the election would be void?

Mr. BLAIR. No, sir. I think there is a very broad distinction between the two cases.

Mr. Commissioner EDMUNDS. What is the distinction?

Mr. BLAIR. The purity of election is *nomen generalissimum*.

Mr. Commissioner EDMUNDS. A very important thing, is it not?

Mr. BLAIR. It is very important, to be sure; but it is not mandatory. It is general. But here is a specific thing that is required. There is manifestly a very broad distinction between an act, even if it be mandatory in its nature, which such acts generally are not, that legislation shall be taken for the preservation of the purity of elections, and a mandatory requirement in the constitution requiring specifically a particular thing to be done. The distinction is recognized all through the books. For example, it has been held that where elections were required to be held by ballot and were not so held, that was a violation of law. Here is an election required to be held by registry. The registry is a preliminary indispensable to the election by the express order of the constitution and its manifest intent.

Mr. Commissioner ABBOTT. Do you find any case where a refusal to carry out the mandate of the constitution requiring registry has ever been sufficient to set aside the election? Are not the cases all confined to the case of a statute being made in reference to a particular election and that not being complied with?

Mr. BLAIR. There is not a case to be found in the books where the constitutional requirement of a registry has ever been defied except in the case of South Carolina.

I thank the Commission for allowing me to trespass upon them so long.

The PRESIDENT. We will now hear from the counsel on the other side.

Mr. SHELLABARGER. Counsel on the other side have decided that they will not ask the Commission to be heard. In view of the value of the time that is now left to complete this count, we deem that it is our duty to omit to consume any part of that time by discussion, and therefore on our part we submit the case without argument.

The PRESIDENT. Counsel for objectors to certificate No. 2 submit the case. It now belongs to counsel on the other side.

Mr. Commissioner BAYARD. The offers of proof are not printed. The Commission might desire to consider them. I suggest that an order for their printing be made. I understand they can be furnished us in the course of an hour or so.

The PRESIDENT. Do you submit the motion that they be printed?

Mr. Commissioner BAYARD. I submit the motion that the offers of proof submitted by Mr. Cochrane be printed.

The motion was agreed to.

Mr. BLACK. Mr. President and gentlemen, I had not and have not now any intention to argue this case. I never heard the objections nor knew what they were until they were read in your presence this morning. It would be presumption in me to attempt an argument before a tribunal like this on such a case as this, having had no previous opportunity to consider it which might put me in a condition better than the judges themselves. You have heard as much of this case and know as much about it as I do.

My idea of the duty which a counselor owes to a court or to any other tribunal, judicial or quasi-judicial, is that he should never open his mouth except for the purpose of assisting the judges in coming to a correct conclusion; and if he is not in a situation to do that, he ought to keep silence.

Besides that, I am, I suppose, the very last man in this whole nation who should be called upon to speak here and now. Everybody has suffered more or less by events and proceedings of the recent past, some by wear and tear of conscience, and some by a deep sense of oppression and wrong. But perhaps I, more than most others, have felt the consciousness that I have lost the dignity of an American citizen. I, in common with the rest, am degraded and humiliated. This nation has got her great big foot in a trap. It is vain to struggle for her extrication.

I am so fallen from the proud estate of a free citizen, you have so abjected me, that I am fit for nothing on earth but to represent the poor, defrauded, broken-hearted democracy. And because I suffer more, they think me more good for nothing than the rest, and conclude to send me out on this forlorn hope, judging, no doubt truly, that it matters nothing what becomes of me. I ought to go gladly if anything which I can do or say might have the effect of mitigating the horrible calamity with which the country is threatened: a President deriving his title from a shameless swindle, not merely a fraud, but a fraud detected and exposed. I know not how I would feel if called upon to suffer death for my country; I am not the stuff that martyrs are made of; but if my life could redeem this nation from the infamy with which she is clothed, I *ought* to go to the grave as freely as I ever went to my bed. I see, however, no practical good that I can do, and it is mere weakness to complain.

We have certain objections to the counting of this Hayes vote from South Carolina which look to me insuperable, but I cannot hope that they will wear that appearance in other men's eyes. Perhaps the feeling which I in common with millions of others entertain on this subject prevents us from seeing this thing in its true light. But you are wise; you are calm. You can look all through this awful business with a learned spirit; no passionate hatred of this great fraud can cloud your mental vision or shake the even balance of your judgment. You do not think it any wrong that a nation should be cheated by false election re turns. On the contrary, it is rather a blessing which Heaven has sent us in this strange disguise. When the omnipotent lie shall be throned and sceptered and crowned, you think we ought all of us to fall down and worship it as the hope of our political salvation. You will teach us and perhaps we shall learn (perhaps not) that under such a rule we are better off than if truth had prevailed and justice been triumphant.

Give, then, your cool consideration to these objections, and try them by the standard of the law. I mean the law as it was before the organization of this Commission. I admit that since then a great revolution has taken place in the law. It is not now what it used to be. All our notions of public right and public wrong have suffered a complete *bouleversement*.

The question submitted to you is whether the persons who gave these votes were "duly appointed." "Duly" of course means according to law. What law? The Constitution of the United States, the acts of Congress passed in pursuance thereof, the constitution of South Carolina, and the authorized acts of her legislature—these taken all together constitute the law of the case before you.

By these laws the right, duty, and power of appointing electors is given to the people of South Carolina; that is to say, the citizens of the State qualified to vote at general elections. Who are they? By the constitution of the State in order to qualify them as voters they must be registered. The registry of a native citizen is a *sine qua non* to his right of voting as much as the naturalization of a foreigner.

Now, the legislature never passed any law for the registration of voters, and no registration of them was ever made. No doubt has been or can be entertained that the object and purpose of this omission was fraudulent and dishonest; for the legislature as well as the executive department of that government has been in the hands of the most redemptionless rogues on the face of the earth. But whatever may have been the *motive*, nobody can doubt that the legal *effect* of this omission is to make the election illegal.

That is hardly the worst of it. The election itself, emancipated from all law and all authority, was no better than a riot, a mob, a general saturnalia, in which the soldiers of the United States Army cut the principal as well as the decentest figure. We offer to prove—the offer will go upon record, and there it will stand forever—that every poll in Charleston County, where they rushed into the ballot-box 7,000 majority, was in possession of the soldiers.

A government whose elections are controlled by military force cannot be republican in form or substance. For this I cite the authority of Luther *vs.* Borden, if perchance the old-time law has yet any influence. Do you not see the hideous depth of national degradation into which you will plunge us if you sanctify this mode of making a President? Brush up your historical memory and think of it for a moment. The man whom you elect in this way is as purely the creature of the military power as Caligula or Domitian, for whom the pretorian guards controlled the hustings and counted the votes.

But then we cannot get behind the returns, forsooth! Not we! You will not let us. We cannot get behind them. No. That is the law, of course. We may struggle for justice; we may cry for mercy; we may go down on our knees, and beg and woo for some little recognition of our rights as American citizens; but we might as well put up our prayers to Jupiter, or Mars, as bring suit in the court where Rhadamanthus presides. There is not a god on Olympus that would not listen to us with more favor than we shall be heard by our adversaries. We are at their mercy; it is only to them that we can appeal, because you gentlemen unfortunately cannot help us. You are bound by the new law which you have made. You are of course addicted like other people to the vice of consistency, and what is done once must be done over again.

In the Louisiana case the people appointed electors in favor of Tilden, recorded their act, finished it, and left their work in such a state that nobody could misunderstand it. But other persons, who had no power to appoint, falsified the record of the actual appointment, partly by plain forgery, and partly by fraud which was as corrupt in morals and as void in law as any forgery could be. You thought it right and legal and just to say that you would not look at the record which the people had made; the forgery, the fraud, and the corruption were too sacred to be interfered with; the truth must not be allowed to come in conflict with the imposture, lest the concussion might be damaging.

This precedent must be followed. It is new law, to be sure, but we must give it due welcome; and the new lords that it brings into power must be regarded as our "very noble and approved good masters." Having decided that electors were duly appointed in Louisiana who were known not to be appointed, we cannot expect you to take notice of any fact similar or kindred to it in South Carolina.

Then, again, the question of "duly appointed" was decided in the case of Levissee, an elector who was an officer of the United States Government at the time he was appointed and continued to be afterward. The Federal Constitution says that no man shall be appointed who is in that relation to the Federal Government. But you held, according to law, mind you, that he was a lawful elector and his vote a good vote. In other words, a thing is perfectly constitutional although it is known to be in the very teeth of a constitutional interdict!

Now, you see why we are hopeless. The present state of the law is sadly against us. The friends of honest elections and honest government are in deep despair. We once thought that the verifying power of the two Houses of Congress ought to be brought always into requisition for the purpose of seeing whether the thing that is brought here is a forgery and a fraud on the one hand, or whether it is a genuine and true certificate on the other.

But while we cannot ask you to go back behind this certificate, will you just please to go *to* it—only to it—not step behind. If you do, you will find that it is no certificate at all such as is required by law. The electors must vote by ballot, and they are required to be on oath before they vote. That certificate does not show that either of those requirements was met, and where a party is exercising a special authority like this he must keep strictly within it, and you are not to presume anything except what appears on the face of the act to be done.

If anybody will cast back his mind a little into the history of presidential elections or look at the debates of less than a year ago, he will remember that Mr. Jefferson was charged when he was Vice-President of the United States with having elected himself by means of, not a fraudulent, but a merely informal vote sent up from Georgia. The informality was not in the certificate inside of the envelope, but in the outside verification. Mr. Matthew L. Davis in 1837 got up that story. It was not true, but it was believed for a while, and it cast great odium on Mr. Jefferson's memory. It was not an informality that was nearly as important as this, nothing like it. But one of the Senators now on this bench referred to it in a debate only a short time ago, and denounced Mr. Jefferson as having elected himself by fraud because he did not call the attention of the Senate and House of Representatives to that fact. If Mr. Jefferson's memory ought to be sent down to posterity covered with infamy because he in his own case allowed a vote to be counted which was slightly informal on the outside of the envelope, I should be glad to know what ought to be done to those who would count this vote which has neither form nor substance, which leaves out all the essential particulars that the electors are required to certify?

This great nation still struggles for justice; a million majority of white people send up their cry, and a majority of more than a quarter of a million of all colors demand it. But we cannot complain. I want you to understand that we do not complain. Usually it is said that "the fowler setteth not forth his net in sight of the bird," but this fowler set the net in sight of the birds that went into it. It is largely our own fault that we were caught.

We are promised—and I hope the promise will be kept—that we shall have a good government, fraudulent though it be; that the rights of the States shall be respected and individual liberty be protected. We are promised the same reformation which the Turkish government is now proposing to its people. The Sultan promises that, if he is sustained in his present contest, he will establish and act upon certain principles :

First, the work of decentralization shall commence immediately and the autonomy of the provinces shall be carefully looked after. Secondly, the people shall be governed by their natural judges; they will not send Mohammedans nor Christian renegades from Constantinople down on them, but they shall be governed by people of their own faith. Thirdly, no subordinate officer when he commits an illegal act shall be permitted to plead in justification the orders of his superior. How much we need exactly that kind of reform in this country; and how glad we ought to be that our Government is going to be as good hereafter as the Turk's.

They offer us everything now. They denounce negro supremacy and carpet-bag thieves. Their pet policy for the South is to be abandoned. They offer us everything but one; but on that subject their lips are closely sealed. They refuse to say that they will not cheat us hereafter in the elections. If they would only agree to that; if they would only repent of their election-frauds and make restitution of the votes they have stolen, the circle of our felicities would be full.

If this thing stands accepted and the law you have made for this occasion shall be the law for all occasions, we can never expect such a thing as an honest election again. If you want to know who will be President by a future election, do not inquire how the people of the States are going to vote. You need only to know what kind of scoundrels constitute the returning-boards, and how much it will take to buy them.

But I think that even that will end some day. At present you have us down and under your feet. Never had you a better right to rejoice. Well may you say, "We have made a covenant with death, and with hell are we at agreement; when the overflowing scourge shall pass through, it shall not come unto us: for we have made lies our refuge, and under falsehoods have we hid ourselves." But nevertheless wait a little while. The waters of truth will rise gradually, and slowly but surely, and then look out for the overflowing scourge. "The refuge of lies shall be swept away, and the hiding-place of falsehood shall be uncovered." This mighty and puissant nation will yet raise herself up like a strong man after sleep, and shake her invincible locks in a fashion you little think of now. Wait; retribution will come in due time. Justice travels with a leaden heel but strikes with an iron hand.

God's mill grinds slow but dreadfully fine. Wait till the flood-gate is lifted and a full head of water comes rushing on. Wait, and you will see fine grinding then.

Mr. Representative COCHRANE. Mr. President, will you permit me to refer the Commission to one or two authorities which I neglected to refer to before?

The PRESIDENT. We shall allow it.

Mr. Representative COCHRANE. I must ask pardon of the Commission for the irregularity. I desire to refer you to section 30 of article 8 of the constitution of the State of South Carolina, as contained in the publication of the Revised Statutes of South Carolina, page 28:

Members of the general assembly and all officers, before they enter upon the execution of the duties of their respective offices, shall take and subscribe the following oath.

Which oath is provided for. Then I desire to call your honors' attention to the provision of the Revised Statutes of the United States on page 22, section 139:

The electors shall seal up the certificates so made by them, and certify upon each that the list of all the votes of such State given for President, and of all the votes given for Vice-President, are contained therein.

It is hardly necessary for me to refer you to the provision of the Constitution requiring the voting to be done by ballot, but I simply call attention to this fact, that the certificate upon the envelopes of certificate No. 1 is not in accordance with this provision of section 139. It does not certify that the envelope contains the list of all the persons voted for for President and Vice-President, but simply that it contains the names of the persons voting.

Mr. Commissioner HUNTON. Will you read that provision referring to the oath to be taken?

Mr. Representative COCHRANE. Yes, sir.

Members of the general assembly and all officers, before they enter upon the execution of the duties of their respective offices, shall take and subscribe the following oath.

Then follows the oath. The certificate upon the back of the envelope is as follows:

We certify that this sealed envelope contains lists of the votes of the State of South Carolina for President and Vice-President of the United States.

And that is all that it says.

Mr. Commissioner EDMUNDS. Your point is that it does not say that it contains all?

Mr. Representative COCHRANE. That it contains all the votes in this certificate. It is said that all the votes were cast for Mr. Hayes and Mr. Wheeler, and that there were no other votes cast except those which are mentioned in this certificate. This certificate is directly opposite in form and terms to the certificates in the cases of Florida, Louisiana, and Oregon.

We further say that certificate No. 2 contains the statement of all these facts, states that the electors were duly sworn under the provisions of the constitution, and that they balloted first for President and next for Vice-President.

The PRESIDENT. I understand that the argument is closed on both sides.

Mr. Representative COCHRANE. I will say to the Commission that if the Commission shall decide to admit the testimony or any part of it offered, the objectors and counsel will be prepared to offer it at once.

Mr. Commissioner EDMUNDS. I move that the public proceedings of the Commission be considered now closed.

The motion was agreed to.

Mr. Commissioner ABBOTT, (at one o'clock and ten minutes p. m.)　I move that a recess be taken until one o'clock and forty-five minutes p. m.

The motion was agreed to; and the Commission accordingly took a recess until one o'clock and forty-five minutes p. m.

After the recess the Commission re-assembled with closed doors for deliberation in the matter of the electoral vote of the State of South Carolina.

After debate,

Mr. Commissioner STRONG moved (at four o'clock and twenty minutes p. m.) that the vote be taken on the question pending in one hour from that time; and, after remarks, the motion was withdrawn.

On motion of Mr. Commissioner EDMUNDS, (at five o'clock and seventeen minutes p. m.,) it was, by a vote of yeas 8, nays 7,

Ordered, That the vote on the pending question be taken by six o'clock p. m.

The time allowed for debate having expired,
Mr. Commissioner MORTON offered the following resolutions:

Resolved, That it is not competent for the two Houses, assembled for the purpose of counting the votes for President and Vice-President, to inquire by evidence whether a State regularly represented in the two Houses of Congress, and recognized as a State of the United States by the other Departments of the Government, has a government republican in form.

Resolved, That while the existence of public disturbance and anarchy in any State, to such an extent as to make it impossible for the State to exercise its right to appoint electors of President and Vice-President, and to express its will in that behalf, is sufficient cause for rejecting any electoral votes purporting to be the votes of electors appointed thereby, yet, that when a State is regularly represented as a State in the Congress of the United States, and is recognized as a State by the other Departments of the Government, and has a government republican in form, and does appoint electors in the manner prescribed by the legislature thereof, evidence cannot be received by the two Houses of Congress assembled to count the votes for President and Vice-President as aforesaid to show that disturbances existed at the time of election which may have interfered, to a greater or less extent, with the freedom of election at the polls in said State.

Resolved, That it is not competent for the two Houses of Congress when assembled to count the votes for President and Vice-President, by taking evidence, to inquire into the regularity of the action of the President of the United States in sending a military force into any State for the preservation of order or the suppression of insurrection and domestic violence, in order by such proof to lay a ground for rejecting the electoral vote of said State.

Resolved, That, in view of the propositions contained in the three foregoing resolutions, the evidence offered to show that the State of South Carolina at the late election did not have a republican form of government, and the evidence offered on the subject of disorder and violence and the presence of troops in said State during said election, is not competent, but that notwithstanding the offer of such evidence the electoral votes of the State of South Carolina ought to be received and counted, if not objectionable on other grounds.

Resolved, That the other objections to certificate No. 1 show no valid cause for rejecting the same.

Mr. Commissioner FIELD offered the following as a substitute therefor:

Resolved, That evidence is admissible to show that prior to and during the election on the 7th day of November, 1876, in the State of South Carolina, there were unlawfully stationed in various parts of the State, at or near the polling-places, detachments of troops of the Army of the United States, by whose presence and interference qualified voters of the State were deprived of the right of suffrage, and a free choice by the people of presidential electors was prevented.

Resolved, That evidence is admissible to show that at the election on the 7th day of November, 1876, in South Carolina, there were stationed at the several polling-places in the State deputy marshals of the United States exceeding one thousand in number, by whose unlawful action and interference, under orders from the Department of Justice, qualified voters of the State were deprived of the right of suffrage, and a free choice by the people of presidential electors was prevented.

The question being on the adoption of the substitute, it was decided in the negative:

Yeas.. 7
Nays.. 8

Those who voted in the affirmative were: Messrs. Abbott, Bayard, Clifford, Field, Hunton, Kernan, and Payne—7.

Those who voted in the negative were: Messrs. Bradley, Edmunds, Frelinghuysen, Garfield, Hoar, Miller, Morton, and Strong—8.

The question recurring on the adoption of the resolutions offered by Mr. Commissioner Morton, it was decided in the affirmative:

Yeas.. 8
Nays.. 7

Those who voted in the affirmative were: Messrs. Bradley, Edmunds, Frelinghuysen, Garfield, Hoar, Miller, Morton, and Strong—8.

Those who voted in the negative were: Messrs. Abbott, Bayard, Clifford, Field, Hunton, Kernan, and Payne—7.

Mr. Commissioner FRELINGHUYSEN offered the following resolution:

Resolved, That Theodore R. Barker, S. McGowan, John W. Harrington, John Isaac Ingram, William Wallace, John B. Erwin, and Robert Aldrich, the persons named as electors in certificate No. 2, were not the lawful electors for the State of South Carolina, and that their votes are not the votes provided for by the Constitution of the United States, and should not be counted.

The question being on the adoption of the resolution, it was decided in the affirmative:

Yeas.. 15
Nays.. 0

Those who voted in the affirmative were: Messrs. Abbott, Bayard, Bradley, Clifford, Edmunds, Field, Frelinghuysen, Garfield, Hoar, Hunton, Kernan, Miller, Morton, Payne, and Strong—15.

Mr. Commissioner MORTON offered the following resolution:

Resolved, That C. C. Bowen, J. Winsmith, Thomas B. Johnston, Timothy Hurley, W. B. Nash, Wilson Cook, and W. F. Myers, the persons named as electors in certificate No. 1, were the lawful electors for the State of South Carolina, and that their votes are the votes provided for by the Constitution of the United States, and should be counted for President and Vice-President of the United States.

The question being on the adoption of the resolution, it was decided in the affirmative:

Yeas.. 8
Nays.. 7

Those who voted in the affirmative were: Messrs. Bradley, Edmunds, Frelinghuysen, Garfield, Hoar, Miller, Morton, and Strong—8.

Those who voted in the negative were: Messrs. Abbott, Bayard, Clifford, Field, Hunton, Kernan, and Payne—7.

Mr. Commissioner MILLER offered the following:

Ordered, That the following be adopted as the final decision and report in the matters submitted to the Commission as to the electoral vote of the State of South Carolina.

ELECTORAL COMMISSION,
Washington, D. C., February 27, A. D. 1877.

To the President of the Senate of the United States, presiding in the meeting of the two Houses of Congress under the act of Congress entitled "An act to provide for and regulate the counting of votes for President and Vice-President, and the decision of questions arising thereon, for the term commencing March 4, A. D. 1877," approved January 29, A. D. 1877:

The Electoral Commission mentioned in said act, having received certain certificates, and papers purporting to be certificates, and papers accompanying the same, of the electoral votes from the State of South Carolina, and the objections thereto, submitted to it under said act, now report that it has duly considered the same, pursuant to said act, and has by a majority of votes decided, and does hereby decide, that the votes of C. C. Bowen, J. Winsmith, Thomas B. Johnston, Timothy Hurley, W. B. Nash, Wilson Cook, and W. F. Myers, named in the certificate of D. H. Chamberlain, governor of said State, which votes are certified by said persons as appears by the certificates submitted to the Commission as aforesaid, and marked "No. 1, N. C." by said Commission, and herewith returned, are the votes provided for by the Constitution of the United States, and that the same are lawfully to be counted as therein certified, namely: seven votes for Rutherford B. Hayes, of the State of Ohio, for President, and seven votes for William A. Wheeler, of the State of New York, for Vice-President.

The Commission has by a majority of votes also decided, and does hereby decide and report, that the seven persons first above named were duly appointed electors in and by the State of South Carolina.

The brief ground of this decision is, that it appears, upon such evidence as by the Constitution and the law named in said act of Congress is competent and pertinent to the consideration of the subject, that the beforementioned electors appear to have been lawfully appointed such electors of President and Vice-President of the United States for the term beginning March 4, A. D. 1877, of the State of South Carolina, and that they voted as such at the time and in the manner provided for by the Constitution of the United States and the law.

And the Commission, as further grounds for their decision, are of opinion that the failure of the legislature to provide a system for the registration of persons entitled to vote, does not render nugatory all elections held under laws otherwise sufficient, though it may be the duty of the legislature to enact such a law. If it were otherwise, all government in that State is a usurpation, its officers without authority, and the social compact in that State is at an end.

That this Commission must take notice that there is a government in South Carolina republican in form, since its constitution provides for such a government, and it is, and was on the day of appointing electors, so recognized by the Executive and by both branches of the legislative department of the Government of the United States.

That so far as this Commission can take notice of the presence of the soldiers of the United States in the State of South Carolina during the election, it appears that they were placed there by the President of the United States to suppress insurrection, at the request of the proper authorities of the State.

And we are also of opinion that from the papers before us it appears that the governor and secretary of state having certified under the seal of the State that the electors whose votes we have decided to be the lawful electoral votes of the State, were duly appointed electors, which certificate, both by presumption of law and by the certificate of the rival claimants of the electoral office, was based upon the action of the State canvassers, there exists no power in this Commission, as there exists none in the two Houses of Congress in counting the electoral vote, to inquire into the circumstances under which the primary vote for electors was given.

The power of the Congress of the United States in its legislative capacity to inquire into the matters alleged, and to act upon the information so obtained, is a very different one from its power in the matter of counting the electoral vote. The votes to be counted are those presented by the State, and when ascertained and presented by the proper authorities of the States they must be counted.

The Commission has also decided, and does hereby decide, by a majority of votes, and report, that as a consequence of the foregoing, and upon the grounds before stated, the paper purporting to be a certificate of the electoral vote of said State of South Carolina, signed by Theodore R. Barker, S. McGowan, Jno. W. Harrington, Jno. Isaac Ingram, Wm. Wallace, John B. Erwin, and Robt. Aldrich, marked "No. 2, N. C." by the Commission, and herewith returned, is not the certificate of the votes provided for by the Constitution of the United States, and that they ought not to be counted as such.

Done at Washington, D. C., the day and year first above written.

The question being on the adoption of the order, it was decided in the affirmative:

Yeas.. 8
Nays... 7

Those who voted in the affirmative were: Messrs. Bradley, Edmunds, Frelinghuysen, Garfield, Hoar, Miller, Morton, and Strong—8.

Those who voted in the negative were: Messrs. Abbott, Bayard, Clifford, Field, Hunton, Kernan, and Payne—7.

So the report of the Commission was adopted; and said decision and report were thereupon signed by the members agreeing therein, as follows:

SAM. F. MILLER.
W. STRONG.
JOSEPH P. BRADLEY.
GEO. F. EDMUNDS.
O. P. MORTON.
FRED'K T. FRELINGHUYSEN.
JAMES A. GARFIELD.
GEORGE F. HOAR.

Mr. Commissioner MILLER offered the following:

Ordered, That the President of the Commission transmit a letter to the President of the Senate in the following words:

"WASHINGTON, D. C., *February* 27, *A. D.* 1877.

"SIR: I am directed by the Electoral Commission to inform the Senate that it has considered and decided upon the matters submitted to it under the act of Congress concerning the same, touching the electoral votes from the State of South Carolina, and herewith, by direction of said Commission, I transmit to you the said decision, in writing, signed by the members agreeing therein, to be read at the meeting of the two Houses, according to said act. All the certificates and papers sent to the Commission by the President of the Senate are herewith returned.

"Hon. THOMAS W. FERRY,
    "President of the Senate."

The question being on the adoption of the order, it was determined in the affirmative; and the letter was accordingly signed, as follows:

"NATHAN CLIFFORD,
    " President of the Commission."

Mr. Commissioner MILLER offered the following:

Ordered, That the President of the Commission transmit to the Speaker of the House of Representatives a letter in the following words:

"WASHINGTON, D. C., *February* 27, *A. D.* 1877.

"SIR: I am directed by the Electoral Commission to inform the House of Representatives that it has considered and decided upon the matters submitted to it under the act of Congress concerning the same, touching the electoral votes from the State of South Carolina, and has transmitted said decision to the President of the Senate, to be read at the meeting of the two Houses, according to said act.

"Hon. SAMUEL J. RANDALL,
    " Speaker of the House of Representatives."

The question being on the adoption of the order, it was decided in the affirmative; and the letter was accordingly signed, as follows:

"NATHAN CLIFFORD,
    " President of the Commission."

THANKS TO PRESIDENT.

Mr. MORTON offered the following resolution:

Resolved, That the thanks of this Commission are due to Commissioner Clifford for the ability, impartiality, and urbanity with which he has presided over its deliberations.

And the same was adopted by a unanimous vote.

OPINIONS OF COMMISSIONERS.

Mr. Commissioner STRONG moved the following order:

Ordered, That the members of the Commission be at liberty to reduce to writing the remarks made by them during the consultations of the Commission, and cause them to be published in the printed proceedings on or before the 15th day of March next.*

* The remarks referred to, as thus reduced to writing by the members, will be found in the Appendix of Opinions.

The question being on the adoption of the order, it was decided in the affirmative:

Yeas 10
Nays 4

Those who voted in the affirmative were: Messrs. Bayard, Bradley, Clifford, Edmunds, Frelinghuysen, Garfield, Hoar, Miller, Morton, and Strong—10.

Those who voted in the negative were: Messrs. Abbott, Field, Hunton, and Payne—4.

REMOVAL OF SECRECY.

On motion of Mr. Commissioner MILLER, it was

Ordered, That the injunction of secrecy imposed on the acts and proceedings of the Commission be removed.

On motion of Mr. Commissioner GARFIELD, (at six o'clock and fifty-four minutes p. m.,) the Commission adjourned until eleven o'clock a. m., Friday, March 2, unless sooner called together by the President.

PROCEEDINGS OF THE TWO HOUSES.

SOUTH CAROLINA.

IN SENATE, *Wednesday, February* 28, 1877.

The recess taken on the previous day having expired, the Senate resumed its session at ten o'clock a. m., Wednesday, February 28.

The PRESIDENT *pro tempore* laid before the Senate the following communication, which was read:

WASHINGTON, D. C., *February* 27, *A. D.* 1877.

SIR: I am directed by the Electoral Commission to inform the Senate that it has considered and decided upon the matters submitted to it under the act of Congress concerning the same, touching the electoral votes from the State of South Carolina, and herewith, by direction of said Commission, I transmit to you the said decision, in writing, signed by the members agreeing therein, to be read at the meeting of the two Houses, according to said act. All the certificates and papers sent to the Commission by the President of the Senate are herewith returned.

NATHAN CLIFFORD,
President of the Commission.

Hon. THOMAS W. FERRY,
President of the Senate.

On motion of Mr. Senator CRAGIN, it was

Ordered, That the Secretary be directed to inform the House of Representatives that the president of the Electoral Commission has notified the Senate that the Commission has arrived at a decision of the questions submitted to it in relation to the electoral votes of South Carolina, and that the Senate is now ready to meet the House for the purpose of laying before the two Houses the report of the said decision, and to proceed with the count of the electoral votes for President and Vice-President.

At eleven o'clock a. m. a message was received from the House of Representatives announcing that it would be ready to receive the Senate at ten minutes past twelve o'clock to proceed with the count of the electoral votes; and at the hour named the Senate proceeded to the hall of the House.

IN THE HOUSE OF REPRESENTATIVES,
Wednesday, February 28, 1877.

The recess taken on the previous day having expired, the House resumed its session on Wednesday, February 28, at ten o'clock a. m.

The SPEAKER laid before the House the following communication, which was read:

WASHINGTON, D. C., *February* 27, 1877.

SIR: I am directed by the Electoral Commission to inform the House of Representatives that it has considered and decided upon the matters submitted to it under the act of Congress concerning the same, touching the electoral votes from the State of South Carolina, and has transmitted its decision to the President of the Senate, to be read at the meeting of the two Houses, according to said act.

NATHAN CLIFFORD,
President of the Commission.

Hon. SAMUEL J. RANDALL,
Speaker of the House of Representatives.

Mr. Representative ATKINS moved a call of the House, which motion was disagreed to—yeas 76, nays 156.

A message was received from the Senate announcing its readiness to meet the House for the purpose of proceeding with the count.

On motion of Mr. Representative SAYLER, the Clerk was directed to notify the Senate that the House would be ready to receive it at ten minutes past twelve o'clock to proceed with the electoral count; whereupon the House proceeded with legislative business until the time named.

JOINT MEETING.

WEDNESDAY, *February* 28, 1877.

At twelve o'clock and ten minutes p. m. the Senate entered the Hall of the House of Representatives in the usual manner.

The PRESIDENT *pro tempore* of the Senate took his seat as Presiding Officer of the joint meeting of the two Houses, the Speaker of the House occupying a chair upon his left.

The PRESIDING OFFICER. The joint meeting of Congress for counting the electoral vote resumes its session. The two Houses, having separated upon the submission to the Commission of the objections to the certificate from the State of South Carolina, have reconvened to consider and act upon the decision of that tribunal. The decision, which is in writing, by a majority of the Commission, and signed by the members agreeing therein, will now be read by the Secretary of the Senate and entered in the Journal of each House.

The Secretary of the Senate read as follows:

ELECTORAL COMMISSION,
Washington, D. C., February 27, *A. D.* 1877.

To the President of the Senate of the United States presiding in the meeting of the two Houses of Congress under the act of Congress entitled "An act to provide for and regulate the counting of votes for President and Vice-President, and the decision of questions arising thereon, for the term commencing March 4, A. D. 1877," approved January 29, A. D. 1877:

The Electoral Commission mentioned in said act, having received certain certificates and papers purporting to be certificates, and papers accompanying the same, of the electoral votes from the State of South Carolina, and the objections thereto submitted to it under said act, now report that it has duly considered the same pursuant to said act, and has by a majority of votes decided, and does hereby decide, that the votes of C. C. Bowen, J. Winsmith, Thomas B. Johnston, Timothy Hurley, W. B. Nash, Wilson Cook, and W. F. Myers, named in the certificate of D. H. Chamberlain, governor of said State, which votes are certified by said persons, as appears by the certificates submitted to the Commission as aforesaid, and marked "No. 1, N. C.," by said Commission, and herewith returned, are the votes provided for by the Constitution of the United States, and that the same are lawfully to be counted as therein certified, namely: Seven votes for Rutherford B. Hayes, of the State of Ohio, for President, and seven votes for William A. Wheeler, of the State of New York, for Vice-President.

The Commission has by a majority of votes also decided, and does hereby decide and report, that the seven persons first above named were duly appointed electors in and by the State of South Carolina.

The brief ground of this decision is, that it appears, upon such evidence as by the Constitution and the law named in said act of Congress is competent and pertinent to the consideration of the subject, that the before-mentioned electors appear to have been lawfully appointed such electors of President and Vice-President of the United States for the term beginning March 4, A. D. 1877, of the State of South Carolina, and that they voted as such at the time and in the manner provided for by the Constitution of the United States and the law.

And the Commission, as further grounds for their decision, are of opinion that the failure of the legislature to provide a system for the registration of persons entitled to vote does not render nugatory all elections held under laws otherwise sufficient, though it may be the duty of the legislature to enact such a law. If it were otherwise, all government in that State is a usurpation, its officers without authority, and the social compact in that State is at an end.

That this Commission must take notice that there is a government in South Carolina, republican in form, since its constitution provides for such a government, and it is and was on the day of appointing electors so recognized by the executive and by both branches of the legislative department of the Government of the United States.

That so far as this Commission can take notice of the presence of the soldiers of the United States in the State of South Carolina during the election, it appears that they were placed there by the President of the United States to suppress insurrection, at the request of the proper authorities of the State.

And we are also of opinion that, from the papers before us, it appears that the governor and secretary of state having certified under the seal of the State that the electors whose vote we have decided to be the lawful electoral vote of the State were duly appointed electors—which certificate, both by presumption, by law, and by the certificate of the rival claimants of the electoral office, was based upon the action of the State canvassers—there exists no power in this Commission, as there exists none in the two Houses of Congress in counting the electoral vote, to inquire into the circumstances under which the primary vote for electors was given.

The power of the Congress of the United States in its legislative capacity to inquire into the matters alleged, and to act upon the information so obtained, is a very different one from its power in the matter of counting the electoral votes. The votes to be counted are those presented by the State, and when ascertained and presented by the proper authorities of the State they must be counted.

The Commission has also decided, and does hereby decide by a majority of votes and report, that, as a consequence of the foregoing, and upon the grounds before stated, the paper purporting to be a certificate of the electoral vote of said State of South Carolina, signed by Theodore G. Barker, S. McGowan, Jno. W. Harrington, Jno. Isaac Ingram, Wm. Wallace, Jno. B. Erwin, and Robt. Aldrich, marked "No. 2, N. C." by the Commission, and herewith returned, is not the certificate of the votes provided for by the Constitution of the United States, and that they ought not to be counted as such.

Done at Washington, District of Columbia, the day and year first above written.

SAM. F. MILLER.
W. STRONG.
JOSEPH P. BRADLEY.
GEO. F. EDMUNDS.
O. P. MORTON.
FRED'K T. FRELINGHUYSEN.
JAMES A. GARFIELD.
GEORGE F. HOAR.

The PRESIDING OFFICER. Are there any objections to the decision of the Commission?

Mr. Representative PHILIPS, of Missouri. I send up an objection signed by Senators and Representatives, and along with it I present the evidence upon which the objection is founded.

The PRESIDING OFFICER. The member from Missouri [Mr. Phillips] having presented an objection, it will be read by the Clerk of the House.

The Clerk of the House read as follows:

The undersigned, Senators and Representatives, do hereby object to counting the votes cast by C. C. Bowen, J. Winsmith, Thomas B. Johnston, Timothy Hurley, W. B. Nash, Wilson Cook, and W. F. Myers, alleged electors of the State of South Carolina, in conformity to the decision of the Electoral Commission, and as reasons therefor assign the following:

I.

Because no legal election was held in the State of South Carolina on the 7th day of November last past for presidential electors in compliance with section 3, article 8, of the constitution thereof requiring a registration of the electors of the State as a qualification to vote.

II.

Because in consequence of frauds practiced in said election, and the interference with and intimidation of the electors in said State by the Federal Government prior to and during said election, stationing in various parts of said State near the polling-places detachments of the Army of the United States, a full and free exercise of the right of suffrage was prevented, in consequence of which there was no lawful election had.

III.

Because in violation of the Constitution of the United States the Federal authorities, at the several polling-places in said State on the day of election, stationed over one thousand deputy marshals of the United States, who by their unlawful and arbitrary action, in obedience to the unauthorized instructions from the Department of Justice, so interfered with the full and free exercise of the right of suffrage by the voters of said State that a fair election could not be and was not held in said State on the 7th day of November, 1876.

IV.

Because the certification of the election held by said electors on the 6th day of December, 1876, was not made by the lawfully constituted governor of said State.

V.

Because the said Electoral Commission, contrary to its duty and the authority vested in it by law, neglected and refused to inquire into the facts and allegations aforesaid, and their said decision is contrary to the law and the truth.

VI.

Because at the time of the pretended appointment of the said electors in the State of South Carolina, it was under duress from the power of the United States unlawfully exerted upon it, and said pretended appointments were made under such duress.

VII.

Because the certificate numbered 1 was and is void.

First. For irregularity in that the electors were not sworn, as by the constitution of the State of South Carolina they were required to be.

Second. The certificate does not state that said electors voted by ballot, as required by the Constitution of the United States.

Third. The certificate upon the envelope in which the said certificate and accompanying papers were inclosed was not the certificate required by the laws of the United States.

> T. M. NORWOOD,
> JAMES K. KELLY,
> HENRY COOPER,
> S. B. MAXEY,
> WM. A. WALLACE,
> *Senators.*
> J. F. PHILIPS,
> HIESTER CLYMER,
> ERASTUS WELLS,
> A. T. WALLING,
> A. M. WADDELL,
> JOHN R. EDEN,
> THOS. L. JONES,
> J. R. TUCKER,
> *Representatives.*

The PRESIDING OFFICER. Are there further objections to the decision of the Commission?

Mr. Representative SOUTHARD. I send up in duplicate an objection, signed by Senators and Representatives.

The PRESIDING OFFICER. The member from Ohio [Mr. Southard] submits an objection, which will be read by the Secretary of the Senate.

The Secretary of the Senate read as follows:

The undersigned Senators and members of the House of Representatives object to the counting of the electoral vote purporting to come from South Carolina, in conformity with the decision of the majority of the Electoral Commission, for the reason that the said electoral votes, as well as the votes of the people of said State at the presidential election on the 7th day of November last, were given under duress caused by the unlawful exercise of Federal power.

A. S. MERRIMON,
GEO. R. DENNIS,
J. E. McDONALD,
WM. A. WALLACE,
C. W. JONES,
Senators.

DAVID DUDLEY FIELD,
M. I. SOUTHARD,
WM. MUTCHLER,
JOHN GOODE, Jr.,
JESSE J. YEATES,
JOHN H. CALDWELL,
S. S. COX,
R. A. DE BOLT,
JOHN B. CLARK, Jr.,
Representatives.

The PRESIDING OFFICER. Are there further objections to the decision? [A pause.] If there be none, the Senate will now withdraw to its chamber, that the two Houses separately may consider and determine the objections.

Accordingly (at twelve o'clock and thirty minutes p. m.) the Senate withdrew.

IN SENATE, *Wednesday, February* 28, 1877.

The Senate having retired from the joint meeting, the President *pro tempore* resumed the chair at twelve o'clock and thirty-five minutes p. m., and caused to be read the objections to the decision of the Electoral Commission as to the electoral votes of the State of South Carolina; whereupon,

Mr. Senator ROBERTSON offered the following resolution:

Resolved, That the decision of the Commission upon the electoral vote of the State of South Carolina stand as the judgment of the Senate, the objections made thereto to the contrary notwithstanding.

Mr. Senator MERRIMON submitted the following resolution:

Resolved, That it is competent to receive testimony to sustain the several exceptions above specified.

Mr. Senator EDMUNDS raised the point of order that, the two Houses having separated to consider objections made to the decision of the Electoral Commission as to what votes returned from the State of South Carolina were the votes provided for by the Constitution of the United States, it was not competent for the Senate, under the provisions of the electoral law, to consider any question or resolution which did not order a concurrence or non-concurrence with such decision, and hence the resolution of Mr. Senator Merrimon was not in order.

The PRESIDENT *pro tempore* submitted to the Senate the question whether Mr. Senator Merrimon's resolution was in order, and it was decided in the negative—yeas 18, nays 43.

Mr. Senator BOGY moved that the testimony submitted with the objections be read, which motion was disagreed to—yeas 21, nays 41.

The question recurring on the resolution of Mr. Senator ROBERTSON, after debate, it was agreed to by a vote of yeas 39, nays 22.

The Secretary was ordered to notify the House of Representatives of this action and of the readiness of the Senate to meet the House to continue the counting of the electoral votes.

At six o'clock and twelve minutes p. m., a message was received from the House of Representatives announcing its action on the objection to the decision of the Electoral Commission upon the electoral votes of South Carolina and its readiness to receive the Senate to continue the count ; whereupon the Senate proceeded to the hall of the House.

IN THE HOUSE OF REPRESENTATIVES,
Wednesday, February 28, 1877.

The Senate having withdrawn from the hall of the House of Representatives, at twelve o'clock and thirty minutes p. m. the House resumed its session.

Mr. Representative SPRINGER moved that the House take a recess till Thursday, March 1, at ten o'clock a. m., which motion was disagreed to—yeas 92, nays 170.

Mr. Representative SHEAKLEY moved that the House take a recess until 7½ o'clock p. m. this day.

Mr. Representative WOOD, of New York, raised the question of order that the motion was not in order under the electoral law.

The SPEAKER sustained the point of order and declined to entertain the motion.

From this decision Mr. Representative SHEAKLEY appealed, and, on motion of Mr. Representative WOOD, of New York, the appeal was laid on the table by a vote of yeas 184, nays 61.

Mr. Representative SHEAKLEY moved that the House take a recess until to-morrow (March 1) at ten o'clock a. m.

The SPEAKER ruled the motion out of order and declined to entertain it.

From this decision, Mr. Representative SPRINGER appealed.

The SPEAKER declined to entertain the appeal, and stated the regular order of business to be the consideration of the objections to the decision of the Commission upon the electoral certificates from the State of South Carolina.

A message was received from the Senate announcing its resolution on the objection to the decision of the Commission in the case of South Carolina and its readiness to meet the House to proceed with the count.

Mr. Representative PHILIPS, of Missouri, demanded the reading of the testimony taken by the Select Committee of the House to investigate the recent election in the State of South Carolina, accompanying the said objections.

Mr. Representative WOOD, of New York, objected to the reading of the testimony called for.

The SPEAKER submitted to the House the question whether the testimony should be read ; and it was decided in the negative—yeas 87, nays 176.

Mr. Representative WALLING moved to reconsider the vote by which the reading of the testimony was refused.

On motion of Mr. Representative WOOD, of New York, the motion to reconsider was laid on the table—yeas 177, nays 73.

Mr. Representative VANCE, of Ohio, moved that parts one and two of said testimony be read.

The SPEAKER held that the motion was not in order, the House having just refused to order the reading of the testimony.

Mr. Representative COCHRANE submitted the following resolution, which was debated for the two hours allowed by the electoral law, viz:

Resolved, That the objections to the decision of the Electoral Commission upon the electoral vote of South Carolina be sustained by the House, and that said votes be not counted.

Mr. Representative WALLING moved to amend the resolution by adding the words " in conformity with the decision of said Commission."

Mr. Representative JONES, of Kentucky, offered the following as a substitute for the pending propositions:

Resolved, That the decision of the Electoral Commission upon the electoral vote of South Carolina be not concurred in by this House.

Mr. Representative WOOD, of New York, demanded the previous question.

Mr. Representative HALE raised the point of order that as the electoral law required the main question to be put at the end of two hours' debate, it was not necessary that the ordinary forms of seconding the previous question and ordering the main question should be observed.

The SPEAKER overruled the point of order and held that "the main question," as used in the electoral law, embraced the original proposition, an amendment, and an amendment to the amendment.

The call for the previous question was seconded; and, on ordering the main question to be put, the yeas were 190, the nays 72.

Mr. Representative WALLING moved to reconsider the vote by which the main question was ordered.

Mr. Representative WOOD, of New York, (unanimous consent being given for the purpose,) submitted the following proposition as a compromise:

The amendment to be withdrawn, and the House to come to a direct vote upon the original resolution as amended by Mr. Walling; the Senate then to be invited to meet the House for the purpose of continuing the count; and when the State of Vermont shall be reached and the two Houses shall separate, then the House to take a recess until to-morrow at ten o'clock.

The proposition was unanimously agreed to.

The question recurring on the amendment of Mr. Representative Walling to the resolution of Mr. Representative Cochrane, the amendment was agreed to, and the resolution, as amended, was adopted.

On motion of Mr. Representative WOOD, of New York, the Clerk was directed to notify the Senate of the action of the House and of its readiness to receive the Senate to proceed with the count of electoral votes.

JOINT MEETING.

WEDNESDAY, *February* 28, 1877.

At six o'clock and eighteen minutes p. m., the Senate entered the House Hall in the usual manner.

The PRESIDENT *pro tempore* of the Senate took his seat as presiding officer of the joint meeting of the two Houses, the Speaker of the House occupying a chair upon his left.

The PRESIDING OFFICER. The joint meeting of Congress for counting the electoral vote resumes its session. The two Houses having separately determined upon the objections to the decision of the

Commission on the certificates from the State of South Carolina, the Secretary of the Senate will read the resolution adopted by the Senate.

The Secretary of the Senate read as follows:

Resolved, That the decision of the Commission upon the electoral vote of the State of South Carolina stand as the judgment of the Senate, the objections made thereto to the contrary notwithstanding.

The PRESIDING OFFICER. The Clerk of the House of Representatives will now read the resolution adopted by the House of Representatives.

Mr. Representative JONES, of Kentucky. I desire to inquire if there is a quorum of the Senate present. The law under which we are acting and the Constitution of the United States require that the certificates shall be opened in the presence of both Houses. If, therefore, there is not a quorum of the House and Senate present, I imagine that this proceeding cannot go on.

Mr. Representative BANKS. That is not a question for the convention to decide; the Senate must decide it for itself.

The PRESIDING OFFICER. The Clerk of the House will read the resolution of the House.

Mr. Representative JONES, of Kentucky. I protest that this proceeding should not go on.

The PRESIDING OFFICER. Debate is not in order.

Mr. Representative JONES, of Kentucky. My protest is entered and should go on the record.

The Clerk of the House read as follows:

Resolved, That the objections to the decision of the Electoral Commission upon the electoral vote of South Carolina be sustained by the House, and that said vote be not counted in conformity with the decision of said Commission.

The PRESIDING OFFICER. The two Houses not concurring in ordering otherwise, the decision of the Commission stands unreversed, and the vote of the State of South Carolina will be counted in conformity therewith. The tellers will announce the vote of the State of South Carolina.

Mr. Representative STONE, (one of the tellers.) South Carolina casts 7 votes for Rutherford B. Hayes, of Ohio, for President of the United States, and 7 votes for William A. Wheeler, of New York, for Vice-President of the United States.

UNDISPUTED STATES.

The count then proceeded, the certificates from the State of—

Tennessee, casting 12 votes for Tilden and Hendricks; and

Texas, casting 8 votes for Tilden and Hendricks—

being opened by the Presiding Officer and read by the tellers, and the votes thereof counted without objection.

VERMONT.

The PRESIDING OFFICER. Having opened the certificate received by messenger from the State of Vermont, the Chair hands the same to the tellers, to be read in the presence and hearing of the two Houses, and the corresponding one received by mail is also handed to the tellers.

Mr. Representative POPPLETON. I ask that the certificate from the State of Vermont be read at length.

The PRESIDING OFFICER. The certificate in full will be read, objection being made to dispensing with reading any portion of it.

Mr. Senator INGALLS (one of the tellers) read in full the certificate from the State of Vermont, to the effect that that State had cast 5 votes for Rutherford B. Hayes, of Ohio, for President, and 5 votes for William A. Wheeler, of New York, for Vice-President.

The PRESIDING OFFICER. Are there any objections to the certificate from the State of Vermont?

Mr. Representative POPPLETON. I desire to inquire of the President of the Senate whether there have been other returns, or papers purporting to be returns, received from the State of Vermont.

The PRESIDING OFFICER. There have been none received except the one submitted.

Mr. Representative POPPLETON. I desire to say that I have prepared objections, upon information by telegraph and otherwise that there were dual returns from the State of Vermont.

Mr. Representative HEWITT, of New York. I desire to make a statement.

The PRESIDING OFFICER. Is there objection to the member from New York [Mr. Hewitt] making a statement? [A pause.] The Chair hears none.

Mr. Representative HEWITT, of New York. I hold in my hand a package which purports to contain electoral votes from the State of Vermont. This package was delivered to me by express about the middle of December last, and with it came a letter stating that a similar package had been forwarded by mail to the Presiding Officer of the Senate. Being informed to-day that no package corresponding to this had been received by mail by the Presiding Officer of the Senate, I called upon him and inquired whether any other than one certificate from the State of Vermont had been received by him by mail, and he informed me that there had been no other received by him than the one which was already in his possession. I then tendered to him this package, the seals of which are unbroken and which is now as it came into my possession. He declined to receive it, upon the ground that he had no authority in law so to do. Under the circumstances, I now tender this package to the Presiding Officer of the Senate as purporting to contain electoral votes from the State of Vermont.

Mr. Representative KASSON. I object to the reception of the package.

Mr. Representative SPRINGER. I offer the following resolution——

The PRESIDING OFFICER. The Chair stated that he had received but one set of certificates from the State of Vermont. He also states that the law prohibits him from receiving any after the first Thursday in February. His duty is to receive and open and have read all certificates that have been received by him up to and on that day.

Mr. Representative SPRINGER. I understand that a third certificate or return from the State of Florida was received on the 30th day of January, and was laid before the two Houses by the Presiding Officer of the Senate when that State was reached.

Mr. Representative KASSON. This is in the nature of debate, and I must object.

The PRESIDING OFFICER. The 30th of January is not the first Thursday in February. The Chair now asks if there are any objections to the certificate from the State of Vermont.

Mr. Representative SPRINGER. I submit the resolution which I send up——

Mr. Representative KASSON. I object.

The PRESIDING OFFICER. If it is an objection to the certificate from the State of Vermont, the Chair will entertain it; but if it is a simple resolution the Chair cannot entertain it.

Mr. Representative SPRINGER. I ask that it be read. It is in reference to "a question arising under the electoral act," which is provided for by tne fourth section of that act, to which I call the attention of the Chair:

That when the two Houses separate to decide upon an objection that may have been made to the counting of any electoral vote or votes from any State, or upon objection to a report of said Commission, *or other question arising under this act,* each Senator and Representative may speak to such objection or question ten minutes, and not oftener than once.

This is a "question arising under this act," and I offer the resolution as such, and ask that it be read at the Clerk's desk.

The PRESIDING OFFICER. The Chair again states that if the member from Illinois [Mr. Springer] submits an objection to the certificate from the State of Vermont, the Chair will entertain it; but the Chair cannot entertain a resolution.

Mr. Representative SPRINGER. I submit it as a question arising under the electoral act.

The PRESIDING OFFICER. The Chair cannot entertain it.

Mr. Representative SPRINGER. I ask that it be read.

The PRESIDING OFFICER. If the member states that it is an objection to the certificate from the State of Vermont, the Chair will direct it to be read.

Mr. Representative SPRINGER. I will read it for information. [Cries of "Object!" "Object!" and "Order!" "Order!"]

The PRESIDING OFFICER. It is out of order.

Mr. Representative SPRINGER. Gentlemen may as well hear it read, because it is a question arising under the electoral act. I ask that it be read.

The PRESIDING OFFICER. Objection is made.

Mr. Representative SPRINGER. I ask that the resolution be read as a question arising under the electoral act. The question is this——

[Renewed cries of "Order!" "Order!"]

The PRESIDING OFFICER. Objection is made.

Mr. Representative SPRINGER. That one of the two returns from the State of Vermont has not been laid before the two Houses.

The PRESIDING OFFICER. The Chair will be compelled to direct the member to be seated.

Mr. Representative SPRINGER. Mr. President, I have rights upon this floor which you cannot take away from me, rights which were given me by the people I have the honor to represent. I desire to submit a "question arising under the electoral act," and now ask that it be entertained by the Chair.

The PRESIDING OFFICER. The Chair has decided that if the member states that it is an objection to the certificate from the State of Vermont, with the signature of one Senator and one Representative, it will be read; but if not, it cannot be read.

Mr. Representative SPRINGER. It is a question arising under the electoral act. It is now in order, and I ask the decision of the Chair upon it.

The PRESIDING OFFICER. The Chair decides that he will not entertain anything except objections to the certificate.

Mr. Representative SPRINGER. I appeal from the decision of the Chair.

The PRESIDING OFFICER. The Chair cannot entertain an appeal. [Applause.] The Chair requires order.

Mr. Representative SPRINGER. I ask that the question be put on my appeal.

The PRESIDING OFFICER. The Chair cannnot entertain any appeal.

Mr. Representative SPRINGER. This objection must be read ; otherwise the count cannot be proceeded with in accordance to law. [Cries of "Order!"]

The PRESIDING OFFICER. The member from Illinois is not in order.

Mr. Representative SPRINGER. Will the Chair allow this to be stated as a question arising under the act—as an objection to the counting of the vote ?

The PRESIDING OFFICER. The Chair has stated, and will state once more, that if the gentleman presents an objection bearing the signature of a Senator and a Representative, the Chair will receive it and submit it to the joint meeting.

Mr. Representative SPRINGER. Then I will submit this as an objection to counting the vote, on the ground that another return has been sent here which has not been laid before the two Houses, and ask time to prepare the objection in due form and present it with the signature of a Senator and a Representative.

The PRESIDING OFFICER. When the member submits the paper in proper form, the Chair will then rule upon it.

Mr. Representative POPPLETON. I send up an objection——

The PRESIDING OFFICER. The Chair will rule upon one case at a time. Let order be restored and gentlemen be seated. We have all night before us. [A pause, during which Mr. SPRINGER was preparing the objection.] The member from Illinois submits an objection to the certificate from the State of Vermont. Has the member a duplicate ?

Mr. Representative SPRINGER. Not now; it will be prepared hereafter.

The PRESIDING OFFICER. The Clerk of the House will report the objection.

The Clerk of the House read as follows :

The undersigned, Senator and Members of the House of Representatives, object to the counting of the vote of the State of Vermont, for the reason that two returns, or papers purporting to be returns, of the electoral vote of said State were forwarded to the President of the Senate, and that only one of said returns has been laid before the two Houses, the President of the Senate having stated that but one return has been received by him from said State ; and a duplicate copy of one of said returns is herewith submitted for the consideration of the Senate and House of Representatives.

A. S. MERRIMON,
Senator.
W. M. SPRINGER,
A. H. HAMILTON,
Members of the House of Representatives.

The PRESIDING OFFICER. Are there further objections to the certificate of the State of Vermont ?

Mr. Representative SPRINGER. I ask that the telegram accompanying this objection be read.

The PRESIDING OFFICER. Is there objection to reading the accompanying telegram ?

SEVERAL MEMBERS objected.

Mr. Representative TOWNSEND, of New York. It will not do any hurt to read it. It is not long.

Mr. Representative SPRINGER. It is a short telegram; only about ten words.

The PRESIDING OFFICER. Is there objection?

Mr. Representative PAGE. I object. [Cries of "O, no."]

The PRESIDING OFFICER. Does the gentleman persist in his objection?

Mr. Representative PAGE. I waive the objection.

The PRESIDING OFFICER. The Chair hears no objection, and the telegram will be read.

The Clerk of the House read as follows:

BURLINGTON, VERMONT, February 28, 1877.

[Received at two o'clock and twenty-six minutes p. m.]

To S. J. RANDALL,
Speaker of the House of Representatives:

Certificate of Amos Aldrich as elector was deposited in this office December 13.

B. B. SMALLEY,
Clerk of the United States District Court for Vermont.

A SENATOR. That is not the post-office. [Laughter.]

The PRESIDING OFFICER. Are there further objections to the certificate from the State of Vermont?

Mr. Representative POPPLETON. Yes, sir. I submit the objection which I send to the desk.

The PRESIDING OFFICER. The member from Ohio submits an objection, which will be read by the Secretary of the Senate.

The Secretary of the Senate read as follows:

The undersigned, Senator and Representatives, object to the return from the State of Vermont on the grounds following, namely:

1. That Henry N. Sollace, who is certified to have been elected on the 7th of November, 1876, was at that day and for a long time before had been a postmaster of the United States, and therefore held an office of trust and profit under the United States, and could not be constitutionally appointed an elector of said State under the Constitution of the United States.

2. That the law of Vermont did not authorize the election of said Sollace to fill the vacancy alleged to have been the result of the absence of said Sollace from the college of electors.

3. It does not appear that said Sollace had resigned his office of postmaster at the date of his appointment by the college of electors.

4. That Amos Aldrich, who received the highest vote at the election on the 7th day of November, 1876, next to that cast for said Sollace, should have been allowed to have cast one of the electoral votes of the State of Vermont.

W. H. BARNUM, Connecticut,
Senator.
E. F. POPPLETON,
J. A. McMAHON,
JACOB TURNEY, Pennsylvania,
JOHN L. VANCE, Ohio,
G. G. DIBRELL, Tennessee,
FRANK H. HURD,
A. T. WALLING, Ohio,
WM. TERRY,
Representatives.

The PRESIDING OFFICER. Are there any further objections to the certificate of the State of Vermont?

Mr. Representative POPPLETON. I submit the following additional objections.

The PRESIDING OFFICER. Has the member from Ohio a duplicate?

Mr. Representative POPPLETON. I will furnish a duplicate hereafter.

The PRESIDING OFFICER. The objections will be read by the Clerk of the House of Representatives.

The Clerk of the House read as follows:

The undersigned, Senator and Members, object to the return No. 1 from the State of Vermont on the ground following, to wit:

I. That Henry N. Sollace, who is certified to have been elected on the 7th day of November, 1876, was at that day, and for a long time before had been, a postmaster of the United States, and therefore held an office of trust and profit under the United States, and could not be constitutionally appointed an elector of said State under the Constitution of the United States.

II. That the law of Vermont did not authorize the election of said Sollace to fill the vacancy alleged to have been the result of the absence of said Sollace from the college of electors.

III. It does not appear that said Sollace had resigned his office of postmaster at the date of his appointment to the college of electors, which fact is proper to be inquired of by the Commission established by law.

IV. It is proper for the said Commission to inquire and report whether Amos Aldrich, who received the highest number of votes at the election on the 7th day of November, 1876, next to that cast for said Sollace, and who is certified as an elector by certificate No. 2, is not a duly appointed elector for the State of Vermont.

W. H. BARNUM, of Connecticut,
Senator.
EARLEY F. POPPLETON, of Ohio,
JOHN A. McMAHON, of Ohio,
JACOB TURNEY, of Pennsylvania,
JOHN L. VANCE, of Ohio,
GEORGE G. DIBRELL, of Tennessee,
FRANK H. HURD, of Ohio,
ANSEL T. WALLING, of Ohio,
WILLIAM TERRY, of Virginia,
Representatives.

The PRESIDING OFFICER. Are there further objections to the certificate of the State of Vermont?

Mr. Representative SPRINGER. I ask that the duplicate return shall now be opened by the Presiding Officer and read by the tellers.

The PRESIDING OFFICER. The original certificate from the State of Vermont has been read.

Mr. Representative SPRINGER. I refer to the dual return submitted with my objections, and referred to in those objections. [Cries of "Order!"] I ask that that second return be opened and now read.

The PRESIDING OFFICER. That is not an objection.

Mr. Representative SPRINGER. That is not an objection, but it is my right to demand that it shall be read as it has been laid before the two Houses. [Cries of "Order!"] It is my right to have it read.

The PRESIDING OFFICER. Does the gentleman refer to the one corresponding with that received by messenger; that is, the one received by mail?

Mr. Representative SPRINGER. I allude to the one submitted by the gentleman from New York, [Mr. Hewitt.]

The PRESIDING OFFICER. So the Chair understood, and rules it out.

Mr. Representative SPRINGER. I ask that the Chair will now order, the State of Vermont having forwarded double returns, that those returns and the objections thereto shall now be submitted to the judgment of the Electoral Commission. [Laughter and cries of "Object!"]

The PRESIDING OFFICER. The Presiding Officer has stated that he has not received any duplicate returns from the State of Vermont.

Mr. Representative SPRINGER. They are now before the joint meeting, presented by the gentleman from New York.

The PRESIDING OFFICER. Are there further objections to the certificate from the State of Vermont? The Chair hears none.

Mr. Representative SPRINGER. Does the Chair decline to receive the return laid on the table with my objections?

The PRESIDING OFFICER. The Chair declines to receive any return from any State at this time.

Mr. WADDELL. As being *aliunde*, I suppose, Mr. President?

The PRESIDING OFFICER. In any form.

If there are no further objections to the certificate from the State of Vermont, the Senate will withdraw to its chamber to separately consider the objections already presented and read.

Mr. Representative SPRINGER. I make the point that the electoral vote of the State of Vermont now goes to the Commission, and cannot be considered separately by the two Houses. [Laughter.] O, yes; you can laugh now, but the laugh will be on the other side after a while. Let me tell gentlemen that the law which they have been so anxious to carry out heretofore is now being disregarded by them. [Laughter.]

The Senate (at seven o'clock and ten minutes p. m.) withdrew.

IN SENATE, *Wednesday, February* 28, 1877.

The Senate having returned from the joint meeting at seven o'clock and fifteen minutes p. m., the President *pro tempore* resumed the chair and caused to be read the objections submitted to the certificate from from the State of Vermont; whereupon

Mr. Senator EDMUNDS offered the following resolution; which, after debate, was adopted by a vote of yeas 47, nays 0:

Resolved, That the vote of Henry N. Sollace as an elector for the State of Vermont be counted together with the other four electoral votes of that State, the objections to the contrary notwithstanding.

On motion of Mr. Senator EDMUNDS, the Secretary was directed to notify the House of Representatives of this action and of the readiness of the Senate to meet the House to continue the count of the electoral votes.

The Senate (being advised that the House of Representatives had taken a recess) took a recess at seven o'clock and forty minutes p. m. until to-morrow at ten o'clock a. m.

IN THE HOUSE OF REPRESENTATIVES,
Wednesday, February 28, 1877.

The Senate having withdrawn from the hall of the House at seven o'clock and ten minutes p. m., the House resumed its session; and the Speaker, acting under the previous unanimous agreement of the House, directed a recess to be taken until to-morrow at ten o'clock a. m.

IN SENATE, *Thursday, March* 1, 1877.

The recess taken from the previous day having expired, the Senate resumed its session on Thursday, March 1, at ten o'clock a. m., transacting no business.

At ten o'clock and fifty minutes p. m., a message was received from the House of Representatives announcing its resolution in regard to the vote of Henry N. Sollace, claiming to be an elector for the State of Vermont;

Whereupon the Senate immediately proceeded to the hall of the House.

IN THE HOUSE OF REPRESENTATIVES,
Thursday, March 1, 1877.

The recess taken from the previous day having expired, the House of Representatives resumed its session on Thursday, March 1, at ten o'clock a. m.

Mr. Representative WOOD, of New York, rose to submit a resolution, and was recognized by the Speaker.

Mr. Representative WALLING moved a call of the House; which motion was disagreed to—yeas 68, nays 169.

Mr. Representative WALLING moved a reconsideration of the vote by which a call of the House was refused.

On motion of Mr. Representative HALE, the motion to reconsider was laid on the table—yeas 173, nays 66.

A message was received from the Senate announcing its resolution on the objection to the vote of Henry N. Sollace as elector of the State of Vermont and its readiness to meet the House to proceed with the electoral count.

Mr. Representative WOOD, of New York, submitted the following resolution:

Resolved, That the vote of Henry N. Sollace, claiming to be an elector from the State of Vermont, be not counted.

Mr. Representative POPPLETON claimed the floor as objector in the joint meeting to the vote of Sollace as an elector for Vermont.

Mr. Representative CAULFIELD claimed the floor on a question of high privilege.

The SPEAKER declined to entertain the claim of Mr. Representative Caulfield at present, as there can be but one question of privilege pending at a time.

Mr. Representative POPPLETON submitted the following:

Whereas, at a joint meeting of the two Houses on the 28th day of February, 1877, a sealed package, addressed to the President of the Senate, purporting to contain the electoral vote of the State of Vermont, was delivered to the said President of the Senate by Mr. Hewitt, a member of this House, who then stated that he received it by express about the middle of December last, and with it a letter notifying him that a similar package had been forwarded by mail to the President of the Senate; and said Hewitt being informed by the said President that no package had been received corresponding thereto, that he, Mr. Hewitt, had, previously to said joint meeting, tendered said package to said President of the Senate, who declined to receive the same, and which statement was not denied;

And whereas it also appeared by a telegram from the clerk of the district court of the United States for the district of Vermont that a duplicate of said return was deposited in that office on the 13th day of December, 1876;

And whereas objections were made pursuant to law to the certificate purporting to be the electoral vote of Vermont which had been opened by the President of the Senate in the presence of the two Houses, and said package was in terms made a part of said objection, and still remains unopened, and said objection cannot be considered until said package is opened according to law;

And whereas the said return then tendered to said President of the Senate in the presence of the two Houses was retained by him or by the Secretary of the Senate, and the said President of the Senate refused to open said sealed package in the presence of the two Houses: Therefore,

Resolved by the House of Representatives, That the refusal of the President of the Senate to open, in the presence of the Senate and House of Representatives, said sealed package, purporting to be the electoral vote of the State of Vermont, was a violation of law and of the privileges of this House, and that, until said package shall be opened pursuant to law in the presence of the two Houses of Congress, the counting of the votes cannot further proceed according to the Constitution and law now in existence for the counting of said electoral votes for President and Vice-President of the United States.

Resolved further, That the Clerk of this House inform the Senate of the adoption of the foregoing preamble and resolution, and request the Senate to meet this House in joint session, to the end that said package purporting to be a certificate of the electoral vote of Vermont be opened by the President of the Senate, and that the proceedings thereafter be held according to law.

Mr. Representative WOOD, of New York, made the point of order that the paper submitted by Mr. Representative Poppleton was not in order under the first section of the electoral act.

The SPEAKER held that, while in his opinion a grave mistake and wrong had been committed in the joint meeting of the two Houses yesterday by the refusal of the Presiding Officer to receive, even for opening and reading for information, a package which had all the surroundings of an authentic and duly-attested paper in relation to an electoral vote for the State of Vermont, he was also of opinion that there was no power in the House to reverse the decision of the Presiding Officer of the joint meeting. In his view, however, so much of the paper submitted by the member from Ohio [Mr. Poppleton] as requests the return of certain papers from the Senate, alleged in the preamble to have been taken away in an undue manner, was in order.

Mr. Representative POPPLETON thereupon modified his resolution to conform to the decision of the Chair.

The SPEAKER decided this to be the pending resolution, and the proposition of the member from New York [Mr. Wood] an amendment thereto.

Mr. Representative KNOTT submitted the following as an amendment in the nature of a substitute for the modified resolution:

Resolved, That this House require that the package tendered by the member from New York [Mr. Hewitt] to the President of the Senate in the presence of the two Houses on yesterday, and purporting to be a certificate of the electoral vote for the President and Vice-President of the United States in the State of Vermont, shall be opened by the President of the Senate in the presence of the two Houses, and if found to be such a certificate, the same shall be submitted, together with the certificate read in the presence of the two Houses, to the Electoral Commission for its judgment and decision, and that the Senate be requested to make a like order, requiring the President of the Senate to open said package in the presence of the two Houses; and until such order be made the House will not be ready to meet the Senate to proceed with the count of the electoral vote.

Mr. Representative POPPLETON accepted the proposed amendment.

The question being raised, the SPEAKER ruled that the two hours' debate authorized by the electoral law would now commence; from which ruling Mr. Representative CAULFIELD appealed; but the Speaker declined to entertain the appeal.

A scene of confusion followed, several members protesting against the action of the Speaker and others insisting that proceedings should continue according to the electoral law.

When order was restored, debate proceeded; and after two hours' debate the proposition of Mr. Representative Knott, accepted by Mr. Representative Poppleton, was rejected—yeas 116, nays 148.

The question recurring on the amendment of Mr. Representative Wood, of New York, to the original resolution submitted by Mr. Representative Poppleton,

Mr. Representative HOPKINS moved to amend the amendment by striking out all after the word "Resolved" and inserting—

That this House requires that the package tendered by the member from New York [Mr. Hewitt] to the President of the Senate in the presence of the two Houses on yesterday, and purporting to be a certificate of electoral votes for President and Vice-President of the United States in the State of Vermont, shall be opened by the President of the Senate in the presence of the two Houses; and, if found to be such a certificate, the same shall be submitted, together with the certificate read in the presence of the two Houses, to the Electoral Commission for its judgment and decision; and that the Senate be requested to make a like order requiring the President of the Senate to open said package in the presence of the two Houses.

The amendment to the amendment was rejected—yeas 115, nays 147.

Mr. Representative LANE moved to reconsider the vote rejecting the amendment to the amendment.

Mr. Representative HALE moved to lay the motion for reconsideration on the table; which was agreed to—yeas 171, nays 80.

Mr. Representative WALLING moved that the pending resolution be laid on the table.

Mr. Representative McCRARY made the point of order that under the electoral law this motion was not in order, but the main question was required to be put.

The SPEAKER overruled the point of order, on the ground that any motions which are allowed by the rules of the House, and which pertain to the main question, are in order at any period of the progress of the main question.

The question being put on the motion to lay on the table, it was decided in the negative—yeas 61, nays 167.

Mr. Representative POPPLETON moved to reconsider the vote last taken.

Mr. Representative WOOD, of New York, raised the point of order that this was a dilatory motion, and therefore not in order at this stage.

The SPEAKER overruled the point of order.

The question being taken on the motion to reconsider, it was decided in the negative—yeas 64, nays 162.

The amendment of Mr. Representative Wood, of New York, was then agreed to—yeas 208, nays 17.

Mr. Representative O'BRIEN moved to reconsider the vote last taken.

Mr. Representative GARFIELD moved to lay the motion to reconsider on the table; which was agreed to—yeas 172, nays 55.

The question recurring on the resolution submitted by Mr. Representative Poppleton, as amended by the substitute of Mr. Representative Wood, of New York, viz:

Resolved, That the vote of Henry N. Sollace, claiming to be an elector from the State of Vermont, be not counted,

Mr. Representative VANCE, of Ohio, moved to lay the resolution on the table; which motion was disagreed to—yeas 53, nays 180.

Mr. Representative MONEY moved to reconsider the vote last taken.

Mr. Representative HALE moved to lay the motion to reconsider on the table; which was agreed to—yeas 170, nays 57.

The question recurring on the original resolution as amended,

Mr. Representative WALLING asked to be excused from voting thereon.

Mr. Representative VANCE, of Ohio, moved that his colleague [Mr. Walling] be excused.

The Speaker declined to entertain the motion.

Mr. Representative WALLING appealed from the decision of the Chair.

The Speaker declined to entertain the appeal.

The resolution, as amended, was then agreed to—yeas 207, nays 26.

Mr. Representative CLARK, of Missouri, moved to reconsider the vote last taken.

Mr. Representative HALE moved that the motion to reconsider be laid on the table; which was agreed to—yeas 174, nays 59.

Mr. Representative O'BRIEN claimed the floor to submit a resolution notifying the Senate of the action of the House.

The SPEAKER stated that he had allowed a vote to be taken on every legitimate legislative motion. He had allowed the motion to reconsider to be voted on whenever made, so that the House might have an opportunity to correct any error it might have committed. The House had had an opportunity to vote on the motion to lay on the table the propositions themselves and on the motions to reconsider the votes upon those propositions. The House, having now advanced to a declaration of its judgment on the objection to counting the vote from the State of Vermont, was brought to the following paragraph of the law as its guide and its mandatory instruction:

When the two Houses have voted, they shall immediately again meet, and the Presiding Officer shall then announce the decision of the question submitted.

The Senate had notified the House of its action on the objection; the House had now reached its judgment on the objection; and it was the duty of the Chair, by the terms of the law, mandatory and ministerial, to notify the Senate to that effect; and he therefore directed the Clerk accordingly.

JOINT MEETING.

THURSDAY, *March* 1, 1877.

The Senate entered the hall of the House of Representatives at ten o'clock and fifty-five minutes p. m., in the usual manner.

The PRESIDENT *pro tempore* of the Senate took his seat as presiding officer of the joint meeting, the Speaker of the House occupying a chair on his left.

The PRESIDING OFFICER. The joint meeting of Congress resumes its session. The two Houses separately having determined on the objection to the certificate from the State of Vermont, the Secretary of the Senate will now read the resolution of the Senate.

The Secretary of the Senate read as follows:

Resolved, That the vote of Henry N. Sollace, as an elector for the State of Vermont, be counted, together with the other four electoral votes of that State, the objections to the contrary notwithstanding.

The PRESIDING OFFICER. The Clerk of the House will now read the resolution of the House.

The Clerk of the House read as follows:

Resolved, That the vote of Henry N. Sollace, claiming to be an elector from the State of Vermont, be not counted.

The PRESIDING OFFICER. The two Houses not having concurred in an affirmative vote to reject one of the votes from the State of Vermont, the whole vote of that State will be counted. The tellers will announce the vote.

Mr. Senator INGALLS, (one of the tellers.) The State of Vermont casts 5 votes for Rutherford B. Hayes, of Ohio, as President, and 5 votes for William A. Wheeler, of New York, as Vice-President.

UNDISPUTED STATES.

The PRESIDING OFFICER. Having opened the certificate received by messenger from the State of Virginia, the Chair hands the same to the tellers to be read in the presence and hearing of the two Houses. The corresponding one received by mail is also handed to the tellers.

Mr. Representative WOOD, of New York. Mr. President, I suggest that the result be announced without the full reading of the papers.

Mr. Representative LANE and others objected.

The PRESIDING OFFICER. Objection is made, and the certificate will be read in full.

The certificate having been read by Mr. Representative Cook, (one of the tellers,) and there being no objection thereto, the vote of Virginia was counted—11 votes for Samuel J. Tilden, of New York, as President, and 11 votes for Thomas A. Hendricks, of Indiana, as Vice-President.

The certificate from the State of West Virginia was next opened; and having been read by Mr. Representative Stone, (one of the tellers,) and there being no objection thereto, the vote of West Virginia was counted —5 votes for Samuel J. Tilden, of New York, as President, and 5 votes for Thomas A. Hendricks, of Indiana, as Vice-President.

WISCONSIN.

The certificate from the State of Wisconsin was next opened; and, it having been read by Mr. Senator Allison, (one of the tellers,)

The PRESIDING OFFICER. Are there any objections to the certificate from the State of Wisconsin?

Mr. Representative LYNDE. I send to the Chair an objection.

The objection was read, as follows, by the Clerk of the House:

The undersigned, Senators and Representatives, object to the counting of the vote of Daniel L. Downs as an elector for the State of Wisconsin upon the following grounds, namely:

That the said Daniel L. Downs held the office of pension surgeon and of examining surgeon for the Pension-Office, by valid appointment under the laws of the United States, prior to the 7th day of November, 1876, the day of the presidential election, and upon said day and upon the 6th day of December, 1876, at the time of his assuming to cast a vote as elector for the State of Wisconsin, and that he has continually held said office from a long period prior to the said 7th day of November, 1876, until the present time; and the undersigned therefore state that said Downs, as pension surgeon and as examining surgeon for the Pension-Office as aforesaid, held an office of trust and profit under the United States on the day of the presidential election and on the day that he voted as an elector for the State of Wisconsin, and therefore could not be constitutionally appointed an elector for the State of Wisconsin or vote as such under the Constitution of the United States.

Wherefore the undersigned aver that the said Downs was not duly appointed an elector for the said State, and that his vote cannot be constitutionally counted. And the undersigned hereto annex the evidence of the facts above stated and to be taken as a part of their objections.

W. H. BARNUM, Connecticut;
J. E. McDONALD, Indiana;
JAS. K. KELLY, Oregon;
HENRY COOPER, Tennessee;
JOHN W. JOHNSTON, Virginia;
Senators.

WM. P. LYNDE, Wisconsin;
J. F. PHILIPS, Missouri;
SAML. D. BURCHARD;
J. R. TUCKER, Virginia;
WM. M. SPRINGER;
A. V. RICE, Ohio;
JOHN L. VANCE, Ohio;
CASEY YOUNG, Tennessee;
H. D. MONEY,
Representatives.

WASHINGTON, D. C., *February* 3, 1877.

DANIEL L. DOWNS sworn and examined.

By Mr. SPARKS:

Question. Were you appointed elector in the State of Wisconsin in the last presidential election?

Answer. I was.

Q. In what district?

A. In the third congressional district.

Q. Did you sit as a member of the electoral college?

A. I did.

Q. And voted?

A. And voted.

Q. For whom were the electoral votes of Wisconsin cast?

A. For Hayes and Wheeler.

Q. You were on the ticket and were elected ?

A. Yes.

Q. Did you hold any office under the Government of the United States at the time you were appointed elector ?

A. I can only give my opinion on that point. I never understood myself as holding an office. I held the position of examining surgeon for the Pension-Office.

Q. Did you hold that position at the time you were elected ?

A. I did.

Q. Did you hold it at the time you acted and voted ?

A. I did.

Q. And hold it now ?

A. Yes, sir.

Q. How long have you held it ?

A. My recollection is that I received the appointment in 1863.

Q. And that has continued up to the present time ?

A. It has continued up to the present time.

Q. Have you your appointment with you ?

A. I have not.

Q. It was in writing ?

A. Yes, sir.

Q. By whom were you appointed ?

A. By the Commissioner of Pensions.

Q. Did you derive any profit from the position ?

A. I did. The compensation is fixed by law. In the first instance, when I was first appointed, I received nothing from the United States Government. The law was then changed so that I received $1.50 for each examination, which was paid by the applicant and was refunded to him on the first payment of his pension. The law has been since changed, so that now I have a fee which is paid by the Government of the United States.

Q. How much from each applicant ?

A. Two dollars from each person referred to me for examination and examined.

Q. How many applicants do you examine a year ?

A. The biennial examination would probably amount to sixty persons. In the other odd year, there would be some fifteen or twenty examinations in the course of a year.

Q. How many examinations would that make annually ?

A. Probably an average of forty.

By Mr. BURCHARD:

Q. There is no salary connected with your position ?

A. No, sir.

Q. Nothing but a fee ?

A. A fee in each case.

Q. At first it was paid by the applicant ?

A. Yes.

Q. When was the law changed ?

A. I cannot tell you.

Q. Are you now paid on a statement of account ?

A. Yes; I render a monthly account, and return the notice of reference with my accounts to the Pension-Office.

Q. Was there any question raised as to your eligibility as a presidential elector ?

A. Not before the election ; there was after the election.

By Mr. LAWRENCE:

Q. It never was mentioned before the election ?

A. Not that I know of.

Q. How many examining surgeons are there in your county ?

A. None, besides myself.

Q. How many in the congressional district ?

A. I cannot answer; I know three or four.

By Mr. SPARKS:

Q. You say that at first the applicant paid a fee of $1.50 ?

A. Yes, sir.

Q. And that was refunded to the applicant by the Government ?

A. That was my understanding of it.

Q. So that the Government paid it.

A. Yes.

Q. When was the law changed that you got $2 for each examination ?

A. I cannot tell you the time ; my recollection is that it was about 1868 or 1870.

Q. Since then the fee has been $2 for each examination, and has been paid by the Government?
A. Yes.
Q. At what period is that paid?
A. Monthly. I make out a monthly statement of the business done by me and send it to the Pension-Office, together with the orders of reference. The Pension-Office approves of the account and returns it, and it goes to the pension agent of the district, and he pays it.

By Mr. BURCHARD:

Q. You did not suppose that you were ineligible as a presidential elector, and do not suppose it now?
A. No, sir; that was not my understanding.
Q. And no one else supposed so, to your knowledge?
A. No, sir; I understand that I was simply an employé of the Pension-Office.

By the CHAIRMAN:

Q. When did you receive your appointment?
A. My recollection is that I received it in 1868. I cannot state positively.

By Mr. BURCHARD:

Q. The examination biennially is of the same or nearly the same persons, is it not?
A. Of the same persons exactly; all persons except those who are termed permanently disabled have to be examined biennially, simply to ascertain whether a continuation of the disabilities exists.

By Mr. SPARKS:

Q. There is a list of persons whom you examine biennially?
A. Yes, sir.
Y. And then there are original applicants constantly coming in for examination?
A. Yes, sir.
Q. And you receive $2 *per capita* for each examination?
A. Yes, sir.
Q. Where is your appointment?
A. I am not positive whether I have it in my possession at home or not. I think I have.
Q. What other duties do you perform besides mere examinations?
A. Not any, except that I make a report after I make the examination. I send the certificate of each examination directly to the Pension Office, excepting the certificates of biennial examination. These go to the pension agent and duplicates to the Pension Office.
Q. Do you make any other report except those certificates?
A. No; except that I make out an account monthly of the names of the persons examined, and return them with the orders of examination in order to get my pay.
Q. You draw your pay monthly on those vouchers?
A. Yes, sir.
Q. By whom were you sworn in as examining surgeon?
A. I think I was not sworn in at all, but I would not state positively, as it is a good many years since.
Q. If it is the rule to swear in examining surgeons, you doubtless were sworn in?
A. Yes, sir; I suppose so. I have no recollection at all on the subject. I know that I never received any commission beyond simply the appointment in writing.

DEPARTMENT OF THE INTERIOR, PENSION OFFICE,
Washington, D. C., February 8, 1877.

DEAR SIR: Yours of the 6th instant, requesting the certificate of the appointment of Dr. Daniel W. Downs as pension surgeon at Richland Center, Richland County, Wisconsin, the time of his appointment, the amount of fees received by him in the years 1875 and 1876, and whether he has ever resigned, and whether he now holds and has held such position since his first appointment, was received on yesterday, but owing to the illness of the medical referee, who has charge of the papers relating to the surgeons employed by the office, I could not sooner get at the information you desired.

Dr. Daniel L. Downs, of Richland Center, Richland County, Wisconsin, was first employed by the Commissioner of Pensions to make examinations to be used in pension cases as early as May, 1863, and, excepting for the period of his service in the Army during the late rebellion, cases have been occasionally sent to him for examination all along down from that date. In 1875 he made twenty-three examinations, and in 1876 he made thirty-five examinations, receiving for his services $2 for each examination. So far as I am informed, he has never declined to make examinations which have been requested; and he is still employed to make examinations in pension cases in his neighborhood. The last order for a claimant to appear before him to be examined was made as late as the 3d instant.

The above statement does not include biennial examinations which he may have made in 1875, the number of which I cannot readily ascertain, as the certificates of such examinations are sent by the examining surgeon to the pension agent who pays the pension.

I suppose you must be in error as to the name being Daniel W., as no other surgeon at that place named Downs has ever been employed as herein stated than the Daniel L. above referred to.

Very respectfully, your obedient servant,

J. A. BENTLEY,
Commissioner of Pensions.

Hon. J. R. TUCKER,
House of Representatives.

The PRESIDING OFFICER. Are there further objections to the certificate from the State of Wisconsin ? If there be none, the Senate will now withdraw to its Chamber, that the Houses separately may consider and determine the objection.

The Senate retired at eleven o'clock and twenty-seven minutes p. m.

IN SENATE, *Thursday, March* 1, 1877.

The Senate having returned from the joint meeting, the President *pro tempore* resumed the chair at eleven o'clock and thirty minutes p. m., and caused the objection to the vote of Daniel L. Downs as an elector for the State of Wisconsin to be read, whereupon

Mr. Senator CAMERON, of Wisconsin, submitted the following resolution, which was agreed to without debate and without a division, viz :

Resolved, That the vote of Daniel L. Downs as an elector for the State of Wisconsin be counted together with the other nine electoral votes of that State, the objections made thereto to the contrary notwithstanding.

On motion of Mr. Senator CAMERON, of Wisconsin, the Secretary was directed to notify the House of Representatives of this action, and that the Senate was ready to meet the House to continue the count of the electoral vote for President and Vice-President.

A message was received from the House of Representatives at three o'clock and fifty-eight minutes a. m., (Friday, March 2,) announcing the action of the House on the objection to the vote of Daniel L. Downs as an elector from Wisconsin, and the Senate immediately proceeded to the hall of the House.

IN THE HOUSE OF REPRESENTATIVES,
Thursday, March 1, 1877.

The Senate having withdrawn from the House hall at eleven o'clock and twenty-seven minutes p. m., the House of Representatives resumed its session.

Mr. Representative MILLS claimed the floor to submit, as a question of privilege, a resolution for the immediate election of a President by the House of Representatives.

Mr. Representative LYNDE moved that the House take a recess till to-morrow (March 2) at ten o'clock.

The motion was not agreed to, yeas 99, nays 148.

A message was received from the Senate, announcing its action on the objection to the vote of Daniel L. Downs as an elector for the State of Wisconsin, and its readiness to proceed with the count.

Mr. Representative LYNDE submitted the following resolution :

Resolved, That the vote of Daniel L. Downs as an elector of the State of Wisconsin should not be counted, because he held an office of trust and profit under the United States, and therefore was not constitutionally appointed an elector by the said State of Wisconsin.

After debate,

Mr. Representative CASWELL moved to amend the resolution by striking out all after the word "Resolved" and inserting—

That the vote of D. L. Downs be counted with the other votes of the electors of the State of Wisconsin, the objections thereto notwithstanding.

After debate,

The amendment was rejected—yeas 77, nays 136.

The question recurring on the resolution of Mr. Representative Lynde, it was agreed to.

JOINT MEETING.

THURSDAY, *March* 1, 1877.

The Senate entered the hall of the House at 4 o'clock a. m. (Friday, March 2) in the usual manner.

The PRESIDENT *pro tempore* of the Senate took his seat as Presiding Officer of the joint meeting, the Speaker of the House occupying a chair on his left.

The PRESIDING OFFICER. The joint meeting of the two Houses of Congress for counting the electoral vote resumes its session. The Houses acting separately having considered and determined on the objection to the certificate from the State of Wisconsin, the Secretary of the Senate will read the resolution of the Senate.

The Secretary of the Senate read as follows:

Resolved, That the vote of Daniel L. Downs as an elector for the State of Wisconsin be counted together with the other nine electoral votes of that State, the objections made thereto to the contrary notwithstanding.

The PRESIDING OFFICER. The Clerk of the House of Representatives will read the resolution of the House.

The Clerk of the House read as follows:

Resolved, That the vote of Daniel L. Downs as an elector of the State of Wisconsin should not be counted, because he held an office of trust and profit under the United States, and therefore was not constitutionally appointed an elector by said State of Wisconsin.

The PRESIDING OFFICER. The two Houses not having concurred in an affirmative vote to reject, the vote of the State of Wisconsin will now be counted. Tellers, announce the vote of the State of Wisconsin.

Mr. Senator ALLISON, (one of the tellers.) The State of Wisconsin casts 10 votes for Rutherford B. Hayes, of Ohio, for President, and 10 votes for William A. Wheeler, of New York, for Vice-President.

THE RESULT.

The PRESIDING OFFICER, (at five minutes past four o'clock a. m., March 2, 1877.) This concludes the count of the thirty-eight States of the Union. The tellers will now ascertain and deliver the result to the President of the Senate.

Mr. Senator ALLISON (one of the tellers) read the list of votes, as follows:

List of votes for President and Vice-President of the United States for the constitutional term to commence on the 4th day of March, 1877.

Number of electoral votes to which each State is entitled.	States.	For President.		For Vice-President.	
		Rutherford B. Hayes, of Ohio.	Samuel J. Tilden, of New York.	William A. Wheeler, of New York.	Thomas A. Hendricks, of Indiana.
10	Alabama		10		10
6	Arkansas		6		6
6	California	6		6	
3	Colorado	3		3	
6	Connecticut		6		6
3	Delaware		3		3
4	Florida	4		4	
11	Georgia		11		11
21	Illinois	21		21	
15	Indiana		15		15
11	Iowa	11		11	
5	Kansas	5		5	
12	Kentucky		12		12
8	Louisiana	8		8	
7	Maine	7		7	
8	Maryland		8		8
13	Massachusetts	13		13	
11	Michigan	11		11	
5	Minnesota	5		5	
8	Mississippi		8		8
15	Missouri		15		15
3	Nebraska	3		3	
3	Nevada	3		3	
5	New Hampshire	5		5	
9	New Jersey		9		9
35	New York		35		35
10	North Carolina		10		10
22	Ohio	22		22	
3	Oregon	3		3	
29	Pennsylvania	29		29	
4	Rhode Island	4		4	
7	South Carolina	7		7	
12	Tennessee		12		12
8	Texas		8		8
5	Vermont	5		5	
11	Virginia		11		11
5	West Virginia		5		5
10	Wisconsin	10		10	
369	Total	185	184	185	184

The PRESIDING OFFICER. In announcing the final result of the electoral vote the Chair trusts that all present, whether on the floor or in the galleries, will refrain from all demonstrations whatever; that nothing shall transpire on this occasion to mar the dignity and moderation which have characterized these proceedings, in the main so reputable to the American people and worthy of the respect of the world.

The whole number of the electors appointed to vote for President and Vice-President of the United States is 369, of which a majority is 185.

The state of the vote for President of the United States, as delivered by the tellers, and as determined under the act of Congress approved January 29, 1877, on this subject, is:

For Rutherford B. Hayes, of Ohio...... .... 185 votes.
For Samuel J. Tilden, of New York............ .... 184 votes.

And the state of the vote for Vice-President of the United States, as delivered by the tellers, and as determined under the act of Congress approved January 29, 1877, on this subject, is :

For William A. Wheeler, of New York..................... 185 votes.
For Thomas A. Hendricks, of Indiana..................... 184 votes.

Wherefore, I do declare—

That Rutherford B. Hayes, of Ohio, having received a majority of the whole number of electoral votes, is duly elected President of the United States for four years, commencing on the 4th day of March, 1877.

And that William A. Wheeler, of New York, having received a majority of the whole number of electoral votes, is duly elected Vice-President of the United States for four years, commencing on the 4th day of March, 1877.

This announcement, together with the list of the votes, will be entered upon the Journals of the two Houses.

The count of the electoral vote being completed, and the result determined, the joint meeting of the two Houses is dissolved. The Senate will now retire to its chamber.

The Senate accordingly retired from the hall of the House of Representatives at ten minutes past four o'clock a. m., March 2, 1876.

ELECTORAL COMMISSION—CLOSING PROCEEDINGS.

FRIDAY, *March* 2, 1877.

The Commission met at eleven o'clock a. m., pursuant to adjournment.

Present, the President and Commissioners Miller, Strong, Field, Bradley, Morton, Frelinghuysen, Kernan, Payne, and Abbott.

The Journal of Tuesday last was read and approved.

Mr. Commissioner FRELINGHUYSEN, from the committee appointed to consider the allowances to be made to the officers and persons who had been employed in the service of the Commission, submitted a report, which was read, considered, and agreed to.

On motion of Mr. Commissioner MORTON, it was

Ordered, That the time heretofore allowed for the filing of opinions by members of the Commission be extended until the close of the month of March.

On motion of Mr. Commissioner MILLER, it was

Ordered, That 450 copies of the RECORD (after all the proceedings, including the arguments of the Commissioners, shall have been published) shall be bound with an index, under the care of the Secretary and his assistants, and distributed equally among the members of the Commission.

At the suggestion of the PRESIDENT, it was

Ordered, That the minutes of to-day's proceedings, after they shall have been prepared by the Secretary, be read by the President, and if approved by him be considered as approved by the Commission.

On motion of Mr. Commissioner PAYNE (at eleven o'clock and thirty minutes a. m.) the Commission adjourned *sine die.*

APPENDIX OF BRIEFS.

The briefs submitted to the Electoral Commission by counsel in the various cases argued before it, are as follows:

BRIEF No. 1.

SUBMITTED BY COUNSEL FOR OBJECTORS TO CERTIFICATE No. 1 IN THE CASE OF THE STATE OF FLORIDA.

Brief as to the conclusive character of lists of the Executive, presented February 3, 1877, by Ashbel Green, of counsel.

This brief is limited to the consideration of the question, how far this Commission can go behind the lists of the Executive, furnished in compliance with the provisions of the United States Revised Statutes, section 136.

It will be convenient to consider—

I. THE POWERS OF THE COMMISSION:

The act approved January 29, 1877, section 2, provides:

"That if more than one *return, or paper purporting to be a return* from a State, shall have been received by the President of the Senate, purporting to be the certificate of electoral votes given at the last preceding election for President and Vice-President in such State, (unless they shall be duplicates of the same return,) *all such returns and papers* shall be opened by him in the presence of the two Houses, when met as aforesaid, and read by the tellers; *and all such returns and papers* shall thereupon be *submitted to the judgment and decision* as to which is *the true and lawful electoral vote of such State*, of a commission constituted" by the act. It then provides, whenever objections presented in the mode pointed out in the act shall be made, that "When all such objections so made to any *certificate, vote, or paper* from a State shall have been received and read, all *such certificates, votes, and papers* so objected to, and *all papers accompanying the same*, together with such objections, shall be forthwith submitted to said commission, which shall proceed to consider the same, *with the same powers*, if any, *now possessed for that purpose by the two Houses acting separately or together,* and, by a majority of votes, *decide* whether any and what votes from such State are the votes provided for by the Constitution of the United States, and how many and what persons were duly appointed electors in such State, and *may therein take into view such petitions, depositions, and other papers*, if any, as shall, by *the Constitution and now existing* law, be competent and pertinent in such consideration."

By the terms of the act, then, the tribunal thus constituted has the same powers which are possessed by the two Houses of Congress acting *separately* or *together.*

This would lead to the consideration of the questions—

1st. Whether the Houses of Congress have any powers either together or separately?

2d. What these powers are?

Have the Houses of Congress any powers separately or acting together?

Three theories have been advanced:

a. That the power of counting or rejection of the votes resides in the President of the Senate.

b. That the two Houses, acting together, shall determine the question.

c. That the two Houses have equal power in ascertaining what votes shall be counted, and that if the two Houses disagree there can be no decision allowing the vote, and that what the two Houses do not agree to count, cannot be counted.

It would seem to be unnecessary to do more than to refer to the debates which have taken place upon the right of the President of the Senate to determine what votes should be counted. It cannot be useful to repeat the argument here; for the act constituting the commission has at least settled the question *pro hac vice,* and must be taken to have decided that the power of counting the vote is not vested in the President of the Senate. The whole theory of the bill is contrary to the idea of the right of that officer. It ignores him except so far as it constitutes him the presiding officer of the joint meeting of the Houses of Congress, grants him the incidental power as such presiding officer to preserve order, and recognizes his duty *to open* the certificates, and to hand them to the tellers appointed previously by the Senate and the tellers previously appointed by the House of Representatives.

The bill would also seem to have settled the point that the concurrence of two Houses is requisite to the counting of any disputed vote. It was adopted by both Houses for their guidance in the emergency now presented, and the necessity of their concurrence and their equal voice in arriving at the determination of the question are involved in the very fact of the passage of the act. Moreover, the act itself recognizes this right of the two Houses and the control of their concurrent action in the premises. For it reserves to the two Houses the absolute power to overrule by their action the solemn adjudication of the tribunal constituted by the act whenever "the two Houses shall, separately, concur in ordering otherwise, in which case such concurrent order shall govern."

It must, therefore, be held that the Houses of Congress have some powers in the counting of the electoral votes, and that the two Houses, acting *concurrently,* and only so acting, have the authority to admit or reject any votes which may be " opened or presented to them for action."

II. WHAT POWERS HAVE THE TWO HOUSES OF CONGRESS TO DECIDE WHETHER ANY AND WHAT VOTES SHALL BE COUNTED ?

Here, again, recourse may be had to the act of January 29, 1877. It cannot be reasonably contended that Congress is to act merely as an accountant to *add up* the numbers of the respective returns and announce the result. If this were true, its action would be paralyzed at the outset; for it would be met by double inconsistent returns, each claiming to be true, and in order to determine which was correct, the exercise of judgment and the adjudication of the question thus presented would be a prerequisite to the mere clerical act of addition and announcement of the result.

Moreover, the examination does not stop here; for it is contemplated by the act that some votes may not be counted at all, and that the whole number of electors which a State has the constitutional right to appoint, may not be appointed. The commission is expressly directed *to decide* whether *any* and *what* votes are the votes provided for by the Constitution, and how *many* and *what* persons were duly appointed electors. This authority is not limited by the clause preceding, giving the commission " the same powers, *if any,* now possessed for the purpose of considering the objections by the two Houses, acting separately or together," but is a legislative declaration, free from the saving doubt therein expressed, that there is a clear right to decide whether any and what votes are votes provided for by the Constitution, and how many and what persons were duly appointed electors.

In this connection, before proceeding to look at the Constitution, and at the laws heretofore enacted, it may be profitable to refer to the previous practice of Congress in this behalf.

I. (*a*) The question whether the State whose vote was presented was a State of the Union or not, arose in the following cases, and the votes *were counted in the alternative:*

    1.—1817, Indiana. (p. 46, House Doc. No. 13.)
    2.—1821, Missouri. (p. 51.)
    3.—1837, Michigan. (p. 72.)

(*b*) The same question arose in the following cases, and *the votes were rejected:* (p. 229.)

    1.—1865, Virginia.
    2.—1865, North Carolina.
    3.—1865, South Carolina.
    4.—1865, Georgia.
    5.—1865, Florida.
    6.—1865, Alabama.
    7.—1865, Mississippi.
    8.—1865, Louisiana.
    9.—1865, Texas.
    10.—1865, Arkansas.
    11.—1865, Tennessee.

II. The question whether a vote was valid on the facts stated in the certificate arose, and was not decided, in·one case:

    1.—Wisconsin, 1857. (p. 88.)

III. The question whether a vote, duly certified, could be rejected because the election was not valid (*i. e.*, on the ground of fraud) has been raised in one case, and the vote was counted:

    1.—1869, Louisiana. (p. 238.)

IV. All of these questions (I, II, III) arose in one case, and the vote was taken in the alternative:

    1.—1869, Georgia. (p. 244.)

V. In the cases of Mississippi, 1873, (p. 378,) and Texas, 1873, (p. 382,) two questions arose:

    1. That the vote was bad on the face of the certificate.
    2. That the certificate was defective in form.

The vote was counted.

In the case of Mississippi the first objection was overruled, on the ground of the provision of the State statute.

VI. In the case of Arkansas, 1873, (p. 389,) two questions arose:

    1. Whether the certificate was good in form.
    2. Whether it agreed with the actual returns of the election.

The Senate and House disagreeing, the vote was rejected.

VII. In the case of Louisiana, 1873, (p. 391,) there were two certificates, and seven objections were raised. Neither vote was counted.

VIII. The vote of Georgia was rejected in 1873, (p. 407,) because cast for a candidate dead at the time of election.

III. THE PROVISIONS OF THE CONSTITUTION IN THIS REGARD ARE—

ARTICLE II.

2. Each State shall appoint, in such manner as the legislature thereof may direct, a number of electors equal to the whole number of Senators and Representatives to which

the State may be entitled in the Congress; but no Senator or Representative, or person holding an office of trust or profit under the United States, shall be appointed an elector.

ARTICLE XII.

1. The electors shall meet in their respective States and vote by ballot for President and Vice-President, one of whom at least shall not be an inhabitant of the same State with themselves; they shall name in their ballots the person voted for as President, and in distinct ballots the person voted for as Vice-President; and they shall make distinct lists of all persons voted for as President and of all persons voted for as Vice-President, and of the number of votes for each, which lists they shall sign and certify, and transmit sealed to the seat of the government of the United States, directed to the President of the Senate; the President of the Senate shall, in the presence of the Senate and House of Representatives, open all the certificates, and the votes shall then be counted; the person having the greatest number of votes for President shall be President, if such a number be a majority of the whole number of electors appointed; and if no person have such majority, then from the persons having the highest numbers, not exceeding three, on the list of those voted for as President, the House of Representatives shall choose immediately, by ballot, the President. But in choosing the President, the votes shall be taken by States, the representation from each State having one vote; a quorum for this purpose shall consist of a member or members from two-thirds of the States, and a majority of all the States shall be necessary to a choice. And if the House of Representatives shall not choose a President, whenever the right of choice shall devolve upon them, before the fourth day of March next following, then the Vice-President shall act as President, as in the case of the death or other constitutional disability of the President.

2. The person having the greatest number of votes as Vice-President shall be the Vice-President, if such number be a majority of the whole number of electors appointed; and if no person have a majority, then from the two highest numbers on the list, the Senate shall choose the Vice-President; a quorum for the purpose shall consist of two-thirds of the whole number of Senators, and a majority of the whole number shall be necessary to a choice.

4. The Congress may determine the time of choosing the electors, and the day on which they shall give their votes; which day shall be the same throughout the United States.

1. The Constitution, therefore, does not prescribe the evidence of the appointment of electors. It does not require certified lists from the governor that persons claiming to have been appointed as electors have in fact been so appointed. It does not require any particular form of proof. It is wholly silent in respect to the evidence by which such an appointment is to be authenticated.

2. In delegating to the State the appointment of electors, and to the legislature of that State the authority to "direct" the "manner" in which such appointment shall be made, the Constitution seems to contemplate that the proof of the appointment should, in the first instance at least, be furnished by the State and its nature and form prescribed by the legislature of the State. "Each State," it declares, "shall appoint, in such manner as the legislature thereof may direct," the electors. It is natural that the power authorized to do an act and to determine the manner in which that act is to be done should also provide for verifying its own act and showing that it was done in the proper manner. The legislative power of the State, in directing the manner in which the act is to be done, might properly direct also the mode of proving that such manner had been followed.

In conformity to the well-established rules of proof, it would seem that the primary and best authority as to what the State had done is the State itself. Its own declarations through its legislature and judicial organs are the most weighty testimony which can be offered.

IV. The provisions of the statutes of the United States are as follows:

Sec. 136. It shall be the duty of the executive of each State to cause three lists of the names of the electors of such State to be made and certified and to be delivered o the electors on or before the day on which they are required by the preceding section to meet.

SEC. 137. The electors shall vote for President and Vice-President, respectively, in the manner directed by the Constitution.

SEC. 138. The electors shall make and sign three certificates of all the votes given by them, each of which certificates shall contain two distinct lists, one of the votes for President and the other of the votes for Vice-President, and shall annex to each of the certificates one of the lists of the electors which shall have been furnished to them by direction of the executive of the State.

The statute of 1792 provided that "It shall be the duty of the executive of each State to cause three lists of the names of the electors of such State to be made and certified, and to be delivered to the electors on or before the day on which they are required by the preceding section to meet;" and one of these lists was directed to be annexed by the electors to each certificate of their votes.

This provision, so far as the State executive is concerned, is little more than a request to the governor to make such lists; for there is probably no mode of compelling him to perform the duty. Its real effect is to provide by act of Congress convenient evidence of the appointment of the electors to be considered by the two Houses of Congress when they come to examine and count the votes. The act nowhere goes beyond that. It does not require even the seal of the State to be affixed, nor the countersigning by the secretary of the State, as in the case of a certificate of election of Senators. It does not make this evidence indispensable. It does not make this evidence conclusive. It does not make this evidence exclusive. It does not shut out other evidence. It does not limit the discretion or fetter the judgment of the authority having the power to count the votes and to decide between several sets of papers purporting to be votes, as to which are in truth genuine and valid votes.

Suppose the governor's certified list should happen to have been unattainable at the time the electors voted. Suppose that accident, disability, or death intervened, or that the governor's conscientious judgment on the case, or his willful refusal to perform his duty, deprived the electors of this evidence, are their votes to be destroyed?

Or suppose that by mistake or fraud the governor should give the certified lists in favor of persons who were not appointed electors and should withhold them from the true electors. Suppose, as was said by Senator Frelinghuysen, "a State had notoriously given its vote for one candidate, and by sheer accident the list of votes had such a heading as to give it for another?" Is there no remedy? Must the State lose its votes? Must the State submit to have its votes cast against its real will, as if by false personation made before its eyes, in the open day, but which it has no power to resist?

If it can be shown that the certificate was corruptly made, by the perpetration of gross frauds in tampering with or altering the returns, must it nevertheless flaunt its falsehood in the faces of us all without the possibility of contradiction?

The answer is that the authority commissioned to count the votes (and, in doing so, to determine what are authentic and valid votes entitled to be counted) will receive other evidence besides the governor's certificate, which evidence may prevail over that certificate, and will receive evidence impeaching the truth of that certificate for mistake or fraud. The tribunal might act on the petition of the persons claiming to have been duly appointed electors and wrongfully interfered with in the exercise of their functions; for it is not limited as to the sources of the evidence it will accept. But especially will it receive evidence from the State itself.

1. The Constitution deals expressly with the subject of authenticating the votes, (Article XII.) And it declares expressly what powers of legislation Congress "*may*" exercise with respect to action within the respective States in the choosing of electors and the casting of electoral votes, (Article II, section 4.) *Expressio unius exclusio est alterius* is a maxim, and it is very doubtful, at best, whether any other compulsory power over the States in these matters can be exercised by Congress.

2. Section 136 of the Revised Statutes was a very suitable precautionary enactment, and it ought to be obeyed. But under the view last stated it is justly subject to many observations.

(*a*) Its framers seem to have understood that it was only directory or as a recommendation, and operative only through the presumable respect of the State authorities for the wishes of Congress.

Certainly there was no power in the United States Government to compel a governor's obedience. A *mandamus* could not be employed in the case by any judicial court.

(*b*) The section does not declare that the lists referred to shall be conclusive evidence, or the only evidence, or *the* evidence, or any evidence as to the appointment of the electors; nor does it define, affirmatively, negatively, or in any way, what shall be the effect of their presence or their absence.

(*c*) If Congress chooses to go behind the governor's certificate and inquire who have been chosen electors, it is not violating the right of the States· to prescribe what shall be the evidence of the election of electors, but it is simply going behind the certificate as prescribed by an act of Congress.

The bill creates a *tribunal* which is to consider the questions and is to decide the issues presented.

1. It is to consider the returns which are double and antagonistic, with the objections of members of Congress, and which thus raise the issues.

2. It is also to *decide* the issues thus raised, and in so doing is to "take into view" *petitions*, which may supplement and fortify the claims or the objections of either of the contestants; also depositions and other papers, which are modes of proof of the facts asserted upon either hand.

a. From the character of the members of the Commission, composed of high judicial officers.

b. From the nature of its attributes and functions, viz, examination, impartiality, decision, and judgment.

c. From the methods pointed out for arriving at its decision, viz, consideration of certificates, votes, papers, objections, and taking into view petitions, depositions, and other papers, which include the most inferior means of evidence.

d. From the oath the members of the Commission are to take, viz, "I, ——, do solemnly swear (or affirm, as the case may be) that I will impartially examine and consider all questions submitted to the Commission of which I am a member, and a true judgment give thereon, agreeably to the Constitution and the laws: so help me God."

e. From the previous course of procedure by both Houses of Congress in inquiring and investigating "whether elections of electors have been conducted in certain States in accordance with the Constitution and laws of the United States and the laws of the said States, and what contests, if any, have arisen as to who were elected as electors."

f. From the language of the commission issued by both Houses of Congress to their investigating committees, to send for persons and papers, and take testimony.

These instructions were in the Senate, viz: "That the said committee be, and is hereby, instructed to inquire into the eligibility to office under the Constitution of the United States of any persons alleged to have been ineligible on the 7th day of November last, or to be ineligible as electors of President and Vice-President of the United States, to whom certificates of election have been or shall be issued by the executive authority of any State as such electors, and whether the appointment of electors, or those claiming to be such, in any of the States, has been made, declared, or returned, either by force, fraud, or other means, otherwise than in conformity with the Constitution and laws of the United States and the laws of the respective States; and whether any such appointment or action of any such elector has been in any wise unconstitutionally or unlawfully interfered with." And in the House, viz: "*Resolved*, That three special committees, one of fifteen members, to proceed to Louisiana; one of six members, to proceed to Florida; and one of nine members, to proceed to South Carolina, shall be appointed by the Speaker of the House to investigate recent elections therein, and the action of the returning or canvassing boards in the said States in reference thereto, and to report all the facts essential to an honest return of the votes received by the electors of the said States for President and Vice-President of the United States, and to a fair understanding thereof by the people, and whether the electoral votes of the said States should be counted; and that for the purpose of speedily executing this resolution, the said committee shall have power to send for persons and papers, to administer oaths, and to take testimony, and, at their discretion, to detail subcommittees, with like authority to send for persons and papers, to administer oaths, and to take testimony; and that the said committees and their subcommittees may employ stenographers, clerks, and messengers, and be attended each by a deputy sergeant-at-arms; and said committees shall have leave to report at any time by bill or otherwise."

g. From the construction already placed by the Commission upon its own powers by its Rule V, viz:

Application for process to compel *the attendance of witnesses or the production of written or documentary testimony* may be made by counsel on either side   *   *   *
Depositions taken for use before the Commission shall be sufficiently authenticated if taken before any commissioner of the circuit court of the United States, or any clerk or deputy clerk of any court of the United States.

From all this, it follows irresistibly—

1. That evidence and proof were heretofore sought for by the Houses of Congress for the purposes of arriving at a judicial determination of the issues which are now remitted for primary decision to the Commission created; and

2. That this Commission must also employ the common modes which the experience of mankind has pointed out for the purpose of arriving at the truth of any matter submitted to the determination of conscientious and intelligent persons, whether clothed with judicial or *quasi*-judicial functions or not.

These methods are knowledge and judgment.

It will not be for a moment contended that the members of this Commission have *knowledge* of the truth of the various disputed questions of fact which are raised by the returns, petitions, and objections.

They must therefore enlighten themselves, and base their judgments upon some evidence outside of themselves.

In so doing they must resort to the ordinary methods by which inquiry after truth is conducted, and must satisfy their consciences and

understandings by such proof as any other tribunal employs in seeking
the same end.

We conclude, therefore, that the Commission is limited as to the kind
of evidence it is to take into consideration by the Constitution and now
existing law, only by the petitions, depositions, and other papers as shall
be competent and pertinent in such consideration.

But it has been contended with great ability and pertinacity that the
certificates of the executive are *conclusive* evidence of the facts stated
in them, and this leads to the consideration of the question—

V. WHAT IS THE NATURE OF THE CERTIFICATES SIGNED BY THE
EXECUTIVE?

It will assist in the solution of this problem to inquire what is the
end sought to be gained by the signing, delivery, and forwarding to
the President of the Senate of these certificates. There can be but
one answer to this inquiry, viz: it is to furnish proof as to what persons the State has, in accordance with the forms of law, appointed
to vote for President and Vice-President of the United States. This
is *the fact* to be determined. There is no inherent virtue in the mode
pointed out by Congress. There is nothing which invests the certificate
with a sanctity superior to legislative and judicial acts.

The *certificate* is not the election. It is only *one* proof of the result
of the election.

The commission of the President of the United States is not an
appointment, but only *evidence* of an appointment. Marbury *vs.* Madison, (1 Cranch, 170.)

The election is the foundation, not the return. (4 Coke, Inst., 49.)

Chief-Justice Whiton, in 4 Wis., 792, commenting upon the effect of
certificates of canvassers, says:

Before proceeding to state our views in regard to the law regulating the canvass of
votes by the State canvassers, we propose to consider how far the right of a person to
an office is affected by the determination of the canvassers of the votes cast at the election held to choose the officer. Under our constitution, almost all our officers are
elected by the people. Thus the governor is chosen, the constitution providing that
the person having the highest number of votes for that office shall be elected. But
the constitution is silent as to the mode in which the election shall be conducted, and
the votes cast for governor shall be canvassed and the result of the election ascertained. The duty of prescribing the mode of conducting the election and of canvassing the votes was, therefore, devolved upon the legislature. They have accordingly
made provision for both, and *the question is whether the canvass or the election establishes
the right of a person to an office.* It seems clear that it *cannot be the former,* because by
our Constitution and laws it is expressly provided *that the election by the qualified voters
shall determine the question. To hold that the canvass shall control would subvert the foundations upon which our Government rests.* But it has been repeatedly contended in the
course of this proceeding that, although the election by the electors determines the
right to the office, yet the decision of the persons appointed to canvass the votes cast
at the election settles finally and completely the question as to the persons elected,
and that, therefore, no court can have jurisdiction to inquire into the matter. It will
be seen that this view of the question, while it recognizes the principle that the election is the *foundation* of the right to the office, assumes that the canvassers have
authority to decide the matter finally and conclusively. We do not deem it necessary
to say anything on the present occasion upon the subject of the jurisdiction of this
court, as that question has already been decided and the reasons for the decision
given. Bearing it in mind, then, that under our constitution and laws it is *the election*
to an office, and not *the canvass* of the votes, which determines the right to the office,
we will proceed to inquire into the proceedings of the State canvassers, by which they
determined that the respondent was duly elected.

The legality of the election, and the rights, powers, and duties of the officer do
not depend upon the fact of the declaration of the board of election. That declaration
is proper and is the usual practice; but withholding it or neglecting, causelessly or
illegally, to make it, will not prevent the installation in and investment with the

office. The authority, rights, and powers of such officers are derived from the election, and not from the returns, which are the usual prescribed evidences of it.—(People *vs.* Killduff, 15 Ill., 492.)

We have, therefore, no ground for our interference but the single one that the return-judges included in their enumeration returns purporting to be from three companies of volunteers, which were mere forgeries. We admit that, in the evidences before us, it appears clear to us all that those returns are forgeries, and that it was only by their inclusion in the enumeration that the defendants have obtained certificates of their election. We admit, therefore, that the evidence proves that these certificates of the election of the defendants are founded in manifest fraud, the forgery of some unknown person, but we do not find that the defendants had any hand in it, and we trust that they had not.

Can we on this account interfere and declare the certificates void ? We think not. According to our laws the election has passed completely through all its forms, the result has been in due form declared and certified, and the defendants have received their certificates of election, and are entitled to seats as members of the common council. The title-papers of their offices are complete, and have the signatures of the proper officers of the law, and if they are vitiated by any fraud or mistake in the process that has produced them, this raises a case to be tried by the forms of "a contested election" before the tribunal appointed by law to try such questions, and not by the ordinary forms of legal or equitable process before the usual tribunals. It is part of the process of political organization, and not a question of private rights, and therefore the constitution does not require that the courts shall determine its validity.

The law has appointed a 'special tribunal to try just such a question, and we can have no right to step in between the case and that tribunal and alter the return of the election-judges and annul their certificates.—(Per Lowrie, C. J.; Hulseman *vs.* Rems, 41 Penn., 396.)

The title to an elective office is derived from the people through the ballot-box. Somebody must declare the will of the electors as thus expressed. Canvassers are provided for that purpose. The certificate of a board of canvassers is evidence of the person upon whom the office has been conferred. Upon all questions arising collaterally, or between a party holding the certificate and a stranger, it is conclusive evidence; but, in a proceeding to try the right to the office, it is only *prima-facie* evidence. In such a proceeding, now regarded as a civil action, it is competent for the court to go behind the adjudication of the canvassers. The whole question is thrown open and extrinsic evidence is allowed to show which was the true state of the votes. In such an action, where the right to the office is the very thing in issue, the court will allow nothing to stand in the way between it and the ballot-box. It will put in requisition all the means within its reach to ascertain the expressed will of the electors, and will conform its judgment to such ascertained will.—(Morgan *vs.* Quackenbush, 22 Barb., 72.)

In deciding the question as to which candidate has received the greater number of votes cast by the electors for a particular office, the court and jury will go behind the canvass to ascertain the intention of the voters, and, when ascertained, will give effect to that intention by giving to each candidate the votes the voters gave him.—(People *vs.* Ferguson, 8 Cow., 102; People *vs.* Cook, 8 N. Y., 67, 83; People *vs.* Pease, 27 N. Y., 45; People *vs.* Love, 63 Barb., 535.; People *vs.* Wilson, 62 N. Y., 186; People *vs.* Vail, 20 Wend., 12.)

The *false* issue, whether a certificate has been issued, cannot be properly substituted for the *true* issue, who have been appointed electors by the State. That is *the* question, and it is only as they assist in the solution of that question that there is any power or authority in the certificates themselves. The fact to be determined is the appointment; the certificate is only the evidence, controvertible or incontrovertible, as may be provided by law. The point to be adjudged and declared is, who has received a majority of valid electoral votes, not who has received a majority of certified votes. A President is to be declared elected not by a preponderance of certificates, but by a preponderance of electoral votes. The end, therefore, to be arrived at by the signing, delivery, and forwarding of the certificates, is proof of the fact of the appointment of electors and who the electors are that have been so appointed. There is nothing in the nature of the lists of the governor which forbids in-

quiry into their verity. They are not revelations from above; they are
papers made by men, fallible always, and sometimes dishonest as well
as fallible; and, if honest, often deceived; made generally in secret and
ex parte, without hearing both sides, without oral testimony, without
cross-examination. Of such evidence it may be safely affirmed that it
is never made final and conclusive without positive law to that express
effect.

Now, it may be competent for the legislature of a State, under its own
constitution, to determine how far one of its own records shall be conclusive between *its own citizens*. It may enact that the certificate of a
judge of a court of record, of a sheriff, county commissioner, a board of
tax-assessors, or a board of State canvassers shall or shall not be open
to investigation. There is, however, no act of Congress on the subject
of the present inquiry, and we are left to the Constitution itself, with
such guide to its true interpretation as is furnished by just analogy
and by history. A President is to be declared elected for thirty-eight
States and forty-two millions of people; the declaration depends upon
the voice, we will suppose, of a single State; that voice is uttered by
her votes; to learn what those votes are, this tribunal is referred to a
certificate, and told that it cannot go behind it. In such case, to assert
that the remaining thirty-seven States are powerless to inquire into the
getting up of this certificate, on the demand of those who offer to prove
the fraud of the whole process, is to assert that we are the slaves of
fraud and cannot take our necks from the yoke.

In the absence of express enactments to the contrary, any judge may
inquire into any fact necessary to his judgment. The certificate is not
the fact to be proved, but evidence of the fact, and one kind of evidence
may be overcome by other and stronger evidence, unless some positive
law declares that the weaker shall prevail over the stronger, the false
over the true. There may be cases where, for the quieting of titles or
the ending of controversies, a record or certificate is made unanswerable; that is, though it might be truthfully answered, the law will not
allow it to be answered. Such cases are exceptional, and the burden of
establishing them rests upon him who propounds them. Let him, therefore, who asserts that the certificate of a returning-board cannot be
answered by any number of living witnesses to the contrary, show that
positive law which makes it thus unanswerable. There is certainly
nothing in the Constitution of the United States which makes it so, as
there is no act of Congress to that effect.

We may formulate the question in this manner: *Whom has the State
appointed to vote in its behalf for President?* The manner of appointment is the vote of the people, for the legislature has so directed. Who,
then, are appointed by the people? To state the question is nearly
equivalent to stating what evidence is admissible; for the question is
not who received the certificate, but who received the votes; and any
evidence showing what votes were cast and for whom is pertinent, and
must therefore be admissible, unless excluded by positive law. The
law by which this question is to be decided is not State, but Federal.
If it were otherwise, the State officers might evade the Constitution
altogether, for this ordains that the appointment shall be by the State,
and in such manner as its legislature directs; but if the State certificate
is conclusive of the fact, the State authorities may altogether refuse
obedience to the Constitution and laws, and save themselves from the
consequences by certifying that they have obeyed them. And they may
in like manner defraud us of our rights, making resistance impossible,
by certifying that they have not defrauded. Indeed, they might make

shorter work of it, and *omit the election altogether, writing the certificate in its stead.*

The nature of the question to be determined, the absence of any positive law to shut out pertinent evidence, the impolicy of such an exclusion, its injustice, and the impossibility of maintaining it, if by any fatality it were for a time established—all these considerations go to make and fortify the position that whatever body has authority to decide how a State has voted has authority to draw information from all sources of knowledge.

It has been asserted that the certificates of the executive partake of the nature of records, and it is sought to be argued therefore that they are conclusive evidence of the facts contained in them. We proceed, therefore, to consider the question:

VI. IS THE CERTIFICATE OF THE EXECUTIVE A RECORD INCAPABLE OF CONTRADICTION?

Records, in the original sense of the word, in which only it is true that they are "authentic beyond all manner of contradiction," include only "the memorials of the legislature and of the king's courts of justice."—Gilbert on Evidence, 7; Plowd., 491; Co. Litt., 260a; 4 Coke, 71a; Finch Law, 230.

These are said to be "*monumenta veritatis et vetustatis vestigia,*" as also the "treasure of the king."—Coke-Litt., 118a; 293b; 11 Edw. IV, 1, cited in Best on Evidence, 5 ed., § 128.

Outside of these two kinds of documents there are others inappropriately called records, but which derive no vigor or efficacy from their own nature, but only from some potentiality impressed upon or imputed to them by positive statutory enactment. There is nothing in the mere fact of a public instrument being engrossed in a book of records, or being uttered by a public official, even of the highest rank in political office, or in its being stamped or verified by the great seal of a sovereign State, which gives the instrument the attributes of a *record* as that word is used in the ancient books.

The proclamation of the President of the United States as to the conclusion of a treaty only derives its power from the Constitution and laws of the United States, and not because it is an official document called a record. So, too, with the other proclamations the President is authorized to issue. Rev. Stat., §§ 4067, 4079, 4228, 4230, 5300, 5301, 5317.

The copies of records, books, or papers in the Executive Departments are only evidence equally with the originals. And the instances in which such originals are evidence—plenary, sufficient, *prima facie*— are rare; and, when having such effect, only derive it from the force of positive enactment, and not from any virtue by reason of being official acts or being recorded in a public office. See Rev. Stat., §§ 862–896, inclusive; Church *vs.* Hubbart, 2 Cranch, 178; The Amiable Isabella, 6 Wheat., 1; United States *vs.* The Amistad, 15 Peters, 595.

Neither does the affixing of the great seal of the State impart to the certificate of the executive such absolute verity that the truth of its statements cannot be inquired into.

The authority of the executive of the State to certify the list of names of the persons appointed as electors rests upon the act of Congress of 1792. The form of the certificate is not prescribed, nor does the act require that it should be under seal; and the fact that the election of Senators must be certified by the executive of the State under the seal of the State, and the certificate countersigned by the secretary of state, (U. S. Stat. at L., p. 3,) is presumptive evidence that the certificate to the list of electors would be sufficient without having affixed to it the seal of State. In other words, that the seal is not necessary to give to the certificate of electors the force and effect intended to be conferred upon that paper. This being so, the fixing of the seal of State is a mere harmless superfluity, or, at furthest, is merely evidence of authenticity of *the signature* to the certificate. In the language of the Chief-Justice, in Marbury *vs.* Madison, 1 Cranch, 158: "It attests, by an act supposed to be of public notoriety, the verity of the (presidential) signature."

A modern writer has defined a record to be "a written instrument made by a public officer authorized by law to perform that function, and intended to serve *as evidence* of something written, said, or done." 2 Bouvier's Law Dic., 41, 429, citing 18 Vin. Ab., 170; 1 Kent., 260; Gresley on Evidence, 99; Coke-Litt., 260*a*; 6 Call, 78; 1 Dana, 595.

But this definition does not imply that the evidence of such records is conclusive. They are intended to serve *as* evidence, but not as the exclusive evidence, unless made so by positive enactment.

There is nothing in the nature of the certificate itself, nor in the object which it is to accomplish, which brings it within the category of records "authentic beyond contradiction."

It is a mere ministerial, not a legislative or judicial, act, issued without the exercise of discretion, founded not upon testimony of witnesses, and given without opportunity to parties interested to be heard as to its truth or falsity.

Its object is to furnish evidence, and this can be accomplished without giving to it that conclusive character which some records are supposed to possess.

VII. EVEN IF THE CERTIFICATE PARTOOK OF THE CHARACTER OF A LEGISLATIVE ACT OR OF A JUDICIAL RECORD, ITS VERITY COULD BE INQUIRED INTO.

1. *As to legislative acts:*

The question how far acts of legislatures may be inquired into has been mooted in the courts of the several States, and the power of the courts asserted to go behind statutes and explore their enactment at every stage. Clare *vs.* State of Iowa, 5 Iowa Reports; Pond *vs.* Maddox, 38 California Reports; Fowler *vs.* Pierce, 2 California, 165; Jones *vs.* Hutchinson, 43 Alabama Reports, 721; People *vs.* Mahoney, 13 Michigan Reports; Illinois Central Railroad *vs.* Wren, 43 Illinois Reports; Cooley on Constitutional Limitations, pp. 135, 177; State *vs.* McBride, 4 Mississippi Reports, 302; Furgusson *vs.* Miners' Bank, Sneed, Tennessee, 609; People *vs.* Campbell, 3 Gilman, Illinois, 466; Spangler *vs.* Jacoby, 14 Illinois, 297; Hurley *vs.* Logan, 17 Illinois, 151; Prescott *vs.* Board of Trustees, 19 Illinois, 324; Supervisors *vs.* People, 25 Illinois, 181; Skinner *vs.* Demming, 2 Indiana, 560; Board of Supervisors *vs.* Heenan, 2 Minnesota, 330; De Bow *vs.* The People, 1 Denio, 9; Bank *vs.* Sparrow, 2 Denio, 97; People *vs.* Purdy, 2 Hill, 31; same case, 4 Hill, 484; 35 New Hampshire, 579; Southwark Bank *vs.* Commonwealth, 26 Pa. State, 446; Miller *vs.* The State, 3 Ohio, 475; Fordyce *vs.* Gadman, 20 Ohio State, 1.

The enrolled act duly authenticated as the Constitution prescribes, and approved and signed by the governor, is not conclusive evidence of the terms of the bill as it passed the houses of the general assembly, but the journals of the houses or other appropriate evidence may be received to show what these terms were; and whenever it appears that the enrolled act differs from the bill as it passed, in a substantial manner, the judiciary department of the State may declare the whole act, or the part affected by the change, unconstitutional and void. (State *vs.* Platt, So. Ca. Rep., 2 Rich, N. S., 150.)

See Jones *vs.* Jones, 2 Jones, (Penn.,) 350; Crouse *vs.* Crouse, 54 Penn. State, 255.

While the motives of the legislature may not be inquired into, nor fraud in the passage of the act proved, yet the fact whether the act was passed at all or in consonance with due formality may be considered, as well as whether the engrossed or enrolled copy contains all of the act or more than the act actually passed. (Fletcher *vs.* Peck, 6 Cranch, 87.)

The Supreme Court of the United States, in Gardner *vs.* The Collector, 6 Wallace, 499, (Miller, J.,) say:

We are of opinion therefore, on principle as well as authority, that whenever a question arises in a court of law of the existence of a statute, or of the time when a statute took effect, or of the precise terms of a statute, the judges who are called upon to decide it have a right to resort to any source of information which in its nature is capable of conveying to the judicial mind a clear and satisfactory answer to such questions, always seeking first for that which in its nature is most appropriate, unless the positive law has enacted a different rule.

2. *As to judicial proceedings.* Noonan *vs.* Bradley, 12 Wall., 121; Jackson *vs.* Ludeling, 21 Wall., 631; *Ex parte* White *vs.* Tommey, 4 Ho. of Lords Cases, 313; U. S. *vs.* Gomez, 23 How., 326; U. S. *vs.* Hughes, 11 How., 566; Maxfield *vs.* Levy, 4 Dallas, 336; 2 Smith Lead. Cases, 634–636.

There are other matters of record which may be inquired into, viz:

1. Letters-patent.

Scire facias lies to repeal letters-patent where the grant is made upon a false suggestion. (4 Coke Inst., 88.)

2. Grants of land by the United States.

The great difficulty in this case consists in the admission of any testimony whatever which calls in question the validity of a warrant issued by the officer to whom that duty is assigned by law. In examining this question, the distinction between an act which is judicial and one which is merely ministerial must be regarded. The register of the land-office is not at liberty to examine testimony and exercise his own judgment respecting the right of an applicant for a military land-warrant. (Miller *vs.* Kerr, 9 Wheat., 1.)

In Brush *vs.* Ware, 15 Peters, 104, the court hold that the acts of the officer being ministerial, and not judicial, the presumption in favor of his acts, if apparently fair and legal, might be impeached by evidence.

The general doctrine is that when the law has *confided* to a special tribunal the authority to hear and determine certain matters arising in the course of its duties, the decision of that tribunal, within the scope of its authority, is conclusive upon all others. That the action of the Land-Office in issuing a patent for any of the public land, subject to sale by pre-emption or otherwise, is conclusive of the legal title, must be admitted under the principle above stated; and in all courts, and in all forms of judicial proceedings, where this title must control, either by reason of the limited powers of the court or of the essential character of the proceeding, no inquiry can be permitted into the circumstances under which it was obtained. On the other hand, there has always existed in the courts of equity the power in certain classes of cases to inquire into and correct mistakes, injustice, and wrong in both judicial and executive action, however solemn the form which the result of that action may assume, when it invades private rights; and by virtue of this power the final judgments of courts of law have been annulled or modified, and patents and other important instruments issuing from the Crown, or other executive branch of the government, have been corrected or declared void, or other relief granted. No reason is perceived why the action of the Land-Office should constitute an exception to the principle. In dealing with the public domain under the system of laws enacted by Congress for their management and sale, that *tribunal* decides upon private rights of great value, and very often, from the nature of its functions, by a proceeding essentially *ex parte* and peculiarly liable to the influence of frauds, false swearing, and mistakes. (Johnson *vs.* Towsley, 13 Wall., 83.)

3. The case of the United States *vs.* The Amistad, 15 Peters, 518, is instructive on this point. The court say:

It is argued that the ship and cargo and negroes were duly documented as belonging to Spanish subjects, and this court has no right to look behind these documents; that full faith and credit is to be given to them, and that they are to be held conclusive evidence in this cause, even although it should be established by the most satisfactory proofs that they have been obtained by the grossest frauds and impositions upon the constituted authorities of Spain. To this argument we can in no wise assent. There is nothing in the treaty which justifies or sustains the argument. We do not here meddle with the point whether there has been any connivance in this illegal traffic on the part of any of the colonial authorities or subordinate officers of Cuba; because, in our view, such an examination is unnecessary, and ought not to be pursued, unless it were indispensable to public justice, although it has been strongly pressed at the bar. What we proceed upon is this: that although public documents of the Government accompanying property found on board of the private ships of a foreign nation certainly are to be deemed *prima-facie* evidence of the facts which they propose to state, yet they are always open to be impugned for fraud; and whether that fraud be in the original obtaining of these documents or in the subsequent fraudulent and illegal use of them, when once it is satisfactorily established, it overthrows all their sanctity and destroys them as proof. *Fraud will vitiate any, even the most solemn, transaction; and an asserted title to property founded upon it is utterly void.* The very language of the ninth article of the treaty of 1795 requires the proprietor to make due and sufficient proof of his property.

And how can that proof be deemed either due or sufficient which is but a connected and stained tissue of fraud? This is not a mere rule of municipal jurisprudence. Nothing is more clear in the law of nations as an established rule to regulate their rights and duties and intercourse than the doctrine that the ship's papers are but *prima-facie* evidence, and that, if they are shown to be fraudulent, they are not to be held proof of any valid title. This rule is familiarly applied, and, indeed, is of every-day occurrence in cases of prize, in the contests between belligerents and neutrals, as is apparent from numerous cases to be found in the reports of this court; and it is just as applicable to the transactions of civil intercourse between nations in times of peace. If a private ship, clothed with Spanish papers, should enter the ports of the United States claiming the privileges and immunities and rights belonging to *bona-fide* subjects of Spain, under our treaties or laws, and she should in reality belong to the subjects of another nation, which was not entitled to any such privileges, immunities, or rights, and the proprietors were seeking by fraud to cover their own illegal acts under the flag of Spain, *there can be no doubt that it would be the duty of our courts to strip off the disguise and to look at the case according to its naked realities. In the solemn treaties between nations it can never be presumed that either state intends to provide the means of perpetrating or protecting frauds,* but all the provisions are to be construed as intended to be applied to *bona-fide* transactions.

VIII. BUT OVER AND ABOVE ALL OTHER CONSIDERATIONS REMAINS THE RULE THAT FRAUD VITIATES EVERY ACT.

The general maxims of the law: "*Dolus et fraus nemini patrocinentur,*" "*Jus et fraus nunquam cohabitant,*" "*Qui fraudem fit frustra agit,*" apply to the decisions of tribunals.

Lord Chief-Justice de Grey, in delivering the answers of the judges of the House of Lords in the *Duchess of Kingston's case,* speaking of a certain sentence of a spiritual court, says:

If it was a direct and decisive sentence upon the point, and as it stands, to be admitted as conclusive evidence upon the court and not to be impeached from within, yet, like other acts of the highest judicial authority, it is impeachable from without; although it is not permitted to show that the court was *mistaken,* it may be shown that they were *misled.*

Fraud is an extrinsic collateral act which vitiates the most solemn proceedings of courts of justice.

In such cases, as has been well expressed, the whole proceeding was "*fabula non judicium.*"

The principle applies to every species of judgments; to judgments of courts of exclusive jurisdiction; to judgments *in rem;* to judgments of foreign tribunals, and even to judgments of the House of Lords.

On an indictment for perjury, the record of the proceedings at the trial, with the finding of the jury and the judgment of the court thereon, in accordance with the evidence given by the accused, is no defense.

It is perhaps needless to add that a supposed judicial record offered in evidence may be shown to be a forgery. (Best on Evidence, § 595, citing 14 Hen. VIII, 8 *a*; 39 Hen. VI, 50, p. 15; 1 Keb., 546; 10 Co., 45 *a*; 2 Rol., 17; 3 Co., 78 *a*; the Duchess of Kingston case, 11 St. Trials, 262; Brownsword *vs.* Edwards, 2 Vez., 246; Earl of Bandon *vs.* Becher, 3 Cl. & F., 479; Harrison *vs.* Mayor of Southampton, IV De G. & M. & G., 148; Meddows Craft *vs.* Hugenin, 3 Curties, 403; *In re* Place, 8 Exch., 704; Bank of Australasia *vs.* Nias, 16 Q. B., 717; Sheddon *vs.* Patrick, 1 Macq. Ho. Lo. cases, 535; Hobart, 201; Titus Oates case, 10 How. St. Trials, 1136; Noell *vs.* Wells, 1 Sid., 359.)

In *Ex parte* White *vs.* Tommey, 4 Ho. of Lords Cases, 313, it is held that though the House of Lords cannot reverse their own judgment, they will *find* a way to protect themselves and parties from fraud, and they annulled their order granting the petition for leave to appeal.

IX. IS THIS TRIBUNAL A CANVASSING BOARD?

For the purpose of the argument, it must be conceded that a wrong exists. It is averred that the highest crimes possible under our Government have been committed, namely: The fraudulent setting aside of the will of the people constitutionally expressed, and the usurpation of the right to choose the chief magistrate of the nation.

It is a maxim recognized in the jurisprudence of every civilized community that there is no wrong without an adequate remedy.

What remedy exists for this alleged wrong?

Will *quo warranto* lie at the relation of a claimant of the presidential office against the actual incumbent?

Certainly not in any State court; no State court could enforce its judgments by ouster, even if it should entertain jurisdiction. It is not useful to inquire whether State courts might not consider the question in a collateral matter.

It is at least doubtful if the Federal courts are not equally powerless. There is no common-law jurisdiction in the Federal courts. Whatever jurisdiction the Federal courts possess to issue writs of *quo warranto* is to be found in express statutory enactment.

The only provisions in the Revised Statutes (pp. 95, 111, 318) would seem to exclude the exercise of this jurisdiction in the case now under consideration.

The doctrine that canvassing-boards " act, for the most part, ministerially only, and are not vested with judicial powers to correct errors and mistakes that may have occurred with any officer who preceded them in the performance of any duty connected with the election, or to pass upon any disputed fact which may affect the result," is founded on the reason that adequate remedy exists for the redress of a wrong, false or fraudulent return, in the courts or other tribunals erected for the trial of contested elections, or in the right of legislative bodies to judge of the election and qualifications of their own members.

Cooley on Const. Lim., 3d ed., 734, *citing—*
State *vs.* Justices of Middlesex, Coxe, 244;
Hill *vs.* Hill, 4 McCord, 277;
Wammack *vs.* Holloway, 2 Ala., 31;
State *vs.* Clerk of Passaic, 1 Dutch, 354;
Marshall *vs.* Kerns, 2 Swan, 68;
Attorney-General *vs.* Barstow, 4 Wis., 567;

Attorney-General *vs.* Ely, ib., 420;
People *vs.* Van Cleve, 1 Mich., 362;
People *vs.* Higgins, 3 Mich., 233;
Dishon *vs.* Smith, 10 Iowa, 211;
State *vs.* Johnson, 17 Ark., 407;
State *vs.* Fetter, 12 Wis., 566;
State *vs.* Avery, 14 Wis., 122;
People *vs.* Jones, 20 Cal., 50;
Newcum *vs.* Kirtley, 13 B. Monr., 515;
People *vs.* Van Slyck, 4 Cow., 297;
People *vs.* Vail, 20 Wendell, 12;
People *vs.* Seaman, 5 Denio, 409;
People *vs.* Cook, 14 Barb., 259, and 8 N. Y., 67;
People *vs.* Matteson, 17 Ill., 167;
Taylor *vs.* Taylor, 10 Minn., 107;
Calaveras County *vs.* Brockway, 30 Cal., 325;
Ex parte Ellyson, 20 Grat., 10.

Justice Christiancy, in People *vs.* Cicotte, 16 Mich., 313, expresses his views as follows:

I cannot go to the extent of holding that no inquiry is admissible in any case into the qualification of voters, or the nature of the votes given. Such a rule, I admit, would be easy of application, and, as a general rule, might not be productive of a great amount of injustice, while the multitude of distinct questions of fact in reference to the great number of voters whose qualifications may be contested is liable to lead to some embarrassment, and sometimes to protracted trials, without a more satisfactory result than would have been attained under a rule which should exclude all such inquiries. Still, I cannot avoid the conclusion that in theory and spirit our constitution and our statutes recognize as valid those votes only which are given by electors who possess the constitutional qualifications; that they recognize as valid such elections only as are effected by the votes of a majority of such qualified electors; and though the election-boards of inspectors and canvassers, acting only ministerially, are bound in their decisions by the number of votes deposited in accordance with the forms of law regulating their action, it is quite evident that illegal votes may have been admitted by the perjury or other fault of the voters, and that the majority to which the inspectors have been constrained to certify, and the canvassers to allow, has been thus wrongfully and illegally secured; and I have not been able to satisfy myself that in such a case these boards, acting thus ministerially, and often compelled to admit votes which they know to be illegal, were intended to constitute tribunals of last resort for the determination of the rights of parties claiming an election. If this were so, and there were no legal redress, I think there would be much reason to apprehend that elections would degenerate into mere contests of fraud.

The person having the greatest number of the votes of legally qualified electors it seems to me has a constitutional right to the office, and if no inquiry can be had into the qualification of any voter, here is a constitutional right depending upon a mode of trial unknown to the Constitution; and, as I am strongly inclined to think, opposed to its provisions. I doubt the competency of the legislature, should they attempt it, which I think they have not, to make the decision of the inspectors or canvassers final under our constitution.

If it be correct to say that no remedy exists for trial of the title to the Presidential office, then it follows that this tribunal must have other powers than those of a mere returning or canvassing-board, for where the reason fails the law ceases.

But it is not necessary even to concede that writ of *quo warranto* will not lie to test the right to the Presidential office. The object of the writ is to try the question of *fact*. This, we submit, is one of the purposes of this tribunal. It cannot be that the people of this country are to be kept in a state of suspense while the tedious process of a trial under *quo warranto* is to be followed. This tribunal can reach a decision more speedily and with equal efficacy, and by the same methods as a court trying the issues raised on the proceeding by *quo warranto*.

BRIEF No. 2.

SUBMITTED BY COUNSEL FOR OBJECTORS TO CERTIFICATE No. 1 IN THE CASE OF THE STATE OF FLORIDA.

1. The Constitution of the United States does not prescribe the evidence of the appointment of electors. It does not require certified lists or certificates from the governor that persons claiming to have been appointed as electors have in fact been so appointed. It does not require any particular proof of form. It is wholly silent in respect to the evidence by which such an appointment is to be authenticated.

2. In delegating to the "State" the appointment of electors, and to the legislature of that State the authority to "direct," the "manner" in which such appointment shall be made, the Constitution seems to contemplate that the proof of the appointment should in the first instance at least be furnished by the State, and its nature and form prescribed by the legislature of the State. "Each State"—it declares—"shall appoint, in such manner as the legislature thereof may direct," the electors. It is natural that the power authorized to do an act and to determine the manner in which that act is to be done, should also provide for verifying its own act and showing that it was done in the proper manner. The legislative power of the State, in directing the manner in which the act is to be done, might properly direct also the mode of proving that such manner had been followed.

The primary and best authority as to what the State has done is the State itself. Its own declarations through its legislative and judicial organs are the most weighty testimony which can be offered.

3. The statute of 1792 provided that "It shall be the duty of the executive of each State to cause three lists of the names of the electors of such State to be made and certified, and to be delivered to the electors on or before the day on which they are required, by the preceding section, to meet;" and one of these lists was directed to be annexed by the electors to each certificate of their votes.

This provision, so far as the State executive is concerned, is little more than a request to the governor to make such lists; for there is no mode of compelling him to perform the duty. (See Note D, post, p. 30.) Its real effect is to provide by act of Congress convenient evidence of the appointment of the electors to be considered by the two Houses of Congress when they come to count the votes. The act nowhere goes beyond that. It does not make this evidence indispensable. It does not make this evidence conclusive. It does not make this evidence exclusive. It does not shut out other evidence. It does not limit the discretion or fetter the judgment of the authority having the power to count the votes and to decide between several sets of papers purporting to be votes, as to which are in truth genuine and valid votes.

Suppose the governor's certified lists should happen to have been unattainable at the time the electors voted. Suppose that accident, disability or death intervened, or that the governor's conscientious judgment on the case, or his willful refusal to perform his duty, deprived the electors of this evidence—are their votes to be destroyed?

Or suppose that by mistake or fraud the governor should give the certified lists in favor of persons who were not appointed electors and should withhold them from the true electors—is there no remedy? Must the State lose its vote? Must the State submit to have its vote cast against its real will, as if by a false personation made before its eyes, in the open day, but which it has no power to resist?

The answer is that the authority commissioned to count the votes, and, in doing so, to determine what are authentic and valid votes entitled to be counted, will receive other evidence besides the governor's certified lists, which evidence may prevail over that certificate; and will receive evidence impeaching the truth of that certificate for mistake or fraud. The tribunal might act on the petition of the persons claiming to have been duly appointed electors, and wrongfully interfered with in the exercise of their functions; for it is not limited as to the sources of the evidence it will accept. But especially will it receive evidence from the State itself.

EVIDENCE OF THE APPOINTMENT OF THE TILDEN ELECTORS.

The evidence that Wilkinson Call, James E. Yonge, Robert B. Hilton, and Robert Bullock, or the Tilden electors, as we shall for convenience call them, were duly appointed by the State of Florida, in the manner the legislature of that State had directed, is complete and conclusive.

GOVERNOR'S CERTIFIED LISTS.

The only defect which can be alleged in the evidence in their favor is that the governor's certified lists specified by the act of 1792 were not furnished "*on* or *before* the day on which" they were required to meet for the purpose of casting and certifying their votes, and therefore were not at that time annexed to their statements of their votes; but that the governor's certified lists were furnished and annexed after that day.

GOVERNOR'S CERTIFIED LISTS NOT ESSENTIAL.

It has already been shown that the permanent absence of the governor's certified lists is not fatal to the validity of the vote of the electors; that this piece of evidence is not made indispensable or conclusive or exclusive, or invested with any particular force or effect, by the statute which provides it. The terms of the statute are remarkable. They do not even say that the certified lists shall be required by anybody or as a condition of anything to be done, but are a mere imposition of a "duty" upon the State executive to furnish the lists, with only the moral force of a recommendation. Language could not be chosen fitter to make the injunction fall within the class called in legal parlance directory, as contradistinguished from mandatory, the neglect of which works no invalidity in the act done, but only an omission of duty on the part of the officer who ought to have complied with the direction. And in this instance the injunction is not addressed to the electors who cast the votes or to the tribunal which counts the votes, but only to a third party to do an act for the convenience of the electors and the counting tribunal. There can be no doubt, then, that the permanent absence of the governor's certified lists would work no invalidity of the votes of the electors.

STATUTORY SPECIFICATION OF TIME FOR DELIVERY OF CERTIFIED LISTS DIRECTORY.

Still less can delay in receiving the governor's certified lists, which the electors have no legal power to obtain, but are wholly dependent on the voluntary action of the governor, or a consequent delay in annexing such lists to the electors' statement of their votes, until the day fixed for the meeting of the electors had elapsed, work an invalidity of the votes, or indeed produce any legal consequences whatever.

The reason the governor is directed to furnish his lists on or before the day the electors meet was doubtless in order that the electors might not be hindered in annexing the lists to their statements of the votes if they chose to do so on the first day of their meeting.

The first Wednesday in December is fixed by the statute for the meeting of the electors. The delivery of the statement by the electors of their votes, by messenger, to the President of the Senate, at the seat of Government, is to be made at any time before the first Wednesday in January. Thirty days are thus allowed for transmission and delivery. No doubt it would be a perfect compliance with this provision if the electors' statement of their votes were made out, and the lists of the governor obtained and annexed at any time, so that the delivery should be made within the thirty days. It is true that the statement of the votes to be forwarded by mail and the statement to be deposited with the district judge are required to be sent forthwith; but the one transmitted by the messenger would be good if the others were never received or never sent. How little the statute regards the times specified in it as of the essence of the transaction is illustrated by the provision directing that whenever neither the statement sent by messenger nor that sent by mail shall have been received at the seat of Government on the first Wednesday in January, the secretary of state shall send a messenger to the district judge, and that he shall forthwith transmit the copy deposited with him to the seat of Government.

No time is fixed by any of the statutes for the arrival at the seat of Government of the statement deposited with the district judge. No doubt if it were received at any time before it was to be used in the counting of the votes, that would be sufficient. The vote could not be objected to because it had not arrived earlier.

Taking all the statutory provisions together, they exhibit careful precautions that the votes shall be received before the count. The Tuesday after the first Monday in November—falling this year on the 7th of November—is fixed for the appointment of electors. The first Wednesday in December—falling this year on the 6th of December—is fixed for the meeting of the electors. They are required to make out three statements of the votes and to transmit one by messenger and one by mail, and to deposit the third with the district judge of the United States for the district in which the electors shall have assembled. The first Wednesday in January—falling this year on the third day of January—is fixed for the arrival of the transmitted statements at the seat of Government, which are to be received by the President of the Senate, or, in his absence, by the Secretary of State as temporary custodian. If the two transmitted statements fail of arriving before the first Wednesday in January, the Secretary of State is directed to take measures to supply the default by means of the statement deposited with the district judge; but no time is fixed for the arrival of that statement, because no subsequent act is dependent on it, and no provision is made to supply the failure of that expedient. And the second Wednesday in February—falling this year on the 14th of February—is fixed for the counting of the votes. The times fixed would be this year as follows:

Appointment of electors, November 7.

Meeting of electors, December 6.

Arrival of transmitted statement of votes, January 3.

Counting of the votes, February 14.

The specifications of the times at which or before which acts shall be done to furnish evidence to the counting tribunal as to who have been appointed electors and for whom those electors have voted, are merely directory. The times are fixed so that each act shall be done in season to enable the next step to be promptly taken, and in season to enable any failures to be remedied. These limitations of time are precautionary and remedial. They are intended to save and give effect to the votes. They are not snares to betray and destroy the votes.

The act of the governor in furnishing certified lists containing the names of the electors; the act of the electors in annexing these certified lists to the statements of their votes; their acts in making out and signing the statements of their votes; in transmitting one set by messenger and another by mail, and in depositing the third set with the judge; the act of the Secretary of State in notifying the district judge, and the act of the district judge in transmitting the set deposited with him, are each and all acts of this nature, intended to furnish evidence of the appointment and votes of the electors. The times when these acts should be done are expressly specified, except in the case of the Secretary of State. But if these acts should not have been done within the times specified, but should be done afterward in season for their object, these acts would not be void, but would be valid and effectual. Take an illustration.

The district judge, who, in the event that the other sets of statements have failed to arrive by the 1st of January, is to transmit the set deposited with him, is required to do so "forthwith."

If he have prompt notice, some six weeks would intervene before the packages could be opened for the counting. If he should happen to transmit them on the last of the six weeks instead of the first, will anybody suggest that his act would be void and the votes should not be counted?

The Constitution commands the electors to seal up their statements of their votes, and orders that the seals shall be broken only in presence of the two Houses when the votes are to be counted. To have them in the possession of the President of the Senate, ready to be opened at that time, is the object; and all the provisions fixing the times when the acts of preparation and transmission shall be successively done are intended to insure that object. They are designed for that purpose and for nothing else. There is no possible utility in having these papers in the hands of their depositaries before they can be opened and used, except to make it certain that they will be there when they are needed for use on the count.

CERTIFIED LISTS FURNISHED AFTERWARD EFFECTUAL.

Such acts of public officers, if not done within the time prescribed by law, do not thereby become incapable of being done afterward. They not only remain capable of being done, but the duty of the public officers to do them subsists in full vigor and obligation, and the right to compel their performance by the public officers accrues for the very reason that the time limited by law has passed. *Mandamus*, resorted to in innumerable instances to coerce by the mandate of judicial courts the performance by public officers of acts enjoined on them by law, begins by alleging that the time fixed by law for the doing of the acts has elapsed. It is on that very ground that the judicial power is invoked. Such is the general doctrine of our jurisprudence and the settled construction of the effect of statutes fixing the time within which official acts shall be done, adopted by courts and governments.

(See authorities cited, *post* p. 750, and note A, *post* p. 756.)

But in the present instance the same result is also established by an enabling and remedial statute enacted by a legislative power having competent jurisdiction over the subject.

CURATIVE STATUTE.

That statute of the State of Florida authorizes and directs the governor of that State to make and certify in due form and under the great seal of the State three lists of electors named in the act, and to transmit the same to the President of the Senate of the United States, and also to make and certify three other like lists and to deliver them to the said electors, who are required to meet and make out new statements of their votes cast on the 6th of December, 1876, and to annex thereto the said certified lists of the governor and the same to transmit and forward to the President of the Senate and to deliver to the district judge in the manner provided by law. And the statute further enacts that the said certified lists of the governor and statements of the votes of the electors " shall be as valid and effectual to authenticate in behalf of this State the appointment of such electors by this State as if they had been made and delivered on or before the 6th day of December, 1876, and had been transmitted immediately thereafter."

Of the competency of the legislative power of the State of Florida to pass a curative statute of this nature, and of the complete efficacy of that statute to remedy such an informality, there can be no doubt. It is simply allowing and requiring a piece of evidence to be supplied after the time within which the law required the public officers to furnish it, but before it is needed for the use intended. It is allowing an act to be done *nunc pro tunc* in furtherance of right and justice, as courts sometimes do, curing a defect of form which the law-making power has a large jurisdiction to do, and frequently and habitually does.

Not only is such a statute clearly within the power of the government of Florida, under the general authority in respect to appointing electors for the said State conferred by the Constitution of the United States, but it is in perfect harmony with the policy indicated by the Federal Government and the rights on the part of the States over this subject, which are recognized in or granted by the legislation of the Federal Government.

In addition to the precautions against, and remedies for, neglects and omissions provided by the acts of 1792 and 1804, which have been already mentioned, the statute of 1845 affords an illustration of the same policy and purpose. That act was intended to execute the power conferred on Congress by the Constitution to " determine the time of choosing the electors " by fixing a uniform day in all the States. But the first proviso, now re-enacted as section 134 of the Revised Statutes, provided for supplying vacancies happening otherwise than by non-election " which may occur in its college of electors when such college meets to give its electoral vote."

And the second proviso, substantially re-enacted as section 135 of the Revised Statutes, provided for supplying vacancies happening from non-election, as follows:

Whenever any State has held an election for the purpose of choosing electors, and has failed to make a choice on the day prescribed by law, the electors may be appointed on a subsequent day in such manner as the legislature of such State may direct.

If a State, by its legislature, may, by itself appointing, or by providing for the appointment of electors, remedy a total failure of election at the time and in the manner prescribed by act of Congress in pursuance of an express authority of the Constitution and may do so after that failure has actually happened, much more may it remedy a delay or omission of a specific piece of evidence of the appointment of electors, not in itself regarded by law as of much significance or value, and not made necessary or conclusive or exclusive, or even expressly, but only by implication, made evidence at all.

THE ILLEGAL PRIOR LISTS.

If the lists made and certified by Governor Drew under this statute would be valid and effectual in the absence of any competing documents, the existence of the prior certified lists can make no difference. Such prior lists are impeached by a statute enacted by the law-making power of the State of Florida testifying to the counting tribunal and declaring that such prior competing lists are illegal and consequently void.

That statute adduces the most absolute proof that such prior lists are false in fact; that the persons whose names are contained in them were not chosen electors according to the laws of Florida; that such persons did not receive the highest number of votes for the electoral offices at the election held on the 7th of November, 1876; that the pretended canvass of the board of State canvassers by which such persons were declared by such board to have been elected has been adjudged by the highest court of the State, after full argument and by a unanimous judgment, to be unlawful and to be in truth no canvass; that, under an enabling statute, a canvass has been conducted in the manner approved and according to the rules prescribed by the supreme court, which showed that such persons had not, but that other persons actually had, the highest number of votes for the said electoral offices at the said election.

Acting on these facts, the legislature of Florida has by statute declared, authenticated, enacted, confirmed, ratified, and renewed the appointment as electors of the said other persons who did receive the highest number of votes at such election, and who are shown by the aforesaid lawful and valid canvass to have been duly chosen. In the mean time, in an action of *quo warranto* duly brought in a court of competent jurisdiction, the said persons named in such prior and illegal certified lists, and called for convenience the Hayes electors, appeared and defended; judgment was rendered ousting the said Hayes electors and affirming the title of the four other persons, who may for convenience be designated Tilden electors.

The competing certified lists of the Hayes electors are thus effectually impeached and shown to be null and void.

The Supreme Court of the United States, speaking by Mr. Justice Story, in the Amistad case, 15 Pet., 594, said:

What we proceed upon is this, that although public documents of the government, accompanying property found on board of the private ships of a foreign nation, certainly are to be deemed *prima facie* evidence of the facts which they purport to state, yet they are always open to be impugned for fraud; and whether that fraud be in the original obtaining of these documents, or in the subsequent fraudulent and illegal use of them, when once it is satisfactorily established, it overthrows all their sanctity, and destroys them as proof. Fraud will vitiate any, even the most solemn transaction; and an asserted title to property founded upon it is utterly void.

The extent to which the courts go in the remedy of default in doing official acts within the time limited by law is illustrated by the following cases: Queen *vs.* St. Pancras, 11 Adolphus and Ellis, 15; (S. C. 39 Eng. Com. Law R., p. 38.)

Facts.—A statute required that " on the day of the annual election," fixed by the act, inspectors should be nominated by the church-wardens and the meeting, and that after such nomination the parishioners should elect vestrymen, &c.

At a meeting held May 6, which was the statute day, the church-wardens, acting as chairmen, prevented a fair choice of inspectors. A mandamus being moved for on June 6, to compel them to hold a new election, and cause shown on November 4, it was objected that the proceeding was too late.

Held, on November 21st, that the mandamus ought to issue.

Opinion of the court :

The difficulty, *or impossibility, rather,* of complying now with the act of Parliament, on account of the lapse of time, was not very strongly pressed.

For, though the election is fixed to take place in May, yet the well-known practice of this court is to set aside vicious proceedings held at the regular period, and direct others in their place afterward. *It would be too great a triumph for injustice if we should enable it to postpone forever the performance of a plain duty only because it had done wrong at the right season.*, (pp. 24, 25.)

Mayor of Rochester *vs.* The Queen, 1 Ellis, Blackburn, & Ellis, 1024.

Facts.—Objections were taken to certain voters, which were unlawfully overruled. After the time limited for holding the tribunal had expired, and its presiding officer, the mayor, had been succeeded by the plaintiff in error, a mandamus was awarded, to which the new mayor returned that he was not the mayor who rejected the objections, but was willing to obey the writ if he could lawfully hold the court. On demurrer to this return, the Queen's Bench sustained the demurrer and issued a peremptory mandamus.

Held : No error.

Opinion of the court, (Martin, B.:)

We are of opinion that the Court of Queen's Bench was right, and ought to be affirmed. It seems to us that Rex *vs.* Sparrow, 2 Strange, 1123, and Rex *vs.* Mayor of Norwich, 1 B. and Adolphus, 310, are authorities upon the point, and that the principle of those cases establishes the doctrine that the Court of Queen's Bench ought to compel the performance of a public duty by public officers, *although the time prescribed by statute for the performance of them has passed ;* and if the public officer to whom belongs the performance of that duty has in the mean time been succeeded by another, we think it is *the duty of the successor* to obey the writ and to do the acts (when required) which his predecessor has omitted to perform ; and we think *all statutes are to be read with reference to this known, acknowledged, recognized, and established power of the Court of Queen's Bench to superintend and control inferior jurisdictions and authorities of every kind.* So, reading this statute, we think it sustains the judgment of the Court of Queen's Bench *as much as if express words were found in it directing what that court has ordered.* (pp. 1031–2.)

(Cited and followed, Queen *vs.* Monmouth, Law Reports, 5 Q. B., 251.)

Ex-parte Heath, 3 Hill R., 42.

Facts.—Ward inspectors of New York City were required by statute to certify the result of the ward election *" on the day subsequent* to the closing of the polls, or sooner." A ward election was held on the 12th of April ; the result was not certified until the 14th.

Held : The return was valid notwithstanding, and a mandamus should go commanding the mayor to administer the oath to the persons returned as elected.

Opinion of the court, (pp. 46, 47 :)

The idea which we understood to be thrown out in argument, that the return from the sixth ward was void because not completed till the 14th of April instead of the 13th, is altogether inadmissible. Nothing is better settled, as a general rule, than that where a statute requires an act to be done by an officer *within a certain time* for a public purpose, the statute shall be taken to be merely directory ; and though he neglect his duty by allowing the precise time to go by, if he afterward perform it, the public shall not suffer by the delay.

This case was affirmed in the court of errors by the unanimous vote of thirty-four members out of the thirty-five constituting the court, one alone being absent.   (3 Hill, 53, *note.*)

(See Note A, *post*, p. 756.)

STATUTE OF AUTHENTICATION AND CONFIRMATION.

The statute "declaring and establishing the appointment of electors," if considered merely as a testimony of what the State of Florida has actually done in respect to the appointment of electors, is an evidence of a higher nature, of greater authority, and of more cogency than a certified list by the governor.

A statute enacted with the concurrence of the two houses of the legislature, and approved by the governor, is, in itself, a more important and weighty thing than a certificate made by the governor in a merely ministerial capacity, and at best but *quasi* official. It has attributes and incidents of a public law, and is in its nature, in the absence of any legal standard of appreciation, entitled to more consideration and credit.

The law-making power, except as limited by written constitutions, is the highest of governmental powers, it is the government itself; and, subject to such limitations, may modify the powers of the governor and direct him in their exercise.

And in respect to the appointment of electors by the State, the legislature of the State is vested by the Constitution of the United States with special and exceptional powers. It may direct the mode in which electors shall be appointed, provided they be in reality appointed by the State, through some of its proper organs. It may appoint those electors itself; and even after it has devolved that function on a popular vote may resume the power.

It creates all the machinery by which the appointment of electors by popular election is made, its powers in this respect being limited by the condition that the election shall be a reality and not a fiction; and it prescribes the whole system of authentication and proof of the persons who are chosen, except only the governor's lists. Curative powers to remedy a failure in the appointment of electors have been specially added to the general authority of the legislature or recognized as a part of that authority by the acts of Congress of 1792, 1804, and 1845. These remedial means have been applied to two classes of cases, the one of vacancies in the electoral colleges arising from every variety of cause subsequent to the original appointment, and the other vacancies occasioned by failure to elect. It is not doubted that the legislature might fill such vacancies by its own direct appointment.

The legislature representing the State stands in some sort as a principal to rectify the errors and wrongs of the subordinate agents by which the State might lose its votes, or, what is worse, be misrepresented in the votes given in its behalf. If, in its extensive and various acknowledged powers over the whole subject, no capacity could be found to prepare and submit fresh proofs of what the State has really done, to authenticate the acts of the State, to correct defects of form and give effect to the will of the State, it would be a solecism in governmental polity. Such remedies appeal to the tribunal which is to count the votes with great force, and are entitled to a benign construction.

This statute of Florida contains words of authentication, words of confirmation and ratification, and words of appointment.

If the Commission shall find, what it is not believed it will find, that there was a failure to make a choice of electors in Florida on the seventh day of last November, or an impossibility of ascertaining what that choice was, then these words of appointment in the new law of Florida must be taken as a new appointment under section 134 of the Revised Statutes of the United States, which does not limit the time within which such appointment can be made, while authorizing it to be made " on a subsequent day." It would follow that the electors appointed could meet and vote, if they had not already done so, even though it were on a later day than the first Wednesday in December, the statute of 1845 thus making an exception to the statute of 1792. But that question is not involved. The power of new appointment is a larger power than that of perfecting and validating official acts which the legislature had the right to authorize, and did authorize, but which had been imperfectly performed.

CANVASS OF THE ELECTORAL VOTES.

The first canvass of the votes cast at the election of November 7, 1876, in the State of Florida, for presidential electors as well as for Representatives in Congress, governor and other State officers, became the subject of discussion before the Supreme Court in the mandamus case brought on the relation of Drew, a candidate for governor, against McLin and others forming the board of State canvassers. Although Drew alone was relator, and the claimants for the other offices were not parties, the questions involved and the principles declared applied equally to other State officers and to the presidential electors. The board of State canvassers, in obedience to the judgment of the court in this case, made a new canvass of the votes for governor. Mr. Drew was declared elected, and entered upon, and ever since has been and is now in his office without opposition. The new canvass was applied to the lieutenant-governor, though he was not a relator, and he was declared elected and was installed.

The votes for presidential electors were likewise canvassed anew by the same board of State canvassers. In making such canvass, the directions of the Supreme Court were obeyed by them in respect to the returns from all the counties which had been the subject of special correction in the opinion pronounced by the court; but they changed the effect of these corrections, and neutralized the judgment by setting aside their own former conclusions in respect to Baker County. In respect to it, they rejected the perfect returns which they had allowed and canvassed on the former occasion, and substituted as a basis of their revision the imperfect returns which they had before rejected.

In this condition of things the old board of State canvassers went out of office and the new board came in. The legislature deeming both the canvasses of the electoral vote, so made by the former board, illegal and therefore void, passed an act to provide for a new canvass, and requiring that the canvass should be conducted according to the rules prescribed by the Supreme Court. A canvass was made accordingly and recorded and reported to the legislature. It shows that the Tilden electors received the highest number of votes, and that they were duly chosen and appointed as such electors.

THE QUO WARRANTO.

I.—In Florida, as in most other States, the local inspectors of election form the first or primary returning-board. They make returns to a county board or officer, and this second returning-board makes a return to the final or State canvassing-board. Neither the first nor the second of these bodies has any power or duty but that which is most purely and simply ministerial. They can merely compute from the documents before them, and, in their respective returns, report the result.

The State board of canvassers in Florida has authority which may be said slightly to exceed this. They have power to judge of the " *returns* " on which they act, so far as to reject them if irregular, false, or fraudulent. They have no power beyond this. They cannot investigate the qualifications of voters, or as to the employment of any force, fraud, or improper influence that might justly defeat or vitiate the ballots cast. The powers and duties of all these officers are essentially ministerial.

Outside of, or beyond this, it is the judicial power alone that can investigate and determine any question of fact.

II.—In Florida, as in most if not all the States, if a deeper investigation be necessary to justice, the judicial power must be invoked through the ancient process commonly called *quo warranto*, or through such other essentially similar judicial process as may be created by statute or established by custom in the particular State. In Florida the *quo warranto* is used.

III.—It may safely be assumed that, in fact there was no fault in the voting process. Any attempt to color a pretense of this sort by affidavit or otherwise will utterly fail from its own internal weakness. It can hardly require the employment of any evidence to overthrow it. And really, the only questions in the Florida case must arise upon an inquiry: 1st, whether the documentary title to their alleged electoral offices set up by the persons who have cast their vote for Mr. Hayes is so strong in the mere technical forms entrenching it that it cannot be gainsaid; and 2d, if that asserted title be not thus impregnable through the absolute force of its formality, whether an adequate impeachment of it is presented by the opposing documents?

IV.—The material elements of the title set up by the Hayes electors and of the impeachment presented against it may easily be stated in a brief and intelligible form, and so as to be free from dispute about matters of detail.

1. The so-called Hayes electors were reported by the State canvassing-board as duly elected. Mr. Stearns, the governor of Florida, gave them the three lists prescribed by the act of Congress (Revised Statutes of U. S., § 136), and on December 6th, 1876, being the proper day appointed for that purpose (R. S. U. S., § 149), they cast the four votes of that State for Mr. Hayes, and in the prescribed form returned their certificates thereof to the President of the Senate. Their title to their asserted offices and their action as assumed electors, conducing to give Mr. Hayes four votes for the Presidency of the United States, would be in all respects perfect, but for the fact that the report of the State canvassing-board was unlawful and untrue. It was unlawful in this, that such canvassing-board, exercising high powers of a judicial nature not granted to them, rejected certain regular, formal, and true returns duly laid before them, and by this means alone were enabled to reach a result favorable to the so-called Hayes electors. If these returns had been included in the computation made by the State-canvassers, the so-called Hayes electors could not have been returned as chosen; and on the contrary four other persons, who may be called Tilden electors, would have been so returned. Independently of the strict technical questions, 1st, whether the mere documentary title of these so-called Hayes electors can lawfully be drawn in question, and 2d, whether such asserted title

has been effectually impeached by stronger and controlling documentary evidence, the correctness of the preceding statement must be conceded.

2. On —————, 1876, and prior to the time when the so-called Hayes electors assumed to cast, and in form did cast, the electoral votes of Florida, proceedings in due form by *quo warranto* were instituted against them in the proper judicial court of that State; and such proceedings having been prosecuted against them with due diligence and all practicable speed; judgment of *ouster* was duly entered against them on —————, 1877.

3. The said four Tilden electors, acting without the triplicate lists prescribed by the act of Congress (R. S. of U. S., § 136), did on December 6, 1876, cast the four votes of Florida for Mr. Tilden as President; and, as well in that respect as in all others, acting in entire and perfect conformity with the Constitution of the United States, they certified the same votes to the President of the Senate.

They did everything toward the authentication of such votes required by the Constitution of the United States or by any act of Congress except the said section 136 of the Revised Statutes. And, in conformity with the aforesaid judgment of the Florida court, a governor of Florida, who had been duly inducted into office subsequently to December 6, 1876, did, on the —— day of ———, 1877, give to the abovementioned Tilden electors the triplicate lists prescribed by said act of Congress (R. S. of U. S., § 136), which they have forwarded as prescribed by the acts of Congress, as a supplement to their former certification in that behalf.

V.—No technical difficulties exist which can prevent the proper authorities of the Union from seeing the invalidity of the title set up by the Hayes electors.

1. It is a fundamental rule that *all* intruders into official positions may be ousted by regular judical action at law in the nature of *quo warranto.*

2. Judgment against the defendants in a *quo warranto* determines conclusively that such defendants were without title, and were usurpers holding by unlawful intrusion, as far back, at least, as the commencement of the proceedings against them. (Note B, *post,* p. 757.)

3. Acts performed by officers *de facto,* holding under color of a regular appointment, are held to be valid so far as may be necessary for the public good and to protect rights and interests acquired in good faith under the formal action of such officers; but this conservative principle, adopted from the necessity of the case, can have no application to the unlawful casting of electoral votes for Mr. Hayes now in question.

(*a.*) Balloting and certifying the votes are preliminary steps only in a process which has no perfection or efficacy until the certificates reach the proper authority at the seat of government, and are there opened and published in the presence of the two Houses.

Until this is done no act of the pretended electors is consummated or perfected. And if, before this act is done, the State of Florida, through its appropriate judicial power, ascertains and condemns the usurpation and ousts the usurpers, the conservative principle in question will not apply. It has never been held that partial and incomplete action during their usurpation by wrongful intruders into an office shall be carried onward to perfection after their *ouster* by *quo warranto.*

(*b.*) The judgment of the circuit court is not impaired or lessened in efficacy by the proceeding to review it in a higher court. At common law

the judgment of a court of original juisdiction takes full effect immediately upon its entry, and until reversed it is as effectual as if pronounced by a court of last resort.

(Note C, *post*, p. 758.)

VI.—Taking into view the action of the Tilden electors, a case of
competition is presented, and their votes should be counted instead of
those cast for Mr. Hayes.

1. The Constitution deals expressly with the subject of authenticating
the votes. (Article XII.) And it declares expressly what powers of
legislation Congress "*may*" exercise with respect to action within the
respective States in the choosing of electors and the casting of electoral
votes. (Article II, § 4.) *Expressio unius exclusio est alterius* is a maxim,
and it is very doubtful, at best, whether any other compulsory power
over the States in these matters can be exercised by Congress.

2. Section 136 of the Revised Statutes was a very suitable precautionary enactment, and it ought to be obeyed. But under the view
last stated it is justly subject to many observations.

(*a.*) Its framers seem to have understood that it was only directory
or as a recommendation, and operative only through the presumable
respect of the State authorities for the wishes of Congress.

Certainly there was no power in the United States Government to
compel a governor's obedience. A mandamus could not be employed
in the case by any judicial court.

(*b.*) The section does not declare that the lists referred to shall be
conclusive evidence, or the only evidence, or *the* evidence, or any evidence as to the appointment of the electors; nor does it define, affirmatively, negatively, or in any way, what shall be the effect of their presence
or their absence.

3. The Tilden electors, on the day prescribed by the act of Congress,
did everything required by the Constitution itself, or by any act which
Congress had authority compulsorily to prescribe to the State or any of
its officers as a duty.

VII.—Neither the omission of the State canvassers to make proper
evidence that the Tilden electors were appointed, nor the want of the
lists prescribed by the Revised Statutes of the United States, § 136, can
work any prejudice.

1. The failure of an officer to perform a duty at or within a time prescribed cannot, except in very special cases or under very peculiar
circumstances, utterly defeat the right which the law intended to secure
by enjoining such performance.

2. Of this proof may be found in the practice of the courts on application for a mandamus to compel performance of official duties.

(Note A, below.)

The time allowed for performance of the duty must always be shown
to have *elapsed* before a mandamus will be granted.

If the duty could never be performed after by any accident or misadventure the time had elapsed, the law would by an absurd technical
rigor defeat its own object.

VIII.—If there be any incurable defects in prior action, the subsequent legislation of Florida was warranted by the Revised Statutes of
the United States, § 134. A just and liberal construction, of the most
liberal kind, should be given to remedial acts of this nature.

Note A.

1. State *vs.* Judges of Bergen County Common Pleas, 2 Pennington
N. J. Law R., 541, (3 ed., p. 308.)

Facts.—A statute required that the trial justice should send the papers on appeal to the clerk of the appellate court *"on or before the first day* of the next term." The trial-justice delayed filing the return until after such first day, whereupon the appellant filed them himself during the term. The appellate court having dismissed the appeal on the ground of this omission,

Held, A mandamus should issue to compel the appellate court to receive the appeal.

Opinion of the court:

The act * * is only directory to the justice, and not conclusive on the court. The mandamus must, therefore, issue.

2. People *vs.* Dodge, 5 Howard's N. Y. Practice R. 47.

Facts.—An inferior court was required by statute to file its decision *"within twenty days* after the court at which the trial took place." In a case where the court had made a decision within, but had been prevented by accident from filing it until after the statutory time,

Held, A mandamus should go to compel the filing after the day.

3. King *vs.* Carmarthen, 1 Maule & Selwyn, 697.

Facts.—A borough charter ordained that no persons should be a burgess except freeholders having specified estates, &c., "so as such person should make application to the mayor, &c., on Monday next after Michaelmas in each year, *and at no other time,* and so as such person did *then* before the mayor so make * * * proof of his qualification; and that *upon such proof* such person should be admitted at the next or any subsequent court," &c.

The prosecutors, some fifty in number, made application on the statute day, and offered proof of their qualifications, but the whole day was consumed in other business, and the mayor, &c., refused to hold an adjourned meeting for taking the proof offered, on the ground of want of power to go beyond the day fixed by the statute.

Held, That the excluding words of the charter did not prevent the issuing of a mandamus compelling the mayor, &c., to record an adjournment and hold an adjourned meeting.

Opinion of the court, (Le Blanc, J. :)

There is no doubt that a peremptory mandamus must go. The provisions of the charter are to enable persons having a previous inchoate right to perfect that right. * * * In this case it seems that from unavoidable necessity the whole day had been exhausted; not before the claims were made, but before the evidence in support of them could be heard. Common sense shows that the charter must have meant that the corporate body should have power to adjourn in order to conclude such business as they had regularly begun; *otherwise it would have been in the power of any person, by contrivance, to protract the business and prevent the claims being effectual.* (P. 702, 703.)

Dampier, J.:

The argument on the (mayor's) side would go to show that if the corporation wrongfully refused the claims, those claims must be suspended until another year; that this case is like the case of no election, or of a colorable election, prior to the statute. But that is pushing the argument much too far. It seems to me, from the very nature of this case, to be absolutely necessary that the corporate body should have the power of adjournment, *in order to give effect to the inchoate rights of the claimants, and to guard against the possibility of their claims being frustrated by collusion.* Therefore, I am of opinion a peremptory mandamus ought to go. (P. 706.)

(See additional authorities cited, *ante,* p. 750.)

Note B.

1. High on *Quo Warranto:*

§ 748. The effect of an absolute judgment of ouster is conclusive upon the person against whom the judgment is rendered, and is a complete bar to his again asserting title to the office or franchise *by virtue of an election before the original proceedings.*

2. King *vs.* Clarke, 2 East., 75.

Facts.—After a judgment of ouster in *quo warranto* had been entered against one claiming to be an alderman duly elected and sworn, he obtained a mandamus to have himself sworn in, and was sworn. On a second *quo warranto* against him, he pleaded that he had been duly elected before the first *quo warranto* and sworn afterward. On demurrer,

Held, That the first judgment was a bar.

Lord Kenyon, C. J.:

The question is abundantly clear of all doubt. * * Upon an information exhibited against the defendant for usurping the office, * * there was judgment of ouster against him, whereby he was actually forejudged and excluded from ever using the office in future. If this were not to conclude him from insisting upon *the same election* again, I know not what would. Suppose, after this, an application had been made to the court for a mandamus to compel the corporation to proceed to a new election to fill up the vacancy, what resistance could have been made to it? And yet if the prior election could be resorted to again it could be of no avail; or there could be two persons filling one office at the same time. If the defendant could insist on the former election, he would also be entitled to a mandamus to swear him in, and thus the proceedings of the court would be utterly inconsistent. (P. 83, 84.)

3. Queen *vs.* Blizard, Law Reports, 2 Q. B., 55.

Facts.—The relator and the defendant were both of them candidates at an election. The relator had a majority of the votes if the defendant was ineligible. The defendant being in fact ineligible resigned the office. Afterward a rule for a *quo-warranto* information was moved for, and this prior resignation was relied on by the defendant to defeat the rule.

Held, That the object of the relator being to substantiate his own claim to the office arising from the election itself, the rule should be made absolute.

Opinion of the court, (Cockburn, C. J.:)

The relator not only denies the validity of the defendant's election, but claims to have been himself elected into the office. * * In order to enable the relator to take that position, it must necessarily be assumed that there never was any election of the defendant. * * * The effect of a resignation would be simply to send the parties to a new election, while *the effect of a disclaimer or judgment for the Crown* upon the final issue of the *quo warranto would be to displace the defendant* FROM THE FIRST, leaving it open—which otherwise it would not be—to the relator to claim the office. (Pp. 57, 58.) Mellor and Lush, JJ., concurred.

Note C.

1. Allen *vs.* Mayor of Savannah, 9 Georgia, 286.

Facts.—Pending an appeal from a judgment declaring a tax ordinance of a city to be unconstitutional and void, the legislature passed an act confirming all the ordinances *in operation* at its date. Afterward the court of error affirmed the original judgment.

Held, That the confirmatory act did not validate the ordinance in question.

Opinion of the court:

The pendency of the writ of error did not affect the judgment. * * It was binding until reversed, and, being affirmed, was binding *ab initio.* * * * The judgment of affirmance * * * relates back and takes effect from the date of the first judgment. (P. 294.)

2. Sage *vs.* Harpending, 49 Barb., 174.

Facts.—After a judgment in favor of a landlord that a tenancy had expired, and while an appeal therefrom was pending, the defeated tenant attempted to oust the landlord, and being repelled by force, sued the landlord for an assault.

Held, That the judgment was a good plea to the action.

Opinion of the court:

The fact that an appeal had been taken to another court did not affect the conclusive nature of the judgment as a bar while it remained unreversed. (Harris *vs.* Hammond, 18 How Pr., 124.)

3. Buzzard *vs.* Moore, 16 Indiana, 107, 109.

Opinion of the court:

The only effect of an appeal to a court of error, when perfected, is to stay execution upon the judgment from which it is taken. In all other respects the judgment, until annulled or reversed, stands binding upon the parties as to every question directly decided. (Cole *vs.* Connolly, 16 Ala., 271.) And it has been expressly decided that "It is no bar to an action on a judgment that the judgment has been removed by writ of error to a superior court." (Suydam *vs.* Hoyt, 1 Dutcher, N. J. R., 230.)

S. P. Bank of North America *vs.* Wheeler, 28 Conn., 441, 442, and cases cited.

Note D.

In this connection the following special message of Governor John Hancock to the senate and house of representatives of Massachusetts, dated November 8, 1792, calling the attention of the legislative power of that commonwealth to the mandatory character of the Federal legislation of March 1, 1792, is most suggestive:

Gentlemen of the senate and of the house of representatives:

By the Constitution of the United States of America, each State is to appoint, in such manner as the legislature shall direct, electors of President and Vice-President. By a late act of Congress it is enacted "that the supreme executive of each State SHALL cause three lists of the names of the electors of such State to be made and certified, and to be delivered to the electors on or before the first Wednesday in December."

I feel the importance of giving every constitutional support to the General Government; and I also am convinced that the existence and well being of that Government depends upon preventing a confusion of the authority of it with that of the States separately. But that Government applies itself to the people of the United States in their natural, individual capacity, and cannot exert any force upon or by any means control the officers of the State governments as such; therefore when an act of Congress uses compulsory words with regard to any act to be done by the supreme executive of this commonwealth, I shall not feel myself obliged to obey them, because I am not, in my official capacity, amenable to that Government.

My duty as governor will most certainly oblige me to see that proper and efficient certificates are made of the appointment of electors of President and Vice-President; and perhaps the mode suggested in the act above mentioned may be found to be the most proper. If you, gentlemen, have any mode to propose with respect to the conduct of this business, I shall pay every attention to it.

Gentlemen, I do not address you at this time from a disposition to regard the proceedings of the General Government with a jealous eye, nor do I suppose that Congress could intend that clause in their act as a compulsory provision; but I wish to prevent any measure to proceed through inattention which may be drawn into precedents hereafter to the injury of the people, or to give a constructive power where the Federal Constitution has not expressly given it.—*Columbian Sentinel, Nov.* 10, 1792.

[NOTE.—The language of the statute of 1792 is: "The executive authority of each State SHALL CAUSE three lists," &c. That of the Revised Statutes, § 136, is: "It shall be THE DUTY of the executive of each State *to cause* three lists," &c.]

Note E.

CURATIVE ACTS.

Thomson *vs.* Lee County, 3 Wallace, 327.

A statute submitted the question to bonding a town to a vote of the municipality. After bonds had been issued, defects in the voting were alleged, and the legislature passed a curative act legalizing the issue.

Held, That the act was valid.

Opinion of the court:

If the legislature could authorize this ratification the bonds are valid, notwithstanding the submission of the question to the vote of the people or the manner of taking the vote may have been informal and irregular. This act of confirmation, very soon after its passage, underwent an examination in the courts of Iowa, and it was held that the legislature possessed the power to pass it, and that the bonds were valid and binding. (6 Iowa, 391.) * * If the legislature possessed the power to authorize the act to be done, it could, by a retrospective act, cure the evils which existed, because the power thus conferred had been irregularly executed. (P. 331.)

St. Joseph *vs.* Rogers, 16 Wallace, 644.

Opinion of the court:

Argument to show that defective subscriptions of the kind may in all cases be ratified when the legislature could have originally conferred the power is certainly unnecessary, as the question is authoritatively settled by the decisions of the supreme court of the State (of Illinois) and of this court in repeated instances. (15 Ill., 203; 34 *ib.*, 405; 3 Wallace, 327; 9 *ib.*, 477; 8 Peters, 111; 24 How., 295.)

Mistakes and irregularities are of frequent occurrence in municipal elections, and the State legislatures have often had occasion to pass laws to obviate such difficulties. Such laws, when they do not impair any contract or injuriously affect the rights of third persons, are never regarded as objectionable, and certainly are within the competency of the legislative authority. (Pp. 663, 664.)

Cooley on Constitutional Limitations, 137:

A retrospective statute curing defects in legal proceedings where they are in their nature irregularities only, and do not extend to matters of jurisdiction, is not void on constitutional grounds, unless expressly forbidden. Of this class are the statutes to cure * * irregularities in the votes, or other action by municipal corporations, or the like, where a statutory power has failed of due and regular execution through the carelessness of officers or other cause. (1 Penn. St., 218; 17 *ib.*, 524; 26 Iowa, 497; 49 Maine, 346; 69 Penn. St., 328; 4 Vroom, 350.)

BRIEF No. 3.

SUBMITTED BY WM. C. WHITNEY, OF COUNSEL IN THE CASE OF THE STATE OF FLORIDA.

In the matter of the electoral vote of the State of Florida.—Argument and authorities in support of the validity of the vote cast by those electors whose title to their office has been established by the decision of the circuit court of Florida.

FIRST.

It is proper and relevant to the determination of the main question— What is the electoral vote of Florida?—to ascertain whether the officers of the State, in the execution and delivery of the certificates or evidences of election, have conformed to the laws of the State governing their action.

There are two classes of State officers whose combined action ordinarily contributes to the determination of the question, How has the State voted?

These are the board of State canvassers, a body which, in the discharge of ministerial and quasi-judicial functions strictly defined and limited by law, enumerates and announces the votes cast, and the Governor, who, in the discharge of a purely executive function, and in response to an invitation from the Federal Government, undertakes to certify the result transmitted by the canvassers.

That the functions of the canvassers are thus limited was determined by the supreme court of Florida in the recent gubernatorial contest of Drew *et al. vs.* Stearns *et al.*, and also with reference to a former election law (in this particular not essentially unlike the present) in the case of the State *ex rel.* Bloxham *vs.* Board of State Canvassers, 13 Fla., 55–73.

The court there says of the canvassers:

Their duties and functions are mainly ministerial, but are quasi-judicial so far as it is their duty to determine whether the papers received by them and purporting to be returns were in fact such as were genuine, intelligible, and substantially authenticated as required by law; in other words, whether they contained within themselves evidence that they were authentic returns of the election.

In this discussion it is assumed that the certificate of the governor adds no strength to the force of the announcement of the canvassers, but is a mere attestation of the result of their enumeration as declared by them.

It is also assumed that if this declaration of the canvassers was in disregard and violation of the laws governing their action, the certificate of the governor founded upon that declaration is equally contrary to the laws of the State.

In this view it is unnecessary to treat of the declarations of the canvassers and the governor separately, for they both proceed from the executive department of the government.

What, then, would be the effect of these certificates, if it can be shown that they were given in disregard and violation of the laws of Florida?

It is clear that these certificates do not themselves constitute a right to the office of elector, but can operate only as an evidence of that right.

It is by the popular expression, by the voters through the ballot-box, that a title is derived to an elective office. The certificate of the board of canvassers is mere *evidence* of the person to whom the majority of the votes was given.—*People vs. Cook*, 8 *New York*, 67–82.

And in the case of Rex *vs.* Vice-Chancellor, &c., of Cambridge, 3 Burr, 647, involving the election of Lord Hardwicke to be chancellor of the university, notwithstanding the contrary declaration of the proctors who canvassed the vote, the court said:

As to the declaration of the proctors, I think it immaterial, for the question depends not upon that, but upon the real majority of legal votes.

But if it is to be held that these certificates, which are mere evidences as to the existence of facts, are not open to question as to their truth, it is of the utmost consequence to determine whether they are certificates. If they are not made according to the laws of the State for which they assume to speak, what authority can they possess?

Would it not be a monstrous perversion of justice and law to accept as conclusive a mere form of law, an assumed instrument of legal evidence, without permitting those who allege its falsity to show that those from whom it emanated executed and delivered it in violation of law?

The certificates assume to speak in the name of the State; they emanate from the executive department of the State; they are, as we have seen, mere instruments of evidence, not judgments of courts; in the absence of any legal provision expressly giving to them a conclusive effect, they cannot defy inquiry as to the legality of the action from which they result.

Neither can it be claimed that there is any infringement upon the independence of the State transmitting the return, if the inquiry be limited, as is now proposed, simply to the question, Has the State itself given formal expression as to the legality of the assumed instrument of evidence ?

If it has so determined, that decision may properly be accepted as the voice of the State instead of the certificate, if such determination proceeds from a body possessing revisory powers over the body from which the assumed instrument of evidence emanated.

It therefore is of consequence to ascertain what the law of Florida provides as to the powers of those making these certificates, and whether these certificates result from a lawful exercise of these powers.

SECOND.

In the examination of the question whether or not the State officers have conformed to their own laws in the execution and delivery of these certificates or instruments of evidence, the decisions, if any, of the courts of the State upon the question are competent evidence.

As we have seen, the certificates emanate from the executive department of the State government; they are consequently subject to the determination of the judicial department of the State as to their validity. This is the theory upon which rests the distribution of power under our system of government.

This proposition as to the prerogative of the judicial department is not liable to the criticism that it asserts the existence of a power liable to injuriously affect the public rights. As was said in the Federalist, No. 78 : " Whoever attentively considers the different departments of power must perceive that in a government in which they are separated from each other, the judiciary, from the nature of its functions, will always be the least dangerous to the political rights of the Constitution, because it will be least in capacity to annoy or injure them."

From the beginning, our courts have held the power not only of construing statutes so as to decide what requirements they impose and what rights they confer upon those to whom they apply, but even the right to determine whether or not the legislative department has conformed to the fundamental law in making its enactments. This last right is possessed by every tribunal in the land as much as by the Supreme Court of the United States, which differs from the others only in being the court of last resort, from whose decision there is no appeal. Dana's Wheaton, eighth edition, p. 79, *n*. 1.

And so the courts have always had the authority to determine as to the lawfulness of the act of any person or officer of the Government when presented before them in an actual case, not involving the question of the exercise by any public officer of a discretionary power.

In fact, as is well said by Mr. Yearman, (*Study of Government*, p. 236:)

Both the legislative and executive departments act independently, not of each other, but of the courts, *up to the point of judicial construction regularly had.* At this point their independence, such as it properly is, does not cease, but a new rule of action is established, or rather the true rule is constitutionally ascertained and established. *A statute is held law only in the sense in which it is construed and applied by the courts.* * * *

If the foregoing observations are well founded, it results that *the office of the executive in all its ramifications is to execute the law* in such a manner as to it seems to be required by the law itself, *subject to ultmiate authoritative judicial construction.* * * * *Competent judicial construction becomes a part of the law,* or the official and authoritative light by which the law must be read and its real meaning discovered.

And so it was recognized by the United States Supreme Court, Shelby *vs.* Guy, 11 Wheat., 367, " that a fixed and received construction of their respective statute laws, (of the several States,) in their own courts, makes in fact a part of the statute law of the country."

The State thus seems to be a political community, organized and existing under a system of law by which the declaration of the courts, in matters submitted to their jurisdiction, becomes the declaration of the State itself.

Let us, then, ascertain how the State of Florida has expressed itself with reference to this question, through its judiciary.

THIRD.

A decision has been given by the circuit court of Florida to the effect that the certificate of the canvassers that the vote of the State was given for the Hayes electors is without foundation in law or fact, and also determining that the vote of the State was given for the Tilden electors.

The record has been produced, and will speak for itself.

FOURTH.

The judgment of the circuit court of Florida conclusively determines that the true electoral vote of Florida was that cast by the Tilden electors.

This proposition involves an examination of the following questions:

First. What is the effect of a judgment of a State court when presented before any other tribunal?

Second. Did the circuit court of Florida have jurisdiction of the subject-matter and parties in this proceeding?

Third. Did it render a judgment?

Fourth. What is the operation and effect of that judgment?

These questions are answered in the following discussion.

By the Constitution of the United States, Art. IV, sec. 1, it is declared that "full faith and credit shall be given in each State to the public acts, records, and judicial proceedings of every other State. And the Congress may, by general laws, prescribe the manner in which such acts, records, and proceedings shall be proved, and the effect thereof.

The act of May 26, 1790, (1 Stats. at Large, 115,) declared that—

The said records and judicial proceedings, authenticated as aforesaid, shall have such faith and credit given to them in every court within the United States as they have by law or usage in the courts of the State from whence the said records are or shall be taken.

This provision of law has been preserved and continued by section 905 of the Revised Statutes.

While the courts of the several States did not invariably, in the years immediately following the adoption of the Constitution and this act of Congress, recognize the full force of these provisions, the courts of the United States never mistook their effect. The Federal tribunals have from the first regarded as final all judgments of State courts of general jurisdiction over matters and persons within their jurisdiction, and the courts of the several States now, without exception, acquiesce in this ruling.

The earliest as well as the leading case on the subject is that of Mills *vs.* Duryee, 7 Cranch, 481, wherein the opinion of the court was delivered by Judge Story.

The learned justice says:

Were the construction contended for by the plaintiff in error to prevail, that judgments of the State courts ought to be considered *prima-facie* evidence only, this clause in the Constitution would be utterly unimportant and illusory. The common law would give precisely the same effect. It is manifest, however, that the Constitution contemplated a power in Congress to give a conclusive effect to such judgments, and we can perceive no rational interpretation of the act of Congress, unless it declares a judgment conclusive when a court of the particular State where it is rendered would pronounce the same decision.

From this decision down to that of Maxwell *vs.* Stewart, 22 Wall., 77, the Supreme Court of the United States has held to this doctrine.

There has been some discussion as to the necessity that certain preliminary questions of jurisdiction in the court rendering the judgment shall be first settled, but even as to these questions the presumption of regularity and jurisdiction is to be invoked in support of the State record.

See 2 Am. Leading Cases, 5th ed., 652; 4th ed., 797.

It is now clearly settled, according to the opinion of the court, by Mr. Chief-Justice Waite, in Maxwell *vs.* Stewart, *supra*, that—

The form of a record of a judgment is regulated by the practice of the court in which the action is prosecuted. To make such a record valid upon its face it is only necessary for it to appear that the court had jurisdiction of the subject-matter of the action and of the parties, and that a judgment had in fact been rendered. All else is form only.

In the supreme court of Connecticut, in the case of The Bank of North America *vs.* Wheeler, 28 Conn., 433–439, the court says:

In Hampton *vs.* McConnell, 3 Wheat., 234, which was declared by Chief-Justice Marshall to be precisely the same case as that of Mills *vs.* Duryee, he states that the doctrine there held was that the judgment of a State court should have the same credit, validity, and effect in every other court in the United States which it had in the State where it was pronounced, and that whatever pleas would be good to a suit thereon in such State, and none other, could be pleaded in any other court in the United States. This principle has since been universally recognized and adopted, with the exception of a single case decided by the county court of Baltimore, in which that court, as we think, misapprehending the decision in the case of McElmoyle *vs.* Cohen, 13 Pet., 312, came erroneously to a different conclusion.

Neither does this conclusive character of the judgment of a foreign tribunal, possessing jurisdiction, depend solely upon the Constitution and laws of the United States. It results from the adjudicated principles of the common law as well.

In 1862 the Court of Queen's Bench, in the case of Scott *vs.* Pelkington, 2 Best and S., 11, which was an action brought to enforce a New York judgment in England, held the judgment of the New York court having jurisdiction over the subject-matter could not be questioned in England on the ground that the foreign court had mistaken the laws of its own country, or had come, on the evidence, to an erroneous conclusion as to the facts. This conclusion was reached notwithstanding the New York judgment had been rendered on the report of a referee, which embraced conclusions of law that would not have been followed in England, and, also, notwithstanding the fact that an undetermined appeal was still pending from such judgment.

It is also decided that the acts of Congress prescribing the mode of authenticating the records of such judgment do not exclude all other evidence thereof.

See Kean *vs.* Rice, 12 S. and R., 203; Bennett *vs.* Bennett, Deady, 299–309.

In order to a determination of the effect of the judgment-record of the circuit court of Florida, it becomes necessary, therefore, to ascertain, according to the rule in Maxwell *vs.* Stewart, 27 Wall., 77—

First. Whether the court has jurisdiction:

(*a*) Of the subject-matter;

(*b*) Of the parties.

Second. Whether a judgment was in fact rendered.

These questions may be considered in their order.

First. (*a*) The court had jurisdiction of the subject-matter.

By the constitution of Florida, adopted February 25, 1868, (Bush's Digest, p. 1,) it is provided in the eighth section of the first article "that the circuit court and the judges thereof shall have power to issue writs of *quo warranto*." This provision has not been affected by the amendments. (Laws 1875, p. 49.)

By the laws of Florida (1868, p. 33; 1872, p. 28) provision has been made for the exercise and the effect of the exercise of this power by the courts. It is also provided by law (chap. 1561, sec. 2) that the circuit court may issue the writ in vacation as well as in term, and, by rule of the court, that the judge will regulate the practice. (Rule 14; 14 Fla., App. 23.)

By the decision of the supreme court of Florida, (which is hereafter shown to be binding upon the tribunals of the United States,) it was held that this grant of power to issue a writ of *quo warranto* embraces and includes the proceeding by information in the nature of a *quo warranto*. It was also held that in absence of statutory regulations as to the mode of procedure, the common-law practice was to be followed. (State *vs.* Gleason, 12 Fla., 190.)

First. (*b*) The court also had jurisdiction of the parties.

In the first place, as to the particular branch of the tribunal and the venue within which the proceedings were had.

The defendants in the proceeding were assembled at the capital of the State, Tallahassee, in the county of Leon. By the third section of the twenty-first article of the constitution of Florida the county of Leon is made part of the second circuit, of which P. W. White, before whom the proceedings were had, is judge. (15 Florida Reports, p. 3.)

In the second place, as to the persons of the defendants.

Their appearance in the proceeding would confer jurisdiction of person if the court also had jurisdiction of the subject-matter,

If, however, it be suggested that the proceeding, being instituted with relation to an official capacity or character which the defendants had assumed, and that such official capacity had been entirely exercised and exhausted before the judgment was rendered, the following answer is made:

The proposition that the office had expired or was exhausted is in no wise conceded, but is in all respects resisted, and denied to be true in fact or sound in law.

The office of elector could not determine and expire so long as any act remained to be done to express the true voice of the State. In this respect the same rule applied to the electors as was announced by the supreme court with reference to the board of canvassers, (13 Florida, 55–73:)

The object of the law is to ascertain the whole number of votes cast and who had received the highest number of such votes, so that the choice of the majority of the voters might be ascertained and respected. If the facts are correctly stated by the relator, the respondents neglected to perform this duty, and therefore did not comply with the law, in which case they did not conclude their duties as canvassers nor put an end to their powers as canvassers by an adjournment *sine die.*

There is no provision of law which determines when the office of elector shall expire, and upon principle it would seem to continue so long as anything could be done by use of the office in accomplishing the object of its creation, the expression of the real and true will of the State.

But even if the claim that the term had expired were true, the judgment of the court would not in consequence be without jurisdiction.

Mr. High, in treating of *quo warranto*, (Extraordinary Remedies,

§ 633,) observes that while under the English practice *leave to file an information* is frequently given, notwithstanding the expiration of the term of office in question, yet in this country a different rule prevails. This is not invariably the case even with reference to the first step in the proceeding, namely, the *granting of leave to file an information*, which is a matter purely in the discretion of the court. Thus, in the case of People *vs.* Tibbetts, 4 Cow., 358–381, leave was granted to file an information notwithstanding the near expiration of the term. But an examination of the cases upon which Mr. High rests his unguarded proposition shows that even they *do not* refer to the initiatory proceeding, the obtaining leave to file the information, and do not indicate the existence of different rules as to the subsequent proceedings. This is shown upon an examination of the two leading cases upon this subject, both decided in the same year, (1807,) and from which every subsequent American decision has drawn its law.

The Commonwealth *vs.* Athearn, 3 Mass., 285, was a case in which the supreme court of Massachusetts declined to grant leave to file an information as against an alleged usurper whose term would expire before judgment could be given. But, in denying the application, Chief-Justice Parsons says:

The court will be understood by this decision to have determined not that they have no authority to grant an information whenever they shall think a case exhibited to them shall require it, but only in the present case it would not be a discreet and proper exercise of their authority.

In The People *vs.* Sweeting, 2 Johns., 184, the supreme court of New York, in denying a similar application, said:

This court has a *discretion* to grant motions of this kind or to refuse them if no sufficient reasons appear for allowing this mode of proceeding.

That this was the sole effect of this decision appears from the subsequent case of The People *vs.* Tibbetts, 4 Cow., 358, 381, bottom. Here the same court granted such a motion for leave to file an information, notwithstanding the former case, which was cited and considered. They say:

Here the motion was brought before us at the term next after the election. We cannot refuse it upon the mere chance that a trial may fail. To do this would be equivalent to a refusal in all cases where the office is annual; a length to which we presume the court did not intend to go, and to which it was not necessary they should go, in The People *vs.* Sweeting. On the whole, we are clear, upon the nature of the case, as to our right of allowing the information to be filed; and that the lapse of time is not such as to require us *in the exercise of a sound discretion* to deny it.

And all the succeeding line of American authorities have arisen upon applications for leave to file informations involving an exercise of pure discretion on the part of the court, or have else been misapplications of the rule laid down in the first cases in Massachusetts and New York, upon which they assume to rest.

But while the courts may and have this discretion with reference to the granting of leave to file an information in the first instance, their discretion is entirely exhausted after that leave is granted. The trial must then proceed like any other.

Says Chief-Justice Ames, in delivering the opinion of the supreme court of Rhode Island, State *vs.* Brown, 5 R. I., 1:

When the information is filed all the discretionary power of the court is expended, and the issues of law or fact raised by the pleadings must be tried and decided under the law, and in the same manner and with the same strictness as in any other case, civil or criminal. (P. 4.)

There is no difference between the authorities of England and America as to the course to be taken after the information is filed—after the discretion of the court has been expended. The only difference has been as to the cases in which the original discretionary power should be exercised.

The circuit court of Florida had passed this point of discretion and had entered upon the actual trial of the issue as to the rights of the contending parties under the laws of Florida. What decision, therefore, was the circuit court bound to give under those laws ?

One of the statutes of Florida provides that any office in the State becomes vacant upon a decision of a competent tribunal, declaring void the election or appointment of the one occupying it, and his removal by said tribunal. (Laws of 1868, p. 34.) Another statute provides that, in the trial of an information in the nature of a *quo warranto*, the court, if requested, must pass upon the title of the claimant as well as that of the defendant. (Laws of 1872, p. 28, ch. 1874.) It is also the practice of the court that an unsuccessful defendant must pay costs.

Vide judgment in The State of Florida *vs.* Gleason, 12 Fla., 267.

The courts of other States have already determined what duties such statutes impose upon the courts administering them. Even the obligation of the defendant to pay costs is sufficient to induce and authorize, nay, to constrain the court to proceed to a determination of all the rights of the parties, with a view to the settlement of this minor and incidental question.

In the action of The People *vs.* Loomis, 8 Wend., 396, 397, the supreme court of New York, speaking by Mr. Justice Nelson, said:

> The remedy must be entirely fruitless in this case, as the term of office of the defend- ant has long ago expired. If application had been made for the *quo warranto* we should have denied it, as was done in The People *vs.* Sweeting. Although judgmen t will be unavailing and the damages, if a suggestion be made, must be very trifling, still I am of opinion we cannot suspend the judgment, as the Revised Statutes are imperative, and give to the prevailing party costs.

The same conclusion was reached by the supreme court of Michigan, in the case of The People *vs.* Hartwell, 12 Mich., 508, 522.

And Mr. High, § 633, *supra*, states that although a *quo warranto* information is concededly not to be granted merely for the purpose of vacating an office which the defendant has already resigned, " yet where the object of the proceeding is not only to cause the respondent to vacate the office, *but also to establish the title of the relator thereto, a different principle prevails.*"

It will be remembered that the Florida statute (Laws 1872, p. 33) especially provides for such a trial of the relator's right.

In illustration of this principle may be cited the recent case, (1866,) decided by the court of King's Bench, in which Lord Chief-Justice Cockburn is very careful to place his decision, not upon the prior authorities, but upon the underlying reasons which he states. (Queen *vs.* Blizard, 7 B. & S., 922.)

The question arose upon an application to make absolute a rule *nisi*, which had been previously obtained, calling upon the defendant to show by what authority he claimed to exercise the office of town councilor of Tewksbury, to which he had assumed to be elected on November 10, three weeks before the hearing. It appeared, also, that the defendant had resigned the office three days before the relator had made his first application. Nevertheless the court made absolute the rule to file the information.

The chief-justice, after saying that at first he thought the resignation avoided the possibility of the proceeding, and that he reached his conclusions independently of the authority of the cases cited by the relator, decides as follows:

If the object were merely to vacate, so that a fresh election might take place, it is obvious that the resignation of the office would effect it as well as the removal from the office by an information in the nature of a *quo warranto;* but in the present case the proceeding is instituted by a relator, who not only denies the validity of the election of the person against whom he moves, but also claims to have been elected and to be admitted into the office. * * * Now, in order to enable the relator to stand in that position and be admitted into this office, it must, as he maintains, necessarily be assumed that there was never any election of the defendant. * * * The effect of a resignation would only be to send the parties to a fresh election, whereas the effect of a disclaimer or judgment for the Crown would be to displace and oust the defendant, leaving it open, which it otherwise would not be, to the relator to claim the office.

This reasoning sustains the circuit court of Florida in proceeding to a determination of the relators' rights.

But still another principle, recognized by the courts both of England and of this country, may be invoked in support of the procedure of the circuit court, notwithstanding the assumption (the correctness of which we always controvert) that the term of office in dispute had expired before judgment. That principle results from the necessity of determining the validity of the acts of the defendants, which were of public concern and were intended to confer rights upon others.

So long ago as 1759 this principle received recognition in the case of The King *vs.* New Radnor, 2 Ld. Kenyon, 498. An information was applied for as against a defendant four years after the expiration of the aldermanic term which the defendant was charged with having usurped. It was held that leave should be granted to try a civil right, for in order to invalidate the " election of other members (chosen while the defendant was in office) it may be put in issue that he was not a legal officer; and, to prove that, it may perhaps be necessary to produce the record of his conviction, as the judge may otherwise say he appeared to have been an officer *de facto,* and the right to his office is not the issue then to be tried."

And this case was followed and approved by the supreme court of North Carolina, which held (Burton *vs.* Patton, 2 Jones's Law, 24) that an information in the nature of a *quo warranto* may be filed against public officers after the expiration of their office, where their conviction is necessary to invalidate their acts, when such acts are of public concern and are intended to confer rights upon others. The court also cites with approval the language of Littledale, J., (*Re* Harris, 6 A. and E., 475–477,) that " there have been instances in which an information issued after the office expired, where something done in the office would have affected the general administration of affairs in the borough."

Even upon the most disputed assumption that the term of the electoral office had expired, it does not seem possible to doubt that the court had jurisdiction of the parties for either one of the following purposes:

1. To award costs to the plaintiffs.
2. To establish the relators' rights with reference to the office.
3. To invalidate the acts of the defendants, which were of public concern and were intended to confer rights upon others.

And, having jurisdiction for these purposes, the court should and did examine and determine the entire question.

In any event, the court had sufficient jurisdiction of the question to determine whether, under the laws of Florida, it had jurisdiction, and its decision that it had is now conclusive and final.

This brings us, in our consideration of the conditions suggested by Chief-Justice Waite, (Maxwell *vs.* Stewart, *supra,*) to the—

Second. Whether a judgment was in fact rendered.

The profert of the record sufficiently establishes the fact of the judgment, and the cases of Bank *vs.* Wheeler, Merchants' Insurance Company *vs.* DeWolf, and Scott *vs.* Pilkington, before cited, sufficiently demonstrate that it is binding and conclusive, notwithstanding the possibility or pendency of an appeal.

But in its essential features this judgment of the circuit court is founded upon the decision of the court of last resort, the supreme court of Florida, in the *quo warranto* proceedings of Drew *et al. vs.* Stearns *et al.*, in which the gubernatorial question was settled. It was there decided, which was the turning-point of the present case, that the board of State canvassers was without judicial functions.

This decision is absolutely controlling upon the courts of the United States, not by reason of any act of Congress or any principle before cited, but upon the ground stated in the cases of Shelby *vs.* Guy, 11 Wheat., 361, and Green *vs.* Lessee of Neal, 6 Peters, 291, with reference to the decisions of the State courts upon a question arising under local law. The court say that "the decision of this question by the highest tribunal of a State should be considered as final by this court; not because the State tribunal, in such case, has any power to bind this court, but because a fixed and received construction by a State in its own courts makes a part of the statute law."

So in the case of Tioga Railroad Company *vs.* Blossburgh and Corning Railroad, 20 Wall., 137–143, Mr. Justice Bradley says, for the court, with reference to the decisions of the New York courts as to the New York statute of limitations: "These decisions upon the construction of the statute are binding upon us, whatever we may think of their soundness on general principles."

And in the very last case upon the subject, (Township of Elmwood *vs.* Macy, 2 Otto, 289–294,) the court says, as to certain Illinois decisions concerning the effect of Illinois statutes:

We are not called upon to vindicate the decisions of the supreme court of Illinois in these cases or approve the reasoning by which it reached its conclusions. If the questions before us had never been passed upon by it, some of my brethren who agree to this opinion might take a different view of them. But are not these decisions binding upon us in the present controversy? They adjudge that the bonds are void because the laws which authorized their issue were in violation of a peculiar provision of the constitution of Illinois. We have always followed the highest court of the State in its construction of its own constitution and laws.

In fact and in law, therefore, the judgment of the circuit court of Florida is final and conclusive.

We have now to consider what was the operation and effect of this judgment.

It is well observed by Mr. High, (§ 750,) following the case of Attorney-General *vs.* Barstow, (4 Wis., 567,) that in this proceeding the judgment itself creates no right, but is merely declaratory of rights already existing, the court being the instrument or medium through which the rights created by law are ascertained and definitely fixed. The judgment, he continues, therefore, neither creates a right in the successful party nor destroys one which formerly belonged to the party ousted.

It appears that in the cited Wisconsin case the claim was made that the substitution by the court of the relator as governor would impose upon the people a governor elected or created by the court. The answer was made by Judge Whiton, for the court, (p. 659:)

As the case now appears upon the record, the respondent has no legal right to the office, and the relator has a perfect right to it by virtue of the clause of the constitution above referred to. If the facts should remain unchanged, a judgment of ouster in this court against the respondent and a judgment establishing the right of the relator would not create a right in the latter or destroy one which belongs to the former. Their rights are fixed by the constitution, and the court, if it has jurisdiction of this proceeding, is the mere instrument provided by the constitution to ascertain and enforce their rights as fixed by that instrument. Its office is the same as in all controversies between party and party, not to create rights, but to ascertain and enforce them. The same argument would apply with equal force to an information in the nature of a *quo warranto* against a sheriff or any other officer. We do not think it well founded.

And so in the Florida case, the judgment in favor of the relators did not create them electors from the day of its rendition, but it declared that from the day of election, November 7, 1876, they were, and had been, the electors of the State of Florida, chosen under its laws, and consequently that all their acts as electors since that time were the acts of the legal and valid electors of the State of Florida.

The position of the assumed Hayes electors was not that of *de facto* officers, whose acts were valid as to the public and third persons until they were ousted. They had merely undertaken to perform an act which had not yet been finally acted upon by others when the court gave its judgment that they had never possessed the authority necessary to the performance of the act.

At the time of this judgment there were in existence and awaiting the acceptance of Congress the returns evidencing action of each of these bodies of electors. When these returns are opened there is presented to the tribunal about to choose between them the judgment of the court declaring that at the time these returns were prepared the Hayes electors were not, and the Tilden electors were, authorized to cast the vote of Florida.

It does not seem possible that the merely ministerial and executive attestation of the official character of the one body can stand for a moment as against the subsequent judicial determination that these ministerial and executive attestations had been given without warrant in law or fact.

There is also another legal principle which may be invoked in support of the proposition that the tribunal should accept the judgment in favor of the Tilden electors as evidence of their official character.

As has been repeatedly demonstrated, the certificates of the governor and canvassers of the State of Florida did not constitute the right, but were simply the evidence of the right of the electors to their office. If they had in fact been elected to the office, they were entitled to the evidence of that fact; and if the prescribed instrument of evidence, the certificate, was withheld without sufficient *legal* reason by the officers whose duty it was to give it to the lawfully-chosen electors, then they could resort to other instruments of evidence to establish the existence of the *fact* of their election.

The judgment of the circuit court thus operates not only to demonstrate that the governor and canvassers were without legal excuse in withholding from the Tilden electors the prescribed evidence of their election, but it also becomes admissible as itself constituting the constituted evidence of such election.

The authorities for the proposition that, in case of the prescribed instrument of evidence being withheld by those whose duty it is to give it, substituted evidence of the fact may be offered, have all arisen upon matters of contract, but they sufficiently demonstrate the principle that the law in all cases seeks to determine controversies according to existing facts, and that it is not to be defeated in this purpose by the unreasonable suppression or withholding of any particular method of proving such facts.

Among these authorities the following may be cited:

United States *vs.* Robeson, 9 Peters, 319–327. In this case the defendant had proved in the court below, as an offset, the payment of certain amounts for which it was provided by the contract that certificates of the commanding officer should be obtained, and such certificates were not produced or offered. On this ground the judgment was reversed, the court saying:

> The defendant cannot compel the payment of this amount unless he shall procure the kind of evidence required by the contract or show that by time or accident he was unable to do so.

> Had the defendant proved that application had been made to the commanding officer for the proper certificates and that he had refused to give them, it would have been proper to receive other evidence to establish the claim.

To the same effect are the decisions of the New York court of appeals in Thomas *vs.* Fleury, 26 N. Y., 26, and The Bowery National Bank *vs.* Mayor, 63 N. Y., 336.

It is also to be noticed that no statute makes the certificate of the governor or canvassers exclusive proof as to the question of the election of the electors; other competent proof would therefore be admissible.

It has been decided by the New York superior court (6 Bosworth, 213) that, though a statute provide that a copy of a certificate of incorporation shall be presumptive legal evidence of the facts therein stated, this does not exclude any other method of proving the fact of incorporation.

FIFTH.

The judgment of the circuit court is not impaired or lessened in efficacy by the proceeding to review it in a higher court, if any such proceeding has been taken. At common law the judgment of a court of original jurisdiction takes full effect immediately upon its entry; and until reversed it is as effectual as if pronounced by a court of last resort.

Allen *vs.* Mayor of Savannah, 9 Georgia, 286.

Facts.—Pending an appeal from a judgment declaring a tax ordinance of a city to be unconstitutional and void the legislature passed an act confirming all the ordinances *in operation* at its date. Afterward the court of error affirmed the original judgment.

Held, That the confirmatory act did validate the ordinance in question.

Opinion of the court:

> The pendency of the writ of error did not affect the judgment. * * It was binding until reversed, and, being affirmed, was binding *ab initio.* * * * The judgment of affirmance * * relates back and takes effect from the date of the first judgment.— (P. 294.)

Sage *vs.* Harpending, 49 Barb., 174.

Facts.—After a judgment in favor of a landlord that a tenancy had expired, and while an appeal therefrom was pending, the defeated tenant attempted to oust the landlord, and being repelled by force sued the landlord for an assault.

Held, That the judgment was a good plea to the action.

Opinion of the court:

> The fact that an appeal had been taken to another court did not affect the conclusive nature of the judgment as a bar, whilst it remained unreversed. (Harris *vs.* Hammond, 18 How. Pr., 124.)

Buzzard *vs.* Moore, 16 Indiana, 107, 109.

Opinion of the court :

The only effect of an appeal to a court of error, when perfected, is to stay execution upon the judgment from which it is taken. In all other respects, the judgment, until annulled or reversed, stands binding upon the parties as to every question directly decided. (Cole *vs.* Connolly, 16 Ala., 271.) And it has been expressly decided that "it is no bar to an action on a judgment that the judgment has been removed by writ of error to a superior court." (Suydam *vs.* Hoyt, 1 Dutcher, N. J. R., 230.)

Bank of North America *vs.* Wheeler, 28 Conn., 441, 462. Suit in Connecticut upon notes. Defendants pleaded that plaintiffs have recovered judgment on them in N. Y.

The plaintiffs finally claim that the judgment in New York is set aside or suspended by the appeal from it to the court of appeals of that State, and that it therefore constitutes no defense in this suit.

The effect of that appeal depends upon the character of the jurisdiction of that court. If, by the laws of New York, a case coming before it by appeal is to be retried by it as upon original process in that court, and it has jurisdiction to settle the controversy by a judgment of its own and to enforce that judgment by its own process, the appeal, like an appeal under our statutes, from a justice of the peace to the superior court, would vacate the judgment of the inferior tribunal.—(Curtiss *vs.* Beardsley, 15 Conn., 518; Campbell *vs.* Howard, 5 Mass., 376.)

But if the appeal is in the nature of a writ of error, and only carries up the case to the court of appeals, as an appellate court, for the correction of errors which may have intervened in the trial of the case below, and for its adjudication upon the question whether the judgment appealed from should be affirmed, reversed, or modified, and that court has no other powers or duties than to affirm, reverse, or modify that judgment, or remit the case to the inferior tribunal that it may conform its judgment to that of the appellate tribunal, then such an appeal, like an appeal under our laws from the probate court to the superior court, does not vacate or suspend the judgment appealed from; and the removal of the case to the appellate court would no more bar an action upon the judgment than the pendency of a writ of error at common law, when that was the proper mode of correcting errors which may have occurred in the inferior tribunal. That such an action would not be barred by the pendency of such a proceeding is well settled. The judgment below is only voidable, and stands good until set aside. (Case *vs.* Case, Kirby, 284; Sloan's Appeal from Probate, 1 Root, 151; Curtiss *vs.* Beardsley, 15 Conn., 523.)

It was accordingly held, and in our opinion correctly, by Judge Nelson, in the United States circuit court for this district, at its September term, 1854, in Seely *vs.* Pritchard, that under the laws and practice of the State of New York a judgment was not impaired by an appeal, but that an action of debt was sustainable thereon while the appeal was pending.

BRIEF No. 4.

SUBMITTED BY MR. MERRICK IN THE CASE OF THE STATE OF LOUISIANA.

AS TO VALIDITY OF ACTS OF OFFICERS DE FACTO.

1. The rule that the acts of a *de facto* officer will be regarded as valid rests upon public policy and the necessities of public convenience. Being an *exception* to the general rule that no official act is valid unless performed by some party having legal authority in that regard, rather than a *rule*, it is limited in its application to those *exact conditions* from which it derives its existence and authority.

2. The acts of an officer *de facto* are regarded as valid *only* when it appears that the officer has been in the exercise of the functions of the office for such a *period of time and with such degree of public notoriety* as to justify the conclusion that those dealing with him had reason to *believe* that he was an officer *de jure.*

3. It follows from the last foregoing proposition that where the function of the office extends to the performance of a *single act*, the exception in favor of the validity of the acts of *de facto* officers can never apply.

4. As the acts of a *de facto* officer are regarded as valid only as regards the public and third parties, it follows that such acts will never be treated as valid *unless* they have, at the time of the inquiry into their validity, already operated to affect the rights of third parties to such an extent as to cause a change in the condition of those to whom such acts may have reference.

5. It follows from the foregoing propositions that when the act of the *de facto* officer has not operated to accomplish some change in the relation of parties to each other or to property, or to the public, such acts will never be regarded as valid, *especially* when the particular act in question was performed by the officer *de jure* at the same time of its performance by the officer *de facto*, and when the inquiry is as to whose performance is to be accepted as valid.

In support of the foregoing propositions the following authorities are respectfully submitted:

An individual coming into office by color of an election or appointment is an officer *de facto*, and his actions in relation to the public or third persons are valid until he is removed, although it be conceded that his election or appointment was illegal. His title shall not be inquired into. The mere claim to be a public officer and the performance of a single act or even a number of acts in that character would not perhaps constitute an individual an officer *de facto*. There must be some color of an election or appointment, or an exercise of the office, and an acquiescence on the part of the public *for a length of time* which would afford a strong presumption of at least a colorable election or appointment. (Wilcox *vs.* Smith, 5 Wend., 231; Heirs of Hildreth *vs.* McIntire's Devisee, 1 J. J. Marshall, 206.)

A road commissioner, declared elected by the court of common pleas, after reversal of that decision by the superior court, but before the declaration by the court of common pleas of the election of another person in obedience to the *mandamus* of the superior court, was *held* to be no longer an officer *de facto*, and his acts as such were void. (Petition of Portsmouth, 19 N. H., 115.)

The act of an officer *de facto* is good wherever it concerns a third person, who had a previous right to the act or had paid a valuable consideration for it. (Savage *vs.* Ball, 17 N. J. Eq., 142.)

Where an officer attempts to enforce a legal right by action, he must show himself properly qualified. But where the action is against the officer, it is sufficient if he is shown to be an officer *de facto*. (Fetterman *vs.* Hopkins, 5 Watts, (Pa.,) 539.)

The acts of officers *de facto* are valid when they concern the public or the rights of third persons who have an interest in the act done. But a different rule prevails where the act is for the benefit of the officer, because he is not permitted to take advantage of his own wrong. Venable *vs.* Curd, 2 Head, Tenn., 582; Patterson *vs.* Miller, 2 Metc., Ky., 493; Gourley *vs.* Hawkins, 2 Iowa, 75.

A person not duly appointed to an office cannot justify his acts on the ground that he was an officer *de facto*. Cummins *vs.* Clark, 15 Vermont, 653.

When suit is brought against individuals who justify as public officers, they must show themselves officers *de jure*, and that they were duly qualified by taking the oath prescribed by law. A record that they were duly sworn is insufficient. Blake *vs.* Sturtevant, 12 New Hampshire, 507; Schlenke *vs.* Risley, 4 Illinois, (3 Scam.,) 483.

1821.   Riddle *vs.* County of Bedford, 7 Sergeant & Rawle, 391:

There are many acts done by an officer *de facto* which are valid.

They are good as to strangers, and all those persons who are not bound to look further than that the person is in the actual exercise of the office, without investigating his title.   *   *   *

Whenever the act done by an officer *de facto* has been declared to be valid, it is where some third person claims an interest or title in the act done; and I have not been able, after much research, to find any decision where such an act has been considered valid in an action by the officer *de facto* claiming for an act done by himself.

1855.   Vaccan *vs.* Maxwell, 3 Blatchford, 368, Judges Nelson and Betts.

Facts.—The plaintiff, an importer, whose entry of goods had been appraised by a general appraiser and a *merchant appraiser* appointed by the collector, and the value of the goods raised by them, protested on paying the duties " that the merchant appraiser was not legally sworn in." Suit to recover back the overcharge.

It appeared that he had not been sworn in, and the court then treats of his acts as a *de facto* officer:

We think, however, that the decisions in relation to the acts of officers *de facto* are reasonably to be restricted to those who hold office under some degree of notoriety, or are in the exercise of continuous official acts, or are in possession of a place which has the character of a public office.

     *   *   *   *   *   *

Merchants called in by the collector to estimate the value of merchandise take no rank as public officers.

1874.   The United States *vs.* Insurance Company, 22 Wallace, 99.

The real nature of the rule as to the validity of the acts of a *de facto* officer is well illustrated in this case.   "Their acts are held valid, as it respects the rights of third persons who have an interest in them and as concerns the public, in order to prevent the failure of justice." Green *vs.* Burke, 23 Wend., 490.

They rather hold the position of referees or trustees, *charged with the performance of a single act or appointed to act in an individual case.*

Held that the act was invalid.

The King *vs.* The Corporation of Bedford Level, 6 East, 368.   Lord Ellenborough, C. J.:

An *officer de facto* is one *who has the reputation of being the officer he assumes to be* and yet is not a good officer in point of law.

1 Lord Raymond, 660.

In this case Gotobed was never more than deputy; and, therefore, after the death of his principal he never could have had the *reputation* of being *more than a deputy*, but such reputation must necessarily have ceased with the knowledge of the death of his principal. When that fact was notorious to the owners of land in this level, no one could have registered his deeds with him under a belief that he was acting as the assistant of one who by the course of nature has ceased to fill the office in the execution of which he was to be assisted by the deputy.

In this case Cole died in December, and the greater part of the conveyances objected to were registered some months after, on the eve of the election.

R. T. MERRICK.

BRIEF No. 5.

SUBMITTED BY MR. MERRICK IN THE CASE OF THE STATE OF LOUISIANA.

THE LOUISIANA RETURNING-BOARD WAS WITHOUT AUTHORITY BECAUSE NOT COMPOSED OF THE FULL NUMBER OF MEMBERS REQUIRED BY THE STATUTES OF THAT STATE.

By the act of November 20, 1872, creating the returning-board of Louisiana, it is provided as follows :

SECTION 2. *Be it further enacted, &c.,* That five persons, to be elected by the Senate and from *all political parties,* shall be the returning-officers for all elections in the State, a majority of whom shall constitute a quorum and have power to make the returns of all elections. In case of any vacancy by death, resignation, or otherwise, of either of the board, then the vacancy shall be filled by the residue of the board of returning-officers.

Where an authority of a public nature is delegated by law to a certain number of individuals, the authority cannot be exercised unless the body created by law is composed of the full number the law requires. It is not contended that a less number than the entire board may not act; but the entire number must be in existence, clothed with authority to act, and have due notice of all proceedings that take place, and an opportunity to attend and participate therein, in order to give such proceedings validity. Wentworth *vs.* Farmington, 49 New Hamp., p. 120.

Especially is this true where different constituent elements of such body are by the law required to *represent* distinct and separate interests to be affected by its action.

Now, it is well known that in the elections that take place in the United States there are contests between two or more political parties, and these contests are more or less exciting.

The laws of Louisiana evidently contemplated the appointment on the board of canvassers of members of the different political parties in the State, in order that each of such parties might have a representative who would be a guard and protection against any evil practices that might be designed or attempted by their associates on the board.

It may be stated as a rule, without exception, that where the law provides for the organization of a body of men to execute a public authority, and requires it to be composed of a certain number of persons representing the different interests in regard to which that authority is to be exercised, such body can never exercise the power conferred upon it unless it is, in every particular, constituted in accordance with the requirements of the statute.

In such cases the requirement that a board should consist of a certain number of individuals taken from the different classes of citizens designated is *mandatory,* and unless so constituted it is not the body created by the law, and therefore not authorized to execute the power conferred by the law.

That one of the individuals composing the organization should, after his appointment and after entering upon his duties, change his political opinions, is no answer to the position assumed. In such a case the statute requirement would have been fully complied with if the appointment had been made in obedience to its mandate in the first instance. Under such circumstances the organization would have been full and complete under the law.

The case now presented is one in which that full and complete organization had not been accomplished, and where those who professed to
exercise the entire power conferred by the statute *persistently* and *stub-
bornly* refused to fill up the number required by the law, although
repeatedly and *earnestly requested to do so by one of the very parties the
act of legislation was designed and intended to protect by giving it a representation on the board.*

The power of a *quorum* to act is not denied, *provided* the body itself
had power to act. But we deny that the body had the power to act,
because of its defective organization.

The subject was fully discussed in the case from New Hampshire
above referred to.

The case is directly in point on the proposition submitted, and the
court, in its opinion, says:

Even if the statute goes no further than the common-law rule, a report signed by
the majority, under the circumstances of this case, would have been good. According
to the case of Grindley *et al. vs.* Barker, 1 B. & P., 228, before cited, it would have been
deemed to be the report of the whole. The real point of the objection is, that at the
time when the report was signed there was a vacancy in the board of commissioners,
caused by the removal of the chairman from the county; and the general doctrine
that in case there be a vacancy in the board the remaining members cannot act, seems
to be unquestionable. Palmer *vs.* Conway, 22 N. H., 148; Mitchell *vs.* Holderness, 34
N. H., 209, 214.

The question here, then, is whether this doctrine applies where, at the time the vacancy occurred, nothing remained to be done but to reduce to writing, and make the
formal report of what had already been determined by the whole board.

In Palmer *vs.* Conway, before cited, it was held that as there were not three members of the board in office at the time, there was no such board as the statute requires,
and therefore there could be no action of the majority.

In that case a report laying out a highway had been recommitted to the same board,
and a hearing notified, and before the time appointed one of the commissioners died,
but the others went on with the hearing and made several changes in the report, and
upon the report being again recommitted, the same two commissioners made further
changes, and the report, upon full consideration, was set aside for want of authority
in those commissioners to act.

In Mitchell *vs.* Holderness, before cited, the full board had decided to lay out a road
and made known their decision, and thereupon a motion was made that the town of
Plymouth be required to contribute to the expense of making the road, and as one of
the commissioners lived in Plymouth another was appointed in his place; afterward
another member of the board removed from the State, and the petitioners thereupon
moved the court to declare his office vacant and appoint another in his stead, but the
motion was denied, and upon exceptions to the supreme court this ruling was held to
be wrong. The court held that while unfinished business was pending before the
board, it became the duty of the court to pronounce the office vacant, and to fill the
vacancy under the statute. The court say that they do not understand that because
a board of commissioners have decided to lay out a road, and then proceed to inquire
whether other towns should defray part of the expense, they may not, upon further
investigation, reconsider their original intention to lay the road; that the statute contemplates but one report, and until that is made to the court, commissioners may
change it if they think proper. The petition of Nashua, 12 N. H., 425, was for leave to
discontinue a highway, and commissioners to whom it was referred reported in favor
of the discontinuance; but as one of the commissioners was a resident of Nashua, the
report was rejected, the court holding that a majority could not act unless the matter
was heard and considered by a full board, all of whom were competent to act.

The court concludes by saying:

Upon the whole, we think that by the removal of the chairman from the county
his office *ipso facto* became vacant, and the others had no power to complete the proceedings by the making of a report.

We should have been glad to have found some satisfactory ground on which the report could have been sustained, but have been unable to do so. What remained to be
done was of a substantial character; and should the report now be sustained, it would
be difficult to fix any limits beyond which the majority of the board could not go, after
the office of one member had become vacant.

The same principle is laid down in the following cases :
Schenck *vs.* Peay, 1 Woolworth, 175.   Opinion Mr. Justice Miller.
Same case, 1 Dillon, 267.
Pell *vs.* Ullman, 21 Barb., 500.
Matter of Beekman, 1 Abbt. Prac., 449.
Matter of Palmer, 31 Hd. Prac., 43.
Pulaski Co. *vs.* Lincoln, 9 Ark., 320.
People *vs.* Coghill, 47 Cal., 361.
Ballard *et al. vs.* Davis, 31 Miss., 525.
Dillon on Mun. Corp., secs. 221, 222.
State *vs.* Deliesseline, 1 McCord, 52, and criticism upon same by Judge Dillon, in note to Dillon on Mun. Corp., sec. 220.
In Schenck *vs.* Peay, (1 Woolworth, C. C. Rep., 175,) Mr. Justice Miller says :

We understand it to be well settled that where authority of this kind is conferred on three or more persons, in order to make its exercise valid all must be present and participate, or have an opportunity to participate, in the proceedings, although some may dissent from the action determined on. The action of two out of three commissioners, to all of whom was confided a power to be exercised, cannot be upheld when the third party took no part in the transaction and was ignorant of what was done, gave no implied consent to the action of the others, and was neither consulted by them nor had any opportunity to exert his legitimate influence in the determination of the course to be pursued. Such is the uncontradicted course of the authorities, so far as we are advised, where the power conferring the authority has not prescribed a different rule. (2 Kent's Commentaries, 293, note *a*, 633, and authorities cited there, note *b* ; Commonwealth *vs.* Canal Commissioners, 9 Watts, 466; Green *vs.* Miller, 6 Johnson, 39 ; Kirk *vs.* Ball, 12 Eng. L. & E., 385 ; Crocker *vs.* Crane, 21 Wendell, 211 ; Dougherty *vs.* Hope, 1 Comstock, 79, 252 ; *ib.*, 3 Denio, 252, 259.)
The case before us goes even beyond this, for, according to the statement of the bill, there never was a board of commissioners in existence until after the proceedings in regard to his title were completed. *The law required three commissioners. A less number was not a board and could do nothing.* The third commissioner for Arkansas, although nominated and confirmed, did not qualify or enter upon the duties of his office until after the sale of the lots to the defendants. *There was, therefore, no board of commissioners authorized to assess the tax, to receive the money, or to sell the property. If Congress had intended to confide these important functions to two persons, it would not have required the appointment of the third. If it had been willing that two out of the three should act, the statute could easily have made provision for that contingency,* as has since been done by the act of 1865.

II.

If William Pitt Kellogg was, at the time of the meeting of the electoral college of Louisiana, governor of that State, he was, under the laws of Louisiana, disqualified as an elector.
Constitution of La., Art. 117.
If, on the other hand, his appointment as an elector vacated his office as governor, the lists certified to by him as governor are ineffectual, because he was not then governor.

R. T. MERRICK,
GEORGE HOADLY,
ASHBEL GREEN,
ALEX. PORTER MORSE,
Of Counsel.

BRIEF No. 6.

SUBMITTED BY COUNSEL FOR OBJECTORS TO CERTIFI-CATE NO. 1 IN THE CASE OF THE STATE OF OREGON.

In the matter of the electoral vote of the State of Oregon.

ARGUMENT.

We claim that the three votes given for Hayes and Wheeler by William H. Odell, John C. Cartwright, and John W. Watts are not the electoral votes of the State of Oregon, but that the three electoral votes cast—two for Hayes and Wheeler and one for Tilden and Hendricks—by E. A. Cronin, J. N. T. Miller, and John Parker—are the true and valid electoral votes of the State of Oregon.

Our inquiry is thus divisible into three branches, viz:

First. Was John W. Watts duly appointed and had he the right to vote as an elector of the State of Oregon at the recent presidential election?

Secondly. Was E. A. Cronin duly appointed, and had he the right to cast a vote as an elector of the State of Oregon at said election?

Thirdly. Which was the electoral college of the State of Oregon, that composed of Odell, Cartwright, and Watts, or that composed of Cronin, Miller, and Parker?

Of these, in their order, we say:

I.

That John W. Watts was not duly appointed, and that he had no right to vote as an elector for the State of Oregon, at the recent election for President and Vice-President of the United States.

His claim of title to this office is twofold. *First*, by force of the votes of the qualified electors of the State of Oregon cast in his favor at the election held on Tuesday, November 7, 1876; and, *secondly*, in virtue of the attempted organization on December 6, 1876, by Odell, Cartwright, and Watts, as the electoral college of Oregon, and his resignation and re-election by Odell and Cartwright to fill a supposed vacancy.

Of these claims, in their order, we say:

1. It is not denied that at the election held in the State of Oregon on Tuesday, November 7, 1876, a majority of the votes of the qualified electors were given in favor of John W. Watts.

It cannot be denied that at that time and at least until November 13, 1876, John W. Watts was the incumbent of the office of postmaster at Yamhill, the county-seat of La Fayette County, in the State of Oregon, an office of trust and profit under the United States.

Our contention is that while Watts held this office he could not be "*appointed*" an elector, and that the attempt to appoint him was during the time when he was laboring under such disqualification.

The provision of the Constitution in this regard (article 2, section 1) is in these words:

> Each State shall appoint, in such manner as the legislature thereof may direct, a number of electors, equal to the whole number of Senators and Representatives to which the State may be entitled in the Congress; but no Senator or Representative, or person holding an office of trust or profit under the United States, shall be appointed an elector.

In *form* this provision of disqualification is mandatory,

First, because it is coupled with the grant of power to appoint electors by the word " but," which indicates that it is a qualification, diminution, and limitation of the powers granted in preceding words.

Secondly, because it is clothed in *negative* language.

Sedgwick on Const. & Stat. Law, 370.

Cooley on Const. Lim., 75.

From these expressions the conclusion is sometimes drawn that " negative words will make a statute imperative," which is incontestable. * * * Negative words will make a statute imperative, and it is apprehended affirmative *may*, if they are absolute, explicit, and peremptory, and show that no discretion is intended to be given, and especially so when jurisdiction is conferred. Potter's Dwarris on Statutes, 228; Rex *vs.* Justices of Leicester, 7 B. & C., 6, 12.

In substance, this provision of disqualification is imperative, and admits of no evasion.

Lord Mansfield distinguished mandatory from directory clauses in statutes by dividing "circumstances which are of the *essence* of a thing required to be done by act of Parliament from clauses merely directory." Rex *vs.* Loxdale, 1 Burr, 447.

First, considerations relating to the character of the provision, as shown by the Constitution itself, fix its meaning. The grant of power is "to each State"—to each State in its organized governmental, or if we may be allowed the expression, corporate capacity; and the limitation, in like manner, is of the action of the State in the same capacity. The restriction in the choice of electors does not merely work a disqualification of the candidate, nor does it bind merely the *voters* of the State; for, by the Constitution, the *manner* of appointing electors may be directed by the legislature of the State, and as was done in Colorado at this election, and formerly in most, if not all the States, need not be left to popular choice at all—it binds the State itself, binds it in its entire action from first to last, binds it in all its departments, binds all its functionaries. This is clearly shown by the distinction taken in the provision itself between the appointing power, which is confided to "each *State*," and the power to direct the *manner* of appointment, which is given to the "*legislature thereof;*" it is further indicated by the subsequent use of the word "State:" "Senators and Representatives to which *the State* may be entitled in the Congress."

Again, the limitation is upon the *action* of the State : " No person holding an office of trust or profit under the United States shall be *appointed* an elector." The State may act so as to appoint electors, but such action shall not have the effect to establish the appointment of any such disqualified person. Again, the limitation works by taking from or carving out of the granted power; it establishes a province into which the power may not extend; it establishes a class of persons from among whom the appointment may not be made, and thus another class from which only it may be made. Each State may appoint, but not from the disqualified class. This is equivalent to saying that each State may appoint from among the whole body of citizens other than the disqualified class.

This, then, is the power as determined by the letter and spirit of the words used, viz: Each State may appoint from among persons not disqualified, in the manner directed by its legislature, a number of electors equal to the whole number of Senators and Representatives to which the State may be entitled in the Congress.

Secondly, this conclusion follows from the consideration of the reasons for the disqualification; of the mischiefs sought to be prevented by its enactment. The purpose of our wise forefathers was to exclude the possibility, so far as this provision could have effect, of the interference of the officers controlling the Federal Government and its agencies, even with the assent of any State or number of States, to perpetuate their own power. The apprehension of our forefathers was that Federal officers might use the power conferred upon them for the purposes of Federal trust, to prevent the free action of the States in the choice of electors.

Time has not weakened the force of their reasoning; experience has not shown the futility of their apprehensions. To-day we are confronted by this danger, grown into colossal proportions by the augmentation of Federal power and the increased number of Federal functionaries. If it be suggested that the plan of our fathers to avert the peril is insufficient, we answer that the suggestion itself requires a liberal construction of the provision, so that it may have at least all reasonable potency in the prescribed direction toward the desired end.

The history of the disqualifying proviso seems to be this: On July 19, Mr. Gerry and Mr. Gouverneur Morris moved "that the electors of the Executive shall not be members of the National Legislature, nor officers of the United States, nor shall the electors themselves be eligible to the Supreme Magistracy." Agreed to *nem. con.* (Madison Papers, 343.)

On Thursday, September 6, Mr. Rufus King and Mr. Gerry moved to insert in the fourth clause of the report, (see the 4th of September, page 507,) after the words "may be entitled in the legislature," the words following: "But no person shall be appointed an elector who is a member of the legislature of the United States, or who holds any office of profit or trust under the United States," which passed *nem. con.* (Madison Papers, 515.)

Several postmasters were chosen electors at the presidential election of 1836, and on January 27, 1837, on motion of Henry Clay, the joint committee of the Senate and House to ascertain and report a mode of examining the votes of President and Vice-President of the United States were instructed by the Senate also "to inquire into the expediency of ascertaining whether any votes were given at the recent election contrary to the prohibition contained in the second section of the second article of the Constitution; and if any such votes were given, what ought to be done with them; and whether any and what provision ought to be made for securing the faithful observance, in future, of that section of the Constitution.

Felix Grundy, Henry Clay, and Silas Wright were appointed to this committee on the part of the Senate; Francis Thomas, Churchill C. Cambreleng, John Reed, Henry W. Connor, and Francis S. Lyon (of whom the latter is still living, at great age, in the State of Alabama) were the members of this committee on behalf of the House.

On February 4, 1837, Mr. Grundy submitted to the Senate the report of the committee, from which we make the following quotations:

That the short period at which they were appointed, before the day on which the vote for President and Vice-President of the United States have to be counted, have prevented them from investigating the facts submitted to their examination as fully as might have been done had more time been allowed. The correspondence which has taken place between the chairman of the committee and the heads of the different departments of the Executive branch of the Government accompanies this report, from which it appears * * * that in two cases persons of the same names with the individuals who were appointed and voted as electors in the State of North Carolina held the office of deputy postmasters under the General Government. It also appears that in New Hampshire there is one case; in Connecticut there is one case; in North Carolina there is one case, in which, from the report of the Postmaster-General, it is probable that at the time of the appointment of electors in these States, respectively, the electors or persons of the same name were deputy postmasters. The committee have not ascertained whether the electors are the same individuals who held or are presumed to have held the office of deputy postmasters at the time when the appointment of electors was made; and this is the less to be regretted, as it is confidently believed that no change in the result of the election of either the President or Vice-President would be effected by the ascertainment of the fact in either way, as five or six votes only would, in any event, be abstracted from the whole number, for the committee cannot adopt the opinion, entertained by some, that a single illegal vote would vitiate the whole electoral vote of the college of electors in which it was given, particularly in cases where the vote of the whole college has been given for the same persons.

The committee are of opinion that the second section of the second article of the Constitution, which declares that "no Senator or Representative, or person holding an office of trust or profit under the United States, shall be appointed an elector," *ought to be carried, in its whole spirit, into rigid execution, in order to prevent officers of the General Government from bringing their official power to influence the elections of President and Vice-President of the United States. This provision of the Constitution, it is believed, excludes and disqualifies deputy postmasters from the appointment of electors; and the disqualification relates to the time of the appointment, and that a resignation of the office of deputy postmaster after his appointment as elector would not entitle him to vote as elector under the Constitution.*

In the debate ensuing in the House of Representatives upon the report of this joint committee, Mr. Francis Thomas, chairman of the House committee, said that "the committee came unanimously to the conclusion that they (the postmasters in question) were not eligible at the time they were elected, and therefore the whole proceeding was vitiated *ab initio.*"

Fortunately or unfortunately, our American habit of not providing by legislation in advance for apprehended dangers controlled Congress in 1837, and inasmuch as the eligibility or non-eligibility of the five postmasters chosen electors made no difference in the result of the election, Congress passed to its more immediate business without legislating, as Mr. Clay proposed, with reference to cases of disqualification.

(See Gales & Seaton's Register of Debates in Congress, vol. 13, part 1, pp. 617, 698; part 2, p. 1583.)

2. *The attempt to elect this disqualified person Watts cannot be treated as if it had any legal effect, unless it were (and this we shall consider in a subsequent part of our argument) to prevent the choice of the next highest competitor.*

It was a mere nullity, incapable of ratification or any process of healing. A violation of the Federal Constitution is a wrong which can never ripen into a right; a malady which must necessarily be fatal to the diseased part. As the provision of the Constitution is not merely a disqualification of the candidate, but a limitation of the power of the State, it follows that the action of the State in the appointment of a disqualified person to be an elector, even if consummate and complete in form, has such defect of substance that in law it is a mere nullity, utterly void, and of no effect. It is in law as if it had not been in fact, at least so far as concerns the election of the disqualified candidate.

Opinion of the Judges, 7 Maine, Appendix, 497.
Spear *vs.* Robinson, 29 Maine, 531.
Opinion of Supreme Court, 38 Maine, 597.
People *ex rel.* Furman *vs.* Clute, 50 N. Y., 451.
Commonwealth *vs.* Cluly, 56 Penn. Stat., 270.
Commonwealth *vs.* Read, 2 Ashmead, 261.
Hutcheson *vs.* Tilden & Bordley, 4 Harris & McH.
Gulick *vs.* New, 14 Indiana, 93.
Carson *vs.* McPhetridge, 15 Indiana, 327.
Price *vs.* Baker, governor, 41 Indiana, 572.
Stewart *vs.* Hoges, 3 Chicago Legal News, 117.

State *vs.* Giles, 1 Chand., (Wis.,) 112.
State *vs.* Smith, 14 Wis., 497.
State *vs.* Boal, 46 Mo., 528.
State *vs.* Vail, 53 Mo., 97.
Whitman *vs.* Malony, 10 Cal., 47.
Saunders *vs.* Haynes, 13 Cal., 145.
State *vs.* Gastinel, 18 Louisiana, 517.
State vs. Gastinel, 20 Louisiana, 114.
Fish *vs.* Collins, 21 Louisiana, 289.
People *ex rel.* Crawford *vs.* Moliter, 23 Mich., 341.
State *vs.* Swearingen, 12 Georgia, 23.
Sublett *vs.* Bidwell, 47 Miss., 226.
Pearce *vs.* Hawkins, 2 Swan, 87.
Patterson *vs.* Miller, 2 Metc., Ky., 323.
Morgan *vs.* Vance, 4 Bush., 323.
Harrison *vs.* Evans, cited in Cowper, 393 note, 535.
Rex *vs.* Monday, Cowper, 536.
Hawkins *vs.* Rex, 2 Dou., 124.
Gosling *vs.* Veley, 7 Ad. & Ellis, N. S., 437.
Regina *vs.* Coaks, 3 Ell. & Bl., 249 ; 14 Jurist, Part 1, 378.
Drinkwater *vs.* Deakin, Law Rep. 9 C. P., p. 626.
French *vs.* Nolan, Irish Rep., 9 Com. Law, 217.
Grant on Corporations, 208.
Cushing's Law and Pr. of Leg. Ass., §§ 177, 178, and 179.
And to this effect are all the cases, English and American, which we shall hereafter cite, as well as those that may be cited against our proposition that the candidate receiving the next highest vote is, under such circumstances, elected. Any other construction would destroy the whole force of the constitutional inhibition. Like the other inhibitory clauses of the Constitution, this is self-enforcing.

3. *The disability relates to the time of the election, and is not cured by subsequent resignation of the disqualifying office.*

By the Constitution the manner of appointing electors is left to the direction of the legislatures of the States, but " Congress may determine the time of choosing the electors, and the day on which they shall give their votes; which day shall be the same throughout the United States."

That the words " choosing " and " appointing " are convertible terms, used in the same sense, is obvious from the fact that the manner of appointing (or choosing) is not specified; " choosing " therefore means appointing in such manner as the legislatures of the States may direct.

Congress has determined the time of choosing the electors, viz, by section 131 of the Revised Statutes, now in force :

SEC. 131. Except in case of a presidential election, prior to the ordinary period, as specified in sections 147 to 149 inclusive, when the offices of President and Vice-President both become vacant, the electors of President and Vice-President shall be *appointed* in each State on the Tuesday next after the first Monday in November in every fourth year succeeding every election of a President and Vice-President.

In the act of March 1, 1792, the same language was used, viz: " Electors shall be *appointed* in each State for the election of a President and Vice-President of the United States within thirty-four days preceding the first Wednesday in December, 1792, and within thirty-four days preceding the first Wednesday in December in every fourth year succeeding the last election."

So also in the act of January 23, 1845, "that the electors of President and Vice-President shall be *appointed* in each State on the Tuesday next after the first Monday in the month of November of the year in which they are to be *appointed*."

It follows that the appointment must be complete on the day prescribed by the act of Congress, and that whatever may be done after that date is not part of the appointment, but is rather the ascertaining who was then appointed. The principle is well stated in McWhirter *vs.* Brainard, 5 Oreg., 426, thus: " The mode of canvassing the vote and the proclamation of the governor are substantially only modes of ascertaining and publishing the result of the vote."

We have already seen what was the opinion upon this subject of Felix Grundy, Henry Clay, and Silas Wright, and of their associates, the members of the committee from the House of Representatives in 1837.

The same doctrine was held in the case of Searcy *vs.* Grow, 15 Cal., 118, where the opinion was pronounced by Baldwin, J.; Cope, J., and Field, C. J., concurring. It was a contest for the office of sheriff of Siskiyou County. Grow had been returned as elected to the office. At the time of the election he was postmaster in the town of Yreka, the compensation of which exceeded five hundred dollars per annum. The court below found for Searcy, and Grow appealed. The constitution of California provides that " no person holding any lucrative office under the United States or in their power shall be eligible to any civil office of profit under this State, provided that offices in the militia to which there is attached no annual salary, or local officers, and postmasters whose compensation does not exceed five hundred dollars per annum, shall not be deemed lucrative." Grow was postmaster at the time of the election, but had resigned at the time of his qualification. The supreme court unanimously confirmed the judgment of the court below.

In the opinion Justice Baldwin says, (page 121,) " The people in this case were clothed with this power of choice. Their selection of a candidate gave him all the claim to the office which he has. His title to the office comes from their designation of him as sheriff. But they could not designate or choose a man not eligible—that is, not capable of being selected. They might select any man they chose, subject only to this exception: that the man they selected was capable of taking what they had the power to give. We do not see how the fact that he became capable of taking office after they had exercised their power can avail the appellant. If he was not eligible at the time the votes were cast for him, the election failed. We do not see how it can be assumed that by the act of the candidate the votes which, when cast, were ineffectual because not given for a qualified candidate, became effectual to elect him to office."

In The People *vs.* Pease, 27 New York, 55, it is said that it is the vote of the people which confers title to an elective officer. " It is not the canvass, or estimate, or certificate which determines the right. These are only evidences of the right."

So, also, in Mayfield *vs.* Moore, 53 Ill., 428, the court say, " Under the law, so soon as a majority of the votes were cast for appellant, at the election held in pursuance to law, he became legally and fully entitled to the office. The title was as complete then as it ever was, and no subsequent act lent the least force to the right of the place. The commission was evidence of the title, but not the title. The title was conferred by the people, and the evidence of the right by the law." To the same effect see Laimbeer *vs.* Swineburne, 48 Illinois, 400; State *ex rel.* Cornwell *vs.* Allen, 21 Indiana, 516; Shannon *vs.* Baker, 33 do., 380; State *vs.* Steers, 44 Missouri, 223.

So also in the case of the State of Nevada *ex rel.* Nourse *vs.* Clarke, (3 Nev., 566,) the supreme court of Nevada held that a person holding the office of United States district attorney on the day of election was incapable of being chosen to the office of attorney-general of the State, because of a provision in the State constitution to the effect that no Federal office-holder " shall be eligible to any civil office of profit under this State." " Which word ' eligible,' " says this learned court, " means capable both of being legally chosen and capable of legally holding."

Since the election of November 7, 1876, the subject has been considered by the supreme court of Rhode Island, in the matter of George H. Corliss. (16 American Law Register, N. S., 15, number for January, 1877.) Corliss was a Centennial commissioner on November 7, 1876, when the qualified voters of Rhode Island cast a majority of their votes for him for the office of presidential elector. The governor, under the laws of Rhode Island, submitted to the supreme court five questions, the answers to which were to guide his action in making the required executive lists of electors appointed. Of 'these the third, upon the assumption that the court should answer that the office was one of trust and profit under the Constitution of the United States, was: " Is the disqualification removed by the resignation of said office of trust and profit?" There was a dissenting opinion of one judge out of five in answer to the first question, but all agreed in answering the third question as follows:

We think the disqualification is not removed by the resignation of the office of trust unless the office is resigned before the election. The language of the constitution is that "no person holding an office of trust or profit under the United States shall be *appointed* an elector." Under our law (Gen. Stats., ch. 11, sects. 1 and 2,) the election by the people constitutes the appointment. The duty of the governor is to examine and count the votes, and give notice to the elector. He merely ascertains, he does not complete, the appointment. A resignation, therefore, after the election is too late to be effectual.

The manner of appointing electors in Oregon is precisely similar to that adopted in Rhode Island. It has been directed by the legislature by section 1 of chapter 44, page 848, of the general laws of Oregon, as follows:

On the Tuesday next after the first Monday in November, 1864, and every four years thereafter, there shall be elected by the qualified electors of the State as many electors of President and Vice-President as this State may be entitled to elect of Senators and Representatives in Congress.

Therefore if Postmaster Watts was not qualified to be "chosen," "appointed," "elected," on November 7, 1876, he was not chosen, appointed, or elected on that day, and no subsequent resignation of his disqualifying office could, by relation, or any *nunc pro tunc* action, avoid the operation of the two peremptory constitutional requirements, viz, that he should be qualified when appointed, and that the time of his appointment should be on the day determined by the Congress.

4. *The disqualification of Watts did not create a case of vacancy, but of non-election, if not of the election of the next highest competing candidate.*

It can hardly be claimed that in principle a different result flows from the disqualification of part of the electoral college, from that which would be the consequence if every elector were disqualified.

If every elector appointed in every State were disqualified, there would be no election.

If every elector appointed in any one State were disqualified, the case would fall within the contingency contemplated in section 134 of the Revised Statutes.

Sec. 134. Whenever any State has held an election for the purpose of choosing electors, and has failed to make a choice on the day prescribed by law, the electors may be appointed on a subsequent day, in such a manner as the legislature of such State may direct.

This is a different power, and relates to a different class of cases from that contemplated in section 133:

Sec. 133. Each State may, by law, provide for the filling of any vacancies which may occur in its college of electors, when such college meets to give its electoral vote.

Omne majus continet in se minus. If it be true that whenever a State has held an election for the purpose of choosing electors, and has failed to make a choice of any qualified electors on the day prescribed by law, the case is governed by section 134, then it follows that the same is true, *pro tanto*, in the case of the failure to make the choice of all the electors to which the State is entitled from among the class of persons qualified under the Constitution; in other words, in the case of the choice of one or more disqualified electors.

The distinction here made is between an election held on the day prescribed by law, resulting in a tie vote, or the election of one or more disqualified persons, (a case governed by section 134,) and an election held at the appointed time, resulting in the election of the full number of qualified electors, after which, and at the time when the electoral college meets to give its electoral vote, a vacancy shall occur. This case is governed by section 133. These provisions of law, now separated from each other by being cast in the revision of the statutes into two sections, may be found in the original form in the act of January 23, 1845, the whole of which is as follows:

AN ACT to establish a uniform time for holding elections for electors of President and Vice-President of the United States.

Sec. 1. *Be it enacted, &c.*, That the electors of President and Vice-President shall be appointed in each State on the Tuesday next after the first Monday in the month of November of the year in which they are to be appointed: *Provided,* That each State may by law provide for the filling of any vacancy or vacancies which may occur in its college of electors, when such college meets to give its electoral vote: *And provided also,* When any State shall have held an election for the purpose of choosing electors, and shall fail to make a choice on the day aforesaid, then the electors may be appointed on a subsequent day in such manner as the State shall by law provide.

Approved January 23, 1845.

And this was the act in force when Oregon adopted its statute relative to vacancies in the electoral college. It will appear that whereas Rhode Island, as shown by the Corliss case, enacted laws to meet both the contingencies named in the act of 1845, Oregon made provision only for the case of vacancy "which might occur in its college of electors when such college meets to give its electoral vote."

Without the election of a qualified candidate, there can be no vacancy. A vacancy only occurs where the office has been once filled by the election of a qualified incumbent.

The case of George H. Corliss, already referred to, is exactly in point. The second question propounded by the governor to the judges of the supreme court of Rhode Island was in these words:

Does such a candidate [one disqualified by holding an office of trust or profit] for the office of elector, who receives a plurality of the legal votes given, and declines said office, create thereby such a vacancy as is provided for in section 7, chapter II of the General Statutes?

This was answered, by the unanimous voice of the judges, thus:

We think a centennial commissioner, who was a candidate for the office of elector, and received a plurality of the votes, does not, by declining the office, create such a vacancy as is provided for in Gen. Stats., ch. 11, sect. 7. Section 7 is as follows:

"If a y electors, chosen as aforesaid, shall, after their said election, decline the said office, or be prevented by any cause from serving therein, the other electors, when met in Bristol in pursuance of this chapter, shall fill such vacancies, and shall file a certificate in the secretary's office of the person or persons by them appointed."

Before any person can decline under this section he must first be elected, and no person can be elected who is ineligible, or in other words incapable of being elected. "Resignation," said Cockburn, C. J., in The Queen *vs.* Blizzard, Law Rep., 2, Q. B., 55, "implies that the person resigning has been elected into the office he resigns. A man cannot resign that which he is not entitled to, and which he has no right to occupy.',

The fifth question propounded to the judges by the governor of Rhode Island was: "If by reason of the disqualification of the candidate who received a plurality of the votes given there was no election, can the general assembly in grand committee elect an elector?"

To which the judges, without dissent, made answer:

Our statute (Gen. Stat., ch. 11, sec. 5) provides that if, by reason of the votes being equally divided, or otherwise, there shall not be an election of the number of electors to which the State may be entitled, the governor shall forthwith convene the general assembly at Providence for the choice of electors to fill such vacancy by an election in grand committee.

We think this provision covers the contingency which has happened, and that, therefore, the general assembly in grand committee can elect an elector to fill up the number to which the State is entitled. The law of the United States provides that "whenever any State has held an election for the purpose of choosing electors and has failed to make choice on the day prescribed by law, the electors may be appointed on a subsequent day, in such manner as the legislature of the State may direct."

A vacancy was defined by Sawyer, Chief-Justice, in People *vs.* Tilton, (37 Cal., 617,) as follows: "A vacancy in the statutory sense is when the party enters upon the duties of the office, and afterwards dies, resigns, or in any manner ceases to be an incumbent of the office before the expiration of the term."

In Miller *vs.* The Supervisor of Sacramento County, (25 Cal., 93,) it was held that "one who has been elected to an office cannot resign the same until the time has arrived when he is entitled by law to possess the same, and has given oath, filed the bond required, and entered upon the discharge of its duties."

In Broom *vs.* Hanley, (9 Penn. St., 513,) it was decided that even death, after a lawful election and before qualification, does not create an incumbent of the office, nor does it create a vacancy which can be filled by appointment, where the law authorizes vacancies to be so filled.

Article 1, section 3, of the Constitution provides that if vacancies happen in the Senate by "resignation or otherwise, during the recess of the legislature of any State, the executive thereof may make temporary appointments until the next meeting of the legislature, which shall then fill such vacancies."

Under this power, it has been held that the State executive cannot fill a vacancy in the Senate unless there has been an incumbent of the term, and the incumbent has ceased to hold during the recess of the legislature.—Lanman's case, Clarke & Hall, 871; Story on the Constitution, sec. 1559; Sergeant's Const. Law, (2d ed.,) 373. See also Schenck *vs.* Peay, 1 Dillon, 267; State *vs.* Benedict, 15 Minn., 199; Battle *vs.* McIver, 68 N. C., 469; People *vs.* Stratton, 28 Cal., 382; Stratton *vs.* Oulton, 2 Cal., 51; People *vs.* Parker, 37 Cal., 639; Dodd *ex parte*, 6 Eng., (Ark.,) 152; State *vs.* Jenkins, 43 Mo., 261.

The statutes of Oregon contemplate but one election of electors. The provision in this regard is express and peremptory:

On the Tuesday next after the first Monday in November, 1864, and every four years thereafter, there *shall be* elected, by the qualified electors of this State, *as many* electors of President and Vice-President as this State may be entitled to elect of Senators and Representatives in Congress.

"*Shall be elected,*" "*as many electors*"—this is the mandate of Oregon. But there were not on November 7, 1876, (unless Cronin was duly elected, of which hereafter,) elected "as many electors" as Oregon was entitled to elect of Senators and Representatives in Congress. There were elected but two electors; whereas Oregon is entitled to elect two Senators and one Representative in Congress. It follows that on November 7, 1876, there was in Oregon a case falling directly within section 134 of the Revised Statutes. Oregon had "held an election for the purpose of choosing electors" and had "failed to make a choice on the day prescribed by law."

But while Oregon has provided by law for "the filling of vacancies which may occur in its college of electors when said college meets to give its electoral vote," as contemplated in section 133, it has taken no steps whatever to meet the contingency which actually happened—happened on November 7, 1876, by the non election of the third elector—happened twenty-nine days before its college of electors met to give its electoral vote.

This provision of Oregon law is to be found in the compilation of the general laws, page 849, chapter 45, section 2, as follows:

The electors of President and Vice-President shall convene at the seat of government on the first Wednesday of December next after their election, at the hour of 12 of the clock at noon of that day, and if there shall be any vacancy in the office of an elector, occasioned by death, refusal to act, neglect to attend, or otherwise, the electors present shall immediately proceed to fill, by *viva voce* and plurality of votes, such vacancy in the electoral college, and when all the electors shall appear, and the vacancies, if any, shall have been filled, as above provided, such electors shall proceed to perform the duties required of them by the Constitution and laws of the United States.

Had the legislature of Oregon intended to authorize any vacancy, however caused, to be filled by the electors present, they would not have used the words: "If there shall be any vacancy in the office of an elector, occasioned by death, refusal to act, neglect to attend, or otherwise," for the words "occasioned by death, refusal to act, neglect to attend, or otherwise," are entirely superfluous upon this theory. For the sentence would then have read: "If there shall be any vacancy in the office of an elector, the electors present shall immediately proceed to fill by *viva voce* and plurality of votes such vacancy in the electoral college." The use of these words, "occasioned by death, refusal to act, neglect to attend, or otherwise," indicates that there are cases of vacancy which the electors may not fill, and this view is strengthened by the character of the vacancies thus described, the three named, death, refusal to act, and neglect to attend, being all the results of events occurring after the election. The words "or otherwise," upon canons of interpretation well known to every lawyer, cannot enlarge the preceding words so as to make them apply to every case of vacancy, but only refer to other like cases depending upon conditions similar to the enumerated cases. The maxim applicable is *noscitur a sociis*. So a statute treating of "deans, prebendaries, parsons, vicars, *and others having spiritual promotion,*" is held not to extend to *bishops*, though they have spiritual promotion, deans being the highest persons named, and bishops being of a still higher order. (1 Blackstone's Comm., 88.)

The word "otherwise" here means "other causes;" but whether *all* other causes, or only *some* other causes, is the question. If "*some* other causes" is meant, as has been already shown, then the maxim already quoted indicates what other causes. "*Ex antecedentibus et consequentibus fit optima interpretatio.*"

If it be said that "otherwise" is a general term, we answer, "*Verba generalia restringuntur ad habilitatem rei vel personam.*"
Broom's Legal Maxims, 565, 620.
Coe *vs.* Columbus, Piq. & Ind. R. R. Co., 10 Ohio St., 377, 378.

In point of fact, Odell and Cartwright did not assume to appoint Watts to a vacancy under the "otherwise" clause of the statute, but accepted his resignation, and then elected him to fill a vacancy created by his voluntary assumption or pretense of office and resignation.

Thus far we have been considering this claim of vacancy as if the quoted section of the Oregon laws were the only statutory provision thereto relating.

It may be claimed, however, that this vacancy is controlled by chapter 13, title 7, "Of vacancies," sec. 45:

> Every office shall become vacant on the happening of either of the following events, before the expiration of the term of such office:
> 1. The death of the *incumbent.*
> 2. *His* resignation.
> * * * * * * *
> 7. The decision of a competent tribunal declaring void *his* election or appointment.

We do not consider this provision of law applicable to electors for vacancies in whose offices special provision is made by chapter 44, section 2, but if it be, we answer, *first*, that Watts was never "the incumbent;" and, *secondly*, that there was and could have been no competent tribunal declaring void his appointment after he became *incumbent;* and, *thirdly*, the constitutional inhibition does not operate through the instrumentality of a judgment of conviction or ouster, but works by self-enforcement, (as we shall more fully show hereafter,) rendering nugatory the conflicting appointment.

5. *The resignation of Watts did not take effect so as to relieve him from* "*holding an office of trust or profit under the United States*" *until his successor was elected and qualified, which was after he had cast his vote as an elector.*
Revised Statutes, section 3836:

> Whenever the office of any postmaster becomes vacant, the Postmaster-General or the President shall supply such vacancy without delay, and the Postmaster-General shall promptly notify the Sixth Auditor of the change; and every postmaster and his sureties shall be responsible under their bond for the safe-keeping of the public property of the post-office, and the due performance of the duties thereof, until the expiration of the commission, or until a successor has been duly appointed and qualified, and has taken possession of the office; except, that in cases where there is a delay of sixty days in supplying a vacancy, the sureties may terminate their responsibility by giving notice, in writing, to the Postmaster-General, and the Postmaster-General may, when the exigencies of the occasion require, place such office in charge of a special agent until the vacancy can be regularly filled; and when such special agent shall have taken charge of such post-office, the liability of the sureties of the postmaster shall cease.

ARE THE INHIBITORY CLAUSES OF THE CONSTITUTION SELF-ENFORCING?

We had not supposed that the negative of this proposition would be maintained, but Groves *vs.* Slaughter has been referred to as if it countenanced such denial.

But Groves *vs.* Slaughter did not relate to an inhibitory, but to a mandatory clause, and, what is even more significant, *mandatory upon the legislature.* The clause construed was in the constitution of Mississippi:

> The introduction of slaves into this State as merchandise or for sale shall be prohibited from and after the first day of May, 1833.

And the passage quoted from Groves *vs*. Slaughter admits "that the constitution is mandatory upon the legislature." But inhibitions are not merely mandates; they are limitations of power, thrown into the negative and inhibitory form for the very purpose of rendering them self-enforcing, so that no legislation might be needed (not but that it might be appropriate in proper cases) for their enforcement, and so that all legislation or public or private action in conflict with them, might be absolutely null and void to all intents and purposes, *de jure et de facto*.

The express inhibitions, such as *ex post facto* laws, laws impairing the obligation of contracts, treaties between States, export duties, titles of nobility, bills of credit emitted by States, State tariffs, these and the like are inhibited, and by reason of the inhibitions, are utterly without legal force, *nec jure neque facto*.

In like manner with the implied inhibitions. When was it ever held that a State law taxing Federal agencies protected anybody? These, also, need no aid of legislation, but all laws, or public or private action in conflict with them, are void *de jure et de facto*.

The inhibitions relating to office are in like manner self-enforcing. They differ only in this, that they point to and operate at different stages, and therefore render the action they inhibit either absolutely void or voidable according to the time at which it may be impugned. Thus—

> No person shall *be* a Representative who shall not have attained to the age of twenty-five years, &c.
>
> No person shall *be* a Senator who shall not have attained to the age of thirty years, &c.
>
> No person shall *be* a Senator or Representative in Congress or elector of President and Vice-President, &c., who, having personally taken an oath, &c., to support the Constitution of the United States, shall have engaged in insurrection or rebellion, &c.

In these cases, the operation of the Constitution is to render the original election voidable, action under it void; in other words, to render the election void, unless the condition of disability be removed before the candidate shall *be* Representative, Senator, or elector.

This is rendered very plain by reference to article 1, section 6.

> No Senator or Representative shall, during the time for which he was elected, *be appointed* to any civil office under the authority of the United States, which shall have been created, or the emoluments whereof shall have been increased during such time; and no person holding any office under the United States, shall *be* a member of either House during his continuance in office.

Read now in connection with this the clause under discussion, and what room is left for controversy?

> But no Senator or Representative, or person holding an office of trust or profit under the United States, *shall be appointed* an elector.

In Morgan *vs*. Vance, 4 Bush, 323, the court of appeals of Kentucky held (p. 330) that—

> So far as the constitution requires of all officers to take the prescribed oath, and so far as it provides disqualifications upon acts and not upon judgment of conviction, the constitution, as the supreme law of the land, executes itself without any extraneous aid by way of legislation, nor can its requirements be so defeated.

The view we are presenting derives strong support from the re-examination of this subject by the court of appeals of Kentucky, in the case of Commonwealth *vs*. Jones, 10 Bush, 725. Section 20 of the article of the constitution of Kentucky provides that—

> Any person, who shall * * either directly or indirectly give, accept, or knowingly

carry a challenge to any person or persons to fight in single combat with a citizen of this State * * * *shall be deprived* of the right to hold any office of honor or profit in this commonwealth, and shall be *punished* otherwise in such manner as this general assembly shall prescribe by law.

The court held this provision

Not self-executing, except to the extent that persons who cannot or will not take the constitutional oath are thereby prevented from holding office.

Upon page 738, the court (Lindsay, J.,) say:

Upon the other hand, if, instead of the phrase "shall be deprived," the word "ineligible," or the phrase "shall not be eligible," had been used in section 20, some of the difficulties attending the argument to show that it is self-executing would have been obviated. We have already shown that the change of language or phraseology in this regard was deliberate and intentional, and that apt and appropriate words are used to show that participation in a duel between citizens of the State was intended to be treated as a public offense, and that the deprivation of the right to hold office is a penalty or punishment to be inflicted upon those who may be guilty of said offense.

Even the third clause of article 4, section 2, providing for the rendition of fugitives from slavery was held by no less an authority than Joseph Story to be self-enforcing.

Prigg *vs.* Pennsylvania, 16 Peters, 613.

See, also, Dill *vs.* Ellicot, Taney's Decisions, 233.

Upon this principle only can be preserved in its full vigor the authority which the second clause of the sixth article declares: "This Constitution * * * shall be the *supreme* law of the land; and the judges in every State shall be bound thereby, anything in the constitution or laws of any State to the contrary notwithstanding."

How can legislation add to the force of the inhibition? Of what character shall it be? Would the repetition of the inhibition or the addition of penalties lend it more vigor? Would an act antecedently passed enable the proof of violation to be more clearly made than the powers of Congress and the act creating this Commission already provide?

If it be sought to support the action of the disqualified candidate by the judgment of the canvassing officer, we answer in the language of the court of appeals of Kentucky, in Patterson *vs.* Miller, &c., 2 Metc. Ky., 497:

The certificate which the examining board issues to a candidate that he is elected to the office of sheriff—although conclusive evidence that he was elected thereto, unless his election be contested before the proper board—is not even *prima facie* evidence that he was eligible to the office.

II.

E. A. Cronin was duly appointed, and had the right to cast his vote as an elector of the State of Oregon.

Watts received 15,206 and Cronin 14,157 votes at the election held upon November 7, 1876. Watts having been shown to have been disqualified, and the votes cast for him therefore being null and void, our contention is that, by the laws of Oregon, Cronin was elected and entitled to cast his vote as an elector.

It will not be contended that it was necessary for Cronin to receive the votes of a *majority* of all the legal voters casting their vote at the November election. Such is the law in some of the New England States at elections for Representatives in Congress and State and county officers; such is the law, also, in the election of United States Senators, (Revised Statutes, sec. 15,) and this principle explains in part the judgment of the Senate in the case of Abbott and Vance. But such is not the rule at presidential elections. It has often happened that the minority of the people have by plurality of votes chosen electors in the States. Thus, in 1848, in Ohio and several other States, the Cass electors were elected by a plurality of votes in preference to the Taylor electors, the Van Buren electors receiving a much larger number of votes than their plurality. There is, therefore, nothing in American public law to prevent the choice of electors by a minority of popular votes in a State any more than to forbid the choice of a President, as in the case of Mr. Lincoln's first election, by a minority of the total popular vote.

Nor, according to our antagonists, is a *majority* voting for an ineligible candidate required to defeat an election. On the contrary, our learned opponents must contend that even if the majority of qualified voters desire to elect, and so vote, yet if they divide their votes among several, so that a mere plurality, less than a majority, has supported the disqualified candidate, this plurality, if insufficient to elect, suffices to defeat the next highest competitor, and to force a new election upon the majority.

It may also happen that more than the number of electors to which a State is legally entitled may receive each more than a majority of the votes cast.

Thus, we may suppose, that in the State of Oregon, where there are three electors to be chosen, twenty thousand votes may be cast, divided among six candidates: A, B, and C receive each 9,800 votes; D, E, and F receive 9,700 votes. The remaining 500 votes may be thus distributed: To A, B, and D 200 votes; to A, C, and D 200 votes; and to B, C, and D 100 votes. The result will be: For A, 10,200; for B, 10,100; for C, 10,100, and for D, 10,200 votes. Supposing, now, that A were disqualified by holding a Federal office, who would be elected, and which rule ought to be adopted? that which rejects A as disqualified, and B and C as not elected, by reason of the votes for them having resulted in a tie, and only D elected; or that which rejects A as disqualified, and returns B, C, and D as elected?

We submit these questions to assist in elucidating the principle which should govern us. Under our present plan, by which the electors are mere *automata*, registering the decrees of party conventions, this case may be said to be unlikely, although the actual state of the vote in Oregon shows variations in the total number of votes given for the several candidates, thus indicating preferences among the voters even of the same party. And, according to the plan of our forefathers, by which the office of elector was to be a personal trust, confided to the wisest citizens, best qualified to judge of presidential capacity and the fitness of candidates, it would not have been at all unlikely that such a result might be developed by the counting of the ballots.

The principle to govern us must be consistent, *first*, with the constitutional mandate, " each State *shall appoint;*" *secondly*, with the constitutional inhibition, " but no person holding an office of trust or profit under the United States shall be appointed;" *thirdly*, with the rule that a majority vote is not necessary, but a plurality suffices for election; *fourthly*, with the possibility that a majority of the voters may vote for more than the legal number of electors; and *fifthly*, with the fact that upon the views of their work entertained by those who made the Constitution, the candidates for electors do not run, like rivals for the office of sheriff, *against* each other, but the choice is made by selection of the successful candidates out of the whole list of those nominated in that connection.

We respectfully submit that the only rule which fulfills these demands is that which treats votes given in violation of the constitutional prohibition as null and void, and not to be used for any purpose, and we believe this proposition to be sustained by the greater weight, if not the greater number, of both the American and English authorities.

The mandate is explicit, "each State *shall* appoint." Are we to adopt a principle which will permit the majority or, it may be, the minority, being a plurality, of the voters to prevent the execution of this mandate, to refuse obedience to this command? Were this majority or plurality to stay away from the polls, the minority attending and performing the duty of voting, as good citizens, would constitute the State, at least for this purpose. If the majority or plurality attend, and insist on doing that which is null and void in law, by casting blank pieces of paper as votes, or those which are equivalent to blanks, by not having force to elect because bearing the name of a disqualified candidate, should not the law-obeying minority still be considered the State?

In Oldknow *vs.* Wainwright, 1 W. Black, 228, S. C., 2 Burr. 1017, it was held by the King's Bench, (Lord Mansfield delivering the judgment,) that where a majority dissent from the election, but vote for no one else, an election by the minority is good.

The mandates of the Federal Constitution, "each State *shall* appoint;" of the act of Congress, (Revised Statutes, section 131,) "the electors of President and Vice-President *shall* be appointed, in each State, on the Tuesday next after the first Monday in November;" and of the State of Oregon, "on the Tuesday next after the first Monday in November, 1864, and every four years thereafter, there *shall* be elected," &c., are equally peremptory. The principle to be adopted must secure, or at least be consistent with obedience to this command. And for this reason, to enforce easy and certain obedience to the command, the public law of the United States has adopted the plurality principle in the choice of electors.

The inhibition is equally explicit. "But *no* person holding an office of trust or profit under the United States shall be appointed an elector." The principle to be adopted must enforce this inhibition in its full vigor and effect.

No other rule has this effect, except that which treats the votes cast for an ineligible candidate as in law blanks, which, not having been given in obedience to the mandate "shall elect," and having been cast in disobedience to the inhibition, have no legal force to elect an ineligible, nor to defeat an eligible candidate, and counts only the efficient votes, votes given to elect, not to defeat an election, to obey, not to frustrate the execution of the constitutional mandate.

And such is the weight of American authority, and to this conclusion, as one of general public law, would this Commission be forced to come, were the question directly before them for consideration, unaided by the action of the competent political authority in Oregon, which, as we shall show, is decisive of the rule as it prevails in that State.

The earliest American decision upon this subject was made by one of the greatest lawyers of the revolutionary period, one of the signers of the Declaration of Independence, Chief Justice Samuel Chase, of Maryland, the attempt at whose impeachment when a judge of the Supreme Court of the United States furnishes such a large item in the early judicial history of this country. That Chief Justice Samuel Chase was a lawyer of the first rank nobody has ever ventured to deny; but his violent temper exposed him to an attack which nearly cost him his high judicial position. In the case of Hutcheson *vs.* Tilden and Bordley, (4 Harris & McHenry's Rep., 279,) the defendants, being judges of the sheriffs' election, on the first Monday of October, 1794, declared Jones and Hall duly elected sheriffs of the county of Kent, although Hutcheson had more votes than either of them, on the ground that he was ineligible to election by want of sufficient qualification in real and personal estate, as required by law, whereupon Hutcheson sued Tilden and Bordley in an action on the case for damages for refusing to return him as sheriff elect. Chief Justice Chase, after stating the qualification required by the constitution, says:

All votes given for a candidate not having such qualifications are to be thrown away and rejected as having no force or operation in law. The plaintiff can only be entitled to such votes as were given after he received the necessary qualifications, all votes in his favor previous being illegal and void.

The report says that—

The plaintiff had received the necessary qualifications about 12 o'clock on the third day of the election, and, from the state of the polls, if he had received all the votes taken after that time, he could not be elected. Therefore there was verdict and judgment for the defendants.

This decision is the law of Maryland to-day, and has been applied in several cases, in more recent times, by the legislative department of that State.

In the constitution of Maryland, as it was in 1865, was contained the following provision of disqualification:

If any person has given any aid, comfort, countenance, or support to those engaged in armed hostility to the United States, or has, by any open deed or word, declared his adhesion to the cause of the enemies of the United States, or his desire for the triumph of said enemies of the United States, he is disqualified from holding any office of honor, profit, or trust under the laws of this State.

In 1865, Hart B. Holton contested the seat of Littleton Maclin as a senator from Howard County, and claimed the same for himself. It was referred to the Committee on Elections, who reported, *first*, that although Maclin had received the highest number of legal votes, nevertheless, being disqualified under the quoted provision, he was not entitled to the seat; and, *secondly*, "that Hart B. Holton, having received the highest number of votes cast for any duly-qualified candidate for senator for Howard County, is declared duly elected, and entitled to a seat in this body as senator from said county."—(Senate Journal, 1865, appendix, document E.)

And on February 14, 1865, this report was adopted by the senate, Maclin unseated and Holton inducted into office.—(Senate Journal, 1865, 116.)

In 1866, in the house of delegates, Thomas A. Spence, now assistant attorney-general for the Post-Office Department in this city, successfully contested the office of John R. Franklin as circuit judge of the twelfth judicial circuit of Maryland, on the double ground of disloyalty and the want of the necessary majority of legal votes.—(House Journal of 1866, 412, and appendix, document H.)

In 1866, before the house of delegates, George E. Gambrill contested the office of Sprigg Harwood as clerk of the circuit court for Anne Arundel County, on the ground of constitutional ineligibility caused by an increase in the profits of this clerkship while Harwood was a senator from Anne Arundel County, in 1865. Harwood had received the majority of the legal votes, but the committee on elections reported that Harwood was ineligible; that it "must be *presumed* to have been known by every voter;" and that Gambrill, the candidate of the minority, was entitled to the place.

And we think—

Say the committee, after stating the rule as we claim it, proceeding to show its convenience—

in a case like this, it would be highly inexpedient to submit this matter to another election. The result of the election of an ineligible person is that he enjoys the office until the legislature meets ; then, if he is declared out of office, he may again offer himself and hold until the legislature may again assemble, receiving the emoluments until again unseated, and perhaps again offer himself as a candidate with the same thing to go through.

The house of delegates, before which contests of this kind are judi- cially prosecuted in Maryland, sustained this report, ousted Harwood, voted down a resolution that the office was vacant, and inducted Gam- brill.—(House Journal, 1866, 279, 280, 281, 282, document G.)

The same rule prevails in the State of Maine, where it was first de- cided in 1831. It was in Maine that Governor Grover, of Oregon, was born and received his education, and thence he bore to Oregon the prin- ciples of law which guided his action in this case. The first elucidation of law upon this subject in Maine may be found in the opinion of all the judges of the supreme judicial court, viz, Chief-Justice Prentiss Mellen and Justices Nathan Weston and Albion K. Parris, published in the appendix to the seventh volume of Greenleaf's Reports, (pages 497 and 501.)

The governor and council submitted to the judges the following among other questions :

Question 4. Can ballots having the names of persons on them who do not possess the constitutional qualifications of a representative be counted as votes under the fifth sec- tion of fourth article, part first, of the constitution of Maine, so as to prevent a majority of the votes given for eligible persons constituting a choice ?

To which the judges, in June, 1831, submitted the following answer, (side page 501 :)

To the fourth question proposed, without a particular statement of reasons, we merely answer in the negative.

The fifth section of the fourth article, part first, of the constitution of Maine, (adopted in 1819,) then in force, was as follows :

The meetings for the choice of representatives shall be warned in due course of law by the selectmen of the several towns seven days at least before the election, and the selectmen thereof shall preside impartially at such meetings, receive the votes of the qualified electors present, sort, count, and declare them in open town meeting and in the presence of the town clerk, who shall, from a list of the persons voted for, with the number of votes for each person against his name, make a fair count thereof in the presence of the selectmen and in open town meeting, and a fair copy of this list shall be attested by the selectmen and town clerk and delivered by said selectmen to each representative within ten days next after such election. And the towns and planta- tions organized by law, belonging to any class herein provided, shall hold their meet- ings at the same time in the respective towns and plantations, shall be notified, held, and regulated, the votes received, sorted, counted, and declared in the same manner. And the assessors and clerks of plantations shall have all the powers and be subject to all the duties which selectmen and town clerks have and are subject to under this con- stitution. And the selectmen of such towns, and the assessors of such towns, and the assessors of such plantations so classed, shall, within four days next after such meet- ing, meet at some place, to be prescribed and notified by the selectmen or assessors of the eldest town or plantation, in such class, and the copies of said lists shall be then examined and compared ; and in case any person shall be elected *by a majority of all the votes,* the selectmen or assessors shall deliver the certified copies of such lists to the person so elected within ten days next after such election ; and the clerks of towns and plantations respectively shall seal up copies of such lists and cause them to be delivered into the secretary's office twenty days at least before the first Wednesday in January annually ; but in case *no person shall have a majority of votes,* the selectmen and assessors shall, as soon as may be, notify another meeting, and the same proceed- ings shall be had at every future meeting until an election shall have been effected :

Provided, That the legislature may by law prescribe a different mode of returning, examining, and ascertaining the election of the representatives in such.

(Constitution of Maine, article 4, section 5, October 29, 1819.)

Spear *vs.* Robinson, 29 Maine, 531, (decided in 1849,) is to the same effect. At a town meeting in the town of Warren it was—

Voted to choose a fish committee; voted to choose three for said committee; chose Robert Spear 2d, John G. Hoffses, and Waldo Brackett; voted that two more be added to the fish committee; Larkin Bogs and Joseph Vaughan were chosen. It being ascertained that John G. Hoffses was not a freeholder, Robert McIntyre was chosen one of the fish committee in his stead. (Page 532.)

The court held (page 541) that—

The case shows that the town voted to choose five as their fish committee, and they made choice of five persons; but it appearing that one of those elected was not a freeholder, another was chosen in his stead, and that the plaintiffs are those who were freeholders, and have acted as that committee.

The choice of the man who was not a freeholder was a *nullity*, and the one last elected was chosen in conformity with the provisions of the act.

The opinion of the judges, published in the appendix to 38 Maine, 597, given in 1855, in answer to questions submitted by the governor, does not bear upon the question under discussion.

The last governor and council had issued a commission to Abel C. Dinslow as county commissioner of Sagadahoc county. It subsequently appeared that there was no such man as Abel C. Dinslow, but there was one whose name was "Abel E. Dinslow," and for whom there was good reason to suppose the voters intended to throw their votes, instead of Abel C. Dinslow.

Upon this state of facts the succeeding governor submitted four questions to the judges, viz: First. Whether the governor and council could revise the doings of the last governor and council so as to receive proof of the eligibility to said office of such a man as Abel C. Dinslow? Secondly. If they found there was no such man as Abel C. Dinslow, but that the voters intended their votes for Abel E. Dinslow, it was competent to issue a new commission to him? Thirdly. If not, could they throw out the votes for Abel C. Dinslow, and issue a new commission to "such person who is eligible to said office as hall appear to have the highest number of votes?" And, fourthly. If not, was there a vacancy in the office which the governor might fill?

The judges reported, in reply, that the new governor and council could not review the proceedings of their predecessors; that they were not authorized by the act to receive any other evidence of the number of votes or names of the persons voted for than what is contained in the copies of the records of votes given in the cities, towns, and plantations of the county. They " *therefore* answered the first, second, and third questions in the negative, and the fourth in the affirmative."

Indeed, it is not possible that Spear *vs.* Robinson, and the opinion reported in 38 Maine, could have any effect adverse to our views, for the reason that the principle of public law enunciated by the judges in 1831, as reported in 7 Greenleaf, was adopted by the legislative department, and is now the law of that State, as shown by the Revised Statutes of Maine of 1840, page 65, section 27, and the Revised Statutes of 1871, page 98, section 32, in the following words:

And in all returns of elections the whole number of ballots given in shall be distinctly stated; *but blank pieces of paper, and votes for persons not eligible to office, shall not be counted as ballots.*

The same rule prevails in the commonwealth of Massachusetts.

By resolves approved May 18, 1852, Luther S. Cushing, C. W. Storey, and Lewis Josselyn were "appointed commissioners to prepare and publish a new edition of the Reports of Contested Elections, prepared and published by said Cushing in pursuance of an order of the house of representatives of March 1, 1834, including therein reports of all cases which have occurred since the time of said publication."

From this work, a volume of 757 pages, we find, on page 576, that, in 1849, it was decided, on a petition against the election of the member returned from the town of Somerset, that "a vote for a candidate who is constitutionally ineligible is not to be counted." The committee to whom the subject was referred made an elaborate report, which was agreed to April 10, 1849. They state (p. 578) that they—

Believe the question to have been settled by the 'decision of the house in the case of the town of Whately, (reported on page 439 of the same volume,) in 1843, but as that decision is perhaps of doubtful authority, having been made at a time of much party excitement, and as it seems desirable that a question so important should be finally settled, they venture to suggest a few reasons in favor of rejecting votes given for ineligible candidates at elections for representatives.

In the first place, it is to be *presumed* that such votes are cast by mistake, as, whenever the names of the persons giving such votes have been ascertained, it has generally been found that their votes had been cast inadvertently.

Again, the policy of the law requires that such a construction should be put upon all proceedings at elections as to make such proceedings valid rather than nugatory. An election is always attended with trouble, inconvenience, and expense, and should not be set aside for light or frivolous causes. If votes cast by mistake for persons not eligible are to be counted, then the intention and will of the voter is defeated; if, on the other hand, such votes are wilfully put into the ballot-box, the person who thus votes indicates so clearly his disregard of the value of the elective franchise that it is only a deserved punishment for his delinquency to deprive his vote of all weight and influence at such election. By so doing a voter is not deprived of any legitimate exercise of his right, because he can always manifest his opposition to any one candidate by voting for some other.

Finally, it seems to the committee that there is no reason why a person who votes for an ineligible candidate should not be put upon the same footing with one who does not vote at all, as in both cases the parties show a disposition to prevent an election, and both of them show an unwillingness to perform their duty by aiding to promote those elections which are absolutely essential to the existence of the government. For if every voter refrained wholly from voting, or voted for an ineligible candidate, the result would be the same—no choice; and, although it is true that no penalty is attached by law to a neglect of this obligation of voting, yet the obligation is not the less plain for that, and the committee believe it to be a duty too important to be neglected and too sacred to be trifled with by voting for fictitious persons or ineligible candidates. It may be urged that, since the Revised Statutes provide that blank pieces of paper shall not be counted as votes, the absence of any provision to reject votes for ineligible candidates is a strong argument that the legislature did not intend that they should be so rejected. The committee, however, believe that it was not at that time contemplated that any provision could be necessary, it being supposed that the practice of rejecting such votes by the legislature was so uniform as to have taken the place of law; otherwise, it is difficult to see why the same section was not made to comprehend both cases.

The voter who puts into the ballot-box a blank piece of paper as clearly indicates his opposition to all the candidates as he who puts in a vote for an ineligible candidate, and there seems to be no reason why the opinion of one should not be entitled to consideration as well as that of the other.

New York, by the unanimous judgment of her court of appeals, has approved the same rule in the case of People on the relation of Furman *vs.* Clute, 50 N. Y., 451, in an elaborate opinion, of which this is the summary:

A minority of the whole body of qualified electors may elect to an office where the majority decline to vote, or where they may vote for one who is ineligible to the office, knowing of the disqualification. Notice of the disqualifying fact and of its legal effect may be given so directly to the voter as to charge him with actual knowledge of the disqualification, or the disqualifying fact may be so patent or notorious as that his knowledge of the ineligibility may be presumed as matter of law; but not only the fact which disqualifies, but also the rule or enactment of law which makes it thus effectual, must be brought home so clearly ·to the knowledge or notice of the elector as that to give his vote therewith indicates his intent to waste it, in order to render his vote a nullity. Where a majority of the electors, through ignorance of the law or the fact, voted for one ineligible to the office, the votes are not nullities; but while they fail to elect, the òffce cannot be given to the qualified person having the next highest number of votes. The election is a failure, and a new election must be had.

Three times has Indiana spoken in emphatic approbation of the doctrine for which we contend: Gulick *vs.* New, 14 Ind, 93, decided in 1860; Carson *vs.* McPhetridge, 15 Ind., 327; Price *vs.* Baker, governor, 41 Ind., 572, decided in 1873.

In Gulick *vs.* New, the principle decided is summarized by the reporter in these words: ·

The governor may determine, even against the decision of a board of canvassers, whether an applicant is entitled to receive a commission or not, where the objection to his right to receive it rests upon the ground that the constitutional prohibition is interposed. If the governor should ascertain that he has commissioned a person who is ineligible to the office, he may issue another commission to the person legally entitled thereto. Where a majority of the ballots at an election were for a person not eligible to the office under the constitution, it was held that the ballots cast for such ineligible person were · ineffectual, and that the person receiving the greatest number of legal votes, though not a majority of the ballots, was duly elected and entitled to the office. The mayor of a city, under the general law, has jurisdiction as a judicial officer throughout the county, and the voters of the county are therefore chargeable with notice of his ineligibility under the constitution to any office other than a judicial one during the term for which he was elected.

Of Price *vs.* Governor Baker, the syllabus is as follows:

Where a majority of the ballots at an election are given to a candidate who is not eligible to the office, the ballots so cast are not to be counted for any purpose. They cannot elect the ineligible candidate or defeat the election of the opposing candidate by showing that he did not receive a majority of the votes cast at such election. It follows that the eligible candidate will receive an office, although less than a majority of the votes are cast for him.

The same principle is supported by the cogent reasoning of the dissenting òpinion of Chief-Justice Thompson in Commonwealth *vs.* Cluly, 56 Penn. St., 277:

But I confess my inability to see, if it must be treated as a preliminary question, why, if the constitutional disqualification of the defendant be established, the relator is not entitled to the office. He had votes enough to elect him, if the votes for the defendant be regarded as thrown away. This cannot be disputed: It seems to me this proposition cannot be controverted; that if the votes cast for the defendant would not confer the office on him, they do not possess the faculty or capacity of depriving the plaintiff of his election, having, as already said, enough votes to elect him. The majority of votes operates only in one direction, namely, to elect, and, by electing, defeat any competitor; but without electing, I deny that the effect is to elect a competing candidate. The thing is not possible. If it were, a majority of votes for a fictitious candidate, or one notoriously ineligible, would defeat an eligible candidate. The elective franchise cannot operate in such a way. If people do not vote, generally they consent that those that do may elect. This is the rule in all popular elections. If, therefore, people do not vote for candidates who can by law exercise the offices voted for, it seems to me to follow that they tacitly consent that those who do vote for such as are eligible shall elect on equivalent principles. If such an excuse were good for anything, it ought to be good to render effective the votes for the ineligible candidate, and thus give him the office in spite of the existing disqualification."

An analogous proposition was adopted and acted upon in Commonwealth *vs.* Read, 2 Ashmead, 264; where the defendant [Read] was held to have been elected treasurer by the county board, having received but one legal vote out of twenty cast. The other nineteen were decided to have been void and ineffectual, because they were cast *viva voce*, and the single vote by ballot to have controlled the election, that being the mode prescribed by law.

The view we present has the support of the best text-writers in England and America.

Judge Luther S. Cushing, in his standard work upon the law and practice of legislative assemblies, states the rule thus:

SEC. 177. In England, where a plurality only is necessary to an election, and where the votes are given orally, it is also held that if the electors have notice of the disqualification of a candidate, every vote given for him afterward will be thrown away and considered as not having been given at all. The effect of this rule is that not only will the election of a disqualified person be held void; but if such election takes place after notice of the disqualification is given to the electors, the candidate having the highest number of votes will be elected. This doctrine, however hard it may seem, is founded in the familiar principle that every man is bound to know the law with reference to any act which he undertakes to do, and consequently that when an elector is apprised of the fact of disqualification of a candidate, and notwithstanding gives his vote for him, the elector takes upon himself the risk of losing his vote if his construction of the law turns out to be wrong.

SEC. 178. In this country it is equally true that an election of a disqualified person is absolutely void, and in those States where a plurality elects and where the votes are given orally, as in England, votes given for a candidate after notice of his disqualification are thrown away, and the candidate having the next highest number of votes is elected.

SEC. 179. In reference to elections by ballot, in which secrecy is the distinguishing feature, and in which, consequently, neither the returning officers nor the electors themselves are supposed to know for whom the votes are given until the result is declared, it seems not unreasonable to consider the votes for ineligible candidates to be thrown away in all cases, and the opposing candidate elected where the electors know, or must be presumed to know, the disability, and in all cases where there is no such actual or presumed knowledge to hold the whole proceeding merely void.

And we are supported by an unbroken array of the expositions of the law made in our mother country, as we shall presently show, as well as the approval of her best text-books.

Mr. Grant, in his work on corporations, at page 208, says:

A disqualification patent or notorious, at once causes the votes given for the candidate laboring under it to be thrown away; the same would probably be held to be the case where the electors had the means of knowledge of the candidate's qualification, or the contrary, and might have ascertained the facts if they had pleased.

These judgments also find a large measure of support in the legislative practice of the country, as may be learned by examination of the speech of Senator Carpenter, of Wisconsin, at the second session of the Forty-second Congress, in the case of the disputed senatorial election in North Carolina. See *Congressional Globe*, part 3, March 19 to April 23, 1872, appendix.

What can be produced to the contrary?

Pennsylvania is vouched in aid, but presents herself with the broken voice of a divided court, speaking however only *obiter*, and conceding that a vote given with knowledge for an ineligible candidate cannot be counted. Commonwealth *vs.* Cluly, *ut supra.*

California is cited in aid of the proposed rule that a plurality may, by voting for an ineligible candidate, defeat the constitutional mandate to elect.

People *ex rel.* Malony *vs.* Whitman, 10 Cal., 38.

Saunders *vs.* Haynes, 13 Cal., 145.

In Malony *vs.* Whitman the question did not require or receive decision. The majority of the court held that Mandeville, the officer whose qualification was in dispute, was not ineligible. The dissenting opinion of Mr. Justice Field abstained from discussion of the question now under debate. He says: "As we hold that Mandeville was eligible, we refrain from the expression of any opinion whether, if he were ineligible, the votes given for him should be thrown out as so many blanks, and Whitman declared elected, as contended by counsel. Much argument may be had against the propriety of a rule which would, in a popular government, give an office to a person who was clearly not the choice of the people, as shown by the election." (See State of Wisconsin *vs.* Giles, 1 Chandler, 117; opinion of the judges of the supreme court of Maine in answer to the questions propounded by the governor, 38 Maine, 597.)

In Saunders *vs.* Haynes, the opinion was pronounced by Baldwin, J., who, as counsel, had argued the case of Malony *vs.* Whitman on the same side, Terry, C. J., concurring. It, however, assumes that the " majority of those voting, *by mistake of law or fact,* happen to cast their votes upon an ineligible candidate," and thus justifies the conclusion that an opposite rule would have been applied, if the result had not been produced *" by mistake of law or fact."*

The decision in State of Wisconsin *vs.* Giles, 1 Chandler, 112, is mere *gratis dictum.* The court held the majority candidate qualified, but added (p. 117):

> *Such being the opinion of the court, it is unnecessary to pass upon the second question— whether in the event of the person receiving the highest number of votes being ineligible, the person receiving the next highest number is elected.* But as the question was fully argued, and as it is one that may arise again, it is proper to say, that we are all of the opinion that the mere ineligibility of a candidate does not, as the law now is, render void the votes cast for him; that such votes should not be rejected, but should be counted by the canvassers, and in the event of such ineligible person having the highest number of votes, the person having the next highest number is not thereby elected. If any public embarrassment is apprehended from this, such as that an office may remain indefinitely vacant, by reason of a majority of the electors obstinately persisting in voting for an ineligible person, it is within the undoubted power of the legislature to prevent it, by enacting that all such votes shall be deemed void, and not to be counted.

This decision was followed by the case of The State of Wisconsin on the relation of Off *vs.* Smith, 14 Wisc. 497, in which the gratuitous and unnecessary observations just quoted were treated, without re-examination, or any even the most superficial consideration, as having settled the law in Wisconsin. The court say, (page 498,) and this is all of their opinion upon this question:

> The last question has been already settled in this State by the case of The State *vs.* Giles, 1 Chand., 112. It was there held, by the unanimous judgment of the court, that in the absence of a statute declaring it so, the mere ineligibility of a candidate does not render void the votes cast for him; that such votes should not be rejected, but should be counted by the canvassers; and that in the event of such ineligible person having the highest number of votes, the person having the next highest number would not be thereby elected.

Georgia is supposed to have pronounced against our proposition, State *ex rel.* Hardwick *vs.* Swearingen, 12 Geo., 23. In this case, also, the remarks of the court upon the matter now under debate are purely *obiter dicta,* for the majority candidate was found to have been free from disqualification. The objection to him was that he was not a corporator and resident within the city of Oglethorpe, as clerk and treasurer, of which he claimed to have been elected. But the court, (Lumpkin, J.,) pronouncing the opinion, held that the objection was not well taken, in that—

> No such restriction was imposed upon the voters of the young and rapidly growing town in their selection of a suitable person to fill the offices of clerk and treasurer. They are at liberty to select from Macon, Columbus, or any other part of the State, the person in their judgment best qualified to discharge these functions.

And thus having decided and disposed of the case, added:

> Under no circumstances could we permit the informant to be installed into these appointments, he not having received a majority of the legal votes of the city. Under such circumstances, if the incumbent be removed, a new eletion will be ordered.

Which addition is about as valuable, without being as true, as this, with which Judge Lumpkin's wisdom follows and concludes the opionion, viz:

> These municipal corporations are the germs and miniature models of free government; and their internal police and administration should not be interfered with for slight causes; not unless some great right has been withheld or wrong perpetrated.

Missouri is claimed to have dissented from our proposition.

State *ex rel*. Kempf *vs*. Boal, 46 Mo., 528.

State *ex rel*. Attorney-General *vs*. Vail, 53 Mo., 97.

But the first of these cases sustains the principle for which we contend. Both relator and defendant were disqualified, and therefore judgment could not be rendered in the relator's favor, but the court say in addition:

> As regards the votes cast for the defendant, they were nugatory. It was as though no such votes had been cast at the election. The constitution distinctly prohibited their being cast up or treated as votes at all, as it also prohibited the issuing a certificate of election because of them. The evident intention of the constitution is that the party receiving the majority of the available votes should have the certificate of election; that is, the majority of votes that "it was permissible for the canvassers to cast up."

The provisions of the constitution of Missouri, here referred to, are the following, (article 2:)

> SEC. 7. Within sixty days after this constitution takes effect, every person in this State holding any office of honor, trust, or profit, under the constitution or laws thereof, or under any municipal corporation, or any of the other offices, positions, or trusts mentioned in the third section of this article, shall take and subscribe the said oath. If any officer or person referred to in this section shall fail to comply with the requirements thereof, his office, position, or trust shall *ipso facto* become vacant, and the vacancy shall be filled according to the law governing the case.
>
> SEC. 8. No vote, in any election by the people, shall be cast up for, nor shall any certificate of election be granted to, any person who shall not, within fifteen days next preceding said election, have taken, subscribed, and filed said oath.

State *vs*. Vail does not withdraw this affirmation of the view for which we contend, although it does limit it to disqualifications other than those personal and latent. The syllabus No. 6 is this:

> The candidate who at an election receives the greatest number of votes, except the successful candidate, is not entitled to the office when the successful candidate is ineligible, *owing to personal disqualifications and such as were not patent to the voters*.

In the course of the very elaborate opinion of Judge Napton, he comments upon and distinguishes the case of Gulick *vs*. New, without disapproving it, in these words:

> But in the case in Indiana, it is conceded that where the candidate receiving the highest number of votes is ineligible by reason of a cause which the voters were not bound to know, such as non-age, want of naturalization, &c., the result is a failure to elect. (P. 115.)

And afterward added, (p. 116:)

> To declare a candidate elected, who has received but few votes, on the ground that his competitor who received, perhaps, twice as many, was disqualified, would not accomplish the will of the electors. The object of an election is to ascertain the choice of the majority. [Query, *plurality?*] If a disqualified candidate receives a thousand votes and his competitor only a hundred, to pronounce the latter elected is not in accordance with any ascertained will of the electors, unless it may be inferred that the votes for the disqualified candidate were cast with a knowledge of his inability to take the office—an inference which could not be drawn *where the disqualifications are such as are enumerated in the pleadings in this case*. [Not a citizen for five years, nor a qualified voter, non-age, and disloyalty.] *It is unnecessary to determine whether it would be the rule, in any case of disqualifications, whether patent or latent.*

The case of Pearce *vs*. Hawkins, 2 Swan, 87, sometimes cited in argument against the view we present, really sustains it. Two sentences in the opinion of the court contain all that is said upon the subject:

> But as he was a resident in the tenth civil district when elected constable for the

eleventh, he was ineligible to the office, and his appointment was *void*. And in an action against him for an alleged trespass, he cannot defend and justify the act as being done in virtue of his office, when it is made to appear that he has no title thereto, and that his asumed appointment *was illegal and void*.

The case of The People on the relation of L. C. Crawford *vs*. Moliter, 23 Mich., 341, was disposed of by an admission in pleading. It was a *quo warranto* to inquire into respondent's title to the office of supervisor. His plea set up that one hundred and fifty votes were cast at the election, of which relator, Leonard Crawford, had two votes, respondent sixty-nine votes, and that seventy-two ballots contained the name, " L. C. Crawford," whereby the relator claimed to be duly elected. The court say they can—

Consider any admissions in the plea as binding on the respondent, and as showing all he can aver in his own behalf; and this plea is an admission that respondent has no title, because it shows, affirmatively, that he did not receive the greatest number of votes cast. The statute in relation to town elections is substantially like those governing other elections. It provides that "the persons having received the greatest number of votes given for any office at such election shall be deemed and declared duly elected." It does not, under any circumstances, allow a minority candidate to be deemed elected—whether the person for whom the majority appear to have voted can or cannot be installed. The majority here *are alleged by the plea* to have voted for some one whom they designated as " L. C. Crawford." Whether there is in fact a person of that name or not does not change the state of the canvass, nor make 69 a larger number than 72.

Fish *vs*. Collins, 21 La. Ann., 289, may be claimed to be, but is not, against us. All things considered, the modesty with which it refrains rom deciding this question is remarkable. Ludeling, C. J., says:

The plaintiff does not allege that he received a larger number of votes cast at the election than either of his competitors ; *but, on the contrary, he admits that the defendant received a greater number of votes than he did.* * * *It is unnecessary in this case to express any opinion as to whether the votes cast for a person who is notoriously known to be ineligible should be rejected or not, as no such allegations are made in the petition.*

In State *ex rel*. Staes *vs*. Gastinel, 18 La. Ann., 517 ; S. C. 20 La., 114, it was shown that Gastinel was not of sufficient age (thirty years) to be eligible to the office of recorder and justice of the peace, and he was accordingly ousted. The court said:

We cannot adopt the theory of the relator, that the ousting of the defendant by means of this proceeding inures to his benefit. *What might have been his rights had he contested the election of defendant in accordance with law, we are not called on to say ;* but we are of the opinion that, having, as a candidate, acquiesced in the result of that election, we must in these proceedings consider him only as a citizen before us, seeking to have the law enforced against the recorder *de facto;* and, under the provisions of the C. P. and the 15th section of the city charter, notify the corporation of the necessity of a new appointment. The law does not authorize us to declare the relator, under the circumstances, to be the choice of the people. Upon his own showing, he did not receive a majority of the votes cast, and but for some action, on the part of some one authorized, the present incumbent would have continued in the performance of the duties of the office, as the duly-elected recorder of the second district of New Orleans.

In Sublett *vs*. Bidwell, 47 Miss., 273, where the candidate was disqualified by having been a registrar of voters at the registration preliminary to the very election, it was held that—

It cannot be said that the candidate has been elected unless he has received a majority of the legal votes cast; he is not the choice of the people. If the majority make choice of candidate under some personal disability, disqualifying him from taking and enjoying the office, the utmost that can be said of it is, that there has been no election. The election, by a majority or plurality of votes, (as the law may be,) is the foundation of the "right" to the office. The certificate or the commission is only evidence of that fact.

If the majority candidate is disqualified, it does not follow that he who has received the next highest vote and is qualified shall take the office. * * * The general principle pervading our election system is that the highest vote entitles to the office, if its recipient can take. There is by implication a negation of the office to the minority candidate in all cases, except those covered by the last section of the schedule to the constitution (sec. 15.) * * * The section is as follows: "If any candidate receiving the highest number of votes cannot take the oath of office preseribed in this constitution, then the candidate receiving the next highest vote shall be entitled to enter the office." * * * The constitution does establish the rule that votes cast for a person *thus* disqualified are void and of no effect, unless the disfranchisement has been removed. The practical interpretation put upon the section has been that it is a *personal* disability to "hold office," and if that be removed before the term begins, the election is made good, and the person may take the office. * * * Without going into the general reasoning, the great weight of American authority, and, as we think, upon the soundest consideration, is, that although the majority vote for a disqualified person, the votes so cast are not illegal, and therefore to be treated as naught; but the result is, if the ineligible candidate cannot take the office, *the electors have failed to make a choice. In truth, there has been no election at all,* and the minority candidate has no right to the office.

The cases cited are State of Georgia *vs.* Swearingen; State *ex rel.* Off *vs.* Smith; State *vs.* Giles; Saunders *vs.* Haynes; 23 Louisiana, 314, and the opinion of the supreme court of Maine in 38 Maine, 597.

And again, (p. 277:)

The votes are ineffective to confer the office, *not because of any legal infirmity in the electors,* but because the individual has not himself the capacity for the office. In such cases as already observed, upon the fact being ascertained, there has been a failure to fill the office, and it is vacant *de jure.*

Rhode Island is the last State which can be cited against us. We refer to the case, in the matter of George H. Corliss, *ut supra.* To the fourth question, the judges of the supreme court of Rhode Island made answer:

We think the disqualification does not result in the election of the candidate next in vote, *but in a failure to elect.*

In England it has been held that where electors vote for an ineligible candidate, knowing his disqualification, their votes are not to be counted any more than if they were thrown for a dead man or the man in the moon; and that in such a case the opposing candidate being qualified, will be elected, although he has had a minority of the votes. (King *vs.* Hawkins, 10 East., 210; Reg. *vs.* Coaks, 3 Ell. & Bl., 253.) But even in England, if the disqualification is unknown, the minority candidate is not entitled to the office, the election being a failure. (Queen *vs.* Hiorns, 7 Ad. & E., 960; Rex *vs.* Bridge, 1 M. & Selw., 76.) And it has been held that to entitle the minority candidate to the office, it is not enough that the electors know of the facts which amount to a disqualification, unless they likewise know that they amount to it in point of law. (The Queen *vs.* The Mayor, &c., Law Rep., 3 Q. B., 629.)

In this country the law is certainly not more favorable to the minority candidate. (State *vs.* Giles, 1 Chandler, Wis., 112; State *vs.* Smith, 14 Wis., 497; Saunders *vs.* Haynes, 13 Cal., 145; People *vs.* Clute, 50 N. Y., 451.) *The question submitted to us does not allege or imply that the electors, knowing the disqualification, voted for the ineligible candidate in willful defiance of the law;* and certainly, in the absence of proof, it is not to be presumed that they so voted. The only effect of the disqualification, in our opinion, is to render void the election of the candidate who is disqualified, *and to leave one place in the electoral college unfilled.*

That this was purely *obiter,* that it was wholly unnecessary for the governor to have submitted such a question to the judges, is shown by the following passage from a letter written by that eminent publicist, William Beach Lawrence, to Senator Kernan, published in the New York World, January 27, 1877:

OCHRE POINT, NEWPORT, R. I., *January 26,* 1877.

DEAR SENATOR KERNAN: When it became known, some weeks since, that one of the republican candidates who had been voted for as an elector was disqualified in consequence of holding an "office of profit or trust," it was supposed that the same question might arise here as is now before you in regard to the Oregon electoral vote. Having been myself at the head of the Rhode Island democratic electoral ticket, I looked into the subject with the intention of claiming the place for the democratic candidate who might have the highest number of votes. The canvass showed, however, that excluding the votes for Mr. Corliss, there had been no election, inasmuch as three of us had the same number of votes, and the fourth man one less than his colleagues—a case for which express provision is made by our State law, which requires the place to be filled by the general assembly "when the votes are divided equally among any of the candidates, or otherwise there shall not be an election of the number of electors to which the State may be entitled." As in the act of Congress of 1845, there is in our law a distinction between a failure to elect and a vacancy arising from the electors chosen declining to serve or failing to attend after the election, in which cases the vacancies are to be filled by the other electors. I note this, because in the Oregon law there is but one provision as to vacancies, and they are to be filled by the electoral college. This provision cannot apply to cases of failure to elect, the term "otherwise" being controlled by the context.

I shall not trouble you with the distinctions between original vacancies and those occurring after an office is filled—a matter so often discussed in connection with the respective powers of the President and Senate in relation to nominations—but I merely allude to the fact that the electoral colleges are in no sense continuous bodies, but that they are created *de novo* for each presidential election. The powers of the canvassers are in the two States substantially the same. In Rhode Island, "the governor, in the presence of the secretary of state, shall examine and count the votes, and give notice to the electors of their election." In Oregon the votes are to be canvassed by the secretary of state in the presence of the governor. "The secretary of state shall prepare two lists of the names of the electors elected and affix the seal of the State to the same. Such lists shall be signed by the governor and secretary, and by the latter delivered to the college of electors at the hour of their meeting on such first Wednesday of December."

The supreme court of Rhode Island are by the constitution required to "give their written opinion on any question of law whenever requested by the governor or by either house of the general assembly." The governor is not, however, bound by it. I inclose the opinion given by the judges under which the governor and general assembly acted on the recent occasion. So much of it as shows that a person cannot decline or resign an office to which he is ineligible or incapable of being elected, that the disqualification is not removed by the resignation of the office of trust unless the office is resigned before the election, and that under our law the election by the people constitutes the appointment in the sense of the Federal Constitution, is applicable to the case before you. For the reason already mentioned—the equality of the votes between the highest democratic candidates—the discussion whether the disqualification resulted in the election of the candidate next in the vote or in a failure to elect any one was wholly irrelevant, as confessedly under the circumstances there was no minority candidate chosen.

The opinion was not published till it was laid before the legislature, and I was surprised to find that a question depending on the fact of one of the democratic candidates having more votes than his colleagues was passed on by the judges or that it had been submitted to them by the governor, inasmuch as he was well aware that, had there been any occasion for considering it, we should have been asked to have been heard on it. As it is, so far as the "opinion" touches on the effect of Mr. Corliss's disability on the claim of the next eligible candidate, it must be regarded in the nature of *obiter dictum*.

Another passage from the letter we desire to submit, because it is in the nature of original and very valuable historical testimony, with reference to the cases of Albert Gallatin and Mr. Bailey, referred to in Commonwealth *vs.* Cluly :

In the debates in Congress as to the effect of the election of a disqualified candidate, the cases of Mr. Gallatin and Mr. Bailey are frequently cited. The one occurred in the Senate, the other in the House ; and in neither case did the question arise on the claim of a competing candidate. Mr. Gallatin's case dates back as far as 1793. Owing to the position which I occupied toward him many years afterward in the diplomatic service, I became entirely familiar with it. Arriving in this country fourteen years previously to his election and consequently during the war of the Revolution, and many years before the adoption of the present Constitution, Mr. Gallatin had become identified with the American people in every way known to the laws of that day. He had as early as 1780 acquired a legal domicile in the State of Massachusetts, the only way in which naturalization could then be effected.

The articles of the Confederation, which were the existing Constitution, provided that " the free inhabitants of the different States in the Union shall be entitled to all privileges and immunities of all citizens in the several States," thus making the terms "inhabitants" and "citizens" equivalent to one another.

Mr. Gallatin, having invested his patrimony in lands which were then supposed to be in Virginia, but were afterward decided to be in Pennsylvania, as a matter of abundant caution in reference to those lands, went through the form of naturalization according to the laws of the State of Virginia, and nine years had not elapsed from the date of that act, which was the assumed ground of disqualification, before he took his seat in the Senate. Even dating from the period of that naturalization, he had been a citizen some five years before the adoption of the Constitution. That the restrictions in that instrument were not intended to be retrospective, may well be inferred from the fact that for the office of President no one who was then a citizen was disqualified, and Mr. Gallatin at the time that he was unseated as a Senator was eligible to the Presidency. These facts I take from what may be deemed an autobiographical notice of Mr. Gallatin, as the paper, though prepared by me, was submitted to his revision. No competitor, as has been stated, petitioned against his return, nor, as far as I am aware, had he any, for he was elected by a legislature the majority of which were his political opponents. In all probability, had he been an ordinary man, there would have been no objection to his election. The petition was made by federalists, who feared the force of his abilities, and he was declared ineligible by a strict party vote of 14 to 12.

Mr. Bailey's case arose several years later. He was chief clerk of the State Department, and notwithstanding the fact that he was at Washington in the public service, and that no residence there could give him more political rights than would be derived from living in a fort or an arsenal of the United States, he was decided to have lost his Massachusetts citizenship and to be disfranchised so as not to be competent to be elected a Representative from that State.

We have thus cited, and endeavored fairly to represent, every American case of which we have any knowledge, and we submit that while there may be *obiter dicta* contrary to the proposition for which we contend, in no one American case has it been ruled that the plurality or majority of voters, by voting with knowledge, actual or presumed, for an ineligible candidate, can defeat an election. In most of the cases the observations upon this subject were entirely gratuitous and uncalled for; and others simply adopt the former without any examination whatever. We find, for instance, the significant fact that the opinions of the judges in 38 Maine are repeatedly referred to as sustaining a doctrine contrary to that which we maintain upon this subject, although in Maine the law has been long settled by the concurring and harmonious action of the judicial and executive departments that votes for an ineligible candidate are mere waste paper, and can perform no legal function whatever.

The gospel of American political action, whatever else it may contain, embraces two great commandments : first, thou shalt elect; and, secondly, thou shalt not elect any disqualified person. The disqualification in this case is attached to the grant; the State, availing itself of the power, must take it *cum onere*, and subject to the disqualification. It is not the voter who appoints the elector ; it is the State; and the State cannot plead ignorance ; she cannot appoint any disqualified person. Even the voter, although the Constitution secures him no right to partake in the appointment, except through the agency of the State, which does appoint, if he be permitted by the legislature of the State, in its control over the manner of appointment, to cast his ballot for electors, must see to it that they are duly qualified. He cannot plead ignorance of the law, as perhaps he might of some lurking and obscure statutory disqualification, for the disqualification is in the very sentence which contains the grant by force of which the State is enabled to permit him to vote, and, except subject to the disqualification, advantage cannot be taken by him of the grant at all.

Nor can he plead ignorance of the fact in this case. The rulings of the Commission forbid our making the proof, and showing, as we otherwise should endeavor to do, that of those who voted for Watts, far more in number than his excess of votes over Cronin knew of his disqualification; that twice, at numerously attended public meetings in Oregon City and Portland, the fact was made matter of public debate between Watts and Cronin ; that it was considered and discussed in a newspaper published at the home of Watts; that Yamhill, where Watts was postmaster, is the county-seat of La Fayette County, to which town the people of the county resort for the transaction of their legal business, marriage licenses, the settlement of the estates of their decedents, the record of their deeds and the payment of their taxes, as well as the purchase of their supplies and the marketing of their produce; and that Watts is no insignificant and unknown person, but a public citizen, whose life and character is known of many—a doctor, a preacher, a politician—a physician of body, soul, and state.

But in lieu of this testimony, which we had expected and hoped to give, until the Commission decided it could hear no proofs other than such as might be contained in the certificates opened by the President of the Senate, and proof of ineligibility, we have the certificate of the governor and secretary of state, under the great seal of the State of Oregon, that "William H. Odell received 15,206 votes, John C. Cartwright received 15,214 votes, E. A. Cronin received 14,157 votes for electors of President and Vice-President of the United States. Being the highest number of votes cast at said election for persons eligible under the Constitution of the United States to be appointed electors of President and Vice-President of the United States, they are hereby declared duly elected electors as aforesaid for the State of Oregon." The maxim applies, " *Omnia præsumuntur rite et solemniter esse acta donec probetur in contrarium.*" (Broom's Legal Maxims, 908.)

As Watts was in fact ineligible, and if this were known (both law and fact) to more than 1,049 voters who voted for him, and we take the New York rule for our guide, then it follows that Cronin was elected. This being so, it became the duty of the governor and secretary, in such case, as we shall hereafter more fully show, to declare the result, and give the official lists to Cronin. To have given them to Watts under such circumstances would have been to violate the Constitution of the United States, which the governor and secretary had each taken a solemn oath to support, (Constitution of Oregon, article 15, section 3,) and to adopt a rule of law which the supreme court of Oregon has never announced. Therefore the fair and reasonable presumption, from the act of the governor and secretary, until the contrary is shown, is that the facts existed which justify the official action taken.

This, then, is the established principle of American public law, that the mandate to elect, obedience to which is essential to the perpetuity of republican self-government, is of such paramount importance, that neither by protests against it, by blank votes, nor by votes for disqualified candidates, can it be frustrated. A plurality vote for an eligible candidate is required; this and nothing more. First expounded in Maryland by one of the greatest of the patriotic jurists of the revolutionary period, sanctioned by judicial judgments in Maine, in Indiana, and (with limitations) in New York, and by legislative adoption in Maine and Massachusetts, it served no inconspicuous purpose in the re-organization of the States after the war of the rebellion, when it became part of the constitutional guarantees of Missouri and Mississippi, and by legislative action served the same end in Maryland.

Shall this Commission say that this is not the law of Oregon? The judiciary of Oregon have not said so. The legislature of Oregon have not said so. The executive of Oregon informs you that this is the law of Oregon. Compelled, in the performance of his duty, to act upon one or the other principle, to act as if it were the law of Oregon that ineligible candidates might be elected, or as if the election failed, or as if the next highest competing candidate were chosen, he heard argument, he took time to consider, and he acted. Had he given the certificate to Watts he would have violated the Constitution of the United States, which he had sworn to support. Had he given it to no one he would have given his assent to the view that the next highest competing candidate was not elected. He was compelled to act. He found that in his native State of Maine, where the constitution quite as emphatically required a "majority of votes," as the laws of Oregon require "the highest number of votes," (General Laws of Oregon, chap. 13, title 4, sec. 33, p. 706,) it was held that just construction determines the meaning to be a majority of efficient, available votes, cast for eligible candidates, and that this interpretation received the approval of the first chief-justice of Maine, that eminent magistrate, Prentiss Mellen, and of his successor in that high office, Nathan Weston, as well as of their associate, Albion K. Parris. We submit that he could not have had higher authority; that he could not have acted more wisely.

He had the right—it was his duty—so to act.

"It is argued," said Chief-Justice Parsons in Kendall vs. Inhabitants of Kingston, 5 Mass., 533, "that the legislature cannot give a construction to the constitution, cannot make laws repugnant to it. But every department of government, invested with certain constitutional powers, must in the first instance, but not exclusively, be the judge of its powers, or it could not act."

See also Martin vs. Mott, 12 Wheat., 29; Opinions of Judges, 49 Mo., 216.

"It follows, therefore, that every department of the government, and every official of every department may, at any time, when a duty is to be performed, be required to pass upon a question of constitutional construction." Cooley on Const. Lim., 41.

Taylor vs. The Governor, 1 Arkansas, 21, was a motion for an alternative *mandamus* against the governor to compel him to show cause why a peremptory *mandamus* should not issue directing him to deliver to John A. Taylor his commission as sheriff for the county of Pulaski, to which office he had been elected by the majority of the votes of the people of that county. The clerk of the county court had issued him a certificate of election; he demanded his commission of the governor, who refused to deliver it upon the ground that he was ineligible to the office, because, in point of fact, Taylor was a defaulter to the State. The supreme court of Arkansas sustained the governor and disallowed the writ. They say, p. 28:

The executive, in common with every other officer, is bound by oath to support the constitution, and whenever an effort is made to evade or violate it, it is not only his privilege but his duty to interpose and prevent it.

See also Hawkins vs. Conway, 1 Pike, 570.

In State ex rel. Bartley vs. Fletcher, governor, 39 Missouri, 388, a *mandamus* was prayed for to compel the governor to issue a commission to Bartley as one of the justices of the county court of Calloway County. The court, (Wagner J.,) after reciting (p. 398) that it is by the constitution of the State made the duty of the governor to commission all officers not otherwise provided by law, that this is clearly an exercise of political power of a ministerial character, proceed to say:

The governor is bound to see that the laws are faithfully executed, and he has taken an oath to support the constitution. In the correct and legitimate performance of his duty he must inevitably have a discretion in regard to granting commissions; for should a person be elected or appointed who was constitutionally ineligible to hold any office of profit or trust, would the executive be bound to commission him when his ineligibility was clearly and positively proven? If he is denied the exercise of any discretion in such case, he is made the violator of the constitution, not its guardian. Of what avail then is his oath of office? Or, if he has positive and satisfactory evidence that no election has been held in a county, shall he be required to violate the law, and issue a commission to a person not elected, because a clerk has certified to the election? In granting a commission the governor may go behind the commission o determine whether an applicant is entitled to receive a commission or not where the objection to the right of the applicant to receive it rests upon the ground that a constitutional prohibition is interposed. *Gulick vs. New*, 14 Ind., 93.

The issuing of a commission is an act by the executive in his political capacity, and is one of the means employed to enable him to execute the laws and carry on the appropriate functions of the State; and for the manner in which he executes this duty he is in nowise amenable to the judiciary. The court can no more interfere with executive discretion than the legislature or executive can with judicial discretion.

The granting of a commission by the executive is not a mere ministerial duty, but an official act imposed by the Constitution, and is an investiture of authority in the person receiving it. We are of the opinion, therefore, that *mandamus* will not lie against the governor in a case like this.

To sustain this view, that *mandamus* will not lie in such case, the court cite also—

Low *vs.* Towns, 8 Geo., 360.
People *vs.* Bissell, 19 Ill., 229.
Houston, &c., R. R. Co. *vs.* Randolph, 24 Tex., 317.
In the matter of Dennett, 32 Maine, 508.
Chamberlain *vs.* Sibley, 4 Minn., 311.
State *vs.* Governor, 1 Dutcher, 331.
Mauran *vs.* Smyth, (in Rh. Isl.,) 4 Am. Law Reg., 630.
State *vs.* Chase, 5 O. St., 528.
Cotton *vs.* Ellis, 7 Jones's Law, 545.

The case of George H. Corliss, in Rhode Island, sustains the action taken by Governor Grover and Secretary Chadwick in Oregon. We quote from the letter of Mr. Lawrence, already referred to, the following cogent passage:

In repudiating the votes for Watts, Governor Grover did precisely what Governor Lippitt did in Rhode Island as to Corliss. The latter governor could only have done it by virtue of the power given to him "to examine and count the vote," and it is impossible to discover any authority which he had to reject the ballots cast for Corliss that Governor Grover did not possess as to Watts. The fact of there being three candidates next to him with equal votes, precluded the question as to the right of a minority candidate in that case; but in the case passed on by Governor Grover, the votes for Watts being absolutely void, Cronin had the highest number of votes, and was consequently, under the provision of the constitution of the State of Oregon, which requires that "in all elections held by the people, the person or persons having the highest number of votes shall be declared duly elected," legally appointed an elector.

Article 10, section 3, of the constitution of Rhode Island is as follows

The judges of the supreme court shall, in all trials, instruct the jury in the law. They shall also give their written opinion upon any question of law whenever requested by the governor, or by either house of the general assembly.

Chapter 28, section 4, of the Revised Statutes of Rhode Island reads thus:

The governor, in the presence of the secretary of state, shall examine and count the same, and give notice to the electors of their election.

To the same effect was the action of the governor and council of Maine in 1831.

Gulick *vs.* New, *ut supra*, is directly in point.

The governor may determine, even against the decision of a board of canvassers whether an applicant is entitled to receive a commission or not, where the objection to his right to receive it rests upon the ground that the constitutional prohibition is interposed.

If the governor should ascertain that he has commissioned a person who is ineligible to the office, he may issue another commission to the person legally entitled thereto.

But we need not go out of Oregon for authority as to the duty of the governor under these circumstances. Only the death of the judge of the supreme court, charged with the duty of preparing it, (Judge Thayer,) has prevented their opinion from appearing in the volumes of Oregon Reports. We submit the following letter in proof of our assertion: (See testimony taken by subcommittee of the Committee on Privileges and Elections of the Senate, pp. 127, 128.)

SUPREME COURT ROOM,
Salem, Oregon, December 20, 1876.

SIR: Your communication of the 18th instant was duly received, and, in reply thereto, I beg leave to submit the following:

The case of the State of Oregon *ex rel.* C. B. Bellinger, appellant, *vs.* A. C. Gibbs, respondent, was heard and determined at the January term, 1873, of the supreme court. The action was instituted in the circuit court of the State of Oregon for the county of Multnomah, and was determined at the March term, 1872, of said court. The complaint alleged in effect that the respondent had been elected to the office of prosecuting attorney in the fourth judicial district in June, 1870, for the term of two years; that he entered upon, held, and exercised the office; that thereafter, and while so holding, he was appointed to the office of United States district attorney for the district of Oregon, and that he qualified and entered upon said office on March 2, 1872. Allegations showing that both offices were lucrative were duly made, and it was further alleged that on March 6, 1872, the governor of Oregon duly appointed the relator to the office of prosecuting attorney for the said fourth judicial district, and that said relator duly qualified on March 8, 1872, and thereupon made demand upon the respondent for the office, which demand was refused.

Respondent demurred to the complaint in the court below, upon the ground, among others, that the complaint did not state facts sufficient to constitute a cause of action. The court below (Upton, J.) sustained the demurrer and entered a judgment against the relator for costs, &c.

An appeal was thereupon taken to the supreme court at the term mentioned. Upon the argument in the supreme court, the respondent, in support of his demurrer, contended "that the governor could not determine for himself that a vacancy existed in the office of prosecuting attorney in the fourth judicial district so as to authorize the appointment of the relator, for the reason that the determination of that fact involved the exercise of judicial functions by the executive.

This was the principal legal question in the case, and the court unanimously declared that the governor was invested with authority, in cases of the kind, to look into the facts and pass upon the same without awaiting the action of the courts.

The justices of the supreme court were, at the time, Hon. W. W. Upton, chief-justice; Hon. A. J. Thayer, P. P. Prim, B. F. Bonham, and L. L. McArthur, associate justices. As the case was from the fourth district, Upton, chief-justice, did not participate in the hearing and decision in the supreme court. The writing of the opinion was assigned to Hon. A. J. Thayer, who died shortly after the adjournment of the term, leaving the duty unperformed. Ex-Chief-Justice Bonham and Justice McArthur authorize me to say that their recollection of the case and the point decided comports with my own.

I have the honor to be your excellency's obedient servant,

P. P. PRIM,
Chief-Justice of Oregon.

His Excellency L. F. GROVER,
Governor of Oregon.

If it be claimed that this was judicial action of Governor Grover, we reply that until the certificate had been delivered, judicial action could not begin. Ministerial political authority ascertains and certifies the result of an election; judicial authority revises and corrects it. Political authority determines in whom the color of right shall rest, by the delivery of the commission. Judicial authority searches that colorable title, and awards the possession of the office according to the real title.

In addition to the cases already cited upon this point, we refer the Commission to the case of Collins *vs.* Knoblock *et al.*, 25 La. Ann., 263:

The adjustment and compilation of election returns, determining the number of legal and illegal votes cast for each candidate, declaring the result of an election and furnishing the successful candidate with the proper certificate; in short, superintending and controlling all the details of an election, belong properly to the political department of the government.

To the same effect is State upon the relation of Bonner *vs.* Lynch, 25 La. Ann., 268.

Except so far as it may have been altered by statute, the common law of England is the law of Oregon.

The following is believed to be a fair statement of the cases which contain the exposition of the common-law doctrine upon this subject. They show that the action of the governor and secretary of Oregon was consistent with the common law. To save labor, we refer for a summary of many of the cases to the opinion of Mr. Justice Blackburn in the case of The Queen *vs.* Tewksbury.

The statute 13 Charles II, ch. 12, enacted that no person should be elected into any corporation office who had not received the sacrament within a twelvemonth preceding the election; and in default of doing so the election, placing, and choice should be void. And in Harrison *vs.* Evans, cited in Cowper's Rep., 393, note, and 535, Lord Chief-Justice Wilmot said:

> The Stat. 13 Car. II, ch. 12, is not only addressed to the *elected* and a prohibition upon them, but a prohibition laid down to the *electors* if they have notice. The legislature has commanded them not to choose a nonconformist, because he ought not to be trusted. * * * Consequently, with respect to any legal effect or operation, it is as if there had been no election.

In Rex *vs.* Monday, Cowper, 536, (in 1777,) Serjeant Buller laid down the law thus:

> Two requisites are necessary to make a good election: First. A capacity in the *electors;* Second. Capacity in the *elected;* and unless both concur the election is a nullity. With respect to the capacity of the *electors,* * * * their right consists in an affirmative, not a negative declaration. Consequently, there is no effectual means of voting *against one man* but by voting *for another;* and even then, if such other person be unqualified, *and the elector has notice* of his incapacity, his vote will be thrown away.

This statement of the law is absolutely accurate.

In Regina *vs.* Boscawen, cited by Burke, ten voted for Roberts, who was a qualified person, and ten for the defendant, who was incapacitated on account of non-inhabitancy. Lord Chief-Justice Parker and the whole court held " that the votes given for the latter were *thrown away,* and Roberts duly elected." That was the case of an *equal* number; but a minority does not vary it.

For in Rex *vs.* Withers, in the King's Bench, five voters out of eleven voted for the defendant upon a *single* vacancy of a burgess for the borough of Westbury; six others voted for two persons jointly; and the court held that the *double* votes were absolutely thrown away.

So in Taylor *vs.* Mayor of Bath, in the King's Bench, 28 electors being assembled, 14 voted for A, 13 for B, and 1 for C. A, who had the 14 votes, was unqualified, and his incapacity known to the electors at the time. Lee, chief-justice, in his direction to the jury, said that the votes given to A, with notice of his incapacity, were thrown away. It afterward came before the court, when Lee, chief-justice, compared it to the case of voting for a dead man, and held that B was duly elected; and Page, justice, said " that in such a case a minority of two only would have been sufficient to elect the other candidate."

After the argument in Rex *vs.* Monday, Lord Mansfield agreed that, in the case of an election for member of Parliament, where the electors *must* proceed to an election, because they cannot stop for that day or defer it to another time, there must be a candidate or candidates, and in that case there is no way of defeating the election of one candidate proposed but by voting for another, and that other, he held, must be a person not incapacitated by law.

In Oldknow *vs.* Wainwright, or Rex *vs.* Foxcroft, 2 Burrow, 1017, in 1760, the same great judge had said:

> The protesting electors had no way to stop the election, when once entered upon, but by voting for some other person than Seagrave, or at least against him.

And Mr. Justice Wilmot quoted Regina *vs.* Boscawen and Taylor *vs.* Mayor of Bath as establishing that votes given for a non-inhabitant, where inhabitancy was necessary, were thrown away.

In Hawkins *vs.* Rex, 2 Dou., 124, in the House of Lords, in error from the Court of King's Bench, in 1813, the case being *quo warranto*, calling on defendant to show by what title he claimed to be an alderman of a borough, notice of ineligibility had been given at the assembly, he not having taken the sacrament within a year. Abbott, for Hawkins, said in argument:

> There were not many cases where it had been decided that the votes of the majority were so absolutely thrown away as to give the election to the minority. That was a strong measure in any case, and it was submitted that it could not hold here unless the notice of disqualification had been given before the commencement of the election. The electors ought to have notice and time to speak and deliberate before they were called on to vote.

He admitted that the votes given *after* notice were thrown away, and he cited Rex *vs.* Coe, Heywood County Elections, 538, where, after *nine* had voted for the opponent of Coe, he was declared disqualified. The rest of his voters polled for another, but there were not enough; and Coe, who would otherwise have been outvoted, was, though he had only a minority, declared elected. But he was ousted by the court. And in Rex *vs.* Budge, 1 Maule & Selwyn, 76, where Sparling had 91 votes and Budge 11, when notice was given that Sparling was disqualified, and the poll proceeding, the numbers were 123 for him and 22 for Budge, the court held that the 91 votes given before notice were not thrown away.

Mr. Abbott further says:

> " In two cases the election by the minority was held sufficient; but there the disqualification was very different from that in the present case. *It was one thing to say that votes were thrown away where there was an absolute disqualification,* and another to say so where the disqualification was not absolute," as he contended it was not in the case he was arguing.

Our constitutional disqualification *is* absolute.

Moreover, he argued that a candidate had not taken the sacrament within a year was a matter of no *public* notoriety, was within his own knowledge alone, was not *presumed* to be known to an elector or to anybody, and therefore it was right to require notice, actual and personal, to put the voter in the position of throwing his vote away.

On the other side the counsel said:

> The general doctrine was clear that after notice of disqualification the votes for the disqualified person were thrown away. There was no necessity for stating particularly the cases where the general doctrine was clearly recognized.

Lord Eldon, giving his opinion to the House of Lords, said that when two persons had voted for each candidate the knowledge of the disqualification appeared. But he said:

> The election proceeded, and the great majority voted for Hawkins; and the election of Hawkins was an absolute nullity by the act. (13 Car., 2, lib. I.) *The majority knowingly voted* FOR THIS DEAD MAN, and that was to be attended to.

The election was held on the 18th of December, 1806. When two persons had voted for each, Hawkins admitted that he had not taken the sacrament within a year. Receiving a majority of the votes, he was sworn in by the mayor, and Spicer was sworn in by two of the aldermen.

The statute (47 Geo. 3) made valid the election of Hawkins if he took the sacrament within a certain time *after* the election. He did that on the 4th of October, 1807. But if the office was at the time of passing that act legally filled up and enjoyed by Spicer, then the act did not help Hawkins; and the Court of King's Bench, giving judgment against Hawkins, held that Spicer was legally in the office; and this decision the House of Lords affirmed. (See also Claridge *vs.* Evelyn, 5 B. & A., 8.)

The result of the English cases was well stated by Lord Denman, in 1847, in deciding the case of Gosling *vs.* Veley, 7 Adolphus & Ellis, N. S. 437, in these words:

The result of the decisions appears to be this: Where the majority of electors vote for a disqualified person in ignorance of the fact of disqualification, the election may be void or voidable, or in the latter case may be capable of being made good, according to the nature of the disqualification. The objection may require ulterior proceeding to be taken before some competent tribunal in order to make it available; or it may be such as to place the elected candidate on the same footing as if he never had existed, and the votes for him were a nullity. But in no such case are the electors who vote for him deprived of their votes if the fact becomes known and is declared while the election is still incomplete. They may instantly proceed to another nomination and vote for another candidate. (It will be remembered that in England elections are all conducted *viva voce.*) If it be disclosed afterward, the party elected may be ousted and the election declared void, but the candidate in the minority will not be deemed *ipso facto* elected. But where an elector, before voting, receives due notice that a particular candidate is disqualified, and yet will do nothing but tender his vote for him, he must be taken voluntarily to abstain from exercising his franchise, and therefore however strongly he may, in fact, dissent, he must be taken in law to assent to the election of the opposing and qualified candidate, for he will not take the only course by which it can be resisted; that is, the helping to the election of some other person. He is present as an elector. His presence counts as such to make up the requisite number of electors, where a certain number is necessary, but he attends only as an elector to perform the duty which is cast on him by the franchise he enjoys as elector; he can speak only in a particular language; he can do only certain acts; any other language means nothing; any other act is merely null; his duty is to assist in making an election. If he dissents from the choice of A, who is qualified, he must say so by voting for some other also qualified. He has no right to employ his franchise merely in preventing an election, and so defeating the object for which he is empowered and bound to attend. And this is a wise and just rule in the law. It is necessary that an election should be duly made and at the lawful time; the electoral meeting is held for that purpose only; and but for this rule, the interest of the public and the purpose of the meeting might both be defeated by the perverseness or the corruption of electors who may seek some unfair advantage by postponement. If, then, the elector will not oppose the election of A in the only legal way, he throws away his vote by directing it where it has no legal force, and in so doing he voluntarily leaves unopposed—*i. e.,* assents to—the voices of the other electors.

Where the disqualification depends on a fact which may be unknown to the elector, he is entitled to notice, for without that the inference of assent could not be fairly drawn, nor would the consequences as to the vote be just. But if the disqualification be of a sort whereof notice is to be presumed, none need expressly be given; no one can doubt that if an elector would nominate and vote only for a woman to fill the office of mayor or burgess in Parliament, his vote would be thrown away; there the fact would be notorious, and every man would be presumed to know the law upon that fact.

It follows from these observations that the true ground of the decision is that stated by Lord Mansfield in the case first cited, Rex *vs.* Foxcroft, 2 Burr., 21021: "Whenever electors are present who do not vote at all, they virtually acquiesce in the election made by those who do." In that case the numerical majority contented themselves with protesting against the election of him for whom the minority voted. In the case of Taylor against the Mayor of Bath, (3 Luders, 324,) the counsel in argument took the distinction between not voting at all and voting for a disqualified candidate. They admitted that silence might be held to give consent, but that voting for the other candidate was an express negative; it was the only way, they said, of voting against one to vote for the other. But the court overruled the distinction; to vote for a person not qualified, they said, was the same thing as not to vote at all, which it was admitted would have been a constructive assent."

Lord Campbell held the same doctrine in very vigorous language in the case of The Queen *vs.* Coaks, 3 Ellis & Blackburn, 249:

"I must say," said he, "that this appears to me to be a very plain case. It is allowed that it depends on the right of Cundall to act as a councilor on the 9th of November, 1852. If he had a right so to act at that time, the present defendant is not duly elected. Now, as to Cundall's right, who was elected a councilor on the 1st of November, 1851, the case is just the same as if Blake had not been the candidate on that occasion. To be sure, he did stand, but then he was ineligible, and that fact was known to the voters. It is a principle of all election law and of good sense that persons who knowingly throw a vote for an ineligible candidate throw away *their votes just as much as if they voted for the man in the moon.*"

In another report of the same case, namely, 18 Jurist, part 1, page 378, Lord Campbell's language is reported thus:

This is clear; it is allowed that it depends upon whether Cundall had a right to act as city councilor of Norwich on the 9th of November. If he had a right so to act, the present defendant was not duly elected mayor, and is a usurper, and the *quo warranto* properly issued. Cundall was elected a city councilor on the 4th of November, 1851; it is the same as if Blake had not been a candidate, because he was ineligible, and that fact was known to the electors, and if the voters know that a candidate is ineligible, they throw away their votes when they vote for him. They do not vote.

This is good corporation law, good parliamentary law, and good sense, and there is nothing in Statute 6 and 7 William IV, chapter 76, to alter it. Then, Blake's votes being disregarded, Cundall had the greatest number of votes, and being duly elected, he ought to have been returned as one of the councilors.

In Queen *vs.* Tewksbury, L. R., 3 Q. B., 636, Blackburn, J., says:

I take this to be the rule of law applicable to this case. I think the knowledge that Blizard was the mayor is clearly brought home to every voter, but the question is not merely whether every vote given for him was thrown away, in the sense that it was given for a disqualified candidate—in that sense it was undoubtedly thrown away; but whether it was thrown away in the same manner as if the vote had been given for a dead man, or had not been given at all. I think that where a voter is informed that a certain circumstance in point of law disqualifies a candidate, even although he may hold a different opinion, yet if he afterward votes for that candidate, his vote is thrown away.

In the present election a voter may possibly have been told by the one party that Blizard being returning-officer could not be elected, by the other party that he could be; if this could be shown the vote would be thrown away; but the case merely shows as a fact that Blizard was returning-officer, from which a lawyer would be aware that he was disqualified, and, in my opinion, the knowledge that Blizard was returning-officer does not, in law, necessarily involve the knowledge that he was disqualified. It must be observed that when a voter is said to have notice of disqualification in a candidate, the word notice is ambiguous.

In Rex *vs.* Hawkins, 10 East, at p. 217, the question is thus stated: "If the law be that at the election of corporate officers, the votes given for an incapable candidate, after notice of such incapacity, are to be considered as thrown away, *i. e.*, as if the voters had not given any vote at all, then this will be a good election of Spicer; unless the time when notice of his incapacity is given, viz, after two persons had given their votes for each of the candidates, can be considered as making any difference."

The general proposition that votes given for a candidate after notice of his being ineligible are to be considered as the same as if the persons had not voted at all, is supported by the cases of Reg. *vs.* Boscawen, Easter, 13 Anne; Reg. *vs.* Withers, Easter, 8 Geo., 2; Taylor *vs.* Mayor of Bath, M. 15 Geo., 2; all which are cited in Cowper, 537, in Rex *vs.* Monday. In the first, Boscawen *vs.* Roberts, the two candidates had an equal number of votes; but because Boscawen was incapable, the votes given for him were considered as thrown away, and the other duly elected.

In the second case Withers had five votes out of eleven; and the other six refusing to vote at all, the court held Withers duly elected, and that the six who refused to vote were virtually consenting to the election of Withers.

In the third case, Taylor, Biggs, and Kingston were candidates, which Biggs had fourteen votes, Taylor thirteen, and Kingston only one. There Lee, C. J., at *nisi prius*, directed the jury that if they were satisfied that the electors had notice of Biggs's want of qualification they should find for the plaintiff, (that was Taylor, who had only thirteen votes,) because Biggs, not being qualified, was to be considered a person not *in esse*, and the voting for him a mere nullity. The jury found for the plaintiff, and the court, on motion for a new trial, agreed with the law as laid down by Lee, C. J., and refused a new trial.

The whole of this reasoning goes to show that those who voted for the disqualified candidate, knowing of his disqualification, were to be treated as voting for a person not *in esse*, so that there must be an actual knowledge of his disqualification in law. And Lord Eldon similarly grounds his decision on the fact that the majority knowingly voted for a disqualified candidate, or, as he terms it, " for a dead man." Rex *vs.* Hawkins, 2 Dou., 124, 148.

Certainly he seems to have thought that the *ratio decidendi* was the knowledge of the disqualification in law, and that the votes given with that knowledge were mere nullities. In Reg. *vs.* Coaks, 3 E. and B., at pp. 253-'4; 23 L. J., (Q. B.,) at p. 136, Lord Campbell, C. J., says: " Blake was, in fact, a candidate, but he was an alderman, and therefore ineligible, and that fact was known to the electors. Now, it is the law, both the common law and the parliamentary law, and it seems to me also common sense, that if an elector will vote for a man who he knows is ineligible, it is as if he did not vote at all, or voted for a non-existent person, as it has been said, as if he gave his vote for the man in the moon." It seems to me that Lord Campbell's opinion was this: The reason why the vote given for a dead man is not to be counted is that the voter knowingly votes for a person whom he knows to be incapable of election, and therefore the result is the same as if he had not voted at all.

Voting for a dead man, or for the man in the moon, are expressions showing that in order to make the vote a nullity there must be willful persistence against actual knowledge. But it does not seem to me consistent with either justice or common sense, or common law, to say that because these voters were aware of a certain circumstance they were necessarily aware of the disqualification arising from that circumstance, and that therefore their votes are to be considered as mere nullities. Upon this ground I do not think that the votes given in ignorance that Blizard was in law disqualified, are made out to have been wholly thrown away, and that Moore is entitled to act as town councilor. Under these circumstances the election ought to be considered as void, and a new election ought to be held.

In the Warwick election petition case, (19 L. T., 616,) Martin, B., said:

The fact that he had forbidden him to bribe is utterly immaterial, if the bribery is committed by him, and the effect would be to destroy his *status* as a candidate, and render him by law incapable of election; and every vote given for him would be void.

Again:

The moment an act of bribery was committed by himself or a person for whom he was responsible, from that moment his *status* as a candidate was annihilated.

Lord Westbury, in the case of Cooper *vs.* Phibbs, L. R., 2 H. L., 170, thus explains the maxim:

It is said *ignorantia juris haud excusat;* but in that maxim the word *"jus"* is used in the sense denoting general law, the ordinary law of the country.

Lord Coleridge, C. J., in Drinkwater *vs.* Deaken (L. R., 9 C. P., 633,) draws the true distinction applicable to disqualification thus:

Was Colonel Deakin then disqualified in point of law at the time of the election? That depends upon the meaning of the word " disqualified," and in this case, as so often happens with regard to the English language, much argument would be prevented by accurately defining the terms to be employed, and always using them in the sense defined. The word " disqualified " may be used in two senses at least—either to signify a person disqualified to be elected, so that, although the great majority of the electors voted for him, his election would be void, or to signify a person disqualified to be a candidate, so that, upon notice of the disqualification, if the great majority of the electors voted for him, his election would be void, with this further consequence, as regards the electors, that they would be held to have intentionally and deliberately abstained from voting, and to have acquiesced in the choice by the other electors of the other candidate, because they would not do what alone could prevent such choice— vote themselves for a candidate duly qualified to be one.

The same principle has been decided in Ireland in the case of Trench *vs.* Nolan, (Irish Rep., 6 Common Law, 464,) where the court of common pleas held that—

Votes given to a candidate who is disqualified, after notice of that disqualification had been given, are thrown away.

The same rule was followed in 1875 in the celebrated case of the Tipperary election, (Irish Rep., 9 Common Law, 217,) where John Mitchel and Stephen Moore were the only candidates for member of Parliament in the county of Tipperary. Mitchel received 3,114 votes and Moore 746. John Mitchel having been convicted in 1848 of treason-felony and sentenced to transportation for fourteen years, having escaped and been naturalized as a citizen of the United States, it was held that he was disqualified to be elected a member of the House of Commons, and that notice of his disqualification having been brought home to the electors who voted for him, their votes were thrown away, and the rival candidate, though numerically in the minority, was entitled to the seat.

III.

The true and valid electoral college of Oregon is that composed of Cronin, Miller, and Parker, and not that composed of Odell, Cartwright, and Watts.

The Revised Statutes provide that—

SEC. 136. It shall be the duty of the executive of each State to cause three lists of the names of the electors of such State to be made and certified, and to be delivered to the electors on or before the day on which they are required by the preceding section to meet.

SEC. 138. The electors shall make and sign three certificates of all the votes given by them, each of which certificates shall contain two distinct lists, one of the votes for President and the other of the votes for Vice-President, and shall annex to each of the certificates one of the lists of the electors which shall have been furnished to them by direction of the executive of the State.

These lists are attached to the votes given by Cronin, Miller, and Parker. No such lists are attached to the votes given by Odell, Cartwright, and Watts. Therefore, at least *prima facie*, the *de facto* electors are Cronin, Miller, and Parker. They had color of title, and, in fact, acted.

If it be said that Odell and Cartwright's names also appear as chosen electors in the certificates annexed to Cronin, Miller, and Parker's votes, we reply :

First. That the statement made by Cronin, Miller, and Parker is, that Odell and Cartwright "refused to act as such electors." This made a case of vacancy under the Oregon statutes; "death, *refusal to act*, neglect to attend, or otherwise," being the enumerated contingencies, in each of which cases "the electors present shall immediately proceed to fill by *viva voce* and plurality of votes such vacancy in the electoral college," &c. Upon the refusal of Odell and Cartwright to act with Cronin, the latter, as was his right, duly proceeded to fill the vacancies by the appointment of Miller and Parker.

Secondly. The certificates filed by Odell, Cartwright, and Watts confirm this statement, as we suppose. For they show that Odell and Cartwright accepted a resignation tendered by Watts, and then elected the latter to fill the vacancy caused by his own resignation, acts which justify the description, "refused to act" with Cronin.

But this is not all. The Commission will notice that section 136 does not *require* any attestation of the executive lists by the secretary of state, or authentication by the great seal of the State.

Chapter 44, section 3, p. 849, of the General Laws of Oregon, provides that:

SEC. 3. The votes for electors shall be given, received, returned, and canvassed as the same are given, returned, and canvassed for members of Congress. *The Secretary of State shall prepare two lists of the names of the electors elected, and affix the seal of the State to the same. Such lists shall be signed by the governor and secretary, and by the latter delivered to the college of electors at the time of their meeting on such first Wednesday of December.*

Chapter 13, title 4, section 33, requires the secretary of state, in presence of the governor, to proceed, within thirty days after the elec tion, and sooner, if the returns be all received, " to canvass the votes given for * * * members of Congress."

The two lists prepared by the secretary, and signed, under the great seal of the State, by the governor and secretary of state, and given to the electors, are, therefore, the " official determination and declaration of their appointments by the board of State canvassers." They are here. The lists required by section 136 of the Revised Statutes, signed by the governor, and which by that section only the governor was *required* to sign, the secretary has made to conform to section 3 of chapter 44, by adding his signature, and the great seal of the State, and thus Cronin, Odell, and Cartwright were furnished at once with the authoritative statement by the secretary of the result of the canvass, and the certificate of the governor.

The case is thus brought directly within the rulings of the Commission in the Florida case. We produce the muniments of title which the secretary, upon completing the canvass, is required to furnish to the "electors elected," and those which the governor is required to cause to be made, certified, and "delivered to the electors." The governor's certificate, based upon the results of the secretary's canvass, as shown by the signature of the secretary and the great seal of the State, vouches for the election of Cronin.

Article 5, section 18, of the constitution of Oregon, provides—

That all commissions shall issue in the name of the State, shall be signed by the governor, sealed with the seal of the State, and attested by the secretary of state.

In Coolidge *vs.* Brigham, 1 Allen, 335, Bigelow, C. J., pronouncing the opinion of the whole court, said :

The magistrate before whom the action was originally brought was an officer *de facto.* He was not a mere usurper, undertaking to exercise the duties of an office to which he had no color of title. He had an apparent right to the office. He had a commission under the great seal of the State, bearing the signature of the governor, with his certificate thereon that the oaths of office had been duly administered, and in all respects appearing to have been issued with the formalities required by the constitution and laws of the commonwealth. He was thus invested with the apparent muniments of full title to the office. Although he might not have been an officer *de jure,* that is, legally appointed and entitled to hold and enjoy the office by a right which could not on due proceedings being had be impeached or invalidated, he was nevertheless in possession, under a commission *prima facie* regular and legal, and performing the functions of the office under a color and show of right. This made him a justice of the peace *de facto.*

Cronin was therefore *de jure et de facto* elector. Odell and Cartwright, although originally *de jure* electors, were not such *de facto,* for they were not clothed with the evidences of title, and by refusing to act with Cronin they divested themselves of their *de jure* right, and made it his duty to appoint others to fill the vacancies.

In Boardman & Perry *vs.* Halliday *et al.,* 10 Paige, 223, it was held that—

Where there is but one office, there cannot be one officer *de jure* and another officer *de facto* in possession of the office at the same time.

To the same effect is Morgan *vs.* Quackenbush, decided by Mr. Justice Ira Harris, 22 Barb., 79, thus :

Again, the common council having, as a board of canvassers, declared Mr. Perry elected to the office, and their decision, however erroneous, remaining unreversed, what evidence has the defendant Quackenbush—however rightfully he may deem the office to belong to him—even of a *color* of right ? Unless the returns of the inspectors can be successfully attacked, in an action to try the right to the office, he must succeed in such an action. But if, as I have attempted to show, the recanvassing of the returns by the new board furnished no more evidence of his right to the office than the certificate of any other equal number of respectable men, there is no determination upon which he can rely to give him even *the color* of right. Indeed I do not understand that two persons *can be* in possession of the same office at the same time. If the certificate of the canvassers declaring Mr. Perry elected vested him with *colorable* title to the office, as I think it did, so that he had a right to enter upon the discharge of its duties, another effect of that decision was, to exclude the defendant Quackenbush, as well as everybody else, from the office. They could not hold as tenants in common—each having a legal right to perform its functions. If Mr. Perry became mayor *de facto*, the defendant Quackenbush, whatever his right, could not be mayor in fact at the same time.

In the absence of proof to the contrary, upon proof that he was an officer *de facto*, the court will presume that he was also an officer *de jure*. (Prell *vs.* McDonald, 7 Kans., 426; see also Willis *vs.* Sproule, 13 Kans., 257 ; Diggs *vs.* State, 49 Ala., 32.)

As to officers *de facto :*

The authorities all concur in recognizing as such any person who exercises the duties of an office under color of an appointment or election to that office.

See also Bowen *vs.* Hixon, 45 Mo., 342.

In conclusion, we claim to have established—

1. That Cronin, Miller, and Parker constituted the electoral college of Oregon, and that their votes should be the votes counted for President and Vice-President of the United States. They were the lawful electors *de jure et de facto.*

2. That if not, at least the vote cast by John W. Watts for Hayes and Wheeler cannot be counted.

First. On the day when by act of Congress electors must be appointed, the State of Oregon could not appoint him, nor could he accept the appointment, because he was then holding an office of profit and trust under the United States.

Secondly. Not having attained to the office *de jure*, he could not resign it into the hands of Odell and Cartwright.

Thirdly. Odell and Cartwright not having themselves attained to the office *de facto*, not being in possession, or acting under the muniments of title, nor *de jure*, having refused to serve with Cronin, who produces the certificates, could not appoint him to fill a vacancy.

Fourthly. Watts could not resign an office which Cronin *de facto* held.

Fifthly. Watts's original disqualification did not create a vacancy, but a case of failure to make choice, for which the laws of Oregon did not provide.

Sixthly. While Cronin held the office *de facto*, Watts's disqualification could not make a case of *ab initio* vacancy. An office cannot be vacant when filled, even if filled *non jure*. Baird *vs.* Bank of Washington, 11 S. & R., 414.

Seventhly. Watts was not an elector *de facto*, for Cronin, who held the muniments of title, the proper certificates, was present and voted, and his vote (sustained by evidence of his title) is presented here for count.

Whether, therefore, the vote of Cronin be counted or not, that of Watts cannot be.

GEO. HOADLY,
ASHBEL GREEN,
R. T. MERRICK,
ALEX. PORTER MORSE,
Of Counsel.

APPENDIX OF OPINIONS.

REMARKS OF MEMBERS OF THE ELECTORAL COMMISSION
IN THE CONSULTATIONS THEREOF, AS REDUCED TO
WRITING BY THEMSELVES, IN ACCORDANCE WITH A
RESOLUTION OF THE COMMISSION.

The remarks of the various members of the Commission, in its consultations, are presented in the order in which they spoke on the Florida case.

[Mr. Commissioner Edmunds, who was the first speaker in the deliberations on the Florida case, was taken ill early in March and obliged to leave the Capital on account of illness, and was unable to write out his remarks by the time limited by the Commission's resolution.]

REMARKS OF MR. COMMISSIONER MORTON.

FLORIDA.

The Electoral Commission having under consideration an offer of evidence to impeach the canvass of the November election in Florida for presidential electors made by the State canvassing-board—

Mr. Commissioner MORTON said:

Mr. PRESIDENT: By the statute of Florida enacted in 1872 the secretary of state, attorney-general, comptroller of public accounts, or any two of them, together with any other member of the cabinet who may be designated by them, were constituted a board of canvassers to canvass the returns of the election, and determine and declare who have been elected State officers and presidential electors. The statute provides that—

If any such returns shall be shown or shall appear to be so irregular, false, or fraudulent that the board shall be unable to determine the true vote for any such officer or member, they shall so certify, and shall not include such return in their determination and declaration; and the secretary of state shall preserve and file in his office all such returns, together with such other documents and papers as may have been received by him or by said board of canvassers.

Under this statute the secretary of state, the comptroller of public accounts, and the attorney-general acted as a board of State canvassers, and on the morning of the 6th of December, 1876, a majority of them returned and certified that Frederick C. Humphreys, Charles H. Pearce, William H. Holden, and Thomas W. Long had been chosen as electors. Afterward, on the same day, the governor of the State, M. L. Stearns, issued to them, as electors, his certificate, and they cast their votes in due form of law for Rutherford B. Hayes for President and William A. Wheeler as Vice-President, and certified the same to the President of the Senate.

Afterward, the supreme court of the State issued a mandamus di-

recting the board of canvassers to make another count of the votes for
governor and other State officers, rejecting all testimony of irregularity
and fraud except such as might appear upon the face of the returns.
Under this order of the court the board of canvassers was reconvened
and recounted the votes in accordance with the order made by the court,
and declared Drew and the other democratic candidates for State offices
to have been elected. They at the same time made a recount of the
votes for electors, and again declared the Hayes electors to have been
chosen. After Drew had been inaugurated governor, and the new secretary of state, attorney-general, and comptroller of public accounts
had taken their offices, the legislature being in session, in January,
1877, passed an act requiring the new secretary of state, comptroller of
public accounts, the attorney-general, and such other members of the
cabinet as they might choose, to reconvene as a board of canvassers to
count the votes for electors. This they did on the 19th day of January,
and declared Wilkinson Call, James E. Yonge, Robert Bullock, and
Robert B. Hilton to have been chosen as electors. The same persons had
assembled on the 6th day of December, and, assuming to have been
chosen as electors, voted for Samuel J. Tilden as President and Thomas
A. Hendricks as Vice-President, and sealed up their votes and sent them
to the President of the Senate, inclosing with them a certificate from
William A. Cocke, attorney-general, certifying to their election as electors.

On the morning of the 6th of December an application was made in
the circuit court of Florida in the name of the State on the relation of
Wilkinson Call, James E. Yonge, Robert Bullock, and Robert B. Hilton, to which the Hayes electors were made defendants and upon whom
process was served at one o'clock on the 6th of December before the
said Hayes electors had cast their votes for President and Vice-President. By the terms of the writ they were required to appear in the
court on the 18th of January, 1877, to show by what right they claimed
to act as electors. This writ was prosecuted to final judgment on the
29th day of January, 1877, and judgment of the court was rendered declaring that the Tilden electors had been chosen as such by the votes
of the people on the 7th of November, and that the Hayes electors had
no title whatever to the office.

The Constitution provides:

The electors shall meet in their respective States and vote by ballot for President
and Vice-President, one of whom, at least, shall not be an inhabitant of the same
State with themselves; they shall name in their ballots the person voted for as President, and in distinct ballots the person voted for as Vice-President, and they shall
make distinct lists of all persons voted for as President, and of all persons voted for as
Vice-President, and of the number of votes for each; which lists they shall sign and
certify, and transmit sealed to the seat of Government of the United States, directed
to the President of the Senate; the President of the Senate shall, in the presence of
the Senate and House of Representatives, open all the certificates, and the votes shall
then be counted; the person having the greatest number of votes for President shall
be the President, if such number be a majority of the whole number of electors appointed; and if no person have such majority, then from the persons having the highest
numbers, not exceeding three on the list of those voted for as President, the House of
Representatives shall choose immediately, by ballot, the President.

Leaving out of view the disputed question who shall count the votes,
and assuming that the power belongs to the two Houses, and was by
them properly vested in this Commission, the question still remains,
what is embraced in the phrase "the votes shall then be counted."

And first, "What votes shall be counted?" I answer, "The votes
recorded in the certificates which the President of the Senate is required to open in the presence of the two Houses." May the two Houses

inquire whether the certificate is a forgery? Certainly; because the President of the Senate is only required to open in the presence of the two Houses the certificates from the electors. If the certificate is a forgery, it is not from the electors. The thing to be ascertained is that the certificate is from the electors of the State, and if it is, then the votes contained in it are to be counted. If the votes were cast by the electors of the State, is it competent for the two Houses or this Commission to inquire whether such persons had the requisite qualifications to be electors as prescribed by the laws of the State, or were eligible under the Constitution of the United States, and if found in the negative, reject their votes? I answer, "No!" Such inquiry and rejection would be inconsistent with the positive command of the Constitution that the votes contained in the certificates "shall then be counted." There is no time provided for such an inquiry, and it is evident that it was not contemplated. The injunction was placed upon the States that they should not appoint as an elector a member of Congress or any person holding an office of trust or profit under the United States; but if the States disregard the injunction, there is no time or place for trial of the question when the votes are counted. We should do violence to the intelligence of the framers of the Constitution if we supposed they intended the result of a presidential election might be changed by the discovery after the election, or after the votes had been cast by the electors, that an elector was disqualified. It is a matter in which the elector has no other interest than that of the whole body of citizens, and we are not at liberty to suppose that the wishes of a State should be defeated by the fact that an elector was ineligible for some cause of which the mass of the voters, or the appointing power, whatever it might be, had no knowledge. The process of counting the votes was intended to be short and simple. The States were to appoint electors in the manner prescribed by their legislatures, and the electors were to meet in the several States and vote upon the same day; the records of their transactions were to be sent to the President of the Senate in sealed envelopes, and by him to be opened in the presence of the two Houses, and the votes were then to be counted.

Whether it is competent for Congress to pass laws under which the title of a President may be tried in the courts upon a writ of *quo warranto*, in which the very right and truth of the election may be examined, is not material for the present inquiry. We cannot by logic or imagination enlarge the simple provision of the Constitution, that the certificates of the electors from the various States shall be opened in the presence of the two Houses and the votes therein contained "shall then be counted." If it should appear when the certificates were opened that the requirements of the Constitution had not been complied with, for example, that the electors did not vote by ballot, or that they did not designate in distinct ballots the persons voted for as President and Vice-President, or that the electors were holding offices of trust and profit under the United States and therefore ineligible, it might be the duty of the two Houses—although upon this point I give no opinion—to reject such votes, for there it would appear affirmatively in the certificate, over the signatures of the electors, that they had not conformed to the Constitution or that they were not eligible. To reject such votes would be going to the limit of the power of the two Houses to disobey the express command of the Constitution that "the votes shall then be counted." But if the certificates were silent as to whether the electors voted by ballot or were ineligible, then such votes must be counted, and the two Houses have no power to make an inquiry whether the electors voted by ballot or were eligible.

The word "counted" means enumerated. Had it been intended to give the two Houses, or whoever counted the votes, any judicial or revisory power over them, beyond mere enumeration, the purpose would have been expressed in words. In the several States the canvassing or returning officers are held to a simple ministerial enumeration of the votes, unless enlarged powers are expressly given by the statute. Strange to say, in this very case, those who insist that this Commission has power to go behind the decision of the Florida returning-board, made at the proper time, before the 6th of December, and to receive testimony impeaching its truthfulness and legality, are compelled to reverse the rule and nullify the principle when considering the action of the returning-board itself, acting under a statute much broader than the provision in the Constitution.

The statute under which they acted contains the provision I quoted at the beginning of my remarks, and, by necessary construction gives the board the power to take testimony to show whether a return was "false or fraudulent."

It is insisted that this statute did not permit the board to look beyond the mere face of the papers and take evidence to show that any return from a county or precinct was irregular, false, or fraudulent. This construction does violence to the language and spirit of the statute, and it is hard to see how any court could maintain it; and yet those maintaining it insist, in the next breath, that the constitutional declaration that "the votes shall then be counted" gives to this Commission the most enlarged powers of inquiry, far beyond any attempted to be exercised by the Florida canvassing-board.

If the Florida statute gives no authority to take testimony or to look beyond the mere face of the returns, what shall be said of the Constitution of the United States, which declares that when the certificates are opened "the votes shall then be counted?" The whole case in favor of the Tilden electors consists in the demand that the returns from the various counties and precincts of the State of Florida shall be received and counted, and that no evidence shall be admitted to show fraud or violence; and this demand is made in the face of a statute evidently giving to the returning-officers power to take testimony and to reject any return if it be shown to have been irregular, false, or fraudulent; and then, reversing the principle absolutely, to demand that this Commission, representing the two Houses, under the brief command of the Constitution "to count the votes," shall go behind the decision of the proper officers of Florida and make inquiries, both of law and fact, and exercise the highest judicial powers.

Aside from the consideration of matters which might appear upon the face of the certificate, there is absolutely but one thing to be done, and that is to identify the certificates as coming from the electors of the States. If they come from the electors of the States, the votes are to be counted. How, then, shall it be known that the certificate comes from the electors of the State? There is no requirement in the Constitution that the electors shall be certified by the governors of the States. That is a plan of identification, which was not devised until five years after the adoption of the Constitution and three years after the first presidential election. The positive requirement of the Constitution that the certificates from the electors appointed by the States shall be opened and the votes therein counted cannot be defeated by an act of Congress making the certificate of a governor necessary to the right of the elector to vote and to have his certificate opened and his vote counted. Should the certificate of the governor be withheld arbitrarily or by accident, or be falsely given to another, it could not defeat the express requirement of the Constitution that the certificate from the electors appointed by the State shall be opened and the votes therein counted.

As before stated, the only issue that can be tried is that the certificate is from the electors. The only certificate which the President of the Senate is bound to receive, and to open in the presence of the two Houses, is from the electors, a fact which he has a right, I think, to ascertain in any way that he can; but as this law requires him to open all certificates purporting to contain electoral votes, and he acts under it, it is the duty of this Commission to ascertain which certificate comes from the electors of the State, and when that is done the duty is performed, and the votes contained therein must be counted. The certificate of the governor is no part of the appointment of an elector, nor is its issue in any sense the act of the State. It is issued by virtue of an act of Congress, and Congress might have devolved the duty upon the secretary of state, the judge of the district court of the United States, or upon any other officer it chose to select. The certificate of the governor is the creation of the act of Congress, intended as a convenient form of evidence, but is not made conclusive, and could not be, for Congress has no power to make it a condition-precedent of the right of an elector appointed under the laws of a State that he shall obtain a certificate from the governor before exercising his right to vote. Such a provision would clearly be an infringement of the Constitution by attaching a new condition to the office of an elector. If it shall be made to appear that the certificate of the governor has been given to an elector who was not appointed in the manner prescribed by the legislature of the State, the certificate is null and void, and is to be utterly disregarded. The certificate of the governor issued under the act of Congress is not the act of the State. The return made by the canvassing-officers of the State is the act of the State and cannot be questioned.

How then shall we know whether the electors executing the certificate No. 1 in this case were the electors for the State of Florida? I answer, first, by the certificate of the governor, which is *prima facie* and sufficient evidence, if unimpeached, but if impeached then by reference to the declarations of those officers who, by the laws of Florida, were authorized to ascertain and certify who have been appointed electors; and when we have found such declarations we are at the end of the inquiry, and must accept them as final and conclusive.

There are some things in government that must depend upon forms, and some kinds of evidence that must be received as conclusive. In those particulars in which the Government deals with States as such, the forms of expression and action adopted by the States must be accepted as final.

It was intended that the States, in the appointment of electors, should be absolutely independent of each other and of the National Government.

The action of the State in the appointment of electors must be declared by officers designated by the legislature for that purpose, and when they have declared it, their declaration must not only be accepted by Congress as final and unquestionable, but be final and conclusive as to themselves and to the State; and they cannot afterward, under the influence of temptation, fear, or any other motive, reconsider their finding and determination.

If it were attempted by an act of Congress to take from the State the determination and ascertainment of the persons appointed electors in the manner prescribed by the legislature, it would be clearly unconstitutional.

The right of a State to appoint electors carries with it necessarily the right to ascertain in form of law who have been appointed. The power of the State to appoint would not be complete without the power to declare finally who have been appointed. If Congress may overrule the State authorities and decide who were elected by the people, the independence of the States in the appointment of electors would be lost, and their power amount to little more than the right to nominate a number of candidates from whom Congress might select. It is the peremptory duty of the governor to give the certificate to those persons who have been decided in the manner prescribed by the law of the State to have been appointed electors; and should he give the certificate to other persons, it would be fraudulent and void.

It is provided in the Constitution that the votes of the electors shall all be cast on the same day, and the history of the clause shows that great importance was attached to it.

The purpose was to prevent fraud, to prevent the electors in one State from waiting until the other States had voted and then so vote as to change or control the result.

How completely would this purpose be defeated if it were in the power of a State, after the electors in all the States had voted, to have a new count of votes in that State, so as to invalidate the votes of the electors and give effect to the votes of another set, who at the time of casting their votes had no title in law and were mere pretenders. This would present the greatest opportunities and temptations to fraud, and reverse the theory and purpose of the framers of the Constitution, who intended that the result of a presidential election should be settled irrevocably in one day, and that no opportunity should be left for intrigue and cabal after that time.

When electors have cast their votes on the 6th of December, and have sealed them up and transmitted them to the President of the Senate, they are *functus officio*. Their office has expired and their functions are gone forever. The power of the State in the election of a President is then exhausted, and the jurisdiction of the State which was absolute before, is thereafter absolutely extinguished. It is not left in the power of a State to undo or impair what she has done, by subsequently declaring that the electors who had voted had not been appointed, and that by a recount of the votes, real or pretended, other persons were shown to have been appointed. Whether such subsequent action on the part of the State is had through the courts, or by the legislature, or by both combined, can make no difference. Either way, or any way, such action, if allowed to prevail, would be fatal to our system of government. The certainty of political action requires that an act once performed in the election of a President shall be irrevocable.

If it be conceded that an elector at the time of the election in November, and at the time he voted as elector in December, held an office of trust under the United States, and was therefore ineligible, the question arises, what effect would it have upon his vote? Having been declared elected by the State returning-officers, and having received the certificate of the governor as an elector, he certainly had the color of office and was an officer *de facto*.

The act of an officer *de facto* is held to be valid so far as it affects the rights of any other person than himself. If his ineligibility had subsequently been established by a court of competent authority, upon a writ of *quo warranto*, it could not affect the validity of his vote.

The ineligibility of a person holding an office of trust or profit under the United States to be appointed an elector is not self-executing, and remains in abeyance until laws are passed providing method and process for ascertaining judicially such ineligibility.

Where the action of a State legislature is provided for or required by the Constitution of the United States, such action when performed cannot be revoked.

Each State is entitled to two Senators, to be chosen by the legislature thereof.

When a Senator has been chosen in the manner prescribed by law, the power of the legislature is exhausted, and it cannot at a subsequent time, when becoming dissatisfied with its choice, annul the first election and enter into a new one, nor can it accomplish the same purpose by resolving that the votes at the first election had not been properly counted and thereupon order a new election or a new count.

Again, the Constitution provides that amendments to it may be submitted by two-thirds of each House of Congress to the legislatures of the several States for their ratification. When the ratification of an amendment has been made by a legislature, it cannot be afterward reconsidered and undone. The legislatures of New York and Ohio attempted by formal votes to reconsider the ratifications before given to the fifteenth amendment, but their action was generally considered as a nullity by the legal mind of the United States.

Each House shall be the judge of the elections, returns, and qualifications of its own members.

Under this power the House may go behind the returns and count the actual number of votes received by a member, and the Senate may go behind the certificate of the governor and inquire whether a Senator received the number of legislative votes necessary to elect, whether h e has the qualifications required by the Constitution, or was guilty of bribery or other misconduct. And here it is claimed that the two Houses, or this Commission in their stead, in the absence of any constitutional provision, have the right to inquire into the election, returns, and qualifications of electors; that together they have the same power over electors that each House has over its own members. How monstrous is this assumption when we remember that the great effort by the framers of the Constitution was to make the executive independent of the legislative, and to place the election of a President beyond the reach or control of Congress. The electors were to be appointed by the States, in such manner as the legislatures might direct, and were thus removed from Congress as far as possible. The only mention of Congress in connection with the subject is, that the President of the Senate shall open the certificates in the presence of the two Houses; and from that is inferred the vast power to judge of the election, returns, and qualifications of electors.

The right of each House to judge of the election, return, and qualification of its members was not left to implication but was expressly conferred, notwithstanding it was so necessary and proper that each House should have that power. And can it be supposed that a similar power in regard to electors, so important and controlling in the choice of a President, would be left to implication had it been intended that the two Houses should have it? Not only is the power not given, but there is no provision from which it can be implied, and the history of the Constitution shows conclusively that the purpose was to put the election of a President beyond the control of Congress. The tenth article of amendment to the Constitution declares that—

The powers not delegated to the United States by the Constitution, nor prohibited by it to the States, are reserved to the States respectively or to the people.

The rule of construction adopted from the first is that the Government of the United States possesses no powers except those that are expressly conferred or such as are necessary to the due execution of those expressly conferred. Not only is the power on the part of the two Houses to judge of the election, returns, and qualification of electors not expressly conferred, and no provision from which it can be implied, but to infer it would be to violate the purpose entertained by the framers of the Constitution, and so often expressed by them, to preserve the independence of the executive department from the control and absorption of the legislative.

As the appointment of electors is to be made by the States in such manner as the legislatures may provide, it is clearly within the power of the States to provide for contesting the election of electors by the people, or to correct any errors or frauds in the return or canvass of the vote, provided such contest or correction is made before the 6th day of December, when the votes of the electors are to be cast; but, because the States have failed to make provision for such contest, or the correction of frauds or errors, it is absurd to argue that the two Houses of Congress or this Commission may step in and do that which the States had power but failed to do. The powers of the two Houses upon this or any other subject are not made to depend upon the failure of States to exercise their constitutional power, but depend upon the positive or implied grants of power in the Constitution.

If the States have a distinct and clearly defined right expressed in the Constitution, it is their perfect freedom from all outside interference in the appointment of electors. In this they are as free and independent as in the choice of a governor or any State officer.

In making an application of the principles of law to this case, certain great purposes should be kept in view:

First. That the process of electing a President shall be progressive, so that when the term of one expires there shall be another ready to take his place and no interregnum occur; and to cut off every method or purpose to retard the process and defeat the great result.

Second. That it was a leading purpose of the framers of the Constitution to preserve the independence of each department of Government, and especially to protect and preserve the independence of the Executive as against the absorbing tendencies of the legislative department.

Third. The judicial power of the Government is vested entirely in the courts, except where the same is expressly given, or by necessary implication, to another department, as where each House is authorized to judge of the election, returns, and qualifications of its own members.

In the organization of government the certainty of political action is an indispensable element, so that every step when taken shall be irrevocable.

After the electors have been appointed by the States, and have voted on the day fixed by law, and their votes have been sealed and transmitted to the President of the Senate, the States, as such, have no longer any connection with the matter. They cannot reconsider their action, appoint new electors, and vote for new candidates, nor can they accomplish the same things by declaring that although their electors were appointed in due form of law, yet in fact the appointment was procured by fraud or by a mistake of law or fact on the part of some of the State officers while in the process of appointment. The appointment of electors, when once made, must, for the very highest reasons of public policy, be irrevocable; for if a State should have the power, after the votes have been cast honestly, to undo a fraud, or correct a mistake, it is manifest that parties or conspirators, under that cover, might seek the perpetration of fraud to change or control the result of presidential elections.

For the reasons given, I believe that the votes contained in certificate No. 1 must be counted, and that the evidence offered to impeach them ought not to be received. The electors therein named were certified by M. L. Stearns, the lawful governor of the State at the time, and their election by the people was declared in due form of law by the officers of the State expressly authorized by the laws of the State to perform that duty. That a new governor, a new legislature, and a new returning-board, coming into office after the 6th of December and after the jurisdiction of the State had passed away, with or without the aid of the courts, can recount the vote, or in any way change the result, is a doctrine most dangerous and absurd.

LOUISIANA.

The electoral votes of Louisiana being under consideration—

Mr. Commissioner MORTON said:

Mr. PRESIDENT: It is not my purpose to go over the ground which was discussed and decided in the Florida case. An offer is made to impeach the decision of the returning-officers of Louisiana by showing that they threw out votes in violation of law; that their rulings were arbitrary and unjust, and that in point of fact the Tilden electors were appointed. The question as to the right to go behind the returns of the proper officers and inquire what was the actual result of an election in the State, and to examine into the conduct of such officers to find whether they acted within their jurisdiction or upon sufficient evidence, was fully settled in the negative in the Florida case. Without pretending that it is legitimate in this case—for I know it is not—to discuss the actual condition of things in Louisiana, yet I wish here to repel the charge of fraud which has been so persistently made by the objectors and counsel who appeared in favor of the Tilden electors.

If I am correctly advised, I believe that if we were to go behind the action of the returning-board of Louisiana we should find that action based upon sufficient evidence, and that the pretended majorities for the Tilden electors in many parishes had been obtained by intimidation produced by murder, violence, and the most dreadful crimes. It is easy to talk about what could be proven in the way of fraud when it is pretty well understood that there will be no opportunity or time to make the proof, and to bring the parties making the charge to the test. During the last ten years Louisiana has been the theater of the most fearful outrages recorded in the annals of our country. According to the testimony taken by investigating committees, and collected by General Sheridan, thousands of men have been killed and wounded on account of their opinions. The most terrible proscriptions have been practiced, and cruelties inflicted, compared to which the warfare of the American savage is civilized and humane.

But we are here to discuss questions of law, and I refer to these features in the recent history of Louisiana only to repel the constant charge of fraud and to rebut the allegations that resistance is made to going behind the returns and entering into the details of the Louisiana election for fear of the proof of these frauds. The appointment of the Hayes electors was duly certified by the governor of the State, and their appointment by the votes of the people was declared in due form of law by the proper returning-officers of the State, who alone were duly authorized to canvass and determine the persons appointed electors by the votes of the people.

To investigate the question whether these officers exceeded their jurisdiction or acted without proper evidence would concede the whole ground, would overturn the decision made in the Florida case, and lead necessarily to an examination of the details of the election in every parish in Louisiana. If the returning-officers were authorized to canvass the votes and make the declaration of the persons elected, we are concerned only with that declaration and not with the grounds upon which it was made. The declaration made by these officers is the act and declaration of the State, and we cannot, under the brief command of the Constitution, "and the votes shall then be counted," examine into the evidence upon which it was made. But to consider this demand in a practical point of view, we know very well that such an investigation could not be made between this and the 4th day of March. It would take weeks and perhaps months; and to enter upon it would be to defeat the presidential election altogether, create an interregnum, and bring confusion, perhaps anarchy, into the Government.

The length of the investigations which would have to be made, if we went behind the returns of the State officers, is an overwhelming argument against the soundness of the doctrine contended for. Taking the four disputed States, it is not possible that the investigations could be made in months, hardly this year; and it is claimed that all this shall be done under the brief command in the Constitution, "and the votes shall then be counted." Never was so monstrous a burden suspended upon so small a peg. It cannot be that the framers of the Constitution intended to authorize the two Houses of Congress, when the votes for President are being counted, to enter upon investigations in any or all the States which, by means of their length and complexity, would enable cunning conspirators to defeat the result of an election every time.

If it were intended by the fathers of the Republic to plant a rock in the straits directly in the path of the ship of state, and upon which she might be wrecked at any time by the carelessness or wickedness of the crew, it could not be done more effectually than by authorizing the two Houses of Congress to enter upon investigations almost interminable in their character and which through their magnitude and nature could be but imperfectly made, no difference how long the time consumed.

But it is alleged that the returning-board of Louisiana was not a legal body, not being composed according to the law of the State. Section 2 of the act of 1872, which is the latest law upon the subject, contains the following provision:

That five persons, to be elected by the senate from all political parties, shall be the returning-officers for all elections in the State, a majority of whom shall constitute a quorum and have power to make the returns of all elections. In case of any vacancy by death, resignation, or otherwise, by either of the board, then the vacancy shall be filled by the residue of the board of returning-officers. The returning-officers shall, after each election, before entering on their duties, take and subscribe to the following oath before a judge of the supreme or any district court, &c.

It is charged that the board at the time it made the canvass and declaration of votes had but four members, and was not, therefore, a legal body. There is nothing in this objection. The law expressly provides that a majority of the five persons "shall constitute a quorum, and have power to make the returns of all elections." Three would constitute a majority and be sufficient by the express terms of the statute "to make the returns of all elections." The law provides that the Supreme Court shall consist of nine judges, but it will not be asserted that the existence of even three vacancies in the court would invalidate its character as a legal body. In every deliberative body which is required to have a quorum, whether of a majority or any other number, its legal character is not destroyed so long as that quorum is maintained. The very object of having a quorum with which any deliberative body may do business is that its legality and capacity for business shall not be detroyed by vacancies or the absence of members so long as the number fixed for a quorum is maintained. It is provided that the Senate of the United States shall consist of two Senators from each State, yet the existence of a dozen vacancies would not impair the legal character of the body.

But it is argued that this rule will not apply in this case, because the remaining members of the board have the power to fill vacancies and it is their duty to do so. While it may be their duty to do so if they can agree upon the person, yet their failure to perform it could no more impair the legality of the body while a quorum remains than if the power to fill the vacancies belonged to the governor or the legislature. It is the duty of the majority to canvass and determine the result of an election when the votes have been placed in their possession, and the failure to perform the duty of filling a vacancy could not discharge them from the performance of the other duty to canvass and determine the result of an election. In point of fact, they may have been unable to agree upon the person, or have failed to fill the vacancy from other cause than a willful disregard of duty; but whether that is so or not is wholly immaterial.

But it is said that the board was illegal because it was not composed of men from all political parties as directed by the statute. The statute in that particular is merely directory and is incapable of rigid enforcement. How many parties or factions there were in the State we are not advised, although we know as a matter of general history that there were two principal parties, and the injunction to make up the board from all political parties is one which rests upon the senate of the State and not upon the board itself, and if the senate, in electing members of the board, disregard the injunction, there is no power lodged anywhere in the government of the State or in the courts to correct the error.

The distinction between *mandatory* and *directory* statutes is very broad, and this one clearly belongs to the latter class. It is like the injunction in the statute creating the office of attorney-general, that the person selected for that office "shall be learned in the law." The legality of the appointment of an attorney-general could not be questioned and the validity of his acts set aside by the allegation that he was not learned in the law, as required by the statute. The injunction that the senate in creating this board should take the members from all political parties should have been observed if it were possible, but the pretense that the validity of the acts of the board would be affected by proof that the senate had failed to observe the injunction is quite absurd.

Although the speeches have been very lengthy and able, and the objections filed against the validity of the action of the returning-board voluminous and elaborate, the whole question comes down to this simple proposition: Is it competent for the two Houses of Congress, or for this Commission acting in their stead, when counting the electoral votes for President, to go behind the decision made by the officers appointed by the legislature of the State for the purpose of canvassing and determining the result of the election, to inquire what was the number of votes cast for one set of candidates or for the other, whether the election was fairly conducted, and whether the officers appointed by the State to conduct the election or to determine its results acted within the limits of the law or upon sufficient evidence. A majority of this Commission decided in the Florida case that we had no such power. and I believe that time and the good sense of the American people will justify the decision in every respect.

OREGON.

The electoral votes of Oregon being under consideration—

Mr. Commissioner MORTON said:

Mr. PRESIDENT: At the late presidental election in Oregon Dr. Watts was a candidate for elector on the republican ticket, and received something more than one thousand majority over his highest democratic competitor. He was, at the time of the November election, postmaster in the little town of La Fayette, in which he lived. This office he resigned on the 13th of November, and on the next day a special agent it the Post-Office Department took possession of the office and removed of to another building, and his resignation was accepted by the Postmaster-General. On the 4th day of December the secretary of state of Oregon, in pursuance of law, canvassed the votes for presidential electors in the presence of the governor, and made out a tabulated statement of the returns from the various counties, which he certified under the seal of the State as being a complete and lawful canvass, showing that Dr. Watts and Messrs. Odell and Cartwright had been appointed electors for the State of Oregon.

On the morning of the 6th of December the governor issued three certificates, in each of which he stated that Messrs. Odell and Cartwright and one E. A. Cronin were the three eligible persons who had received the highest number of votes, and were duly appointed electors. These certificates he placed in the hands of Cronin, who refused to deliver them to Odell and Cartwright, but kept them in his possession, and after professing to read their contents, or a part of them, in the hearing of Odell, Cartwright, and Watts, retired to another part of the room in which they were assembled, and appointed two persons to act as electors instead of Odell and Cartwright; and assuming to act as electors, the three voted, Cronin for Tilden and the other two for Hayes. When Odell and Cartwright met at twelve o'clock on the 6th of December, Dr. Watts resigned the office of elector, and was immediately thereafter elected by them to fill the vacancy in the college of electors, and the three then cast their votes for Hayes for President and Wheeler for Vice-President.

The governor refused to give the certificate of election to Watts for the alleged reason that Watts was ineligible to be voted for on the 7th of November because he was a deputy postmaster, and gave it to Cronin upon the ground that he had received the next highest number of votes. He assumed that he had judicial power to judge as to Watts's eligibility, and decided that he was ineligible at the time of the election and that his competitor having the next highest number of votes was elected. This assumption on the part of the governor was entirely erroneous. His business under the statute of the United States was simply to give the certificate of appointment as electors to those persons who had been declared by the proper returning-officers of the State to have been appointed. He had no more power to pass upon the question of the eligibility of an elector, and refuse to give a certificate upon that account, than he had to pass upon the eligibility of a person who had been elected as a member of Congress. His duty was simply ministerial. In the next place, if he had the judicial power and the right to pass upon the question, his decision was directly in conflict with the law. The meaning of the Constitution is that an elector shall not be a member of Congress or an officer under the United States at the time he takes the office and casts his vote. If on the 6th of December, when the electors voted, Dr. Watts was eligible, having before resigned his office as postmaster, it was of no importance that he had been postmaster when voted for in November. This question has often been decided, and it has always been held that members of Congress who were ineligible from any cause, from want of age, of citizenship, or disability under the fourteenth amendment, at the time of their election by the people or by the legislature, but whose disabilities were removed at the time the term of office began and they took their seats, were eligible, and their ineligibility on the day of the election was of no importance. But whatever may be the law upon this subject, it became unimportant from the fact that on the 6th day of December Watts resigned his office of elector to the college of electors and was immediately re-elected to fill the vacancy at a time when he was unquestionably eligible. The power of the college of electors to fill the vacancy occasioned by his resignation appears from the following provision of the Oregon statute:

SEC. 59. The electors of President and Vice-President shall convene at the seat of government on the first Wednesday of December next after their election, at the hour of twelve of the clock at noon of that day, and if there shall be any vacancy in the office of an elector, occasioned by death, refusal to act, neglect to attend, or otherwise, the electors present shall immediately proceed to fill by *viva voce* and plurality of votes such vacancy in the electoral college, and when all the electors shall appear, or the vacancies, if any, shall have been filled as above provided, such electors shall proceed to perform the duties required of them by the Constitution and laws of the United States.

By this statute the college of electors is expressly authorized to fill " any vacancy in the office of an elector, occasioned by death, refusal to act, neglect to attend, or *otherwise.*" So that they could fill a vacancy arising from non-election as well as from death or resignation. The object of the statute is remedial, and it should be liberally construed, so as to give the State her full voice in the election of a President and Vice-President. In any view of the case, whether the vacancy in the college of electors arose from non-election by reason of Watts's ineligibility on the 7th of November, or by reason of his resignation on the 6th of December, the college of electors had the right to fill it. The doctrine upon which the governor assumed to act, that where a candidate is ineligible the person having the next highest number of votes is elected, is in conflict with the general current of judicial decisions in the United States. Each House of Congress, after the fullest deliberation, has expressly decided that in such a case the minority candidate is not elected, and that the election is a failure.

In England it has been held that where it was known to the voters that the majority candidate was ineligible at the time they voted for him, the minority candidate was elected. But these decisions were put upon the express ground of actual knowledge upon the part of the voters of the ineligibility, and that the voters not only knew the fact which in law made the candidate ineligible, but knew also that the fact did make him ineligible under the law. The English courts have held that in such a case the voters are not presumed to know the law, but it must be shown affirmatively that they knew not only the fact which made the candidate ineligible, but also knew that under the law the fact made him ineligible. The statute of Oregon provides in section 60 that—

> The votes for the electors shall be given, received, returned, and canvassed as the same are given, returned, and canvassed for members of Congress. The secretary of state shall prepare two lists of the names of the electors elected, and affix the seal of the State to the same. Such lists shall be signed by the governor and secretary, and by the latter delivered to the college of electors at the hour of their meeting on such first Wednesday of December.

Here it is provided that "the votes for the electors shall be given, received, returned, and canvassed as the same are given, returned, and canvassed for members of Congress." By turning to section 37 we find the provision for canvassing the votes given for Representatives in Congress as follows:

> The county clerk, immediately after making the abstract of the votes given in his county, shall make a copy of each of said abstracts, and transmit it by mail to the secretary of state at the seat of government; and it shall be the duty of the secretary of state, in the presence of the governor, to proceed within thirty days after the election, and sooner if the returns be all received, to canvass the votes given for secretary and treasurer of state, state printer, justices of the supreme court, member of Congress, and district attorneys; and the governor shall grant a certificate of election to the person having the highest number of votes, and shall also issue a proclamation declaring the election of such person.

By the above provision, the secretary of state is made the canvassing and returning officer for member of Congress and *all the State officers*. He is to canvass the votes in the presence of the governor, but the governor is simply a witness and takes no part whatever in the canvass, and is positively required to issue a certificate of election to the person having the highest number of votes as certified by the secretary. Upon this subject the governor has no discretion whatever. His duty is purely ministerial, and the certificate of election for member of Congress and *every State officer* is to be issued to the person having the highest number of votes. All questions of eligibility are taken from him. His duty is imperative to certify to the person having the highest number of votes; and what he is to do as to the member of Congress and the State officers, he is by the other section required to do as to presidential electors.

By section 60, above quoted, the secretary is to canvass and return the persons appointed electors; is to prepare two lists of the names of the persons appointed, and affix to them the seal of the State. The governor is then commanded to sign these lists, and the secretary to deliver them "to the college of electors at the hour of their meeting on such first Wednesday of December." When the secretary has canvassed, certified, and returned the votes of electors to his office, their appointment is complete. All that the governor has to do with the matter thereafter under the statute is purely ministerial. He has no judicial power upon the subject. He has no discretion whatever reposed in him by the law. It is his peremptory duty to sign the lists made out by the secretary, and the secretary is to certify to the election of the persons having the highest number of votes. Taking the two sections of the statute together, it is the absolute duty of the secretary to return as appointed those persons having the highest number of votes, and the absolute duty of the governor to give the certificate to the persons thus returned by the secretary.

The title of the persons appointed electors, as shown by the certificate of the secretary made out on the 4th day of December, and deposited in his office, was complete, and could not be impaired or affected in any way by the refusal of the governor thereafter to issue the certificate as he was required to do by law. The secretary of state in Oregon is the canvassing officer, and has the same duties devolved upon him as those which belong to the canvassing-officers in Florida or to the returning-board in Louisiana, except that he has no judicial or discretionary powers given to him as are conferred by the statutes of Florida and Louisiana, his duty in all cases being to return as elected the persons having the highest number of votes. The certificates signed by the governor of the appointment of electors having been withheld from the electoral college, the electors procured from the secretary, under the seal of the State, a copy of the certificate of the vote of the State, as tabulated and prepared by him on the 4th of December, and inclosed it in the certificate containing their votes and the record of their action on the 6th day of December, transmitted by them to the President of the Senate.

I may here repeat what I said in the Florida and Louisiana cases, that the question of eligibility of electors belongs to the States, and if it is disregarded by the States there is no way when the votes are counted in the presence of the two Houses or by this Commission to try and settle such question. In the case of Cæsar Griffin, Chief-Justice Chase decided that the fourteenth amendment to the Constitution making certain persons ineligible to office was not self-executing, and could not be carried into effect in the absence of an act of Congress providing for the adjudication and settlement of questions arising under it. There are few provisions of the Constitution that are self-executing, and clearly this is not one; but in any point of view the question of eligibility as it has been raised in this and the Louisiana and Florida cases is wholly unimportant. Here Dr. Watts was re-elected elector by the college, in pursuance of the statute, after the alleged ineligibility had been removed ; but if at the time of his re-election on the 6th of December he had still been postmaster it could not have affected the validity of the vote which he cast as an elector. It has been held that the official acts of one who was ineligible to hold the office were valid although after that time a court of law in the proceeding upon *quo warranto* found the fact of ineligibility and ousted him from the office. In one case the judgment and findings of a court were held to be valid, although it was subsequently decided by the proper tribunal that the judge was ineligible under the fourteenth amendment to hold the office. But this doctrine is so well understood and so universally applied that there ought to be no argument upon this subject.

The very highest interests of society require that the validity of official acts shall not be disturbed because of the ineligibility of the persons performing them to hold the office. And the reasons for this doctrine apply as strongly in this case as in any other. If the vote of an elector can be stricken out by a subsequent decision that he was ineligible, the evil is without remedy, the State has lost the vote, and the spirit of the Constitution has been violated. The theory of the Constitution when it was formed was that the electors were to be an independent body of select men who were to be perfectly free, and without committals or entanglements of any kind, to act as they thought best for the good of the country ; and to secure this independence they were to vote by ballot, so that one should not know how the other voted. We all know in practice how completely this purpose upon the part of the framers of the Constitution has been swept away. They are pledged in every case in advance to cast their votes for the candidates of a particular party, and if they should disregard this pledge they would be infamous, and it is a matter of no importance whatever whether they are members of Congress or officers of the United States. Not only are they pledged in advance for whom they shall vote, but under the practical working of our institutions this previous pledge is the greatest security the country has against their corruption and the improper exercise of so great a power.

In the State of Oregon there was no dispute as to the result of the vote by the people on the 7th of November. The action of the governor was clearly illegal and in violation of the plainest provisions of the statutes of the State as well as of the United States. The secretary in the performance of the duty imposed upon him counted the vote and certified to it under the seal of the State, and when he issued his certificate showing who had received the highest number of votes, the law of the State declared that such person was elected, and was entitled to be ministerially certified to by the governor, and no failure or refusal upon the part of the governor could affect his title. The certificate of the governor of the appointment of the electors is *prima facie* evidence of their appointment, unimpeached, but it may always be impeached by showing that it is in conflict with the canvass and return made by the officers authorized by the law of the State to make such canvass and return, and in this case the certificate of the secretary of state inclosed in the certificate made by the electors and transmitted to the President of the Senate shows clearly that the State of Oregon had appointed Watts, Odell, and Cartwright as electors.

SOUTH CAROLINA.

The electoral votes of South Carolina being under consideration—

Mr. Commissioner MORTON said:

Mr. PRESIDENT: In this case it seems hardly necessary to say a word. It is not denied that the Hayes electors received a majority of all the votes at the late election in South Carolina. This fact was found by a democratic investigating committee sent into the State by the House of Representatives. The republicans contend that but for the most monstrous frauds practiced in Edgefield and Laurens Counties and in many other localities in the State, their majority would have been thousands where it is now conceded to be hundreds. There are but two points made in the argument against the validity of the vote of the Hayes electors which I will notice.

First, it is alleged that the election in South Carolina was void because there had been no registry made of the voters as required by the constitution of the State. The provision of the constitution of South Carolina has never been executed by a law passed by the legislature, and repeated elections have been had and the legality of them has never been questioned, notwithstanding the absence of a registry law. If the absence of such a law invalidates all elections in the State, then South Carolina has had no legal government since 1868, and the recent pretended election of Hampton is a fraud.

But whatever might be the legal effect of the absence of a registry law upon the election of State officers, it is absurd to pretend that it could have any upon the appointment of electors. They are to be appointed in the manner prescribed by the legislature of the State and not by the constitution of the State. The manner of the appointment of electors has been placed by the Constitution of the United States in the legislature of each State, and cannot be taken from that body by the provisions of a State constitution. If the constitution of a State should provide that electors should be appointed by the supreme court of the State, that could not prevent the legislature from providing that electors might be appointed by the vote of the people. The Constitution of the United States provides that Senators shall be chosen by the legislature of each State, and it is not competent in the constitution of a State to require that Senators shall be elected by the people at a general election, and thus take from the legislature the right to elect.

The power to appoint electors by a State is conferred by the Constitution of the United States and does not spring from a State constitution, and cannot be impaired or controlled in any respect by a State constitution. It is competent for the constitution of the State to provide that State officers shall be chosen at an election where the voters have been registered, but it is not competent to make any such requisition as to the appointment of electors. If the legislature provides that electors may be appointed by the people at the polls without having been previously registered, it has a clear right to do so.

Second, it is alleged that there is no republican government in the State of South Carolina, and, therefore, no legislature which can provide for the appointment of electors or direct and control an election by the people. My answer to this is, that it is not true.

There is and has been a republican government in the State of South Carolina ever since reconstruction in 1868, and although it has been surrounded with great difficulties and has often been disturbed by violence and threatened with revolution, it has maintained a continued existence since its re-establishment after the rebellion. The Constitution provides that the United States shall guarantee to each State a republican form of government. If there is not a republican form of government in South Carolina it is for the two Houses of Congress acting in a legislative capacity to declare that fact and provide for the establishment of one; but until that takes place I must assume that South Carolina has a republican form of government, and as much right as any other State to appoint electors and participate in the presidential election. It seems to me I should be trifling with the intelligence of the Commission to argue this question further.

REMARKS OF MR. COMMISSIONER THURMAN.

FLORIDA.

The Commission having under consideration the electoral votes of the State of Florida—

Mr. Commissioner THURMAN addressed the Commission. Ill-health has prevented his writing out his remarks. The following is a synopsis of them:

Mr. President, in the discharge of its duties, this Commission, by the act creating it, is vested with the same powers, in the count of the electoral votes, now possessed by the two Houses of Congress acting separately, or together; and it is required to ascertain and decide whether any and what votes from a State are the votes provided for by the Constitution of the United States, and how many and what persons were duly appointed electors in such State. We are thus brought to the question, What are the powers of the two Houses of Congress in counting the electoral vote? It has been contended that we are concluded by the certificate of the governor that A B, &c., were duly appointed electors of the State of Florida, but this proposition cannot be maintained. There is nothing in the act of Congress requiring the governor's certificate, nor in any statute of Florida, that makes his certificate conclusive. It is, therefore, subject to be rebutted, and the question now is upon what grounds can it be contested. I understand it to be asserted by those who claim the election or the appointment of the Hayes electors, that the governor's certificate is not conclusive unless made in accordance with the decision of the canvassing-board; but that, when so made, it is conclusive. This raises the question whether the decision of that board can be impeached. I maintain that it can. I shall not in this case, because it is unnecessary, go into an inquiry as to all the causes for which a decision of a canvassing-board may be impeached. It will be found sufficient for the decision of this case that it is impeachable for want of jurisdiction in the board to do that which it did; and the effect of which was to change the apparent result of the election. I know of no tribunal, high or low, whose acts, without jurisdiction or beyond its jurisdiction, are not absolutely void.

Now, upon the county returns it is not denied, and, indeed, appears by evidence already before us and not controverted, that the Tilden electors received a majority of the votes of the people of Florida; and it also appears that it was only by throwing out the votes of counties or precincts that an apparent majority was shown for the Hayes electors. Had the canvassing-board of Florida any authority to throw out these votes? This question has been decided by the highest judicial tribunal of that State, interpreting the statute creating that board and defining its powers. In the case of Drew against Stearns the supreme court of Florida held that the canvassing-board had no judicial powers whatsoever; that its powers were simply ministerial; that it was bound to count the votes *given* and could not inquire into the legality or illegality of the votes thus given. Consequently, the decision of the canvassing-board that Stearns was elected governor, which decision was effected in the same manner by which that board declared the Hayes electors to be chosen, was declared by the supreme court of the State to be unauthorized by the statute and a plain usurpation of power. That decision is as applicable to the case of the presidential electors as to the case of Drew and Stearns, the rival candidates for governor. It is perfectly conclusive of the meaning of the statute, as much so as if it were written in the statute in so many words. It follows then that if we are to respect the statute of Florida, which everybody admits must govern the case, the canvassing-board, in throwing out the votes for the Tilden electors and thereby giving an apparent majority to the Hayes electors, acted without jurisdiction, and their act was, therefore, absolutely null and void.

But the above is not the only decision of the Florida courts. In a *quo warranto* sued out by the Tilden electors against the Hayes electors, the circuit court of Florida, having admitted jurisdiction, has decided that the Tilden electors and not the Hayes electors were duly appointed. Moreover, the legislature of the State has affirmed this view of the State statute and the present governor of the State has given to the Tilden electors certificates of their appointment. So that every department of government in Florida, executive, legislative, and judicial, has decided against the pretension of the Hayes electors. And I think it is impossible for any fair-minded lawyer to carefully examine the Florida statutes without being brought to concur in the correctness of these decisions of her authorities.

And here it is proper to remark that there is nothing in the Constitution or laws of the United States, or in the constitution or laws of Florida, that makes the canvassing-board the sole judge of its own jurisdiction. On the contrary, the decisions to which I have referred distinctly hold that it is not the sole judge, and, in Drew against Stearns, the supreme court compelled it to recount the votes and reverse its first decision. And here I would further observe that to remedy the injustice perpetrated by that board in the count of the votes for presidential electors, is not, as has been suggested, to invade the right of the State. It is precisely the reverse. It is to uphold the statute of the State and to protect her from the consequences of a violation of her laws and a usurpation by her officers. The votes cast for Hayes by the Hayes electors have not yet been counted. Effect cannot be given to them until they be counted. The proceeding is, therefore, still *in fieri* and the two Houses of Congress, to whom it belongs to count the votes, must of necessity determine—as this Commission is required by the act creating it to determine—

Whether any and what votes from such State are the votes provided for by the Constitution of the United States, and how many and what persons were duly appointed electors in such State.

In executing these powers the two Houses of Congress cannot, and therefore this Commission cannot, shut their eyes to the fact that the statutes of Florida, as construed by her courts, required the certificate of election to be given to the Tilden electors, and that it was only by a gross usurpation of power that the canvassing-board decided in favor of the Hayes electors.

But if it be said that the remedy can be provided by the State alone, and that if she has not provided a remedy the wrong is remediless, I answer—

First. That the electors being a creation of the Federal Constitution, it is the duty of the two Houses of Congress, who count the votes, to see that they are appointed consistently with the provisions of the Constitution. And, consequently, no State can, by neglecting to provide a remedy, compel the Houses to count votes given by usurping electors who are not appointed in the mode contemplated by the Constitution; that is to say, in the manner prescribed by the State legislature.

Second. That the other States and the whole people of the United States are parties interested in the proceeding, and the question whether there shall be a remedy is not left to the discretion of the State alone.

Third. That if the remedy must be a State remedy, it has been applied in this case, and the decision is adverse to the claim of the Hayes electors.

If I am right in these propositions, it follows that the testimony on the question of jurisdiction ought to be received.

I also think that proof of fraud is admissible. The canvassing-board was neither a legislature nor a judicial court, and I know of no principle of law, or manifest public policy, that shields it from an inquiry into the *bona fides* or *mala fides* of its acts.

It is said that if we go behind the decision of the canvassing-board we must go to the bottom, and may thus be led to investigate the doings of hundreds of thousands of election-officers in the United States and the qualification of millions of voters. I reply, *non constat.* It is not sound logic to say, that because we cannot investigate everything we shall investigate nothing; that because we cannot correct all errors and frauds we shall correct none. The law never requires impossibilities, but it does require what is possible.

But the argument upon which the greatest stress has been laid to sustain the vote for Hayes is that the Hayes electors were, when they cast their votes, electors *de facto*, and that consequently the doctrine in relation to the acts of officers *de facto* applies to them. I deny that that doctrine has any application in this case. I am not prepared to admit that presidential electors are officers at all. They are what the Constitution calls them—"electors" who have but a single act to perform, and their existence as electors may be as ephemeral as the life of an insect. In this case it was so. The canvassing-board declared the appointment of the Hayes electors on the very day that the electoral vote was to be cast, and in two or three hours after that declaration the vote was cast. What time was there to institute legal proceedings and carry them into judgment between the decision of the canvassing-board and the casting of the electoral votes? Manifestly none at all. To require, therefore, as the argument does, that these men should have been ousted from their office by judicial proceedings before they cast their votes, and that if not so ousted they were officers *de facto*, and their acts are valid, is a simple mockery of justice that it is difficult to contemplate without a feeling of contempt. All that could be done in the way of judicial proceedings was done in this case. A writ of *quo warranto* was issued by a court of competent jurisdiction and served upon the Hayes electors before they cast their votes. Of course no decision could be had upon that writ within the two or three hours that elapsed after its service and before the votes were cast. But the case was prosecuted to final judgment, and the judgment was that the Hayes electors were usurpers who never had any title to be called electors of Florida, and although no judgment of ouster could be pronounced, because the votes had been already cast, yet the decision is a judicial determination that the Hayes electors had no title whatsoever.

The power of the two Houses to go behind the governor's certificates and the decisions of canvassing-boards has been again and again asserted by the Houses and carried into execution. Thus in 1865 Congress resolved that no votes for presidential electors should be received from the States of Florida, Louisiana, Tennessee, Mississippi, North Carolina, Virginia, South Carolina, Alabama, Arkansas, Texas, and Georgia. In 1873 the votes of the States of Arkansas and Louisiana, and certain electoral votes of the State of Georgia, were rejected. But these instances are familiar to the members of the Commission, and it is unnecessary to dwell upon them.

LOUISIANA.

The Commission having under consideration the electoral vote of the State of Louisiana—

Mr. Commissioner THURMAN addressed the Commission. Ill-health has prevented his writing out his remarks in full. The following is a synopsis of them:

Mr. President, it is my opinion—

1. That the votes for presidential electors, cast in the State of Louisiana at the last election, have never been canvassed by any lawful authority. I deny that the returning-board of Louisiana has any lawful existence. I deny that the constitution of that State, or anything in the Federal Constitution, confers upon her legislature the power to create *such* a board. To understand this proposition we must look at the constitution and powers of that board as defined in the statute creating it. And we must consider them not in an abstract and theoretical manner, but with a clear view of their practical effect. It is not true that every law that might upon its face seem to be unobjectionable is necessarily constitutional. Laws are not mere abstract things. They are meant to be practical, and if the inevitable practical

result of a law directly conflicts with the admitted principles or provisions of the Constitution, the law cannot stand.

Let us then see what is the Louisiana returning-board. It is a board consisting of five persons holding their offices without any limitation of time and filling all the vacancies that occur in their own body. It is, therefore, a kind of perpetual, self-preserving and self-perpetuating corporation. Neither its existence nor its powers can be affected except by a repeal or modification of the law creating it. But no such repeal or modification can take place without its permission; for, by conferring upon it, in plain violation of the constitution of the State, the power to canvass the votes for members of the general assembly, the board is enabled to constitute the legislature, whenever it sees fit, so as to contain a majority of its friends. It is of no use to say that it will not corruptly or unlawfully exercise this power. Again and again it has corruptly and unlawfully exercised it. It has so corruptly and unlawfully exercised it after every election that has taken place since the board was created. In 1872, a majority of conservatives, or fusionists as they were then called, were elected to the general assembly. The returning-board threw out large numbers of them and gave their places to men who were notoriously not elected, and thus created a republican majority in both branches of the assembly. In 1874 precisely the same thing occurred. In 1876 it occurred for the third time, and these are the only years since the creation of the board in which elections for members of the assembly have taken place. In the same way the board has defeated the election of State officers by the people in each one of these years, and to cap the climax of its infamy it has thrown out thousands of votes given for the Tilden electors, and thereby changing the vote of the people, has declared the Hayes electors to be duly appointed. And if its power can be sustained, there is obviously no end to its rule over the people of Louisiana. It is made, by the statute creating it, the returning-board for *all* elections held in the State for all officers from the highest to the very lowest, and it executes its powers in the interest of its party and itself without shame and without remorse. Take a map of Louisiana, mark upon it the democratic precincts whose votes for members of the assembly were thrown out last December, and you will find as many blotches on the map as there are scars upon the face of a victim of the small-pox. Why was this done? Not merely to affect the result of the presidential election, or of the election for officers of the State—for the republican electors and State officers could have been counted in without running all over the State to throw out a democratic precinct here and another one there. It was done to give the republicans the majority in the legislature; and to do it, precinct after precinct was thrown out where there was no pretense whatever that the election was not fair and peaceable; no pretense whatever of bribery, intimidation, or employment of any corrupt means. In short, the powers given to this board are more transcendent in their practical operation than the powers of the whole body of the people of the State. The board is in effect constituted the State—to govern it according to its own arbitrary will and discretion. There is no republican government in Louisiana. There can be no republican government in that State so long as this returning-board is upheld. An oligarchy more corrupt, more odious, more anti-republican, never before existed on this globe.

I repeat, that the constitution of Louisiana confers no authority upon the legislature of that State to create any such board. Nay, more, its power to canvass the votes for members of the general assembly is in direct conflict with that constitution, which makes each house of the assembly the sole judge of the election, returns, and qualifications of its members. And such was the view taken by the Senate Committee on Privileges and Elections in 1873, in the elaborate report presented by Mr. Carpenter, and which was dissented from by but one member of the committee. The returning board of that day was denounced as unconstitutional; but if that board was unconstitutional, *a multo fortiori* is the board of to-day, created by a subsequent statute, and with the powers of self-perpetuation to which I have alluded, unconstitutional. Now, it is upon the canvass made by this unconstitutional returning-board, it is upon its assumption of power to throw out from six to ten thousand votes given for the Tilden electors, that the advocates of the Hayes electors claim the vote of the State. I deny that this decision of that board has any legal effect whatsoever. Being unconstitutional, it had no right to canvass those votes, no more than any other four citizens of the State of Louisiana.

Another objection to the constitutionality of the board was made by counsel [Mr. Carpenter] and argued with great force, and seems to me to deserve our serious consideration. It is the objection that the statute clothes the board with power to *disfranchise* voters—the innocent as well as the guilty—and to do so without any trial or hearing to which the voter is a party. That the power to disfranchise is a *judicial* power that could not be conferred upon the board ; the constitution of Louisiana expressly declaring (article 94) that "No judicial powers, except as committing-magistrates in criminal cases, shall be conferred on any officers other than those mentioned in this title, (title 4,) except such as may be necessary in towns and cities ; and the judicial powers of such officers shall not extend further than the cognizance of cases arising under the police regulations of towns and cities in the State." The officers mentioned in title 4 are judges, justices of the peace, an attorney-general, sheriffs, and coroners.

II. But if the law creating the board is not unconstitutional, yet the board that canvassed the votes in question was not legally constituted. The statute creating it required that the board should consist of *five* persons taken "*from all political parties*," and this provision requiring the different political parties to be thus represented is of the very essence of the law. But the board that canvassed the votes for electors after the late election consisted of but four members, all of the same political party, namely, all republicans. These four were applied to, again and again, to execute the statute by filling the vacancy in the board with a democrat. They utterly refused or neglected to do so, and, without filling the vacancy at all, proceeded to canvass the returns, throw out thousands of votes, and pronounce a decision in favor of the Hayes electors. It has been argued that because a majority of the board constituted a quorum, therefore the board could proceed without filling the vacancy, and it has been said that if a dozen or more members of the Senate of the United States were absent or dead, but a quorum were present, there would be a lawful Senate ; or that if four of the judges of the Supreme Court were absent, but five were present, there would be a lawful court. Nobody doubts either of those propositions; but they have not the remotest application to the present case. If the Constitution required that the Senate should consist of different *classes* of persons and gave to the Senate the power to fill all vacancies in its own body, and there were vacancies, and the members present refused to fill them, there would be some analogy between that case and this. And so of the Supreme Court. But no such requisition or power is contained in the Constitution, and hence the illustrations are of no value whatsoever. Here we have a plain statute that requires the returning-board to be constituted from all political parties. The reason of the requirement is perfectly obvious. It was to secure fairness and justice in the canvass. It was enacted for the same reason that in some of the States the judges or inspectors of election are required to be of different parties, as, for instance, in Louisiana, whose statute requires—

That the election at each poll or polling-place shall be presided over by three commissioners of elections, residents of the parish for at least twelve months next preceding the day of election, who shall be selected from different political parties, and be of good standing in the party to which they belong.

The requirement is, therefore, as I have already said, of the very essence of the statute. As well might it be said that the jury known to the common law as the jury *de medietate linguæ* could be lawfully constituted of but one nationality and of jurors speaking but one language, as to say that the returning-board of Louisiana could be lawfully constituted of members of but one political party. For this reason, then, even if the law creating the board is constitutional, the board itself that canvassed the votes in question was not legally constituted, and its canvass has no legal effect.

III. But if I am wrong in both these propositions, yet the canvass of that board must be rejected. I need not repeat here what I said in the Florida case, that the doings of any tribunal, however high, acting without jurisdiction, are absolutely null and void. This is elementary law, and I know of no exception whatever to the rule.

This brings us to the inquiry, had the returning-board jurisdiction to cast out the thousands of votes given for the Tilden electors which it did cast out, and by the casting out of which the majority in the State was reversed? To answer this question we must recur to the election law of that State. By section 2 of that law the returning-board is created. Section 26 of that law provides as follows:

That in any parish, precinct, ward, city, or town in which, during the time of registration or revision of registration, or on any day of registration, there shall be any riot, tumult, acts of violence, intimidation, and disturbance, bribery, or corrupt influences at any place within said parish or at or near any poll or voting-place or place of registration or revision of registration, which riot, tumult, acts of violence, intimidation, and disturbance, bribery, or corrupt influences shall prevent or tend to prevent a fair, free, peaceable, and full vote of all the qualified electors of said parish, precinct, ward, city, or town, it shall be the duty of the commissioners of election, if such riot, tumult, acts of violence, intimidation, and disturbance, bribery, or corrupt influences occur on the day of election, or of the supervision of registration of the parish, if they occur during the time of registration or revision of registration, to make in duplicate and under oath a clear and full statement of all the facts relating thereto and of the effect produced by such riot, tumult, acts of violence, intimidation, and disturbance, bribery or corrupt influences in preventing a fair, free, peaceable, and full registration or election, and of the number of qualified voters deterred by such riots, tumult, acts of violence, intimidation, and disturbance, bribery or corrupt influences from registering or voting; which statement shall also be corroborated under oath by three respectable citizens, qualified electors of the parish. When such statement is made by a commissioner of election or a supervisor of registration, he shall forward it in duplicate to the supervisor of registration of the parish, if in the city of New Orleans to the secretary of state, one copy of which, if made to the supervisor of registration, shall be forwarded by him to the returning-officers provided for in section 2 in this act, *when he makes the returns of election in his parish. His copy of said statement shall be so annexed to his returns of elections, by paste, wax, or some adhesive substance, that the same can be kept together,* and the other copy the supervisor of registration shall deliver to the clerk of the court of his parish for the use of the district attorney.

Section 8 provides, as I have already shown, that the election at each poll or polling place shall be presided over by three commissioners of election of different politics.

Section 13 enacts, among other things, that—

The vote shall be counted by the commissioners at each voting-place, *immediately after closing the election* and without moving the boxes from the place where the votes were received, and the counting must be done in the presence of any bystander or citizen who may be present.

Section 43 is as follows:

That immediately upon the close of the polls on the day of election, the commissioners of the election at each poll or voting-place shall proceed to count the votes as provided in section 13 of this act, and after they shall have so counted the votes and made a list of the names of all the persons voted for, and the offices for which they were voted for, and the number of votes received by each, the number of ballots contained in the box, and the number rejected, and the reasons therefor, duplicates of such lists shall be made out, signed, and sworn to by the commissioners of election of each poll, and such duplicate lists shall be delivered, one to the supervisor of registration of the parish and one to the clerk of the district court of the parish, and in the parish of Orleans to the secretary of state, by one or all such commissioners in person *within twenty-four hours after the closing of the polls.* It shall be the duty of the supervisor of registration, *within twenty-four hours after the receipt of all the returns for the different polling-places,* to consolidate such returns, to be certified as correct by the clerk of the district court, and forward the consolidated returns, with the originals received by him, to the returning-officers provided for in section 2 of this act, the said report and returns to be inclosed in an envelope of strong paper or cloth, securely sealed, and forwarded by mail. *He shall forward a copy of any statement as to violence or disturbance, bribery or corruption, or other offenses specified in section 26 of this act, if any there be,* together with all memoranda and tally-lists used in making the count and statement of the votes.

From these provisions it appears—

1. That if any statements of riot, tumult, acts of violence, intimidation and disturbance, bribery or corrupt influences, are made by the commissioners of election, they must be made before the commissioners make their return to the supervisor of registration and must accompany that return, and that return must be made within *twenty-four hours after the closing of the polls.*

2. That the supervisor of registration *within twenty-four hours after the receipt of all the returns* for the different polling-places shall consolidate such returns, to be certified as correct by the clerk of the district court, and forward the consolidated returns, with the originals received by him, to the returning-board, and therewith " *shall forward a copy of any statement as to violence or disturbance, bribery or corruption, or other offenses specified in section 26 of this act, if any there be.*"

3. *That the statement of violence, &c., shall be so annexed to the returns of the supervisor, by paste, wax, or some adhesive substance, that the same can be kept together.*

It is thus apparent that all statements of violence, &c., made by commissioners of election must be made within twenty-four hours after the close of the polls, and that all such statements made by supervisors of registration must be made not later than forty-eight hours after the close of the polls. The reasons for this requirement are very apparent and very weighty. The jurisdiction of the returning-board to throw out votes depends, as I will presently show, upon these statements being made; but it would obviously open a wide door to fraud if such statements could be made after it was ascertained what was the general result of the election in the State, and an inducement thereby created to throw out the votes of particular parishes or precincts in order to change that result. And, therefore, the statute requires the statements, or protests, as they are sometimes called, to be made as soon as possible after the election—by the commissioners within twenty-four hours after the close of the polls, by the supervisors of registration not later than forty-eight hours after such closing. The practical effect of this provision is to require the statements to be made before the general result of the State election can be known, and thus to avoid any inducement to make false and fabricated statements. But not only were the statements of the commissioners or supervisors necessary; the third section of the act also required an affidavit of three or more citizens to the fact of riot, tumult, &c.

We now come to the powers of the returning-board. They are given by sections 2 and 3 of the act, which I will quote in full as follows:

SEC. 2. That five persons, to be elected by the senate *from all political parties*, shall be the returning-officers for all elections in the State, a majority of whom shall constitute a quorum, and have power to make the returns of *all elections*. In case of any vacancy by death, resignation, or otherwise, by either of the board, then the vacancy shall be filled by the residue of the board of returning-officers. The returning-officers shall after each election, before entering on their duties, take and subscribe to the following oath before a judge of the supreme or any district court:

"I, A B, do solemnly swear (or affirm) that I will faithfully and diligently perform the duties of a returning-officer as prescribed by law; that I will carefully and honestly canvass and compile the statements of the votes, and make a true and correct return of the election: so help me God."

Within ten days after the closing of the election said returning-officers shall meet in New Orleans to canvass and compile the statements of votes *made by the commissioners of election*, and make returns of the election to the secretary of state. They shall continue in session until such returns have been compiled. The presiding officer shall, at such meeting, open in the presence of the said returning-officers the *statements of the commissioners of election*, and the said returning-officers shall, from *said statements*, canvass and compile the returns of the election in duplicate; one copy of such returns they shall file in the office of the secretary of state, and of one copy they shall make public proclamation by printing in the official journal and such other newspapers as they may deem proper, declaring the names of all persons and officers voted for, the number of votes for each person, and the names of the persons who have been duly and lawfully elected. The return of the election thus made and promulgated shall be *prima facie* evidence in all courts of justice and before all civil officers, until set aside after contest according to law, of the right of any person named therein to hold and exercise the office to which he shall by such return be declared elected. The governor shall, within thirty days thereafter, issue commissions to all officers thus declared elected, who are required by law to be commissioned.

SEC. 3. That in such canvass and compilation the returning-officers shall observe the following order: They shall compile first the statements from all polls or voting-places at which there shall have been a fair, free, and peaceable registration and election. *Whenever, from any poll or voting-place, there shall be received the statement of any supervisor of registration or commissioner of election, in form as required by section 26 of this act, on affidavit of three or more citizens, of any riot, tumult, acts of violence, intimidation, armed disturbance, bribery, or corrupt influences, which prevented, or tended to prevent, a fair, free, and peaceable vote of all qualified electors entitled to vote at such poll or voting-place,* such returning-officers shall not canvass, count, or compile the statement of votes from such poll or voting-place until the statements from all other polls or voting-places shall have been canvassed and compiled. The returning-officers shall then proceed to investigate *the statements* of riot, tumult, acts of violence, intimidation, armed disturbance, bribery or corrupt influences, at any such poll or voting-place; and if from the evidence of *such statement* they shall be convinced that such riot, tumult, acts of violence, intimidation, armed disturbance, bribery or corrupt influences, did not materially interfere with the purity and freedom of the election at such poll or voting-place, or did not prevent a sufficient number of qualified voters thereat from registering or voting to materially change the result of the election, then, and not otherwise, said returning-officers shall canvass and compile the vote of such poll or voting-place with those previously canvassed and compiled; but if said returning-officers shall not be fully satisfied thereof, it shall be their duty to examine further testimony in regard thereto, and to this end they shall have power to send for persons and papers. If, after such examination, the said returning-officers shall be convinced that *said* riot, tumult, acts of violence, intimidation, armed disturbance, bribery or corrupt influences, did materially interfere with the purity and freedom of the election at such poll or voting-place, or did prevent a sufficient number of the qualified electors thereat from registering and voting to materially change the result of the election, then the said returning-officers shall not canvass or compile the statement of the votes of such poll or voting-place, but shall exclude it from their returns: *Provided,* That any person interested in said election by reason of being a candidate for office shall be allowed a hearing before said returning-officers upon making application within the time allowed for the forwarding of the returns of said election.

It is perfectly obvious from the provisions of section 3, above quoted, that the returning board has no power whatever to reject any vote unless a statement of riot, tumult, &c., has been received from the officers of election as provided in the other sections of the law which I have quoted, that is to say, statements made within the time and in the manner, and transmitted in the mode, and supported by the affidavits of three or more citizens, as provided by the law. I do not understand this proposition to be seriously disputed. I have heard no argument against it, and it seems to me that none can be made which would have even a show of plausibility. Now, I have said, and it is not denied, that the returning-board threw out many thousand votes and thereby changed the result of the election. Were there in each of the cases, that is to say, in each of the precincts or parishes whose votes were thus thrown out, statements of violence, &c., made and supported as required by the law? We have an offer to prove that in no instance whatever, that from no parish or precinct whatever, was any such statement transmitted. In other words, that no such statement accompanied any return transmitted to the returning-board or was made or sent from any precinct or parish in the State, within the time and in the mode required by law, to the returning-board. And, further, that if any statements of violence, &c., were laid before the returning-board, they were corruptly fabricated in the city of New Orleans, weeks after the election, and known to be so corruptly fabricated by the board when it received them. If such are the facts, and upon the question of admissibility of proof it must be assumed that they are facts, can there be any doubt of the illegality of the action of the board in throwing out the votes in question? Is it not perfectly plain that the statements and affidavits required by the statute are necessary to give *jurisdiction* to the board to throw out any votes whatever? They are the very foundation of the jurisdiction, without whose existence no power to throw out votes exists. It is not a question of error of judgment or of *bona fides* or *mala fides* on the part of the board. A question of jurisdiction goes far deeper than that. The judgment of the tribunal may be ever so righteous and correct, the tribunal itself may be ever so pure and enlightened, yet if it lack jurisdiction to pronounce the decision which it does pronounce, or to do the act which it does do, its decision and its acts are absolutely null and void. It would be vain to say that the returning-board is the sole judge of its own jurisdiction. There is nothing in the statute that makes it such sole judge. On the contrary, the statute itself declares that its decision shall only be *prima facie* evidence. But I have said enough on this point, and I proceed to consider another.

IV. The statute, section 2, gives to the returning-board the power and imposes upon it the duty "to canvass and compile the statement of votes made by the *commissioners of election* and make returns of the election to the secretary of state," and provides that "they shall continue in session until *such* returns have been compiled." The only things, then, that the board had authority to canvass and compile were the statements of votes made by the commissioners of election, and it was upon *them* that they were to decide and make returns of the election to the secretary of state. They had no right to make their decision and returns upon the consolidated statements of the supervisors of registration. Nowhere in the statute is any such power given to them. Nowhere are they expressly required to even look at the consolidated returns of the supervisors of registration. Certain it is that in no case are they authorized to found their decision upon any such papers. Now, the objectors to the votes of the so-called Hayes electors offer to prove that the board did not canvass or compile a single return made by the commissioners of election; that the only returns they looked at, the only returns upon which they formed their decision and made their return to the secretary of state, were the consolidated returns sent to them by the supervisors of registration. If this be true, then the board have not canvassed the votes as they were expressly required by the statute to canvass them. They have canvassed nothing which the law required them to canvass. They might as well have canvassed the returns of the election as published in the newspapers and made their decision upon them as to make it upon the supervisors' returns alone. No canvass known to the law of Louisiana has taken place, and the pretended return by the board to the secretary of state is a fabrication and a falsehood. In my opinion, evidence to prove these allegations ought to be admitted, and, if proved, they are in my judgment fatal to the so-called canvass of the board.

V. Testimony is offered to prove that the decision of the returning-board was procured by conspiracy, forgery, fraud, and bribery. I think the testimony admissible for the reasons I stated in the Florida case.

VI. Testimony is also offered that two of the Hayes electors, Brewster and Levissee, were, at the time of the election, officers of the United States, whose appointment as electors is expressly prohibited by the Constitution. I think this testimony should be received. The Constitution makes such officers ineligible to appointment. It is not a mere ineligibility to hold an office or trust, but it is ineligibility to be appointed to the office or trust. Nor, if I am correct in my interpretation of the Louisiana statutes, is the matter helped by the appointment of Brewster and Levissee, by the remaining electors, to fill the supposed vacancies created by the non-attendance of Brewster and Levissee. Upon a careful review of those statutes, I am brought to the conclusion that they nowhere confer upon a portion of the electoral college the power to fill vacancies occurring in that body.

Mr. THURMAN here read the provisions of the statutes relating to this point, and commented upon them at some length.

VII. But it is argued, as it was heretofore argued in the Florida case, that the Hayes electors had color of title and that, unless ousted before they cast their votes, they must be regarded as electors *de facto* and full effect given to their votes. I shall not repeat what I said upon this proposition in the Florida case. I adhere to the opinion I then expressed, and call attention to the fact that here is another case in which it was impossible to oust the so-called Hayes electors by any judicial proceeding before they cast their votes. They were declared by the returning-board to be appointed on the very day on which they voted, and it was manifestly impossible in the few hours that elapsed between that declaration and the casting of their votes to oust them by judicial proceedings. To hold then that they had color of title, were electors *de facto*, and that Congress is bound to count their votes, is to declare that no matter by what usurpation of power, fraud, or corruption a man may be declared by a returning-board to be an elector, and no matter how ineligible he may be to receive an appointment as elector, or to be an elector *de jure*, yet, unless he be ousted before he casts his vote for President, (though to do so is manifestly impossible,) that vote must be counted; and neither the State nor Congress can right the wrong or remedy the evil. I utterly dissent from such a proposition. In my humble judgment, it is destructive of the right of the States, of the powers of Congress, of constitutional provisions, of the principles of justice, of purity in elections, and of popular rule.

In saying this I attribute improper motives to no one; it is not with persons but with judgments that I am dealing. Of them and of what appears to me their probable effect, it is my right and duty to speak; and, thus speaking, I cannot help expressing the fear that if this Commission shall decide in accordance with the above proposition of *de facto* title, its decision will have the effect of a proclamation to dishonest returning-boards to perpetrate whatever villainies their interest or their inclinations may dictate, with an absolute certainty that they will prove successful.

REMARKS OF MR. COMMISSIONER FRELINGHUYSEN.

The following are the remarks and opinion of Mr. Commissioner FRE-LINGHUYSEN:

I. The important question to be decided by the Commission, as both political parties distinctly understood when the bill creating the Commission was passed, is whether the Commission has jurisdiction or right to look behind and reverse the determination of that tribunal which in the several States has by law been established finally to decide who have been elected presidential electors.

This Commission has, in the language of the act creating it, "the same powers, if any, now possessed for that purpose, [the purpose of counting the electoral vote,] by the two Houses acting separately or together."

The question then is, What powers have the two Houses of Congress, acting separately or together, when counting the electoral vote for President? The Commission has the same; no less, no more.

When the two Houses meet to count the votes of the electors for President, they do not act in their legislative capacity, but as a tribunal upon which is imposed that special duty. The legislative powers of Congress are specified in the Constitution, and counting the electoral votes is not among them. The President of the United States, whose concurrence is essential to all legislative action, has no part in this procedure. The two Houses in counting the vote not only have no legislative power, but also have none of those powers so constantly used, and which only exist as and because they are incident to the legislative power; such as sending committees of Congress to investigate the condition of affairs in different parts of the country, that Congress may possess information on which to base future legislation. Neither has Congress in counting the votes such power to investigate by committees or otherwise the election of presidential electors as it possesses for the purpose of ascertaining whether its members have been fairly elected, because while the Constitution expressly declares that "each House shall be the judge of the elections, returns, and qualifications of its own members," it nowhere declares, either expressly or by implication, that Congress shall be such judges as to the election of presidential electors; and this clear provision conferring the power to investigate elections for Senators and Representatives, and the absence of any such provision as to electors, is significant and emphatic of the truth that no such power exists as to electors. Neither do the two Houses possess the judicial power belonging to a court when trying the title to an office, because by the Constitution the judicial, legislative, and executive powers of the Government are carefully kept separate and distinct. The legislative branch possesses no judicial power excepting in the two specified cases of judging of the election of members of Congress and trials of impeachment. The two Houses when they meet to count the votes do not assemble as a joint convention, but as two distinct Houses, and separate to vote on any question that arises; and the very nature of this special tribunal, consisting of two distinct Houses, is inconsistent with having a jury, with having confronting witnesses; there are no parties, and there is nothing about the procedure that is judicial.

What power, then, do the two Houses of Congress possess? Just that power named in the Constitution when it says, "the votes shall then be counted." And what votes are then to be counted? Surely not the votes that have been given for the presidential electors by some seven millions of voters over a vast continent, but the votes cast by the presidential electors for President and Vice-President which the Constitution provides shall be certified to the President of the Senate and by him opened in the presence of the two Houses.

The two Houses in counting the votes of the electors may determine whether the State is in such relations to the Federal Government as to be entitled to vote; whether the votes were cast on the day prescribed by the statutes of the United States; whether the governor's certificate is genuine; whether that certificate is true in its statement as to who have been appointed electors by the State; but the truth of the statement of the governor's certificate in this regard is to be decided only by looking to the determination of the tribunal which the laws of the State say shall finally determine that fact, and not by a canvass of the popular vote of the State. The two Houses may inquire into anything consistent with the nature of the procedure, and which the Constitution has not devolved on the States to regulate.

The reasons why the Constitution does not either expressly or by implication provide or intend that Congress shall inquire into or canvass the election of presidential electors are apparent.

The framers of the Constitution, as its history shows, did first decide that the President and Vice-President should be chosen by Congress; but on full debate and mature deliberation they saw the evil of placing one co-ordinate branch of Government under the control of another—the executive under the control of the legislative branch—and they determined that, except to prevent a failure to elect, (in that event the House voting by *States* should elect,) Congress should have nothing to do with the choice of President or Vice-President. The Constitution casts that duty on the States. It says that each State, large or small, shall have two votes, and also as many additional votes as it has Representatives, and that each State shall appoint the electors in such manner as the legislature thereof shall direct. Under this power, the legislature might direct that the electors should be appointed by the legislature, by the executive, by the judiciary, or by the people. In the earliest days of the Republic, electors were appointed by the legislatures; in Pennsylvania they were appointed by the judiciary. Now in all States except Colorado they are appointed by the people. And in contemplation of the Constitution the electors were not, as the agent of a party, to *elect*, but as independent men, responsible to no one, were to *select* the President and Vice-President.

More completely to separate Congress from all connection with the election of President and Vice-President, the Constitution provides that no Senator or Representative or person holding an office of trust or profit under the United States shall be appointed an elector. And it would be an anomaly indeed if, after the Constitution had thus carefully excluded Congress from any intermeddling with the choice of the Presi dent further than to ascertain whom the State said it had appointed, that yet Congress had absolute control over the whole subject, and could while engaged in this summary proceeding of counting the vote adjudge and determine who should be President. If the claim now put forth was to reverse the decision of New York or Massachusetts as to who had been appointed the electors of those States respectively, the claim would hardly secure a patient hearing; but the public have become so accustomed to disorderly proceedings in some of the Southern States, that the determinations of those States do not challenge full respect, and yet the law is the same as to all the States.

The impracticability of the two Houses when met to count the votes of the presidential electors going behind the final decision of the States, and attempting to find out which set of electors in very truth have received the most votes, is a conclusive argument against the existence of any such power in the two Houses. If Congress enters upon the work of investigating which of two or more sets of electors have been chosen, it must do its work thoroughly, or it does gross injustice. It would not answer for Congress to examine the returns of the county canvassing-boards for the purpose of reversing the decision of the State canvassing-board, and then refuse to examine the returns of the precincts when invited to do so, for the purpose of showing that the county boards were in error. It would not answer for the two Houses to examine the state of the vote of Florida, Louisiana, and South Carolina for the purpose of showing that the Hayes electors were not elected, and then refuse to examine the vote of Mississippi, Alabama, and Georgia, when so requested, for the purpose of showing that the Tilden electors were not chosen. How, by possibility, could this investigation into the popular vote be effected? There are probably seven millions of popular votes. On the first Wednesday of December the electors give votes as required by the Constitution by ballot, and that imports their secrecy. The list of the votes is then transmitted sealed (secrecy again) to the President of the Senate, and these lists are first to be opened when the two Houses meet to count the votes. According to the theory of the Constitution, no one is to know until the two Houses are thus assembled what has been the action of the electoral college. And to claim that in the February before the 4th of March, when the President is to be inaugurated, the two Houses are to go behind the final determinations of the States and make a canvass to find out the very truth as to which set of electors have the majority of lawful votes, is an absurdity, because an impossibility. An investigation by the two Houses behind the final determination of the States would lead to anarchy and to nothing better.

It is urged that without such investigation by the two Houses the President may be elected by fraud. Then change the laws. It would, however, be found that the opportunity for fraud would be multiplied many fold if the regulation of the election was transferred from the States to the General Government.

It is said that if we take as final the determination of the State board the result may be that, while one citizen has a popular majority, another citizen will be inaugurated President. Our Government is not that of a mob. It is not majorities, but *legal* majorities that control. Under our system many complex functions are invoked to obtain an expression of the constitutional will. Thus Delaware casts one electoral vote for every 40,000 inhabitants, and New Jersey only one electoral vote for every 110,000 inhabitants. The democratic majority in New York is 50,000, and the State government by the same election is republican.

We have agreed to the Constitution, and if the expression of the will of the people is according to that instrument it is right. The complaint that one possibly, and I do not say probably, having a popular majority will not be inaugurated, seems a pretense.

I conclude that a State is as sovereign in its right finally to determine who have been elected presidential electors as it is to determine who have been elected legislators or governor, or to decide what shall be the punishment of crime within its borders, or what law shall regulate the transfer of property; and as this nation extends and grows the wisdom of making the States the final judges in this and many other things will become year by year more apparent.

I am confirmed in the correctness of my conclusions by the impressions of distinguished public men who differ from me in political views, and even by my own opinion expressed in the Senate when the question had not possibly any partisan significance.

Recently, when this question was before the country, Chief-Justice Church, of the court of appeals of the State of New York, made this expression in a letter which he gave to the public:

I have always expressed the opinion that the authentication of the election of presidential electors according to the laws of each State is final and conclusive, and that there exists no power to go behind them.

And Senator Bayard, on the 25th Frebruary, 1875, when the Senate had under consideration the bill to provide for counting the votes for President and Vice-President, after reading the twelfth amendment to the Constitution which makes provision for counting the electoral vote, said:

There is nothing in this language that authorizes either House of Congress or both Houses of Congress to interfere with the decision which has been made by the electors themselves and certified by them and sent to the President of the Senate. There is no pretext that for any cause whatever Congress has any power, or all the other departments of the Government have any power, to refuse to receive and count the result of the action of the voters in the States in that election, as certified by the electors whom they have chosen. That questions may arise whether that choice was made, that questions may arise whether that election was properly held or whether it was a free and fair election, is undoubtedly true; but there is no machinery provided for contest, and no contest seems to have been anticipated on this subject. It is *casus omissus*, intentionally or otherwise, upon the part of those who framed this Government, and we must take it as it is; and if there be necessity for its amendment, for its supplement, that must be the action of the American people in accordance with the Constitution itself; and I am free to say that some amendment on this subject should be had.

Senator Thurman in the Senate on January 7, 1873, when the resolution authorizing an investigation as to whether the election for President and Vice-President had been conducted in Louisiana and Arkansas in accordance with the laws of the United States, expressed views similar to those above quoted from Mr. Bayard's subsequent speech.

It is proper to state that both of these distinguished Senators stated these views as a matter of first impression, reserving their final judgment on the question; but first impressions with minds as well furnished as theirs are often more valuable than more carefully considered conclusions.

In the debate of January 7, 1873, I had the honor to follow the Senator from Ohio, [Mr. Thurman,] and said:

There seems to be no way provided by Congress, and no way I believe that Congress, as the Constitution stands, can provide to try the title of an elector to his office. * * * I take it that the entire control over the manner of appointing the electors is one of the reserved rights of the States; that they never surrendered the right of determining who should be these electors. The States possess the right of determining who shall be elected and who has been elected as entirely as the United States Government has the right to decide who shall represent the country in England.

These views I had occasion to express again in January last when the bill creating this Electoral Commission was before the Senate, and when I had no idea of being a member of this Commission; and I have seen no reason for changing those views.

And, as still further authority to show that the final decision of the question whether electors have been appointed is with the States, let me call attention to the fact that those who aided in framing and those who lived at the time of the adoption of the Constitution did not consider that Congress, even when acting with the President as a Legislature, had the constitutional power to pass a law under which the two Houses of Congress, or any commission created by the Federal Legislature, could inquire into the number of votes by which electors have been elected.

This whole subject was thoroughly considered in 1800, and a bill passed both Houses of Congress, but amendments not being agreed to, did not become a law. That bill provided that a grand committee, in its organization not unlike this Commission, might make inquiry and decide as to everything relative to the election of President and Vice-President over which the Constitution gave the General Government jurisdiction, but did not provide for any investigation or decision as to the procedure which the Constitution has devolved upon the States.

It provided that the grand committee should examine and decide: (1) as to the qualifications of persons voted for as President and Vice-President; (2) as to the constitutional qualification of electors; (3) whether the appointment of the electors was authorized by the State legislature; (4) whether the mode prescribed by the State legislature had been followed; (5) whether improper means had been used to influence the votes of the electors; (6) as to the truth of the returns of the electors; (7) as to the time and place of giving their votes. And that is all. Congress did not assume that it had any constitutional right to investigate or review the vote on which the electors had been appointed, further than to see that it was according to the mode prescribed by the States. On the contrary, fearing that the very claim which is now set up, of making an investigation as to whether the electors had been duly elected in the States, might be inferred, they guarded against such inference by providing that the grand committee should " not draw in question the number of votes on which any elector should have been appointed."

If Congress when acting in its sovereign legislative capacity had not the constitutional right to confer on the two Houses of Congress when performing the subordinate duty devolved on them of counting the vote, or upon the grand committee, the power " to draw in question the number of votes on which any elector should have been appointed," *a fortiori* the two Houses of Congress, or this Commission without such legislation, do not possess such power.

Thus authority fortifies the conclusion that the two Houses of Congress, and consequently this Commission, cannot go behind or reverse the determination as to who has been appointed electors as made by the lawful tribunal of the State.

It has been said that although the Constitution does not give to Congress the right to question the determination of the tribunal which by the laws of the State is finally to decide who has been elected an elector, in this case the offer is made to prove fraud in that final decision of the State tribunal; that we must assume that the offer is made in good faith, and that fraud vitiates and renders void everything. It is true that fraud, when proven before a tribunal having jurisdiction over the question in controversy, will vitiate all transactions except such as are judicial or legislative. Without raising the inquiry whether the counting the votes is a procedure that comes within the exceptions, I ask whether it was ever heard that a charge of fraud made before a tribunal that otherwise had no jurisdiction over the question at issue conferred jurisdiction to try the question? Does fraud give power? I knew that it rendered void, but not that it created. Can it be claimed that while under our system of government the determination as to who has been appointed an elector is with the States and not with the Federal Government, the allegation of fraud is potential in changing our system, and transfers the decision of the question as to who has been elected elector from the State to the Federal Government? I think not.

II. The Constitution provides that " no Senator or Representative, or person holding an office of trust or profit under the United States, shall be appointed an elector," and it is claimed that some holding such offices were appointed electors and were therefore ineligible, and that their votes should not be counted.

The real object of this provision of the Constitution ceased when the electors came to exercise no volition in choosing a President and became the mere agents of a party, but still the Constitution stands and must be enforced if it can be. The provision, I think, is equivalent to saying that no one who holds an office of trust or profit under the United States shall be an elector; and no one has been. In every instance the elector who happened to hold an office of trust or profit under the United States resigned such office before assuming to perform the functions of his office as an elector, or resigned as an elector and another was according to law appointed in his stead.

To my mind it is a sufficient answer to all the charges of ineligibility against electors that the provision of the Constitution on which the charges are based does not execute itself, and no law has been enacted to execute it. It is said that other provisions of the Constitution execute themselves. I think not. Courts are established by law, where the provisions can be vindicated, but this requirement of the Constitution cannot be enforced in the courts after the count before the two Houses has commenced, and after the electors have voted. Neither can the two Houses stop the count for the purpose of ascertaining whether some one or more of the three hundred and sixty-nine electors, thousands of miles away, did or did not thirty years ago accept a commission as a United States commissioner or other unimportant office which he had forgotten he held, and of which his constituency were ignorant. The Houses of Congress have no machinery enabling them to carry on such an investigation, and if a law should be passed to enforce the provision of the Constitution referred to, the penalty for its infraction would not be that the State should be deprived of its vote. And further, the functions of the office of elector are required by law to be performed and in fact were discharged on the first Wednesday of December last, and if the elector were subsequently declared ineligible such decision would not invalidate the act performed on the day fixed. If a State constitution required that a sheriff should have a freehold estate worth $5,000, and if after he had performed the duties of his office for a year he was on *quo warranto* ousted because of its being proven that he had no estate of any kind at any time, no one would claim that his acts as *de facto* sheriff were invalid. The acts of the State governments in the States formerly in rebellion, except those acts that were in hostility to the United States Government, have been recognized by the Supreme

Court of the United States as valid, because they were the acts of *de facto* governments. I think there is nothing in the objection founded on ineligibility.

III. Should the votes for President and Vice-President, given by what are called the Hayes electors, in Florida, Louisiana, Oregon, and South Carolina, duly authenticated by those States respectively, be counted?

The legislature of Florida, as authorized by the Constitution of the United States, directs that the presidential electors shall be appointed by the lawful voters of that State voting at their respective precincts; that the inspectors of election at those precincts shall report the result to the county board of canvassers; and in the act of February 27, 1872, it is enacted that the board of county canvassers shall report to a board of State canvassers, who " shall proceed to canvass the returns of such election, and determine and declare who shall have been elected, as shown by said returns. If any such returns shall be shown or shall appear to be so irregular, false, or fraudulent that the board shall be unable to determine the true vote for any such officer or member, they shall so certify, and shall not include such return in their determination and declaration."

This board of State canvassers, which was to that end created, made its final determination and then declared that the Hayes electors had been elected by about nine hundred majority; and these electors on December 6, 1876, cast their vote for Rutherford B. Hayes. All of which is certified to us by the electors and by the undisputed governor of Florida. On this statement, the votes of the electors should be counted for Governor Hayes.

And what reasons are urged against their being so counted? They are these: The attorney-general of Florida was by law a member of the State board of canvassers, and he certifies that the Tilden and not the Hayes electors were duly appointed. But it is clear that his certificate has in law no more validity than a letter from any other citizen of Florida would have, and cannot be recognized by this Commission.

Another reason urged why the vote of the Hayes electors should not be counted is, that after the Hayes electors had cast their votes on December 6, 1876, and about the 1st of January, 1877, Mr. George F. Drew succeeded Governor Stearns as governor of Florida; and on the 26th of January, 1877, fifty days after the electors of Florida had and must, if ever, have cast their votes, Governor Drew certified that the Tilden electors had been elected. It is he who is the governor of Florida when the electors were appointed who must by law certify to their appointment, and not he who is inducted after they have been appointed and have discharged all their duties. Governor Drew bases the declaration of his certificate that the Tilden electors had been appointed on the adjudication of the court of Florida to that effect, given on a proceeding in the nature of a *quo warranto* on the 25th of January, 1877. If a State court under a *quo warranto*, fifty days after the electors have according to the Constitution and laws of the United States cast their vote, can invalidate the acts of the electors, then the State courts can control the succession to the Presidency of the United States. It would be strange, indeed, if this Commission should disregard the determination of the State board of canvassers, which the laws of the State say shall determine and declare who have been appointed electors, and should be bound to adopt the conclusions of a State court clothed with no such power. The Commission should, in my opinion, count the vote of Florida for Rutherford B. Hayes.

The laws of the State of Louisiana as to the election of electors are similar to those of Florida. The returning officers, consisting of five persons appointed by the State senate from all political parties, constitute the tribunal finally to determine who has been elected, and have authority to reject returns from any place in which they are satisfied that by reason of fraud or violence there has not been a fair election.

It has been claimed that these returning-officers have improperly rejected certain returns so as to change the result in the State.

It has been sufficiently shown that neither the two Houses of Congress nor this Commission have jurisdiction to go behind and reverse the determination of the tribunal which the State has said shall finally decide who has been elected, and that the allegation of fraud in the action of the returning-board does not give jurisdiction over the subject to the two Houses of Congress or to this Commission.

It has been questioned whether there were sufficient laws in Louisiana to authorize the election of electors. It has been shown by others that the objection is not well taken. The revision of the laws—the digest of the laws—the courts of the State, and all the people properly treat their election laws as sufficient, and we, while engaged in the summary process of counting the vote, may so accept it.

It is said that affidavits of fraud and violence were not filed within the time fixed by the statutes of the State, and that consequently the returning-officers had no jurisdiction to decide whether certain returns should or should not be rejected. There may have been abundant reasons why the affidavits were not filed within the prescribed time, and of that the returning-officers were to judge. The provision as to time is at best only directory. The affidavits were not jurisdictional; if they were, Louisiana for the want of the affidavits might have been without any determination of the result of the election, and either anarchy must have followed or the result not have been according to the truth as intended by the statute.

It is urged also that the laws of Louisiana require that the final tribunal, called in this State "returning-officers," should consist of five members, and of different political opinions, and that in fact it consisted of only four members, and these all of the same political opinion.

If the provision that the board must consist of those having different political opinions were constitutional, which I much doubt, the requirement is clearly only directory. It can hardly be claimed that if one member changed his opinion in a night, the determination of the board thereby became void, and that the confusion therefrom resulting must be accepted.

If the board should have consisted of five members, the fact that there were only four does not invalidate its decisions; the law says a majority shall be a quorum. The Supreme Court of the United States consists of nine judges, but it does not cease to be a court because by death or resignation there are only eight. It is seldom that a board of directors is full, but no one ever questioned the authority of the board on that account. If the fifth member of the canvassing-board was *not* appointed from unworthy motives, all will condemn it, but no one would say that the penalty for this impropriety is that the State shall lose its vote.

It has been urged, too, that the votes of Louisiana should not be counted because, as alleged; it had no State government, and Kellogg, who signed the electors' certificates, was not in truth the governor of that State. And yet, in November and December, when the electors were appointed, and when the electoral vote was cast, a State government with Kellogg as governor existed by the consent of both political parties, was represented in both Houses of Congress, had been recognized by every branch of Government, and regulated the public affairs of society in that State.

I see no good reason why the vote of Louisiana, as determined by the State returning-officers and as certified by the recognized governor and as cast by the Hayes electors, should not be counted.

There are returned here from the State of Oregon two sets of electoral votes, one from Cartwright, Odell, and Watts, certifying that they had cast their votes for Governor Hayes; the other from Cronin, Miller, and Parker, certifying that they had cast two votes for Governor Hayes and one vote for Governor Tilden. The question is, which is the true return? I am satisfied the former is, and for these two reasons:

First. By the sixtieth and thirty-seventh sections of the election law of Oregon, it is made the duty of the county clerk to send an abstract of the votes cast in the county for electors to the secretary of state, and it is made his duty, in the presence of the governor, to canvass the votes. The secretary of state is the final and sole canvassing-officer.

To ascertain who are the true presidential electors from Oregon, we must discover whom the tribunal that the laws of Oregon enact shall finally determine that question has adjudged to be such electors; that adjudication may be certified to us by the governor or be made known to us by the record of such final determination. The governor's certificate is only valuable as evidence of what the final tribunal has adjudicated, and may have been forged, or may from design or mistake be untrue. The two Houses of Congress, or this Commission, will be controlled by the State's decision as to who has been elected. In this case the canvass of the secretary of state, which is the final determination of the question as to who have been elected electors, has been sent in the package containing the list of votes cast for President and Vice-President, and the electoral bill has given us authority to consider papers so presented to us, but without such specific authority, we certainly would look to a record that is controlling.

The canvass of the secretary of state, the State's final determination, being thus before us, shows that Cartwright, Odell, and Watts received 15,200 votes, being a thousand more votes than were received by any other candidates for electors. And the fortieth section of the election laws of Oregon provides as follows, namely:

That in all elections in this State the person having the highest number of votes for any office shall be deemed to have been elected.

I am at a loss to see how this Commission can do otherwise than deem Cartwright, Odell, and Watts elected electors.

Second. By the very showing of those who claim one vote from Oregon for Governor Tilden, he is not entitled to it. Watts, one of those who had a majority of votes, was, when elected, a postmaster, and Governor Grover therefore concluded that he was authorized to give a certificate of election to Cronin, who had the next highest vote. The governor will find few to agree with him that, when a majority of the people declare by their ballots that they do not want a citizen to hold one of their offices, such a vote gives him a title to the office. But Watts, though a postmaster, when elected, resigned that office before December 6, 1876. On that day Cartwright and Odell met, and as Oregon was entitled to three votes, there was a vacancy. Cronin *met*, and he found two vacancies. All three persons whom the governor certified were elected electors, Cartwright, Odell, and Cronin, unite in informing us that there was one vacancy in the college. Cronin says there were two. Under this state of facts Cartwright and Odell filled the vacancy by appointing Watts, who, if ever ineligible, had ceased to be so by resigning the office of postmaster.

Cronin, on the other hand, filled the two vacancies that he found, by appointing Miller and Parker electors; and the only question is whether Cartwright and Odell, or Cronin, had the right to fill vacancies. And that question is solved by deciding whether two or one is a quorum and majority of a college of three.

I think the three electoral votes from the State of Oregon for Governor Hayes should be counted.

The first objection made to the vote of the Hayes electors from South Carolina is that the Constitution of the United States guarantees to that State a republican government, which it is claimed means a government under which the people exercise the supreme power, and that the State did not have such government.

When the Constitution was being framed, Edmund Randolph offered this resolution:

Resolved, That a republican government ought to be guaranteed by the United States to each State.

After the debate this resolution was rejected, and the following adopted:

Resolved, That a republican *form* of government shall be guaranteed to each State.

Few of the States would consent to change the Constitution so that the Federal Government could constitutionally interfere with the State governments further than to see that their *form* of government was republican. Such a change would seriously affect the sovereign character of the State. The government of South Carolina was in November, 1876, unquestionably republican in *form,* and that for us is the only proper inquiry.

Another objection to counting this vote is that the constitution of South Carolina requires that there shall be a registration law, and that there was none, and that consequently the election of electors is void. It is sufficient answer to this objection that the Constitution of the United States provides that the electors of each State shall be appointed "in such manner as the *legislature* thereof shall direct," and not in such manner as the constitution of the State shall direct. The legislature in this regard acts under the authority of the Constitution of the United States, and is entirely untrammeled by State constitutions.

Another objection is that the Federal troops prevented a free election. The two Houses of Congress and this Commission will not withhold from the Federal Government the presumption that its high officers have acted in accordance with the Constitution, laws, and best interests of the nation, a presumption which in the summary procedure of counting the vote for President and Vice-President will be held to be conclusive.

The two thousand and second section of the Revised Statutes of the United States provides by necessary implication that troops may be detailed to keep the peace at the polls. If troops were present at the polls the presumption is, and for the purpose of this proceeding the conclusive presumption is, that they were so present to keep the peace. We are not required to go into evidence on this point; especially when we know that to do so would be to delay the inauguration of the citizen who has been elected President until after the 4th of March, and thus as the law stands entirely defeat his inauguration.

My opinion is that the votes of the Hayes electors of South Carolina should be counted.

REMARKS OF MR. COMMISSIONER BAYARD.

The following remarks by Senator BAYARD, of Delaware, in the course of the private consultations of the Electoral Commission, are prepared for publication in accordance with a resolution of the Commission and by the aid of such notes as were made during its sessions. The action of the majority of the Commission prohibited the presence of a stenographer during these debates, and as a consequence but a comparatively imperfect and unsatisfactory report can now be given.

The case of the State of Florida was the first which was transmitted by the two Houses of Congress for the consideration of this tribunal under the electoral act, and two returns purporting to be certificates of electoral votes cast in that State for President and Vice-President having been made to the President of the Senate, and, in accordance with the provisions of the law, submitted by him on the 1st day of February to the Commission,

On the motion of Mr. Justice MILLER, it was resolved that the Commission should hear counsel on the question whether any evidence will be considered by the Commission that was not submitted to the two Houses by the President of the Senate, and, if so, what evidence can properly be considered; and also the question, What is the evidence now before the Commission?

After debate by counsel, Mr. Justice MILLER moved the following order, on the 7th of February:

That no evidence will be received or considered by the Commission which was not submitted to the joint convention of the two Houses by the President of the Senate with the different certificates, except such as relates to the eligibility of F. C. Humphreys, one of the electors.

Which order was determined in the affirmative—yeas 8, nays 7. In the affirmative: Messrs. Bradley, Edmunds, Frelinghuysen, Garfield, Hoar, Miller, Morton, and Strong; in the negative: Messrs. Abbott, Bayard, Clifford, Field, Hunton, Payne, and Thurman.

On the 9th of February Mr. Representative HUNTON, of Virginia, offered the following resolution:

That the electors named in certificate No. 2, to wit, Wilkinson Call, J. E. Yonge, Robert Bullock, and Robert B. Hilton, are the four persons who were duly appointed electors by the State of Florida on the 7th day of November, 1876, and that their votes as certified in such certificate are the votes provided for by the Constitution of the United States.

This was decided in the negative—yeas 7, nays 8. In the affirmative: Messrs. Abbott, Bayard, Clifford, Field, Hunton, Payne, and Thurman; in the negative: Messrs. Bradley, Edmunds, Frelinghuysen, Garfield, Hoar, Miller, Morton, and Strong.

On the 9th of February the following order was adopted by a vote of 8 yeas to 7 nays:

That the following be adopted as the final decision and report on the matters submitted to the Commission as to the electoral vote of the State of Florida:

ELECTORAL COMMISSION,
Washington, D. C., February 9, A. D. 1877.

To the President of the Senate of the United States, presiding in the meeting of the two Houses of Congress, under the act of Congress entitled "An act to provide for and regulate the counting of votes for President and Vice-President, and the decision of questions arising thereon, for the term commencing March 4, A. D. 1877," approved January 29, A. D. 1877:

The Electoral Commission mentioned in said act having received certain certificates and papers purporting to be certificates, and papers accompanying the same, of the electoral votes from the State of Florida, and the objections thereto submitted to it under said act, now report that it has duly considered the same, pursuant to said act, and has decided, and does hereby decide, that the votes of Frederick C. Humphreys, Charles H. Pearce, William H. Holden, and Thomas W. Long, named in the certificate of M. L. Stearns, governor of said State, which votes are certified by said persons, as appears by the certificate submitted to the Commission, as aforesaid, and marked "number one," by said Commission, and herewith returned, are the votes provided for by the Constitution of the United States, and that the same are lawfully to be counted as therein certified, namely: Four (4) votes for Rutherford B. Hayes, of the State of Ohio, for President, and four (4) votes for William A. Wheeler, of the State of New York, for Vice-President.

The Commission also has decided, and hereby decides and reports, that the four persons first before named were duly appointed electors in and by said State of Florida.

The brief ground of this decision is, that it appears, upon such evidence as by the Constitution and the law named in said act of Congress is competent and pertinent to the consideration of the subject, that the before-mentioned electors appear to have been lawfully elected such electors of President and Vice-President of the United States, for the term beginning March 4, 1877, of the State of Florida, and that they voted as such at the time and in the manner provided for by the Constitution of the United States and the law.

The Commission has also decided, and does hereby decide and report, that, as a consequence of the foregoing and upon the grounds before stated, neither of the papers purporting to be certificates of the electoral votes of said State of Florida numbered two (2) and three (3) by the committee, and herewith returned, are the certificates or the votes provided for by the Constitution of the United States, and that they ought not to be counted as such.

Done at Washington the day and year first above written.

The question being on the adoption of the report of the committee, it was decided in the affirmative:

Yeas.. 8
Nays.. 7

Those who voted in the affirmative were: Messrs. Bradley, Edmunds, Frelinghuysen, Garfield, Hoar, Miller, Morton, and Strong—8.

Those who voted in the negative were: Messrs. Abbott, Bayard, Clifford, Field, Hunton, Payne, and Thurman—7.

So the report of the committee was adopted; and said decision and report was thereupon signed by the members agreeing therein, as follows:

> SAM. F. MILLER,
> W. STRONG,
> JOSEPH P. BRADLEY,
> GEO. F. EDMUNDS,
> O. P. MORTON,
> FRED'K T. FRELINGHUYSEN,
> JAMES A. GARFIELD,
> GEORGE F. HOAR,
> *Commissioners.*

CASE OF FLORIDA.

In the course of the private deliberations of the Commission, Senator BAYARD said:

Mr. President and gentlemen of the Commission, I would not conceal from you, even if I could, the deep anxiety with which I have approached the decision of this question, the difficulties surrounding which have been apparent since the foundation of our Government, and their consideration postponed from generation to generation until we find ourselves now compelled for the first time to make a decision which includes in its consequences the possession of the executive power of the Government of the United States for the ensuing four years; and to the natural and constitutional difficulties surrounding this much debated question is superadded the fact that we are acting not in view of an uncertainty yet veiled by the future, but upon facts exhibited in the clear light of the past, after an exciting and heated controversy between two great political parties, the result of which when established must be full of disappointment to one or the other. I can only say that while I feel a just and natural distrust in my powers to deal competently with such issues, yet I am at least conscious that I approach the duties imposed upon me by the oaths I have taken, both as a Senator of the United States and a member of this Commission, in a spirit deeply solicitous to act worthily in my place.

In order properly to consider the question of receiving evidence other than that contained in the papers submitted by the President of the Senate to the two Houses, and by them sent to this Commission, we must examine the constitution of this tribunal.

I hold that for the purpose of this decision the two Houses of Congress are now present in this tribunal. I am here not only as a member of this Commission but as a Senator, and come here with all the knowledge which I have derived as a member of the Senate from the testimony taken by committees appointed by both the Senate and the House for the investigation of affairs in the State of Florida during the past winter. I cannot divest myself of this knowledge; to do so were impossible and in direct violation of my duty. The knowledge so obtained by me is incidental to the powers and duties of a member of either House; and this Commission and every member of it are by the express language of the second section of the law under which it is organized, invested " with the same powers * * * now possessed * * * by the two Houses acting separately or together." Whatever, therefore, is open to the knowledge or inquiry of one Commissioner, whether Senator, Representative, or judge of the Supreme Court, is open to all. Their functions and powers are equal in all respects. Under the language of the law creating this Commission " all the certificates and papers purporting to be certificates of the electoral votes" shall be opened by the President of the Senate and by him presented to the two Houses, whose tellers shall read the same in the presence and hearing of the two Houses.

Upon such reading of any such certificate or paper, when there shall be only one return from a State, the President of the Senate *shall call for objections*, if any. Every objection shall be made in writing, and shall state clearly and concisely, and without argument, the ground thereof, and shall be signed by at least one Senator and one member of the House of Representatives before the same shall be received. When all objections so made to any vote or paper from a State shall have been received and read, the Senate shall thereupon withdraw, and *such objections shall be submitted to the Senate for its decision;* and the Speaker of the House of Representatives shall, *in like manner, submit such objections to the House of Representatives for its decision;* and no electoral vote or votes from any State from which but one return has been received shall be rejected except by the affirmative vote of the two Houses. When the two Houses have voted they shall immediately again meet, and the presiding officer shall then announce *the decision of the question submitted.*

As a member of the Senate, it will be observed, I am thus called upon to vote in cases of single returns from a State upon objections so made. The jurisdiction of the two Houses over the question of receiving or rejecting electoral votes is unmistakably and clearly assumed by the language of the law which I have read. It recognizes the power of the Senate and the House, by the action of a single member of each body, to raise objections to the reception of an electoral vote, and it provides for the decision of the two Houses upon those objections. If there was no jurisdiction and power in the two Houses over the question of reception or rejection of the votes sent up, it would have been worse than an idle form to have enacted this law calling for objections and providing for their decision. When, therefore, members of the Senate or the House are called upon to vote intelligently and conscientiously upon objections to the reception of electoral votes, what are they necessarily "to take into view," and what is to guide them in the decision they are to make? Necessarily everything that is known as evidence in parliamentary law and usage, all public facts of which both Houses must have knowledge, all reports of committees of either House, all depositions accompanying the same, petitions, and such other papers as contain information necessary and proper for the consideration and determination of the question. This course of proceeding and scope and character of information is essential for the performance of the duties assumed by the two Houses of Congress and each member thereof under the first section of the act.

Let us now consider the duty of this Commission under the second section of the act, which provides—

> That if more than one return, or paper purporting to be a return from a State, shall have been received by the President of the Senate, purporting to be the certificates of electoral votes given at the last preceding election,   *   *   *   all such returns and papers shall be opened by him in the presence of the two Houses when met as aforesaid, and read by the tellers, and all such returns and papers shall thereupon be submitted to the judgment and decision, as to which is the *true and lawful electoral vote of such State*, of a Commission constituted as follows.

The composition and formation of this Commission is then set forth The section provides for the opening and reading by the tellers of all such certificates and papers; and the President of the Senate is directed *to call for objections*, and the description of the objections so called for is in precisely the same language as is provided in the first section in case of single returns. All such objections, together with the certificates, votes, and papers so objected to, and all papers accompanying the same shall forthwith be submitted to this Commission—

> Which shall proceed to consider the same, *with the same powers * * * now possessed for that purpose by the two Houses acting separately or together,* and, by a majority of votes, decide whether any and what votes from such State are the votes provided for by the Constitution of the United States, and how many and what persons were duly appointed electors in such State, and may therein take into view such petitions, depositions, and other papers, if any, as shall by the Constitution and now existing law, be competent and pertinent in such consideration.

The section also provides that when such decision by a majority of the Commission shall have been read and entered in the Journal of each House, " the counting of the votes shall proceed in conformity therewith, unless, upon objection made thereto in writing by at least five Senators and five members of the House of Representatives, the two Houses shall separately concur in ordering otherwise."

Thus it will be observed that on the part of those who have denied that evidence of any character can be considered by the Commission which was not contained in the certificates submitted to the two Houses by the President of the Senate, the following result would be reached: that members of this Commission being also members of the Senate and the House, shall be at liberty to receive, and in fact must receive and consider, evidence in relation to objections to *single* returns of electoral votes when voting in their respective Houses which they will not receive or consider when sitting in this Commission in cases of *double* returns; that evidence of the truth shall be brought home to my mind and bind itself on my conscience in the case of a single return that is to be denied to me in case of a double return. It will scarcely be denied that the extent of inquiry and difficulties of ascertainment as to which is the true return of *two* returns involves an equal or indeed much greater difficulty in the investigation than where a single return is alone under consideration; and it will also be observed that after the Commission shall have refused to receive any evidence outside of the papers submitted by the President of the Senate, and have thus made their decision in the dark and without information, ten of its members withdrawing to their places in the Senate and the House and being called upon to vote upon the question of concurring or non-concurring in the decision of the Commission, shall have both the power and the duty to receive and consider as Senators and Representatives evidence which as Commissioners they had excluded.

This statement of the case would seem to me to make it apparent that this Commission must necessarily have opened to them all avenues and means of information which were open to either or both Houses of Congress; and that the members cannot, by taking seats in the Commission, denude themselves of the powers and duties and the means of information which belong to them as members of either House of Congress.

It is, therefore. my judgment that when I entered this chamber as a member of the Commission I brought with me all the knowledge concerning the late election in Florida of which I had become possessed as a member of the Senate; and whatever were my powers or duties as a member of the Senate in relation to this subject of counting the electoral votes, they are not diminished or altered by my becoming a member of this Commission; and as a corollary of this proposition, I hold the power and jurisdiction of each and all members of the Commission to be necessarily equal in every respect.

It has been alleged as a reason for not hearing evidence that injustice would follow if every possible topic of inquiry were not pursued and every fact probed to its very bottom. So unqualified a proposition cannot be received without the risk of reducing our proposed duties to impossibillity, if not absurdity.

As I have stated, the duty devolved upon the two Houses in relation to single returns in section 1 of the act is in precisely the same frame of words as in section 2 is provided for cases of double returns when submitted to this Commission. In the case of single returns two hours are given for debate, followed by a peremptory order to vote at the termination of that time; and then "immediately" the two Houses are to meet and announce the result. Certain it is the two Houses will not vote in ignorance of the facts upon which their action is to be taken. They have and will certainly "take into view such petitions, depositions, and other papers" as are on their files. They will consider the reports of their committees and listen to the debates, before reaching a decision. To this Commission is expressly confided the same means of information, of the same knowledge in extent or character which is possessed by the two Houses, with this addition, that the Commission is not limited as to time for its ascertainment and determination of facts, but more time and infinitely better opportunities, after listening to objectors and counsel on both sides, are allowed to us in coming to our decision.

For what object, let it be asked, was this enlarged opportunity for examination, hearing, and determination given to this Commission? Plainly because the questions submitted to us were of a more complicated nature than cases of single returns. It was because the law and the facts were supposed to be more in controversy in cases of double returns that this Commission was formed for the purposes of justice and convenience deliberately and fully to examine and justly to decide the vexed questions of law and fact raised by the objections called for by the Presiding Officer and made by the members of the Senate and the House. If no evidence was to be received, then argument would be useless, objections would be useless; the two hours given to the two Houses for debate in single returns would have been reasonably sufficient for this Commission, who in the seclusion of this court-room could more rapidly reach a decision than the two Houses in general debate.

What is meant by *"objections"* and the provision that they are to be "called for" and be "submitted for decision" and "be decided?" Objections must be to the form or the substance of the return. It is difficult to state a valid objection as to the *form* of a return, because no form is prescribed by the Constitution, and as to "*the State*" is confided "the manner" of appointment of the electors, it is to a failure to obey her statutes prescribing form of certificate that consideration alone could be given, and an inspection of the State constitution and laws would settle that. To be of *substance* the objections must arise under the provisions of the Constitution, and be based upon a violation of the requirements of that instrument and the limitations imposed by it upon the State in the selection of persons to *vote* or to *be voted for.*

The call for objections is a distinct recognition in the law under which we are now proceeding of the fact that *valid* objections can exist, and when presented must be decided, and that electoral votes may for just cause be excluded "under the Constitution and existing law."

The Constitution requires in mandatory phrase that—

First. *"Each State* shall appoint."—

Second. *"In such manner* as the legislature *thereof* may direct"—

Third. *"A number* of electors—*equal* to *the whole number* of Senators and Representatives to which the State may be entitled in the Congress."

Fourth. *"But no* Senator or Representative, *or person* holding an office of trust under the United States, *shall be appointed an elector."*

Fifth. The electors shall meet *in their respective States.*

Sixth. They shall vote *by ballot* for President and Vice-President—

Seventh. One of whom *shall not be* an inhabitant of the same State with themselves.

Eighth. They shall make *distinct lists* of all the persons voted for as President and Vice-President—

Ninth. And of the *number of votes for each*—

Tenth. Which lists they shall sign and certify, and transmit sealed to the seat of Government of the United States, directed to the President of the Senate.

Eleventh. The Congress may determine the time of choosing the electors, and *the day* on which they shall give their votes, *which day shall be the same throughout the United States.*

Twelfth. The qualifications of the President and Vice-President are prescribed.

Is it not manifest that in calling for "objections" to the count of the electoral votes, constitutional objections, such as a disregard of any of the foregoing requirements, were plainly contemplated?

What votes are to be counted? "The votes *provided for by the Constitution of the United States."* (See section 2 of electoral bill.) And what votes are to be rejected from the count? Plainly the votes *not* provided for by the Constitution; and "objections" to *such* votes and for such reasons are the only objections "called for" by the terms of the act, and are to be decided under its provisions.

It seems to me, therefore, that upon the very face of this act we are called upon to exercise a jurisdiction involving, first inquiry, and next determination of facts and law, which we cannot abdicate or avoid without rendering the law under which we act a sham and a dead letter. Unless the two Houses have the power to decide upon objections, it is an idle waste of time and a mockery of law to call for objections. Unless his Commission has the power and the duty to consider and determine

objections in cases of double returns, it was an idle form to refer those
returns to us. If limitation upon the time allowed us for investigation,
argument, and consideration was not removed for the purpose of giving
us full and ample opportunity to inquire, to ascertain the truth both of
law and fact involved in these questions of double returns and suggested
by the objections filed, then the formation of this Commission and its
sessions were worse than a mere waste of time; they were a deception of
honest and reasonable public expectation; and the submission of our
decision to the two Houses of Congress was an idle preliminary which
might as well or better have been dispensed with.

Our duties upon this Commission are those of substance or else of
mere form only; and holding them to be of substance, and that substance
to consist in the ascertainment of which is "the true and lawful electoral
vote of such State," it seems to me impossible that we can reach such a
decision without prior inquiry; and inquiry involves the reception and
consideration of all that is evidence "competent and pertinent under
the Constitution and existing law."

It is plain that the object and intent of this law is to reach a decision,
and that this is not to be defeated by delay or prolongation of examination and debate so as to spin out the month allotted to us. The case is
not *inter partes*, in a legal sense. It is a public *res*. The two Houses
have been the known and public tribunal for the consideration and
decision of these vexed questions for months past. They have severally
recognized and acted upon this assumption, and sent forth their committees during the past winter, who, after laborious sessions, have come
back with full reports and testimony of the transactions in question and
have reported their conclusions. In the State of Florida the courts of
that State have themselves taken jurisdiction of the question now before
us, as under the constitution and laws of that State they were empowered, and have reached a decision. The record of those judicial proceedings is before us, and tells its own story. It is true, this fact
appears in the papers submitted for our consideration by the two Houses,
but it is asked that no other or further evidence be received.

It is plain to me that from the very nature of this proceeding all the
testimony, all the information known to parliamentary law and usage
which was and is in the possession of either or both Houses of Congress,
must necessarily be considered as being to-day before this Commission
and subject to its examination; and also that if other and further testimony is needed by us in relation to any fact to satisfy our minds prior
to reaching a decision, it is our duty and power to take it, having always
in view that it shall be competent and pertinent, and regulating our
action so that the law under which we proceed will not be defeated by
prolonged delays.

I recognize expedition as a necessary feature in our proceedings. This
duty is marked all over the law, curtailing as it does debate in the two
Houses, preventing adjournments, limiting the hours of recess, and providing that no separation of the two Houses shall take place during the
execution of the law except as expressly provided. Expedition is inherent in the very nature of the act and its objects. Therefore the
time allowed by this Commission for taking testimony, hearing counsel
and objectors, all will be measured by a due sense of proportion to the
great end in view, which is a decision between all the contested returns
by the 3d day of March next. It is no answer to say that because we
cannot hear everything we must therefore hear nothing; and the hearing in each case will be regulated by reason and a sense of the fitness of

things which is supposed to accompany the intelligent execution of every duty.

The very statement of the question submitted in section 2 of the act for the decision of this Commission is, as I have said, indicative of the duty and in great degree of the power which is vested in the Commission for the performance of that duty. We are to decide "how many and what persons were *duly appointed* electors in such State." These are the precise facts set forth in the Constitution of the United States, which provides that each State shall appoint a certain number ("how many") of electors, but certain persons holding office ("what persons") shall not be appointed.

By the Constitution so *many* persons only and *such* persons only shall be appointed electors, and no more. No other persons than those authorized by the Constitution can be appointed. If a greater number be appointed, the appointment is absolutely void *quoad* the excess beyond the number prescribed. If persons prohibited be appointed, such appointment is absolutely void. The regulation by the Constitution as to numbers and qualifications of the electors is contained in the same sentence, and by no warrant can its grammatical construction be destroyed or the natural alliance of the words used be severed so as to alter its effect or meaning. Its obligation is equal throughout, and no more force can be ascribed to one of its mandates than to the other. The duty of obedience by the States to these two limitations upon the number and qualification of electors is equally plain and distinct. There is no more power in a State to disregard one limitation than the other. The breach of the Constitution by a State in appointing a person forbidden is equally unwarranted and dangerous as to appoint *more* persons than the Constitution permits. The action of any State in the appointment of electors is directly of importance to all her sisters of the Union. The offices in view are the chief executive offices of the entire Union. The safety, rights, and welfare of each State are directly affected by the action of every other State. It is the right and it is the duty of all the other States to see that no State shall have a more numerous or different college of electors than the Constitution provides.

It will scarcely be urged that any State can at its will send up to be counted a greater number of electoral votes than the Constitution allows, and that there is no "counting power" in the Senate or House of Representatives to arrest and defeat such an attempt. To admit the power of any State to increase at its will the number of its electoral votes is surely to reduce the Constitution and our system of government to an absurdity. "No Senator or Representative shall be appointed an elector." Can it be that such votes would be counted in the presence and with the aid of the very persons who in defiance of the Constitution have assumed to act as electors? The exclusion of such persons is contained in the very sentence which limits the number of electors; yet if a State can violate the mandate of the Constitution as to the qualifications of electors and appoint persons electors who, holding offices of trust and profit under the United States, have used their official powers as stepping-stones to exalt themselves and the President, who is the fountain of all executive power of the Government, to a renewed lease of authority, it is evident the wound inflicted upon the Constitution and upon free government is equally deep and dangerous.

There can be no safety unless all the avenues to places of power under the Contitution shall be equally well guarded, and the same measure of duty and with it the same measure of power be given to the two Houses over the count of electoral votes to "decide whether any and what votes from such State are the votes *provided for by the Constitution of the United States,* and how many and what persons were duly appointed electors in such State."

Nothing in this proposition detracts from the just powers of the State, whose voice alone is to be heard and obeyed in the choice of her electors. All interference by the citizens of one State with the elections in another, or by the Government of the United States with the elections or manner of election by a State, is clearly in violation of the letter and spirit of the Federal Constitution. The confusion and dangers which now surround us in connection with the late election have their real origin in the mischievous and utterly unwarranted interference by the President of the United States and his subordinates in office with the process of election in Florida and other Southern States. The official powers and emoluments of the Government have been openly used as an engine of party influence in the late canvass; and finally the military arm of the Government has been sent down upon partisan application to overawe the political opponents of the present administration and abet and encourage its party friends and agents in the commission of violations of the laws of the State. It never was intended that the Federal power should be felt in the State elections, whether for presidential electors or State officers. There never will be peace and safety to the people individually or in their communities as States until the pretensions to the exercise of such power on the part of the Federal administration shall have been abandoned.

I have always voted against inquisition by the Federal Government into the management of their affairs by the States, and would no more do it in case of presidential electors than of State officers. No one can be more averse than I to the invasion of the powers of the State to elect, and then to authenticate according to its own laws the result of its free choice, as provided by the Constitution of the United States. But the very question in the case of Florida is, *did the State* appoint any and what persons electors? Two sets of votes are before us and only one can be the lawful return. Which shall we accept? Surely that which the State has declared to be true. Both sets certainly cannot be counted and the State has a right to have one set counted.

Florida has by the Constitution the power and duty of appointing four electors, no more. Two certificates are before us, one of Humphreys and his three associates, certifying that as electors they had voted on December 6, 1876, for Hayes and Wheeler, which is accompanied by the certificate of Stearns, the late governor, pursuant to the laws of the United States, that Humphreys and his associates were chosen electors. Certificate No. 2 is by Wilkinson Call and his three associates, that they on the 6th of December, 1876, had voted for Tilden and Hendricks. This is accompanied by the certificate of William Archer Cocke, attorney-general of Florida and one of the board of State canvassers, that by the returns of the votes cast in the State of Florida at the general election held on November 7, 1876, Call and his associates were chosen electors for President and Vice-President. Accompanying the certificates of Call is a duly authenticated copy of the act of the legislature of Florida, reciting the judicial proceedings in the courts of that State, whereby it appears that upon a canvass of the true votes of the State, made under order of the court, Call and his associates had been duly chosen electors on the 7th day of November, 1876; and these proceedings are accompanied by the certificate of Drew, the present governor of Florida, verifying the same.

This double return is an abnormal fact, and one that has been caused not by the State of Florida or her people, but by the mischievous and unlawful intervention of the exterior power to which I have before alluded. The power of self-government is awarded to the State to hold her elections free from exterior influences. If her citizens and officials shall send up two returns, then they have necessarily sought a decision at the hands of a third party and made it necessary by their own act. The Constitution provides that the electoral votes shall be counted in the presence of the two Houses of Congress, and not otherwise. When this count shall have been completed the result is to be ascertained, and by whom? Necessarily by the two Houses of Congress, because it is made their duty to recognize and declare the persons found by the count of the electoral votes to have been duly elected; and if no such election shall be by them found to have been accomplished, then in the event of a majority of persons appointed electors not having been found to have voted for any candidate, "*immediately*" upon the House of Representatives is devolved the high duty of doing what the electoral colleges have failed to do, *i. e.*, elect a President, and simultaneously a like duty is devolved upon the Senate to elect a Vice-President, as provided by the twelfth article of amendment to the Constitution. The two Houses of Congress have thus in a certain contingency, of the arrival of which they must inform themselves, the duty of filling the chief executive offices of the Republic. If this shall become their great and high duty, must they not necessarily inquire and ascertain whether events have justified their proceeding? To this end the Constitution provides that—

The President of the Senate shall, in the presence of the Senate and House of Representatives, open all the certificates, and the votes shall then be counted.

It must be in the presence of the two Houses, who, in order to perform their duty and protect the avenues to the great offices in question, must carefully scrutinize and supervise this "count." To this end the two Houses must see that the count is true; true in all that the word implies; accurate in number and lawful in itself; not *more* votes than should be counted; not *other* votes than should be counted; no votes to be counted for a prohibited person; no votes to be counted when cast by persons forbidden by law to cast such votes.

The choice of electors is by the Constitution confided to the State. The language is plain:

Each State shall appoint, in such manner as the legislature thereof may direct, a number of electors, equal to the whole number of Senators and Representatives to which the State may be entitled in the Congress.

The two Houses of Congress have no right or power to question the choice of the State, but they have a right and a duty to insist that the Constitution shall be obeyed by the State in the performance of the act of appointment.

I have been unable to discover any better chart of the power which may be and which must be exercised by the two Houses of Congress in scrutinizing the votes which are brought before them to be counted under their supervision, than to hold that the States whose electoral votes are sent up to be counted shall be controlled by the same limitations of the Constitution as control the two Houses themselves when called upon to elect a President and Vice-President in the absence of a majority of the electoral votes having been found to be cast for any candidate. Thus, if the Constitution of the United States forbids Congress to elect any one President except a natural-born citizen, or a citizen of the United States at the time of the adoption of the Constitution, or any person " who shall not have attained to the age of

thirty-five years, and been fourteen years a resident within the United
States," they surely will not be at liberty to count votes for candidates
so rendered ineligible, and for whom they would themselves have been
debarred from voting; and their duty in this regard is based upon the
inhibitions of the Constitution.

The obligation to support the Constitution is equal as respects all its
provisions. No one provision can be selected from its context and supported and held sacred and those which surround it be treated with
contempt and disregard. If the qualifications of the persons to be
voted for as President and Vice-President are to be respected by the
two Houses of Congress when they are called upon to elect them, it is
their right and duty to insist that they shall be respected by the electoral colleges. The obligation is not greater to support the provisions
of the Constitution which prescribe qualifications for the candidate, than
to support those equally express qualifications of the officials who can
vote to elect a candidate. If the two Houses cannot vote for a person
of foreign birth for President, they have no power to count electoral
votes for such a person. Whether the provisions of the Constitution
define the qualifications of the person who shall vote or the person
who shall be voted for, they are equally obligatory upon those who have
the supervision of the ultimate fact of ascertaining and declaring the
lawful President and Vice-President of the United States.

In the case before us two voices pretend to speak for the State of
Florida. To us is confided the duty of discovering which is the true
and which is the false. We cannot avoid this duty, and all that is implied in its performance. The organic act of this Commission expressly
provides for a count of the votes by the two Houses, and by no one
else. To count means to count truly, and to count truly we must have
knowledge of what is the truth.

The question before us is whether we will hear proof tending to show
that one and not the other of these returns is the true return. How
can we execute this duty without hearing the facts? The Constitution
has directed the State to "appoint, in such manner as the legislature
thereof may direct, a number of electors." If this essential fact be
brought in question, then the constitution and the laws of the State
must be consulted in order to ascertain what is the "manner directed."
This Commission is invested with all the powers of the two Houses of
Congress acting separately or together. It is in its essence, therefore,
and in the purview of its power and contemplated action, a parliamentary body, with parliamentary powers and methods. We are not sitting
as a judicial court of general or statutory jurisdiction, but to exercise
judgment undoubtedly, and to that end to prosecute inquiry into the
subject-matter, not by technical methods, but by the general methods and
usages well known to the history of parliamentary proceeding, to take
such views as are a fit basis for legislation, and to be governed in our
judgments here by the same kind of proofs as would enlighten legislative discretion and judgment. The very language of the section of the
act creating this Commission commands that we shall proceed to consider and decide "what votes from such State are the votes provided
for by the Constitution of the United States, and how many and what
persons were duly appointed electors in such State, and may therein
take into view such petitions, depositions, and other papers * * *
as shall, by the Constitution and now-existing law, be competent and
pertinent in such consideration." Where, except in legislative bodies,
are "petitions" used as evidence? Where are "other papers" received as means of information? The technical rules of evidence

would exclude all such, and yet this law clearly contemplates their reception and use. The very word " law" is advisedly in the singular, because it is used in its broadest and most embracing sense, which would not be extended if the additional words "parliamentary, common, or statutory" had been annexed.

It will be observed that I have omitted in my citations the words "if any," which are to be found in many places throughout the act. I have done so because in proceedings such as this no one will gravely contend that such words are to have the slightest force in giving or excluding jurisdiction. No one has said, here or elsewhere, that such words would impair or assist the operation of law. If, in the jurisdiction of a justice of the peace over the property in a shilling, such words would be without force to control jurisdiction, surely their furtive and petty presence will hardly be recognized in the consideration of such issues as confront us now and upon which the executive power over a nation of forty millions of people may be said to depend. This Commission stands admittedly in the place of, and armed with all the powers and discretion over this subject which are vested in, the Senate of the United States representing the people in their organized polities called States, and in the Representatives in Congress representing every individual person in the United States.

I say nothing here of the new-fangled claim for power in the President of the Senate to count the electoral votes. Such a pretension had late birth and a speedy death. It was advanced in opposition to the unbroken line of precedent of the history of the Government from its foundation. It had no warrant in the express or implied meanings of the Constitution. It was in opposition to the nature and the spirit of our popular government. Discussion and public opinion soon settled its fate. It no longer exists as a subject for consideration.

An examination of the history of congressional precedent over this subject of the count of the votes has given me more knowledge than I had when the discussions took place in the Senate two years ago. Since that time the proceedings of the two Houses in the year 1800 in relation to " a bill prescribing the mode of deciding disputed elections of President and Vice-President of the United States" have been disinterred from the archives of the Senate. The bill in question originated in the Senate, and proposed that either House of Congress should have power to reject an electoral vote. It provided for the creation of an electoral commission of which the elements were the same as the present, consisting of members of the House and Senate and presided over by the Chief-Justice of the Supreme Court. This " grand committee," as it was then called, in the eighth section of the bill was invested with "power to inquire, examine, decide, and report upon the constitutional qualifications of the persons voted for as President and Vice-President of the United States, upon the constitutional qualifications of the electors appointed by the different States, and whether their appointment was authorized by the State legislature or not; upon all petitions and exceptions against corrupt, illegal conduct of the electors, or force, menaces, or improper means used to influence their votes ; or against the truth of their returns, or the time, place, or manner of giving their votes; *provided, always,* that no petition or exception shal granted or allowed by the grand committee which shall have for its object to draw into question the number of votes on which any elector in any of the States shall have been declared appointed."

And the preceding section, 6, was as follows:

That the grand committee shall have power to send for persons, papers, and records, to compel the attendance of witnesses, to administer oaths or affirmations to all persons examined before them, and to punish contempts of witnesses refusing to answer as fully and absolutely as the Supreme Court of the United States may or can do in causes depending therein; and the testimony of all witnesses examined before the committee shall be reduced to writing by the secretary of the committee, and shall be signed by the witness after his examination is closed. And if any person, sworn and examined before this committee, shall swear or affirm falsely, such person thereof convicted shall incur the pains, penalties, and disabilities inflicted by the laws of the United States upon willful and corrupt perjury.

At the close of the seventh section is a proviso that the number of votes on which any elector in any of the States shall have been declared appointed should not be inquired into. By the ordinary rules of construction, it would appear that the power of inquiry would have embraced this subject but for the express exception.

The bill passed the Senate and was reported to the House of Representatives, by which body it was also passed with an amendment requiring the concurrence of the two Houses to reject a vote. It was upon this point of difference, to wit, whether the Houses acting separately should have power to reject a vote or whether it required their concurrent action to reject a vote, that the disagreement took place and became final. But the claim of power over the counting of the votes and of instituting inquiry as to the lawfulness of the electoral votes was upheld in both Houses of Congress by large majorities. Among those so voting to exercise the jurisdiction by Congress over this question were found many persons who had sat in the convention which framed the Constitution of the United States. Among the chief actors was Mr. John Marshall, soon after the Chief-Justice of the United States; and the record of the vote discloses the names of well-known characters in American history who as constitutional lawyers are entitled to great weight. It is proper to say that the argument of Mr. Charles Cotesworth Pinckney was strongly in opposition to the exercise of such power by Congress, and his speech is more fully reported than any other, to which may be added that it is the only speech in the same direction. The concession of power in Congress to control the count of the electoral votes according to the Constitution, and to institute such inquiries and take such evidence as would be necessary to secure the end in view, was apparently affirmed by a great majority of both House.

In 1824 a bill was introduced in the Senate by Mr. Van Buren, of New York, to regulate the count of the votes, and providing that the concurrence of both Houses should be necessary for the rejection of a vote. No provision dealing with double returns is made in the bill. The bill introduced by Mr. Van Buren passed the Senate without amendment, was referred to the Committee on the Judiciary of the House, and reported back without amendment by Mr. Webster, but no further action was ever taken on it, and it never became a law.

February 8, 1865, President Lincoln sent the following message to Congress, which is to be found on page 229 of the compilation, of the action of Congress on this subject:

To the honorable the Senate and House of Representatives:

The joint resolution entitled "Joint resolution declaring certain States not entitled to representation in the electoral college" has been signed by the Executive in deference to the view of Congress implied in its passage and presentation to him. In his own view, however, *the two Houses of Congress, convened under the twelfth article of the Constitution, have complete power to exclude from counting all electoral votes deemed by them to be illegal;* and it is not competent for the Executive to defeat or obstruct that power by a veto, as would be the case if his action were at all essential in the matter.

He disclaims all right of the Executive to interfere in any way in the matter of canvassing or counting electoral votes, and he also disclaims that, by signing said resolution, he has expressed any opinion on the recitals of the preamble or any judgment of his own upon the subject of the resolution.

ABRAHAM LINCOLN.

EXECUTIVE MANSION, *February* 8, 1865.

The joint twenty-second rule, adopted on the 6th of February, 1865, by the two Houses without division, assumed in either House the existence of the power to reject at will and without debate any electoral vote; in other words, the concurrent vote of the two Houses was necessary for the counting of any electoral vote. This rule continued in force until February, 1875, and was then rescinded by the action of the Senate. Under it the count of electoral votes had been thrice made, in 1865, in 1869, and in 1873; and the power of excluding electoral votes was claimed and exercised by each House acting separately on these three occasions.

On the 6th of January, 1873, on the motion of Mr. Sherman, of Ohio, the following resolution was adopted:

Resolved, That the Committee on Privileges and Elections is directed to inquire and report to the Senate whether the recent election of electors for President and Vice-President has been conducted in the States of Louisiana and Arkansas in accordance with the Constitution and laws of the United States and with the laws of said States, and what contests, if any, have arisen as to who were elected as electors in either of said States, and what measures are necessary to provide for the determination of such contests and to guard against and determine like contests in the future election of electors for President and Vice-President. That for the purpose of speedily executing this resolution the said committee shall have power to send for persons and papers, to take testimony, and at their discretion to send a subcommittee of their own number to either of said States with authority to take testimony; and, if the exigency of this service demands, the said committee may appoint and employ suitable disinterested and unprejudiced persons not resident in either of such States, with authority to take such testimony as may be material in determining any pending contest growing out of the election of electors in either of said States.

Under this resolution the committee, presided over by Mr. Morton, of Indiana, one of the present Commission, made investigation, and on the 10th of February following made a report accompanied by voluminous testimony on the subjects embraced in the resolution, in the course of which report it is said:

The certificate of the secretary of state is not required, and the certificate of the governor, as provided for in this section, seems to be the only evidence contemplated by the law of the election of electors and their right to cast the electoral vote of the State. If Congress chooses to go behind the governor's certificate, and inquire who has been chosen as electors, it is not violating any principle of the right of the States to prescribe what shall be the evidence of the election of electors, but it is simply going behind the evidence as prescribed by an act of Congress; and, thus going behind the certificate of the governor, we find that the official returns of the election of electors, from the various parishes of Louisiana, had never been counted by anybody having authority to count them.

Under the twenty-second joint rule and this report the electoral vote of the State of Louisiana was not counted, there being two returns from said State.

On December 6, 1876, the following resolutions, introduced by Mr. Edmunds, of Vermont, a member of this Commission, passed the Senate:

Resolved, That the Committee on Privileges and Elections, when appointed, be, and it hereby is, instructed to inquire and report as soon as may be—

1. Whether in any of the elections named in said amendment, in said States, in the years 1875 or 1876, the right of any portion of such inhabitants and citizens to vote as aforesaid has been in any wise denied or abridged.
2. To what extent such denial or abridgment has been carried.
3. By what means such denial or abridgment has been accomplished.)

4. By whom has such denial or abridgment been effected.

5. With what motives and for what purposes has such denial or abridgment been carried on.

6. By what authority or pretended authority has such denial or abridgment been exercised.

Resolved further, That the said committee have power to employ such number of stenographers as shall be needful, and to send for persons and papers, and have leave to sit during the sessions of the Senate, and to appoint subcommittees with full power to make the inquiries aforesaid, and report the same to the committee.

Resolved further, That said committee, in order to the more speedy performance of its duties, have power to provide for the taking of affidavits on the subjects aforesaid before any officer authorized by the laws of the United States to take affidavits; and to receive and consider the same.

Resolved further, That the said committee be, and is hereby, instructed to inquire *into the eligibility to office under the Constitution of the United States of any persons alleged to have been ineligible on the 7th day of November last, or to be ineligible as electors of President and Vice-President of the United States,* to whom certificates of election have been or shall be issued by the executive authority of any State as such electors, and whether the appointment of electors, or those claiming to be such in any of the States, has been made either by force, fraud, or other means *otherwise than in conformity with the Constitution and laws of the United States and the laws of the respective States;* and whether any such appointment or action of any such elector has been in any wise unconstitutionally or unlawfully interfered with; and to inquire and report whether Congress has any constitutional power, and, if so, what and the extent thereof, in respect of the appointment of, or action of, electors of President and Vice-President of the United States, or over returns or certificates of votes of such electors; and that said committee have power to send for persons and papers, and to employ a stenographer, and have leave to sit during the sessions of the Senate.

These resolutions are embodied in report No. 611 of the Forty-fourth Congress, second session, made by Mr. Sargent, of California, from the Committee on Privileges and Elections, and which (a significant commentary upon the argument of those who have denied the right or power of this Commission to hear any evidence not contained in the papers presented by the President of the Senate to the two Houses) has been used as a paper-book in the course of the debates before this Commission, and copies of which are now and have been throughout the consideration of this case in the hands of every member of the Commission. Mr. Sargent's report, made to the Senate on the 29th of January, 1877, contains thirty printed pages, which embody abundant extracts from the testimony in relation to the election of electors in the State of Florida in November last. Mr. Sargent reports, on page 2, that, in pursuance of these resolutions introduced by Mr. Edmunds, the committee had " thoroughly examined *all returns of the election, the evidence received and considered by the State canvassing-board,* having especially investigated the contested cases before the board, and having taken the testimony of four hundred and forty-two witnesses concerning the election, the canvassing of the votes thereof, the denial or abridgment of the right of any portion of the inhabitants of Florida to vote, by force or fraud, *and the other objects named in the resolution of the Senate.*"

No action was ever taken by the Senate upon this report, but the report of the committee of the House of Representatives was accompanied by a resolution declaring that the actual returns substantiated by evidence showed that Wilkinson Call and his three associates had been duly chosen electors, and had duly cast their votes for Tilden and Hendricks on December 6, 1876, which resolution was adopted by the House by a vote of 142 yeas to 82 nays.

The resolution of December 6, 1876, from the hands of Mr. Edmunds, of Vermont, contained these words:

That the said committee be, and is hereby, instructed to inquire *into the eligibility to office under the Constitution of the United States* of any persons alleged to have been ineligible on the *7th day of November last,* or to be ineligible as electors of President and Vice-President of the United States, to whom certificates of election have been or shall be issued by the executive authority of any State, and whether the appointment of electors has been made otherwise than *in conformity with the Constitution and laws of the United States and the laws of the respective States.*

Compare these last words with the language of the present act:

SEC. 2. * * * decide whether any and *what votes* from such State are *the* votes *provided for by the Constitution of the United States,* and *how many* and *what persons* were *duly appointed* electors in such State.

The inquiry under the Senate resolution and under the present law is precisely the same, and the exercise of the same measure of power is required for a decision under either.

In the face of this history of congressional precedent, disapproving of much of it as I do, especially as to the claim of power in the two Houses under the late twenty-second joint rule, I cannot but be amazed at the present attitude of members of the Commission and others in denying all power, in the name of State rights, to investigate the facts of an election sufficiently to ascertain what were its true results, to enable this Commission to come to a decision as to which of these two returns before us now was the true and lawful electoral vote of the State of Florida, as settled by the election on the 7th of November last, according to the Constitution and laws of the United States and of the State of Florida.

The introduction of the Senate document to which I have referred, being the report of one of its committees and containing part of the testimony taken before it, and its natural and apparently unconscious use by counsel, by objectors, and members of the Commission, all confirm to me the correctness of my opinion that all the evidence of every nature which was in the possession of the two Houses of Congress, or either of them, was, *ipso facto*, in the possession of this Commission, who are bound to give due weight and consideration to the same. Some of the facts testified to before these committees, both of the Senate and the House, in relation to the Florida election, came to my knowledge before I was appointed a member of this Commission. It dwells still in my memory and cannot be dismissed. At my table in the Senate I have several volumes of this printed testimony. It was furnished to me by order of the Senate, that I might intelligently and conscientiously vote upon the subjects to which it related. When I shall return to the Senate and vote upon any objection which may be offered in cases of single returns from any State, I must cast that vote in the full light of all the knowledge and information within my power. When I leave this Commission, after its decision shall have been made, and vote upon the question of concurrence or non-concurrence in that decision, I shall cast my vote in the full light of all the information of every nature which as a Senator I have derived from every paper and from every source competent and pertinent for the decision of the case. If everything thus properly laid open to me as a member of the Senate, and which binds me as a Senator, is to be shut out from my mind as a Commissioner, how anomalous and absurd, how illogical must be my position in one capacity or the other: as a member of the Senate bound to receive evidence and information; as a member of the Commission to shut my eyes to all evidence except that which the papers presented by the President of the Senate shall contain!

Mr. President and gentlemen of the Commission, I cannot so comprehend my duty nor yours. The law under which we act plainly throws upon us the duty of decision. Inquiry and ascertainment necessarily must precede that decision. We cannot justly decide without evidence and we cannot lawfully refuse to hear evidence.

I not only consider the weight and influence of this decision as important in defining the jurisdiction of the two Houses of Congress and the rights of the candidates to exercise the functions for which they have been lawfully chosen, but I feel there is a moral weight attending the decisions of this Commission which is to sink 'deeper into the hearts and consciences of the American people. The question is one of law, but it is a question of law sustained by sound morals. It is justice and truth under the law which is the object for which this tribunal was created; and therefore I would open wide every door and window of this case through which light and truth may enter, in order that justice and law may be recognized as the same thing in the minds of the people of this country, who will respect and love their Government only when they are satisfied that it is just.

I can scarcely suppose that this Commission would refuse to hear evidence that the certificates of a governor and of a college of electors were in fact forgeries, or that the governor and electors had been compelled under duress and coercion to sign their names to those certificates. Why would we receive such evidence? Because the proof would be that the papers presented were not in truth those which upon their face they professed to be. Go a little further. Suppose the governor had signed willingly and in good faith and without force, but was himself the victim of fraud and deception under which only his signature had been obtained, or that the board of canvassers whose actions he certified had also been induced by the fraud and forgery of others to make a certificate of facts which were afterward discovered to be false, is it to be said that either or both of these things cannot be corrected and that we have no power to do so; that there is no power in the State to do so? Now, if the fraud shall be the fraud of the governor and the board of canvassers combined, does that make it any more binding on us than if they had been the innocent victims themselves of the fraud or force of others?

I understand that proof is offered to this Commission to show that the certificate of Humphreys and his three associates, the Hayes electors, is not the true and lawful vote of the State of Florida; that it is the result of the action of a State board of canvass, ministerial only in its powers, acting beyond its jurisdiction, in fraud and in error certifying an untruth; and, on the other hand, that evidence is offered to show that the State of Florida at the election held November 7, 1876, did elect Wilkinson Call and his three associates, all duly qualified under the Constitution of the United States, and elected in accordance with the constitution and laws of the State of Florida; and that being so elected they did, on the day appointed by act of Congress, in pursuance of the Constitution, meet as an electoral college and cast the votes of that State for Tilden and Hendricks. This, it seems to me, is the question which this tribunal was created to decide, and that in the power and duty of the decision are necessarily embraced the power and duty of inquiring and hearing before determination.

The order of this Commission has been made to hear testimony in the case of Mr. Humphreys, who was alleged to be ineligible to be appointed an elector because on the day of election he held an office of trust and profit under the United States. I do not comprehend, as I have said before, why one provision of the Constitution relating to this subject should be more obligatory upon us than another. I concur that it is our right and duty to hear testimony on this subject, and equally so in all other questions where the true performance of the requirements of the Constitution are brought in question.

FLORIDA.

The Commission having resolved on the 7th of February " that no evidence will be received or considered by the Commission which was not submitted to the joint convention of the two Houses by the President of the Senate, with the different certificates, except such as relates to the eligibility of F. C. Humphreys, one of the electors," the case was argued by counsel, and the order heretofore stated was adopted on the 9th of February. Before the vote was taken on the adoption of this order Senator BAYARD said:

After hearing the testimony of witnesses admitted by the Commission and reading the documents produced by them, I am satisfied that Mr. Humphreys was not ineligible to the office of elector on the 7th of November, 1876. The office of shipping-commissioner formerly held by him had, in my judgment, been resigned early in the month of October preceding. This resignation was not required by law to be in any particular form, but I believe that he did in fact divest himself of all official power and emolument in connection with the said office, and that under the laws of the United States the duties of the said office were assumed on the 5th of October, 1876, by the collector of customs at the port of Pensacola, in Florida, after which time the said Humphreys did not perform or attempt to perform any of its duties. The technicality suggested, of want of form in his resignation, or that it was not made to the court by whom he was appointed, but only to the presiding judge of that court, does not seem to me sufficient to disqualify him from being appointed an elector for President and Vice-President, as I do not consider that he held the office of shipping-commissioner after the 5th of October, 1876.

The Commission having refused to admit any evidence *aliunde* the certificates, I proceed to consider the law and the facts of the case as so presented. The power of choosing electors is vested in the State, who, " in such manner as her legislature may direct," is to appoint them. The *fact* of the election is not required to be established by any form of proof. The electors themselves are required to " make distinct lists of all persons voted for as President, and of all persons voted for as Vice-President, and of the number of votes for each; which lists *they* shall sign and certify, and transmit sealed to the seat of the Government of the United States, directed to the President of the Senate."

On the 7th of November an election was held in the State of Florida for four persons as electors for President and Vice-President. Two sets of candidates were voted for, one headed by Humphreys and one headed by Call. The fact *which was elected* will determine which was entitled to cast the vote of that State for President and Vice-President on December 6, 1876.

We have heard the argument that because the board of State canvassers, whether in disregard and defiance of duty or no, saw fit to certify to Governor Stearns that Humphreys and his associates had been chosen electors, these last-named persons were thereby invested " with the insignia of office," and that they became officers *de facto*, if not *de jure*, and that their acts as such officers *de facto* are valid as to all third parties under the common rule. An important qualification of this rule, however, is that it stops with preventing mischief to such as confided in their power, and it is simply adopted to that extent as a matter of public policy, for the protection of innocent third persons; but the reasoning applicable to officers *de facto* is entitled to no place in the present consideration, no such facts existing here.

The office of elector is confined to a single function, that of casting a vote on a certain day. In Florida there was no such thing as an elector *de facto* as distinguished from an elector *de jure*. Two separate bodies of men assumed the office and executed the function of voting for President and Vice-President on the same day under alleged color of law. One body only were the rightful electors *de jure* and *de facto ;* the other were neither *de facto* nor *de jure* electors. If the certificate and the possession of a certificate can be substituted for the fact of election, then we may hear something of the "insignia of office." It is the *election* that determines the right to the office, and not the *certificate*, which is merely one form of evidence of the election. The principle of *de facto* action and the necessity of protecting the public who have confided in the acts of the *de facto* officer has no place whatever in a proper consideration of the case of the State of Florida and the two sets of rival electors, both of whom assumed equally to execute the office at the same time ; and the only question now is which set was elected.

It is manifestly the duty of the two Houses to secure to the State of Florida her right of choice, as established by the Constitution. It is a case of State action in relation to a Federal or national object. The State of Florida is not alone concerned, but all the other States are concerned, and the two Houses of Congress have been made the verifying witnesses of the truth of this national transaction. The meaning and the nature of our Government must not be forgotten, and we must adopt no construction inconsistent with either. If we propose to secure to each State the right to appoint its electors, do we do it by accepting the action of a set of conspiring and faithless officials who, on the eve of losing office, falsify their duty and deliver over the insignia of the office of electors to persons not entitled to receive them, and who, being thus fraudulently clothed with robes of office, proceed to defeat the real will of the people? It seems to me that with as much justice could it be said that if Colonel Blood had gotten safely away with the scepter-crown, and jewels of England and the coronation robes, he was there, fore the king of England, he who was merely a robber of her regalia, as to say that McLin, the secretary of state, and Cowgill, the comptroller, conspiring with Stearns, the governor, could, by falsifying the returns of the election, and breaking the law under which they made the canvass, thereby say that they spoke the voice of Florida in such manner as her legislature had directed. It is observed in the certificate, No. 2, of Call and his associates that they did notify Governor Stearns, the executive of the State, of their appointment as electors, and did apply and demand of him to cause to be delivered to them three lists of the names of the electors of said State according to law, and the said governor did refuse to deliver the same to them.

There is no doubt that by the conspiracy of McLin, Cowgill, and Stearns the customary certificate of the election of Call and his three associates was withheld from them, *but did the withholding of the certificate destroy the fact of the election?* Suppose no board of canvass had met and no certificates had been issued, but, nevertheless, the two sets of electors had met on December 6, 1876, and each set assumed to discharge the functions of the office by balloting for President and Vice-President, and each had sealed and certified and sent on to Washington the results of their action. If it was made subsequently to appear to the satisfaction of the two Houses of Congress, or to the satisfaction of a court of competent jurisdiction in the State of Florida, that one of these sets of electors had in fact been lawfully elected, and was entitled to vote on the day they did vote, would not such vote and such vote alone be valid, whether accompanied by certificates or not?

The fact of election and who were really chosen by the citizens of Florida as electors for President and Vice-President on the 7th of November, 1876, is certified to this Commission in a manner conclusive under the Constitution and laws of the United States and of the State of Florida. The power of appointment given to the State involves necessarily the power to determine the manner in which the act is to be done and also the power to verify its own act, and showing that it was done in a proper manner. The State is its own best authority. To adopt the language used in argument before the Commission, the State is a political community organized and existing under a system of law by which the declaration of the courts in matters submitted to their jurisdiction *becomes the declaration of the State itself.* The law of a State is the statute of a State as construed and applied by its courts. The public laws of a State promulgated by its authority, bind with absolute notice all persons within the State, and form the very highest means of proof of the action of the State. By the constitution of the State of Florida, the circuit court and the judges thereof shall have power to issue writs of *quo warranto.* The election in Florida was held under the laws of the State, controlled and managed by officers of the State; the canvass of the votes of the State was under the laws of the State performed by officers of the State. Over those officers and under those laws, the courts of the State had by its constitution jurisdiction to examine and determine whether those laws had been construed and executed properly by its executive and ministerial officers.

To use the definition of these powers of the State board of canvass as given by the supreme court of Florida in the case of The State *ex rel.* Drew, in December, 1876:

They are authorized to enter no judgment, and their power is limited by the express words of the statute, which gives them being, to the signing of a certificate containing the whole number of votes given for each person for each office, and *therein declaring the result as shown by the returns.*

The action of the board of canvassers in certifying that Humphreys and his associates had been chosen electors was brought under review in the circuit court for the second judicial circuit of the State of Florida by information in the nature of a writ of *quo warranto,* wherein Wilkinson Call and his three associates were relators, and Humphreys and his three associates were respondents, and the circuit court, after full consideration and proofs produced on behalf of the parties, including a careful and accurate recanvass of *all* the votes cast, determined that the said relators were in fact and in law elected said electors as against the said respondents and all other persons.

By the record of the judicial proceedings in the courts of Florida having jurisdiction of the subject-matter, and having all these parties claiming to have been chosen electors for President and Vice-President before them, it is made known to this Commission that the certificate of a majority of the State board of canvass of Florida that Humphreys and his three associates had been chosen electors was not true; but by the circuit court of said State it was—

Therefore considered and adjudged that said respondents, Frederick C. Humphreys, Charles H. Pearce, William H. Holden, and Thomas W. Long, were not, nor was any one of them elected, chosen, or appointed, or entitled to be declared elected, chosen, or appointed as such electors or elector, or to receive certificates or certificate of election or appointment as such electors or elector, and that the said respondents were not, upon the said 6th day of December, or at any other time, entitled to assume or exercise any of the powers and functions of such electors or elector; but that they were, upon the said day and date, mere usurpers, and that all and singular their acts and doings, as such, were and are illegal, null, and void.

And it is further considered and adjudged that the said relators, Robert Bullock, Robert B. Hilton, Wilkinson Call, and James E. Yonge, all and singular, were at said election duly elected, chosen, and appointed electors of President and Vice President of the United States, and were, on the said 6th day of December, 1876, entitled to be declared elected, chosen, and appointed as such electors, and to have and receive certificates thereof, and upon the said day and date, and at all times since, to exercise and perform all and singular the powers and duties of such electors, and to have and enjoy the pay and emoluments thereof.

It is further adjudged that said respondents do pay to the relators their costs by them in this behalf expended.

By the Constitution of the United States, article 4, section 1, it is provided that :

Full faith and credit shall be given in each State to the public acts, records, and judicial proceedings of. every other State. And the Congress may by general laws prescribe the manner in which such acts, records, and proceedings shall be proved, and the effect thereof.

In section 905 of the Revised Statutes of the United States, it is provided that :

The said records and judicial proceedings so authenticated shall have such faith and credit given to them in every court within the United States as they have by law or usage in the courts of the State from which they are taken.

The courts of the United States have, from the origin of the Government, regarded as final all judgments of the highest State courts over matters and persons within their jurisdiction. It is not necessary for me in this presence to review the authorities in the Supreme Court decisions from Mills *vs.* Duryee, 7 Cranch, 481, to Township of Elmwood *vs.* Macy, 2 Otto, 289, in their unbroken effect.

The opinion of the court in the last-named case was delivered by Mr. Justice Davis, who said :

We are not called upon to vindicate the decisions of the supreme court of Illinois in these cases, or approve the reasoning by which it reached its conclusions. If the questions before us had never been passed upon by it, some of my brethren who agree to this opinion might take a different view of them. But are not these decisions binding upon us in the present controversy ? * * * We have always followed the highest court of the State in its construction of its own constitution and laws.

Striking out the name of "Illinois" and inserting the name of "Florida" in this last citation, what effect must be given by this Commission to the judgments of the courts of that State to which I have referred, and the record of which attached to the certificate is now before us? How can the laws of a State be expounded with more authority than by its courts of law? The judiciary of the State is one of the co-ordinate branches of its government. The interpretation of the statutes of a State by its superior court is binding everywhere, if the judgment is conclusive in the State where it was pronounced.

Did the jurisdiction attach in Florida in the proceeding against Humphreys and others? There can be no doubt that under the constitution and laws of Florida the court had jurisdiction, had the parties before it, and entered judgment in accordance with the law and the facts. This proceeding was commenced on the day on which both sets of electors assumed to act, on which day the board of canvass rendered a decision which was declared by the courts to be erroneous and fraudulent, but which did not prevent the true electors from acting upon the fact of their election and casting the votes according to the Constitution and laws of the United States. There was in this case no retroactive force of law. The fact had been determined on the 7th of November, 1876, by the citizens of Florida at the polls, who were the electors ; the function of elector was discharged by those whom that election has proven to have been elected, on the 6th of December. It is no case, as has been suggested, of reconsideration by the tribunals and legislature of a State, changing the result of an election; it is no question of violation of the requirement of the Constitution that the votes should all be cast upon the same day throughout the United States. The votes were cast on the day named by act of Congress, and shall it be because some false votes were cast by pretended electors on the same day that the true votes were cast by the real electors, that, therefore, the action of the latter is to be nugatory? There is no want of performance of every constitutional and legal requirement by Call and his three associates. By the judgment of the courts of Florida the fact is conclusively fastened upon the knowledge of this tribunal, and its effect is binding upon them, that on the 7th day of November, 1876, Wilkinson Call and his three associates were duly and truly chosen, in the manner prescribed by the legislature of the State of Florida, electors for President and Vice-President, and that on December 6, 1876, they lawfully performed the functions of their said office, which they certified duly to the two Houses of Congress.

The subsequent action of the legislature of Florida in ordering a recanvass of the votes and confirming the action of the board of canvass under the decree of the court does not change in any degree the result of the election held on the 7th of November, nor is it claimed that the result of that election could be in any respect changed by the subsequent action of the judiciary or the legislature; but it is plain that by the certificates and records before this Commission the State of Florida has done all in her power to rid herself of the fraud perpetrated by a board of ministerial officers in falsely canvassing and certifying the votes cast at the election held on November 7, 1876. By proceedings in her courts the same board of canvass in Florida, under the order of the supreme court in the case of the State of Florida *ex rel.* George F. Drew, were compelled to return the true vote showing the election of George F. Drew as governor and the other State officers. Prior to the action of the supreme court, this canvassing-board had erroneously and fraudulently returned Stearns as governor, two·republican members of Congress, and a republican legislature. The recanvass being ordered by the supreme court has resulted in seating Drew, the governor, a majority of the legislature, and the entire board of State officers, who are now regularly and peaceably in the control of that State. The construction given by the supreme court of the State to the statute under which the State board of canvass has assumed to act has defined their duties and their powers, and declared in substance that they were ministerial and not judicial, and that in the rejection of the " true " votes returned to them they had exceeded their authority, and their action was consequently void. It is not necessary here to recite the decision of the court in respect to all the powers of this board, except to say that they had assumed powers not given to them by the statute under which they acted, and in regard to which their action was absolutely void; and upon review of their action, under the statute as construed and interpreted by the court, the certificate made by them of the election of Humphreys and his associates (the Hayes electors) was found to be unwarranted in law and false in fact.

If the State of Florida is to be held to have the power to choose these electors, how shall the voice of that State be expressed? It was expressed by the election on the 7th of November and the votes of her citizens cast thereat. What that vote was, and who were elected, are proven to this Commission by the judgment of the judicial branch of the government of Florida. They have reached conclusions of law and of fact in relation to that election which bind this tribunal as much as they bind every citizen of the State of Florida. In confirmation of the truths disclosed by an honest examination of the votes actually cast at the late election for presidential electors in the State of Florida, comes the public law of the legislature of Florida, not assuming to change the result of that election, but to declare, after careful canvass made, what the result was when the polls closed on the 7th of November, 1876.

Thus this State has struggled to have its own voice heard. Her people have spoken through the ballot-box; the State has spoken through her courts; the State has spoken through the legislature, and the present governor has joined his certificate of regularity as to all these proceedings. The electors, declared by the courts to have been the true electors on the 6th day of December, 1876, Wilkinson Call and his three associates, have certified to you the result of their votes for President and Vice-President. I know not how a State can speak save as Florida has spoken. Her laws have been construed by her courts. The facts of the election of November 7, 1876, have been adjudicated according to that interpretation of her laws. The record of those judicial proceedings in due form is now before this Commission and appended to the certificates of the Tilden electors. Shall they be received or shall they be rejected? Will this Commission take heed of the true fact of election, or will they hold themselves bound by a certificate of ministerial officers, which has been proven in the judicial courts of the State to be erroneous, if not fraudulent, and which by the laws of the State is declared to be *prima-facie* evidence only? Whatever of force that certificate would have had *prima facie* has disappeared forever under the judgment of a court of competent jurisdiction, in which the facts set forth in that certificate were brought into controversy and have been determined according to the laws of the State of Florida.

It seems to me that in deciding which of these two returns is the true and lawful return, there cannot be in the mind of lawyer or layman any reasonable doubt. If a State cannot succeed by the united voices of its three branches, executive, legislative, and judicial, in establishing a fact transacted under its own laws and within its own limits, it is idle to talk of State existence or State rights. By the three departments of her government Florida has essayed to make her will known. Those mute witnesses of the truth of the late election in Florida, those silent pieces of paper upon which were written or printed the names of the persons voted for, are in existence. They have been canvassed and compiled, and the result is before this tribunal; and that result proclaims that in fact and in law Call and his three associates did receive a majority of the true votes cast on November 7, 1876, for the office of electors of President and Vice-President. The question is whether the State of Florida shall have her vote received or not. At any rate I would ask if this Commission will not suffer Florida to be represented by those votes which by every department of her government she has certified to you to be true; will you not at least spare her the additional wrong of *mis*representation? If her true voice is to be smothered, do not, I beg of you, permit the false voice to be heard.

CASE OF LOUISIANA.

On Tuesday, February 13, the Commission met at eleven o'clock to consider the case of the electoral votes of the State of Louisiana, two certificates purporting to be the certificates of electoral votes having been opened by the President of the Senate in the presence of the two Houses, certificate No. 1 of William Pitt Kellogg and his seven associates claiming to have been duly chosen electors for President and Vice-President for that State, certified by the said Kellogg as governor of the State, and certificate No. 2 of Robert C. Wickliffe and his seven associates, certified by John McEnery as governor of the State of Louisiana. Objections to the Kellogg certificate were duly made by members of the Senate and House of Representatives, stating in substance that there was on the 7th day of November, 1876, no law or joint resolution of the legislature of Louisiana in force directing the manner in which the electors for said State should be appointed, because if any law was in existence directing the appointment of electors it was an act of the legislature which directed that the electors should be appointed by the people of the State in their primary capacity at an election held on a day certain at particular places and in a certain way; that the people of the State, in accordance with the legislative direction, had elected Robert C. Wickliffe and his seven associates by a very large majority of the votes; that the said William Pitt Kellogg and his seven associates were not in fact and in law chosen electors, but that the said certificate of their election by the said Kellogg was false in fact and fraudulently made by him with the full knowledge of his seven associates claiming to be electors; that the pretended canvass of the votes of the people of the State of Louisiana, made by Madison Wells, Anderson, Casanave, and Kenner, as returning-officers of said election, was without jurisdiction and void; that the statutes under which the said returning-officers claimed to have derived their authority gave them no jurisdiction whatever to make the returns or canvass and compile the statements of votes cast for electors for President and Vice-President; that even if the statutes should be construed as conferring such jurisdiction upon the returning-officers to appoint electors, they are in conflict with the constitution of the State of Louisiana, which requires the electors to be appointed by the State; that the said returning-board was not constituted according to law, because it did not contain the elements required by law; that the action of the said returning-officers was false and fraudulent; that perjury was committed with the knowledge, and at their instance, by which the lawful vote of the people of Louisiana was overthrown and disregarded; that the lawful returns of votes were subtracted and suppressed and their places supplied by forged returns made at the instance and request of the said members of the returning-board; that two of the persons claiming to have been appointed electors, A. B. Levissee and O. H. Brewster, were at the time of their alleged election, on the 7th of November and subsequently, persons holding offices of trust and profit under the United States; that there was no canvass of votes of the State of Louisiana made in accordance with the constitution and laws of that State on which certificates of election were issued unto the said Kellogg and his seven associates; and that the alleged canvass on which the certificates were issued to said Kellogg was founded on an act of usurpation by the board of returning-officers, and was fraudulent and void.

Senator BAYARD said:

The Constitution of the United States provides that "each State shall appoint, in such manner as the legislature thereof may direct, a number of electors." The same Constitution requires that each State of this Union shall have a government republican in form, which is guaranteed by the United States. The power to appoint electors is thus plainly vested in that political entity of our system called a republican State, a government popular in form and representative in its character, and which can speak only by its agents and through its laws. The fundamental law of a State exists, under our system, in a written constitution, which is created by the sovereign power of the people acting in their primary capacity of self-government, and represented under our republican theory by a majority of the citizens. Until the fundamental law represented in the written constitution of a State shall have been repealed, it must be accepted as the highest expression of the will of the State upon the subjects to which it relates. The limitations it contains over the powers of the various departments and officers of the State are all to be maintained and respected.

In this view the execution of the power and duty of the State to appoint electors for President and Vice-President is the substantial fact, and the action of the State's legislature is the mere *modus* or manner of the State's performance. I do not hold that the Constitution of the United States contemplated the deposit in the "legislature" of a State of the control of the appointment of electors as a body distinct from the State itself, with power to act independently and regardless of the arrangements of the constitution of the State. All power vested in the legislature of a State is defined and limited by the State constitution, and all laws passed by any State legislature in violation of the constitution of the State are as absolutely void as if passed in violation of the Constitution of the United States, which is the supreme law of the land. The legislature of a State, being therefore merely one department of the State government, and clearly subordinate to the will of the State, as expressed in its constitution, cannot give validity to any statute which violates the principles of republican government in the State or deprives the people of that State of their rights intended to be secured against encroachment by any of their rulers or officials by the terms of their written constitution and charter of powers.

The constitution of the State of Louisiana, in article 98, prescribes that—

> Every male person, of the age of twenty-one years or upward, born or naturalized in the United States, and subject to the jurisdiction thereof, and a resident of this State one year next preceding an election, and the last ten days within the parish in which he offers to vote, shall be deemed an elector, except those disfranchised by this constitution, and persons under interdiction.

Article 103 prescribes that—

> The privilege of free suffrage shall be supported by laws regulating elections, prohibiting under adequate penalties all undue influence thereon from bribery, tumult, or other improper practice.

Under these safeguards and qualifications the right of suffrage in Louisiana is intended to be exercised, and cannot lawfully be diminished or destroyed by the action of the legislature or its agents. The right to vote would be an empty and idle form if not accompanied by the right to have such vote counted; and yet the result of the arguments to which we have listened, and the examination of the constitution and laws of the State of Louisiana which it has induced me to make, has been to satisfy me that the provisions of the constitution of Louisiana intended to secure and promote the privilege of free suffrage in that State are utterly nugatory if the law of November 20, 1872, entitled "An act to regulate the conduct and to maintain the freedom and purity of elections," &c., shall be executed as it evidently has been by the State board of canvass created by the second section, simply because it is shown by the offers of evidence made in this case to this Commission, and which, for the purpose of the present argument, must be considered as proven, that, notwithstanding upward of five thousand State officials, registrars, and commissioners of election were appointed, being an average of nearly one official for every thirty voters in the State, all selected under the authority of the governor of the State and removable at his will, all selected to obey and represent the will of one only of the political parties in the State, notwithstanding that in addition to this force nearly twenty-five hundred United States marshals were selected from the same party and for the same political interest, notwithstanding the presence of large detachments of troops of the United States under the same control; having thus entire control of the registration of all the voters of the State, in which no interference by the courts was permitted, having every voting-place, every registration-list, and all police authority exclusively in the hands of their own party, a returning-board, imperfect in its numbers and still more imperfect in its political composition under the law was enabled not only to obstruct but wholly to overthrow the results of the exercise of that free suffrage which the constitution of the State was intended to secure to its citizens, and to convert a majority of nearly ten thousand votes in favor of the candidates of one of the political parties, as clearly established by the ballots cast and still in existence, as well as by the duplicate returns of the elections which did not reach the hands of the State returning-board of canvass, into a majority of three thousand and upward for the defeated candidates. In such a state of facts, which, let me ask, shall be held to represent the State of Louisiana; her constitution, commanding "that the privilege of free suffrage shall be supported by laws regulating elections, and prohibiting under adequate penalties all undue influence thereon from *power, bribery, tumult, or other improper practices,*" or an act of the legislature, practically overthrowing the constitution and placing the whole power and result of elections in the hands of a board of returning-officers, whose duty is succinctly defined and expressed in their oath of office to "carefully and honestly canvass and compile the statements of the votes," and from whom the constitution expressly withheld judicial powers?

What is the "manner" in which the State of Louisiana has directed her electors for President and Vice-President to be chosen? By the popular vote according to the provisions of her·constitution; and if it shall appear that the legislature have disregarded and violated this provision of the constitution, is it not our plain duty to respect the constitution and not the law passed in violation thereof?

But in the case before us we are not called upon by the facts offered to be proven to us to decide between a law and the constitution under which it is assumed to have been passed, because we are asked by those who propose that we should receive the certificate of William Pitt Kellogg and his seven associates as being the true and lawful electoral votes of the State of Louisiana to shut our eyes to the plainest violations and overthrow, not only of the constitution of the State, and the system of free popular government it was intended to secure, but also of the statute under which the returning-board profess to find warrant for their action.

It has been admitted that the election of November 7, 1876, in Louisiana was held under the law of November 20, 1872, and I propose briefly to consider the powers and duties of the State returning-board of canvassers under that act. In the first place, as to the quorum who assumed to act. The general object of the law (see section 103 of the constitution) is alleged to be "to support the privilege of free suffrage." Section 2 provides that the number of the board shall be five persons, and that it shall be composed of "all political parties." A majority of the board " shall constitute a quorum, and have power to make the returns of all electors."

In case of any vacancy by death, resignation, or otherwise, by either of the board, then the vacancy shall be filled by the residue of the board of returning-officers.

It is a public fact and embraced in the offers of proof to this Commission that four persons only for two years and upward have composed the board, which, by the language of the act, shall consist of five persons; that all of these four were members of the republican party; and that although 86,000 registered voters and citizens of the democratic party are in the State of Louisiana, not one of them has ever been elected to fill the vacancy, although it is also shown the demand has been made frequently, and always in vain, on the part of the democratic party to have the vacancy on the board filled by one of their members.

In thus requiring the board to consist of "all political parties," there was a recognition of the usage and actual state of affairs throughout the United States as to party lines. No one denies that this country is potentially governed by political parties, and that party organization is usually necessary for the success of any public object. The laws of every State in the Union, in response to the American demand for fair play and justice, and in recognition of the existence of political parties, provide that all parties shall be represented upon a political board of canvass or of election. The laws of the United States appointing supervisors by the circuit courts of the United States provide that they shall be of different political parties. It is therefore reasonably argued by the objectors to the action of the Louisiana returning-board that their refusal to obey the mandate of the law to fill the vacancy so that all parties should be represented in the board is of itself proof of fraud. The law upon this subject was well laid down by Mr. Justice Miller, a member of this Commission, in the case of Schenck vs. Peay, 1 Woolworth's Circuit Court Reports, 175:

We understand it to be well settled that where authority of this kind is conferred on three or more persons in order to make its exercise valid, all must be present and participate, or have an opportunity to participate, in the proceedings, although some may dissent from the action determined on. The action of two out of three commissioners, to all of whom was confided a power to be exercised, cannot be upheld when the third party took no part in the transaction and was ignorant *of what was done, gave no implied consent to the action of the others, and was neither consulted by them nor had any opportunity to exert his legitimate influence in the determination of the course to be pursued. Such is the uncontradicted course of the authorities, so far as we are advised,* where the power conferring the authority has not prescribed a different rule.

In order to constitute a valid quorum of the returning-board, which, under the act, may consist of three persons, such quorum shall contain the different and integral parts necessary for the composition of the original board; in other words, that the quorum of three in order to act in accordance with the law shall contain " all parties " in its composition, and for want of such composition its action would be invalid. All four of the members of the board being republicans and no democrat being allowed to take part in its action, it was defective in an element essential to its lawful existence, and which was equally demanded by common decency as well as the law.

The duty of the board when duly organized is " carefully and honestly to compile the statements of the votes, and make a true and correct return of the election," as is set forth in their official oath. They are to meet within ten days after the closing of the election to canvass and compile " *the statements of votes made by the commissioners of election,* and make returns to the secretary of state. The canvass and compila tion shall be made from the statements of the commissioners of election, whose returns are to be opened by the presiding officer of the board in its presence. From *such statements* the canvass is to be made; and no authority is given for any compilation excepting from the statements of the *commissioners of election.* They shall canvass and compile the returns of election from all polls or voting-places at which there shall have been a fair, and free, and peaceable registration and election; and no jurisdiction is given to them to question the statements of the commissioners of election as returned, except as provided by section 26 of the same act. By section 26 it is provided that if riot, tumult, acts of violence, intimidation, and disturbance, bribery or corrupt influences shall occur and prevent or tend to prevent a fair, free, peaceable, and full vote of all the qualified electors, it shall be the duty of the commissioners of election, if such occurrences shall take place on the day of election, or of the supervisor of registration of the parish, if they have occurred during the time of registration, (which is sixty days prior to the day of election,) to make *in duplicate and under oath* a clear and full statement of all the facts relating to such riot, tumult, &c., and state the effect produced by such riot, tumult, &c., and the number of qualified voters who were deterred by such acts of riot and tumult from registering or voting; and *such* statements shall *be corroborated under oath by three respectable citizens,* qualified electors of the parish, and shall be forwarded by the commissioner of election or supervisor of registration *in duplicate* to the supervisor of registration in the parish, and if in the city of New Orleans, to the secretary of state, one copy of which shall be forwarded to " the returning-officers provided for in section 2 of this act." The commissioner of election shall annex *his copy* of such statement " to his returns of election, by paste, wax, or some adhesive substance," so that the same can be kept together; and the *other* copy shall be delivered to the clerk of the court of the parish for the use of the district attorney.

It will therefore be observed that, in order to institute any question by the returning-board or to give them any pretense for the exercise of any other than the ministerial power to canvass and compile the votes from the statements before them under the hand of the commissioners of election, it is essential that they shall have such statements corroborated under oath, as is provided by the law, and in the absence of such statements made and returned according to law they are wholly without authority or jurisdiction to examine into or determine any facts that occur on the day of the election in any part of the State, or to exercise any power whatever in changing the result of the votes as sealed and certified under the statements of the commissioners of the election.

A commissioner of election, it will be observed, can make no statement of riot, &c., unless it occurs on *the day of the election,* and he must make it at the time and in the manner provided by law. It must be made while the facts are fresh upon his mind, and his statement must accompany his return of the vote, which shall be within twenty-four hours after the closing of the polls. His return shall be forwarded to the supervisor. The supervisor shall consolidate and forward the said report and returns to the returning-board within twenty-four hours; giving therefore forty-eight hours after the close of the election for the returns to be forwarded to the board of canvass, accompanied by the statements of the commissioners of election, the presence of which affidavits and statements of riot and disorder can alone create any juris-

diction or warrant for any examination into the facts attending the
election by the board of State canvassers.

The statements of the registrars of election must relate to occurrences
within the sixty days preceding the day of the election; and such statements must be forwarded within forty-eight hours after the polls have
closed, as is prescribed for the statements of the commissioners of election, and likewise a copy filed in the office of the county clerk for the
use of the district attorney, and, it may here be remarked, not only for
the use of the district attorney, but as a notification to any person,
being a candidate for office and interested in the election, who shall,
under the provisions of section 3, be allowed a hearing before the returning-officers upon making application within the time allowed for
the forwarding of the returns of said election, that is, within forty-eight
hours after the close of the election.

It is therefore obvious that in order to warrant any examination as is
provided by section 3 into allegations of riot, tumult, violence, &c., at
the different voting-places by the board of returning-officers, and justify
the slightest alteration of the returns or rejection of votes, it is essential
for the protection of the citizens, of the rights of the candidates, for the
purpose of public justice, that such statements shall be made in substance, and within the time, and authenticated in the manner provided
by the law, and not otherwise.

Chief-Justice Marshall, in Thatcher *vs.* Powell, 6 Wheaton, 119, lays
down the rule for the execution of statutory power, even when exercised
by a *judicial* court:

In summary proceedings, where a *court* exercises an extraordinary power under a
special statute prescribing its course, we think that course ought to be *exactly* observed
and *those facts which give jurisdiction* ought to appear in order to show that its proceedings are *coram judice.* Without this act of assembly the order for sale would have been
totally void. This act gives the power *only on a report* to be made *by the sheriff. This
report* gives the court jurisdiction, and *without* it the court *is as powerless* as if the act
had never been passed.

The offer of proof to this Commission goes to the extent that *not a
single jurisdictional fact existed* to authorize the action of the returning-
board in excluding votes in the several parishes.

In the case before the supreme court, above cited, the power of sale
could only be exercised upon a "*report made by the sheriff.*"

In the case of Louisiana the investigation by the returning-board of
alleged riot, &c., at the polls could *only* be made upon the sworn and
corroborated statements sent up within forty-eight hours after the
closing of the polls by the commissioners of election, or the registrars.

No such sworn statement as is provided by law accompanied the returns in a single instance, and no jurisdiction consequently existed to
investigate and exclude polls or votes except "*in the course exactly*" provided by the statute.

The proceedings of the returning-board show that they disregarded
the statute under which they pretended to act and under which alone
they had any claim to jurisdiction, in almost every particular; not
only did they refuse to elect any member of the democratic party,
representing more than one-half of the voters of the State, to fill the
vacancy existing for two years in the board; but they did not in
a single case canvass and compile the returns of election from the
"statements of the commissioners of election" as prescribed by law;
in the case of every poll and voting-precinct they compiled their returns from the consolidated statements of the supervisors of registration, which they had no right to consider, disregarding entirely the
statements of the commissioners of election which alone they were

warranted to consider. The powers of investigation given them in section 3 of the act could only be exercised in such cases in which the returns of the commissioners had been accompanied by statements under oath from the commissioners of election or the supervisors of registration; yet it is proven that in not a single case were the returns accompanied by such statements as alone could warrant the returning-board in instituting investigation into the facts of alleged riot and disorder at the voting-places; that in fact the returning-board in making its pretended canvass did not receive from any poll, voting-place, or parish in the State, nor have before them any statement as required by section 26 of the law and which was an essential prerequisite to the assumption or exercise of any jurisdiction whatever by the board in the investigation or consideration of any alleged disorders at the polls. Not only so, but in the prosecution of their unwarranted investigations they refused to receive or consider evidence which is now offered to this Commission to show that the supervisors of registration fraudulently omitted from their consolidated statements any mention of votes given at certain polls and voting-places within their respective parishes, so that in canvassing and compiling the returns of election from the consolidated statements of the supervisors of registration, (for which they had no legal warrant,) the returning-board carried into their canvass and compilation the numerous and glaring frauds committed by the supervisors of registration in making their consolidated statements.

It is clear that the law of Louisiana required the canvass and compilation of the returns of election to be made from the returns of the *commissioners of election,* and which only could be questioned by the returning-board when they were accompanied by statements of violence, riot, &c., made and forwarded in accordance with the law; but by unlawfully adopting the consolidated statements of the supervisors of registration the returning-board willfully adopted the known frauds of omission of votes cast in several parishes committed by the supervisors; and when such frauds, contained in the consolidated statements, were exposed and shown to the returning-board, and compared with the statements of the commissioners of election, they willfully and fraudulently refused to make any canvass of the true majorities shown by the statements of the commissioners of election; that not having any statements by supervisors of registration or commissioners of election, supported by affidavit as required by law, the returning-board, without pretense of authority, threw out the entire vote cast at different voting-places, and sometimes that of an entire parish; and that in fact the only returns being those of the commissioners of election, which by the laws of Louisiana should have been canvassed and compiled, never were canvassed or compiled by the returning-board at all.

The offers of proof contain a catalogue of specified crimes, embracing perjury, forgery, subornation of perjury, and conspiracy, resorted to by this returning-board for the purpose and with the result of defeating the constitution and the laws of the State of Louisiana and of depriving that State of her right under the Constitution to appoint electors for President and Vice-President.

The case presented for our consideration is whether we will sustain the Constitution and the right of the State of Louisiana under it to have the voice of her people, as proclaimed at the election held on November 7, 1876, hearkened unto and obeyed, or whether we will permit this false personation of the State, a band of infamous men and treacherous officials, to palm off upon the State of Louisiana and upon every State in this Union eight false electoral votes, and by such votes determine the possession of the executive power of this Government for the next four years, and whether we as men sworn to examine and consider all questions submitted to this Commission agreeably to the Constitution and the law, shall in the full view of such a condition of law and fact as I have described set our hands to the statement that the electoral votes of Kellogg and his seven associates, so manufactured by this usurping and lawless returning-board, are " the votes provided for by the Constitution of the United States," and that these eight persons were " duly appointed electors in such State."

It is beyond my comprehension how, in the name of the State of Louisiana and the rights of her people, such a decision can be reached, or how in the name of the people of all the States of this Union, under the Constitution of the United States we can say, as members of this Commission or in our respective places in either House of Congress, that *such* votes are the lawful votes provided for by the Constitution and laws, and that they should be counted. Such a decision, I must frankly say, will shock the moral sense of the country and startle all men who believe in law and justice as controlling influences in this Republic.

It has been stated by counsel who appeared before this Commission on behalf of the Kellogg electors that the gross and fraudulent disfranchisement of many thousands of citizens of Louisiana by the returning-board has been equaled or surpassed in its effect upon the popular vote in Louisiana by the bloody hands of the democratic party. Without pausing to comment upon this allegation of facts, of which no evidence has been offered—and certainly none is attached to the papers opened by the President of the Senate in the presence of the two Houses and transmitted to this Commission—without doing more than merely to note the strange inconsistency of nearly every speaker, whether counsel or objector, whether Senator or Member of the House of Representatives, who has appeared before us, whose arguments or speeches have invariably closed with the most wholesale assertions of violence and intimidation throughout the State of Louisiana, always alleged to have been committed by one party, the democratic, as against the other party, the republican, and who, while protesting against the admission of any evidence, whether of fraud or violence within that State, yet have lost no opportunity to assert and re-assert the existence of extreme violence and intimidation within that State as an excuse, in the nature of a set-off and compensating influence to the admitted frauds of the State officers of election and the returning-board acting in collusion with them — it seems to me that the necessary logic of all such statements and arguments, admitting them to be true, should not be permitted in any way to strengthen the claim of those whose title is imbedded in fraud as against those whose title is said to have been created only by violence, because if the facts of fraud which are offered to be proven, and which for the purposes of this argument are to be taken as established, are to be considered, and in connection with them a wholesale system of riot, violence, and bloody intimidation, the result of these charges combined, if established, would be to prove that there was no such thing as a State government existing in Louisiana; that there was no State, in the American sense of the word, existing there to choose, in such manner as the legislature thereof may direct, a number of electors; but a community in which there is no government of law, republican in form or otherwise, which is in a condition of anarchy, and cannot with safety to the remainder of this Union be treated as a State or suffered to be represented by electors in the choice of a President. Such electors, if these facts be true, are the offspring and representatives of anarchy, and not of republican government; and the argument of the counsel and the objectors who have here appeared for the Kellogg electors, if it is to prevail, must necessarily exclude from the count of electoral votes both of the certificates and votes certified from the State of Louisiana by the respective claimants.

But it is also offered to be proven, and for the purpose of this argument must be considered as proven, that two of the Kellogg electors, O. H. Brewster and A. B. Levissee, held offices at the time of the election on the 7th day of November, 1876, of profit and trust under the United States, the said Levissee being a commissioner of the circuit court of the United States for the district of Louisiana, and the said Brewster being the surveyor-general of the land office of the United States for the district of Louisiana. By the certificate of the Kellogg electors it appears that on calling the roll at the State-house in the city of New Orleans on the 6th day of December, 1876, Levissee and Brewster were found not to be present, and—

At the hour of four p. m. the said Aaron B. Levissee and Orlando H. Brewster, having failed to attend, the electors present proceeded to supply such vacancies by ballot, in accordance with the statute of the State of Louisiana in such case made and provided, which is in words and figures as follows:

"If any one or more of the electors chosen by the people shall fail, from any cause whatever, to attend at the appointed place at the hour of four p. m. of the day prescribed for their meeting, it shall be duty of the other electors immediately to proceed by ballot to supply such vacancy or vacancies."

The six then proceeded to fill the vacancies occasioned by the failure of Levissee and Brewster to attend, and the said Levissee and Brewster were declared unanimously elected to fill such vacancy, and being sent for, soon after appeared, and were in attendance as electors.

The statute of the State of Louisiana under which the alleged "vacancies" were thus attempted to be filled was the act of 1868, which was re-enacted in the precise words on the 14th of March, 1870, the date of the act of revision, which by its terms was to go into effect on the 1st day of April, 1870. Two days after the passage of the act of revision and on the 16th day of March, 1870, a general election law of the State of Louisiana was passed, to take effect from and after its passage. There can be no doubt that the later act repealed the former wherever the provisions of the two were inconsistent or where the repeal shall be found to have been effected in express terms. It cannot be doubted that it was not competent for the legislature by passing a law to take effect at a future day to prevent its repeal by subsequent legislation. The provisions of the act of 1868 and of the revised statutes respecting the election of electors and the filling of vacancies have been read. The law of the 16th of March, 1870, in section 26, provides—

That all elections held in this State to fill any vacancies shall be conducted and managed, and the returns thereof shall be made, in the same manner as is provided for general elections.

And section 35 provides that the election for electors of President and Vice-President—

Shall be held on the Tuesday next after the first Monday in the month of November, in accordance with an act of the Congress of the United States, approved January 23, 1845, entitled "An act to establish a uniform time for holding elections for electors of President and Vice-President in all States of the Union;" and such elections shall be held and conducted, and returns made thereof, in the manner and form prescribed by law for the general elections.

These are the only two provisions respecting vacancies or the election of presidential electors contained in the act. The final section of the act, section 85, provides:

That all laws or parts of laws contrary to the provisions of this act, *and all laws re-*

lating to the same subject-matter, are hereby repealed, and that this act shall take effect from and after its passage.

It appears, therefore, that the act of March 16, 1870, was *in pari materia* with the act of 1868, and the act of revision of March 14, 1870. It provided for the filling of vacancies by election. It provided for the election of electors for President and Vice-President. Whether as fully as prior acts or not is not the question; but the law controlled *the subject*, and by the terms of section 85 repealed expressly "all laws *relating* to the same subject-matter."

But on November 20, 1872, was passed the general election law under which the election of November, 1876, was held. The provisions of this last act which relate to the subject of the election of presidential electors, or to the subject of filling vacancies in office, are to be found in sections 24, 28, 29, 30, and 32.

Section 28 provides only for a new election to be held in case of vacancy caused by death or otherwise in the office of Representative in Congress.

Section 30 provides for filling by election vacancies in the seat of any senator or representative in the general assembly.

Section 29 provides—

That in every year in which an election shall be held for electors of President and Vice-President of the United States, such election shall be held at the time fixed by act of Congress.

Section 32 provides—

That the provisions of this act, *except as to the time of holding elections*, shall apply in the election of all officers whose election is not otherwise provided for.

Section 24 provides—

That *all elections* to be held in this State *to fill any vacancies* shall be conducted and managed, and returns thereof shall be made, in the same manner as is provided for general elections.

Section 71 provides—

That this act shall take effect from and after its passage, and that *all others on the subject of election laws* be, and the same are hereby, *repealed*.

It cannot be denied that the election of electors for President and Vice-President was provided for in the act of 1872, and that by section 32 the provisions of that law, except as to the time of holding elections, were made applicable to all officers whose election was not otherwise provided for. There is no other provision, whether for original election or filling vacancies, than those to which I have referred. It is therefore subsequent legislation in relation to the same subject as to the acts of 1868 and 1870 and the act of revision of 1870; and hence it would appear by the ordinary rules of construction that a repeal had been effected of all the provisions of the earlier acts which related to the same subject. But how can we escape the force of the repealing clause of section 71 (which provides that all other acts *on the subject of election laws* shall be and hereby are repealed) construed in connection with sections 24, 29, and 32?

If this view of the statutes of Louisiana be correct and the act of November 20, 1872, is to be considered the sole and complete regulation of the subject of the appointment of electors and filling vacancies, should any exist, an inspection of its terms will show that it contains no provisions whatever on the subject of filling vacancies in the post of elector except by new elections, and no authority whatever for the remaining electors to fill vacancies in their college.

But the Constitution of the United States, as I have before stated when considering the case of the State of Florida, in authorizing the appointment by each State of its number of electors, inhibits the appointment of either more or different persons than is there described.

The State of Louisiana shall appoint eight electors, " but no Senator or Representative, *or person holding an office of trust or profit under the United States, shall-be appointed*." The inhibition is plain and unmistakable. If an appointment be made by the State in violation of this provision of the Constitution, such appointment is absolutely void. The State can no more appoint a disqualified person an elector than she can appoint a person in excess of her constitutional number of electors; and those who count the electoral votes can no more disregard the provisions of the Constitution in respect of qualification than they can in regard to number. The votes of Levissee and Brewster, both being holders of offices of trust and profit under the United States on the 7th of November, the time of their appointment, can no more be counted than if they had both died the week previous. They are not eligible. The Constitution of the United States in affixing the qualification of Senators and Representatives distinguishes between ineligibility *at the time of election* and ineligibility *at the time of filling the office.* Thus:

No person *shall be* a Representative who shall not have attained the age of twenty-five years, and been seven years a citizen of the United States, and who shall not, *when elected,* be an inhabitant of that State in which he shall be chosen.

And so of a Senator:

No person *shall be* a Senator who shall not have attained to the age of thirty years, and been nine years a citizen of the United States, and who shall not, *when elected,* be an inhabitant of that State for which he shall be chosen.

Frequent decisions by either House of Congress have shown that if when the person elected comes forward "*to be*" a Representative or Senator he shall then, *by that time,* have attained the constitutional age, he is considered as qualified; but if it should be shown that *when elected* he was not an inhabitant of that State for which he was chosen he could not be admitted.

So, in the sixth section of the first article of the Constitution:

No Senator or Representative shall, *during the time for which he was elected,* be appointed to any civil office under the authority of the United States, which shall have been created or the emoluments whereof shall have been increased during such time.

We find an absolute prohibition of the appointment during the time in question. Therefore it is plain that as Levissee and Brewster both held offices of trust and profit under the United States on the 7th of November, 1876, and for some days subsequently, the State of Louisiana was inhibited by the Constitution from making such appointment.

As to the suggestion that these inhibitory clauses of the Constitution are not self-enforcing, it would be very difficult to imagine how legislation can add to the force of the inhibition. Its repetition in a different frame of words would not make it clearer or more powerful. In the clause under consideration it is a limitation upon the power of the State to do a certain act. Each State shall appoint a number of electors, but she shall *not* appoint certain classes of persons. It has been held too often by the Supreme Court of the United States that the inhibitory clauses of the Constitution are all mandatory and self-executing, to make it necessary to produce the various cases affirmative of this doctrine. Perhaps it may be said that by far the greater number of the clauses of the Constitution are self-executing, such as the power of the two Houses over their respective members, the power of impeachment, and the inhibitions upon States:

No State shall enter into any treaty, alliance, or confederation; grant letters of marque and reprisal; coin money; emit bills of credit; make anything but gold and silver coin a tender in payment of debts; pass any bill of attainder, *ex post facto* law, or law impairing the obligation of contracts, or grant any title of nobility.

All these inhibitory clauses and many others have been held self-executing, and are recognized by every court in the land, State and Federal, as controlling legislation. It can scarcely be treated as an invasion of the rights of the State of Louisiana in the count of the electoral votes to see that the Constitution, which controls the subject, has not been violated. There is no difference in the result of voting for an ineligible man, or voting for a dead man, or voting in blank. The result in all such cases is the same, to wit, *a failure to elect*. It has been lately determined in a case growing out of the late election in the State of Rhode Island, in which a centennial commissioner of the United States received a majority of the votes cast in the State of Rhode Island for the office of presidential elector, and in response to the inquiry of the governor the judges of the supreme court of the State advised him that, having held an office of trust under the United States, Mr. Corliss was ineligible to be appointed on November 7, and that the failure to elect had not created a vacancy, but that, under the provisions of section 134 of the Revised Statutes of the United States, whenever any State has held an election for the purpose of choosing electors and has failed to make a choice on the day prescribed by law, the electors may be appointed on a subsequent day in such manner as the legislature of such State may direct; and under this authority the legislature of the State of Rhode Island was convened by the governor and an eligible person appointed elector to supply the failure to elect on the 7th of November.

Section 133 of the Revised Statutes provides that—

Each State may, by law, provide for the filling of any vacancies which may occur in its college of electors when such college meets to give its electoral vote.

From the review just made of the statutes of Louisiana, I am of opinion that no statute exists authorizing the filling of a vacancy in the office of elector; and even should it be held that the statute of 1868 is still in force as respects the office of presidential elector, yet it is manifest that there were no vacancies in the case of Levissee and Brewster, who being ineligible at the time of their original appointment such attempted appointment was utterly void; and that if the failure to elect which had thus occurred in these two cases was to be remedied, it was under the authority of section 134, and not otherwise.

The constitutional limitation upon the power of the State to appoint as electors such office-holders as Levissee and Brewster is equally binding upon this Commission in exercising the powers of the two Houses of Congress over the count of the electoral vote. I do not see how we can decide that these votes are to be counted "agreeably to the Constitution and laws," when they are so plainly forbidden by both.

In full view therefore of the combined and separate exercise of powers by the Senate and House of Representatives over the acceptance or the rejection of electoral votes, I cannot comprehend the abdication of all power whatever by a commission so plainly and expressly endowed with powers over this subject, and the issues plainly framed and submitted for their consideration and decision under the terms of their organic law and under the Constitution and existing law. To "take into view" petitions, not petitions to this Commission, but petitions to either or both Houses of Congress; to "take into view" depositions, not merely depositions taken under the order of this Commission, but depositions, which include affidavits (held by both Houses to be synonymous therewith) taken under the order of either or both Houses of Congress; "and other papers," such papers as parliamentary bodies create and receive and consider, which may "be competent and pertinent," for what and to what? To the decision of parliamentary and legislative subjects; for it is with the powers and duties of two parliamentary bodies that this Commission is invested. To circumscribe these methods of broad and substantial examination to the proportions of mere technical proceedings in courts of common pleas, would be simply to ignore the law and to refuse to exercise our plain duties and powers under it. I will not assume that this Commission will commit so grave an offense.

I have felt very deeply the necessity of not only deciding this case according to law and justice, but also of satisfying the moral sense of our fellow-countrymen. Montesquieu has told us that, as honor is of vital essence to a monarchy, so is morality to a republic. I am perfectly aware of the real condition of the State of Louisiana. I am aware that what they are pleased to term "the rights of the State of Louisiana" have been most loudly proclaimed and sought to be protected in argument before this Commission against the slightest invasion by many who view with complacency her government and her people to-day in absolute subjection to the Army of the United States and its official head. I recognize fully the abnormal condition of affairs that grew out of and has succeeded a period of civil war and wide-spread revolution. I have had no object so near to my heart, and none which has drawn from me more of my energies, than the restoration of all parts and sections of this country to their former harmonious and normal relations to each other and to their common government. I cannot shut my eyes to the fact that the disorder and crime of all grades which mark the history of the last few years in Louisiana, and yet which I believe have been shockingly and shamelessly exaggerated for political purposes, has been chiefly, almost wholly, the result of the destruction of local self-government in that State by the constant interference of Federal power, invariably in favor of that one of the political parties of that State whose interest it has thus been made to produce disorder in order to procure that armed assistance without the aid of which it would long since have disappeared. The eyes of the American people must not be closed to the fact that if the voting material of a community is corruptible, it will be corrupted; if it is purchasable, it will be bought; if ignorant, it will be deceived; and if timid, it will be intimidated; if elections are put up at auction by placing their control in vile hands, whom will you blame? Those who have created such an order of things; surely not those who seek to abolish it. On the one hand you see property seeking protection from plunder in the garb of law, and on the other plunderers in the garb of law offering to sell their official powers; and thus property seeks to buy immunity from plunder by bribing men in office, or, impoverished and despairing, strikes down the robbers with fierce blow.

Tribute was paid to the Moors on the rock of Tarifa, and was only held disgraceful on the part of the merchant or trader who paid it because it implied want of manhood in him to submit. If the men of Louisiana rise up and overthrow Kellogg and his crew, thrust them out of their places, as they did in September, 1874, they are instantly to be denounced and suppressed with a strong hand. If they undertake to buy their peace and protect the remnant of their property by paying part of it to their plunderers, they are denounced as corrupt, and the results of their purchase are taken away from them in the name and for the sake of honesty in elections!

The people of the United States have witnessed this tor years. They have desired to test the real will of the people of that State and give it an opportunity for fair exhibition in public election according to the rules of honest republican government.

The election has been held; and under every disadvantage which the official power of the State and the United States combined could create to overcome the public sentiment, the result is known to have been a clear and undoubted majority of from six to ten thousand votes in favor of the entire democratic or conservative ticket, including the electors for President and Vice-President. And in the face of this fact the contrary is formally certified by Kellogg and his associates. The frauds— open, glaring, and astounding—which have been committed by this returning-board and other officials into whose hands the entire control of the election has been delivered, stink in the nostrils of the public. The election in Louisiana no longer is confined in its effects to the people of the State. It has become a national scandal and shame. The prolonged interference by the Federal Government in the affairs of that State has been all on one side and always with the same bad results; and now the people of the United States demand that the question shall be decided by the two Houses of Congress according to law and justice.

In this case I believe that the certificates of Kellogg and of the returning-board are absolutely and thoroughly false and fraudulent. I believe that the will of the State of Louisiana has been misrepresented and falsified by the action of her officials, and that the means of proof as to what was the choice of that State in the election of November 7 are attainable, capable of production, capable of reduction to a certainty, and that we have no right in law or morals to declare that electoral votes in such palpable defiance of the constitution and laws of the State, in defiance of the express and proven will of the lawful voters of the State, in defiance of the plain inhibitions of the Constitution of the United States, should be counted in the choice for President and Vice-President of the United States.

THE CASE OF OREGON.

On Wednesday, the 21st of February, the case of Oregon came before the Commission. There were two certificates, one signed by Odell, Watts, and Cartwright, certified by themselves alone as presidential electors; the other return signed by Cronin, Miller, and Parker as electors, accompanied by the certificate of La Fayette Grover, the governor of Oregon, stating that William H. Odell, John C. Cartwright, and E. A. Cronin had received the highest number of votes cast at the general election held in Oregon on the 7th day of November, 1876, *for persons eligible* under the Constitution of the United States to be appointed electors of President and Vice-President of the United States. This certificate was attested by S. F. Chadwick, secretary of state of Oregon, and to it was affixed the great seal of the State.

Senator BAYARD said:

The facts of the case are that J. W. Watts, who was voted for as one of the Hayes electors, received 15,206 votes, W. H. Odell received 15,206 votes, J. C. Cartwright received 15,206 votes, E. A. Cronin received 14,157 votes. These facts do not appear in either the governor's certificate of electors provided by act of Congress or the certificate of the electors themselves required by the Constitution of the United States, but are derived from papers and evidence on file in the office of the secretary of state of Oregon, who by law is made the custodian of the same, and has certified to their existence and correctness in the usual manner, having been applied to by Odell, Cartwright, and Watts for copies of the same, and the same having been furnished by him in accordance with their request.

In the cases of Florida and Louisiana, this Commission, by a vote of 8 to 7, refused to receive any evidence *aliunde* the certificates of the officials of the State containing what has been characterized as "the final determination" of the State by its board of canvassing-officers of the result of the election. Therefore, after argument and deliberation in the cases of Florida and Louisiana, it was decided that the certificate of a State board of canvass must be taken as conclusive of the facts it alleged, and could not be in any way impeached either for fraud or error, nor would they permit investigation and proof to be made of the tabulated returns from the various precincts of the State upon which the compilation and canvass by the board had been made. Offers of proof were made to this Commission to show that the board of canvass in Florida had reached an erroneous result by exceeding their jurisdiction, and that the courts of Florida having competent jurisdiction had decided this fact; but this Commission refused to hear or consider any evidence tending to show the erroneous basis upon which the board of canvass in Florida had proceeded.

In the case of Louisiana this Commission refused to hear or consider evidence showing that the board of canvass in that State had proceeded wholly outside of their statutory jurisdiction, had made their pretended canvass without any regard whatever to the law under which they should have acted, had been guilty of the grossest frauds in making their returns, and that the result of their action was wholly fraudulent and unjust, completely defeating the will of the people of the State of Louisiana as expressed by them at the polls. This refusal to consider evidence *aliunde* the certificates was based by the majority of the Commission upon the ground that the rights of the State should be sedulously guarded and protected against the counting power of the two Houses of Congress, and that even were it to be admitted that certificates were falsely and fraudulently furnished to persons not in law and in fact chosen as electors, this being done by the official organs of the State for certifying the result of elections, such persons so furnished with false certificates became nevertheless *de facto* if not *de jure* the possessors of the insignia of office, and not being dispossessed of such insignia until after the functions of the office had been executed on the 6th day of December, 1876, their acts as electors *de facto* must on the ground of public policy be sustained, and that the remedy must be found elsewhere than in the two Houses of Congress to punish them for their misconduct and repair the injury they had committed.

The State board of canvass in Florida consisted of three persons, the attorney-general, the secretary of state, and the comptroller of public accounts, whose duty it is "to canvass the returns of election and declare who shall have been elected, * * * *as shown by such returns.*" The supreme court of the State of Florida have given a construction to the statute under which the State board of canvass acts, and held the powers of that board to be ministerial in their nature, and that they were not invested with such discretion as enabled them to make a declaration of "the legal vote" as distinguished from "the true vote actually cast."

Yet this Commission held itself bound by the certificate of the State board of canvass of Florida, and, refusing to regard or consider the judicial proceedings in that State deciding the very question and fact of the true election of electors, refused to go behind the said certificate or suffer the same to be questioned or in any way impeached, because they alleged that the action of the officers of the State of Florida to whom the duty of canvassing and certifying the result had been committed by the laws could not be questioned, however erroneous or fraudulent or unwarranted by the laws of the State the same may have been.

In the State of Louisiana the board of canvass consists, under the law, of five persons. This Commission refused to hear or consider evidence showing that four men, unlawfully assuming to exercise the powers of the said board, had falsely certified the results of said election, and that their action in pretending to canvass and compile the returns from the State of Louisiana was, in fact, a wicked conspiracy against the rights of the people of that State, her constitution, and her laws; and this refusal to allow the certificate of the returning-board of Louisiana to be impeached for fraud and other illegality was based upon the fact that it was not competent for this Commission to impeach or question the final determination of the officials to whom had been committed the canvass of the returns of the election in the State.

Let us now apply these decisions of the Commission to the case of Oregon.

In section 37 of the election laws of Oregon it is provided that—

The county clerk, immediately after making the abstract of the votes given in his county, shall make a copy of each of said abstracts, and transmit it by mail to *the secretary of state* at the seat of government; and it shall be the duty of the *secretary of state, in the presence of the governor*, to proceed within thirty days after the election, and sooner, if the returns be all received, *to canvass the votes* given for secretary and treasurer of state, State printer, justices of the supreme court, *member of Congress*, and district attorneys.

Section 58 of the same law provides:

On the Tuesday next after the first Monday in November, 1864, and every four years thereafter, there shall be elected by the qualified electors of this State as many electors of President and Vice-President as this State may be entitled to elect of Senators and Representatives in Congress.

Section 60 provides that—

The votes for the electors shall be given, received, returned, and *canvassed* as the same are given, returned, and canvassed for *members of Congress. The secretary of state* shall prepare two lists of the *names of the electors elected*, and affix the seal of the State to the same. *Such lists* shall *be signed by the governor and secretary*, and by *the latter* delivered to the college of electors at the hour of their meeting on such first Wednesday of December.

Thus it will be observed that the secretary of state in Oregon is the canvassing-officer, whose duties are in substance the same as those imposed upon the boards of canvass in Florida and Louisiana. It is provided that the governor is to be present at the canvass, but the canvass itself is to be made by the secretary of state; and when he has canvassed the votes he is to prepare two lists of the names of the electors elected and affix the seal of the State to the same. Whatever powers of judgment and discretion are incident to the power to canvass returns and certify the result are, therefore, as plainly committed to the secretary of state of Oregon, under the laws of that State, as to the boards of canvass of either Florida or Louisiana, under the laws of those States respectively.

" The secretary of state shall prepare," not lists of *votes* such as are on file in his office, but " *lists of the names of the electors elected*." Therefore in the preparation of those lists, in ascertaining the names of the electors elected, the secretary of state necessarily determines and declares what persons were, by the laws of Oregon and by the returns which he has canvassed, chosen the true electors of that State. Such lists so prepared by him shall be signed by the governor and by the secretary, have the seal of the State affixed thereto, and be delivered by the secretary to the college of electors at the hour of their meeting on the first Wednesday in December.

The only certificate thus made in accordance with the laws of Oregon by the board of canvass of that State, authorized to express the final determination of the State of Oregon, is certificate No. 2, by which it appears that William H. Odell, John C. Cartwright, and E. A. Cronin had received the highest number of votes cast at said election for persons eligible under the Constitution of the United States to be appointed electors. Criticism has been made upon the insertion of the words "for persons eligible." These words certainly would be mere surplusage, and the certificate would be as true without them as with them, for if it read that they had been "duly elected" it would have stated the same fact in a different form of words.

Persons not eligible cannot be elected; but the presence of these words, "for persons eligible," is mere surplusage, not affecting the form or the substance of the fact of election certified. Suppose the words "for persons eligible" to have been omitted, and suppose the number of votes stated to have been cast for Cronin and the other candidates had been wholly omitted (and no law requires them to be stated) or had been falsely stated, then according to the rule laid down by this Commission in the cases of Florida and Louisiana we would have been without power to hear evidence *aliunde* the certificate or to exclude the votes so falsely certified. The decision of the Commission was to the effect that no error, intentional or unintentional, on the part of the board of canvass, no excess of jurisdiction, no fraud, however glaring, could be questioned or redressed; yet it is now proposed to examine the powers and proceedings of the canvassing-officer of final determination of the State of Oregon, after having refused to do the same thing in regard to the States of Louisiana and Florida.

To the secretary of state of Oregon are confided the duty and power to make out the lists of electors elected. To enable him to ascertain who are elected, he must canvass and decide. The proof of his decision is to be found in the names of the persons contained in the lists so prepared by him, and to whom, as the college of electors, he delivers such lists. No persons other than those whose names appear on such lists are by the laws of Oregon armed with the insignia of the office of elector. If by fraud or mistake the secretary of state should insert the wrong names upon the lists or deliver the lists to the wrong parties, yet it is done by him under the discretion necessarily involved in the execution of his duties, and according to the decisions of this Commission his action cannot be impeached for error in law or fraud or mistake in fact. Thus if the secretary of state had altered the abstracts of votes sent up to him by the clerks of the various counties, this Commission, according to their decisions in the Louisiana and Florida cases, would have refused to hear evidence to prove it. If the clerks in the various counties had sent up forged and false abstracts, this Commission, according to their decisions, would have refused to allow it to be proven.

The case may be stated thus: The secretary of state of Oregon, seated at his desk and having before him the abstracts of votes from the various counties, may tabulate and compile them upon a sheet of paper, and having finished this canvass and compilation he can transfer the results of his arithmetical calculation to the "lists of electors elected," also prepared by him. If in his canvass of the abstracts of votes he shall commit the most serious errors in adding up the columns of figures representing the votes cast, or if he shall fraudulently alter and misstate the abstracts of the votes before him in his canvass, his certificates, which if allowed to stand will completely overthrow the will of the people of Oregon as expressed at the polls, are, according to the decisions of this Commission in Louisiana and Florida, unimpeachable and impregnable. But it is said his fraud or error in the canvass, however gross, having been completed, cannot be inquired into, but when he comes to make out his lists of electors elected upon the basis of his fraudulent canvass, the accuracy of his transfer of figures from one paper to the other may be inquired into; in other words, a canvassing-officer having a consecutive series of acts to perform under a statute, all of which lead to and form a single result, can be impeached as to one of these acts and not as to any that precede it.

As a matter of fact the canvass and compilation of the votes of Oregon and the preparation of the lists of electors elected are performed by the same official at the same time, and probably within the space of a single hour; and yet if we adopt the reasoning of the majority in the Louisiana and Florida cases, we may scrutinize his returns to see that he has correctly transferred, from his canvass of the votes to the lists of electors elected, certain arithmetical results, but we have no power to scrutinize the features of the transaction which immediately preceded the statement of those results, and his final certificate is a shield that completely protects and covers any and all fraud that lurks behind it.

I cannot bring my mind to assent to such a proposition.

In the case of Louisiana offers were made to this Commission to produce the final canvass of the returns of the election, but they were refused. The certificate of that board of canvass was held to be impenetrable to the rays of truth. I cannot comprehend why the last act of a canvass should be more open to impeachment than equally essential acts which immediately preceded it. Such a decision implies that the fraud of the same individual committed at different stages of his duty is subject to different rules, although those stages are immediately annexed to each other; that you can impeach one act but not its associates.

The certificate of the State of Oregon, under the seal of the State, and signed by the secretary of state and the governor, is as complete and accurate in form and in as substantial accord with the laws of that State as that of Louisiana or Florida which this Commission has refused to permit to be inquired into or impeached; and yet it is now proposed to impeach it and overthrow it because other records of the election of the State of Oregon are produced and certified in opposition to the regular certificate. This evidence is in my judgment admissible. It is both competent and pertinent for us to know the true facts attending the Oregon election, and I shall vote in the case of Oregon, as I did in the cases of Louisiana and Florida, for the admission and consideration of all evidence tending to show which are the true and lawful electoral votes of that State provided for by the Constitution of the United States.

One feature of difference between the cases of Florida and Louisiana and that of Oregon is that no allegation from any quarter is made of fraud in the canvassing officers. It is admitted on all sides, and contradicted nowhere, that the election was fair and free in that State, and that a majority of more than one thousand votes was cast by the people of that State for Odell, Watts, and Cartwright as presidential electors; but it is proven to us that John W. Watts, one of the persons so voted and for whom the highest number of votes were cast, was on the 7th of November, 1876, and until the 13th day of the same month, a postmaster of the United States at the town of La Fayette, in Oregon. Holding, therefore, an office of trust and profit under the United States, he could not under the provision of the Constitution be appointed an elector. Having already considered this quest on in the cases of in eligible electors in Louisiana, I shall not repeat ¹my remarks on that subject.

I have not yet been able to comprehend the force of the argument that the provisions of the Constitution prohibiting the appointment as electors of certain official classes can be held self-executing on the 6th of December but not self-executing on the 7th of November; and this in the teeth of the plain words affixing the disqualification upon the person and the limitation upon the power of the State. It has seemed, however, satisfactory to some minds to hold that this provision of the Constitution grows in power and changes in nature within the hirty days which lie between the appointment of the elector and the time fixed for the performance of his single function; that the Constit utio1 executes itself on the 6th of December, but cannot do so without aid of legislation in the month of November.

What was the result of a majority of the people of Oregon casting their votes for a person thus holding office under the United States? We find in the papers annexed to the certificate of Watts and his associates that on the 6th day of December, at the meeting of Cartwright and Odell as electors, the resignation of Watts as an elector for President and Vice-President of the United States for the State of Oregon was presented by Odell, and after being duly read was " unanimously " accepted; that by this resignation and the acceptance thereof a vacancy n the electoral college was said to have been created, which vacancy, under the provisions of section 59 of the election laws of Oregon, the said Odell and Cartwright assumed the power to fill; that they proceeded to fill such " vacancy " by electing the said John W. Watts, and the college being so filled the three proceeded to cast their votes by ballot for Hayes and Wheeler as President and Vice-President of the United States.

According to my views of the Constitution and laws as heretofore expressed, the failure of the people of Oregon to elect an eligible person to the office of elector did not create a vacancy; but they having failed to elect on the day appointed by law, it was requisite, if the failure was intended to be remedied, to resort to the means prescribed by the one hundred and thirty-fourth section of the Revised Statutes of the United States. There has been no legislation by the State of Oregon on this subject, nor did her legislature on any subsequent day appoint an elector to fill her electoral college.

Section 48 of the election laws of Oregon provides for vacancies in office, and is in the words following:

Every office shall become vacant on the occurring of either of the following events before the expiration of the term of such office:

1. The death of the incumbent;
2. His resignation;
3. His removal;
4. His ceasing to be an inhabitant of the district, county, town, or village for which he shall have been elected, or appointed, or within which the duties of his office are required to be discharged;
5. His conviction of an infamous crime, or of any offense involving a violation of his oath;
6. His refusal or neglect to take his oath of office, or to give or renew his official bond, or to deposit such oath or bond within the time prescribed by law;
7. The decision of a competent tribunal, declaring void his election or appointment.

None of the vacancies above described is the case now under consideration. It is true that Mr. Watts tendered his resignation of the office of elector claiming to have been elected on the 7th of November; but in opposition to that view is the plain mandate of the Constitution of the United States that *he should not be appointed*, consequently he could not resign an office he had never held, nor by any act of *his* could he create a vacancy in such office.

Therefore, I hold that the State of Oregon had no power to appoint John W. Watts, holding then an office of trust and profit under the United States, one of her electors; that his attempted election was absolutely void; and that the failure to elect a third elector has not been remedied according to the Constitution and laws of the United States and the laws of the State of Oregon.

The question then arises as to the right of E. A. Cronin, who by the certificate of the secretary of state and governor, attested by the seal of the State, is certified to have been one of the persons who received the highest number of votes cast at the said election for persons eligible to be appointed electors. The certificate of Governor Grover and the secretary of state is honest and true according to the facts. The number of votes stated in this certificate as having been received by Cronin was 14,157; but it is also made known to us by evidence *aliunde* the certificate, and in *this* case received by the Commission, that a greater number of votes were cast for John W. Watts. Governor Grover has been assailed in terms of unmeasured violence and reprobation for issuing the certificate which is before us, in which he has adopted a construction of the sixteenth section of article 2 of the constitution of Oregon, which provides that—

In all elections held by the people under this constitution the person or persons who shall receive *the highest number of votes shall be declared duly elected.*

Following the unbroken current of decision in the courts of the country from which our institutions have chiefly been derived, and the repeated decisions of courts of the highest jurisdiction in many of the States of this Union, Governor Grover decided, in the execution of the discretion reposed in him as the executive branch of the government of Oregon, that he was bound to issue the certificate of election to the next highest competing candidate in a case like the present, where the candidate who had received the highest number of votes was ineligible to be appointed; and it is very difficult to answer the authorities and arguments by which this position has been supported before us.

The very able arguments which we have heard upon this subject and the elaborate briefs of authorities submitted for our instruction, if they are not adequate to control us in the adoption of the view taken by Governor Grover in this case, are more than sufficient to place his action upon a high plane of conscientious discretion, which lifts him to a level with as sound and reputable jurists as have adorned the bench of England or of the United States. If he has erred in his decision, his error has been justified by learned and able decisions and reasoning which must appeal strongly to the judgment of any who have considered the subject; and yet I have not been able to find, under the laws of Oregon or in my conception of the general American law relating to popular elections, grounds which will enable me to concur in the decision reached by him.

The underlying theory of our republican rule is the residence of power in the majority. That minority candidates should fill places by popular election is contrary to our American theory, although sometimes by constitutional arrangements such a result is reached. But the meaning, nevertheless, of our popular elections is simple and clear, and a vote by one thousand men for A and a vote by five hundred men for B, his opponent, proves not only that the majority desire that A shall fill the office, but also that B should *not* fill it. Where election is free, it is plainly in the power of the popular will to express favor or condemnation, and if it should turn out that the candidate receiving the majority has been ineligible the popular will is sufficiently defeated without the addition of a still further defeat by seating the person *against* whom they have cast their votes.

It is evident to my mind that the statutes of the various States, providing as they do for the filling of vacancies and sometimes for failures to elect, were all intended to prevent the seating of minority candidates; that the policy and intent of our systems of government, both State and Federal, is in substance that none but those who represent the will of the majority are to hold office under a popular rule. If two men are running for the same office and the successful candidate dies on the day after the election, a vacancy would be thus created, and it would have to be filled in some manner provided by law, but the defeated candidate could gain nothing by the death of his opponent. If a candidate receives a majority of the votes, and upon inspection turns out to be ineligible, the rule under the United States statute and by the statutes of the States is to provide for the failure to elect, but not to seat the minority candidate.

Therefore, to give effect to the will of the people fairly expressed according to law at the polls, I would not be willing to vote to seat a minority candidate because of the ineligibility of his opponent, unless the laws of the State should expressly provide that, in the event of the ineligibility of the successful candidate, the person who had received the next highest number of votes should be considered as elected. I do not understand that this is provided for by the laws of Oregon or that any construction of her constitution to this effect has been given by her courts. I repeat that there are strong authorities the other way, in view of which Governor Grover can readily be understood to have felt himself justified in believing that Mr. Cronin was entitled to the place, and certain it is that his certificate that Cronin was one of the three *eligible* candidates for the office who received the highest number of votes is precisely true and is sustained by all the facts in the case.

The Constitution of the United States is the supreme law of the land, and Governor Grover's official oath bound him to sustain it; and it was his duty to refuse to certify the fact of an election of a United States official to the office of elector when the same was distinctly prohibited by the Constitution. As the governor of the State he represents in his own person the executive branch of the State government, and is bound in all respects to see that the laws are faithfully executed; and I therefore consider that, having personal and official knowledge that Watts was a postmaster of the United States, it was his duty to refuse to certify that he had been duly elected presidential elector. It is, therefore, my judgment that but two votes of the State of Oregon can be counted, and that they are the votes of Odell and Cartwright, the Hayes electors.

CASE OF SOUTH CAROLINA.

On the 26th of February the case of the State of South Carolina was reached, there being two certificates, No. 1, of C. C. Bowen and his six associates, certified by D. H. Chamberlain as governor; No. 2, of Theodore R. Barker and his six associates, the Tilden electors, not having any gubernatorial certificate attached. Objections were made under the law to both of the certificates. It was offered to be proven before this Commission that the free election and power of appointment by the State of her electors was interfered with and controlled by the Army of the United States to the number of several thousand men, and by the employment and presence at the polls of an army of United States deputy marshals.

Senator BAYARD said:

It is a public fact of which this Commission will take notice that the executive power of the State of South Carolina was wholly in the hands of Governor D. H. Chamberlain, who was himself a candidate for re-election and had by law the power of appointment and removal of every officer of election throughout the State; and that it was at his instance and in the absence of such a state of facts as under the Constitution of the United States alone would have warranted it, that the State of South Carolina was filled with troops of the United States for months prior to the election, which military occupation continues until this day. The presence and influence of the troops were wholly lent to the support of the political party to which Chamberlain belongs, and were in aid of his re-election and the success of the presidential electors who have obtained his certificate.

The Constitution provides that the electors shall be appointed *by the State;* and in the present case it is offered to be proven to this Commission that the actual power which influenced the appointment of the electors was extraneous to the State, and that in truth and fact the result of the election of electors in the State of South Carolina, on the 7th of November, 1876, was caused and controlled by the unlawful presence of the agents and officials of the Government of the United States; so that the choice was not that of the State or its people, but of Federal officers who had neither right nor color of right to interfere in the election of that State.

It appears that the Tilden electors, Mr. Barker and his six associates, did endeavor by a writ of *quo warranto* to dispute the election of Bowen and his six associates, claiming that the board of State canvassers had made an erroneous, imperfect, false, and fraudulent statement of the result of the election; but the said suit is now pending in the court and undecided. They had previously made application in the supreme court of the State for a writ of mandamus to compel the board of State canvassers to correct the count according to the true vote of the people as cast at the election; but pending that proceeding the board determined and certified the persons elected upon their fraudulent and erroneous count, and after making a return to the court, and just before the decision thereof, they secretly and unlawfully adjourned in defiance and contempt of the authority of the supreme court.

This Commission will also take notice of the illegal and unwarranted interference by Judge Bond, of the circuit court of the United States, who by the most flagrant usurpation and outrage, without having any jurisdiction over the subject-matter or the persons, discharged from custody the board of canvass while they were imprisoned for contempt of the supreme court of the State of South Carolina, having disregarded and disobeyed its mandates in respect of the lawful and regular canvass of the votes cast at said election.

While I am making these remarks Senator Frelinghuysen lays before me and invites my present commentary upon certain expressions made by me in the course of debate in the Senate two years ago when the question of the jurisdiction and powers of the two Houses of Congress over the count of the electoral votes came up for consideration. The passage he has marked is in the Congressional Record, February 25, 1875, page 160, volume 3, part 3:

Mr. President, from the foundation of the Government up to the year 1865 the American people had managed to conduct the count of the electoral votes for President and Vice-President of the United States without any other aid than the constitutional provision and a single statute that had been passed during the first presidential term of George Washington. In 1792, on the 1st of March, an act was passed "relative to the election of a President and Vice-President of the United States, and declaring the officer who shall act as President in case of vacancies in the office both of President and Vice-President." One thing is observable in this act of Congress, as in all acts of that period of our country's history, that great care was taken to assume no power not distinctly granted or necessarily implied by the terms of the Federal Constitution.

Therefore in this law (which is to be found on pages 305, 306, 307, and 308 of the last compilation of the Constitution, Rules, and Manual provided by the Senate) there will be found no attempt to transcend the grant of power of the Constitution as to the reception and count of the electoral votes. It provided the method of certification of the results ; and it will be observed that not only was the manner of the election of the electoral college confided to each State, and to the discretion of the legislature of each State, but that the certification, the authentication of the electoral vote was confided wholly and unreservedly by the Constitution to the States. And nowhere is power given to either House of Congress to pass upon the election, either the manner or the fact, of electors for President and Vice-President ; and if the Congress of the United States, either one or both Houses, shall assume, under the guise or pretext of telling or counting a vote, to decide the fact of the election of electors who are to form the college by whom the President and Vice-President are to be chosen, then they will have taken upon themselves an authority for which I, for one, can find no warrant in this charter of limited powers.

I am very glad that this extract from my former speech has been thus brought to my attention, because I am aware that it has been furnished before now to members of this Commission, although I will not suggest that the object in bringing it now to my notice is to impale me upon a supposed inconsistency between my views as expressed in 1875 and now. To the doctrine, however, contained in these remarks I can only give my renewed approval and assent, although I must frankly admit that within the two years which have elapsed I have had a better opportunity for the study and attention of this subject, which had been denied me then, and which has given to my mind information and light not obtained before. I trust the time will never come when I shall cling obstinately to an error which can only grow into a wrong by becoming willful, nor do I believe that I shall be found to lack the courage to retract an opinion when I am convinced that it is erroneous.

No one believes more than I in the necessity of preserving the rights of the State from invasion by the authority of the General Government, and this it is not necessary for me now to repeat. I consider the election of electors to be the act of the States, who are the sole judges of the manner and the fact of such election, and that Congress has no right to interfere with such choice either by military power or by coercion of swarms of deputy marshals or of the official influence in any shape of any branch of the Federal Government. What I now contend for is that the act of election, which I am called upon thus to respect as the act of the State, shall be the act of the State, and not the act of a false personation of a State. Thus, when in the case of Florida that State, by the voice of every department of her government, legislative, judicial, and executive, came here before us to entreat us to hear her voice, and to prove to us that the electoral votes sent up here for Hayes and Wheeler under the certificate of Governor Stearns were in violation of the State's constitution and laws and in opposition to the will of her people declared at the polls, I felt it to be my duty to that State to hear her complaint. and not allow her rights to be usurped by false men.

In 1875, in the debate in question, I was considering a case where "*the State*" had chosen her electors in fact, and I was endeavoring to protest against congressional interference with the exercise of her free will in making such choice under the Constitution of the United States. I was not then considering a dual government or dual claims to represent that government. When two South Carolinas appear, each claiming to cast votes for President and Vice-President, one must be false, and that question must be decided or the vote of the State rejected.

Again, such a proposition as was stated by me in the debate referred to, was applicable only to the admitted election of a State. The presence of fraud and its effect in qualifying every proposition was not then considered. The most solemn judgments and decrees of courts; pardons by kings and rulers; every treaty or compact between nations or individuals, alike lose every quality of obligation when touched by fraud. I know of no human contract more irrevocable and binding upon the parties than that of Christian marriage, in which civil and religious obligation combine to secure its performance. The sanction under which marriage is entered into is the most solemn known to civilized men; yet who ever denied that the tie could be and ought to be dissolved upon proof of fraud by one of the parties in obtaining the marriage? Fraud is a universal solvent and destroys whatever it touches, and it ought to be hunted down and crushed whenever possible, in order to protect human society. Every proposition as to legal or moral obligation must be considered as made in the absence of fraud, because fraud admitted as an element displaces all the reasoning which guides men in the ordinary conduct of life or in the administration of human laws and justice.

Thus while I hold that the State of South Carolina had the sole power of choosing her electors and of certifying her choice in her own manner, and that no other power can lawfully obstruct and interfere with her choice, when two voices attempt to speak for that State we must ascertain which is the false voice and which is the true. The power to decide which is the true voice has been assumed by Congress to be vested in the two Houses, and by the law under which we are now proceeding this Commission is invested with "the same powers now possessed for that purpose by the two Houses acting separately or together."

The power and duty of decision thus being imposed upon us, the only remaining question is whether we shall execute that power intelligently or blindly; whether we shall receive and consider such evidence as in the nature of things will enlighten our decision or whether it shall be excluded, and the false certificates and usurpations of power be suffered to stand between us and the real State and people whom they falsely assume to represent.

I will admit, whatever may be my personal belief on the subject, that the fact is not established before us by competent testimony that Mr. Barker and his six associates (the Tilden electors) did receive a majority of the votes actually cast at the election in November last in South Carolina, and therefore I shall not vote in favor of such votes being counted; but, on the other hand, the fact is before me as a matter of public knowledge coupled with specific tenders of evidence to establish it, and which must be accepted as true in the consideration of this case, that between the State of South Carolina and her free choice of electors for President and Vice-President was interposed a will and a physical power stronger than her own, and that the election of Bowen and his six associates as certified by Chamberlain, the governor, was not the election of the State of South Carolina and her people, but the election controlled by the President of the United States and the official and political agents of the party in favor of whom he unlawfully lent the great powers intrusted to his control, in disregard of the Constitution, of the law, and the spirit of free government.

The voice which comes up to us in the certificate of Bowen and his associates is the voice of the United States Army, of swarms of deputy United States marshals, aided and abetted by the profligate abuse of judicial power by Judge Bond of the United States circuit court. It is because I am a true friend and defender of the rights of the State of South Carolina that I object to this false expression of her will, and this military mockery of free republican government which is imposed upon her unfortunate people.

We have been urged to reject the vote of this State upon the ground that no registration of her electors has ever been made or provided for by the legislature in conformity with section 3 of article 8 of the constitution of that State, which provides that—

It shall be the duty of the general assembly to provide from time to time for the registration of all electors.

It is contended that by reason of the failure of the legislature to provide such registration no valid election has been held in that State since the time of the formation of its constitution in 1868. To this proposition I am unable to agree. The second section of the same article fixes the qualifications of all persons who "shall be entitled to vote for all officers that are now, or hereafter may be, elected by the people, and upon all questions submitted to the electors at any election;" and among these registration as a voter is not enumerated. It may be doubted whether any new and additional qualification could be imposed by the legislature upon the voters in that State, the section of the constitution to which I have just referred having enumerated the qualifications, and by two provisos having enumerated all classes and persons who are excluded from the right of suffrage.

REMARKS OF MR. COMMISSIONER HUNTON.

FLORIDA.

Mr. Commissioner HUNTON said:

Mr. PRESIDENT: I approach the consideration of the questions involved in this case with profound diffidence. We are sitting as a court, the highest and most august in the history of the world. Dynasty is the subject-matter of the suit to be tried; forty-four millions of people are the parties, and the civilized people of the world are the spectators.

We are to try a disputed presidential election in which it is alleged that fraud and force strangled the true voice of several States of this Union.

We are to determine, when two or more parties have spoken for a State, which is the true voice of that State. In the case of the State of Florida now before us, three papers purporting to be certificates of electoral votes of that State have been sent to the President of the Senate, and under the law they have been by him opened, objected to, and referred to this Commission. One gives the votes of the State to Hayes, the other two to Tilden; which shall be counted?

In order to determine how we shall proceed and what are our powers, it is necessary to examine the law under which we are acting.

In the second section it is provided that—

All the certificates and papers purporting to be certificates of the electoral votes of each State shall be opened, in the alphabetical order of the States, as provided in section 1 of this act; and when there shall be more than one such certificate or paper, as the certificates and papers from such State shall be so opened, (excepting duplicates of the same return,) they shall be read by the tellers, and thereupon the President of the Senate shall call for objections, if any. Every objection shall be made in writing, and shall state clearly and concisely, and without argument, the ground thereof, and shall be signed by at least one Senator and one member of the House of Representatives before the same shall be received. When all such objections so made to any certificate, vote, or paper from a State shall have been received and read, all such certificates, votes, and papers so objected to, and all papers accompanying the same, together with such objections, shall be forthwith submitted to said Commission, which shall proceed to consider the same, with the same powers, if any, now possessed for that purpose by the two Houses acting separately or together, and by a majority of votes decide whether any and what votes from such State are the votes provided for by the Constitution of the United States, and how many and what persons are duly appointed electors in such State, and may therein take into view such petitions, depositions, and other papers, if any, as shall, by the Constitution and now existing law, be competent and pertinent in such consideration.

This Commission has all the powers now possessed for this purpose by the two Houses of Congress or either one. If the two Houses or either one has any power to look into and decide these matters, then that power is conferred on this Commission.

This Commission is to decide whether any and what votes from this State are the votes provided for by the Constitution, and how many and what persons were duly appointed electors in this State, and shall take into view such petitions, depositions, and other papers, if any, as shall by the Constitution and now existing law be competent and pertinent in such consideration.

What are the powers of the two Houses, or either one?

This law was enacted on the theory and concession that the President of the Senate has no power to *count* the electoral vote, and that power in case of double returns was committed to this Commission.

What is this power to count? Is it merely to add up and declare the number of votes from a State? This cannot be, because we should be stopped at the beginning by the appearance of two or more returns. We must determine which of these returns is the true return, which of these votes " are the votes provided for by the Constitution," and " how many and what persons were *duly* appointed electors in such State." To do this demands examination, scrutiny, and consideration of all the facts on which the several sets of electors proceeded to cast their votes. The law gives the powers possessed by the two Houses or either one of them, and makes a legislative declaration of the right and imposes the duty to decide whether any and what votes are the votes provided by the Constitution. The two Houses of Congress possess this power or they have been on many occasions guilty of gross usurpation of power. Doubts arose in 1817 about the right of the electors of Indiana to cast their vote, in 1821 in Missouri, and in 1837 in Michigan. (See House Document 13, pages 46, 51, and 72.) In each of these cases the votes of the States were counted in the alternative. In 1865 the electoral votes of the eleven seceded States were rejected by both Houses in the electoral count. (Page 229.) In 1869 the vote of Louisiana was objected to on the ground of fraud, and the same was considered and counted. (Page 238.) In 1873 there were two certificates and seven objections raised to the vote of Louisiana. The vote of that State was not counted. (Page 391.) In 1873 the vote of Georgia was not counted because it was cast for a dead man. (Page 407.)

The action of the two Houses of Congress on these several occasions shows that this power in the opinion of these Houses did exist. They were precedents in existence when the law framing this Commission was enacted and must be considered in construing the law. But what are the constitutional provisions on this subject?

ARTICLE II.

Each State shall appoint, in such manner as the legislature thereof may direct, a number of electors, equal to the whole number of Senators and Representatives, to which the State may be entitled in the Congress; but no Senator or Representative or person holding an office of trust or profit under the United States, shall be appointed an elector.

ARTICLE XII.

The electors shall meet in their respective States and vote by ballot for President and Vice-President, one of whom, at least, shall not be an inhabitant of the same State with themselves; they shall name in their ballots the person voted for as President, and in distinct ballots the person voted for as Vice-President, and they shall make distinct lists of all persons voted for as President and of all persons voted for as Vice-President, and of the number of votes for each; which lists they shall sign and certify, and transmit sealed to the seat of Government of the United States, directed to the President of the Senate. The President of the Senate shall, in the presence of the Senate and House of Representatives, open all the certificates and the votes shall then be counted—the person having the greatest number of votes for President shall be the President, if such number be a majority of the whole number of electors appointed; and if no person have such majority, then from the persons having the highest numbers not exceeding three on the list of those voted for as President, the House of Representatives shall choose immediately, by ballot, the President. But in choosing the President, the votes shall be taken by States, the representation from each State having one vote; a quorum for this purpose shall consist of a member or members from two-thirds of the States, and a majority of all the States shall be necessary to a choice. And if the House of Representatives shall not choose a President whenever the right of choice shall devolve upon them, before the 4th day of March, next following, then the Vice-President shall act as President, as in the case of death or other constitutional disability of the President.

The person having the greatest number of votes as Vice-President shall be the Vice-President, if such number be a majority of the whole number of electors appointed; and if no person have a majority, then from the two highest numbers on the list the Senate shall choose the Vice-President; a quorum for the purpose shall consist of two-thirds of the whole number of Senators, and a majority of the whole number shall be necessary to a choice.

The Congress may determine the time of choosing the electors, and the day on which they shall give their votes; which day shall be the same throughout the United States.

These are the constitutional provisions on this subject, and by them the power to *appoint* electors is given to the States to be exercised in such manner as the legislature may direct, and the only limitation on this power to appoint is that " no Senator or Representative, or person holding an office of trust or profit under the United States, shall be appointed."

It is conceded that the power to appoint belongs to the State, but it is our power and duty under this law to decide who has been appointed by the State. The State appointed, if at all, on the 7th of November, 1876. The question for us to decide is whom did she appoint or who were duly appointed electors and which are the votes provided for by the Constitution.

I cannot doubt our power to go into the inquiry which set of electors uttered the true voice of the State of Florida.

It is offered in proof by counsel for objectors to the certificate of the Hayes electors as follows:

First. On December 6, 1876, being the regular law day, both the Tilden and the Hayes electors, respectively, met and cast their votes and transmitted the same to the seat of Government. Every form prescribed by the Constitution, or by any law bearing on the subject, was equally complied with by each of the rival electoral colleges, unless there be a material difference between them in this respect: The certified lists provided for in section 136 of the Revised Statutes were, as to the Tilden electors, certified by the attorney-general, and were, as to the Hayes electors, certified by Mr. Stearns, then governor.

All this appears of record; and no additional evidence is needed in respect to any part of it.

Secondly. A *quo warranto* was commenced against the Hayes electors in the proper court of Florida on the said 6th of December, 1876, before they had cast their votes, which eventuated in a judgment against them on January 25, 1877, a determination that the Tilden electors were duly appointed. The validity and effect of this judgment is determinable by the record, and no extrinsic evidence seems to be desirable on either side, unless it be thought—

1. That the Tilden electors should give some supplemental proof of the precise fact that the writ of *quo warranto* was served before the Hayes electors cast their votes, or

2. It be desired on the other side to show the entry and pendency of an appeal from the judgment in the *quo warranto*.

With these two possible and very slight exceptions, the whole case in this branch of it depends upon the record.

Thirdly. To show what is the common law of Florida, and to show also the true construction of Florida statutes, the Tilden electors desire to place before the Commission the record of a judgment of the supreme court in that State on a *mandamus* prosecuted on the relation of Mr. Drew, the present governor of that State, by force of which Mr. Stearns was ousted and Mr. Drew was admitted as governor. This judgment, together with the court's opinion, are matters of record and they require no other proofs, nor is there any technical rule as to the manner in which this Commission may inform itself concerning the *law* of Florida.

Fourthly. The legislation of Florida authorizing a new canvass of the electoral vote and the fact of such new canvass, the casting anew of the electoral votes and the due formal transmission thereof to the seat of Government, in perfect conformity with the Constitution and laws, (except that they were subsequent in point of time to December 6, 1876,) are all matters of record and are already regularly before the Commission.

Fifthly. The only matters which the Tilden electors desire to lay before the Commission by evidence actually extrinsic will now be stated:

1. The board of State canvassers, acting on certain erroneous views when making their canvass, by which the Hayes electors appeared to be chosen, rejected wholly the returns from the county of Manatee and part of returns from each of the following counties, to wit: Hamilton, Jackson, and Monroe.

In so doing the said State board acted without jurisdiction, as the circuit and supreme courts in Florida decided. It was by overruling and setting aside as not warranted by law these rejections that the courts of Florida reached their respective conclusions that Mr. Drew was elected governor, that the Hayes electors were usurpers, and that the Tilden electors were duly chosen.

No evidence that in any view could be called extrinsic is believed to be needful in order to establish the conclusions relied upon by the Tilden electors, except duly-authenticated copies of the State canvass and of the returns from the above-named four counties, one wholly and the others in part rejected by said State canvassers.

2. Evidence that Mr. Humphreys, a Hayes elector, held office under the United States.

Sixthly. Judging from the objections taken by those supporting the Hayes electors, and the opening arguments here offered in their behalf, it is believed that no evidence is needed or intended to be offered by the supporters of the Hayes electors, unless it be—

1. That the above-mentioned appeal was taken.

2. That Mr. Humphreys, one of the Hayes electors, had resigned his office under the United States before his appointment as an elector.

This is the proof they offer to us. They say they can make good this offer by the production of evidence, and they propose to *satisfy* the minds of this tribunal, if allowed, that the State of Florida, on the 7th day of November, 1876, appointed Tilden electors, and that they, and they alone, are "the duly-appointed electors of the State."

One would suppose, when the past action of Congress on this subject and the provisions of the electoral bill are considered, that there would be no voice raised here against hearing this evidence; but it was maintained by counsel, and is insisted on here, that the Hayes electors, having the governor's certificate, based on the certificate of the returning-board, we cannot go behind these certificates to inquire whether they contain the truth or are false and fraudulent.

It must be conceded that there may be cases which will force an examination into the truth of these certificates.

Suppose it were alleged that these certificates are forged, it will hardly be maintained that they would present a conclusive case. Can a forged certificate be less powerful than a fraudulent one? Would any one desire to uphold a fraud any more than a forgery?

By the laws of Congress it is provided:

SEC. 136. It shall be the duty of the executive of each State to cause three lists of the names of the electors of such State to be made and certified, and to be delivered to the electors on or before the day on which they are required, by the preceding section, to meet. (1 Mar., 1792, c. 8, s. 3, v. 1, p. 240.)

The laws of Florida also provide for certificates from the returning-board and from the governor to the electors. I deny under the precedents (already cited) of the action of the two Houses and under the authorities that these certificates are conclusive. I maintain that they furnish evidence of the action of the State in the appointment of electors not conclusive but *prima facie*, and that we have the right to go behind them to ascertain whether they speak the truth or are fraudulent and false.

Chief-Justice Whiton, in 4 Wisconsin, 792, commenting on the effect of certificates of canvassers, says:

Before proceeding to state our views in regard to the law regulating the canvass of votes by the State canvassers, we propose to consider how far the right of a person to an office is affected by the determination of the canvassers of the votes cast at the election held to choose the officer. Under our constitution, almost all our officers are elected by the people. Thus the governor is chosen, the constitution providing that the person having the highest number of votes for that office shall be elected. But the constitution is silent as to the mode in which the election shall be conducted, and the votes cast for governor shall be canvassed, and the result of the election ascertained. The duty of prescribing the mode of conducting the election and of canvassing the votes was, therefore, devolved upon the legislature. They have accordingly made provision for both, and *the question is, whether the canvass, or the election, establishes the right of a person to an office.* It seems clear that it *cannot be the former,* because by our constitution and laws it is expressly provided *that the election by the qualified voters shall determine the question.* To hold that the canvass shall control would subvert the foundations upon which our government rests. But it has been repeatedly contended in the course of this proceeding that although the election by the electors determines the right to the office, yet the decision of the persons appointed to canvass the votes cast at the election settles finally and completely the question as to the persons elected, and that, therefore, no court can have jurisdiction to inquire into the matter. It will be seen that this view of the question, while it recognizes the principle that the election is the *foundation* of the right to the office, assumes that the canvassers have authority to decide the matter finally and conclusively. We do not deem it necessary to say anything on the present occasion upon the subject of the jurisdiction of this court, as that question has already been decided and the reasons for the decision given. Bearing it in mind, then, that under our constitution and laws it is *the election* to an office, and not *the canvass* of the votes, which determines the right to the office, we will proceed to inquire into the proceedings of the State canvassers by which they determined that the respondent was duly elected.

The title to an elective office is derived from the people through the ballot-box. Somebody must declare the will of the electors as thus expressed. Canvassers are provided for that purpose. The certificate of a board of canvassers is evidence of the person upon whom the office has been conferred. Upon all questions arising collaterally, or between a party holding the certificate and a stranger, it is conclusive evidence; but, in a proceeding to try the right to the office it is only *prima facie* evidence. In such a proceeding, now regarded as a civil action, it is competent for the court to go behind the adjudication of the canvassers. The whole question is thrown open, and extrinsic evidence is allowed to show which was the true state of the votes. In such an action, where the right to the office is the very thing in issue, the court will allow nothing to stand in the way between it and the ballot-box. It will put in requisition all the means within its reach to ascertain the expressed will of the electors, and will conform its judgment to such ascertained will. (Morgan *vs.* Quackenbush, 22 Barb., 72.)

In deciding the question as to which candidate has received the greater number of votes cast by the electors for a particular office, the court and jury will go behind the canvass to ascertain the intention of the voters, and when ascertained, will give effect

to that intenion by giving to each candidate the votes the voters gave him. (People
vs. Ferguson, 8 Cow., 102 ; People *vs.* Cook, 8 N. Y., 67, 83 ; People *vs.* Pease, 27 N. Y., 45 ;
People *vs.* Love, 63 Barb., 535 ; People *vs.* Wilson, 62 N. Y., 186 ; People *vs.* Vail, 20 Wend.,
12.)

These authorities and many more that might be cited prove that the
certificates are not the election. They only form evidence in one form
of the result of it.

It is further submitted that no law that could be enacted in Florida
could make these certificates conclusive and absolutely binding on the
two Houses or this Commission in the electoral count. That State could
by law make a certificate binding and conclusive between her own citizens, but cannot give it this effect out of the State between persons not
her citizens.

It has been declared that to go behind these certificates and to find
contrary to them would be a violation of State rights. I am an advocate for State rights of the straitest sect. I did not, I do not expect
to learn a lesson in that direction from those who have proclaimed it in
this case. Indeed, it is feared that it is used here to cover up a great
wrong to a State. But in this case these new-made converts to the doctrine need have no apprehension, because the State of Florida, through
the executive, legislative, and judicial departments of her State government, has labored to convince us and the country that the Hayes electors are not the duly-appointed electors of that State. She has done
what she could to correct this great wrong, and she relies on us to do
the balance.

When the Hayes electors met and before their vote was cast, the Tilden electors commenced a *quo warranto* proceeding against them, which
it is offered to prove was served before the vote was cast. On the 25th
of January, 1877, judgment was rendered in the case, declaring that the
Hayes electors were usurpers and that the Tilden electors were duly
appointed. From this judgment there was an appeal, but it has never
been reversed. The vote for the Tilden electors was about the same as
the vote for Drew, the democratic candidate for governor. If one was
duly elected the others were. This same returning-board that gave certificates to the Hayes electors also gave certificates to Stearns, the opponent of Drew.

On a mandamus prosecuted by Drew against Stearns in the highest
court of Florida, Mr. Stearns was ousted and Mr. Drew installed as governor.

The effect of these two decisions is to declare by the courts of Florida
what the laws of Florida are, and when so declared these decisions bind
all other courts as fully as if the decisions had been incorporated into
the law.

But it is said that the electors became *functus officio* before the judgment in *quo warranto.* Although the electors had voted before the
judgment in *quo warranto*, yet that judgment was rendered in time to
instruct us on the point which we are to decide and determine, to wit,
which set of electors has been duly appointed.

The court had jurisdiction to proceed to judgment after December 6,
according to the current of authorities both in England and this country. When the office shall expire before judgment, the court may in
its discretion refuse the writ ; but when once granted it must go on to
judgment.

In The People *vs.* Sweeting, 2 Johns., 184, the supreme court of New
York, in denying a similar application, said :

This court has a *discretion* to grant motions of this kind or to refuse them, if no sufficient reasons appear for allowing this mode of proceeding.

That this was the sole effect of this decision appears from the subsequent case of The People *vs.* Tibbetts, 4 Cow., 358, 381, bottom. Here the same court granted such a motion for leave to file an information, notwithstanding the former case, which was cited and considered. They say :

Here the motion was brought before us at the term next after the election. We cannot refuse it upon the mere chance that a trial may fail. To do this would be equivalent to a refusal in all cases where the office is annual; a length to which we presume the court did not intend to go, and to which it was not necessary they should go, in The People *vs.* Sweeting. On the whole, we are clear upon the nature of the case as to our right of allowing the information to be filed ; and that the lapse of time is not such as to require us *in the exercise of a sound discretion* to deny it.

Says Chief-Justice Ames, in delivering the opinion of the supreme court of Rhode Island, State *vs.* Brown, 5 Rhode Island, 1 :

When the information is filed all the discretionary power of the court is expended, and the issues of law or fact raised by the pleadings must be tried and decided under the law and in the same manner and with the same strictness as in any other case, civil or criminal. (P. 4.)

According to these decisions the court in Florida had jurisdiction to issue and try this *quo warranto*, and the judgment that the Tilden electors were the duly appointed electors of Florida until reversed binds all courts in the United States.

This judgment and that in mandamus settle the question that according to the laws of Florida the canvassing-board committed an error (to use no stronger term) in granting certificates to the Hayes electors and that their certificate and that of the governor founded on it gave the said Hayes electors no valid title to their office, and that the Tilden electors were duly appointed.

But the State of Florida did not stop here. Upon the decision of the mandamus Governor Drew was installed into office with his democratic associates on the State ticket, and also a democratic legislature. The old returning-board, consisting of the secretary of state, attorney-general, and comptroller of public accounts, died, and the new board under mandamus came into office.

Under a law of the new legislature passed in January, 1877, a new canvass was held and the Tilden electors declared elected ; this was followed by the certificate of the governor. About the same time another act was passed declaring that the Tilden electors were the duly appointed electors of that State. Thus the State of Florida has, through all of its three several departments, declared that according to her laws the Tilden electors were duly chosen. In the face of all this accumulated evidence of the truth shall we shut our eyes and say we will hear nothing on the subject ? We are acting under a law which requires us to decide " what persons were duly appointed electors " in Florida, and yet we are urged to decide this grave question in favor of one set of electors on the governor's certificate and that of the returning-board, when before our eyes stands evidence which must be satisfying to all that the other set was duly elected. They also offer to produce for our consideration the actual vote of the State that we may revise the canvass for ourselves and decide according to the laws of Florida and the very right of the case. If this offer of proof be rejected, let it not be on the affectation of regard for the rights of the State of Florida. She is suffering under a grievous State wrong, and through all her departments has tried to correct it, and is now stretching out her hands to us for relief. I cannot believe this Commission will refuse to hear this testimony, and (if it comes up to the offer of proof) to correct this foul wrong.

But it has been maintained that though the Hayes electors may not have been duly appointed and though the Tilden electors may have been duly appointed on the 7th of November, yet as the Hayes electors had some color of authority under the governor's certificate, they became *electors de facto*, and their action in casting the vote of the State for Hayes was binding on all persons. What a monstrous doctrine! It must shock the moral sense of every member of this Commission.

It will be recollected that both sets of electors, each claiming to be the duly appointed electors of Florida, met according to law at the same time and with the same forms cast their votes—the one for Hayes, the other for Tilden. We are told we cannot inquire which was the true set of electors, because one set had the governor's certificate, and because they were the *de facto* electors. This seems an entirely new application of the doctrine, and common sense will answer and repudiate it. Where two persons both claiming to hold an office attempt to discharge the duties of the office at the same time, there can be no claim on the part of either that he is a *de facto* officer. One or the other is *de jure*, and his acts must be respected and those of the other repudiated.

The doctrine of the authorities on this subject seems to be this: If the act of the *de facto* officer has not operated to accomplish some change in the relation of parties to each other or to property or to the public, such acts will not be regarded, especially if a like act was performed by the officer *de jure* at the same time. (Wilcox *vs.* Smith, 5 Wend., 231. Hildreth *vs.* McIntire, 1 J. J. Marshall, 206. Green *vs.* Burke, 23 Wend., 490.)

It cannot be that the fact that the Hayes electors acted can give validity to their acts when there could be no inquiry here unless they had acted and the very question to decide is which of the two parties acting had the right to act, and before the act of either was accomplished by the count here this action on the part of the Hayes electors was declared void by the court of Florida.

But the proof is also offered that one of the Hayes electors, Mr. Humphreys, held an office of trust and profit under the United States Government at the time of his appointment.

Surely we cannot refuse to hear this proof.

The Constitution says in article 2, section 1:

The executive power shall be vested in a President of the United States of America. He shall hold his office during the term of four years, and together with the Vice-President, chosen for the same term, be elected as follows:

Each State shall appoint, in such manner as the legislature thereof may direct, a number of electors, equal to the whole number of Senators and Representatives to which the State may be entitled in the Congress; but no Senator or Representative, or person holding an office of trust or profit under the United States, shall be appointed an elector.

The right and power to appoint electors is not an original State right, not one of those rights reserved to the State in the formation of the Constitution. Without the Constitution and the Union it formed, there would have been no such thing as presidential electors. It was a power and a right secured by the compact to each State and owed its existence to the compact. The power, then, must be exercised in conformity to the compact. If there is a limitation on this right or an inhibition on its exercise, this limitation or inhibition must be respected or the exercise of the right is void. The power to appoint electors in the Constitution is subject to the limitation on that power in these words: "But no Senator or Representative, or person holding an office of trust or profit under the United States, shall be appointed an elector." This is an express limitation on the right to appoint electors, and if the State does appoint any of the prohibited class, it is void. She has under the Constitution no more right to appoint such than she would have to appoint any if this section of the Constitution had not been adopted.

The States can now fail or refuse to appoint electors. If so, then they decline to take part in electing a President. If Florida appoints three eligible electors and one who is ineligible, then she can only give three votes for President instead of four.

It is plain that the object of this prohibition or limitation of the power of appointment was wise. It was to prevent the interference of Federal officers in the presidential election—to make the electoral colleges independent of the existing President and prevent him from re-electing himself or naming his successor.

It has always been considered a wise and salutary provision which should be rigidly adhered to.

In the presidential count of 1837 it was suggested that several postmasters had been appointed electors. A committee was raised to ascertain and report on this matter. Felix Grundy, Henry Clay, and Silas Wright were members of this committee on the part of the Senate, and the following is an extract from the report, submitted by Mr. Grundy:

The committee are of opinion that the second section of the second article of the Constitution, which declares that "no Senator or Representative, or person holding an office of trust or profit under the United States, shall be appointed an elector," *ought to be carried, in its whole spirit, into rigid execution, in order to prevent officers of the General Government from bringing their official power to influence the elections of President and Vice-President of the United States. This provision of the Constitution, it is believed, excludes and disqualifies deputy postmasters from the appointment of electors; and the disqualification relates to the time of the appointments, and that a resignation of the office of deputy postmaster, after his appointment as elector, would not entitle him to vote as elector under the Constitution.*

In the debate ensuing in the House of Representatives upon the report of the joint committee, Mr. Francis Thomas, chairman of the House committee, said that " the committee came unanimously to the conclusion that they (the postmasters in question) were not eligible at the time they were elected, and therefore the whole proceeding was vitiated *ab initio.*"

These great men, considering it most important that this provision should be strictly adhered to, gave strong and convincing reasons for it, and declared that the appointment of such was a void act; that the disqualification relates to the time of appointment, and that subsequent resignation of Federal office before voting in the electoral college did not entitle one to vote as elector. Unfortunately, the votes of those ineligible electors did not affect the presidential count of 1837, and no legislation followed; but the principle then declared is as true to-day as it was when declared. Ever since the Wilkes case in the British Parliament, it has been held in a long and almost harmonious current of decisions, both in this country and in England, that the election or appointment of an ineligible person is a void act. Authorities differ as to whether the next highest candidate is elected, but I know of no case in which the ineligible candidate was held to be elected.

I beg leave to refer to some of the leading cases in which this doctrine was held.

The doctrine was held in the case of Searcy *vs.* Grow, 15 Cal., 118, where the opinion was pronounced by Baldwin, J., Cope, J., and Field, C. J., concurring. It was a contest for the office of sheriff of Siskiyou County. Grow had been returned as elected to the office. At the time of the election he was postmaster in the town of Yreka, the compensation of which exceeded $500 per annum. The court below found for

Searcy, and Grow appealed. The constitution of California provides that "no person holding any lucrative office under the United States or in their power shall be eligible to any civil office of profit under this State, provided that officers in the militia to which there is attached no annual salary, or local officers and postmasters whose compensation does not exceed $500 per annum, shall not be deemed lucrative." Grow was postmaster at the time of his election, but had resigned at the time of his qualifications. The supreme court unanimously affirmed the judgment of the court below.

In the opinion, Justice Baldwin says, (page 121:)

The people in this case were clothed with this power of choice. Their selection of a candidate gave him all the claim to the office which he has. His title to the office comes from their designation of him as sheriff. But they could not designate or choose a man not eligible—that is, not capable of being selected. They might select any man they chose, subject only to this exception: that the man they selected was capable of taking what they had the power to give. We do not see how the fact that he became capable of taking office after they had exercised their power can avail the appellant. If he was not eligible at the time the votes were cast for him, the election failed. We do not see how it can be assumed that by the act of the candidate the votes which, when cast, were ineffectual, because not given for a qualified candidate, became effectual to elect him to office. (Price *vs.* Baker, 41 Ind., 572; Stewart *vs.* Hayes, 3 Chicago Legal News, 117; State *vs.* Giles, 1 Chand., Wis., 112; State *vs.* Boal, 46 Mo., 426; Saunders *vs.* Haynes, 13 Cal., 145.)

The electors must be all appointed on the same day under the act of Congress, Revised Statutes—

SEC. 131. Except in case of a presidential election, prior to the ordinary period, as specified in sections 147 to 149 inclusive, when the offices of President and Vice-President both become vacant, the electors of President and Vice-President shall be *appointed* in each State on the Tuesday next after the first Monday in November in every fourth year succeeding every election of a President and Vice-President.

The appointment must be complete on that day. The canvass and certificate made after are only evidence of appointment, and cannot be said in any sense to be an appointment. These questions were well considered in a case in Rhode Island growing out of the appointment on the 7th of November, 1876, of George H. Corliss as an elector. Corliss was at the date of election (the day of appointment) a Centennial commissioner. The question of his eligibility was submitted by the govenor to the supreme court.

The following is a history of the action of the court in the matter of George H. Corliss, (16 American Law Register, N. S., 15, number for January, 1877.) Corliss was a Centennial commissioner on November 7, 1876, when the qualified voters of Rhode Island cast a majority of their votes for him for the office of presidential elector. The governor, under the laws of Rhode Island, submitted to the supreme court five questions, the answers to which were to guide his actions in making the required executive list of electors appointed. Of these the third, upon the assumption that the court should answer that the office was one of trust and profit under the Constitution of the United States, was: "Is the disqualification removed by the resignation of said office of trust and profit?" There was a dissenting opinion of one judge out of five in answer to the first question, but all agreed in answering the third question as follows:

We think the disqualification is not removed by the resignation of the office of trust unless the office is resigned before the election. The language of the Constitution is that "no person holding an office of trust or profit under the United States shall be *appointed* an elector." Under our law, (General Statutes, chapter 11, sections 1 and 2,) the election by the people constitutes the appointment. The duty of the governor is to examine and count the votes, and give notice to the elector. He merely ascertains—he does not complete—the appointment. A resignation therefore, after the election is too late to be effectual.

Upon reason and authority both, Humphreys, if a Federal officer on the day of election, could not act as elector, even though he resigned his Federal office before the 6th of December, when he attempted to vote.

Shall we then refuse to hear evidence to show that he held Federal office on the 7th November, 1876?

An attempt is made to liken this provision of the Constitution to the third clause of the third section of article 1:

No person shall be a Senator who shall not have attained to the age of thirty years, and been nine years a citizen of the United States, and who shall not, when elected, be an inhabitant of that State for which he shall be chosen.

This provision it is claimed has never prevented a person from being Senator who is at the time he is sworn in thirty years of age and who has then been nine years a citizen of the United States.

But how different is the language of these two provisions. In the former the language is, "no person shall be appointed." In the latter, "no person shall be a Senator." He is not a Senator until he is sworn in, and then the qualifications apply. He cannot be called Senator until he assumes the duties of that high position. He is only a Senator-elect and may never become a Senator. There is much more similarity in the last prohibition as to Senator, to wit, "and who shall not when elected be an inhabitant of the State for which he shall be chosen." No case can be found where this ineligibility of non-residence at date of election has been removed by afterward becoming an inhabitant. He must at the date of election be an inhabitant, or he is forever disqualified. Nothing occurring subsequently can remove this ineligibility. So with an elector—he must not *when appointed* be a Federal officer. If he is, no resignation can make him eligible.

Suppose the State of Florida had attempted to appoint her two Senators and two Representatives her four electors, and they had met, formed an electoral college, and cast their votes for President and Vice-President, will any one maintain that such votes could be counted or that we could not go behind the certificates to ascertain if those four men were her Senators and Representatives? Could we, who have sworn to support the Constitution, and have also sworn to decide what are the votes of the State of Florida *provided for by the Constitution of the United States*, decide that these Senators and Representatives had cast the votes provided for by the Constitution, which in terms prohibits them from being electors?

The statement of the case is the answer to the proposition.

Mr. President, when I consider the past action of the two Houses of Congress, the phraseology of the law under which we are acting, the offers of proof, and the authorities which I have examined, I have no doubt left on my mind that it is not only our right but our duty to hear the proof offered and to decide which certificate contains the true and lawful electoral vote of Florida. Any other course would disappoint the expectations of the country, looking to us to solve this vexed presidential election according to the very right of the case. Any other course dwarfs this high Commission into a tribunal to ascertain merely whether the four votes of Florida have been correctly added up or not, and whether the governor's certificate accompanies the votes. This duty might as well have been performed by a page of either House. The business of the two Houses would not then have been interrupted by withdrawing five members from each House, and waiting for days for us to arrive at the *most difficult decision* that Florida had really cast four votes and that the electors who cast the four votes had the governor's certificate. The business of the Supreme Court would not then have been entirely suspended by the withdrawal of five of its associate justices, to form this Commission, and play the rôle of boys in primary arithmetic. No, sir, this Electoral Commission was designed (as the law creating it directs) to "decide whether any and what votes from such State are the votes provided for by the Constitution of the United States, and how many and what persons were duly appointed electors in such State." To do this and to discharge our duties under the bill and satisfy our consciences under the oaths we have taken, we must go behind these certificates and ascertain whether they represent the persons duly appointed electors.

LOUISIANA.

Mr. Commissioner HUNTON said:

Mr. PRESIDENT: We have reached the second State in the history of this Commission, and it remains to be seen whether the frauds, forgeries, and perjuries by which the certificate of the returning-board of Louisiana was sustained are to be upheld by this Commission; whether the vote of this State is to be counted for Hayes on the certificate of the governor, based on the certificate of the returning-board, when proof is offered that these certificates are founded on fraud, forgery, and perjury; whether the vote of Louisiana is to be counted for Hayes when the proof is offered that she voted for Tilden by from six to nine thousand majority.

There are features in this case that distinguish it from that of Florida, and I shall address myself to these points, in the hopes that the Commission will undertake in this case to arrive at the true vote of Louisiana, without regard to the certificates of governor and canvassing-board, except so far as they may afford one character of evidence as to how the State voted.

Three papers purporting to be certificates of the votes of this State were opened and referred to this Commission. Two are votes for Hayes and Wheeler and the other for Tilden and Hendricks. The electors who certified in the first two certificates have the certificate of W. P. Kellogg, who certified as governor of Louisiana that the Hayes electors were chosen according to law. The electors who certified in the third certificate have the certificate of John McEnery, who signs himself governor of Louisiana, that they, the Tilden electors, were duly and legally appointed, &c. We have to determine between these which set has been duly appointed.

Objections have been filed to each of these certificates, and on behalf of the objectors to the certificates of the Hayes votes it is offered to prove as follows:

I.

We offer to prove that William P. Kellogg, who certifies, as governor of the State of Louisiana, to the appointment of electors of that State, which certificate is now before this Commission, is the same William P. Kellogg who, by said certificate, was certified to have been appointed one of said electors. In other words, that Kellogg certified his own appointment as such elector.

2. That said Kellogg was governor *de facto* of said State during all the months of November and December, A. D. 1876.

CONSTITUTION OF LOUISIANA.

"ART. 117. No person shall hold or exercise at the same time more than one office of trust or profit, except that of justice of the peace or notary public."

II.

We offer to prove that said William P. Kellogg was not duly appointed one of the electors of said State in A. D. 1876, and that the certificate is untrue in fact.

To show this we offer to prove—

(1.) By certified copies of the lists made out, signed, and sworn to by the commissioners of election in each poll and voting-place in the State, and delivered by said commissioners to the clerk of the district court wherein said polls were established, except in the parish of Orleans, and in that parish delivered to the secretary of state, that at the election for electors in the State of Louisiana on the 7th day of November last, the said William P. Kellogg received for elector 6,300 votes less than were at said election cast for each and every of the following-named persons, that is to say: John McEnery, R. C. Wickliffe, L. St. Martin, E. P. Poché, A. De Blanc, W. A. Seay, R. G. Cobb, K. A. Cross. (Sec. 43, act 1872.)

(2.) In connection with the certified copies of said lists we offer to prove that the returning-board, which pretended to canvass the said election under the act approved November 20, 1872, did not receive from any poll, voting-place, or parish in said State, nor have before them, any statement of any supervisor of registration or commissioner of election in form as required by section 26 of said act, on affidavit of three or more citizens, of any riot, tumult, acts of violence, intimidation, armed disturbance, bribery, or corrupt influences which prevented or tended to prevent a fair, free, and peaceable vote of all qualified electors entitled to vote at such poll or voting-place.

(3.) We further offer to show that in many instances the supervisors of registration of the several parishes willfully and fraudulently omitted from their consolidated statement, returned by them to the State returning-board, the result and all mention of the votes given at certain polls or voting-places within their respective parishes, as shown to them by the returns and papers returned to said supervisors by the commissioners of election, as required by law; and that in consequence of this omission the said consolidated statements, on their face, omitted majorities against the said Kellogg, and in favor of each and every the said McEnery, Wickliffe, St. Martin, Poché, De Blanc, Seay, Cobb, and Cross, amounting to 2,267, but that said supervisors of registration did, as by law required, return to the said returning-board, with their consolidated statements, the lists, papers, and returns received by them, according to law, from the commissioners of election at the several polls and voting-places omitted as aforesaid from said consolidated statements of said supervisors.

And that the said returning-board willfully and fraudulently neglected and refused to make any canvass of the majorities so omitted, or estimate them in any way, in their pretended determination that the said Kellogg was duly elected an elector at the election aforesaid.

(4.) We offer to show that by the consolidated statements returned to said returning-board by the supervisors of registration of the several parishes of the State of the result of the voting at the several polls or voting-places within their parishes respectively, it appeared that said Kellogg received at said election 3,459 less votes for electors than the said McEnery, Wickliffe, St. Martin, Poché, De Blanc, Seay, Cobb, and Cross, and each and every of them.

(5.) We further offer to show that the said returning-board willfully and fraudulently estimated and counted as votes in favor of said Kellogg 234 votes which were not shown to have been given at any poll or voting-place in said State, either by any consolidated statement returned to said returning-board by any of the said supervisors, nor by the statements, lists, tally-sheets, or returns made by any commissioners of election to any of said supervisors, or which were before said returning-board.

(6.) We offer to prove that the votes cast and given at said election on the 7th November last for the election of electors, as shown by the returns made by the commissioners of election from the several polls or voting-places in said State, have never been compiled nor canvassed; and that the said returning-board never even pretended to compile or canvass the returns made by said commissioners of election, but that said returning-board only pretended to canvass the returns made by the said supervisors. (Act of 1872, section 43: "Supervisor must forward." Act of 1872, section 2: "Board must canvass.")

(7.) We offer to prove that the votes given for electors at the election of November 7 last at the several voting-places or polls in said State have never been opened by the governor of the said State in presence of the secretary of state, the attorney-general, and a district judge of the district in which the seat of government was established, nor in the presence of any of them; nor has the governor of said State ever, in the presence as aforesaid, examined the returns of the commissioners of election for said election to ascertain therefrom, nor has he ever, in such presence, ascertained therefrom, the persons who were, or whether any one was, duly elected electors, or elector, at said election; nor has he ever pretended so to do. (Revised Statutes, section 2826.)

(8.) We further offer to prove—

That the said William P. Kellogg, governor as aforesaid, when he made, executed, and delivered the said certificate, by which he certified that himself and others had been duly appointed electors as aforesaid, well knew that said certificate was untrue in fact in that behalf, and that he, the said Kellogg, then well knew that he, the said Kellogg, had not received, of the legal votes cast at the election of November 7, 1876, for electors, within five thousand of as many of such votes as had at said election been cast and given for each and every of the said McEnery, Wickliffe, St. Martin, Poché, De Blanc, Seay, Cobb, and Cross; and that he, the said Kellogg, when he made and executed the afore-Said certificate, well knew that of the legal votes cast at the popular election held in the State of Louisiana on the 7th day of November last, for the election of electors in said state, as shown by the lists, returns, and papers sent, according to law, by the commissioners of election, who presided over and conducted the said election at the several polls and voting-places in said State, to the supervisors of registration, and as shown by the said lists, returns, papers, and ballots deposited by said commissioners of election in the office of the clerks of the district courts, except the parish of Orleans, and deposited for the parish of Orleans in the office of ecretary of state, according to law, that each and every the said McEnery, Wickliffe, St. Martin, Poché, De Blanc, Seay, Cobb, and Cross had received more than five thousand of the legal votes cast at said election for electors, more than had been cast and given at said election for the said Kellogg as elector, and that the said McEnery, Wickliffe, St. Martin, Poché, De Blanc, Seay, Cobb, and Cross had been thus and thereby duly appointed electors for said State in the manner directed by the legislature of said State.

(9.) We further offer to prove—

That at the city of New Orleans in the State of Louisiana, in the month of October, A. D. 1876, the said William P. Kellogg, J. H. Burch, Peter Joseph, L. A. Sheldon, Morris Marks, A. B. Levissee, O. H. Brewster, Oscar Joffrion, S. B. Packard, John Ray, Frank Morey, Hugh J. Campbell, D. J. M.A. Jewett, H. C. Dibble, Michael Hahn, B. P. Blanchard, J. R. G. Pitkin, J. Madison Wells, Thomas C. Anderson, G. Casanave, L. M. Kenner, George P. Davis, W. L. Catlin, C. C. Nash, George L. Smith, Isadore McCormick, and others, entered into an unlawful and criminal combination and conspiracy to and with each other, and each to and with each of the others, to cause it to be certified and returned to the secretary of state by the returning-board of said State, upon their pretended compilation and canvass of the election for electors, to be thereafter held on the 7th day of Nov ember, A. D. 1876, that the said Kellogg, Burch, Joseph, Sheldon, Marks, Levissee, Bre wster, and Joffrion, had received a majority of all votes given and cast at said election for electors, whether such should be the fact or not; and

That afterwards, to wit, on the 17th day of November, A. D. 1876, after said election had been held, and it was well known to all of said conspirators that said Kellogg and others had not been elected at said election, but had been defeated, and their opponents had been elected at said election, the said returning-board assembled at the city of New Orleans, the seat of government of said State, to pretend to compile and canvass the statements of votes made by the commissioners of election from the several polls and voting-places in said State for presidential electors, and make returns of said election to the secretary of state, as required by an act of the legislature of that State, approved November 20, 1872; that when said returning-board so assembled, said Wells, said Anderson, said Kenner, and said Casanave, who are all members of one political party, to wit, the republican party, were the only members of said board; there being one vacancy in said board, which vacancy it was the duty of said Wells, said Anderson, said Kenner, and said Casanave, as members of said board, to fill, then and there, by the elec tion or appointment of some person belonging to some other political party than the republican party; but that the said Wells, Anderson, Kenner, and Casanave then and there, in pursuance of said unlawful and criminal combination aforesaid, then and there neglected and refused to fill said vacancy, for the reason, as assigned by them, that they did not wish to have a democrat to watch the proceedings of said board; and that although frequently during the session of said board, assembled for the purpose aforesaid, they, the said Wells, Anderson, Kenner, and Casanave, were duly, and in writing, requested by said McEnery, Wickliffe, St. Martin, Poché, De Blanc, Seay, Cobb, and Cross to fill said vacancy, they refused to do so, and never did fill the same, but proceeded as such board, in pursuance of said combination and conspiracy, to make a pretended compilation and canvass of said election without filling the vacancy in said returning-board; and

That said Wells, Anderson, Kenner, and Casanave, while pretending to be in session as a returning-board for the purpose of compiling and canvassing the said election, and in pursuance of said combination and conspiracy, employed persons of notoriously bad character to act as their clerks and assistants, to wit, one Davis, a man of notoriously bad character, who was then under indictment in the criminal courts of Louisiana, and said Catlin, and said Blanchard, and said Jewett, three of said conspirators, who were then under indictment for subornation of perjury in the criminal courts of Louisiana ; the said Jewett being also under indictment in one of the criminal courts of Louisiana for obtaining money under false pretenses ; and Isadore McCormick, who was then under indictment in the criminal court of said State charged with murder.

And that, in pursuance of said unlawful combination and conspiracy aforesaid, the said Wells, Anderson, Kenner, and Casanave, acting in said returning-board, confided to their said clerks and employés, said co-conspirators, the duty of compiling and canvassing all returns which were by said returning-board ordered to be canvassed and compiled ; and, although thereto particularly requested by a communication, as follows—

" *To the honorable returning-board of the State of Louisiana :*

" GENTLEMEN : The undersigned, acting as counsel for the various candidates upon the democratic-conservative ticket, State, national, and municipal, with respect show :

" That the returns from various polls and parishes are inspected by this board, and the vote announced by it is merely that for governors and electors ;

" That the tabulation of all other votes is turned over to a corps of clerks, to be done outside of the presence of this board ;

" That all of said clerks are republicans, and that the democratic-conservative candidates have no check upon them, and no means to detect errors and fraudulent tabulation, or to call the attention of this board to any such wrongs, if any exist ;

" That by this system the fate of all other candidates but governor and electors is placed in the hands of a body of republican clerks with no check against erroneous or dishonest action on their part ;

" That fair play requires that some check should be placed upon said clerks and some protection afforded to the said candidates against error or dishonest action on the part of said clerks ;

" Wherefore they respectfully ask that they be permitted to name three respectable persons, and that to such parties be accorded the privilege of being present in the room or rooms where said tabulation is progressing, and of inspecting the tabulation and comparing the same with the returns, and also of fully inspecting the returns, and previous to the adoption by this board of said tabulation, with a view to satisfy all parties that there has been no tampering or unfair practice in connection therewith.

" Very respectfully,

"F. C. ZACHARIE.
"CHARLES CAVANAC.
"E. A. BURKE.
"J. R. ALCÉE GAUTHREAUX.
"HENRY C. BROWN.
"FRANK McGLOIN.

" I concur herein.

"H. M. SPOFFORD.
"Of Counsel"—

they, the said Wells, Anderson, Kenner, and Casanave, acting as said board, expressly refused to permit any democrat, or any person selected by democrats, to be present with said clerks and assistants while they were engaged in the compilation and canvass aforesaid, or to examine into the correctness of the compilation and canvass made by said clerks and assistants as aforesaid.

And that said returning-board, in pursuance of said unlawful combination and conspiracy aforesaid, and for the purpose of concealing the animus of said board and inspiring confidence in the public mind in the integrity of their proceedings, on the 18th day of November, A. D. 1876, adopted and passed a preamble and resolution, as follows :

"Whereas this board has learned with satisfaction that distinguished gentlemen of national reputation, from other States, some at the request of the President of the United States and some at the request of the national executive committee of the democratic party, are present in this city, with the view to witness the proceedings of this board in canvassing and compiling the returns of the recent election in this State for presidential electors, in order that the public opinion of the country may be satisfied as to the truth of the result and the fairness of the means by which it may have been attained ;

"And whereas this board recognizes the importance which may attach to the result of their proceedings, and that the public mind should be convinced of its justice by a knowledge of the facts on which it may be based : Therefore,

"*Be it resolved,* That this board does hereby cordially invite and request five gentlemen from each of the two bodies named, to be selected by themselves respectively, to attend and be present at the meetings of this board while engaged in the discharge of its duties under the law, in canvassing and compiling the returns and ascertaining and declaring the result of said election for presidential electors, in their capacity as private citizens of eminent reputation and high character, and as spectators and witnesses of the proceedings in that behalf, of this board."

ELECTORAL COUNT OF 1877.

But that said returning-board, being convinced that a compilation and canvass of votes given at said election for presidential electors, made fairly and openly, would result in defeating the object of said conspiracy, and compelling said returning-board to certify that said McEnery, Wickliffe, St. Martin, Poché, De Blanc, Seay, Cobb, and Cross had been at said election duly chosen, elected, and appointed electors by the said State of Louisiana, and in pursuance of said unlawful combination and conspiracy, did afterward, to wit, on the 20th day of November, A. D. 1876, adopt and pass the following rules for the better execution and carrying into effect said combination and conspiracy; that is to say:

"VII.

"The returning-officers, [if they think it advisable, may go into secret session to consider any motion, argument, or proposition which may be presented to them; any member shall have the right to call for secret session for the above purpose."

"X.

"That the evidence for each contested poll in any parish, when concluded, shall be laid aside until all the evidence is in from all the contested polls in the several parishes where there may be contests, and after the evidence is all in, there turning-officers will decide the several contests in secret session; the parties, or their attorneys, to be allowed to submit briefs or written arguments up to the time fixed for the returning-officers going into secret session, after which no additional argument to be received unless by special consent."

That the proceedings thus directed to be had in secret were protested against by the said McEnery, Wickliffe, St. Martin, Poché, De Blanc, Seay, Cobb, and Cross; but said board thereafter proceeded and pretended to complete their duties as such returning-board; and did perform, execute, and carry out the most important duties devolving upon said board in secret, with closed doors, and in the absence of any member of their board belonging to the democratic party or any person whatever not a member of said board not belonging to the republican party.

That the said Wells, Anderson, Kenner, and Casanave, acting as said returning-board, while engaged in the compilation and canvass aforesaid, were applied to to permit the United States supervisors of election, duly appointed and qualified as such, to be present at and witness such compilation or canvass.

That application was made to said returning-board in that behalf, as follows:

"To the president and members of the returning-board of the State of Louisiana:

"GENTLEMEN: The undersigned, of counsel for United States supervisors of election, duly appointed and qualified as such, do hereby except, protest, and object to any ruling made this 20th day of November, 1876, or that hereafter may be made, whereby they are deprived of the right of being present during the entire canvass and compilation of the results of the election lately held in the State of Louisiana, wherein electors for President and Vice-President and members of the Forty-fifth Congress were balloted for, and the result of which said board are now canvassing.

"That under the fifth section of the United States act of February 28, 1871, they are 'to be and remain where the ballot-boxes are kept, at all times after the polls are open, until each and every vote cast at said time and place shall be counted, and the canvass of all votes polled be wholly completed, and the proper and requisite certificate or returns made, whether said certificate or returns be required under any law of the United States, or any State, territorial, or municipal law.'

"That under said law of the United States, District Attorney J. R. Beckwith, under date of October 30, 1872, gave his written official opinion for the instruction and guidance of persons holding the office now held by protestants, wherein said United States district attorney said:

"'It cannot be doubted that the duty of the supervisors extends to the inspection of the entire election from its commencement until the decision of its result. If the United States statutes were less explicit, there still could be no doubt of the duty and authority of the supervisors to inspect and canvass every vote cast for each and every candidate, State, parochial, and Federal, as the law of the State neither provides nor allows any separation of the election for Representatives in Congress, &c., from the election of State and parish officers. The election is in law a single election, and the power of inspection vested in law in the supervisors appointed by the court extends to the entire election, a full knowledge of which may well become necessary to defeat fraud.'

"In which opinion the attorney-general of the State of Louisiana coincided. Whereupon protestants claim admittance of board to amend their rules by making them all open sessions, with leave to a reasonable number of citizens of the State directly interested, or their counsel, and of press reporters to attend, which would furnish the best guarantee possible against the consummation of fraud and the perversion of the popular will.

"The undersigned respectfully asks that the foregoing protest be entered upon the minutes of the board.

"HENRY M. SPOFFORD,
"Of Counsel."

But that said Wells, Anderson, Kenner, and Casanave, acting as such returning-board, in further pursuance and execution of said unlawful combination and conspiracy, then and there refused to permit said United States commissioners of election to be present for the purpose aforesaid, but proceeded in their absence to the pretended compilation and canvass aforesaid.

That the said returning-board, while in session as aforesaid, for the purpose aforesaid, to wit, on the 20th day of November, 1876, adopted the following rule to govern their proceedings; that is to say:

"IX.

"No ex parte affidavits or statements shall be received in evidence, except as a basis to show that such fraud, intimidation, or other illegal practice had at some poll requires investigation; but the returns and affidavits authorized by law, made by officers of election, or in verification of statements as required by law, shall be received in evidence as prima facie."

But that said board subsequently, while sitting as aforesaid, for the purposes aforesaid, having become convinced that they could not, upon other than ex parte testimony, so manipulate the said compilation and canvass as to declare that said Kellogg, Burch, Joseph, Sheldon, Marks, Levissee, Brewster, and Joffrion were elected electors at said election, and in further pursuance of said unlawful combination and conspiracy, did subsequently modify said rule, and declare and decide that, as such returning-board, they would receive ex parte affidavits, under which last decision of said board over two hundred printed pages of ex parte testimony was received by said board in favor of said Kellogg and others; and afterward, when the said McEnery and others offered ex parte evidence to contradict the ex parte evidence aforesaid, the said returning-board reversed its last decision, and refused to receive ex parte affidavits in contradiction as aforesaid.

And that in pursuance of said unlawful combination and conspiracy the said returning-board, in violation of a law of said State, approved November 20, 1872, neglected and refused to compile and canvass the statements of votes made by the commissioners of election which were before them according to law for canvass and compilation as aforesaid in regard to the election of presidential electors, but that said board did, in pursuance and further execution of said combination and conspiracy, canvass and compile only the consolidated statements and returns made to them by the supervisors of registration of the several parishes of said State.

And that said returning-board, in pursuance and further execution of said unlawful combination and conspiracy, did knowingly, willfully, and fraudulently refuse to compile and canvass the votes given for electors at said election in more than twenty parishes of said State, as was shown and appeared by and upon the consolidated statements and returns made to them by said supervisors of said parishes.

And that said returning-board did, in said canvass and compilation, count and estimate, as a foundation for their determination in the premises, hundreds of votes which had not been returned and certified to them either by the commissioners of election in said State or by the supervisors of registration in said State, they, the said members of said board, then and there well knowing that they had no right or authority to estimate the same for the purpose aforesaid.

And that said returning-board, in further pursuance and execution of said unlawful combination and conspiracy, knowingly, willfully, falsely, and fraudulently did make a certificate and return to the secretary of state that said Kellogg, Burch, Joseph, Sheldon, Marks, Levissee, Brewster, and Joffrion had received majorities of all the legal votes cast at said election of November 7, 1876, for presidential electors, they then and there well knowing that the said McEnery, Wickliffe, St. Martin, Poché, De Blanc, Seay, Cobb, and Cross had received majorities of all the votes cast at said election for presidential electors, and were duly elected as the presidential electors of said State.

And that the said returning-board, in making said statement, certificate, and return to the secretary of state, were not deceived nor mistaken in the premises, but knowingly, willfully, and fraudulently made what they well knew when they made it was a false and fraudulent statement, certificate, and return, and that the said false and fraudulent statement, certificate, and return, made by said returning-board to the secretary of state in that behalf, was made by the members of said returning-board in pursuance and execution of, and only in pursuance and execution of, said unlawful combination and conspiracy.

And that said returning-board, while in session as aforesaid for the purpose aforesaid, in further pursuance and execution of said unlawful combination and conspiracy, did alter, change, and forge, or cause to be altered, changed, and forged, the consolidated statement and return of the supervisor of registration for the parish of Vernon, in said State, in the manner following, to wit: The said consolidated statement, as made and returned to said board, showed that of the legal votes given in said parish for electors at said election of November 7, 1876, said McEnery received 647, said Wickliffe received 647, said St. Martin received 647, said Poché received 647, said De Blanc received 647, said Seay received 647, said Cobb received 647, said Cross received 647 ; and that said Kellogg received none, said Burch received none, said Joseph received 2, said Brewster received 2, said Marks received 2, said Levissee received 2, said Joffrion received 2, said Sheldon received 2 ; and said board altered, changed, and forged, or caused to be altered, changed, and forged, said consolidated statement so as to make the same falsely and fraudulently show that the said McEnery received 469, said Wickliffe received 469, said St. Martin received 469, said Poché received 469, said De Blanc received 469, said Seay received 469, said Cobb received 469, said Cross received 469 ; and that said Kellogg received 178, said Burch received 178, said Joseph received 178, said Sheldon received 180, said Marks received 180, said Levissee received 180, said Brewster, received 180, said Joffrion received 180 ; and that said returning-board, while in session as aforesaid for the purpose aforesaid, to pretend to justify the alteration and forgery of said consolidated statement, procured and pretended to act upon three forged affidavits, purporting to have been made and sworn to by Samuel Carter, Thomas Brown, and Samuel Collins, they, the said members of said returning-board, then and there well knowing that said pretended affidavits were false and forged, and that no such persons were in existence, as purported to make said affidavits. And that said members of said returning-board, acting as said board, in pursuance and execution of said unlawful combination and conspiracy, did, in their pretended canvass and compilation of the legal votes given at said election on the 7th day of November, A. D. 1876, for presidential electors in said State of Louisiana, as shown to them by the statements, papers, and returns made according to law by the commissioners of election presiding over and conducting said election at the several polls and voting-places in said State, all of which votes were legally cast by legal voters in said State at said election, knowingly, willfully, and fraudulently, and without any authority of law whatever, exclude and refuse to count and estimate, or compile or canvass, votes given at said election for electors, as follows, which papers, statements, and returns were before them, and which it was their duty by law to compile and canvass, that is to say : for said John McEnery, 10,280 ; for said R. C. Wickliffe, 10,293 ; for said L. St. Martin, 10,291 ; for said F. P. Poché, 10,280 ; for said A. De Blanc, 10,289 ; for said W. A. Seay, 10,291 ; for said R. A. Cobb, 10,261 ; for said K. A. Cross, 10,281 ; they, the said members of said returning-board, then and there well knowing that all of said votes which they neglected and refused to canvass and compile had been duly and legally cast at said election for presidential electors by legal voters of said State ; and then and there well knowing that had they considered, estimated, and counted, compiled and canvassed, said votes, as they then and there well knew it was their duty to do, it would have appeared, and they would have been compelled to certify and return to the secretary of state, that said Kellogg had not been duly elected or appointed an elector for said State, but that at said election the said McEnery, the said Wickliffe, the said St. Martin, the said Poché, the said De Blanc, the said Seay, the said Cobb, and the said Cross had been duly elected and appointed presidential electors in said State.

And that by false, fraudulent, willful, and corrupt acts and omissions to act by said returning-board as aforesaid, in the matter aforesaid, and by said nonfeasance, misfeasance, and malfeasance of said returning-board, as hereinbefore mentioned, the said returning-board made to the secretary of state of said State the statement, certificate, and return upon which the said Kellogg, as *de facto* governor of said State, pretended to make his said false certificate, certifying that himself and others had been duly appointed electors for said State, as hereinbefore mentioned ; and that said statement, certificate, and return made by said returning-board, and that the said certificate made by the said Kellogg, as *de facto* governor, each, every, and all were made in pursuance and execution of said unlawful and criminal combination and conspiracy, as was well known to and intended by each and every of the members of said returning-board when they made their said false statement, certificate, and return to the secretary of state of said State, and by the said Kellogg when, as governor *de facto* of said State, he made his said false certificate hereinbefore mentioned.

III.

We further offer to prove—

That Oscar Joffrion was on the 7th day of November, A. D. 1876, supervisor of registration of the parish of Pointe Coupee, and that he acted and officiated as such supervisor of registration for said parish at the said election for presidential electors on that day; and that he is the same person who acted as one of the electors for said State, and on the 6th day of December, A. D. 1876, as an elector, cast a vote for Rutherford B. Hayes for President of the United States and for William A. Wheeler for Vice-President of the United States.

IV.

We further offer to prove—
That on the 7th day of November, A. D. 1876, A. B. Levissee, who was one of the pretended college of electors of the State of Louisiana, and who in said college gave a vote for Rutherford B. Hayes for President of the United States and for William A. Wheeler for Vice-President of the United States, was at the time of such election a court commissioner of the circuit court of the United States for the district of Louisiana, which is an office of honor, profit, and trust under the Government of the United States.

V.

We further offer to prove—
That on the 7th day of November, A. D. 1876, O. H. Brewster, who was one of the pretended electors in the pretended college of electors of the State of Louisiana, and who in said college gave a vote for Rutherford B. Hayes for President of the United States and for William A. Wheeler for Vice-President of the United States, was at the time of such election as aforesaid holding an office of honor, profit, and trust under the Government of the United States, to wit, the office of surveyor-general of the land office for the district of Louisiana.

VI.

We further offer to prove—
That on the 7th day of November, 1876, Morris Marks, one of the pretended electors who in said college of electors cast a vote for Rutherford B. Hayes for President of the United States and a vote for William A. Wheeler for Vice-President of the United States, was, ever since has been, and now is, holding and exercising the office of district attorney of the fourth judicial district of said State, and receiving the salary by law attached to said office.

VII.

We further offer to prove—
That on the 7th day of November, A. D. 1876, J. Henri Burch, who was one of the pretended electors who in said pretended electoral college gave a vote for Rutherford B. Hayes for President of the United States and a vote for William A. Wheeler for Vice-President of the United States, was holding the following offices under the constitution and laws of said State, that is to say: member of the board of control of the State penitentiary, also administrator of deaf and dumb asylum of said State, to both of which offices he had been appointed by the governor with the advice and consent of the senate of said State, both being offices with salaries fixed by law, and also the office of treasurer of the parish school board for the parish of East Baton Rouge; and that said Burch, ever since the said 7th day of November, (and prior thereto,) has exercised and still is exercising the functions of all said offices and receiving the emoluments thereof.

VIII.

We further offer to prove the canvass and compilation actually made by said returning-board, showing what parishes and voting-places and polls were compiled and canvassed, and what polls or voting-places were excluded by said returning board from their canvass and compilation of votes given for presidential electors; and we also offer to show what statements and returns of the commissioners of election and of the supervisors of registration were duly before said returning-board.

IX.

We further offer to prove—
That the affidavits on which the allegations of tumult were made were forged and false.

X.

One member of the board offered to receive a bribe.

XI.

That they agreed to and did receive, as follows, votes never cast for any elector.

In the first place, there seems to be some confusion as to what election laws were in force in Louisiana on the day of election, and I desire to ascertain what laws the canvassing-board acted under, so as to be able to judge of their conduct under the law.

In 1868 there was a general election law passed in the State, which provided for all elections, including State and presidential.

In 1870 the laws of Louisiana were revised, and the election law of 1868 was embraced in these revised statutes under two heads, or chapters, each making a distinct and separate act. One provided for State and the other for presidential elections.

In 1872, November 20, an act was passed on the subject of both State and presidential election, the seventy-first section of which is in these words:

SEC. 71. *Be it further enacted, &c.,* That this act shall take effect from and after its passage, and that all others on the subject of election laws be, and the same are hereby, repealed.
Approved November 20, 1872.

Under this repealing clause all other acts on the subject of election were repealed, and this left the act of 1872 the only election law of Louisiana.

The following provisions will be found in this law of 1872:

SECTION 1. *Be it enacted by the senate and house of representatives of the State of Louisiana in general assembly convened,* That all elections for State, parish, and judicial officers, members of the general assembly, and for members of Congress, shall be held on the first Monday in November; and said elections shall be styled the general elections. They shall be held in the manner and form and subject to the regulations hereinafter prescribed, and in no other.

SEC. 2. *Be it further enacted, &c.,* That five persons, to be elected by the senate from all political parties, shall be the returning-officers for all elections in the State, a majority of whom shall constitute a quorum, and have power to make the returns of all elections. In case of any vacancy by death, resignation, or otherwise, by either of the board, then the vacancy shall be filled by the residue of the board of returning-officers. The returning-officers shall, after each election, before entering on their duties, take and subscribe to the following oath before a judge of the supreme or any district court:
"I, A B, do solemnly swear (or affirm) that I will faithfully and diligently perform the duties of a returning-officer as prescribed by law; that I will carefully and honestly canvass and compile the statements of the votes, and make a true and correct return of the election: so help me God."
Within ten days after the closing of the election said returning-officers shall meet in New Orleans to canvass and compile *the statement of votes made by the commissioners of election,* and make returns of the election to the secretary of state. They shall continue in session until such returns have been compiled. The presiding officer shall, at such meeting, open, in the presence of the said returning-officers, the statements of the commissioners of election, and the said returning-officers shall, from said statements, canvass and compile the returns of the election in duplicate; one copy of such returns they shall file in the office of the secretary of state, and of one copy they shall make public proclamation, by printing in the official journal and such other newspapers as they may deem proper, declaring the names of all persons and officers voted for, the number of votes for each person, and the names of the persons who have been duly and lawfully elected. *The return of the election thus made and promulgated shall be prima facie evidence in all courts of justice and before all civil officers, until set aside after contest according to law, of the right of any person named therein to hold and exercise the office to which he shall by such return be declared elected.* The governor shall, within thirty days thereafter, issue commissions to all officers thus declared elected, who are required by law to be commissioned.

SEC. 3. *Be it further enacted, &c.,* That in such canvass and compilation the returning-officers shall observe the following order: They shall compile first the statements from all polls or voting-places at which there shall have been a fair, free, and peaceable registration and election. Whenever, from any poll or voting-place, there shall be received the statement of any supervisor of registration or commissioner of election, in form as required by section 26 of this act, on affidavit of three or more citizens, of any riot, tumult, acts of violence, intimidation, armed disturbance, bribery, or corrupt influences, which prevented, or tended to prevent, a fair, free, and peaceable vote of all qualified electors entitled to vote at such poll or voting-place, such returning-officers shall not canvass, count, or compile the statement of votes from such poll or voting-place until the statements from all other polls or voting-places shall have been canvassed and compiled. The returning-officers shall then proceed to investigate the statements of riot, tumult, acts of violence, intimidation, armed disturbance, bribery, or corrupt influences at any such poll, or voting-place; and if from the evidence of such statement they shall be convinced that such riot, tumult, acts of violence, intimidation, armed disturbance, bribery, or corrupt influences did not materially interfere with the purity and freedom of the election at such poll or voting-place, or did not prevent a sufficient number of qualified voters thereat from registering or voting to materially change the result of the election, then, and not otherwise, said returning-officers shall canvass and compile the vote of such poll or voting-place with those previously canvassed and compiled; but if said returning-officers shall not be fully satisfied thereof, it shall be their duty to examine further testimony in regard thereto, and to this end they shall have power to send for persons and papers. If, after such examination, the said returning-officers shall be convinced that said riot, tumult, acts of violence, intimidation, armed disturbance, bribery, or corrupt influences did materially interfere with the purity and freedom of the election at such poll or voting-place, or did prevent a sufficient number of the qualified electors thereat from registering and voting to materially change the result of the election, then the said returning-officers shall not canvass or compile the statement of the votes of such poll or voting-place, but shall exclude it from their returns: *Provided*, That any person interested in said election by reason of being a candidate for office shall be allowed a hearing before said returning-officers upon making application within the time allowed for the forwarding of the returns of said election.

In the first place, it is offered to prove that this canvassing-board was not legal because it should have consisted of five whereas it only consisted of four; that these four persistently refused to fill the board and give the democrats a representation in said board; and that such refusal was for the purpose of concealing from the opposite party the fraudulent acts of said board by which they gave the returns to the Hayes electors.

Was it a legal board?

The general doctrine seems to be that when authority of a public nature has been delegated to a certain number the authority cannot be exercised by less than the full number, and although a quorum shall consist of a majority, yet all of the five must have the opportunity to attend if they please.

This is especially true when the board is to consist of the representatives of the different political parties and only one of them is represented in an incomplete board.

This question was well considered in the case of Wentworth *vs.* Farmington, 49 N. Hamp., 120.

The case is directly in point on the proposition submitted, and the court, in its opinion, says:

Even if the statute goes no further than the common-law rule, a report signed by the majority, under the circumstances of this case, would have been good. According to the case of Grindley *et al. vs.* Barker, 1 B. & P., 228, before cited, it would have been deemed to be the report of the whole. The real point of the objection is that at the time when the report was signed there was a vacancy in the board of commissioners caused by the removal of the chairman from the county; and the general doctrine that in case there be a vacancy in the board the remaining members cannot act seems to be unquestionable. (Palmer *vs.* Conway, 22 N. H., 148; Mitchell *vs.* Holderness, 34 N. H., 209, 214.)

The question here, then, is whether this doctrine applies where, at the time the vacancy occurred, nothing remained to be done but to reduce to writing and make the formal report of what had already been determined by the whole board.

In Palmer *vs.* Conway, before cited, it was held that as there were not three members of the board in office at the time, there was no such board as the statute requires, and therefore there could be no action of the majority.

In that case a report laying out a highway had been recommitted to the same board, and a hearing notified, and before the time appointed one of the commissioners died, but the others went on with the hearing and made several changes in the report, and upon the report being again recommitted, the same two commissioners made further changes, and the report, upon full consideration, was set aside for want of authority in those commissioners to act.

Reference is also made to Pell *vs.* Ullman, 21 Barb., 500; Pulaski Co. *vs.* Lincoln, 9 Ark., 320; People *vs.* Coghill, 47 Cal., 361.

I desire on this point also to refer to an able opinion pronounced on this question by Associate Justice Miller, a member of this Commission, which has been furnished me by Mr. Representative Abbott. It will be found in 1 Woolworth's Circuit Court Reports, 175, and was pronounced in the case of Schenck *vs.* Peay. Mr. Justice Miller says:

We understand it to be well settled that where authority of this kind is conferred on three or more persons, in order to make its exercise valid all must be present and participate, or have an opportunity to participate, in the proceedings, although some may dissent from the action determined on. The action of two out of three commissioners, to all of whom was confided a power to be exercised, cannot be upheld when the third party took no part in the transaction and was ignorant of what was done, gave no implied consent to the action of the others, and was neither consulted by them nor had any opportunity to exert his legitimate influence in the determination of the course to be pursued. Such is the uncontradicted course of the authorities, so far as we are advised, where the power conferring the authority has not prescribed a different rule. (2 Kent's Commentaries, 293, note *a*, 633, and authorities cited there, note *b*; Commonwealth *vs.* Canal Commissioners, 9 Watts, 466; Green *vs.* Miller, 6 Johnson, 39; Kirk *vs.* Ball, 12 Eng. L. & E., 385; Crocker *vs.* Crane, 21 Wendell, 211; Dougherty *vs.* Hope, 1 Comstock, 79, 252; *ib.*, 3 Denio, 252, 259.)

The case before us goes even beyond this, for, according to the statement of the bill, there never was a board of commissioners in existence until after the proceedings in regard to his title were completed. *The law required three commissioners. A less number was not a board and could do nothing.* The third commissioner for Arkansas, although nominated and confirmed, did not qualify or enter upon the duties of his office until after the sale of the lots to the defendants. *There was, therefore, no board of commissioners in existence authorized to assess the tax, to receive the money, or to sell the property. If Congress had intended to confide these important functions to two persons, it would not have required the appointment of the third. If it had been willing that two out of the three should act, the statute could easily have made provision for that contingency,* as has since been done by the act of 1865.

This reasoning seems perfectly conclusive, and I take it for granted will satisfy the mind of at least one of this Commission that this board of four had no right to canvass the Louisiana returns, and that their determination amounts to nothing—absolutely nothing.

But this is not all. By the law of 1872, above quoted, in the third section the order to be observed by the returning-officers is specifically laid down. They shall compile first the statements from all polls where the election was fair, free, and peaceable. This is a mere addition or summarizing of the results of each poll, and shall be continued through the entire list of polls or parishes in the State, unless there shall be received from some poll or polls a statement required by section 26, and then these last polls are not to be canvassed until all the others are compiled.

Section 26 is as follows:

SEC. 26. *Be it further enacted, &c.,* That in any parish, precinct, ward, city, or town in which during the time of registration, or revision of registration, or on any day of election, there shall be any riot, tumult, acts of violence, intimidation, and disturbance, bribery, or corrupt influences, at any place within said parish, or at or near any poll or voting-place, or place of registration, or revision of registration, which riot, tumult, acts of violence, intimidation, and disturbance, bribery, or corrupt influences shall prevent or tend to prevent a fair, free, peaceable, and full vote of all the qualified electors of said parish, precinct, ward, city, or town, it shall be the duty of the commissioners of election, if such riot, tumult, acts of violence, intimidation, and disturbance, bribery, or corrupt influences occur on the day of election, or of the supervisor of registration of the parish, if they occur during the time of registration or revision of registration, to make in duplicate and under oath a clear and full statement of all the facts relating thereto and of the effect produced by such riot, tumult, acts of violence, intimidation, and disturbance, bribery or corrupt influences in preventing a fair, free, peaceable, and full registration or election, and of the number of qualified voters deterred by such riot, tumult, acts of violence, intimidation, and disturbance, bribery, or corrupt influences, from registering or voting, which statement shall also be corroborated under oath by three respectable citizens, qualified electors of the parish. When such statement is made by a commissioner of election or a supervisor of registration, he shall forward it in duplicate to the supervisor of registration of the parish; if in the city of New Orleans to the secretary of state; one copy of which, if made to the supervisor of registration, shall be forwarded by him to the returning-officers provided for in section two of this act, when he makes the returns of election in his parish. His copy of said statement shall be so annexed to his returns of elections, by paste, wax, or some adhesive substance, that the same can be kept together, and the other copy the supervisor of registration shall deliver to the clerk of the court of his parish for the use of the district attorney.

Now, unless this twenty-sixth section is complied with and the affidavit therein prescribed is made within twenty-four hours after the election and shall accompany the returns from the polls attached to the certificate, the returning-officers are absolutely without jurisdiction to inquire into any alleged riot, tumult, or acts of violence. It is offered to be proved that the returning-officers did inquire into and throw out polls when no such affidavits accompanied the returns, and that by thus throwing out polls and parishes, the majority for the Tilden electors was overcome and a majority made to appear for the Hayes electors. We must act on this offer to prove in a motion to admit the evidence as if the proof would come up to the offer. If this be so, then the returning-officers—granting for the sake of the argument that they had the right to proceed without filling the board—proceeded without jurisdiction and had no more right to throw out parishes than any other persons had to act in the premises. If the offer of proof is made good, these returning-officers did not commit an error of judgment in a matter committed to their discretion, but proceeded without jurisdiction and were mere usurpers. It is alleged in the offers of proof that the affidavits provided for by the twenty-sixth section did not accompany the returns from the polls, but were supplied in New Orleans long after the time prescribed by that section, and were made by persons who knew nothing about the facts they were swearing to; that fraud and perjury were resorted to to afford these returning-officers a chance or pretext for throwing out these returns.

To confirm my view of the powers and duties of these returning-officers, under the third and twenty-sixth sections, I quote from a report of a House committee dated February 23, 1875, and signed by George F. Hoar, William A. Wheeler, and W. P. Frye.

After quoting said sections the report proceeds to state:

Upon this statute we are clearly of opinion that the returning-board *had no right to do anything except to canvass and compile the returns which were lawfully made to them by the local officers, except in cases where they were accompanied by the certificate of the supervisor or commissioner provided in the third section.* In such cases the last sentence of that section shows that it was expected that they would ordinarily exercise the grave and delicate duty of investigating charges of riot, tumult, bribery or corruption, on a hearing of the parties interested in the office. It never could have been meant that this board of its own motion, sitting in New Orleans, at a distance from the place of voting, and without notice, could decide the rights of persons claiming to be elected.

This construction of the powers of the returning-board of Louisiana has been acquiesced in by both Houses of Congress, and the electoral vote of Louisiana cast in 1872 was rejected by the concurrent action of the Senate and House of Representatives, because the laws of said State had not been complied with in the canvass and return of the votes cast for the appointment of the electors. See pages 396–407 Compilation of Proceedings of Counting the Electoral Votes.

Of the votes actually cast at the late election for the appointment of electors in Louisiana, the democratic electors received majorities ranging from 5,300 to 8,990; on the face of the returns as made by the supervisors of registration to the board of returning-officers their majorities ranged from 3,459 to 6,405, but by the canvass and the return made by the returning-officers majorities were certified in favor of the republican electors, ranging from 3,437 to 4,800. To produce this result, sixty-nine polls were rejected, embracing twenty-two parishes in whole or in part.

It is believed that in no single instance did the returning-officers have this foundation laid for inquiring into and rejecting the returns from any parish. This board was of special jurisdiction, and its action, according to well-settled principles, must show on its face jurisdiction. In Thatcher vs. Powell, 6 Wheaton, 119, the court, by Marshall, C. J., say:

In summary proceedings, when a *court* exercises an extraordinary power under a special statute prescribing its course, we think that course ought to be *exactly* observed, and those facts especially which give jurisdiction ought to appear in order to show that its proceedings are *coram judice*. Without this act of assembly, the order for sale would have been totally void. This act gives the power only on a report to be made by the sheriff. This report gives the court jurisdiction, and without it the court is as powerless as if the act had never passed. (Walker vs. Turner, 9 Wheat., 541; Atkins vs. Brewer, 3 Cowen, 306; 2 Lord Raymond, 1144.)

I have endeavored to show that this board of returning-officers had no right to act because it did not consist of the statutory number and because they refused to fill the vacancy in it from fraud; that if empowered to act they had no jurisdiction to throw out parishes, and that their action was a mere usurpation. In addition to all this, it is proposed to prove that this board was corrupt, that its action was fraudulent, that they proceeded upon forged papers and affidavits knowing them to be forged, that they encouraged and promoted perjury and forgery in their criminal attempt to rob the State of her true electoral vote, that they offered to sell their services to one of the political parties contending for the vote. This fraudulent and most wicked conduct of the returning-officers reflects a flood of light on their refusal to fill the vacancy in the board with a political opponent, who would have exposed and denounced their conduct on the spot and prevented the consummation of their hellish purpose. It also reflects light on their assumption of jurisdiction to throw out parishes when by the law under which they were acting they had no such jurisdiction.

Taken altogether, the offer of proof shows that there was a damnable conspiracy to cheat the people of this State out of their vote and to elect a President against the wishes of the people by the most disreputable and fraudulent means. This, too, in a State where the whole election machinery was in the hands of republicans, and not the remotest chance given to their opponents to use unfair means to carry the State if they had been disposed to use them. Now, how shall we discharge our duty under this bill if we shut our eyes to these monstrous acts of fraud, perjury, and forgery, by which the votes of this State have been certified for Hayes? Can we say the Hayes votes are the true votes of the State and such as are provided for by the Constitution, in the face of these facts offered to be proved? Heaven forbid that this Commission shall by its action legalize and confirm these outrageous acts, and make fraud respectable and potent in shaping the political destinies of the American people.

Under pretense that we cannot interfere with State action, for God's sake do not let us inflict this grievous wrong on the already down-trodden people of that State. Let us not by our action make these despicable and corrupt returning-officers a power in the land, and give to returning-boards in future elections, instead of to the people, the power to elect a President.

This is a question that does not concern the people of Louisiana alone. It affects the political destiny of the whole American people. Thirty-seven States besides Louisiana are looking to our action and are interested in our decision. If a corrupt returning-board can cheat that State of her vote, the same fate may await any other State in this Union.

But they also offer to prove that two of the pretended electors who cast their votes for Hayes, to wit, A. B. Levissee and O. H. Brewster, were holding offices of trust and profit under the United States when they were appointed. They did not attend the meeting at first, and were elected by the others to fill the vacancy. I will not repeat here the remarks I made on this subject in the Florida case. They commend themselves to my judgment the more I reflect on them. I will only add a few remarks which seem peculiarly applicable to this case. It seems that these two persons felt that they had not been legally appointed, and that the Constitution prohibited their appointment. They therefore failed to attend, and the college proceeded to fill the vacancies caused by their failure to attend. If I am right that the only election law in force in Louisiana is the law of 1872, which repealed all other acts on the subject of election, then there is no law of that State which provides for filling these vacancies in that way. The only provision on the subject of filling vacancies will be found in the twenty-fourth section, as follows:

SEC. 24. *Be it further enacted, &c.*, That all elections to be held in this State to fill any vacancies shall be conducted and managed, and returns thereof shall be made, in the same manner as is provided for general elections.

This is a provision to fill vacancies by a popular election, and confers no power on the board to fill vacancies.

Nor does any law of Congress confer this power. All the provisions on this subject will be found in the following sections of the Revised Statutes:

SEC. 133. Each State may, *by law*, provide for the filling of any vacancies which may occur in its college of electors when such college meets to give its electoral vote.

SEC. 134. Whenever any State has held an election for the purpose of choosing electors, *and has failed to make a choice* on the day prescribed by law, the electors may be appointed on a subsequent day, in such a manner as the legislature of such State may direct.

I beg leave to conclude what I have to say on this subject by quoting from the brilliant and able speech of Hon. Matt Carpenter:

After quoting the two sections from the Revised Statutes as above, he says:

Two cases are here provided for: one, the case of a vacancy occurring after the election; the other, a failure to make an election. Waiving at present the question whether as between two candidates, the one receiving the greater number of votes being ineligible, his opponent is elected, in virtue of a smaller number of legal votes, and assuming that he is not, then it is unquestionable that the election is void.

In the case of the contested seat in the Senate between Vance and Abbott from North Carolina, there was a very full discussion upon this subject. Vance, who received the largest number of votes, was ineligible under the fourteenth amendment to the Constitution, and Abbott, who received the next highest number of votes and *was* eligible, claimed the seat. The Senate decided that Abbott was not entitled to the seat, and, of course, that the State had failed to make an election of Senator.

The Constitution of the United States, article 2, section 1, authorizes each State to appoint an elector, but provides that no person holding an office of trust or profit under the United States shall be appointed.

This provision of the Constitution applied to the case in hand is this: The State of Louisiana may appoint eight electors; but A. B. Levissee and O. H. Brewster shall not be appointed. Hence any attempt to appoint Levissee and Brewster is unconstitutional and void. And hence it follows that the State appointed but six electors; in other words, they failed to elect the full number to which the State was entitled. This is the case provided for by the last section quoted from the Revised Statutes of Congress, which declares that the State may by law provide for subsequent appointment. If the act of 1868 was not in force, the only provision in relation to filling such a *vacancy* was by subsequent popular election. (Election law of 1872, section 24.) If the act of 1868 was in force, it *only* provided for *filling a vacancy* occurring after the officer had been elected. So then, whether the act of 1868 was or was not in force, there was no law of the State which authorized the appointment in place of Levissee and Brewster, as to whom there had been a failure to elect.

And therefore, in any event, two of the votes given by the Hayes electors must be rejected.

The case of the United States *vs.* The Amistad, 15 Peters, 518, is instructive on this point. The court say it is argued "that the ship and cargo and negroes were duly documented as belonging to Spanish subjects, and this court has no right to look behind these documents; that full faith and credit is to be given to them, and that they are to be held conclusive evidence in this cause, even although it should be established by the most satisfactory proofs that they have been obtained by the grossest frauds and impositions upon the constituted authorities of Spain. To this argument we can in no wise assent. There is nothing in the treaty which justifies or sustains the argument. We do not here meddle with the point whether there has been any connivance in this illegal traffic on the part of any of the colonial authorities or subordinate officers of Cuba; because, in our view, such an examination is unnecessary and ought not to be pursued, unless it were indispensable to public justice, although it has been strongly pressed at the bar. What we proceed upon is this: that, although public documents of the Government accompanying property found on board of the private ships of a foreign nation, certainly are to be deemed *prima-facie* evidence of the facts which they propose to state, yet they are always open to be impugned for fraud; and whether that fraud be in the original obtaining of these documents, or in the subsequent fraudulent and illegal use of them, when once it is satisfactorily established, it overthrows all their sanctity and destroys them as proof. *Fraud will vitiate any, even the most solemn, transactions;* and *an asserted title to property founded upon it is utterly void.* The very language of the ninth article of the treaty of 1795 requires the proprietor to make due and sufficient proof of his property. And how can that proof be deemed either due or sufficient, which is but a connected and stained tissue of fraud? This is not a mere rule of municipal jurisprudence. Nothing is more clear in the law of nations as an established rule to regulate their rights and duties and intercourse than the doctrine that the ship's papers are but *prima-facie* evidence, and that if they are shown to be fraudulent they are not to be held proof of any valid title. This rule is familiarly applied, and indeed is of every-day occurrence in cases of prize, in the contests between belligerents and neutrals, as is apparent from numerous cases to be found in the reports of this court; and it is just as applicable to the transactions of civil intercourse between nations in times of peace. If a private ship clothed with Spanish papers should enter the ports of the United States claiming the privileges and immunities and rights belonging to *bona-fide* subjects of Spain under our treaties or laws, and she should in reality belong to the subjects of another nation which was not entitled to any such privileges, immunities, or rights, and the proprietors were seeking by fraud to cover their own illegal acts under the flag of Spain, *there can be no doubt that it would be the duty of our courts to strip off the disguise and to look at the case according to its naked realities. In the solemn treaties between nations it can never be presumed that either State intends to provide the means of perpetrating or protecting frauds,* but all the provisions are to be construed as intended to be applied to *bona-fide* transactions."

OREGON.

Mr. Commissioner HUNTON said:

Mr. PRESIDENT: The Commission has decided the cases of Florida and Louisiana. The votes of those States have been given for Hayes under the decision of this Commission sworn to decide what persons were duly appointed electors. This requirement of the law and this obligation of the oath have been met by a decision that this Commission could not go behind the governor's certificates, based on the certificates of returning-boards, although the proof was offered that these certificates were, in Florida, in violation of the law of the State; that the three departments of that State government had declared in solemn form that these certificates were illegal and void; that the people of the State of Florida in the mode prescribed by the legislature had by a decided majority appointed Tilden electors.

In Louisiana the votes of that State have been given to Hayes on the same ground of the conclusive effect of the governor's certificate based on the certificate of returning-board, notwithstanding the evidence was at hand and offered that these certificates were the result of a most fraudulent conspiracy to count the vote for Hayes; that counsel were ready to prove that these certificates were procured by perjury and forgery; that the returning-board illegally discarded many thousand votes cast for the Tilden electors, without even the color of authority; that the board offered to sell the return of the State to one of the political parties; that the State had, by about eight thousand majority, appointed the Tilden electors in the mode prescribed by her legislature.

Notwithstanding all this, a majority of this Commission shut their eyes to these monstrous facts and decided that they must count according to certificates, and that they, representing the powers of the two Houses of Congress, were yet powerless to examine into and correct these gross wrongs, in deciding what persons were duly appointed electors in such States. These decisions must shock the minds of the legal profession and paralyze the love of the American citizens for their institutions when these acts of fraud, forgery, and perjury can be committed with impunity, the Constitution violated and the guardians of the people's rights declared impotent to defend and correct!

In this case of Oregon the technical advantages seem to be on the Tilden side of the case, and I am curious to see whether they are as potential in that direction as the other. It seems that a majority of votes were cast for Odell, Watts, and Cartwright on 7th November, 1876. One of these, Mr. Watts, was on the day of election a postmaster, and the governor, acting under the best legal counsel, decided that Watts was not, and that Cronin, the next highest, was, appointed, and gave the certificates required by law to Odell, Cartwright, and Cronin, the last having possession of them.

On December 6, according to the offer of proof, Cronin proposed to act with Odell and Cartwright in the formation of the electoral college. They refused. He then proceeded to act alone; filled the vacancies by the appointment of Miller and Parker, and they cast two votes for Hayes and one for Tilden. Odell and Cartwright proceeded by themselves to fill the vacancy caused by the resignation of Watts by the election of Watts, and they cast the three votes for Hayes.

Which are the constitutional votes and who are the duly-appointed electors of Oregon? If the strict technical rule applied to Florida and Louisiana be applied to Oregon, then the vote of the Cronin college must be recognized as the constitutional vote of Oregon. By the election law, it is provided:

SEC. 37. The county clerk, immediately after making the abstract of the votes given in his county, shall make a copy of each of said abstracts, and transmit it by mail to the secretary of state at the seat of government; *and it shall be the duty of the secretary of state, in the presence of the governor, to proceed within thirty days after the election, and sooner if the returns be all received, to canvass the votes given for secretary and treasurer of state, State printer, justices of the supreme court, member of Congress, and district attorneys; and the governor shall grant a certificate of election to the person having the highest number of votes, and shall also issue a proclamation declaring the election of such person.* In case there shall be no choice, by reason of any two or more persons having an equal and the highest number of votes for either of such offices, the governor shall by proclamation order a new election to fill said offices.

SEC. 60. The votes for the electors shall be given, received, returned, and canvassed as the same are given, returned, and canvassed for members of Congress. *The secretary of state shall prepare two lists of the names of the electors elected, and affix the seal of the State to the same.* Such lists shall be signed by the governor and secretary, and by the latter delivered to the college of electors at the hour of their meeting on such first Wednesday of December.

These provisions make the governor and secretary of state the returning-board of Oregon, and the certificates held by Odell, Cartwright, and Cronin will be found on examination to comply strictly with the above provisions of law. The secretary of state in presence of the governor did canvass the votes according to section 37. He did prepare two lists of the persons elected and affixed the seal of the State to the same, and the governor and secretary did sign the same, as required by section 60, and all of this will be found in the governor's certificate, attested by the secretary of state, which accompanies the Cronin certificate No. 2.

It seems to me, therefore, that the votes in the Cronin certificate, according to the ruling of the majority in Florida and Louisiana, are the constitutional votes of Oregon. If the ruling in Florida and Louisiana was right, I demand at the hands of the majority of this Commission a similar ruling in this Oregon case. But, sir, I do not believe that ruling was right. I am more convinced it is wrong the more I think of and study it. I do not believe it is right to smother the voice of a State in a presidential election on such technical quibbles. I do not believe we are discharging our duty to the country and to the law creating this Commission, in refusing to hear evidence to determine the constitutional and duly-appointed electors of a State. I believe that the State of Oregon by a decided, though not large majority, voted for Hayes, and I am not willing to have any part of her vote cast for Tilden. I shall not, therefore, maintain that the vote cast by the Cronin college is the constitutional vote of Oregon.

In taking this position I do not mean to reflect on the conduct of the governor in giving a certificate of election to Cronin instead of Watts, who by concession was a Federal officer on the day of election.

I think the governor was bound by his oath to refuse a certificate to Watts. The votes cast for him were absolute nullities, and according to many of the best-considered authorities these votes for Watts were thrown away—considered as not given to anybody—and Cronin, the next highest candidate or the highest eligible candidate, was duly elected.

While I feel it would not be proper to give one vote in Oregon to Tilden, the oath I have taken as a member of this Commission will prevent me from giving more than two of the three votes to Hayes.

Watts was by concession a Federal officer on the day of election and was ineligible, could not be appointed. See authorities cited in Florida case. Watts, Odell, and Cartwright all seemed to have felt and acknowledged this ineligibility by Watts's resignation and its acceptance. The other two at once proceeded to fill the vacancy by the election or appointment of this same Watts. Now, was there a vacancy? I will not repeat the argument made or attempted in the Florida case, but content myself with referring to it and to some of the authorities, most of which are familiar to the members of this Commission. Clark & Hall, 871. Story on the Constitution, sec. 1559. Sergeant's Const. Law, (2d ed.,) 373. Schenck *vs.* Peay, 1 Dillon, 267. State *vs.* Benedict, 15 Minn., 199. Battle *vs.* McIver, 68 N. C., 469. Stratton *vs.* Oulton, 28

Cal., 51. People *vs.* Stratton, 28 Cal., 382. People *vs.* Parker, 37 Cal., 639. Dodd *Ex parte*, 6 Eng., (Ark.,) 152. State *vs.* Jenkins, 43 Mo., 261.

These authorities establish to my mind that there was no vacancy, but failure to elect if Cronin was not elected. These authorities are greatly strengthened by the statutory definition of a vacancy in Oregon.

The laws of Oregon bearing on this subject are as follows:

TITLE VI—OF VACANCIES.

SEC. 48. Every office shall become vacant on the occurring of either of the following events before the expiration of the term of such office:

1. The death of the incumbent;
2. His resignation;
3. His removal;
4. His ceasing to be an inhabitant of the district, county, town, or village for which he shall have been elected or appointed or within which the duties of his office are required to be discharged;
5. His conviction of an infamous crime, or of any offense involving a violation of his oath;
6. His refusal or neglect to take his oath of office, or to give or renew his official bond, or to deposit such oath or bond within the time prescribed by law;
7. The decision of a competent tribunal, declaring void his election or appointment.

SEC. 49. The governor shall also declare vacant the office of every officer required by law to execute an official bond, whenever a judgment shall be obtained against such officer for a breach of the conditions of such bond.

TITLE IX—OF THE ELECTION OF PRESIDENTIAL ELECTORS.

SEC. 58. On the Tuesday next after the first Monday in November, 1864, and every four years thereafter, there shall be elected by the qualified electors of this State as many electors of President and Vice-President as this State may be entitled to elect of Senators and Representatives in Congress.

SEC. 59. The electors of President and Vice-President shall convene at the seat of government on the first Wednesday of December next after their election, at the hour of twelve of the clock at noon of that day, and if there shall be any vacancy in the office of an elector, occasioned by death, refusal to act, neglect to attend, or otherwise, the electors present shall immediately proceed to fill, by *viva voce* and plurality of votes, such vacancy in the electoral college, and when all the electors shall appear, or the vacancies, if any, shall have been filled as above provided, such electors shall proceed to perform the duties required of them by the Constitution and laws of the United States.

In all cases of vacancy under this law there must first have been a legal and eligible incumbent; and no vacancy can exist, then, in an office unless the office has first been duly filled.

So also the authority given to the electors to fill vacancies by the fifty-ninth section looks merely to a vacancy caused by death, refusal to act, neglect to attend, or otherwise, that is, by any other like cause.

I am constrained to believe that Odell and Cartwright had no authority to elect Watts or any other person as an elector, and consequently that Watts had no right to cast his vote for President.

SOUTH CAROLINA.

Mr. Commissioner HUNTON said:

Mr. PRESIDENT: We have now reached the last case to be submitted to this Commission. That it has disappointed public expectation in its decisions, I need not declare. By a vote of eight to seven, this Commission has decided on purely technical grounds that Florida and Louisiana voted for Hayes, and by the same vote of the same members have, as I think, discarded these same technical grounds to give the one disputed vote of Oregon to Hayes. I say this Commission has disappointed public expectation, because the country expected of it that it would decide who had been elected President and Vice-President by the people. They did not expect of us that we would merely confirm the judgment of corrupt and illegal returning-boards, who were ready to put the Presidency up to the highest bidder in the public market.

But our action in the three cases has become a part of the history of the country, and we must stand or fall by the judgment of the forty-four millions of people who have been anxious, interested, and discontented witnesses of our conduct.

In the case of South Carolina different facts are presented from any heretofore offered. We have heretofore been called on to protect States from corrupt returning-boards who have stifled the voice of the people on election-day, and to protect the Constitution of the United States from infraction by the attempt to appoint persons electors when the States are expressly inhibited by the Constitution from making such appointments.

The South Carolina case will be better understood by reference to the offer of proof, as follows:

In support of the objections to certificate No. 1, it is proposed to prove by competent evidence the following facts, which said facts are offered separately and as a whole:

First. That by reason of the failure and refusal of the legislature of South Carolina to provide for a registration of electors, as required by article 8, section 3, of the constitution of said State, and by reason of the acts passed by said legislature in violation of the spirit of such constitutional provision, great frauds were perpetrated by colored republican voters; that at least 3,000 illegal votes were cast for the Hayes electors, which said votes being excluded would give a large majority to the Tilden electors.

Second. That immediately after the adjournment of Congress, to wit, in the month of August, A. D. 1876, a large number of United States soldiers, under command of General Ruger, were sent by the President into said State; that on October 16, General Ruger telegraphed to the authorities at Washington that all was quiet; that there was no need for further troops; that if he (Ruger) deemed a further force necessary he would call for the same; that he never did call for more troops; but that on October 17 the President issued a proclamation declaring that the people of said State were in a condition of insurrection, and that immediately thereafter large numbers of United States soldiers were sent into said State; that at no time prior to the last-mentioned date was there a condition of violence or insurrection which the authorities of the State were unable to control; that at no time during the year 1876 did such a state of affairs exist in South Carolina as justified the intervention of the Federal Government.

Third. That the troops were sent into said State without any action of the legislature thereof, although the same could have been readily convened.

Fourth. That the troops were sent into said State, not for the purpose of quelling insurrection and preserving peace and good order, but for the purpose and with the design of overawing the voters of said State; that said troops were stationed at and near the polls on election-day, and that their presence before and on the day of the election did obstruct and interfere with an expression of the popular will and prevent a free election.

Fifth. That the presence of said troops served to embolden the more desperate of the negroes. Being assured by their party leaders that said troops were there for the purpose of protecting them in any act of violence, the blacks throughout the counties of Beaufort and Charleston inaugurated a condition of riot and lawlessness; that public officials incited them to the commission of every character of crime; that murder was committed, and the perpetrators allowed to escape punishment; that justices refused to issue warrants for the arrest of criminals charged even with the crime of murder, and sheriffs refused to execute such warrants if issued; that the police force of the city of Charleston, composed almost entirely of republican negroes, employed its time in shooting down upon the public streets quiet and inoffensive white men, members of said force being in many instances leaders in the riots which occurred.

That upon election-day the negroes assembled at the polls armed with rifles, shotguns, and other weapons, and prevented negroes who desired so to do from voting the democratic ticket. That the State militia, composed of the worst element of the negro population, and supplied with State arms, was also at the polls aiding and abetting in the violation of law and in the intimidation of voters. That the sheriff of Charleston County, one of the republican electors, without warrant or authority of law, appointed hundreds of so-called "deputy sheriffs," all negroes and republicans, investing them with the power to make arrests at their pleasure. That these deputy sheriffs swarmed about the various polls on election-day, and by their threats and violence did hinder and prevent many citizens from voting, and did arrest and imprison, without information or warrant, many of those who attempted to vote the democratic ticket. That persons styled "United States deputy marshals" were also stationed at the polls aiding and assisting said "deputy sheriffs." That throughout the State the negroes believed that the United States soldiers had been sent to shoot them if they did not vote the republican ticket.

Sixth. That such violence and lawlessness existed throughout the counties of Charleston and Beaufort shortly before and on the day of the election, which said lawlessness was primarily attributable to the occupation of said State by United States soldiers, that no free election could be or was held in said counties, but that, upon the contrary, the popular will found no expression at the polls; that by reason of the lawlessness which existed in the county of Charleston alone the republican electors secured a majority of about 7,000 votes.

The well-understood rule must be applied. In passing upon the admissibility of evidence we must assume that all that is offered to be proved can be proved.

Applying this rule, I ask, What was the condition of South Carolina on the day of election and for several weeks preceding?

There was no condition of violence or insurrection which the State authorities were unable to control. There was nothing to justify the intervention of the Federal Government in the affairs of South Carolina. On the 16th October General Ruger, commanding the Federal troops in that State, reported all quiet and that there was no need for further troops.

Notwithstanding, on the very next day the President, without authority, declared by proclamation that the people of the State were in a condition of insurrection, and forced Federal troops into that State.

These troops were sent into the State, not for the purpose, as avowed, of preserving the peace and quelling insurrection, but to over-awe the voters. The troops were stationed near the polls on the day of election, and did obstruct the free expression of the popular will.

The presence of troops emboldened the desperate colored men, who, incited to deeds of violence by party leaders, committed all sorts of acts of intimidation on colored men who wished to vote the democratic ticket.

The police force of Charleston, composed mainly of republican negroes, shot down on the public streets quiet white men.

Scenes of violence and bloodshed occurred at many of the polls.

All this and much more was done by the public authorities and protected by the troops of the Federal Government with the design to deter men, and especially colored men, from voting the democratic ticket.

If the half of this is true and can be proved as they offer to do, can it be said there was a free election in that State? Can it be said that the apparent small majority for Hayes expressed the true voice of the State of South Carolina?

Can the electors thus chosen be said by us to be duly appointed? Can we say their votes are the votes provided for by the Constitution?

It is very certain if this state of affairs existed in South Carolina on and before the day of election, that the Hayes electors were chosen by force brought to bear by the Federal Government for the purpose of compelling the result; that a state of anarchy and lawlessness prevailed which absolutely prevented, as it was designed to do, a free and fair expression of the political preferences of the voters of the State; that this condition of affairs in that unhappy State was deliberately planned and persistently and wickedly carried out to coerce the voters of that State for Hayes.

We should be most culpable, nay criminal, if we allowed this wicked design to culminate here by counting the vote of the State for Hayes.

There was such a state of affairs existing there that there could not be said there was on the day of election a republican government in the State.

I am, therefore, for admitting the evidence, and, if the proof comes up to the offer, for deciding that no persons were *duly* appointed electors in that State, and that no votes have been cast for President and Vice-President which are the votes provided for by the Constitution of the United States.

REMARKS OF MR. COMMISSIONER ABBOTT.

FLORIDA.

The Commission having under consideration the electoral vote of Florida—

Mr. Commissioner ABBOTT said substantially:

Mr. PRESIDENT: I understand the Senator from Vermont claims that it is not within the power of this Commission to take evidence to contradict the governor's return made in pursuance of the act of Congress, while the Senator from Indiana is of the opinion that the governor's return under the act of Congress may be inquired into, but that any return, whether of the governor or any other State officer, required by State laws is conclusive and cannot be controlled or in any way contradicted, varied, or explained. I readily understand the position of the latter Senator; it is taken not only for this case, but for one that may be before us in the future, for in so deciding as to get the vote of Florida, it would not do to render it impossible to count the vote of Oregon. I agree with the Senator from Indiana that the return of the governor under the act of Congress may be controlled, indeed set aside and disregarded, by proving it to be false in fact. The act of Congress does not make that return either conclusive or *prima facie* evidence, or even evidence at all, in express terms. If it had undertaken to make it conclusive evidence, it certainly would have been unconstitutional. Clearly, Congress has no authority to prescribe what shall be conclusive evidence in such a case, and, probably, it would be held, had no right to impose such a duty upon the chief executive of a State.

But upon the Senator's second proposition I by no means agree with him. He claims, as I understand him, that in no event can a return made under the laws of a State be controlled, inquired into, varied, or shown to be wrong, not according to the fact, whether this falsity arise from innocent mistakes—a mere error in the addition of figures, for example—or from fraud and corruption; nay, further, if the return is once made by the officers appointed under the State law to count the votes and determine the persons elected, it cannot be shown that such officers have exceeded the jurisdiction given them by that law, have done what the law forbade them to do, so that in fact their return is not an execution of the State law, but a direct violation of it.

Under this claim we are told that both Houses of Congress must count the votes given by electors from any State who are certified to be elected by State officers appointed by the law of the State to count the votes and determine the persons elected, although it may be proven beyond all question that the return is untrue in fact, either because the officers making it had made an innocent mistake in adding up a column of figures, or because, actuated by the grossest and most fraudulent of motives, even to the extent of having been paid so to do, they deliberately and willfully made an utterly false return, even certifying persons to be elected who never had been voted for.

I understand the claim goes even further than this, which would seem to be going far enough in all conscience. We are told that if this return is once made, the certificate of election once given, there is no power to recall it, to show that it is false either from fraud or mistake; that it must stand; that the persons in whose favor it is made must cast the vote of the State for President; and that such votes must be counted by the two Houses of Congress, although known to every man, woman, and child in the land to be false and wrong, and although it may have been declared false and wrong by the parties making it, by the highest courts, by the legislature and the executive of the State! Such a claim is most extraordinary and startling. It is abhorrent to the sense of justice and right of every fair-minded man in the land. Nothing but the strongest, clearest, and most incontrovertible reasons can ever compel the public conscience and judgment to assent to it.

We are told that the two Houses of Congress, for it is admitted that this Commission has all their powers in the premises, have no power to do anything more than simply to perform an arithmetical operation in ascertaining the persons voted for as President; that they are to count the votes and nothing more. I agree that they are to count the votes; but, in order to count the votes, they must first determine whether there are any votes to count, and whether those votes have been cast by duly-appointed electors, or by impostors. They not only have the power, but it is a duty imposed upon them, to inquire into and to authenticate the votes, and, where there are several returns claiming to be votes, to determine which are the true votes and which truly declare the real will of the State according to the State law.

Each and every State has the greatest interest not only in its own vote for President but in the vote of each of the other States. No greater wrong could be done to the people of all the other States than to have a President imposed upon them, not by the honest, real vote of a single State, but by a fraudulent and wicked misrepresentation of that vote, so that the high office should be filled by one never elected by the people or the States.

The Constitution meant to give the power of determining the greatest political question that could ever arise, namely, who should be Chief Magistrate, to some persons or bodies of persons; it was not intended to be left unprovided for; it must be determined every four years; and it is absurd to claim that no provision was made by the organic law for so doing. It is a question which does not determine itself; it must be done by human means; and if provision had not been made, the Government would not have survived the first election, for it could never have been decided who had been elected. Nor is this determination confined merely to the arithmetical duty of counting what are claimed to be votes. Each and every State, as I have said, has the same interest in the vote of every other State as in its own; each State has the highest interest, nay, right, that the vote of every other State should be the real vote of that State according to its law, and should not misrepresent its true voice. Without the power somewhere to determine this question, to decide which are the true votes to be counted, both the spirit and letter of the Constitution could be violated with impunity, and both the States and the people grossly defrauded and deprived of the rights guaranteed to them by their organic law. There was no meeting together of all the electors from the different States provided for, so that all could pass on the question who were entitled to cast the vote of each State. No power was given to the electoral college of each State to pass upon or determine the election of its members. And still that question must be determined or the Government could never have got itself even launched. And to whom should that most vital power be granted but to the two great legislative bodies to which are intrusted most of the powers to be exercised under the Constitution ; upon one of which is imposed the great duty of choosing the President, if none has been chosen by the States and the people, and upon the other the like duty of choosing a Vice-President in the same contingency? The language of the Constitution is amply sufficient to impose this duty of determining who has been elected President upon the two Houses of Congress. If those two Houses refuse to perform this duty, confine themselves merely to the arithmetic of the count instead of discharging their great obligation to the people and to the States of determining what is the real, honest vote of each State according to the law of that State, then they are unworthy of the great trust confided to them. This trust can only be discharged by ascertaining whether the vote offered from each State is the vote of that State according to its law; nothing more, nothing less is the measure and requirement of that trust.

Let me not be misunderstood. It is claimed by the Senator from Indiana and those agreeing with him, that the doctrine of State rights bars the way to any inquiry into the question whether the persons from any State claiming to cast its vote are the true electors, and compels Congress to confine itself merely to counting. I have always been a true and faithful disciple of the great doctrine of State rights. I have always believed in it, and always expect and hope to remain steadfast in my faith. From day to day I am the more assured that there is no way known to man by which our Government can be preserved except by the strictest and firmest maintenance of all the rights of the States. I yield to no one in my fidelity to the doctrine of State rights, but I am not willing to carry it to the extent of doing in its name the greatest wrongs to States, instead of upholding their rights. There never was a clearer case of stealing "the livery of the court of Heaven to serve the devil in," than in thus attempting to wrest the doctrine of State rights to excuse and justify this great wrong to States.

Those with whom I agree do not desire to interfere in the slightest degree with the smallest right of a State. We agree that each State by its legislature can prescribe the manner of the appointment of its electors, and that Congress can in no way interfere. We agree, further, that the State legislature may prescribe the manner of voting for the electors, the method of counting the vote and of ascertaining and determining who has been elected, and Congress cannot interfere. We agree that, if the law of the State has been followed out and complied with, and a return made according to and complying with its provisions, Congress must take and give full effect to such a return.

Much has been said here by those opposed to us about " going behind the returns," and the terrible consequences of such an act. You would suppose that if it was once established that so terrible a crime as to go for a moment " behind the returns" could be perpetrated, we should wander in the great wilderness which the imagination of our friends on the other side has conjured up as lying beyond that mysterious limit for as many years as did the Israelites in the deserts of arid and burning sands before they entered into the promised land. It is a chimera conjured up not to enlighten but rather to darken and mislead counsel.

In no real, proper, true sense is it proposed to go " behind the returns." On the contrary, it is only proposed to go *to* the returns, not *behind* them ; to go to them, I say, and near enough to them to ascertain whether they are real, true, honest returns ; whether they are made according to and in conformity with the laws of the State, or in conflict with and in violation of such laws; whether they are true and honest, or the mere results and creations of fraud and bribery and corruption on the part of those making them; for if in making them the makers were simply endeavoring to perpetrate a fraud, to establish a lie, instead of certifying to the facts and the truth, then they are no returns by any law ever recognized by any civilized people who ever lived on the earth.

Is it not as clear as the sun in the heavens that, if we do not inquire whether the returns are the returns in truth and fact, whether they are in accordance with the law of the State instead of in conflict with it, whether they certify the truth or a lie, whether they are honest or steeped in fraud, we are not only doing a great wrong to all the other States, but a greater to the State whose vote is the subject of inquiry, depriving it indeed of one of its greatest rights?

Let it not be said, then, that we propose "to go behind the returns" in the popular acceptation of the words, or in the sense here claimed. We have no occasion to go behind them, but we can go *to* them. We *can* examine them, whether they are returns in fact and in truth, whether they are made in accordance with and not in violation of law, whether the makers of them executed the law under which they acted and certified the truth; or whether, being corrupt and fraudulent, they not only refused to execute it and certify the truth, but on the contrary put a lie in its place.

Take the case under consideration. What is proposed? Fraud is not directly and in terms alleged, I agree; but it is alleged that the return is not made in accordance with, but in direct violation of the law of the State of Florida, and that the persons making it exceeded and went beyond any jurisdiction given them by law in the premises.

What are the facts offered to be proved—indeed proved by the copies of records and papers before us? Why, by the law of Florida the secretary of state, the attorney-general, and the comptroller-general are made a board of State canvassers to canvass the county returns and to determine and declare who have been elected. They are to make a certificate of such determination, which is to be filed in the office of the secretary of state, and that officer is to send to each person elected a certificate of his election, which is made *prima facie* evidence, nothing more. This board, if *the return from any county* is so irregular or fraudulent that the truth cannot be ascertained from it, have power to reject the whole return, nothing more. Two only of the canvassers joined in the certificate of the Hayes electors; the third refused to do so on the ground that the statements in the certificate were not true.

It is offered to be proved that the two canvassers did not execute the law which gave them their only jurisdiction to act, but violated that law, exceeded their jurisdiction, and in and by their return stated not the truth but a lie. Here is no attempt to go behind the return, only to go to it, to see if it is a return under and by virtue of the State law, or whether it is in fact no return. To show that it is no return by which any one could be bound, it is offered to be proved that the supreme court of Florida has passed upon and decided the question— in fact, decided that in making the return the canvassers went outside of and beyond their jurisdiction. It is also offered to be proved that a circuit court, having jurisdiction under the State constitution, in a process of *quo warranto* instituted by the Tilden electors against the Hayes electors and served upon the latter before they had cast their votes, has given judgment that the Hayes electors were not, but that the Tilden electors were legally elected, and has also given judgment of ouster against the former. It is further offered to be proved, and we have the proof before us, that by judgment of the supreme court of Florida all the State officers, from governor down, who were voted for at the same election and on the same ticket with the Tilden electors, and who received substantially the same number of votes, have been declared legally elected, and been put in possession of their respective offices, although the candidates upon the Hayes ticket for State officers had been declared elected by the State canvassers at the same time they had declared the Hayes electors to be elected.

It is offered to be proved, and here again we have the proof before us, that the legislature of the State of Florida has passed an act requiring the board of canvassers to make a new canvass of the votes cast for electors in conformity with the principles laid down by the supreme court; that such canvass has been made, by which it appears that the Tilden electors were elected; that in consequence of such new canvass the legislature has passed another act declaring that the Tilden electors were duly elected and were the only persons authorized to cast the vote of the State, that the Hayes electors had no authority to cast such vote, and ratifying and adopting the vote of the Tilden electors, and directing the governor to certify to the President of the Senate the election of the last-named electors, together with the act itself, which the governor has done.

Thus it is offered to be proved that the certificate of the State canvassers is false in fact; that in making it they exceeded their jurisdiction and authority; that this has been so decided by the supreme court of the State; that the Hayes electors have been ousted from office by the judgment of a court of competent jurisdiction; that the legislature of the State has intervened and declared that the Hayes electors do not represent the true voice of the State; that the governor has so declared; and that in fact the Hayes electors never were elected, or declared to be elected, in accordance with the laws of the State. And still we are told that this false certificate, made by two men with purely ministerial functions—the appointees of a governor who was himself a candidate for re-election—and which is by law made *prima facie* evidence only, must stand and cannot be in any way controlled. All powers, all rights, all persons, and bodies of persons, courts, legislature, governor, people, the State itself, pale and stand powerless before this false certificate of two men. No power on earth, we are told, is broad and high and great and strong enough to cope with these two men and their false certificate. They have the power to make a President of a person who confessedly was never elected, while two and forty millions of people and their representatives in Congress and all the States have no power to prevent it. Such a proposition is monstrous. It is abhorrent to all sense of right and justice. It is shocking to the conscience of the whole people and ought not to be entertained. It is a scandal upon all law and would bring it into deserved contempt. By it law would be made to uphold wrong and fraud, instead of right and honesty. The establishing of such a doctrine would offer a premium to fraud; it would tell the world that fraud may be perpetrated with impunity, and that there is no help for it, no way of preventing it, and that the guilty persons may enjoy the fruits of their guilt.

Consider for a moment this claim. The Hayes electors have voted; and we are asked to declare their vote the true vote of Florida, because two irresponsible ministerial officers, keeping back their decision till the day the vote was to be cast, have so declared; and this although the court having jurisdiction of the case has adjudged that they had no right to cast the vote and were not electors either in fact or in law; although the supreme court of the State has in fact so declared; although the legislature and the governor have joined in so finding and declaring; and although these men have never been in fact elected by the voters of Florida. We are told that neither the two Houses of Congress, nor, if I understand it rightly, any other authority on earth, have power against this simple certificate signed by two ministerial officers—the creatures of the governor—and made by law *prima facie* evidence only; that we must sanction it, declare it sacred, although we know it to be a lie, and thus, in fact, permit two obscure men to elect a person to the high office of President. This is not only to encourage fraud—it is to sanctify it. Instead of declaring, as heretofore we have been taught to believe—foolishly it would seem—that fraud vitiates everything it touches, it is proclaiming that the greater the fraud the more sacred is the act.

Here in Florida we have this strange spectacle: The governor and all the State officers having been voted for on the same ticket with the Tilden electors, having received substantially the same vote, and having been counted out by the same board of canvassers, have been declared elected by the highest judicial authority of the State, and are now exercising the powers of their respective offices peaceably and to the general contentment of the whole people, while the Tilden electors, we are told—although they too have been declared elected by the courts— have no power to act, and their vote must not be counted. What greater scandal upon the law could be imagined?

Why have not the State courts full authority and right to construe the State statutes? Is there any doubt that such is the law? It is so admitted everywhere. I appeal to the members of the Supreme Court upon this board if such is not the inflexible rule which governs the action of that court in construing any statute of a State? Is not the construction put upon a statute of a State by the supreme court of that State as controlling as if such construction had been in express words incorporated into and made a part of the law?

Apply, then, this rule to the Florida case. The supreme court of that State have construed the statute under which the State canvassers act and which alone gives them any authority to act. By their construction the canvassers in giving a certificate to the Hayes electors exceeded and went beyond any jurisdiction and power conferred upon them, and their action is therefore void and of no effect. Tell me why we, why all the world are not bound by that construction. Where do we get the right to set up our construction, or rather the construction of the board of canvassers, of a statute of Florida against the judgment of the supreme court of Florida? Yet, by giving effect to their certificate, we do in fact declare that the judgment of the two canvassers as to what the law is shall prevail over that of the highest judicial authority of the State.

But it is claimed that these Hayes electors having received certificates of election and having voted are *de facto* officers, and that therefore their acts must be held to be legal and valid. Indeed! But how are the Hayes more than the Tilden electors *de facto* officers? Both voted at the same time. The vote of neither has been followed by any consequences affecting the rights of any person. The effect of the votes is to be determined in the future, and it is to determine it that we are now here.

The doctrine of *de facto* officers in no way applies to presidential electors or to their votes. The act of voting affects nobody; it has no power or vitality until they are given by the votes being counted by the Houses of Congress.

A strange perversion is it of the equitable rule that the acts of a *de facto* officer shall be considered valid as to third persons, to apply it in this case. That rule was established for the protection of innocent third persons who have trusted to and acted upon the fact that an officer was in open and apparently peaceable possession of an office, and to whom great injustice would be done by permitting the acts of such a person to be held void because of a subsequent determination that he was not a legal officer. This rule, that official acts are valid although performed by one having no legal right in that regard, is, however, but an exception, and is applied only in favor of those who have trusted to and acted upon such acts as official, and in order to prevent great wrong to innocent third persons. But in the case of the vote of these electors nobody has trusted to or acted upon it; nobody's rights have been affected by it; nobody's condition has been changed by it; it is inoperative until counted; its whole force and effect is derived from the act and determination of other authorities. We are to give it effect now for the first time.

Besides, this doctrine of the validity of the acts of *de facto* officers and authorities has never been applied or extended to their political action. While very many of the acts of the governments of the States while in rebellion, and of their officers, have been held valid on the ground that they were *de facto*, if not *de jure*, entitled to act in the premises, none of their political action has ever been recognized as binding on any one. And this has been the rule adopted by the Supreme Court of the United States.

I submit that there is no ground upon which the votes of the Hayes electors can be counted. They were, in fact, never elected. To count their votes would be to set aside the judgment of the supreme court, the legislature, and the governor of the State of Florida; it would be to give to the certificate of two ministerial officers, made by law merely *prima facie* evidence, a power and effect and conclusiveness not given to the judgments of the highest courts of law; a result never before heard of in the administration of justice. To count those votes would be to declare elected to the high office of President a person who never received the votes of the people as required by the Constitution, but whose title would depend simply on the illegal, fraudulent action of two State canvassers in Florida. If it were intended to encourage fraud and to show that there was no way known to the law to prevent its perpetration, no better way to do it could be devised.

To count the votes of the Hayes electors would be the grossest outrage, equally upon the dearest rights of the State and people of Florida, and upon those of all the other States. By it wrong and injustice would be put in the place of right and justice.

If this attempt to authorize these two irresponsible officers, not the State or people of Florida, to appoint presidential electors for that State, is by the judgment of this Commission to be crowned with success, we shall in effect proclaim to all the world that the whole armory of the law and the Constitution contains no weapon of offense or defense by which the high office of Chief Magistrate of the greatest civilized nation on earth can be successfully protected and defended against being seized upon and held by means of the grossest fraud. Such a judgment would proclaim to the world that, to obtain and enjoy the office of President of the United States, it is not now, as in the olden time, necessary to be constitutionally elected by the States and the people, but that a candidate and party, as lacking in principle as they are rich in money, can, by buying a few weak, wicked, and irresponsible State canvassers, gain possession of and hold that high office; and that such an act will be justified and sanctified by the two Houses of Congress. In fine, such a judgment would proclaim that this Government is no longer one of the people, under the Constitution and law, but that it is a Government of returning-boards and their creatures.

LOUISIANA.

The Commission having under consideration the electoral vote of Louisiana—

Mr. Commissioner ABBOTT said substantially:

Mr. PRESIDENT: I desire to correct a mistake which Mr. Justice Miller has made in reference to the grounds and effect of the decision of the court in Schenck *vs.* Peay, 1 Woolworth, C. C. Rep., 175, just referred to.

That decision settles the question that the Louisiana returning-board was not a legally constituted board; that it was, in fact, no board at all; and that its acts are not entitled to respect, and are of no force and effect.

That judgment was by no means put solely or mainly upon the ground that, where three persons are made a board or commission, and two undertake to act without notice to the third, or without the third knowing of or having any opportunity to participate in their doings, the action of the two cannot be sustained. That was not the chief reason for the decision.

The question at issue was the validity of the action of a board of tax-commissioners in Arkansas, I think. The law of Congress provided that three persons should be appointed such commissioners by the President; and three had been appointed, but only two had qualified under the appointment. The two had acted, and under their action certain lands had been taken for the payment of taxes; and the question to be decided was the validity of the action of the two.

The court, Mr. Justice Miller, rightfully, I think, and in accordance with principle and the authorities, held that, where the law provides that three shall constitute a board, a less number cannot make a legal board at all, and that the law having required three commissioners, there was no board until the three were appointed and qualified. Hear what he says on page 188:

The case before us goes even beyond this, for, according to the statement of the bill, there never was a board of commissioners in existence until after the proceedings in regard to this title were completed. The law required three commissioners. A less number was not a board and could do nothing. The third commissioner for Arkansas, though nominated and confirmed, did not qualify or enter upon the duties of his office until after the sale of the lots to the defendant. There was, therefore, no board of commissioners in existence authorized to assess the tax, to receive the money, or to sell the land. If Congress had intended to confide these important functions to two persons it would not have required the appointment of a third. If it had been willing that two out of the three should act, the statute could easily have made provision for that contingency as has since been done by the act of 1865.

After the passage of the law creating the tax-commissioners another act was passed by Congress giving power to a majority of the board to do any and all acts which could be done by the whole board. This, it was claimed, legalized the action of the two commissioners; but Mr. Justice Miller held that, if the last act was retroactive, it did not affect the case, for the clear and plain reason that it applied only to cases where there was a legal board in existence, and that, where the law provided for a board of three, two did not constitute a board at all, and so the act did not apply. If there had been three commissioners in existence, then the act might take effect and confirm the action of the two; but not otherwise. Hear what Mr. Justice Miller says on this point, at page 190:

But if the section we have cited could be held to have a retrospective effect, the case before us does not come within its purview, for it requires a board of tax-commissioners to be in existence, and then provides that a majority of that board can act. We have already shown that, according to the allegations of the bill, no such board was in existence; that none had ever been organized when the two commissioners assessed the tax and sold the defendant's property. The act of 1865 does not pretend to hold that the sale shall be valid when there is no board in existence, where one of the commissioners never qualified, and where, consequently, no authority was ever vested in three which might be exercised by two.

In the case of Schenck vs. Peay, Mr. Justice Miller decides another matter to which I wish to call the careful attention of the Commission, because his decision is so admirably expressed and applies with such directness and force to this case of the constitution of the Louisiana returning-board. It is holden that whenever the rights of property are to be affected by proceedings *in pais*, *i. e.*, by any board of ministerial officers, their proceedings must be proved to be exactly and strictly in accordance with the law authorizing them. In the case before him the title to a parcel of land was to be affected by the action of the tax-commissioners. I read what he says, at page 188:

Nothing is better settled in the law of this country than that proceedings *in pais*, for the purpose of divesting one person of his title to real estate, and conferring it upon another, must be shown to have been in exact pursuance of the statute authorizing them, and that no presumption will be indulged in favor of their correctness. This principle has been more frequently applied to tax-titles than to any other class of cases. We cannot presume, therefore, that Congress intended that less than three commissioners could conduct these proceedings, and still less that they intended that, in regard to the important matters confided to the board, any action should be taken when there was no legally organized board in existence.

Apply the rule, thus so well and so forcibly laid down, to the case of the Louisiana returning-board. It is not a court; its action is *in pais*; it is a *ministerial*, not a *judicial* body. The law constituting it requires five members taken from *different* political parties, the functions of the board being political and to affect parties. As constituted, it consisted of *four*, not *five* members, all of the *same*, not *different* parties. Upon the action of this board depended the highest rights of the State and of the United States; nay, the very liberties of the people! Shall greater strictness be required in the case of the title to a parcel of land than when the highest rights and dearest liberties of a whole people are concerned?

But the whole decision is applicable to this case of the constitution of the returning-board of Louisiana; and if it is law—and no one doubts it is—it forever settles the question that there was no legally-constituted board in that State with any power to act. The Louisiana case is, by all odds, the strongest; for not only is the law fixing the number of members violated, but the much more important provision requiring the board, in order to protect the rights of all, to be made up of different political parties, is utterly disregarded, apparently that the grossest frauds might be committed.

The fact that in the Schenck vs. Peay case the third tax-commissioner, though appointed, had never qualified, makes no difference in principle. The decision is put solely on the ground that when the law requires one number to constitute a board, a less number will not make a legal body. And so it is held in other cases of the highest authority, especially in that of Wentworth vs. Farmington, 49 N. H. Rep., 120.

I commend to the Commission this decision of Mr. Justice Miller for their careful examination.

The Commission having under consideration the electoral vote of Oregon—

Mr. Commissioner ABBOTT said substantially :

Mr. PRESIDENT : I wish to call the attention of the Commission to the position of this case in reference and relation to the decisions heretofore made by the majority in the two cases of Louisiana and Florida. In both those cases it has been holden that the certificate of the officers appointed and acting under the State law for the purpose of canvassing the returns and determining who have been elected as presidential electors cannot be questioned, controlled, or contradicted for any cause whatever; that it is final and conclusive, and must be so taken and considered by the two Houses of Congress ; in fact that it imports absolute verity.

With that doctrine I did not and do not agree. I protested against it when it was under consideration, and I shall always protest against it. But by its adoption and maintenance by a majority of this Commission the votes of two States have been counted for a person who never received the true and honest votes of those States, but only false certificates from corrupt and fraudulent returning-boards. Unless the majority are prepared in this case to reverse their former action—to change their judgments as the necessities of the case may require—certificate No. 2, given by the governor to Cronin and his associates, must prevail and be declared to be the only conclusive evidence of the appointment of electors for the State of Oregon. There is no escape from such a decision, if consistency is to govern and the same rules which were established in the former cases are to be applied now. In those cases it was held and determined by the majority beyond all peradventure that the certificate of officers appointed under the State law to canvass returns and determine who were elected could, under no circumstances, be controlled, contradicted, or varied ; but that it must stand as the conclusive evidence of the appointment of electors against any and all objections. Let us apply this rule to the Oregon certificates numbered 1 and 2, the former being in favor of Watts and his associates, and the latter in favor of Cronin and his associates. In the first place, let us see what is the law of Oregon on the subject of determining the persons chosen as presidential electors. It, in substance, provides that the secretary of state, upon receiving the returns from the different voting-precincts, shall proceed to canvass the votes given for State officers and members of Congress *in the presence of the governor ;* and that *the governor shall grant certificates of election* to the persons having the highest number of votes, and shall also issue a proclamation declaring the election of such persons. Another section provides that votes for presidential electors shall be given, received, returned, and canvassed in the same manner as those for members of Congress are given, returned, and canvassed ; and that the secretary of state shall prepare two lists of the names of the electors elected, shall affix thereto the seal of the State, and that such lists shall be signed by the governor and the secretary of state, and delivered to the college of electors.

The certificate of election to be given to members of Congress and State officers is not to be given to the electors ; but it is well to consider this provision in determining who are the canvassing-officers for that State. Upon any fair construction of the law the canvassing-officers are the governor and the secretary of state. Neither of them alone has this power, but it resides in both, acting together. As to members of Congress and State officers, the secretary is to canvass the votes *in presence of the governor*, who alone, from this canvassing, is to certify and proclaim the result. The secretary is subordinate; he is to do the mechanical work, but in the presence of the highest officer of the State, the governor, who alone is to act on the canvass. Where the governor was to make one of the canvassing-board this would be the natural form of expression. It would hardly be provided that the governor should do the work while his secretary was present; but that would be done by the latter in the presence and under the supervision of the governor. The presence of the governor could be required only as canvasser, one who was to be responsible, to see that the work was rightly done. To make him a member, it is by no means necessary that he should do any of the manual or arithmetical work of the canvass; it is sufficient that he is there to see that the right results are reached. Can it with any show of reason be claimed that, if in his presence the secretary should make a mistake or should attempt to commit a fraud, the governor would have no power to set it right, but must make his certificate according to the fraudulent or erroneous canvass by the secretary? His presence is provided for that he may prevent any fraud or mistake in the canvass, and it would be preposterous to claim that he could not correct any such fraud or mistake and make his certificate according to the fact. Indeed, as to Congressmen and State officers he is vested with the sole authority to act. The canvass is made in his presence by the secretary; but the governor alone gives a certificate; he alone determines and proclaims the persons elected.

Now, although the governor is not to make proclamation or alone to give the certificate in the case of electors, his duty with respect to State officers ought to be considered in determining who compose the board of canvassers. In the case of electors the votes are to be canvassed as in the case of State officers, by the secretary of state in the presence of the governor. The canvass can be made by neither without the other; for its validity the governor is just as necessary as the secretary. A canvass made by the secretary alone would be just as illegal, just as void as it would be if made by the governor without the secretary. Both officers are absolutely necessary to make a complete legal canvass. It is of no consequence what part each is to take in the canvass. One may do the mechanical and arithmetical work; the other may be present to see that it is rightly done; both together compose the board of canvassers, not one alone. The test is that both are required to be present when the canvass is made, and that it cannot be made in the absence of either.

Here the canvass is to be made by the secretary and the governor; the secretary is to prepare two lists of the persons elected, to which he is to affix the great seal of the State, and which are to be signed by the governor and himself and delivered to the electors. Can there be any stronger evidence that the governor and secretary are the canvassers of the votes for electors?

The secretary is to canvass the votes in the presence of the governor; both are to ascertain and determine the result—that is, who are elected; and both are to sign a certificate of that result. Both ascertain and determine the fact of election, and both must agree in that ascertainment and determination, for both are required to sign a certificate of it. Both must be present at the canvass, and the absence of either would vitiate it. Both must certify to the result of the canvass, and the refusal of either to do so would destroy the certificate. Can anything show more conclusively that the two—not one—are to canvass the votes, determine who are elected by the canvass, and certify that determination? No certificate of election under the law of Oregon is sufficient unless it is signed by the secretary of state and the governor, and, if it is so signed and the great seal is affixed, it is full and complete—the precise evidence required by law to prove the vote of the State for President. And that certificate must give the result of a canvass of the votes made by both, not one, of the officers signing it.

The certificate of Cronin and his associates fully and exactly answers the requirements of the laws of Oregon. It certifies that Cronin and his associates were elected. It is under the great seal of the State, and is signed by the governor and the secretary of state.

These are all the requirements of the law of Oregon. It is of no consequence what else the certificate may contain; the form of expression is immaterial, for no particular form is prescribed. All that is necessary is that there should appear in it the names of the persons elected as electors; that it should be under the great seal, and be signed by the governor and the secretary of state. All this appears fully and clearly in the Cronin certificate.

The governor certifies that Cronin and his associates are elected, and the secretary of state signs in attestation and affixes the great seal of the State. This is all that is necessary. The fact that it is stated in the certificate that the persons named received the highest number of votes cast for persons eligible under the Constitution of the United States to be appointed electors, and are duly elected, does not affect the validity of the certificate. To be sure, all that was required was to certify the persons duly elected; but because the certificate contains another statement, certainly not contradictory of the first, it does not vitiate it or destroy its effect. This certificate fully meets, too, the requirements of the act of Congress, which directs the governor to cause three lists of the names of the electors of the State to be made, certified, and delivered to the electors; it is certified by the governor under the great seal, and attested by the secretary of state. We have here, then, a certificate of election which in itself fully and exactly complies with and fulfills all the requirements of the law of Oregon and of the act of Congress.

If the Senator from Vermont still adheres to the opinion he expressed in the Florida case, that the certificate of the governor under the act of Congress is final and conclusive, he has such a certificate here. If the Senator from Indiana and the rest of the majority of the Commission propose still to adhere to their decision that the determination of the persons elected as electors and the certificate thereof under and by virtue of the State laws is final and conclusive and cannot be controlled, contradicted, or varied, they have here such a certificate, and it must stand and determine the persons elected unless it is proposed to change that rule of construction. I maintain that, if the decisions of the majority in the Florida and Louisiana cases are to stand and serve as guides in this case to govern it in fact, then Cronin must be declared a duly-appointed elector for Oregon.

To be sure, if you look behind the returns, another person appears to have received some 1,100 more votes than did Cronin; but what of that? If you had looked behind the returns in the Louisiana case you would have found that eight persons received from six to ten thousand votes more than did the persons whom you decided to be elected. Why be troubled at a paltry 1,100 votes, when you have faced without blenching

10,000 votes? When the camel of Louisiana has been swallowed, why strain at the gnat of Oregon?

But let us now examine the certificate of Watts and his associates and see if it comes up to the requirements of any law, State or Federal. Clearly it does not. It contains no certificate of election; it is not signed by the governor, both of which are necessary under the State law; and, not being signed or made by the executive, it in no respect complies with the act of Congress. There is, as I have said, no certificate of election, signed by any one, produced by Watts and his associates. There is, however, a certified statement of the votes cast for electors at the election, from which it is claimed that we, not the secretary of state and governor of Oregon as required by law, are to ascertain and determine who had been elected. That is to say, we are to make ourselves into a returning-board and do the duty of the State officers. The certificate does not state, nor does it appear, that all the votes were legally cast or legally returned. Indeed, no facts are stated from which we can determine who were elected, even were it competent for us to usurp the duties of the State canvassers. It is clear that this is not, and was never intended by the secretary of state to be, a certificate of election under the law of Oregon, and that the one signed by the governor and secretary was so intended. By looking at the affidavit of Watts and his associates, which is attached to Certificate No. 1, you will find them swearing as follows: That they demanded "of the governor and of the secretary of state certified lists of the electors for President and Vice-President of the United States for the State of Oregon, but both L. F. Grover, governor of the State of Oregon, and S. F. Chadwick, secretary of state of said State, then and there refused to deliver to us or either of us any such certified lists or any certificate of election whatever. And being informed that such lists had been delivered to one E. A. Cronin by said secretary of state, we each and all demanded such certified lists of said Cronin, but he then and there refused to deliver or to exhibit such certified lists to us or either of us. Whereupon we have procured from the secretary of state certified copies of the abstract of the vote of the State of Oregon for electors of President and Vice-President at the presidential election held in said State November 7, A. D. 1876, and have attached them to the certified lists of the persons voted for by us and of the votes cast by us for President and Vice-President of the United States, in lieu of a more formal certificate."

Here, then, several things are clear from this sworn statement: First, that the secretary of state and the governor never intended, but always refused, to give any certificate of election to Watts; and that both of these officers did intend to give, and in pursuance of that intent did give, to Cronin a certificate of election in accordance with both State and national law. Second, that all parties interested understood it to be the only legal certificate given. It is claimed here now that the secretary of state, and the governor of Oregon, and all parties interested, together with the citizens of that State, did not know and understand their own law, and that it is left for this Commission to discover that the certificate of election given by the secretary of state and the governor under the great seal, and intended and supposed to be the legal and rightful certificate under State and Federal law, was, in fact, no certificate at all and must be set aside and held of no effect; while a mere abstract of votes, containing no certificate of election and signed only by the secretary of state, and not intended to be given or received as such certificate, answers fully the requirements of the State law, which requires such certificate to certify to the election and to be signed by the governor and the secretary of state.

If the certificate of Cronin is rejected, it is simply reversing the decisions in the Florida and Louisiana cases, and adopting a rule exactly opposite to the one governing those cases.

But even if it is held that the secretary of state alone is the person to canvass the votes and determine who are elected, the Cronin certificate is the only one that meets the requirements of the law. That is the only certificate of election. There is no other. It is under the great seal of the State and is signed by the secretary of state. That it is also signed by the governor does not in any way detract from its legality or effect. So that, whatever construction is put upon the State law, whether it is holden that the secretary of state alone or the governor and secretary together constitute the board of canvassers of votes, that certificate is the only one made in conformity with law—in fact, the only certificate of election at all.

But do not misunderstand me. I do not believe that Cronin was duly elected an elector for the State of Oregon, and I shall so vote. I agree that the weight of American authorities, including especially those of my own State, are in his favor; but I believe the true, the fair, the just rule to be this: When a person ineligible for election is voted for and receives the largest number of votes, it must be held that there is no election, unless it can be proved that the electors knew of his ineligibility when they voted for him, and in that case their votes are to be treated as mere blanks, not votes at all. In this case I am not satisfied that the people of Oregon can be fairly said to have known that Watts held the office of postmaster. Some of them did undoubtedly know it; but in a State so large territorially as is Oregon, it is not reasonable to suppose that any considerable number of the citizens of that State knew that he was postmaster in a small town, and I therefore think it must be held that, Watts being ineligible, there was no election of one elector.

That Watts held an office of profit under the United States at the time he was voted for is not denied. It has been held here that if such a person receives the certificate of election from the proper authorities his vote must be counted, and that the two Houses of Congress have no power to inquire whether he is by the Constitution prohibited from being elected or not. This seems to me a most monstrous proposition, one equally strange and dangerous. The prohibition of the Constitution is absolute.

No person holding an office of trust or profit under the United State. shall be appointed an elector.

Nothing could be stronger. The voting for President is a right created solely by the Constitution; before that was adopted it had no existence; it depends therefore entirely on the terms of the grant, and must be exercised according to its mandates and provisions. If a reason for this prohibition was sought for, it could be easily found. It was not intended that Federal officers should be candidates for appointment, so that they might not be tempted to use their power and influence as such officers to affect or control an election. The Constitution must be construed as saying in terms to the people of Oregon, "You shall not vote for J. W. Watts." It, in effect, so says to the people of any State in reference to any candidate who holds an office of trust or profit under the United States. To claim that this prohibition upon the States is left to them, the very parties prohibited, and to them only, to enforce, is against all logic and reason. It amounts to this: a party is prohibited by a superior authority from doing a particular act which affects that superior authority, and still the party prohibited is alone to determine whether it will regard the prohibition, and if it does not regard it, the superior authority, although affected by such determination, has no right or power to enforce the prohibition. The statement of the claim is a sufficient refutation of it. Until the hearing before this Commission began, it was never heard or even dreamed that a State could against the prohibition of the Constitution appoint a person elector and have his vote counted, there being no power in Congress to prevent it.

Why, look for a moment at the provisions of the law under which we are acting. Consider them, and then say, who can, that we are compelled to count the vote of a person whom the Constitution prohibits the State from appointing as an elector! By that law the duties of this Commission are expressly and carefully defined. This Commission is to "decide whether any and what votes from such States are the votes provided for by the Constitution of the United States"—mark it, and consider it well—"*whether they are the votes provided for by the Constitution.*" Could anything be plainer? Again, the Commission is to "decide how many and what persons were duly appointed electors in such State." We have each taken an oath that "we will impartially examine and consider all questions submitted to the Commission of which we are members, and a true judgment give therein."

It is proven to us that a person who was by the Constitution absolutely prohibited and forbidden to be elected has voted as an elector. Can we find and determine under the law and our oaths that his vote is the one "provided for by the Constitution of the United States" when he is by that instrument expressly prohibited from casting a vote? Can we say that such a person "was duly appointed an elector" when the Constitution expressly declares that he shall not be so appointed?

Speaking for myself alone, I can only say that if I, as a member of this Commission and having in mind the oath I have taken to honestly discharge the duties imposed upon me by the law creating it, decided in favor, as a presidential elector, of the vote of a person who held an office of trust or profit under the United States at the time of his election, I should be morally, if not legally, guilty of perjury. I should be doing precisely that which I had solemnly sworn I would not do.

But it is claimed that Watts, although holding an office of profit under the United States when he was appointed and for some time after, resigned that office and also the office of elector before casting his vote, and that he was subsequently by the other electors chosen to fill his own vacancy. At the best, this is but a gross evasion both of the spirit and the letter of the Constitution. But let us examine and see if the prohibition of the Constitution can be gotten rid of so easily.

The act of Congress, Revised Statutes, section 133, provides that—

Each State may by law provide for the filling of any vacancies which may occur in ts college of electors when such college meets to give its electoral vote.

Section 134 provides—

That whenever any State has held an election for the purpose of choosing electors and has failed to make a choice on the day prescribed by law, the electors may be aϸpointed on a subsequent day in such manner as the legislature of such State may direct.

The law of Oregon provides that "the electors shall convene at the seat of government on the first Monday of December next after the election, at the hour of twelve of the clock at noon of that day, and if there shall be any vacancy in the office of an elector occasioned by death, refusal to act, neglect to attend, or otherwise, the electors present shall immediately proceed to fill by *viva voce* and plurality of votes such

vacancy in the electoral college." It is claimed that under these provisions of the law Watts could resign, thus create a vacancy, be immediately elected to fill it, and cast one vote of the State for President.

An examination of the affidavits and returns of this Watts and his
associates shows a queer state of facts—something, indeed, almost mysterious. The affidavit of Watts and his associates, Odell and Cartwright,
to which they all make oath, says that—

At the hour of twelve o'clock m. of the 6th day of December, A. D. 1876, we duly assembled at the State capital, in a room in the capitol building at Salem, Oregon, which
was assigned to us by the secretary of state; that we duly on said day and hour demanded of the governor and secretary of state "certain certified lists of electors,
which were then and there refused."

Now, in the certificate of their vote for President and Vice-President
two of these same gentlemen, Odell and Cartwright, say that at precisely twelve o'clock noon on the same 6th day of December they two,
alone, met at the seat of government; that they organized by the choice
of one as chairman and the other as secretary; that one of them presented the resignation of Watts, which was read and accepted; that
there were but two electors present, namely, said Odell and Cartwright;
that the two thereupon declared one vacancy to exist in the college, and
elected Watts to fill the vacancy occasioned by his own resignation.
Put together the affidavit of the three and the certificate of the two,
and this is the result: the three swear that at twelve o'clock m. they
were all three present at a certain place and there did certain acts; but
two of the three certify that at the same hour and place the third was
not present, and on account of his absence the two performed certain
other and different acts. This is like a game of "thimble-rig," and
Watts is the "little joker;" "now you see him and now you don't."
When required at a certain point of time to be in a certain place, he is
sworn to be present; when not wanted he is certified to be absent at
precisely the same place and time. A very convenient personage this,
who can thus make himself visible and invisible whenever the necessities of the case require it.

This seems to me to be clear: Section 133 of the law of Congress has
reference only to a college of electors which has been once filled and a
vacancy has occurred subsequently. The words indicate that the intent was to provide for such a case only. This is rendered certain by
the fact that the next section provides for the case of no election having been had, clearly showing that the word "vacancy" when used in
the preceding section applied simply to the case where there had been
an election and the place of a person elected had subsequently become
vacant. Without this, indeed, it might be claimed, with much show of
reason for the construction, that a vacancy could only happen when the
office had been once occupied.

The statute of Oregon clearly meant to deal with the "vacancy" indicated in section 133 of the act of Congress, and not with the case of
the office never having been filled, provided for in the next section.
The phraseology shows this clearly and excludes any other construction. "If there shall be any vacancy occasioned by *death, refusal to act,
neglect to attend, or otherwise*" by no means refers to a case of the office
never having been filled at all. "Or otherwise" must be taken with its
surroundings, and construed in the light of those surroundings and of
the whole statute taken together. The old maxim "*noscitur a sociis,*"
if it could ever apply in any case, applies here. The "other causes"
creating a vacancy must be like causes; for no one can, without violating all the rules of construction applicable to statutes, hold that the in-

tent was to provide by these two words in the connection in which they are used for the case of a failure to elect—a case so entirely different from that of a vacancy occurring after election by reason of death or any other cause. This construction is fortified by the opinion of the supreme court of Rhode Island, a most respectable tribunal, upon a case almost exactly like this both in spirit and letter, and by the action of the legislature upon that opinion. That court held that where there had been no election because the person voted for· at the time held an "office of trust under the United States" there was no " vacancy," and that the place must be filled by the legislature as in the case of a failure to elect.

It seems clear to me that, inasmuch as Watts held an office of trust and profit under the United States at the time of the election, he was "ineligible" to be elected; that there was no election of one elector; that he could not resign an office which he had never held; that there was no " vacancy" within the meaning of the law of Oregon; and that, consequently, but two votes from Oregon can be counted for President and Vice-President. To me it seems clear and beyond all question that to count more than two votes would be a direct violation of the Constitution and a violation of the oath we have here taken "to decide whether the votes are those provided for by the Constitution and what persons were duly appointed electors."

It seems to me certain beyond all controversy that to set aside the certificate of the governor and the secretary of state under the great seal, and to accept in its stead a mere certified statement of votes with no certificate of election, is to openly and directly reverse and overrule the decisions pronounced by the majority of this Commission in the cases of Florida and Louisiana; thus establishing different rules, applicable to the same facts, in different cases.

SOUTH CAROLINA.

The Commission having under consideration the electoral vote of South Carolina—

Mr. Commissioner ABBOTT said substantially:

Mr. PRESIDENT: I desire to say something, after what has been said here, upon the questions raised in this case of South Carolina.

Of course no one claims that the vote of the Tilden electors should be counted. The Hayes electors undoubtedly received a majority of the votes as they were actually cast. There were, no doubt, many irregularities in conducting the election and making returns of votes from the many different precincts, which, if they had been insisted upon, might have altered the result; but ascertaining as nearly as could be done the number of votes as actually cast and disregarding all irregularities connected with the conduct of the elections and the returns thereof, a majority of the votes cast, was for the Hayes electors; therefore, of course, no question can fairly arise in reference to counting the vote of the Tilden electors.

But such a conclusion by no means settles the case. There still remains to be determined the question, shall the vote of the Hayes electors be counted?

The settlement of it involves several considerations and issues quite as important and interesting as any which have been examined and decided in either of the other cases before the Commission.

And first let me consider an objection to counting these votes raised by my friend from Virginia, Mr. Hunton. The objection is this:

The Constitution expressly requires that the electors shall vote for

President and Vice-President by ballot; that they shall name in their ballots the persons voted for as President, and in distinct ballots the persons voted for as Vice-President; and that they shall make distinct lists of all persons voted for as President and of all persons voted for as Vice-President, and of the number of votes for each, which lists they shall sign and certify, and transmit to the President of the Senate.   The acts of Congress merely provide the details for carrying this requirement of the Constitution into effect.   It is clear that, if the Constitution is to be regarded, no vote for President not by ballot is legal or can be counted.   No matter what may have been the reason for this requirement, certain it is that it was considered important enough to put it into the Constitution, and we must regard it, unless we are prepared to say this Commission is not bound by that antiquated instrument.   I think the majority have practically set aside, nullified in fact, the mandate that no person holding an office under the United States shall be appointed an elector, and it may be considered that we can with equal right disregard the mandate that all votes shall be by ballot.   If the Constitution is to prevail, however, not only must the voting be by ballot, but lists must be made of the persons thus voted for, and sent to the President of the Senate.   By fair construction these lists must show that the votes were by ballot, because by the Constitution nothing but ballots are recognized as votes.   By the law establishing the Commission we are to decide what votes " are the votes provided for by the Constitution," and as no vote is recognized by that instrument as a vote for President except it be by ballot, it seems clear that we must be satisfied whether the votes under consideration were, as required by the Constitution, by ballot or otherwise.

It is clear beyond any question that it does not appear from the certificate of the Hayes electors that they voted by ballot; there is nothing in it from the first to the last word which in any manner indicates that the voting was *viva voce* or by ballot.   We therefore have not even a scintilla of evidence before us upon which we can decide as required by law " which are the votes provided for by the Constitution;" that is, whether the votes were by ballot or otherwise.   That is a question that must be settled by evidence; we cannot know it by instinct or intuition, and there is no evidence at all bearing upon it.

We are told by Mr. Justice Bradley that this objection is not even plausible; certainly a somewhat strong word to apply to an objection made by a member of this Commission upon his official responsibility. Not " plausible," forsooth, to inquire whether the votes have been cast in the manner commanded by the Constitution !   Perhaps by some it may not be considered sensible, "plausible" even, to permit the requirements of the Constitution to be regarded at all in this matter of determining who is to be President, but then there are others of us who do consider that some evidence should be furnished to show that the provisions and requirements of the organic law have been complied with before we give judgment in so important an issue.   Therefore, at the expense of not being considered even "plausible" by the learned justice, I venture to discuss and consider this question.

When it is considered important, vital enough to make it a constitutional mandate, that the vote for President should be cast in a particular manner, why must we not in some way, by some evidence, be satisfied that this requirement has been complied with ?   Certainly when we are appointed by law to decide " which are the votes provided for by the Constitution " some evidence should be furnished on the point at issue, so that we may be able to decide that question.   As I have said, when the Constitution requires that the electors shall make and certify lists of the persons voted for as President and Vice-President and of the number of votes for each, a fair construction would require the cer-tificate to state that the votes were by ballot, they being the only votes that could be legally cast. I do not claim that the certificate should contain any set form of words, but that it is necessary that in some form of expression it should set forth the fact that the votes were cast as required by the Constitution.

Now, by looking at the return by the Hayes electors of their acts, there is nothing in it even to indicate that they voted by ballot; on the con-trary, the inference from it would be that they did not so vote. It is not even stated that the vote was duly cast, or according to law, which might be sufficient in the absence of anything to control such a state-ment. Again, the list purports to be of " those voted for by the elec-toral college of the State of South Carolina," rather indicating the result of action by the college as a board than that of each individual member of it. Certainly there is nothing in the return which gives me the slightest intimation that the votes were cast by ballot and nothing from which I can fairly infer that such was the fact, and if I decide they were so cast, I do it absolutely without evidence. Indeed, from the wording of the certificate, I should be strongly inclined to believe that the voting was not by ballot.

Having had some opportunity to know how affairs are conducted by the party in power in South Carolina, that knowledge by no means leads me to believe that any regard would be paid by these electors to either law or Constitution. Several of them I saw when in South Carolina this winter as a member of the committee of investigation on the part of the House of Representatives, and one at least came before that committee and was examined as a witness, and in his examination disclosed facts which would prevent any fair mind from putting the slightest faith in his honesty, integrity, or intelligence. From the certificate itself, from what I know of the persons who signed it, and their disregard of all law, right, and even decency, I am strongly inclined to believe that the voting in this case was not by ballot; certainly no member of the Commission can say there is the slightest evidence that the votes were so cast. Although it may please Mr. Justice Bradley to say of the objection of my friend from Virginia that it is not even " plausible," I defy him to give, not merely a plausible, but any reason, for finding that the votes of the South Carolina electors were cast in the manner required by the Constitution.

How then can we find they were cast by ballot? We must so find in order to determine that they " are the votes provided for by the Consti-tution of the United States," which we are bound to do by our official oaths.

By one Commissioner it is said this objection is not even " plausible," by another that it is merely technical and so ought not to weigh in the consideration of questions so great and important as are here at issue. The answer is plain. The objection is founded on the Constitution itself, and its only purpose is to require a compliance with its express man-dates. If the objection is not plausible, if it is technical, it is the fault of the Constitution in being technical and not even plausible in its requirements.

But there are other objections to the votes of the Hayes electors which involve some of the most important questions and issues that can ever present themselves for consideration and determination where the gov-ernment is constituted as is ours—questions and issues fundamental, and involving the very existence of our institutions in their present form. If you decide to reject the proofs offered in this case, and count the vote, you will establish a principle by which, if acted on in the future, there may never be another free election of President of the United States by the people thereof; a precedent by which any person or party in power may forever perpetuate that power by the use of the Army of the United States.

Consider the proofs which are offered here, and which we are told by the majority we must reject, and count the vote of South Carolina, notwithstanding the facts offered to be proved.

In the first place it is alleged, and proof of the allegation is proffered, that although the constitution of the State which was adopted in 1868 commands the legislature to establish a registration of voters, the legislature has persistently refused to obey this mandate, it being largely republican, for the sole purpose of keeping possession of the government by a resort to repeating and double voting. Certainly the laws of that State regulating voting, if intended expressly to encourage repeating and frauds at elections, could not be better contrived to accomplish such a purpose. The counties are each divided into many voting-precincts, one into over fifty, and every citizen of the county can vote in any precinct without regard to the parish, precinct, or town in which he resides. But although this is reprehensible in the highest degree, and shows the fraudulent intent of the party in power, I agree that it does not furnish sufficient reason to reject the vote of the State. The law certainly is mandatory upon the legislature; but if that body refuses to obey, to do its duty and execute the mandate by making a law to provide registration, such refusal, however wicked and fraudulent, cannot deprive the State and its people of the right to vote. Any other construction would put an end to the government and prevent the people from electing any officers, State or national.

The next offer of proof is, that the troops of the United States were sent to South Carolina before and stationed near the polls at the election, by the President of the United States, solely for the purpose of overawing a portion of the people, and compelling them to vote to sustain the republican party, and that this purpose for so sending and stationing the troops was accomplished; that the people were overawed and compelled to vote to sustain the party so using the troops, and that there was in consequence thereof no free election, no such election as is required by the law and Constitution of both the State and United States.

It is further offered to be proved that the State militia, composed almost entirely of ignorant negroes, was stationed at many of the polls, in fact surrounding them, to prevent a portion of the people from voting the democratic ticket, and by violence did succeed in so doing; that armed bands of negroes also surrounded the voting-places in some counties, and by violence and force prevented thousands of persons from voting with the democrats—a much larger number, in fact, than the majority claimed for the Hayes electors.

The only answer made to all this is that the two Houses of Congress have no right to inquire into these allegations, no right to ascertain whether these offers of proof can be substantiated.

In the Florida and Louisiana cases we were told, and a majority of this Commission has so decided, that by the Constitution, by our organic law, neither the two Houses of Congress, the States, nor their legislatures, nor their courts, nor their executives, had any power to inquire whether the votes of any State had been cast by persons never in fact elected, but who obtained a certificate of election by the grossest frauds and bribery of the State returning-boards; and that Congress, the whole country indeed, must look on in quiet and contentment, able to do nothing to prevent their Chief Magistrate being seated in office not by law and the voice of the people, but by fraud and corrupt practices.

Those decisions, by which fraud is justified and sanctified, are bad enough, but the proposed resolutions are even worse. By the first, the Presidency can be bought and sold, even put up at auction, openly and in the face of the world, and so weak and powerless are our Constitution and laws that it cannot be prevented or remedied.

Some one has said—Gibbon, I think—that when the imperial purple at Rome was sold by the pretorian guard, it was conclusive evidence that all reason for the Roman empire continuing to exist had ceased. No people who submit to have their chief magistracy bought and sold have any right to exist as a nation. What shall we say, then, of our own condition? In the Louisiana case it was offered to be proved, and the offer being rejected it must be taken as true, that the vote of that State for the republican candidate was obtained by bribery, perjury, and forgery, and this Commission decided that a vote so obtained was as good as one absolutely pure and honest, and that the people must submit to a President, though he might owe his election to such crimes. By that decision we are told that a candidate may openly buy the vote of any State from such a returning-board as has been established in perpetuity in Louisiana, and agree that the money therefor shall be paid when the sale is consummated by the count of the two Houses of Congress; and, for aught I can see, he can deposit the money to be paid on the Speaker's desk, to be delivered when the count is complete, and call upon the assembled Senators and Representatives to witness the payment. All this we are told would be constitutional and right under the law. And now, as if it was not quite enough of infamy and disgrace to the country to have it established that the Presidency can be bought without hinderance or objection, we are told that the President, to perpetuate himself or his party in power, may use the military forces of the United States to compel the people of a State to vote as he desires; that the militia of a State may be used to the same end; and that votes so obtained by an election controlled and dominated by military force must be counted precisely as pure and honest votes are counted; and again, that there is no power in Congress, or in any other person or bodies of persons, to prevent such a consummation of wrong and wickedness. If any doctrine more utterly destructive to a free government and free institutions—to a government of the people, for the people, and by the people—could be devised and put forth to the world, I certainly cannot conceive of it. The doctrine is utterly and entirely damnable. It will bear the palm for unmitigated wickedness for all time to come. By it a free goverment may be turned into the worst of despotisms. By it the people may be deprived of all their rights and liberties, and military force and power be made to usurp the place of law and justice. It is a high crime against liberty and good government. It proclaims to the world that our system of government is a failure; that it has ceased to be one regulated by law, and administered according to the will of the people expressed under and according to the law, and has become a despotism, where law has given place to force and the will of the people exists only in name, not as a controlling factor, not in verity and fact.

Indeed, this doctrine, if established, caps the climax of wrong. We have had bribery, forgery, perjury, and all manner of corrupt practices justified by the decision of a majority of this Commission as a proper means to obtain the Presidency. We are now told that the Army of the United States may be used to force the people to vote, not as they wish, but as others wish. If this doctrine is adopted and established, the measure of our woes, and disgrace as well, is full to the brim.

Its greatest foes never before have claimed that our Constitution was so miserably. weak and defective, such a piece of bungled, botched work, as we are now told it is by a majority of this Commission.

In a free government, professing to be a government of the people by the people, whose boast is that the rights and liberties of all are equally protected by and under the law and that all wrongs and abuses are to be righted peaceably by an appeal to the ballot-box, how strange, indeed how criminal it is to claim and act upon the claim that the military arm may be used with impunity, against all law and right, for the very object and purpose of putting an end to free elections—which means nothing more nor less than putting an end to the government of the people; and that there is no way of preventing it, known to man, that the Constitution and law furnish no defense against so great an offense against freedom and free government.

Such a doctrine would not and ought not to be tolerated for a moment where even the smallest show is kept up of a regard for the will of the people in governmental affairs. A doctrine like this put forth and acted on by the King of Great Britain would change the reigning dynasty as effectually as did no worse attempt to establish despotism change it in 1688.

In addition to this employment of the Army of the United States, we have the offer of proof that the State militia were used for the same purpose, that armed bands of negroes surrounded the polls, preventing people of their own race from voting as they wished to do, and resorting to all manner of violence to accomplish such a result; in fact, the offer of proof is such that, if substantiated, an election holden under such circumstances is worse than a farce, it is a disgrace to any civilization however imperfect, and would bring our form of government into most justly merited contempt. Indeed, if it be true that such an election is to be tolerated and its results are to be established and prevail, it furnishes conclusive proof that our institutions, of which so much is boasted, have failed; and it might, with a show of reason, be claimed they ought to give way to some other form of government which will at least give peace and protection to persons and property.

From all I could learn while in South Carolina, the allegations in the offers of proof are substantially true, certainly as to parts of the State, and I am sure no such election was holden the results of which ought to affect in any way the rights of the people of the other States.

The colored people were told and believed that the United States troops were sent into the State to compel them to vote the republican ticket and shoot all who attempted to vote with the democrats. This belief I have no doubt was general among the blacks. Of course there were many too intelligent to give it credit, but the great mass gave it full faith and credence. Any negro who manifested a desire to act with the democrats was completely ostracized, and in addition assaulted and beaten by those of his own race whenever the opportunity to do it occurred. Negro wives left their husbands if the husbands left the republican party. Negro men attempting to vote the democratic ticket were attacked at the polls by negro women, beaten, stripped naked, and driven off. In many places the polls were surrounded by organized bands of armed blacks, who assaulted, beat, and forcibly drove off all of their own race who attempted to vote against the republicans, or compelled them to vote that ticket. I have no doubt that many thousands of colored voters would have voted the democratic ticket had they not been either driven off or compelled by violence and fear to vote for the republicans, and but for that lawlessness and violence the Hayes electors, instead of receiving a majority of some eight hundred, would have been defeated by some thousands.

But one answer suggested to this is, that the democrats, too, resorted to force, violence, threats, and intimidation to compel the blacks to vote their ticket.

Does not this tend, if the charge be true, to prove conclusively the proposition we support, that the vote of the State should not be counted, because by the illegal and unjustifiable acts of both political parties a free election was rendered impossible?

The answer is no answer. Its reason and logic is the reason and logic of the boy charged by his fellow with wrong-doing, who replies to it, "You are another."

I have no doubt the charge, to some extent, is well founded. It would be strange if it was not so. The provocations were so great, the evils to be remedied were so terrible, the wrongs to be righted so subversive of all governments, that no doubt many things were done by the democrats that would not be tolerated in a different condition of affairs, and cannot be justified. But I believe ten negroes were compelled to vote for the republicans by the violence and lawlessness of their own race for one who was compelled to vote against his will for the democrats by their unlawful practices.

But while I admit that there was to some extent a resort to unjustifiable means by democrats to control the colored vote, beyond all question this was not sanctioned by their candidates for office or by any of the leading, influential men of that party. Governor Hampton, Colonel Haskell, the chairman of the State committee, and every other candidate and leading man of the party, I am satisfied, exerted all their power and influence in favor of peace and a perfectly free election. But such was the condition of things in the State, what with the United States troops and the State militia, composed mainly of the most ignorant blacks, what with armed bands of negroes in many precincts, dominating and abusing all their own race who dared even to try to act independently, urged on by bands of carpet-baggers, thieves, and native "scalawags," as they are called, who knew if they were defeated flight or the penitentiary was their only safety, a free election was an utter impossibility. Certainly no election holden under such circumstances and with such surroundings ought ever to affect the rights of a single human being outside the limits of the State; to impose on the other States a Chief Magistrate by the means and appliances there resorted to would bring our whole system of elections into merited contempt and disgrace.

Let me say a few words in reference to another justification put forth for the presence of the Federal troops in South Carolina. It is said that the people of South Carolina were in a state of insurrection against the Government, that the governor was powerless to suppress it, and called on the President for aid under the provisions of the Constitution. This is offered to be proved to be false; but for the purpose of considering the justification, and its effect on the election, let it be taken to be true. The State, then, was not only controlled by turbulence and violence, but an insurrection against the Government and the execution of the laws prevailed over the constituted authorities, which was be-

yond their power to quell and suppress. Such is the justification for
sending the troops. The governor, it is said, asked for them, for he,
with all the authority of the State and its laws, was powerless.

Is an election holden when the people of the State are in open insurrection against its authorities, so general and wide-spread that they are
powerless and the United States are called on to suppress it, an election
at all, in any sense known to our law? How can it be claimed with any
show of reason that when the people of a State are in actual insurrection against its authorities they can hold a valid election, by which the
rights of not only their own State, but of all the other States, are to be
affected, nay, possibly controlled? To hold such an election valid to
affect the rights of the whole country is against the whole
spirit and theory of our Government.

Therefore, whether the troops were rightfully sent to South Carolina
because there existed there an insurrection too strong to be put down
by the State authorities, or whether no such insurrection existed, and
the troops were wrongfully sent there to overawe a part of the voters
and compel them to support the party in power, is perhaps unimportant
to determine, for in either case the reason is equally strong against
giving effect to an election holden under such circumstances and with
such surroundings.

In whatever light, then, you look upon the election in South Carolina
for presidential electors on the 7th of last November, and its result,
with the allegations and offers of proof before you, to count the vote of
the Hayes electors would be a crime against freedom and free governments—as great an offense, if possible, as that committed by counting
the votes of Louisiana.

<hr style="width:15%;" />

REMARKS OF MR. COMMISSIONER HOAR.

FLORIDA.

The Electoral Commission having under consideration the question of counting
the electoral vote of the State of Florida—

Mr. Commissioner HOAR said:

Mr. PRESIDENT: The question before the Commission is not who
have been lawfully elected President and Vice-President of the United
States. We are to decide who were appointed electors by the State of
Florida; and are now to consider one only of the steps required in
arriving at that decision.

The election of President is accomplished by a mechanism wholly
created by the Constitution, unlike anything else in the world, by
which the executive power of the country is to be continued without
interruption, and rendered perpetual, by elections to take place once in
four years by persons appointed by thirty-eight other sovereignties; the
appointment, election, ascertainment of the result, and induction into
office of the person elected being all required to be completed within the
space of a few weeks. Whatever aid we may derive from the common
or parliamentary law, or from the practice of courts, it is obvious that
the best test of the question whether a particular process belongs in
this complicated machine is the inquiry whether if it be introduced the
machine will work; whether it will help or prevent the accomplishment
of the result.

The Constitution provides that the electors of President and Vice-

President shall be appointed by the States in such manner as their legislatures may direct. These electors, when appointed, become clothed with a right of suffrage which they are to exercise on the same day in all the States. There must enter into the act of appointment the exercise of the power of determining who is appointed. This power is also lodged in the State and must be exercised as it provides and before the casting the vote. The vote cannot be cast first and the appointment consummated afterward.

The law of the State of Florida provides that the due appointment of electors shall be ascertained and determined by a board composed of certain designated State officers, who, having made a canvass, " shall determine the result of the election as shown by the returns ;" * * * " shall make and sign a certificate and declare who shall have been elected, which certificate shall be recorded." * * * " When any person shall be elected to the office of elector of President and Vice-President, the governor shall make out, sign, and cause to be sealed with the seal of the State and transmit to such person a certificate of his election." It seems to me that this determination of the canvassing-board is in the nature of a judgment. It must be performed before the electors receive their authority or cast their votes. It is the conclusive evidence of their authority. When the tribunal on whom the State has imposed the duty has ascertained and declared who have been lawfully appointed electors, and such electors have cast their votes and duly certified the result, the State has performed its whole constitutional office, and is *functus officio* in that regard.

I do not think that any evidence can be received to overcome the effect of this determination of the State authority as to who were lawfully appointed, made before the electors cast their vote on the 6th of December. Further, I do not think that the evidence offered or suggested by the counsel or objectors tends to overcome it.

It is true that *votes* are to be counted. But it is the votes of those persons whom the proper authority has determined and certified were entitled to cast them, and not the votes of those persons whom the two Houses of Congress or either of them may think were so entitled.

It seems to me clear that the power to judge of the elections, returns, and qualifications of presidential electors is not given by the Constitution to the two Houses of Congress, or either of them. The power which it was deemed necessary carefully to express in regard to their own members, it could hardly have been intended to bestow by implication from the right to be present when the certificates are opened, or even from the right to count the votes. It is a power which it is utterly impracticable for Congress to exercise between the time when the certificates are brought officially to its knowledge and the time when it must be determined who has been chosen President. Indeed, the distinguished counsel who closed for the Tilden electors conceded this difficulty, to which his only answer is the suggestion that such an inquiry, like the right to the writ of *quo warranto*, must be limited by discretion; in other words, that the two Houses may go as far into the inquiry, who were duly chosen electors in any State, as they in their discretion think fit, or as time will permit.

The statement of this position seems to be its refutation. We are now discussing a question of jurisdiction. In whom is the power to determine who have been appointed electors—in Congress or in the State? It is gravely answered that it is in Congress when the State to be investigated is near the seat of Government, or the inquiry relates to a few election-precincts only, but is to be left to the State in other cases; that Congress may exert a power of inquiry into an election in Delaware which is impossible as to California, or may inquire into one election-district in New York, but cannot into twenty or a hundred. This claim would never have arisen in any man's mind before the days of railroads and telegraphs. Such investigations, possible only in the most limited degree now, would have been wholly impossible as to most of the States when the Constitution was adopted.

It is asked, is there no remedy if the officers to whom the States intrust the power of ascertaining and declaring the result of the election act fraudulently or make mistakes? The answer is that the Constitution of the United States gives no jurisdiction to Congress, when the certificates are opened and the votes are to be counted, to correct such mistakes or frauds. A like question may be put as to every public authority in which a final power of decision is lodged. The danger of mistake or fraud is surely quite as great if the final power be lodged in Congress, and the framers of the Constitution acted in nothing more wisely than in removing from Congress all power over the election of President.

But it is said that the State board of canvassers had no jurisdiction to reject the votes of certain precincts, and that their decision is only binding when they acted within their jurisdiction. This is an erroneous application of the term "jurisdiction." The jurisdiction of that board is to determine and declare who were chosen electors. The rejection or computation of certain votes, whether right or wrong, was but a determination what evidence or elements they would take into account in the exercise of their jurisdiction.

Some of the arguments have proceeded on the supposition that the question is whether evidence that the certificate of the governor was fraudulent might be received. But the certificate of the governor was, on the admission of both sides, exactly what his duty required of him. It will not be claimed that the governor in his single capacity could re-examine the action of the canvassing-board and certify to anything other than the effect of its record. The offer in substance is that stated by Mr. O'Conor under his fifth head, "that the board of State canvassers, acting on certain erroneous views in making their canvass, rejected certain returns." But this seems to me immaterial, first, because the question whether those views were sound or erroneous, must be determined by the judgment of that board and not of Congress; and second, because the evidence would not affect the count of the vote unless it were further shown that the actual result of the election was declared otherwise than truly, to show which must open to both sides the whole question as to the votes actually cast for electors in Florida, a question which the two Houses of Congress cannot investigate or determine.

The suggestion made by the counsel is that the canvassing-board "acted on certain erroneous views." The counsel in their oral argument propose to show that the action of the State canvassers was fraudulent; by which I suppose they mean that they knew that these views were erroneous when they acted on them.

It is vehemently urged that to refuse to go behind the decision of the State authority, however affected by mistake or fraud, and inquire into the truth, may lead to the establishment of the most flagrant injustice and wrong. But the position of our opponents leads them to a like result. Commissioners Clifford and Field, in their written opinions, each distinctly assert that they hold that the judgment of the supreme court of Florida rendered long after the votes for President were cast by the electors, is conclusive as to who were duly chosen such electors, and that no evidence whatever can be received against such judgment. Mr. Commissioner Bayard, in answer to my question put to him in the presence of the Commission, frankly answered that he deemed such judgment conclusive. Both sides, then, agree in this, that the decision of a State tribunal upon this matter is conclusive and binding upon all mankind, and that Congress has no power to go behind it. The difference between these gentlemen and myself is this: they attribute that conclusive effect to the judgment rendered afterward, when all the electors had cast their votes, of a court deriving its authority only by implication from the general power to issue writs of *quo warranto*, while I attribute it to the determination made before the electors discharged their office, at the time when the State law expressly required it to be made, and by the persons in whom the State had expressly reposed that authority.

It does not seem to me that the proceedings of the State legislature or of the State court which have been offered in evidence are of any validity whatever; and this without reference to the question whether the judgment of the court has been vacated by an appeal, or whether the statute of Florida confines the effect of judgment on *quo warranto*, to which the attorney-general is not a party, to private rights. I think the function of elector, under the Constitution of the United States, must be performed and ended on a day certain, and that when the act has been performed its validity cannot be affected by anything which occurs afterward. The right of a State to withdraw the vote of its electors for President in obedience to the decree of a court entered afterward will not bear discussion.

I do not rely upon the doctrine which recognizes as valid in law the acts of public or corporate officers who without rightful title perform the functions of an office with which they are in part clothed. Unless the decision of the canvassing-board and the certificate of Governor Stearns to them thereupon issued made the persons so found and certified to be chosen the *de jure* electors of Florida on the 6th of December, I do not see that they were any more fully clothed with the office than their competitors. Each of the sets of electors who claim to have cast their votes in Florida did everything which was necessary to the entire execution of the office of presidential elector.

The presidential electors of a State are required by the Constitution to meet, and were doubtless in the beginning expected to consult. They are required by the Constitution jointly to make, sign, and certify lists, and jointly to seal and transmit them; they are required by the act of Congress jointly to make certain certificates on the back of their lists and a majority of them jointly to appoint a messenger. It may well be that one person or more, less than the majority of the whole number, meeting with the others, recognized by the others as entitled to take part with them in their consultations and in these joint acts and actually so taking part, may be held to be an elector or electors *de facto*. But where two boards, contesting for an office whose functions by law expire when one act has been performed and certified, each at the lawful time and place does everything which is necessary to the entire execution of the office, there being no corporate or official property or seal or function from which either excludes the other, it seems to me that that board or college which is the board or college *de jure* is also the board or college *de facto*.

Upon the whole matter, therefore, I am of opinion that the appointment of electors and the ascertaining who has been appointed is the sole and exclusive prerogative of the State. The State acts by such agencies as it selects. The powers conferred by the State upon these agencies cannot be exercised by Congress. To usurp them for the purpose of righting alleged wrongs would be for this Commission, which has only the powers of Congress, to commit the very wrong which is imputed to the returning-boards in some of the States. When the agencies which the State has selected have acted, the State has acted ; no power can reverse its action for mistake in law or fact, for fraud, or for any cause whatever, unless it be a power higher than the State, on whom the Constitution has expressly conferred such authority. But there is for this purpose no such power higher than the State, and the President of the Senate and Congress are but the mere servants of the State's will and registers of its action, with power only to open the certificates and count the votes of the electors whom the State authority has appointed and certified.

REMARKS OF MR. COMMISSIONER GARFIELD.

FLORIDA.

The Commission having under consideration the request of counsel to present evidence to prove that the State board of canvassers of Florida acted upon erroneous views in canvassing the returns of votes from the several counties—

Mr. Commissioner GARFIELD said :

Mr. PRESIDENT : We are called upon to determine a rule of evidence upon a proffer of testimony by counsel. This is purely a question of law, to be decided within the limitations of the statute which created this Commission. We cannot go beyond those limitations for any purpose whatever. We are bound by our oaths to search the meaning of the statute and make our answer to the proffer on its merits under the law, without regard to the consequences which may result from the decision.

Such being my view of our duty, I have been pained to notice that, running through all the arguments of the counsel who offered this testimony, and through the remarks of those members of the Commission who favor its reception, has appeared the assumption that those who offer the testimony are able to prove great and manifold frauds, and that those who oppose its reception do so because they do not wish to expose fraud. I wish to repel this assumption as being not only outside of the law we are seeking to administer, but as being gratuitous and wholly unfounded in fact. It may not be out of place to call the attention of the Commission to the fact that four counts of the electoral vote of Florida have been made, as appears in the several congressional reports on that subject. Without vouching for the correctness of any of them, I will state by whom they were made and what is the alleged result of each.

First. On the 28th day of November, the secretary of the State of Florida laid before the canvassing-board the returns of the votes for electors from all the counties of the State; and a count of this gross vote, before any canvass was made by the board, before any vote was rejected or any correction was made, is declared to have shown that the Hayes electors had 43 majority over the Tilden electors.

Second. On the 6th day of December, the board of State canvassers made their official report of the vote as canvassed and compiled by themselves according to law; and that report declared that the Hayes electors had received 925 majority.

Third. On the 10th of January, in obedience to the order of the supreme court, which had issued to the board of canvassers a peremptory writ of mandamus, ordering them to recanvass the votes for governor and to include in the count some polls which they had thrown out, the board reconvened and recanvassed the vote for governor. That canvass resulted in the declaration that Drew was elected governor and Stearns was not. Although the order of the court did not disturb the former canvass, so far as related to the presidential electors, yet if the order had applied to the presidential electors the result would have been 211 majority for the Hayes electors.

Fourth. After Governor Drew was inaugurated and the new legislature had assembled, proceedings in *quo warranto* before the district court were had, which resulted, late in January, in an order for the new board of State canvassers, which had been appointed by Governor Drew, to recanvass the votes for presidential electors. That canvass was made, and the result was forwarded to the President of the Senate, and was received by him less than two weeks ago. According to that count the Tilden electors received a popular majority of 87. But this count was made long after the electoral college had met, given its votes, and dissolved. Some discredit is attached to this result from the allegation that this count was made by a board specially appointed to achieve a special result, after its importance became known. The confirmation of this count by the legislature of Florida has the same *post hac* character.

Here then we have four real or pretended counts of the popular vote of Florida for electors; and three of them give the Hayes electors a majority ranging from 43 to 925; and the fourth, which was made nearly two months after the electoral college had voted and had become *functus officio*, showed for the Tilden electors less than 90 majority. I do not vouch for the accuracy of any of these counts; but they are sufficient to show how unfounded and unjust is the pretension that virtue and right are on the side of the Tilden electors, and that frauds and false counting are to be attributed to the other side. The extremest claim made on behalf of the Tilden electors is but a majority of 90; and that is set up against three counts on the other side, as *prima facie* evidence of the truth.

I have referred to these facts only for the purpose of repelling the assumption that those who deny the authority of this Commission to canvass the popular votes of a State do so because of any desire or willingness to cover up fraud or prevent its exposure. I will add that while one political party charges errors and frauds on the part of the State board of canvassers in declaring the result of the election, the other party charges fraud, violence, and intimidation at the polls to prevent a full and fair vote at the popular election. We must resolutely turn away from the passionate outcries of both parties, and from every consideration except the law which we have sworn to obey, and in the light of that law determine what evidence, if any, we can consider in reaching a decision of the case.

But first let us consider what class of evidence is offered and what allegations are sought to be established that we may more intelligently measure the offer by the provisions of the law under which we are acting.

Let us survey the boundaries of the field which we are invited to enter.

First. In the opening of his speech before us, one of the objectors, Mr. Field, said he " should have occasion to mention canvassers in only one county," and "that county was decisive of the result." He asked us to hear evidence that the county canvassers of Baker County threw out the votes of two polls, one in the Darbyville precinct and another in the Johnsonville precinct. (See Congressional Record, February 3, page 46.)

Thus, at the first step of the contest, we are asked not only to go behind the certificate of the governor and behind the determination of the State board of canvassers, but we are asked to review and correct the alleged errors and wrong-doings of a county judge, a county clerk, and a county sheriff, in making up their returns of votes to the secretary of state. How shall we do this? Certainly no member of this Commission will deny that if we enter the door opened by Mr. Field, we must hear both sides. We must summon the judge, the clerk, and the sheriff, to learn precisely what they did and the reason for it, and must have before us the returns from Johnsonville and Darbyville in order to ascertain whether they were lawful and regular returns, such as the county officers were required by law to include in the general returns of Baker County. Probably, in order to get at the very truth, we should be compelled to summon the election-officers of Darbyville and Johnsonville and examine the ballots and poll-lists, and any contest arising in reference to them.

Second. But while Mr. Objector Field is willing to rest his case upon the polls in one county, Mr. O'Conor, the leading counsel for the Tilden electors, asks us to enter a much larger field. He offers evidence to show that the State board of canvassers, acting "on certain erroneous views in making their canvass, by which the Hayes electors appeared to be chosen, rejected wholly the returns from the county of Manatee and part of the returns of each of the following counties: Hamilton, Jackson, and Monroe." Mr. O'Conor adds that he trusts he has omitted none, but has had no consultation. This extends the area over which evidence is offered to election-precincts in five counties.

Third. Mr. Evarts, at the close of his speech, refers to the votes of five counties, one of which was not named by Mr. Field or Mr. O'Conor.

Fourth. From the reports of the committees of the Senate and House on the subject of the Florida election, I observe that testimony has been taken in reference to polls in seventeen different counties of the State. A portion of that testimony I have no doubt is contained in the large packages brought before us, but not yet opened. Much of the testimony referred to in the Senate report, relates to the proceedings at polling-places, to alleged frauds on the part of voters, and to errors on the part of officers who conducted the election.

This summary of the evidences proffered is sufficient to show that we cannot take one step beyond the final determination which the State itself has made without going to the bottom of the poll; in brief, this Commission must assume to be the canvassing and returning board of Florida. A bare statement of the proposition shows that its accomplishment by us is not merely inconvenient; it is utterly impossible. But if the law under which we are acting commands us to undertake it, we must obey. Though I opposed the bill in the House, and regarded it, as I still do, in conflict with the constitutional plan of counting the electoral vote, my opinion was overruled by the two Houses; and I shall do all in my power to carry out the provisions of the act in its letter and spirit. And this brings me to search the act itself to ascertain our powers and duties under it.

This law is based on the assumption that it is the right and the duty of the two Houses of Congress, meeting together, to count the votes for

President and Vice-President. It prescribes the order of proceeding to perform that duty. When the certificates of any State are opened, if no objection be made, the votes of that State shall at once be counted. If objection be made two modes of procedure are provided, one for a single return, and another for a double return. The two Houses pass upon objections to a single return ; this Commission is required to act in cases of double returns. In either case the action is to be according to the Constitution and the law. In each the object to be reached is to count the lawful votes of the State. The provisions of the act which regulate the conduct of the two Houses in cases of single returns will throw light upon the duty of the Commission in cases of double returns. The first section of the act provides that in cases where there is but one return from a State and an objection is made to the count, the two Houses shall separate and each shall act upon such objection. The fourth section provides that—

When the two Houses separate to decide upon an objection that may have been made to the counting of any electoral vote or votes from any State, or upon an objection to a report of the Commission, or other question arising under this act, each Senator or Representative may speak to such objection or question ten minutes, and not oftener than once; but after such debate shall have lasted two hours, it shall be the duty of each House to put the main question without further debate.

Can it be claimed that this provision implies the hearing of testimony and the trial of a contest ? The whole time allowed to the two Houses to decide the gravest objections that may be raised to the counting of the vote of any State or of any elector is but two hours; and that brief period is devoted, not to the hearing of evidence, but to debate. There is ·no provision in the section for taking testimony or trying disputed questions of fact. The reasonable construction of the section is that the two Houses decide any questions of law or any matter of informality which may appear on the face of the certificates opened by the President of the Senate. It has been said by an honorable member of the Commission that, in deciding upon an objection to a single return, the two Houses may exercise their acknowledged power of inquiry by sending for persons and papers, and may use testimony already taken by their committees; but it must be remembered that the contents of the certificate on which the objection is based can be known by neither House nor by any member of either House until it is opened in their presence; for the objection provided for in the act is " to any vote or paper from a State." Certainly it will not be claimed that any testimony taken, before the contents of the sealed package are made known, can be valid and lawful testimony to sustain an objection made afterward. Such testimony might be *ex parte*, misleading, and false ; and yet in the two hours allowed by the bill it might be wholly impossible to procure evidence to overcome it.

If, then, we take the proceedings of the two Houses, under the first and fourth sections of the act, as a precedent for our action here, we find no warrant for receiving the evidence offered. Again, if we take the proceedings of the two Houses under the first and fourth sections as a precedent, we should compare the time granted to the two Houses with the time we have already consumed on this case. We are far into the sixth day of our proceedings. This is the first of four cases to be submitted ; and we are now debating, not the merits of the case, but a preliminary question of procedure. It is not too much to say that the admission of the evidence proffered will wholly defeat the object of the bill.

But the learned Commissioner [Mr. Bayard] who has just spoken calls attention to the clause of the act which confers upon us our powers. It is in these words:

All such certificates, votes, and papers so objected to, and all papers accompanying the same, together with such objections, shall be forthwith submitted to said Commission, which shall proceed to consider the same, with the same powers, if any, now possessed for that purpose by the two Houses, acting separately or together, and by a majority of votes decide whether any and what votes from such State are the votes provided for by the Constitution of the United States, and how many and what persons were duly appointed electors in such State, and may therein take into view such petitions, depositions, and other papers, if any, as shall, by the Constitution and now existing law, be competent and pertinent in such consideration.

This clause declares what questions we are to decide, and prescribes the rule of evidence by which the decision is to be reached. The rule of evidence is that we " may take into view *such petitions, depositions, and other papers, if any, as shall, by the Constitution and now existing law, be competent and pertinent in such consideration.*" In applying this rule we have *" the same powers, if any, now possessed for that purpose by the two Houses acting separately or together.*" That is, the Commission is clothed with the powers of the two Houses in reference to counting the votes of electors, but in nothing else.

The act speaks of " petitions and depositions;" but it does not permit us to consider them unless we find that the Constitution and the law, as it existed before the passage of this act, authorized the two Houses to employ them in counting the votes.

This act confers no new powers upon the two Houses; but it makes this Commission the interpreter of the powers which they possessed before its passage. It is well known that the framers of the act were unable to agree upon the question whether the Constitution confers upon the two Houses authority to challenge, for any purpose, the determination of the State authorities in reference to the appointment of electors; and, because they could not agree, they purposely left it an open question to be decided by the Commission. For one, I did not consider it an open question; and I was unwilling to place it in the power of any commission to declare that the two Houses possess such authority. But the act permits us to decide and pass upon the question; and we are bound to decide it in accordance with the Constitution and existing law. Let us fully understand the precise question which we are to decide.

The law of Florida provides that the secretary of state, the attorney-general, the comptroller of public accounts, together with any member of the cabinet who may be designated by them, shall " form a board of State canvassers, and proceed to canvass the returns of the election and determine and declare who shall have been elected as shown by such returns. If any such returns shall be shown or shall appear to be so irregular, false, or fraudulent that the board shall be unable to determine the true vote for any such officer or member, they shall so certify, and shall not include such return in their determination and declaration." (Section 4 of act of February 27, 1872.)

This board, thus authorized to " determine and declare " what persons have been chosen by the State, did determine and declare that four persons had been appointed electors of President and Vice-President; and the certificate of the governor, now before us, is acknowledged to be in accordance with the determination. On this state of the law and the facts, assuming that the Constitution empowers the two Houses, or either of them, to count the electoral votes, does this authority to count carry with it the authority to take testimony or to consider evidence to show that the State board of canvassers acted upon erroneous views of the law of the State, or made errors and mistakes in determining and declaring who were elected ?

This is the main question we are now called upon to decide. If the two Houses possess such authority, we may hear the testimony. If they do not, we could not consider it if it were here in our hands.

The distinguished Commissioner [Mr. Bayard] who has just spoken, claims this authority for the Commission, on the ground that the words " existing law " include the *lex parliamentaria* under which each House may send for persons and papers, and may take testimony upon any subject it pleases ; and that, as a matter of fact, each House has already taken testimony in reference to the election in Florida and in other States.

This authority to take testimony is not expressly conferred upon either House by the Constitution. It belongs to the class of implied powers. It is incidental to the power to make laws. Because Congress has authority to enact laws, it is a necessary incident to that power that each House may procure such information as will enable it to act with intelligence. Incidental authority cannot exceed the express authority from which it is derived. Where the authority to legislate ends, there the incidental authority to take testimony also ends.

The testimony taken for purposes of legislation is not testimony in the judicial sense. It is not taken in accordance with the rules of evidence which regulate a trial before a jury or court ; but it is rather the information obtained by a special inquiry made for the purpose of ascertaining the opinions and wishes of intelligent citizens upon questions requiring the action of Congress. I doubt if one deposition in ten, taken by the committees sent to Florida, would be admissible in any judicial inquiry.

Besides the testimony taken in aid of legislation, each House may also take testimony in the case of a contested election of a member, in proceedings to censure or expel a member, or in the still more strictly judicial proceeding in impeachment. But these are authorized by the clauses of the Constitution which provide for the trial of impeachments, and those which empower each House to " be the judge of the election, returns, and qualifications of its own members," and to punish or expel its members for disorderly behavior. These clauses confer no authority whatever upon this Commission. They do not relate to the subject-matter which has been referred to us.

It will not do for us to claim the same powers which we should possess if the Constitution made the two Houses the judge of the elections, returns, and qualifications of electors of the President and Vice-President. The fact that no such power is expressed in the Constitution, is strongly against our right to infer it, and virtually amounts to the denial of such a power.

But I base my opinion on the rule of evidence upon other clauses of the Constitution which seem to me conclusive of the question. I cannot better state my position than to summarize the argument which I made in the House of Representatives three weeks ago.

I will read the only two clauses from which it is claimed that Congress derives any power whatever to inquire into the action of the States in appointing electors of the President and Vice-President. The second clause of the first section of article 2 provides as follows :

Each State shall appoint, in such manner as the legislature thereof may direct, a number of electors, equal to the whole number of Senators and Representatives to which the State may be entitled in the Congress; but no Senator or Representative, or person holding an office of trust or profit under the United States, shall be appointed an elector.

And the third clause of the same section provides—

The Congress may determine the time of choosing the electors, and the day on which they shall give their votes; which day shall be the same throughout the United States.

These two clauses contain all the powers conferred upon the States in appointing electors, and contain also all the limitations upon these powers. There are five expressed or implied limitations upon the power of the States, and only five. The limitations are either absolute in the Constitution itself, or such as authorize Congress to fix limitations. And if Congress has any authority whatever to interfere with the action of the States in the appointment of electors, that authority must be found in some one or more of the five limitations.

Now what are these limitations?

First. It must be a State that elects the electors; and, as Congress alone has the authority to admit new States into the Union, if there should be any political organization, not a State, that shall cast a vote for presidential electors, and if such pretended electors send a certificate of their vote for President and Vice-President, the Congress would undoubtedly have the right to inquire into the authority of such political organization to participate in the election.

Second. No State can have more electors than the number of Senators and Representatives to which that State is entitled in Congress at the time of the presidential election. If any State presumes to elect more, no doubt that can be inquired into. The surplus votes cannot be counted. That is the second limitation.

Third. The Constitution provides that no person shall be appointed an elector for President and Vice-President who is either a Senator or Representative in Congress, or holds any office of trust or profit under the United States. Without doubt, a violation of this provision may be inquired into; for it is distinctly declared as a limitation of the authority of the State. Whether that inquiry can be made without special legislation prescribing a mode of procedure, is a question aside from the topic I am now discussing.

Fourth. Congress is empowered by the Constitution to fix the day when the States shall vote for electors; and as Congress has fixed a day, the Tuesday after the first Monday in November, the State has no right to vote for electors on any other day, except that, in case a State, having held an election on that day, has failed to make a choice, its legislature may provide for holding an election on a subsequent day, in accordance with the act of Congress approved January 23, 1845. Doubtless the inquiry may be made whether the election was held on the day fixed by law.

Fifth. The Constitution provides that Congress may determine the day on which the electors in all the States shall give their votes for President and Vice-President. By the act of March 1, 1792, that fixed day is the first Wednesday of December—within thirty-four days of the date of the general election. From this it follows that all the steps which are necessary to complete the appointment of the electors must have been taken by the first Wednesday in December, when the electors are to vote for President and Vice-President. For the purposes of my argument, I do not follow the process of electing a President beyond the appointment of the electors.

To sum up these limitations in brief, Congress, in obedience to the Constitution, fixes the day for choosing the electors, and the day when they must vote. The Constitution prescribes that *States* only shall choose electors. It prescribes the number of electors for each State, and limits their qualifications. These are the only limitations upon the authority of the States in the appointment of electors of the President. Every other act and fact relating to their appointment is placed as absolutely and exclusively in the power of the States, as it is within their power to elect their governors or their justices of the peace. Across the line of these limitations Congress has no more right to interfere with the States than it has to interfere with the election of officers in England. To speak more accurately, I should say that the power is placed in the legislatures of the States; for if the constitution of any State were silent upon the subject, its legislature is none the less armed with plenary authority, conferred upon it directly by the national Constitution.

It is insisted by those who oppose the view I am taking, that, though the Constitution authorizes the States to appoint electors in such manner as the legislatures thereof may direct, yet the two Houses of Congress, in counting the electoral votes, may inquire whether the State authorities proceeded in accordance with their own laws, and may correct any errors in the process, or any violation of the State law. To this I answer that the power to appoint includes the power to do all those things necessary to complete the appointment, and to determine and declare who have been appointed. In pursuance of its authority to appoint electors, the State may not only provide for holding a popular election, as the mode of choosing them, but it may also provide by what means the result of such election may be verified and declared; and we have already seen that the legislature of Florida has made such provision. The laws of that State prescribe all the steps, from the casting and counting of the ballots at the several polling-places to the final determination and declaration of the result by the board of State canvassers. If any revision of that result be possible, it is the right of the legislature of Florida to provide for it, not the right of the two Houses of Congress or either of them.

The final determination of the result of the election having been declared by the authority empowered to determine and declare it, that act becomes the act of the State; and the two Houses of Congress can no more question such declaration than they can question the primary right of appointment by the State.

For these reasons, Mr. President, I shall vote against receiving the evidence offered. In conclusion, I will add that the preservation of the right of the States under the Constitution to appoint electors and declare who have been appointed, is, in my judgment, a matter of much greater importance than the accession of any one man to the Presidency.

LOUISIANA.

On Friday, February 16, the Commission having under consideration the electoral vote of Louisiana—

Mr. Commissioner GARFIELD said:

Mr. PRESIDENT: The rule of evidence adopted by the Commission in reference to Florida was in fact decisive of that case. The same will doubtless be true in the case before us. The discussion has disclosed the fact that the rule of evidence and the merits of the case stand together, and I shall proceed upon that understanding in my remarks.

There can be no difference in principle between the Florida and the Louisiana cases, so far as the rule of evidence is concerned, unless it be that the allegation of fraud and the offer to prove fraud on the part of the returning board brings this case under principles different from those which the Commission applied to the Florida certificate. In that case, the counsel proffered evidence to show that the State board of canvassers had proceeded upon an erroneous view of the law. In this case, they allege not only error on the part of the returning-board in the construction of the law under which they acted, but they offer to prove actual fraud.

I have listened with great pleasure to the clear and able argument of the distinguished Commissioner [Senator Thurman] who has just spoken. He has aided us in the discussion by making the strongest possible presentation of the argument in favor of admitting the evidence. I will follow the order he has adopted, and will offer some suggestions in reply.

He holds:

First. That, assuming the law of Louisiana which created the returning-board to be constitutional, the board was itself not lawfully organized, because the vacancy was not filled as required by the act of November 20, 1872, which provides that "in case of vacancy by death, resignation, or otherwise, by either of the board, the vacancy shall be filled by the residue of the board." Authorities have been cited to sustain this view. It is no doubt true that where the law creates a board, unless otherwise specially provided, its membership must be full before it can become a legal board. But the rule is otherwise where it has once been full and a vacancy has subsequently happened. In the case before us, however, it is not necessary to go into the general doctrine; for we are able to determine the point in the controversy by the laws of Louisiana, as construed by the courts of that State. I remind the Commission of the point so well made a few days since by Mr. Commissioner Field, in the Florida discussion, that the construction given to a statute of a State by its supreme court is binding upon all other States and upon the United States; and that, for all practical purposes, the construction so given becomes as much a part of the statute as though the language of the court were incorporated into the text of the law. There can be no doubt of the correctness of this position.

In Bank of Hamilton vs. Dudley, 2 Peters, 492, Chief-Justice Marshall, delivering the unanimous opinion of the court, said:

The judicial department of every government is the rightful expositor of its laws, and emphatically of its supreme law.

Again, in Elmdorf vs. Taylor, 10 Wheaton, the same great judge says, at page 159:

This court has uniformly professed its disposition, in cases depending on the laws of a particular State, to adopt the construction which the courts of the State have given to those laws. This course is founded on the principle, supposed to be universally recognized, that the judicial department of every government is the appropriate organ for construing the legislative acts of that government. * * * We receive the construction given by the courts of a nation as the true sense of the law, and feel ourselves no more at liberty to depart from that construction than to depart from the words of the statute. * * * On the same principle, the construction given by the courts of the several States is received as true, unless they come in conflict with the Constitution, laws, or treaties of the United States.

The later decisions of the Supreme Court are all in accordance with this doctrine. (See 12 Wheaton, 167, 168; 6 Peters, 291; 7 Howard, 818; 8 Howard, 558, 559; 11 Howard, 318; 14 Howard, 504; 2 Black, 599; 1 Wallace, 175.)

Now apply this doctrine to the point under consideration. The supreme court of Louisiana has decided that the returning-board of 1872, created under the act of March 16, 1870, and consisting of but four

members, (there being one vacancy,) was the lawful returning-board of
the State. The court also decided that the clause of the act of 1870
requiring vacancies to be filled, which is precisely the same as in the act
of 1872, is not mandatory, and a failure to fill the vacancy does not render unlawful the acts of a remaining quorum. I refer to the case of
Bonner *vs.* Lynch, 25 Louisiana Annual Reports, 267, and to the cases
therein cited. At page 268 the court say:

> We decided in the case of Kennard *vs.* Morgan, and again in the case of Hughes *vs.*
> Pitkin, that the board of returning officers, composed of John Lynch, George E. Bovee,
> James Longstreet, and Jacob Hawkins, was the legal returning-board of the State at
> the late November election. That board, it appears, returned the defendant, Lynch, as
> elected judge of the fourth district court of New Orleans; and upon that return the
> acting governor issued a commission to him according to law.

The court held the returns of the election by that board valid; and
upon the principle so long and so well settled by the Supreme Court of
the United States we are concluded on the question. As a matter of
right and fairness, the board ought to have filled the vacancy by appointing a democrat; but their failure to do so did not invalidate their
acts done in pursuance of the law.

Second. The distinguished Commissioner [Mr. Thurman] holds that
if the board had been full, and organized in accordance with the law,
yet the law itself and the board created by it are unconstitutional and
unrepublican.

Here again I appeal for my answer to the authority of the supreme
court of Louisiana, which is conclusive upon this Commission and upon
all courts. I quote again from Bonner *vs.* Lynch, 25 Louisiana Annual
Reports, 268, where the court says:

> The legislature has seen proper to lodge the power to decide who has or has not been
> elected in the returning-board. It might have conferred that power upon the courts,
> but it did not. Whether the law be good or bad, it is our duty to obey its provisions
> and not to legislate. * * * Having no power to revise the action of the board of
> returning-officers, we have nothing to do with the reasons or grounds upon which they
> arrived at their conclusion.

The court declares the law valid; and that alone ends the controversy.
But I submit that it is not necessary to have recourse to the constitution of the State to find authority for the legislature to prescribe the
mode of appointing electors of President and Vice-President. The national Constitution confers that power directly upon the legislature of
the State. In 1796, at the time of the presidential election, there was
no provision in the constitution or laws of Vermont for choosing electors.
But the legislature of that State, of its own motion, appointed the electors; and Congress did not question the validity of the transaction.

Whether the acts of the returning-board were in conflict with the constitution of Louisiana or not, they were in accordance with the mode of
procedure prescribed by the legislature; and the national Constitution
confers upon the State legislature the sole and exclusive authority to
prescribe the mode of appointment.

In view of the other clause of the objection, that the law is unrepublican, it may be worth while to consider the causes which led to its enactment.

If I were framing a body of election laws for Ohio, I certainly should
not adopt the Louisiana law as my model. But it is difficult to see how
the election laws that prevail in most of the States could be made effective to repress the evils that have afflicted Louisiana. No State of the
Union has passed through an experience so sad and so calamitous.

It is not necessary to repeat the history of the tragic events which
for several years threatened to dissolve the bonds of society and to de-

stroy both liberty and law in that State. It is sufficient for my present purpose to call the attention of the Commission to article 103 of her present constitution adopted in 1868. It is in these words:

The privilege of free suffrage shall be supported by laws regulating elections and prohibiting under adequate penalties all undue influence thereon from power, bribery, tumult, or other improper practice.

I doubt if a similar provision can be found in the constitution of any other State in the Union. It is probable that no other State has found, by terrible experience, that such a provision was necessary to its peace. Will any one say that it is unrepublican for a State to require its legislature to protect its voters against "bribery and tumult" at elections?

The law under which the returning-board acted at the late election was passed in pursuance of this provision of the constitution. In its title it is declared to be "An act to regulate the conduct and to main, tain the freedom and purity of elections; to prescribe the mode of making the returns thereof; to provide for the election of returning-officers to define their powers and duties, and to enforce article 103 of the constitution."

It is a general law, applicable to all elections held within the State. If its provisions are unrepublican, then the State itself is unrepublican; for all the officers which the State has elected during the last seven years have been chosen and declared elected in pursuance of this or a law substantially like this. We are told that the powers granted to the returning-board are unrepublican. It should not be forgotten that the power to canvass, determine, and declare the result of elections must be lodged somewhere; that some authority or authorities of a State must finally determine who have been elected.

In Ohio, for example, the duties of the state board of canvassers are wholly ministerial. They can do nothing but add up the returns sent from the counties and announce the result. The actual work of canvassing and judging is left, not to one board, but to four or five thousand boards, called judges of election, who sit behind the ballot-boxes, clothed with power to administer oaths and prevent the casting of unlawful ballots. When the polls are closed, each of these local returning-boards proceeds to determine and declare the result. But they do not count as lawful votes "all the ballots actually cast." If they find two votes so folded together that in their judgment both were cast by the same voter, such ballots are thrown out and constitute no part of the lawful vote. If they find a printed name pasted over another name on the ticket, they reject the name on the paster. If they find, on completing the count, that the number of ballots in the box exceeds the number of names on the poll-lists, they draw out, by lot, a number of ballots equal to the excess, and reject them wholly from the count. It may be that every fraudulent ballot was put in by one political party, and that every vote drawn out and rejected by the judges was lawfully cast by the other party. But the judges are ministers of the law, and they purge the poll before declaring the result. It is not the count of ballots actually cast, but the result as declared by these judges, which constitutes the lawful vote of the precinct. The declarations made and certified to, at the four thousand ballot-boxes of Ohio, are forwarded through the county officers to the designated State officers, and there remains only the ministerial work of addition and declaration.

In Louisiana it was found impossible to preserve peace and order at all the polls of the State, if the local officers of elections were intrusted with the quasi-judicial powers which are exercised by such officers in Ohio. And hence, in the matter of counting votes, the Louisiana statute enjoins only ministerial duties upon the local election officers. They must count what they find in the ballot-boxes, and must forward the result, together with the poll-lists, through the parish officers, to the State returning-board. In that board the law has vested the quasi-judicial powers, without which no popular election can be conducted. To that board are delivered the unpurged polls of the State, and the law requires them—

To canvass and compile the returns of the election and declare the names of all persons and officers who have been duly and lawfully elected.

In making that canvass and compilation the board must proceed in the order laid down in the statute :

They shall compile, first, the statements from all polls or voting-places at which there shall have been a fair, free, and peaceable registration and election.

And whenever proof is made to the board as required by the statute—

Of any riot, tumult, acts of violence, intimidation, armed disturbance, bribery or corrupt influences, which prevented, or tended to prevent, a fair, free, and peaceable vote of all qualified electors entitled to vote at such poll or voting-place, such returning-officers shall not canvass, count, or compile the statement of votes from such poll or voting-place until the statements from all other polls or voting-places shall have been canvassed and compiled. The returning-officers shall then proceed to investigate the statements of riot, tumult, acts of violence, intimidation, armed disturbance, bribery or corrupt influences, at any such poll or voting-place.

And for that purpose they have power to send for persons and papers and examine witnesses.

The statute then declares that—

If, after such examination, the said returning-officers shall be convinced that said riot, tumult, acts of violence, intimidation, armed disturbance, bribery or corrupt influences, did materially interfere with the purity and freedom of the election at such poll or voting-place, or did prevent a sufficient number of the qualified electors thereat from registering and voting to materially change the result of the election, then the said returning-officers shall not canvass or compile the statement of the votes of such poll or voting-place, but shall exclude it from their returns.

Here, then, is a board upon whom the State of Louisiana has conferred those quasi-judicial powers which, in other States, are usually conferred upon the judges of election in the several voting-precincts. Who shall say that it is unrepublican for a State of the Union to adopt the Louisiana mode of conducting elections rather than the Ohio mode? Certainly each State has the right to choose that method which it deems best for its own protection.

Third. The distinguished Commissioner [Mr. Thurman] holds that if the returning-board, in making their returns, exceeded the jurisdiction conferred upon them by law, all their acts in excess of such jurisdiction are void; and that this Commission may examine and decide whether the board did in fact exceed its jurisdiction.

He does not insist, as some have done, that the two Houses of Congress have authority to question the real voice of a State in declaring who have been chosen as electors; but he holds that they may inquire whether the returning-board did utter the true voice of the State. This proposition is strongly put, but I believe it to be unsound. Its real meaning is obscured by the use of the word "jurisdiction." If, under cover of inquiring into the jurisdiction of the returning-board, Congress may go behind the determination of that board, it follows that the power of Congress is not limited to the counting of the electoral votes, but extends to the counting of the popular vote by which the electors themselves were chosen.

The authority of the State to appoint electors, as I tried to show in the Florida case, carries with it the authority to do every act necessary to complete the appointment, and to determine and declare who has been appointed. It must also carry with it the authority to decide whether the board, created for the purpose of determining and declaring the result, has acted within its jurisdiction.

If the State has made no complaint of excess of jurisdiction on the part of the board, it is difficult to see how the two Houses of Congress can do so. Jurisdiction in general may depend upon territory, upon time, or upon subject-matter. In this case the only question relates to subject-matter. But the very subject-matter upon which the board is authorized to act is summed up in a single sentence: "They are to determine what persons have been elected according to law." That they did determine and declare. But the learned Commissioner says they made an unjust decision, they excluded votes which ought to have been counted, and, in arriving at the result, adopted methods which were beyond their jurisdiction. But, like every other tribunal, they were the judges of their own jurisdiction, unless the law itself provided another tribunal to determine that question.

It will not do to say that because a judgment is erroneous, it is therefore beyond the jurisdiction of the tribunal that declares it. Jurisdiction to decide a case implies jurisdiction to decide it wrong. Hundreds of cases before the Supreme Court have turned on the question of jurisdiction, and that question has often been decided by a divided court. The distinguished members of this Commission who are justices of that court will probably admit that that great tribunal may sometimes have passed upon the merits of a case of which it was erroneously held that they had jurisdiction. But as their judgments are final, even such erroneous decision was valid.

Now, it is not denied that the law of Louisiana confers upon the returning-board the power "to determine and declare" who have been appointed its electors. That duty is their jurisdiction. In the case of the governor and other State officers, the legislature may revise the finding of the board; but in determining who have been appointed electors, no such power of revision is conferred upon the legislature. It follows that the determination of the board, if not overruled by the courts of that State, is the final and conclusive decree of the State itself. That decree we have no power to question or review. The State appoints electors and declares who have been appointed. The utmost that can be claimed for the two Houses of Congress is the authority to count the votes cast by the electors. In doing that they may inquire whether the certificates of votes are genuine; whether they are signed by the recognized officers of the State; in short, may inquire if the certificates do, in fact, represent the determination of the State. But beyond that determination Congress cannot go. In issuing the certificates, the governor does not represent the State. He acts at the request of Congress. The act of 1792 makes it his duty to certify to the President of the Senate what the State has done in reference to the appointment of electors. If his certificate does not testify truly, the authority which counts may go behind the certificate until the actual declaration of the State is found; but there the inquiry ends. To go one step further, is to evade the exclusive domain of State authority.

I am no champion of State sovereignty as that doctrine has sometimes been taught in our political history. But there are rights so clearly and exclusively conferred upon the States, that to invade them is to break up the solid foundation of our institutions; and if one act can be more sovereign than another, it may fairly be said that the most sovereign act which a State of this Union can perform is the act of choosing the men who shall cast its vote for President and Vice-President. Against the theory now urged upon us, that we may review all the processes by which Louisiana has given her vote for President at the late election, I oppose this highest and most unquestioned right of each State of the Union.

It has been said, in the course of our deliberations, that this view of the case is technical; that what is asked on the other side is to ascertain the very right and truth of this matter; to ascertain who was in fact really voted for by the people of Louisiana. I might respond by saying that the objections to the finding of the returning-board are themselves in the highest degree technical. We are asked to go behind the decree of the returning-board; but for what purpose? For the purpose of adding to the count some votes actually cast but which were rejected by the board as unlawful. We are told that some of these polls were improperly rejected; and why improperly? Because it is alleged that, in rejecting these polls, certain technical formalities were not complied with. For example, it is alleged that the protests against the validity of these rejected ballots were not filed within forty-eight hours after the closing of the ballot-boxes; and if protests were not filed within that time, the board could not consider them, no matter how corrupt and fraudulent the ballots might be. They say we stand upon a technicality; but they ask us to break through one only to rest upon another.

If this Commission has authority to go behind the decree of the returning-board for any purpose, it must have the power to go behind it for all the purposes of ascertaining the truth; and if we enter upon such an inquiry, if we open the testimony that both sides will proffer, we shall find a group of allegations like these: that in forty-two parishes of Louisiana, where both sides agreed that there was a fair and free election, the Hayes electors received an aggregate of 6,000 majority; that in two groups of parishes where the validity of the returns was contested, there existed such a state of intimidation and terror, violence and murder, that the voice of the republican party was almost wholly suppressed; that, for example, in the parish of East Feliciana, which for years had cast a large republican majority, not one republican vote was cast at the late election; that in many precincts within the disturbed districts, hundreds of negroes were forced by the coercion of threats and intimidation to vote the democratic ticket against their will; and that on the whole, within the terrorized districts, the voice of the republican voters was so effectually stifled as to produce an apparent majority for the democratic electors, sufficient to overcome the 6,000 republican majority in the undisturbed portions of the State.

If we take one step behind the determination of the State authorities, we must go to the bottom of the case. It will not do to go just far enough to find votes actually cast, and shut our eyes to the violence and outrage that put such votes in the boxes. The duty of purging the polls, and finding the real result of the election, was, by law, enjoined upon the returning-board of the State. That duty they performed. Whether wisely or unwisely, justly or unjustly in every instance, I am not prepared to say; but I take the liberty to remark that after a careful study of the history of that election, and considering the turbulence and irregularities which have long prevailed in that State, I am of the opinion that, on the whole, the decree of the returning-board is in accordance with substantial justice. I have no doubt that thousands of voters were prevented from the exercise of their suffrage. For that evil the laws of Louisiana provide no remedy. But they do command the rejection of polls that are tainted by violence, intimidation, and fraud. And, in doing that, the State has, in part, repaired the wrong sought to be committed upon her people.

Before concluding, I must refer to the single feature in which the Louisiana case is said to differ from the case of Florida. There counsel offered evidence to show that the board of canvassers had acted upon an erroneous view of the law, and had made errors and mistakes in determining the result of the election. Here they offer evidence to show that the returning-board acted fraudulently in determining the result. On the doctrine that fraud vitiates everything, we are told that if fraud be proved in this case, it vitiates the determination of the board.

But the allegation of fraud does not confer jurisdiction of a subject which the law does not authorize a tribunal to consider. The real question is whether the allegation of fraud in the processes of the returning-board confers upon the two Houses of Congress, or upon this Commission acting in their stead, the jurisdiction to inquire into those processes and hear evidence to prove fraud.

A case decided by the Supreme Court of the United States in 1870, and which has already been referred to by one of the commissioners for another purpose, applies so strikingly to the point under consideration that I will cite its leading feature. I refer to the case of Virginia *vs.* West Virginia, 11 Wall., 39.

In adjusting the boundary between the States of Virginia and West Virginia an agreement was made that the counties of Jefferson and Berkeley might become a part of West Virginia, on condition that a majority of the votes cast on that question in the two counties should be found in favor of annexation. A special statute regulated the mode of conducting the election and determining the question, and provided, among other things, that—

The governor of this State, if of opinion that the said vote has been opened and held, and the result ascertained and certified pursuant to law, shall certify the result of the same, under the seal of this State, to the governor of the said State of West Virginia.

The election was held and the result declared by the governor. But subsequently the State of Virginia filed a bill in chancery against West Virginia to recover back the jurisdiction of those counties, upon the ground that the vote was not fairly taken, and that the returns upon which the governor issued his certificate were false and fraudulent. The bill alleged, in terms, "that the vote taken was not a fair and full expression of the people of those counties, and that the officers who made their returns to the governor falsely and fraudulently suggested and falsely and untruly made it to appear to the governor of the commonwealth that a large majority of the votes was given in favor of annexation ; and that his determination of the result, being based upon such false and fraudulent returns, was illegal and void."

These allegations are strikingly analogous to the offers of proof now pending before this Commission. In reference to the allegations of fraud, Mr. Justice Miller, delivering the opinion of the court, said :

But waiving these defects in the bill, we are of opinion that the action of the governor is conclusive of the vote as between the States of Virginia and West Virginia. He was, in legal effect, the State of Virginia in this matter. In addition to his position as executive head of the State, the legislature delegated to him all its own power in the premises. It vested him with large control as to the time of taking the vote, and it made his *opinion* of the result the condition of final action.

Even upon an allegation of fraud the court would not go behind the determination of the officer on whom the State had conferred the authority to declare the result of the election. This is precisely the case before us. The State of Louisiana had empowered the returning-board to determine and declare who had been appointed electors, and having provided no appeal from its decision, its action became the final and conclusive determination of the State; and neither Congress nor this Commission has any authority to inquire whether there was fraud or error in the process by which the determination was reached.

To sum up the points already made:

In appointing her electors, the State of Louisiana has followed the method prescribed by her legislature. That method has been reviewed by her supreme judicial tribunal, and has been declared to be in accordance with her constitution. It is also in accordance with the Constitution of the United States. Of all the steps leading to that appointment, the State, through her chosen organs, is the sole determining power. She has determined and declared that the persons named in certificate No. 1 were duly and lawfully appointed her electors of President and Vice-President.

Those persons met at the time required by law; finding vacancies in their number they filled such vacancies in the manner prescribed by the law of the State; and, in pursuance of the national Constitution, they cast their votes and certified the same to the President of the Senate. These certificates have been opened in the presence of the two Houses of Congress; and there remains but one duty more: that is, to obey the imperial command of the Constitution, which declares, " the vote shall then be counted."

Certificate No. 2 comes with no semblance of authority. It is signed by a man who for three years has not even pretended to be governor. It is based upon no finding or declaration of any officer or pretended officer of the State. It has no validity whatever. It carries upon its face all the indications of worthlessness.

I shall vote against receiving the proffered evidence, and in favor of counting the votes reported in the first certificate.

REMARKS OF MR. COMMISSIONER FIELD.

FLORIDA.

On the 7th of February the Commission having under consideration the electoral vote of Florida—

Mr. Justice FIELD said:

Mr. PRESIDENT: After the elaborate arguments made yesterday by the members of the Commission from the Senate and House of Representatives, I cannot hope to throw much light on the subject under discussion. I shall, therefore, confine myself, in the brief observations I propose to make, to a statement of what I deem to be the law applicable to the case before us.

The main question submitted to us, the one to which all other inquiries are subordinate, is, whom has the State of Florida appointed as electors to cast her vote for President and Vice-President. The electoral act, under which we are sitting, makes it our duty to decide " how many and what persons were *duly appointed* electors" in that State.

The Constitution declares that each State shall appoint electors

" in such manner as the legislature thereof may direct." It fixes the number to be appointed, which is to be equal to the whole number of Senators and Representatives to which the State may be entitled in Congress. It declares who shall not be appointed; that is, no Senator or Representative, or person holding an office of trust or profit under the United States. With the exception of these provisions as to the number of electors and the ineligibility of certain persons, the power of choice on the part of the State is unrestricted. The manner of appointment is left entirely to its legislature.

What, then, was the manner of appointment directed by the legislature of Florida? This is manifestly a proper subject for our inquiry, for if another and different manner from that directed by the legislature has been followed in the appointment of persons as electors, such persons are not " duly appointed" in the State, and we must so decide. Any substantial departure from the manner prescribed must necessarily vitiate the whole proceeding. If, for example, the appointment of electors should be made by the governor of a State, when its legislature had directed that they should be chosen by the qualified voters at a general election, the appointment would be clearly invalid and have to be rejected. So, too, if the legislature should prescribe that the appointment should be made by a majority of the votes cast at such election, and the canvassers, or other officers of election, should declare as elected those who had received only a plurality or a minority of the votes, or the votes of a portion only of the State, the declaration would be equally invalid as not conforming to the legislative direction; and the appointment of the parties thus declared elected could only be treated as a nullity.

In inquiring whether the manner prescribed by the State has been followed, we do not trench upon any authority of the State, or question in any respect her absolute right over the subject, but, on the contrary, we seek only to give effect to her will and ascertain the appointment she has actually made.

What, then, was the manner directed by the legislature of Florida? It was by popular election. It was by the choice of a majority of the qualified voters of the State. When their votes were cast on the 7th of November, the electors were appointed, and all that remained was to ascertain and declare the result. The appointment was then completed and could not afterward be changed. What subsequently was required of the officers of election and canvassing-boards was an authentic declaration of the result. For this purpose the votes in each county were to be canvassed by certain designated officers of the county within a prescribed period after the election, and duplicate certificates were to be made and signed by them, containing the whole number of votes given for each officer, the names of the persons for whom they were given, and the number of votes given to each person. A record was to be made of the certificate, and one of the duplicates was to be forwarded to the secretary of state, and the other to the governor. On the thirty-fifth day after the election, or sooner, if the returns from the several counties were received, the secretary of state, the attorney-general, and the comptroller of· public accounts, or any two of them, together with any other member of the cabinet who might be designated by them, were required to meet at the office of the secretary of state, pursuant to notice to be given by him, and form a board of State canvassers, and proceed to canvass the returns of the election and determine and declare who were elected *"as shown by such returns."** The duty of the canvassers under the law of the State was ministerial, involving only the exercise of such judgment as was required to determine whether the papers returned were genuine, and were executed in conformity with the requirements of the law. Such was the construction given to the statute by the supreme court of the State in the proceeding against the canvassers taken on the relation of Mr. Drew, who was a candidate for governor at the same election, at which the electors for President and Vice-President were chosen, and votes for whom were thrown out by the canvassers upon the same assumed power that votes for the Tilden electors were thrown out by them. In giving its decision in that case, the supreme court said:

> The view that the board of State canvassers is a tribunal having power strictly judicial, such as is involved in the determination of the lelgaity of a particular vote or election, cannot be sustained. All of the acts which this board can do under the statute must be based upon the returns; and while in some cases the officers composing the board may, like all ministerial officers of similar character, exclude what purports to be a return for irregularity, still everything they are authorized to do is limited to what is sanctioned by authentic and true returns before them. Their final act and determination must be such as appears from and is shown by the returns from the several counties to be correct. They have no general power to issue subpœnas, to summon parties, to compel the attendance of witnesses, to grant a trial by jury, or to do any act but determine and declare who has been elected as shown by the returns. They are authorized to enter no judgment, and their power is limited by the express words of the statute, which gives them being, to the signing of a certificate containing the whole number of votes *given* for each person for each office, and therein declaring the result *as shown by the returns*. This certificate thus signed is not a judicial judgment, and the determination and declaration which they make is not a judicial declaration, that is, a determination of a right after notice, according to the general law of the land as to the rights of parties, but it is a declaration of a conclusion limited and restricted by the letter of the statute. Such limited declaration and determination by a board of State canvassers has been declared by a large majority of the courts to be a ministerial function, power, and duty, as distinct from a judicial power and jurisdiction. Indeed, with the exception of the courts in Louisiana, and perhaps another State, no judicial sanction can be found for the view that these officers are judicial in their character, or that they have any discretion, either executive, legislative, or judicial, which is not bound and fixed by the returns before them. The duty to count these returns has been enforced by mandamus so repeatedly in the courts of the several States of the Union, that the power of the courts in this respect has long since ceased to be an open question.

The only clause of the statute, which would seem to invest the canvassers with something more than mere ministerial authority, is the one

---

* The following is the text of the law, being section 4 of the act of February 27, 1872:
"SEC. 4. On the thirty-fifth day after the holding of any general or special election for any State officer, member of the legislature, or Representative in Congress, or sooner if the returns shall have been received from the several counties wherein elections shall have been held, the secretary of state, attorney-general, and the comptroller of public accounts, or any two of them, together with any other member of the cabinet who may be designated by them, shall meet at the office of the secretary of state, pursuant to notice to be given by the secretary of state, and form a board of State canvassers, and proceed to canvass the returns of said election and determine and declare who shall have been elected to any such office or as such member, *as shown by such returns*. If any such returns shall be shown or shall appear to be so irregular, false, or fraudulent that the board shall be unable to determine the true vote for any such officer or member, they shall so certify, and shall not include such return in their determination and declaration; and the secretary of state shall preserve and file in his office all such returns, together with such other documents and papers as may have been received by him or by said board of canvassers. The said board shall make and sign a certificate containing, in words written at full length, the whole number of votes *given* for each office, the number of votes *given* for each person for each office and for member of the legislature, and therein declare the result, which certificate shall be recorded in the office of the secretary of state in a book to be kept for that purpose; and the secretary of state shall cause a certified copy of such certificate to be published once in one or more newspapers printed at the seat of government."

which provides that, " if any such returns shall be shown or shall appear to be so irregular, false, or fraudulent, that the board shall be unable to determine the true vote for any officer or member, they shall so certify, and shall not include such return in their determination and declaration." Great stress was placed by counsel, in the argument before the Commission, and by Mr. Commissioner Morton yesterday, upon this clause, as though it gave unlimited discretion and power to the canvassers to exclude, in their count, such votes as they might judge from any cause to have been illegally or irregularly cast. But it is evident from the language used and its context, that the clause never contemplated the exercise of any such undefined and arbitrary power over the returns, but only intended to authorize the exclusion from the count of a return whenever, from evidence, intrinsic or extrinsic, of its irregularity, falsity, or fraudulent character, the canvassers were unable to determine the actual vote cast for any officer. It gave no authority to reject the votes actually given, except when the canvassers were unable to ascertain for whom they were intended, much less to enter upon any judicial investigation into the legality of the votes. In considering this clause the supreme court of the State, in the case of Drew, already cited, held that the words *true vote* meant the vote *actually* cast as distinct from the *legal* vote; and that this followed from the clear general duty of the canvassers to ascertain and certify the " *votes given* " for each person for each office ; and because *to determine whether a vote cast was a legal vote, was beyond the power of the board.*

We have, then, a decision of the supreme court of Florida giving an authoritative construction to the act under which the electors for President and Vice-President were chosen, to the effect that the powers of the canvassers under the act were purely ministerial, and that their whole duty consisted, whenever they were enabled to determine the actual vote given for any officer, in simply computing arithmetically the number of votes cast, as shown by the returns, and declaring the result by a certificate of the fact over their signatures. Whatever beyond this was done by them was in excess of their authority and void. And I hardly need add, in this presence, that whatever was done by them in excess of their authority was not done in any manner directed by the legislature of the State.

The construction given to a statute of a State by its supreme court is, as we all know, considered as part of the statute itself, as much so as if embodied in its very text. Such is the language of the Supreme Court of the United States in all its decisions. Thus, in Leffingwell *vs.* Warren, reported in 2d Black, the court said:

The construction given to a statute of a State by the highest judicial tribunal of such State is regarded as a part of the statute and is as binding upon the courts of the United States as the text.

And again, in Christy *vs.* Pridgeon, reported in 4th Wallace, the court said :

The interpretation within the jurisdiction of one State becomes a part of the law of that State, as much so as if incorporated into the body of it by the legislature.

Having thus briefly stated the requirements of the law of Florida, providing for the appointment of electors, and thus shown the *manner* of appointment directed by its legislature, I will proceed to state the course actually pursued by the canvassers, from which it will appear whether there was any departure by them, and, if any, how great a departure, from the direction given.

The returns sent from the several counties to the State canvassers all disclosed for whom the votes were cast. It is not pretended that any of them appeared, or was shown to be, either so irregular, false, or fraudulent that the canvassers were unable to determine the actual votes given for any officer. The pretense is that some of the votes returned were illegally or irregularly given, not that there was any doubt for whom they were intended. Under these circumstances the duty of the canvassers, according to the decision of the supreme court, and according to the express language of the statute, was simply to add together the votes and declare, under their certificate, the result *as shown by the returns.* In so doing they would have carried out the direction of the legislature. Being added together, the returns would have shown that the Tilden electors were chosen. But the canvassers, instead of discharging the simple ministerial duty devolved upon them, undertook to exercise judicial functions and pass upon the legality of votes cast at various precincts in different counties, hearing evidence and counter evidence upon the subject, consisting partly of oral testimony, but principally of *ex-parte* affidavits, and in numerous instances, upon one pretense or another, throwing out votes given for the Tilden electors, thereby changing the result. In this way a majority of the canvassers came to the conclusion that the Hayes electors were chosen. In no other way could such a result have been reached.

Now, it matters not, for the purpose of my argument, whether, in taking these proceedings and in exercising judicial functions, the canvassers were actuated by honest or by corrupt motives; whether their conduct was the result of a mistaken conception of their powers, or, as is alleged, of a conspiracy to defraud the State of her choice. In any view that may be taken, it is clear that in deciding upon the legality of votes embraced in the returns, and in rejecting votes from their count on the ground of their asserted illegality or upon any other ground, they exceeded their jurisdiction, and their action in that particular was without any validity whatever.

A result declared, after the returns were altered by the elimination of votes embraced therein, was not a result obtained in the manner directed by the legislature of the State. It was not a result which gave the offices to those who had received the highest number of votes, as required by the law of the State, but to those who had received only a minority of the votes. The whole proceeding, instead of being in accordance with, was in direct contravention of the will of the legislature. Surely it would not be pretended that if a portion of the returns had been feloniously abstracted from the office of the secretary of state, a canvass founded upon the returns remaining would show an appointment of electors in the manner prescribed by the legislature of the State. A felonious abstraction and an unauthorized exclusion of votes are in legal effect the same thing.

By the act of Congress the electoral colleges were required to meet on the first Wednesday in December, which was the 6th of the month. The canvassers commenced their labors on the 27th of November, the returns from the several counties being at that time all received, but did not complete the count until the morning of the day appointed for the meeting of the electoral college. Two of them then certified to the election of the Hayes electors; and the governor issued to them a certificate of their election. One of the canvassers, the attorney-general, certified that by the authentic returns of the votes in the several counties on file in the office of the secretary of state, and seen by him as a member of the board, the Tilden electors were chosen. The two sets of electors met on the same day, and at the same time, and in the same building, and both sets voted, and transmitted their respective certificates of their proceedings in duplicate to the President of the Senate at Washington, one copy by a special messenger and one by mail. Which of these two sets of electors was *duly appointed* by the State? Both were not thus appointed. After the statement I have made of the character of the returns, and the manner in which they were altered, there can be no reasonable doubt that the Tilden electors were thus appointed. They received a majority of the votes cast, as shown by the returns, and the law of the State declares that parties receiving the highest number of votes for any office shall be elected to such office.

Mr. President, I have spoken of the matters appearing by the returns, and of the proceedings of the canvassers, as facts in proof before us. I have done so because the evidence contained in the documents transmitted to us with the papers received and opened by the President of the Senate, if we are allowed to look into them, establishes beyond controversy the facts which I have stated. Why, then, should we not consider that evidence and act upon it? We are answered that the certificate of the governor is the only evidence which the Commission can receive of the appointment of the electors. The Constitution does not prescribe the evidence which shall be received of the appointment. That only provides for the voting of the electors, and the transmission by them of a list of the persons voted for to the seat of Government, directed to the President of the Senate. Congress has, therefore, enacted that the governor shall issue a certified list of the electors to them before the time fixed for their meeting. The language of the act is that—

It shall be the duty of the executive of each State to cause three lists of the names of the electors of such State to be made and certified, and to be delivered to the electors 'of such State on or before the day on which they are required by the previous section to meet.—*Revised Statutes*, section 136.

There is nothing in this act which declares that the certificate thus issued shall be conclusive of the appointment. It does not say that the evidence thus furnished is indispensable, or that other evidence of the appointment may not be received. Its only object was simply to provide convenient evidence of the appointment for the consideration of the two Houses of Congress when called upon to count the votes. It was not its purpose to control their judgment in deciding between different sets of papers purporting to contain the votes of the State. A compliance with the act is not obligatory upon the executive of the State. He is not in that respect subject to the control of Congress. He could not be compelled to give the certificate, nor could he be subject to any punishment for refusal to act in the matter. And certainly, when Congress can furnish no means to control the action of a State officer, it cannot render his action either indispensable or conclusive of the rights of the State. Instances may be readily imagined where, from accident, disability, or sickness of the governor, the certified lists could not be obtained, or be obtained and delivered in time, or, if obtained, might be lost or destroyed before delivery. In such cases would there be no remedy? Would the State in such cases lose its vote? Surely, no one will seriously contend for such a result. Suppose, further, that the governor, by mistake or fraud, should deliver certified lists in favor of persons not appointed electors; for instance, to persons who had not received a majority of the votes cast for those officers, (the persons having such majority of votes being eligible to the office under the constitution;) would it be pretended that the will of the State should be thwarted through the force of his certificate? I feel confident that no lawyer in the country would hold that the truth could not be shown in such case against the face of the certificate; and I will never believe in the possibility of this Commission so holding until I see its decision to that effect.

The truth is, a certificate is only *prima-facie* evidence of the fact certified. Indeed, I venture to assert, without fear of successful contradiction, that in the absence of positive law declaring its effect to be otherwise, a certificate of any officer to a fact is never held conclusive on any question between third parties; it is always open to rebuttal. There are, indeed, cases where a party who has been induced to act upon the certificate of a fact may insist that the truth of the certificate shall not be denied to his injury, but those cases proceed upon the doctrine of estoppel, which has no application here. The fact here to be ascertained is, who have been duly appointed electors of the State of Florida, not who have the certificates of appointment. It is the election, and not the certificate, which gives the right to the office. The certificate being only evidence, can be overcome by any evidence which is in its nature superior. And this is equally true of the certificate issued under the law of the State as of the certificate issued under the act of Congress. And it is equally true of the certificate of the board of canvassers. Those officers exercised mere ministerial functions; they possessed no judicial power; their determination had none of the characteristics or conclusiveness of a judicial proceeding; it has been so decided by the supreme court of the State. And yet, in the opinion of the distinguished Commissioner from Indiana, [Senator Morton,] and some other Commissioners from the Senate and House appear to concur with him, the determination of those canvassers, as expressed by their certificate, is more sacred and binding than the judgment of the highest court of the land, incapable of successful attack on any ground whatever.

I put, yesterday, to these gentlemen this question: Supposing the canvassers had made a mistake in addition in footing up the returns, a mistake that changed the result of the election, and acting upon the supposed correctness of the addition they had issued a certificate to persons as electors who were not in fact chosen, and such persons had met and voted for President and Vice-President and transmitted the certificate of their votes to Washington; and afterwards, before the vote was counted by the two Houses of Congress, the mistake was discovered—was there no remedy? The gentlemen answered that there was none; that whatever mistakes of the kind may have been committed must be corrected before the vote was cast by the electors or they could not be corrected at all. If this be sound doctrine, then it follows that by a clerical mistake in arithmetical computation a person may be placed in the Chief Magistracy of the nation against the will of the people, and the two Houses of Congress are powerless to prevent the wrong.

But the gentlemen do not stop here. I put the further question to them: Supposing the canvassers were bribed to alter the returns, and thus change the result, or they had entered into a conspiracy to commit a fraud of this kind, and in pursuance of the bribery or conspiracy they did in fact tamper with and alter the returns, and declare as elected persons not chosen by the voters, and such persons had voted and transmitted their vote to the President of the Senate, but before the vote was counted the fraud was detected and exposed—was there no remedy? The gentlemen answered, as before, that there was none; that whatever fraud may have existed must be proceeded against and its success defeated before the electors voted; that whatever related to their action was then a closed book. If this be sound doctrine, it is the only instance in the world where fraud becomes enshrined and sanctified behind a certificate of its authors. It is elementary knowledge that fraud vitiates all proceedings, even the most solemn ; that no form of words, no amount of ceremony, and no solemnity of procedure can shield it from exposure and protect its structure from assault and destruction. The doctrine asserted here would not be applied to uphold the pettiest business trans- action, and I can never believe that the Commission will give to it any greater weight in a transaction affecting the Chief Magistracy of the nation.

But the gentlemen do not stop here. I put the further question to them : Supposing the canvassers were coerced by physical force, by pistols presented to their heads, to certify to the election of persons not chosen by the people, and the persons thus declared elected cast the vote of the State—was there no remedy? and the answer was the same as that given before. For any wrong, mistake, fraud, or coercion in the action of the canvassers, say these gentlemen, the remedy must be ap- plied before the electors have voted; the work of the electors is done when they have acted, and there is no power under existing law by which the wrong can be subsequently righted.

The canvass of the votes in Florida was not completed until the morn- ing of the day of the meeting of the electoral college, and within a few hours afterward its vote was cast. To have corrected any mistake or fraud during these hours, by any proceeding known to the law, would have been impossible. The position of these gentlemen is, therefore, that there is no remedy, however great the mistake or crime committed. If this be sound doctrine, if the representatives in Congress of forty-two millions of people possess no power to protect the country from the in- stallation of a Chief Magistrate through mistake, fraud, or force, we are the only self-governing people in the world held in hopeless bondage at the mercy of political jugglers and tricksters.

This doctrine, which seems to me to be as unsound in law as it is shocking in morals, is supported upon the notion that if we are permitted to look behind the certificate of the governor, and of the canvassing- board upon which that certificate is founded, we shall open the door to an investigation which may not be brought to a close before the 4th of March. The argument is that as the new President is to be installed on that day, and the votes of the electoral colleges are to be counted in February, all inquiry as to the truth of that certificate is forbidden, because it may be impracticable to carry the inquiry to a termination in time for the installation. This position was taken by counsel before the Commission, and presented in every possible form, and was repeated yesterday by Commissioners Hoar and Garfield, and dwelt upon by them as though it were conclusive of the question. The argument amounts only to this, that the difficulty of exposing in time a mistake or fraud of the canvassing-board is a sufficient reason for not attempting the exposure at all, and for quietly submitting to the consequent perpe- tration of a monstrous wrong.

It is true that the machinery for the election of President, devised by the framers of the twelfth amendment to the Constitution, contemplates the induction of the successful candidate into office on the 4th of March, and that the office shall not on that day be either vacant or disputed. I admit, therefore, to the fullest extent claimed by gentlemen, that no proceedings can be permitted which will postpone the counting of the votes so as to prevent a declaration within that period of the person elected, or a reference of the election to the House of Representatives

But this limitation of time, so far from being a reason for submitting to a mistake or to a fraud, is a reason for immediate action to correct the one and expose the other. Whatever is done to overthrow the *prima-facie* evidence presented by the certificate of the governor must be commenced, carried forward, and completed, so that the result of the proceeding can be considered by the two Houses of Congress when the certificates are opened in their presence and the votes are counted. The countervailing evidence must be presented in some authentic form, like the judgment of a competent tribunal, or the legislative declaration of a State, or the finding of an appropriate committee approved by the House appointing it; and then it will constitute a basis for the action of the Houses without delaying their proceedings. If, for example, the certificate of the governor were forged, or designated as electors persons for whom no votes were cast, the fact, if it were desired to ask the action of the two Houses upon it in counting the vote, should be presented in such a conclusive form as to be the subject of consideration as a fact found. If an investigation is then required to establish the fact alleged, I admit that the proceeding cannot be had, *except by permission of the two Houses*, by reason of the delay it would occasion. The two Houses cannot be required to stop the count to take testimony and investigate the truth of mere allegations; but if the fact of forgery or falsity has already been found by competent authority, and the finding is laid before the two Houses, the finding would not only be a proper subject of consideration by them, but it would be their manifest duty to act upon the finding, in order that the nation might not be defrauded in its choice of a Chief Magistrate.

In the view which I take of this subject there would be no great delay in the counting of the electoral votes if Congress were permitted to look behind the action of the governor or of the canvassing-board; for the facts to be brought to the attention of the two Houses would have to be presented in the manner indicated before they could be received and acted upon, unless the two Houses should consent that testimony be be taken at the time. If the fact alleged could be readily established without seriously delaying the count, it is not probable that testimony upon the subject would be refused. For example, testimony would hardly be refused as to the ineligibility of an elector, or the constitution of a canvassing-board, or the condition of a State as under military rule at the time of the election. But where the fact alleged is one of conflicting evidence, and is not susceptible of proof within reasonable limits, then, I think, the fact must be presented properly authenticated, as I have stated.

Evidence in this form, impeaching the correctness of the certificate of the governor and canvassing-board, can be furnished by the State or by either House of Congress; by the State, which is interested that it shall not be defrauded of its vote in the election; and by either House of Congress, which is interested that the forty-two millions of people composing the nation shall not be deprived of the President of their choice.

In this case the State of Florida has furnished evidence in an authentic form and conclusive in its character, that the Hayes electors were never appointed and that the certificate of the governor and of the canvassing-board in that respect is false; and that the Tilden electors were duly appointed. It has furnished the declaration of its legislature in a statute affirming such to be the fact, and it has furnished a judicial determination of its courts to the same effect.

Soon after the canvass of the State board was closed, and its certificate of the result was filed, Mr. Drew, who had been a candidate for the office of governor at the same election, against Stearns, the incumbent, and had been declared defeated by the action of the canvassers in excluding votes for him, instituted proceedings by mandamus in the supreme court of the State to compel the canvassers to count the votes given, as shown by the returns. In his petition for the writ he averred that, according to the returns received at the office of the secretary of state, and on file there, a majority of the votes for the office of governor were cast for him; and charged against the canvassers the same disregard of the law of the State which is alleged against them in the count for the electors. Indeed, their action affected equally the candidates for governor and for electors. The canvassers appeared to the writ, and proceedings were conducted to a judgment on the merits. The supreme court adjudged that the canvassers had no authority to exclude the votes, by which exclusion alone Stearns had been declared elected, and directed them to restore the votes. In obedience to this judgment they restored the excluded votes, and certified a majority for Drew, who went into office and has ever since been the accepted governor of the State. It was the exclusion of the same votes for electors that enabled the canvassers to declare the Hayes electors chosen. In deciding this case the court gave a construction to the statute under which the canvassers acted, and delivered the opinion from which I have already quoted.

As soon as it was known that the canvassers had certified to the election of the Hayes electors, the Tilden electors filed an information in the nature of a *quo warranto* against them in one of the circuit courts of the State, to determine the validity of their respective claims to the office of electors. This proceeding was commenced upon the day on which the canvass was completed, and process was served on the Hayes electors before they had cast their votes. The circuit court had jurisdiction of the proceeding by the constitution of the State, the eighth section of which provides in terms that the circuit court and the judges thereof shall have power to issue writs of *quo warranto*. In the information the Tilden electors alleged that they were lawfully elected to the office of electors, and that the Hayes electors were not thus elected, but were usurpers. The Hayes electors appeared to the writ, and, first upon demurrer, and afterward upon an investigation of the facts, their right to act as electors was determined. And it was adjudged that the Hayes electors were never appointed, and were never entitled to assume and exercise the functions of that office, and were usurpers; but that the Tilden electors were duly appointed at the election on the 7th of November, and were entitled on the 6th of December to receive certificates of election, and on that day and ever since to exercise the powers and perform the duties of that office. It matters not that this judgment was not reached until after the Hayes electors had voted; it was an adjudication by a competent court upon the validity of their title as electors at the time they assumed to cast the vote of the State. That judgment remains in full force; the appeal from it neither suspends its operation nor affects its validity. It is certainly entitled to great, if not conclusive, weight upon the subject before us, especially when considered in connection with the action of the legislature of the State. That action seems to me to be conclusive of the case.

After the supreme court in the Drew proceeding had given a construction to the election law, and decided that the canvassers had disregarded its plain provisions, exercised judicial functions which they never possessed, and unlawfully rejected votes, the legislature took steps to have their count corrected with respect to the electors, as it had been with respect to the governor. And on the 17th of January last it passed "an act to provide for a recanvass according to the laws of the State of Florida, as interpreted by the supreme court, of the votes for electors of President and Vice-President cast at the election held November 7, 1876." This act required that the secretary of state, the attorney-general, and the comptroller of public accounts, or any two of them, together with any other member of the cabinet who might be designated by them, should meet forthwith at the office of the secretary, pursuant to a notice from him, and form a board of State canvassers, and proceed to canvass the returns of election of electors of President and Vice-President held on the 7th of November, and determine and declare who were elected and appointed electors at that election, as shown by the returns on file. The act directed the canvassers to follow the construction of the law given by the supreme court defining the powers and duties of State canvassers. It directed that their certificate of the result should be recorded in the office of the secretary of state and a copy be published in one or more newspapers printed at the seat of government. The canvassers accordingly met and made the canvass directed, and certified that the Tilden electors, naming them, had received a majority of the votes and were duly elected.

Subsequent to this, and on the 26th of January, the legislature passed another act in relation to the Tilden electors. That act recited, among other things, that—

Whereas the board of State canvassers constituted under the act approved February 27, 1872, did interpret the laws of this State defining the powers and duties of the said board in such manner as to give them power to exclude certain regular returns, and did in fact under such interpretation exclude certain of such regular returns, which said interpretation has been adjudged by the supreme court to be erroneous and illegal;

And whereas the late governor, Marcellus L. Stearns, by reason of said illegal action and erroneous and illegal canvass of the said board of State canvassers, did erroneously cause to be made and certified lists of the names of electors of this State, containing the names of said Charles H. Pearce, Frederick C. Humphreys, William H. Holden, and Thomas W. Long—

The Hayes electors—

and did deliver such lists to said persons, when in fact the said persons had not received the highest number of votes, and, on a canvass conducted according to the rules prescribed and adjudged as legal by the supreme court, were not appointed as electors or entitled to receive such lists from the governor, but Robert Bullock, Robert B. Hilton, Wilkinson Call, and James E. Yonge—

The Tilden electors—

were duly appointed electors, and were entitled to have their names compose the lists made and certified by the governor, and to have such lists delivered to them:

Now, therefore, the people of the State of Florida, represented in senate and assembly, do enact, &c.

The act then proceeded to declare that the Tilden electors, naming them, were on the 7th of November duly chosen and appointed by and on behalf of the State of Florida in such manner as the legislature thereof had directed, and were from that day entitled to exercise all the powers and duties of the office of electors and had full power and authority on the 6th of December, 1876, to vote as such electors for President and Vice-President, and to certify and transmit their votes as provided by law. The statute then ratified, confirmed, and declared as valid, to all intents and purposes, the acts of such electors. It also authorized and directed the governor to make and certify in due form and under the seal of the State three lists of the names of the electors, and to transmit the same, with an authentic copy of the act, to the President of the Senate, and declared that such lists and certificates should be as valid and effectual to authenticate in behalf of the State the appointment of such electors by the State as if they had been made and delivered on or before the 6th of December, 1876, and had been transmitted immediately thereafter, and that the lists and certificates containing the names of the Hayes electors were illegal and void. The act further authorized and directed the governor to cause three other lists of the names of the Tilden electors to be made and certified and forthwith delivered to them, and required those electors to meet at the capitol of the State and to make and sign three additional certificates of the votes given by them on the 6th of December, to each of which should be annexed one of the lists of the electors furnished by the governor, and that one of the certificates should be transmitted by messenger, and one by mail, to the President of the Senate, and the third delivered to the judge of the district, as required by law.

Pursuant to this act, the governor of the State made and certified three lists of the Tilden electors and delivered the same to them, and the said electors assembled and certified that they had met on the 6th day of December at the capitol and given their votes as electors for President and Vice-President by distinct ballots, the votes for President being for Mr. Tilden and the votes for Vice-President being for Mr. Hendricks, and signed three certificates of their action, which were forwarded as required by law. These certificates were accompanied by the certified lists of the governor, by a certified copy of the two acts of the State, and by a certified copy of the returns on file in the office of the secretary of state, with a tabulated statement annexed showing the result of the votes. The third certificate, which is before us, embraces all these proceedings.

Here, then, we have the highest possible evidence of the action of the State of Florida. The two sets of electors both conformed to every requirement of the law in their proceedings. One set, the Hayes electors, have the certificate of Governor Stearns of their election, based upon a certificate of the canvassing-board, which in its nature is mere *prima facie* evidence; the other set, the Tilden electors, have an adjudication of a State court of competent jurisdiction, that they alone were the legally-appointed electors. They have the authoritative declaration of the legislature of the State that they alone were entitled to act as electors and vote for President on the 6th of December; and they have a certificate of Governor Drew, based upon a recanvass of the votes, that they were duly appointed. And accompanying this evidence they have a certified copy of the returns, showing that they received a majority of the votes cast at the election.

Under these circumstances can it be possible that there is any serious question as to which of the two sets of electors was *duly appointed?* As the legislature was alone authorized to determine the manner in which the electors should be appointed, it could furnish in its own way evidence of their acts as agents of the State, whatever may be the power of Congress for its convenience in requiring a certificate of the governor. Were this transaction one that involved merely questions of property, instead of a matter of great public and political interest, I do not think there is a lawyer on this Commission who could hesitate a moment as to the conclusive character of the evidence in favor of the Tilden electors.

In addition to this action of the State, Congress has moved in the matter, and very properly so; for the entire people are interested in the election of their Chief Magistrate. No other officer can exercise so great an influence for good or for evil upon the whole country. He is not only the Commander-in-Chief of our Army and Navy, but he is the executor of our laws, the organ of intercourse with foreign nations, the bestower of offices of honor and trust, and is charged with the duty of maintaining and defending the Constitution. Of all the obligations resting upon the representatives of the people none is greater than that of seeing that no one takes that high office with a defective and tainted title. Acting upon this obligation the House of Representatives early in the session, when it was rumored that irregular and fraudulent proceedings had characterized the election in some of the States, and in Florida among others, appointed committees of investigation to ascertain the facts and report who in truth had been appointed electors by those States. One of those committees proceeded to Florida and took there a large amount of testimony on the subject, which it has returned to the House with its conclusions as to the result. This committee has reported that the Tilden electors were duly appointed, concurring in that respect with the action of the State tribunals and the State legislature. Their report and its conclusions, if adopted by the House, would undoubtedly have a controlling influence upon its action in counting the vote of the State, if this Commission had not been created, and for that reason they should be received, and if not accepted as final, at least be considered by us.*

We are invested with all the powers of the two Houses of Congress to ascertain and decide what persons were "duly appointed" electors of Florida. By the law which has governed legislative bodies from their earliest existence, matters upon which they may be called to act can be investigated by committees appointed for that purpose. And either House may receive the testimony taken by its committee and proceed upon that, or accept the finding of its committee as its judgment, and act upon that as conclusive. And not until now has it ever been questioned that the power of each House to take testimony in that way was not as extensive as the subjects upon which it could act. One of the gentlemen on this Commission [Mr. Edmunds] introduced into the Senate during the present session resolutions for the appointment of committees to inquire into the matters which we are now considering, and Senators Morton and Frelinghuysen voted for them. One of the resolutions authorized the committees to inquire, among other things, "whether the appointment of electors, or those claiming to be such, in any of the States has been made by force, fraud, or other means otherwise than in conformity with the Constitution and laws of the United States and the laws of the respective States;" and in compliance with the resolutions the committees have passed weeks in their investigations. It certainly provokes surprise and comment to hear these gentlemen now deny that either House of Congress has any power to go behind the certificate of

---

* The committee presented to the House their report on the 31st of January, in which they declared that the evidence was perfectly conclusive that the State of Florida had cast her vote for the Tilden electors, and they closed with recommending the passage of the following resolution:

"*Resolved*, That at the election held on November 7th, A. D. 1876, in the State of Florida, Wilkinson Call, J. E. Yonge, R. B. Hilton, and Robert Bullock were fairly and duly chosen as presidential electors, and that this is shown by the face of the returns and fully substantiated by the evidence of the actual votes cast; and that the said electors having, on the first Wednesday of December, A. D. 1876, cast their votes for Samuel J. Tilden for President and for Thomas A. Hendricks for Vice-President, they are the legal votes of the State of Florida, and must be counted as such."

This resolution was subsequently adopted by the House by a vote of 142 yeas to 82 nays.

The Subcommittee on Privileges and Elections of the Senate also made an investigation of the Florida case, and a report which was adverse in its conclusions to those of the House committee, but the report was never adopted by the Senate.

the governor and that of the canvassing-board of the State, and to inquire into the matters for which those committees were appointed.

It is said that the Hayes electors were *de facto* officers, and, therefore, that their action is to be deemed valid until they were adjudged usurpers. But they were no more *de facto* officers than the Tilden electors. Both sets of electors acted at the same time and in the same building. The doctrine that the validity of the acts of *de facto* officers cannot be collaterally assailed, and that they are binding until the officers are ousted, is usually applied where there is a continuing office, and then only on grounds of public policy. Private individuals are not called upon, and in most cases are not permitted, to inquire into the title of persons clothed with the insignia of public office and in apparent possession of its powers and functions. They are required, for the due order and peace of society, to respect the acts of such officers, and yield obedience to their authority, until in some regular mode provided by law their title is determined and they are ousted. As a consequence of the respect and obedience thus given, private individuals can claim, in all that concerns themselves and the public, for the acts of such officers, the same efficacy as though the officers were rightfully clothed with authority. The doctrine may be applied even to a single act of an officer where the office is a continuing one, but it may be doubted whether it is applicable to the case of a person simply charged with the performance of a single act. In such performance it would seem that the person could properly be regarded only as the official agent of the State, and if, therefore, he was without authority, his acts would be void. If the doctrine is ever applicable to such a case, it cannot be applied where the act performed has not accomplished its purpose before the want of right in the officer to do the act in question is determined. None of the reasons upon which the doctrine rests, of policy, convenience, or protection to private parties, has any application to a case of this kind. It does not seem, therefore, to me that there is any force in the position.

Nor is there anything in the language used in the petition in the *quo warranto* case which can affect the status of the Tilden electors, as is supposed by one of the counsel on the other side, [Mr. Matthews.] Of the two sets of electors each claimed to be lawfully entitled to act, and for the purpose of having a judicial determination of the question in controversy, one set brought the writ. Any allegations they may have made cannot alter their right or title; that depended upon the vote of the people, and no consent or language of theirs could change their position to the State or to the United States.

Mr. President, I desire that this Commission should succeed and give by its judgment peace to the country. But such a result can only be attained by disposing of the questions submitted to us on their merits. It cannot be attained by a resort to technical subtleties and ingenious devices to avoid looking at the evidence. It is our duty to ascertain if possible the truth, and decide who were in fact duly appointed electors in Florida, not merely who received certificates of such appointment. That State has spoken to us through her courts, through her legislature, and through her executive, and has told us in no ambiguous terms what was her will and whom she appointed to express it. If we shut our ears to her utterances, and closing our eyes to the evidence decide this case upon the mere inspection of the certificates of the governor and canvassing-board, we shall abdicate our powers, defeat the demands of justice, and disappoint the just expectations of the people. The country may submit to the result, but it will never cease to regard our action as unjust in itself, and as calculated to sap the foundations of public morality.

After the Electoral Commission had decided to exclude all testimony respecting the vote of Florida except that furnished by the papers opened by the President of the Senate, the following memorial from the legislature of the State was presented to the Houses of Congress :

Concurrent resolution embodying a memorial to Congress relative to the counting of the electoral vote.

Resolved by the assembly, (the senate concurring,) That Hon. Charles W. Jones be requested to present the following memorial to the Senate of the United States, and that Hon. Jesse J. Finley be requested to present the same to the House of Representatives of the United States :

The people of the State of Florida, represented in the senate and assembly, memorializing the honorable Senate and House of Representatives of the United States, respectfully represent that the final counting of the four electoral votes of Florida for Rutherford B. Hayes and William A. Wheeler, when the said votes had been actually and honestly cast for Samuel J. Tilden and Thomas A. Hendricks, is a grievance of such magnitude to your memorialists that in their view this appeal is not only fully warranted, but cogently demanded by the voice of duty. Your memorialists hold themselves to be justified in treating as established and unquestionable the fact that the said electoral votes were diverted from their true course and employed to defeat the end which they had been set forth to accomplish, because the knowledge of this fact has been communicated to your honorable bodies by solemn acts of all departments of the government of Florida. While it is true that the executive branch of said government had previously averred the contrary, it has been made known to your honorable bodies, and is rapidly becoming known throughout the civilized world, that according to the highest judicial authority of the State that averment is false.

Your memorialists may be forced to admit that there is no remedy for the specific wrong of which they herein complain, but they implore the early and earnest attention of your honorable bodies to the vices or defects in the Constitution or laws of the United States by reason of which such a wrong became possible. If it is true that under the Federal Constitution an exigency may arise in which one fraudulent act performed, or one mistake committed by a majority of a canvassing-board, must necessarily defeat the will of the American people and determine the occupancy of the highest position open to human ambition, your memorialists fear that the great instrument which they have been accustomed to regard as the unapproachable master-piece of statesmanship will become an object of derision and scorn.

Your memorialists venture to express the hope that the wisdom which characterizes your honorable bodies will be speedily applied to the devising of some expedient whereby it shall be made certain that the nation will never again prove utterly impotent to protect itself against the illegal action of a board of canvassers. And your memorialists will ever pray, &c.

Adopted by the assembly, February 12, 1877.
Adopted by the senate, February 13, 1877.

STATE OF FLORIDA,
    Office of Secretary of State, ss :

I, William D. Bloxham, secretary of state, do hereby certify that the foregoing is a correct transcript of the original now on file in this office.

Given under my hand and the great seal of the State of Florida, at Tallahassee, the capital, this 26th day of February, A. D. 1877.

[SEAL.]
                        W. D. BLOXHAM,
                            Secretary of State.

OREGON.

On the 23d of February, the Commission having under consideration the electoral vote of Oregon—

Mr. Justice FIELD said :

Mr. PRESIDENT : I have but a few words to say in this case, and they will be said, not in the expectation of affecting the judgment of any one of the Commission, but in order to explain the reasons which will govern my action.

It appears that Odell, Watts, and Cartwright received at the election in Oregon, in November last, a higher number of votes for electors of President and Vice-President than the candidates against them. Odell and Cartwright were accordingly elected; of that there is no question. Watts would also have been elected had he been at the time eligible to the office. He was then and for some time afterward a postmaster at La Fayette, in the State. The office he held was one of trust and profit under the United States; it imposed trusts, and was one to which a pecuniary compensation was attached. He was, therefore, ineligible to the office of an elector; he was at the time incapable of being appointed to that office. Such is the language of the Constitution, which declares that "No Senator or Representative, or person holding an office of trust or profit under the United States, shall be appointed an elector." The prohibition here made is unqualified and absolute. All the power of appointment possessed by the State comes from the Constitution. The office of elector is created by that instrument. Her power of selection is, therefore, necessarily limited by its terms; and from her choice the class designated is excluded. The object of the exclusion was to prevent the use of the patronage of the Government to prolong the official life of those in power.

The clause in question is one that operates by its own force. Like the prohibition against passing an *ex post facto* law, or a bill of attainder, or a law impairing the obligation of contracts, it executes itself; it requires no legislation to carry it into effect. As applied to Watts, it must be read as if his name were inserted in the text, and was as follows: "The State of Oregon shall appoint, in such manner as the legislature thereof may direct, a number of electors equal to the whole number of Senators and Representatives to which the State may be entitled in the Congress; but Watts shall not be appointed one of them." The power to appoint him not existing in the State, the votes cast for him availed nothing; he was incapable of receiving them. He was not, therefore, appointed the third elector.

The provision of the Constitution excluding from the choice of the State as electors certain classes of officers is very different from those provisions which create a mere personal disqualification to hold particular offices. Thus the clause declaring that "No person *shall be* a Representative who shall not have attained to the age of twenty-five years." and the clause that "No person *shall be* a Senator who shall not have attained to the age of thirty years," do not forbid an election of persons thus disqualified; they only prohibit them from holding the office so long as the disqualification exists. They can take the office whenever that ceases. But with respect to electors the case is different; there is an incapacity on the part of the State to appoint as electors certain classes of officers. This distinction between ineligibility to an office and disqualification to hold the office is well marked. The one has reference to the time of election or appointment; the other to the time of taking possession of the office. The ineligibility existing at the date of the election is incurable afterwards; the disqualification to hold may be removed at any time before induction into office. If, therefore, at the time of the election persons are within the classes designated, their appointment is impossible. The Constitution prohibits it, and unless the prohibition is to be frittered away whenever conflicting with the wishes of political partisans, it should be enforced equally with the provision fixing the number of electors. One clause of the same section cannot be disregarded any more than the other, and surely the appointment of a greater number of electors than the State was entitled to have would be a vain proceeding.

The ineligibility of Watts was a fact known to the governor. He had held the office of postmaster for years, and was in its possession and ex-

ercise at the time of the election.   This was a fact of public notoriety,
and was not denied by any one.   It was asserted by parties who protested
against the issue of a certificate of election to him, and it was abundantly proved.   Besides this, the rule of law is that, whenever the ineligibility of a candidate arises from his holding a public office within the
State, the people are chargeable with notice of the fact.   The governor
is, of course, bound by the Constitution, and whenever the performance
of a duty devolved upon him is affected by the existence of public offices
under the United States, he may take notice officially of such offices and
ascertain who are their incumbents.   This is a doctrine which I had not
supposed open to question.   But I find that I am mistaken; and I am
told by some gentlemen on this Commission that it was not competent
for the governor to consider the question of the ineligibility of the candidate, though made known to him in every possible way ; and that its
determination involved the exercise of judicial functions, with which he
was not invested.   The general position advanced by them is that the
duty of the governor, as a commissioning officer, is to issue his certificate of election to any one who may obtain, according to the determination of the canvassers, the highest number of votes, however ineligible
the person and however imperative the prohibition may be against his
taking the office.

To test this doctrine I put this question to these gentlemen: Supposing the law declared that only white persons should be eligible to an office, and the highest number of votes, according to the canvassers, should
be cast for a colored man, would the governor be bound to issue a commission to him ?   The gentlemen answered that he would be thus bound ;
that the governor could not in such case decide the question of the colored man's ineligibility.   Mr. Senator Thurman put this further question :
Supposing the law of the State declared that only males should be
elected to an office, and the highest number of votes were cast, according to the report of the canvassers, for a female, would the governor be
bound to issue a commission to her ?   The gentlemen replied, as before,
that he would be thus bound ; that the governor could not determine
the ineligibility of the party on the ground of her sex.   There is something refreshing in these days of sham and pretense to find men who will
thus accept the logic of their principles, to whatever result they may
lead.

A different doctrine, I think, prevails in this country.   Every department of Government, when called upon to apply a provision of the Constitution, must, in the first instance, pass upon its construction and determine the extent of its obligation.   A just man empowered to issue a
certificate of election will, it is true, hesitate to decide on the question
of the ineligibility of a candidate, where there is any serious doubt on
the subject, and for that reason to refuse his certificate.   He will in
such a case leave the matter to the determination of the judicial tribunals.   But where there is no doubt on the subject, and the language of
the Constitution forbidding the appointment is clear and imperative, he
cannot, without violating his oath of office, disregard its mandate.

The law is laid down in numerous adjudications in conformity with
these views.   In the case of the State of Missouri on the relation of
Bartley against the governor, which is cited by counsel, (39 Missouri,
399,) the doctrine for which I contend is stated with great clearness and
precision.   There a mandamus was prayed against the governor to compel him to issue a commission to the relator as one of the justices of the
county court.   The supreme court refused the writ on the ground that
the issuing of a commission was the exercise of political power, and no t

a mere ministerial act. After reciting that by the constitution the duty devolved upon the governor to commission all officers not otherwise provided by law, the court said :

> The governor is bound to see that the laws are faithfully executed, and he has taken an oath to support the constitution. In the correct and legitimate performance of his duty he must inevitably have a discretion in regard to granting commissions; for should a person be elected or appointed who was constitutionally ineligible to hold any office of profit or trust, would the executive be bound to commission him when his ineligibility was clearly and positively proven? If he is denied the exercise of any discretion in such case, he is made the violator of the constitution, not its guardian. Of what avail then is his oath of office? Or, if he has positive and satisfactory evidence that no election has been held in a county, shall he be required to violate the law and issue a commission to a person not elected, because a clerk has certified to the election? In granting a commission the governor may go behind the certificate to determine whether an applicant is entitled to receive a commission or not, where the objection to the right of the applicant to receive it rests upon the ground that a constitutional prohibition is interposed.

In Gulick against New, also cited by counsel, (14 Indiana, 93,) the supreme court of Indiana used language substantially to the same effect, holding that the governor, who was authorized to commission officers, might determine even against the decision of a board of canvassers whether an applicant was entitled to receive a commission or not, where the objection to his right to receive it rested upon a constitutional prohibition.

Other adjudications might be cited, but I believe these express the law as recognized generally throughout the country.* The question then arises, Watts being ineligible, whether the person receiving the next highest number of votes, he being eligible, was elected. Governor Grover held that such person was elected and issued a certificate of election to him. In his action in this respect he followed the rule which obtains in England, where, if the voters having knowledge of the ineligibility of a candidate persist in voting for him, their votes are considered as thrown away, and the eligible candidate receiving the next highest number of votes is declared elected. There are numerous decisions by courts of the highest character in this country to the same effect. They have been cited to us by counsel in their elaborate arguments, and in view of them an honorable and conscientious man might well have acted as the governor did. But I do not yield my assent to them; they

---

* In the debate which took place in the Senate on the 16th of December, 1876, on the electoral vote of Oregon, Senator Thurman replied to some remarks of Senator Morton upon the action of Governor Grover, as follows :

"The Senator from Indiana says that the question whether Watts was eligible or not was a judicial question, and that the sole duty of the governor was a ministerial duty, that he had no judicial function whatever, that it was therefore his duty simply to certify to the person who received the highest number of votes. He states that in the most absolute manner. If his statement be correct, then, if, instead of voting for Watts, the voters who cast their votes for him had voted for Queen Victoria, it would have been the duty of the governor to issue a certificate of election to Her Majesty the Queen that she was chosen elector of President and Vice-President for the State of Oregon. * * * It is very true in Oregon, as in every State in the Union and in the Federal Government, that there is a department of government which is called the judiciary, and another department called the executive, and another the legislative, and the constitutions endeavor to partition out the great powers of government between these three departments; but does it follow from that that no power to judge in any case can be devolved either upon the legislative department or upon the executive department of the government or an executive officer? We could not get along with the government one day on such an idea as that. The judicial power which the governor of Oregon cannot exercise, which the legislature cannot exercise; the judicial power that Congress cannot exercise, that the President cannot exercise, is the power of deciding litigated cases that arise in jurisprudence, and is a wholly different thing from the exercise of that quasi-judicial power which executive officers are called upon every day to exercise and which they must exercise."

are not in harmony with the spirit of our system of elections. The theory of our institutions is that the majority must govern; and their will can only be carried out by giving the offices to those for whom they have voted. In accordance with this view, the weight of judicial opinion in this country is, that votes given for an ineligible candidate are merely ineffectual to elect him, and that they are not to be thrown out as blanks, and the election given to the eligible candidate having the next highest number of votes. It is fairer and more just to thus limit the operation of votes for an ineligible candidate than to give them, as said in the California case, "the effect of disappointing the popular will and electing to office a man whose pretensions the people had designed to reject." (Saunders *vs.* Haynes, 13 California, 154.)

I cannot, therefore, vote that Cronin, the candidate having the next highest number of votes to Watts, "was duly appointed" an elector of the State at the election in November. As there was, in my opinion, a failure to appoint a third elector, the question arises whether a vacancy was thus produced which the other electors could fill. In a general sense, an office may be said to be vacant when it is not filled, though this condition arise from non-election, or the death, resignation, or removal of an incumbent. Cases have been cited before us where the term "vacancy" is used in both these senses. But the question for us to decide is whether there was a vacancy within the meaning of the legislation of Congress. That legislation distinguishes between cases of non-election and cases of vacancy, evidently treating the latter as only occurring after the office has been once filled. I refer to sections 133 and 134 of the Revised Statutes, which are as follows:

SEC. 133. Each State may by law provide for the filling of any vacancies which may occur in its college of electors when such college meets to give its electoral vote.

SEC. 134. Whenever any State has held an election for the purpose of choosing electors, and has failed to make a choice on the day prescribed by law, the electors may be appointed on a subsequent day in such manner as the legislature of such State may direct.*

Under this legislation the State of Oregon has provided for filling vacancies in its electoral college, treating, as does Congress, a vacancy as arising only after the office has once been filled. Its code of general laws declares when vacancies in any office shall be deemed to have occurred, as follows:

Every office shall become vacant on the occurring of either of the following events before the expiration of the term of such office:
1. The death of the incumbent;
2. His resignation;
3. His removal;
4. His ceasing to be an inhabitant of the district, county, town, or village for which he shall have been elected or appointed, or within which the duties of his office are required to be discharged;
5. His conviction of an infamous crime, or of any offense involving a violation of his oath;

---

* These provisions are taken from the act of January 23, 1845, which is as follows:

An act to establish a uniform time for holding elections for electors of President and Vice-President of the United States.

SECTION 1. *Be it enacted, &c.*, That the electors of the President and Vice-President shall be appointed in each State on the Tuesday next after the first Monday in the month of November of the year in which they are to be appointed: *Provided*, That each State may by law provide for the filling of any vacancy or vacancies which may occur in its college of electors, when such college meets to give its electoral vote: *And provided also*, When any State shall have held an election for the purpose of choosing electors, and shall fail to make a choice on the day aforesaid, then the electors may be appointed on a subsequent day, in such manner as the State shall by law provide.
Approved January 23, 1845.

6. His refusal or neglect to take his oath of office, or to give or renew his official bond, or to deposit such oath or bond within the time prescribed by law;

7. The decision of a competent tribunal declaring void his election or appointment. —*General Laws of Oregon,* page 576, section 48.

On the subject of vacancies in the electoral college, the same code of general laws provides that when the electors convene—

If there shall be any vacancy in the office of an elector, occasioned by death, refusal to act, neglect to attend, or otherwise, the electors present shall immediately proceed to fill, by *vira voce* and plurality of votes, such vacancy in the electoral college.—*General Laws of Oregon,* page 578, section 59.

It seems evident from these provisions that there could be no vacancy in the office of elector unless the office had once been filled. The events, upon the occurrence of which the statute declares that a vacancy shall occur in any office, all imply the existence of a previous incumbent.

The word " otherwise," used with respect to a vacancy in the electoral college, does not enlarge the scope of that term. The code having enumerated under one title the events upon which a vacancy may arise, including death, resignation, and other causes, proceeds to declare, under another title of the same chapter, that when a vacancy occurs in the office of elector by death, refusal to act, or *otherwise,* meaning thereby any other cause which would remove an incumbent, the electors present may fill the vacancy. As here there never had been an incumbent, there could be no vacancy in the sense of the statute by death or *otherwise.*

The two electors, Odell and Cartwright, undertook to appoint Watts as the third elector upon the assumption that he had resigned the office, and that a vacancy was thereby created. But inasmuch as he had never been elected, he had nothing to resign. The case was not one of a vacancy, but of a failure to elect; and the legislature of the State had made no provision for a subsequent election in case of such failure, as it might have done under the legislation of Congress.

For these reasons, Mr. President, I shall vote in this case as follows:

First. That, as Watts held on the day of election an office of trust and profit under the United States, he was then ineligible as an elector within the express terms of the Constitution;

Second. That, as of the three persons who received the highest number of .votes for electors at the election, only two of them, Odell and Cartwright, were then eligible, they were the only persons " duly appointed" electors, and there was a failure on the part of the State to appoint a third elector; and

Third. That, as the legislature has made no provision for the appointment of an elector under the act of Congress where there is a failure to make a choice on the day prescribed by law, the attempted election of a third elector by the two persons chosen, as in case of a vacancy, was inoperative and void.

I have prepared resolutions expressive of these views which I shall in proper time present to the Commission for its action.

Upon the question whether Watts, by his appointment to fill a supposed vacancy, or by virtue of the election in November, was a *de facto* officer, whose act is to be treated as valid, I have only a word or two to say:

First. There could be no filling of a vacancy if no vacancy within the meaning of the statute existed. As already said, Watts could not create such a vacancy by assuming to resign an office which he had never held. There could be no *de facto* officer where there was no office.

Second. The doctrine that the acts of officers *de facto* are to be held

63 E C

as valid is usually applied to cases where the office filled is a continuing one, like that of a judgeship of a court, or a directorship of a corporation, or a commissionership of a county; and is properly applicable only to such cases, and to cases where the functions of the office consist in supervising or recording the acts of numerous parties, like an inspectorship or clerkship of an election, or a registership of deeds; and then is applied simply on grounds of public policy, for the protection of the public and parties who have relied upon such acts. It is not properly applicable to cases where the entire function of the office consists in the performance of a single act; although there are *dicta* that it has been so applied. The only instances mentioned of such application are those where there was colorable appointment of a deputy, or other under-officer, to do a particular act for his principal; and the acts of the subordinate officers in those instances were sustained on other grounds. In the case of a continuing office, a single act of the officer may be upheld, as for instance the order of a judge *de facto*, though he should exercise his authority in no other instance. But where there is no continuing office, and an isolated act is to be performed, the person undertaking the execution of the act as agent of the State must be legally invested with authority, or his action will be void. All the authorities cited in the argument of one of the objectors [Mr. Mitchell] relate to cases of the former kind, and have no application to a case like the one before us.

Third. If Watts can be considered as having acted by virtue of the election in November, a position which is not claimed for him in the certificate transmitted to the President of the Senate, then the doctrine asserted is not applicable to his acts, for the further reason that such application would nullify an express provision of the Constitution. The doctrine invoked is that if a person whose appointment is prohibited is, nevertheless, permitted to act upon a certificate of election, the prohibition as to him is abrogated, and his acts are as valid as though the prohibition had never existed. He shall not be appointed, says the Constitution; but if he is appointed, says this doctrine, that fact will make no difference; the prohibition will not impair the validity of his action; the prohibition is a dead letter.

REMARKS OF MR. COMMISSIONER STRONG.

FLORIDA.

The Electoral Commission having under consideration an offer of evidence to impeach the canvass of the November election in Florida for presidential electors made by the State canvassing-board—

Mr. Commissioner STRONG said:

Mr. PRESIDENT: If the evidence offered can have any legitimate and constitutional bearing upon the decision of the questions sent to this Commission by the act of Congress which has conferred upon us our powers, it is pertinent within the meaning of the act, and it ought to be received. But if, on the other hand, it has no such bearing—if, when received, it could not lawfully affect the decision we are empowered to make, it is impertinent, and it should not be admitted. It is, therefore, a vital inquiry for what precise purpose the evidence is offered. Without undertaking to call attention to it in detail, it may be said that, primarily and substantially, the attempt of those who offer it is to show that the persons who, for convenience, are called the Hayes electors were not in fact elected by the people of Florida; that the return of their election, and the governor's certificate founded on the return, were not a true representation of the votes cast, but that the Tilden electors were elected, and that the canvass and decision of the board of State canvassers should have so declared. What we are asked to do, then, is to recanvass a State election for State agents or officers, or, rather, to try a contested election for presidential electors, such a contested election as is provided for in most of the States by established tribunals created for the purpose of determining election contests, on which courts of law frequently decide in cases of *quo warranto.*

Hence, the question that meets us at the outset is: Has this Commission power to try a case of contested election in a State? It has, by virtue of the act which created it, all the powers over the Florida election for electors which Congress itself has, and all which either House has, as well as all which the two Houses in convention have. It can have no more. Congress could have conferred no more, and it has made no attempt to confer more. The statute directs us to consider all certificates, votes, and papers from a State objected to, and all papers accompanying the same, with the objections, and directs us to consider them " with the same powers, *if any*, now possessed for that purpose by the two Houses, acting separately or together, and by a majority of votes decide whether any and what votes from such State are the votes provided for by the Constitution of the United States, and how many and what persons were duly appointed electors in such State, and [we] may therein take into view such petitions, depositions, and other papers, *if any*, as shall by the Constitution and now existing law be competent and pertinent in such consideration." We are, therefore, to have whatever powers Congress has, *if any*, under the Constitution for the purpose of considering the papers laid before us, and the same powers for deciding what are the votes provided for by the Constitution. In making our decision and report, as well as in receiving extrinsic evidence, we can only act within the limits of the constitutional power conferred upon Congress. This is plain from the language of the act, as I have quoted it.

The question, then, restated and carried back one step, is this: Has Congress power to recanvass the votes and returns of votes given in a State for presidential electors, or has it power to try a contested election in a State? The answer to this must be sought in the Constitution. Congress, confessedly, has no powers which the Constitution has not conferred upon it, either expressly or by fair implication from the grant of some express power. This will not be questioned by any one.

Now, if it be that Congress, or either House of Congress, has any power to canvass the votes cast for electors, or the returns of such votes, that power must be found in the clause of the Constitution which ordains that the President of the Senate " shall, in the presence of the Senate and House of Representatives, open all the certificates " [of the lists of persons voted for for President and Vice-President, and of the number of votes for each,]" and the votes shall then be counted." The opening of the certificates and the counting of the votes is not the election. Nor is the voting done on the second Tuesday in November the presidential election. It is only preparatory to such election. The presidential election takes place on the first Wednesday of December, when the appointed electors meet and cast their votes, and all that the President of the Senate and the two Houses of Congress have to do after that time is to ascertain the result. And it is worthy of notice that in this constitutional provision, which alone is the basis of all claim set up for congressional power to canvass the votes and returns of the November State election, there is no reference to that election, or to anything antecedent to the act of voting by the electors. The reference is exclusively to matters that must occur after they have performed their duties.

Now, certainly no one can contend that the direction that the votes (that is, the votes of the appointed electors) shall be counted in the presence of the Senate and House of Representatives is an express bestowal of power upon any body to inquire and determine whether a State canvass of the election of electors was correct or not. The framers of the Constitution well understood what was necessary to confer upon Congress, or upon either House, power to canvass elections or returns, and the subject did not escape their attention. When such power was intended to be granted, it was given in plain language. Each House was made a judge " of the elections, returns, and qualifications of its own members." No such language was used respecting electors, and for what appears to me to be the plainest reason. The scheme of the Constitution was to make the appointment of electors exclusively a State affair, free from interference of the legislative department of the Government, excepting only that Congress was permitted to determine the time for choosing electors, and the day on which they shall give their votes, with this limitation, that the day shall be the same throughout the United States. And it was ordained that no Senator or Representative shall be appointed an elector.

The States, as such, were required to appoint, in such manner as their legislatures might direct; the plain object of which was to make State governments, in the matter of choosing a President, as independent as possible of any possible action by the General Government.

It will, then, I think, be admitted that the power claimed for Congress, and of course for this Commission, by the proponents of the evidence offered, has not been expressly granted. Is there any implication of such a grant? I am unable to find it in the Constitution. I have already remarked that when the grant of such a power was intended to be made it was given in unmistakable language, expressly making each House a judge of the elections, returns, and qualifications of its members. The express gift in that case tends to repel the idea of an implied grant of the same power in any other. I think it may safely be said that no powers were granted to Congress by the Constitution, either expressly or impliedly, that were not intended to be granted, and it is difficult to believe there was an intention to grant to Congress by implication power to canvass and judge of elections and returns of elections of State electors when it was thought necessary to grant that power expressly in cases of elections of Senators and Representatives.

An implication of power must have something upon which it can rest, and certainly there is in the Constitution no basis for an implication such as is sought to be made here, except it be found in the required presence of the two Houses when the electoral votes are to be opened and counted. I know of no other implication of congressional power which rests on so shadowy a foundation, and I find it impossible to infer from that any grant of power of canvassing elections in the States. Yet if we receive the evidence offered we shall be claiming and exerting the exact power which Congress would have possessed if the Constitution had expressly declared that Congress shall be the judge of the elections, returns, and qualifications of presidential electors.

The truth is, the framers of the Constitution seem never to have contemplated the possibility of disputes respecting the appointment of electors, and hence they made no provision for the decision of such controversies. They were wise men, but they did not foresee everything. They would have been more than human if they had. I doubt whether they had in mind at all the idea of a popular election as a mode of appointing State electors. They used the word "appoint," doubtless thinking that the legislatures of the States would themselves select the electors, or empower the governor or some other State officer to select them. The word "appoint" is not the most appropriate word for describing the result of a popular election. Such a mode of appointment, I submit, is allowable, but there is little reason to think it was contemplated, and still less reason to suppose that the idea of a contested popular election for electors had any existence in the minds of its framers when the Constitution was formed. It was not until years afterward that the electors were chosen by popular vote. It is altogether improbable, therefore, that any necessity was felt in the constitutional convention for giving to Congress, or any other branch of the new Government, the decision of contests over the results of such elections, and hence it is not surprising that we find no provision made for determining them.

And it seems to me, if such contest had been foreseen, that it is by no means clear the convention would have provided for their decision by any Federal tribunal. There are inherent difficulties in the way. As I have said, the appointment of electors, however it may be made, is peculiarly and exclusively a State affair. The action of electors after their appointment has relation to the General Government, but the appointment itself is a different matter. Before the first Wednesday of December, when the electors cast their votes, neither Congress nor any Department of the General Government has anything to do with them, or with the proceeding for appointing them. The State confessedly has. She has entire control over the elections, over the returns, and over the canvass. And so, after the votes of the electors have been cast, if there be any power over the election, the returns, or the canvass, confessedly the State has it. Now, if Congress had power also to enter upon a recanvass, or to try a contest over the results, its exercise might lead to untold confusion and difficulty. Congress might decide that one set of electors had been appointed, while the State, which has undoubted authority, might decide another set were the true appointees. If the decision of Congress is to prevail, where then is the right of the State to appoint in its own manner? I cannot believe the Constitution justifies any such possible conflict, or any such invasion of the domain of a State. The implication of such a power ought to be clear, if it exists at all. It ought not to rest on any other than a substantial foundation. Somebody ought to be able to put his finger on some clause in the Constitution that justifies it. No such clause has been pointed out, and I can find none. The present juncture sometimes tempts me to wish I could find some power in Congress and in this Commission to explore to the bottom the election and returns in Florida; and could I find anything upon which to build a fair implication of such a power, I would exert it. But I cannot construe the Constitution as I may wish it to be; I must construe it as I find it.

If, then, Congress has not the power to enter into the consideration of the evidence offered, it would be idle to admit it.

But we are asked, Is there no way of avoiding the possibility of having electoral votes cast on the faith of false returns of elections? Can no inquiry be made into the correctness of such returns? To such questions I reply, there is ample power in the State. She may provide in any way to purify her elections, and may devise means to correct an erroneous canvass, or rectify false returns, or throw out illegal votes.

She may do this in the most summary way. She may accomplish it completely before the day for casting the electoral vote arrives. But I find no power in Congress, either express or implied, to do this work which the State may do.

There may be a necessity for its lodgment somewhere outside of the State, but when Congress undertakes to act it must find a warrant for its action in some provision of the Constitution. There are many things the experience of ninety years has taught us it would be desirable to have, some things that seem to be necessary, which the Constitution has not given.

In all elections there are and there must be finalities. There must be an ultimate canvass and ascertainment of the result. That must be final and conclusive until reversed, though it may not be in exact accordance with the actual facts.

The statute of Florida provides that its presidential electors shall be appointed by a popular vote, and it directs that the result of that vote shall be *determined* and *declared* by a State board of canvassers constituted as directed. That board is made by the statute the ultimate determinant and declarant of what the vote was and of its result, and it has power in certain cases to exclude county returns. The board is to *determine and declare*. Such is the plain direction of the act. Determination is a quasi-judicial act; the declaration which is to follow is an announcement of the determination; and after the determination and declaration the governor is required to give a certificate to the persons elected electors. But how is he to know who has been elected, except from the determination and declaration of the board? He has no authority to canvass the returns, and he cannot overrule the action of the board. He must be governed by that action if he obeys the law and certifies as required.

I admit the declaration and determination of the board may be set aside by any authority the State may designate to try contested elections. It may be shown to be erroneous on the trial of a *quo warranto*. But until thus reversed, it is and must be final, obligatory upon the governor as upon all others. The certificate he is required by law to give is a certificate of a fact, and of a fact which can appear only in that determination of the State board of canvassers, which is in existence unreversed when the certificate is to be given. Surely, he cannot certify that a person has been elected who, at the time of his certificate, is shown by the determination of the State board not to have been elected. Such a certificate would be a palpable falsehood and fraud.

Now, in this case, it is not offered to be shown that Governor Stearns's certificate of the election of what are called the Hayes electors did not truly represent the conclusions and determination of the State board; and if it did truly conform to that determination, it was such a certificate as he was authorized and required to make. It was neither untrue nor fraudulent.

I admit the governor's certificate is not unimpeachable. It may be shown to be untrue by proof that it does not correspond with the determination of the canvassing-board. It may be proved to be a forgery. But in the present case these things are not alleged. The certificate must be, therefore, at least *prima-facie* evidence that the persons certified to be elected were in fact elected, and, therefore, that they were the State's appointees. They derived their title from the election, and what was the result of the election was determined by the State canvassing-board. The determination, I have said, may have been subject to revision by process of State law, but until annulled it was the pronounced action of the State.

Are, then, persons who have received a governor's certificate that they have been appointed electors, a certificate which the governor is required by law to give, and which is founded on a quasi-judicial determination of the results of the election, incapable of acting until it shall be decided by another tribunal, in some proceeding which may or may not afterward be commenced, whether the determined and declared result of the election was erroneous or not?

Must every person who has received a commission to fill an office, the duties of which are to be performed immediately, if at all, decline acting under the commission because subsequent investigation may have shown that he was not entitled to it? No such doctrine, I think, has ever been asserted by any tribunal.

Now, then, the persons who voted for Hayes on the 6th day of December had all the insignia of title when they voted. They had the governor's certificate of their right. They had the judicial determination and declaration of the State canvassing-board that they had been elected. No other persons had even a *prima-facie* right. The Tilden electors had no decision in their favor of any board or tribunal authorized by law to ascertain and declare the results of the election. They had no certificate from anybody empowered to certify that they were electors. They were not even electors *de facto*.

I do not care to discuss the question how far the acts of officers *de facto* are effective. It is admitted that they generally are valid as against, or for, others than themselves. But I maintain that the *acts* of such officers are *de jure*. When they have at the time of their action all the evidences of right known to the law, their right is absolute and perfect until annulled or revoked. I do not see how anybody can contend that *acts* of officers who have received certificates of their election from the authority empowered and directed to issue such certificates—certificates truly representing the final returns of the election, as determined and declared by the ultimate board constituted by law for making such determination—are not *de jure*. How can it be maintained that such officers are personally responsible for acts done in pursuance of their apparent right, even though it may subsequently be shown that they were not in fact elected? Could the Hayes electors have been sued for intrusion? If they had been, would not the governor's certificate and the determination of the State canvassing-board have been a complete protection? If a sheriff has a commission from a governor, are his acts, while he holds the commission, rendered invalid by a subsequent judicial decree that he was not entitled to the office? Surely this will not be claimed. And if it cannot be, it is because the acts of such officers are rightful, or *de jure*.

In my judgment, it follows inevitably that what was done in Florida after the 6th of December is immaterial. Neither the action of the legislature, nor a *post hac* decision of a court, can affect an act rightfully done, when it was done and completed before the legislature and the court attempted to annul the authority for it.

Mr. Commissioner THURMAN. Are we not now counting the vote? Is it not a matter *in fieri?*

Mr. Commissioner STRONG. We are now counting the electoral vote. But the offer of evidence assumes that we may count the State vote for electors, an antecedent matter. I have already attempted to show that there is no constitutional power in Congress, and consequently none in us, to count the votes of States, or to review a State canvass.

But to return to the subject I was considering. There must be a finality in ascertaining the results of an election, and when the election is a mode of appointment of persons to cast a vote for a State on an appointed day, the finality must be on or before that day, else nothing can be settled. The electors of the State of New York cast the votes of the State on the 6th of December last. Can those votes now be nullified by any subsequent action of the New York legislature declaring that the persons who voted were not elected, or creating a new board to make a new canvass, or by the judgment of an inferior court, or any other court, that other persons were entitled to cast the votes of the State? If that is possible, the new President to be installed on the 4th of March next can be ousted by the declaration of a State legislature or the judgment of a State court. There is no statute of limitations to bar such action by any State. If the votes of electors can be destroyed by State action after they have been cast, it may be done next July as well as it can be now.

But I have detained the Commission too long. I will only add some references to a few decisions that bear directly on the question before us, and show the conclusive effect of the decision of a statutory canvassing-board.

In 25 Maine Reports, 567, may be found a unanimous opinion of the supreme judicial court in answer to a question propounded to the court by the governor. The question was, " Is it competent for the governor and council, in counting votes for county officers, under the provisions of the. act providing for the election of county officers, approved February 22, 1842, to receive from the town clerk and selectmen evidence to show that the return made by them does not correspond with the records?" The constitution and statutes of the State required, in the choice of county officers, that the votes of towns and plantations should be received by their selectmen and assessors respectively, in the presence of their respective town and plantation clerks, and that the clerks should make a list of the persons voted for with the number of votes for each against his name, and that the same should be recorded in the presence of the selectmen and assessors respectively, in the open town and plantation meetings, and that fair copies of the lists should be attested by the selectmen and assessors of their respective towns and plantations, and by the clerks of each, and sealed up in open town and plantation meetings. The votes so sealed up are required to be transmitted to the governor and council within thirty days thereafter, who are to "open and count the votes returned." Open and count the votes— such is the language of the law. The court was of opinion that the governor and council had no authority to receive any other evidence in relation to the votes than what the certificates so prepared, transmitted, and received, may contain—not even evidence that the township records differ from the return-lists. A similar decision was made in Bacon vs. The York Commissions, 26 Maine, 494; and a like opinion was given in 1867, reported in 54 Maine, 602.

In The People ex rel. Bailey vs. The Supervisors of Greene, 17 Barb., 217, it was held that after a board of county canvassers has met and organized according to law, and proceeded to estimate the votes of the county, and to make the statement prescribed by the statute, and to determine who have been elected county officers, and a copy of their determination has been published and filed and become a matter of record, and the board has dissolved, a mandamus will not lie requiring them to reorganize and correct the estimate of votes of the county, by allowing counting, canvassing, and estimating the votes of an election-district.

alleged to have been improperly omitted by the board at its former meeting.

In Hadley *vs.* The Mayor of Albany, 33 New York (Court of Appeals), 603, it was ruled that when the law has committed to the common council of a city the duty of canvassing the returns and determining the result of an election from them, and the council have performed that duty and made their determination from them, they have exhausted their power and cannot afterward reverse their decision by making a different determination. It was also held that the question as to the effect of the returns is not open for determination by a jury in an action to which the title to the office comes up collaterally. In that case an offer was made to show that the returns in fact showed (as is alleged in the case now before us) that the person determined and declared elected was not elected. But the evidence was ruled inadmissible, and Denio, the eminent judge who delivered the opinion of the court, said:

> If the question had arisen upon an action in the nature of a *quo warranto* information, the evidence would have been competent. But it would be intolerable to allow a party affected by the acts of a person claiming to be an officer to go behind the official determination to prove that such official determination arose out of mistake or fraud.

So in Clark *vs.* Buchanan, 2 Minnesota, 346, it was held that a canvassing-board, having made a canvass and adjourned *sine die,* was *functus officio* and had no right to reconvene and correct errors in its decisions. I know of no authorities in conflict with these. There are very many that assert the same doctrine.

My conclusions, then, are that neither Congress nor this Commission has authority under the Constitution to recanvass the vote of Florida for State electors; that the first determination of the State canvassing-board was conclusive until it was reversed by State authority; that while it remained unreversed it conferred upon the persons declared by it to have been chosen electors rightful authority to cast the vote of the State; and that the act which those electors were appointed to do having been done, it was not in the power even of the State afterward to undo the act and call in question the authority by which it was done.

It follows, in my judgment, that the evidence now offered is impertinent to any question we can decide, and, therefore, that it ought not to be admitted.

OREGON.

The electoral votes of Oregon being under consideration—

Mr. Commissioner STRONG said:

Mr. PRESIDENT: I do not propose to present an extended argument in support of the opinions I have respecting this case. The condition of my health forbids that; but I wish to state very briefly what my opinions are, together with the conclusions at which I have arrived. I still think, as I thought when we had the Florida and Louisiana cases under consideration, that when the laws of a State have appointed a tribunal, either a board, a council, an officer, or any authority, to ascertain, decide, or determine what have been the results of an election for presidential electors, the decision of that board, officer, or authority is conclusive, so long as it remains unreversed by a judicial tribunal empowered by State law to reverse it. If I could have had any doubts upon this subject they would have been removed by the very able argument of Judge Hoadly, submitted to us night before last, and by the numerous authorities he cited. Those authorities show that it is everywhere held that the decision or ascertainment of the result of an election by the appointed canvassing authority is final, and that it must be accepted as such. Not a single authority has been adduced which asserts any other doctrine. The right of a person claiming to have been elected is to be tested, then, by the results of the State canvass, not by what preceded it, and not by what followed it. The State canvass is the determination by the State, acting through its appointed agents, of the question who was elected. I have never doubted that when the legal profession of the country shall come to examine the subject coolly, as they will after the present excitement has passed, they will agree that this is a perfectly sound doctrine. But I had not expected the doctrine would, at this early period, in the midst of an excited party struggle, receive the assent and complete vindication it has received from the counsel who have addressed us on behalf of the Tilden electors.

In view of this principle, to which there appears to be universal assent, let us examine the statutes of Oregon and see what provision that State has made for ascertaining and determining the results of elections for presidential electors. The sixtieth section of its election laws enacts that " the votes for electors shall be given, received, returned, and canvassed as the same are given, returned, and canvassed for members of Congress," and former sections of the act prescribe how the returns and canvass of votes for members of Congress shall be made. In each county the county clerk is required to make an abstract of the votes cast in the county and send it to the secretary of state; and the thirty-seventh section of the law directs as follows:

It shall be the duty of the secretary of state, in the presence of the governor, to proceed, within thirty days after the election, and sooner if the returns be all received, to canvass the votes given for * * * members of Congress.

This provision plainly makes the secretary of state the sole canvassing officer. It may not be proper to call him a board, but he is the sole officer designated and appointed by the law to make the canvass and ascertain the result of the election. It is true he must make the canvass in the presence of the governor, but no duties in regard to the canvass are assigned by the law to the governor. His presence is required to insure an open canvass, and for no other apparent reason. Had it been intended he should take part in the canvass, the language of the act would have been, it shall be the duty of the secretary of state and of the governor to proceed to canvass the votes, &c. But the words actually used have no such meaning. It is worthy of notice that in the thirty-fifth section, where provision is made for a county canvass, and for making up the abstract of votes to be sent to the secretary of state, it is enacted that the county clerk, "taking to his assistance two justices of the peace of the county, shall proceed to open the [returns received] and make abstracts of the votes." There the two justices selected are made part of the county canvassing-board, because they are to be active participants therein, but the provision in regard to the State canvass is widely different, and the different language employed respecting that indicates clearly a difference of intention. I think, therefore, that it is beyond any reasonable doubt that by the law of Oregon the secretary of state is made the sole canvassing-officer to ascertain, from the county abstracts sent to him, and to determine the results of an election for member of Congress, and also for presidential electors.

This canvass was made in the present case, and we have it before us. The secretary of state has certified and affixed the seal of the State to his certificate that the tabulated statement to which he certifies is the result of the vote cast for presidential electors at a general election held in and for the State of Oregon on the 7th day of November, A. D. 1876, as opened and canvassed in the presence of his excellency L. F. Grover, governor of the State, according to law, on the 4th day of December, A. D. 1876, at two o'clock of that day, by the secretary of state. That certificate shows that each of the three Hayes electors received over 15,200 votes, and that each of the Tilden electors received less than 14,200. The secretary has also made out and certified, over the seal of the State, a list of the names of the three persons who received the highest number of votes, as it appears by the returns of the election on file in his office, and those three persons are the three Hayes electors.

This result of the canvass, thus made to appear, was the final determination of the officer appointed by the State to make such a determination. I agree with the honorable Senator from Delaware that there is no essential difference in the authority of the State canvassing-boards of Florida and that of the State canvassing-officer of Oregon. The duty of each is to ascertain, as a finality, who have been elected by the popular votes. But in Oregon there is a most important statutory provision. It is found in the fortieth section of the law regulating elections, as follows:

In all elections in this State, the person having the highest number of votes for any office shall be deemed to have been elected.

When, therefore, the secretary of state, on the 4th day of December, 1876, canvassed the vote of the State, and ascertained, as he did, that Odell, Cartwright, and Watts had received the highest number of votes for presidential electors, the law declared them to be elected. It required that they should be deemed elected. Deemed by whom? Deemed elected by the secretary of state, by the governor, and by everybody else. Apart, then, from the question respecting the alleged ineligibility of Watts, of which I shall speak hereafter, the appointment of those three electors was complete on that day, so soon as the secretary of state had completed his canvass. Now, had nothing more been done; had no certificate of their election ever been given by the secretary or by the governor, the three electors, having been ascertained by the State's appointed officer to have received the highest number of votes and having been required by law to be deemed elected, would have had a complete and unquestionable right to cast the vote of the State for President and Vice-President. No one doubts or denies this. Their right was founded upon the election as determined by the law, and not upon any certificate of their having been elected or of their being electors.

But the sixtieth section of the statute imposes upon the secretary of state an additional duty, to be performed after he has completed the canvass. He is required to prepare two lists of the names of the electors elected, and affix the seal of the State to the same. These lists are required to be signed by the secretary and the governor, and to be delivered by the secretary to the college of electors at the hour of their meeting on the first Wednesday of December. This, I say, is no part of the canvass. It is a simple ministerial act, which may be performed, and which was performed in the present case, days after the canvass and determination of the question who had the highest number of votes, and days after the time when, by force of law, the persons ascertained to have received the highest number were deemed to have been elected. These lists, then, are in no sense the commission of the electors and their warrant for action. Their authority is complete before the lists are made out. Nor can there be any pretense for saying that the lists are the decision of the canvassing-officer. Nobody claims that. What, then, are they, and what purpose were they designed to subserve? They are not required to give notice to the electors that they have been appointed. This is clear, for they are not to be delivered to the college of electors until the hour of their meeting. As notices, therefore, they would be nugatory. The chosen electors might reside hundreds of miles from the capital. Had the lists been intended for notice of appointment, service of them must have been required before the hour of meeting. It is evident they are intended to be evidence, *on the count here*, of a previous appointment, and they are made out in duplicate that they may accompany the two certificates of votes required by the act of Congress of 1792 to be sent to the President of the Senate. These lists, it is true, are required to be signed by the governor as well as by the secretary of state. They are not to be made out by the governor or delivered by him. He, as well as the secretary, signs to furnish evidence required at Washington to show here that the State had previously appointed the persons electors whose votes have been sent.

The truth is, the law of Oregon confers on the governor no authority to canvass the returns of votes for presidential electors, or to commission those who by the ascertainment and decision of this canvassing authority are to be deemed elected, or to certify who have been appointed. He may grant such a certificate of election to the person having the highest number of votes for certain other offices and may issue a proclamation declaring the election of such person. This power is conferred by the thirty-seventh section. But the provisions in regard to presidential electors are entirely different. His certificate of their election is wholly unauthorized. When, therefore, he certified that Odell received 15,206 votes, Cartwright 15,214 votes, E. A. Cronin 14,157 votes for electors, being the highest number of votes cast at the election for persons eligible to be appointed electors, and declared them duly elected electors for the State of Oregon, he did an act which the law conferred upon him no power to do, and he certified what was untrue, for the law declared that the persons who had the highest number of votes should be deemed elected.

This unauthorized certificate, which alone is the foundation of all claim the Tilden electors set up, was the act of the governor. It was attested, it is true, by the secretary of state, and the seal of the State is attached, but it is not the certificate of the secretary any more than the attestation of Mr. Secretary Fish to a presidential proclamation of a thanksgiving day makes it Mr. Fish's proclamation. The attestation is to the fact that the governor signed the certificate. It is not an assertion that the certificate is true. The secretary of state of Oregon has never certified that Cronin was an elector, or that any persons were other than Odell, Cartwright, and Watts.

Even where the law of the State directs the governor to give to electors certificates of their election, as the law of Florida does, I have never contended, and no one has contended, that the certificate is conclusive. I said distinctly, more than once, when remarking upon the Florida case, that the governor's certificate is not unimpeachable. It may be shown to be untrue, and it is so shown when it is proved to be different from the conclusions of the State canvassing authority or board. I say so now. Unless the decisions of all courts are to be disregarded, the result of an election for electors is that ascertained and determined by the State canvassing-board or officer designated by law for that duty. That is what we held in both the Florida and Louisiana cases, and that I hold now. But if such were not the law, an unauthorized certificate of the governor can be evidence of no fact asserted in it.

A few words in regard to the ineligibility of Watts. I believe that neither this Commission nor Congress has any power under the Constitution to judge of the qualifications of a State elector, no more than we have to judge of the State election and returns. Ineligibility is a disqualification. But I will not discuss the question of our power; I have sufficiently discussed it heretofore. If it be conceded that Watts was ineligible on the 7th of November, the day of the election, his disqualification for appointment ceased on the 14th of that month, and there was nothing in the way of his appointment on the 6th of December. Concede, for the sake of the argument, that he was ineligible on the 7th of November, and, therefore, was not elected, though he received a higher number of votes than any competitor, then there were two chosen, and the college consisting of three was not full. One elector was wanting. There was a vacancy, and that vacancy was filled on December 6, by the action of the two electors who were chosen, who then appointed Watts to fill it. Our friends, however, whose opinions do not concur with mine, earnestly insist that the deficiency in the college having been caused by a failure to elect more than the two electors, there was no vacancy within the meaning of the law which the two electors could fill. A vacancy, they say, can only exist when the office has had an incumbent. Rather technical, I think! The statute of Oregon declares that if, at the hour of twelve o'clock at noon on the first Wednesday of December after their election, "there shall be any vacancy in the office of an elector, occasioned by death, refusal to act, neglect to attend, or otherwise, the electors present shall immediately proceed to fill, by viva voce and plurality of votes, such vacancy in the electoral college, and when all the electors shall appear, or the vacancies, if any, shall have been filled, as above provided, such electors shall proceed to perform the duties required of them by the Constitution and laws of the United States." The language is very broad—as comprehensive as possible. It is not only vacancies occasioned in specified ways that may be filled, but vacancies occasioned otherwise. The statute is plainly remedial, and the mischief or evil it was intended to remedy was a college of electors only partly filled when the time for voting came. If there was a vacancy then, if there were not in being the entire number of electors to which the State was entitled, the State would lose her just share in the choice of a President and Vice-President. This was the mischief the statute proposed to remedy, and the mischief was precisely the same, whether the incompleteness of the college was caused by the death, refusal to act, or neglect to attend of one of the persons elected, or whether it was caused by a failure to elect a sufficient number of electors.

Now, if there be any rule of construction which no one doubts, it is that remedial statutes are to be liberally construed, and that such effect is to be given to them, if possible, as to remove the whole mischief they are intended to cure. In view of this principle, I cannot see how it can be maintained that Odell and Cartwright were not authorized to appoint a third elector, as they did, and thus complete the college. The argument that they had no such right is based, if it has any basis, upon the most refined technicality. Together with those who act with me, I have been charged with standing on technicalities to defeat justice. If to stand on the Constitution of the United States and the decisions of all the courts, as I have done, is to be technical, what is to be said of the argument that under the Oregon statute two admittedly chosen electors had no right to fill the electoral college, if its incompleteness was occasioned by a failure of the people to elect more than two electors?

Mr. President, such are my opinions respecting the principal questions in this case. They lead inevitably to the conclusion that, under the law of Oregon, Odell, Cartwright, and Watts were the duly-appointed electors of the State, and that the votes cast by them should be counted.

REMARKS OF MR. COMMISSIONER MILLER.

FLORIDA.

The Commission having under consideration the electoral vote of Florida—

Mr. Commissioner MILLER said:

Mr. PRESIDENT : As all the members of the Commission have spoken to the matter before us but you, my brother Bradley, and myself, and as I am aware that before the vote is taken both you and he desire to give expression to your views, it seems appropriate and it is probably expected that I shall do the same.

The only question which I consider to be properly before the Commission is the one propounded by us to counsel, namely, whether any other evidence can be received and considered by the Commission than that which was submitted by the President of the Senate to the two Houses of Congress, being the different certificates and the papers accompanying the same. The other members of the Commission who have taken part in this discussion have not limited themselves to this, but have inquired into the effect of the action of the State courts of Florida, and of her legislature, and the certificates of Attorney-General Cocke, and Governor Drew, as found in those papers; and in considering the effect of the certificate of Governor Stearns and the action of the returning-board of the State, in excluding other evidence of the appointment of electors, it was not easy to keep wholly out of view the papers I have mentioned.

I shall therefore give them a few moments' consideration. But as they, with another matter much insisted on, lie outside of the general and what I believe to be the more legitimate course of reasoning, on which the true solution of the question must rest, I will dispose of them first.

It is strongly urged upon us that a large pile of papers, a half-bushel perhaps in quantity, of the contents of which both this Commission and the two Houses of Congress are profoundly ignorant, has become legitimate evidence and must necessarily be considered by us, because they are in a very general way referred to in the paper filed by certain members of the two Houses as their objection to what has been familiarly referred to as certificate No. 1, by which I understand the certificate of Governor Stearns that the electors who have since cast their votes for Hayes and Wheeler were the duly-appointed electors for the State of Florida. This proposition has been defended by Mr. Commissioner Hunton on the ground that by analogy to the exhibits accompanying a bill or answer in chancery, these, being exhibits to the objections which the statute requires to be made in writing, become part of those objections. But if the principle were sound the analogy wholly fails, because every exhibit referred to in a bill in chancery must not only have its pertinency shown by describing its nature or character in the bill, but the exhibit itself must be identified by a mark or reference, as a number, a letter, or some other mode by which that identity is clearly established. Nothing of the kind is done here. No statement of the character, or nature, or source of a single paper, out of perhaps a hundred, is made. No reference is made to anything by which these papers can be identified. There is nothing to hinder alterations or substitutions among them. They may be *ex parte* affidavits taken in the morasses of Florida, the slums of New York, or the private office of retained counsel in this city. It would be very strange indeed if the act of Congress, under which we sit, intended to furnish in this manner the materials on which our decisions must be founded. Such, however, is the argument of Mr. Commissioner Thurman, who, construing, as I venture to say erroneously, an important phrase in that act, insists that all the papers accompanying *the objections must be* considered by us. The language he relies on is this:

When all such objections so made to any certificate, vote, or paper from a State shall have been received and read—

In the joint meeting of the two Houses—

all such certificates, votes, and papers so objected to, *and all papers accompanying the same*, together with said objections, shall be forthwith submitted to said Commission, which shall proceed to consider the same, &c.

The good sense of the framers of this bill is vindicated by the critical accuracy with which they have clearly expressed that the certificates, votes, and papers so objected to, and all papers accompanying *them*, are to be considered, and the objections also, the latter only on *their* merits, with no directions to consider any papers filed with them, even if fully described and identified. This seems so clear to me that I shall pass from the consideration of the point without further remark.

Another matter, much relied on by counsel and urged again in the Commission, is the action of the courts of Florida in two cases which are supposed to affect the right of the electors mentioned in the first certificate.

The first of these was the suit between Stearns and Drew, rival candidates for the office of governor at the same general election in which the electors are said to have been chosen. It is not claimed that this suit of itself determined who were the lawfully-appointed electors, but that the opinion of the supreme court of the State settles principles of law, binding on us, which show that the action of the returning-board is not conclusive. I am not satisfied that the principles laid down in that opinion, if applied to the action of that board in the case of the electors, would have the effect claimed for it now. But whether this be so or not, I am very clear that the opinion of the court in that case is not of the class which binds this body in construing the statute of Florida on that subject. It is the well-settled doctrine of the Supreme Court in case of writs of error to the decisions of the State courts, that where the matter to be considered is the constitutionality or validity of a State law, the Supreme Court must for itself determine that question, and that to follow implicity the State decision on the construction of the statute is to abdicate the power and refuse to perform the duty devolved on it in that case. (Bridge Proprietors *vs.* Hoboken Company, 2 Wallace, 116.) Such is precisely the case here. If Congress or the two Houses, whose power, neither more nor less, we exercise to-day, had a right to determine on the validity and effect of the certificate of the returning-board to these electors, it was a power called into existence before any action of the State court of Florida, and could not be forestalled, nor could the principles on which it must be decided be concluded by any anticipatory action of the courts of Florida, whether had with that view or not. The effect of that opinion on our action must, therefore, be limited to the force of its reasoning and the weight of character which the court brings to its support.

I confess that if the opinion is fairly construed to hold that the returning-board of elections of that State had no other than the mere ministerial function of adding up and comparing the columns of votes, and could exercise no judgment on questions of fraud or other matters, and was wholly without power in reviewing and rejecting the poll of any voting-precinct, it is so much at variance with the language and spirit of the statute it was construing as to have little weight with me in forming a judgment on the same subject.

The other case in the State courts was a proceeding in *quo warranto*, brought in person by those whom I shall, to avoid circumlocution, call the Tilden electors against the Hayes electors, in the local circuit court of Leon County, to test the title to said office.

Of this suit no record is before us. We know nothing of it except a very short statement in a certificate given by Governor Drew that such a suit had been instituted in the circuit court of the State for the second judicial district, and resulted in a judgment in favor of the relators. It is not stated when the suit was commenced, or when the judgment was rendered. It seems to have been conceded in argument that service of the writ or notice of the suit was made on the 6th day of December, the day on which by act of Congress the electors everywhere must cast their vote, and the day on which the electors declared by the returning-board and by Governor Stearns—the governor then in power by undisputed right—did cast the electoral vote of the State of Florida; but whether the notice was before or after they had voted is not shown. Can the right to cast one of the electoral votes of a State for President be thus tried in a court of law? It is not asserted that any such right is found in any act of Congress or in any statute of Florida.

The single function of an elector is to give one of the votes to which the State is entitled for President and Vice-President. His powers begin there and end there. He has no permanent office with continuing functions, in which he may repeatedly perform acts of authority unless prevented by the courts. There is, therefore, no necessity for the application of such a writ. An injunction would be much more appropriate, if any judicial remedy existed at all, for by that writ the single act which he can perform might be prohibited. If a county which had taken stock in a railroad company should attempt to appoint an agent to cast its vote in the election of directors, would a *quo warranto* lie to test his authority? Yet he is exercising a function precisely similar to an elector, except that one represents a State and the other a county.

It is perhaps not the most satisfactory test of the soundness of a principle to look to its consequences, but where the principle rests on no statute, but on some general common-law doctrine, this is usually a very fair test of its correctness. If the doctrine be true of Florida, it must be equally so of other States. In New York there are thirty-two judges of the supreme court of that State, a court which exercises original jurisdiction all over the State. Under the principle asserted any one of these thirty-two judges may issue his writ of *quo warranto*, or of injunction, or other appropriate writ, the day before the votes must by law be cast for President and Vice-President, and by this exercise of his power prevent the 35 votes of the State from being given or counted in the election. And if you say it is only the final judgment which is effectual, *that* may be delayed until after the 4th of March, when it will be of no avail to give any judgment, whether it be right or whether it be wrong. It is safe to say that no such power exists in any man or in any tribunal, unless it is placed there by the expressed will of the law-making power.

The Constitution declares that no person holding an office of trust or profit under the United States shall be appointed an elector, and the objectors to certificate No. 1 propose to give evidence to show that Mr. Humphreys, one of the electors named in that certificate, was at the date of his election holding the office of shipping-commissioner under the appointment of the circuit court of the United States for the district of Florida. There are two reasons why I do not think such evidence admissible. The first is that the inquiry comes too late, because Mr. Humphreys, acting under the credentials which the law prescribes as his authority, has already cast his vote for President and Vice-President. That vote being a fact accomplished, cannot be annulled by any subsequent proceeding to question his eligibility. The second is, that like many other provisions of the Constitution, it is not self-executing; and as no means of enforcing it have been provided it remains ineffectual, save as its directions shall be observed by those who appoint the electors. In this regard the provision of the Constitution in question is not singular. A very large residuum of the powers conferred by the Federal Constitution has never been called into action by appropriate legislation. As regards the grant of judicial power by that instrument, it has been the frequent subject of comment that a large—perhaps until very recently the largest—part of this power has never been called into exercise because Congress has not conferred the necessary jurisdiction on any court or other judicial tribunal. It was early decided that the provision for the rendition of persons held to service in one State escaping into another was inoperative because no statute to enforce it had been enacted. And after the fugitive-slave law had been supposed to provide ample means to secure the object of the constitutional provision, it was decided in the case of Kentucky vs. Dennison, governor of Ohio, 24 Howard, 66, Chief-Justice Taney delivering the opinion of the court, that while the party might arrest his slave or recover damages for his detention or for aiding in his escape or concealment, the duty of the governor of the State to cause his rendition was not capable of enforcement by any judicial proceeding, and had only the sanction of a moral and political obligation.

In the case before us, neither the Constitution of the United States, nor any act of Congress, nor any statute of the State of Florida has created a tribunal or provided a mode of procedure by which the question of the eligibility of an elector may be inquired into and determined.

Having disposed of these extraneous matters, I now proceed to the consideration of others which, from their essential nature, are, in my judgment, conclusive of the questions before us.

The business of electing a President and Vice-President, as it is laid down in the Constitution, may be divided into three distinct acts or stages of the grand drama. They are the appointment of electors, the voting of those electors, and the counting of their votes. The first of these acts or functions belongs by the Constitution wholly to the States, "who shall appoint in such manner as the legislature thereof may direct" the number of electors to which each respective State is entitled. The casting of this vote must be by the persons so appointed, and can be cast by no one else.

These propositions are very clear; but who is to count the votes after they are given is matter of grave dispute, into which I do not propose to enter. But the power of counting does not reside with the States nor with the electors, but somewhere within the domain of Federal power, as represented by the President of the Senate and the two Houses of Congress-

What we are mainly concerned to ascertain just now is the proper evidence to be furnished of the appointment of electors by the appointing power, the nature and effect of that evidence, and the nature and extent of the inquiry which the counting power can make into the fact of appointment.

It is manifestly the duty, and therefore the right, of the State, which is the appointing power, to decide upon the means by which the act of appointment shall be authenticated and certified to the counting power and to the electors who are to act on that authority. To this proposition I have heard no dissent from any quarter. This evidence of appointment must in its nature vary according to the manner in which the electors are appointed. If elected by the legislature, as they may be, an appropriate mode would be the signatures of the presiding officers of the two Houses to the fact of such appointment, or a certified copy of the act by which they were elected. If appointed by the governor, his official certificate with the seal of the State would be an appropriate mode. If elected by popular suffrage, that election should be ascertained and authenticated in the mode which the law of the State prescribes for that purpose.

In the case before us they were elected by popular suffrage, and the statute of Florida prescribes a well-defined mode of ascertaining the result of that election, and of giving official expression to that result.

By the fourth section of the act of February 27, 1872—

The secretary of state, the attorney-general, and the comptroller of public accounts, or any two of them, together with any other member of the cabinet who may be designated by them, shall constitute a board of State canvassers for any general or special election of State officers, who shall canvass the returns of said election, and determine and declare who shall have been elected to any such office, or as such member, as shown by such returns. If any such return shall be shown, or shall appear to be, so irregular, false, or fraudulent, that the board shall be unable to determine the true vote for any such officer or member, they shall so certify, and shall not include such return in their determination and declaration.

The board shall make and sign a certificate * * * and therein declare the result, which certificate shall be recorded in the office of the secretary of state in a book to be kept for that purpose.

By another act the governor is required to make out, sign, and cause to be sealed with the seal of the State, and transmit to each person so elected elector or Representative in Congress, a certificate of his election.

These two provisions prescribe the manner in which the result of an election for electors shall be "determined and declared" and how that result shall be duly authenticated. When the canvassing-board herein mentioned has canvassed the returns of the election, has determined who is elected, and has declared that fact by signing the certificate, which is to be deposited with the secretary of state, the person named in that certificate is from that moment a duly appointed elector. The fact of his appointment, that is, his election, has been ascertained and declared by the tribunal, and the only tribunal, to which the duty and power of so declaring has been confided by law. I have already shown that this power belonged to the State of Florida—to its legislature. It cannot be vested in two independent and distinct bodies. It rests with the State of Florida. The law is clear, perspicuous, methodical.

It is said by way of impeachment of this certificate that the board of canvassers exceeded its jurisdiction by rejecting returns which were neither irregular, false, nor fraudulent; and that this can now be shown by proof before this Commission. But what is the *jurisdiction* of this board? It is not merely to count up and compare the returns, but upon all the facts submitted to them to determine, that is, to decide, who is elected. This is its duty, and its jurisdiction is commensurate with its duty. If it mistakes the law, or does not properly weigh the facts, these do not affect the jurisdiction, or invalidate the judgment which it renders.

Jurisdiction is the power to examine and decide, to hear and determine, the subject-matter submitted to the tribunal by which the jurisdiction is to be exercised. When jurisdiction is given over the whole subject, as in this case, to decide who are elected, it cannot be limited to that which is directory in the mode of proceeding. It may not follow that mode, yet its decision be valid. Its decision may be erroneous, but it is nevertheless the decision of the only tribunal having jurisdiction, and it must be conclusive. I say it must be conclusive, because there is no other tribunal which is by law authorized to review this decision or to correct its errors if any exist. I shall presently consider the claim here set up that this Commission, in the exercise of powers belonging to the two Houses of Congress, can do this, and I lay out of view the right of the State to oust an officer declared by this board to be elected, by a writ of *quo warranto*, because that writ by its very nature admits that the party against whom it is directed is in office, and is exercising its functions, and demands of him by what authority he does so.

In all governments where rights are secured by law, it has been found necessary where those rights, whether public or private, depend upon the existence of certain facts, to appoint an officer, a commission, a tribunal, by whatever name it may be called, to ascertain these facts and declare the rights which they give. This is a necessity of civil society, and on it courts of justice are founded. It is also a principle necessary to the existence of law and order and to the security of these rights, that the decision of this tribunal should be respected, whether those rights be public or private. And except where there is a provision in the law for an appeal from such decision, or a review of it in some recognized legal mode, it *must* be conclusive. As regards courts of justice, this principle is everywhere recognized and is acted on every day. There is no reason why it should not be equally applicable to all other tribunals acting within the scope of their authority, and it is so. As illustrations I will cite a few instances from the highest judicial authority in this country with whose decisions I am familiar. We have had in that court a vast number of suits founded on bonds issued by counties, cities, towns, and townships, in which the defense was that the bonds were issued without authority of law, and by frauds practiced by the officers who issued them. In most of these cases the authority to issue the bonds could only be given by the vote of the majority of the citizens of the municipality. In the case of Knox County *vs.* Aspinwall, 21 Wallace, 539, when this question first came up, the court decided that inasmuch as the commissioners who issued the bonds were also authorized to ascertain and determine whether there had been such a vote and whether the election had been lawfully held, their action in issuing the bonds was conclusive on both these questions, and could not be afterward questioned in any action to recover the amount of the bonds against the counties.

Perhaps no decision has been more controverted than this. At every term of the court, for now nearly twenty years, similar cases have come up and been so decided from the date of that case to the case of The Town of Coloma *vs.* Eaves, 92 Supreme Court R., 484, at the recent term of the court; and by those decisions millions of dollars of debt have been fastened upon the citizens of these municipalities to the ruin of many of them, which they were denied the privilege of showing were created without authority and by fraud and chicanery. These decisions are all based upon the principle that the decision of the tribunal created for that purpose, on the existence of the facts necessary to make valid the issue of bonds, is final and conclusive as to the existence of those facts.

Again, in the administration of the system of public lands of the United States, questions of conflicting rights are perpetually arising which by the acts of Congress are to be decided by the officers of the Land Department of the Government. Many applications have been made to the courts to control the action of these officers by writs of mandamus to compel them to do something, or of injunction to restrain them; but the Supreme Court has uniformly held that in the performance of their functions, which required the exercise of judgment or discretion, they were beyond the control of the courts, because to them, and to them alone, had the law confided the exercise of that judgment, and, except as by appeal from one officer of that department to another, no right of reviewing that judgment had been provided. (Gaines vs. Thompson, 7 Wallace, 347; Litchfield vs. Register and Receiver, 9 Wallace, 575; Secretary vs. McGarrahan, 9 Wallace, 248.)

The same principle has been repeatedly asserted when contests for titles to lands derived from the Government have arisen after the action of these officers has been ended, and the title passed from the Government to a private claimant. A very recent case of that kind instructive in the matter before us is that of French vs. Fyan, decided at the present term of the Supreme Court.

A contest for a quarter-section of land in Missouri arose between a party claiming title under the swamp-land grant of 1850 and another who claimed under a grant to railroads of 1852. Both parties had regular evidence of title, each under his own grant, and as the swamp-land grant was the elder, it must, if valid, prevail. To show that it was not valid the plaintiff offered to prove by parol evidence that the land was not in fact and never had been "overflowed and swamp land, made thereby unfit for cultivation," which is the description of the lands granted by the act of 1850. But the circuit court first, and the Supreme Court on writ of error, held that this could not be done. The swamp-land act made it the duty of the Secretary of the Interior to make out accurate lists of these swamp-lands and certify them to the States and issue patents therefor when required, and the Supreme Court held that his action in so doing was final and conclusive and could not be impeached by parol testimony. And this it founds, as it says, on "the general doctrine that where the law has confided to a special tribunal the authority to hear and determine certain matters arising in the course of its duties, the decision of that tribunal, within the scope of its authority, is conclusive upon all others," and it cites the previous case of Johnson vs. Towsley, 13 Wallace, 72, from which the extract is taken. That the same principle applies to affairs of more public character is shown by the cases of Luther vs. Borden, 7 Howard, 1, and the Commonwealth of Virginia vs. West Virginia, 11 Wallace, 39.

In the former case where the issue in an action of trespass depended upon which was the true government of the State of Rhode Island, that set up and known as the Dorr government, which was alleged as in the case before us to have the support of a majority of the popular vote, or the ancient government which was resisting overthrow by the Dorr movement, this court shut its eyes resolutely to any inquiry into the facts on which either government claimed to be the right one, and said that the Constitution of the United States had confided to the political department of the Government the right to determine that question, and that though the private rights before the court were judicial in character, the court was bound by the action of President Tyler, who in issuing a proclamation requiring the supporters of the so-called Dorr government to disperse had treated them as insurgents and had recognized the ancient government as the true one. Behind this action the court could not inquire, but must accept it as decisive of the question.

In the latter case, in the process of constructing the State of West Virginia out of certain counties of the commonwealth of Virginia, it had been determined to refer the question of which State should include the counties of Berkeley and Jefferson to the popular vote of these counties. By a statute of the commonwealth the governor of that State was authorized to call such an election by proclamation to ascertain the result, and, if carried, to certify the same to the governor of West Virginia, whereupon those counties became part of the new State. All this was done. But a few years after the commonwealth filed her bill in chancery in the Supreme Court of the United States against West Virginia, claiming to recover back jurisdiction of those counties upon the grounds, among others, that no fair vote had been taken, that the majority was the other way, and that the governor was imposed upon by false and fraudulent returns. The case was heard on demurrer, and on this subject the court said:

> We are of the opinion that the action of the governor is conclusive of the vote as between the States of Virginia and West Virginia. He was in legal effect the State of Virginia in this matter. In addition to his position as executive head of the State, the legislature had delegated to him all its own power in the premises. It vested him with large control as to the time of taking the vote, and it made his *opinion* of the result the condition of final action.

This language is eminently applicable to the case before us. The legislature of Florida has vested in her board of canvassers the authority to determine who are elected electors. It has conferred no power on any tribunal to revise that decision. The board in this respect represents the State. Its judgment is her judgment and its official certificate is her authorized expression of what she has done in the matter, and it is conclusive.

Mr. President, I might well rest here, but as I have said that I would consider the question of the right of *this Commission* exercising the powers of the two Houses of Congress to review or inquire into the truth of the certificate of the board of canvassers, I will say a few words on that point. It has, however, been so clearly presented by my brother Strong, and I concur so entirely in what he has said, that it is hardly necessary that I should do so.

Conceding for the present, for that is the theory on which is framed the bill creating this Commission, that by the Constitution to the two Houses of Congress has been confided the duty of counting the votes of the presidential electors and declaring the result, it is difficult to see what right this duty of counting gives those bodies to inquire into the means by which the electors whose votes they are to count obtained their appointment. The whole basis on which this right of the two Houses to inquire into the fraudulent or honest character of the vote, the conduct or misconduct, the mistakes, errors, or corruption of the judges of election at every polling place in an entire State is this short and single sentence of the Constitution:

> The President of the Senate shall, in the presence of the Senate and House of Representatives, open all the certificates, and the votes shall then be counted.

The votes here mentioned are the votes of the electors of President and Vice-President, and not the votes by which these electors were appointed, and the certificates are the evidence of their appointment.

I have endeavored to show, and I think successfully, that this latter counting belongs solely to the State authorities, as well as the mode of authenticating the result.

It is not asserted by any one that express power to make this inquiry is conferred on the two Houses by the language quoted or by any other. The argument is founded on two implications, both of which are very remote and very unnecessary.

The first of these, and the one which I think is mainly relied on, is that in order to count the votes it is necessary to know who are the electors. Before you can make a correct count of the votes for President you must ascertain who are authorized to vote for President. Undoubtedly the reasoning thus far is sound. But since the Constitution says that those who can cast such votes are those who are appointed by the State in such manner as the legislature thereof shall direct, it amounts to nothing more than ascertaining who are appointed electors.

Congress has nothing to do with this appointment,—neither with the manner of appointment nor the manner of authenticating the appointment.

If, then, a body of electors present with the vote which they cast for President and Vice-President the evidence which the State has prescribed of their appointment, the inquiry of the two Houses is answered. They have been legally and officially informed who are entitled to vote as electors for that State. There exists neither in the nature of the duty they are to perform nor in any language of the Constitution the right to inquire into the validity of that appointment, the means by which it was brought about, the fairness of the election by which it was determined, or the misconduct of the tribunal which the State had created to determine the result. Much has been said of the danger of the device of returning-boards, and it may be that they have exercised their power in a manner not always worthy of commendation. But I take the liberty of saying that such a power lodged in one or in both Houses of Congress would be a far more permanent menace to the liberty of the people, to the legitimate result of the popular vote, than any device for counting these votes which has as yet been adopted by the States.

Neither at the time of the adoption of the Constitution nor at any time since would the people of the States have placed in the hands of Congress the power to constitute itself a returning-board as to the votes for presidential electors, and then upon the vote cast by those whom *they* declare to be electors, decide who are to be President and Vice-President of the United States; but that is precisely the power claimed for the two Houses of Congress and for this Commission representing them.

The other implication is that because the House of Representatives is authorized, in the event of a failure to elect a President by the prescribed method, to proceed itself to make such an election, it must therefore have the power of deciding all questions relating to the appointment of electors. I confess I do not see the force of the implication or of the argument. If it had any force otherwise, it is liable to the serious objection that it makes that body the sole judge of its right to exercise the most important power residing in the domain of the Federal Government. The Senate would have a corresponding power in regard to the Vice-President, and thus each House for itself, and not the two Houses, would count the vote. I do not consider the argument worth further attention, and therefore dismiss it.

These are the reasons, Mr. President, which have determined me to vote that none of the testimony offered in this case outside of that submitted to the two Houses of Congress by the President of the Senate, can be lawfully received or considered by the Commission.

OREGON.

The electoral votes of Oregon being under consideration—

Mr. Commissioner MILLER said:

Mr. PRESIDENT: Having on the occasion of the papers referred to this Commission in the Florida case, upon the question of the admissibility of any testimony outside of the certificates and accompanying papers as they were laid before the two Houses of Congress by the President of the Senate, expressed the views which governed my action on that question, as well as on the final vote, I took no part in the discussion of the Louisiana case in conference, because I was of opinion that the principles laid down by me in the former, and which received the approval of the Commission, must govern its action in the latter. In this I was not mistaken, as will be seen by an examination of the brief grounds of the decisions of those cases, as reported to the two Houses of Congress under the statute.

It is the purpose of the few remarks which I propose to make now to show that the same principles, when applied to the one before us, must govern this as it did the two former cases.

We have, however, now as then, an extraneous question of the eligibility of one of the electors, rendered more important because it was made the ground of a refusal by the governor of the State to certify to the election of J. W. Watts, whose election was otherwise beyond controversy, and of the substitution in his certificate of the name of E. A. Cronin, who certainly was *not* elected.

On this subject I remain of opinion, as I expressed it in the Florida case, that the fact that Watts held an office of trust and profit under the United States at the date of his election did not render that election void. I concede, as I did then, that his title to the office could have been avoided, if there had been any tribunal competent to try the question of his ineligibility and it had been so tried and found before he gave his vote for President and Vice-President. In this case it is said that the governor of the State was such a tribunal, and that he did decide that Watts was ineligible, and therefore his refusal to certify him as an elector is justified. But I look in vain in the Constitution of the United States, in the laws of Congress, and in the constitution and laws of Oregon, for any support for such authority in the governor. In the absence of such authority in one or the other of these places, the action of the governor in that respect was the merest assumption of power without any legal right. If he had such authority, by what mode of procedure was he to be governed? Under what rules of law or of evidence did he act? Was Watts notified of the trial? Had he opportunity to be heard? How were the facts ascertained? There is not a shadow of pretense that any such trial or hearing was had.

The question of the disqualification to hold an office has almost always arisen in courts of justice after the party has been commissioned or has entered upon the duties of his office. Even in cases of members of legislative bodies, which are by express constitutional provision judges of the qualification of their own members, it is nearly always tried after admission to a seat. This concurrent course of proceeding, whether in courts or in the legislature, is strong evidence that the title is recognized until the disability is established. And this is logically just. There can be no presumption of law that a person elected is disqualified. The disqualification is a fact to be averred and established before some tribunal legally authorized to inquire into that fact. I am therefore clearly of opinion, notwithstanding the cases cited from the courts of Indiana, that Governor Grover had no more right to determine the ineligibility of an elector who has the required popular vote than any other citizen of the State of Oregon. I have already discussed the right of this Commission to do so.

If Watts's election was not void, his subsequent resignation and failure to attend made a vacancy in the electoral college which the other members were by statute authorized to fill, and his appointment by them to fill that vacancy was valid, because he had then ceased to hold the office of postmaster, which had been the source of the controversy.

It is urged, however, in opposition to counting the vote of Watts for President and Vice-President, that he has no certificate of his appointment by the governor, and that in the only certificate given by that officer his name is omitted and that of Cronin is substituted, and it is contended that this certificate of the governor, under the seal of the State, attested by the secretary of state, is the official and conclusive evidence of the right to act as electors for the State. In support of this proposition it is strongly asserted that such was the effect given to the governor's certificates in the Florida and Louisiana cases.

This is a strange misconception, if it be honestly believed by those who assert it, as to the grounds of the decision in those cases. Neither by any of the counsel who argued the case on both sides nor any member of the Commission in conference was any such sanctity claimed for the certificate of the governor. The counsel for the Tilden electors insisted, as it was necessary they should insist, that these certificates interposed no legal barrier to an investigation of the facts on which the certificates were or ought to have been founded. The other side agreed to this, and the only difference of opinion was where that inquiry should end. The majority of the Commission, both in argument and in the reasons attached to their decision, as required by the statute, said this inquiry could go so far as to see what officer or tribunal was by the laws of the State authorized to ascertain and declare who were elected electors by the popular vote and what declaration they had made on the subject, and could go no further. The minority of the Commission, and the counsel with whom they agreed, made their principal assault upon this position, and argued manfully for the right to go behind the action of that tribunal, to reconsider the evidence on which it had acted, and to review and reverse its decision. The majority were of opinion that the tribunal authorized to determine finally and conclusively who were appointed to act as electors was the board which in Florida is called the board of State canvassers, and in Louisiana the returning-officers; and it was against what was charged to be the mistakes, the usurpations, the frauds, and corruption of these officers that arguments of counsel and of the minority of this Commission were mainly directed. Over the question of their power and the finality of their decisions, the battle was fought, and it is idle now to assert that it was over the effect of the governor's certificate.

But, Mr. President, while I am not willing to have my position in the Florida case perverted or misrepresented and in this perverted shape thrust upon me as a rule of action in this case, I can have no right to complain and do not complain if those who in that case regarded the governor's certificate as of no weight shall in the present case insist upon it as a document against which nothing is to be said, and which must conclude this Commission. If the statute of Florida had made the governor the officer to canvass the returns of the elections and declare the result, I am not able to see how we could go behind his official certificate of that result. If the statutes of Oregon, which all must concede differ from those of Florida, give him that power, then, according to my view, his certificate must prevail here and with me, whatever may be the change of front, if there be such a change, in others.

I proceed to that inquiry.

The first clause of section 60 of title IX, concerning the election of presidential electors, declares that " the votes for the electors shall be given, received, returned, and canvassed as the same are given, returned, and canvassed for members of Congress." The remainder of this section directs what is to be done after this canvass, and will be considered further on. But I turn now to section 37 of title III, which governs the canvassing of the returns for members of Congress:

The county clerk—

It says—

immediately after the abstract of votes given in his county, shall make a copy of each of said abstracts and transmit it by mail to the secretary of state, at the seat of government; and it shall be the duty of the secretary of state, in the presence of the governor, to proceed, within thirty days after the election, and sooner if the returns be all received, to canvass the votes.

This is all of that section which has any applicability to the electors. Returning then to the sixtieth section of the law, concerning electors, we find that after making this canvass—

The secretary of state shall prepare two lists of the names of the electors elected and affix the seal of State to the same. Such lists shall be signed by the governor and secretary, and by the *latter* delivered to the college of electors at the hour of their meeting on such first Wednesday of December.

When we have added to these extracts the last sentence of section 40 of the general election law of the State, we have all that I deem essential to this inquiry. It is as follows :

In all elections in this State, the person having the highest number of votes for any office shall be deemed to have been elected.

I am of opinion that these statutory provisions of the law of Oregon make it the duty of the secretary of state, and of no one else, to canvass the returns of all the votes given for electors, to ascertain the result, and to deliver to the persons elected a certificate of that fact. It follows from what I said in the Florida case, and which I do not desire to repeat, that his action in the matter, within the scope of his authority, that authority being commensurate with the duties I have mentioned, is binding and conclusive. If he has made a canvass of the votes, and ascertained who was elected, no other canvass can be made and no other person is elected. If that canvass shows who had the highest number of votes, so many as the State is entitled to, and who had that number of votes the *law* declares them to be elected ; that is, appointed.

If, in addition to this, he has filed a full and official statement of this canvass in his office, as the law requires, and has delivered to the persons thus found to be duly elected a certificate under the seal of the State and his official signature showing this statement and this result, their title to the office and the right to exercise its functions are complete.

The argument in opposition to this view is, that the governor is the person who must do all this; or if he alone cannot do it, that he and the secretary of state must do it jointly; that the provision that the returns must be canvassed in his presence, and that he must sign the certificate to be delivered to the person elected, establish this proposition.

Let us examine into this a little more critically. If we separate what the governor is to do in the matter of canvassing the vote from what he is to do afterward, we shall see that his duty in the former, if indeed it be a duty at all, is merely that of being present as a witness to the canvass made by the secretary. The returns are to be transmitted to the secretary by mail. They are to be received by him at his office; to be opened by him. The time of making the canvass is to be determined by him as soon as all the returns are received, but in no event later than thirty days after the election. The canvass is to be made by him. The returns on which this canvass is to be made, the canvass itself, the result, are all to remain in his office under his official control. When this is done, the law applies to the result the declaration that the persons possessing the highest number of votes are elected. That is, their election is then determined. No one has a right to review this canvass or to declare a different result. The right of the successful candidate is established and is perfect. And it is here on this action I rest, as I did on the action of the board of canvassers of Florida, the decision of the question submitted to us, Who are the lawful electors of Oregon, and whose votes are the constitutional votes of that State for President and Vice-President?

Now, in all this matter what part has the governor of the State to play? He receives no returns, he counts no votes, he has custody of no papers, he controls no one in the matter; and if it were true, as maintained by some, that he alone can execute the official certificate mentioned hereafter, it would still remain, as I have already said, that such a certificate is not conclusive nor its absence fatal, but, as in the cases of Florida and Louisiana, this tribunal can go behind it and inquire if it is in conformity to the action of the board or officer who has the right to decide on the result of the votes as returned to him.

It may be asked, Why is he required to be present at the canvass? I answer, as a witness to the transaction, as a protection to its fairness, by having some one to watch the secretary. He may have a right to make objections, suggestions, to file a protest, to institute proceedings against the secretary, to furnish evidence of his mistake or grosser injustice, but no right to dictate, to control, or assist in the process.

The canvass being made, the next step is to certify the result to the persons elected. And what part does the governor perform in this? " The secretary shall prepare two lists of the names of the persons elected electors, and affix the seal of the State to the same." In doing this the governor takes no part. " Such lists shall be signed by the governor and secretary, and by the *latter* delivered to the college of electors." The making out this certificate, the affixing to it the seal of the State, its delivery to the electoral college, are all acts of the same officer who received and canvassed the returns and in whose custody and control they remained. The governor is required to place his signature to this paper, prepared to his hand, as a mere official attestation of the result arrived at—a formal act, adding to the paper prepared by the secretary, in addition to his own name and the seal of the State, the dignity of the governor's verification.

Though lacking the governor's name, the persons who received the highest number of votes, and whom the statute declares to be elected, present to the President of the Senate and the two Houses of Congress a certificate from the secretary of state, under the seal of the State, and signed by him in his official capacity, showing that, in pursuance of the statute, he did, on the 4th day of December last, in the presence of the governor, canvass the votes given for electors; that the result of that canvass was that Odell, Cartwright, and Watts having received the three highest numbers of votes were elected electors; that all this appears from the canvass so made by him and on file in his office on the 6th day of December, the date of this certificate. This certificate he delivered as directed by law to the electors on the first Wednesday in December, and thereupon they proceeded to give their votes for President and Vice-President. What is wanting to their authority to do so? They had a majority of votes. They were duly elected. This fact was ascertained in the mode and by the officer intrusted with that duty by law. They have his official certificate of that fact under the seal of the State.

I cannot believe that the willful refusal of the governor to sign that certificate is sufficient to nullify everything else that was done, and make it of no effect. No such force has been attributed to it in the other cases, and I do not see how it can be here.

As to the certificate of the governor given to Cronin, Odell, and Cartwright, if it was perfect on its face, no one has yet held that it was conclusive. No one in the Commission has asserted that it is valid as to Cronin, and this is a full admission that it is not conclusive in any case.

I will only add that on its face this certificate shows that the governor undertook to decide the question of some person's eligibility to the office, and when taken in connection with the certificate of the secretary it establishes the fact that he refused to certify Watts because he held him ineligible, and did certify Cronin who was never elected. Of this paper no more need be said, nor is it necessary for me to detain the Commission longer.

REMARKS OF MR. COMMISSIONER BRADLEY.

[The following opinions and remarks have been somewhat abbreviated, and repetition of similar arguments in the different cases has been omitted.]

THE FLORIDA CASE.

Statement.

In this case the objectors to the certificate No. 1 (which was authenticated by Governor Stearns, and contained the votes of the Hayes electors) proposed to prove by the papers accompanying the certificates that a writ of *quo warranto* had been issued from a district court in Florida against the Hayes electors on the 6th day of December, 1876, before they gave their votes for President and Vice-President, which on January 26, 1877, resulted in a judgment against them, and in favor of the Tilden electors; also an act of the legislature passed in January, in favor of the Tilden electors; and also certain extrinsic evidence described by the counsel of the objectors as follows:

"Fifthly. The only matters which the Tilden electors desire to lay before the Commission by evidence actually extrinsic will now be stated:

"I. The board of State canvassers, acting on certain erroneous views when making their canvass, by which the Hayes electors appeared to be chosen, rejected wholly the returns from the county of Manatee and parts of returns from each of the following counties: Hamilton, Jackson, and Monroe.

"In so doing the said State board acted without jurisdiction, as the circuit and supreme courts in Florida decided. It was by overruling and setting aside as not warranted by law these rejections, that the courts of Florida reached their respective conclusions that Mr. Drew was elected governor, that the Hayes electors were usurpers, and that the Tilden electors were duly chosen.

"II. Evidence that Mr. Humphreys, a Hayes elector, held office under the United States."

The question was argued as to the admissibility of this evidence.

Mr. Commissioner BRADLEY said:

I assume that the powers of the Commission are precisely those, and no other, which the two Houses of Congress possess in the matter submitted to our consideration; and that the extent of those powers is one of the questions submitted. This is my interpretation of the act under which we are organized.

The first question, therefore, is, whether, and how far, the two Houses, in the exercise of the special jurisdiction conferred on them in the matter of counting the electoral votes, have power to inquire into the validity of the votes transmitted to the President of the Senate. Their power to make any inquiry at all is disputed by, or on behalf of, the President of the Senate himself. But I think the practice of the Government, as well as the true construction of the Constitution, has settled that the powers of the President of the Senate are merely ministerial, conferred upon him as a matter of convenience, as being the presiding officer of one of the two bodies which are to meet for the counting of the votes and determining the election. He is not invested with any authority for making any investigation outside of the joint meeting of the two Houses. He cannot send for persons or papers. He is utterly without the means or the power to do anything more than to inspect the documents sent to him; and he cannot inspect them until he opens them in the presence of the two Houses. It would seem to be clear, therefore, that, if any examination at all is to be gone into, or any judgment is to be exercised in relation to the votes received, it must be performed and exercised by the two Houses.

Then arises the question, How far can the two Houses go in questioning the votes received, without trenching upon the power reserved to the States themselves?

The extreme reticence of the Constitution on the subject leaves wide room for inference. Each State has a just right to have the entire and exclusive control of its own vote for the Chief Magistrate and head of the republic, without any interference on the part of any other State, acting either separately or in Congress with others. If there is any State right of which it is and should be more jealous than of any other, it is this. And such seems to have been the spirit manifested by the framers of the Constitution. This is evidenced by the terms in which the mode of choosing the President and Vice-President is expressed: "Each State shall appoint, in such manner as the legislature thereof may direct, a number of electors equal to the whole number of Senators and Representatives to which the State may be entitled in the Congress; but no Senator or Representative, or person holding an office of trust or profit under the United States, shall be appointed an elector. The electors shall meet in their respective States and vote by ballot," &c. Almost every clause here cited is fraught with the sentiment to which I have alluded. The appointment and mode of appointment belong exclusively to the State. Congress has nothing to do with it, and no control over it, except that, in a subsequent clause, Congress is empowered to determine the time of choosing the electors, and the day on which they shall give their votes, which is required to be the same day throughout the United States. In all other respects the jurisdiction and power of the

State is controlling and exclusive until the functions of the electors have been performed. So completely is congressional and Federal influence excluded, that not a member of Congress nor an officer of the General Government is allowed to be an elector. Of course, this exclusive power and control of the State is ended and determined when the day fixed by Congress for voting has arrived, and the electors have deposited their votes and made out the lists and certificates required by the Constitution. Up to that time the whole proceeding (except the time of election) is conducted under State law and State authority. All machinery, whether of police, examining boards, or judicial tribunals, deemed requisite and necessary for securing and preserving the true voice of the State in the appointment of electors, is prescribed and provided for by the State itself and not by Congress. All rules and regulations for the employment of this machinery are also within the exclusive province of the State. Over all this field of jurisdiction the State must be deemed to have ordained, enacted, and provided all that it considers necessary and proper to be done.

This being so, can Congress or the two Houses institute a scrutiny into the action of the State authorities and sit in judgment on what they have done? Are not the findings and recorded determinations of the State board or constituted authorities binding and conclusive since the State can only act through its constituted authorities?

But it is asked, must the two Houses of Congress submit to outrageous frauds and permit them to prevail without any effort to circumvent them? Certainly not, if it is within their jurisdiction to inquire into such frauds. But there is the very question to be solved. Where is such jurisdiction to be found? If it does not exist, how are the two Houses constitutionally to know that frauds have been committed? It is the business and the jurisdiction of the State to prevent frauds from being perpetrated in the appointment of its electors, and not the business or jurisdiction of the Congress. The State is a sovereign power within its own jurisdiction, and Congress can no more control or review the exercise of that jurisdiction than it can that of a foreign government. That which exclusively belongs to one tribunal or government cannot be passed upon by another. The determination of each is conclusive within its own sphere.

It seems to me to be clear, therefore, that Congress cannot institute a scrutiny into the appointment of electors by a State. It would be taking it out of the hands of the State, to which it properly belongs. This never could have been contemplated by the people of the States when they agreed to the Constitution. It would be going one step farther back than that instrument allows. While the two Houses of Congress are authorized to canvass the electoral votes, no authority is given to them to canvass the election of the electors themselves. To revise the canvass of that election, as made by the State authorities, on the suggestion of fraud, or for any other cause, would be tantamount to a recanvass.

The case of elections of Senators and Representatives is different. The Constitution expressly declares that "each House shall be the judge of the elections, returns, and qualifications of its own members." No such power is given, and none ever would have been given if proposed, over the election or appointment of the presidential electors. Again, while the Constitution declares that "the times, places, and manner of holding elections of Senators and Representatives shall be prescribed in each State by the legislature thereof," it adds, "but the Congress may at any time by law make or alter such regulations, except as to

the places of choosing Senators." No such power is given to Congress
to regulate the election or appointment of presidential electors. Their
appointment, and all regulations for making it, and the manner of making it, are left exclusively with the States.

This want of jurisdiction over the subject makes it clear to my mind
that the two Houses of Congress cannot institute any scrutiny into the
appointment of presidential electors, as they may and do in reference
to the election of their own members. The utmost they can do is to
ascertain whether the State has made an appointment according to the
form prescribed by its laws.

This view receives corroboration from the form of a bill introduced
into Congress in 1800 for prescribing the mode of deciding disputed
elections of President and Vice-President, and which was passed by
the Senate. It proposed a grand committee to inquire into the constitutional qualifications of the persons voted for as President and Vice-
President, and of the electors appointed by the States, and various
other matters with regard to their appointment and transactions; but
it contained a proviso, in which both Houses seem to have concurred,
that no petition or exception should be granted or allowed which should
have for its object to draw into question the number of votes on which
any elector had been elected.

This bill was the proposition of the federal party of that day, which,
as is well known, entertained strong views with regard to the power of
the Federal Government as related to the State governments. It was
defeated by the opposition of the republican side, as being too great
an interference with the independence of the States in reference to the
election of President and Vice-President. And taken even as the federal view of the subject, it only shows what matters were regarded as
subject to examination under the regulation of law, and not that the
two Houses of Congress, when assembled to count the votes, could do
the same without the aid of legislation. The bill was rather an admission that legislation was necessary in order to provide the proper machinery for making extrinsic inquiries.

It is unnecessary to enlarge upon the danger of Congress assuming
powers in this behalf that do not clearly belong to it. The appetite for
power in that body, if indulged in without great prudence, would have a
strong tendency to interfere with that freedom and independence which
it was intended the States should enjoy in the choice of the national
Chief Magistrate, and to give Congress a control over the subject which
it was intended it should not have.

As the power of Congress, therefore, does not extend to the making
of a general scrutiny into the appointment of electors, inasmuch as it
would thereby invade the right of the States, so neither can it draw in
question, nor sit in judgment upon, the determination and conclusion of
the regularly constituted authorities or tribunals appointed by the laws
of the States for ascertaining and certifying such appointment.

And here the inquiry naturally arises, as to the manner in which the
electors appointed by a State are to be accredited. What are the proper
credentials by which it is to be made known who have been appointed?
Obviously, if no provision of law existed on the subject, the proper
mode would be for the governor of the State, as its political head and
chief, through whom its acts are made known and by whom its external intercourse is conducted, to issue such credentials. But we are not
without law on the subject. The Constitution, it is true, is silent; but
Congress by the act of 1792 directed that "it shall be the duty of the
executive of each State to cause three lists of the names of the electors

of such State to be made and certified and to be delivered to the electors on or before the day on which they are required to meet;" and one of these certificates is directed to be annexed to each of the certificates of the votes given by the electors. And if it should be contended that this enactment of Congress is not binding upon the State executive, the laws of Florida, in the case before us, impose upon the governor of that State the same duty. I think, therefore, that it cannot be denied that the certificate of the governor is the proper and regular credential of the appointment and official character of the electors. Certainly it is at least *prima-facie* evidence of a very high character.

But the Houses of Congress may undoubtedly inquire whether the supposed certificate of the executive is genuine; and I think they may also inquire whether it is plainly false, or whether it contains a clear mistake of fact, inasmuch as it is not itself the appointment, nor the ascertainment thereof, but only a certificate of the fact of appointment. While it must be held as a document of high nature, not to be lightly questioned, it seems to me that a State ought not to be deprived of its vote by a clear mistake of fact inadvertently contained in the governor's certificate, or (if such a case may be supposed) by a willfully false statement. It has not the full sanctity which belongs to a court of record, or which, in my judgment, belongs to the proceedings and recorded acts of the final board of canvassers.

In this case, it is not claimed that the certificate of the governor contains any mistake of fact, or that it is willfully false and fraudulent. It truly represents the result of the State canvass, and if erroneous at all, it is erroneous because the proceedings of the canvassing-board were erroneous or based on erroneous principles and findings.

It seems to me that the two Houses of Congress, in proceeding with the count, are bound to recognize the determination of the State board of canvassers as the act of the State, and as the most authentic evidence of the appointment made by the State; and that while they may go behind the governor's certificate, if necessary, they can only do so for the purpose of ascertaining whether he has truly certified the results to which the board arrived. They cannot sit as a court of appeals on the action of that board.

The law of Florida declares as follows:

On the thirty-fifth day after the holding of any general or special election for any State officer, member of the legislature, or Representative in Congress, or sooner if the returns shall have been received from the several counties wherein the elections shall have been held, the secretary of state, attorney-general, and the comptroller of public accounts, or any two of them, together with any other member of the cabinet who may be designated by them, shall meet at the office of the secretary of state, pursuant to notice to be given by the secretary of state, and form a board of State canvassers, and proceed to canvass the returns of said election and *determine and declare who shall have been elected to any such office or as such member, as shown by such returns.*

The governor's certificate is *prima-facie* evidence that the State canvassers performed their duty. Indeed, it is conceded by the objectors that they made a canvass and certified or declared the same. It is not the failure of the board to act, or to certify and declare the result of their action, but an illegal canvass, of which they complain. To review that canvass, in my judgment, the Houses of Congress have no jurisdiction or power.

The question then arises, whether the subsequent action of the courts or legislature of Florida can change the result arrived at and declared by the board of State canvassers, and consummated by the vote of the electors and the complete execution of their functions?

If the action of the State board of canvassers were a mere statement of a fact, like the certificate of the governor, and did not involve the exercise of decision and judgment, perhaps it might be controverted by evidence of an equally high character; like the return to a *habeas corpus*, which could not, in former times, be contradicted by parol proof, but might be contradicted by a verdict or judgment in an action for a false return.

Looking at the subject in this point of view, I was at one time inclined to think that the proceedings on *quo warranto* in the circuit court of Florida, if still in force and effect, might be sufficient to contradict the finding and determination of the board of canvassers—supposing that the court had jurisdiction of the case. But the action of the board involved more than a mere statement of fact. It was a determination, a decision quasi-judicial. The powers of the board as defined by the statute which created it are expressed in the following terms: "They shall proceed to canvass the returns of said election and determine and declare who shall have been elected to any office;" and "if any such returns shall be shown, or shall appear to be, so irregular, false, or fraudulent that the board shall be unable to determine the true vote for any such officer or member, they shall so certify, and shall not include such return in their determination and declaration." This clearly requires quasi-judicial action. To controvert the finding of the board, therefore, would not be to correct a mere statement of fact, but to reverse the decision and determination of a tribunal. The judgment on the *quo warranto* was an attempted reversal of this decision and the rendering of another decision. If the court had had jurisdiction of the subject-matter, and had rendered its decision before the votes of the electors were cast, its judgment, instead of that of the returning-board, would have been the final declaration of the result of the election. But its decision being rendered after the votes were given, it cannot have the operation to change or affect the vote, whatever effect it might have in a future judicial proceeding in relation to the presidential election. The judicial acts of officers *de facto*, until they are ousted by judicial process or otherwise, are valid and binding.

But it is a grave question whether any courts can thus interfere with the course of the election for President and Vice-President. The remarks of Mr. Justice Miller on this subject are of great force and weight.

The State may, undoubtedly, provide by law for reviewing the action of the board of canvassers at any time before the electors have executed their functions. It may provide any safeguard it pleases to prevent or counteract fraud, mistake, or illegality on the part of the canvassers. The legislature may pass a law requiring the attendance of the supreme court or any other tribunal to supervise the action of the board, and to reverse it, if wrong. But no such provision being made, the final action of the board must be accepted as the action of the State. No tampering with the result can be admitted after the day fixed by Congress for casting the electoral votes, and after it has become manifest where the pinch of the contest for the Presidency lies, and how it may be manipulated.

I am entirely clear that the judicial proceedings in this case were destitute of validity to affect the votes given by the electors. Declared by the board of canvassers to have been elected, they were entitled, by virtue of that declaration, to act as such against all the world until ousted of their office. They proceeded to perform the entire functions of that office. They deposited their votes in a regular manner, and on the proper and only day designated for that purpose, and their act could not be annulled by the subsequent proceedings on the *quo warranto*, however valid these might be for other purposes. When their votes were given, they were the legally-constituted electors for the State of Florida.

The supreme court of Florida said in the Drew case, it is true, that the board of canvassers exceeded their jurisdiction, and that their acts were absolutely void. In this assertion I do not concur; and it was not necessary to the judgment, which merely set aside the finding of the board and directed a new canvass. Under the Florida statute, the board had power to cast out returns. They did so. The court thought they ought to have cast out on a different principle from that which they adopted. This was at most error, not want or excess of jurisdiction. They certainly acted within the scope of their power, though they may have acted erroneously. This is the most that can be said in any event; and of this the Houses of Congress cannot sit in judgment as a court of appeal.

The question is asked, whether for no cause whatever the declaration and certificate of the board of canvassers can be disregarded? as if they should certify an election when no election had been held, and other extreme cases of that sort. I do not say that a clear and evident mistake of fact, inadvertently made, and admitted to have been made by the canvassers themselves, or that such a gross fraud and violation of duty as that supposed, might not be corrected, or that it might not affect the validity of the vote. On that subject, as it is not necessary in this case, I express no opinion. Such extreme cases, when they occur, generally suggest some special rule for themselves without unsettling those general rules and principles which are the only safe guides in ordinary cases. The difficulty is that the two Houses are not made the judges of the election and return of the presidential electors.

I think no importance is to be attached to the acts performed by the board of canvassers after the 6th day of December, nor to the acts of the Florida legislature in reference to the canvass. In my judgment, they are all unconstitutional and void. To allow a State legislature in any way to change the appointment of electors after they have been elected and given their votes, would be extremely dangerous. It would, in effect, make the legislature for the time being the electors, and would subvert the design of the Constitution in requiring all the electoral votes to be given on the same day.

My conclusion is that the validity of the first certificate cannot be controverted by evidence of the proceedings had in the courts of Florida by *quo warranto*, and that said evidence should not be received.

It is further objected that Humphreys, one of the Hayes electors, held an office of trust and profit under the Government of the United States at the time of the general election, and at the time of giving his vote. I think the evidence of this fact should be admitted. Such an office is a constitutional disqualification. I do not think it requires legislation to make it binding. What may be the effect of the evidence now produced, I am not prepared to say. I should like to hear further argument on the subject before deciding the question.

[It being shown that Humphreys resigned his office before the election, the question of ineligibility became unimportant. Justice Bradley held, however, that the constitutional prohibition, that no member of Congress or officer of the Government should be appointed an elector, is only a form of declaring a disqualification for the electoral office, and does not have the effect of annulling the vote given by one who, though disqualified, is regularly elected, and acts as an elector; likening it to the case of other officers *de facto*.]

THE LOUISIANA CASE.

Statement.

The objections to the votes of the electors certified by Kellogg as governor of Louisiana, being condensed, are in substance as follows:

First. That the government of Louisiana is not republican in form.

Second. That Kellogg was not governor.

Third. That at the time of the election, in November last, there was no law of the State directing the appointment of electors.

Fourth. That so much of the election law which was in force as relates to the returning-board was unconstitutional and void.

Fifth. That the board was not constituted according to the law; having only four members of one political party, when there should have been five members of different political parties.

Sixth. That they acted fraudulently and without jurisdiction in casting out and rejecting the returns or statements of various commissioners of election, without having before them any statement or affidavit of violence or intimidation as required by law to give them jurisdiction to reject returns; that they neglected to canvass the returns of the commissioners and canvassed those of the supervisors of registration—that is, the parish abstracts instead of the precinct returns; that they did not canvass all of these, (which would have elected the Tilden electors,) but falsely and fraudulently counted in the Hayes electors, knowing the count to be false; and that they offered to give the votes the other way for a bribe; and that the certificate given by Kellogg to the Hayes electors was the result of a conspiracy between Kellogg and the returning-board and others to defraud their opponents of their election and the State of her right to vote; and that the Hayes electors were not elected, but their opponents were.

Seventh. That two of the electors certified by Kellogg were ineligible at the time of the election by holding office under the Government of the United States; and that others were ineligible by holding State offices, and that Kellogg could not legally certify himself as an elector.

FEBRUARY 16, 1877.

Mr. Commissioner BRADLEY said:

The first two objections, that the State is without a republican form of government, and that Kellogg was not governor, are not seriously insisted upon.

The question whether the State had any law directing the appointment of electors of President and Vice-President, and regulating their proceedings, depends upon whether the presidential electoral law of 1868 was or was not repealed by the general election-law of 1872, which is admitted to have been in force at the time of the last election.

The repealing clause relied on is in the last section of the act, and is in these words:

That this act shall take effect from and after its passage, and that all others on the subject of *election laws* be, and the same are hereby, repealed.

The question is, whether the act relating to presidential electors is an act " on the subject of *election laws* " within the meaning of this repealing clause. I am entirely satisfied that it is not, and that no part of it is repealed by the act of 1872, except one section which relates to the mode of returning and ascertaining the votes for electors. My reasons are these:

In the session of 1868, an act was passed, approved October 19, 1868, which professed to be a general election law, regulating the mode of holding and ascertaining the result of all elections in the State, making provision for preserving order thereat, and for executing generally the one hundred and third article of the constitution, which declares that " the privilege of free suffrage shall be supported by laws regulating elections and prohibiting under adequate penalties all undue influence thereon from power, bribery, tumult, or other improper practice." A distinct act was passed at the same session, approved October 30, 1868, which is the act relating to presidential electors, before referred to. It certainly was not supposed that one of these acts conflicted with the other. The one regulated the manner of holding and ascertaining the results of elections generally; the other prescribed the mode of appointing the presidential electors to which the State was entitled, namely, that they should be elected on the day fixed by Congress, two for the State at large, and one for each congressional district; prescribed their qualifications, and the time and place of their meeting to perform their duties; authorized them when met to fill any vacancies caused by the failure of any members to attend; and regulated their pay. One section, it is true, directed the manner in which the returns should be canvassed, namely, by the governor in presence of the secretary of state, the attorney-general, and a district judge; and the first section directed that the election for electors should be held on the day appointed by the act of Congress, and that it should be held and conducted in the manner and form provided by law for general State elections.

At the same session (1868) provision was made for revising all the general statutes of the State under the direction of a committee appointed for that purpose. This committee appointed Mr. John Ray to make the revision. It was duly reported and adopted during the session of 1870. It contained, under the title of "Elections," the act of October 19, 1868; and under the title "Presidential Electors," the act of October 30, 1868, showing conclusively that at that time the two acts were not deemed incompatible with each other.

A new election law was passed at the same session as a substitute for that of October 19, 1868, repealing all conflicting laws; but it was not inserted in the revised statutes, because they did not contain any of the laws of that session. A law was passed, however, authorizing the reviser (Mr. Ray) to publish a new edition, under the name of a digest, which should embrace the acts of 1870. This was done, and the new election law was inserted under the title "Elections" in the place of the old law. The act relating to presidential electors was untouched, except to insert in it the new method of making the returns of the elections by the returning-board, which was the only part of the new law which conflicted with it. It is apparent, therefore, that the election law of 1870 was not deemed repugnant to the law relating to "Presidential Electors," except in the one particular mentioned.

Now, the act of 1872, which it is alleged does repeal the law relating to presidential electors, is simply a substitute for the general election law of 1870, going over and occupying exactly the same ground, and no more, and making very slight alterations. The principal of these is the reconstruction of the returning-board. With this exception it does not in the least conflict, any more than did the act of 1870, with the provisions of the law relating to "presidential electors." And as the repealing clause therein (before referred to) is expressly confined to "acts on the subject of *election laws*," it seems to me most manifest that the intent was to repeal the election law only, and not that relating to "presidential electors." This view is corroborated by the sixty-ninth section, which has this expression: "The violation of any provision of the act, or section of *the act repealed by this act*, shall be considered," &c. Repealing clauses should not be extended so as to repeal laws not in conflict with the new law, unless absolutely necessary to give effect to the words. And when we consider the consequences which a repeal of the law relating to presidential electors would have in depriving the State of its power to have vacancies in its electoral college filled, in introducing confusion and uncertainty as to the districts they should be chosen from, and by leaving no directions as to the time and place of their meeting, it seems clear that it could never have been in the mind of the legislature to repeal that law.

There is a section in the act of 1872 relating to vacancies which it has been suggested is repugnant to the authority of the electoral college to fill vacancies in that body. It is section 24 which enacts, " that all elections to be held in this State to fill any vacancies shall be conducted and managed, and returns thereof shall be made, in the same manner as is provided for general elections." But this is explained by the fact that both the constitution and the election law itself direct vacancies in certain offices named (including that of members of the legislature) to be filled by a new election. The twenty-fourth section means only, that where elections are to be held to fill vacancies, they shall be held in the usual manner. It cannot mean that all vacancies shall be filled by another election; because the constitution expressly gives to the governor the power to fill vacancies in certain cases.

I am clearly of opinion, therefore, that the law relating to presidential electors has not been repealed, except as to the mode of canvassing the returns; and that that is to be performed by the returning-board created by the act of 1872, in lieu of the Lynch returning-board created by the act of 1870, and in lieu of the method originally prescribed in the law relating to presidential electors.

This disposes of the objection, that the electoral college has no power to fill vacancies in its own body, since the electoral law has a section which expressly authorizes the college to fill any vacancy that may occur by the non-attendance of any of the electors by four o'clock in the afternoon of the day for giving their votes.

But it is insisted that that part of the election law of 1872 which re-establishes the returning-board, and gives it its powers, is unconstitutional. The act declares " that five persons, to be elected by the Senate from all political parties, shall be the returning-officers for all elections. In case of any vacancy by death, resignation, or otherwise, by either of the board, then the vacancy shall be filled by the residue of the board of returning-officers."

The powers and duties of the board are, to meet in New Orleans within ten days after the election, canvass and compile the statements of votes made by the commissioners of election, and make returns of the election to the secretary of state, and publish a copy in the public journals, declaring the names of all persons and officers voted for, the number of votes for each person, and the names of the persons who have been duly and lawfully elected. It is declared that the returns thus made and promulgated shall be *prima facie* evidence in all courts of justice and before all civil officers, until set aside after contest according to law, of the right of any person declared elected. On receiving notice from any supervisor of election, supported by affidavits, and being convinced by examination and testimony that by reason of riot, tumult, acts of violence, intimidation, armed disturbance, bribery, or corrupt influences, the purity and freedom of election at any voting-place were materially interfered with, or a sufficient number of qualified voters to change the result were prevented from registering and voting, it is made the duty of the board to exclude from their returns the votes given at such voting-place.

Why this law is unconstitutional, I cannot perceive. The powers given may be abused, it is true, but that is the case with all powers. The constitutionality of the board has been considered by the supreme court of

Louisiana, and has been fully sustained. It is said that the term of office is indefinite, and might continue for life. But where no period is fixed for the tenure of an office, it is held at the will of the appointing power, which may at any time make a new appointment. So that no evil consequences can ensue from this cause. If the members of the board were appointed for a term, the senate could re-appoint them. Allowing them to remain when power exists to remove them at will, is substantially the same thing.

The objection that there were only four members constituting the board at the canvass in December last is met by the general rule of law in regard to public bodies, that the happening of a vacancy does not destroy the body if a quorum still remains. The Supreme Court consists of nine justices; but the court may be legally held though there are three vacancies, only six being required for a quorum. A vacancy in a branch of the legislature, in the board of supervisors of a county, in the commissioners or selectmen of a town, in the trustees of a school district, does not destroy the body nor vitiate its action, unless there be an express law to make it do so.

But it is said that the power given to the board to fill vacancies in its own body is mandatory. It is in exactly the same terms as those contained in the election law of 1870 on the same subject. In several cases arising under that act, the supreme court of Louisiana decided that this language was not compulsory, or at least did not affect the legal constitution of the board if not complied with; but that the board was a legal board though only four members remained in it. Had the board never been filled at all, it might be urged with more plausibility that it was never legally constituted. If a court be created to consist of five judges, although if once legally organized a single judge might hold the court in the absence of the others, yet if only one judge were ever appointed, it might very properly be said that no legal organization had ever taken place. In this case the vacancy in the board occurred after it had been duly constituted by the appointment of the full number of members. Afterward the vacancy occurred. And if it be the correct view, as was decided by the supreme court of Louisiana in regard to the Lynch board, that the power given to the remaining members to fill the vacancy is not mandatory, a neglect on their part to fill it does not, it seems to me, destroy the existence of the board or deprive it of power to act. If it be true, as alleged, that members of only one political party remained on it, it may have been an impropriety in proceeding without filling the vacancy, and the motives of the members may have been bad motives, corrupt, fraudulent, what not; but with improprieties and with the motives of the members we have nothing to do. We are not the judges of their motives. The question with which we have to do is a question of power, of legal authority in four members to act. And of this I have no doubt. The board was directed " to be elected by the senate from all political parties," it is true. It does not appear that this was not done. Can it be contended that the resignation or death of one of the members, who happened to be alone in his party connections, deprives the remainder of the power to act? I think not. If the four members remaining were all of different politics, the objection would lose all its force. So that it is resolved to this: that the power to fill a vacancy is mandatory when any political party ceases to be represented by the death or resignation of a member, and is not mandatory in any other case. Suppose, instead of dying or resigning, the member changes his party affiliations; is there a vacancy then? Can the other members oust him, or can he oust them? The senate, with whom resides the power of appointing a new board whenever it sees fit, might be in duty bound to act; but the same cannot be said of the board itself. If this were not Louisiana, but some State in which no charges of fraud and disorder were made, the objection would hardly be thought of as having any legal validity.

The next question relates to the alleged illegality and fraud in the proceedings of the returning-board. Can the two Houses of Congress go behind their returns and certificate and examine into their conduct? I have already discussed this subject to some extent in the Florida case. I shall now only state briefly the conclusions to which I have come in this case:

First. I consider the governor's certificate of the result of the canvass as *prima facie* evidence of the fact, but subject to examination and contradiction. This point has already been considered in the Florida case.

Secondly. The finding and return of the State canvassers of the election are, in their nature, of greater force and effect than the governor's certificate, being that on which his certificate is founded and being the final result of the political machinery established by the State to ascertain and determine the very fact in question. *"Each State shall appoint,"* is the language of the Constitution. Of course the two Houses must be satisfied that the State has appointed and that the votes presented were given by its appointees. The primary proof of this, as prescribed by the laws of the United States, is the certificate of the governor. But, as before stated, I do not deem that conclusive. It may be shown to be false or erroneous in fact, or based upon the canvass and return of a board or tribunal that had no authority to act. This was conceded in the proceedings which took place with regard to the votes of Louisiana in 1873.

Was the returning-board of Louisiana a tribunal, or body, constituted by the laws of the State, with power to ascertain and declare the result of the election, and did that board, in the exercise of the jurisdiction conferred upon it, ascertain and declare that result? This, it seems to me, is the point to be ascertained.

This involves an examination of the laws of the State to ascertain what that tribunal is and what general powers it is invested with, not for the purpose of seeing whether all the proceedings of the board, or of the election-officers whose action preceded theirs, were in strict compliance with the law, but for the purpose of seeing whether the result comes from the authorities provided by the State, acting substantially within the scope of their appointment. This is necessary to be done in order to see whether (whatever irregularities may have occurred) it was the State which made the appointment or some usurping body not authorized by the State at all.

The examination to be made is somewhat analogous to that made into the jurisdiction of a court when its judgment is collaterally assailed. If the board declared the result of the election, and in so doing acted within the general scope of its powers, it seems to me that the inquiry should there end. The constitutional power of the two Houses of Congress does not go further.

On the question of jurisdiction, I think it competent for the Houses to take notice of the fact (if such was the fact) that the returning-board had no returns before it at all, and, in effect, (to speak as we do of judicial proceedings,) without having a case before it to act on; or of the fact (if such was the fact) that the board which pretended to act was not a legal board. This view was taken by both Houses, if I understand their action aright, in the count of 1873 in rejecting the electoral votes from Louisiana on that occasion. (Document on Electoral Counts, 407.)

Anything which shows a clear want of jurisdiction in the returning-board divests its acts of authority, and makes it cease to be the representative of the will of the State. But it must appear that there was a clear and most manifest want of authority; for, otherwise, the State might be deprived of its franchise by mere inadvertence of its agents or an honest mistake made by them as to the law.

In the case before us, the board had ample powers, as we have seen. These powers have frequently been sustained by the supreme court of the State. The law of Louisiana not only gives the board power to canvass the returns, but to reject returns whenever in their opinion, upon due examination had, they are satisfied that the vote was affected by violence and intimidation. They did no more in this case, supposing them to have done all that is alleged. It is said that they proceeded without jurisdiction, because they did not canvass the statements of the commissioners of election, but only the abstracts of the parish supervisors of registration. It is not denied that they had both and all of these statements before them. If they acted wrongfully in relying on the abstracts and not examining the original statements, it may have been misconduct on their part, but it cannot be said that they were acting beyond the scope of their jurisdiction. If, in a single case, and without coming to an erroneous result, they took the abstracts instead of the original returns, it would be just as fatal as a matter of jurisdiction (and no more so) as if they relied on the abstracts in all cases. It would only be error or misconduct, and not want of jurisdiction. And the Houses of Congress, as before said, are not a court of errors and appeals, for the purpose of examining regularity of proceedings.

It is also said that they acted without jurisdiction in rejecting returns without having before them certificates of violence or intimidation. It is admitted that they took a large quantity of evidence themselves on the subject; but it is contended that they had no jurisdiction to enter upon the inquiry without a supervisor's certificate first had. Is this certain? The one hundred and third article of the constitution made it the duty of the legislature to pass laws regulating elections, to support the privilege of free suffrage, and to prohibit undue influence thereon from power, bribery, tumults, or other improper influences. The election law was passed to carry out this article. As one means of carrying it out in spirit, the returning-board were prohibited from counting a return, if it was accompanied by a certificate of violence, until they had investigated the matter by examination and proof. Receiving such a certificate, they could not count a return if they wanted to. Now, is it certain that under such a law, if the board had knowledge from other sources than a certificate that violence and intimidation had been exercised and had produced the result, they could not inquire into it? And more, is their whole canvass to be set aside, because they made an investigation under such circumstances? There is no other tribunal in Louisiana for making it. The supreme court has decided that the courts cannot go behind these returns. In my judgment, we have no more authority to reject their canvass for this cause than for that of not using the original statements. It is as if a court having jurisdiction of a cause used a piece of evidence on the trial which it had no jurisdiction to take. It would be mere irregularity at most, and would not render its judgment void in any collateral proceeding.

I cannot bring my mind to believe that fraud and misconduct on the part of the State authorities, constituted for the very purpose of declaring the final will of the State, is a subject over which the two Houses of Congress have jurisdiction to institute an examination. The question is not whether frauds ought to be tolerated, or whether they ought not to be circumvented; but whether the Houses of Congress, in exercising their power of counting the electoral votes, are intrusted by the Constitution with authority to investigate them. If in any case it should clearly and manifestly appear, in an unmistakable manner, that a direct fraud had been committed by a returning-board in returning the electors they did, and if it did not require an investigation on the part of the two Houses to ascertain by the taking of evidence the truth of the case, I have no doubt that the Houses might rightfully reject the vote—as not being the vote of the State. But where no such manifest fraud appears, and fraud is only charged, how are the two Houses to enter upon a career of investigation? If the field of inquiry were once opened, where is its boundary? Evidently no such proceeding was in the mind of the framers of the Constitution. The short and explicit directions there given, that the votes shall be first produced before the Houses when met for that purpose, and that "the votes shall then be counted," is at variance with any such idea. An investigation beforehand is not authorized and was not contemplated, and would be repugnant to the limited and special power given. What jurisdiction have the Houses on the subject, until they have met under the Constitution, except to provide by law for facilitating the performance of their duties? An investigation afterward, such as the question raised might and frequently would lead to, would be utterly incompatible with the performance of the duty imposed.

At all events, on one or two points I am perfectly clear. First, that the two Houses do not constitute a canvassing-board for the purpose of investigating and deciding on the results of the election for electors in a State. The proposed act of 1800 carefully excluded any inquiry into the number of votes on which an elector was elected; and I think it cannot well be pretended that the Houses have power to go further into the inquiry than was proposed by that bill. Secondly, that the two Houses are not a tribunal, or court, for trying the validity of the election-returns and sitting in judgment on the legality of the proceedings in the course of the election. The two Houses, with only their constitutional jurisdiction, are neither of these things; though as to the elections, qualifications, and returns of their own members, they are certainly the latter, having the right to judge and decide.

I have thus far spoken of the power of the two Houses of Congress as derived from the Constitution. Whether the legislative power of the Government might not, by law, make provision for an investigation into frauds and illegalities, I do not undertake to decide. It cannot be done, in my judgment, by any agency of the Federal Government without legislative regulation. The necessity of an orderly mode of taking evidence and giving opportunity to cross-examine witnesses would require the interposition of law. The ordinary power of the two Houses as legislative bodies, by which they investigate facts through the agency of committees, is ill adapted to such an inquiry.

It seems to me, however, the better conclusion, that the jurisdiction of the whole matter belongs exclusively to the States. Let them take care to protect themselves from the perpetration of frauds. They need no guardians. They are able, and better able than Congress, to create every kind of political machinery which human prudence can contrive, for circumventing fraud, and preserving their true voice and vote in the presidential election.

In my judgment, the evidence proposed cannot be received.

Then, as to the alleged ineligibility of the candidates. First, their alleged ineligibility under the laws of the State, I think we have nothing to do with. It has been imposed for local reasons of State policy, but if the State sees fit to waive its own regulations on this subject, it is its own concern. If the State declares that no person shall hold two offices, or that all officers shall possess an estate of the value of $1,000, or imposes any other qualification, or disqualification, it is for the State to execute its own laws in this behalf. At all events, if persons are appointed electors without having the qualifications, or having the disqualifications, and they execute the function of casting their votes, their acts cannot be revised here.

Two of the electors, however, Levissee and Brewster, are alleged to have held offices of trust and profit under the United States, when the election was held on the 7th of November. It is not alleged that they did so on the 6th of December, when they gave their votes. Being absent when the electoral college met, their places were declared vacant, and the college itself proceeded to re-appoint them under the law, and sent for them. They then appeared and took their seats. So that, in point of fact, the objection does not meet the case, unless their being Federal office-holders at the time of the election affects it.

Though not necessary to the decision of this case, I have re-examined the question of constitutional ineligibility since the Florida case was disposed of, and must say that I am not entirely satisfied with the conclusion to which I then came, namely, that if a disqualified elector casts his vote when disqualified, the objection cannot be taken. I still think that this disqualification at the time of his election is not material, if such disqualification ceases before he acts as an elector. But, as at present advised, I am inclined to the opinion that if constitutionally disqualified when he casts his vote, such vote ought not to be counted.

I still think, as I thought in discussing the Florida case, that the form of the constitutional prohibition is not material; that it is all one, whether the prohibition is that a Federal officer shall not *be* an elector, or, that he shall not be *appointed* an elector. The spirit and object of the prohibition is to make office-holding under the Federal Government a disqualification. That is all. And this is the more apparent when we recollect the reasons for it. When the Constitution was framed, the great object of creating the office of electors to elect the President and Vice-President was to remove this great duty as far as possible from the influence of popular passion and prejudice, and to place it in the hands of men of wisdom and discretion, having a knowledge of public affairs and public men. The idea was that they were to act with freedom and independence. The jealousy which was manifested in the convention against the apprehended influence and power of the General Government, and especially of the legislative branch, induced the prohibition in question. It was feared that the members of the Houses of Congress and persons holding office under the Government would be peculiarly subject to these influences in exercising the power of voting for Chief Magistrate. It was not in the process of appointment that this influence was dreaded, but in the effect it would have on the elector himself in giving his vote.

It seems to me, therefore, that if a person appointed an elector has no official connection with the Federal Government when he gives his vote, such vote cannot be justly excepted to; and that substantial effect is given to the constitutional disqualification if the electoral vote given by such officer is rejected. And my present impression is that it should be rejected.

Circumstances, it is true, have greatly changed since the Constitution was adopted. Instead of electors being, as it was supposed they would be, invested with power to act on the dictates of their own judgment and discretion in choosing a President, they have come to be mere puppets, elected to express the preordained will of the political party that elects them. The matter of ineligibility has come to be really a matter of no importance, except as it still stands in the Constitution, and is to be interpreted as it was understood when the Constitution was adopted. Hence we must ascertain, if we can, what was its original design and meaning, without attempting to stretch or enlarge its force.

[It may be proper that I should here add that I concede that there is great force in what is urged by other members of the Commission respecting the difficulty which still remains, of the two Houses, when assembled to count the votes, undertaking an investigation of facts to determine a question of ineligibility, which might be extended in such a manner as materially to interfere with the main duty for which they assemble. This was probably seen when the law of 1800 was proposed for the purpose of having such matters determined by a grand committee preparatory to the meeting of the two Houses in joint convention. The passage of some law regulating the matter is on all accounts desirable.]

THE OREGON CASE.

Statement.

The laws of Oregon do not provide for a board of State canvassers, but direct as follows:

"It shall be the duty of the secretary of state, in presence of the governor, to proceed within thirty days after the election, and sooner if the returns be all received, to canvass the votes given for secretary and treasurer of state, State printer, justices of the supreme court, members of Congress, and district attorneys."

And then, with regard to State officers, directs: "The governor shall grant a certificate of election to the person having the highest number of votes, and shall also issue a proclamation declaring the election of such person."

But with regard to presidential electors, it directs: "The votes for the electors shall be given, received, returned, and canvassed as the same are given, returned, and canvassed for members of Congress. The secretary of state shall prepare two lists of the names of the electors elected, and affix the seal of the State to the same. Such lists shall be signed by the governor and secretary, and by the latter delivered to the college of electors at the hour of their meeting on such first Wednesday of December."

When the electors are met on the day for casting their votes, the law directs: "If there shall be any vacancy in the office of an elector, occasioned by death, refusal to act, neglect to attend, or otherwise, the electors present shall immediately proceed to fill, by *viva voce* and plurality of votes, such vacancy in the electoral college."

Watts, one of the electors having the highest number of votes, was a postmaster at the time of the election, November 7, 1876, but resigned that office during the month.

On the 4th of December, the secretary of state, in presence of the governor, canvassed the votes for presidential electors, made a statement of the result, authenticated it under the seal of the State, and filed it in his office. The following is a copy of this document:

Abstract of votes cast at the presidential election held in the State of Oregon November 7, 1876, for presidential electors.

Counties.	W. H. Odell.	J. W. Watts.	J. C. Cartwright.	Henry Klippel.	E. A. Cronin.	W. B. Laswell.	D. Clark.	F. Sutherland.	B. Carl.
Baker	318	319	319	549	550	549	1	1	1
Benton	615	615	615	567	567	567	77	77	77
Clackamas	949	950	950	724	724	724	17	17	17
Clatsop	432	432	432	386	385	386			
Columbia	157	156	157	179	179	179	22	22	22
Coos	571	571	571	512	516	515			
Curry	131	131	131	124	124	124	3	3	3
Douglas	1,002	1,002	1,003	847	847	847	43	43	43
Grant	315	314	316	279	279	277	3	3	3
Jackson	585	585	586	827	840	840	5	5	5
Josephine	209	209	209	252	252	252	4	4	4
Lane	949	949	949	946	946	946	33	33	33
Lake	173	173	173	258	258	258			
Linn	1,323	1,324	1,323	1,404	1,404	1,404	140	141	140
Marion	1,780	1,782	1,781	1,154	1,154	1,155	24	23	22
Multnomah	2,124	2,122	2,122	1,525	1,528	1,525	2	2	2
Polk	607	608	608	542	542	542	54	55	54
Tillamook	119	119	119	76	76	76	1	1	1
Umatilla	486	486	486	742	742	742	42	42	42
Union	366	366	366	525	525	525	32	32	32
Wasco	491	491	493	621	621	619			
Washington	693	692	693	423	424	423			
Yamhill	811	810	812	674	674	674	6	6	6
Total	15,206	15,206	15,214	14,136	14,157	14,149	509	510	507

Simpson, 1; Gray, 1; Saulsbury, 1; McDowell, 1.

SALEM, STATE OF OREGON:

I hereby certify that the foregoing tabulated statement is the result of the vote cast for presidential electors at a general election held in and for the State of Oregon on the 7th day of November, A. D. 1876, as opened and canvassed in the presence of his excellency L. F. Grover, governor of said State, according to law, on the 4th day of December, A. D. 1876, at two o'clock p. m. of that day, by the secretary of state.

[SEAL.]   S. F. CHADWICK,
Secretary of State of Oregon.

The statute of Oregon declares, " in all elections in this State the person having the highest number of votes for any office shall be deemed to be elected."

On the 6th of December, when the electors met to give their votes for President and Vice-President, Watts resigned as elector, and was re-appointed by Odell and Cartwright to fill the vacancy. The governor refused them the usual certificate, but certified that Odell, Cartwright, and Cronin received the highest number of votes cast for persons *eligible* under the Constitution of the United States, and declared them duly elected. As Odell and Cartwright refused to meet with Cronin, he assumed to fill two vacancies. This proceeding of the governor and of Cronin raised the principal question in the Oregon case.

FEBRUARY 23, 1877.

Mr. Commissoner BRADLEY said:

This case differs from the two cases already heard in this : By the laws both of Florida and Louisiana, the final determination of the result of the election was to be made by a board of canvassers invested with power to judge of the local returns and to reject them for certain causes assigned. In Oregon, no such board exists. The general canvass for the State is directed to be made by the secretary of state, in presence of the governor, from the abstracts sent to him by the county clerks. This canvass having been made, the result is declared by the law. The canvass is the last act by which the election is decided and determined. This canvass was made in the present case on the 4th day of December, 1876; the result was recorded in a statement in writing made by the secretary and filed by him in his office. This statement or abstract thus became the record evidence of the canvass. It remains in the secretary's office to-day as the final evidence and determination of the result. We have before us, under the great seal of the State, a copy of this statement, which shows the result to have been a clear plurality of over a thousand votes in favor of the three electors, Odell, Cartwright, and Watts; and there is added thereto a list of the votes.

This document, after exhibiting a tabulated statement of the votes given for each candidate in each county of the State, footing up for Odell, 15,206; Watts, 15,206; Cartwright, 15,214; Klippel, 14,136; Cronin, 14,157; Laswell, 14,149, and a few scattering votes, was certified and authenticated at the end, as follows:

SALEM, STATE OF OREGON:

I hereby certify that the foregoing tabulated statement is the result of the vote cast for presidential electors at a general election held in and for the State of Oregon, on the 7th day of November, A. D. 1876, as opened and canvassed in the presence of his excellency L. F. Grover, governor of said State, according to law, on the 4th day of December, A. D. 1876, at two o'clock p. m. of that day, by the secretary of state.

[SEAL.]   S. F. CHADWICK,
                                              Secretary of State of Oregon.

This document, with this certificate and authentication upon it, was filed by the secretary in his office on the 4th day of December.

To the exemplified copy of it, which was sent to the President of the Senate, (and which we have before us,) is added another document, entitled "List of votes cast at an election for electors of President and Vice-President of the United States in the State of Oregon, held on the 7th day of November, 1876," which contains the votes given for each candidate, (the same as in the canvass,) written out in words at length, and certified by the secretary of state, also under the great seal of the State, to be the entire vote cast for each and all persons for the office of electors as appears by the returns of said election on file in his office.

Having made this canvass, recorded it, and filed it in his office, the secretary of state was *functus officio* with regard to the duty of ascertaining the result of the election. He could not change it; he could not tamper with it in any way. By his act and by this record of his act, the ascertainment of the election in Oregon was closed. Its laws give no revisory power to any other functionary and give none to the secretary himself. And this, as we have seen, was done and completed on the 4th day of December, at two o'clock in the afternoon, in the presence of the governor, according to the law of Oregon.

Now, what is the decree of the law on this transaction? It is clear and unmistakable:

In all elections in this State the person having the highest number of votes for any office shall be deemed to be elected.

It is not left for any functionary to say that any other person shall be deemed to be elected. No discretion, no power of revision is given to any one, except as the general law of the State has given to the judicial department power to investigate the right of persons elected to hold the offices to which they have been elected.

Now, what is the next step to be performed? It is this:

The secretary of state shall prepare two lists of the names of the electors elected, and affix the seal of the State to the same. Such lists shall be signed by the governor and secretary, and by the latter delivered to the college of electors at the hour of their meeting on such first Wednesday of December.

This direction seems to be intended as a compliance with the act of Congress of 1792. It is true that this act requires three lists instead of two to be delivered to the electors; but the number required by the State law was probably an inadvertence. Be this, however, as it may, what names was the secretary required by law to insert in his certificate?

He made out his certificate on the 6th day of December, two days after his canvass had been completed, recorded, and deposited in the public archives. In making this certificate he was performing a mere ministerial duty. It was his clear duty to insert in his certificate the names of the persons whom the law declared to be elected. Doing otherwise was not only a clear violation of duty, but he made a statement untrue in fact; and the governor putting his name to the certificate joined in that misrepresentation. It may not have been an intended misrepresentation, and the use of the word "eligible" may have been thought a sufficient qualification; nevertheless it was a misrepresentation in fact and in law, and it all appears from the record itself. It needs no extrinsic evidence.

But it is said that the governor has the power to disregard the canvass and to reject an elector who he is satisfied is ineligible. There is no law in Oregon which gives him this power. In my judgment, it was a clear act of usurpation. It was tampering with an election which the law had declared to be closed and ascertained.

It is said, however, that he may refuse a commission to an ineligible person elected to a State office. If so, it does not decide this case. And it seems to me that such an act, even with regard to State officers, would be an encroachment on the judicial power. A case is referred to as having been decided in Oregon in which the appointment by the governor to fill a vacancy in a State office caused by the incumbent being appointed to a United States office was sustained. But surely the judgment in that case must have been based on the fact that there was a vacancy, and not on the fact that the governor assumed to judge whether there was a vacancy or not. His executive act, whether in determining his own action he had the right to decide the question of eligibility or not, was valid or not according as the very truth of the fact was.

But in the case before us he had a mere ministerial act to perform. He had no discretionary power.

If any one could have taken notice of the question of supposed ineligibility, it was the secretary of state when making his canvass. Had he taken it upon himself to throw out the votes given for Watts, he would have had a much more plausible ground of justification for his act than the governor had, to whom no power is given on the subject.

But it is said, no matter whether the governor and secretary acted right or wrong, they were the functionaries designated for giving final expression to the will of the State, and their certificate must be received as such, under the decision in the cases of Florida and Louisiana. To this view, however, there is a conclusive answer. As I said before, the certificate to be given by the secretary and governor to these electors was not intended as any part of the machinery for ascertaining the result of the election, but as a mere certificate of the fact of election, as a credential to be used by the electors in acting as such and transmitting their votes to the President of the Senate of the United States, as required by the act of Congress of 1792. As such it is *prima facie* evidence, it is true; but no person has contended that it cannot be contradicted and shown to be untrue, especially by evidence of equal dignity. We did not so decide in the other cases. We held that the final decision of the canvass by the tribunal or authority constituted for that purpose could not be revoked by the two Houses of Congress, by going into evidence behind their action and return.

The only remaining question is, whether there was a vacancy in the college at the time when Odell and Cartwright assumed to fill a vacancy on the 6th day of December, 1876. It seems to me that there was, whether there was a failure to elect on account of the ineligibility of Watts or on account of his resignation afterward.

It is agreed by a large majority of the Commission that Cronin was not elected. Some of this majority take the ground that Watts was duly elected, whatever effect his ineligibility, had it continued, might have had on his vote. Others take the ground that there was no election of a third elector. It seems to me that it makes no difference in this case which of these views is the correct one; there was a clear vacancy in either case.

The act of Congress of 1845 declares that "each State may by law provide for the filling of any vacancies which may occur in its college of electors when such college meets to give its electoral vote;" and also, "that whenever any State has held an election for the purpose of choosing electors, and has failed to make a choice on the day prescribed by law, the electors may be appointed on a subsequent day in such manner as the legislature of such State may direct."

The first contingency would occur when some of the electors were elected and could meet and fill any vacancy in their number. The second contingency would occur when no electors were appointed, and therefore no meeting could be held. It is evident that these are two very different cases, and that the one before us does not belong to the latter, but to the former. It is the difference between a college which is not full and no college at all. In Oregon, according to the exigency supposed, the case belonged to that of a vacancy under the act of 1845.

The act of Oregon in relation to vacancies in the electoral college was evidently passed in view of the act of Congress upon which it was based; and its terms are so broad and comprehensive that I cannot doubt that it was intended to apply to every case of vacancy. The words are that "if there shall be *any* vacancy in the office of an elector, occasioned by death, refusal to act, neglect to attend, *or otherwise*, the electors present shall immediately proceed to fill," &c. This clearly covers every supposable case, and must be intended to be as broad as the corresponding section of the act of Congress. It is more general in its terms than the act relating to vacancies in State offices, which specifies only certain classes of cases.

As the electors Odell and Cartwright filled the vacancy in a regular manner, I cannot avoid the conclusion that they, together with Watts, were the true electors for the State of Oregon on the 6th day of December, and that their votes ought to be counted.

Their credentials are not signed by the governor, it is true; but that is not an essential thing and was not their fault. They have presented the records of the State, found in its archives; and these show that the act of the governor was grossly wrong; and they have also presented the certificate of the secretary of state, under the great seal of the State, conclusively showing their election. They have also shown by their own affidavit that they applied to the governor for his certificate and that he refused it. I think their credentials, under the circumstances, are sufficient.

It is urged that the distinction made between this case and that of Florida and Louisiana is technical and will not give public satisfaction. My belief is that when the public come to understand (as they will do in time) that the decision come to is founded on the Constitution and the laws, they will be better satisfied than if we should attempt to follow the clamor of the hour. The sober second thought of the people of this country is in general correct. But while the public satisfaction is always desirable, it is a poor method of ascertaining the law and the truth to be alert in ascertaining what are the supposed wishes of the public. And as to deciding the case on technicalities, I do not know that technicalities are invoked on the one side more than on the other. In drawing the true boundary-line between conflicting jurisdictions and establishing certain rules for just decision in such cases as these, it is impossible to avoid a close and searching scrutiny of written constitutions and laws. The weight due to words and phrases has to be observed, as well as the general spirit and policy of public documents. Careful and exact inquiry becomes a necessity. And in such a close political canvass as this, in which the decision of a presidential election may depend not only on a single electoral, but a single individual vote, the greatest strain is brought to bear on every part of our constitutional machinery, and it is impossible to avoid a close examination of every part. There is a natural fondness for solving every doubt on some " broad and general view" of the subject in hand. " Broad and general views," when entirely sound and clearly applicable, are undoubtedly to be preferred; but it is extremely easy to adopt broad and general views that will, if adhered to, carry us into regions of error and absurdity. The only rule that is always and under all circumstances reliable is to ascertain, at whatever cost of care and pains, the true and exact commands of the Constitution and the laws, and implicitly to obey them.

THE SOUTH CAROLINA CASE.

Mr. Commissioner BRADLEY said:

It is not pretended that the votes of the Tilden electors, as presented in certificate No. 2, in this case, are legal. The entire controversy arises upon the objections to certificate No. 1, containing the votes for Hayes and Wheeler.

These objections are—

First. That the November election in South Carolina was void because the legislature of that State has never passed a registration law as required by the constitution of the State, article 8, section 3, which is as follows:

It shall be the duty of the general assembly to provide from time to time for the registration of all electors.

This constitution was passed in 1868, and from that time to this elections have been held, and the various elective officers of the State, as well as the office of Representative in Congress, have been filled without a registration law having been passed. If the effect of the omission has been to render all these elections absolutely void, South Carolina has for some years been without any lawful government. But if the effect has only been to render the elections voidable, without affecting the validity of the acts of the government in its various departments, as a government *de facto*, then the election of presidential electors and their giving their votes have the same validity as all other political acts of that body-politic. But, in my opinion, the clause of the constitution in question is only directory, and cannot affect the validity of elections in the State, much less the official acts of the officers elected. The passage of a registration law was a legislative duty which the members on their oaths were bound to perform. But their neglect to perform it ought not to prejudice the people or the State.

The objection that it does not appear by the certificate that the electors voted by ballot, or that they took an oath of office as required of all officers in South Carolina, are so formal and manifestly frivolous that I shall not discuss them. The presumption is that all due formalities were complied with.

The only objections of any weight are those which charge that there was such anarchy and disturbance in the State during the election, and such interference of United States troops and others therewith, that no valid election was held in the State, and it is impossible to know what the will of the State was. This is placing the objections and the offer of proof to support them, in their strongest light.

I think it unquestionably true that such a state of things as this objection contemplates ought to exclude any vote purporting to come from the State, for no such vote can be regarded as expressing the will of the State. But that is not the only question to be considered.

The first and great question is as to the constitutional power of the two Houses of Congress, when assembled to count the votes for President and Vice-President, to institute an investigation by evidence such as is necessary to determine the facts to be proved. This power of canvassing the electoral votes is constantly confounded with that of canvassing the votes by which the electors themselves were elected—a canvass with which Congress has nothing to do. This belongs to the jurisdiction of the States themselves, and not to Congress. All that Congress has to do with the subject is to ascertain whether the State has or has not appointed electors—an act of the State which can only be performed by and through its own constituted authorities.

It seems to be also constantly overlooked or forgotten that the two Houses, in their capacity of a convention for counting the electoral votes, have only a special and limited jurisdiction. They are not at all invested with that vast and indefinite power of inquisition which they enjoy as legislative bodies. Until met for the specific purpose of the count, they have no power over the subject, except to pass such laws as it is competent for the legislative branch of the Government to pass. The electoral votes are in sealed packages, over which the two Houses have no control. They have not, constitutionally, any knowledge of these until they are opened in their presence. Their jurisdiction over the subject of the count, and the votes, and the appointment of electors, commences at that moment. They have no power before this to make investigations affecting the count. Could it have been in the contemplation of the Constitution that the two Houses, after commencing the count, should institute such an investigation as the objectors propose, involving (as it would be likely to do) many weeks in the process? It seems to me impossible to come to such a conclusion.

When the state of things in a State is of such a public character as to be within the judicial knowledge of the two Houses, of course they may take notice of it and act accordingly, as was done in the times of secession and the late civil war, or as might have been done at any time, so long as the seceding States were not in harmonious relations with the General Government. But when a State is in the enjoyment of all those relations, when it is represented in both Houses of Congress, is recognized by the other departments of the Government, and is known to have a government republican in form—in other words, when all the public relations of the State are the same as those of all other States, how can the two Houses in convention assembled (and assembled for such a special purpose) go into an investigation for the purpose of ascertaining the exact state of things within the State, so as to decide the question (perhaps a very nice question to be decided) whether the tumults and disorders existing therein at the time of the election, or the presence of the troops sent there by the President for the preservation of the public peace, had such an influence as to deprive the State of its autonomy and the power of expressing its will in the appointment of electors? Such an investigation, or one of any such character and extent, was surely never contemplated to be made while the votes were being counted.

That South Carolina is a State and that she has a republican form of government are public facts of which the two Houses (and we in their stead) must take judicial notice. We know that she is such a State. That she is capable of preserving the public order, either with or without the aid of the Federal authority, and that the executive interference, if made at all, was made in the exercise of his proper authority for the reasons set forth in his public proclamations and orders, are facts to be presumed. At all events the two Houses, under their special authority to count the electoral votes, are not competent to take evidence to prove the contrary.

I do not doubt that Congress, in its legislative capacity, with the President concurring, or by a two-thirds vote after his veto, could pass a law by which investigation might be had in advance, under proper regulations as to notice and evidence and the cross-examination of witnesses; the results of which could be laid before the two Houses at their meeting for the count of votes, and could be used by them as a basis for deciding whether such a condition of anarchy, disturbance, and intimidation existed in a State at a time of the election of its electors as to render its vote nugatory and liable to be rejected. But without the existence of a law of this sort, it is, in my judgment, impracticable and unconstitutional for the two Houses to enter upon such an inquiry. The investigations made by legislative committees, in the loose manner in which they are usually made, are not only not adapted to the proper ascertainment of the truth for such a purpose, but are totally unauthorized by the Constitution. As methods of inquiry for ordinary legislative purposes or for the purpose of laying the foundation of resolutions for bringing in an impeachment of the President for unconstitutional interference, of course they are competent; but not for the purpose of receiving or rejecting the vote of a State for the presidential office. They are not made such by any constitutional provision or by any law. Legislation may be based on the private knowledge of members, and a resolution to bring in an impeachment may rest on *ex parte* affidavits or on general information; and, therefore, the evidence taken by a committee cannot be deemed incompetent for such a purpose, but is often of great service in giving information to the Houses as legislative bodies, and to the House of Representatives as the grand inquest of the nation. But the decision to receive or reject the vote of a State is a final decision on the right of the State in that behalf, and one of a most solemn and delicate nature, and cannot properly be based on the depositions of witnesses gathered in the drag-net of a congressional committee.

For these reasons I am clear that the evidence offered in support of the objections made to the electoral votes of South Carolina cannot be received.

These are, in brief, the views which I entertain in reference to this case; and under them I am forced to the conclusion that the objections made to the votes given by the electors certified by the governor of the State, and the evidence offered in support of the same, are insufficient, and that the said votes ought to be counted.

REMARKS OF MR. COMMISSIONER CLIFFORD.

INTRODUCTORY EXPLANATIONS.

More than one return, purporting to be certificates of the electoral votes of the State of Florida, having been received by the President of the Senate and opened by that officer in the presence of the two Houses, and objections thereto having been filed in the manner required by law, the certificates, votes, and all papers accompanying the same, together with such objections, were duly submitted to the judgment and decision of the Electoral Commission to decide which, if either, was the true and lawful vote of the State from which the returns were received.

Prior to the commencement of the hearing the Commission adopted certain rules to regulate the course of its proceedings, to two of which it is proper to refer in order to a better understanding of what took place. They are in substance and effect as follows: (1) Objectors to a certificate may select two of their number to support their objections and to advocate the validity of any one or more of the other certificates, under the prescribed limitations. (2) Counsel, not exceeding two on each side, may afterward be heard on the merits of the case.

Pursuant to the rule first named, the objectors to the Hayes certificate, called certificate No. 1, were fully heard, and the objectors to the Tilden certificates, called certificates Nos. 2 and 3, were also fully heard. Special leave was given by the Commission that three counsel might speak on each side, and the time allowed by the rule was enlarged.

Pending the argument it was suggested to counsel that if they proposed to introduce evidence to support their objections, it would facilitate the hearing if they should make known to the Commission in some proper form what the evidence was that they proposed to introduce. Offers of proof were accordingly made by the counsel supporting the objections to certificate No. 1, as appears in the published proceedings of the Commission. No offer of proof was submitted to the Commission by the counsel supporting the objections to the other two certificates, at that stage of the hearing.

Without entering into details, suffice it say that a portion of the time allowed under the rule for the discussion of the merits of the case having been spent before the offer of proof was made, it was moved by Mr. Justice Miller "that counsel be allowed two hours on each side to discuss the question whether any evidence will be considered by the Commission that was not submitted to the two Houses by the President of the Senate, and, if so, what evidence can properly be considered, and also what is the evidence now before the Commission." Debate ensued, but the motion was adopted and the argument proceeded under that regulation and restriction.

Both sides were heard, and at the close of the arguments all persons present, except the members of the Commission and the officers thereof, retired and the Commission went into consultation with closed doors. Opportunity for debate was extended to every member of the Commission and all participated in the discussion before the final votes were taken. Certain remarks were made at the close of the debate by Mr. Justice Clifford, in substance and effect as follows:

REMARKS.

Since the case was submitted to the Commission, pursuant to the recent act of Congress, I have carefully examined the several certificates in question and all the written objections to the same transmitted here by the President of the Senate, in order to ascertain what the matters in controversy are and what questions are presented to the judgment and decision of the Commission. Beyond doubt, those documents, with the accompanying papers, were intended by the act of Congress to present the matters in contestation to be submitted to the judgment and decision of the tribunal created for the purpose of hearing and determining such controversies. Fifteen commissioners have been appointed for the purpose, and they, as required by the act of Congress, have severally been sworn impartially to examine and consider all questions submitted to the tribunal, and to render a true judgment in the premises, agreeably to the Constitution and the laws.

Sitting under that act of Congress I shall assume that it is a constitutional act and that it correctly describes and defines the duties and the jurisdiction of the Commission.

Differences of opinion existed upon that subject before the act of Congress creating the Commission was passed. Two theories were advanced: one that the power to decide what persons were duly appointed electors in a State is vested in the President of the Senate, and the other that the sole power in that regard is vested in the two Houses of Congress. Discussion upon that topic is closed by the act of Congress, which makes it the duty of the Commission, in a case submitted to it under the second section of the act, to "decide whether any and what votes from such State are the votes provided for by the Constitution of the United States, and how many and what persons were duly appointed electors in such State."

Appointed, as the members of the Commission have been, under that act, they are bound by its provisions, and it is the duty of the tribunal to perform in good faith the duties which it prescribes.

Three returns or certificates are submitted to the Commission from the State of Florida, and the tribunal is required to decide what persons are duly appointed electors from that State. Certificate No. 1, if unexplained, shows that the Hayes electors are duly appointed, and certificates Nos. 2 and 3 show that the Tilden electors were duly elected by a majority of the votes cast at the election.

Such an issue must be decided by the Commission, and all just and intelligent persons must admit that it cannot be properly decided without an inquiry into the facts and a hearing of the parties. Inquiry to a very limited extent, it is admitted, may be made, but the amazing proposition is advanced that the inquiry cannot extend beyond the examination of the papers presented by the President of the Senate to the two Houses and which were subsequently submitted to the Commission. Attempt is made to support that proposition chiefly by the argument of inconvenience. Should the inquiry be opened to a wider investigation the argument is that the Commission would not be able to close its duties in season to render the electoral votes effectual for the purpose prescribed by the Constitution.

Support to that view is attempted to be drawn from the most extravagant suppositions that ingenious minds can devise or imagine. If the suggestions were well founded, they would be entitled to weight; but a few observations, I think, will be sufficient to show that the supposed dangers are merely imaginary and without any foundation whatever.

Arguments unsupported by fact are entitled to no weight and may be dismissed without consideration as mere sound and fury, signifying nothing. Judging from the issues presented by the certificates and the objections thereto filed in behalf of the contestants, I assume that the Commission is not expected to enter into any scrutiny of the votes cast at the general election of the State, nor of the qualifications of the voters who voted for President and Vice-President at that election. Nothing of the kind is suggested in any one of the written objections and no such extravagant proposition has been advanced by any member of the Commission. Matters of that sort may, therefore, be dismissed without further remark; and it is equally clear that no attack is made upon the local officers who presided in the precincts, nor does any one of the objections filed in the case impeach their conduct in receiving, sorting, or counting the votes, or in declaring the result. Questions of the kind sometimes arise in other forums, which give rise to difficult and protracted investigations, but no question of that character is involved in this investigation, nor can it be without a willful departure from the issues presented in the written objections filed in the case.

Impartial men everywhere must admit that the act of Congress makes it the duty of the Commission to decide "what persons were duly appointed electors" in that State; and if so, it may be assumed that no member of the Commission is willing to be deterred from performing the prescribed duty by any imaginary dangers, which have no real foundation in fact.

Sufficient has already been remarked to show that none of the objections to the certificates requires any scrutiny into the votes cast at the primary election or calls in question the returns made by the officers who presided in the precincts. Throughout, the controversy has respect to the conduct of the State board of canvassers in dealing with the returns made by the county canvassers to the secretary of state.

Precinct inspectors are required to make duplicate certificates of the result and deliver one of the same, with the poll-lists, to the clerk of the circuit court, and the other to the county judge. Six days later the county canvassers are required to meet and to make and sign duplicate certificates containing in words and figures, written in full length, the whole number of votes, the names of the persons voted for, and the number of votes given to each person for each office. Duplicate returns must be made and recorded, and the requirement also is that one of the duplicates shall be transmitted by mail to the secretary of state and the other to the governor. Provision is also made for a board of State canvassers, whose duty it is, within a prescribed period, to canvass the returns of election received from the several counties, and to determine and declare who shall have been elected to such office or as such member, *as shown by such returns.*

The State canvassers are to determine and declare who have been elected, as shown by the county returns received from the county canvassers.

Unless these views can be successfully controverted—and I submit with entire confidence that they cannot—then it follows that there are but three questions involved in the main feature of the resolution adopted by the Commission on motion of Mr. Justice Miller, which I assume is the proper guide of the Commission in the present consultation.

1. Whether the certificate No. 1 is absolutely conclusive of the election of the Hayes electors and has the effect to exclude all evidence to

prove the matters charged in the written objections submitted to the Commission at the same time with the certificate?

Charges of the kind involve the imputation of fraud, perjury, and forgery; and if evidence to sustain such imputations cannot be admitted, then the Congress, the President, and the Supreme Court have been misled and deceived.

2. Whether the action of the board of State canvassers is conclusive that the Hayes electors were duly appointed, and has the effect to shut out evidence to show error, fraud, perjury, or willful forgery?

3. Whether certificates Nos. 2 and 3 are valid, supported as they are by the action of all the branches of the State government, which, if admissible in evidence, show to a demonstration that the Hayes electors were never duly appointed, and that they are mere usurpers.

When a person is elected to the office of elector, the requirement of the State statute is that the governor shall make out and sign a certificate of his election, cause the same to be sealed with the seal of the State, and transmit the same to the person elected to such office. Certificates of the kind to persons chosen to any State office are made out by the secretary of state, whose duty it is to transmit the same to the person having the highest number of votes cast, and the provision is that the "certificate shall be *prima facie* evidence of his election to such office."

Votes cast for electors are canvassed for the same purpose as votes cast for State officers, and the certificate given by the governor to an elector is given for the same purpose that the certificate of the secretary of state is given to a person supposed to be elected to a State office, and there is no reason for holding that the certificate of the governor was intended to have any other or different effect than the certificate of the secretary of state when given to a State officer, as required by the same statute.

Truth and justice, it is admitted, ought to prevail, but the argument is that such an investigation is impracticable for the want of time to complete it, and in order to give plausibility to that theory it is assumed that the objectors to certificate No. 1 propose to enter into a scrutiny of the qualification of the voters, and of the votes cast at the primary election, and of the conduct of the officers who presided in the precincts, and of their returns. Assumptions of the kind are entirely without foundation, as sufficiently appears from the certificates and the written objections filed to the same, which clearly present the issues to be tried and determined by the Commission.

1. Certificate No. 1, dated December 6, 1876, signed by M. L. Stearns, governor, certifies that Frederick C. Humphreys, Charles H. Pearce, William H. Holden, and Thomas W. Long have been chosen electors of the State, agreeably to the laws of the State and in conformity to the Constitution of the United States.

Six specifications of objections were duly filed to that certificate, which in substance and effect are as follows: (1) That the persons therein named as electors were not appointed as such in the manner directed by the legislature of the State. (2) That they were not appointed electors of President and Vice-President in such manner as the legislature of the State directed. (3) That the qualified voters of the State did, on the 7th of November, 1876, execute the power of appointing such electors, and did appoint Wilkinson Call, James E. Yonge, Robert B. Hilton, and Robert Bullock to be such electors. (4) That certificate No. 1 is untrue, and was corruptly procured, and made in pursuance of a conspiracy therein more particularly described. (5) That the papers falsely purporting to be votes are fictitious and unreal, and were made out and executed in pursuance of the same fraudulent conspiracy. (6) That the printed certificate has been annulled and declared void by the executive and by the legislature and judiciary of the State.

Apart from that, the objectors also allege that certificate No. 1 was annulled by the subsequent certificate to the Tilden electors, by which the latter were declared duly appointed in the manner provided by the legislature of the State and the Constitution, the legislature having declared that the title of the persons named as electors in the last-named certificate is good and valid. Nor do the objectors rest the case entirely upon the certificate of the governor and the legislative act, but they also set up the judgment of the circuit court rendered in the suit in the nature of *quo warranto*, and allege that it was adjudged by the court in that case that the four persons named in certificate No. 1 were not elected, chosen, or appointed electors for the State, and that the court also decided that they were mere usurpers, and were not entitled to assume or exercise any of the powers or functions of electors of President and Vice-President.

Superadded to these general specifications, they also file a special objection to one of the four persons named in certificate No. 1, to wit, that Frederick C. Humphreys was ineligible as an elector because he held at the time of the election the office of shipping-commissioner, which, under the act of Congress of the 7th of June, 1872, is an office of trust and profit within the meaning of the Constitution.

II. On December 6, 1876, the attorney-general of the State, one of the board of State canvassers, executed a certificate to Wilkinson Call, James E. Yonge, Robert B. Hilton, and Robert Bullock, called certificate No. 2, that it appears by the authentic returns on file in the office of the secretary of state that they, on the 7th of November, 1876, were chosen the four electors of the State, and that the law of the State makes no provision whereby the result shown by those returns can be certified to the executive of the State. Under that certificate the persons therein named as electors on the same day met and cast their votes for Samuel J. Tilden for President and Thomas A. Hendricks for Vice-President.

Two objections are filed to that certificate: (1) That it is not authenticated according to the Constitution and laws of the United States, so as to enable the votes given by those four persons to be counted. (2) That the package inclosing that certificate, when opened in the presence of the two Houses, did not contain any paper from the executive of the State showing that the persons therein named were the electors appointed by the State, nor is said certificate accompanied by any lawful authentication that they were appointed to cast the electoral vote of the State.

Florida, on the 17th of January, 1877, enacted a statute creating a board of State canvassers, and by the same statute directed that board to proceed to canvass the returns of the election of electors held on the 7th of November, 1876, and to determine and declare who were elected and appointed electors at said election, as shown by such returns on file in the office of the secretary of state. By the second section of the statute the new State board was required to canvass those returns according to the fourth section of the election law which was in force at the time the election was held for the choice of electors, as construed by the supreme court of the State. Pursuant thereto, the said State board was duly constituted, consisting of the secretary of state, the governor of the State, the comptroller of public accounts, and the treasurer of the State, and they met at the capital of the State on the 19th of January in the same year, and made the canvass of the said returns on file in the office of the secretary of state, by which it appears that the four persons designated as the Tilden electors received a majority of all the votes cast for electors in the several precincts of the State, and that they were duly appointed such electors.

Enough also appears to show that those persons claimed title as electors duly appointed under certificate No. 2, and that they, on the 6th of December, 1876, instituted a suit in the circuit court of the second judicial circuit, in the nature of *quo warranto*, against the Hayes electors, alleging that the respondents were not entitled to those offices, and praying judgment of ouster against them as wrongfully in possession of the same. Service was made and the respondents appeared and filed an answer. Proofs were subsequently taken, and the court rendered judgment in favor of the relators.

Contemporaneous action upon the subject was also taken by the legislature. On the 26th of the same month the legislature passed a statute declaring that the four persons called the Tilden electors were, on the 7th of November preceding, duly chosen and appointed electors, and that they were from that time entitled to exercise all the powers and duties of the office of electors, and had, on the 6th of December then next, full power and authority to vote as such electors and to certify and transmit their votes as provided by law.

Explicit recognition of their power and authority is there declared, and the statute proceeds to ratify, confirm, and declare valid all their acts as such electors to all intents and purposes, and to declare that they are thereby appointed electors as of the day of the prior general election.

Section 2 of the same act authorizes and directs the governor to make and certify in due form and under the great seal of the State three lists of the names of those persons as such electors, and to transmit the same, with an authenticated copy of that act, to the President of the Senate of the United States. Three lists of like character were also directed to be certified by the governor, and he was directed forthwith to deliver the same to the said electors.

III. These directions were obeyed by the governor, and on the same day he made and delivered to the said electors the certificates designated in the proceedings before the Commission as certificate No. 3, which, as well as No. 2, was given to the Tilden electors.

Three grounds of objection are stated in the paper filed in opposition to that certificate: (1) That it is not duly certified by any one holding the office of governor at the time the electors were appointed, nor at the time when they exercised their functions, nor until after their duties had been fully discharged. (2) Because the alleged preceedings are *ex post facto* and do not confer any right to those persons to cast the electoral vote of the State. (3) Because the proceedings, being retroactive, are null and void and of no effect.

Mention should also be made that an objection was also filed in the case applicable to both of the two preceding certificates, in which the objectors deny the validity of those certificates upon the ground that certificate No. 1 is in all respects regular, valid, and sufficient, and that the electors therein named were duly appointed to cast the electoral vote of the State.

Properly analyzed and construed, it is clear, from the several objections filed to the certificates, that the returns of the State canvassers, including that made by the attorney-general, are the only returns called in question, the charge being that the return of the State board, which is the basis of the Hayes certificate, is false, forged, and counterfeit.

Exception is also taken by the other side to certificates Nos. 2 and 3, but it is not alleged that they are false or forged, nor that the returns on which they are based are false or manufactured, nor that the election to which they refer was not lawfully held and properly conducted.

Intelligent inquirers will see at a glance that all of the certificates refer to the same election, to wit, to the election held on the 7th of November, and that no one of the objections calls in question either the validity or the regularity or fairness of that election. Neither side proposes to institute any scrutiny into the votes cast or to require any investigation as to the qualification of the voters who cast the votes, nor do they attack the conduct of the officers who presided in the precincts, nor the returns which the precinct officers made to the county canvassers. Everything of that sort may be dismissed from consideration as not within the jurisdiction of the Commission, because not submitted to its judgment and decision, and the remarks apply with equal force to the returns made by the county canvassers, for the reason that none of the objections attack either the truthfulness or fairness of those returns, nor do they propose any inquiry into the conduct of the officers who made those returns.

Strenuous opposition is made to certificate No. 1, and those who object to it insist that the return of the State canvassers on which it is founded is false, and the offers of proof point out more particularly the specific grounds of the charge. Decided opposition is also made to the other two certificates, chiefly that the officers who made the instruments were unauthorized to give any such certification, and that the certificates are of no legal validity.

Viewed in the light of these suggestions, it is clear that the argument of inconvenience is a mere hollow pretense, and that it is entitled to no weight.

Precinct returns were duly made to the county canvassers and the county canvassers made due returns to the secretary of state, where they still remain on file, as appears by the certified copies of the same among the papers submitted to the Commission by the two Houses. What the objectors to certificate No. 1 charge, when expounded in the light of the offers of proof, is that the State canvassers unlawfully rejected the entire return from the county of Manatee and parts of the respective returns from the counties of Hamilton, Jackson, and Monroe; that the State board by those unlawful acts changed the result of the election, and created the unlawful basis on which certificate No. 1 is founded.

Both the certificate of Governor Stearns and the certificate of the attorney-general are founded upon the same county returns, except the returns from the county of Manatee, and parts of the respective returns from the counties of Hamilton, Jackson, and Monroe, which were excluded from the basis on which Governor Stearns issued his certificate. He adopted the basis formed by the State canvassers, excluding the whole of the return from one county and parts of the returns from the three other counties.

All the county returns, as before remarked, are on file in the office of the secretary of state, and the attorney-general, who was one of the State canvassing-board, denying the right of the board to reject a county return without good cause shown, or to mutilate or tamper with such returns under any circumstances, dissented from the acts of the other two members of the board. Apparently, his conduct was open and frank, and he, on the same day, canvassed the entire county returns, and finding that the returns when honestly counted elected the Tilden electors, he executed certificate No. 2, and it appears that the four persons therein named met on the same day in the same building with the persons named in certificate No. 1, and cast their votes for President and Vice-President.

None of these facts can be successfully controverted, as all the returns are on file in the office of the secretary of state, and duly certified copies of the same, together with the original certificates, are now before the Commission, having been submitted by the order of the two Houses in the regular course of their action.

Few, I presume, will deny that it is competent for the Commission to take notice of the statutes of the State relating to the matter in controversy without any formal proof of their legal authenticity. Suppose that is so, then there are no matters involved in the issues presented which may not be thoroughly examined in a very few hours. Differences of opinion may exist as to the legal effect of the evidence if admitted, but I have yet to learn that any one denies that the alleged facts are capable of being proved by authentic documents in the archives of the State. Certified copies of the record and judgment of the court in the *quo warranto* proceedings are also here, ready to be introduced, and no one, I suppose, will deny that a duly exemplified copy of a record and judgment between the same parties would be admissible in this case, unless it be held that the action of the State canvassers or the certificate of the governor closes the door to all investigations and is sufficient to show that this Commission is so high that it has no power to investigate either fraud, perjury, or forgery.

Extended argument to show that the certificate of the governor is not conclusive seems to be unnecessary, as the opening counsel supporting certificate No. 1 disclaims that proposition, and very properly admits that it is only *prima facie* evidence of what it certifies to be true. Such a certificate made by an officer charged with the duty of making it imports verity, and it is doubtless true that it affords a *prima facie* right in the holder in the absence of any showing whatever to the contrary.

Grant that, but I suppose it was never heard that evidence of a mere *prima facie* right could have the effect to exclude all opposing testimony to show that the right did not exist, or that it had no other foundation than fraud and forgery. Fraud, it is said, will vitiate everything, and it is a maxim which has fewer exceptions than any other known to the common law.

Evidence of error is sufficient to overcome a *prima facie* presumption, but it was never heard that such a presumption is sufficient to shut out all proof of fraud. With all respect to those who advocate that proposition, I must be allowed to say that such a decision was never made, and it is presumed never will be, by any just and intelligent tribunal. Considerable time was spent in argument by counsel who support the Hayes certificate to convince the Commission that they do not maintain any such proposition, and I am convinced that if they do, it cannot properly be adopted by the Commission.

Concede that, and it follows that evidence in a proper case may be admitted to prove fraud or forgery in the certificate given in such a case by the governor of the State. Credentials of the kind are founded upon a prescribed basis, regulated by law, which is usually dependent for its accuracy not upon the doings of the governor, but upon the acts of other public agents. Whether that basis is truth or error, he does not know, and consequently the legal effect of his certificate is, whatever may be its form, that it appears to him, in view of that prescribed basis, that the party interested is duly elected to the particular office in question, which is sufficent to show that it would be monstrous to hold that such a certificate is a muniment of title which cannot be contradicted.

Even suppose that is so, still it is insisted by the same counsel that the action of the State canvassers, pursuant to the fourth section of the State act of the 27th of February, 1872, is conclusive, and that this Commission, in view of the action of that board and of the provision of the State law, is not authorized to admit evidence of any kind to show that their return is not true or that it is fraudulent, nor even that it is a forgery. Startling as the proposition is, it will require careful examination in view of that statute.

Certain persons are designated in the introductory part of the fourth section of the statute to meet at a prescribed time, at the office of the secretary of state, to form a board of State canvassers, and that board is required to canvass the returns of the election—meaning the county returns filed in the office of the secretary of state—and to determine and declare who shall have been elected * * * *as shown by such returns.*

Obviously, they are required to canvass the county returns filed in the office of the secretary of state and to determine who are elected, *as shown by such returns.* If the provision stopped there, it would be clear that the sole duty of that board would be to canvass and declare the result shown by those returns; but it does not stop there, and consequently it becomes necessary to examine the residue of the section.

They are required to examine those returns and no others, and the further provision is that if any such return shall be shown, or shall appear to be *"so irregular, false, or fraudulent"* that the board shall be unable *to determine the true vote* for any such officer or member, they shall so certify, and shall not include such return in their determination and declaration. Unless the return shall be shown or shall appear to be *so irregular, false, or fraudulent* that the board is unable to determine the true vote, they have no authority to reject such a return, and they have no jurisdiction to mutilate or alter it under any circumstances. Where the return is so irregular, false, or fraudulent that they cannot determine the result without rejecting such a return, they shall not include it in their return, but they must certify that fact. It is difficult to see why they are required to certify the fact unless their action is subject to review. Confirmation of that view is also derived from the fact that the secretary of state is required to preserve and file in his office all such returns, with such other documents and papers as he may receive.

Proof that any such irregular, false, or fraudulent return from a county was filed in the office of the secretary of state is entirely wanting, and noshing of the kind is suggested in the objections filed by either party; nor would it afford any argument to exclude investigation if it were otherwise, as the case shows that all the evidence is preserved in the office of the secretary of state, and certified copies of the same are among the papers transmitted to the Commission.

Beyond question, the provision assumes that a county return may be so irregular, false, and fraudulent that the board will be unable to determine the true result unless such defective return be rejected; and, if so, they shall so certify and shall not include such return, but the return is to be filed and preserved in the office of the secretary of state.

None of the objections set up any such state of things, nor does any one pretend, I think, that any of the returns filed in the office of the secretary of state come within the category of that provision. Should it be said that the presumption is that the board performed its duty, the answer to that is that such a presumption is merely a *prima facie* one, which may be overcome by competent proof, and that a brief examination of the documents will be sufficient to enable the Commission to determine whether the board, in order to change the result of the election, were or were not guilty of fraud, perjury, or forgery. Opportunity to introduce evidence is asked, and the proper response to the request, in my judgment, is, let the evidence determine the issue between the parties.

Candid men everywhere will agree, I think, that the board were directed to include regular returns, and that they had no right to exclude any one unless it was so irregular, false, or fraudulent that if included they would be unable to ascertain and determine the true vote or result. Those supporting the objections to certificate No. 1 allege and propose to prove that the board threw out returns which were neither irregular, false, nor fraudulent, in order to change the result of the election, and in my opinion they are entitled to that privilege if the evidence offered is competent and tends to prove the charge.

Imputations of the kind are explicitly made, and the main question, under the order adopted by the Commission, is whether evidence is admissible to prove the accusation. No one here, I suppose, will deny that in general such evidence in an issue between party and party is admissible, but the argument is that in the case under consideration neither Congress nor the Commission has jurisdiction to try such an issue.

Electoral votes are to be transmitted to the President of the Senate, and the provision of the Constitution is that the President of the Senate shall, in the presence of the Senate and the House of Representatives, open all the certificates, and that "the votes shall then be counted."

Wide differences of opinion prevailed, pending the passage of the act creating the Commission, as to the meaning of that clause; one side maintaining that the votes should be counted by the President of the Senate, and the other that it was both the right and the duty of the two Houses to inquire and determine whether the votes returned and opened in the presence of the two Houses are the true votes given by "the duly appointed electors" of the State. Discussion, rarely ever surpassed, followed. Suffice it to say, the bill became a law almost by general consent. Parties and counsel seem indisposed to open that discussion, nor is it my purpose to enter that field, except to say that in my judgment the verdict of posterity will be that it is the duty of Congress to count the votes and to solve every question involved in the performance of that duty.

Under the act creating the Commission, the provision is that where more than one return from a State has been received by the President of the Senate, the same shall be opened by him in the presence of the two Houses, and shall be submitted to the Commission to determine which is the true and lawful electoral vote of the State. Written objection may be made to such certificates, and when made, if there be more than one, the requirement is that all such certificates, votes, and papers, and all papers accompanying the same, together with the objections, shall be forthwith submitted to the Commission, which shall proceed to *consider the same*, with the same powers, if any, now possessed for that purpose by the two Houses acting separately or together.

Important duties are required of the Commission, as follows: (1)

they are required to consider all such certificates, votes, and papers objected to, and all papers accompanying the same; (2) they are required to decide by a majority of votes whether any and what votes from such State are the votes provided for by the Constitution of the United States, and how many and what persons were duly appointed electors by such State.

Express requirement is made that the Commission shall perform those duties, and the act further provides that they " may therein take into view such petitions, depositions, and *other papers*, if any, as shall by the Constitution and now existing law be competent and pertinent in such consideration."

Duties such as those required cannot be properly performed without evidence nor without hearing the parties interested. By the express words of the act the Commission may take into view such petitions and depositions, if admissible by the Constitution and the existing laws, provided they are pertinent to the matter under consideration, which shows to a demonstration that Congress never intended that the Commission should determine the questions submitted without evidence, any more than without giving the parties an opportunity to be heard.

Conclusive support to that view is also derived from the form of the oath the Commissioners are required to take and subscribe before entering upon the duties prescribed by the act. Every member of the Commission solemnly engaged by that oath that he would impartially examine and consider all questions submitted to the Commission and a true judgment give thereon, agreeably to the Constitution and the laws.

Two of the questions submitted are as follows: (1) What votes from the State are the true votes? (2) What persons were duly appointed electors in such State? You are all sworn to impartially examine and consider those questions and a true judgment give thereon, agreeably to the Constitution and the laws. How can you comply with that requirement unless you admit in evidence the documentary evidence from the office of the secretary of state and an exemplified copy of the record and judgment in the suit between these contestants?

Jurisdiction is the power to hear and determine, and it is to me past comprehension how any person accustomed to legal investigation can read the act of Congress creating the Commission and still entertain a doubt that the Congress intended that the Commission should examine and consider those two questions and give a true judgment thereon agreeably to the Constitution and the laws. Common experience is sufficient to convince every person of ordinary intelligence that a true judgment cannot be given without evidence nor without a hearing. Tribunals of justice are not expected to shut their eyes to evidence and decide blindly without hearing the parties.

Unless parties are allowed to give evidence they are not benefited by being heard upon the merits of the controversy. By the terms of the order under which they have been heard the merits are excluded, and if the Tilden electors are not permitted to give evidence the merits must be decided in favor of the other party without any hearing. Worse than that; the case was practically decided before it was submitted to the Commission, and it must be sent back without any one of the questions presented in the objections having been examined or considered by the Commission.

Congress never would have passed the law if those who favored its passage had supposed that the only duty the Commission had to perform was to certify to the two Houses the enumeration made by the State board of canvassers. Nor would the President of the United States have considered it his duty to send a special message to Congress commending the measure if he had supposed that the jurisdiction of the Commission was limited to a mere clerical enumeration of the votes certified and transmitted to the President of the Senate.

Two branches of the Government were stopped to enable the members of the Commission to sit and hear these cases, and now it is gravely contended by members of the tribunal that the Commission can neither hear evidence nor decide the questions presented in the written objections submitted to the Commission by the two Houses, beyond the mere enumeration of the votes. Duties of the kind are usually performed by a county judge upon the desk before him, without referring the cause to a master. Others may argue such a question if they see fit, but I cannot, as it seems to me that the proposition calls in question the wisdom of Congress and involves a theory which is past belief.

Both Houses of Congress knew full well that there were in the contested cases charges of fraud, perjury, and forgery, and it is clear to a demonstration, in my judgment, that those charges in respect to the returns made by the State board should be examined, considered, and decided by this tribunal, so far as the charges are involved in the objections filed to the certificates submitted to the Commission by the two Houses of Congress.

When the Commission was organized the whole country expected that those charges would be heard and that a true judgment would be given thereon, and sound discretion and a due regard to the words of the act of Congress forbid the conclusion that the action of the State board in rejecting the county returns from the county of Manatee and parts of the returns from the three other counties named is a matter the Commission cannot examine, consider, and decide, the charges, as alleged, involving fraud, perjury, and forgery. Such a decision, in my judgment, is forbidden by every consideration of law and justice, and if made, I fear that it will shock the public sense, and when the knowledge of it reaches other lands I shall be greatly disappointed if it does not shock the wise and just throughout the civilized world.

Without the right to introduce evidence, a trial in any case is a mockery, and in this case the refusal to hear evidence is the height of injustice, as it amounts to an *ex parte* decision in favor of the persons claiming title under certificate No. 1, without having examined or considered any one of the objections filed to that supposed muniment of title.

Explanations to sustain that proposition are unnecessary, as it is obvious that they claim title under the certificate of Governor Stearns founded upon the return of the board of State canvassers. Unlike that, the Tilden electors allege that the return which constitutes the basis of that certificate is false and fraudulent and that the canvassers tortiously and unlawfully excluded from the count the votes of one county and part of the votes from three other counties, for the express purpose of changing the result and of defeating the well-known choice of the people at the general election.

Formal charges of the kind are made in the objections, and are also contained in the offers of proof, and the counsel opposing the certificate in question allege that authentic documents are at hand to prove those charges, and to show that the certificate signed by the attorney-general, which is also based upon the county returns filed in the office of the secretary of state, expresses the true result of the election, the sole difference being that the attorney-general in his computation included the return from the county of Manatee and the votes from the other three counties which were excluded by the board of State canvassers, and assertions of the kind may be investigated without difficulty and in a brief period.

Contest arose at the same time between the rival candidates for governor, in consequence of which a suit was commenced in the supreme court of the State on the relation of George F. Drew, one of the candidates, against Samuel B. McLin and others, which was decided on the 25th day of December, 1876, the court holding to the effect that the State canvassers had no authority to reject a county return or the votes given, except when the canvassers were unable to ascertain for whom they were cast, for the reason specified in the fourth section of the act prescribing their duties.

Acquiescence in that decision was universal, and the legislature, on the 17th of January following, passed a law creating a new board of State canvassers, and directed that a new canvass should be made of the county returns of the election held on the 7th of November in the preceding year. Agreeably to that law the board was organized, and they recanvassed the same returns and came to the same result as that previously reached by the attorney-general of the State.

By the third section of the act they were required to make and sign a certificate containing the whole number of votes given at the election and to declare the result, and the further requirement is that the certificate shall be recorded in the office of the secretary of state. Requirements of the kind were all fulfilled and the certificate was duly made and signed, which is the basis of certificate No. 3, executed by the present governor of the State.

Viewed in any light, it must be admitted that it is "confirmation strong as proofs of Holy Writ" that certificate No. 2, signed by the attorney-general, is true, and that it gave the true and honest result of the election. Investigations made by the legislature induced that body to come to the same conclusion, and on the 26th of January following the legislature passed a statute, in which it is enacted that the Tilden electors, on the 7th of November previous, were duly chosen and appointed electors by and on behalf of the State and in the manner directed by the legislature. "Each State shall appoint, in such manner as the legislature thereof may direct," the number of electors to which the State is entitled, subject to the exception therein contained.

None of these proceedings were intended to choose new electors, but merely to ascertain who were elected at the antecedent general election, and they show beyond peradventure that the return of the first board of State canvassers was false and fraudulent, and that the result could only have been reached by perjury and forgery.

Power is certainly vested in a State to appoint electors in such manner as her legislature shall direct, and all agree that the statute of the State required that the electors should be chosen by the qualified voters of the State; nor is it controverted by any one that the election held on the 7th of November, 1876, was duly notified and regularly conducted, nor that the returns of the local officers were regularly and in due form of law made to the county canvassers.

Prescribed duties are to be performed by the county canvassers, and they are required to transmit their returns to the secretary of state, and it is certain that the objections filed to the respective certificates do not impugn the county returns, nor is there any evidence before the Commission to justify any one in calling those returns in question as irregular, false, or fraudulent. Imputations of the kind are explicitly made against the returns of the board of State canvassers, as before fully explained.

Electors are to be appointed by the State, and the State very properly claimed the right to inquire and ascertain who had been chosen at the election held for that purpose. Charges of fraud, perjury, and forgery hanging over the old board, the legislature, by a public law approved by the governor, made provision for a new board, and directed the new board to canvass the same county returns on file in the office of the secretary of state, and to report the result of their doings. They performed that duty, and the legislature by a public act ratified their doings, and enacted that the Tilden electors were duly chosen on the 7th of November previous, and that they are the electors duly appointed by the State.

Opposed to this there is nothing to support the pretensions of the Hayes electors except the certificate of Governor Stearns, founded upon the return of the old board of State canvassers.

These proceedings constitute the basis of certificate No. 3, and they show that the proceedings and the certificate were intended to confirm as true what is certified in the certificate of the attorney-general, and it is clear, in my judgment, that they are properly admissible and amply sufficient for that purpose.

Matters of the sort may be readily investigated in a very brief space of time, as every impartial person must see from the very nature of the transactions.

States may appoint electors in such manner as their legislatures may direct, and the judiciary of the State may interpret such laws, and the decision of the State court in such a case must be regarded as the rule of decision, as appears by the express enactment of Congress (1 Stat. at Large, 92 ; McKeen *vs.* Delancy, 5 Cranch, 22.) Circuit courts in that State have power to issue writs of *quo warranto* and all other writs proper and necessary to the complete exercise of their jurisdiction. (State Const., art. 6, sec. 8.)

Proof of the most satisfactory character is exhibited in the papers transmitted to the Commission, that the old board of State canvassers did not complete their canvass until the 6th of December, 1876, and that the certificate given to the supposed Hayes electors bears date on that day. It appears, also, that the certificate given to the Tilden electors and signed by the attorney-general bears the same date as exhibited in the documents printed by order of the Commission. Both sets of electors met at the capital of the State on that day, as required by law, for the purpose of executing the functions of electors, but the Hayes electors, before they voted, were served with process in *quo warranto* sued out from the circuit court of the second judicial circuit of the State by the Tilden electors. They sued in their own behalf as well as in behalf of the people of the State, as they had a right to do under the law of the State, inasmuch as the attorney-general refused to institute the proper proceeding.

Service being made, the respondents appeared and filed an answer. Subsequently proofs were taken on both sides, and the parties having been fully heard, the court, on the 25th of January following, entered a decree in favor of the relators.

By that decree the court adjudged : (1) That the Hayes electors were not, nor was any one of them, elected, chosen, or appointed electors. (2) That they were not, on the said 6th of December, or any other time, entitled to assume or exercise any of the powers and functions of such electors. (3) That they were upon the said day and date mere usurpers, and that all and singular their acts and doings as such were and are illegal and void. (4) That the Tilden electors all and singular were at said election duly elected, chosen, and appointed electors of the State, and were, on the said 6th of December, entitled to be declared elected, chosen, and appointed as such electors, and to have and receive certificates to that effect, and at all times since to exercise and perform all and singular the powers and duties of such electors.

Prior to the rendering of the decree in this case, the new board of State canvassers had made their report, and on the following day the legislature passed the act to delare and establish the appointment of electors, by which it is enacted that the Tilden electors were, on the 7th of November previous, duly chosen and appointed as such, with all the powers incident to such offices.

Repeated admissions have been made during the discussion that a State may determine what persons the qualified voters have chosen and appointed electors of President and Vice President, but the proposition is advanced that the determination must be made before the electors meet and cast their votes, and that it cannot be made at any subsequent time. Antecedent investigation could not be made in this case before the electors voted, for the reason that the old board of State canvassers did not make their return until the day when the votes were cast, nor were the Hayes electors furnished with the certificate of the governor until that day. All that could be done by the way of investigation before that time was done, as appears by the certificate of the attorney-general, which was also given to the Tilden electors on the same 6th of December. Without a moment's delay the Tilden electors sued out a writ of *quo warranto* against the usurpers, and by extreme diligence caused it to be served on them one hour before they cast their votes.

Weighed in the light of these suggestions, the proposition that subsequent investigation cannot be made is monstrous, as it shows a mockery of justice. You may investigate before the votes are cast when it is impossible for want of time, but you shall not after that, as you would then have an opportunity to ascertain the truth!

Canvassers may, if they see fit, keep back their report until the day appointed for the electors to meet, and if they do so, the effect of the proposition is that there can be no investigation, no matter how enormous the fraud has been. Forgery and fraud ought not to go unexposed; but if the proposition submitted is correct, it necessarily follows that the State is powerless to protect itself from the consequences of such crimes.

Whatever could be done by every branch of the State government to establish the truth was done, and if it now be decided that their efforts are fruitless, the effect must be to offer impunity in the future to all scheming officers who may tamper with subordinate returns in order to change the result of an election.

Opposing candidates for governor of the State were in the field at the same election, and it appears that the board of State canvassers threw out sufficient of the county returns to elect the incumbent who gave the certificate to the Hayes electors. His opponent, the present governor, (Drew,) brought mandamus against the members of the canvassing-board, praying that they might be decreed to correct their return. Process was served, and the respondents appeared and filed an answer. Both sides took proofs, and the parties went to trial.

Authority to issue mandamus is vested in all the courts of the State. The proceedings in this case was in the supreme court, and that court decreed that all that the State board of canvassers can do in such a case under the statute creating it must be based upon the returns; that everything they are authorized to do is limited to what is sanctioned by the authentic and true returns before them; that their final act and determination must be such as appears from and is shown by the returns from the several counties to be correct; that they have no general power to issue subpœnas, to summon parties, to compel the attendance of witnesses, to grant a trial by jury, or to do any act but determine and declare *who has been elected as shown by the returns.* (State *ex rel.* George F. Drew *vs.* Samuel B. McLin *et al.*, 15 Florida R.)

Special reference is made in that case to the return from the county of Manatee and to those from the three counties of Hamilton, Jackson, and Monroe. By that opinion, it appears that the answer set up that there was such irregularity and fraud in the conduct of the election that the board could not ascertain the true vote. Responsive to that defense, the court say that—

The facts stated in the answer present a judicial question beyond the power and jurisdiction of the board; that a return of votes cast in a county at such a general election, duly signed by the proper officers, and regular in form, * * * is a return which the State officers must count, as it is neither irregular, false, nor fraudulent within the meaning of the statute.

Comment is also made in the same opinion upon the action of the State board in respect to the other three counties, and the decision is to the effect that if the return is genuine and in due form, the question whether the irregularities shown to have existed at the election are sufficient to reject the same is a question of law, not within the power of the board to determine; that what is fraud in such an inspector is a question of law, so also is the question whether such a fraud by inspectors can vitiate an election. Both are judicial questions, beyond the power of the board to determine.

Unless it be denied that the construction of a State statute given to it by the supreme court of the State furnishes the rule of decision, it would seem to follow that the board of State canvassers exceeded their jurisdiction; and, if so, all must concede that their acts are null and void.

Five years before that, the supreme court of the State decided that the object of the statute in question is to ascertain the whole number of votes cast and who had received the highest number of votes, so that the choice of the majority of the voters might be ascertained and respected; that if the facts stated by the relator were correct, that returns made had not been included in the canvass, then the board of State canvassers had not performed their duty; that their duties are ministerial beyond that of determining that the papers received by them as returns are genuine authentic returns of the election; that they are required by law to meet on a given day for the purpose, and may adjourn from day to day until their duties are accomplished, and in case legal returns are received by them at any time before they complete the canvass which would have been counted if received before the canvass was commenced, it is their duty to include such in the canvass and certificate, and if they refuse they may be compelled by the writ of mandamus to complete the canvass of all the returns received, and to certify the result according to law. (State *ex rel.* Bloxham *vs.* The Board of State Canvassers, 13 Florida, 73.)

Proper opportunity to investigate such charges ought to be permitted at some time, and if it is not possible to accomplish that object before the day appointed for the meeting of the electors, justice and necessity demand that it shall be allowed subsequent to that time, for it would be too great a triumph for injustice to hold that it must be postponed forever because the outrage was committed so near to the time designated for the performance of the duty that it was impossible to institute and close the scrutiny before the accessories in guilt have actually enjoyed the stolen privilege which belonged to the complaining party. (Queen *vs.* Vestrymen of Pancras, 11 Ad. & Ell., 25.)

Three points were decided by the exchequer chamber in Rochester *vs.* The Queen, (1 Ell., Bl. & Ell., 1031,) which support the proposition that it was not too late to make the investigation : (1) That the court ought to compel the performance of a public duty by a public officer although the time prescribed by statute for the performance of the same has passed. (2) That if the public officer to whom belongs the performance of such a duty has in the mean time quitted his office and has been succeeded by another, it is the duty of the successor to obey the commands of the court. (3) That all statutes are to be construed with reference to the known, acknowledged, recognized, and established power of the proper court to superintend and control inferior jurisdictions and authorities of every kind.

Due service of process in the *quo warranto* suit was made at the earliest possible moment, and it is not even suggested that any greater diligence could have been employed in bringing the litigation to a close. Prompt investigation was made by the new board of State canvassers, and the legislature enacted the statute declaring that the Tilden electors were duly chosen and appointed the next day after the decree was entered in the *quo warranto* suit. Neither the public nor the citizens have any power to defeat the machinations of fraud, perjury, and forgery if the measures adopted for that purpose in this case are held to be ineffectual and insufficient.

For these reasons I am of the opinion that the evidence offered should be admitted and that the other side should be permitted to give evidence in reply.

Debate being closed, the Commission adopted the following order, moved by Mr. Justice Miller :

Ordered, That no evidence will be received or considered by the Commission which was not submitted to the joint convention of the two Houses by the President of the Senate with the different certificates, except such as relates to the eligibility of F. C. Humphreys, one of the electors.

Adopted—yeas 8, nays 7.

Commissioner Abbott moved the following :

Ordered, That in the case of Florida the Commission will receive evidence relating to the eligibility of Frederick C. Humphreys, one of the persons named in certificate No. 1, as elector.

Adopted—yeas 8, nays 7.

Notice was given to counsel of the result, and that the Commission was ready to proceed with the case. Witnesses were examined on both sides in respect to the eligibility of Frederick C. Humphreys as an elector, and their testimony is fully reported in the record of the proceedings. The testimony being closed, counsel were heard upon the merits under the third rule prescribed by the Commission, and at the conclusion of the argument the spectators retired and the Commission went into consultation with closed doors. Discussion ensued, in which several of the members of the Commission participated. During the discussion as to the eligibility of Frederick C. Humphreys, Mr. Justice CLIFFORD stated his conclusions on the matter, as follows:

1. That no person is eligible as an elector, or can be lawfully appointed

as such, who holds an office of trust or profit under the United States at the time of the election or appointment.

2. That the office of shipping-commissioner is an office of trust and profit under the United States.

3. That Frederick C. Humphreys was legally appointed to that office.

4. That the evidence introduced fails to show a complete legal resignation of the office by the incumbent before the 7th of November, 1876.

5. That if he had performed official acts after the date of the correspondence between him and the judge of the circuit court, his acts would have been legal.

6. That if the incumbent had subseqently decided, with the consent of the judge, to retain the office, he might have done so without a new appointment, because his letter to the judge had never been filed.

7. That inasmuch as the evidence shows that both the judge and the incumbent regarded the resignation as complete, and it appears that the incumbent never did perform any subsequent official act, I am of the opinion that, in an equitable view, the person named ought to be regarded as having been eligible as an elector on the day when the election was held.

Other members of the Commission discussed the whole case in view of the papers submitted to the Commission by the President of the Senate, but Mr. Justice CLIFFORD, believing that discussion would be unavailing and useless, took no further part in the debate.

Commissioner Hunton moved an order to the effect that the Tilden electors were duly appointed by the State, and their votes as certified in certificate No. 2 are the votes provided for by the Constitution. Rejected—yeas 7, nays 8.

When that result was announced, Commissioner Garfield moved that the Hayes electors were duly appointed and that the votes cast by them are the votes provided for by the Constitution; also, that Commissioner Edmunds, Mr. Justice Bradley, and Mr. Justice Miller be appointed a committee to draught a report of the action of the Commission, as required by law. Adopted—yeas 8, nays 7.

None of the subsequent proceedings in the case need be reproduced, as they are given in full in the Congressional Record.

Like submissions were made to the Commission in the cases of Louisiana, Oregon, and South Carolina, the proceedings in which cases are also published in the same Record, but Mr. Justice CLIFFORD did not participate in those discussions, having become thoroughly convinced that nothing he could say would be of any public benefit.

INDEX TO ELECTORAL COUNT OF 1877.

A.

Page.

1078 INDEX.